The Memoirs of
COUNT
WITTE

The Memoirs of
COUNT
WITTE

Translated and Edited by
SIDNEY HARCAVE

M. E. Sharpe, Inc.
Armonk, New York
London, England

Available in the United Kingdom and Europe from
M. E. Sharpe, Publishers, 3 Henrietta Street, London WC2E 8LU.

Photographs courtesy of the Slavic and Baltic Division,
the New York Public Library.

Library of Congress Cataloging-in-Publication Data
Vitte, S. I͡U. (Sergeĭ I͡Ul'evich), graf, 1849–1915.
The memoirs of Count Witte.

Rev. translation of Vospominaniia,
which includes text of the unpublished Zapisi Grafa Vitte.
Includes bibliographical references.
1. Vitte, S. I͡U. (Sergeĭ I͡Ul'evich), graf, 1849–1915.
2. Statesmen—Soviet Union—Biography.
3. Soviet Union—Politics and government—1894–1917.
I. Harcave, Sidney, 1916- . II. Title.
DK254.W5V5   1990   947.08'092   89-43534
ISBN 0-87332-571-0

Printed in the United States of America

MV 10 9 8 7 6 5 4 3 2 1

Contents

VOLUME III, 1906–1912

Part I
My Life, 1906–1911

Part II
My Times, 1906–1912

Introduction
Sidney Harcave

This translation of the memoirs of Count Sergei Iulevich Witte (1849–1915) is based on the original texts of his memoirs which are held in Columbia University's Bakhmeteff Archive of Russian and East European History and Culture. Since this is not the first translation, one may ask why another is called for. Before dealing with this question, it is necessary to look briefly at the man and his memoirs.

Witte was the most notable and controversial minister to serve under the last two emperors of Russia. A huge, ungainly man, a brilliant mind, a tireless worker, plain-spoken, sometimes coarse, he evoked and provoked extreme characterizations, ranging from "Russia's evil genius" to "Russia's John the Baptist."

All agreed that he was remarkably able, but how able? A genius? The only statesman in Russia since Peter the Great? A Bismarck without a William I? A Colbert in the wrong century? The verdict is not yet in, and may never be, but there is no question that Witte was the ablest minister of the twilight years of Russian tsarism.

There is even less agreement about his character. There were many, in high places and low, who, prey to fearful fantasies, saw in him a sinister figure, one "of the angels who were not for God or God's enemies, but fought for themselves alone," a power-hungry man who conspired with Jews and revolutionaries for his own purposes. There were also many, in high places and low, who saw in him a devoted subject who alone among the emperor's ministers had the ability to cope with Russia's problems. The latter were closer to the mark than the former. No doubt Witte was extremely ambitious and sometimes devious, but he was devoted to Russia and the Romanov dynasty.

Witte was born in Tiflis, the administrative center of the Caucasus. His father was a Russified Baltic German, a bureaucrat who gained admission to the hereditary nobility by virtue of the rank he achieved in the civil service. His mother was a Russian, a member by birth of the hereditary nobility. Witte received his early schooling in Tiflis, and went on to study at Novorossiisk University in Odessa.

After receiving his degree he began a career in railroading, quickly demonstrating his ability to assume great responsibility and to act with daring and breadth of vision. In 1889 he became director of the Department of Railroad Affairs of the Ministry of Finance, a position from which he was soon to advance with remarkable speed. His rise was due to a combination of great talent and great luck, the luck to find an enthusiastic supporter in Alexander III. In February 1892 the emperor named Witte acting minister of ways and communications. A year later he appointed Witte acting minister of finance, and in January 1893 he raised him to the rank of minister of finance.

By this time Witte was seen as a rising star, an ambitious, brash, young (by bureaucratic standards) man. To what might be called the establishment, he seemed to have come out of nowhere. But there he was, solidly in favor with Alexander III, steadily becoming more visible and more powerful. Nicholas II, who came to the throne in 1894, was not as taken with Witte, this diamond in the rough who talked down to him, as his father had been, but for nearly a decade he would back his finance minister's hand.

During that decade Witte became the most powerful minister of the realm, his finger in almost every pie, virtually master of a state within a state. Then, in 1903, because he had become too powerful, had made too many enemies in high places, had opposed too many of his sovereign's initiatives, he was abruptly shunted to the dead-end position of chairman of the Committee of Ministers by Nicholas II. Whether or not the emperor had by then come to give credence to the spurious allegation that Witte was part of a Jewish-Masonic conspiracy is not certain, but within the year he came to suspect that such was the case. As far as he was concerned, Witte would be allowed to wither away in his new post.

When the time came to appoint a chief plenipotentiary to negotiate peace with Japan, in 1905, he said "anyone but Witte." But, for lack of any other candidate both willing and able, Nicholas had to choose him. Witte performed brilliantly at the peace conference, winning better terms for Russia than she had a right to expect. When Witte returned to Russia in late September his star was once more in the ascendant. Impressed by Witte's performance, his suspicions of him temporarily stilled, the emperor bestowed the title of count on him and was persuaded to name Witte chairman of the Council of Ministers, a post hitherto held by the sovereign, to coordinate the work of the executive branch and to implement the many reforms that had been squeezed out of the government during the preceding, turbulent months. Those in the know predicted that Witte would accept the post if it were offered because it would be his last opportunity to return to power, and went on to predict that if he did he would regret it, given the emperor's basic hostility toward him. Witte, too, had misgivings and, probably at the urging of his wife, tried by circuitous means to have himself appointed ambassador to France.

Had he succeeded, he and his wife would have been spared much grief, but that was not to be. Nicholas II needed him in Russia even before the outbreak of the general strike early in October. The strike only increased that need.

In the view of many in a position to influence the emperor, Witte was the only man capable of saving the throne at this juncture. Accordingly, Nicholas II accepted Witte's counsel that the only way out was to grant reforms that would in effect, but not in name, transform Russia into a constitutional monarchy. This he did in a manifesto issued on October 17. Witte, who had unofficially been acting as chairman (premier) of the Council of Ministers, was now officially installed in that post, his responsibility being to carry out the reforms and place the government on an even keel. Six hectic months later, Nicholas II parted with his chief minister, privately convinced that the man was a traitor and determined never again to entrust him with any responsibility.[1] At the same time he promised Witte the next available ambassadorship and was publicly effusive in his appreciation of Witte's work. And, quite reluctantly, he appointed Witte to the State Council, the usual honor (really a pension, a kind of "bonbon" as the dowager empress called it) given to departing ministers. The ambassadorship would never come. Witte's career was over.

When Witte left office he was a sick and embittered man and, what is more, for the first time in thirty-six years without real employment. He now had time on his hands and much on his mind, much that he wished to say about recent events, beginning with the course of action that had led to what he, and not he alone, called "that disgraceful war with Japan," a war that would have been avoided, in Witte's opinion, had his counsel been followed; a war that, in his opinion, had led to the revolution of 1905. Of course, it would be impolitic for him to publish what he had to say during his lifetime, but he could arrange to have it published after his death.

First, however, he had to get some rest and medical attention. Shortly after leaving office, he and his wife went abroad. While he was out of the country two events occurred that served to intensify the bitterness he already felt toward Nicholas II. The first was a message that the emperor thought it best, given the political turmoil in Russia, for Witte to remain abroad for a time. Witte took this advice as a veiled form of banishment and reacted in characteristically angry fashion, offering to leave government service. The offer was ignored and Nicholas II in effect retreated, but the incident could not help but reinforce Witte's conviction that his sovereign was a weak and treacherous man. Then came a telegram from the notorious Prince Andronikov, a highly connected busybody, warning him that if he returned to Russia he would be killed. Witte took the telegram to mean "that because the Emperor's efforts to induce me to remain abroad had failed, an attempt was now being made to frighten me into remaining abroad." He refused to be frightened and with his wife returned to Russia in the fall.

Soon after his return he set about preparing an account of what he considered to be the truth about the origins of the war with Japan. In the course of the next months, with the aid of former colleagues in the Ministry of Finance, relying on documents in his personal archive, he prepared a three-volume typewritten work, consisting of two volumes of text and one of documents. This work, entitled "Vozniknovenie russko-iaponskoi voiny" (The Origins of the Russo-Japanese War), opens with the plan for construction of a trans-Siberian railroad and closes with the failure of efforts to resolve differences between Russia and Japan by peaceful means.

In form and style this work resembles the "colored" books that governments issue in time of war to justify themselves. In this case, however, it was an individual, Witte (who appears here in the third person), whose conduct and counsel are being justified. This work is not included in this edition of the memoirs (although it is briefly excerpted on pp. 348–49), nor has it been included in other editions, but its existence must be kept in mind, for, in writing his memoirs, Witte assumed that his readers would have at hand a published version of the work and that he would therefore not have to deal with the minutiae of the prewar diplomacy.[2]

On January 27, 1907, while he was still at work on this project, he accidentally and providentially discovered a bomb planted in his home that had failed to go off. The investigation of this attempt on his life, the work of agents in the extreme right, was to drag on for years, with no charges filed, no arrests made. The investigation of a later attempt on his life would also lead to nowhere. From the first Witte was convinced that senior officials in the Ministry of Interior had foreknowledge of these efforts to kill him and had no intention of solving these cases. Also, he believed that some courtiers were implicated and that Nicholas II, although not implicated, was not distressed by the news of the attempts on Witte's life. It requires no great effort to imagine how Witte felt about the emperor after this. Also helping to exacerbate Witte's hostility toward and contempt of his sovereign was the "*coup d'état*" of June 3, 1907, when the second State Duma, which had proved so hostile to the government, was dissolved and a new electoral law, ensuring that the next Duma would be a docile one, was issued. Witte thought then that the "*coup d'état*" was the brain child of the emperor, engaging in one of his typical leaps in the dark.

It was shortly after the "*coup d'état*" that Witte, while in Frankfurt am Main for a minor operation, began to write his memoirs. He began with these words: "I have set forth the history of the origins of the Russo-Japanese War in a separate, systematic, and documented narrative: it ends with my departure from the post of minister of finance and my appointment as chairman of the Committee of Ministers." His recollections start with that appointment. During the next five months—in Frankfurt am Main, Bad Homburg, Cauteret, Biarritz, and Brussels (where his son-in-law served in the Russian legation)—he continued his account, bringing it up to October 1905 by the time he was ready to return to Russia. In concluding this section of his memoirs, he wrote:

> Until recently I have had neither the time nor the inclination to write my memoirs. Now, cut off from political life, I have decided to set down my recollections. I think that they may serve to illuminate many events. On the

whole I do not like to write, hence I must force myself to do so, as I have just been doing, abroad, with no documents at hand, writing from memory. For that reason I may have made some errors in dates and names. My memory for dates and, even more so, for names, has weakened, but concerning facts and essential matters everything is set forth *with complete truth and accuracy*.

I am writing these recollections in a very desultory fashion, in sessions of five or ten minutes. Therefore the exposition is not only not literary but is sometimes quite fuzzy. I ask that my heirs publish these memoirs and in doing so *correct the style* where necessary but not touch the essence of the exposition.

I am leaving this part of my memoirs with my son-in-law, in Brussels. If it appears possible, I will continue to write in Russia, where I will have some of the documents at hand. Whatever the case, I *will number* all my recollections *consecutively*.

In January 1908, now back in Russia, Witte was able to resume work on his memoirs, turning now to the events leading to the publication of the Manifesto of October 17, 1905. By the spring, time for his annual trip abroad, he was almost finished with this section. Thereafter, try as he might, he would never again be able to write his memoirs at home because he would find the political atmosphere too dispiriting for this kind of effort. Also, there was the fear that the secret police might attempt to lay its hands on what he had written.

As a consequence, whatever writing he did thereafter on his memoirs he did abroad, in such places as Biarritz, where he and his wife had the use of a villa, in Vichy and Bad Salzschlirf, where the two went for the cure. During the summer and fall of 1908, when he was much concerned about the health of his wife, he accomplished little. The next four seasons of writing were more productive. By October 5, 1912, he had just completed his account of his departure from office in April 1906 and was touching on the attempts on his life in 1907 when he decided to bring his work to a halt, declaring that if he resumed writing he would deal with contemporary events. As far as we know, he never did.

This set of memoirs, which he entitled "Zapisi Grafa Vitte" (Memoirs of Count Witte), hereafter referred to as the "handwritten memoirs," comes to some 750 handwritten pages and a typewritten insert consisting of memoranda prepared by Witte, Vuich, and Obolenskii concerning the Manifesto of October 17.

When he began to write, Witte had no intention of later embarking on yet another set of memoirs, but that is what he did: toward the end of 1910, while at home, he began dictating an account of his life and times. These he entitled "Vospominaniia (rasskazy v stenograficheskoi zapisi) Grafa Sergeia Iulevicha Vitte" (Recollections of Count Sergei Iulevich Witte, in stenographic transcription), hereafter referred to as the "dictated memoirs."

In embarking on this task Witte appeared to be acting impetuously and with some sense of urgency, for, although he had a mountain of documents at his fingertips, he relied primarily on his memory as he dictated. Of this set of memoirs he wrote that they "make no claim to being systematic or being completely accurate, but it is justified to claim that . . . all that is told is the unquestionable truth and the circumstances are presented impartially and honestly.''

Witte worked diligently at his new task. By May 20, 1911, he had dictated 1,029 pages, reaching the end of the reign of Alexander III. He and his wife then went abroad. On December 12, once more at home, he resumed dictating. As before, he worked at a fairly rapid pace. On March 5, 1912, he dictated the last entry in this set of memoirs:

> Thus I have reached 1912 in my stenographic memoirs. For the time being I am discontinuing this work. As is evident from the preceding pages, I have omitted from these memoirs the period when I was premier because it is dealt with in my handwritten memoirs, which I wrote usually while I was abroad. I have not finished the handwritten memoirs and shall try to complete them either by hand or by dictation.

At this point he had reached page 2,438 in the dictated memoirs. As far as we know this was the last page.

Seven months later, on October 12, a week after he had decided to discontinue work on his handwritten memoirs, Witte decided that he was not likely to resume work on either set of memoirs. In a postscript to his handwritten memoirs he directed that both sets of memoirs, except for some ''references to living persons,'' and his work on the origins of the Russo-Japanese War be published after his death.[3]

The two sets of memoirs are the basis of all editions of the memoirs thus far published and of this one as well. These texts present some problems for any editor. First is the fact that they are first drafts, poorly organized and quite repetitive. Then there is the difference in tone between the two sets of memoirs. This is particularly striking in the treatment of Emperor Nicholas and Empress Alexandra. In the handwritten memoirs Nicholas is a spineless, treacherous man whose shortcomings are masked by an air of breeding and Alexandra is ''a strange creature,'' a neurasthenic who, instead of compensating for the shortcomings of her husband, brought out his worst qualities. In contrast, the Nicholas of the dictated memoirs is basically decent, his shortcomings as a ruler the result of lack of preparation for his task, the inadequacies of those who served him, and lack of firmness on his own part. The Alexandra of the dictated memoirs is virtually a cipher, young, pretty, a bit unsure of herself, an angry look on her face. The differences between these sets of portraits is accounted for by the fact that Witte felt he could dare to be franker in his handwritten memoirs than in his dictated memoirs. What is an editor to do?

Witte left the work of editing to his heirs. That was hardly a wise decision, as Joseph Dillon, the British journalist with whom he was close, pointed out to him. Dillon writes: ''For the last time, in the spring of 1914, I admonished Witte that unless he prepared his reminiscences carefully for the press, correcting slips of memory and errors and leaving the manuscript quite ready for the printer, his reputation would surely suffer.''[4] But by then it was too late to follow such advice even if Witte had been inclined to do so. A few months later war broke out, finding Witte, his wife, their daughter Vera, and their grandson Lev abroad. They, of course, rushed back to Russia. By this time, as Countess Witte noted in the foreword, the memoirs were in a French bank vault. In February 1915 Witte died after a short illness, leaving the responsibility for publishing his memoirs to his widow.

It was not until after her angry departure from Bolshevik Russia that Countess Witte could arrange for publication. At the end of May 1919, the memoirs now in her possession, she sailed from Copenhagen to New York, where she had reason to believe she could receive a substantial sum for publication rights.[5] There she contracted to have the memoirs published in translation, reserving the right to see the copy before publication and to make suggestions; the publisher, however, was under no obligation to follow them.[6]

The publisher then engaged Avrahm Yarmolinsky, of the New York Public Library's Slavonic Division, to translate and edit the memoirs. The work went rapidly. Excerpts from Yarmolinsky's translation began to appear in periodicals in November 1920. Then, on March 19, 1921, the publisher informed the book trade that *The Memoirs of Count Witte* would be published on March 30.

> This is acknowledged as the most important book yet published on the Russian problem and on the whole international situation. It is being brought out simultaneously in England, France, Spain, Germany, Russia, and the United States. It has been translated from the hidden memoirs of Russia's greatest and most powerful minister. Advance newspaper articles, appearing from day to day, are giving the book vast publicity, and the publishers are sparing no effort to make it known the country over.[7]

The American, English, French, and Spanish editions appeared on schedule, but the German and Russian editions, which were to have been published by the Ullstein Publishing House, of Berlin, did not appear then or ever.

Why Ullstein acted as it did is a bit of a puzzle. A good guess is that Countess Witte was unhappy over the way the memoirs had been edited and expressed her feeling to I. V. Hessen, an old acquaintance of the Wittes, who was chief of an Ullstein subsidiary, the recently established Slovo Publishing House.[8] Whatever the explanation, the fact is that Ullstein decided to make a fresh start. Hessen would publish the memoirs in Russian, using the original texts, supplied by Countess Witte. Subsequently, a German translation of this edition would be made.

Hessen and his associates wasted no time.[9] The first volume of a two-volume edition appeared on October 17, 1921, the sixteenth anniversary of the October Manifesto, the second volume a few months later. These two volumes included Witte's memoirs for the period from 1894, the date of Nicholas II's accession, on. There is good reason to believe that, initially, Hessen did not intend to publish the first part of the memoirs, covering the period before 1894, but that, encouraged by the sales of the two-volume edition, he changed his mind. In 1923 a third volume, covering the earlier period, appeared.[10] In the same year Ullstein published an abridged German translation of the first two volumes.

All of the many editions of the memoirs that have appeared since then have been based on either the Yarmolinsky or the Hessen redaction. Why? Because until recently these were the only ones available. The story is this: After Hessen returned the original texts of the memoirs to Countess Witte, she placed them under lock and key, together with others of her husband's papers.[11] There they remained until 1951, when her daughter Vera transferred these texts and the other papers to Columbia University's Bakhmeteff Archive of Russian and East European History and Culture, with the stipulation that they be kept under seal, their presence at Columbia a secret, until 1965. As it turned out, several years passed after the seal was "broken" before the papers were made accessible. To be sure, Hessen had made a copy of the handwritten memoirs for deposit in the State Public Library in Petrograd, but that copy seems to have disappeared without a trace. All this meant that anyone wishing to prepare a new edition or a new translation had to turn to either the Yarmolinsky or the Hessen redaction, as so many have in the last sixty or so years.

Which brings us to the question, why a new English translation? Why not continue using Yarmolinsky's translation? It is readable, exciting, valuable. For over six decades it has served tens of thousands of readers, ranging from those with zero knowledge of Russia to specialists. Yet, as has long been realized, it is not without its faults.

In the first place, the Yarmolinsky redaction, which is about one-fifth the length of the original texts, omits most of what Witte wrote, which is why those with the necessary language facility have relied on the Hessen redaction. In the second place, Yarmolinsky's purplish prose is a far remove from Witte's. To be sure, a translation need not be literal, but it should be close to the original. In the third place, the Yarmolinsky redaction contains a number of errors of transcription and translation.

Granted that Yarmolinsky's work can be improved upon, why bother? Is anyone still interested in Witte's memoirs? The answer is an emphatic yes.

For most of the fifteen years of his service under Alexander III and Nicholas II, Witte was close to the center of power, deeply involved in foreign as well as domestic affairs, with greater access to information about affairs of state than virtually anyone but the emperor. Consequently, his memoirs are a major source for the history of Russia during this crucial period of rapid industrialization, foreign expansion, war, revolution, and fundamental political change. For many important events his memoirs provide the only source of information. In addition, the memoirs tell us much about his times in general.

The importance of the memoirs is attested to by the fact that they have been translated into seven languages and have gone through many editions and printings, one a run of 75,000 three-volume sets. The memoirs have been read and studied with microscopic care. There is no sign that interest in the memoirs has flagged.

The memoirs are important not only for what they say about the past but also for their relevance to the present. Consider the following thoughts expressed by Witte: Finland must not be allowed to become another Poland, kept under Russian control only by force of arms; Americans who call for a strong and independent Poland are naive; Afghanistan must serve Russia as a buffer; Russian annexation of northern Persia is inevitable; Russia needs a naval base in Murmansk; a northeast passage to the Far East is desirable; a pleasant manner and an imposing figure are negative rather than positive qualities in a public official; Russia has excellent natural resources, but they are poorly located; the Russian peasant must go through "the crucible of individual ownership" of the land before he can come to believe that collective ownership is preferable. Consider:

> Our peasantry labors the way it drinks. It does not drink much, but it gets drunk more often than other people. It works little, but sometimes it is overworked. To make sure the peasantry does not starve, that its labor becomes efficient, it must be given the opportunity to work, it must be freed from tutelage, it must achieve equality under the law, it must be assured that it can enjoy the fruits of its labor.

Consider also the following:

> For a thousand years, beginning in the time of Rurik, we have been swallowing up non-Russian peoples. As a consequence the Russian Empire is a conglomerate of nationalities. Despite this fact we now have a semi-comic nationalist party in the State Duma which insists on Russian for the Russians, i.e., for those whose surnames end in "ov" and who read *Russkoe znamia* and *Golos Moskvy*.

These are but a few examples of the striking freshness of what Witte had to say.

Also, many of Witte's unfulfilled hopes and expectations must continue to engage our attention: his hope for a disarmed, unified Europe; his expectation that sooner or later Russia would become "a truly constitutional state, like other civilized states," either through evolution or revolution.

I have long been aware of the need for a new translation of Witte's memoirs. Incidentally, when I learned from Mr. Yarmolinsky in 1966 that his translation would soon be reprinted I suggested that this would be a good opportunity to make some changes in what he had done, only to be told that the arrangement for a reprint permitted no changes. Of course, it was possible for me then to prepare a new translation on the basis of the Hessen redaction, as the Japanese have done, but one couldn't be sure how reliable the redaction was. Now that it is possible to compare that redaction with the original texts, it is apparent that, good and useful though that redaction is, it is no substitute for the original texts. In the first place, it omits a good deal of substantive material—concerning Witte's first marriage, members of the imperial family, important officials and private individuals, Russo-American relations. Such material should be in any edition of the memoirs that claims to be full. In addition, the Hessen redaction, which was largely produced by the use of scissors and paste, sometimes does violence to Witte's line of reasoning and to his chronology.

Consequently, I feel fortunate to have been given the opportunity by the administrative committee of the Columbia University Bakhmeteff Archive of Russian and East European History and Culture to use the original texts of Witte's memoirs. And, I am beholden to the late Lev Magerovsky, the first curator of the archive, to William Corsyn, his successor, and to Marc Raeff, the honorary curator, for their help in the course of my work. I owe thanks to Mark Kulikowski, of State University College of Oswego, for valuable bibliographical assistance.

Also, many thanks to the staff of the Manuscript Center of State University of New York at Binghamton for its help in preparing copy.

I have profited greatly from the work of Hessen and Yarmolinsky, as well as from the work of B. V. Ananich, R. Sh. Ganelin, H. Mehlinger, J. M. Thompson, and T. von Laue.

*   *   *

Some notes concerning the editing and translation. First, the translation is faithful but not literal. The text has been edited to reduce verbosity, to eliminate repetition, and to improve clarity. Simple errors, e.g., mistakes in dates, have been corrected without the change being noted. Complex errors have been noted but not corrected. The footnotes are Witte's own.

Wherever feasible, the two sets of memoirs have been kept distinct from one another and the order in the original has been followed as closely as possible. Where exceptions have been made, they are noted (see Sources, pp. 837–840).

The English equivalents of Russian given names have been used where they seem more pleasant to the eye and ear than the Russian. Thus Nikolai appears as Nicholas, but Fedor remains Fedor, because its English equivalent, Theodore, seems out of place. Patronymics, however, have been retained in Russian form. Sergei G. Pushkarev's excellent *Dictionary of Russian Historical Terms* has been followed in the translation of historical terms unless there seemed reason not to do so.

Library of Congress rules for transliteration from the Cyrillic to the Latin alphabet have been followed (omitting diacritical marks), with some exceptions. The major exception is in the rendering of surnames of non-Russian origin. Where it seemed appropriate and the information was available, such names have been given in their original spelling, e.g., Witte, Hessen, Richter, Schwanebach, and (alas) Freedericksz. Witte's usage in capitalizing imperial terms and titles has been followed, to preserve the monarchist flavor of the writing. However, his rendering of titles and honorifics has been contracted, e.g., His Imperial Majesty has become His Majesty and Sovereign Emperor has become merely Emperor.

Unless otherwise indicated, dates have been given according to the Julian calendar.

The editor's notes will be found at the back of the book, beginning on page 745.

Countess Witte's Foreword

It is not without hesitation that I have decided to say a few words in the form of a foreword to the memoirs of my late husband. I am not able to be impartial in evaluating this work, to which Count Witte attached so much importance, and a partisan evaluation on the part of a wife can hardly be of interest to the reader.

But I would like to tell the reader what importance my late husband attached to the work and what prompted him to set forth his thoughts and recollections in the form of a book which was intended for publication after his death and the death of his contemporaries. Count Witte was not a courtier who sought favor from the throne, nor a demagogue who catered to the mob. Although he belonged to the nobility he did not defend its privileges; although he believed that the chief task of the state was to provide a just foundation for the peasantry, he was too much of a statesman to embrace theoretical populism, as did so many of the Russian intelligentsia. He was not a liberal, inasmuch as he did not share the impatience of liberals, who wished to reconstruct the entire governmental structure at one stroke; neither was he a conservative, for he scorned the coarseness and backwardness that characterized the political thought of Russia's ruling bureaucracy. Many times my husband said to those close to him: "I am neither a liberal nor a conservative; I am simply a civilized man. I cannot send someone to Siberia simply because he doesn't think as I do, and I cannot take away his civil rights simply because he does not worship God in the same church as I."

This attitude earned S. Iu. Witte many enemies in both the conservative and liberal camps, and he was everywhere regarded as an "outsider." He went his own way in seeking the good of the fatherland and for that reason had few faithful companions. A sense of fairness compels me to say that my husband's remarkable gifts as a statesman were not denied and were in fact appreciated in all of Great Russia. Nonetheless, for the reasons already stated, no Russian official was the subject of such passionate, yet varied and contradictory, attacks as was my late husband. At court he was accused of republicanism; in radical circles he was charged with trying to undermine the rights of the people for the benefit of the monarch. The large landowners accused him of trying to ruin them for the benefit of the peasantry, while the radical party accused him of trying to deceive the peasantry for the benefit of the large landowners. S. Iu. Witte, the creator of the constitution of October 17, with which the modern history of Russia begins, was a very tempting object for slander and intrigue; also, the nature of this great statesman was so complex and many-sided that it gave rise to errors of judgment about him, even, on occasion, on the part of well-intentioned persons.

My husband did not wish to turn to the press in order to engage in polemics with his opponents, to answer slander, to clear up misunderstandings.[1] He stood above the ongoing gossip. Moreover, censorship under the old regime, which was more severe for the prime minister of the Tsar than for the ordinary citizen, as well as the desire to spare the feelings of many of his contemporaries, made it impossible for Count Witte to express his thoughts fully and frankly. For that reason he wrote these memoirs for a later generation, for it to pass judgment on his work.

My husband kept these memoirs abroad, for he had no assurance that his study on Kamenno-Ostrovskii Prospekt, in Petrograd, was sufficiently safe from the eyes and fingers of the secret police. At any moment a search could easily deprive him of his manuscripts. He knew that this work was of interest to too many powerful people. The manuscripts were kept in a foreign bank in my name until my husband expressed fear that in the event of his death, the [Imperial] court and the government would seek to take possession of his archive and asked me to act in time to safeguard the security of his memoirs. I did this by transferring the manuscripts from Paris to Bayonne, to be kept in the bank there under another name.

The precautions turned out to be warranted. Immediately after my husband's death, in February 1915, his study was sealed and everything found in it examined and taken away by the authorities. A few days later a general-adjutant, acting on behalf of the Emperor, said that as a result of having become acquainted with the table of contents of the memoirs the Emperor would be interested in reading the memoirs.[2] I replied that it was not possible to permit the Emperor to read the memoirs, because they were being kept abroad. The spokesman of the Emperor did not insist, but soon thereafter an official from the Russian embassy in Paris entered our villa in Biarritz and, in the absence of its owners, carried out a thorough search. He was looking for the memoirs, which as I have said, were then in a safe in Bayonne.

Countess Matilda Witte

I. V. Hessen's Introduction

Excerpt

Without a doubt, Count Sergei Iulevich Witte occupies the first place among our leading governmental figures. His name is firmly linked with the major reform of our monetary system and the basic reorganization of the government budget, which enabled Russia rapidly to become an equal partner in international trade. The critical role played by Count Witte in carrying out these reforms calls attention to the fact that he had no preparation for such tasks: a mathematician by training, he himself recognized that he was self-taught in the fields of political economy and finance.

He began with no specific, preconceived program. At the beginning of the 1890s he was a committed supporter of the village commune, but subsequently became an uncompromising opponent of that institution and was to come to grief several times in disputes with I. L. Goremykin over the question. The well-known professor A. S. Posnikov, as Witte tells us, taught him that the question of value and price was nonsensical and that the theory of supply and demand is simply a human invention. In response to such human inventions he set forth what he considered reality: "What is demanded above all from a 'government banker' is the ability to come to grips with the financial mood."

Consequently, it is not surprising that immediately after Count Witte's death a great dispute began: Was he a great man (some compared him to Peter the Great), or was he, as some insisted, simply a man who had the good fortune to be in the right place at a time of great historical importance? It is obvious that if I permitted myself, on the basis of my long acquaintance with Count Witte, to offer my own characterization of the man, this would only add fuel to the fire of controversy, because I, too, would be unable to claim to be objective. We know that many hold him responsible for the tragic circumstances Russia has experienced, and he, for his part, often asserted in his memoirs that Russia was headed for catastrophe because his program was not being carried out.

But it is possible to assert with complete objectivity that from the very beginning of his career in government Count Witte attracted attention because of his exceptional gifts. It is not often that one can say of an individual that it is he who confers distinction on the office he holds rather than the reverse, but with Count Witte this is precisely the case. He lent distinction to whatever position he occupied and always left evidence of his activity and tireless initiative. Therefore it was no accident that he consistently rose in the ranks, and it was inevitable that he become a minister. If one considers another major figure, that of P. A. Stolypin, to whom Count Witte devotes a great deal of hostile attention in his memoirs, one can confidently assert the opposite: before his appointment as minister, Stolypin had the reputation of being a very limited, ordinary bureaucrat whose advance up the governmental ladder was the result of influence. And when he was appointed minister it seemed accidental, unexpected, the product of exceptional circumstances. But it should be noted that in addition to having great ability, Witte came into prominence at a time propitious for the application of his gifts.

As we know, the reign of Alexander II is considered an age of major reforms and also of tensions. Serfdom had kept Russia at the stage of natural economy, separating her from the West by an insuperable wall. Emancipation and the shift to wage labor tore down this wall, resulting in the need for changes in the entire political structure—the courts and the organs of local self-government. But there was no creative, constructive principle behind these reforms, which merely removed obstacles that kept Russia from entering the European scene. The reforms only established the foundation but not the structure to be built on it.

The challenge posed by the reforms of Alexander II brought to the fore several prominent statesmen, but it is significant that their biographies invariably emphasize that, in keeping with the tasks they faced, these men displayed high moral qualities and noble character in the implementation of the principle of civil equality. Also emphasized is their spirit of self-denial with respect to the privileges of the nobility for the benefit of their "lesser brethren."

Subsequent to the laying of the foundation, a period of reaction ensued that affected society as well as government. Nonetheless, the question of what kind of a structure should be placed on the new foundation was insistently raised, leading to heated debates over whether Russia should follow the path already taken by Western Europe or, given her later arrival in the world, she should follow an indigenous route. The book by V. V. (Vasilii Vorontsov) called *The Fate of Capitalism in Russia*, which spoke for the latter view, became the gospel of our students during the 1880s, but subsequently the views of the intelligentsia, influenced by Marxism, which was making considerable inroads in Russia, began to shift to the former view, that Russia ought to follow the path of capitalist evolution that was so marked in Western Europe. The practical task of cutting this Gordian knot would fall to Count Witte, who would do so, perhaps with greater impetuosity than consistency.

It is difficult to imagine a person more suited for the resolution of so complex a problem under such transitional circumstances as then obtained in Russia. Of course, it would have been better if such a task had been given to a man coming from our developing industry, a man with a knowledge of commerce, but in those days the thought of such an appointment would have been considered blasphemous, at a time when our bureaucracy, whose roots were so intertwined with those of the nobility, took little pleasure in the transition to capitalism: to permit some sort of commoner into the holy of holies was unthinkable.

Count Witte not only belonged to the nobility but was always boasting of his noble origins. At the same time, his amazingly clear and practical mind alienated him from what he referred to in his memoirs as the passive, decadent, ruined nobility. His was of a different mentality: his railroad service, his provincialism, his varied and extensive circle of acquaintances, a circle that he was constantly enlarging, all permitted him to look at things from the viewpoint of a commoner, thus creating the possibility of communication between the two worlds.

In short, Count Witte seemed to qualify as an "insider" on the bureaucratic Mount Olympus, one who spoke their language, yet at the same time to have all the qualities required for leading Russia in a new direction, one required by the times. By the way, it is interesting to note that Count Witte was appointed minister of finance in 1892, a year after a very bad harvest, which so tragically underscored Russia's urgent need to develop her economy.

In his memoirs Count Witte tells of the difficulties he encountered in his efforts to establish the gold standard, which was clearly not in the interests of the provincial nobility: those who exported grain considered it to their advantage to continue to see the value of the ruble fluctuate in foreign markets. Count Witte protected himself from such people by helping some get "loans" and by the activities of the Nobles' Land Bank, but, even so, had to make [larger] compromises about which he later expressed regret in his memoirs.

But, far more important, the transition to capitalism required extension of the basic political changes begun during the reign of Alexander II, namely, the strengthening of the rule of law, the extension of education, as well as broad social reforms, all of which were met with hostility. For example, there was opposition to the establishment of the factory inspectorate, and after it was established, there were those who considered its activities to be subversive. In his memoirs Count Witte noted that the factory inspectorate "had always been regarded with suspicion because it allegedly favored the interests of the workers against those of the capitalists" and "it was only with great difficulty that I was able to get a workmen's compensation law approved by the State Council, a law that was less liberal in its provisions than those in comparable laws abroad." But Count Witte had to follow such a course, which earned him the reputation of being a dangerous liberal and, what is more, raised suspicions about him in the ruling circles. In his interesting memoirs, D. N. Shipov relates that when Prince Sviatopolk-Mirskii suggested to the Emperor that he summon a conference to consider the state of the country, the Emperor said he would not invite Witte to attend because he was a Freemason. In 1906, Baron Freedericksz, in the name of the Emperor, suggested to Count Witte that he not return to Russia because his presence there might cause unrest. It was in this that Count Witte perceived the tragedy of his career.

Probably the most important theme in his memoirs is his loyalty to the principle of autocracy, how untiring were his efforts to protect monarchical prerogatives. And there can be no question that all of Count Witte's actions bear proof that by both inclination and habit he was a deeply committed supporter of autocracy. Suffice it to note that his major reform, the establishment of the gold standard, was enacted without the participation of the State Council, in violation of established procedure. Yet, and this is typical of him, he charges P. A. Stolypin with being contemptuous of the Fundamental Laws. Although at heart he supported the principle of autocracy, he was compelled to be a liberal *malgré lui* because that was his lot in building the political structure of Russia. Yet he had not the slightest doubt that the solidity of such a structure could be ensured without political guarantees as long as he had the leading role in government.

When I became acquainted with Count Witte in 1903, I was able to talk with him, a representative of the government, about a constitution. That I could do so was a sign of the times, but my remarks produced nothing but bewilderment that was reflected in his contemptuous remark that such a conversation with him was pointless. It was in keeping with this attitude that in December 1904, at the last moment, he was able to have excluded from the proposed decree the point providing, for the first time, for the summoning of elected representatives. This we know from his memoirs, as well as from those of D. N. Shipov. Prince Sviatopolk-Mirskii, who had initiated the proposal for the decree, reacted to the exclusion of this point by asking to be relieved of his duties, and it fell to Count Witte to implement what was left of the decree. At this point he was firmly convinced that he would be able to implement the proposed reform program. (He said: "I will do it so effectively that it can't be rescinded.") Nonetheless, as he states in his memoirs, his confidence was misplaced, and the decree of December 12 came to nought.

Yet, when the so-called Bulygin conference concerning the convocation of elected representatives began, he relates that he was silent. Subsequently, with the issuance of the October Manifesto, which should have been ceremoniously hailed as a transition to a constitutional regime, he once more adopted an ambivalent position. In his memoirs, personal statements, and otherwise he tried to show that, in any case, he had not been in favor of issuing the manifesto. Even more telling was the fact that his effort to bring public men into his cabinet failed because he wanted as his minister of interior P. N. Durnovo, a notable representative of the old order, who had been the subject of Alexander III's famous command: "Get rid of this scoundrel in twenty-four hours." Yet Count Witte considered the inclusion of Durnovo more important than gaining the cooperation of the public men. Several months later, just before the opening of the Duma, Count Witte gave as his reason for asking to be relieved of his duties that he could not accept the burden of assuming responsibility for Durnovo's actions before the Duma. It was as if some historical Nemesis were taking revenge on him.

It should be noted that just before leaving office, during the discussion of the Fundamental Laws, Count Witte, as he tells us, considered his chief task to be the protection of the prerogatives of the monarch and the limitation of the rights of the representatives of the people. This points up an historical irony: here was a man who, as he clearly put it, believed that the revolution had been the fault of "the police-nobility regime" yet acted at the crucial moment to protect that regime. Ironical, too, is the fact that the ruling circles had been fearful of entrusting the office of premier to a man they considered a Freemason, a man from whom they had parted with relief not so long ago, and now they believed that by taking such a bold step they were making a major concession to the forces of society. Yet these forces of society, having refused to support him, at the same time proved insufficiently inspiring to induce him to break with the past and openly take the constitutional route.

By the way, Count Witte himself acknowledged in his memoirs that there were two opposing souls in him, one believing in unlimited monarchy, the other, influenced by what he had seen and experienced, being convinced that limitations had to be imposed on the monarch. Count Witte argued that the only trouble with unlimited monarchy came when the throne was occupied by an unsuitable monarch, that if Alexander III could have been brought back to life all might have been well. Such an argument suggests that Count Witte believed that even under an unsuitable monarch, unlimited monarchy could show its good side if that monarch had a suitable adviser at his side. It was therefore natural that when Count Witte was in power or was seeking to gain power he should be deeply affected by such feelings and by the traditions to which he adhered. It would hardly be fair, however, to reprove him for this striking lack of historical perspective, a failing he shared with other major figures who, like him, held a mistaken belief in the importance of the individual.

All this explains what was for Count Witte a happy circumstance, that until the end of his days he remained deeply convinced in the absolute correctness of all he had done. In the course of these memoirs, which deal with such turbulent and varied governmental activities, there is not one instance in which Witte admits a mistake on his part, instead constantly placing the blame on others for mistakes.

Because his chief concern in these memoirs is to defend his record, he slights the financial and economic reforms which have earned him a place in history. Thus, in speaking of the establishment of the gold standard he dwells primarily on superficial matters, without giving the slightest attention to the extreme excitement which this reform aroused in society, as shown by the heated debates that took place in the Free Economic Society, debates that attracted large crowds and aroused widespread interest. Also, he deals only slightly with the reform of the government budget, about which so much was written in the press. Moreover, he casts very little light on the Russo-German commercial treaty. It seems that on such matters, which were clear and evident, he did not feel that he could spread his wings.

Yet, in writing about fields outside his competence, for example, foreign affairs, he goes into great detail. Thus, he shows great enthusiasm and interest in recounting his talks with Li Hung-chang, which led to a favorable treaty with China, about his talks with Marquis Ito, about his efforts to prevent the taking of reckless steps in the Far East, efforts that ended in his removal from the post of minister of finance. He gives special attention to the Treaty of Portsmouth, which we owe to his brilliant gifts. Most of all he devotes the power of his passion, his indignation, and his distinct and unwieldy dialectic to the failure of October 17, 1905. Torn between attraction toward the police-nobility regime and recognition of the need for a regime based on the rule of law, Count Witte divides the blame for that failure between the police-nobility regime and the Constitutional Democratic (Kadet) party.

It is therefore obvious that one will not find in Count Witte's memoirs an objective account of those major events of Russian history in which he was a central figure. But it is not difficult to fill in what is missing in these memoirs by comparing them with the memoirs of other writers. Yet, even without such recourse, one will find these memoirs of real historical value because their very subjectivity enhances our ability to evaluate the higher circles.

These memoirs take us almost up to the World War which led to our revolution, an event about which the last word has not yet been spoken. It is therefore obvious that these memoirs contain a wealth of material necessary for an understanding of the catastrophic course of events, for answers to many alarming and painful questions produced by contemporary life. . . .

A. L. Sidorov's Introduction

Excerpts

Count S. Iu. Witte, the most eminent statesman of tsarist Russia during the latter part of the nineteenth century and the early part of the twentieth, did much for the development of capitalism in Russia. His great abilities were displayed during his tenure as minister of finance, chairman of the Committee of Ministers, and chairman of the Council of Ministers, as well as in the diplomatic field.

He has been compared to Speranskii and Kankrin, but he lived in a more complex time than they did and, what is more, was a better-rounded man than they. Witte served in a period of transition from the capitalist to the imperialist stage of history, a period of the flowering of revolution, during the stormy days of the first Russian revolution of 1905–1907. Although a convinced monarchist, he recognized that the nobility alone could not continue to rule the country and understood the need of making concessions to the bourgeoisie, whose representatives he sought to bring into the government.

Witte's memoirs provide us with a broad historical canvas, at the center of which stands the author. His perception of events, his relationship to the major political events of the period and to individuals, most of them close to the throne, are of great value for understanding the evolution of tsarism and of the class that held power then.

On the whole, Witte adheres to the principle of historicism in his exposition of events. But in some chapters, especially in his characterization of certain personages, he allows himself to digress: sometimes he follows the fate of his heroes for entire decades. When not adhering to a strict chronological order he sometimes repeats himself. . . . And matters of incidental interest often cause him to digress from the basic themes of his account. . . . He was a bit careless and sometimes hasty in his use of words. Although, as Witte himself admitted, what he wrote was "a rough draft," "notes of recollection," his memoirs retain the freshness and

xxxii   A. L. SIDOROV'S INTRODUCTION

originality associated with the author. Sometimes a sharp phrase written by the way, for example, "Plehve is a scoundrel and Sipiagin a fool," hits the nail on the head. He soberly characterizes those around him. He provides a restrained, but sometimes outrightly critical, view of grand dukes and high court officials, with, in some cases, sarcastic characterizations of their religious mysticism and sancti- moniousness, their emptiness and their general limitations. Such observations show the author to be a man of considerable and independent intellect and demonstrate his well-known independence of judgment, all this lending a special interest to the memoirs.

Witte's accurate and original characterizations of his associates are clearly of historical interest because they present an entire portrait gallery of representative members of the ruling classes in positions of power. Also, the memoirs contain interesting characterizations of Emperors Alexander III and Nicholas II. Al- though the devoted Witte idealizes and ennobles Alexander III, under whom he enjoyed such a dazzling rise in position and by whose favor he became so power- ful, he does not spare Nicholas II, the instrument of his unexpected departure from office in 1903. This wise courtier, who did not forget the shame inflicted on him, reveals the web of behind-the-scene influences on Nicholas II, describing his intellectual limitations, his lack of will, and his unsuitability for governing. Such revelations may explain why Witte, fearing that there would be a search for and seizure of his memoirs, kept them abroad.

During the years that have passed since the memoirs were first published, Soviet historical science has achieved much in the study of modern Russian history. Now we have in print thousands of hitherto unknown documents which provide detailed insight into the economic development of the country, its foreign policy at the end of the nineteenth century, and the events of the first Russian revolution. Using these documents as well as the published work of Soviet histori- ans, it is possible to determine exactly how closely the author of these memoirs adheres to the truth.

One of the features of the memoirs which had previously been considered a minus, the result of the author's bureaucratic limitations, was Witte's inclusion in his work of the record of as many persons as possible and his review of their careers in the bureaucracy. Nowadays, from our point of view, this feature seems a plus, because it permits the reader to see that the selection of officials under tsarism was not as random and haphazard as might appear but was, in fact, determined by the class interests of the aristocratic nobility. Witte himself affirms that certain indi- viduals were not suitable for government service yet were appointed to positions of responsibility. This large gallery of individuals depicted by Witte shows what an obstacle autocracy was in the path of historical progress and the degree to which the nobility provided the base upon which tsarism rested and how slowly that base changed. To the contemporary Soviet reader it may seem strange that such an archaic situation could have existed as late as a half-century ago.

Witte provides us with a picture of postreform capitalist Russia. His interests and point of view put him closer to the capitalist class and to those strata of the nobility who were on the road to capitalism than to the upper nobility, by whose interests the life of the country was determined. By the way, Witte was driven out of political life precisely because of the power of that stratum. All of this explains the contradictions within Witte, why he had to be opportunistic: he had to be because of his recognition of the need to reconcile the interests of landowners and bourgeoisie. This explains why his program of innovation was limited by his effort to reconcile his desire for bourgeois reconstruction of Russia and the acceleration of capitalist development with his recognition of the fact that the state expressed the interests of the nobility. Thus, Witte gave expression to and defended that degree of capitalist progress that was feasible as long as the masses were docile. Witte believed that the preservation of the power and the grandeur of the autocratic state required that capitalism grow, that industry be strengthened, that railroads be constructed, that the landlord economy take on a capitalist character. Only under such circumstances would it be possible to preserve the political and economic independence of the state and the might of the army.

S. Iu. Witte was of noble origin and reflected the interests of the nobility as a whole, a body favorable to capitalist development of the country, rather than the interests of the privileged semi–serf-owning [upper] nobility. Such a "broad" understanding of the interests of the nobility inexorably implied governmental stimulation of bourgeois development, protectionism, stimulation of native industry, development of commercial banking, and the strengthening of capitalism in the noble and peasant economy.

In his memoirs Witte portrays capitalist-nobility Russia as it experienced the revolution of 1905–1907. Naturally, he draws this picture from the point of view of his own class, the interests of which he represents. The picture is a distorted one, as if drawn from what one sees in a concave mirror. Here Witte was incapable of being objective, but he could not ignore reality completely, whether in dealing with the general facts of Russian economic development or with the growth of the revolutionary movement.

Witte's limitations as a statesman came into prominence when he sought to characterize the revolutionary movement after having come into conflict with the revolutionary masses. Although he believed that the government should make concessions to the capitalists and to those landowners who were becoming bourgeois, he favored the unstinted use of force against the revolutionary masses. And he believed that the revolutionary uproar was the result of the personal inadequacies of Nicholas II.

The limitations and poverty of such a bourgeois-liberal philosophy can be traced directly to Witte's social origins. A landless noble, a man who had been through a long school of capitalist business operations, a railroad man, then a minister with ties to the banking world, he tried to introduce bourgeois methods into the administration of the government of Russia. He favored encouraging the capitalist development of the countryside, opposed the exclusive claims and privileges of the upper nobility, although he continued to encourage that stratum at the expense of the treasury. With respect to the relationship between nobility and

bourgeoisie, he favored the latter, but understood full well that it was impossible
to conduct a governmental policy that went against the nobility. This is the source
of Witte's political opportunism, his shifting from one side to another that is so
evident in his memoirs.

The Russian bourgeoisie, being as closely linked to tsarism as it was, was
incapable of putting forth any kind of revolutionary program. Even less radical
was the social program of Witte himself. He favored bourgeois development of
Russia only to the degree that it could be achieved by means of reform under the
aegis of tsarism, reform to which the nobility agreed. Beyond these limits he would
not go. In this connection it is quite impossible to agree with P. Struve's view (as
expressed in *Russkaia mysl*, March 1915) that Witte understood the inevitability of
"the great reform" of October 17, 1905, but was unable to implement it because
of personal shortcomings, which prevented him from understanding the situation
and led him into confusion and apathy. The unavoidability of enactment of reform
derived from the temporary balance of forces, not from complete victory of the
revolution. The impact of revolution forced tsarism into concessions, the limits of
which were determined by the class interests of the nobility. . . .

The memoirs of Witte, this major figure, whose great intelligence and ability
were completely devoted to the service of a regime on its way off the historical
stage . . . clearly demonstrate why Russia then had to be economically and
politically backward. The efforts of Witte to revitalize the failing body of the
Russian Empire were useless. These efforts did not and could not have produced
significant results primarily because they did not alter the economic condition of
the country's basic classes—the workers and the peasants, who represented the
major remnants of feudalism in the empire. Under such circumstances, even
given the progressive thoughts and efforts of Witte in connection with the growth
of capitalism in industry and in railroad construction, growth was aided by the
government only to the degree that it conformed to the interests of the nobility.

In these memoirs we do not find objective information about the growth of the
working class or the development of the labor and peasant movements. The facts
about these movements are presented under the rubric of "rebellion" rather than
that of "revolution." A loyal servant of the landowners and capitalists, Witte
could not perceive matters otherwise. Nonetheless, his memoirs are instructive, of
great importance, rich in facts, an historical document. Before the reader's eyes
passes the life of a human being and there is presented a panorama of historical
events written in a fascinating and keen manner. Unquestionably, it will be read
with great interest and profit. . . .

VOLUME I

1849–1903

I

My Family

Parentage

I was born in Tiflis in 1849 and am now sixty-two.[1] My father, Julius Fedorovich Witte, a member of the nobility (the *dvorianstvo*)[2] of Pskov province, was born a Lutheran, in the Baltic provinces. His ancestors were Dutch who had settled in the Baltic provinces when they still belonged to Sweden.[3] After graduating from the University of Dorpat,[4] he studied agriculture and mining in Prussia. It was as an agricultural expert that he went to Saratov, where he fell in love with my mother, Catherine Andreevna Fadeeva. She was one of four children of the governor of Saratov province, Andrei Mikhailovich Fadeev, and Princess Helen Pavlovna Fadeeva, née Dolgorukaia, the last of the senior branch of the Dolgorukii princes; she was descended from Gregory Dolgorukii, a senator during the reign of Peter I, the brother of the famous Jacob Fedorovich Dolgorukii.

My grandparents were married when they were very young. Where, I do not know, but I know that my grandmother's relatives belonged to the nobility of Penza province. When they married, my grandmother's father, Paul Vasilevich Dolgorukii, blessed them with an ancient cross that, according to family tradition, had belonged to Michael of Chernigov. It is said that Michael died a martyr's death (for which he was canonized) for refusing to bow before the idols carried by a Tatar khan who was marching on Moscow. It is further said that, as he went to his death, he entrusted a cross to some boyars with instructions that it be given to his children; this cross, according to tradition, was handed down from father to son in the senior Dolgorukii line.*

---

*My grandmother left the cross to her son, General Fadeev, a bachelor, who left it to my mother. When she died, it went to my aunt Nadezhda, who entrusted it to me two years ago, when I was in Odessa, because she was very old. The cross is now in my home. I have shown it to two experts, Academician Kondakov and Kobeko, director of the Public Library. They agree that the cross is very old and that it has holy power, but they are unable to affirm or deny that this was the cross that Michael of Chernigov had with him when he died.

Grandfather Fadeev was under his wife's moral domination, so that, in fact, she was the head of the family.

For her time she was an exceptionally well-educated woman. She was a great nature lover and put together a large collection of Caucasian flora, which her heirs were to give to Novorossiisk University. It was she who taught my brothers and me to read and write and who instilled in us the fundamentals of the Orthodox faith. She was already paralyzed by the time I was a boy, and I always remember her as being seated.

The eldest of their four children, Helen, was fairly well known in the Belinsky era as a writer, under the pseudonym of "Zinaida R." My mother was the second of the four. The third, Nadezhda, is about eighty-three, and lives in Odessa with my surviving sister. The fourth was the eminent writer on military themes, General Rostislav Fadeev.

My grandparents were ardent members of the Orthodox faith (genuinely Orthodox and not Orthodox in the Black Hundreds sense of the word) and would not hear of their daughter marrying out of the faith. So my father was converted to Orthodoxy, either before marrying or shortly thereafter. Because my father became an integral part of the Fadeev family and did not retain close ties with the Witte family, and because he enjoyed several decades of marital bliss with my mother, he became completely Orthodox in spirit.

When grandfather accepted a post in the Chief Administration of the Caucasian Viceroyalty[5] and moved to Tiflis [in 1846], my parents joined the Fadeevs in their move. In time father was to become the director of the Department of State Domains. This was at a time when few were eager to take civilian posts, even very high ones, in the Caucasus, because it was an isolated region, ablaze with uprising, where the mountain passes were still held by hostile tribes, a region marked by frequent conflicts with the Turks. However, military men and others who liked to be where there was fighting were attracted to the Caucasus. Perhaps my grandparents were eager to go there for that reason.

The Wittes and the Fadeevs shared the same household, which was one of the largest and most hospitable in Tiflis. It was located on a side street, the name of which I do not recall, that ran from Golovinskii Prospekt to Mount Davidovskaia. Grandfather lived on a lordly scale. Even though I was very young then, I can clearly recall that just the household serfs (most of them Dolgorukii serfs) numbered eighty-four.

The Witte Children

I was one of five children, three boys and two girls. The oldest was Alexander [b. 1844].[6] He studied at the Moscow Cadet Corps and spent almost all of his career with the Nizhegorodskii Dragoons, who still sing songs about the brave Major Witte, whose eyes radiated kindness.

Alexander was rather stout and awkward, of average height, average intelligence, average education. But he possessed a remarkably fine soul. He was a very sympathetic, good-natured person. All of his brother officers—even those with whom he occasionally quarreled—loved him.

Sometime before the Turkish War [1877–78] Alexander killed Westmann, an officer in the Severskii Regiment, in a duel. (Westmann's father served as assistant minister of foreign affairs under Gorchakov.) At the time of the duel both Alexander's and Westmann's regiments were stationed in Piatogorsk, a popular spa. The duel arose over a young lady whose family was visiting Piatogorsk and with which Alexander was on close terms. Westmann was in love with the young lady, and although he was handsome and Alexander was not, he saw him as a rival.

According to Alexander, the incident that led to the duel took place during a ball at the officers' club, of which he was chairman. He had been sitting at a table with the young lady, when he was called away on business. On his return he found Westmann sitting in his chair, but now there was an additional chair beside the young woman, which she had evidently ordered to be placed there for him to sit in when he returned. After Alexander sat down, Westmann asked if he had done so to overhear their conversation. Alexander replied that he didn't think there was anything to overhear and that, in any case, he was quite ready to leave. Westmann then called him a scoundrel.

The next day Alexander sent two of his fellow officers to inform Westmann that he, Alexander, knowing that Westmann had been drunk when he had insulted him, would take no further action if he apologized to him before the officers. Westmann refused, saying that he had intended his remark to produce the usual result. Alexander thereupon issued a challenge to a duel, which was accepted.

The two agreed that the duel would continue until one of them was killed or so severely wounded that he could not hold his pistol. The first signal to fire was given when they were eighty paces apart. Alexander told me (and this was later confirmed at his trial) that at the first signal he fired into the air, but that Westmann's shot just missed his ear. When my brother sent his seconds to see if Westmann was ready to apologize, Westmann refused. Each then advanced ten paces and fired on signal: again Alexander fired into the air; Westmann's shot grazed his other ear. By this time my brother was very angry, but once more he sent his seconds to ask Westmann to apologize. Again a refusal. They advanced once more and fired on signal. Westmann's shot was close; Alexander's was fatal.

My brother was then tried and sentenced to six months' imprisonment, but, as I recall, he had served no more than two months when war with Turkey broke out and he was released on the order of the Grand Duke Michael Nikolaevich, viceroy of the Caucasus, so that he could join his regiment in combat.

Alexander distinguished himself during the war, in which he first commanded a squadron, then a battalion. Best known among his exploits was one that took place near Kars. General Loris-Melikov, the corps commander, sent him on a reconnaissance mission, with two Cossack companies under him. Using a map provided by the General Staff, they were to proceed toward Kars by one route and return by another. En route they suddenly encountered several Turkish battalions. Since Alexander's orders were to proceed on that route, he ordered his men to attack. They broke through, with few casualties, and galloped on till they came to a deep ravine not shown on their map. There was no way to go around the ravine. Faced with a choice of riding into it, which would have meant certain death, or turning around and attacking the Turks, who had just arrived with reinforcements, he ordered his men to attack. Again they were successful, but this time at the cost of heavy casualties. Throughout the engagement Alexander held on to his unit's flag.

According to regulations Alexander should have received the St. George[7] for his courage under fire, but if he had it would have come out that the officers of the General Staff had prepared a faulty map and it would have been necessary to try them. So Grand Duke Michael Nikolaevich, who liked my brother, summoned him and told him they would have to ''pretend that the whole episode had never occurred.'' However, amends were made after the war, when the facts could be revealed. At the first St. George celebration after the war, which my brother attended with other officers from the Caucasus, Emperor Alexander II (who had been told of the facts by the Grand Duke) took off his own small St. George decoration and gave it to my brother, saying that he had long ago earned it.

Despite the constant dangers to which he had been exposed, Alexander had gone unscathed until the very end of the war, when he suffered a concussion from a Turkish bomb and was presumed to be dead when he was taken to a hospital. In fact the Grand Duke sent a telegram of condolence to my mother. But Alexander regained consciousness in the hospital and was able to leave it soon. Unfortunately, the concussion left him unable to open his eyes in daylight, and he had to sit with his eyes shut during the daylight hours. I consulted the finest doctors about his condition and was warned that he could die of a stroke at any time.

Because of his disability he was given no more than the command of a reserve cavalry cadre stationed in Rostov. One sad day I received a telegram from Dr. Pisarenko, the unit's doctor, informing me that my brother had died in his sleep, of a stroke.

I loved Alexander more than I did any other member of my family.

We often talked about fighting. Alexander told me not to believe those who said they did not experience fear before going into battle: everyone was afraid, at least until the fighting started. That, he said, was his experience. Before the battle he would be anxious, but once the fighting began he would slash away at the enemy with less feeling than if they were sheep. General Skobelev, whom I knew, had much the same experience: he was always frightened before the battle, but once he took his place before his men and the shooting began, his fears would vanish.

I experienced similar feelings during the six months that I was premier when I was in constant danger. I would be warned to remain at home for a few days or not to go to this place or that, but I ignored the warnings and when I was advised to avail myself of a guard I would not. Yet I must admit that many a night I went to bed frightened and shaking, thinking of the next morning when I would have to go downstairs, get into my carriage, and go somewhere where there would be a crowd. But as soon as I would take my seat in the carriage and it would begin to roll my fears would vanish and I would feel as calm as I do now, dictating these lines. It was at such times that I truly understood the feelings about which my brother had spoken.

My other brother, Boris [my elder by a year], did not distinguish himself. He graduated from the faculty of jurisprudence of Novorossiisk University and was chairman of the Odessa Superior Court at the time of his death.

My two sisters, Olga and Sophia, were younger than I. They were very close and lived most of their years together, in Odessa. Sophia, the younger sister, who contracted tuberculosis, is alive but is very ill. Olga, who nursed her, contracted the disease and died of it, two years ago. Those of the Fadeev family who are still alive are I, Sophia, and my aged aunt Nadezhda, who lives with Sophia.

I was my grandfather's favorite and Alexander my grandmother's. The family treated me kindly but, on the whole, with indifference. Boris was my parents' favorite and was more spoiled than the rest of us. Olga, too, was favored by my parents, being their first daughter after three sons. Sophia, although treated affectionately by everyone, was not spoiled.

I clearly remember a few events from my early childhood. I remember that when I was a few months old and there was an epidemic in Tiflis, my father took me in his arms and mounted his horse, on which we rode to a place outside the city. My mother and my sisters would laugh at me when I spoke of this recollection, saying that I could not possibly have remembered this incident, but my old wet nurse, whom I saw only a week ago (she lives with my sister in Odessa, where I go on holidays), thinks that I am not imagining it.

I recall another episode from my very early years. I was in a room with my nanny when first my mother, then my grandfather, my grandmother, and my aunt came into the room sobbing over the news of the death of Emperor Nicholas Pavlovich. This made a strong impression on me; one can sob like this only when one has lost someone very close. My family was always extremely monarchist, and this trait is part of my inheritance.

The Zhelikhovskiis

My mother's oldest sister, Helen, who married Colonel Peter Hahn, died at an early age leaving a son and two daughters, Helen and Vera. The son was a nonentity; he was a justice of the peace in Stavropol at the time of his death. Helen and Vera were taken into my grandfather's home after their mother's death. Shortly thereafter Helen married Blavatskii, the lieutenant-governor of Erivan, and Vera married Iakhontov, a landowner in the province of Pskov.

After Vera's husband died, she returned to the Fadeev household in Tiflis. There she fell in love with Zhelikhovskii, a local *gimnaziia* teacher. The Fadeevs, who were not devoid of a kind of boyar arrogance, naturally would not hear of her marrying the man. So she fled home, married him, and never again set foot in the Fadeev household. It was only after the death of my grandparents that my parents began to receive the Zhelikhovskiis.

Vera wrote books for young people. To this day mothers talk to me about her books and express regret that she is gone and that books suitable for young people are no longer written. I must confess that I have never read any of her books.

She is survived by two sons and three daughters. One son is a colonel in a dragoon regiment. The eldest daughter married an American journalist named Johnson; when I was in the United States they called on me.

The other daughters live in Odessa; one of them married a seventy-year-old corps commander a few weeks ago. They are the kind of women my sisters would not receive, nor would I. My sister Sophia calls them disgraceful types. Even though I am not especially censorious about morals I consider them contemptible: they may in fact be Okhrana [political police] agents, and they were on very good terms with Tolmachev, the prefect of Odessa.

Blavatskaia

Now I want to dwell on the personality of Vera's sister and my cousin, Helen Petrovna Blavatskaia [Madame Blavatsky], who for a time made quite a stir as a Theosophist and writer.[8]

I have no recollection of her in the years just following her marriage [1848], but from stories I later heard at home I know that she soon abandoned her husband and returned to the Fadeev household. No sooner had she appeared there than Grandfather Fadeev sent her packing to her father, who then held a military command somewhere near Petersburg. Since there were no railroads then in the Caucasus, he sent her in a hired coach-and-four, accompanied by a steward chosen for his reliability and three other servants. They were to go by coach to Poti and from there to a southern Russian port, and from there proceed to her father's residence.

When they arrived in Poti they put up in a hotel. Somehow Blavatskaia managed to find a cooperative English steamship captain who took her in the hold of his ship to Constantinople. There she joined a circus as an equestrienne. While in Constantinople she fell in love with the famous basso Metrovich and soon forsook the circus to go off with him to Europe, where he had accepted an engagement.

Soon grandfather began to receive letters from his "grandson" Metrovich, who assured him that he was married to his granddaughter, although she had not been given a divorce by Blavatskii. Time passed and, lo and behold, a letter came from a new "grandson," some sort of an Englishman, who wrote that he was married to Helen and that they were engaged in some kind of commercial operation in America.

Subsequently she returned to Europe and became a close follower of the well-known spiritualist Home, an adroit and talented trickster, from whom she learned many of the techniques she was to use later. Then the Fadeevs learned from newspaper accounts that she was giving pianoforte concerts in London and Paris. Later she became conductor of a choir organized by Prince Milan of Serbia.

All in all, she spent ten years in these travels. [In 1858], she asked permission from grandfather to return to Tiflis, vowing that she would behave properly, even return to her lawful husband, Blavatskii. Although I was a boy then, I remember her appearance when she returned to Tiflis. It was obvious that she had once been pretty and her face was still extraordinarily expressive, but it bore the marks of a tempestuous life and she was already showing signs of aging. Also, she had become quite stout and frowzy.

Although she was no longer attractive, she captivated many in Tiflis society with the seances she conducted in our home. The cream of local society, including several of the viceroy's dashing adjutants—Count Vorontsov-Dashkov, the two Counts Orlov-Davydov, and Perfilev—would take part, sometimes deep into the night, in table turning, table rapping, and spirit writing. It seemed to me that my mother, my aunt, and my uncle were fascinated by all this and, to a degree, believed in it. But all these goings-on were kept more or less secret from my grandfather and grandmother, who like my father were unsympathetic to such things.

Although I was a mere boy then, I was already quite critical of Blavatskaia's performances, sensing a degree of charlatanism in them. But she carried them out quite skillfully. I recall being present once when, at the request of one of the guests, a pianoforte in an empty room, its keyboard covered, began to play. Nowadays, public opinion in Europe, including Russia, considers such exploits the work of charlatans. Unfortunately, another kind of spiritualism has recently begun to flourish in Russia, a pathological belief that the dead can manifest themselves in various forms and through various signs; this kind of spiritualism has even had some unfortunate consequences for our political life.

During this period of her life Blavatskaia resumed living with her lawful husband, in Tiflis, but not for long. One day, on the street, she unexpectedly met Metrovich, now nearly sixty, who had accepted an engagement at the Tiflis Italian opera. The attitude of this toothless lion toward her was remarkable: although she was by now elderly, stout, and slovenly, he still worshiped her. Also, he considered her his lawful wife, and after he had created a scene on the street, she returned to him and they both made a hasty departure from the city.

They then took up residence in Kiev, where Metrovich, who did not know Russian, was engaged by the local opera to perform in such Russian operas as *A Life for the Tsar* and *Rusalka*. Being talented, and profiting from Blavatskaia's direction, he learned his roles easily and, despite his age and despite some deterioration in his voice, he gave good performances.

Their stay in Kiev was a brief one because of a quarrel between Blavatskaia and Governor-General Prince Dondukov-Korsakov, with whom she was acquainted from the days when he had commanded the Nizhegorodskii Dragoons. I do not know what the quarrel was about, but I know that she wrote some verses that were very objectionable to the governor-general, which we found pasted on street corner walls. As a result she and Metrovich had to leave the city.

Next the two appeared in Odessa, where our family was then living. To earn her bread she opened an ink store and factory. After that failed, she opened an artificial flower shop. Naturally she visited my mother often, and I called on her at the store several times.

By this time I was mature enough to look at Blavatskaia with a critical eye and to form an objective conception of this remarkable and, to a degree, demoniacal person. As I became better acquainted with her I was struck by the extraordinary facility with which she learned. Never having studied music, she taught herself to play the pianoforte and gave concerts, in Paris and London. Without having studied musical theory she became conductor of the choir of Prince Milan of Serbia. Although she never seriously studied foreign languages, she was able to speak French, German, and other European languages as well as she could speak Russian. And although she never seriously studied Russian grammar or literature, I have seen her write lengthy letters in verse more rapidly than I could write them in prose, and she could fill whole pages with frivolous verse that flowed like music. With great facility she wrote articles on the most serious subjects without having a basic knowledge of the subject about which she was writing.

She could look you straight in the eye and tell you the most fantastic things, lies if you will, with the conviction of a person who has never told anything but the truth. Therefore, I can't help but wonder if there had not been something demonic in her, or, to put it bluntly, witchlike, although in essence she was a good, gentle person.

Never in my life have I seen such large, blue eyes as hers; they sparkled wondrously when she began to tell a tale, particularly if it were fantasy. So it was no surprise to me that she exercised considerable influence over those who were inclined toward crude mysticism, toward the extraordinary; that is, over those who find life on this earth a burden and who, in seeking the meaning of life beyond the grave and being unable to find a true understanding of it, are taken in by a false image of that after-life.

One would think that a man like the publisher Katkov, clever as he was, with a realistic appreciation of the facts of life, would have been able to see through her, had he met her. But he had not, and he was carried away by her bewitching collection of stories *In the Jungles of Hindustan*, which he published in his *Russkii vestnik*: he considered her an exceptional person and was quite amazed when I told him that, although she possessed some supernatural talent, one could not take her seriously. Even now, decades after these stories appeared, I still occasionally hear the most enthusiastic praise of them.

It goes without saying that the flower shop went bankrupt. She and Metrovich then left for Cairo, where he had an engagement in the Italian opera. As they neared Cairo their ship sank. With the help of other passengers Metrovich saved her, but drowned in the effort. She arrived in Cairo with nothing but a soaked blouse and skirt, without a penny to her name.

How she managed to leave Cairo I don't know; but I know that soon she was in England, where she established a new Theosophical society. In order to provide the society with a firm [dogmatic] basis she went to India to study her secrets. By the way, it was her stay in India that provided her with the theme for *In the Jungles of Hindustan*, which she obviously wrote to make money. By the time she returned from India she had already attracted followers for her teachings. She then settled down in Paris, as the leader of all Theosophists, but she did not have long to live. [She died in 1891.]

Even after her death Theosophical belief continued to flourish in many parts of the world. Even today Theosophical societies are to be found in many places. And, not long ago, a Theosophical journal was established in Petersburg.

When all is said and done Blavatskaia serves as proof, if proof is required, that man is not an animal created out of matter. There can be no question that she possessed a soul that was independent of matter. The only question is what kind of a soul? If one accepts the view that life hereafter is divided among heaven, hell, and purgatory, then the question arises: from which of these did this soul, which inhabited Blavatskaia during her earthly sojourn, come?

II

General Fadeev and His Times

Rostislav Andreevich Fadeev

Because Uncle Fadeev was an only son, it was natural that he should be the center of his father's love. He was sent to a cadet corps in Petersburg to prepare for an army career. But he did not remain there long, because he struck an instructor who, on seeing that his hair was unkempt, seized him by the hair and told him to go and comb it.[1]

Emperor Nicholas I was, of course, immediately informed of the incident and sentenced Fadeev to serve as a private in an artillery battery in Bender. By the standards of those days the punishment should have been more severe, but Uncle Fadeev was saved from worse punishment thanks to the intervention of a relative, Prince Dolgorukii, the chief of the military educational institutions, who enjoyed the Emperor's favor. While in Bender, Uncle Fadeev carried out his duties faithfully. After he had served his sentence he returned to Saratov, where his father was governor.

Being without employment he spent his time in Saratov in reading and in scholarly work, under his mother's guidance. As will be seen, he was to have considerable influence on my education and on my intellectual development, particularly after my graduation from university, when I was quite close to him and intellectually receptive.

I can say that never in my life have I met anyone better educated or more talented than Rostislav Andreevich Fadeev, a fact that should be evident to all educated persons in Russia, for he wrote many remarkable books on military questions as well as on domestic and foreign affairs. And he knew French so well that he wrote for the *Revue des deux mondes* and other French periodicals. With all his gifts and education he should have had a brilliant career, but he was hampered by his fantastic enthusiasms, which he permitted to run away with him. In this he resembled his niece Blavatskaia, but he was, of course, more honorable and better educated than she. In any case, the two serve as evidence that certain traits are hereditary.

Although he loved books, he could not endure remaining unemployed and living with his parents. Moreover, his somewhat eccentric behavior made him a source of embarrassment to his parents: sometimes he strolled stark naked through the streets of Saratov, in the early hours to be sure; sometimes he would fire his gun in public, fortunately without serious consequences.

So he volunteered to serve as a soldier in the Caucasus, which [as I have said] in those days attracted those who preferred to live where there was fighting. He soon earned a commission and took part in virtually all of the campaigns fought there during the viceroyalties of Prince Vorontsov [1844-1853], Muravev [1853-1856],* Prince Bariatinskii [1856-1862], and during the first years of the viceroyalty [1863-1881] of Grand Duke Michael Nikolaevich.

It was during Muravev's tenure, at the siege of Kars [1855], that my uncle, who had been an atheist, became a believer, under the influence of Skobelev, the father of the famous Skobelev and of Princess Beloselskaia-Belozerskaia, who now lives on Krestovskii Island. My uncle, by then a captain, told me that when the order to take Kars, by whatever means, was received, many officers followed the custom of the times by becoming very drunk on the night preceding the attack, but that Skobelev spent the night in solemn and reverent prayer, preparing himself for death. Skobelev, who was much older than my uncle and had taken a liking to him, so inspired my uncle by his example that from that time on he believed in God and in the after-life and was a fervent adherent of the Orthodox church (in which, of course, he was born).

All the rest of his life, Uncle Fadeev remained faithful to the holy Orthodox church, a highly educated and erudite adherent, steeped in religious history in general and in the history of our church in particular. It goes without saying that his support of the Orthodox church was not like that found these days in our highest circles, particularly the higher clergy; he would have been disturbed by the current tendency of the hierarchs to occupy themselves less with God than with Black Hundreds politics. He always admired that volume of Alexis Khomiakov's works that contains his articles on theological matters. This volume could not be sold in Russia, and I do not know whether or not its sale is now permitted. I read it when I was a young man and was more impressed by it than by any other theological work. (Alexis Khomiakov's son Nicholas, the former chairman of the State Duma, is a fine man, but a great chatterbox.)

---

*I was too young to remember Prince Vorontsov, but I know that he was respected in the Caucasus, primarily for his work in organizing civilian administration. I do remember Muravev, who was not well liked. I recall that he was very stout and cut a poor figure on horseback. In those days the viceregal palace had no bathing facilities. Muravev, attired like Fadeev in the streets of Saratov, would stroll to a nearby Russian bathhouse when he wanted to bathe.

In speaking about the assault on Kars, Uncle Fadeev told me about Prince Orbeliani, a close relative of the Princess Orbeliani who later became wife of Field Marshal Prince Bariatinskii. In the course of the assault, Orbeliani's horse was impaled by enemy bayonets, but the prince continued to brandish his saber to encourage his men to press on: his horse, said my uncle, looked as it if were mounted on a pedestal made of bayonets. To be sure, such an event was not remarkable in time of war; what was remarkable was that Orbeliani survived, with only a few bayonet wounds to show for it. I was to meet him later and was on friendly terms with his son Nicholas, with whom I attended university.

Fadeev played an important role under Prince Bariatinskii, who succeeded Muravev as viceroy of the Caucasus in 1856. [I shall have more to say about Prince Bariatinskii further on.] One of the new viceroy's first acts was to appoint Fadeev adjutant. I can testify that Fadeev was closer to Prince Bariatinskii than any other member of his suite.

My uncle took an important part in Bariatinskii's campaign against Shamil, who surrendered following the capture of Guniba [in 1859]. On the eve of the siege of Guniba, Fadeev argued heatedly for assault, in the face of the many who favored starving Shamil out, insisting that an assault might cost thousands of lives. Bariatinskii agreed with Fadeev.

Uncle played a very active role in the assault, being constantly at the disposal of Bariatinskii. When Shamil surrendered, he handed over, as an act of submission, the banner he always carried with him. (Lithographs of the scene are still preserved.) That evening Bariatinskii summoned Fadeev and gave him the banner, saying that the capture of Guniba had been largely due to his counsel. After Fadeev's death this banner was turned over to his sister Nadezhda; when we last met, she entrusted it to me and it now hangs in my library.

In those days Bariatinskii's closest advisers were his chief of staff, Dmitrii Miliutin,* later minister of war, and my uncle. The two were contrasting types. Fadeev was largely self-educated, something of an amateur, sparkling with talent, a man of passion, with more than his share of fantasy; he was more the fighting man who preferred the sound of guns to military routine, a great and lively writer who wrote like a human being, not like an academic automaton. Miliutin, in contrast, was a bit of a dry stick, a military academician, a man of broad but uninspired ideas, presented systematically; in short, his mind was orderly, disciplined, systematic, qualities that Bariatinskii lacked. It was easy to see why he could not get along with Fadeev. Subsequently they were to be at logger-

---

*I have known Count Miliutin since my boyhood days. I was on good terms with his son, whom he loved dearly. When my brother and I visited Miliutin, we would race about his study with his son. The son, a very fine, but quite ordinary individual, was to become governor of Kursk.

In those days I was very impressed with Miliutin, but later, because of the differences that arose between him and my uncle, a coolness developed between the Miliutin family and mine and for many decades I did not meet him at all. However, when I became minister of finance and spent autumn in Yalta [near Miliutin's home], I visited him and had many opportunities to speak with him about many matters.

heads over the long-term military program that Russia should follow.

Fadeev remained in the Caucasus after Bariatinskii left, but not for long, because he offended Grand Duchess Olga Fedorovna (née Princess of Baden), the wife of the succeeding viceroy, Grand Duke Michael Nikolaevich. On the eve of the ceremonial entry of the new viceroy and his wife into Tiflis, my uncle, who had a sharp tongue that he did not always keep in check, remarked that the Grand Duchess, being stingy, would be pleased by the fact that the viceregal carriages would be showered with flowers: she would have the flowers collected and fed to her horses, thus saving the cost of several days' feed. I did not see the point of the remark at the time, but I did learn that the remark reached her ears. She was thereafter very antipathetic to uncle, and that is one of the reasons he was to leave the Caucasus.

Later I understood the point of the remark when I learned her natural father was a [Jewish] banker (Baron Haber, if my memory is correct) living in Karlsruhe, and not the man listed as her father, the Grand Duke of Baden.[2] Thus, it appears that she had a considerable degree of Jewish blood in her and that is what uncle had in mind; and this explains why his remark made such an unpleasant impression on her that she was hostile toward Fadeev for the rest of his days. Later, when I became minister and made my acquaintance with Petersburg society, I heard rumors about her origins from the most trustworthy sources, relatives of the Grand Duke.

After leaving the Caucasus, Uncle Fadeev spent many years in the company of Prince Bariatinskii, who, as will be seen, was to remain abroad for some time. Fadeev took an active part as a writer in support of Prince Bariatinskii's views about military organization [about which I shall write somewhat later], thus coming into conflict with the Ministry of War and its head, Dmitrii Miliutin. He thereby deprived himself of the opportunity of continuing his military career in Russia. In fact, Emperor Alexander II was annoyed with my uncle; once on encountering my uncle in the park of Tsarskoe Selo and on being told who he was, he said: "What is all this that you are writing; when will you stop?" I have this story from my uncle.

Uncle Fadeev's retirement from the army was precipitated by his book *Vostochnyi vopros* (The Eastern Question), which exacerbated Austro–Russian relations. As a result, the chancellor, Prince Gorchakov, complained to the Emperor about Fadeev, and this led to his retirement.

My uncle was then invited by the khedive of Egypt to organize his army. In effect, uncle became minister of war, but without the title. As far as I know, this invitation was arranged by Count Ignatev, the ambassador to Constantinople.

Thus Fadeev came to spend some time in Egypt, but things did not turn out well because the khedive was soon forced to declare war on the Abyssinians— who follow the teachings of Christ, in a somewhat distorted form. Since it would have been against his conscience to fight in such a war, he left the khedive's service, but remained on very good terms with him. Fadeev then returned to Odessa, where we were then living, a man without a post. It was at that time that he wrote *Chem nam byt?* (How are We to Exist?).

When we went to war with Turkey [in 1877], Fadeev wrote to War Minister Miliutin saying that his military spirit rebelled against remaining inactive. As a result Miliutin and my uncle were reconciled. Miliutin sent him to serve with the Prince of Montenegro as representative of the Russian army in the Montenegrin forces.

After the war, the Prince of Montenegro presented my uncle with a small estate near Antivari, which he subsequently sold. Fadeev was a man of limited means. He had declined his part of the modest inheritance left by his father and mother in favor of his sisters and thus was in straitened circumstances.

During these, the final years of his life, Fadeev remained close to Prince Bariatinskii. Also he was very intimate with the Vorontsov-Dashkov family, or more properly speaking, with Count Vorontsov-Dashkov, the current viceroy of the Caucasus. Since Fadeev had been Bariatinskii's senior adjutant, Vorontsov-Dashkov had, to a degree, come under my uncle's influence and direction. The count often visited us at our home, where Fadeev was staying. The closeness between the two endured for life.

Early in the 1880s, Fadeev began to experience stomach trouble (I believe it was cancer), and my mother and sister took him to Karlsbad; I was then taking the cure at Marienbad and often visited him. The stay at Karlsbad made him feel better and he returned to Odessa, where he stayed with my mother, on Khersonskii Street (I do not remember the number of the house), and died there, in 1883.

Prince Bariatinskii

As I have said, Fadeev played an important role under Prince Bariatinskii, and I learned much from him and others about the prince. As a young man the prince served in the Life Hussar Regiment, in Petersburg, and was on *tutoyer* terms with the Tsesarevich Alexander, the future Emperor Alexander II. Prince Bariatinskii was remarkably handsome and was considered the leading Don Juan of Petersburg high society. There is a rumor, apparently well founded, that Bariatinskii was very much in the good graces of one of the daughters of Emperor Nicholas I—Olga Nikolaevna, I believe. Since the Emperor could see for himself that the relationship had gone beyond permissible bounds, he sent the prince off to the Caucasus, where he served as commander of the Kabardinskii Regiment and showed remarkable courage. During the campaign against the rebellious mountaineers he was hit by gunfire so often that it was said that he had a stomach like a sieve. It was during this campaign that he first became acquainted with Fadeev.

Soon after Emperor Alexander II ascended the throne, he appointed Prince Bariatinskii, still a young man, as viceroy of the Caucasus, partly because they were friends, partly because of the prince's military prowess. I remember those days well, and I must say that everyone was delighted with the appointment, because nobody liked his predecessor, Muravev, and because he was, so to speak, a native son, while Muravev was considered an outsider, and viceroys who were outsiders never enjoyed any special affection in the Caucasus.

I have a vivid recollection of Prince Bariatinskii, after his pacification of the Caucasus and his being made field marshal. I remember being with the choirs at the great balls he gave at the viceregal palace. He had a magnificent presence, and many of his adjutants, typical of the Petersburg *jeunesse dorée*, added splendor to his balls. In those days many young men came to Tiflis from Russia for the sport, others to get a taste of war, some simply to enjoy themselves.

On the whole, the young people around Bariatinskii led rather exciting and striking lives. For example, I recall the following incident involving the viceroy's escort (which was commanded by Vorontsov-Dashkov); they dropped an egg in the street and rode around it, taking shots at it; whoever hit the egg received some sort of a prize.

Also, I recall the case of Pozen, also an adjutant, of Jewish origin, who was later appointed intendant of the Caucasus because of his probity. Well, the adjutants took turns entertaining one another. On one such occasion, at a party at Vorontsov-Dashkov's quarters, the adjutants, thoroughly soused, decided to draw Pozen's profile on the wall with bullets. They seated the poor man in a chair next to the wall and took shots at him for half an hour, while he sat there quaking with fear. Fortunately, such extravaganzas ended happily.

After the capture of Shamil and the pacification of the mountaineers there was nothing of particular interest to keep Bariatinskii in the Caucasus. It was at this time that the prince, who was on the very best of terms with Emperor Alexander II, prepared a plan to reorganize the army.[3]

What he proposed was to reorganize the Russian military machine according to the Prussian model. Under the Prussian system, the army is under the jurisdiction of the chief of the general staff, not the minister of war; the chief of the general staff is subject only to the monarch, who deals with him through his field chancellery. Under this system only military-administrative functions remain under the jurisdiction of the war ministry. Bariatinskii submitted the plan orally to the Emperor and received his approval. The prince expected that he would become chief of the general staff in the reorganized army; Fadeev would be chief of the chancellery of the general staff, that is, his righthand man, and Dmitrii Miliutin would become minister of war.

Before going to Petersburg to preside over the reorganization of the army, Bariatinskii, who was beginning to suffer from gout, asked for and received permission to go abroad for a rest. Unfortunately for his career and his relations with the Emperor, the prince took with him, virtually by force, the wife of Colonel Davydov, one of his adjutants.[4]

Mme. Davydova, née Princess Orbeliani, was neither tall nor pretty, but she

was of the feline type, with a vivacious face, typical of the Caucasus. When Bariatinskii, a bachelor, had begun to court her, no one had thought that anything
serious would come of it because he was known as a lady's man, but they were
wrong.

While abroad he fought a duel with the husband. My uncle, who went abroad
with Bariatinskii, told me about it but I have forgotten the details and remember
only that Davydov behaved shamefully.

Obviously, Bariatinskii could not return to the Caucasus after this duel, nor
could he, in fact, quickly return to Russia. Also, his relations with Emperor
Alexander II deteriorated, although the Emperor did make it possible for him to
reside in Skierniewice, where the prince sometime stayed with his wife, the former
Mme. Davydova, and her younger "sister."*

The Emperor turned to Bariatinskii only at the end of the so-called Eastern
War [1877–1878]. When the war ended, with the Treaty of San Stefano, the
European powers, notably Austria, were displeased with it. War with Austria was
in the air. At this point the Emperor asked Bariatinskii to become commander-in-
chief of the army in the event of war with Austria. Despite the fact that he was very
ill, Bariatinskii accepted. He proposed to have General Obruchev as his chief of
staff, General Annenkov as commander of the armies in the rear, and me as chief
of railroad communications. I agreed. As we know, the Treaty of San Stefano was
superseded by the Treaty of Berlin, eliminating the possibility of war with Austria
and thus removing the possibility of the prince's assuming command.

[Bariatinskii died soon thereafter, in 1879.] He was buried at his estate, in
Kursk province. Tsesarevich Alexander, later Emperor Alexander III, who had
shown Bariatinskii many marks of favor, attended the burial service.

The Fate of the Bariatinskii Plan

About the time that Bariatinskii left the Caucasus [in 1861], his former chief of
staff Dmitrii Miliutin was appointed minister of war. Instead of carrying out the
army reorganization plan proposed by Bariatinskii, Miliutin followed a plan
based on the French model, under which the war minister is in fact chief of the
entire military system. I believe that Miliutin acted as he did out of conviction and
not to advance his own career, but, nonetheless, there was an intrigue against
Bariatinskii.[5]

Obviously, the Miliutin plan provided no military role for Bariatinskii. So a
quarrel developed between Fadeev and Miliutin's supporters, a quarrel that
sometimes reached the press. Fadeev's supporters included such prominent generals as Cherniaev, Count Kotzebue, and Count Liders. But virtually all that
appeared in the press in support of Fadeev's position was his work and that of
Komarov, whose thinking was close to his.

*The younger "sister" was an adopted child who had been given the Orbeliani surname and title. It
was at Skierniewice that Vasilii Lvovich Naryshkin, father of my son-in-law, and then immensely rich,
met this "sister," fell in love with her, and married her.

Komarov established a newspaper through which to carry on the struggle: I don't recall the name under which it first appeared, but I do know that it was later renamed *Svet* and that it is still in existence.[6] After General Komarov died, only two years ago, *Svet* took on a purely civilian character and is no longer concerned with military questions, but in the 1870s and 1880s it was largely devoted to military articles, a few by Cherniaev, some by Komarov, most by Fadeev. In the official periodicals of the War Ministry, men such as Generals Obruchev, Onuchin, and Annenkov spoke out against the view of the Fadeev party; they were, for the most part, former general staff officers. Thus, it can be said that the debate in those days was between those whose ties were with the general staff and those who had seen action. As we know, disagreements on fundamental military questions continue to this day.

After ascending the throne, Emperor Alexander III reopened consideration of Bariatinskii's plan. But by this time Bariatinskii was no longer among the living, and it could easily have been predicted that nothing would come of the effort. The new minister of war, Vannovskii, was under the influence of Obruchev, the new chief of staff. Obruchev, who had been closely associated with Miliutin, was better equipped for the [bureaucratic] battle than Vannovskii, and it was evident that the war minister would look at matters through Obruchev's eyes.

Nonetheless, the Bariatinskii plan was reviewed at a special conference presided over by Count Kotzebue, a supporter of the plan. The conference accomplished nothing because Vannovskii and Obruchev insisted that it was inadvisable to carry out the proposed reorganization at once, since to do so would upset the entire military structure. True, Vannovskii undertook to carry out reorganization gradually, but in the end nothing was done.

III

Some Caucasian Memories

Grand Duke Michael Nikolaevich

As I have already noted, Grand Duke Michael Nikolaevich, one of the younger brothers of Emperor Alexander II, succeeded Prince Bariatinskii as viceroy. The Grand Duke was no stranger to the region, having visited it a few years earlier with his brother Grand Duke Nicholas Nikolaevich, when they were still quite young and unmarried. Although I was only a child at the time I vividly remember their coming to Tiflis.

I remember, too, the visit of the Tsesarevich Nicholas Aleksandrovich; it was not long after the Grand Duke's appointment as viceroy. I remember the ball given in the Tsesarevich's honor and how young and handsome he was.

I recall that the Tsesarevich was accompanied by Count Adlerberg, later minister of the Imperial court, and how the viceroy's adjutants predicted that Adlerberg would take everybody's money! It was common knowledge that although Adlerberg was very intelligent and a decent person in all respects, he was a spendthrift and always in debt.

When the news came that Grand Duke Michael Nikolaevich had been appointed viceroy, everyone was very pleased because this was the first time that a grand duke, and an emperor's brother at that, had been given the post. The Grand Duke brought two adjutants, Prince Trubetskoi and Count Levashev (later to be prefect of Odessa). Of course, those of Bariatinskii's adjutants who had not left after his departure stayed on to serve under the new viceroy. My father, in addition to being director of the Department of State Domains, was a member of the viceroy's Council of the Chief Administration and played an important role in the civilian administration of the Caucasus during this period.

As viceroy the Grand Duke did well, although he was a man who let others (among them his wife) guide him. But he was a man of tradition, grand ducal tradition. By conviction he was a true son of his father, Emperor Nicholas I, and worshiped his memory. He had the good sense to surround himself with men of long experience in the Caucasus, who identified themselves with the region. As a result he continued the wise policy of his predecessors according to which the Caucasus was treated as part of the Empire, and its natives, particularly those of the Christian faith, were treated in the same fashion as Russians. This was so because most of the population of the Caucasus had voluntarily become subjects of Russia and because its Christian population in general, and its Orthodox population in particular, had long been loyal to Russia.

Thus the Caucasus lived under Grand Duke Michael Nikolaevich as it had under his predecessors, except that it received more attention, for the simple reason that he was the brother of Emperor Alexander II and the uncle of the succeeding sovereign, Emperor Alexander III. Both sovereigns had a close and kindly feeling toward the Grand Duke, and rightly so because he was a good man.

To be sure, he had a somewhat excessive interest in money and land, even government land, for example, Borzhom, which was later granted him by the Emperor, something that did not add luster to his tenure as viceroy. But everyone in the Caucasus knew that he was under the influence of his wife, who was very mercenary for the reason noted earlier, her Semitic origin.

The Grand Duke spent his first summer in the Caucasus at Belyi Kliuch, a few dozen miles from Tiflis, where the famous Georgian Regiment was stationed. At that time the Wittes and the Fadeevs spent their summers there. I and my brothers, who had begun to ride as children, rode in the Caucasus style, using Cossack saddles. I remember that when the Grand Duke saw us riding, on the parade ground, he would sometimes call us over and try to teach us to ride as the cavalry did, but we could not get used to that style, which Caucasian riders disdained. In later years (and I rode regularly until very recently) I changed my mind and decided that the cavalry style was preferable to the Caucasian.

Under the Grand Duke the subjugation of the western Caucasus, which Bariatinskii had not finished, was brought to a successful conclusion. For this he received a St. George around the neck.[1] And, in the war with Turkey [1877–78], he was nominally in command of our army on the Transcaucasian front, but the actual commander was Loris-Melikov, who was made a count for his part in this war.

Both in war and in peace the Grand Duke was largely a figurehead, but that does not detract from his stature as viceroy. When he left the Caucasus, in 1881, to become chairman of the State Council, he left excellent memories of him behind. He was the exception to the rule that viceroys who had had no previous identification with the Caucasus were not liked there.

The Grand Duke's Successors

The Grand Duke's successors were Caucasians, that is, they had had some previous experience in the Caucasus and were therefore not considered outsiders. Prince Dondukov-Korsakov [1882–1890], noted for the drinking bouts he organized, did not distinguish himself, but he was well liked. So was his successor, Sheremetev [1890–1896], who also did not distinguish himself. Prince Golitsyn [1897–1904] was disliked, even hated, because he was the first to seek to Russify the Caucasus by police methods rather than by moral authority; he is responsible for much of the disorder we have experienced during the recent years in that region.[2] In contrast, his successor, the current viceroy, Count Vorontsov-Dashkov, is well liked and respected.

Count Vorontsov-Dashkov, whom I have known from childhood, is a fine man, of ordinary education, who belongs to high society. It is remarkable that although he became viceroy during the midst of our so-called revolution, when bombings were a daily occurrence in Tiflis, he was probably the only official in the area who could travel, whether on horseback or by carriage, throughout the city without being harmed or hindered. He is probably the only official in this troubled area who in recent years has not been the object of an assassination attempt or of insult. And, he is probably the only high official in the area who enjoys general respect and sympathy.

I dare say that an official who enjoys general respect from a population as varied as that of the Caucasus must have outstanding qualities. These qualities derive from the fact that he is, in the full sense of the word, a genuine Russian nobleman, with all its noble and chivalrous traits.

Like all of us who have lived in the Caucasus, Count Vorontsov-Dashkov understands the spirit of this region and can never forget that although the Caucasus was conquered by Russian soldiers, many who commanded these men were native Caucasians. I well remember the time when the great majority of officers were natives—Georgians, Armenians, Tatars—who, wearing Russian uniforms, led Russian soldiers in those battles that brought glory to the Caucasian army. It is enough to mention the names of such Armenian generals as Prince Bebutov, Lazarev, and Ter-Gusakov and such Georgian generals as Chavchevadze and Orbeliani, generals who left behind them glorious pages in the military history of Russia. Therefore, to say now, as many do, only a few decades after the pacification of the Caucasus, that we do not need the kind of people who brought honor to our army in the military or civil service is short-sighted, to say the least.

Some Caucasian Officers

There were some differences between the Armenian and Georgian officers. Both types were, at best, half educated, but the Armenians tended to be intelligent as well as brave, while the Georgians tended to be stupid, but compensated for their lack of intelligence by their courage and their sense of honor.

One of the Armenian generals I remember was Lazarev, to whom we owe the taking of Kars. At a meeting of the military council shortly before the storming of that city, various opinions were expressed about how the operation should be conducted. As usual, the most voluble at the meetings were the officers of the general staff. Finally came the turn of Lazarev, who had the task of storming Kars. When asked how he thought it should be done, he asked to be shown the map which had been lying all this time on the table, and on which generals had been making notations. He then asked to be shown on the map where we were and then where Kars was. He then said: "I shall proceed from where we are to Kars and take it." That was all the explanation he would give. A few days later he took Kars, but at a heavy price in men.

Among the Georgian officers I particularly remember Chavchevadze, who commanded the cavalry in the war against the Turks. I recall seeing him when he was in command of the Severskii Dragoons; I was to meet him again, in Petersburg, when I was minister. He was a very brave man, very strong, huge, with shoulders nearly two yards wide [sic] and a waist that a young girl might envy. Some in the army solemnly declared that he seemed to be made of steel; my brother told me, although not in earnest, that he had seen Chavchevadze ignore bullets that bounced off his skull.

Also, I recall the last descendant of the Georgian tsars, Prince Erekle. He served in the cavalry as an ordinary colonel and even acted as adjutant to the viceroy. Everyone called him Prince Erekle-tsarevich.

Now I would like to set down a few more recollections about some other notable people and events I recall from my childhood and youth in the Caucasus.

Count Evdokimov

One of the generals I met when young whose reputations were made in the Caucasian campaigns of the 1860s was General Evdokimov, who was later made a count. He rose from the ranks and left a name in Caucasian military history as an extraordinarily brilliant commander, one of Prince Bariatinskii's most important associates.

I met him when he visited my relatives in Tiflis. For the most part he lived in such places as Groznyi and Vladikavkaz, close to the scene of uninterrupted war with the mountaineers. He left no offspring.

General Heimann

Then there was General Heimann, a very original personality. He, too, had risen from the ranks, in this case the ranks of the Jewish soldiers, and he was typically Jewish. Even as a boy I heard of him as one of the heroes of the Caucasus.

I became acquainted with him under peculiar circumstances. I had spent my first vacation from the university with my family in Tiflis. At the end of the vacation, my Uncle Fadeev took me along for troop inspection in the Black Sea region. Since there were no railroads then [in the Caucasus], we went by post-chaise to Poti by way of Kutais, then by steamer to Sukhumi, where we found cholera raging. There we went straight to the quarters of General Heimann, commander of the region, and found him in his bedroom, surrounded by bottles of wine. After greeting my uncle in friendly fashion, he asked us to sit down and drink with him, insisting this was the only protection against cholera. After keeping us up all night, drinking, the general, weak and half drunk, took us back to the steamer. My uncle went on to Novorossiisk and I to Odessa, to the university.

During the war with Turkey [1877–78], General Heimann distinguished himself as commander of one of the units under General Loris-Melikov.

My brother Alexander later told me various stories about Heimann. I have forgotten most of them but I remember one, how Alexander, Heimann, and some Cossacks, riding, came upon two English journalists, also riding. Heimann could not endure journalists and wanted to have any he met flogged. Well, when he learned that these two were journalists, he wanted to have them flogged on the spot, but my brother barely succeeded in dissuading him.

In truth, Heimann was a very simple, barely literate, soldier, but his name will always remain fresh in the pages of the history of the conquest of the Caucasus.

General Roop

My brother also told me about General Roop, who is still alive and is virtually the oldest member of the State Council. As we know, a grenadier division, under the general, which was sent from Moscow to reinforce the Caucasian troops, fled in panic during the storming of Kars. While his men were fleeing, a native whose name I don't remember kept shouting the vilest curses at him. Naturally, the division had to be sent back to Moscow.

The authorities feared that the Tiflis natives, given their courage and their highly developed sense of honor, would be very hostile when this division, called the Roopskaia in honor of its commander, marched through the city. So it was arranged that it pass through at night.

The Tiflis Meat Riot

I recall another incident in Tiflis involving the military. After I had completed my leave-taking examination at the Tiflis *gimnaziia*, I was playing billiards in a Caucasian inn on Theater Square when a mob of angry residents gathered in the square, determined to find and kill a meat contractor and his family: the civilian administration had placed the entire sale of beef in his hands and he had taken advantage of the people he served. When the authorities learned what was afoot, they ordered the Georgian and Erivan regiments into the city to deal with the problem. I don't recall the name of the commander, but I remember that his chief of staff was Colonel Cherkasov, who prepared elaborate plans, based on the fundamentals of military science, for surrounding and subduing the mob.

Just as these regiments, marching at quick step, were entering the city, my father reached the square in a carriage. Seeing the mob, he hurried to a nearby fire station and ordered the fire hoses brought out and used against the mob, which thereupon fled without laying a hand on my father, who was very popular. He quietly returned to his carriage and went home.

By the time the troops arrived at the square, most of the mob was gone, in search of its quarry. The troops fired a few salvoes over the heads of those who remained, managing to kill a young employee in the pharmacy opposite the inn where I was playing billiards. As a result of the incident Cherkasov became the laughing-stock of the military. (As a rule, general staff officers had no prestige whatsoever in the Caucasus.)

Georgian Exarchs

When I was a very young boy, the exarch of Georgia was Isidor, a fine old man, later metropolitan of Petersburg. He had the reputation of being a wise prelate, an outstanding administrator, and a true monk in his way of life. He often dined at our house.

He was succeeded by Evsevii, whose life was not quite as monkish. For example, while still a boy I learned that Evsevii was living with my nanny's niece. He was later transferred to a minor post in Russia and remained in that post, in total obscurity, until the end of his career.

Baron Nikolai and His Brother

One civilian who was later to play a somewhat important role in the central government was Baron [Alexander Pavlovich] Nikolai, then the head of the Chief Administration for Civil Affairs in the Caucasus. He was a red-headed German, or rather a Finn, a very stiff and intelligent man, whose wife was Georgian. He owned a small estate near Kazhiore, where fairly prominent and well-to-do civilian officials resided during the summer.

Before coming to the Caucasus he had been superintendent of the Kiev School District. He left the Caucasus [in 1881] to become minister of education, but he soon gave up the position because he was unsympathetic to the new university regulation, enacted in 1884, which rescinded many of the rights that had been granted under Emperor Alexander II.[3]

His brother's life had a strange ending. The brother [Baron Leontii Pavlovich Nikolai], already a general-adjutant when I was still a boy, was known as a brave soldier. Suddenly, after the Caucasian war, he was converted from Lutheranism to Catholicism and went to Rome to become a monk.

He is buried in the cemetery of a Catholic monastery not far from Aix-les-Bains that has been closed by the French government. Three years ago, when I was near

Aix-les-Bains, I visited the monastery, a beautiful place that attracts many visitors. When I arrived I asked to see his grave, but was told that monks are buried as nameless "slaves of God." However, one old workman who had known Nikolai pointed out the spot where he was buried.

Some Civil Servants

I remember Staritskii, a civil servant who was later to play a fairly prominent role in government. He served as chief of the judicial institutions of the Caucasus before the judicial reforms. After the reforms he was appointed senior chairman of the Superior Court. Subsequently he was appointed a member of the State Council and chairman of its Department of Laws.

Insarskii served as chief of chancellery under Prince Bariatinskii, who was well disposed toward him because of certain personal ties. I remember Insarskii not because he distinguished himself, but because of his peculiarities, which made him the butt of many jokes on the part of the viceroy's adjutants. He was a very decent and honorable man, but a very limited and bombastic one, who combined the characteristics of grandee and bureaucrat. After a few minutes conversation with no matter whom, he would address the person as *ty* [the familiar of you] and as "my dearest friend."

When Bariatinskii left the Caucasus, he used his influence to get Insarskii the position of Moscow post office director, then an important position because Russia was not yet covered with a network of railroads. Insarskii felt completely at home in Moscow and was on excellent terms with all of the local commercial aristocracy, whom he treated in a *haut en bas* manner, pompously addressing everyone as *ty*.

Because they had little education, few of the native nobility went into the civil service. One exception was Prince Mukhranskii, a remarkably intelligent man who, if I remember correctly, succeeded Staritskii.

Dumas *Père*

Although I was very young when Alexandre Dumas *père* visited the Caucasus, I remember his visit very well. As soon as he arrived, he put on a *cherkeska* (Caucasian tunic), wore it everywhere he went, meanwhile consuming huge quantities of wine. On his return to France, he wrote all sorts of fantastic things about the Caucasus, typical of his usual buffoonery.

Tengoborgskii

Also, I remember the visit to the Caucasus of Tengoborgskii, the well-known economist of the 1850s. He had a great deal to do with the adoption of the free trade policy in Russia and it was not until the reign of Emperor Alexander II that we were able to get rid of it and enter the road of straightforward and open protectionism.

Doctor Andreevskii and Prince Shervashidze

I am reminded too of Doctor Andreevskii, who was in the Caucasus during my childhood. He was known in the Caucasus not as a mere doctor but as "the doctor of Prince Vorontsov," the viceroy. Because the prince was then well along in years, Andreevskii gained considerable influence over him and used it to his own financial advantage. When Prince Vorontsov left the Caucasus, Andreevskii, by then in comfortable circumstances, moved to Odessa.

Later on Prince Shervashidze, a member of the former royal family of Georgia and adjutant to Bariatinskii, married one of Andreevskii's daughters, for her money. They were married in the church of Novorossiisk University, which I was then attending. It was a high society wedding and I went to it out of curiosity. When the bride and groom entered, I was astonished to see that he was neither in uniform nor in formal attire, but in the costume of a French marquis of the time of Louis XIV. To this day I cannot understand the reason for this dress. When I asked his cousin, now an official in the court of the Dowager Empress, for an explanation, he had none.

Mining in the Caucasus and the Family Fortune

While Bariatinskii was viceroy, he became interested in exploiting the natural resources of the Caucasus, at a time when such exploitation was only in its infancy. [An indirect result of his efforts was the ruin of the Witte family fortune. It happened the following way.]

When Bariatinskii became interested in the production of iron from the ore in the Chetakh fields, near Tiflis, he turned to a certain Lippe, the consul of the Grand Duchy of Baden in Odessa. Lippe in turn invited Russian mining engineers, the chief of them being Bernuli, to direct operations there. Since the fields were on state lands, under the supervision of the Department of State Domains, father would sometimes inspect the operations there, taking me and my brother Boris along.

We boys suffered somewhat on these trips because we couldn't eat the strange dishes that the Germans there provided, dishes such as prune soup and game with preserves. So we would go to the local tavern and stuff ourselves, chiefly on bread and butter and coffee.

After Lippe fell from a horse and fractured his skull, the foundries at Chetakh, which had just begun operation and were still losing money, closed down. Bariatinskii then asked my father to take them over, promising to arrange everything later on. For the time being the enterprise was to be carried on as a commercial [private] venture, money for its operation to be supplied by father, with the expectation that the state would reimburse him later when things had smoothed out.

So father, who had some training in mining, agreed or rather acceded to Bariatinskii's request. Father had no fortune of his own, but he had received a large dowry when he married and, with my mother's permission, put the money into the operation. But his was not enough, so he borrowed additional money from private lenders, to whom he gave promissory notes.

When Grand Duke Michael Nikolaevich became viceroy and was informed about the Chetakh operations, he asked father to continue handling them, telling him that he would write to the Emperor about the matter and that things would therefore be placed on a proper footing and the money that father had invested would be returned to him.

Father's unexpected death (while I was a student at the university) led to our financial ruin. He left huge debts, but few assets, chiefly a large estate in Stavropol province that had been granted to him during Bariatinskii's tenure as viceroy, which we were supposed to inherit. But Gorbunov, one of my father's assistants, who had been appointed guardian because we were still minors, advised us to refuse the inheritance on the grounds that father had left greater debts than assets.

Thus, father's death reduced us from a position of affluence to one of straitened circumstances. All mother had to live on was a pension, which she received through the good offices of the viceroy, and that part of the inheritance from her father [who died in 1867] which Uncle Fadeev had refused in favor of her and her sister. As for Boris and me, we could not have completed our university education without the stipend of fifty rubles a month granted us by the Caucasian viceroyalty.

Alexander, Boris, and I were saddled with huge debts, my share, as I recall, being 2 million rubles. While I was manager of the Southwestern Railroad I was dunned for the money on several occasions. Each time I replied that even if the debt were only 200 rubles there was nothing I could do, because my resources (at the time) were very small.

This business dragged on until the first years of the reign of Emperor Alexander III. By this time Grand Duke Michael Nikolaevich was chairman of the State Council and the aged Staritskii, whom we knew from the Caucasus, was chairman of one of the council's departments. Both men took a hand in the matter. Finally, the Committee of Ministers, with the approval of the Emperor, annulled our debts.

Now, so that my memoirs will be more or less organized, I will deal with my training and education.

IV

My Education

Early Training and Education

As an infant I was looked after by a wet nurse (a free woman) and a nursemaid (a household serf). The wet nurse, a fine woman who also nursed my sisters, is the one who lives with my surviving sister in Odessa; her husband, named Vakula, a private in an infantry battalion stationed in Tiflis, was an inveterate drunkard who often quarreled with her in my presence, when he came to visit her. Our nursemaid's husband, a serf, waited on tables and like Vakula was a quarrelsome drunkard. The wet nurse was to become my second nursemaid.

When we were a little older, I and Boris were placed in the care of a *diadka*,[1] a retired Caucasian soldier with twenty-five years of service, who was partial to the bottle. He was succeeded by a tutor named René, a retired French naval officer. René not only loved to drink but also, although sixty, was still a lecher, as we had occasion to observe.

René came from France with his wife, whom he placed as governess with Chermak, the director of the Tiflis *gimnaziia*, father of the famous scientist N. K. Chermak and of three daughters. When René would take me and my brothers for a walk, he would invariably visit his wife at the Chermak home. There, he became friendly with Chermak's eldest daughter and entered into an affair with her. Chermak complained to the viceroy, and one fine day gendarmes came to our nursery and took René away. Acting on administrative orders, they escorted him by post-chaise to a port on the Black Sea and put him aboard a ship leaving the country.

His poor wife had to leave the Chermak household and come to serve as nursery-governess to my sisters. She was a stupid Frenchwoman, almost an idiot, but essentially a good woman. She soon left us to rejoin her husband.

René was succeeded by a French Swiss named Shavan and René's wife by a young Frenchwoman named Demulian. Lo and behold, these two became lovers and had to be dismissed, but not before she had seduced my eldest brother.

I tell all this to show how difficult it is to protect children from corrupting influences, even in families of means, if their parents do not take a keen interest in their training.[2]

Mr. Shavan was succeeded by a Mr. Paulson, a Baltic German from Dorpat, whom my father hired. He instructed us in history, geography, German, and other subjects. German did not come easily to me, and I did not learn to speak it. At the same time that we were taught by Mr. Paulson, we were coached by a horde of teachers from the Tiflis *gimnaziia*; their task was to prepare us for entrance to their school.

There were three categories of students in the *gimnaziia*—boarding students, day students, and auditors, the last admitted only under special circumstances. In view of our family status, I and my brother Boris were admitted as auditors, I to the fourth class, he to the fifth. Since it was a seven-year school, I had to spend four years there, but I profited little from these years because of my indifference to schoolwork. I would report to school in the morning and then, after an hour or so, sneak out through a window and return home.

My chief interest, as well as Boris's, lay elsewhere, in music, on which we spent more time than on our schoolwork. At first a flutist from one of the local regiments taught us to play the flute and other wind instruments. Subsequently we studied at the conservatory under performers from the local Italian opera.

Other extracurricular interests were riding and fencing. Uncle Fadeev was particularly interested in our fencing and provided us with a fencing instructor from the military. By the way, this instructor came to a tragic end: he cut the throats of his common-law wife and their children and then cut his own. We were the ones who found him and his family dead when we went to his quarters one morning.

At school I was regularly promoted without examination. The teachers did not consider themselves responsible for our deportment and educational progress because we were auditors. But, for extra compensation, they came to our home during these four years to tutor us in those subjects on which we would be examined for our school-leaving certificate required for graduation from *gimnaziia* and entrance to a university.

At last [1865], the time came to take the school-leaving examinations. I would not have passed them had I not been coached for four years. As it was, I barely passed. I did not mind the fact that most of my examination grades were low, but I was greatly annoyed by the comparatively low grade (three) that I and Boris received in French. At home we chattered in French most of the time so it was only natural that we spoke it fluently, more fluently, if you will, than Russian.[3] We were examined in French by Guguberidze, a science teacher, and Zakharov, a mathematics teacher, both of whom spoke French with a barbaric accent. And they dared to find that we had a poor command of the language.

This shocked us. Being rascals, we waited for them outside the *gimnaziia* and followed them, shouting curses and throwing filth at their backs. Despite this incident we were graduated and given our school-leaving certificates, but with a grade of one for deportment. I was not yet seventeen.

Entry into University

Off we went to the university, accompanied by our father and mother, on what was my first trip away from the Caucasus. Our destination was Kiev, where my uncle, Senator F. F. Witte, was school district superintendent. It was father's intention that we enroll at the University of Kiev, with his brother's help. But, while we were in the Crimea, en route to Kiev, father received a telegram telling him that his brother was going to leave Kiev to become superintendent of the Warsaw School District, a step up for him. Because our uncle would not be in Kiev to help us and because the trip there would be difficult (there was no railroad then between Odessa and Kiev), we decided to stop in Odessa, where the Lycée Richelieu had just been transformed into Novorossiisk University.[4] A. A. Artsimovich, a Pole, who was superintendent of the Odessa School District and a close acquaintance of the senator, would use his influence to have us admitted. Despite his efforts we were refused because of our low grades in deportment. Moreover, I was not yet seventeen, the minimum age for admission. So father enrolled us in the Richelieu *Gimnaziia* and then he and mother returned home. I began to attend the *gimnaziia*, but Boris enrolled in the university as an auditor.

Now that we were on our own I began to take life seriously for the first time. I realized that I and Boris had wasted our years in play, had learned nothing but to chatter in French, and that if we continued in this way we would come to nothing. So I began to strengthen my character, began to become my own man and have been so ever since. It was a different story with Boris: having been my parents' favorite he was spoiled and he did not have as strong a character as I. So, although he was a year older than I, I took him in hand, to a considerable degree.

Once I became convinced that we had to change our way of life, I urged that we go to Kishinev, to board with a teacher who would prepare us once more for the school-leaving examinations. I argued that if we went to a city where no one knew us and engaged a teacher who would have a stake in providing us with adequate preparation, and if we worked hard, we would be sure to earn high grades and be accepted by the university.

Boris was convinced. He went to Kishinev, where he located a mathematics teacher at the local *gimnaziia* named Beloussov, who agreed to let us board with him. A day after Boris's return we left for Kishinev—traveling part way by post-chaise because the railroad there had not yet been completed—and established ourselves in the Beloussov household.* When father learned of our move, he was astonished, but he offered no objection and continued to supply us with the necessary money. We hired teachers and for six months studied literally day and night.

During those months Beloussov discovered that I had a gift for mathematics and told the director of the *gimnaziia*, K. P. Iannovskii, also a mathematician, about my gift. Iannovskii promised me that if I received a five in each of the physico-mathematical subjects—arithmetic, geometry, algebra, physics, mathematical physics, meteorology, physical geography, and mathematical geography—he would see to it that I received good grades in all the other subjects included in the school-leaving examinations.

Well, when I took the examinations, he examined me in all the mathematical subjects and I earned fives in each. Then, in his capacity as director, he appeared at all my other examinations and was the one who put the questions to me. To tell the truth, these questions were very elementary and he gave me good grades. Boris did not do as well as I in the mathematical subjects, in which he was weak, but he did better than I in the other subjects, to which he had given primary attention during those six months. We passed our school-leaving examinations and were able to enter Novorossiisk University [in 1866].

A year after I entered the university Grandfather Fadeev died. His death made a great impression on me, for I was his favorite and loved him dearly. Grandmother Fadeeva, née Princess Dolgorukaia, had died some years earlier, after many years of illness. Not long after grandfather's death came the news of the premature death of my father, who was just over fifty.

As I have noted, his death left us in reduced circumstances. After he was gone, my mother, my two sisters, then still girls, and their nursemaid joined us in Odessa, where they made their permanent home. My brother Alexander, of course, remained with the military, in the Caucasus.

University Years

At the university I enrolled in the Physico-Mathematical Faculty and Boris in the Faculty of Jurisprudence. In the former it was impossible to get by without studying; in the latter little studying was done then nor is it now. I studied so diligently that I graduated [in 1870] at the top of my class, with an average grade of 5.5. I knew my subjects so well that I did not have to prepare for the yearly promotion examinations. Instead, I helped my fellow students prepare for theirs. My brother, in contrast to me, was not a diligent student and earned his degree by the skin of his teeth.

*Our host, Beloussov, had only one vice—he drank, as did his wife. When they were both in their cups, they would quarrel, often in our presence. And sometimes drink kept him in his rooms for two or three days.

For my degree (candidate in the physico-mathematical sciences) I wrote a dissertation entitled "On Infinitesimal Quantities," an original piece of work, which, although on pure mathematics, consisted exclusively of philosophical conclusions and contained not a single equation. A few years ago I was astonished to see a French translation of this dissertation on display in a bookstore window.

I could have earned a gold medal on graduation had I been willing to do an additional dissertation, on a set subject in astronomy. But by this time I was in love with the actress Sokolova and didn't feel like writing any more dissertations. Thus, although I graduated at the head of my class, I was not awarded the gold medal, which went to the second-ranking student.

Nonetheless, I definitely wanted an academic career—to become a professor in the Department of Theoretical Mathematics at the university. One of my closest friends at the school, Ligin, planned to stay on, too, in the Department of Mechanics. How it came about that I did not embark on an academic career, I will explain later. Now I would like to share some of my recollections of university life.

In those days Pisarev, Dobroliubov, and Chernyshevsky were the idols of the youth, and the atheistic point of view prevailed among them. Two of the students, the Miller brothers, had already experienced exile in Siberia and were consequently worshiped as martyrs. I took little part in politics at the university, because I was so busy with studies, but to the degree that I did take part, it was to oppose the radical tendencies because by training I was a thoroughgoing monarchist and a believer and still am.[5]

Nowadays, and for some time past, the idol of the youth has been Count Leo Tolstoy, whose basic ideas include belief in God and in the immortality of the soul. Therefore, I am always amazed by the senseless assertions made by officials of the government, as well as by reactionaries outside of it, that his teachings have a subversive effect on the youth. Anyone who experienced university life in the 1860s can appreciate the great service that Tolstoy performed, by directing the Russian youth toward God, to be sure not the God of that fanatic Iliodor or that buffoon Purishkevich.

The Student Fund

My fellow students respected me because of my seriousness and learning and showed their respect by electing me a member of the council which administered student funds. Another member was E. F. Turau, rather a liberal at the time, but now, in the State Council, much further to the right than I on many questions. Among the other members was one of the Miller brothers and G. E. Afanasev, later professor of world history at the university.

Without warning someone challenged the legality of the fund, and as a result, legal proceedings were initiated against the members of the council by a certain Orlov, procurator of the Superior Court. Had we been found guilty we would have been exiled to Siberia. Fortunately, the English Club indirectly saved us.[6]

It did so by blackballing Orlov when his name was put up for membership. This shocked Pahlen, the minister of justice, who wanted to know how it could be that a procurator of a superior court could be blackballed. He was told that the action was taken because Orlov had begun proceedings against well-known, upstanding young people, proceedings that could lead to exile. Consequently, a new investigation was begun. It was followed by a hearing before a justice of the peace who fined us twenty-five rubles each.

Fellow Student: G. E. Afanasev

One of my fellow students, as I have noted, was Afanasev, who was to become a professor at the university. As professor he was attacked as being too liberal, for concentrating on the French Revolution, a subject on which he often gave public lectures. As a result he had to leave the university.

When I was minister of finance I arranged for his appointment as manager of the Kiev branch of the State Bank.[7] Once on a trip to the Crimea with His Majesty, the then court commandant General-Adjutant Hesse told us that he had information that Afanasev was too liberal, that he gave lectures on unsuitable topics and should therefore be dismissed.

I wrote about the matter to Dragomirov, the governor-general of Kiev. He replied that he knew Afanasev well, thought him a worthy person, and that he had attended and would continue to attend his lectures. Dragomirov said further that Afanasev was unable to hide the fact that there had been a revolution in France and that his only sin was to utter the words "French Revolution."

The denunciation of Afanasev came from the scoundrel, Iuzefovich (who now plays a very shady role in Kiev that includes his work with the Union of the Russian People), a man of "the very lowest character" as Dragomirov characterized him in the letter. Dragomirov expressed astonishment that Hesse should pay any attention to Iuzefovich's denunciations. I thereupon conveyed the substance of this letter to His Majesty. Afanasev is still manager of the Kiev office of the State Bank and continues to be a moderate, very law-abiding liberal, just as he was at the university.

Fellow Student: Ligin

I want to say a few words about V. N. Ligin, one of my closest friends at the university, whom I have mentioned before, because he was a remarkable man.

He was the illegitimate son of a German doctor who served as a physician at the court and Kozlova, the favorite lady-in-waiting of Empress Alexandra Fedorovna, wife of Emperor Nicholas I. When it became evident that Kozlova was in an "interesting condition," she admitted to having had intimate relations with this young doctor, but she would not marry him. He immediately left Russia and she left Petersburg, for Odessa.

In what were the outskirts of the city, she established a convent and took a house nearby. There she bore a son, who was listed in official documents as Kozlov, of the artisan estate. And it was as Kozlov that we knew him when we were students at the university. But when he graduated we learned that his surname had been legally changed to Ligin (if you reverse the spelling you get *nigil* [nihil], i.e., nobody's).

Although Kozlova led an ascetic life, she spared no expense in assuring her son a fine education. She engaged Korystelev, later professor of theoretical mechanics at the university, as tutor for the boy. (Korystelev was not a gifted teacher, as I discovered when I studied under him.) Well, it was Korystelev who nearly became the cause of preventing Ligin from becoming a professor. It happened in the following manner.

After graduation from the university, Ligin went abroad for advanced work in preparation for a professorship. On his return to Odessa he prepared a dissertation on the new geometry, which he submitted for a master's degree in mechanics. In those days, our universities were caught up by the "democratic" principle, according to which students would be treated equally, without regard to the status or wealth of their families. Of course, this is a perfectly just principle, but in trying to adhere to it professors sometimes overcompensated by being unfair toward those students who had means or who came from fairly good families. Ligin was a victim of this overcompensation.

With one exception—Umov (who now teaches at the University of Moscow)— the learned professors, men such as Mechnikov (botany), Semenov (physiology), Sokolov (chemistry), and Tsinkovskii (botany), before whom Ligin was to defend his dissertation, did not have the knowledge to judge it. But they knew of the tie between Ligin and Korystelev, by then head of the Mathematics Department, and suspected that the members of that department, who were enthusiastic about Ligin's work, were motivated by personal rather than professional reasons. So these professors engaged in childish attacks on Ligin during his dissertation defense, and each declared the dissertation utterly unsatisfactory. Even Umov, who knew better, was so caught by the "democratic" spirit that he took the same position. Because there was no faculty of mathematics at the university (nor is there one now), it was the council of the Physico-Mathematical Faculty, in which the examiners were full members, that declared the dissertation unacceptable.

Even though I had left the university by then I took a hand in the matter. I told one of the professors, either Mechnikov or Semenov, that the decision was unfair, and I advised that the dissertation be sent to Chasles, in Paris, the creator of the new geometry. He was sent a French translation.

After some time Chasles gave his opinion: Ligin's dissertation was so "excellent" that its author deserved a doctor's degree, rather than a master's. The university thereupon awarded Ligin a master's degree. He subsequently wrote another dissertation for which he received the doctorate. He was appointed to the university and served there for twenty-five years, as professor of mechanics. Subsequently he served two terms as head of the Odessa Municipal Duma.

By that time I was minister of finance. When the superintendency of the

Warsaw School District became vacant [in 1897],* I was instrumental in securing Ligin's appointment to it because I was on good terms with Prince Imeretinskii, the governor-general of Warsaw. The prince did not know Ligin but he had complete faith in my recommendation.

In fact, I nearly succeeded in having Ligin appointed minister of education. After minister of education Count Delianov died [in 1897], Constantine Petrovich Pobedonostsev came to me in great distress. He felt that the man the Emperor had in mind to succeed Delianov was quite unsuitable, but had excellent connections. He asked me to dissuade the Sovereign from making this mistake, but I declined on the ground that I could not meddle in what was not my business. I suggested instead that he make the effort since his relations with the Emperor were closer than mine. He agreed and then discussed with me who would be a suitable candidate for the post. He favored Bogolepov, superintendent of the Moscow School District, and I favored Ligin. It was agreed that he would suggest these two. The Emperor decided on Bogolepov, who was personally known to Grand Duke Sergei Aleksandrovich. Although the Emperor did not select Ligin, he was even more favorably disposed toward him than he had been.

Ligin did not have long to live. When he was still a young man he had gone to Vienna, where his natural father was an eminent psychiatrist, to have a tumor removed from his lip. Several decades later the tumor reappeared: this time it proved malignant and fatal.

By the way, Ligin's father was of assistance to me, in helping me get treatment for my throat and nasal passages, which have long troubled me. When I asked Ligin for help, he wrote a few words to his father, who received me cordially when I went to Vienna, even though I was then an unknown young man, without any means. He provided me with letters to several very eminent Viennese doctors, who treated me attentively.

Ligin's widow, an Odessa girl, the daughter of a merchant, is still alive, as are their two sons. One is the vice-governor of one of the provinces of the Kingdom of Poland. The other is the chief doctor of the Nikolaevskii Military Hospital; he is said to be an able man.

Some Professors

In addition to the other professors I have mentioned, there were other outstanding men at the university, among them Grigorovich, a specialist in Slavic dialects. Later there was Professor Jagič, who is now at the University of Vienna and is something of a celebrity. Also, there was Professor Leontovich, in the Department of Russian Law, who died recently, in Warsaw.

When I was at the university all the professors in the Philological Faculty were required to have an excellent command of Latin. Also, the defense of dissertations

*The incumbent, A. L. Apukhtin, who had succeeded my uncle Witte on the latter's death, left because he could not get along with the governor-general.

in that faculty was in Latin, a fact that warmed the heart of Professor Grigorovich. Above all, he loved scholarly disputes conducted in Latin.

There were no especially eminent men in the Mathematics Department in those days. Korystelev was undistinguished. Andreevskii, professor of theoretical mathematics, was only remarkable for his youth: he was twenty-two when he came to the university. He later became professor at the University of Warsaw and died at a very early age.

Then there was Lapshin, professor of physics, who enjoyed great popularity because of his advanced age. But he was an utter nonentity. Also, there was Shedov, professor of physics and later rector of the university; he was a very knowledgeable and talented professor, but not a particularly eminent one.

Professor Sabinin

Among the more gifted professors was E. G. Sabinin. Just last year he sent me a pamphlet of his on geometry, which he described as marking a great advance in the subject, and asked that I give him my opinion of it, since, so he wrote, I was the only one capable of evaluating the work. Being somewhat rusty in the subject, I asked Academician B. B. Golitsyn to ask his colleagues what they thought of the pamphlet. After some time they responded that they considered it proof that Sabinin was old and could no longer think straight.

But when Sabinin was younger he was a very able professor. Unfortunately, he had a weakness for drink that very often kept him from lecturing. Since I was the only student for whom he had a high opinion he had me help out. I would be summoned to his home when he was suffering from the effects of alcohol: he would barely explain what he intended to lecture on and give me some sources. Thus armed, I would prepare a lecture on, let us say, integral calculus. When he felt better, he would correct what I had done; I would then lithograph the lecture and distribute copies of it, bearing Professor Sabinin's name as author. I still have copies of his lectures. Although he was rarely in condition to lecture, he had an immense influence on the mathematical awareness of the students because he was, in fact, a gifted mathematician.

There are two kinds of mathematicians: (1) mathematician-philosophers, whose interest is in mathematical ideas and who regard numbers and calculations as nothing more than tools of the trade; (2) mathematician-calculators, for whom the be-all of mathematics is numbers and calculations. Major mathematicians such as Ostrogradskii, Chebyshev, and Sabinin belong to the first category. Unfortunately, Sabinin was unable to develop his great gifts because of his addiction. Most contemporary mathematicians, for example, Academician Markov, fall into the second category.

Mathematician-philosophers, and I consider myself one of them, look upon mathematician-calculators with disdain. The latter, many of them quite notable, consider mathematician-philosophers a bit "touched."

The Meaning of a University

Having studied at a university, I am far better attuned to the needs of universities than are graduates of [specialized] higher schools such as the Imperial School of Jurisprudence. A genuine university is characterized by academic freedom and intellectual and scholarly breadth. When I say "academic freedom" I do not mean the license to ignore the quest for knowledge in favor of politics, particularly the politics of the moment, which is always poisoned by passions, lies, and coarse cynicism. I mean the freedom to pursue truth and knowledge. Without such freedom a university will not encourage intellectual development, will not advance knowledge. A university without academic freedom, one in which professors and students are rigidly controlled, is not worthy of the name and should be transformed into a higher school that trains narrow specialists.

Genuine universities do not turn out narrow specialists. By devoting themselves to all branches of knowledge, they provide the kind of environment necessary for the development of intellectual breadth. For example, although one specializes in mathematics at a university, one comes into contact with other branches of knowledge. From morning till night a university student lives with students from other faculties and comes into contact with a variety of ideas. For instance, even though I specialized in mathematics, I was very interested in the subjects taught in the Faculty of Jurisprudence. Also, students would flock to hear the lectures of talented professors, no matter what their own area of specialization might be. Thus, students in a university worthy of the name are exposed to a variety of scholarly and intellectual influences and develop intellectual breadth and maturity, which are even more important than scholarly knowledge.

Those to whom the university is alien can never understand what is indispensable for a university to fulfill its purpose. Such men judge universities as they would higher schools or look at universities from the point of view of the military and have brought great harm to the universities.

The Teaching of Theology

In speaking of universities, I recall that theology, which is required of all students, is badly, even shamefully, taught. For example, when I was a student at the university, the administration found it difficult to round up as many as four students to attend Father Pavlovskii's lectures in theology. And, in all my four years at the university, I attended lectures in theology no more than three or four times.

And, when I appeared for my final examination in theology, I was completely ignorant and unprepared. One of my examiners was Palimpsestov, professor of agriculture, who wanted me to pass with a high grade because I was the best student in the university. When I drew a question about marriage he saw that I was lost and tried to rescue me by asking if I had read Debu's *The Physiology of Marriage*. I had, because this work, although to some degree scientific, was salacious. The other examiners—a lay professor, Father Pavlovskii, and a local prelate—were amazed by the question, but they accepted Palimpsestov's assurance that it was a fine book and that since I had read it, it meant that I knew theology well. They passed me with a four.

An exception to the rule that professors of theology are dreary was Father Petrov who taught at the Petersburg Polytechnic Institute, of which I was the founder. He was very popular, as I discovered on one of my visits to the institute. It was my custom, when I visited, to choose a lecture to attend, but on this occasion I was told that there was only one lecture scheduled for the hour, that given by Father Petrov. I was told that no other lectures were scheduled when Father Petrov lectured because all other lecture halls would be deserted when he was to speak. The last thing I wanted to hear was a lecture on theology, but having no choice, I heard him. I was enchanted, as were all the other professors and students. Without a question his was the best lecture I have ever heard.

When I saw His Majesty a few days later, I told him of Petrov, of whom he had already heard, and pointed out that if all professors of theology were like Petrov, our students would be as fascinated by theology as they are by other subjects. I had no idea at the time that Petrov, a very fine and talented man, would be ruined as a priest solely because of his interest in politics.[8]

He is now a writer, whose work appears chiefly in *Russkoe slovo*. He writes for the money involved. How he will fare, I do not know, but I suspect that he will not do well, because of where he writes and why he writes. Although his articles show marks of talent, they will be quickly forgotten.

V

The Odessa Railroad, 1870–1879

Change of Plan

When I graduated from the university, it was my firm intention to become a professor there. But both my mother and my Uncle Fadeev, who was visiting us, took a dim view of my ambition: they did not think that the calling of a professor was suitable for a noble.[1] In those days such an attitude was common among those of high society who clung to old values, and my uncle was one of them. My arguments that such members of the nobility as Chicherin and Kavelin, then quite prominent, were professors, did not sway them. So, I let my uncle persuade me to accept a post—official on special assignment (*chinovnik osobykh poruchenii*)— with no duties or salary, in the chancellery of Governor-General Count Kotzebue,* while at the same time preparing myself for a professorship.[4]

The Franco-Prussian War was then in progress and military men would gather at Count Kotzebue's to plot the course of the war and engage in armchair strategy. Most, including my uncle, let sympathy for France cloud their judgment, but Kotzebue, a Russian German,† took a more realistic view of the war.

---

*In those days the government correctly took the position that it would not tolerate pogroms of any kind, be they against Jews or Russians, and took firm steps to stop such outbursts. Count Kotzebue adhered to this policy.

I was living at the Naples Hotel,[2] across the way from the Greek church, when spontaneous disorders broke out against Jews in Odessa. Troops were soon summoned to stop the rioting. First a drum-beat warning was given. If it was not heeded, troops advanced on the crowds with drawn bayonets and, in some instances, as I saw, used them. Also, troops rounded up rioters in the courtyard under the windows of my hotel and proceeded to beat the ruffians. During the pogrom Count Kotzebue rode around the city on horseback to see that his orders were carried out.[3]

†Like a true German, he followed a set schedule, to the hour and minute. Every day, at a fixed time, he and his wife would take an hour-and-a-half drive around Odessa. When he became ill, the aged

It was at one of these gatherings that I met Count Vladimir Bobrinskii, then minister of ways and communications. Evidently prompted by my uncle, Count Bobrinskii prevailed on me to forget about being a professor and to choose instead the field of railroading.

In agreeing to Count Bobrinskii's suggestion, I thought that my next step should be to go to Petersburg and there to prepare for the examinations for a degree of engineer of ways and communications. Since I already knew mathematics, all that would be required of me by way of preparation would be to spend six months studying drawing and a few other specialized subjects. Imagine my astonishment when he sternly criticized the course I proposed to follow.

He said that he considered the caste of engineers of ways and communications a great evil: such engineers should be excluded from all aspects of railroad operations except the technical. No, he decidedly did not want to see me become an engineer of ways and communications. He had fixed on me, he said, because I was a university graduate, with a broad education, as well as a specialization in mathematics, someone who would not be infected by the corporate spirit of the engineers. Instead of my spending six months preparing for the engineering examinations, I should spend six months in on-the-job training, serving in every position, from the lowest up, to learn the practical side of railroad operations. I agreed and accepted employment with the Odessa Railroad.

The Odessa Railroad

At the time I began to work for the Odessa Railroad (which was then government-operated), not all of its lines had been completed. The sections from Razdelnaia to Kishinev and from Balta to Elizavetgrad were still under construction, under the direction of Baron Ungern-Sternberg, who had contracted with the government to do the work and would turn over the completed sections to the Odessa Railroad. In those days it was believed that government operation was preferable to private operation.

The chief of the railroad was Klimenko, an undistinguished man, a *military* engineer who had exchanged his army uniform for the uniform of the Ministry of Ways and Communications. In those days the highest positions on the railroads were held by military engineers, graduates of the Institute of Ways and Communications. On their uniforms they wore insignia indicating their military rank, whereas civilians, such as I, did not have such insignia on their uniforms.[5]

Kotzebue (he was about seventy) summoned Professor Mering from Kiev to treat him. When Professor Mering told him to discontinue his daily drive until his health improved, Kotzebue insisted that he could not give up his daily drive. So Mering suggested that the count and his wife sit in their carriage but not drive. And so it was done. Every day, at the regular hour, the carriage would be hitched up in the courtyard of the residence. Count and Countess Kotzebue would then sit in the carriage for the allotted time.

Later, when I was living in Kiev, I learned from Professor Mering that he had suggested the alternative because Count Kotzebue, being an old man, fixed in his ways, might not have been able to survive a change in his way of life.

During my first six months with the railroad I became acquainted with operations at all levels: I sat in cashiers' offices of freight stations and in ticket offices of passenger stations; I studied the work of assistant station chiefs; I served as assistant station chief at freight and passenger stations. Although I worked at various levels, I received a salary of 200 rubles a month from the beginning (as had been agreed to beforehand), at a time when the salary for these positions was a few dozen rubles a month. After having served in all these positions I was appointed chief of the traffic office, replacing Fedor Moiseevich Shtern.

Mr. Shtern

Shtern, who died a few months ago (in Odessa), was the son of a local watchmaker. He was a fine man, as everyone in the city knows. He was Jewish, obviously so, and made no effort to hide his nationality, but quite the contrary.

Although Shtern had little education, he had the polish so characteristic of the young people of Odessa. He had very gallant manners and, although he was somewhat Jewish in cast, he was the handsomest man I have ever met. He had considerable success with the ladies, many of them titled, who used to come to Odessa for the winter.

He was an able man and had advanced from one position on the railroad to the next, some say with the aid of Mme. Klimenko, a former lady-in-waiting to Empress Marie Aleksandrovna. (She also furthered her husband's career.) Finally, he had been promoted to traffic chief. It was odd to see someone so obviously Jewish in such a position on a *government* railroad.

He was able, but he had one shortcoming: like so many Jews, he was insolent. It was this trait that helped bring him down after the railroad passed into private hands.

Chikhachev and My Appointment
as Traffic Chief

In keeping with a growing tendency to move from government to private operation of the railroads, the Odessa Railroad was sold to the Russian Steamship and Commercial company, which was headed by Nicholas Matveevich Chikhachev.[6] He was an aide-de-camp to the Emperor and held the rank of captain, first class, in the navy. This fine man is now eighty-four and, like me, is a member of the State Council, whose meetings he attends faithfully. By a strange coincidence I sit almost next to him in that body.

When his company assumed control of the Odessa Railroad, he took an immediate dislike to Fedor Moiseevich Shtern, partly because of his insolence. So Shtern had to go and I replaced him.

In fact, Chikhachev had a higher position than that of traffic chief in mind for me, that of manager of the railroad. But I was still very young and, in any case, the Ministry of Ways and Communications would not have confirmed me as manager (and its confirmation was required), because by that time Count Bobrinskii was no longer minister and power was in the hands of engineers of ways and communications.

So I advised Chikhachev to offer the post of manager to Andrei Nikolaevich Gorchakov, director of the Kursk to Kiev Railroad, a man of somewhat inflated renown. Gorchakov was a fine man and not a bad engineer, but he was narrow and stubborn and was not temperamentally suited for business management. He wanted changes that required a great deal of money, this at a time when the railroad was not doing well. He and Chikhachev soon clashed, for Chikhachev was a practical and economical man. So Gorchakov had to leave before two years were up.

Once more Chikhachev tried to have me appointed manager, but the Ministry of Ways and Communications would not confirm me. So once more an engineer, Baron Ungern-Sternberg, was selected as manager. There was no harm to him, but he was not the man for the job. As it turned out, he was only a figurehead and I the manager in all but name, at least of the railroad's operational branch, with a resulting lack of harmony between the two branches. Things went on in this way until the outbreak of war with Turkey, in 1877.

Once the war began, Chikhachev, by now admiral à la suite to His Majesty, gave up direction of the company for the duration of hostilities to assume command of the Black Sea defenses. His temporary replacement was van-der-Flit, a member of the company's administration. As I have noted, I was the real head of the Odessa Railroad, which by now had lines reaching to the Rumanian border. The railroad was placed under the jurisdiction of the commander-in-chief, Grand Duke Nicholas Nikolaevich.

Now I would like to tell of some of the interesting events that occurred while I was with the railroad.

Imperial Contacts

During this period the railroad had not yet reached the Crimea. Consequently, when Emperor Alexander II traveled there, he would come by rail to Odessa and then go on by ship to Sebastopol. As a result I had several opportunities to see him and even to travel on Imperial trains on which he was riding.

On one such occasion, his train stopped at Birzula for a few minutes and he took the opportunity to leave the train for a walk. To avoid being seen by the public, the Emperor descended from the right side of the train, rather than from the left, which led to the exit, where the public was waiting to see him. The station chief and the chief conductor had not noticed that the Emperor had left the train, and when the time came for it to depart, they sent it off without him. Of course, this was immediately noticed: the train returned and the Sovereign continued his journey, taking a kindly view of what had occurred.

Also, I recall another incident. One day I received a telegram advising me that a lady of high station was on her way back from Yalta to Petersburg and that she should be given special attention. She was to arrive by ship at Odessa harbor and we were to take her by private railroad car to the passenger station and attach her car to an express bound for Petersburg.

The ship was late. When the passengers disembarked, I saw a pretty woman among them, with a rather full figure, in the company of the lady I was expecting. I was told that the lady was Princess Dolgorukaia, later to be the wife of the Emperor. To make sure that we did not miss our connection, we rushed her private car to the passenger station. In so doing we narrowly missed a head-on collision with a train that the stationmaster, thinking we were not coming, had permitted to proceed in our direction on the track we were using.

How many times have I thought of how different the subsequent history of Russia might have been had there been a collision that would have taken the princess's life. Would there have been a March 1 [1881]? I often think how insignificant events, how a minute's difference, can affect the fate of nations, the course of history.

I remember another incident about Emperor Alexander II's travels on the Odessa Railroad. We were waiting at Zhmerinka, where the Odessa Railroad line began on the Petersburg–Odessa route, for the arrival of the Imperial train, when the Emperor appeared on foot! It turned out that the train had left the rails just outside the station. The Emperor was told that there had been no foul play behind the derailment. He accepted the explanation with good grace, and when the train was back on the rails he continued his journey.

Speaking of Imperial trips, I recall once receiving a telegram informing me that the Emperor's young sons, Grand Dukes Sergei Aleksandrovich and Paul Aleksandrovich, would be coming on a regular passenger train; they were en route to see their father, in the Crimea. I met the train at Zhmerinka. The two young Grand Dukes, still wearing dresses, were accompanied by the then all-powerful chief of the gendarmerie, Count Peter Shuvalov: I was surprised to see that he was looking after them as if he were their tutor. The three of them and I lunched at Kryzhopole. The brothers seemed very close. Sergei Aleksandrovich appeared to be a bit effeminate. I was not to see them again until I became minister. By that time Grand Duke Sergei Aleksandrovich was in command of the Preobrazhenskii Regiment and Grand Duke Paul Aleksandrovich of a squadron in the Horse Guards.

I had occasion to escort the Emperor to the theater of war during the conflict with Turkey, from Zhmerinka to Jassy, via Kishinev. He was accompanied, among others, by his Heir, several Grand Dukes, and Chancellor Gorchakov. This was the second time I saw the Heir; the first had been while I was a student and he had visited our university.

En route we stopped for several hours at Proskurov, to review several units there. By morning we were at Velikii Kut. The Heir, the future Emperor Alexander III, was in good spirits, which he expressed by teasing chancellor Prince Gorchakov, who had not yet completed his toilet when the train arrived at the station. Outside the prince's compartment was a mess that looked the product of seasickness. So the Heir said to the prince, still in his compartment, that he must have suffered from motion sickness during the night; those around him laughed loudly. The Heir, of course, knew that the mess really consisted of the debris left from the prince's toilet and was evidently having a joke. Gorchakov was quite obviously not amused.

I saw the prince before and after his toilet. Before, he looked like a decrepit old man, toothless, no eyebrows, face deeply wrinkled; after—face made up, fine teeth and eyebrows.

The following day we arrived in Kishinev, where the Emperor inspected several military units. Then we went on to Jassy, which was as far as my journey with the Imperial train took me. We were amused and astonished to find a Russian Imperial throne at the Jassy station, which was on the Rumanian railroad line. Evidently, Rumanian railroad officials believed that a Russian emperor could sit on nothing but a throne. To tell of the tragic events connected with this throne, it is necessary for me to back up a bit.

Captain Kuzminskii

As we know, our war with Turkey grew out of the Serbo-Turkish conflict. Everybody, I among them, was caught up by the Serbian cause, by the idea of Slavonic unity, the idea of taking Constantinople.[7] It was this spirit, to tell the truth, that forced Emperor Alexander II to declare war on Turkey.

While we were still at peace, masses of Russian volunteers went off to fight on the Serbian side in ships provided by the Odessa Slavonic Society, of which I was vice-chairman. Our efforts were helped by the sympathetic attitude of gendarmes and other officials who dealt with passport formalities.

One of the volunteers who came to us for help was a Captain Kuzminskii, a brave soldier with three St. George crosses, one of them gold. He struck me by the regular features of his face, which seemed carved from marble, and his extreme pallor. He was, he said, an officer in a guards regiment stationed in the Kingdom of Poland and was very anxious to join the Serbians. We were to meet again in Jassy, some time later, after we had gone to war with Turkey.

When the Imperial train arrived in Jassy, the Emperor remained in his carriage while the rest of us left the train and stood near his window. He opened his window, leaned his elbows on the ledge, and stared off in the distance, breathing heavily because his asthma was worse than usual that day.

Then we noticed that he was staring intently at someone nearby. It was Captain Kuzminskii, in a *cherkeska* [Caucasian tunic], wearing all his St. George crosses.

The Emperor, breathing heavily, asked: "Are you Captain Kuzminskii?"

"Yes, Your Majesty," Kuzminskii replied and went close, evidently to ask to be pardoned.

The Emperor then said: "You are a deserter; you left my army without my permission or that of your superiors." Turning to General Katalei, commander of the forces in the rear, who had been standing next to me, the Emperor said: "Arrest him and confine him in the fortress."

Suddenly I saw Kuzminskii plunge a dagger into his heart. To prevent the Emperor from seeing what had happened, we surrounded Kuzminskii, but it was too late to save him, for he had driven the dagger halfway into his heart. Keeping him upright, we slowly edged the dying man into the station and placed him on the step of the throne.

The Emperor, who was still at the window, could not understand what had happened and kept asking what was going on. To keep the Emperor from learning the facts I asked the local railroad chief to send the Imperial train off as quickly as possible. As the train began to move, the Emperor, now even more perplexed, asked me why the train was beginning to move, was it time to leave? I told him that I was not in charge there, and it must obviously be time for the train to leave. After the Imperial train departed, we went to look at Kuzminskii. He was dead. Someone pulled the blood-covered dagger out of his chest.

In a very depressed mood we got on our train taking us back to Kishinev. En route we received a telegram to Katalei, signed by either Miliutin or Adlerberg, from the Imperial train, rescinding the order for Kuzminskii's imprisonment because the Emperor had decided to pardon him. Evidently the Emperor had had a change of heart after being informed of Kuzminskii's exemplary service in the Serbian army.

Nonetheless, Kuzminskii had committed a serious breach of discipline by leaving the Russian army without permission. It is true that, while in Serbia, Kuzminskii had applied to the Russian army for permission to serve with the Serbs, but his request had been denied because war between Russia and Turkey was in the offing.

The Kuzminskii episode reminds me of how I met the famous Stambulov while I was working with the Odessa Slavonic Society. Late in the afternoon, after having attended to my regular work, I would go to the society office, located in Krivtsov's quarters. Every time I entered, one of the clerks would rise to his feet, although I was still very young and had neither high social nor high official status. At the time I paid no attention to him. Some years later Krivtsov told me that the clerk was Stambulov, at that time a seminarist in Odessa.

Stambulov was the one who wrought such havoc in Bulgaria. He was the man who was to become Russia's enemy, who was to help drive Battenberg from his princely throne; he was the man who helped put Ferdinand on the throne; ultimately he was assassinated. He played an important role in the fate of Bulgaria, whether for good or for evil only time will tell.

The Tiligul Catastrophe

The Tiligul catastrophe, in which I was deeply involved, took place in December 1875. At the time our railroads were in a primitive condition, not as they are now: the trains were slow, stations poor, damage and spoilage of freight common, roadbeds poorly constructed. The circumstances of the catastrophe were as follows.

In December 1875, a train carrying recruits was scheduled to travel from Balta to Odessa. The first station after Balta was Birzula, and the engineer of the troop train had been assured that the track between the two was clear. But what he did not know was that a section of track, along the Tiligul embankment, was being replaced: such work was not considered a major repair and nearby stations had not been informed of it. But it was the practice to place red warning flags on either side of the work area, to warn trains to stop. This time the road master in charge had failed to put out such flags. To make matters worse, a howling blizzard had forced him and his men to leave the scene before they could replace the section of track they had removed; they had gone to a nearby hut, to take shelter.

When the train reached the work area, it left the roadbed and rolled down the steep embankment; when it came to rest, part of it lay below a conduit used to carry off melted snow and rain water. A fire in the wrecked train, probably starting in the locomotive, spread rapidly through the cars below the conduit and was fanned by the howling winds, which were even stronger below the conduit than above.

We, in Odessa, 110 miles away, were immediately notified. I and Baron Ungern-Sternberg rushed in a special train to the scene of the accident. When we arrived, we found nothing but ashes left of some of the cars and its occupants. Fortunately, some cars had escaped complete destruction and had been raised and some of the wounded had already been taken to Birzula. We took others to a military hospital in Odessa. I don't remember how many died, certainly more than a hundred. Since this was a major accident, it attracted a great deal of attention.

In those days educated, liberal people felt a strong antipathy for persons who stood out from the crowd because of their wealth or position. The seeds of this antipathy had been sown by Pisarev, Dobroliubov, and Chernyshevsky. And, if truth be told, it is this antipathy which still animates anarchists and socialists,[8] in fact the whole revolutionary crowd. It was this spirit that was to culminate in the foul murder of so great an Emperor as Alexander II.

So, in order to appease that segment of public opinion which held such views, there arose a movement to make scapegoats of highly placed persons. But who were they to be? Naturally, N. M. Chikhachev, admiral à la suite of His Majesty, the highly paid head of the company. Then there was I. Although I was subordinate to both Chikhachev and Ungern-Sternberg, I was considered to be the leading figure in the railroad. Actually, I had no control over road maintenance, and in any case, the immediate responsibility for the accident belonged to the road master, who was not under my jurisdiction. I and Chikhachev bore some degree of responsibility, but ours was indirect and remote. If action had been taken on the basis of *degree* of responsibility, the first to have been held accountable would have been the road master, then his immediate superior—the section chief, then the chief engineer for road maintenance, then I. But that was not the way it was to be. I and Chikhachev were unable to influence the course of the investigation, which was conducted in a prejudiced manner that catered to the mood of the time.

A special investigator named Kessel, as I recall, was brought from Petersburg to supervise the judicial investigation of responsibility for the accident. First, the road master was charged with responsibility, but he had lost his mind as a result of the disaster and had disappeared; I do not know to this day if he ever showed up again. Then they turned to me and Chikhachev.

Kessel carried out his work in an openly prejudicial manner. Thus, although he resided in Odessa during the course of the investigation, he had the two of us go to a small village near the Borshchi station, not far from Birzula, to give our testimony, when he could just as easily have questioned us in Odessa, but, in this way, he showed the railroad employees what his attitude toward us was.

The investigation resulted in indictments against the road master, me, and Chikhachev, which were sent to the Odessa District Court and there placed in the hands of Smirnov, the procurator of the Superior Court. This was the same Smirnov who had served as prosecutor in the notorious case of Mother Superior Mitrofania.[9] Since by this time most courts and officials, as a result of the judicial reforms, had attained complete freedom of judgment, Smirnov in the end decided that there was no case against us: We could not be held indirectly responsible for the actions of the road master; we could not be considered the road master's accomplices since one could not be an accomplice to an unpremeditated crime, and the road master was not charged with premeditation. But the matter did not end there.

Under the influence of the liberal mood prevailing in Petersburg, our case was then transferred to the Kamenets-Podolsk Criminal Court, a prereform court[10] on which administrative pressure could be brought to bear. Since I and Chikachev knew what would happen there, we neither appeared before the court nor did we send lawyers to represent us. The road master, I, and Chikhachev were each sentenced to prison for four months.

But soon war was declared. Chikhachev was appointed chief of the Black Sea defenses. I was placed in virtual charge of the railroad and in that capacity went to Bucharest to take part in working out the preliminary convention with the Rumanian railroads concerning transportation of our troops on their lines. Then I returned to Odessa.

About that time Grand Duke Nicholas Nikolaevich arrived in Kishinev to assume his duties as commander-in-chief. I went to see him to tell him that I would not be able to carry out my duties because I had decided to serve my jail term. Naturally, he was astonished and asked for an explanation.

I told him that I thought it more prudent to serve my term then than to wait until the end of the war to serve it. If I waited I would have the responsibility of getting the troops to and from the theater of war. If all went well, I would have a four-month jail term waiting for me. But, if by mischance anything went wrong, and that was likely, given the chaos then prevailing on the railroads, and even one unit for which I was responsible met with a mishap, I would be faced with additional punishment.

The Grand Duke then promised me that if I succeeded in transporting the entire army to its destination and back without any hitch he would ask his brother the Emperor to annul my sentence; he was certain that the Emperor would agree. Naturally, I remained on the job and devoted all my efforts to handling troop transportation successfully.

Operations of the Odessa Railroad during the War, 1877-1878

In carrying out my task I faced great difficulties which I overcame, if I may say so, because my character, particularly when I was young, was strong and decisive.

The chief difficulty was that the railroads and other means of transportation were in a sorry state. To make matters worse, the transportation plans of the chief of staff, by which we were guided, were unrealistic ones that did more harm than good. They provided precisely, by the hour and minute, for the coordinated mobilization of troops and trains so that the army could be sent expeditiously to the theater of war.

But things did not work out according to plan for the Odessa Railroad, so I had to use my own judgment and act on my own initiative in dealing with the problems I encountered. When the first cavalry units arrived in Zhmerinka it was evident that if I permitted them to go on as planned, to Kishinev, in the trains in which they had arrived, I would not have enough rolling stock for the troops being assembled. So without any authorization from the military, I ordered these cavalry units off the trains and had them proceed by horse to Kishinev. I was later to be called to account for this action.

Then, as rolling stock began to arrive from other railroads, I was faced by still another problem. Although there were enough cars coming in, we did not have enough locomotives to pull them. This was because our railroads followed the general European practice of assigning only one engineer to a locomotive: when he rested, as rest he must, his locomotive was idle. Using my common sense I introduced a different system, which, as I later learned, was used in America, that of keeping locomotives in continuous use, except for water, fuel, and maintenance stops.* This entailed the use of engineers' assistants to operate locomotives because there were not enough qualified engineers to implement the new system. Since my action in this case did not require authorization from the military, I was not likely to be taken to task by them for my act. As for the Ministry of Ways and Communications, it was in such a state at the time that it paid no attention to privately owned railroads.

Still another obstacle to be overcome in my work arose from the fact that we were using single-track lines, with no electricity-operated semaphores to warn engineers that there were trains ahead of them. Lacking such signals, we had followed the practice of permitting only one train at a time on the track between two stations, let us say Stations A and B. Only when Station B notified Station A that the train which had left it had arrived would the next train be permitted to depart for Station B. Had I adhered to this practice, the fighting would have come to a halt, given the huge number of troops pouring in, given the delays in their arrivals. Therefore, I began to have trains sent at fifteen- to twenty-minute intervals without waiting for notification that the track ahead was clear.

This action, too, did not attract official attention, but my taking a cavalry unit off a train and sending it on by horse provoked complaints that brought on an investigation by General Annenkov, who was in charge of troop movements throughout the empire. He was, moreover, a close associate of the minister of war. After investigating my action, he concluded that although I had exceeded my authority in this case (I should not have acted without an order from the commander-in-chief), I had had no choice but to act as I did.

General Annenkov conducted another investigation of my actions because of my policy of transporting wounded soldiers, who began to arrive in Jassy after our first engagement. At the time we had only five, rather luxurious, hospital trains (one the gift of the Empress, another of the present Dowager Empress),[12] which among them could carry no more than three hundred wounded to military hospi-

---

*My use of the "American" system of keeping locomotives in continuous use reminds me of the International Railroad Congress held in Brussels to mark the fiftieth anniversary of the establishment of railroads in Belgium. It was a gala occasion, with Belgian high society, including the king and queen, attending as spectators. I was there as a member of the Russian delegation.[11]

One of the questions discussed at the congress was which system of locomotive use, the American or European, was preferable. The question was first considered at a closed session, where, with the support of the French engineer Sartiaux, I defended the American system. (I still see Sartiaux, who is now the chief director of the Chemin du Fer de Nord, from time to time.)

Then the question was discussed at a general session. Belpaire, an old, well-known Belgian engineer, spoke in favor of the European system. Like all French-speaking Belgians, he spoke eloquently, all the more so because King Leopold was in the audience. Rather floridly, and with some pathos, he compared the locomotive and its engineer to a wife and her husband and spoke almost tearfully of how painful it would be to separate the two, how much happier a wife was when she was close to her husband.

Then came Sartiaux's turn. He complimented Belpaire on his speech, but expressed surprise that Belpaire, although he lived not far from Paris, had never visited the city, for if he had, he would have spoken differently. In Paris, said Sartiaux, everyone knew that a woman with several husbands was happier than the woman who has only one. The audience howled with laughter at this. King Leopold, who did not take his marital vows very seriously, found the discussion very amusing.

tals and then return for more wounded that were coming in from the front. Yet Petersburg took the view that wounded should be carried only on hospital trains.

Here again I acted on my own authority. When, after our first battle, many of our wounded were laid out like logs, on straw, in Jassy, with no place there to take care of them and no hospital trains to take them to military hospitals, I ordered that the sick and wounded be bedded on straw in freight cars (the weather was still summery) and sent back to Russia. Soon, several thousand wounded a day were passing through my hands.

This manner of transporting the wounded roused a storm; I was accused of treating the wounded as if they were logs, not humans. So Annenkov was sent to investigate what I had done. When he was through he reported that, all things considered, it was better that I had done what I had done than to have left the wounded in Jassy, where they all would have died. Further, he recommended that if the policy were to be that wounded be carried only on hospital trains, the number of such trains be increased to thirty or forty.

Grand Duke Nicholas Nikolaevich kept his word to me. At the tail-end of the war, after he had turned over the command to Totleben, he interceded on my behalf, as well as Chikhachev's, with the Emperor to have our jail sentences annulled. He informed the Emperor that I had brilliantly performed my task of transporting the army to the theater of war and back. As a result Chikhachev and I received a telegram from War Minister Miliutin telling us that the Emperor had ordered our sentences annulled. I assumed, mistakenly as it turned out, that with this the Tiligul case was closed.

VI

St. Petersburg, 1879–1880

Service on the Southwestern Railroad,
My First Marriage,
the Baranov Commission,
Railroad Kings

Transfer to Petersburg
and My First Marriage

Following the war with Turkey, the Odessa, the Kiev–Brest, and the Brest–Gaev
railroads were merged to form the Southwestern Railroad, with Ivan [Jan] Bloch
as chairman of the board, the aim being to produce a profitable operation.
Naturally, some officials had to be let go and some had to be shifted as a result of
the merger. I might have become traffic chief of the new road if Bloch had not
offered the position to Danilevich, who had been his traffic chief when he had been
head of the Kiev–Brest Railroad. I was offered the post of chief of the operational
section of the new road, with my office to be in Petersburg, and accepted it for two
reasons. First, another position might have taken me to Kiev, and that would have
been uncomfortable for me, as I shall explain. Second, I wanted to be in Petersburg to work with the so-called Imperial commission to investigate the condition
of the railroads, about which I will speak later.

   It would have been uncomfortable for me to live in Kiev then because of
unpleasant circumstances, well known in the city, connected with the first marriage of my wife-to-be, Mme. Spiridonova, née Ivanenko. She had married
Spiridonov, the son of a military doctor, when the two of them had been very
young.[1] He was a wastrel who, after piling up large gambling debts that he was
unable to repay, persuaded her, then still a girl of sixteen, to steal an expensive
bracelet from her sister, assuming that the sister-in-law would not make a fuss
about it. He was wrong: the matter was taken to the Kiev Criminal Court. Since it

was a prereform court, the case did not come up for more than a year, but come up it did. In desperation my future wife went to the chairman of the court, Goncharov (at present a member of the State Council), told him the whole story, and threw herself on his mercy. Goncharov did not let her down: he handled the case so that she was acquitted. Nonetheless, many of the unpleasant details became common knowledge in Kiev.

So, with her young daughter Sonia, she left her husband and came to Odessa, where I met her. After my repeated pleadings, she sued her husband for divorce, to which he agreed, in return for a rather small sum of money. Thus, because my future wife was well known in Kiev, the thought of moving there amidst all the talk was unpleasant. She left Sonia in Kiev, in the care of the girl's grandmother, and came to Petersburg. We were married at the Vladimir Church not long after I had assumed my new position.

End of the Tiligul Case

As I have said, one of my reasons for wanting to be in Petersburg was to work with the Imperial commission to investigate the conditions of the railroads. Count Baranov was the head of the commission, and General Annenkov, about whom I have already spoken, was its administrative chief. General Annenkov had tried very hard to get me to join or, at the very least, to participate in the work of the commission, but before I could get well started on that work I was arrested.

We were living on Troitskii Street, off Nevskii Prospekt, when, in the middle of the night, my manservant roused me to tell me that a gendarme officer and some police were at my door, waiting to take me away. I dressed and went to talk to them. When I asked for an explanation, they had none, saying simply that they had orders to arrest me.

At first I was mystified. Then, it occurred to me that I might somehow be implicated in the wave of revolutionary activity with which the government was then contending: I remembered that my secretary in Odessa, Gerto-Vinogradskii, who wrote under the pseudonym of Baron X, had been exiled to one of the northern provinces. Perhaps he had implicated me: if so, I had nothing to fear since I knew nothing about the matter.

I was first taken to a police station, then to headquarters on Sadovaia Street, where I learned that the police had orders to take me to the court commandant Adelson at the Winter Palace. As we drove along the Moika, the officer accompanying me in the carriage permitted me to stop at the home of Nicholas Nikolaevich Sushchov, to have his concierge transmit a message to my frightened wife that I was being taken to the commandant at the palace and to tell her that I didn't know why.

When we arrived at the Winter Palace, I was informed that on the night before Emperor Alexander II had ordered Chikhachev to be placed under house arrest for two weeks. (Chikhachev was then staying at the Hôtel de l'Europe, and it was there that he was to serve his sentence.) As for me, I was to spend two weeks in the Haymarket guardhouse.

As soon as I heard the name Chikhachev I guessed that our arrest was related to the Tiligul catastrophe. This guess was confirmed after I had been taken to the guardhouse, now some sort of municipal laboratory. A few hours after my arrival there, General Annenkov, representing Count Baranov, came to tell me what had happened.

He told me that after the Emperor returned from the war he was informed by Minister of Justice Nabokov that while he could grant pardons, he could not annul sentences. Nabokov's position was supported by the Tsesarevich Alexander. Nabokov also told the Emperor that the public was still upset over the Tiligul catastrophe and would be disturbed if no one connected with the case were punished. The Emperor responded by saying that if he could not annul our sentences, he would punish us in "a paternal manner," and this he did with our new sentences.

Count Baranov, who was liked by the Emperor and had easy access to him, then told the Emperor he needed me, because there was a great deal of work for me to do on his commission. That is why within three days[2] after my incarceration an Imperial order arrived permitting me to leave the guardhouse during the day but requiring that I spend my nights there for the remainder of my sentence.

My Work with the Baranov Commission

If the truth be told, I was the guiding spirit of the Baranov Commission,[3] because most of its members knew nothing about railroading and those who did, from the Ministry of Ways and Communications, were unsympathetic to the commission out of fear that it would reveal irregularities in their ministry.

The head of the commission, Count Baranov, who was then serving as chairman of the State Council's Department of the State Economy, was an honorable man. Although he spoke in a pompous, Pythian manner, he was, in fact, kindly and unassuming. His mother, born plain Barangof, had been the Emperor's governess and had been granted the title of countess. She and Count Adlerberg, the minister of the Imperial court, were good friends and her son had a deep, but platonic, love for the elderly wife of Count Adlerberg. He devoted his life to her, visiting the Adlerberg home every day.

Naturally, Count Baranov, who owed his position to his friendship with the Emperor, knew nothing about railroading, or for that matter, of anything else of importance. And neither did General Annenkov know anything about railroading: he was a typical general staff officer, a great chatterbox, who was quite capable of departing from the truth.

Two well-known jurists, Koni and Nekliudov, participated in the work of the commission. Nekliudov was later to be over-procurator of the Holy Synod and subsequently assistant minister of interior under Goremykin.

As we know, all that the commission accomplished was the preparation of the Railroad Charter, which is still the basis for regulations of the railroads.[4] I wrote almost the entire charter; Nekliudov did the final editing. The charter is now being reviewed by a commission modeled after the Baranov Commission.

My Transfer to Kiev

Meanwhile, the Southwestern Railroad was losing money. So the board of directors decided to send me to Kiev as chief of operations, with a free hand. Because more than a year had passed since my marriage to Spiridonova, I agreed to go.

Railroad Kings

[Before I deal with my work in Kiev, I would like to say something about the railroad kings about whom I was able to learn something during this period in St. Petersburg.]

In those days there were still railroad kings in Russia because the government still favored private ownership and operation of railroads and provided them with generous support. Chief among these "kings" were Poliakov, Bloch, and Kronenberg—converted Jews; Gubonin and Kokorev—former tax farmers; Derviz—a former Senate official; von Meck—a former engineer. They were aided in their rise by favorable governmental practices, but they would not have achieved their positions if they had not been intelligent, clever, and, to some degree, unscrupulous.

Bloch

As I have noted, the head of the Southwestern Railroad was Bloch, who, like many Jews, began his career as a small-scale entrepreneur. He was remarkably able and had a very interesting career. I tell about it so that one can see how railroad kings became what they were in those days, how they amassed large fortunes and achieved great influence and power through their railroads, and banks. Once a man became head of a railroad, it was natural for him to become the head of a bank, since all the financial operations of the railroads were carried out through the banks. In this way such persons were able to gain powerful social influence, even in the upper levels of the propertied class.

Bloch came from the Kingdom of Poland. When he began his career he had very little education. He worked as a subcontractor with old S. V. Kerbedz, who was building the Kiev–Warsaw Railroad. After saving some money, he had the good sense to go abroad for a few years to acquire polish and education. He even attended lectures at German universities. When he felt that he had completed his self-education, he returned to the Kingdom of Poland, by this time a proper sort of young man. Back in Poland he met a rather beautiful, clever, and very fashionable young lady, the daughter of Doctor Kronenberg. But she was Catholic; to marry her Bloch was converted to Catholicism. They made their home in Warsaw, where Bloch acquired a large bank.

He had become so rich that he could build railroads, for example, the Lodz Railroad, with his own capital. Also, he acquired a major interest in the three railroads that were merged to form the Southwestern Railroad and was thus able to become chairman of its board.

But because he resided in Warsaw and the railroad's headquarters were in Petersburg, he delegated the day-to-day administration of the company's affairs to the vice-chairman of the board, Ivan Alekseevich Vyshnegradskii, whom I was to succeed as minister of finance. Earlier on Vyshnegradskii had, so to speak, been Bloch's lawyer and was, one could say, nothing more than Bloch's hired hand. Vyshnegradskii was an exceptionally able man, with a broad mathematical education, a strong but harsh man who was obviously at home in his position. But, with one exception, the other members of the board were nonentities who knew nothing about railroading. The exception was Feldman, who had previously been secretary of the Council of the Main Company of Russian Railroads. He was old, very kind, well educated. Undoubtedly he was of Jewish origin, but he had long ago become so Germanized that he was accepted as Russian.

Although Vyshnegradskii knew his work, he was too busy to give it his full attention: he was at the same time director of the Technological Institute, a member of the Council of the Ministry of Education, the major figure in the Petersburg Water Supply Company and many other privately owned companies. Some days he did not appear at all at company offices; when he did appear it was for no more than two or three hours. In fact the chief administrator was a young engineer, S. I. Kerbedz, nephew of the old Kerbedz I mentioned earlier. I was in charge of operations, but the technical part was in the hands of Kerbedz.

Young Kerbedz, who died only a few months ago, was a highly gifted engineer. When I was minister of finance and began construction of the Chinese Eastern Railroad, I put him in charge of the undertaking, although his title was only that of vice-chairman of the company. He married the daughter of old Kerbedz, who inherited a large estate from her father, thus making him a wealthy man.

During my days in Petersburg with the Southwestern Railroad, Bloch would stay at the Grand Hotel when he came to the city, and there he would give dinners to which he would invite his associates. It was at these that I was struck by the way Vyshnegradskii humbled himself before Bloch. After all, Vyshnegradskii was by then a well-known professor, a privy councillor, and a member of the Council of the Ministry of Education. However, even as a young man without means or position, I would not humble myself before anyone; I always looked men in the eye and said what I thought. Rather than humble myself before a Bloch as the price of holding a position, I would rather have gone begging in the streets. It was not that Bloch was a Jew, but it was because he himself was nothing: the entire power of such gentlemen is in their pockets. He tolerated me, but he did not find me sympathetic and always complained of my harshness, or, as he called it, my arrogance.

As I have said, Bloch was very able and well educated, but like most Jews he was insolent and tended to put on airs. He was already putting on airs and trying to make a name for himself when I began to work for him and had become interested in matters other than the railroad or his bank. By appointing subordinates to act for him (Vyshnegradskii in Petersburg and two very able Poles, whose names I have forgotten, in Warsaw), he was able to spend his time on scholarship and his peace crusade.

His major scholarly work was a multivolume history of Russian railroads, published about thirty years ago and now quite out of date. Actually the scholarly works that appeared under his name were written by hired writers and specialists. All that he did, with the aid of assistants, was to work out the general nature of the books that were to appear under his name.

I remember how once, when I was visiting the elder Kerbedz, a servant announced that Bloch was calling on him. The servant was told to show Bloch in. So in he came, with a presentation copy of his finely bound history of the Russian railroads. Thereupon, Kerbedz, who had known Bloch when he was still a young Jew-boy (*zhidok*) and had always *tutoyered* him, thanked him profusely and then, in mock naiveté, said: "Ivan Stanislavich, please tell me, have you read these books?" Bloch was very offended; I was taken aback.

In later years Bloch sought fame by energetically propagating the ideal of universal peace. In this connection he wrote, or rather had written for him, a number of books, bearing his name, that strove to show that the salvation of Europe and all mankind lay in universal disarmament and peace. Also, he organized conferences devoted to peace and hoped to establish a museum, in Switzerland I believe, to keep the idea of peace alive. While I was minister of finance he tried to win Emperor Nicholas and Empress Alexandra Fedorovna to his cause, but it appears that he received little encouragement, partly because he was of Jewish origin. As I have suggested, he was more infatuated with the idea of winning fame than with the ideal of peace. He died without achieving any results.

It goes without saying that the ideal of disarmament and peace is a magnificent one and that any man who devotes his energy and strength to it deserves great respect. But I must say that this ideal is so ambitious that it will take many centuries before it can be realized.

It is true that we have fewer wars now than in the past. Also, we now live in a state of permanent war—a war of universal armament races, with all their attendant evil. The vast sums spent on armaments come from the sweat of the poor;

they sap our productive strength while poverty, sickness, and mortality increase. What we have is continuing war in the midst of peace.

Gubonin

During those years in Petersburg I met other railroad kings, among them Gubonin, a typical potbellied Russian peasant (*muzhik*), almost totally uneducated, but a man of good common sense. As I have noted, he began his career as a tax farmer. He then went on to become a contractor and railroad builder and ultimately a star in the railroad firmament.

The Poliakovs

The most famous of the railroad kings was, of course, Samuel Poliakov, who established a veritable dynasty. He had been the proprietor of several postal stations somewhere in Kharkov province when he was able to perform some kind of important service for Ivan Tolstoi, the minister of postal and telegraph services, who happened to be traveling along a post road. It appears that Poliakov later handled some of Tolstoi's business affairs and that Tolstoi, in turn, launched Poliakov on his career.

Samuel Poliakov's brother Lazar was a well-known figure in the Moscow banking world, but he had largely gone to rack and ruin. Another brother, Jacob, rose to the rank of privy councillor and was thus ennobled, but not one assembly of nobles would have him as a member. He, too, went to rack and ruin; he died a year ago, in Biarritz.

Samuel Poliakov's son never engaged in useful employment and spent a good part of his fortune. He married a very pretty, nice, educated Jewish girl and now rarely visits Petersburg, preferring to spend most of his time in Paris. While still quite young I met him in Petersburg, at a conference of railroadmen. When he began to speak insolently to me I cut him off completely. This startled him so that he kept asking people who I was. I never met him again.

Derviz and von Meck

I believe that Derviz was a graduate of the Imperial School of Jurisprudence. After Reutern, a schoolmate, became minister of finance, he gave him the concessions to build the Moscow–Riazan and Riazan–Kozlovka lines. In those days there were few takers for concessions because few made money in railroading. However, Derviz, who was without doubt a clever man, amassed a good deal of money in the course of building these lines, or rather in the course of collecting the capital for construction. Also, in collaboration with von Meck, he built the Kursk–Kiev line.

After salting away a fortune, Derviz had the good sense to retire from business, went to Italy, built himself a mansion, and settled down to enjoy his wealth. When von Meck invited Derviz to join him in building the Libau line, Derviz replied that he was not such a fool that after having accumulated a fortune he would start risking it. He would rather enjoy the life of a Maecenas. In rejecting von Meck's offer Derviz showed good judgment, for von Meck was to lose a great deal of money on the construction of this line, the reason being that the government had learned, through experience, to impose increasingly burdensome conditions on railroad contractors; some even went bankrupt.

In the course of enjoying his millions, Derviz became mentally unbalanced. For example, he employed an entire opera company, which gave daily performances in his mansion for virtually his exclusive benefit. When his brother Nicholas, a tenor in the Petersburg opera who sang under the name of Ende, spent a summer in Italy, Derviz invited him to sing but would not invite him to call socially. At the end of the season, Derviz sent Ende a purse filled with gold, in addition to his fee. I heard this from Ende himself.

Derviz's odd behavior was also illustrated by his conduct at his twenty-fifth wedding anniversary, to which he invited many friends and relatives. He had long lost interest in his wife, a very nice, but ordinary, old lady, and had been paying court to various prominent ladies, who took advantage of him. Well, sometime in the course of the dinner he stood up and expressed gratitude toward his wife for having been so devoted to him for all those years; then, to show his gratitude he ordered a servant to hand her a tray carrying an anniversary gift—a million rubles worth of gold. Then, he thanked her once more and asked her to leave because he no longer wanted her to be with him. Clearly, money had unsettled his mind.

K. F. von Meck, an engineer of ways and communications, was a very proper German. Although he amassed a large fortune, he lived rather modestly. His oldest son was a heavy drinker who spent his entire youth among the gypsies and died at an early age. Two sons survived K. F. von Meck. One who lives in Moscow is chairman of the board of the Moscow–Riazan and Riazan–Kazan lines; the other is a landowner who lives in Kiev with his wife, the granddaughter of the Decembrist Davydov.

Steingel

Baron Steingel was one of the lesser railroad kings, a man who made his fortune solely by being in the right place at the right time. He was just an ordinary engineer of ways and communications, working for the Tsarskoe Selo Railroad, who happened to be at the Tsarskoe Selo station when Count Alexis Bobrinskii,* the minister of ways and communications, saw him and decided that he would be a suitable man to receive the concession to build the Rostov–Vladikavkaz line. It happened this way.

Princess Dolgorukaia, with whom the Emperor was already on intimate terms,

---

*Alexis Bobrinskii succeeded his cousin Vladimir as minister. Vladimir Bobrinskii was the head of the Bobrinskii family, which had large landholdings in the province of Kiev. Alexis Bobrinskii owned a great deal of land in the province of Tula.

had no qualms about accepting large gifts [from prospective concessionaires]. She pressed the Emperor to grant the Rostov–Vladikavkaz concession to someone whose name I can't recall: it could have been the engineer Felkerzam or some other railroad concessionaire, perhaps even Poliakov.

But Count Bobrinskii, a man of principle, was very upset that the concession should be granted in such a manner and opposed it by every means. Not afraid to speak up, he had it out with Emperor Alexander II one day at Tsarskoe Selo. When the Emperor asked why he opposed the person chosen, Bobrinskii replied that he did so because he considered that person to be an untrustworthy man who lined his own pockets, and he though it improper to squander the government's money in such a fashion. The Emperor became very angry, made many unpleasant remarks, and ended by telling him to submit the name of a man he considered honorable and to do it that very day. That is how the minister came to propose Baron Steingel. After a few hours' consideration, he wrote to the Emperor, suggesting the baron: a man well thought of in the ministry. And that is how Baron Steingel came to build the Rostov–Vladikavkaz line and make a great deal of money, not millions, but several hundred thousand rubles.

Alexis Bobrinskii was to pay for his temerity. Sometime later the Emperor, who was traveling on the Warsaw line, encountered the count, who was not in proper uniform. Thereupon the Emperor ordered the count to the guardhouse. Naturally, after his stay in the guardhouse Bobrinskii went into retirement and returned to his village, in the province of Tula, where he became a Radstockite.[5] He rarely ventured forth from his village, and if he had to go to Petersburg he went incognito. His son Vladimir Alekseevich Bobrinskii now sits in the State Council. From what little I know of him he seems like a decent, but somewhat odd and unbalanced, man.

Sushchov

One of the more prominent and interesting persons I met in my work with the Odessa and Southwestern Railroads was Nicholas Nikolaevich Sushchov, to whom I have referred earlier. [He was not a railroad king but he deserves to be mentioned here.] It is true that he accomplished nothing of significance, but it seemed during the 1860s, 1870s, and early 1880s that Sushchov was everywhere, that no railroad or commercial enterprise could come into being without his participation. He typifies the Russo-Tatar character: a man of great ability and good solid sense, yet a man who used his gifts unproductively from the point of view of the state.

His wife was a member of the very aristocratic Kozlov family: one of her brothers was adjutant to the Heir and Tsesarevich Alexander Aleksandrovich, later Emperor Alexander III; another brother was general à la suite of His Majesty. Sushchov himself had a court title—gentleman of the chamber. Also he achieved some prominence in government, first as director of the chancellery under minister of justice Zamiatnin, then as over-procurator of the Senate. But he had to leave government service because he had become involved in business dealings and this was not proper for an over-procurator and a gentleman of the chamber.

In the 1860s and 1870s, when he first became involved in business dealings, Russia was just beginning to become used to the intricacies of corporations, banks, and industry. Sushchov, a gifted man and an able jurist, had his hand in everything and became quite adept at such things as drawing up charters for new companies. Nowadays such work is so routine that any chief clerk in a government office can prepare a charter, but in those days the ability to do so was considered a special talent: for drawing up such a charter he would receive 25,000 or 30,000 rubles, this for work that required a few hours spread over two days. In addition, he served on the boards of many established companies, such as the boards of the Southwestern Railroad and the Russian Steamship and Commercial Company, as well as on the boards of companies that were only projected. For such work he received a great deal of money.

A great deal of money passed through his hands, but he spent it freely, and when he died, a year ago, he left only a small estate.

I first met him in the early 1870s, when I was with the Odessa Railroad. It was my first trip to Petersburg and I was there on business. One of my first calls was Sushchov, who had a large apartment in a house owned by Count Zubov, opposite St. Isaac's Cathedral. As soon as he was informed that I was calling, he received me, despite the fact that it was a reception day and many people were waiting to see him. This was the first of several visits, during which I discussed the establishment of tariff schedules for the Odessa Railroad and other railroad matters. (It was in Petersburg that I worked out the first reasonably organized tariff schedule for my railroad.)

I have rarely met anyone as fat as he, so fat that he could hardly move. His was a very distinctive physiognomy: with his red hair and huge, remarkably brilliant eyes, he seemed like a red-headed Tatar.

On these visits I had the opportunity of learning what a good heart he had and what an original way he had of showing it. On my first call I noticed a sad, old man who waited in vain to see him. On my second call the old man, with tears in his eyes, asked me to ask Sushchov to see him. I did. At my next visit, the old man was waiting for me and thanked me for "saving" his son. I never saw him again.

When I asked Sushchov what the old man had wanted, he told me in his most serious manner that the man had asked him to help his son, a graduate of the Imperial School of Jurisprudence,* who had embezzled 50,000 rubles from the company for which he worked as cashier, could not replace the money, and was fearfully awaiting an audit. On learning that the son had had free access to the company's funds, he told the old man to have the son take another 100,000 rubles

*As we all know, graduates of this school help one another, forming a kind of Jewish *kahal*.[6]

and bring them to him, Sushchov. Sushchov then went to the company's board of directors, told them how easy it was to embezzle money from the company, gave them the 100,000 rubles, and suggested that if they wanted to avoid a scandal they make up the other 50,000 rubles from their own pockets. He said that he was acting this way as a favor to a fellow alumnus of the Imperial School of Jurisprudence. According to Sushchov they agreed, made up the 50,000 rubles, the cashier left the firm, and there the matter ended.

Sushchov's was a typically expansive Russian nature. Although he could barely stand, he loved to dance, well into his fifties. He would give feasts to which he would invite actresses, feasts which invariably concluded with drinking bouts and dancing. Well, this tub of a man would invite an actress to dance and with astonishing spryness would first dance with her in the Russian fashion and then move into a waltz.

Also, I recall an interesting card game I played with him on a train journey, while I was with the Odessa Railroad. When he asked me if I played cards, I said that I rarely did. Would I play preference with him? I said I would if it were for small stakes and he agreed. As I recall I lost three rubles to him during the first day of our trip and won two during the second. When I noticed he was making notes of the outcome of the games, I asked him why. He replied:

> Ginzburg, Kokorev, Gubonin, and I have agreed that if one of us plays with someone else for smaller stakes, he will act as if he were playing with one of the others for larger stakes. Well, I was playing this one with Kokorev. Since your net loss to me is one ruble, he owes me a hundred rubles.

I remember another characteristic incident involving Sushchov. Once as I was about to return to Petersburg from Moscow I noticed that there was a private car attached to the train. When I asked who was traveling on it, I was told that it was a party of eminent Muscovites. As I watched I saw Kokorev and Gubonin arrive, wearing long-flowing coats (their dress was half-merchant, half-peasant). Then the engineer Danilov arrived. Finally, Sushchov came shambling along. They had with them huge containers of champagne and cucumber kvass and spent the whole night's journey drinking and playing cards.

This strange mixture of champagne and cucumber kvass is not to my taste, but the taste for it evidently spread from Moscow to other cities. Some years later, when I was seated next to General-Adjutant[7] Richter at a dinner given by the Emperor, I noticed that he was drinking a mixture of champagne and what I discovered to be cucumber kvass.

VII

Kievan Years, 1880–1889
Service with the Southwestern Railroad

Chief of Operations

[As I have already noted] I was transferred to Kiev in 1880 as chief of operations of the Southwestern Railroad. Subsequently, the company board decided that I should be promoted to the position of manager, but the Ministry of Ways and Communications would not confirm my appointment because I was not an engineer of ways and communications. As a result the engineer Andreevskii was given the position. Although he was a man of strong character, was far more independent then my former chief Baron Ungern-Sternberg, and although he knew something about the work, it was I who provided the ideas and initiative for the reorganization of the railroad's administration, to make it a more centralized operation than it had been before.

Manager

When Vyshnegradskii became minister of finance, Andreevskii was invited to take over his functions on the Southwestern Railroad, that is, to act as chairman of the board since Bloch did not concern himself with the company's operations.[1] Consequently, I was again nominated as manager of the railroad, which year after year had been losing money or, at best, showing a slight profit. This time [September 1886], as a result of the prestige I had acquired in railroading, the Ministry of Ways and Communications was no longer in a position to reject me. Thus, I became the first, and last, person to be made manager of a major railroad without being an engineer of ways and communications.

If I understood anything of railroading it was because I was a good mathematician and because I had practical experience in railroading. During my tenure as manager [1886-1889], I was able to put the railroad on a solid financial footing: under me the company began to pay regular dividends and its shares rose in price.

On the whole I was well satisfied with my position. I received a large salary, much larger than the one I was to receive as premier. I was in charge of a large enterprise, with 1,800 miles of road, and I was my own master, because the board of directors, knowing my nature, did not interfere with me in my operation of the railroad.

My Associates

In whatever post I have served I have been fortunate enough to be surrounded by a galaxy of able and talented subordinates. This is the case because I have the highly developed knack of finding the right people, of evaluating their strengths and weaknesses. Such a knack is indispensable for an administrator with major responsibilities. The able men whom I selected and trained, particularly while I was minister of finance, can be found in prominent positions in government and business. All the ministers of finance who succeeded me—Pleske, Shipov, Kokovtsev—were men I nurtured, so to speak. The major banker in Petersburg today, Alexander Ivanovich Vyshnegradskii (son of the minister of finance), served and advanced under me; he was to leave the Ministry of Finance for private banking because, as he told me, he couldn't adjust himself to the rigidity of Kokovtsev. Another prominent banker, Alexis Ivanovich Putilov, chairman of the board of the Asiatic Bank, also served under me; when I left the post of premier he retired from government service. And then there is Bark,[2] manager of one of the major banks in Petersburg, whom I sent to Mendelssohn, in Berlin, to learn the banking business.

Exactly in the same way did I pick a brilliant array of eminent railroadmen while I was manager of the Southwestern Railroad. Some are still alive and prominent. Many of the able men who served with me were engineers, whose knowledge and skills I needed in improving the condition of our lines and stations: I, in turn, provided them with the knowledge I had gained from general railroad experience, as well as from my knowledge of mathematics and mechanics.

One such man was Ziegler, a very capable and young engineer. When I left the railroad to become director of the Department of Railroad Affairs, he went with me as an official on special assignment. Later, when I became minister of finance, he became my director of railroad affairs and remained in the ministry after my departure: he was Kokovtsev's guide on all railroad questions because Kokovtsev knows nothing about railroading. Ziegler, a fine and honorable man, died a year ago.

Another able young engineer who served under me was Abragamson, who was of Jewish origin. (There were many Jews and Poles working on the Southwestern Railroad because there were many Jews and Poles in the southwestern region and it was natural to want to work close to home.) He is one of the many Jews and Poles on the railroads now being forced out of their posts because of the current

Black Hundreds policy, not because they are less trustworthy than Russians, but as a sop to a senseless political trend. Abragamson, who was recommended to me by Chikhachev, is better qualified than most other engineers in Russia because he is a graduate of one of the higher engineering schools in Germany.

I appointed him chief of road and building repairs, and he performed ably and reliably; he earned the affection of his subordinates, most of them of the common people—guards, workers, and foremen. He had no interest in politics. Nonetheless, he was recently transferred to a less important line by Rukhlov, our current minister of ways and communications, solely because of his Jewish origins. He was transferred rather than dismissed (the Southwestern Railroad is now government-owned) because dismissal would have been too crass. I can see no rational explanation of how he can be fit to serve on one line and not the other. There is good reason to believe that he will soon decide to retire.

Another example of the stupid policy now being followed is the dismissal of Katulskii, whom I had appointed as stationmaster at Port Odessa, one of the largest stations on the Southwestern Railroad. A few months ago, while I was in Odessa to see my sick sister, he called on me to tell me that he was no longer stationmaster and would I help get his pension increased. When I expressed surprise that he was no longer working, he told me that he had been dismissed, probably because he was believed to be Polish. Had he explained that he was not? He had, but to no avail.

I learned later from chief of the road that Tolmachev, the prefect of Odessa, had called for the dismissal of all persons of Polish origin: Katulskii had been dismissed because his name ends in "skii."[3] Although the Ministry of Ways and Communications had been advised that Katulskii could not possibly be Polish because he was the son of a [Russian Orthodox] priest, the ministry would not restore him to his position because to have done so would have been an admission that it frivolously dismissed employees on the basis of the ending of their surnames.

One of the interesting engineers who served under me was Demchinskii. Although he was not a good engineer and was of little use to me, I write about him because he is representative of a type of talented but unstable Russian who goes from one enthusiasm to another.

After being forced to leave his post on the Moscow–Kursk line because of a marital scandal, he came to me, begging for any kind of work under me. I appointed him to an engineering post in which he served directly under me. Although he was not of much use as an engineer, he could write well and was good at preparing proposals.[4]

One day, out of the blue, he informed me that the law was the best of all possible careers, one that would suit his nature. He said that he wanted to become a lawyer and would I free him from work for a few months so that he could prepare for the final examination in the Faculty of Jurisprudence at the University of Kiev. I did not see how he could prepare himself in so short a time, but I agreed and did not give him any assignment for a few months. He surprised me by passing his examination. He became a lawyer and left the railroad to pursue his new career.

But his enthusiasm for the law did not last long. He soon decided that the courts were debased, this at a time when the courts were, in fact, independent and honorable, not as they are today under our current minister of justice, that rogue Shcheglovitov.[5]

Demchinskii then moved to Petersburg, where he was the first to open a photozincographic establishment. He claimed that zincography was his invention and, in fact, received some kind of patent on the process, although it is probable that something like it had already been invented abroad. But he did not stay long with this business. He sold it for a few hundred thousand rubles and with the proceeds went into farming.

During his farming phase, he decided he could revolutionize the art of weather prediction and thus revolutionize farming. He began writing articles for *Novoe vremia* in which he predicted the weather and gave advice on how to apply these predictions in agriculture.

So accurate were his forecasts that many urged that his work be subsidized, among them landowners close to the Emperor. I must admit that I agreed with them and I successfully urged that Demchinskii be given an annual subsidy of 15,000 rubles to publish a meteorological journal.

Once Demchinskii began publishing this journal, experts started questioning his methodology. Academician Rykachev, whose opinion I solicited, decided after some investigation that Demchinskii's success in prediction was the result of luck, that his methods were worthless. I passed these conclusions on to Dmitrii Ivanovich Mendeleev, our distinguished but unappreciated scientist. He agreed with them, but added that Demchinskii had a great, God-given talent and that if he managed to live a few more decades he might come forth with a major discovery. Meanwhile, Demchinskii's success in prediction declined and his meteorological journal failed.

Demchinskii then became a foreign correspondent. During the war with Japan he went to the front as a well-paid correspondent for several newspapers, chief among them *Birzhevye vedomosti*. On the whole his articles were sensible, but uneven.

While in China he became entranced with the Chinese method of growing grain in beds, the method we use for cabbage and other vegetables. The Chinese yields were so much higher than our own that he became convinced that we could revolutionize our agriculture by adopting the Chinese method. Somewhat later he was to become a propagandist for that method.

Meanwhile, on his return from the East, he began a new career, that of newspaper publisher, but without any capital. In this career, too, he had his troubles. First, he often failed to pay his employees, not because he was dishonest but because he was irresponsible. Then he ran afoul of the government when his newspapers began to publish sharp attacks against it, following my departure from the post of premier.

He was coaxed out of publishing by Kryzhanovskii, the assistant minister of interior, who, realizing that Demchinskii was both fickle and venal, arranged (obviously by the use of money) for Demchinskii to travel around the country and abroad to proclaim the virtues of the seed-bed method of cultivating grain. And, it should be noted, Demchinskii had been successful in winning support.

There are, of course, those who criticize this method. I have not investigated it thoroughly, but I believe that it is more suitable for large landowners than for peasants and therefore cannot be of any importance under present circumstances. But Demchinskii is obviously very pleased with the results of his efforts. Just the other day he wrote me from Moscow to say that he had been too busy to call on me or to write to me, but now that his affairs were well in hand, his first thought was to thank me, for he had always been obliged to me.

VIII

Kievan Years, 1880–1889
The Holy Brotherhood

The most important event that occurred during my years in Kiev was the assassination of Emperor Alexander II on March 1, 1881. That evening I and my wife were at the theater when an acquaintance, Mme. Mering, in the next box, informed us that the Emperor had been killed. I immediately left the theater and wrote a letter to my Uncle Fadeev, then living in Petersburg. In this letter, in which emotion prevailed over reason, I said that our government had failed in its efforts against the anarchists because it had used inappropriate methods, as if it were trying to crush a microscopic grain of sand with the kind of steam hammer we have in our railroad shops. Although the revolution then was not comparable to the revolution of 1905–1906, it had managed to achieve some successes, culminating in the assassination of our Emperor. I argued that we must fight the anarchists with their own weapons, which could not be employed by the government but could be employed by a society of men of the utmost probity. Every time the anarchists prepared or made an attempt on the life of the Sovereign, the society should respond by ruthlessly killing them. This was the only way, I said, we could fight them and succeed in frightening them out of their efforts to hunt down our Sovereign.[1]

A few days later I received a reply from my Uncle Fadeev informing me that my letter was on Emperor Alexander III's desk and that I would probably soon be summoned to Petersburg.[2] And, in fact I soon received a letter from Count Vorontsov-Dashkov, whom I had known from boyhood, asking me to come to Petersburg. (At that time he was temporarily in charge of protecting His Majesty.)

When I met him, he asked if I had any second thoughts about what I had written. I replied that I did not. At this he presented me to his aide-de-camp,

Count Paul Shuvalov, and told me to accompany him to his home.* As soon as I entered his study, he asked me to take an oath of loyalty on the Bible to the Holy Brotherhood, a secret society which had been organized in accordance with the idea I had suggested in my letter. Since I could have no objection I took the oath.

Then Shuvalov told me that I would be in charge of the Kievan branch of the society: I was to organize a group of five; each of the five would in turn organize a group of five known only to him, and so on. He gave me a list of rules, several codes, and some signs by which I could, if the need arose, make myself known to or recognize other members of the society. Evidently the model for the society was one that existed in medieval Venice to fight enemies with arms and, even, poison.

When I returned to Kiev I heard a disturbing rumor that a certain low-class character, the proprietor of an employment agency for servants and governesses, was connected with some sort of a secret society [the Holy Brotherhood].

I had not been back long when I received instructions to leave for Paris, where I would receive further instructions. I went there and registered at the Grand Hotel, across from the opera. Once there, I received word that Polianskii, who was also staying at the hotel, had been instructed by our society to kill Gartman, who two years earlier had tried and failed to assassinate Emperor Alexander II. It was believed that he was now planning to kill Emperor Alexander III.

I knew Polianskii from my Odessa days when, still a bachelor, I was often in the company of actresses. Polianskii, then an Uhlan officer, had been paying court to the very beautiful and fairly well-known actress Glebovaia.

My encounter with him in Paris was in the spirit of comic opera. Our first meeting was at lunch, in the closed terrace. When he asked me for whom I was waiting, I naturally gave him an evasive reply. We met again the following day and again nothing happened. On the third day he gave me the society's recognition sign and I responded with the same sign. Thereupon he said:

> Undoubtedly you have been sent to kill me if I fail to kill Gartman.[3] I have not killed him because I was told not to act until I had received the order from Petersburg. Evidently, you were expected. If you go with me tomorrow morning at five, I can show you that I can have him killed at any time.

I said that I knew nothing.

The following morning I went with him to a place in the Latin Quarter, near a house from which we saw Gartman emerge. Two apaches, whose task it was to pick a fight with him and kill him, had been waiting nearby. They followed him a short distance and then returned to complain to Polianskii. This was their third day on the job, they said, and although each was receiving a hundred francs a day, they were becoming impatient: if Polianskii did not give then the signal to finish

*The Shuvalov home is of historical interest because Marie Antonovna Naryshkina, the intimate friend of Emperor Alexander I, had lived there. It had subsequently passed into the hands of Shuvalov, her husband's nephew, and is now occupied by Shuvalov's widow, Countess "Betsy" Shuvalova.

Gartman off on the following day, they vowed to wash their hands of the whole business.

After this encounter Polianskii told me once more that he had been ordered by Petersburg not to act. When I asked who had given him the order, he told me that it was Zografo.* He suggested that we go to Voisin's, where Zografo would be waiting, possibly with word from Petersburg. Zografo was there when we arrived. I gave him the recognition sign and he replied in kind. We then sat down at his table and Polianskii said to him: "I know why Sergei Iulevich has come; I took him with me today and convinced him that there is some kind of misunderstanding, that I do not know why I am being held back from acting."

Zografo replied that General-Adjutant Wittgenstein was coming to Paris "to liquidate the undertaking." I responded by saying that I had no intention of waiting for Wittgenstein and was leaving immediately for Kiev. And so I did.

I returned to Kiev disgusted over the stupid Gartman episode. My disgust grew when I learned that the Holy Brotherhood had become "the talk of the town," what with rumors that all sorts of riff-raff were joining it to further their careers. I felt that I had to get out of this half-comic, half-odious business. So I wrote Vorontsov-Dashkov that I wanted to leave this society, which I had helped inspire, because within its brief existence it had been transformed into a ludicrous, possibly shameful, affair, with which I did not want to be associated any longer.[4] Yet, I continued, I was honor bound by oath not to leave the society. Therefore, I suggested a way out: the publication of the aim of the society and the names of its members in *Pravitelstvennyi vestnik* and other newspapers. I was certain that the only ones who would agree to have their names published, and thus risk becoming targets of anarchists and revolutionaries, would be those who had joined out of a sense of honor. I knew that many, perhaps the majority, would refuse to have their names published and we would thus be rid of the unworthy elements in our midst. I advised Vorontsov-Dashkov that if I did not receive a reply within a month I would no longer consider myself a member of the society.

After a month passed without a reply, I sent him all the society's documents, including signs and codes, that I had. With this my part in the comic-opera episode came to an end.[5]

I can't help recalling an amusing incident that happened while I was staying at the Grand Hotel.

A young merchant from Ivanovo-Voznesensk, who was staying at the hotel, had had too much to drink on his first day there and had had to be helped to his room, where he was undressed and put to bed. This was after dinner. He did not leave his room the next day or the day after. Meanwhile telegrams from home were arriving for him. Because the Grand Hotel is such a large establishment that no attention is paid to new arrivals, it was not until the

---

*Zografo, a friend of Vorontsov-Dashkov since childhood, and the son of the former envoy to Greece, was the father of Countess Orlova-Davydova, whose husband is one of the richest men in Russia.

third day that, as the merchant's compatriot, I was asked for advice about what to do about his nonappearance. I suggested that we enter his room.

We found him sleeping peacefully, but then he woke and asked how long he had been asleep. With difficulty I convinced him (by the way, he did not speak a word of French) that he had been asleep for nearly three days. He then said that he had awakened from his sleep several times, but finding it dark (the shutters on the windows did not admit any light), he had gone back to bed. After he read a telegram from his wife in which she cursed him out and insisted that he return home, he took the next train back to Russia.

IX

Kiev in the 1880s

More or Less Interesting Personalities

When I lived in Kiev, I met some more or less important people who were to have some effect on subsequent events. I want to say a few words about them, as well as about some who are of interest for other reasons.

Governor-General Chertkov

[About the time that I moved to Kiev] Chertkov was about to leave his post of governor-general of Kiev and commander of the Kiev Military District; his departure followed a senatorial investigation by the well-known A. A. Polovtsov, who made a sensation by immediately taking up arms against Chertkov.[1] I don't think he was worse than the run-of-the-mill governor-general, of whom there are so many. After leaving his post he was out of favor at court for many years and did not receive another administrative appointment until well into the reign of Emperor Nicholas II. During the intervening years he lived on his estate, in the province of Kiev.

Chertkov was quite wealthy, belonged to high society, and had close ties with the Petersburg aristocracy. His arrogance contributed to his fall from favor, but the chief reason for that fall was his marriage to Olga Ivanovna Vereshchagina, a divorcée, whose divorce he had arranged while governor of Voronezh. In those days, in contrast to the present, the court took an unfavorable view of such things as divorce.

Olga Ivanovna, whom I knew in Kiev, was remarkably beautiful and always enjoyed herself. She had many admirers, most of them platonic, among Chertkov's adjutants. It was said, and with good reason, that she is of Jewish origin, the daughter of a liquor dealer, but this is in no way a minus for her. She is a very fine, well-educated, and very cheerful person.

She had a son and a daughter by her first husband, Vereshchagin. The son is in the State Chancellery. The daughter was well along in years when she married Kovalevskii, the procurator of the Warsaw Superior Court; it will soon be two years since he shot himself. Olga Ivanovna had two daughters by Chertkov. Both are in their thirties. One is married to Count Tolstoi, the other to Prince Gagarin.

Although Olga Ivanovna is now an elderly lady, she still gets about in society. People find her an amusing and original person.

Governor-General Drenteln

[Chertkov's successor was General-Adjutant Drenteln.][2] Both Drenteln and his wife, Marie Aleksandrovna, were well thought of in Kiev. He was far superior to Chertkov as governor-general, took a greater interest in his troops than did Chertkov, and enjoyed far more prestige than he.

Drenteln did not see combat in the war with Turkey, but he was an excellent peacetime general who knew his work well and kept the Kiev Military District in brilliant order. He was strict with his troops and harsh toward non-Russians, but he was respected by Russian and non-Russian alike because he was fair, honest, and decent. Although Poles and Jews complained about his harshness toward them, they now acknowledge that his period was one of the best they have experienced because he was very fair.*

Drenteln was very stout, with practically no neck. I was present just after his death [in 1888] of a stroke. He died while on horseback, reviewing his troops. I was just leaving his palace (for some reason the governor-general's residence in Kiev is called a palace) when I saw him being carried in by two of his adjutants: one was Trepov, the current governor-general of Kiev; the other was Afonasopul, who had nothing to distinguish him but his height. I walked behind as his body was taken into his study, and I attended the first memorial service for him.

Drenteln was survived by his wife, now nearly eighty (with an excellent memory for one of her age), a young daughter, and a young son. The daughter married a staff officer Romanenko, who is now a corps commander in Odessa. The son, known as Sasha, attended the University of Kiev, where he did very well. After he graduated, he married Popova, whose father, chairman of the Superior Court, had come into a fortune by marrying a merchant's daughter.

After Drenteln's death Marie Aleksandrovna and her children moved to Petersburg, where young Drenteln enrolled in the Preobrazhenskii Guards Regiment. He is now assistant chief of His Majesty's Field Chancellery and is very close to the Emperor. I mention all this because Drenteln is destined to become one of the major figures at court because of the following circumstances: The

---

*There were attacks on Jews in Kiev during my stay there, but they were not incited by the government. How they started and what provoked them I do not recall. But I remember that when I heard of the attacks I went to watch them and saw a drunken mob marching about the streets, pillaging Jewish stores and homes. Then I saw Cossacks arrive and vigorously use their knouts to break up the mob.[3]

Sovereign and he served in the same regiment; the Sovereign knows that his father, Emperor Alexander III, was very favorably disposed toward Drenteln; being a university graduate, Drenteln is a very cultivated man; also, he is not vulnerable to the petty intrigues that come from having a wife, and this is the most important circumstance that helped establish him firmly at court.

When I became minister of finance, I was able to do Marie Aleksandrovna a slight favor. I had known her even before my first marriage, and after I married she was very kind toward my wife. After her husband's death she received what was a rather small pension for someone in her position; this was because, being very modest and proper, she did not intercede on her own behalf and she had no one to intercede for her, since her son, Sasha, was not yet in a position of influence. So, knowing that her means were limited, I considered it right to supplement her pension, using government funds. (I do not remember the exact sum, but it was not large.)

Speaking of Governor-General Drenteln, I recall an amusing incident involving the lawyer Andreevskii that occurred during his tenure. Andreevskii was the nominal editor of the local liberal newspaper *Zaria*; the real editor was Kupernik, a lawyer of Jewish origin whose daughter is a well-known writer.

Andreevskii was a very witty and frivolous profligate. He had married the daughter of Setov, the impressario of the Kiev opera, expecting that her father would provide her with a large dowry. Instead, complained Andreevskii, she brought with her nothing but the scenery for the fourth act of *Aida*.

He wrote feuilletons for the Sunday edition of *Zaria* in which he poked fun at members of Kievan society. One of these was an honorable artillery colonel whose beautiful wife was pursued, sometimes successfully, by many men. One of these was Prince Constantine Gorchakov, about whom I shall have something to say later. Then Andreevskii began to write a *roman à clef*, which appeared serially in the paper, depicting the colonel's wife and her pursuers, including Prince Gorchakov. This exhausted the patience of the poor colonel, who complained to Drenteln.

In those days journalists were treated as roughly as they are today, under Stolypin. Then, as now, a journalist who printed something offensive would be summoned to the chief of the press department, who would threaten him with unpleasant consequences if he did not behave. Well, Drenteln summoned Andreevskii to his office and said to him: "Is it true that you are writing all sorts of foul things about decent ladies? Well, I am telling you to stop, and I promise you that if you don't, I will deal with you in a way that will surprise you." Andreevskii replied: "Your excellency, you know that I always carry out your instructions, but I ask you to be kind enough to let me have the hero of the novel die quietly. I give you my word that he will die in the next installment, and with his death the novel will come to an end."

Drenteln laughed and sent Andreevskii away.

Governor-General Radetskii

The next governor-general was Radetskii, the famous hero of the last Turkish war, the same Radetskii who held out for so long a time at Shipka (one of the highest peaks in the Balkan Mountains) and kept sending out bulletins stating that all was quiet at Shipka when, in fact, his comparatively meager forces were being bombarded by the Turks. He had prestige as a military man, but he knew nothing of civilian affairs. In any case, he was quite senile by the time he came to Kiev.

The Iuzefovich Family

The Iuzefoviches were a highly respected family in Kiev. The family head was far to the right in his views, but he was a serious, well-read, and learned man. He had two sons. One of them was director of Count Loris-Melikov's chancellery when the count was minister of interior.

The other son now lives in Kiev, where he is a prominent figure in the Black Hundreds. This one is an egregious scoundrel and a man of abnormal passions. While I was minister of finance, I met this Iuzefovich several times at the home of P. P. Hesse, the court commandant. Because I knew of Iuzefovich's bad habits I once asked Hesse how he could permit the man in his home. Hesse replied: "I know him from childhood. He has an excellent style and writes remarkably well. I often have him prepare my memoranda for the Emperor. As far as his vices are concerned, I never permit him to be with my sons."

One can only wonder how fine parents such as this Iuzefovich had could have had a son like him.[4]

Loris-Melikov

Now I want to say a few words about Loris-Melikov, lest I forget to tell about him later on.

I may have seen Loris-Melikov in Tiflis, when I was a boy, but if I did I do not remember. However, most of my family knew him quite well. It was not long after I moved to Kiev that I met him in connection with my work on the general charter of the Russian railroads. After the work on the charter had been completed, Count Baranov presented it to the State Council, where it met strong opposition, directed particularly against the section providing for an autonomous council on railroad affairs, under the nominal control of the minister of ways and communications.

At the time of which I am speaking, Count Loris-Melikov was minister of interior and chief of the supreme commission, a very powerful man whom Katkov called "dictator of the Sovereign's heart." He was in a position to decide whether the charter would be adopted without change or modified. It was about the charter that he summoned me to see him.

He was then staying at Tsarskoe Selo, in a wing of the Great Palace, where Emperor Alexander II was then in residence. When I arrived at the palace, Loris-Melikov was too busy to see me immediately, but he invited me to have lunch with him, just the two of us.

At lunch he immediately began to talk business. "Tell me, dear boy (*dusha moia*)," he asked, "did you (*ty*)* prepare the charter?"

When I said that I had, he replied: "Of course, who else? Baranov is a fine man, but he couldn't prepare it, nor could Annenkov. I have heard that you prepared the whole thing?" I said that I had. Then he said:

> Tell me what you think. You see, no one is strongly opposed to the charter as a whole, but there is opposition to the council. You see, Minister of Ways and Communications Poset is raging against the council, while good old Baranov insists that it is indispensable. So please be candid with me and tell me what you think.

I replied that a council was needed because, since the introduction of railroads, no minister of ways and communications had known his business or had been an authority on railroads. "Under the circumstances," I said, "collegial direction, i.e., a council on railroad affairs, will do better than a minister of ways and communications."

Then he asked me if I had any suggestion for a [suitable] minister of ways and communications. I put forward the name of Ivan Grigorevich Derviz, brother of the Derviz I have spoken about. Ivan Grigorevich was a graduate of the Imperial School of Jurisprudence. He was intelligent and well informed and knew all the ins and outs of the ministry, a hotbed of intrigue. But because I correctly presumed that Loris-Melikov would not have Derviz appointed minister, I continued to insist that the charter be passed without change, to ensure that the council would be able to limit the power of the minister and not be a toy in his hands.

My insistence obviously irritated Loris-Melikov. He said:

> My dear fellow, how you keep insisting—get the charter passed, get it passed. It is easy for you to talk, but to get it passed is easier said than done. Here, let me tell you a story.
>
> When I was a very young officer in the Life Hussar Regiment, the sergeant-major and other non-commissioned officers exercised a great deal of influence on us younger officers. We could not do anything without them and but for them I would have always been in the guardhouse.
>
> Once the sergeant-major of our squadron invited several of us younger officers to his daughter's wedding. After the wedding there was a dinner followed by a ball. We had no trouble with the first dances, a polka and a quadrille,

---

*Like most Armenians and Georgians, Count Loris-Melikov *tutoyered* acquaintances, or those he considered acquaintances. And since he knew my family very well, he took it that he knew me well.

but when they played a mazurka none of us could dance to it and we stood around like mummies. Then the sergeant-major said: ''I will teach these clerks (most of the men there were clerks) how to do it.'' He assembled the clerks and told them that all the ladies had to do in order to dance the mazurka was run, while the men had to keep time in their heads and let their legs take care of themselves.

You keep chattering about getting done, but I must keep time (*takt*)[5] in my head, for if I don't, the Emperor might get rid of me.

In the end, the charter was approved but with such changes as to give the minister of ways and communications more power over the council than I had proposed.

Grand Duchess Alexandra Petrovna and the Oldenburgs

During my stay in Kiev I became acquainted with Grand Duchess Alexandra Petrovna, her two sons, Grand Dukes Nicholas Nikolaevich (the younger) and Peter Nikolaevich, as well as with her brother Prince Constantine Petrovich Oldenburg.

The Grand Duchess was honorable and had a good heart. She was not stupid, but she displayed some of the abnormalities of the Russian Oldenburgs,[6] who, as we all know, are descendants of Grand Duchess Catherine Pavlovna, daughter of Emperor Paul I, and Prince George Oldenburg. One of their children, Peter Georgevich, is known for his philanthropic work during the reigns of Emperors Nicholas I and Alexander II: he established the Imperial School of Jurisprudence, which has given us so many honorable jurists, although it should be noted that graduates of privileged schools have an unfinished air about them.

Prince Peter Georgevich had one daughter, Alexandra Petrovna, and three sons. One of these, Alexander Petrovich, is still among the living and manages to do useful work despite his abnormality. The second son, Constantine Petrovich, died a few years ago, in Nice, after a life of heavy drinking. I will return to Alexandra Petrovna in a moment.

We know that the abnormality of the Russian Oldenburgs can be traced back to Emperor Paul I, who inherited it from his father Emperor Peter III. Why this abnormality did not show itself in the Grand Duchess Catherine Pavlovna, a very normal and intelligent person, is a secret of nature. But it is an unquestionable fact that the abnormality sometimes does not appear in their immediate offspring and then appears in the female, but not the male, line!

The Grand Duchess Alexandra Petrovna was married to Grand Duke Nicholas Nikolaevich (the elder) and bore him two sons, whom I have already mentioned. She was not especially happy in her marriage. As we know he had an affair with the dancer Chislova, who bore him a daughter, now married to Prince Cantacuzene, and is accepted as a relative, at least by the Mikhailovich branch of the Imperial family.

Why Grand Duchess Alexandra Petrovna's marriage was unsuccessful is difficult for an outsider to judge, even for one who knows all the circumstances; only surmise is possible. Perhaps it was because the Grand Duke had an inclination for a free and easy life. Perhaps it was because the Grand Duchess was somewhat abnormal: she was very religious, in a markedly sanctimonious way; and she suffered from a nervous condition that left her legs paralyzed. In Kiev, I had occasion to see her get up suddenly and walk, but not for long; later, in Petersburg, I saw her walking for long periods. Whatever the reason for her unhappiness with her husband, the fact is that she was finally to leave and take up residence in Kiev.

She came to Kiev while I was there, after a long sea voyage from Petersburg to Odessa. According to the newspapers, she had taken the voyage in the hope that the sea air might relieve the paralysis that affected her legs. But nasty tongues in Petersburg had it that her association with the priest Lebedev, who enjoyed her special favor, had led Emperor Alexander II to advise her to take a sea voyage.

Whatever the facts about her sea voyage, it is a fact that after completing it she took up residence in Kiev, in an imperial palace beautifully located above the Dnieper in Lipki [a fashionable part of Kiev]. Her master of the court was Alexander Aleksandrovich Rostovtsev, formerly her husband's adjutant—a fine, well-bred, very cheerful and amusing man who, unfortunately, was virtually without the use of his legs. Her priest was Lebedev, who came with her to live at the palace.

Everyone living in Lipki, among them I and my wife, benefited from the high status of the Grand Duchess. She asked me and my wife to visit in the evenings, even without an invitation. She invited others as well. This was evidently for the benefit of the priest Lebedev, an ardent card player. We would play vingt, for small stakes. Sometimes, while we were playing, the Grand Duchess would be brought in on an easy chair. Usually, though, if we saw her at all, it was at evening services, and then only fleetingly.

This priest Lebedev conducted services very well and had an excellent choir. But he was an ugly, rough-hewn, boorish man who dressed as foppishly as it was possible for a priest to dress. It was evident that he exercised tremendous influence on the Grand Duchess. She felt love for him, of a psychopathological character, typical of the Oldenburg abnormality, but from what I was able to observe, her relationship to this priest was platonic. Also, I came to know her sons.

One son, Grand Duke Peter Nikolaevich, I found to be a very nice young man. But he was and is a man of limited ability and is not capable of performing any useful function.

The other son, Grand Duke Nicholas Nikolaevich [then called "the younger" to distinguish him from his father], currently the commander of the Petersburg Military District, stood out from the other grand dukes in those days because he was a general staff officer, i.e., he allegedly had graduated from the General Staff

Academy. How seriously he had studied there I do not know. In any event he was and is much more intelligent than his brother, but he has inherited a generous amount of Emperor Paul's abnormality.[7] And with the passage of the years that abnormality has become more evident. In the past five or so years it has had a baneful effect on several governmental matters and an even more baneful effect on the life of the Imperial family. Perhaps I shall have more to say later about this aspect of the Grand Duke. In any case, I have already dealt with it in part in my "political memoirs," and I will have more to say there.

When the two brothers came to visit their mother, we would usually play vingt every evening—Grand Duke Nicholas Nikolaevich, I, the priest Lebedev, Rostovtsev, and occasionally, another invited Kievan. Because the visits were usually during the summer, when it was very hot, we would play without our jackets. I remember that at one game the priest Lebedev said something about Emperor Nicholas I that Grand Duke Nicholas Nikolaevich considered to be too familiar. Up jumped the Grand Duke and screamed, "Remember you are speaking of my grandfather." Then he sat down and calmly resumed play.

Well, in the end Emperor Alexander III felt compelled to act because of the rumors he had heard about the Grand Duchess and the priest Lebedev. He did not like to have any member of the Imperial family be the subject of unpleasant rumors. And evidently he did not relish the idea of a priest such as Lebedev living in the palace. So, the Grand Duchess was asked to vacate it to make room for the Emperor, who was coming to Kiev for a visit. (I shall speak later about the visit.) Actually, there was more than enough room for both of them.

The Grand Duchess and the priest then moved to another house in Lipki. She built a private chapel at her new home, and the priest Lebedev continued to play his accustomed role and to be the source of such rumors that he was transferred to Petersburg, to serve in the private chapel of the Grand Duke Nicholas Nikolaevich (the elder).

Some time later, by which time I was back in Petersburg, she bought a large estate in Kiev, on which she established something in the nature of a hospital and a convent, and gave her time to them. We remained on good terms; when I had occasion to be in Kiev I would usually visit her. Also, she would write me kindly and attentive letters, and I, for my part, would help her with her affairs, largely through advice. The institution which she established was undoubtedly useful. She was buried there.

If she were alive today, she would be astonished to learn of my recent disputes with her son the Grand Duke Nicholas Nikolaevich.

Prince Constantine Petrovich Oldenburg

As I have noted, I became acquainted with Prince Constantine Petrovich at the home of his sister. His abnormality: addiction to drink. Also, one had to talk only once with him to realize that he was up to his ears in debt. While in Kiev he became acquainted with Lev Brodskii, a very rich Jew, from whom he naturally borrowed money. Whether or not he repaid it, I do not know.

When I met him, he was in command of a regiment in Kutais, in the Caucasus, where he had been sent because of his heavy drinking. In the Caucasus he had fallen in love with an Imeretian woman, the wife of one of the native officers, and had had to marry her after she divorced her husband. She was given the title Countess Zarnikau. She was very gentle and decent and far from stupid, but not a cultivated person: for example, she spoke French poorly.

In later years they were permitted to return to Petersburg. I know the prince obtained money on several occasions from Emperor Nicholas II, who is far less strict with the Imperial family than was his father. This is understandable, given the fact that he became Emperor when he was very young.

Prince Constantine Petrovich had three daughters and, I believe, three sons. I knew the sons when they were boys, but have not seen them for a long time. The youngest daughter married Plen, a navel officer of no particular distinction. The second daughter was a semi-idiot to start with and later went completely mad: she is now somewhere in a sanatorium.

The eldest daughter was first married to Prince Iurevskii. She subsequently left him and married Lev Naryshkin, my son-in-law's brother. I meet her abroad quite often. She is a very nice woman, but, in my opinion she is abnormal like the rest of the Oldenburgs.

Prince Alexander Petrovich Oldenburg

[It is appropriate to say something here about Grand Duchess Alexandra Petrovna's brother Prince Alexander Petrovich Oldenburg.] He is a remarkable type.

His name is linked with several institutions established through his efforts or those of his father: the Institute of Experimental Medicine, the psychiatric hospital on Udelnaia, the Imperial School of Jurisprudence, the special *gimnaziia* of the Twelfth Company of the Izmailovskii Guards Regiment, the Petersburg People's House, and the health resort at Gagri.

Most Russians believe that the institutions established through the efforts of Prince Alexander were paid for from his pocket. Not so. They were paid for by the government. And there is no question that if the government's money used for these institutions had been given to ordinary mortals there would have been far less waste and inefficiency. However, ordinary mortals would not have been able to get money for such institutions. He, on the other hand, could, for he is the kind of highly placed zealot who can badger officials, and even the Emperor, into parting with hundreds of thousands of rubles from the state treasury just to be rid of him. Also, one should note in fairness to the prince that if there is something that has to be done rapidly, particularly something out of the ordinary, he is the man for such a task.

If one accepts what history has to say about the personality of Emperor Paul, one must say that no one in the Imperial family resembles him more closely than does Prince Alexander Petrovich Oldenburg. Prince Alexander is not an evil man.

In fact, he is a good man, but, to put it mildly, he has inherited an "unusual" personality and temperament.[8]

As a minister of finance I was to have several unpleasant encounters with him. Once, for example, he told me that His Majesty had ordered that he be given a hundred thousand rubles from government funds for something or other. When I asked if he had been empowered as a general-adjutant to state this officially, he answered ambiguously. Usually he managed to get what he asked for by putting His Majesty and me, especially, in an unpleasant position.

Also, I had unpleasant encounters with him on the commission to combat the plague.* In 1897, while he was inspecting the situation in the Kirghiz steppe, I, as senior member of the commission, served as chairman in his absence. Well, we received a telegram from him, couched in his usual imperious terms, stating that because of the appearance of the plague, the export of certain food products from certain regions should be prohibited. Naturally, I could not agree to such an action, under any circumstances, for if I had, all Europe would have been alarmed and would have felt fully justified in banning the import of many food products originating in Russia. The other members of the commission agreed with me, as did the Emperor. Prince Oldenburg took grave offense and after he returned to Petersburg would have nothing to do with me for a long time. I returned the compliment.

When my good friend D. S. Sipiagin became minister of interior, he persuaded me to take the initiative in renewing relations with the prince. I then made an appointment by telephone to call on the prince. When I saw him, I found him as eccentric as ever.

After I had said that everything had ended well with the plague because of the actions he had taken on the spot and that, after all, the prohibition of the export of some food items had not been necessary, he replied with tears in his eyes that the episode had brought on heart trouble, from which he was still suffering.

While we were talking, the prince walked nervously around the room. Twice his manservant appeared, said something to him, received an order, and left the room. Then the manservant returned once more, and the prince, without saying a word to me, rushed from the room. Ten minutes passed before he returned, this time in good spirits, shouting: "She is awake, she is awake." When I asked what had happened, he told me that they had a very old nurse whom they had been unable to rouse from her sleep for a few days, but that a huge enema had awakened her. This put Prince Oldenburg in a good frame of mind, and we parted on excellent terms.

I also had some differences with Prince Oldenburg over the consumption of liquor. It came about this way. When I introduced the liquor monopoly in Peters-

*In 1896 isolated cases of the plague began to appear in India and on our soil, in the province of Astrakhan and on the Kirghiz steppe. On January 11, 1897, the Special Commission to Prevent the Entry of the Plague into Russia was established, with Prince Alexander Petrovich Oldenburg as chairman. I and other ministers concerned with public health were appointed as members.

burg, an official temperance board was established in this city. At my suggestion, His Majesty appointed the prince chairman of the board, a post he still holds. I did this because I wanted a man as chairman who had access to the Emperor, a man who could do what no ordinary mortal could. Without him the board could not have received the extensive funds it did, for the State Council would not have agreed to the expenditure of so much money, but, as I have said, he has ways: he has organized large enterprises without any money at hand, but in the knowledge that one way or another the money will be provided, for if all else fails, he could ask the Emperor to order it done.

It was thanks to the prince that the so-called People's House was constructed and still functions—it is a special place for wholesome diversion, if not for all the people, at least for the poorer classes of Petersburg. But the two of us had some differences over the fact that he permitted the consumption of strong drink at certain festivities for the common people, something which I have always opposed.

His son Prince Peter Aleksandrovich Oldenburg, a fine young man, does not take after him psychologically, but his health is poor. Because of his poor health, his marriage to Grand Duchess Olga Aleksandrovna, in July 1901, was not applauded in high society. They were married solely because it was the young Grand Duchess's wish and the Dowager Empress may be criticized for not exerting sufficient influence on her kindly but capricious daughter to keep her from marrying the prince.

D. I. Pikhno

When I came to Kiev, Dmitrii Ivanovich Pikhno was already publisher of the newspaper *Kievlianin*, which in those days took a somewhat liberal position. In addition he sometimes wrote for Katkov, in the *Moskovskie vedomosti*, and for Aksakov, in *Rus*. I found Aksakov's position more to my taste than Katkov's.[9] During my stay in Kiev we quarreled over numerous issues, which I will deal with later. We still quarrel, in the State Council, over the question of introducing zemstvos in the western provinces. In the 1880s he was to the left of me; now I am to his left.

In point of fact Pikhno has his good points: he is intelligent, was a good newspaper man, was a professor, of statistics I believe, at the University of Kiev. But he is not well educated, in the Western sense: he knows little of the outside world, in which he has traveled but little, knows no foreign languages. On the whole, he is prominent in Russian public life, but he will be forgotten a few months after his death.

Pikhno is the son of a rich merchant. He completed a military *gimnaziia* and then entered the Faculty of Jurisprudence of the University of Kiev. While a student he earned extra money by giving lessons and serving as a reporter for the *Kievlianin*.

Vitalii Shulgin, the publisher of the newspaper, was a well known professor of history who taught at the university, the Institute for Noble Girls, and other institutions. He published a textbook on general history which I, like most *gimnazia* students in the late 1860s, used in my studies. He was not a distinguished scholar, but he was a very able and popular lecturer. Although he was a hunchback, the girls at the institute found him enchanting. One of them, a very beautiful girl (whose maiden name I do not recall), fell in love with him and married him just after her graduation. This was a June and December wedding that soured after she learned some facts of life.

By this time Shulgin was the publisher of *Kievlianin*, a newspaper with a small circulation, but one that was widely read because of Shulgin's talent. Soon after Pikhno became a reporter for the paper, he and Mme. Shulgina became lovers, although she was older than he. It is said that [Vasilii Vitalevich] Shulgin, now a member of the State Duma, is, in fact, the natural son of Pikhno and Mme. Shulgina.[10]

When [Vitalii] Shulgin died, his fortune went to his widow, for the duration of her life; after her death the bulk of the fortune was to go to his daughter, who was deformed as he was, the rest to his son.

Pikhno succeeded Shulgin as editor and, to boot, married his widow. The marriage was not a happy one. Because my office was opposite the Pikhno home, I was witness to several scenes between them. Several times I saw Mme. Pikhno running out of the house, disheveled, hatless, and Pikhno, also hatless, running after her. Evidently she had run out of the house because they had quarreled and he had run after to see that she did not harm herself. Because she suffered from consumption she did not have long to live. After her death, he married the deformed daughter.

Because all Kiev knew the story the city became too small for Pikhno, so he turned to Bunge,* his former teacher at the university, by now minister of finance. As rector of the university, Bunge had helped Pikhno win a professorship at the university. Now, as minister of finance, he helped secure Pikhno a position on the Council of Railroad Affairs, in Petersburg.

Bunge had also brought another Kievan, Kartavtsev, to Petersburg, to serve as director of the Peasants' and Nobles' Banks. Bunge was considered very liberal in those days and for that reason became the indirect target of the conservative Constantine Petrovich Pobedonostsev. Pobedonostsev began a direct attack on Kartavtsev and Pikhno, and thus an indirect attack on Bunge, by accusing the two

---

*Thanks to me, Bunge, one of the best professors of financial law in Russia, had left the rectorship of the University of Kiev to become assistant minister of finance and later minister of finance.

At the meeting with Count Loris-Melikov about which I have spoken, the question of a replacement for Admiral Greig, one of the weakest of our finance ministers, had arisen. I suggested Bunge because he was an able man and, more important, because he was a strong supporter of the gold standard, without which we could not have put our finances on a sound basis. Count Loris-Melikov put Bunge's name before Emperor Alexander II, but the Emperor, not wishing to hurt Greig's feelings, appointed Bunge assistant minister. Greig soon left his post and was replaced by Abaza, whose tenure was short. He was succeeded by Bunge.[11]

of being extreme liberals. As we know Kartavtsev lost his position because all the nobles complained against him, and Emperor Alexander III supported their interests. But it was more difficult to find grounds for forcing Pikhno out. Finally, Constantine Petrovich unearthed the fact that Pikhno's marriage to his step-daughter was in violation of church law, and hence invalid. After he brought this fact to the attention of the Emperor, Pikhno had to leave Petersburg and return to Kiev, where he resumed his previous activities.

The Establishment of *Kievskoe slovo*, My Polemics with Pikhno, and My Book—*Principles of Railroad Tariffs*

Because Pikhno used *Kievlianin* to attack our railroad policy in general and the Southwestern Railroad in particular and because we disagreed on financial and other matters, I established a newspaper of my own, *Kievskoe slovo*, through which I could present my views. Since I did not feel that it was in keeping with my position to be listed officially as publisher, I chose a stand-in, Professor Antono-vich, a typically cunning Little Russian [Ukrainian] who had been Pikhno's assistant on *Kievlianin* and had long dreamed of parting company with him be-cause of their differences. Many years later Antonovich was to be my assistant minister of finance.

In *Kievskoe slovo* we conducted polemics with Pikhno on many issues, but most of all concerning railroad operations. Pikhno favored government opera-tion of railroads and governmental intervention in the affairs of privately owned companies, particularly in the setting of tariffs. I took a quite different position.

These disputes finally led me to expound my theory of railroad tariffs in a book, *Principles of Railroad Tariffs*, which I wrote while taking the waters at Marienbad. After the first edition sold out, I prepared a second, enlarged edition, again doing the writing while taking the waters abroad. A year ago a third edition appeared. Although the book is somewhat out of date, it continues to serve as a guide for all railroad officials who deal with tariffs and other economic aspects of railroading.

Our polemics had provided Pikhno with material for his doctoral dissertation, which had earned him a professorship.

After I left Kiev I was not to see Pikhno again until I invited him to take part in the Special Conference on the Needs of Rural Industry, of which I was chairman. He was still fairly liberal, arguing, for example, that only laws approved by the majority of the State Council should be submitted to the Emperor for approval or disapproval; this would preclude the Emperor from approving a minority decision.

Subsequently, during our so-called revolution, he rushed like a madman over to the right, became an adherent of the Union of the Russian People, and began to espouse reactionary views in *Kievlanin*. Thanks to his new political orientation, he was made a member of the State Council, in which he now speaks for the views of the Black Hundreds. Compared to him I am now an extreme liberal.

Interestingly enough, Pikhno and Antonovich became reconciled after 1905, when both became ardent supporters of the Black Hundreds, in order to further their careers. Pikhno's career was furthered, Antonovich's was not: I believe that he now lives on a pension.

There are some differences between the two. Antonovich was somewhat superior to Pikhno as a professor, and his books showed more talent than did Pikhno's, but Pikhno is unquestionably more intelligent, firmer in his convictions, has a stronger character.

University Professors

In the 1880s there were several fairly prominent professors at the University of Kiev.

One of them was the physician Mering, who treated Count Kotzebue while I lived in Odessa. He played the kind of role in Kiev that Botkin now plays among us in Petersburg. Professor Mering was born in Germany, studied medicine abroad, then came to Russia at the invitation of a landowner, to serve as doctor at his sugar factory, not far from Kiev. He quickly learned Russian, but retained a sharp German accent. When his practice expanded he moved to Kiev, passed the medical examinations, and became professor of internal medicine at the university. He married one of the Ivanenkos (my first wife's family), who where well known in the south because many of them served as marshals of the nobility in Chernigov province.

Gradually he gained a reputation both as professor and practitioner, with a large practice and a clinic at the university, which had the reputation of being an outstanding research center. One could say that he was one of the medical luminaries of the south.

Over the years he accumulated a considerable fortune, not from his medical practice, but from real estate, which he bought and sold on the advice of poor, grateful Jews whom he treated without fee. They would tell him of business enterprises, houses, estates, and the like, that could be purchased and sold at a profit. When we lived in Lipki, he had a house on the Kreshchatik, the main street, and behind it a parcel of land that stretched almost up to Lipki. As the city grew, the parcel was subdivided and developed and Mering's fortune grew and grew.

Mering's son, who was to marry Sonia, my first wife's daughter, graduated from the university, then went abroad to study astronomy. His father hoped he would become a professor of astronomy, but he would not take the examinations to become a docent, and returned instead to Kiev during the time that Vyshnegradskii was minister of finance. I recall how Professor Mering would complain about his son's refusal to become a professor, about his penchant for gambling. He was afraid that his son would come to a bad end, and he was right.

Professor Mering could hardly walk because he suffered from a disease that he called "elephantine legs." Because of his inability to walk he would go about the city in a phaeton drawn by two horrible nags. Everybody in Kiev knew and respected him. When his phaeton, looking like a canopy, and its two nags appeared on the horizon everyone knew that it was Professor Mering who was coming.

One time when he came to our house to see my wife, who was ill, I noticed that he was smiling and asked him why. He said:

> Because of something that happened to me. My coachman is ill and the gardener took his place. As we were driving along he suddenly became frightened and shouted at me that the horses were running away. At that one of the horses turned its head to me and laughed: he thought it was funny that the man should be frightened at horses that could barely move their legs.

Mering's disease proved to be fatal. A few days before his death, he described the disease to me in the most dispassionate terms. It was as if he knew death were near and he was pleased to be able to describe the disease so well.

Another medical luminary in Kiev was Professor Karavaev, professor of surgery at the university, whose ability had been recognized by the famous surgeon and public figure Pirogov. Karavaev was also well known abroad: I know that he was summoned to Paris to remove a cataract from the eye of a member of the family of Emperor Napoleon III.

Yet another well known professor at the university was the surgeon Hübbenet, whose brother was chief of police in Kiev. It was said that Hübbenet was not a bad surgeon, that he had performed many successful operations during the Crimean War, but he was marked by that unbelievable German stupidity that permits a man to be clever in his own field, yet otherwise stupid.

Once when Emperor Alexander II came to Kiev, and visited the university, Hübbenet was among those presented to him. The Emperor, who *tutoyered* everyone, asked Hübbenet: "Are you (*ty*) the brother of the local chief of police?" Hübbenet was very insulted and replied: "Your Imperial Majesty, he is not my brother, I am his." The Emperor laughed heartily but did not reply.

Still another eminent professor at the university was Rennenkampf, professor of the philosophy of law and of international law, who succeeded Bunge as rector. On the whole there were more eminent men at the university then than are to be found there today, and most of those who are now eminent are past their prime.

The University Rector Rennenkampf
and Adjutant Trepov

While I lived in Kiev, there were many disturbances at the university. I want to tell about one of them. On this occasion Governor-General Drenteln and his adjutant

F. F. Trepov (the present governor-general of Kiev), drove over to the university because a certain professor had told the governor-general that the students were rioting and were threatening to besiege the rector's quarters.[12] While Drenteln was in the rector's office, Trepov waited in the anteroom with Professor Subbotin, a man of mediocre intellect and of no particular distinction. When Subbotin made some rather critical remarks about Drenteln, Trepov could think of no better response than to slap him. This Trepov is not a bad sort at all, but he is very limited, probably the most limited of the Trepovs.*

The Brodskiis

Israel Brodskii was the most prominent and one of the wealthiest among the many Jews in Kiev. A fine old man, with the look of a Biblical patriarch, he did not look like a Jew. His fortune came from his many sugar factories and from the sugar beet estates that supplied them. He was probably one of the major capitalists of the southwestern region. There is an unfounded, but firmly held, belief that he began to build his fortune by forging treasury notes during the Crimean War. I often had business dealings with him and found him a highly intelligent, but uneducated, man.

Also, I met his brother when I worked in Odessa. The brother was very rich, but not quite as rich as the Kievan Brodskii. In contrast to the Kievan Brodskii, the Odessa Brodskii made a repulsive impression: without going into his morals, one can say that his physiognomy, his mannerisms, even his speech were entirely Jewish.

The Kievan Brodskii was survived by three sons. The oldest, who was insane and lived at home under the supervision of a servant and a doctor, did not live long after his father's death. The second son, Lazar, who did not live long either, left part of his inheritance to his children, part to his sisters, and the rest to the third of Israel Brodskii's sons, Lev.

Although Lev Brodskii still lives in Kiev, he spends much of his time in spas that provide roulette. I often meet him in Biarritz, where he spends part of the year because the card playing there is heavy. Just recently I was visited by someone who had just returned from Nice. When I asked who was there from Russia, he told me that he had seen Lev Brodskii lose 600,000 francs there in the course of a week.

Potocki and His Son

Few Poles lived in Kiev, but a number of Polish landowners would come to Kiev for the contract fair,[13] among them Count Potocki, the Potocki who had served as governor of Galicia. A typical Polish magnate, his manners were graceful, his French excellent, his attitude toward peasants, particularly Russian peasants,

*F. F. Trepov was the oldest son of the Trepov who was prefect under Alexander II.

was that shown toward cattle. In fact, Polish magnates consider their cattle superior to their peasants.

When he came to town he would stay at a small house that belonged to him. I had business dealings with him because he owned a good deal of land and I was sometimes invited to dinners that he gave at his house.

When he died, he left two sons. One owns all the Potocki estates in Austria. The other, a deputy to either the First or Second State Duma, is married to the daughter of Prince Radziwill, a former general-adjutant to William I. He lives on a luxurious scale. During the past few winters he gave many large parties in Petersburg. This winter he is living on his large estate, after receiving the concession to build a railroad from Shepetovka to Proskurova, which runs through his estate.

A. A. Polovtsov

While I lived in Kiev the very wealthy and well-known senator Polovtsov came there to conduct a senatorial investigation, to which I have referred. I had few contacts with Polovtsov then, but later, after becoming minister of finance, I became better acquainted with him.

Polovtsov is a remarkable man. He came from a minor noble family, graduated from the Imperial School of Jurisprudence, and, but for his marriage, might have ended up as nothing but a minor official. To be sure, there is a possibility that he might have gone higher because graduates of that school always help one another.

Polovtsov was an almost penniless bureaucrat when he successfully courted the adopted daughter of Stieglitz,[14] one of the richest bankers in Russia. She was his only heir and, incidentally, very beautiful. When Stieglitz died [in 1884], he left his entire fortune—50 million rubles in government notes and considerable real estate—to his adopted daughter. This made Polovtsov a very rich man, for he now owned, or at least had at his disposal, his wife's entire fortune, which produced a yearly income of a few million rubles.

Thanks to his wealth and to the support of several grand dukes, notably Grand Duke Vladimir Aleksandrovich, he was able to go far in the official world. After the Grand Duke was appointed to the Senate, Polovtsov, too, became a senator. Then followed Polovtsov's appointment as Imperial secretary, member of the State Council, member of the Finance Committee. He was one of the most intelligent members of the council.

I found him to be an interesting, but unsympathetic person, a *parvenu* in every sense of the word: he was very obsequious and pleasant toward highly placed persons or persons whose good will he needed or thought he might need, but toward persons in inferior positions he was arrogant, even insolent. On the whole, he was not a nice person, and I say that he was not even a decent man, not the kind one could trust completely.[15]

Also, I found Polovtsov something of a puzzle. Although he was intelligent and well rounded, even in government affairs, he managed to squander most of his wife's fortune through speculation. How could so intelligent a man be so frivolous and stupid in his own affairs?

Prince Gorchakov

I first met Prince [Constantine Aleksandrovich] Gorchakov in Kiev, an extraordinarily handsome man who was considered quite attractive even up to recent times. He now lives not far from me and is a grandfather. (He had been married to the daughter of Prince Sturdza, of Rumania, but they were divorced.)

Prince Gorchakov is very rich, having inherited a large estate from his father, Chancellor Gorchakov, and from his older brother, Prince [Michael Aleksandrovich] Gorchakov, the former minister of Madrid, who died a bachelor. How Chancellor Gorchakov amassed a fortune is something of a mystery. It is said, although I have no proof of it, that he speculated with the Russian ruble. In any event, it is known that the chancellor died a rich man although he had not inherited any kind of fortune from his relatives.[16]

I find Prince [Constantine Aleksandrovich] Gorchakov, as I did Polovtsov, very unsympathetic. I often ask myself: what do these people need? They have position and money, yet it is in their nature to lick the boots of the powerful, of such men as grand dukes, and they do so in a manner that decent people must find offensive and repellent.

As for the older brother, he was quite abnormal. First of all, he had quite unnatural instincts, for a man. Moreover, he was a Pliushkin[17]—pathologically stingy, even though he was very rich. The secretary of our Madrid legation told me that Prince Gorchakov would walk the streets of Madrid picking up cigar and cigarette butts, which he would save.

As I said, he left his money to his younger brother, who, far from squandering the inheritance, managed to add to it.

X

Kiev in the 1880s

Contacts with Emperor Alexander III and His Family

My First Trip with Emperor Alexander III

While I was in Kiev I had several occasions to travel with Emperor Alexander III on trips through the area served by the Southwestern Railroad. The first was not long after he had ascended the throne. He had come to Kiev with several members of his family for a few days. Andreevskii, then still the manager of the railroad, had accompanied the Imperial party to Kiev. For some reason he could not accompany the party when it was to depart and I was to take his place.

I remember the scene in the Imperial waiting room at departure time as if it were today. The first to arrive were the Emperor's brothers Grand Dukes Vladimir and Alexis. A few minutes later the Emperor, the Empress, and their boys Nicholas (the present Emperor) and George arrived. A large group, in full dress uniform, had gathered to see the Emperor off. The boys were very playful and kept running between the legs of the assembled guests. Suddenly Grand Duke Vladimir Aleksandrovich grabbed Nicholas by the ears, dragged him off, telling him emphatically to behave. I remarked to someone that when Nicholas would become emperor, in a few decades, he might remember this episode and that, if he did not, someone would remind him of it.

Unfortunately the time for Nicholas to ascend the throne was to come much sooner than I expected, only eleven years after this incident. Because Emperor Nicholas II is naturally kind, particularly toward his relatives, it would not have occurred to him to remind Vladimir Aleksandrovich of the suffering he had endured at his hands. Emperor Nicholas II loved Vladimir Aleksandrovich very much, and the latter, for his part, held the Emperor in high respect, but being a more experienced, more cultivated, and more intelligent man, could not but be aware of many shortcomings in the administration of the state, shortcomings which, unfortunately, weakened the empire, a matter about which I shall have occasion to speak many times. For the present I will say only that Emperor Nicholas II ascended the throne completely unprepared for the role he had to assume. Emperor Alexander III bears much of the responsibility for this because he did not prepare him adequately, but then he did not expect to die so soon and, therefore, put off the preparation of his son, whom he considered very young, in order to concentrate on the affairs of state.

To return to my account of Emperor Alexander III's departure from Kiev, I should relate that the train left late at night and that the following morning the two boys would dash off the train at every stop, ignoring their tutor's admonitions, to inspect the train's journal boxes. I was in constant fear that they might be left behind.

Emperor Alexander III's Trip to Maneuvers

Several years later I accompanied Emperor Alexander III to a small station north of Brest, to observe army maneuvers. For this occasion he made his base at a nearby mansion that belonged to a Polish noble.

Accompanying the Emperor was Grand Duke Nicholas Nikolaevich (the elder), of whom the Emperor was not particularly fond, first because the two had had differences during the war with Turkey, second because of differences in temperament: the Emperor was a very simple, modest, and gentle man, while the Grand Duke was a noisy sort. I recall how at one station the Grand Duke used the crook of his cane to grab Baron Taube, an engineer, by the neck and nearly knocked him off his feet. Such obstreperous actions did not sit well with the Emperor.

Also, I recall two incidents involving William, Crown Prince, later Emperor, of Germany.* On learning that Emperor Alexander III would be present at the maneuvers, the prince's grandfather William I asked for permission to send his grandson there with greetings for our Emperor. Our Emperor did not wish the crown prince to attend the maneuvers, which by this time were almost over, and decided to head him off by meeting him at Brest. But he wanted to meet him in his Prussian uniform, which was in Petersburg. So General-Adjutant Cherevin, chief of Imperial security, asked me how long it would take for a courier to bring the uniform. I replied that it could be done in forty-eight hours, by express. Cherevin gave the necessary orders and the uniform arrived on time, just as the Emperor was ready to leave for Brest. Of course I accompanied the Imperial party.

The scene at Brest, minor but revealing, is etched in my memory. Our Emperor, in his Prussian uniform, wearing a Russian military greatcoat, had just

---

*The first time I ever saw William was at Ems, shortly before the death of his grandfather William I. The old Emperor was staying at the Kurhaus and, as was his custom, usually sat near a large window overlooking the square, thus permitting everyone to see him at work. I was surprised to see that the young William was constantly at the side of his grandfather, acting like an office boy, very respectfully opening and sealing envelopes, providing pens and pencils and the like.

managed to alight from his train when the train bearing the prince arrived from Warsaw. The Emperor took off his greatcoat and handed it to his Cossack escort before advancing to meet the prince. Upon completion of the greetings by the ceremonial honor guard, the Emperor shouted for his greatcoat. At that, William, who understood a few words of Russian, dashed over to the Cossack, snatched the greatcoat out of his hands, carried it back, and placed it around the Emperor's shoulders.

In those days I paid little attention to politics, but seeing this I thought to myself that William must stand in awe of the Emperor. In fact, even after he became emperor, William remained in awe of our Emperor and told me after Emperor Alexander III's death: "There, truly, was an autocratic Emperor."

In many respects Emperor Alexander III did not look like an emperor. A tall but flabby man, not handsome, an unaffected, slovenly, bearlike man, one could imagine him a Russian peasant from the central provinces by seeing him in one's mind's eye in a sheepskin coat and bast shoes. In many respects he was not majestic. But his fine heart, his strong character, his calmness, his sense of fairness were all reflected in his face, giving him the look of true majesty. Dress him however you like and put him in a room of strangers who did not know his position, and you would find that he would still be impressive and attract everyone's attention. Therefore, I understood that Emperor William II had caught a glimpse of the truly imperial nature of Emperor Alexander III.[1]

But, to return to the meeting at Brest.

The Emperor took Prince William to the fortress at Brest, where a large dinner was served. I did not have a high enough rank then to be invited to dine, but I could observe Prince William. In most respects he was different from Emperor Alexander III. William, like Grand Duke Nicholas Nikolaevich (the elder), was a foppish guards officer. He was the typical Prussian guards officer, with his turned up mustache, his mannerisms in walking, his affected elegance.

After dinner everyone watched the fireworks provided by the artillery. The following morning the Emperor accompanied William back.

Emperor Alexander III's Journeys on the Southwestern Railroad in 1888

In the summer and early fall [of 1888] the Emperor traveled several times on the lines of the Southwestern Railroad, en route to the maneuvers at Elizavetgrad and back, then once again en route to the Crimea or the Caucasus (I do not remember which). A month or so later he was to return to Petersburg, but not on the lines of the Southwestern Railroad: it was on this trip that the terrible accident at Borki was to occur.

I would meet the Emperor's train at the point where it entered the lines of the Southwestern Railroad and supervise the journey from there on, but I had no control over the schedule, which was usually prepared by the Ministry of Ways and Communications without consulting the manager of the railroad. It was but a few hours before I was to accompany the Emperor, who was en route to maneuvers, from Rovno to Fastov, that I was given a schedule that could be safely met on our road only by a light passenger train. But the cars of the Imperial train were heavy, and the speed called for could be met only by having two heavy freight locomotives pull the train. I saw that it would be quite possible that the locomotives could break up the road and jump the track. That night, after we left Rovno, I was almost in a fever, expecting an accident at any moment, while the others were sleeping. And there I was, assigned to the rear car in the train, with no way of communicating with the engineers.

When we reached Fastov and I turned the train over to the management of the next railroad on the line, I was unable to get any message to Admiral Poset, the minister of ways and communications, or to Baron Sherval, the chief inspector of railroads, about my fears. So when I returned to Kiev, I immediately wrote a report to Admiral Poset, explaining why the speed at which we had traveled was unsafe: the rails were too light (considerably lighter than those on foreign lines); we had wooden ties in contrast to the steel ties used abroad; we used sand for ballast, abroad they generally used crushed stone. Under such circumstances, I wrote, a heavy train could knock the rails loose. I said that I had not had the speed changed for fear of provoking an incident, but that I had no intention of assuming responsibility for the train's safety on its return trip along our stretch of the road, from Fastov to Kovel, if the speed were not reduced. (I believe that I asked that the schedule from Fastov to Kovel be increased by three hours.) I concluded by saying that I would not accompany the train if the schedule were not changed. In reply I received a telegram ordering the schedule lengthened as requested.

When the time arrived for the Imperial train to pull into Fastov, on its return trip, the passengers aboard were asleep, but they soon awakened, began to leave the train and walk around the platform. I found the attitude toward me rather chilly. Admiral Poset looked askance at me. Count Vorontsov-Dashkov acted as if we were strangers. Then General Cherevin began to convey a message to me that the Emperor was displeased with the Southwestern Railroad. As he spoke, the Emperor himself came up and listened to our conversation. When I tried to tell Cherevin what I had reported to Admiral Poset, the Emperor said to me: "What are you talking about? I have traveled on other roads and nowhere else has my speed been reduced; your railroad is an impossible one because it is a kikish (*zhidovskaia*) road." (This remark was inspired by the fact that Bloch, the chairman of the board, was a Jew.) Naturally, I did not reply.

Later, within earshot of the Emperor, Admiral Poset implied that the railroad must be in poor condition, for no other road had "dared" demand that the Emperor travel at a reduced speed. I could not contain myself and told him: "Your Excellency, let others do as they please, but I do not wish to break the Emperor's neck." The Emperor overheard my reply and, of course, was displeased at my impudence, but, being a kind and calm man, said nothing.

The next time the Emperor traveled along our line, his train maintained the speed I had asked for. Naturally I accompanied the train on our stretch of road. And again I was in the rear car, the car of the minister of ways and communications. This time I noticed that the car listed to the left. The reason for this I discovered was that the minister had a passion for what one might call railroad gadgets—instruments for measuring speed, heaters of various kinds, all of these heavy and fastened down on the left side of the car.

So, at the next station I had the train stopped and had the car inspected by specialists on railroad car construction. They decided that the list did not constitute a danger, counseled that an eye be kept on it. I then noted in the car's service record that although the car was listing, I was permitting the train to proceed and counseled that unless instruments and heaters were removed or moved to the right, the car should always be placed at the rear of the train. I then crossed myself, happy to be done with these Imperial trains, for they were always associated with trouble and danger.

The Borki Train Wreck, October 17, 1888

Two months passed. In the middle of the night my manservant knocked on my door to tell me that there was an urgent telegram for me. (My residence had a telegraph room, with operators always on duty.) The telegram was from Baron Sherval, informing me that because of a change in route the Imperial train would enter our road at Fastov. I quickly ordered a special train to be made ready to take me there and then waited to receive the train's schedule. Instead I received a second telegram informing me that the route had once more been changed, that the Imperial train would not be traveling on our stretch of line.

There came alarming rumors that the Imperial train had been in an accident, which had been the reason for the change in route.[2] But, because the train was continuing on its journey, I assumed that if anything had gone amiss it must have been trifling. However, a few hours later a third telegram arrived, asking me to proceed immediately to Kharkov, to serve as expert in an investigation of an accident to the Imperial train. When I reached Kharkov I found Baron Sherval in a bed at the station, his arm broken. Also, his courier had sustained a broken arm and leg. (This same courier was to serve me when I became minister of ways and communications.) From Kharkov I went on to the scene of the accident, Borki.

There I found other experts—several engineers of ways and communications and Kirpichev, the director of the Technological Institute. Kirpichev, who is still among the living, had and still has a considerable reputation as an engineer, as a professor of mechanics, and, generally, as an authority on railroad construction, but never having worked on a railroad, his knowledge is purely theoretical. Naturally I and Kirpichev played the chief roles in the investigation. Later we were joined by Koni, who was sent by Petersburg. This was my first meeting with him.[3]

We learned that the Imperial train, pulled by two freight locomotives, had been traveling at the same high rate of speed originally called for when it was on the

Southwestern Railroad line. Also, the minister's car, although relieved of some of its paraphernalia, had not been thoroughly gone over. Moreover, it had been placed directly behind the second locomotive. What I had warned against had happened: because of their weight the locomotives began to sway when they reached the speed called for, then loosened some rails and jumped the track, taking the rest of the train with them down an embankment.

Although several aboard were injured, the Emperor and his family escaped injury. In fact the Emperor and his family might have been killed but for his tremendous strength.[4] They were in the dining room when its roof collapsed, but he was able to support it on his back, thus permitting the others to leave the car safely. Then, in his characteristically calm and gentle manner, he left the car and gave comfort and aid to those who were suffering. It was only because of his strength, calm, and kindness that nothing worse happened.

I and Kirpichev disagreed about the cause of the accident. As I have said, I believed that it had been caused by the excessive speed at which the train had been traveling. Kirpichev, on the other hand, believed that the wreck had been caused by rotten ties, demonstrating his ignorance of the practical side of railroading. The wooden ties we use in Russia will become rotten on the outside in a few months if they are not treated, but their cores, which hold the spikes, remain thoroughly sound.

Koni, for his part, wished to put the blame on the officials of the railroad on whose line the train had been traveling and to exonerate the government officials and those in charge of the train itself. Naturally he was not pleased by my expertise, which led me to conclude that the only culprits were the inspector of Imperial trains and higher officials in the ministry. As it turned out, within a few months the Emperor parted with Poset, Sherval (a decent man but a mediocre engineer, with the typically dull mind of a Finn), and Salov, chief of the ministry's railroad administration. The Emperor felt no rancor toward Poset or Sherval, but let them go in deference to public dissatisfaction aroused by the accident. He did, however, feel rancor toward Salov, whom he considered the chief culprit, and justifiably so.

Salov was intelligent, solid, and knowledgeable in many respects, but he knew little of the practical side of railroading. And like most engineers of ways and communications, he believed that fellow engineers were suitable for any position and that those who were not engineers were good for nothing. Moreover, like Stolypin today, he amassed power by giving positions to people beholden to him, no matter how stupid or incompetent they might be. And he was adroit enough to have kept both Admiral Poset and Baron Sherval under his thumb. The Emperor, with his characteristic common sense, understood all this.

Salov was to remain in disfavor until three years ago, when he was appointed vice-chairman of a railroad commission and made a member of the State Council, but the commission had just begun its work when he fell ill and died.

XI

Director of the
Department of Railroad Affairs,
1889–1891

My Role in the Regulation of Railroad Tariffs

After Vyshnegradskii became minister of finance, and while I was still manager of the Southwestern Railroad, he asked me for ideas on how to deal with railroad deficits, which were costing the government 40 million rubles a year. My efforts were to lead to legislation dealing with railroad tariffs, to the establishment of the Department of Railroad Affairs, and to my appointment as its first director.

I suggested that one must first bring order out of the existing chaos in freight tariffs if one were to deal with the deficits. In those days all railroads in Russia were privately owned, and all were free to set any tariffs they wished, to publish or not publish their tariff schedules, to offer discounts to preferred customers, to engage in cutthroat tariff-cutting where there was competition. These practices left many shippers bewildered, hurt commerce, were a heavy burden to the government, which guaranteed returns on much of the capital of the railroad companies. In the end it was the common people who had to pay for the railroad deficits. Clearly, such a situation could not continue indefinitely.

In America, where similar practices existed and to some extent still exist, a number of laws have been passed against arbitrary reduction of tariffs, against the practice of not publishing tariffs, against secret rebates, and against the orgy of competition. But we had to take a more active role in regulation than America did and does, for there the railroads are private in fact as well as in name, and if they sustain losses, the government is under no obligation to make the losses good while our government was obliged to make them good.

So, I proposed a railroad tariff law that would give the railroads some leeway in setting tariffs, but that would stipulate that no tariff could be effective unless it were in a published schedule; that would give the government the right to supervise the setting of tariffs. It would therefore be necessary to establish a new department, in the Ministry of Finance rather than in the Ministry of Ways and Communications. I did not believe that supervision of tariffs was the proper business of the latter; and if it were, it could not be entrusted with such a task because it was virtually moribund and, moreover, dependent, to some degree, on the railroad kings.

I proposed that the new department be called the Department of Railroad Affairs, to distinguish it from the Department of Railroads of the Ministry of Ways and Communications, which dealt only with the technical side of railroad operations. The new department would have two divisions, one to deal with tariffs, the other with finance. The finance division would handle the financial relations between the government and the railroads as long as the government owed money to railroad companies under the system of guarantees.

Also I proposed the creation of a Tariff Committee that would include representatives from the Ministries of Finance, Ways and Communications, Agriculture, and Interior. It would be chaired by the director of the Department of Railroad Affairs. It would have the right to raise questions about setting and rescinding of certain tariffs, and, more important, it would review all proposed tariffs.

Disputes among members of the Tariff Committee or between members of the committee and the railroad companies would be mediated by a tariff council, which would also deal with matters requiring legislative action. The council would consist of high-ranking representatives from various ministries, among them the Ministry of Finance; the director of the Department of Commerce and the director of the Department of Railroad Affairs would be members *ex officio*; the council would be chaired by the minister of finance.

At the wish of the Emperor, the tariff bill that I worked out was considered by a special conference, to which I was invited. Its chairman was Dmitrii Martynovich Solskii, who died only recently; this was my first meeting with him. General Paucker, the minister of ways and communications, also took part in the conference. A fine man who knew nothing about railroading, he agreed to everything, although in so doing he was agreeing to the reduction of the powers of his ministry: obviously, he agreed because he was on friendly terms with Vyshnegradskii. Also, one or two members of the State Council later participated in the work of the conference. In the end all my proposals were approved.

My Appointment as Director
of Railroad Affairs

After the work of the conference was over I returned to Kiev, with Vyshnegradskii's thanks for my contribution. Then, when the Department of Railroad Affairs was established, he offered me the departmental directorship. Of course I refused: I had no intention of leaving an important position, with a high salary, a position that gave me independence, for a bureaucratic post, although one of high status.[1]

He replied that I could not refuse because it was the Emperor who wanted me to take the post and that, moreover, the Emperor had other work in mind for me. According to Vyshnegradskii, the Emperor had said:

> This is the Witte who was so insolent in my presence when I traveled on the lines of the Southwestern Railroad, the man who told the minister of ways and communications that he did not want to break my neck. I pretended I did not hear this highly insolent remark. Because Witte turned out to be right I have big plans for him.

I then wrote to Vyshnegradskii:

> If the Emperor so directs I will accept the post, but please tell him that my present salary is fifty thousand rubles and that being married I would find it difficult to live on the eight or ten thousand rubles that a department director receives. I can't presume to expect the salary I now receive, understanding as I do that no one in the government receives as much, but I would like at the very least a salary on which I could live comfortably.

As I learned the Emperor then agreed to supplement the 8,000 ruble salary of a director with another 8,000 rubles from his own funds. And I was told that when he asked what my [civil service] rank (*chin*) was, he was informed that I had the rank of titular councillor, but that I was out of service[2] because of my insolence.

The story of my "insolence" is this. As manager of the Southwestern Railroad I had frequent contact with the management of a line running from Graevo to the Prussian city of Königsberg. As a result I often joined German railroad men at conferences. One day the Ministry of Ways and Communications informed me that Emperor William I was bestowing the Order of the Prussian Crown on me (a man who has never had a desire for decorations) and wanted to know why.

I did not know the answer for I was not aware of having performed any services for the Emperor or for Prussia. Because I was angry with the ministry for having earlier refused to confirm me as manager, I replied tartly that it should ask Emperor William for an explanation since he was bestowing the order on me, not I on him. When he was informed of the nature of my "insolence," Emperor Alexander III said that he liked people with that kind of spirit.

I am aware that I have a sharp tongue but that fact did not hurt my relations with Emperor Alexander III. I always felt free to express myself without restraint in his presence, knowing that he would not show any sign of displeasure or reprimand me. Emperor Nicholas II is very unlike his father: he is well bred (more so than any man I have ever met), is always dressed to the nines, never uses rough language, never behaves in a rough manner. It was to be expected that my manners and my kind of speech would not please him and would, in fact, often irritate him. This is one of the chief reasons he was so cool toward me. I must admit that I should have been more restrained in speaking to him. In fact, I was reproached by some for speaking as sharply and daringly as I did in his presence: my reply to such was that I had grown accustomed to speaking in that way to his father and found it difficult to change my ways.

In appointing me director, the Emperor bestowed on me the rank of actual state councillor. Thus I advanced from the rank of titular councillor [9th class] to that of actual state councillor [4th class].[3] This was an exceptional advancement and, I believe, an unparalleled one. Thus, I began a new career.

My wife was not at all happy over our move to Petersburg, because it was obvious that we could not live there in as grand a manner as we lived in Kiev. We made our new home in Kolokolnaia Street.

My wife's daughter, Sonia, who had just graduated from the Kiev Institute for Noble Girls, came to live with us, and, at my wife's request, I adopted her, permitting her to use my surname. I agreed to this step out of affection for my wife, but I did so with the provision that Sonia would not inherit if we had children of our own.[4]

(My wife was pretty, one might even say beautiful, but Sonia is plain, almost repellent in appearance, and, what is more, unsympathetic, like her father. While we lived in Kiev, Sonia would spend no more than a few days a year with us. I hardly knew her and felt no attachment for her, all the more so because my wife had no particular affection for the girl.)

My Presentation to Emperor Alexander III

In accordance with custom I was presented to the Emperor following my appointment as director. My rank was still not high enough for me to be presented alone, and I was to be one in a group of ten. Although I had the rank of actual state councillor, I had no decorations [to wear on my uniform] because I had not really been in government service before.[5]

Our group went by train to Gatchina and from the station by carriage to the palace, where the Emperor was then residing. Because of his insistence on living modestly, he lived on the palace's second story, whose low ceilings and small rooms remind one of an entresol, rather than on the top story, which is luxurious. We were conducted through the entire length of the palace, from the right wing to a reception room in the left wing, where we were to wait for the Emperor.

The Emperor entered the reception room alone, dressed very modestly as usual, in uniform of course, but a rather shabby one. He walked with a heavy tread—for he was a rather big and heavy man—but with a majestic gait, greeting each one of us as we were presented to him, first the military, then the civilians.

One of the military was a colonel, and when the Emperor spoke to him he asked him to stay behind. When the Emperor came to me, he told me how happy he was to see me and how happy he was that I had agreed to accept the position of director. Then he returned to the colonel and began to talk quietly to him. Finally, the Emperor's aide-de-camp told the rest of us that we could leave.

We were then escorted back to the right wing of the palace, where, in accordance with custom, we were served lunch. According to the place cards, the colonel was supposed to sit next to me, but he did not appear until lunch was half over. When he returned, I restrained my impulse to ask why the Emperor had kept him, because it would have been gauche to ask at that time. However, when the two of us were alone in a carriage taking us back to the station, I said: "Forgive me if I am indiscreet, but could you tell me why the Emperor kept you?" He smiled and replied: "Because I am now thin and the Emperor knew me when I was fat, he wanted to know how I had lost weight; he does not like being fat and wants to follow my example." And I had thought that the Emperor had been asking him about some state secret!

P. M. Romanov

On assuming the directorship my first task was to organize the administration of the department.

I chose Peter Mikhailovich Romanov of the Credit Chancellery to be my vice-director. He is a very honorable man, widely respected, works hard, but is too gentle and lacks spirit. A few years ago he married a comparatively young woman, the sister of Pokotilov, our former minister to China, one of those whom I helped get ahead.

When I later became minister of finance, Romanov went along with me as my assistant minister. After I left that position, he continued on as assistant minister under my successor, Pleske. After Pleske's death, he served briefly as acting minister, then was succeeded by Kokovtsev, who intrigued against him. I may deal later on with how Kokovtsev came to be appointed.

V. I. Kovalevskii

Also, I brought Vladimir Ivanovich Kovalevskii, of the Department of Tax Collection, into my department as a member of the Tariff Committee. I did so despite the fact that in higher administrative circles he was considered politically unreliable. I acted as I did because he is a remarkably talented, very lively, remarkably hard-working man.

He had a stain on his reputation because of his association with the well-known anarchist Nechaev, while both were students at the Petrovskii Academy.[6] It seems that after an attempt on the life of Emperor Alexander II, Nechaev spent the night at Kovalevskii's quarters. Kovalevskii had no notion of what Nechaev had done, but that did not save him from being under a cloud thereafter.

When I became minister of finance I appointed him director of the Department of Commerce and Manufacture. I found him very useful, but ultimately I would have to part with him because of his incomprehensible weakness for the ladies, particularly the wrong kind. It was a weakness that made its appearance when he was in his fifties.

While still a student, he married a *kursistka* [a student in the Women's Higher Courses].[7] This was in the "Pisarev" era, when *kursistki* felt that they had to wear glasses and keep their hair short, in the belief that that was how free-thinking women should look. Naturally, by the time Kovalevskii was in his fifties, his wife was an old woman, and dull to boot. He then became entangled with Shabelskaia, who is not a very decent woman. In recent times she has attracted attention as one of the Black Hundreds collaborators on Dubrovin's *Russkoe znamia*.

I remember her from my Odessa days, when I would see her, in the company of merrymakers, at the restaurant in the Severnaia Hotel. A general's daughter, she fled from home while very young. When I met her she was still very young and amusing, in the sense that she drank a great deal and was very familiar. Her ambition was to be an actress. She first went to Vienna to act, then to Berlin, where she lived quite *maritalement* with the well-known publicist Harden, the publisher of *Zukunft*.

This is the Harden who considers himself the defender of the heritage of Prince Bismarck. In my opinion Harden is not a particularly honorable man, but he is a very able publicist, and he has performed a public service by raising questions that have attracted the attention of all Germany. For example, it was his work that led to the sensational trial a year ago of Prince Eulenberg, a friend of Emperor William.

Well, Kovalevskii met Shabelskaia while she was still "Mme. Harden," by which time, I am told, Harden was ready to palm her off on someone else. She snared Kovalevskii by appearing to be very liberal, very much in favor of women's emancipation.

After the two became lovers, Kovalevskii began to have trouble at home. That was no concern of mine, but it was a concern of mine that Shabelskaia began to engage in shady business that involved trading on his name.

Also he began to act out of character. For example, he took money from Nobel and used it to engage in a strange speculation with an estate somewhere across the Volga. Then he divorced his wife, although they had a son and a married daughter.

The whole nasty business came to a head with the appearance of some kind of promissory notes, allegedly signed by Kovalevskii, but, in fact, forgeries produced at Shabelskaia's home. At the inevitable trial, she falsely swore that the notes were genuine. Such an unpleasant picture emerged from the case that it was clear that Kovalevskii would have to go.

So I had a talk with him and told him that he must ask to be permitted to leave government service. Had he not done as I asked that master of intrigue Grand Duke Alexander Mikhailovich, with whom he was not on the best of terms, would have passed on the story, with embellishments, to the Emperor, who would surely have dismissed Kovalevskii. (The Grand Duke was then chairman of the Committee for the Merchant Marine, which was within the jurisdiction of Kovalevskii's department.)

After this episode Kovalevskii parted with Shabelskaia and took up with another woman, to whom he is now married. She, too, is not above reproach. She had been married twice before this, once to a man whose name I can't recall, the second time to Ilovaiskii, commanding officer of the Ataman Regiment, stationed in Petersburg. He was tried for embezzling some 60,000 rubles, either with her help or, in any case, to satisfy her many wants. She divorced him and then set her cap for Kovalevskii. She and her children by her first two marriages now live with him. I do not think that this union will last, because she is one of those ladies who cannot live without being involved in escapades.

All in all, I consider Kovalevskii a very gifted, but impressionable, person whom one cannot trust very far because of his weakness for the ladies, especially the wrong kind of ladies.

Maksimov, Gatsintsov, and others

Some of those I brought in to man the newly established Department of Railroad Affairs came from the Petersburg bureaucracy, some were men with practical experience in railroading, from the Southwestern Railroad. One railroad man was Maksimov, one of Bunge's most brilliant students, who had served under me in Kiev: I brought him in as a member of the Tariff Committee. He is a well-rounded, very knowledgeable, comparatively modest family man and, by the way, a friend of Pikhno. He succeeded me as director when I became minister of ways and communications and stayed as director after I became minister of finance, until I had to part with him, because of the well-known Mamontov affair,[8] involving the construction of a railroad to Archangel.

The Mamontov affair was investigated by a Moscow court, with Mamontov being placed under arrest and almost ending up in prison. Maksimov appears to have behaved improperly, or, at least, unwisely, in becoming involved with Mamontov. Consequently, it was to become necessary for me to ask him to leave the service [in 1899].

In addition to Maksimov I brought in Gatsintsov, who is now the director of the department, and Shabunevich, now an actual state councillor, and many others, some dead, some still alive and holding positions in private railroad companies. In this fashion I established the Department of Railroad Affairs and the Tariff Committee.

My Work as Director

When I became director and began to implement the law on railroad tariffs, all the railroad companies were hostile to me because they felt their interests being threatened, their hitherto unbridled powers in setting tariffs curtailed. It did not take long before they changed their minds about me, first because they recognized me as an authority on tariffs and also because they began to see that they were gaining rather than losing from the establishment of order in the setting of tariffs. I soon brought order into the setting of tariffs and gradually eliminated the railroad deficit, which was 48 million rubles when I took office. All the rules and principles which I established continue to be followed, without significant modification.

During these years all aspects of railroad affairs, except the purely technical, came to be concentrated in the hands of the Ministry of Finance and its Department of Railroad Affairs: this meant control over all construction of new railroads, granting of charters to railroads, and establishment of standards according to which railroads are to be constructed. On the whole this state of affairs still maintains.*

As director of the Department of Railroad Affairs, and later as minister of finance, I had to deal with many members of the Petersburg aristocracy who were interested in building railroad lines and came to know what they were like. They differ from ordinary people both in their virtues and in their vices, particularly in their greed, which is a hundred times greater than the greed of ordinary people.

When ordinary people are greedy they are fighting for survival and thus obeying nature's law. But aristocrats are greedy out of love of luxury and wealth, particularly the power that wealth confers. At Imperial processions and balls these aristocrats would put on such airs that a stranger might think that business was beneath them, yet these same people would come to my office and virtually grovel on their hands and knees for some advantage that might net them a few thousand rubles.

Of course, this is not true of the entire aristocracy: many individuals and families are not greedy, are decent and honorable, and fully worthy of the illustrious names they bear, but many of the aristocracy are unbelievably avaricious hypocrites, scoundrels, and good-for-nothings. I do not wish to name names.[9] Many of them now occupy important positions at court, as they did under Emperor Alexander III, and are very close to the Imperial family, at least with respect to the formal aspects of that family's life.

I will, however, mention one individual, General Mavrin, a fine old man, who was not of that kind although he was a product of the Petersburg world. He often

*When the Ministry of Commerce and Industry was established [in 1905], on my initiative, the Department of Railroad Affairs was transferred to its jurisdiction. But I soon began to have second thoughts, because of the continuing rise in railroad deficits and the tendency of the minister Timiriazev to accede to requests from businessmen for lower tariffs. Lower tariffs were in some cases to the good, but not at a time of rising deficits. They were rising because of the construction of many railroads purely for political and strategic purposes, railroads that could not show a profit for decades. So, I felt it best to return the department to the jurisdiction of the Ministry of Finance. This was done while I was still premier, by Imperial decree, with the consent of the Council of Ministers.

came to see me and would annoy me with petty railroad business, about this or that tariff, the construction of a station near some estate, etc. He did all this at the behest of his son, but he himself was a very honorable man, and quite amusing.

Once, when he told me that he had taken part in a parade on the preceding day and that in a few hours he was going to Krasnoe Selo, with the Emperor, to review the troops, I asked him if he did not find it tiring to be on horseback for several hours on end.

He replied that he didn't find it tiring at all, but that during the preceding year he had begun to feel his age in another respect. When I asked him how, he replied sadly: "Until a year ago I loved to pay court to the ladies, but an entire year has passed without my feeling any desire for that sort of thing."

I was amazed by a statement like this from an eighty-four-year-old man.

XII

St. Petersburg, 1889–1891
People and Incidents

A. A. Abaza

During my tenure as director of the Department of Railroad Affairs I had the opportunity of becoming well acquainted with Alexander Ageevich Abaza, the chairman of the Department of State Economy of the State Council,[1] a major figure in government at the time and, of all the men I have ever met in government service, the one with the greatest common sense. Unfortunately, he had a weakness for gambling, a matter to which I shall return.

He graduated from a university, but it had left little mark on him, probably because he had been bored there and had studied little. Then he served for a time in the Life Hussar Regiment. Subsequently he embarked on a successful career in the civil service. He owed his success to his fine appearance, his fine breeding, his solid sense, and the backing of Grand Duchess Helen Pavlovna, who exercised an enormous influence on Emperor Alexander II.*

When I say "backing," I mean it in the best sense of the word, for the Grand Duchess is deservedly remembered as a highly moral, proper, and intelligent woman. She is remembered too for her role in Emperor Alexander's decision to emancipate the serfs, the fiftieth anniversary of which was recently celebrated, bringing back memories of her role.

He was married to a woman (she was either French or German) whom he met at the home of the Grand Duchess. She was one of the many young women musicians who performed for the Grand Duchess and served as companions to

---

*Abaza's views were formed in the salon of Grand Duchess Helen Pavlovna: as a result he was very liberal, but he would not have sacrificed one evening of card playing to carry out any kind of liberal measure.

her. He had been forced to marry the young lady because he had engaged in hanky-panky with her. The marriage had not turned out well. This was quite understandable, for a person such as she—a musician and a lady's companion— could not satisfy a nature such as his. Although they occupied the same house, they lived separate lives.

He lived almost *maritalement* with the widow of General Nelidov (she had three sisters: one married Vogüé, the French academician; the second married Prince Golitsyn; the third married Struve, who served as our minister to America). She was a very intelligent woman, at whose salon virtually the entire liberal wing of Petersburg's upper officialdom would meet during Loris-Melikov's so-called dictatorship of the heart. These were the men who wanted to introduce a constitution but failed because of the greatest of all historical misfortunes, the murder of that greatest of monarchs, Emperor Alexander II.

The Department of State Economy was a very important one. Also, it was the senior department, so that Abaza frequently substituted for the chairman of the council. He was rarely prepared when he came to meetings, but he had a mousy secretary who would provide him with a summary of the business at hand. Because of his remarkable ability he grasped things quickly: after the others had spoken, he would form his opinion and take the floor to express his views. He would do so with such good sense, authority, and knowledgeability that he seemed to have studied the matter at hand very thoroughly.

We first met while I was still manager of the Southwestern Railroad, in connection with the extensive estates he owned in the region served by the railroad. As a result, after I became director of the Department of Railroad Affairs, he asked Vyshnegradskii to appoint me as chief administrative assistant[2] of a special commission that reviewed military and naval appropriations too secret to be discussed in the State Council: the commission, of which Abaza was the chairman, included the general-admiral of the navy,[3] the director of the Ministry of the Navy,[4] the army chief of staff,[5] and the state controller.

Customarily the commission met at the beginning of the administrative year, in October or November, and then at its end, in June. Usually it met at night, and after a session I would go home and prepare the minutes. Then, in the morning before going to my office, I would stop by to see Abaza, who lived on the Fontanka, off Nevskii Prospekt, not far from the home of Count Shuvalov.

It was eleven in the morning one day when I stopped at Abaza's house to give him the minutes of one such session. He had just gotten out of bed. It was his custom after arising to go into his reception room, still in his dressing gown: he would be handed a long Turkish pipe and thus arrayed, feeling at ease, he would receive callers. This was the time he liked to chat, probably for the sake of his digestion.

That morning, as I was on my way into Abaza's study, I met General Alexis Nikolaevich Kuropatkin, with whom I was acquainted, leaving the study. He was still rather young and had only the orders of St. George and St. Stanislas. He had

XII ■ ST. PETERSBURG 107

just been named governor of the Trans-Caspian Region and was calling on bigwigs before leaving: Abaza was the first of these. When Kuropatkin recognized me, he apologized for not having called on me, saying that he had to leave immediately for Central Asia, but that I would be the first he would call on when he returned. Then, as he took his leave, he kissed me, as was his custom with people he knew.

When I went into Alexander Ageevich's study, he asked me if I knew Kuropatkin well, obviously having seen us in the mirror opposite him. I told him that when Kuropatkin served in the chief of staff's Asiatic section, I had had some dealings with him. Then I told of my first meeting with Kuropatkin, during the war with Turkey.

I had come to Kiev in the small railroad carriage I used when traveling to deal with troop movements. There I met Colonel Skobelev, who had already distinguished himself in the conquest of Ferghana and was soon to become a major hero in the war with Turkey. Although I had met him earlier, at the home of my Uncle Fadeev, I barely knew him. When he asked if he could share my carriage, I replied that I was glad to. Then he asked if Captain Kuropatkin, who had been his chief of staff in Central Asia, could join us. I agreed, but pointed out that the sleeping quarters were too cramped for three. Skobelev replied that in that case the two of them would sit up.

During the course of our journey I was astonished to note that Skobelev treated Kuropatkin with a mixture of friendliness and contempt. I never heard directly from Skobelev how he felt about Kuropatkin, but his sister Princess Beloselskaia-Belozerskaia told me that her brother was of the opinion that Kuropatkin was brave, in the sense of being able to face death in battle, but that he was afraid to make decisions and assume responsibility. For that reason, she said, her brother considered Kuropatkin unfit to hold a command in time of war.

Some time after I had told Abaza about my acquaintance with Kuropatkin, he made a prediction about Kuropatkin that would have earned him the title of prophet if he had lived in ancient times. He said:

I will not live long enough to see the realization of my prediction, but you will. General Kuropatkin is a clever and brave general and he will have a remarkable career. He will some day become minister of war and he will be even more than minister of war, but in the end everyone will be disappointed in him. They will be disappointed in him because although he is a clever and brave general, he has the soul of a staff clerk.

It was on this occasion that Abaza asked if I knew the Rafalovich banking house. I said that I did, because I did a good deal of business with it.[6] He said that he understood that I had a high opinion of Rafalovich. I replied that I had known the elder Rafalovich, Fedor, very well. I said that he had been converted to Orthodoxy and had been very devout and had become an elder in a church not far from the Hotel Naples, where I had lived. I added that he had been a very fine man and that this firm was one of the best and largest in Odessa, that when he died his sons, led by Alexander Fedorovich, had assumed direction of the firm and that I did not know how the firm was faring.

I mention this conversation because when I come to tell about the Rafalovich affair, I will have occasion to refer to it.

My Trip to Central Asia with Vyshnegradskii

In the early fall of 1890, I accompanied Vyshnegradskii, his son Alexander, and Alexander's friend Alexis Ivanovich Putilov on a trip to Central Asia. On our way there we stopped at Nizhnii Novgorod for the fair, then went down the Volga, part way by steamship, part way by railroad. In the northern Caucasus we stopped off for a few days in Kislovodsk, a spa, where my wife was staying and where Vyshnegradskii's oldest daughter, the wife of the well-known musician Safano, was living. The daughter was living there because her father-in-law, a Cossack general and a speculator, had a large hotel and summer home in that city.

My wife, who had kidney trouble, was there for the Narzan mineral waters, on the advice of the eminent Moscow physician Zakharyn. Naturally, I stayed with her in the small cottage that she had rented.

Bathing in the Narzan waters strengthens the body and increases animation, but, as I was to learn, too much animation can strain the heart and people were warned against staying too long in the Narzan waters. (For that reason the local inhabitants were amazed when Prince Dondukov-Korsakov, son of the Dondukov-Korsakov I mentioned earlier, was able to stay in the waters a long time and drink a bottle of champagne while in them, all with no ill effect.) My wife said that the Narzan waters were helping her. She was very happy and animated when we parted. Her plan was to return to Petersburg about the same time that I would.

Nothing very striking occurred during our trip to Central Asia, but a few events and impressions remain in my memory.

From Kislovodsk our party continued on to Tiflis, where we stayed at the palace of the then governor-general, Sheremetev. When we arrived there something happened (perhaps my being awarded my first order) that prompted me to telegraph my wife. In her return telegram, which surprised me, she predicted virtually everything that has since happened to me.

It was in Tiflis that Vyshnegradskii's servant came to me saying that his master had received a telegram that had made him angry and had told him to give me twenty kopeks and to tell me that my prediction had come true. We were then considering going on the gold standard, and the minister's policy then was to buy gold with paper rubles and moreover to keep the exchange value of the paper ruble at somewhere between sixty-five and seventy-five kopeks in gold rubles. But, as a result of a good harvest and increased exports, the paper ruble was going up while Vyshnegradskii was trying to keep it down. While on the Volga, I was sending dispatches to Petersburg on Vyshnegradskii's behalf ordering the sale of paper rubles. I had predicted that his efforts would not prevent the paper ruble from rising to something like eighty gold kopeks, and I had expressed the view that it might be better to permit the exchange rate of the paper ruble to rise so that we might be able to buy gold more cheaply. My prediction had angered him and he had bet me twenty kopeks that it would not come true. It had and that is why his servant had brought me the money. However, following its rise, the paper ruble began to fall, and when it had gone down to sixty-five kopeks, we stopped selling paper rubles. I mention this incident because I shall return to it, in connection with the Rafalovich affair.

From Tiflis we went to Baku and from Baku to Central Asia. There we visited Merv, Cherdzou, Bukhara, Samarkand, Tashkent, and Ferghana. In Central Asia we inspected the Trans-Caspian Railroad. We returned home by way of the Caucasus. I was impressed by the vast, untapped resources of Central Asia, which I was seeing for the first time. Although cotton production has increased there in the intervening years, its resources are still largely untapped.

We saw Kuropatkin, who, as I have said, had become governor of the Trans-Caspian region. One must give credit where credit is due: he may have been the best governor the region ever had. Subsequently, as we know, he became governor-general of Turkestan, but soon left to become minister of war.

The governor-general of Turkestan at the time of our visit was Baron Vrevskii, a decent enough man but totally inconsequential. He had been chief of staff of the Odessa Military District and had gained the position of governor-general with the help of Obruchev, his classmate at the General Staff Academy.

In Tashkent I briefly met Grand Duke Nicholas Konstantinovich, the eldest son of Grand Duke Constantine Nikolaevich and Grand Duchess Alexandra Iosifovna. (She is still alive, but is blind.) I was amazed by him: here was a man who was obviously intelligent, hard-working. He accomplished much in Central Asia with respect to irrigation projects and cotton cultivation, and is well regarded in the area. Yet he is abnormal in that he is given to bizarre actions. To put it bluntly, he stole valuable jewels from his mother when he was still a very young officer. The doctors had declared him abnormal because he stole despite the fact that he had everything.[7]

He had at first been exiled to the province of Orenburg, where he had married the daughter of some police chief or other. Then he had been sent to Tashkent. Subsequently, after the accession of Emperor Nicholas II, he would be permitted to live in the Crimea for a time, but would then be sent back to Tashkent.

He was always in mufti, so he must have been stripped of his military rank. When I saw him he was not particularly striking in appearance; he was already bald. He was unaffected and there was nothing repellent about him.

As we started on our return trip, from Tashkent, Vyshnegradskii received a telegram from Count Vorontsov-Dashkov, the minister of the Imperial court, informing him that the Emperor wished him to go to the Imperial estate at Murgab, to inspect its sluices and canals.

Emperor Alexander II had acquired this large estate following the conquest of the region, with the aim of raising cotton and other crops of high value on it, as an example to the inhabitants. That he had taken possession of this estate was unfortunate for two reasons. First, it was hardly in the spirit of the times for a ruler to take so large an area won by Russian blood for his private use. Second, to raise crops on the estate required irrigation, that is, diversion of water from the nearby Amu-Daria River, this in an arid region where every drop of water is precious, where the entire well-being of the local inhabitants depends on irrigation.

As was to be expected the local population was very hostile to this undertaking. To his credit Kuropatkin also was critical, even hostile, to the Murgab estate and for that reason did not accompany us on our visit to it.

Of course, neither Emperor Alexander II nor Emperor Alexander III knew of the local hostility and neither was the sort to take something that belonged to the state or to the people for his own benefit. They had probably acted on the basis of erroneous reports and explanations from those close to them, one of the culprits, I believe, being Count Vorontsov-Dashkov.

We spent a whole day at Murgab, giving most of our attention to the sluices, which had been constructed by the military engineer Kozel-Poklevskii, an able man.* I had some knowledge of construction from my railroad experience. Both Vyshnegradskii and I considered the construction to be defective. We then asked to see the plans and came to the conclusion that the dike designed to hold back the water could not stand up to the pressure once water was released from the river. Kozel-Poklevskii insisted that we were wrong, as would be proven when the water was released.

After we left Murgab we telegraphed our report, couched in very careful terms, to Vorontsov-Dashkov for transmittal to the Emperor. In it we said that cotton could be grown there, with irrigation, but that the local population, and Kuropatkin, were unfavorably disposed toward the enterprise because it would reduce the volume of water available to the inhabitants for irrigating their own lands. We also expressed our doubts about the dike. The telegram irked Vorontsov-Dashkov because it could only trouble so noble and honorable a man as Emperor Alexander III. I believe that he either kept the telegram from the Emperor entirely or informed him of it in such a way as to soften its argument.

Our fear about the dike proved justified. After we returned to Tiflis we received a telegram informing us that two days after our departure, when the sluices had been opened, the dike collapsed.

I and Vyshnegradskii stopped in Bukhara and were presented to the emir at his

---

*I believe that he and his brother had been exiled to Siberia for their part in the Polish revolt of 1863. He gained a reputation as an engineer; why he had chosen this kind of work I don't know. His brother was also well known, for amassing a fortune in Siberia.

palace. We spent a whole day in the old city, which impressed us with its customs and mores as a completely Asiatic city of the old kind. For example, I saw a large tower (which is still standing), from which criminals were hanged for certain crimes and then tossed into the square. This kind of punishment has long existed in Asiatic countries.

In Tiflis, en route back, local young Georgian nobles organized a drinking bout for young Vyshnegradskii, to which Putilov and I were invited. Young Vyshnegradskii attended and spent the whole night carousing, but I, who wasn't feeling well, and Putilov went instead to the famous sulphur baths.

At the baths we were massaged by vigorous Tatars who could make one's bones crack, although there is no noticeable pain in the process. I told Putilov's masseur to give him a good massage. When he began to hear his bones crack, Putilov began to scream like a madman, calling on me to have the masseur stop. The masseur who, needless to say, did not understand a word of Russian, just smiled and continued, and Putilov continued to scream until it was over. Twenty years have passed since that incident, but even today when I remind him of the Tiflis baths he falls into a panic.

Of course one gets to know people better on journeys. I already knew a good deal about the elder Vyshnegradskii, having worked with him for many years. But this trip underlined two things about him for me. First, that he was stingy. He was so mean in his tips to servants, coachmen, et al. that I was embarrassed and added an extra amount to my tips in his name. Also I noticed that although he was fluent in French, his accent was atrocious.

My First Wife's Death

As I have said, my wife and I had agreed to return to Petersburg at about the same time. But she changed her plans and went from the Caucasus to her brother's estate, in the province of Chernigov, and wrote me from there that she was having a pleasant time. Then she intended to go on to Kiev, to see her mother for a day or two, after which she would return to Petersburg.

Soon after my return to Petersburg I received word that she had died unexpectedly, of a heart attack. I have no doubt that she died as a result of taking the Narzan cure. When I went to Kiev to arrange for her burial, I took her daughter Sonia along. Sonia then returned to Petersburg and I hired a fine woman to be a combination of governess and companion to her.

The Rafalovich Affair

After my return to Petersburg, Abaza told me that the Rafalovich banking house was in trouble and should be helped, since, as I myself had said, it was a very reputable house. Wouldn't I talk to Vyshnegradskii about it? I replied that he had more influence with Vyshnegradskii than I, and, besides, I knew nothing about the matter.

When I spoke to Vyshnegradskii about my conversation with Abaza, it was evident that Abaza had already spoken to him. He told me that he had recommended an 800,000 ruble loan from the State Bank to be used to pay the firm's creditors, explaining that he needed Abaza's support in the State Council for a protective tariff, the first in the country's history; without Abaza's support it would not be approved.

To round out my account of the Rafalovich affair I have to leap ahead to my first months as minister of finance. Almost immediately after my appointment Alexander Fedorovich Rafalovich, the head of the firm, called on me to ask for a large loan. I told him that it was out of the question. I was not going to ask the Emperor for approval of such a loan and added that, even if I asked, I would be refused. He advised me not to make a hasty decision and to look carefully into the matter: I would find that unless a loan were granted, there would be a scandal.

When I asked for an explanation, he told me that his firm had been unable to pay its creditors and that the 800,000 ruble loan arranged for by Vyshnegradskii had been used to pay some creditors in full, but that the loan had been insufficient to permit payment of anything to some creditors and those creditors were threatening to go to court. If the matter went to court, he continued, it would be revealed that the State Bank had acted improperly, by not arranging for all the creditors to receive their proportionate share of the 800,000 rubles.

I agreed that the State Bank had acted improperly, but then he had misled Vyshnegradskii by not telling him that the 800,000 rubles would not cover all claims. I suggested that his failure to disclose the full facts would be the source of any scandal.

Not so, he said. If the matter went to court, he would not play the game of fraudulent bankruptcy and would explain everything: his books would show that he had deposited 900,000 rubles to Abaza's account. I was astonished: did that money represent a bribe? Rafalovich said that it did not and explained what had happened in roughly the following words:

> In the spring Abaza summoned me to his estate, at Shpola. The ruble was then rising rapidly and he wanted to speculate that it would fall by buying foreign currency. He would use a code in sending me orders. If, for example, he telegraphed an order to buy so many *puds* [a Russian unit of weight] of corn, I would know that he wanted me to buy such an amount of French francs.
>
> Knowing that he was chairman of the Finance Committee I assumed that he knew for certain that the ruble would fall. So I did as he did: when he bought francs, I bought francs on my own account. But the ruble continued to rise and after several months Abaza's account showed a loss of almost 800,000 rubles and so did mine. So I traveled to Shpola once more, to tell him of his losses and to ask if he had not been mistaken in his expectations. He told me that it was no

concern of mine and for me to continue to execute his orders. However, I thought that he was mistaken and instead of executing his orders I bought paper rubles for his account. Then the ruble began to fall rapidly so that had I carried out his orders completely his account would have shown a net profit of 900,000 rubles.[8] In the end I lost several million rubles and my firm failed. Thus, I will not get a kopek from any loan that may be made to me: it would all go to pay my creditors. If the loan is not granted and if the matter goes to court it will become public knowledge that Abaza, chairman of the Finance Committee, actual privy councillor, state secretary, chairman of the Department of State Economy, has been speculating on the rise and fall of the ruble.

I didn't believe Rafalovich at first and asked him to bring any evidence he had on the following day. The next day he appeared and showed me his correspondence with Abaza, which left no doubt that he had been acting on the latter's orders.

I then began making inquiries in the Ministry of Finance and learned that before embarking on his campaign of buying gold with paper rubles, Vyshnegradskii had decided to ask the Emperor for authorization to do so. But, fearing that the Emperor would rebuff him, he had first solicited Abaza's support and received it in writing. Vyshnegradskii had then gone to the Emperor, armed with Abaza's statement of support, and won Imperial approval. From the dates that I had found, it was clear that Abaza had speculated on the fall of the ruble on the basis of definite [inside] knowledge. Clearly we were dealing with a scandalous matter.

Consequently, when I next reported to the Emperor, I told him of Rafalovich's request for a loan and recommended that it be granted. The Emperor said that he granted the first loan at Vyshnegradskii's insistence, but that, in general, he did not see why kikes should receive loans. I informed him that the Rafaloviches were not kikes, that their father had been of the Russian Orthodox faith. When the Emperor would not change his mind I told him why there would be a major scandal if the loan were refused. Finally, he was convinced and the loan was granted, with many conditions attached, among them that the Rafaloviches put up everything they had as security.

By this time Abaza had returned from abroad. Usually he would spend some time in Monte Carlo, gambling. And if he happened to spend some time in Paris, he would play heavily at cards in one of the clubs there. I recall that while I was still in Kiev, he went to Paris to negotiate a government loan and that while there he incurred large gambling debts, which were paid for by Herman Rafalovich, who had chosen to make his home in that city.

Well, when Abaza returned he was supposed to present himself to the Emperor, in his capacity as chairman of the Department of State Economy, but the Emperor would not receive him, a clear sign of his displeasure with Abaza. Meanwhile rumors about the Rafalovich affair were circulating. Abaza's friends would not believe that Abaza was guilty of any impropriety; they believed that I had defamed him, either out of malice or ignorance. When I attended sessions of the State Council, his friends would turn their backs on me. I was even warned by the minister of interior that Abaza's nephew (the one who was to play such a lamentable role in the events leading to our war with Japan) would either challenge me to a duel for slandering his uncle or would shoot me on sight. Of course nothing happened.

It was all very unpleasant for me, so I asked the Emperor to appoint a commission to investigate the allegation that I had defamed Abaza. He replied that what people said did not matter to him: he trusted me completely. But when I told him that I would not be able to deal with the members of the State Council unless my name were cleared, he agreed to appoint an investigating committee. Whom would I suggest as members? I proposed Bunge and Filippov, who had served under Abaza at one time, and Chikhachev, a friend of Abaza. I further suggested that Bunge serve as chairman. The Emperor agreed, adding that he wanted minister of justice Muravev to serve as over-procurator and for me to be present at sessions of the commission.

When the commission met I presented documentary evidence which convinced its members that I had not defamed Abaza and that his behavior could be characterized as improper, if not worse. As far as I can recall no minutes were kept.

The Emperor told me, with a smile, that when Bunge had reported the commission's findings to him, Bunge had argued that Abaza had done no harm to the state, because in speculating on the ruble's fall he was doing as Vyshnegradskii did; had Abaza speculated on the ruble's rise, it would have been a different matter. I tried to explain to the Emperor that what Vyshnegradskii had done was for the benefit of Russia but that what Abaza had done was for personal gain, based on his knowledge of state secrets. But the Emperor cut me off, saying that Bunge had probably been joking.

Before another two weeks had passed I saw the Emperor again, at the Anichkov Palace. As usual, he smiled kindly at me. (I can see him now.) He told me that he had received a letter from Abaza, which he read to me: in it Abaza admitted that he had acted impulsively in what he had done, asked the Emperor's pardon, and vowed never to repeat the offense. After reading the letter, the Emperor said that he would like to believe Abaza but that once before, after an incident involving gambling,* Abaza had promised never to gamble again. He said that he would never forgive the man again.

[The Rafalovich affair was to be brought up again a year ago.][9]

As a result of the Rafalovich affair, Abaza had to leave his post as chairman of the Department of State Economy. Since the work of this department is closely linked with that of the Minister of Finance, the Emperor asked me whom I would recommend as a replacement. I suggested Solskii, who had given up the post of

---

*There was a scandal over Abaza's winning a large sum of money at the Yacht Club. There had been a complaint that reached the Emperor who called Abaza in. Abaza at first denied everything, then admitted it and promised he would never gamble again.

state controller partly because of a stroke, partly because he seemed inclined to the so-called liberal tendency of Emperor Alexander II. (The mistaken view was held that this tendency had permitted things to get out of hand and had led to the Emperor's assassination.) I thought that Solskii would make a good chairman because the office did not require initiative, but an ability to act as a force for calmness, to act as mediator. As it turned out, Solskii, as chairman, smoothed things over, brought calm to the proceedings, and in general acted as a moderating influence. On the whole he was a very decent, honorable, cultivated, and intelligent man, but he could not take a firm position and failed to carry out any reform in his entire life.

Literary Figures

As a result of my contacts with Vyshnegradskii in Petersburg I met a whole pleiad of fairly prominent literary men with whom he was acquainted.

One was the late A. N. Maikov, an eminent poet, with whom he often took counsel on general questions. Maikov was a very fine and intelligent man who held to a rather reactionary point of view.

Because of his friendship with Maikov, Vyshnegradskii appointed his son N. A. Maikov as director of the Tsesarevich Nicholas Trade School, for which he was not qualified. N. A. Maikov did a very poor job of directing the school: he let the students get out of hand and would spend nights drinking with students from the senior class. When I became minister of finance and head of the society under whose jurisdiction the school functions, I had to dismiss him.

Subsequently he joined the Union of the Russian People and worked closely with Dubrovin in all his ugly undertakings, including the killing of Herzenstein. And it was through this organization that young Maikov was able to further his career. Now as vice-chairman of the society I mentioned, he oversees the very school from which I had to remove him as director.

Another well-known literary figure I met at Vyshnegradskii's was the poet Polonskii, a more liberal, more worldly, more sympathetic figure than A. N. Maikov. Polonskii was lame and had to use crutches.

Polonskii is no longer among the living but the so-called Polonskii Society, which he endowed, holds literary readings in his memory several times a year.

Also at Vyshnegradskii's I met the eminent novelist Grigorovich, who had been one of Turgenev's friends. He was of quite a different stamp compared to Maikov and Polonskii. He was a man of the world, very witty, much more brilliant. And even though he was quite old then, he still enjoyed the social life.

Also at Vyshnegradskii's I met Nicholas Nikolaevich Strakhov, half philosopher, half critic. He often spoke of Count Leo Tolstoy, with whom he was quite close. However, it appears from the recently published letters of Tolstoy that relations between the two cooled off later.

Princess Radziwill

At Vyshnegradskii's I became acquainted with the interesting and notorious Princess Radziwill, née Rzewuska, a beautiful woman married to a nonentity. Apparently Vyshnegradskii courted her or, at least, was infatuated by her. After his death, possibly even before, she became close to General-Adjutant Cherevin, the chief of Imperial security. To put it bluntly she lived with him and through him had some influence in Petersburg society. After Cherevin's death she left Russia for England because it turned out that she had been involved in improper dealings.

In England she took up with and lived completely *maritalement* with an English banker and speculator whose name, I believe, was Rhodes, a man, it seems, of Jewish origin. He had amassed a large fortune from African gold, before the Boer War. Then the two went to his gold mines in Africa. There he died, so unexpectedly that nothing of substance was left for her. But then, lo and behold, a promissory note made out to her and signed by this man came to light. A court found the note to be a forgery and sentenced her to prison.

After leaving prison she wrote her recollections of this affair, thus earning some fleeting notoriety. Now, she is, of course, forgotten. I saw her not long ago, at Aix-les-Bains. She is very aged, but has managed to snare a young and comparatively penniless Englishman, who obviously married her for her money.[10]

XIII

Minister of Ways and Communications, 1891–1892

My Predecessors

I have already told how Admiral Poset, minister of ways and communications, was obliged to retire after the Borki catastrophe. He had been appointed minister because he had been tutor as well as mentor to Grand Duke Alexis Aleksandrovich. It was he who provided the Grand Duke with naval instruction and commanded the frigate on which the Grand Duke made his round-the-world voyage.

On one occasion, with the Grand Duke aboard, Poset's ship collided with another vessel. He was found guilty, to a degree, but being a general-adjutant, a man of high position, his career did not suffer. Emperor Alexander II liked him very much: when Poset left the navy, the Emperor wished, but was unable, to appoint him minister of the navy and, instead, appointed him minister of ways and communications.

As minister Poset was universally respected as an honorable and straightforward man, but everyone knew that he was very limited. For example, when he inspected railroads, he was interested in little but the station facilities labeled "men" and "women." When we on the Southwestern Railroad learned that he was coming to inspect us, we saw to it that these places were clean and in proper order. This was the only preparation we made for his coming, for the first thing he did on arriving at a station was to inspect these places. If he found something wrong, there would be a good deal of unpleasantness, followed by penalties, but if these places were in perfect order he gave little attention to anything else (probably because he knew nothing of other matters). Why he considered himself a specialist on this one matter I do not know.

I recall the following incident in Poset's tenure as minister. Once, while I was still with the Odessa Railroad, I was traveling with him on the Moscow–Kursk Railroad, then just a single-track line. Just as we were leaving some station or other, a freight train came at us from the opposite direction. Fortunately, this was seen in time and the freight train backed up slowly to the next station and we followed it.

When we arrived at the next station, Poset poured out his anger on the stationmaster, who received it all in silence. Had he replied, Poset's temper would have cooled, but by remaining silent, he further infuriated the minister, who finally said: "Why don't you say something?"

The station manager replied:

> Your high excellency does not understand how one can be so careless as to let trains approach each other. Of course there was an error; two trains on the same track approaching each other must collide. You are astonished at this, your high excellency, but isn't it even more astonishing when two ships, with so much room to pass each other, collide? You yourself, your high excellency, commanded a frigate when such an event occurred.

Poset became very angry and demanded that the stationmaster be dismissed. Then we continued our journey.

But for the Borki accident, Poset would have stayed on as minister because Emperor Alexander III had probably met this honorable admiral while still a young man and was favorably disposed toward him because of his brother Alexis.

As I have said, General Paucker replaced Poset, but soon fell ill and died. He was a fine old man.

He was succeeded by Hübbenet, who had served as assistant minister under Poset and Paucker.* It appears that Count Dmitrii Tolstoi, the minister of interior, helped Hübbenet win the appointment. Hübbenet was an average sort of official. He was not a bad sort, although he loved to speak in a pompous tone and was very touchy to boot. He did not have the ability to exercise any influence on railroad operations. Before long, complaints were pouring in from landowners and businessmen about freight piling up on the railroads. In time these were to lead to his dismissal.

At this time Colonel Wendrich, a military engineer, appeared, or rather leaped, on stage. I should say a few words about him, because he has been fairly prominent in recent years and to this day enjoys some prestige in certain circles.[1] (He is now a senator.)

Wendrich is fine man, and on the whole honorable and proper, but he is very

---

*In those days the man chosen to be assistant minister was usually an experienced civil servant, often a senator. Hübbenet's predecessor was Senator Silfontov, who went on to become presiding officer in the Senate.

limited, in a way peculiar to Germans. People such as he have a "blinkers" mentality, a dull, narrow vision. Where a Russian would write a page, a German such as he would write several volumes. I recall hearing him speak at railroad congresses about his specialty, freight-car turnaround. He would speak in his habitual dull, narrow, and stupid manner, and we would listen condescendingly and impatiently.

He had held positions on various railroad lines, but not for long. Then he joined the ministry as a railroad inspector. When the problem of freight pile-ups became pressing he was given special authority. As he went about his work he managed to irritate those he dealt with by his stupidity, his narrowness, his pigheaded insolence, and his often impossible demands. But although he did more harm than good, he did achieve some results by stimulating the activity of some railroads that were in a state of somnolence.

Although Wendrich owed his appointment to Hübbenet, he soon began to by-pass the minister and send reports, unjustly criticizing certain officials, directly to the Emperor. He was able to do so because he had connections with persons in the military who had access to the Emperor. Needless to say, relations between Wendrich and Hübbenet soon became strained. When the minister ignored several orders from the Emperor to dismiss certain officials, he had to go.

There was some talk of Wendrich as a possible successor to Hübbenet, but almost all who knew him were frightened at the thought—he might be acceptable as an inspector but under no circumstances as a minister—and sought to dissuade the Emperor. But there was no need to convince the Emperor because he had long had me in mind for the post. I was appointed minister of ways and communications on February 15, 1892,[2] to the astonishment of everyone in Petersburg.

Staff and Other Changes

On the whole I tend to avoid making personnel changes unless they seem necessary. In this case, although my tenure was short, I had to make a few changes. My first task was to deal with Wendrich because of the harm he was doing by his impossible demands and by the severity of his attitude, by his Germanic "wildness" (*shalost*), which is so unlike Russian "wildness." For example, when I became minister I found among the papers on my desk an unfavorable report from Wendrich to the Emperor about Pechkovskii, the manager of the Kharkov–Nikolaevskii line (and now chairman of the board of the Rostov–Vladikavkaz line). The Emperor, who as usual was outspoken and direct, had written on the report: "When will you get rid of this scoundrel?" As a result, Pechkovskii had had to leave his post. What had probably occurred was that Wendrich had made some tactless demands, which had been rejected; the result—an unfavorable report.

In one of my first reports to the Emperor I said frankly that although Pechkovskii was not a very sympathetic person, he was a good engineer, a fine and knowledgeable man, and not the kind of man Wendrich made him out to be. He replied very kindly, saying that he had acted on the basis of what he had been told and had done so in order "to force the ministry to be energetic" about the freight pile-ups, which were provoking so much complaint.

I was anxious to shunt Wendrich to a position where he could do no harm, but I was afraid that the Emperor would not agree, because he had confidence in him. However, when I broached the subject the Emperor said, of course, Wendrich should be shunted aside: he had given him authority to deal with the problem because Hübbenet knew nothing about railroading, but I, he said, was considered one of the leading railroad experts. As a result Wendrich was removed from his assignment and made a member of the ministry's council.* In addition, I made a number of other changes.

I brought in Anatolii Pavlovich Ivashchenkov, who had been the director of a department in the state controller's office, to serve as assistant minister. I did so because of his reputation for honesty: he was the kind of man I needed to help me in dealing with abuses in the highway and waterway departments.

Ivashchenkov is no longer among the living. He was a remarkably honorable man, although not generously endowed with talent or intelligence. He was unassuming, well balanced, with a great capacity for work, very sensible: in short, a fine, outstanding civil servant.

In addition, I brought in two experienced railroad managers, both of them engineers—Sumarokov, manager of the Moscow–Kursk Railroad, and Adádurov, manager of the Libau Railroad, the first to be chief of railroad administration, the second to be chief of railroad construction. Also I appointed a number of men with experience in railroading, particularly its commercial side, to fill less important posts. Among them were Shabunevich, who is still with the ministry, and Gordon, now dead.

As one of the leading railroad experts I felt at home in dealing with railroading, the most important area in the ministry's jurisdiction. Other areas, such as highways and waterways, were a different matter because I knew comparatively

---

*Wendrich spent most of the next twelve years abroad, writing books about the role of railroads in Germany during troop mobilization.

He became prominent once more soon after Stolypin became premier and the railroads were in the grip of sedition (kramola), a time when the minister of ways and communications, Schaufuss, could not cope with the problem. At that point, Grand Duke Nicholas Nikolaevich pushed Wendrich (by now a general) forward as the man to restore order on the railroads, arguing that under Emperor Alexander III he had been used to end freight pile-ups.

So Wendrich was called in to deal with the problem. For a whole year he made a nuisance of himself, proposing grandiose schemes, the most grandiose of which was a railroad corps, modeled on the Corps of Gendarmes. Wendrich personally submitted this proposal to Emperor Nicholas II, evidently without Stolypin's knowledge. According to Wendrich, the Emperor approved the proposal and wrote on it: "General Wendrich to be appointed chief of the railroad corps."

Wendrich told all his acquaintances that he had been appointed chief of the corps, but he did not release the Emperor's statement of appointment. Almost all officials opposed the creation of such a corps, with a chief who would report directly to the Emperor, because it was not in keeping with the proper organization of railroad operations. As a result Wendrich fell into disfavor and instead of being made chief of the corps was appointed to the Senate and went abroad.

little about them. Yet these areas were the ones that gave me the greatest concern. The departments of highways and waterways had been in bad repute for good reason since time immemorial, even in the time of Melnikov [1865-1869]. It was known that there was a great deal of impropriety on the part of engineers and other employees in these departments, and I undertook to get rid of abuses in them, but I had only begun the effort when I left the ministry. After I left, the struggle petered out.

Rules for Imperial Train Movement

Even before I became minister, work began on the preparation of new rules for the movement of Imperial trains. And I, as member of the Council on Railroad Affairs, had taken part in that work, but it had encountered many delays, in part because many court officials, and particularly those who accompanied the Imperial trains, feared the infringement of their prerogatives, and many in the ministry catered to these people because they valued the good will of those in the court or sought favors. This is how Baron Sherval became a chamberlain and master of the court. And Salov was always dreaming of becoming a state secretary.

In light of the Borki accident, I was determined when I became minister to complete the preparation of the rules quickly. It goes without saying that as soon as the Emperor learned why there had been delays, he immediately approved the rules that I prepared. The aim of the rules, which dealt with such matters as the speed of the train, the number of cars in relation to the power of the locomotive, the speed in relation to the condition of the track—was to guarantee, insofar as rules could do it, the safety of trains carrying the Emperor and his most august family.

These rules are still in force, but, as I discovered recently on my way to Odessa, they are not always followed to the letter. This is a pity, because once one begins to deviate from the rules, especially in matters of substance, the result may be worse than an accident.

The Cholera Epidemic

In the spring of 1892, not long after my appointment as minister, the Emperor sent me to the Volga region, where a cholera epidemic was raging, with full power to see if all the necessary steps against the dread disease were being taken. He told me that he was sending me because I was the youngest of the ministers. Another consideration in my appointment was the fact that the fight against cholera involved railroads and waterways, both within the jurisdiction of my ministry.

Before I left, several doctors of my acquaintance advised me of various methods for protecting myself against the disease. (At the time they did not know as much about cholera in Russia as has been the case in recent years.) One doctor, the well-known Badmaev, a Buriat, gave me some powders to take with food, but I did not use them.

My first stop was in Samara. I arrived there with a secretary. There I met Professor Pavlovskii, of Kiev University, one of the directors of the medical personnel sent there earlier on. He was to accompany me during my entire tour of the Volga region.

I spent two days in Samara, going first to hospitals, infirmaries, and receiving stations, where, for the first time, I saw large numbers of cholera victims. I was amazed to note that there were no doctors to be seen: I was told that some were on leave and others refused to treat the victims out of fear of contracting the disease. Instead, medical students were in charge, treating and nursing the sick with utter selflessness. Naturally, I showed great kindness to these young people.

Having to spend a good deal of time with the cholera victims, touching them, and speaking with them, could not but affect my nerves. When I returned to the Imperial rooms at the railroad station, where I was staying, I must admit that the first thing I did was give my clothes to my servant for disinfection and then get into a bath prepared with mercuric chloride and soap myself thoroughly. During the first days, I was always anxious to get into the tub, have my clothes disinfected, etc. And, I found myself washing my hands very frequently. After a few days, however, I became so used to my surroundings that I dropped these precautions, but I did follow Professor Pavlovskii's advice on diet: not to eat fruit or, in general, anything raw, and to drink nothing but weak tea, which we would drink instead of wine or water.

Next we went to Saratov, where a few days earlier the so-called cholera riots had taken place. An ignorant mob had accused the doctors of being responsible for the disease and attacked those who were trying to provide medical aid. One doctor saved himself from being torn to pieces by climbing up a fire observation tower and spending the night there.

In Saratov, as in Samara, I visited the hospitals, infirmaries, and receiving rooms, and there too I found medical students in charge, with hardly any doctors in evidence. I was struck, too, by the fact that the governor of the province was not at the dock to meet me, as is the custom when a minister arrives. In fact, I did not see him at all during my stay at Saratov: I was told that he was away.

Our next stop, at Tsaritsyn, was an extended one. Here the scene was even more depressing: when our ship docked we saw many bodies of cholera victims waiting to be removed. Only a policeman and a doctor were at the dock to receive me. I visited all the hospitals in the company of the doctor, who turned out to be a railroad doctor, who was on the spot because all the other doctors had gone. (I learned from him that the other doctors were either on leave or absent without leave.) And, because there were few medical students there, the main burden fell on the nurses.

When we arrived at the main cholera ward, a nurse met us with tears in her eyes and whispered something to the doctor, who appeared to be embarrassed. When I asked what she was whispering about, he said that, because he had been in a hurry to meet me, he had taken the wrong flask from the pharmacy, a flask containing carbolic acid. He had given instructions that a certain patient was to be given drops from that flask and the patient had died, in horrible pain. I tried as best I could to console them, but this incident made a painful impression on me. It clearly showed how few medical personnel were available.

From Tsaritsyn I went by train to Nizhnii Novgorod, stopping at several stations en route without finding any cases of cholera. I was received in Nizhnii Novgorod by General N. M. Baranov, governor of the province.

A former naval officer, he had commanded the *Vesta*, an armed merchant vessel, in a famous engagement during our war with Turkey. He and his crew claimed, and the claim was officially accepted, that they had put a Turkish ship to flight. For this feat Baranov and his assistant Rozhdestvenskii were awarded the St. George and the rest of the crew received various other honors. (Had Rozhdestvenskii not been considered a hero as a result, he might not have come to command our fleet at Tsushima many years later.)

To be sure there were skeptics who claimed that the *Vesta* had fled from Turks, not vice-versa, that Baranov made up the story of a heroic victory. I was in Odessa at the time and heard a great deal about the episode. It is my impression that the crew of the *Vesta* acted heroically, but that the story of the engagement had been inflated and embroidered. But it was difficult to judge because the only witnesses were aboard the ship and it was to their advantage to support the story of the commanding officer.

In addition to receiving the St. George, Baranov was made an aide-de-camp to the Emperor, a marked honor in those days. After the war he was much in evidence in Petersburg, thanks to the fact that he spoke well, was very quick-witted and intelligent, as well as being something of a careerist, with no firm moral principles. But, on the whole, he was not a bad sort. And he got along well until he clashed with Grand Duke Constantine Nikolaevich, then general-admiral of the navy.

Baranov aroused the anger of the Grand Duke by writing articles, pseudonymously I believe, in which he criticized the fleet and the naval ministry. As one would expect from Baranov, the articles, which were scathing, showed an intelligent mind and some knowledge, but they were very self-serving: Baranov sought to move ahead by undermining some powerful men in the ministry.

After the publication of one such article—and everybody knew who the author was—he was confronted by the Grand Duke, who, in the presence of others, asked if he were the author of the article. Baranov replied that he was. Thereupon the Grand Duke said that such an article could have been written only by a scoundrel. Baranov responded: "Your Imperial Highness, I do not answer insults from French *cocottes* or Grand Dukes."

Naturally, Baranov had to leave the navy after this. But apparently he had the backing of the Tsesarevich, who worked with him and Pobedonostsev in creating the Volunteer Fleet. Shortly before the death of Emperor Alexander II, he was given the rank of general and appointed governor of Grodno. After the assassination of the Emperor, Baranov was brought to Petersburg to deal with the revolutionary threat there, but he did some foolish things: he formed an association of homeowners and tenants to consider matters over which they had no jurisdiction, and in those days Russia was not accustomed to such activity. So he had to leave the post, although he continued to enjoy the support of Pobedonostsev. From Petersburg he returned to Grodno, as governor, and then went on to Nizhnii Novgorod, where I met him.

As soon as I arrived in Nizhnii Novgorod, Baranov took me in his carriage and for the whole day dragged me around to all the hospitals, where I had to sit near the sick, speak with them, come into contact with them. I was later told that it had been Baranov's aim to frighten me and thus have some fun at my expense. But I was already hardened by now, and no matter how much he dragged me around, no matter what scenes I was made to observe, I did not flinch. In the end he had to admit to those close to him that his attempt to upset me had been in vain.

I should say that unlike the governors of Samara and Saratov, Baranov acted energetically and effectively in dealing with the epidemic. In short, he was an efficient governor and was therefore regarded by the residents with confidence and gratitude.

During the course of my trip I kept the Emperor informed of all that I saw, including the services performed by the medical students. When I returned to Petersburg I had the pleasure of hearing him say that because of my reports about the noble and selfless service of the students, he had experienced a change of heart toward them. Before he had taken a dim view of the university youth because of its part in the assassination of his father; now he saw that it was probably the noblest part of the Russian intelligentsia. It should be noted that after this the Emperor looked upon the students with sympathy and good will. And the students sensed this and appreciated it.

In fact, even a few years before this, when the Emperor returned to Petersburg following the Borki accident and went to the Kazan Cathedral, students, upon whom Borki had made a great impression, wanted to unharness his carriage and pull it.

In short, Russian [student] youth, despite its shortcomings and its lack of balance, sometimes approaching barbarism, is very sincere and senses who loves it and who hates it; even then it had a sense of what a noble and honorable man the Emperor was.

The Trans-Siberian Railroad

It was Emperor Alexander III's dream to have a railroad constructed from European Russia to Vladivostok. At one of my first reports following my appointment as minister of ways and communications, he talked to me of this dream, but complained that its realization had been delayed by individual ministers, by the Committee of Ministers, and by the State Council. In effect, he asked me for my word that I would complete the undertaking. Therefore, both as minister of ways and communications and as minister of finance I strove energetically to compensate for the delays and to complete the railroad. Unfortunately, it was not possible to complete the railroad during his lifetime. That it was finally completed was due, I say this without exaggeration, to my energy, and, of course, to the support I received from Emperor Alexander III and Emperor Nicholas II, who had become interested in the undertaking while still Tsesarevich. (As we know the Tsesarevich inaugurated the construction of the Ussuri Railroad, from Vladivostok to Khabarovsk, on May 18, 1891, while he was in the Far East.)

Had I remained minister of ways and communications the work would not have gone as rapidly as it did, for the undertaking required a great deal of money and I would have encountered resistance on that score from the minister of finance. After becoming minister of finance I gave my heart and soul to completing the railroad.

To speed up its construction I proposed the establishment of the Siberian Railroad Committee, a committee that would have sufficient authority to overcome efforts at delay by the Committee of Ministers and the State Council, sufficient authority to deal also with decisions concerning construction that required legislative actions. Emperor Alexander III approved my proposal and then one Friday, my regular day to report to him, at the Anichkov Palace, he told me that Alexander Ageevich Abaza had been suggested as chairman of the committee, but that he found the idea to be disagreeable. Whom would I suggest? I suggested the Tsesarevich. The Emperor was astonished and asked if I knew him. I replied that, of course, I did. When he asked if I had "ever talked with him about serious matters," I said that I had "never had the pleasure of talking with the Tsesarevich about anything." The Emperor responded by saying: "He is nothing but a boy, whose judgments are childish." How, he wanted to know, could he serve as chairman?

Since it was customary to introduce a Tsesarevich to governmental affairs by having him present when ministers reported to the Emperor and by appointing him to high government posts[3] I said:

> Yes, Your Majesty, he is a young man and like many young people he may not have a serious interest in governmental affairs. But you see, Your Majesty, if you do not begin to train him in governmental affairs, he may never learn. This would be his first schooling in administration.
>
> As you say, Your Majesty, he is inexperienced. That being the case, why not appoint Bunge [chairman of the Committee of Ministers] as his vice-chairman. Since Bunge had served as one of his teachers, their relationship is such that the Heir will not be offended if Bunge explains matters to him and to a degree directs him in how to manage matters.

The Emperor said that he wanted to think about my advice. At my next report he told me that he had decided to follow it.

I must say that idea turned out well, because the Tsesarevich was entranced by his appointment and took it seriously.[4] It was soon evident that he was equal to the task. This is not remarkable for he has a quick mind and learns easily. In this respect he is far superior to his father, who, however, had different qualities, qualities that made him an outstanding Emperor.

When the Tsesarevich became Emperor he retained the chairmanship of the committee and continued to be interested in its work. With his support I was able to push construction along so that within a few years Petersburg, or, to put it another way, Paris, had a direct link with Vladivostok.

The Tsesarevich and the Far East

That the Tsesarevich was enamored of his role as chairman suggests that he and the Far East seemed linked by fate.

When he reached his majority, before his appointment as chairman, it was decided to send him abroad, to round out his political development. At this point Emperor Alexander III had the idea of sending the Tsesarevich to the Far East. The Tsesarevich was accompanied on the trip by his brother George, who had to return home before the trip was over because he began to show signs of having consumption, brought on either by a cold or through some kind of carelessness. Also accompanying the Tsesarevich was Prince George of Greece, whose behavior could not serve as a model for grand dukes or princes. There were three other young men along—Prince N. D. Obolenskii, of the Horse Guards, Prince V. S. Kochubei, of the Chevalier Garde, and E. N. Volkov, of the Life Hussars—all very fine persons, but they were not in a position to represent any kind of authority. The entire expedition was under the supervision of General Prince V. A. Bariatinskii, not a bad sort, but a nonentity, unable to exert any moral authority on the Tsesarevich or his brother.

Also accompanying the Tsesarevich was Prince E. E. Ukhtomskii, quite a decent man, who now edits and publishes *Peterburgskie vedomosti*. He wrote a book about the journey, which Emperor Nicholas II himself censored.[5] Everyone who wishes to become acquainted with the superficial aspects of the journey should turn to this book. But because it is an official publication, prepared under Imperial censorship, it could not deal with the most significant aspects of the trip, the consequences of the attempt on the life of the Tsesarevich.

As we know, when the Tsesarevich arrived in Japan, a Japanese fanatic named Va-tsu struck him in the head with a sword. I was told by eyewitnesses that if this had been a drama, the circumstances of the attack would not have aroused sympathy for either the assailant or his victim on the part of the spectators. This incident produced a painful effect in Petersburg, particularly on Emperor Alexander III and, naturally, on the Tsesarevich. It seems to me that the attack left the Tsesarevich with an attitude of hostility toward and contempt for Japan and the

Japanese, as can be seen from official reports in which he refers to the Japanese as "*macacques.*"

If not for his belief that the Japanese are an unpleasant, contemptible, and powerless people who could be destroyed at one blow from the Russian giant, we would not have adopted a policy in the Far East that led us into the unfortunate war with Japan. It was a disgraceful war, the consequences of which are not entirely behind us.

The Tsesarevich's journey, as I have said, was to have fateful consequences for Russia, producing in him an unbalanced view of Russia's world interests and destiny, concentrating his attention on the East in general and on the Far East in particular, instead of on the Near East and the West. In addition to leaving him with a hostile feeling toward the Japanese, the journey produced in him an unreal sense about the East. The atmosphere of the journey of the heir to the throne of the greatest empire in the world could not help but influence this impressionable young man.[6] And the return home, by way of Siberia, along the post roads, could not help but leave him with a sense of the great role which God had predetermined for him. This journey was to put its stamp on Emperor Nicholas II's reign.

When the young Tsesarevich unexpectedly became Emperor because of the untimely death of his father, it seems justifiable to believe that as a result of the impressions produced on him by the journey he dreamed of expanding the great Russian Empire in the Far East by subordinating the Chinese Bogdykhan (Emperor), as the Emir of Bukhara had been subordinated, and possibly adding such titles as Bogdykhan of China and Mikado of Japan to the titles he already held.

I have heard it said that Emperor Alexander III made a mistake in sending the Tsesarevich to the Far East rather than to the interior of Russia and to Western Europe. It was a mistake, and a fatal one, but it would not have been a great mistake had the Emperor not died prematurely.

Tsion's Memorandum about Vyshnegradskii

Toward the end of my tenure as minister of ways and communications, at the conclusion of my regular report to him, at Gatchina, the Emperor handed me some sort of pamphlet, asked me to give him my opinion of its allegations. I took it back with me and on reading it saw that it was an attack by Tsion on Vyshnegradskii, alleging that the minister of finance had taken a 500,000 franc bribe from Rothschild for having negotiated a loan from him. The pamphlet included what was unquestionably a copy from entries in the Rothschild books that showed a payment of the alleged sum to Vyshnegradskii.

At my next report to the Emperor I told him that although the pamphlet proved that Vyshnegradskii had received the sum in question, I did not believe that it represented a bribe. When asked why I thought so, I told him that I knew the man intimately and that, although he was not very scrupulous and although in work outside the government he made a good deal of money in ways not befitting a man in his position, I knew that in his position as minister he would not commit any misdeed. I said that it is impossible for a minister of finance to take a bribe without a few others knowing about it, and if a few knew, all would eventually know, for ministers of finance, even more so than other ministers, have many enemies as well as many friends.

The Emperor thanked me for my opinion, said that he believed me, and asked me to keep the pamphlet. I kept it until I left the Ministry of Finance, when I destroyed it. Later I will explain how the matter of the 500,000 francs was cleared up. Now, I want to say a few words about Tsion.

Tsion was a physiologist who early in his career was forced to leave his post as professor of physiology at the Military-Medical Academy in Petersburg because, being a dishonorable man, he had great difficulties with his colleagues. He was said to be a very fine lecturer, but not a profound scholar.

In the late 1870s, Tsion, a convert, of Jewish origin, realized that the extreme conservative spirit, represented by Katkov,* was in the ascendancy and decided to adopt the Katkov view. So, he began writing articles for Katkov's *Moskovskie vedomosti* and *Russkii vestnik*.

On the whole, Katkov had nothing against Jews and was even on good terms with some. Thus, the well-known Katkov Lycée (the so-called Tsesarevich Nicholas Lycée) was established with the help of Poliakov and other Jewish money. So it was not remarkable that Katkov was favorably inclined toward Tsion.

It was through Katkov that Tsion gained a foothold in the Ministry of Finance. After Katkov, together with the entire ultraconservative party, had succeeded in replacing the somewhat liberal Bunge† with their candidate Vyshnegradskii in the post of minister of finance, the new minister being indebted to Katkov, agreed [in 1887] to the appointment of Tsion as an official on special assignment in the ministry. Vyshnegradskii then sent Tsion to Paris to negotiate a loan from a group of French financiers, headed by Hoskier, a man of minor importance and still among the living.

This was the first substantial loan we had floated in France. Hitherto the French government and the French financial community had not looked favorably on having financial dealings with us, in part because of our friendship with Germany, in part because of memories of the Sebastopol [Crimean] War. But since the accession of Emperor Alexander III we had begun to recognize that the tradition of blind unity with Germany had outlived its day and were slowly moving toward an alliance with France. As a result, the French money market was opening up for us, at a time when the English money market, once open to us, was now less open.

---

*Katkov's conservatism was far milder than that of our contemporary Black Hundreds and is quite unlike it.

†Bunge was more suited to academic life than to being a minister of finance. Because Emperor Alexander III respected him as a person, Bunge left office with honor.

After the loan was concluded, Vyshnegradskii learned that Tsion had received a commission of nearly 200,000 francs from the bankers with whom he had dealt. Thereupon he forced Tsion to leave government service [with a pension]. At the time Tsion had the rank of either privy councillor or actual state councillor.

Tsion was able to stay on his feet thanks to the money he had received. He remained in Paris and from there began to attack Vyshnegradskii through pamphlets and anonymous denunciations. The pamphlet the Emperor had shown me dealt with Vyshnegradskii's conversion loan, which had been negotiated through a group of French bankers, headed by Rothschild. (For a long time Rothschild had refused to have any dealings with Russia because of the Jewish question.)

Immediately after I succeeded Vyshnegradskii as minister of finance, Tsion wrote me a letter expressing his joy at Vyshnegradskii's departure and my appointment, and offered me his services, which, he said, would be of great value to me. Having already formed my opinion of the man, I did not reply.

Naturally, he began to write books, pamphlets, and articles in which he attacked me;[7] most of his work appeared in a magazine published by the notorious Mme. Adam.[8] Also, he distributed denunciations of me to the Emperor, to interested fellow ministers, and to others. There was no filth that he did not write about me.

Finally, during the reign of Emperor Nicholas II, I directed the attention of the minister of interior to Tsion's activities. He held some sort of meeting, [in 1895], that resulted in Tsion's losing his pension and being forbidden to return to Russia.

A decade later, while I was in Paris on my way back from Portsmouth, Tsion called on me. This was the first time in my life I had seen him. Characteristically, this gentleman began to praise me to the skies, apologizing profusely for his earlier activities, saying that he hadn't known me. Then he advised me on how to act in the face of the revolution we were experiencing. Apparently he knew, or guessed, that on my return to Russia I would assume the reins of government. But I was quite cold toward him. Then, after my return to Petersburg, I received several letters from him to which I did not reply. Thereafter he faded completely from view.

This Tsion, who as I have noted was of Jewish origin, married a Jewess from Odessa. After he had squandered her meager fortune, he divorced her, under scandalous circumstances. Subsequently, pretending that he had made money on the stock exchange, he married a beautiful actress in Paris. After she had become old and penniless, he parted from her in a manner that was not quite proper.

I tell all this to show what kind of a person Tsion is.

Both the left and the right produce scoundrels. Both left-wing and right-wing scoundrels profess that they are acting for the sake of principle when they do vile things. Left-wing scoundrels tell the truth when they make such professions. Right-wing scoundrels, and the majority of right-wingers who have gained re-nown since 1905 are scoundrels, are in fact actuated not by principle but by baseness and greed when they do vile things. At least that is the case in Russia.

XIV

Family Matters

My Second Marriage

About a year after the death of my first wife, while attending the theater, I saw a lady who made a very powerful impression on me, although at the time I had no interest in finding out who she was. Later, when I met her, I learned that she was the wife of Lisanevich, nephew of the wife of General-Adjutant Richter,[1] director of the Commission of Petitions.

After I became acquainted with the Lisaneviches and visited their home, I noticed that her husband treated her abominably and that theirs was an unhappy marriage. I decided to persuade Mme. Lisanevich to divorce her husband and marry me.[2] Given her husband's behavior, a divorce would be easy to obtain.

Only when the divorce was nearly completed did it occur to me that if I married her I would have to leave the government, for in those days, in contrast to the present, it was rarely permitted for one in my position to marry a divorcée. In view of this I decided to leave the government and return to private life.

But, since the thought of explaining the matter to the Emperor was unpleasant, I first spoke to Ivan Nikolaevich Durnovo, the minister of interior, who knew the Richters and the Lisaneviches.[3] I told him that I was planning to marry and that my intention to do so was irrevocable, but that I found it unpleasant possibly to put the Emperor in an awkward position. I said that it might appear inconsiderate of me, having only recently been appointed minister, to act as I intended to. But, said I, I had no choice. I added that it would help my situation if he acquainted himself with the particulars of the case, which he could learn from General Richter, his close friend, and from the Holy Synod, where the divorce was being considered. What Durnovo reported to the Emperor I do not know.

At my next report to the Emperor I came armed with my request to be permitted to leave the service. At the conclusion of my report I took out my request and said:

> Your Majesty, however unpleasant and difficult it may be, I must, nonetheless, ask Your Majesty for permission to leave the service, because I plan to marry a divorcée and I understand that it would not be proper for me to continue as minister of ways and communications under the circumstances.

The Emperor replied:

> I know all the details about your wish to marry from the chief of the gendarmerie and from Richter. Your intention to marry only demonstrates that you are an honorable man and serves to deepen my respect for and confidence in you. If you did not marry after all that has happened, I would not respect you. I must say that you have no reason to leave the service.

Naturally, I was very grateful to the Emperor, and within a few days I was married, in the church of the Institute of Ways and Communications (in those days there was no church in the residence of the minister of ways and communications) which is next to the garden of the minister's residence. My best man (shafer)[4] was Baron Volf, then an officer in the Horse Guards, and now master of the horse [at court]. My wife's best man was her friend Captain Tatishchev, then adjutant to Grand Duke Vladimir Aleksandrovich, and now general à la suite, representing our Emperor at the court of Emperor William II.*

The day after my marriage I had to attend a dinner, presided over by General-Adjutant Richter, at the Winter Palace. Everyone stared at me with great curiosity and watched to see how I got along with Richter. My relations with him remained excellent to the end of his life, but I have not been on speaking terms with Mme. Richter, who is still alive, since my marriage.

My marriage created quite a furor among the ladies of society and all sorts of slanders about us were circulated.[5] The furor and the slanders haunted me far less than they did my wife, because I paid little attention to them.

Things changed in 1905, when everyone at court was reconciled with her. Since then Petersburg high society has come to accept this event in my life. Now my wife is cordially received everywhere in the highest society, particularly since I am no longer engaged in political life.[6]

My second wife had a baby daughter, Vera, whom I grew to love as my own. I adopted her, conferring on her all the rights of an only daughter. I raised her and

---

*It appears that Tatishchev is in the good graces of both emperors. In any event, whenever there is talk of replacing our ambassador to Berlin, Count Osten-Sacken, because of his age, the name of General Tatishchev always comes to the fore.

In fact, he is a very fine and decent man, well bred and educated, but he is very, very limited. What puzzles me is this: does Emperor William want him because he is a fine man or because he is limited?

had her with me until she married. Thus, she considers me as her father because she virtually did not know her own father.

Sonia, My First Wife's Daughter, and Her Husband

Not long after my second marriage, my first wife's daughter, Sonia, and M. F. Mering, vice-director of the Credit Chancellery of the Ministry of Finance (son of the Mering I have mentioned earlier), announced that they wished to be married. They had met at our home. I and my wife gave Sonia as substantial a dowry as we could then afford—not that she needed it, for Mering was a rich man. I did this to clear my conscience, so to speak.

Soon after their marriage the couple moved to Kiev, where Mering became director of the Commercial Bank and indulged his passion for speculation. Later, after I became minister of finance, I heard rumors that he was taking advantage of our relationship, by exploiting my name in his affairs, although I had never discussed business with him, nor had I maintained correspondence with him or his wife.

Finally, when word reached me that the bank was in trouble and that this state of affairs was being tolerated because he made it appear that he was close to me, I summoned him and Sonia to Petersburg. I asked them if the bank were in a critical condition, as I had heard. Young Mering gave me his word that the bank was in excellent condition, that he was not involved in speculation, and that Sonia was well acquainted with his affairs. Sonia supported him and swore that everything being said about them was a damnable lie. I said that I had no choice but to accept their word, but if it turned out that they were not telling the truth, I would have nothing further to do with them.

They were not telling the truth. A few months after they had returned to Kiev, it turned out that Mering's speculations had pushed the bank to the verge of bankruptcy. It would have failed had not some wealthy Kievan bigshots come to the aid of the bank in the mistaken notion that their actions would please me. Because of Mering's and Sonia's behavior, my feelings toward them turned from indifference to hostility.

Subsequently, Mering went abroad. He now lives in Paris, in bad company. Thanks to his speculations his fortune has been frittered away. I have heard nothing of him in recent years, except that he keeps the lowest kind of company.

Sonia left him when he moved to Paris. I feel more embittered toward her than ever because she goes about referring to me as her "daddy" (*papasha*), uses my name everywhere, and claims that my feelings toward her have changed not because of what she did but because of my wife's influence. Sonia is her father's daughter—dishonest and sly.

XV

Prince Vladimir Petrovich Meshcherskii

The most interesting man with whom I dealt while minister of ways and communications was the sadly famous Prince Vladimir ("Vovo") Petrovich Meshcherskii, editor and publisher of *Grazhdanin*.

I first met him in Moscow at the home of Ivan Grigorevich Derviz, with whom I was well acquainted. Ivan Grigorevich, whose brother was the famous railroad king, served as chairman of the board of the Riazan–Kozlovskii Railroad. Twice, while in Moscow for railroad congresses, I met Meshcherskii at the Derviz home. Ivan Grigorevich and Meshcherskii, who had been fellow students at the Imperial School of Jurisprudence, were on *tutoyer* terms, yet I was astonished to note that Derviz received him in his study, but not in his drawing room. Derviz's wife, Marie Ivanovna (née Princess Kozlovskaia),* told me when I asked if she knew Meshcherskii that he was "a dirty man" whom she would not receive, even though her husband and the prince had been schoolmates. She did not explain what made him dirty.

When I became director of the Department of Railroad Affairs and moved to Petersburg, I met Prince Meshcherskii once or twice, in the summer, at suburban parks and summer theaters. Each time he would try to strike up an acquaintance with me, but I discouraged him.

When I became minister of ways and communications, Meshcherskii called on me and, in his very saccharine and servile manner, directed my attention to [Iosif Iosifovich] Kolyshko,[1] an official on special assignment in the ministry, saying that he was very able. Therefore I took time to learn something about Kolyshko.

---

*After the death of Derviz, she married General of the Infantry Dukmasov, the senior member of the military council, who died a few weeks ago.

He had been an officer, in the Uhlans, I believe, and was married to Princess Obolenskaia. Before coming to my ministry he had been an official on special assignment in the Ministry of Interior, under Tolstoi. Because of this background I made no special inquiries about him. As I came to know him, I was pleased by the fact that he was a facile writer.

Subsequently, after calling attention in *Grazhdanin* to improprieties in the operation of my ministry's Department of Roads and Waterways, Meshcherskii urged me to permit Kolyshko to demonstrate his ability by sending him to investigate alleged wrongdoing in the Mogilev District of Ways and Communications. Knowing that there was substance to such accusations, and there still is, I sent Kolyshko that summer to investigate the Mogilev district and other officials to investigate other districts.

Kolyshko found so much amiss in his inquiries that I decided to dismiss the Mogilev district chief and turn him over to the courts, but first I had to go to the Senate. But I was frustrated there by Senator Fadeev, the former director of the Department of Roads and Waterways, who persuaded his colleagues not to agree to such an action. However, I then went to the Emperor, who overrode the decision of the Senate. (In the course of the investigation, I was told, Kolyshko behaved like a Khlestakov,[2] representing himself as a major Petersburg figure.)

Subsequently I became more closely acquainted with Meshcherskii. He had me over to his home for dinner on several occasions, where I met Durnovo, minister of interior, Krivoshein, who was to succeed me as minister of ways and communications, Filippov, Colonel Wendrich, and many others. I invited Meshcherskii to my home for dinner on two or three occasions.

As I came to know him I was puzzled about Meshcherskii's source of money for *Grazhdanin*, a paper with a small circulation. I was to find out when I became minister of finance. Because I want to tell the story of Prince Meshcherskii here, a long and rather interesting story, I am jumping ahead to the time when I became minister of finance.

After I became minister of finance Durnovo came to see me and told me that in my new capacity I would receive a yearly request for 80,000 rubles for the editor-publisher of *Grazhdanin*, the money to be charged to the fund for extraordinary needs.* It had been the practice, he said, for the money to be turned over to the Ministry of Interior, which would then transfer it to Meshcherskii. But, for the future, the Emperor thought it best for the minister of finance to transfer the money directly to Meshcherskii. Durnovo added that he had asked the Emperor to relieve him of the duty because, on the whole, he had become disappointed in the prince. At my next report the Emperor confirmed that he wished me to give the money directly to Meshcherskii. Naturally I carried out the Emperor's instructions.

*I recall that when I was minister of ways and communications I met Meshcherskii at Vyshnegrad-skii's.

I could not help but become interested in the personality of the publisher of *Grazhdanin*: what sort of a man was he and why did he have such ties with the Emperor? I asked both Pobedonostsev and Vorontsov-Dashkov about him. Vorontsov-Dashkov told me he wouldn't shake hands with that man.

Pobedonostsev told me that Meshcherskii was simply a scoundrel, a dirty man whom he had once known and with whom he wished to have nothing to do. He told me that Meshcherskii belonged to high society and came from an illustrious family, his maternal grandfather being Karamzin, the famous historian. And because Karamzin had been close to the Imperial family, he, Meshcherskii, had been one of a handful of young persons chosen to be companions to the Tsesarevich Nicholas Alexandrovich [1843–1865]. As one of the teachers of the Tsesarevich, Pobedonostsev had traveled with him and his companions on a journey across Russia. This explained how Pobedonostsev had come to know Meshcherskii. He said: "Just wait and see how he repays you for any favor you may show him."

Then he told my why Emperor Alexander III behaved toward Meshcherskii as he did.[3] The Emperor, if one may use a schoolgirl term, worshiped his brother Nicholas. And when the Tsesarevich died, he felt an attachment for everyone who had been close to his brother. This was especially true in the case of Meshcherskii, because he and Emperor Alexander were nearly the same age and had played and studied together with the Tsesarevich. And for a time the future Emperor Alexander III and his adjutant Vorontsov-Dashkov were on friendly terms with the prince. It should be noted that the Emperor was firm in his attachments.

However, I was struck by the fact that Meshcherskii rarely called on the Emperor and that when he did, it was, so to speak, by way of the back door. I wondered why and was told that while the Emperor was still heir to the throne his wife had become so offended by the prince's behavior that she referred to him as a scoundrel and had said that she never wanted him to cross her threshold again. Thereafter whatever contact there was to be between Emperor Alexander III and Meshcherskii had to be maintained, more or less, through the back door.

The Emperor did not break off contact completely because of his attachment to those who had been close to his brother, also because he had a fairly high opinion of Meshcherskii's writing, and it must be admitted that he has a considerable, even outstanding, talent as a writer. Also, there is the fact that no one could outdo Prince Meshcherskii at begging and wheedling. He was always going on at great length about his sad life and thus was able to get the Emperor's commitment to an annual subsidy of 80,000 rubles for *Grazhdanin*, which I had the Department of the Treasury pay out in 1893 and 1894, as my predecessor, Vyshnegradskii, had done before me, informing the Emperor each time of my action.*

*In this connection I should note that I. N. Durnovo became the target of criticism in *Grazhdanin* after he refused to continue as an intermediary in providing Meshcherskii with the subsidy. Also, after relations between Vorontsov-Dashkov and the prince had cooled, Meshcherskii attacked Vorontsov-Dashkov in his paper whenever he could, but not harshly enough to offend the Emperor. The same was true of the paper's treatment of Pobedonostsev after relations between the prince and the over-procurator had become strained.

The situation in which I found myself with respect to Meshcherskii spurred him to establish close ties with me, and so he was constantly trying to ingratiate himself with me. I, for my part, used the opportunity to get to know him better.

I soon became convinced that he rarely saw the Emperor but that he did communicate with him by sending him something on the order of a diary, in which he wrote in great detail about all the major political events. And the Emperor sometimes wrote to Meshcherskii. The Empress, however, grew increasingly hostile toward Meshcherskii as reports of his scandalous behavior reached her.

One scandal of which she was probably aware, because it was the talk of Petersburg, involved the relationship between Meshcherskii and a young trumpeter in the Life Rifle Battalion. When the battalion commander, Count Keller, told the trumpeter to stop seeing Meshcherskii, the prince began to denounce the count in the pages of *Grazhdanin*, as a consequence of which Count Keller was forced to give up his command.[4] Later, an investigation cleared the count's name completely and showed Prince Meshcherskii's role in the case to have been a very nasty one. Count Keller was then able to resume his career. He was appointed director of the Corps of Pages; later he became governor of Ekaterinoslav. During the war with Japan, as is well known, Count Keller died an honorable death in battle.

Prince Meshcherskii was usually surrounded by an entourage of young men, who were close to him on the basis of dirty, unnatural passions. He was their energetic patron: he pushed them forward, pleaded for them, and, if an official did not show the interest in his protégés that he sought, he did not hesitate to defame that official in *Grazhdanin*.

In Prince Meshcherskii's entourage there is always one young man who enjoys his special favor, one whose career moves forward rapidly thanks to his patron's support. Kolyshko was one of these. He graduated from an officers training school and began his career as an ordinary officer, but was able to find positions in the Ministry of Interior and the Ministry of Ways and Communications under the patronage of Prince Meshcherskii. After I left the ministry, his position there improved under my successor, Krivoshein, until he was accused of taking a bribe. He claimed that the charge against him was without foundation, but he had to leave government service. Although I did not look into the case, I am inclined to believe that the charge was well founded and that he escaped more serious punishment only because of the special protection of Prince Meshcherskii. As I have noted, Kolyshko is a talented man, but he is a man of little education and a man of elastic morals.

In time Kolyshko was displaced as Meshcherskii's favorite by Burdukov, a young officer, who completely conquered the prince's heart and to this day dominates his life, does anything he wishes with this old roué, much as a pretty young woman can do as she wishes with an old man who has lost his faculties. Under Meshcherskii's patronage Burdukov advanced even more rapidly than Kolyshko.

A man of no education, no talent, an utterly inconsequential person, Burdukov began his career, like Kolyshko, as an ordinary officer. Yet now he holds the title of chamberlain [at court], represents the Ministry of Interior on the Tariff Committee of the Ministry of Finance, and is an official on special assignment with the Ministry of Interior. Moreover, he has been able to put aside money from lucrative assignments arranged for by his patron. For example, Burdukov has been to Turkestan for the Ministry of Agriculture on several occasions to study the carpet industry there, and for each trip he received several tens of thousands of rubles. I am told that on one occasion he even received money for a trip he didn't make.

Prince Meshcherskii was very distressed when Emperor Alexander III died, partly because no one who had the good fortune to be close to the Emperor could refrain from being grieved over the death of so fine and majestic a person, partly because he feared that his material position might change for the worse. Consequently, he entreated me to speak as favorably as possible to the new Emperor about his annual subsidy.

When I reported to Emperor Nicholas II about the subsidy, including its history as I have related it here, I found him unfavorably disposed toward Prince Meshcherskii. Evidently he had never spoken with his father about the prince, but he had heard about him from his mother. He said that he did not consider *Grazhdanin* to be of any significance and had no intention of continuing to subsidize it. I said that it was impossible to liquidate the newspaper at one stroke, that it should be kept in mind that Meshcherskii had published it for many years with the support of the Emperor's father, and that, in any case, Meshcherskii should be given time to shut down the publication. The Emperor agreed to give Meshcherskii one more grant of 80,000 rubles, but I was to tell him that there would be no more. Also I was to tell the prince that the Emperor did not wish to have any contact with him, written or otherwise. I did as I was told.

This did not deter Meshcherskii, who, as I learned, employed General Vasilovskii, the superintendent of the Anichkov Palace, as his intermediary for communication with the Emperor. He wrote the Emperor a personal letter, enclosing with it all the letters he had received from Emperor Alexander III, as a way of demonstrating how close he had been to him. Emperor Nicholas II later told me that he had returned all these letters to Meshcherskii and asked him never again, under any circumstances, to get in touch with him.

Meshcherskii was in despair and came to me many times, begging me to intercede with the Emperor on his behalf. I don't doubt that he made similar requests of other ministers, particularly of Count Delianov, because he, Meshcherskii, had a nominal position in the Ministry of Education. However, all his efforts were in vain until Dmitrii Sergeevich Sipiagin, who was distantly related to the Meshcherskiis, became minister of interior.

Meshcherskii was able to play on family ties and succeeded in persuading Sipiagin to intercede on his behalf. As a result the Emperor gave Meshcherskii permission to write to him and agreed to provide him with an annual subsidy of

18,000 rubles, which I was to transmit and about which I was to report annually.*
As far as I know, Meshcherskii continues to receive the subsidy.

Once he had permission to write to the Emperor,[5] he was able to establish close
ties with him, so close that the Emperor even *tutoyered* him, as I could see from
letters that he showed me. As we know, Emperor Alexander II *tutoyered* subordinates and those close to him, while Emperor Alexander III *tutoyered* no one but his
relatives. This was even more the case with Emperor Nicholas II because, as I
have already said, he is very well bred, in the European sense of the word, at least
with respect to externals. Thus, for him to *tutoyer* Prince Meshcherskii was a
particular mark of favor, one that he did not show toward ministers or to others
with whom he was in constant contact. Meshcherskii told me that he begged for
this favor, in memory of the tie he had had with Emperor Alexander III, who had
tutoyered him, his faithful servant.

After the tragic assassination of Sipiagin, Meshcherskii wrote to the Emperor
recommending Plehve to succeed Sipiagin. He said that Plehve was a man who
could strengthen public order and eliminate the revolutionary hydra that had
destroyed that fine and decent man Sipiagin. On the strength of this recommendation Plehve was appointed. That he should have recommended Plehve, of all
people, seemed odd, for only a few months earlier when I, Meshcherskii, and
Sipiagin were having dinner (at either Sipiagin's or Meshcherskii's home), Sipiagin, who was talking of leaving his post, said if Plehve were to succeed him, it
would be a great misfortune for Russia and Meshcherskii had agreed.

Meshcherskii got along well with Plehve after he became minister. He visited
him frequently and almost every request he made was honored. It was during
Plehve's tenure that Burdukov was chosen to represent the Ministry of Interior on
the Tariff Committee of the Ministry of Finance. And when Meshcherskii visited
Plehve he would offer him advice about how to administer the country and in
return would receive various bits of news he could use in *Grazhdanin*.

From its inception *Grazhdanin* was able to influence a limited group of readers,
partly because Meshcherskii is a talented and experienced writer, partly because
he was able to publish certain items of information not available to other journalists and publishers. Also of importance was the fact, as I have reason to know, that
he has influence in high places. So, it is understandable that there are those who
buy and read this newspaper because they know of his influence.

Meshcherskii also exerts influence through his weekly soirées. I have never
attended one, but I am told they attract many who seek his support or favor. Some
even aspire to an appointment to the State Council, and I know of two, Platonov
and Shevich, who managed to get into the State Council with his help. Some have
attained governorships with his help.

Take the case of Zasiadko, one of the young men loved by Prince Meshcherskii.

---

*Under Emperor Alexander III, *Grazhdanin* was a daily. With the end of the 80,000 ruble subsidy it
became a weekly, as it is to this day.

Well, while I was minister of finance, this Zasiadko was an inspector and Me-shcherskii was constantly badgering me to put him in charge of a provincial revenue department. I held out for a long time, but when such a position became vacant in Polotsk, in the Kingdom of Poland, I appointed him to it. Then, as soon as he became minister of interior, Plehve made Mr. Zasiadko chairman of the Tver provincial zemstvo board. (This was after an Imperial order had made the post an appointive one.) After I became premier, I found Mr. Zasiadko adminis-tering the province of Samara; naturally, he lost this post within a few months. But subsequently, after my departure from office, he was appointed governor of one of the provinces of the Kingdom of Poland, with Meshcherskii's help; he is still in that position.

This Zasiadko is far from stupid and is not a particularly bad sort, but he has advanced not on the basis of his ability or of his work, but on the basis of his closeness to Prince Meshcherskii while a young man.

When Prince Sviatopolk-Mirskii, that fine man, became minister of interior, Meshcherskii sought my help in his efforts to become close to him, but I would not cooperate. So, Meshcherskii had to write to the Emperor, asking that he intercede on his behalf with Sviatopolk-Mirskii. When the Emperor did so, Sviatopolk-Mir-skii said that even for the Emperor to utter that man's name was to sully his lips. Naturally, Meshcherskii played no role whatsoever during Sviatopolk-Mirskii's short tenure and devoted himself to defaming him in print and in letters to the Emperor. Meshcherskii had no better luck with the next minister of interior, Bulygin, or with Trepov, Bulygin's assistant minister (in fact, dictator), both of whom despised the man.

During the tenure of these three men, Meshcherskii lost much of his access to the Emperor, but not solely because of them. In part it was because, to give Me-shcherskii his due, he had the courage to oppose Bezobrazov and his gang. I recall perfectly well how on May 6, 1903, Meshcherskii showed me a letter from the Emperor, which went roughly as follows:

> I am grateful to you for writing candidly to me and for warning me against those who, in your opinion, are leading me into war. I am very grateful to you for such communications, but I am committed to my position. Tomorrow you will see evidence of this.

When I asked Meshcherskii what had occasioned this kind of reply, he read to me what he had written to the Emperor. In his letter, naming names and writing in a very witty and caustic manner, he warned the Emperor against those who were carrying on a vile and dangerous intrigue that was driving us into war. (I do not consider it possible to cite the letter here.)

When Meshcherskii asked what the last sentence in the Emperor's letter meant, I could not offer him any enlightenment. It came on the following day, when we read that Bezobrazov had been appointed state secretary and that General Vogak, one of his associates, had been appointed to His Majesty's suite. In addition there were other honors. In short, Bezobrazov had become one of the most influential men around the Emperor.

It was Meshcherskii's critical attitude toward our Far Eastern policy and his sharp letters on the subject that put him in disfavor with the Emperor. And he remained in disfavor for several years. In the last year or so the Emperor has softened toward him, by receiving him twice and showing him other marks of favor.

But as for me, I have had nothing to do with Prince Meshcherskii since leaving the post of premier because of his attacks on me. Earlier, on my return from Portsmouth [September 1905], he wrote all kinds of dithyrambs to me. He came to visit me and wept, saying that all that could save Russia was a constitution. But after October 17 [1905], when a very moderate and conservative constitution was granted and especially after my leaving the office of premier, Meshcherskii began to write all sorts of filth about me.

I was particularly upset by one article in which he said that while Russia was suffering and bleeding, I had somehow acquired the means to live abroad and would spit on everything. Then, adopting the Black Hundreds point of view, which was gaining strength, he declared that at the time of the issuance of the October 17 Manifesto and of the constitution I had been quite mad and irresponsible and that it was while in such a condition that I had led the Emperor to agree to such acts.

Yet after writing an article of this kind, Meshcherskii and Mr. Burdukov, his adjutant, or, to put it bluntly, his lover, had the gall to attempt to call on me just after I left the post of premier. Of course I would not receive them. Later, when I went abroad to Bad Homburg, Meshcherskii went there, too, on the pretext of going there for the cure, but in fact to keep in contact with me, thinking that there was a possibility that I might return to power. Naturally, he failed and I have had nothing to do with him since then. I have treated his efforts, as well as those of Mr. Burdukov, to get back into my good graces with contempt.

All his life Meshcherskii has made a trade out of politics, trafficking in it, without conscience, for his benefit and that of his favorites. When someone is in power and seems useful to him, he writes dithyrambs about that person, proclaiming that if this person goes, Russia will perish, but no sooner is this person out of office than he begins to fling mud at him. That is why everyone considers him a terrible man.

Virtually everyone who had anything to do with him agrees. Early on, as I have said, Count Vorontsov-Dashkov and Pobedonostsev warned me against him and could think of no term for him other than scoundrel. Filippov and Durnovo were also against him. Meshcherskii's brother, the superintendent of the Moscow School District, his daughters, and his sons-in-law (outstanding men of good social position, e.g., Prince Golitsyn and Vasilchikov) will have nothing to do with him.

This then is Prince Meshcherskii. One cannot help but grieve that a man of this sort should have had entrée to such decent people as our monarchs.[6] Clearly what we have here is tremendous deception on one side and delusion on the other.

XVI

Fellow Ministers and Other High Officials, 1889–1894

Count Dmitrii Tolstoi, Minister of Interior

Count Tolstoi died while I was director of the Department of Railroad Affairs. I saw him no more than twice, once as a student and again, when, as director, I paid him a courtesy call.

He was an exceptional man, a powerful personality, a man of strong will, well educated, and a fairly honorable man. Politically, he was on the extreme right. Emperor Alexander III appointed him to succeed Count Ignatev precisely because of his political views. I did not agree with him on many matters, and I believe that many of the reforms he introduced, both as minister of education and as minister of interior, are to a considerable degree responsible for the disorders Russia has experienced in the past few years. It is noteworthy that even many conservatives, among them Constantine Petrovich Pobedonostsev, opposed a number of his reforms.

One of Tolstoi's harmful reforms was the establishment of the institution of land captains, with the Emperor's strong support. The Emperor was attracted by the idea of having the peasantry of each rural district under the supervision of a land captain, an honorable noble landowner, who would look after the peasants in his district, act as their judge, and lay down the law to them. It was assumed that the land captains would be the "best" members of society, men qualified to look after and lead the peasantry.

Even if the idyllic vision of the "best" serving as land captains could have been realized, the idea of land captains was fundamentally wrong because it was based on the union of administrative and judicial functions in one person. However, for a society to be civilized there must be separation of the administrative and judicial

branches. The courts at all levels must be completely independent of the administrative branch. Once this separation is breached, rule of law is replaced by
arbitrary action, as we can see nowadays when our judiciary has completely lost
its independence and Minister of Justice Shcheglovitov is nothing but an errand
boy for Stolypin.

Constantine Petrovich Pobedonostsev, being a very learned and cultivated
man, naturally could not accept the mixing of administrative and judicial functions and therefore opposed the law establishing the institution of land captains,
as did the State Council. That the law was enacted was largely the result of the
influence, among others, of Prince Meshcherskii.

The expectation that the "best" would serve as land captains proved to be an
illusion. At first there were a few decent and competent land captains; now there
are hardly any. Typically, the office is filled by second-rate men—retired officers
with no higher education.

Thus, one can say that the institution of land captain has been unsuccessful
and has brought Russia much harm. Yet it has been decided to retain the institution, as a bulwark of order, a bulwark of conservatism. But this notion is based on
illusion. Solid conservatism and order can exist only on the basis of the rule of law.
And as long as the entire population does not enjoy the rule of law, one can expect
the unexpected.

This was the same Count Tolstoi who raised the question of reorganizing the
zemstvos. He was not destined to complete the undertaking—that was done by his
successor, Durnovo—but it was he who laid the foundation for the law of 1890
that reorganized the zemstvos. The essence of the change was to increase the
representation of the nobility and to reduce that of the peasantry; it might be said
that the zemstvos were "ennobled." This change, too, was unsuccessful.

There is no question that Russia has to replace the institution of land captain
and the zemstvos, as reorganized in the 1890s. Instead of being under the jurisdiction of land captains, the peasants should be subject to the same courts that exist
for all other subjects; the rule of law should prevail in peasant life. Likewise, the
zemstvos should be democratized by giving the peasantry its due influence and
voice. It is to be hoped that the government will be wise enough to see to it that
these changes come about peacefully while there is still time, rather than wait
until it must be done under the gun, that is, as a result of mass unrest.

When Count Tolstoi was minister of education he replaced the university
statute of the 1860s with a reactionary one, [in 1884], which eliminated such
autonomy as professors had enjoyed and placed university professorial councils
under the jurisdiction of superintendents of school districts and of the minister of
education. Although Constantine Petrovich Pobedonostsev was a conservative he
strongly opposed the new statute, because, as a cultivated man, he understood
that a university without academic freedom is not a university. The new statute
proved unsuccessful, being responsible for much of the unrest we have experienced in recent years.

However, it can be said on Count Tolstoi's behalf that under his administration the government did not go to the extremes that it does nowadays in its treatment of Jews, Poles, and other non-Russian subjects. Moreover, he was a strong administrator who kept his ministry in proper order.

I. N. Durnovo, Minister of Interior

Ivan Nikolaevich Durnovo, Tolstoi's successor, had served as assistant minister under him, and as such he had played a significant role, especially in being able to smoothe over unpleasantness.

Durnovo graduated from a military school, then served for a time as an artillery officer. After leaving the army he looked after his small estate, in the province of Chernigov, where he was elected marshal of the nobility. Subsequently he was appointed governor of Ekaterinoslav. From that post he moved on to become assistant minister of interior under Count Tolstoi's predecessor, Count Ignatev.

Because of Durnovo's good nature, his ability to get along with people, his ability to be very pleasant, his very imposing figure—all negative rather than positive qualities in a public official—he was an agreeable marshal of the nobility, an agreeable governor, and an agreeable assistant minister of interior. He was a gentle, hospitable man, but was very sly, with that slyness of the *khokhlatskii.*[1] He was married to Leokadiia Aleksandrovna, the very gentle and beautiful daughter of the supervisor of some sort of educational institution in Petersburg. Leokadiia Aleksandrovna, who survived her husband, is a very fine woman, but she has the mind of a chicken.

Naturally, Ivan Nikolaevich Durnovo could have served as minister of interior only under a strong, definite personality such as Emperor Alexander III. With respect to politics, he did what the Emperor told him to do and tried to get along with everybody. In administering his ministry he relied on his subordinates, particularly on his assistant minister, Viacheslav Konstantinovich Plehve, an intelligent and gifted man who in effect ran the ministry.

My relations with Ivan Nikolaevich Durnovo were reasonably satisfactory. To be sure, we disagreed on many subjects, such as the reorganization of the zemstvos, the role of the peasantry in the political scheme of things, and, even more so, the role of the nobility, but neither as minister of ways and communications nor as minister of finance did I have any conflicts with him.

Toward the end of the reign of Emperor Alexander III, Ivan Nikolaevich Durnovo began to feel that his position was shaky because he was in disfavor with Empress Marie Fedorovna. Of course, she had no influence on the Emperor's conduct of government, for although he dearly loved his wife, he did not permit her or anyone else to dominate him. Nonetheless it was somewhat unpleasant for Durnovo to be in disfavor with her.

I found it difficult to understand why this should be so, since early in the reign he had worked closely with her, as head of the Chancellery for Empress Marie

Fedorovna's Institutions. Once when he told me that he would like to give up his position as minister, I asked him why. He replied, ''She thinks that I perlustrate her letters and that is why she is not overfond of me.'' I thought to myself: if the Empress thinks so, she must have good reason to, for all ministers of interior love to read other people's mail, especially that of influential people.

Durnovo told me that he had already informed the Emperor of his wish to leave. When the Emperor asked him to suggest a successor, Ivan Nikolaevich replied that he had a candidate who was ready to assume the post—Plehve. The Emperor said that he would never appoint Plehve to a ministerial post. Durnovo told me that he was amazed at the Emperor's attitude toward Plehve and asked me to put in a good word for the man. Well, I happened to know that the Emperor was not overfond of Plehve, or, to put it more accurately, he looked at him with distrust because he considered him insincere.

When the post of Imperial secretary became vacant [in 1894], the Emperor immediately appointed Plehve to it and replaced Plehve as assistant minister of interior with Dmitrii Sergeevich Sipiagin, against Durnovo's wishes: it was the Emperor's intention to replace Durnovo with Sipiagin, but he did not live long enough to do so.

Vannovskii, War Minister, and Obruchev, Chief of Staff

When I was appointed minister of ways and communications General-Adjutant Vannovskii was already minister of war and was to continue to serve in that capacity throughout the reign of Emperor Alexander III. He had commanded a detachment in the war with Turkey and had been chief of staff to the Emperor when he was heir to the throne. The Emperor, who liked him very much, had selected him from among the corps commanders in Kiev. Although neither well educated nor highly cultivated, Vannovskii was a strong personality, a somewhat bilious man who liked order and was very loyal to the Emperor.

When Vannovskii became minister of war, he asked that Obruchev be appointed chief of staff.[2] It should be noted that Obruchev had been one of the closest associates of Miliutin and that while heir to the throne the Emperor had been very ill disposed toward Miliutin and his liberal subordinates. Thus, no one expected that he would appoint Obruchev chief of staff, but he did as Vannovskii asked. The Emperor did so because the war minister said that while he was thoroughly acquainted with the practical side of military affairs, he was deficient in military theory and science and that Obruchev was the only man qualified to help him make up for that deficiency. As for Obruchev's liberalism, said Vannovskii, there would be no need to fear it because he would not be influenced by it.

The combination of Vannovskii and Obruchev worked out well because they complemented each other: Obruchev supplied the mind and Vannovskii the strength of character. Between them they kept the ministry in good order all during the reign of Emperor Alexander III.

After the Emperor's death, several grand dukes began to interfere in the ministry's operations and it began to be reorganized, first in accordance with one model, then another. Then came the unfortunate Japanese war, following which Grand Duke Nicholas Nikolaevich began to exert a major influence in the ministry. For years it was in turmoil, with almost yearly reorganizations, with continual change in the upper echelons.

In recent times these childish experiments have been abandoned. Every Russian should hope that the ministry is once more on the right path, because our entire future depends on it. If, God forbid, we again have to defend the honor, dignity, and soil of Russia by force of arms, will we be equal to the task or will we cover ourselves with shame, as we did on the fields of Manchuria?

N. A. Manasein, Minister of Justice

The minister of justice when I became minister of ways and communications was Manasein, an intelligent, knowledgeable man, but of no particular distinction. He was appointed to his post because he pleased Petersburg, notably, Count Dmitrii Tolstoi and Emperor Alexander III, by investigating and reorganizing the judicial institutions of the Baltic provinces from the so-called nationalist point of view. In so doing he acted not so much to defend the dignity, interests, and ways of life of the Russians, but to prejudice the interests of the non-Russians. (It should be said that although the Emperor loved his Russian subjects more than he did his non-Russian ones, he understood that he was sovereign of all his subjects.)

Manasein was a very run-of-the-mill minister who did not distinguish himself in any way. [In 1894] he left office after developing cancer. At the time of his leaving he was not highly regarded by the Emperor, who replaced him with Nicholas Valerianovich Muravev.

N. V. Muravev, Minister of Justice

Muravev was a graduate of Moscow University.[3] After leaving the university he served as procurator of the Moscow Superior Court and lectured on criminal law at the university. He first came into prominence when he very ably prosecuted the assassins of Emperor Alexander II.

In most respects he was a highly gifted man, an excellent jurist, an outstanding orator, a man who had a very successful career. He was successful in part because of his ability, in part because of the patronage of Grand Duke Sergei Aleksandrovich, governor-general of Moscow, with whom he found great favor. It was the Grand Duke who directed the attention of Emperor Alexander III to Muravev, so that when the post of Imperial secretary became vacant the Emperor gave the appointment to Muravev. In fact it may be said that the vacancy was created—by the appointment of Polovtsov, who was not in the Emperor's favor, as member of the State Council—to make way for Muravev. He was a brilliant Imperial secretary but he did not serve long, for as soon as Manasein left, he was named minister of justice, at the early age of forty-three. (I was younger, forty-two, when I was appointed minister.)

Muravev was an outstanding minister of justice in most respects, but to a degree he compromised the principle of the independence of the judiciary by supporting that pro-noble tendency (with which the Emperor sympathized) that found expression in the institution of land captains. That was a mistake on his part. Another mistake was to snatch the administration of the prison system from the Ministry of Interior. All the same, Muravev held the banner of judicial independence high, at least in comparison with the current minister of justice, that worthless Shcheglovitov, who, I believe, had served under Muravev.

Muravev was an adroit man, with a practical mind. When the shameful war with Japan broke out, he sensed that there was trouble ahead, and he instinctively chose to separate himself from that trouble lest his career be endangered. So, with the aid of Grand Duke Sergei Aleksandrovich (just in time, for the Grand Duke was soon to be assassinated), he sought a quiet place as ambassador far from the storm that was on Russia's horizon. He would have preferred to go to Paris, but this being impossible, he accepted an appointment to Rome. (He considered his successor as minister of justice, S. S. Manukhin, a scoundrel and would not call on him or even leave his card when he visited Petersburg.)

Soon he was summoned back to Russia to serve as chief plenipotentiary in our peace negotiations with Japan. But he sensed that he would reap no benefit in that role. So, pleading ill health, he declined the appointment and returned to Rome, where he died under circumstances that I will soon relate.

As I have said, Nicholas Valerianovich Muravev was a remarkably gifted man but there was a dark side to his character that showed itself throughout his life in his relations with women.* He was married three times, the first time when he was young and married against the wishes of his mother and of most older members of his family. His first wife bore him a son, who, as a young man, shot himself, it is said, because of his father's callous attitude toward him. This marriage ended in divorce, as did the second. His second wife subsequently married Count Henckel von Donnersmarck, a Prussian, on whose estate Emperor William sometimes stayed. Although she is one of the richest and most prominent ladies in Germany, thanks to her husband, she thinks of Muravev with love, I am told.

His third marriage was to the divorced wife of Mr. Akkerman, a judicial official. This wife, who held him in great respect, finally took him in hand. It may be said that she was the only person he feared and listened to. She brought with her a daughter and a son from her previous marriage. He was affectionate toward

---

*Muravev had expected to inherit the title of count from his childless uncle Count Muravev-Amurskii, but he forfeited the right by virtually bringing suit against his mother (or was it his stepmother) following his father's death. The count was so annoyed with N. V. Muravev that he passed over him in favor of Nicholas Valerianovich's brother, a colonel of the general staff, now retired, I believe.

both. He adopted the daughter and gave her his surname. The son, who is now, I believe, in the judicial administration, retained the surname of Akkerman. Nonetheless, Muravev was very helpful toward this son, whose natural mother would not receive him. Such delicacy of feeling on the part of Muravev was very touching, considering the circumstances.

N. V. Muravev's third wife bore him two daughters and a son, toward whom he was very affectionate and loving; the same cannot be said of the wife's attitude toward her children, for she was something of a virago.

I saw Muravev a few months before his death. I had been staying with my wife near Lausanne, waiting for a surgeon, who was to operate on her, to return from vacation. October 20, the anniversary of the death of Emperor Alexander III, was approaching, and I always attended a requiem on the occasion. I decided to go to Rome this time for the services.

When Muravev learned of my presence in Rome, he immediately called on me at my hotel, and we spent most of the next few days together (his wife was away and did not return until the day before my departure) reminiscing about the past. For a number of years he had a slight grudge against me, because he mistakenly believed that I had prevented his being appointed to succeed Goremykin as minister of interior, in 1899.[4] Although our relations had continued to be friendly on the surface, his real attitude toward me had been less than kindly. And when he had backed out of the task of serving as chief plenipotentiary at Portsmouth, I had been quite annoyed with him, for as a diplomat he was duty bound to undertake this difficult task.

As we reminisced, I told him about several things, explaining my actions in those cases in which he had been under a misapprehension, attributing motives to me that had never entered my mind. Finally, Muravev admitted that some of his actions as minister of justice had not always been correct.

While in Rome I noticed that he had established himself well as ambassador. He worked hard at his task, although as we know, an ambassador is under no obligation to work hard. He gave a good deal of attention to his work and enjoyed some prestige in Rome, for, as I have already said, he was an extraordinarily gifted man. His French had always been good. Now it was excellent, and he was even beginning to speak Italian reasonably well.

At his request the Italian government provided me with a large, private compartment for my return journey and he escorted me to the station. The last words I said to him were:

What a fortunate man you are, Nicholas Valerianovich. Since the last time we parted in Petersburg I have experienced much anguish and danger, have suffered from the malice of so many, while here you are, in Rome, in an excellent climate, untouched by all that we have experienced in Russia, except to the degree that it has touched every Russian.

It is true that he seemed a bit off-color, but he told me that he felt well. A few months later came the news that he died, under circumstances consistent with his life.

I have already said that all the abnormalities of his life, all his misfortunes, were connected with women. And so it was in his way of dying. He died in the hotel room of a young French woman and was found in such an unattractive state that it is best not to speak of it.

N. K. Giers,
Minister of Foreign Affairs

During the entire time that I served under Emperor Alexander III, Giers was minister of foreign affairs. He was of Jewish origin and to a degree he looked Jewish.[5] He was a calm, peaceful man: even when we disagreed, our relations remained excellent. He was a man of good judgment, well balanced, but he was obviously not a man of great ability. He was a man of narrow outlook, perfectly suited to serve as foreign minister under a ruler such as Emperor Alexander III, who once said: "I am my own minister of foreign affairs." The Emperor, who trusted and liked Giers, thought of him as his secretary for foreign affairs. This does not mean he never listened to him, for there were times when Giers pointed out things that he had overlooked.

I found him especially appealing because of his attachment to the Emperor, about which I learned during the Emperor's final illness. Giers was ill at the time and kept to his rooms. Because I had to see the foreign minister about some business I went to his rooms and, without thinking, blurted out the news, which I had been the first to hear, that there was no hope for our Sovereign. At this the old man began to weep bitterly. I was astonished because I had not imagined that this old, dried up bureaucrat could feel attachment for anyone. Of course, everyone who had the good fortune to know him would have paid homage to this great Tsar, but I had not expected such emotion from Giers.

C. P. Pobedonostsev,
Over-Procurator of the Holy Synod

The over-procurator of the Holy Synod while I served under Emperor Alexander III was Constantine Petrovich Pobedonostsev.[6] As a human being he was not bad. Undoubtedly, he was a highly gifted and very cultivated man and truly a learned one. He had a keen, critical mind, but he was totally uncreative.

When I assumed direction of the Ministry of Finance, one of my first tasks was to deal with a bill that my predecessor had prepared concerning responsibility of factory owners for the death of workers or injuries to them. When the bill came up for consideration in the State Council, Pobedonostsev argued at length against it, declaring it to be socialist in nature, a sign of growing socialist pressure from abroad. He said Russia did not need such a bill because there already existed a patriarchal relationship between employers and workers, that, moreover, our workers were, strictly speaking, agriculturalists who had not broken their ties with the land. And, he continued, the bill was aimed at creating a proletariat in Russia, a proletariat without any fixed abode, that could move from one factory to another.

This speech impressed the State Council. Although its tenor was in keeping with Pobedonostsev's views, I believed, correctly as it turned out, that it had been inspired by Polovtsov, who had opposed the bill at preliminary discussions. Polovtsov, unlike Pobedonostsev, was motivated by self-interest: he had some money (he had not yet dissipated his fortune) invested in industry and was afraid that if the bill became law his income would be reduced.

In view of the objections raised to the bill, and in view of the fact that I had not prepared the bill and was not fully conversant with it, I stated that although I did not share C. P. Pobedonostsev's opinion, I was willing to take the bill back for reconsideration, taking into account the points that had been made. The chairman of the State Council, Grand Duke Michael Nikolaevich, was obviously pleased by my statement.

The Emperor as usual received a summary of what took place at the general assembly of the State Council. So, the next Friday, when I appeared to give him my report, he asked me why I had taken the bill back. I explained that I had done so because given the fact that I had not prepared the bill, was not thoroughly versed in the matter, that Pobedonostsev who commanded great respect was strongly opposed to it, I had not considered it possible to quarrel with him. I said that I had taken the bill back in order to study it thoroughly.

The Emperor said that he had no objection to my action, but that he did want the bill enacted, quickly. Then he advised me against submitting to Pobedonostsev's influence. To be sure, said the Emperor, the man is a very learned and fine person, but he had decided on the basis of long experience that Pobedonostsev, although an excellent critic, was not a creative person, that one cannot live by criticism alone. Pobedonostsev had been of help in the troubled times following the death of Emperor Alexander II, but now one must move forward, one must create, and in this respect Pobedonostsev and those who shared his views could be of no more use. Said the Emperor: "I have long stopped paying attention to his advice."

It is remarkable that Pobedonostsev proved unable to leave any intellectual or moral heritage. Nonetheless, I must say that during my governmental career, which, although not long, was spent in a period marked by striking events, Constantine Petrovich Pobedonostsev was easily the most distinguished of all the officials I dealt with, with respect to his talent, or rather his mind and education. I found him more agreeable to talk to than any other Russian official I had occasion to meet.[7]

T. I. Filippov, State Controller

The state controller during the years I served under Emperor Alexander III was Tertii Ivanovich Filippov, a religious type who busied himself with church and literary matters, particularly literary matters of a mystical nature. He was not stupid, but he was a second-rate official who paid little attention to his duties. He was appointed to his post because of his nationalistic tendencies, but it can be said that his vision of Russian nationalism was far broader than that of our current scoundrelly nationalists.

Unquestionably, Tertii Ivanovich was far less able and far less educated than Pobedonostsev, who was quite contemptuous of him. The two disagreed over everything, most sharply over the status of the Bulgarian Orthodox church. Filippov considered the patriarch of Constantinople to be the head of the entire Orthodox church and believed that all Orthodox churches, except the Russian, should recognize him as their head and that even the Russian church should do so, if only nominally. Pobedonostsev favored autonomy for the Bulgarian church, and, as we know, that is what it received.

The following incident, which occurred while I was minister of finance and resided on the corner of Moika and Nevskii Prospekt, is typical of Tertii Ivanovich. When he heard that Lavrovskii, superintendent of the Riga School District, might be appointed assistant procurator of the Holy Synod, he rushed to see Pobedonostsev, at his residence, on the corner of Liteiny and Nevskii Prospekt, to ask if it were true. Pobedonostsev asked, "What if it were true?" Tertii Ivanovich said that Lavrovskii was a scoundrel. Pobedonostsev replied: "Who isn't a scoundrel nowadays?"

Thereupon T. I. Filippov left and called on Delianov, the minister of education, who lived nearby, on Nevskii Prospekt. As usual there was a large crowd of favor-seekers waiting to see Delianov, who would give his card to anyone who asked for it, and even to those who didn't ask, on which he would write a few words recommending that the recipient be given a position or receive a favor. (Because this practice was well known the card did little good.)

Well, Filippov saw Delianov and somewhat agitatedly told him of the conversation with Pobedonostsev. Delianov reproved him for calling Lavrovskii a scoundrel, saying he wasn't a scoundrel but was "merely two-faced."

Dissatisfied with this response, Tertii Ivanovich left. As he was walking on Nevskii Prospekt he remembered that my residence was nearby. Still upset, he stopped off to see me, expecting reassurance. Instead of reassuring him I laughed heartily and suggested that it was none of his business.

As I have said, Tertii Ivanovich concerned himself mainly with matters that had no relation to his office. Most of the work he should have done, was done by Cherevanskii, the assistant state controller, and by Cherevanskii's successor, Anatolii Pavlovich Ivashchenkov, about whom I have already spoken.

N. M. Chikhachev,
Director of the Ministry of the Navy

In my years as minister to Emperor Alexander III, the director[8] of the Ministry of the Navy was Nicholas Matveevich Chikhachev, with whom my early career was closely tied. At that time the ministry was under the direct control of the general-admiral.

Chikhachev is a fine man, well-meaning on the whole, and far from stupid. As director he concerned himself more with the administrative side of the ministry than with the fighting capacity of the navy, a subject for which he had no bent. His ideas about [naval] warfare came from General Obruchev, who transmitted them through Obruchev's brother,* a colonel in the Admiralty, who was one of Chikhachev's closest associates.

I believe that Chikhachev's appointment was a mistake because of his lack of attention to the fighting capacity of the navy. And it seems to me that part of the blame for the inadequacy of our fleet, which came to light at the unfortunate battle of Tsushima, rests on the shoulders of this man.

Grand Duke Alexis Aleksandrovich,
General-Admiral

The general-admiral in those days was Grand Duke Alexis Aleksandrovich. Because he was the beloved brother of the Emperor, he exercised a great deal of influence.

The Grand Duke was a very fine and decent man, but he was more interested in his private pleasures than in the affairs of state and had no serious ideas of his own. His trouble was that he was a bachelor who was under the influence of the lady with whom he was having an affair at the time. Perhaps I will have occasion later to mention several episodes that occurred before the war with Japan, in which he showed extreme weakness although he was aware that war would do us more harm than good.

Count I. D. Delianov,
Minister of Education

Count Delianov, whom I have mentioned earlier, was an Armenian. He succeeded Baron Nikolai as minister of education in 1882 and served in that post for the rest of the reign of Emperor Alexander III and the first years of Emperor Nicholas II. He was a very kind, nice person who knew his work. He was a cultivated, educated man, but was in the full sense of the word an *armiashka*.[9] He was meek, ingratiating, adroit, always maneuvering, always supporting the position in favor

---

*As a youth Colonel Obruchev had been exiled to Siberia for some sort of transgression. After his return, he had been able to reestablish himself with Chikhachev's help.

at any given moment. When he was assistant minister of education under Count Tolstoi, he supported the position of his superior. After Baron Nikolai vacated the post of minister, it was Count Dmitrii Tolstoi, by then the powerful minister of interior, who arranged for Delianov to succeed the baron.

It is true that Count Delianov trimmed his sails, but I must say that he was able to maintain some semblance of order in the universities and other higher schools; in any case, he did not follow the kind of harsh and absurd policies we have seen applied to higher education in the last five years.

General O. B. Richter,
Director of the Chancellery for Petitions

The director of His Majesty's Chancellery for the Receipt of Petitions, a position equivalent in rank to that of minister, was General-Adjutant Richter, to whom I have referred earlier. He had been tutor to the Tsesarevich Nicholas Aleksandro-vich and his brother Grand Duke Alexander Aleksandrovich, the future Emperor Alexander III. After the death of the Tsesarevich, Richter stayed on for a time with his brother.

But then he fell into something like disfavor at court when he married his niece, a former lady-in-waiting at the court of Grand Duke Michael Nikolaevich. I saw her in the Caucasus during the viceroyalty of the Grand Duke.

At the time of Emperor Alexander III's accession to the throne, General Richter was corps commander in Simferopol. The new Emperor soon appointed him director of the Chancellery for Petitions, a post he was to hold until the beginning of the reign of Emperor Nicholas II, when he was forced to leave because of ill-health.

General Richter was a very fine, educated, and cultivated man, and was extremely close to Emperor Alexander III. I believe that he had some influence over the Emperor, but he behaved in such a manner that his influence was not visible, and he played no particular role in the life of the state.

Directors of His Majesty's
Personal Chancellery

Sergei Aleksandrovich Taneev, director of His Majesty's Personal Chancellery, was succeeded, [in 1889], by Rennenkampf, his assistant director. [When Ren-nenkampf died, in 1896], he was succeeded by the son of S. A. Taneev, Alexander Sergeevich, who received the post as if by right of inheritance. I did not know the father, who was said to be a very intelligent, businesslike man, something that cannot be said about the son, whose only claim to fame is that he is nothing.[10]

M. N. Ostrovskii,
Minister of State Domains

The minister of agriculture, or, as he was called in those days, the minister of state domains,[11] was Michael Nikolaevich Ostrovskii. He was an intelligent and educated man, cultivated in the Russian, but not the foreign, sense of the word. A conservative, Ostrovskii had some influence on Emperor Alexander III because of his good mind, or rather his solid common sense and his strong, definite, and consistent point of view.

Neither Ostrovskii nor his assistant minister, Veshniakov, also a fine man, had any knowledge of agriculture. This fact prompted Alexander Ageevich Abaza to say that the only fields (*polia*) the two had ever seen were the brims (*polia*) of their hats.

A. S. Ermolov,
Minister of Agriculture and State Domains

When Ostrovskii gave up his post [in 1892], I suggested Count Bobrinskii, the former minister of ways and communications, as his replacement. At the Emperor's direction Count Vorontsov-Dashkov asked Count Bobrinskii if he would accept the position. Count Bobrinskii declined, saying he had to look after his estate, but unwisely offered to advise the next minister. The Emperor told me about the reply, saying that Count Bobrinskii "wants to assume part of my obligations."

When the Emperor asked me to suggest someone else, I proposed Ermolov, my assistant minister, because before coming to the Ministry of Finance, he had spent many years in the Ministry of State Domains. The Emperor agreed and appointed him.

Alexander Sergeevich Ermolov is a fine, intelligent, well-educated man, but he has no strength of character and was consequently a weak minister of agriculture. He was constantly complaining that I, as minister of finance, would not give him enough money. I thought then and I think now that he should not have received any money, because he does not know how to manage it.

On several occasions I said [roughly] the following to him:

> I understand perfectly that a great deal of money is required to develop and administer the Ministry of Agriculture, but we have to agree from the beginning as to how you will administer the ministry. In my opinion a Russian minister of agriculture should concern himself primarily, almost exclusively, with the needs of peasant agriculture because the big landowners either have the means to look after themselves, or know how to acquire the means.

It should be noted that all of Ermolov's predecessors from the time of emancipation on had ignored the needs of the peasants and had concerned themselves exclusively with the needs of the landlords, or rather with the needs of a few hundred landlords. Alexander Sergeevich also confined himself to catering to the needs of various groups of landowners.

Nowadays, he is a prominent member of the so-called Center of the State Council. He is a gentle and, as I have said, an educated man who can do nothing creative. I call him *bozhia korovka* [ladybug], but those who are hostile to him call him *navoznyi zhuk* [dung beetle].[12]

Ministers of the Imperial Court

When Emperor Alexander III ascended the throne, Count A. V. Adlerberg, to whom I have referred earlier, was the minister of the Imperial court. Count Adlerberg was a remarkably intelligent, gifted, and cultivated man, a close friend of Emperor Alexander II, upon whom he exercised considerable influence. Because he lived beyond his means, being something of a playboy, he was always in financial trouble, and it was rumored that he was guilty of financial improprieties. But the fact that he left no estate when he died proved that these rumors were untrue.

It was believed that Adlerberg had a hand in arranging the liaison between Emperor Alexander II and Princess Dolgorukaia. If this was not the case, it was at least true that he concealed the fact of the affair and that he, together with Count Loris-Melikov, was a witness at the marriage of Emperor Alexander II and the princess [following the death of the Empress]. (The best men were Count Baranov, because he was unmarried, and someone else, whose name I can't recall.)

Of course, the heir to the throne, later Emperor Alexander III, being a man of staggeringly high morality and a very fine family man, could not help but be indignant over the marriage. Therefore, it is understandable that he did not entertain kindly feelings toward those, notably Count Adlerberg, who took such a prominent part in the affair.

For that reason, as well as because of Adlerberg's financial reputation, and also, it seems, because as Heir he had been treated with indifference by Adlerberg, he soon replaced him as minister of the Imperial court with Count Vorontsov-Dashkov, who had been serving as his chief of security. Count Vorontsov-Dashkov was not as intelligent, educated, or cultivated as his predecessor. But, as I have said, he is a typical Russian noble of the old school, a man of firm principles, an honorable and worthy official, quite unlike today's trash. He was then and still is somewhat liberal in his views and picked subordinates of the same inclination. This did not sit well with the Emperor, who, nonetheless, remained friends with Vorontsov-Dashkov as long as he lived.

I recall one episode involving Count Vorontsov-Dashkov and Emperor Alexander III which illustrated the character of the Emperor.

Until Vorontsov-Dashkov arrived on the scene, ministers sent recommendations concerning honors and decorations to be awarded their subordinates directly to the Emperor. These recommendations were based on the personal judgment of the minister and were not governed by any specific rules.

There were arguments for and against this system. On the one hand the minister was the person best able to evaluate the achievements of his subordinates and, moreover, was the person responsible for the operation of his ministry. On the other hand, the career of a subordinate could easily be affected by how the minister regarded him, as well as by how much influence the minister had with the Emperor.[13]

Count Vorontsov-Dashkov wanted to change the system. He prepared a decree for the Emperor's signature whereby a committee would be established to review recommendations concerning honors and decorations. It would be the chief of the committee, and not the ministers, who would submit recommendations in these matters to the Emperor. Apparently he wanted to strengthen his influence in personnel decisions.

I and my fellow ministers were disturbed when we heard about the proposed decree. We were disturbed first of all by its substance. We thought it wrong for the recommendations to come from the outside and not from the appropriate ministers. Also, we were disturbed by the fact that Vorontsov-Dashkov had not consulted us before submitting the decree to the Emperor. We learned what was afoot only when the decree was ready for publication.

When we heard about the decree we decided to inform the Emperor that this decree was inappropriate and inexpedient. Muravev, the minister of justice, who had just received the decree for publication, undertook to hold up publication. And since I was to make my regular report to the Emperor on the day following our decision, I was delegated to explain to him why the decree should not be published, i.e., why it should be rescinded.

So, on the following day, as I began my report, I asked the Emperor to pardon me for bringing up the matter of the decree, stating that I was speaking for the group. I explained why we thought that changes proposed by the decree would diminish the ability of ministers to get good work from their subordinates. The Emperor expressed regret that he had not heard these objections earlier, for if he had he would not have signed the decree. Unfortunately, he said, he could not withhold publication of the decree because Count Vorontsov-Dashkov had left for his estate on the strength of his assurance that the decree would be published in his absence.

This was typical of the Emperor. If he made a decision on the basis of a minister's report, he would never rescind the decision. Or, to put it another way, he never betrayed a minister on the basis of whose report he authorized some measure.

As I have noted earlier, Princess Iurevskaia,[14] née Princess Dolgorukaia, both while she was living out of wedlock with Emperor Alexander II and after her marriage, had a hand in some sordid financial dealings. What follows is an example.

During the war with Turkey, the firm of Varshavskii, Greger, Gorvitz, and Kogan was one of the major contractors that dealt with the quartermaster service.

Greger had longtime ties with General Nepokoichitskii that went back to the time the two lived in Odessa and the latter was chief of staff to Count Liders.*

During the war General Nepokoichitskii arranged matters so that Greger's firm received a large military contract. It was rumored, probably not without justification, that for his efforts Nepokoichitskii received either a large sum of money or stock in the firm, which, of course, profited handsomely from the contract.

However, after the war, after a commission had settled accounts with the firm, the firm claimed that the government had underpaid it by several million rubles and attempted to recover the money through the courts. When it became evident that the firm was not likely to win its case, it turned to a Jewish lawyer named Serebrianyi.

He was a very intelligent man and, what is more, a very witty one, who handled civil cases with great dispatch, providing it was not necessary to go to court. He did most of his work by sending letters, petitions, and such. Well, he managed to get in touch with Princess Iurevskaia, and thanks to her the firm recovered most of the money it claimed due it. Naturally, Princess Iurevskaia, or persons close to her, received suitably large sums of money for this.

I recall an amusing incident connected with the affair that occurred after the case had been settled.

It happened in Marienbad, where I, Serebrianyi, and a certain Nizguritser were staying at the same hotel. In the evenings I loved to listen to the stories told by these two old, well-educated, and very witty Jews.

Once Serebrianyi asked if I would care to eavesdrop on a conversation with Varshavskii. Hadn't they had a falling out, I asked? They had. Serebrianyi claimed that Varshavskii had failed to pay him the 500,000 rubles he had promised if he won the claim. Now Varshavskii, who resided in Karlsbad, was coming to patch things up.

The following day I eavesdropped on the conversation, from a room next to the one in which the two were talking. It turned out that Varshavskii's firm was being sued for nearly a million rubles and needed a deposition. Would Serebrianyi help him? The lawyer then offered advice on how to proceed, but Varshavskii wanted more than advice. Would Serebrianyi prepare the deposition? With pleasure, said the lawyer, and in fifteen minutes completed his work. Varshavskii was very grateful and expressed regret over their misunderstanding but insisted that he had been in the right. Serebrianyi replied that he didn't want to discuss the matter and on that note they parted.

*Count Liders had an affair with Mrs. Popudova, a beauty and a well-educated woman, the wife of an old Greek who had grown rich from military contracts he had received through the good offices of the count and Nepokoichitskii.
Rumor has it that Mrs. Popudova received more comfort from Greger, an extraordinarily handsome man of the world, than she did from the aged Count Liders.

I had been amused by Varshavskii's intonation and gestures, but otherwise I had not found the conversation interesting and told Serebrianyi so afterward. He told me that he was pleased with what had happened because if Varshavskii used the deposition he had prepared he would lose the case, and that would be Serebrianyi's revenge for not being paid the 500,000 rubles.

I am telling about this incident because it is an example of the customs that prevailed among these people.

XVII

Minister of Finance

Appointment and Personnel

Vyshnegradskii

Vyshnegradskii suffered a stroke in 1892. I was very sorry for him, for I had worked closely with him for many years. As minister of ways and communications I was on the best of terms with him although I disagreed with him, on a number of matters. One was the Siberian Railroad. In accordance with my instructions from the Emperor, I was trying to complete it as quickly as possible, while he, although unable to oppose me openly, hampered my efforts by not providing me with the necessary funds.

We were different personalities. I tend to be bold and to see things broadly, while he was narrow and cautious, a man who concerned himself with detail, more so, I must admit, than do I, but he was unable to think and visualize at a high level, and one who is unable to do so cannot be creative in dealing with major questions that are important for the life of the state.

Take our views on mathematics. I recall a conversation I had with him while we both served on the Southwestern Railroad. Both of us could consider ourselves mathematicians, but everything that I considered significant in mathematics—its philosophy, its abstract side—he considered insignificant. He attached importance only to the practical application of mathematics. One can put it this way: he was more of an arithmetician than a mathematician and I more a mathematician than an arithmetician. Once, while we were speaking of mathematics, I happened to express admiration for several of the ideas of Auguste Comte. He thereupon informed me that Comte was nothing but an ass, with no understanding of mathematics. No one, he said, who did not understand mathematics could be a good philosopher. Nor did he believe that philosophy, which he considered to be

160

nothing but nattering, had a place in mathematics. I, of course, take a different view.

For Vyshnegradskii the greatest joy was to do mathematical equations. His colleagues in the ministry amused themselves by asking him to do all the calculations related to loans, and he would do them with the greatest pleasure, even though this was not proper even for a chief clerk, let alone a minister. I must admit that he did have a good head for figures. Once he made and won a wager that he could memorize an entire page of logarithms in an hour.*

Unlike Vyshnegradskii I never once, while minister of finance, took pencil in hand to make calculations or to check figures in my dealings with bankers and in the negotiation of loans and contracts, even though I had to engage in financial operations on a larger scale then he ever did because I served longer than he did.

Vyshnegradskii experienced the stroke I have mentioned on a Thursday, while attending a meeting of the Department [of State Economy] of the State Council. As he was speaking there he felt a pain in the head, then stood up unsteadily and was helped to his carriage. When I went to call on him, his doctors told me that he had suffered a comparatively mild stroke, but said that I couldn't see him.

We were both scheduled to give our weekly reports to the Emperor on the following day, at Gatchina. I assumed that he would be unable to give his, so I was astonished to find him the next day traveling on the train to Gatchina with me. When I asked him if his business was so urgent that he had to give his report, he replied that a minister could no more refuse to deliver his report to the Emperor than a soldier could refuse to go to war. Accompanying him was Dr. Loboiko (the nephew of Mrs. Vyshnegradskii), who cautioned me to leave Vyshnegradskii in peace. During the entire trip Vyshnegradskii remained in his compartment, carefully going over his report.

Vyshnegradskii was scheduled to report before me. I was afraid that the Emperor might not know of the stroke and might inadvertently precipitate a second one by making an upsetting remark if Vyshnegradskii should happen to become confused. Accordingly, when the train reached Gatchina, I rushed ahead of him to the palace and told the Emperor's valet that I would like to see his master for a moment before he received the minister of finance.[1] The Emperor seemed anxious when I entered his study and asked what had happened. I told him about the stroke, how Vyshnegradskii insisted that it was his duty, like that of a soldier going into battle, to do his duty and give his report. Also I expressed my fear of a second stroke. The Emperor thanked me for my warning. I then left by a door other than the one through which I had entered, lest Vyshnegradskii see me and become upset.

Later, when I gave my report, the Emperor told me that Vyshnegradskii had

*I recall an incident that Rothstein, of the International Bank, told me about. Once, in connection with a loan, he and Vyshnegradskii independently made calculations about one aspect of the loan. Rothstein arrived at a figure that differed by 300,000 francs from the one Vyshnegradskii had arrived at, using logarithms. Vyshnegradskii was very angry and told Rothstein that he had been doing calculations before Rothstein was born.

experienced no difficulty in giving his long report, although he noted that the minister was nervous and walked a bit unsteadily as he left. The Emperor assured me that he had said nothing that would discomfit the minister. Subsequently, when I was ready to return to Petersburg, I found that Vyshnegradskii had left before me. Usually, we returned together.

Some time later Vyshnegradskii was given a few months' leave, in the expectation that a rest would permit him to regain his health. While he was on leave, the administration of the ministry was of course entrusted to his assistant minister, Fedor Gustavovich Thörner.

Even before coming to Petersburg I knew of Thörner because of a widely disseminated verse dealing with his odd belief that coffee was the chief, possibly the only, nourishment required for the development and proper functioning of the brain and that the backward Russian mind was in particular need of such nourishment. The verse had been inspired by a long speech he had made before a commission that was considering the tariff on coffee: it had been his contention that not only should the tariff on coffee not be raised, as some wished, but also that it should be eliminated altogether, to encourage the consumption of coffee.

His surname would not lead one to expect him to be of the Orthodox faith; in fact, he was fervently Orthodox. (He came from a Lutheran family, but I do not know whether it was he or his father who had been converted.) Like Filippov, he wrote theological treatises, of which both Filippov and Pobedonostsev were critical. Thörner liked to write, but everything he wrote was vapid.

Nonetheless, he was an admirable man, an educated man of the highest principles. But he had a limited mind and would adapt his convictions to match those of his superior, not because of a lack of principle, but precisely because he was limited: his was a dull, German mind, the kind that prevents one from seeing the forest for the trees.

My Appointment as Minister of Finance

During the summer [of 1892] Vyshnegradskii returned to Petersburg feeling better, but far from well. He realized that he was quite ill and wanted to leave his post for a less demanding one. He had the idea of transferring everything related to commerce and industry and the customs administration to the Ministry of Ways and Communications (i.e., under my jurisdiction), thus transforming it into a Ministry of Commerce. The Ministry of Finance would consequently have a more limited scope. Further, Thörner would be the minister of finance, working under the general direction of Vyshnegradskii.[2]

I heard of this proposal from Vyshnegradskii himself. Whether or not he presented it to the Emperor I do not know for certain. But I recently learned from excerpts from Thörner's memoirs (he is now dead) that Vyshnegradskii presented a memorandum on the subject to the Emperor, who did not take to the idea. Naturally, the Emperor, as a monarch with unlimited power, could not agree to an intermediary between himself and a minister, as would have been the case had he accepted Vyshnegradskii's proposal.

Be that as it may be, during one of my reports the Emperor asked me if I were willing to accept the post of minister of finance. I replied that this was not a case of being willing or unwilling; I would do whatever he ordered me to do. He thanked me.

For several weeks, while the Emperor was away, there was no word of my appointment. I had to wait until August 30, 1892, for my appointment as [acting] minister of finance. [I was appointed minister of finance on January 1, 1893.]* My family and I had to wait some time for Vyshnegradskii to clear his things out before we could take occupancy of the residence provided for the minister of finance. Our former residence had been palatial, but the new one resembled the officers' quarters in a barracks: my wife was not very happy over the change, but I did not mind for I have never paid attention to where I live.

Now I would like to say a few words about my associates in the Ministry of Finance.

Assistant Ministers

To my regret Thörner did not wish to stay on as assistant minister,[4] for two reasons. First, as I learned later, he had been put forward as a candidate for minister by Vyshnegradskii. Second, he was my senior in all respects. He left shortly after my appointment and was appointed to the Senate. At my suggestion, Alexander Sergeevich Ermolov, the director of the Department of Indirect Taxation, was appointed to succeed Thörner.[5] Anatolii Pavlovich Ivashchenkov, my assistant minister in the Ministry of Ways and Communications, was appointed as the other assistant minister of finance.

As I have noted earlier, Ermolov left the Ministry of Finance after six months, to become minister of state domains. There was a candidate ready to replace him in the person of my old Kievan associate Professor Antonovich. When I became minister of finance he entreated me to make him assistant minister, so when Ermolov left I was able to have him appointed. I was glad to do so because during

---

*When the Emperor asked me whom I would suggest to replace me as minister of ways and communications, I replied that I could think of no one at the moment. When he then asked what I thought of A. K. Krivoshein, I said that I did not know him well, but that as far as I could judge he was an intelligent man. (Krivoshein was the director of one of the departments of the Ministry of Interior and represented it on the Council on Railroad Affairs and on the Tariff Committee of the Ministry of Finance.) Krivoshein received the appointment, helped, as I discovered, by the support of Prince Meshcherskii and of Durnovo, the minister of interior.[3]

I decided that Prince Meshcherskii had a hand in the Krivoshein appointment because Kolyshko played a more important role under Krivoshein than he had under me or Hübbenet. As for Durnovo, he and Krivoshein had been on close terms for many years, dating to the time when Durnovo had been governor of the province of Ekaterinoslav and Krivoshein the head of the Rostov municipal government. Krivoshein was married to a prominent member of the Strukov family, which owned a great deal of land in the province of Ekaterinoslav. It has been said by nasty gossips that Durnovo had ardently courted Krivoshein's wife before her marriage.

our earlier association he had made a favorable impression on me by his simplicity and by his *khokhol*[6] cleverness. Also, I had been influenced by several of his books, particularly the one on monetary standards. In it he spoke out for a solid currency based on a metallic standard, and no knowledgeable expert could think otherwise. Unfortunately, he was to prove a disappointment, a matter about which I will write later.[7]

The Chancellery of the Ministry of Finance

The director of the [ministry's chancellery][8] at the time of my appointment was Dmitrii Formich Kobeko, now director of the Petersburg Public Library. He is an able man, with something of a reputation in literature and scholarship: for example, he wrote a rather interesting book about Emperor Paul.

A graduate of the [Imperial Alexander] Lycée, he had become director of the chancellery while quite young, in the days when Reutern was minister. He might have gone on to a successful career if not for a scandal. Being married to a very unattractive woman, he became entangled with some Frenchwoman, the owner of a fashionable store, who became involved in a nasty financial venture. Kobeko was innocent of any wrongdoing, but because she had traded on his name he had had to leave the post of director, a position of some importance in those days, and was relegated to an inferior position in the ministry. When Vyshnegradskii became minister he appointed Kobeko director of the administration of the Russian Steamship and Commercial Company, on whose board he had been representing the ministry.

After the death of Emperor Alexander III, I recommended Kobeko's appointment to the State Council. Emperor Nicholas II expressed reservations about Kobeko because he had heard about the scandal with the Frenchwoman. After I explained that Kobeko had been guilty of no more than a youthful lack of caution and was seconded in this by the minister of interior, the Emperor agreed to appoint him.

Kobeko was succeeded as director of the chancellery by Peter Mikhailovich Romanov, who had served as vice-director of the Department of Railroad Affairs under me. After a few years, he was appointed assistant minister of finance and stayed on in that post after I left the ministry. He might ultimately have become minister if not for the fact that Count Solskii disliked him and supported the candidacy of Kokovtsev.

State Bank

When I became minister, the manager of the State Bank was Shukovskii, who did a mediocre job. He had something of the reputation of being a leftist because he had written for *Sovremennik* in the 1860s. As far as I could see, he posed no threat to the state: had this been the case, Vyshnegradskii would not have kept him. When he left his post, [in 1894], because of poor health, he was appointed to the Senate, at my recommendation. As his successor I suggested Pleske, director of the Credit Chancellery—an honorable, decent, very self-possessed man, but saddled with a typically narrow German mind, but who was to replace Maleshevskii, one of the most interesting of my associates.

Credit Chancellery

I knew Maleshevskii from my Odessa days, when he was chief of control of the Kiev–Brest Railroad. Although he is only a few years older than I, he is now almost senile, but in those days he had an exceptionally fine mind, which, like those of geniuses such as Dostoevsky and Tolstoy, was on the borderline between normalcy and madness. For that reason I used to refer to him as Umalishevskii (madman).

Maleshevskii, a Pole, lost his parents when he was young and was under the guardianship of Mr. Zatler,* or, properly speaking, his fine wife. He attended a cadet corps (military school), then the University of Warsaw. After his graduation from the university he went to work for Ivan Bloch.

While working for the railroad, Maleshevskii, who has an excellent mathematical education, helped establish an old-age insurance fund for employees of the railroad. When the Ministry of Ways and Communications, under Poset, decided to establish an old-age insurance company for all railroad employees, Maleshevskii was asked to prepare the plans for such a company.

As we know, every properly established old-age insurance fund is based on the theory of probability. To establish such a fund calls for considerable mathematical knowledge, although such knowledge alone is inadequate in the absence of sufficient statistical data. For example, although the old-age insurance fund of the War Ministry was established with the aid of so eminent a mathematician as the late Academician Buniakovskii, the estimates used were not confirmed by experience.

Well, Maleshevskii started with the theoretical work and wrote a book on the subject, for which he received a prize from the Academy of Sciences. Then he prepared estimates for an old-age insurance fund for the entire railroad system; for this work he was given the civil service rank of state councillor and the "Vladimir" [Order of St. Vladimir]. (In those days such an honor was rarely given, in contrast to present practice.)

Maleshevskii was obviously able, reliable, honest, and politically trustworthy. Also, he knew something about finance, as a result of having served in the administration of the Southwestern Railroad. But I feared that the fact that he was a Pole might be a hindrance to his appointment. But when I told the Emperor of his qualifications and then raised the question of his being a Pole, an ardent Pole yet a loyal subject, he replied that there would be no difficulty in making such an

*This is the Zatler who, while intendant in the Sebastopol war, was tried for misconduct in office. However, according to the evidence of many who knew him, he was a thoroughly honorable man who left no estate.

appointment: that he did not conceal the fact that he was a Pole and yet was a thoroughly loyal subject showed that he was a fine and decent man.*

Maleshevskii served as director of the Credit Chancellery throughout the rest of my tenure as minister of finance and continued to serve my successors until two years ago, when he left the post and was appointed to the Senate. As I have said, his mental faculties are rather weak now, and he looks older than his years.

When Pleske became manager of the State Bank, he asked for Timashev (then vice-director of the Credit Chancellery) to be his assistant manager. His wish was granted. Then Bunge, chairman of the Committee of Ministers, and Anatol Nikolaevich Kulomzin, the chief administrative assistant of the committee, both recommended Ivan Shipov, chief of the division of the chancellery of the committee, to replace Timashev. I had dealt with Shipov and had found him to be a competent young man who was close to Bunge because he was able to please him. Also, I knew that at Bunge's suggestions he had written, or rather translated, a little book on John Law† from French into Russian and had written a foreword to it. Shipov wrote, or rather translated, this little book rather well and thus attracted attention to himself.

Shipov succeeded Romanov as director of the chancellery [in 1897]. When the post of director of the treasury became vacant [in 1902], I transferred him to that post, which he held until I became premier and, on my recommendation, was named minister of finance. After I left office, Shipov had to give up his position but was subsequently named minister of commerce and industry under Stolypin.

As we know, Stolypin, especially at the beginning, advanced those who had served with me in the expectation that he would profit from the knowledge they had gained under me. But Shipov did not turn out to be a satisfactory minister of commerce and industry and is now a member of the State Council.

What kind of a civil servant is Shipov? He is a very able, even gifted man who works hard, keeps abreast of his field, has a quick mind, and does not make mistakes in his work. But he does not have strong political views; in fact, one can say that he has no political views at all. Although he is an honorable man, he likes, as the French say, *manger à deux rateliers*. He is always subservient to his superiors, praises them to the skies, but when they lose power, he gradually dissociates himself from them.

---

*When Emperor Alexander III visited the Kingdom of Poland, he was very kind toward the Poles. This did not mean that he did not hold completely to the historical Russian policy toward the Kingdom of Poland or that he would be indulgent toward the Poles. But it did mean that he believed that its residents were entitled to be treated like all other subjects and to be permitted to live in peace, in consonance with the interests of the entire empire.

†Every financial expert associates the name of John Law with paper money and with the harm its introduction brought to France. In suggesting that Shipov translate this little book Bunge had an ulterior motive: he was afraid that his successor, Vyshnegradskii, would be won over to the idea of paper money and thus bring harm to Russia. When I became minister of finance Bunge had the same fear about me.[9]

The following incident is illustrative. After I had signed the Portsmouth Peace Treaty, Shipov, who had accompanied me to Portsmouth, came to see me and, without saying a word, kissed my hand and left. I was dumbfounded by this action. Later, when I asked him what had possessed him to do this, he replied that he had been so overjoyed that he could not restrain himself. But I do not know whether or not he continued to feel joy after we returned to Petersburg and found that some newspapers were demanding that I be hanged for signing the treaty.

By the way, Emperor Nicholas II, who does not, as a rule, like people who are unable to look him in the eye, did not care for Shipov for that reason. It is true that Shipov can't look people in the eye and looks a bit shifty, but that is because he has an eye defect.

Treasury Department

The director of the Department of the Treasury at the time of my appointment was Golindo, an honorable old civil servant with the brain of a chicken. He died soon after I assumed office.

To replace him I selected Dmitriev, vice-director of the department. I had appointed him vice-director because he had served under me as assistant director of the Chancellery of the Ministry of Ways and Communications. Prior to that he had served in the State Controller's office and, consequently, had a good knowledge of the technical side of finance.

Department of Indirect Taxation

Markov, a fine man with a military background, was chosen to replace Ermolov as director of the Department of Indirect Taxation. Markov was a stronger, more decisive man than Ermolov, but he had a narrow education and suffered from a limited imagination. Working with Markov, I introduced the liquor monopoly, a major and unparalleled reform.

Department of Customs

The director of the Department of Customs when I became minister was a certain Tukholka, a Bunge appointee. He had achieved some prominence during the war with Turkey, when he had served as director of the Chancellery of Prince Dondukov-Korsakov. As director he was an utter cipher. After his death I appointed Beliustin as his replacement. He held the post during the remainder of my tenure as minister of finance. He died the year before last.

Department of Commerce and Industry

The director of the Department of Commerce and Industry when I became minister was a certain Bähr, a decent old man and a fairly experienced civil servant, but on the whole a man of no distinction. The Emperor knew Bähr well because he was very interested in the home for poor children of which Bähr was chairman and he the [honorary] head.

Soon after I became minister, Bähr died and was replaced by Vladimir Ivanovich Kovalevskii, about whom I have already spoken.

Board of Weights and Measures

When I became minister, the Board of Weights and Measures was directed by the eminent chemist Mendeleev. He had served as professor at the University of St. Petersburg, but because of his exceedingly quarrelsome nature he had left the university as soon as he had become eligible for a pension. It is to the discredit of the Academy of Sciences that when it came to choose a chemist to fill a vacancy in its ranks it would not elect him because of his contentious personality and the fact he had been critical of its work; instead it chose a chemist of little reputation.

Mendeleev was a man of both theory and practice. He contributed greatly to the development of our oil and other industries. But, as often happens with outstanding men, he was the subject of wide and bitter criticism, partly because of his personality, partly because he was more intelligent, more talented, more learned than those around him. His writings on economic development, which favored protectionism, were the object of derisive criticism, of [unfounded] charges that he was in the pay of industrialists.

It was only after his death that we began to proclaim that we had lost a great scientist in him. That is to the good, but it would have been better if his achievements had been honored in his lifetime.

Vyshnegradskii, a friend of his, had made him head of the board, which was in a poor state, and Mendeleev himself was in disfavor when I became minister. Naturally, I could not fail to appreciate the fact that a man as distinguished as Mendeleev was head of the board, and I gave him all the assistance I could without meddling in the scientific aspect of his work. (I could not have meddled had I wanted to, for I lacked the necessary knowledge.) With my support, he put the board back on its feet.

Department of Railroad Affairs

I forgot to mention that when I became minister of ways and communications I had wanted Romanov, my vice-director, to succeed me as director of the Department of Railroad Affairs. For some reason Vyshnegradskii had not wanted Romanov and had chosen Maksimov instead.[10]

Maksimov is an able and knowledgeable man and is much more energetic than Romanov, but he has an inclination for questionable business dealings, as was shown by his involvement in the Mamontov affair, to which I have already referred. Whether he became entangled in it because of stupidity or because of poor judgment I do not know, but he did compromise himself and I had to part with him. He was succeeded by my old associate Ziegler, about whom I have already spoken. As for Maksimov, he is now engaged in a number of business operations: I believe that, among other things, he is chairman of a spur line company.

XVIII

Emperor Alexander III

General Observations

I have already spoken of Emperor Alexander III's great and noble personality. It is a great pity that his reign was so short, only thirteen years. Yet, although he came to the throne unprepared for his task, he matured fully as a sovereign during those brief years. All Russia and the rest of the world recognized this fact on the day of his death. Unfortunately, he was not fully appreciated either by his contemporaries or by the succeeding generation.

This is unfair, for he was a great emperor. To assess his reign fairly, one must keep in mind the fact that his education was neglected because he was a younger son and therefore not expected to rule. Also, one must note the circumstances that prevailed in the years following his older brother's death, in 1865, when he became heir to the throne.

First of all, during the sixteen years that he served as Heir-Tsesarevich, the future Emperor could not help but notice, as he began to take an interest in political matters, the vacillating and occasionally reactionary policies pursued by his father, the Great Liberator, and the growing revolutionary movement that they provoked. Influenced by his former teacher Pobedonostsev and by certain Petersburg circles led by Stroganov,[1] he could not help but believe that the revolutionary movement must be dealt with harshly.

Moreover, given his probity, Tsesarevich Alexander Aleksandrovich could not help but be shocked by the improprieties of various officials. Equally shocking for him was the behavior of his father's morganatic wife, Princess Iurevskaia, who, as I have said earlier, helped some shady operators win favors from the government. Even more disturbing to this pure, even saintly man, was the fact that his father, a man in his sixties, with grown children, and even grandchildren, should even marry the princess.[2]

It should be noted, too, that the future Emperor was deeply affected by our war with Turkey and its consequences, a war in which he himself commanded a detachment. Although this war was not as disgraceful militarily as our war with Japan, it was disappointing both in its conduct and in its results.

We won the war not because of superior military ability but because of our superior numbers. And to achieve numerical superiority we had to deplete our forces at home. To be sure, we were able to gain a fairly advantageous and honorable peace, at San Stefano, but when we were threatened by a new war as a result of the refusal of the European powers, notably Austria, to recognize the treaty, we were not prepared to fight. As a result, the Congress of Berlin annulled much of what we had gained at San Stefano. All these unfortunate developments were dispiriting for all Russia and could not but tell on the future Emperor.

Also, one should not forget that the war undid the work of minister of finance Reutern, who had been trying to establish the gold standard in Russia, by attempting to raise the exchange rate of our paper money to par, after its fall as a result of the Sebastopol [Crimean] War. The [1877–78] war completely disrupted our finances, which could not be put in order for another twenty years. It was only I, as minister of finance, who was finally able to establish a sound monetary system and put our finances on a sound basis.

And then, following the war, came a series of anarchist, terrorist acts that culminated in the assassination, on March 1, 1881, of the Tsesarevich's father. Thus, it can be said that Emperor Alexander III ascended a throne stained by his father's blood. There can be no question but that this circumstance left a strong mark on him.

Therefore, in order impartially to judge Emperor Alexander III and his actions during the first five or six years of his reign, when he pursued a reactionary policy under the influence of such prominent men as C. P. Pobedonostsev, one must keep in mind the psychological and historical circumstances under which he came to the throne.

Those who did not know the Emperor unjustly picture him as limited, slow of mind. It is true that he was below average in intelligence and education. As we know, he had not been trained to be emperor. His older brother, Tsesarevich Nicholas Aleksandrovich, his superior in appearance, ability, and brilliance, had received all the attention of their parents, while he, Alexander, had, so to speak, been given a back seat, with little attention paid to his education and upbringing. But the Tsesarevich truly appreciated his worth. It is known from reliable sources that when Tsesarevich Nicholas was on his death bed (in Nice, where he died of consumption), and knew that he was dying, someone asked him: "Who will govern Russia if something happens to you? Your brother Alexander is completely unprepared for the task." Nicholas replied: "You do not understand my brother Alexander: his heart and character are more than enough to make up for all other qualities with which a man may be endowed.''

It is not enough to say that Emperor Alexander III had a noble heart! He had a tsar's heart! Such nobility can exist only when it is innate, when one's life is innocent. Such unmarred purity of heart can blossom only in the environment in which Russia's tsesareviches and tsars find themselves, in which an individual is not compelled to act against his own conscience or to close his eyes to what he does not want to see, either because of self-interest or the interests of those close to him. They do not have the same interests as ordinary mortals, those egotistical material interests that often corrupt the human heart.

For the Emperor there was no difference between word and deed. If he were not certain of what he thought or would do, he would hold his tongue, but if he said something, one could have absolute confidence in his word. For that reason he enjoyed the confidence and respect not only of those close to him, but, more important, of the entire world.

I will not dispute the assertion that the Emperor was not well educated, but I do deny what is often said, that he did not have a good mind. Of course, one has to define what is meant by mind. Perhaps he did not have a good mind if the word is taken to mean mind-intellect (*um-rassudka*). But he had an outstanding mind in the sense of mind-heart (*um-serdtsa*), the kind of mind that enables one to look ahead, to sense what is coming. Such a mind is more important than mind-intellect.

Emperor Alexander was a model in many ways, among them in the economical care of his government's money, as well as his family's money, not because of greed, but because of his sense of duty. Never have I encountered such respect for the government's money, either among the members of the Imperial family, or among bigwigs, as that shown by the Emperor. He respected every ruble, every kopek that came from the Russian people. He was an ideal husbander of the government's money. It was he who resisted all the efforts to squander the government's money, money produced by the sweat and tears of the Russian people. It was thanks to his strength that first Vyshnegradskii and then I were able to put our country's finances in order.

The Emperor had the same respect for his own money that he had for that of the government. I recall that when I accompanied him on railroad trips, I would notice after the others had gone to bed (naturally I did not go to bed when I was on such trips), his valet Kotov (now Emperor Nicholas II's valet) would be repairing tears in his master's trousers. When I asked Kotov why he did not take along spare trousers to replace the torn ones, he replied that the Emperor did not like to throw anything away, that ''once he has begun to wear a pair of trousers or a frock coat, he will wear it till it bursts at the seams.'' He would not tolerate excessive luxury or waste in his household and, in fact, as I have noted, he lived very modestly.

To be sure, given the circumstances under which the Emperor lived, some of his economies seemed a bit naive. For example, while I served as minister, the food at his court was terrible. Although I had no occasion to eat at the Emperor's table and cannot speak from personal experience about the food served there, I can speak about the food served at the so-called court marshal's table; to eat it was to endanger one's stomach. But I have heard that the food served at the Emperor's table was even worse. In fact, he preferred the plainest of food, and when his regular fare palled on him, as it did during the last year or so of his reign when he was ill, he would ask for an ordinary soldier's dinner brought from a nearby barracks.

When he became Emperor, Alexander III ordered changes in military uniforms that made them simpler and, therefore, cheaper. He liked the Russian style of uniforms—blouse, roomy trousers, and high boots.

This change in uniforms endured until the end of the war with Japan. Since then, apparently as a reward for the shame we endured on the fields of Manchuria, our army has been issued handsome uniforms, like those seen on the backs of playing cards. What this change is supposed to signify is beyond me.

Emperor Alexander III's greatest achievement was that, except for the negligible expedition to Akhaltek, he gave Russia thirteen years of peace, not by being weak, but by being fair and unswervingly firm. He had no dreams of conquest or of military laurels. Other nations knew this, but they knew too that under no circumstances would he besmirch the honor and dignity of the Russia entrusted to him by God.

He hated war and said to me during one of my reports:

> I am glad that I took part in war and saw all the horrors inescapably connected with it. I believe that no human being who has a heart can desire war. I believe that one who has been entrusted by God with the government of a people must do all he can to avoid the horrors of war, but that if he is forced into war by his opponents, then the guilt and the consequences of war should fall on the heads of those who brought it on.

Emperor Alexander III was not a phrasemonger like some rulers who utter beautiful phrases which they quickly forget. He said little, but what he said he meant, and he never retreated from his word. This man, with his gigantic awkward figure, his kindly face, and his utterly friendly eyes filled Europe with awe and bewilderment. Would this giant suddenly begin to growl? And when he died, all Europe realized that with him there had disappeared a man who, by his moral strength, had kept Europe calm and peaceful, a man who had contributed much to international peace. Having assumed the reins of power at a time that seemed unpropitious for Russia, he raised his country's prestige without having shed a drop of Russian blood.

Emperor Alexander III did much to undo the harm done by the war with Turkey. It was he who, to a considerable extent, helped restore the army after the disorganization in it that resulted from the war.

And it was because of his strength of character that his finance ministers were able to shore up the finances of Russia. It fell to me to complete that work under Emperor Nicholas II, who supported my program not so much because he believed in me as because he knew that his father had approved it and had had complete confidence in me. It was only for this reason that I was able to stay on as minister of finance for more than eight years after his father's death, despite the dirty tricks that were played on me.

Under Emperor Alexander III, particularly after I became director of the Department of Railroad Affairs, railroad construction, which had come to a halt during the last years of his father's reign, began once more.[3]

Under Emperor Alexander III, our system of tariffs changed from one based on free trade to one based on protectionism. This shift, carried out by Vyshnegradskii with my help, took place only because the Emperor understood that Russia could not be great without a developed industrial system.

Was this the work of a man lacking in intelligence? With his tsar's heart, the Emperor understood what the country entrusted to him by God required. And once he did, he firmly supported a protectionist policy, thanks to which Russia possesses a well-developed industry that will enable her, in the not too distant future, to become one of the greatest of industrial nations.

To appreciate what an achievement the shift to protectionism was, one must recall that it was met by opposition from the public at large as well as from the ruling circles. What that shift required was a man of stature who could go against prevailing attitudes and opinions, and that man was our wise and firm Emperor.

Debits

Emperor Alexander III has been reproached for his approval of the university statute of 1884. I admit that it was a mistake, but I must note that he acted under the influence of Count Dmitrii Tolstoi and a small group of conservatives.

Mistaken though the statute was, its application was not accompanied by the excesses we see in university life nowadays. True, in the first years of the reign several well-known professors, among them Mechnikov, lost their chairs because Count Delianov, the minister of education, considered them too liberal. But, on the whole, university life proceeded quietly under the Emperor, because he was neither a liberal nor a reactionary, but an honorable, noble, straightforward man.

The Emperor has also been criticized for agreeing to the zemstvo statute of 1890, with its patriarchal view of the peasantry, about which I have already spoken. I cannot deny that this was a mistake on his part, but it was a mistake made in good conscience, for he was a truly autocratic Russian tsar who understood that he must be the sympathetic guardian of the Russian people, the defender of the weak, including the peasantry. The prestige of the Russian tsar is based on Christian principles, on the ideals of Orthodoxy, which call for defense of the weak, of those who are in need, not for the protection of the Russian bourgeoisie or of us, the Russian nobility. (As a whole the Russian bourgeoisie does not live up to the ideals of Orthodoxy. Many of our nobles do, but some are inclined to seek a life of luxury for themselves while denigrating the labor and the hearts of others.)

Changing Views

I am convinced that if Emperor Alexander had had a reign of twenty-six rather than thirteen years, his would have been one of the greatest reigns in the history of the Russian Empire.

During the last years of his reign, after he had acquired experience, he realized that the unrest that had existed at the end of his father's reign had resulted from his father's wavering and not from Russia's desire for revolution. He realized that Russia wanted a quiet existence. As a result, his attitudes toward many questions were quite different at the end of his reign from those he had held at the beginning. One can put it in popular terms: he had become distinctly liberal.

Had Emperor Alexander III lived on there would have been no war with Japan. We would have enjoyed peace, peace that would have permitted us to move along the road of gradual liberalization, toward a life in which the state exists for the good of the people. But it was not given to Emperor Alexander III to achieve this, for God summoned him to Himself.

The Emperor as Head of
the Imperial Family

Emperor Alexander III was truly the head of the Imperial family and kept the grand dukes and grand duchesses in their places.[4] They not only respected and admired him, but also feared him. It would have been unthinkable for any of them to act then as some do now.

Wisely, the Emperor understood that one cannot expect ordinary mortals to behave better than do members of the Imperial family. He understood that members of the family must be models of proper behavior in their private as well as public lives. It was unacceptable to him that anything in their lives should serve as the subject of unfavorable gossip.

For example, members of the family, and other high personages for that matter, were not permitted to divorce their spouses or marry persons who were divorced. That is why, as I have said, I asked the Emperor for permission to leave the service when I planned to marry a divorcée. And during the period that my wife was not received at court, I considered it right that it should be so, for in those days divorced women were not received at court.

Unfortunately a striking change has occurred since the death of Emperor Alexander III. Many grand dukes and grand duchesses, and other high personages, receive divorces, marry divorced persons, even arrange divorces so as to be free to marry. What is remarkable is that what once was considered unthinkable is now permitted under an Emperor who is himself a model family man.

Also, it would have been unthinkable under Emperor Alexander III for grand dukes to make spectacles of themselves while abroad. A grand duke who had done so would have received a talking to that he would never have forgotten.

One reason that the Emperor was ill disposed toward Grand Dukes Constantine Nikolaevich and Nicholas Nikolaevich [the elder] was that they lived *maritalement* with ballerinas and had illegitimate children. Even worse, Grand Duke Constantine Nikolaevich and his mistress Kuznetsova traveled abroad as if they were husband and wife.* The Emperor could not endure such behavior, and even though the Grand Duke was his uncle, and older than he, he would not permit him to live in Petersburg. It was only when Grand Duke Constantine Nikolaevich was close to death that he was permitted to return to the capital and take up residence with his legitimate family, in Pavlovsk. The Emperor then visited the dying man and behaved very kindly and respectfully toward him, as nephew to uncle. It was only then, close to death, that the Grand Duke realized how kind and honorable the Emperor was. I have been told that, unable to speak, the Grand Duke kissed the Emperor's hand as a sign of homage to the head of the Imperial family.

As for Grand Duke Nicholas Nikolaevich, even had his private life been exemplary, he would not have been in the Emperor's good graces because of his conduct during the war with Turkey. The Emperor, having served under him in the war, was critical not only of the orders issued by his uncle and his uncle's suite but also over the various financial improprieties that occurred, a matter about which I have already spoken. But he was far more upset by the fact that the Grand Duke lived with the ballerina Chislova, who bore him several children. (Only one of these children was beautiful, with features that reminded one of Emperor Nicholas I; she married Prince Cantacuzene.) The Grand Duke, who stood in fear of the Emperor, was given little to do during the last years of his life. As for the Grand Duke's wife, Grand Duchess Alexandra Petrovna, I have already mentioned the Emperor's attitude toward her.

À propos of the Emperor's attitude toward improper behavior by members of the Imperial family, I recall the following.

I had gone to give my regular Friday report to the Emperor and found that he was still receiving. I overheard him ask of one man who had recently returned from Biarritz if there were many Russians there. The man replied that there were many, among them Prince George Leuchtenberg.[5] The Emperor, who sometimes did not exercise restraint in expressing himself, said: "Do you mean to say that the prince washes his dirty hide in the ocean?"

I was very astonished by the crudity of the remark and later asked General

---

*Another reason for the Emperor's displeasure with him was over the fact that Grand Duke Constantine Nikolaevich was a bit of a liberal. I think that his liberalism was beneficial for Russia with respect to the reforms that he supported. However, as viceroy of Poland, the Grand Duke's liberalism prompted him to follow policies that were not in the interests of the Russian empire.

Cherevin, chief of security, what the point of it was. He told me that the Emperor had expressed himself as he did because the prince continued to live with his French mistress after he had married Princess Anastasia Nikolaevna of Montenegro. (By the way, the prince still lives with his mistress.)

The Emperor also looked unkindly at Prince George's brother Eugene, first because he was frivolous, second because his morganatic wife [Countess Zinaida Beauharnais], a sister of the famous General Skobelev, would be seen in public with Grand Duke Alexis Aleksandrovich[6] and not with her husband.

The Emperor took a more favorable view of the older brother, Prince Nicholas, because, although he too had married morganatically, his family life was above reproach. Another reason that the Emperor favored Prince Nicholas over his brothers was that there was no doubt that he was the legitimate son of Grand Duchess Marie Aleksandrovna and Prince Maximilian Leuchtenberg, but that there was some question about the paternity of the brothers, particularly George: there was reason to believe that his real father was Stroganov, whom the Grand Duchess married after the death of Prince Maximilian.

Prince Nicholas had inherited the entailed family estate, which consisted of precious stones. On his death bed the prince asked that the Emperor recognize his children as princely [although they were born of a morganatic marriage] and thus permit them to inherit the estate. Acting on a report by Count Vorontsov-Dashkov, the Emperor decided that the estate go to the prince's children. Also he recognized them as princely.

Prince Eugene protested. He believed that the estate should go to him and, after his death, to Prince George. Consequently, Emperor Alexander III appointed a commission of inquiry, consisting of the minister of the court, the over-procurator of the Holy Synod, the minister of justice, and the minister of finance, me. We decided that the estate should remain with the heirs of Prince Nicholas because such an entail had no status in Russian law: it had force only as a result of a family decision made by Emperor Alexander II, and if the reigning Emperor decided to annul the entail, for whatever reason, there was no legal obstacle to such an act. The Emperor approved the finding of the commission and the estate passed to the sons of Prince Nicholas. (Much of what I learned of the Leuchtenbergs came from my work on the commission.)

As I have said, Emperor Alexander III led a model family life. He had three sons and two daughters. (There may have been a sixth, who died early on.)[7] His oldest son is now happily our reigning emperor, Emperor Nicholas II. I knew him when he was Heir to the throne: as I have said I had some dealings with him in connection with the Siberian Railroad Committee; I will have more to say about it later. He was to marry the Grand Duchess Alice of Darmstadt, now Empress Alexandra Fedorovna; some years before the marriage, she had visited Russia as a possible bride for the Heir: she obviously pleased the future Emperor Nicholas II, but it appears that on that visit she was not successful.

I did not know the second son, the Grand Duke George Aleksandrovich, at all. He died of consumption, in Abastuman.

The third son, Michael Aleksandrovich, was his father's favorite. Why one loves this one or that is a secret of the soul, and so I find it difficult to explain why the Emperor preferred his Misha to the others, but he did. Unlike the other children, Michael Aleksandrovich felt completely free with his father, as shown by the following incident, about which I heard from the Grand Duke's valet.

The Emperor liked to go walking with Misha and to be playful with him. Once, it was in the summer, as they were walking, they stopped where a gardener was watering the flowers. It seems that Michael Aleksandrovich did something to annoy his father: perhaps he had disobeyed an order not to walk into the water. Whatever the case, the Emperor took the hose and thoroughly drenched the boy. Then they returned home and Misha changed his clothes.

Later that day, after lunch, the Emperor happened to be leaning out of the window of a room just below that of Michael Aleksandrovich. On seeing this the boy poured a pitcher of water over his father's head. Only his Misha could have played such a trick with impunity; anyone else would have received what for.

I remember talking to the Emperor's elder daughter, Grand Duchess Xenia Aleksandrovna when she was a little girl. It was at a family lunch, with few outsiders. I was with her at a separate table. It was difficult for me to start a conversation with her because she was very shy and did not know what to talk about. She has grown up to be a fine woman.

When the time came for her to marry her choice fell on Grand Duke Alexander Mikhailovich, whom the Emperor disliked.* The Grand Duke was a very handsome young man and still is handsome, with a somewhat Jewish appearance. In the course of my clashes with him I have become convinced that he not only looks Jewish but also that he has some of the negative traits found among Jews. That is not to say there are no good sides to the Jewish character: I am not one of those who do not consider Jews to be human beings. Well, the Emperor objected to the idea of his daughter marrying the Grand Duke but in the end gave his consent because she was smitten with him.

The Grand Duke was aware of the Emperor's dislike for him. Once, during his engagement to Grand Duchess Xenia Aleksandrovich, he accompanied the Emperor on his annual voyage to the Finnish skerries. During the trip something went wrong with the Emperor's bath and the Grand Duke offered him the use of his own rubber bath. After bathing in it, the Emperor praised it highly. At last, said the Grand Duke to one of the Emperor's aides-de-camp, the Emperor had found something about him to praise. I believe the Emperor foresaw that the Grand Duke would not be a fit husband for the daughter of an Emperor such as he.

*In part he disliked him because of the belief that the Grand Duke's mother, Grand Duchess Olga Fedorovna, had a Jewish father (Baron Haber). Sometimes the Emperor referred to her "Aunt Haber." Once the Emperor used a Jewish surname ending in "sohn" in referring to the Grand Duchess, whom he disliked as much as he did her son Alexander Mikhailovich. However, he was fond of her husband, Grand Duke Michael Nikolaevich, because his private and public life were exemplary. He was the only uncle whom the Emperor looked on with kindness.

XIX

My Work as Minister of Finance under Emperor Alexander III

Old Business: Tsion and Vyshnegradskii

As soon as I became minister of finance I made it my business to get to the bottom of Tsion's allegation that Vyshnegradskii had taken a bribe from Rothschild.

On learning that the negotiations for the loan had been conducted by Laskin, the director of the International Bank, and by Rothstein, later the director of the bank, I summoned Rothstein to give me the facts.

He told me that Vyshnegradskii had felt that the Hoskier group, which had handled the first loan, was not equal to dealing with major operations and had therefore turned to Rothschild for the second loan, but since he had made an oral promise to Hoskier that his group would participate in subsequent dealings, he wanted the group included in the consortium that Rothschild would lead. Vyshnegradskii was determined to keep his promise, even though it was not in writing, because reputable bankers regard an oral promise as binding as a written one. (During my eleven years as minister of finance I never dealt with a banker who did not keep his word, just as I never failed to keep any word that I gave as minister of finance.)

Rothschild, however, categorically refused to permit the Hoskier group to join his consortium because he was not on good terms with it and had never done any business with it. Vyshnegradskii deferred to Rothschild's wishes.[1]

Then, after the conclusion of the negotiations, Vyshnegradskii summoned Rothstein and Laskin and told them that since the consortium would be making a profit from arranging the loan, it should pay him a commission of 500,000 francs. Rothstein told me that this request saddened him because when abroad he heard repeated allegations about corruption, allegations that he preferred not to believe, and here he was hearing the minister of finance ask for a bribe. He said that he and Laskin reluctantly telegraphed Rothschild to place the money in Vyshnegradskii's account. When they told Vyshnegradskii that the transaction had been completed, he rubbed his hands and said, with his usual sarcastic smile:

> Distribute this money to the members of the Hoskier group, in proportion to their part in the first loan. This is to make up for the commission they would have received had they been admitted to the consortium. I think that it is only proper that the money come from Rothschild and his associates, but knowing that Rothschild would not give this money to the Hoskier group, I asked for it on my behalf.

I was very surprised by this subterfuge and asked Rothstein if he had proof that the money had in fact been distributed to the members of the Hoskier group. Within a few days he brought me receipts to support his statement. I, in turn, showed the receipts to the Emperor, who was very pleased to have it established that his minister of finance had not taken a bribe.

However, the Emperor correctly felt that the subterfuge employed by Vyshnegradskii had been highly improper. I, of course, agreed completely with him. This kind of subterfuge was a vestige of the days before Vyshnegradskii had become minister, when he sometimes acted with impropriety in his dealings with bankers and other businessmen.

The Creation of the Separate Corps of Border Guard

When I became minister of finance, our border guard, a military formation, was under the jurisdiction of the Department of Customs, i.e., under civilian control. The director of the department was *ex officio* chief of the guard and the chiefs of the customs districts were *ex officio* chiefs of the border guard units in their respective districts. (The inspector of the border guard, Lieutenant General Baron Gan, a nonentity, was the vice-director of the department.)

I was unhappy over the fact that the border guard, which was composed of soldiers, serving under the same condition as other soldiers, should be under civilian administration, which meant that civil servants had greater influence over the soldiers than did their officers. Consequently, one could say that the prestige of the military uniform had fallen.

At the first opportunity I suggested to the Emperor that the border guard be removed from civilian control. Evidently he had held the same view for some time, for he told me that he had brought up the idea with my predecessors, Bunge and Vyshnegradskii, to no avail. They had argued that the border guard must remain under the jurisdiction of the Department of Customs because its chief duty was to deal with contraband, a matter of direct concern to the department.

With the Emperor's support, and despite opposition from the director of the

Department of Customs, other civilian officials, and General Gan, I went about preparing a statute to change the status of the border guard. In this work I had the help of several military men. After we had done our work, we had a draft statute that provided for a Separate Corps of Border Guards, organized like a regular army corps, except that it would have a fairly large medical division since it would be larger than an ordinary army corps. This body, which would be independent of the Department of Customs and linked to the Ministry of Finance only through the person of the minister, would be responsible for surveillance over contraband and, in general, over cases involving the use of force.

When I submitted the draft of the statute to the Emperor, he objected to the word "separate" in the title of the unit. I argued that I had chosen the word because every corps that had indeed been separate had indeed been called "separate," as had been the case with the Loris-Melikov "separate" corps in the Caucasus. To this the Emperor replied that, nonetheless, Loris-Melikov had been subordinate to the viceroy of the Caucasus. The Emperor completely approved all the rest of the draft and added that he wanted the minister of finance to be the [titular] chief of the corps, obviously as a sign of gratitude for my work.[2]

Then came the task of selecting a commander of the corps. I presented to the Emperor the names of three generals, men whom I did not know, suggested by General Vannovskii on the basis of their records. Of the three I preferred Svynin because he had been in combat, having distinguished himself at the taking of Plevna. The Emperor, who knew all three, agreed to appoint Svynin.

I had a very warm feeling for the corps, partly because, never having been in the military, it pleased me to have an entire corps under my jurisdiction, partly perhaps because I had spent so much of my youth among the military in the Caucasus, partly too because I had met so many prominent military men at the home of my uncle General Fadeev. Whatever the reason, the fact is that I gave a good deal of attention to the corps and felt that I was well liked by both officers and men. I had many occasions to inspect the border guards in my capacity as chief, but I must say that I always found playing this role a strain.

Emperor Nicholas II later gave me a semi-military uniform to wear when I acted in my capacity as chief. When I left the Ministry of Finance he was kind enough to permit me to retain my uniform, in view of the fact that I had established the corps, under the direction of his father.

By the way, when we began to construct the Chinese Eastern Railroad, I provided it with a railroad security guard, consisting of "temporarily retired" soldiers from the border guards and retired soldiers. The term "temporarily retired" was a subterfuge, since it was not possible for soldiers on active duty to serve with the railroad. Subsequently, when we began, so to speak, to act more openly, I transformed the railroad security guard into the Trans-Amur District of Border Guards, one of the largest units in the corps.

This unit distinguished itself during the recent Japanese war and drew praise from all commanding officers. This is understandable because the unit was more homogeneous than other army units, consisting as it did of men and officers who had served together for many years; also its men and officers knew Manchuria quite well, from their years of service there. Unfortunately, I was no longer minister of finance by that time and could not have the pleasure of being associated with this unit, which it had been my privilege to organize.

Our First Commercial Treaty with Germany, 1894

On becoming minister of finance it fell to me to negotiate the first commercial treaty Russia ever made with Germany. Previously there had been no such treaties between our two countries because the traditional ties between the ruling dynasties of the two countries had been such that commercial treaties had not seemed necessary. After all, Russia had contributed her blood to the preservation of the Kingdom of Prussia and to the establishment of the German Empire.

Given such political ties, the question of a commercial treaty did not arise until the political and economic interests of the two countries began to diverge. As a result Emperor Alexander III began to become friendly toward France. At the same time economic relations between us and Germany began to deteriorate as a result of policies adopted by the great German Chancellor, Bismarck, as well as changes brought about by the desire to develop our own industry.

Chancellor Bismarck, inspired by the ideas of the well-known economist Frederick List (about whom I wrote a short pamphlet),[3] began to impose duties on agricultural products in an effort to protect German agrarian, particularly Junker, interests. (The idea of a protective tariff on foodstuffs, particularly our daily bread, would have been considered not merely heretical but also insane in the first half of the century and here comes along a statesman who imposes a protective tariff on the most necessary food products.)* We, in turn, as the result of our economic needs, began to impose duties on German iron and steel products in the early 1880s. Ignoring the fact that Germany had set a precedent by imposing duties on agricultural products, Chancellor Bismarck once warned our foreign minister Giers (while taking the waters in Karlsbad, or was it Marienbad?) that this new direction in Russian economic policy did not correspond to German economic interests and that Germany might respond by imposing protectionist duties on agricultural imports from Russia.

In 1891 Emperor Alexander III established the basis of our protective tariff system, which was worked out by Vyshnegradskii, a system maintained to this day. As a result many German industrial goods imported into Russia were made

*The last word on whether or not such protection is in accord with the principles of economics has not yet been uttered by economic history. I think that economic history will rule in the negative, but, of course, economics is not an exact science. Its principles are not absolute and change with the interplay of world economic forces. That major European powers employ broad protectionist policies clearly indicates this to be the case. But there is another side to such a policy: it unquestionably encourages the growth of socialism.

XIX • MY WORK AS MINISTER OF FINANCE   183

subject to the payment of duty for the first time. Germany, for its part, was by this time subjecting agricultural imports from Russia to higher duties than those imposed on the agricultural imports from countries with which Germany had commercial treaties. This meant that the Russian Empire was virtually the only country subject to the higher (maximum) duties; as a result we were at a competitive disadvantage in exporting grain to Germany.

Clearly we needed a commercial treaty with Germany, all the more so because in the past, when we had relied on oral agreements with the Germans, they had interpreted promises made to them in the broadest possible sense and promises made to us in the narrowest. Under Vyshnegradskii the first steps toward negotiating a commercial treaty with Germany had been begun through our ambassador in Berlin, Count Paul Shuvalov, and the German ambassador in Petersburg, General Werder.

General Werder, although in good standing with our Emperor, was incapable of playing a political role and did nothing to further the negotiations. Count Shuvalov, on the other hand, was of more help. He was a fine person, a distinguished soldier, a man of the world, combining good Russian common sense, inherited from his father, and Polish cleverness (in the good sense of the word), inherited from his mother, a Pole. He was an outstanding ambassador who had been in the good graces of Emperor William I and was in the good graces of the then Emperor, William II. He was strongly in favor of concluding a commercial treaty with Germany, but hoped that the process would involve no friction. Also, because he was not at home with economic and broad political questions, he did not quite realize what the costs of concluding a treaty would be. Despite his help, little progress had been made in negotiating a commercial treaty by the time I became minister.

To help our embassy in Berlin we sent Vasilii Ivanovich Timiriazev, who, it goes without saying, knew what he was doing because he was vice-director of the Department of Commerce and Industry and was quite capable of conducting negotiations, but only up to a point, for he lacked the mind and character to make proper judgments. Also, he put us at a disadvantage by trying to conclude a treaty by all possible means: in response the Germans were unyielding and sought advantages without offering concessions.

As I have said, Germany had imposed maximum duties on our products, thus in effect presenting us with an ultimatum: if you want the benefit of the minimum rates you must agree to our terms. In this connection I should note that the minimum rates were quite nominal, while the maximum rates were simply impossible.

I saw that we would have to take strong action if we were to gain satisfactory terms. So, I asked the Emperor for permission to request the approval of the State Council for two sets of duties on most manufactured goods, one set already in force under the existing tariff and another, higher than those by several dozen percent. Thus we would be able to retaliate: we could threaten to impose our higher duties on Germany unless she applied her minimum duties to our products. The Emperor agreed to my proposal and empowered me to present it before the State Council.

As soon as I did, and my action became generally known, there was widespread alarm and opposition. Many members of the State Council feared that the imposition of higher duties would involve us in diplomatic, and even military, difficulties. Giers opposed my action because I had not consulted with him or gained his prior approval. Count Shuvalov warned Petersburg that this step might result in diplomatic difficulties.

The Emperor, in keeping with his firm and loyal nature, supported me. He paid no attention to Giers's complaints and let Count Shuvalov know that he considered my position entirely correct and had full confidence in me in this matter.

In presenting my proposal to the State Council, I assured it that the higher duties would be imposed only as a last resort. I told the members that I hoped that the Germans would see that we could not continue to negotiate as long as they continued to behave as they did. If they would grant us the minimum rates and grant us various privileges, we would agree not to impose the higher duties, but we would not agree to any substantial reduction in the existing [1891] tariff. I was thus able to win approval from the State Council.

As soon as the Emperor approved this dual tariff system, I informed Germany of it, but Berlin apparently assumed that I would not impose the higher duties and continued to be stubborn. When I realized that Germany would not yield, I discontinued negotiations and imposed higher duties on all German goods, much to that country's discomfiture. The Germans replied by raising their duties on agricultural products: with the permission of the Emperor, I countered by sharply raising our duties on their imports. Thus, we embarked on a merciless tariff war. We were in a better position to endure such a war, which falls harder on nations with a more developed industry and commerce than upon a less developed nation such as Russia.

This war aroused a great deal of hostility against me in the official circles of Petersburg. They were saying that because of my irrepressible nature and my youth and frivolity I could drag us into a war with Germany, which would then turn into a general European war. I recall the way I was received in Peterhof in the midst of this bitter tariff war on the occasion, as I recall, of Empress Marie Fedorovna's nameday, July 22. There they were—the ministers, the ladies-in-waiting, the entire Imperial suite, the grand dukes—assembled in the Great Palace at Peterhof, where the ceremonies to mark the occasion were to be conducted. When I entered the hall everyone, except General Vannovskii, avoided me like the plague. He was virtually the only minister who supported me in my firm and decisive position, knowing that if we did not show strength we would always find ourselves under the German thumb. Naturally, at such a time there were those who tried to frighten the Emperor and to lower me in his eyes. But anyone who knew his character knew that such efforts would prove fruitless. He supported me completely during that tariff war.

In response to our action, Germany declared that she would not resume the negotiations that had begun in Berlin unless we discontinued our measures against German imports. But in the end it was Germany that yielded and resumed negotiations. When I saw that negotiations were going smoothly, I canceled our maximum duties on German industrial goods, and Germany, in turn, applied her minimum rates on imports from us.

Negotiations then proceeded fairly quickly to a successful conclusion. They were conducted on behalf of Russia by Timiriazev and other officials from my ministry, who acted only in accordance with my instructions and authorization. And Count Shuvalov must be given his due: once he saw the German government begin to retreat, he recognized that he had been mistaken in his warnings and that I had been right in insisting that if we bared our teeth Germany would quickly soften her position. Thereafter we were good friends.

Caprivi, Bismarck's successor as chancellor, and Marschall, state secretary for foreign affairs, acted on behalf of Germany in the negotiations. And their Emperor, young William II, played a positive role during the entire course of the negotiations. He obviously had not wanted a rupture with Russia, and when he saw that I would not yield and that my Emperor supported me and had faith in me, he began to pursue a conciliatory policy. And to give him his due, he helped calm German public opinion in general and the Reichstag in particular, where there were some difficulties with the treaty because it was not advantageous to Germany.

The commercial treaty, which covered many matters, including political ones insofar as they related to economic questions, was concluded [in March 1894] for a term of ten years, subject to renewal. Of course, both sides made concessions and it was fair to both sides, but Germany conceded more than we did; in fact Germany had never had to yield as much as she did in this case.

Soon after the treaty went into force, Caprivi left office. The treaty was not the cause of his departure. Neither his extreme propriety and calm nor his liberalism suited the German Emperor. But if his leaving was not the result of the treaty, its timing had something to do with it, for William used the occasion to throw a sop, for the German setback, to German public opinion, or rather Prussian Junkerdom, whose interests had not been served by the treaty.

Emperor Alexander III was very grateful to me for my handling of this affair and for its successful outcome. When he talked of bestowing an honor on me for my role in the affair, I easily dissuaded him and said that all I desired was for him to confer an honor—the uniform of an admiral in the Russian navy—on Emperor William. I said this because the German ambassador had hinted broadly that this was what his Emperor wanted.

The Emperor smiled in good-natured mockery at my suggestion, as if to say: that is just like him. For to the degree that the love of orders, uniforms, and decorations was foreign to him, it was abnormally developed in Emperor William. The Emperor then said good-naturedly to me: ''I will fulfill your request at the first possible moment because I recognize he behaved very properly and, for the first time, I actually saw that he sincerely does not wish to break with us completely.'' But the Emperor died before he could find the occasion to bestow the uniform.

After Emperor Nicholas II ascended the throne, I told him of his father's promise. He smiled, but did not reply. A few years later he bestowed the uniform of a Russian admiral on Emperor William, perhaps because he recalled what I had said, or perhaps for another reason. (This was before the war with Japan, when the uniform possessed greater prestige than it was to have after that unfortunate conflict.)

Thus I made my debut on the world scene and all Europe marveled.

Some time later, the well-known German writer Maximilian Harden, whom I mentioned earlier, came to Petersburg to become acquainted with me. He told me that Bismarck, who was well disposed toward him, had urged him to see me because in the former chancellor's opinion no one in the last few years has shown ''such strength of character and the will to achieve what he seeks'' as I and, moreover, predicted that I would ''have a tremendous political career.'' I told Harden to tell Bismarck that I was flattered to hear his opinion of me and particularly to hear his prediction about my future. I was never to have the opportunity of meeting Bismarck, but I was told by Count Shuvalov and Count Muravev, then the counsellor of our embassy in Berlin, that whenever he spoke to Russians he inquired about me.

The commercial treaty of 1894 served as a model for other commercial treaties which I concluded while minister of finance. In 1904, at the expiration of this treaty, I was to conduct negotiations for its renewal, at a time when we were weak because of the senseless war with Japan. I shall probably write about these negotiations later.

The Siberian Railroad Committee and the Question of Migration

I do not wish to speak here of all the minor and major matters considered by the Siberian Railroad Committee, but I feel obliged to speak of the response to my proposal that with the construction of the Siberian Railroad there should come greater migration from European to Asiatic Russia. According to my way of thinking, the construction of the Great Siberian road was inextricably linked with the question of migration to Siberia. Such a movement would help thin out the population of European Russian and thus make it easier to improve the peasant lot there and, in the long run, help the railroad pay for itself by developing Siberia.

Yet the idea, far from receiving support, met with hidden opposition, of a kind appropriate to the mentality of the days of serfdom, of the Middle Ages. Many of our influential landowners and their supporters among the Petersburg bureaucracy, particularly minister of interior Ivan Nikolaevich Durnovo, considered my idea harmful. They claimed that migration might produce harmful political consequences, but it was evident from conversations with them that they were concerned over the effect on their economic interests: if peasants were to leave in any number the price of land would go down and the wages paid to agricultural workers would go up. They, of course, preferred a dense peasant population that would be forced to pay high prices for land or accept low agricultural wages, under the goad of hunger.

I had first presented my ideas on migration in a memorandum prepared for the special conference that decided on the speedy construction of the railroad. The memorandum was later considered, in its broadest aspects, at a meeting of the Siberian Railroad Committee. Despite the efforts of several members, led by Durnovo, to bury the idea of migration, it was approved by the committee. What is more important was the approval of the Tsesarevich, for which I had Bunge to thank. This was the first occasion on which the future Emperor Nicholas II had to express himself definitely on a major political question, and he did so in a manner considered liberal, even revolutionary, in those days. It goes without saying that Emperor Alexander III approved the minutes of that meeting, in which the committee agreed that migration was in the interests of the state and that efforts to hinder it by artificial means were harmful.

Nowadays, of course, no one denies that migration to Siberia is beneficial. I think that many will find it hard to believe that less than twenty years ago it was considered harmful.

The Liquor Monopoly: First Efforts

Soon after I became minister of finance, the Emperor told me that he had a task for me, in addition to the completion of the Siberian Railroad, that was close to his heart: the establishment of a government monopoly on the sale of liquor.[4] He was very grieved that the Russian people squandered so much money on liquor and saw a liquor monopoly as a means of reducing drunkenness.

The problem of drunkenness had been recognized toward the end of the reign of Emperor Alexander II, and many conferences had been held to devise means of dealing with it, but only palliative measures had been adopted. This was so because the existing excise system of regulating the manufacture and sale of liquor was considered superior to the earlier farming-out system and therefore unchangeable. Consequently, since the excise tax system did not permit regulation of the distillation and sale of alcohol, the conferences were doomed to failure.

Since Emperor Alexander III was determined to curb drunkenness, he was ready to take the bold step of replacing the excise tax system with one under which the government as the exclusive purchaser of liquor from distillers could regulate liquor production and then be the sole seller of liquor to the public. This idea was unprecedented and extraordinarily bold.

Where did the Emperor get this idea? Some say from the publicist Katkov. It is true that in those days Katkov wrote articles for *Moskovskie vedomosti* arguing for the idea of a liquor monopoly, but I am inclined to think that the inspiration for the liquor monopoly came from within the Emperor, because such an idea was totally in keeping with his kind of mind. His was the kind of mind that did not recognize complexities, ambiguities. For him everything had to be simple, clear, pure. Perhaps this is characteristic of the mind of a child. This kind of mind-soul was the basic strength of the Emperor. It might embarrass some, but it compelled all who were close to him to pay homage to him.

Once the Emperor complained to me about the difficulties he had encountered with my predecessors in advancing the idea of a liquor monopoly. Bunge, an orthodox financial expert (or, as the Emperor put it, a scholar or financial theoretician), had candidly criticized the idea, declaring it if not impossible, at least very difficult, to implement. Thus, under Bunge nothing was achieved in this respect, except possibly the departure of Grot, the director of the Department of Indirect Taxation and the creator of the excise tax system. With Grot there could, of course, be no talk of replacing the excise tax system with a liquor monopoly. But even with Grot gone, Bunge did not take to the idea of a liquor monopoly.

The Emperor told me that when Vyshnegradskii succeeded Bunge he raised the question of a liquor monopoly with him. After investigating the matter a bit, Vyshnegradskii had given him an equivocal opinion, not completely negative but very evasive.

So, the Emperor earnestly asked me to study the proposal and to implement it, saying that he relied heavily on my youth, my character, my loyalty to him. Thus, he virtually made me give him my word that I would realize his wish.

During the few years that remained of his reign I was able to take the first steps toward establishing the liquor monopoly. In this I was helped by Markov, the director of the Department of Indirect Taxation. He was an effective person, but was completely under the influence of my personality, blindly obeying and carrying out all my wishes.

What we undertook to do was to place rectification of liquor and its sale in the hands of the government, leaving the first stages of distillation in the hands of private entrepreneurs, who would distill only as much as the government required. When I submitted the proposal for a liquor monopoly to the State Council I, not unexpectedly, encountered opposition there, particularly from Grot, who was a member recognized as an authority on the subject of liquor and my ardent opponent. Moreover, the notion of a liquor monopoly was so novel that it inspired fear in many of the gray-haired members of the council, partly because it did not fit into the framework of orthodox financial teaching, partly because they feared my youthful enthusiasm and saw in me a young man who might upset everything.

They did not realize that although I was comparatively young, not quite forty-three, I was more mature, more experienced in practical matters than most of them. I had had twenty-one years of experience in the world of private enterprise, while most of their wisdom and knowledge came either from books or from the Petersburg salons.

As I have said, I took the first steps toward establishing the liquor monopoly under Emperor Alexander III. I was to continue the work under Emperor Nicholas II, and I shall probably write about it when I come to write about his reign.

Monetary Reform and the Reorganization of the State Bank

I have already noted that the first steps toward the establishment of the gold standard were taken during the reign of Emperor Alexander III.[5] The conversion of our monetary system to the gold standard, which I was to implement during the reign of Emperor Nicholas II, would enable us to weather the unfortunate consequences of the war with Japan and to reach our present state of financial well-being.

However, I must admit that although I believed in a metallic money standard when I became minister of finance, I had not studied the question thoroughly. One of my first actions was not consistent with the belief in a metallic standard. I had just been appointed acting minister of finance, when Golindo, the director of the Treasury, informed me that there was not enough money to meet the next payroll, on September 20, and asked for my orders. (Our resources were exhausted because we had been through the worst harvest in decades in 1891.) Having just assumed my post and not being thoroughly at home with the finances of the empire, I saw no alternative to printing more money. So, I told Golindo to have the Government Printing Office run off from 10 to 20 million rubles in paper money to meet the payroll. When my act became public knowledge, my predecessor Bunge remarked to me that here I was fresh in my post and already I was embarking on a dangerous course that would lead Russia to complete financial ruin.

I said: "Nicholas Khristianovich, I can assure you that I am in no way a proponent of paper money and I consider it an evil, but not being reasonably at home in my position I had no other choice. I can assure you that I will not rush to employ such means."

His reply made me laugh and left me speechless:

> I believe you are sincere in saying you will not do it, but you will. You are like the French girl who sinned and when she was told that it was improper to sin, swore that this was the first time she had sinned and that she would never sin again. I would not believe such a girl nor would I believe the assurance of a finance minister who could issue 20 million paper rubles, with no backing in silver or gold, with no value that any exchange would recognize. You will do it again.

Several years later, after I had succeeded, with some help from Bunge and in the face of hostile Russian public opinion, in establishing the gold standard, I often reminded him about the story and his lack of confidence in my commitment to a sound monetary system.

It is not surprising that at first I took some actions inconsistent with a metallic standard. After all, ever since the Sebastopol [Crimean] War, Russia had lived under a monetary system based on paper money and had no knowledge, or experience, of a metallic-based monetary system. Neither in the universities nor in other higher schools was there sound instruction about the principles of such a system. And except for the works of Bunge and Wagner (formerly of the University of Dorpat and now an authority on financial policy in Germany), there were no solid monographs or textbooks in Russian on the subject. How well I remember a conversation I had with Bunge just before a session of the Finance Committee where I was beginning the task of carrying out the monetary reform. Just before the meeting he said to me: "Sergei Iulevich, you will have trouble in getting this reform approved because not a single person on the committee has any practical or theoretical knowledge of the subject."

I was hampered in quickly finding the right path by depending too much on Professor Antonovich, my assistant minister, whom I had selected chiefly because of his book on monetary systems. I had read the book before becoming minister of finance, at a time when I was not particularly interested in the subject, and I had the impression that he was in favor of a metallic standard. I was right in that respect, but my mistake was in not giving enough weight to his character, which was weak: thus, when he saw that Petersburg, and in fact all Russia, was opposed to monetary reform, he began to waver and ultimately would come out against it. Moreover, he was coarse, uncouth, and more interested in his petty personal interests than in carrying out monetary reform.

Also, he put me on the wrong track in matters of detail. Take the reorganization of the State Bank, for which he helped prepare a revised charter. The new charter was supposed to reflect our intention of adopting a metallic monetary standard. And to a degree it did, but the commitment to such a standard was weakened by Antonovich's introduction in the charter of provisions permitting the State Bank to grant long-term loans without solid security. And it was I who would be criticized for permitting such actions, but I would have no choice under the terms of the revised charter.

In addition, the task of getting on with monetary reform was made difficult by the lack of consensus among those foreign financial experts, some of whom supported a metallic standard, others the silver standard, and still others the bimetallic standard. Subsequently, after I had almost completely mastered the subject and had come close to having the gold standard adopted, I was to have many discussions with experts on the subject, among them Alphonse Rothschild and Léon Say, minister of finance in the early days of the French republic and son of a famous economist. They favored the silver standard, as did the aged Loubet, former president of the republic. I was well acquainted with, and on good terms with, Loubet, a fine man and a major figure, but no financial expert. It was not so long ago that he was still arguing with me about this subject, still trying to justify his views, although it is not really a matter for debate any more. Also opposing me on the gold standard was to be the French premier Méline, a well-known economist, who implemented a protectionist policy. He had working for him a prominent economist and journalist named Theuriet, who presented his views with vigor.

Such attitudes were quite understandable. France had nearly 3 billion silver francs in circulation at the time, and the price of silver was going down, but there was still hope that its price would be stabilized, particularly if Russia adopted the silver standard. So this was a question that affected French pocketbooks. It should be noted that although France preferred the silver standard, it would have found the bimetallic standard acceptable, but not the gold standard.

Emperor Alexander III gave me full support in the question of monetary reform, at least in the preliminary measures that I undertook. Of course, he did not understand this highly specialized question, one that only a handful of people in Russia at the time understood. He supported me because he had confidence in me and believed that any policy I supported vigorously could not be harmful to Russians.

I shall have more to say about the adoption of the gold standard when I come to the reign of Emperor Nicholas II.

Parochial Schools

Among the tasks I, as minister of finance, undertook, was to carry out the wish of Emperor Alexander III to see that the parochial school system grow and be placed on a firm footing. The parochial schools were not popular with many members of the State Council, who tended to support those ministers of finance who were indifferent to or hostile to such schools.

I have always been sympathetic to the idea of parochial schools and still am, although these schools are very much out of fashion nowadays. My chief reason for being sympathetic is that I considered it my sacred duty to carry out all wishes expressed to me by the Emperor.

In addition, I support the parochial schools out of personal conviction, for I think that they can play an important part in our primary school system. I believe that any state that claims to be civilized must have an adequate system of primary education, and it is my deepest conviction that Russia's chief shortcoming is lack of primary education. Nowhere among civilized people are there as many illiterates as in Russia. If the Russian people, with all its illiteracy, its lack of the most elementary education, were not Christian and Orthodox, it would be completely savage. What distinguishes the Russian people from beasts are the religious principles which have been transmitted to them mechanically or which they have inherited in their blood.

Therefore, the question of which is superior, secular or parochial education, is completely irrelevant under present circumstances and will be for a long time to come. I believe that any kind of primary education is to the good and that any honest person who is not misled by political bias should support any kind of education. I am not antipathetic to secular schools, be they under the jurisdiction of the zemstvos or the Ministry of Education, but I believe it a mistake to scorn the asset that parochial schools represent in bringing education to the people. If rabbis can have a great influence on the education of Jews, Moslem clergy on the education of their people, [Catholic] priests on the education of Poles, then it would be criminal, if it were not foolish, to prevent our clergy from exerting influence on the education of the Russian people. Be that as it may be, we have tens of thousands of clergymen, meaning tens of thousands of [potential] teachers. And it should be noted that many laymen are glad to offer money and property for the benefit of parochial schools. And last but not least is the fact that in many localities the people themselves prefer parochial to secular schools.

That is why, as minister of finance, I gave Constantine Petrovich Pobedonostsev complete support in the promotion of parochial schools. As I have said, this was not a popular position to take in the State Council. It seems that I was the first minister of finance to take a completely sympathetic position toward parochial schools, and with me helping him in the State Council, Pobedonostsev was able to win larger appropriations for these schools.

Railroad Policy
under Emperor Alexander III

As indicated earlier, under Emperor Alexander III we began a shift from private to governmental construction and operation of the railroads, a shift that was to be completed in the reign of Emperor Nicholas II. The new policy was and is based on the belief that railroads have a major importance for the state and that private enterprise, which is basically concerned with private interests, cannot adequately serve the interests of the state in this field. Consequently, both as minister of ways and communications and as minister of finance, I carried out a policy of buying up privately owned railroads as well as promoting construction and operation of new railroads by the government. There may be a difference of opinion concerning the respective merits of this or that system of railroad construction and operation, but those who attach great value to governmental construction and operation—and they are almost in the majority in continental Europe—cannot help but recognize the great service performed in this connection in the reign of Emperor Alexander III.

The chief concern of the Emperor in carrying out the new railroad policy was for the weak, for the masses, but his decision to implement this policy rapidly was partly due to the fact that he was shocked to see that there existed within his realm private railroad realms ruled by little railroad kings such as Poliakov, Bloch, Kronenberg, and Gubonin.

As an example of shocking behavior by a railroad king let me note the following. In the second year of his reign, following the end of the period of mourning for his father, Emperor Alexander III held a soirée at Gatchina, to which he invited many guests, among them the brother of the Polovtsov about whom I have already spoken. This Polovtsov was head of the Main Company of Russian Railroads, which owned the line serving Gatchina. When the time came for the guests to depart, they assembled at the station to take an express train especially provided for them. The departure of this train carrying the Emperor's invited guests was held up because Polovtsov and his party chose to leave first, in his special train. Polovtsov behaved so rudely, one can say, insolently, because the Main Company of Russian Railroads was, so to speak, in his pocket.

My Journey to the Murman Littoral, 1894

Emperor Alexander III was fascinated by the Russian north, partly because the peasantry there represented a special, pure Russian type, pure as a result of blood and history, partly because as Tsesarevich he had had close contact with the north when he had served as chairman of a committee to aid famine victims in the area.

Possibly because his interest in the area was known, the Murmansk Steamship Company was later organized. Since I was not in Petersburg at the time, I cannot say for certain that some persons close to the Emperor organized the line or merely invested in it. Among them was General S. A. Sheremetev, who was very close to him and served him as chief of convoy when he became Emperor. In any event it was a fact that the Emperor was sympathetic toward the company.

My journey to the north was the result of the decision to increase our naval strength in the Baltic, and this required the construction of a major naval base. Admiral Chikhachev, director of the Ministry of the Navy, together with General Obruchev, chief of staff, recommended that the base be established in Libau. The general-admiral of the navy, Grand Duke Alexis Aleksandrovich, who, as I have said, did not take his work seriously and was under the influence of Chikhachev, naturally favored Libau. But the real inspiration for Libau as a major base was General Obruchev, who transmitted his ideas to Admiral Chikhachev through his brother, who was the admiral's secretary.

General Obruchev was indeed a distinguished military theoretician, and on several occasions I was to talk to him about the question of a naval base at Libau. Knowing his fine mind and his ability, I am certain that his position was not without merit, that in supporting a base at the city he was looking at it not as an independent factor of our military strength, but as part of his general system for the defense of the realm. However, the majority of naval men believed that the construction of a naval base at Libau would be a complete waste of money—as turned out to be the case. They argued that we should seek a naval base on one of the open seas, a base that could not be blockaded in time of war.

At first Emperor Alexander III had accepted the position recommended by Chikhachev and Obruchev, but then he began to have second thoughts about the desirability of Libau for a base and began to come around to the view of establishing a base at a site that was ice free the year round and that gave out to the open sea. But such a site, he said, could be found only on the Murmansk coast, i.e., in our far north.

Thus it came about that he commissioned me to go to the north to become acquainted with the area, to see if it had a site suitable for the fleet's chief naval base, a site where a large fleet could be constructed. Strictly speaking this was not a matter in the normal jurisdiction of the minister of finance, but apparently he turned to me because he knew that Obruchev and Chikhachev would be totally opposed to Murmansk because of their commitment to Libau. Although such a matter was not technically in my jurisdiction, he could justify sending me to the north on the basis of the fact that my ministry's Department of Commerce and Manufacture had jurisdiction over steamship companies, including the Murmansk line.

I decided to carry out the journey to the north in the summer of 1894, taking with me P. M. Romanov, director of my chancellery; the journalist E. L. Kochetov, of *Moskovskie vedomosti*, who had been close to Katkov, and who had written about our war with Turkey under the pseudonym Evgenii Lvov;[6] A. A. Borisov, a young painter, who was added to our group at the last moment and about whom I shall have something to say later. Naturally I was also accompanied by naval experts: they were M. I. Kazi and A. G. Konkevich. Before going on I want to say something about these two.

I knew Kazi from my Odessa days, when he was Chikhachev's assistant for the division of steamships and I his assistant for the division of railroads. He had studied at the Nikolaevskii Naval School and had gone on to become navigator and then captain in a privately owned steamship line. Subsequently he became manager of the Sebastopol shipbuilding yard of the Russian Steamship and Commercial Company. He and Chikhachev later parted company because he had a strong bent for intrigue. In this he was true to his heritage—he was of Greek origin, looked like a Greek, but a handsome one—and we know intrigue is the essence of life to a Greek. After leaving the company he became manager of a naval shipbuilding yard. He was a very intelligent and able man, more able than Chikhachev. He spoke well, wrote well, had been abroad many times, including trips to England, where he observed the construction of ships for the Russian Steamship and Commercial Company. To repeat, he was a very able man, but with a bent for intrigue.

I knew that Emperor Alexander III had heard of Kazi, who opposed a base at Libau, and had read several of his articles. The Emperor had a good opinion of him, but he had no personal contact with him. Being a very upright and straightforward man, the Emperor did not have behind-the-scenes ties with subordinates, a weakness that is, unfortunately, found in some monarchs.

Konkevich is a graduate of the Petersburg Naval Cadet Corps who later was compelled to give up his career as a naval officer because of differences with his superiors and because he wrote articles critical of the Ministry of the Navy.*

Konkevich looks like an "old salt," a genuine sailor, and is considered a competent sailor and even a competent fighting man. He is a fine, intelligent man. He writes often and well in the newspapers.

We went by train to Velikii Ustiug, by way of Vologda, from there by ship to Kotlas, from Kotlas again by ship, on that magnificent waterway, the Northern Dvina, to Archangel. There we stayed at the residence of Governor Engelgardt. From Archangel we sailed on one of the fine steamships of the Murmansk Steamship Company to Solovetsky Monastery, where we spent two days.

As I have noted, a last-minute addition to our party was the young painter Borisov, a student at the Academy of Arts in Petersburg. When his father, an Archangel peasant, had noted that the son, then a boy, had a passionate interest in painting, he arranged for him to attend the icon-painting school at the Solovetsky Monastery. It was there that General Goncharov discovered young Borisov, recognized his talents, and arranged for him to enroll at the Academy of Arts; and it was Kazi who collected money from me and others to pay for Borisov's tuition. It was because Borisov had studied at the Solovetsky Monastery that we took him along; while there he did many sketches.

Everybody at the monastery recognized this young man, who not so long ago had been painting icons there. He has since become a well-known artist whose favorite subject is the north, which he visits frequently; a few years ago he visited Novaia Zemlia. I have helped him arrange showings of his pictures in Berlin, London, and America. (He went to America a few years ago, when I still enjoyed popularity there, with a letter of recommendation to President Roosevelt that I provided. The president received him cordially. All of this has served to make his showing a brilliant success everywhere.)

I have visited many monasteries, among them the well-known monastery (called Mangobi, I believe) outside of Tiflis, near which I would go hunting and in which I sometimes spent the night, and the Kievan Lavra, but I must say that Solovetsky Monastery made a more powerful impression on me than these be-

*After leaving the service he unsuccessfully tried to earn a living as a writer, using the pseudonym of Belomor; he then became a police official in Libau, where I was to meet him some years after this trip. I was able to find him a place in the Maritime Section of the Department of Commerce and Manufacture, which was later to be under the jurisdiction of the "celebrated" Grand Duke Alexander Mikhailovich. Being an honorable man, Konkevich shared my opinion of the Grand Duke and could not get along with him. Konkevich now serves in the council of the Ministry of Commerce and Industry, and I see him from time to time.

cause of its severity, the simplicity of the life there, which is so completely in keeping with monastic life. And there is its natural setting—magnificent and very severe.

We traveled from Solovetsky Monastery to Murmansk to investigate the harbors there. We had been told in advance that we would find Ekaterinskaia harbor to be the best of them. This proved to be the case. It is an excellent harbor—large, deep, ice-free because of the Gulf Stream, well protected. I had never before seen such a magnificent harbor. It was even more impressive than the port and harbor of Vladivostok.

Also several features of this region made a powerful impression on me as a newcomer. I was impressed by the fact that the sun never sets there during the summer, making it possible to light a cigarette [at night] by use of a magnifying glass. I was impressed too by the whaling I was able to observe. It was a striking sight to see the whales "blowing," being harpooned, the long struggle to haul the whale in.

From Murmansk we sailed to the North Cape, then south along the Norwegian coast, stopping at Christiana and other cities, then to Sweden, spending several days in Stockholm. From Stockholm we sailed to Finland and entrained there for Petersburg.

En route I began to prepare my report on the journey so that on my return to Petersburg it could be printed for presentation to the Emperor.[7] I reported to the Emperor about the trip on my regular report day, Friday. He was then in residence at Peterhof, where he occupied several small rooms upstairs in the small palace, which was little more than a simple bourgeois home. To get to his study, where he heard reports, it was necessary to go through his dressing room. During the report he would sit at one end of a table and the one reporting at the other.

As I was delivering my report it was evident that he was agitated, anxious to see what I had in my packet of papers. When I reached the end and he noted a printed report in my packet, he cheered up and said:

> Undoubtedly that is your report, and I am waiting for it impatiently. Because I knew that you were having your report printed, I waited until you finished without asking any questions. I am very grateful to you for having made the trip and, even more, that you are submitting the report to me before my departure.

This was the last report I was ever to make to him and the last time that I would see him alive. He was quite evidently a sick man, and to see him in this condition was particularly painful for me, for I worshiped him. He soon left for Belovezh Forest. From there he was to go on to Skierniewice and then on to Yalta, where he died. I will probably write about his death and, when I come to deal with the first months after the ascension of Emperor Nicholas II to the throne, I will have occasion to return to my report about Murmansk.

I am certain that had Emperor Alexander III lived on we would have had a naval port at Ekaterinskaia harbor. Had this happened, we would probably not have become involved with Port Arthur in a search for an ice-free, open port and would have escaped all the unfortunate consequences of our frivolous venture in Port Arthur, the effects of which we still feel. I shall return to the question of Port Arthur when I speak of the reign of Emperor Nicholas II.

For the present let me say that in my report I described all that I had seen, all that deserved special attention, but emphasized the advantages and disadvantages of constructing a base at Ekaterinskaia harbor. On the plus side were the facts that the port is ice free, is easily defended, and has direct access to the ocean. On the minus side were the facts that there is virtually no summer there and that it is distant from sources of food.

I pointed out that if it were decided to construct a naval base there it would be necessary to build a general network of railroads including a double-track road from Petersburg. If such a railroad were built, Murmansk would be closer to central Russia than Archangel, but, more important, in direct contact with sources of food. Also, it would be necessary to construct sources for powerful electrical illumination for the sailors, who would be living in a place where there were nearly six months without daylight.

Before I left the Emperor he told me that it was his dream to see the completion of a railroad to the north so that in the event of famine the victims could be supplied with food. He told me of how many had died during a famine because it had been impossible to reach the famine-stricken area in time. It was his hope that this region, whose interests were close to his heart, would not remain without railroads.

It was only during the reign of his son that I was able to fulfill the dream, in part. At my initiative and insistence a railroad between Archangel and Moscow was built by the Moscow–Iaroslav Railroad, under a concession. Subsequently, the line was bought out by the government.

Also I was to succeed in connecting the Siberian Railroad with Kotlas, via Perm. This made it possible for Siberian grain to reach the Northern Dvina, i.e., the region where navigation could be further developed. In constructing this link I knew that not all members of the Siberian Railroad Committee would be won over to the project simply because it was in fulfillment of the late Emperor's dream, so I explained that the link would open a market for Siberian grain. This would help keep Siberian grain off the market in central Russia and thus help landowners in that region get a higher price for their grain.

XX

The Imperial Court

Persons Close to the Emperor
—Cherevin

I have already spoken of Count Vorontsov-Dashkov, who served as chief of security to Emperor Alexander III at the beginning of his reign and then went on to become minister of the Imperial court.[1] He was succeeded as chief of security by General-Adjutant Cherevin, who enjoyed the favor of both the Emperor and the Empress. Cherevin had only an ordinary education (he was a guards officer), but he had good sense and was a witty man of the world. His manner and speech were quite sharp, which suited the Emperor. I have no doubt that he had occasion to give good advice.

I would like to relate several incidents that shed light on his character as well as on his relations with the Emperor.

Cherevin was addicted to strong drink.[2] Once, after dinner, following maneuvers, as he and the Emperor were playing cards, a bit maudlin under the influence of alcohol, he kept annoying the Emperor: he said that he felt that he had not long to live and was pained not so much by the thought of death as by the thought of the pain his death would cause his Sovereign. Would he grieve and cry? The Emperor told Cherevin to leave him alone. Then Cherevin tried another tack, pestering the Emperor to bestow the Order of St. Alexander Nevskii on him while there was still time, noting how many of his contemporaries had received the order while he, Cherevin, had nothing more than the Order of the White Eagle. (The Emperor, as we know, was rather niggardly in awarding decorations and honors, particularly on those close to him.)

Once, after the marriage of the son of A. A. Polovtsov to Countess S. V. Panina, Cherevin was given a "diplomatic" assignment by the Emperor. The story is this.

Countess S. V. Panina was the last of her line, and her mother (who was married to I. I. Petrunkevich) was resolved that the Panin name and title should be bestowed on the man who married her daughter. This fact was undoubtedly of considerable importance to A. A. Polovtsov, a man with a weakness for honors and titles. He asked Cherevin to remind the Emperor of the mother's wish that her son-in-law be given the title of Count Panin. When the Emperor was so reminded, he told Cherevin to inform A. A. Polovtsov, whom he disliked intensely, that he did not wish to bestow the title.

After carrying out his assignment, by this time a bit tipsy, Cherevin stopped by at my place while we were at lunch. We provided him with a bottle of champagne and then asked what had brought him into town. (The Emperor resided in Gatchina most of the time.) When he said that he had been to see A. A. Polovtsov on a "diplomatic" assignment, I asked him about it.

Cherevin replied that he had carried out his task rather adroitly. He had told Polovtsov that the Emperor did not want his son "to bear the worthy name of Panin," but that if he wished his son to be a count he could be called Polovtsov-Count Petrunkevich. "Well," continued Cherevin, "since the name of Petrunkevich is almost synonymous with the word 'revolutionary,' you can imagine how Polovtsov greeted the proposal."

On another occasion, Cherevin, somewhat under the influence of drink, stopped by at our place to tell us about his conversation with Prince N. S. Dolgorukii* over lunch at the Yacht Club. The prince, he told us, was after him to ask Empress Marie Fedorovna to help him be named minister to Denmark. (The post was a stepping stone for diplomatic advancement because Denmark is the Empress's homeland and she and the Emperor took a good deal of interest in those who served in that post.)

Some time later I asked Cherevin if he had passed on Dolgorukii's request. He had, and the Empress had asked how Dolgorukii could hope to be appointed to a post that was already filled. Simply, replied Cherevin to the Empress: if Dolgorukii were told that he could have the post when it became vacant, he would go immediately to Denmark and poison the incumbent. When I asked Cherevin if he had told Dolgorukii what he had told the Empress, he said that he had, advising the prince that if he wanted the post he should go to Denmark and do away with the minister.

*He lost his post as minister to Persia because the Emperor rightly considered him two-faced and took a dim view of him. Prince Dolgorukii is now our ambassador to Rome.

Other Persons at Court Close
to Emperor Alexander III

When the Emperor ascended the throne, the marshal of the court was Colonel Vladimir Obolenskii, who was close to the Emperor. When he died, his loss was strongly felt by the Emperor, others in the Imperial family, and in the court.* The place of his death was almost a premonitory sign: he died in the very room at Yalta where Emperor Alexander III was to die. He was replaced by General Goleni- shchev-Kutuzov.

The general, a fine man who had previously served as military attaché in Berlin, was probably offered the post of marshal of the court because his sisters had served as ladies-in-waiting to the Empress Marie Fedorovna. The general did not have long to live. When he died, he was replaced by a comparatively younger man, Count P. K. Benckendorff.

Count Beckendorff held the rank of captain then. Now he is a general-adjutant and is still marshal of the court. He is an ardent Catholic, but he is, nonetheless, a decent man.

I mention his Catholicism because nowadays, given the ultra-Orthodox ten- dency at court, it seems very strange that the marshal of the court should be a Catholic and the minister of the court, Baron Freedericksz, also a very fine man, should be a Lutheran.

It is odd to see these two, men who hold such high positions at court, standing like statues at divine services, while everyone else is crossing himself. Although this does not hurt their positions, their behavior is completely out of keeping with the superficial ultra-Orthodox tendencies that have crept into high places since the revolutionary unrest of 1905.

Count Benckendorff married the sister of Prince Alexander Dolgorukii . . . a woman much older than he.[3] She has a good head, but her past is such that it is almost impossible to believe that she should be close to the throne, as she is these days. I recall that during the coronation of Emperor Nicholas II, about the time of the marriage, Vorontsov-Dashkov, then minister of court, protested against their living in the Winter Palace, because of her reputation. Now she is one of the first ladies of the court. . . .

Her brother, Prince Alexander (Sandi) Dolgorukii, is a clever man with a practical turn of mind, the kind of mind found especially at court. He is always involved in business operations, in clever deals, in which his name, his ties, his special position at court enable him to dispense favors that appeal to the egos of vain people.

He dispenses these favors carefully, to people who are in a position to repay him

---

*When the Emperor was Tsesarevich, General V. V. Zinovev, a well-bred man of the world, served as his marshal of the court. When the Tsesarevich became Emperor, Zinovev continued to manage the business of the court but without having the title. General Zinovev, who died early in the reign, was close to the Emperor.

by engineering such favors as arranging to have a feeder line run near his estate or arranging for the Peasants' Bank to buy land from him on terms favorable for him. In short, he belongs to the type that depends on the kind of connections that are so peculiar to the Russian court and uses these connections for operations that do not go too evidently beyond proper bounds.

While I was minister he was constantly playing up to me to help him with an appointment to the State Council. In those days an appointment depended primarily on Grand Duke Michael Nikolaevich, or those close to him, men like Dmitrii Martynovich Solskii, with whom I was on good terms. After I had made several requests to Solskii, he received the appointment, which he still holds.

Dolgorukii's power has been derived chiefly from the fact that, first as a chief master of ceremonies, now as honorary chief marshal, of the court, he has been, so to speak, an indispensable fixture at all major events at court. He is everywhere at such events, but always visible to the Emperor, moving around him like a tiny satellite around a great, radiant sun.

I recall an Imperial procession at the Winter Palace when I was new to Petersburg court life and knew only a few of its types. As Emperor Alexander III and his retinue were passing through the room where I was present, Count Vorontsov-Dashkov, referring to Dolgorukii, who was part of the retinue, said to me: "Look at Sandi, standing there like a pointer." And indeed Dolgorukii looked like a pointer, standing close to the Emperor, on the alert to perform any service the Sovereign might require, for example, picking up a dropped handkerchief. Whenever I see Dolgorukii, and the last time I saw him was a few days ago, at Tsarskoe Selo, I cannot help but smile and recall Count Vorontsov-Dashkov's words.

The Character, Customs, and Mode of Life of Emperor Alexander III

As I have said, the Emperor preferred to live simply. For that reason he preferred the Anichkov Palace (where he had resided as Tsesarevich) to the Winter Palace when in residence in Petersburg. He put up with the splendors of the court only because it was required of him.

The Emperor was not afraid of death, but he was afraid of horses and for that reason it was difficult to provide him horses on which he would feel at ease. (Empress Marie Fedorovna had no fear of horses and was a good rider.) The Emperor's difficulty with horses grew in the last years of his reign as he put on weight. I recall that a year or so before the Emperor's death, Baron Freedericksz, who was then in charge of the court stables, complained how difficult it was to find a suitable horse for the Emperor and how difficult it was to persuade him to mount a new horse.

Visit of the Emir of Bukhara

There were a few visits by heads of state during the reign. One such visitor was the Emir of Bukhara, who died a year ago. When he visited our country he was accompanied by Dr. Pisarenko, his personal physician. Pisarenko, who had been the doctor of my brother Alexander's unit, had somehow gotten to Bukhara and became the Emir's personal physician. I knew the Emir, having been presented to him, together with Vyshnegradskii, on our visit to Central Asia.

Visit of the Shah of Persia

Another royal visitor was Nasir un-Din, Shah of Persia. In Asiatic countries only a person with a harsh, strong, and well-defined character can maintain order. Shah Nasir un-Din was such a man.* His two successors were not and for that reason chaos and disorder have been the rule since his death [in 1879], leading to the total anarchy in which Persia finds herself.

Shah Nasir un-Din may have been an outstanding ruler, but his table manners were poor. For example, he would use his fingers to help himself from a serving plate. And when asparagus was being served, instead of putting some asparagus on his plate, he cut the stems of the asparagus on the serving plate and placed them on his plate. Also, once when he was sitting next to the Empress Marie Fedorovna, as a result of some remark that I did not hear, he reached over to her plate with his fork, took something from it, and put it in his mouth.

The Visit of Prince Nicholas of Montenegro

Of all the visits of crowned heads to St. Petersburg during the reign of Emperor Alexander III, that of Prince Nicholas of Montenegro made the greatest sensation. It made a sensation because at a dinner the Emperor offered a toast to "my only friend the Prince of Montenegro." It was generally assumed that by this toast the Emperor meant that he esteemed Prince Nicholas more than he did any other ruler. The toast buoyed up the prince but threw other European rulers into a state of bewilderment.

I believe that the toast did not have the meaning ascribed to it. I believe that the Emperor offered it deliberately to show that Russia needed no political friend-

*When Shah Nasir un-Din died and his sickly son, Muzzafar un-Din, ascended the throne, Emperor Nicholas II sent General Kuropatkin, then governor of the Trans-Caspian region, to congratulate the new shah.

After performing this duty, Kuropatkin returned directly to Petersburg and presented a memorandum about Persia to the Emperor. This memorandum is of historic interest because it is evident from it that in those days it was perfectly natural for us to look at Persia as totally under our influence and protection, a country with which we could do anything we thought useful for us. If we compare our position vis-à-vis Persia now with our position then, we cannot help but be astonished at the metamorphosis that has taken place in less than fifteen years. And this change, too, is the result of the unfortunate war with Japan which has weakened us everywhere and diminished our prestige.[4]

ships, that Russia was powerful enough to influence world politics alone and that those who wanted an influence in world politics should desire to seek the friendship of Russia and of her ruler, Emperor Alexander III. Therefore the toast should be interpreted to mean: I have but one friend, one political friend that is, the Prince of Montenegro, ruler of a country that is smaller than a small district in one of Russia's provinces.

Perhaps the Emperor had in mind some measure of praise for Prince Nicholas as a person, but if he had at the time, I do not believe that he still would have praised him subsequently, for there is no question that Prince Nicholas is an opportunist who is friendly toward those who can benefit him, be it Austria-Hungary or Russia. And when it seemed in his interest to appear to be ultra-Orthodox, he would condemn Catholicism for its errors, but when the heir to the Italian throne wanted to marry one of his daughters, he gladly agreed, accepting his daughter's conversion to Catholicism without any qualms.

Whenever he came to Russia, it was with a scheme to put a few hundred thousand rubles into his pocket, pretending that the money he asked for was for military purposes, to permit his country to help Russia in the event of war in the Balkans. But the money would go into his pockets, as I can attest from my experience as minister of finance; I believe that the relevant documents will be found in the Ministry of Foreign Affairs.

On the whole, Prince Nicholas of Montenegro has earned remarkably little confidence, but he has persuaded himself that he has been able to mislead people into believing that he is loyal to Slavdom, Russia, and Orthodoxy. His loyalty, in fact, is for the most part to money.

Grand Duchess Catherine Mikhailovna

Grand Duchess Catherine Mikhailovna,[5] who died [in 1894],* improperly bequeathed the Mikhailovskii Palace, in which she and her father before her had resided, to her sons. I say "improperly" because although she had resided in the palace, it was not her property but that of the Imperial family. Yet Pobedonostsev, a friend of her family, had prepared a will treating it as if it were her property. When she was on her death bed, the Emperor went to see her, at her request, and had witnessed the will without reading it, because it had been prepared by Pobedonostsev: he trusted Pobedonostsev, who, after all, was a jurist and a professor of civil law.

When the Emperor learned, after her death, what was in the will, he was annoyed with Pobedonostsev for letting him down, yet having witnessed the will he would not contest it. Nonetheless, he wanted the palace to remain in the hands of the Imperial family and therefore authorized me to negotiate for its purchase,

*Although Emperor Alexander III was a pious man, he could be stern with the higher clergy. I recall that at the funeral of the Grand Duchess he became upset at the dirty clothing worn by members of the choir and scolded the aged Metropolitan Palladius for their attire. The poor old man was quite shaken by the scolding.

adding that if no member of the Imperial family wanted to live in it, it should house an educational institute to be named after his daughter Xenia Aleksandrovna. Unfortunately, the Emperor died before the transaction could be undertaken.

But Emperor Alexander III's wish remained on my mind, and shortly after Emperor Nicholas II came to the throne, I told him of his father's desire to purchase the palace and was authorized to take care of the matter. As I recall, the sons of the Grand Duchess Catherine Mikhailovna were paid 4 million rubles. After they had vacated the palace it turned out that they had taken with them all the expensive doors, fireplaces, and decorations of the palace, although such items were not considered part of the removable furnishings.

When the Emperor asked what I thought should be done with the palace, I suggested that he use it as his Petersburg residence since his mother was residing in the Anichkov Palace, in which he had lived while Tsesarevich. I suggested that the palace would be a suitable residence, also that its park, when restored, would provide him with an excellent place to take the air.

But the Emperor had other plans. He told me that he preferred to make the Winter Palace his Petersburg residence. This prompted me to point out that the Winter Palace lacked a park in which his children could walk. Subsequently he had part of the Palace Square fenced off and turned into a park in which he could walk and his children could play, at least until we experienced revolutionary unrest. (By the way, fencing off part of the square led to some disagreement with the city government.)

There still remained the question of what to do with the Mikhailovskii Palace. When the Emperor asked me for a suggestion, I reminded him of his father's wish that it become the Xenia Institute. However, he preferred that the institute be located in the palace of the late Grand Duke Nicholas Nikolaevich (the elder), which his sons wanted to sell to pay off their debts. Fearful that the palace might be sold to private persons and be turned into a theater or a *café-chantant*, he authorized me to purchase the palace for the government. This I did and in March 1895 the palace became the Xenia Institute.

After this palace had been purchased, it occurred to me that in addition to erecting a statue to Emperor Alexander III,* the Mikhailovskii Palace might be turned into an additional monument to the late Emperor. When I suggested to Emperor Nicholas II that this be done, he agreed. The Mikhailovskii Palace now houses the Emperor Alexander III Museum, which will in time become a major art museum, a fitting memorial to the greatness of Emperor Alexander III.

*The statue, which stands on Znamenskaia Square, was first proposed by me after the Emperor's death, but it was not until 1909 that it was completed and unveiled.[6]

XXI

Last Days of Emperor Alexander III

Those who believe in omens can find one in an event that occurred at the Winter Palace on the last Easter Sunday before the Emperor's death. As usual on Easter Sunday there was an Imperial procession (*vykhod*) at the palace. Just as the Emperor and Empress left their quarters, to begin the procession, the electricity went off in most of the palace, forcing us to use candles and kerosene lamps for illumination.

The Emperor always looked anemic, but by this time it was evident that he was quite ill. Soon after Easter Sunday the famous Professor Zakharyn was summoned from Moscow to see the Emperor, then residing at Gatchina. After this visit it became known that the Emperor was suffering from nephritis. Not that one needs a doctor to diagnose this disease, from which my first wife suffered: it is a kidney disease, marked by extreme pallor and puffiness of the body. Many believed that the Emperor's kidney trouble could be traced back to his effort in supporting the dining car roof in the accident at Borki, about which I have written.

It was either late in July or early in August that the Emperor left Gatchina and, as I have noted, went first to Belovezh Forest, then on to Skierniewice, and from there to Yalta, where, as was his custom, he chose not to stay in the Imperial palace but in the small house next to it. The palace has since been razed to make way for a larger one, but the house has not been touched, and I hope that it will be preserved as a sacred historical shrine. Whenever I am in Yalta I visit this small house, where Emperor Alexander III spent his last days.

After the Emperor's departure from Gatchina, I went to Vichy, for my wife's sake. It was my first visit to that spa. After a few weeks there I returned to Russia. Since it is customary for a minister who returns from leave to ask permission to resume his duties, I telegraphed the Emperor from Verzhbolovo of my return asking for such permission. I received an immediate reply granting permission: this was the last word I was to receive from him. After his death I asked for the original of the telegram he sent me, first because I wanted it as a memento, second because I was interested to know if it had been written by him or by a member of his suite. My request was granted and I now have it in my archive: it was written by him, in a firm hand.

Emperor Alexander III, even more so than other members of his family, hated to admit that he was sick and tried if possible to keep from being treated. However, it was so evident that the Emperor was very sick when he arrived in Yalta that Dr. Leyden, the famous Berlin professor, was sent for. (The Emperor's personal physician, Veliaminov, to whom the Emperor was quite attached, was already in attendance.) Dr. Leyden later said that the Emperor had made a most gratifying impression on him, but that he obviously had no faith in medicine and was one of the most uncooperative patients he had ever treated. Professor Zakharyn had the same opinion of the Emperor as a patient.

As the Emperor's condition grew worse and he felt that death was near, he decided to have the Tsesarevich Nicholas marry his fiancée, Princess Alice of Darmstadt, as soon as possible. Accordingly he gave his son permission to bring her to Yalta. Although he had not taken an especially favorable view of the young lady before, the Emperor was now anxious, with that impatience characteristic of the sick, to see her. I am told that he was very happy to see her when she arrived. This was some ten days before his death.

As word of the Emperor's grave condition spread, the attention of all Europe was centered on Yalta. Newspapers everywhere, whatever their political persuasion, published dithyrambs to the Emperor; all acknowledged his great significance in world affairs and paid homage to his fine, noble, and honorable character. The entire world recognized that it had enjoyed peace during his reign only because of his great love of peace, a love expressed not in words—he did not prattle about peace or initiate international peace conferences[1]—but through action, by his firmness and his devotion to peace.

On October 19, because of alarming news from Yalta, prayers were offered at Kazan Cathedral for the Emperor's recovery, in which not only officials but also ordinary citizens, among them students, took part. Despite their prayers, the terrible news came the following day.

Emperor Alexander III died as he had lived, a true Christian, a devoted son of the Orthodox church, a simple, strong, honorable man. As he lay dying, he was less concerned with himself than with the fact that his death would disturb his beloved family, now clustered about him. He died peacefully. Immediately after his death, the oath of allegiance to the new Emperor, Nicholas II, was taken.

The body of the late Emperor was taken by funeral train to Moscow, where it lay in state in Uspenskii Cathedral, for a day, I believe. Then the body was taken to Petersburg, where high officials, I among them, met the train, at Nicholas Station. I was on the platform when the train arrived, and I remember the scene as if it were today.

Emperor Nicholas II, still a young man, left the train, followed by two blond women. Naturally, I was eager to see our future Empress, whom I had never seen before, and mistakenly thought that the prettier of the two was she. I was astonished when I was told that the prettier one was her aunt, Princess Alexandra, wife of Edward, Prince of Wales.* The young lady who turned out to be our future Empress seemed not only less good-looking, but also less sympathetic than her aunt. Of course, she too was pretty then, and still is, but her mouth always seems to be set in anger.

The streets outside the station and the sidewalks along the route which the funeral procession would follow to the Cathedral of SS. Peter and Paul were overflowing with people. And as the coffin was removed from the train, those of us in the funeral procession took our places in accordance with protocol, the ministers in pairs preceding the coffin. I was depressed and do not remember with whom I was paired, but I remember two minor incidents that occurred en route.

As we marched along Nevskii Prospekt I suddenly heard the command "Attention" and raised my head. I saw that it was a young officer who had given the command to his squadron, as the carriage bearing the coffin approached. This command was followed by "Eyes right, look lively."

The second command seemed so odd that I asked my partner who "that fool" was. It was Captain Trepov,[2] who was to play a remarkable role in my career and was to be the chief reason for my leaving the post of premier.

The other incident occurred while we were on Liteinii Bridge. I was astonished to see Ivan Nikolaevich Durnovo, our minister of interior, leave the procession and issue orders to the police about how the onlookers should behave. Of course, these orders dealt only with outward behavior. But no untoward action was expected from any quarter, not even from the extreme left,

---

*The Prince of Wales was with her.

Prince Edward led a rather profligate life—a round of heavy eating, drinking, card playing, et sim., which provided the press with a steady source of unfavorable news. But this kind of life gave him an opportunity of getting to know people, to come into contact with representatives of various professions—in short, to become acquainted with real life, not life as it appears to members of ruling families who are reared exclusively in the environment of the court. As a result he was to be an outstanding monarch, against all expectations. Unfortunately for England he did not reign long.

Following the death of Emperor Alexander III, the prince spent several months in Petersburg. As we know, he was the uncle of our present Empress and as a result was quite intimate in his manner toward her. Once, at lunch, he suddenly turned toward her and said quite undiplomatically: "Your husband's profile is quite similar to that of Emperor Paul," a remark that both the Emperor and the Empress found quite displeasing. I heard of this from someone close to Prince Edward, who in telling of the episode admitted that he had committed a "gaffe."

During his stay in Petersburg, Prince Edward showed sincere familial friendliness toward the Dowager Empress and the Emperor.

for everyone was deeply shocked by the death of the Emperor.

Speaking of Durnovo, I recall that when I received the news of the death of Emperor Alexander III, I called on him to discuss a number of questions. We were both attached to our late Sovereign and were naturally depressed. Suddenly Ivan Nikolaevich asked me what I thought of our new Sovereign. I replied candidly, saying that from what little I knew of him he seemed well bred, well intentioned and likable, and would be a worthy successor to his father, but that he had not sufficient experience to be prepared for the role that fate had thrust on him. Ivan Nikolaevich looked at me slyly and said: ''Well, it appears that you do not know the young Emperor well. I think that I know him better than you do: you will see how much misfortune we will experience during his reign.'' I did not see the point of the remark at the time. And since I considered Ivan Nikolaevich a very limited man, I ascribed this remark to his limitations.[3]

It was about this time that I visited Constantine Petrovich Pobedonostsev. He, too, was upset over the Emperor's death. He liked the new Emperor, whose teacher he had been, but he was uncertain about him. Above all he feared that because of his youth and inexperience Emperor Nicholas II would be susceptible to harmful influences. I chose not to prolong the conversation.

The body of the deceased Emperor lay in state at the Cathedral of SS. Peter and Paul. I stood watch beside the body several times, once for a whole night, as throngs came to pay homage to their departed ruler.

Then came the lengthy burial service, which the Dowager Empress Marie Fedorovna bore stoically, except at the end of the Metropolitan's lengthy eulogy, when her nerves snapped for a moment and she cried hysterically: ''Enough, enough, enough.''

A few days later I called on her. She had been rather pleasant toward me during the first years of her late husband's reign, but after my marriage her manner toward me had become frigid. This time, however, she received me very kindly and said, among other things: ''I think that you are very distressed by the death of the Emperor. He liked you very much.''

My subsequent recollections will deal with the reign of Emperor Nicholas II.

XXII

A New Reign Begins

The New Emperor

Undoubtedly, the new Emperor had loved his father very much and was consequently very grieved by his death; but, in addition, he was distressed at the thought of his new responsibilities, for which he was totally unprepared. Moreover, he was very much in love with his bride-to-be. Thus, he was subject to various and strong impressions.

On November 2, the new Emperor received all the members of the State Council, and its chairman, at the Anichkov Palace, where he was then in residence. Since ministers were *ex officio* members of the State Council, we, too, were present. The Emperor, who appeared very agitated, uttered a few deeply felt words in memory of his father. On the whole he was very cordial to all present.

I noted that among those present was Alexander Ageevich Abaza, about whom I have spoken earlier. Although he was a member of the State Council, he had been living on his estate or in Monte Carlo ever since the exposure of his financial speculations. I was not amazed at the fact of his presence, for it was quite natural for him to come to Petersburg on the occasion of the death of Emperor Alexander III and the accession of the new Emperor, but I was amazed to see Emperor Nicholas treat him with exceptional kindness and gentleness. I guessed immediately that Polovtsov, the [former] Imperial secretary, a close friend of Abaza's (as was Grand Duke Michael Nikolaevich), was trying to rehabilitate Abaza and place him in the favor of the new Emperor.

As I have said earlier, I had virtually nothing against Abaza and I had a high opinion of his abilities, but I feared that he could be rehabilitated only if the charges made against him during the reign of Emperor Alexander III were now to be considered unfounded. And what I did not want was a repetition of the time when the entire State Council accused me of slandering Abaza and it had been necessary to form an investigative commission under Bunge, which had found the charges to be completely true.

Consequently, at one of my first reports to Emperor Nicholas II, I briefly told him the whole story of why A. A. Abaza had lost the confidence of Emperor Alexander III and had gone abroad. And, since Bunge was still alive, I asked the Emperor to get the full details from him if he had any doubts about what I said.

A few days later the Emperor received his generals-adjutant and his aides-de-camp. Then he received deputations from foreign powers that had come to Petersburg for the funeral. Among those he received was General Boisdeffre, the very one who had concluded the military convention with General Obruchev which established our alliance with France.[1]

On November 14, the marriage of Emperor Nicholas II and the Darmstadt Princess, who was given the name of Alexandra Fedorovna, took place, in the Winter Palace. Ministers, members of the State Council, the highest officials of the court, and representatives of the armed forces were among the guests. Because full mourning was still in effect, the wedding was a very simple affair.

After the wedding the Emperor and his bride went to Tsarskoe Selo, which has ever since served as his chief residence. Before his marriage, he resided at the Anichkov Palace when in Petersburg, but after it he chose the Winter Palace for his Petersburg residence, at least until the ill-starred war with Japan. Since then he has rarely stayed at the Winter Palace and has resided chiefly at Tsarskoe Selo. He spends his summers at Peterhof or Livadia, except when he goes abroad, and most of his foreign trips were made in the early years of his reign.

The Emperor was especially attentive to the Empress when she was expecting their first child. They were in residence then at Peterhof, in the new summer residence built for the Emperor while he was the Tsesarevich. I often saw the Emperor pushing the Empress in a wheelchair from their residence to the nearby residence of the Dowager Empress. The first child of the Emperor and Empress, Grand Duchess Olga Nikolaevna, was born on November 3, 1895.

Influences on the New Emperor

[I quickly learned that the young Emperor, unlike his father, would permit members of his family to influence his decisions. Take the case of the decision to build a naval base in Libau.]

At my first report to the new Emperor, shortly after his father's death (and, as always, on Friday), I was received with great kindness. He knew that his father had been favorably disposed toward me. Moreover, he was grateful to me for having spoken up at the Siberian Railroad Committee, of which he was chairman.

He asked to see the report I had written concerning my trip to the Murmansk coast. When I told him that his father had not returned the report to me, he said that his father had read (or shown) him the report while they were at Belovezh and that his father had written some comments on it. I said again that the report had not been returned to me. The Emperor was very astonished at this and said that he would search for it.

The following Friday the Emperor told me that he had found the report and wished to issue a decree immediately to implement the chief recommendation of the report, that a major naval base be constructed at Ekaterinskaia harbor, on the Murmansk coast, and linked to Petersburg by rail. Also, he proposed canceling plans for constructing a base at Libau, which could be blockaded in time of war.

Although I favored such a decree, I advised His Majesty to hold off issuing it, for to do so so soon after his father's death might offend his uncle, Grand Duke Alexis Aleksandrovich, who favored the Libau site. I knew that the Grand Duke, being the only bachelor among Emperor Alexander's brothers, had always been close to Empress Marie Fedorovna; now that she was a widow, she would be even more attached to him. I was afraid that if the decree were issued then, it might lead to a division in the Imperial family, something that obviously should be avoided. Furthermore, it would be said that the Emperor, having just ascended the throne and therefore unacquainted with the matter, was acting under some kind of [outside] influence. The Emperor replied that there could be no allegation of influence since his father's comments were on the report, but he agreed to wait a bit before issuing the decree.

Two or three months later I was astonished to see a decree in *Pravitelstvennyi vestnik* according to which the base would be established in Libau and named after Emperor Alexander III, in recognition of the fact that the site had been chosen by the late Emperor. I was, of course, amazed, knowing what the late Emperor's wish had been, as the personal archives of Emperor Nicholas II would most likely show.

Several days later Kazi, who was very close to Grand Duke Constantine Konstantinovich, told me that the grand dukes were misusing their influence over the young Emperor, who, so to speak, had not yet found himself. He said that after issuing the decree, the Emperor had gone to Grand Duke Constantine Konstantinovich and, with tears in his eyes, complained over the fact that Grand Duke Alexis Aleksandrovich[2] had forced him into issuing the decree by threatening to give up his position as general-admiral if Libau were not chosen.

As I have said earlier, Grand Duke Alexis Aleksandrovich was under the influence of Chikhachev. So, in view of what Kazi told me about the circumstances of the young Emperor's decision and knowing something of his character, I thought to myself that he would not forget this episode and that in the end Chikhachev would have to pay for it. In fact, little more than a year later the Emperor insisted on Chikhachev's removal from his post. (Chikhachev's successor, Admiral Tyrtov, was a fine, intelligent man, but below average in ability; under him the ministry functioned as badly as it had under Chikhachev. Tyrtov's successor, Avelan, was no improvement.)

Because the decision to construct the base at Libau had unfortunate consequences, I came to regret having dissuaded the Emperor from immediately issuing the decree for a base at Eketerinskaia harbor, which, by the way, had been recommended by Kazi. I was to become convinced from subsequent experience that sometimes, especially when dealing with wavering personalities, it is important to seize the moment, for if you lose it there may not be another opportunity.

I say that the decision had "unfortunate consequences" because, if we had used Ekaterinskaia harbor, we undoubtedly would not have sought an ice-free port with access to the open sea in the Far East, we would not have taken the ill-starred step of seizing Port Arthur, an act that would lead us step by step on the road to Tsushima.

Having ascended the throne so unexpectedly, the young Emperor was quite understandably not ready for it and found himself under all kinds of influences. During the first year of his reign it was his mother, the Dowager Empress, who exercised the dominating influence on him, but her influence did not endure long. At the same time three of his uncles, Grand Dukes Vladimir Aleksandrovich, Alexis Aleksandrovich, and Sergei Aleksandrovich, who occupied fairly important posts, exercised considerable influence and continued to do so for many years. They were all first-rate man and quite suitable as grand dukes. Grand Duke Vladimir Aleksandrovich, in particular, was a highly cultivated and educated man. They are all dead now, and some younger grand dukes have come to influence the Emperor, although to a lesser degree because by now the Emperor is convinced, and not without some justification, that he is far more experienced and knows more than the many members of the Imperial family who surround him, since he has reigned for many years, has experienced much in his life, has seen much, and therefore has acquired training in administration that no other member of his family now has.

Even with respect to the abler grand dukes, one can only regret that generally grand dukes played the roles they did only because they were *grand dukes*, when in fact they did not have the knowledge, the ability, or the education for these roles. For the most part, their influence on the Emperor has been quite unfortunate.

By the way, the recent assassination of Premier Stolypin,[3] the effects of which are still being felt, might not have taken place if the ill-fated brothers Grand Dukes Alexander Mikhailovich and Nicholas Mikhailovich had not interfered in matters that did not concern them. When Stolypin threatened to leave his post over the dispute concerning introduction of zemstvos in the western provinces, it was they who persuaded the Emperor to retain Stolypin by following his recommendations. Had these Grand Dukes not intervened, the Emperor would quietly have told Stolypin that if he felt he must leave, he should do so. And I feel that if Stolypin had left the government he might still be alive today, because those who considered him a menace, to be removed by force, would not have considered him a source of harm once he was out of office.

We must remember that Emperor Alexander III kept the grand dukes on a tight rein. He respected them, but he did not permit them to interfere in matters that did not concern them; moreover, they were under his complete authority even in their respective spheres of jurisdiction. The grand dukes loved him, but at the same time they feared him.[4]

With the accession of Emperor Nicholas II all this changed, something that is quite naturally explained by the differences in age and experience between them and the young Emperor, who respected his elders in the family, as well as by his weak character. This fact was one of the causes of the many unfortunate events and, I will go so far as to say, the disaster of the reign of Emperor Nicholas II, particularly of the first years of his reign, when, so to speak, he had not fully matured.[5]

War minister Vannovskii told me that early in the reign, when he noticed that the grand dukes were gaining influence in matters, particularly military ones, outside their province, he once said to Emperor Nicholas II: "Your Majesty, do not reintroduce the appanage system, which your late father destroyed."*

When the Emperor asked what appanage system he was referring to, Vannovskii replied: "An appanage system like the one that prevailed in ancient Rus, when each grand duke was sovereign, when Russia had not yet become the unified Muscovite tsardom." The Emperor, according to Vannovskii, smiled at this and said: "Peter Semenovich, I, too, will clip their wings."

Unfortunately, this was not done energetically, and several grand dukes continue to exercise an unfortunate influence on the Emperor. Among these are his brother-in-law Grand Duke Alexander Mikhailovich, whose influence has been the most unfortunate of all. I venture to suggest that if not for this Grand Duke we might not have experienced all the misfortunes in the Far East that proved to be our lot.

When Emperor Nicholas II ascended the throne, he had, if one may put it this way, an aura of resplendent good will. He truly desired happiness and a peaceful life for Russia, for all his subjects, whatever nationality they might belong to. There is no question that he has a thoroughly good, kind heart. If he displayed other characteristics in later years it is because he experienced many tribulations. Perhaps he brought on some of these tribulations by placing his faith in unsuitable people, but he acted as he did in the belief that he was doing the right thing. In any case he is kind and remarkably well bred. I may say that in all my life I have never known a person of better breeding than our Emperor Nicholas II.

*A modified form of the appanage system had reappeared under Emperor Alexander II, when grand dukes had once more begun to interfere in matters that did not concern them, but this had been brought to an end by Emperor Alexander III.

XXIII

The New Emperor's First
Personnel Changes, 1894–1895

Governor-Generalship of
the Kingdom of Poland

On December 13 [1894], General Iosif Vladimirovich Gurko was unexpectedly replaced by Count Paul Andreevich Shuvalov as governor-general of the Kingdom of Poland. As will be seen, General Gurko's departure from office was typical of him; it also revealed something of the new Emperor's character.

General Gurko was an outstanding soldier, both in time of peace and in time of war. As we know, there were many outstanding commanders in the last Turkish war—Totleben, Skobelev, Mirskii, Loris-Melikov, Dragomirov, and Gurko—but Gurko stood out among them for the manner in which he conducted a very skillful, very difficult, and very dangerous cavalry campaign in the Balkans. After the war he was appointed temporary governor-general of Odessa and later was named to succeed Count Kotzebue as governor-general of the Kingdom of Poland.

He was the most outstanding governor-general seen in Warsaw in the last three decades. For one thing, he held the Russian banner high.[1] For another, he brilliantly maintained the prestige of our forces there. He took a great interest in the forces under his command and enjoyed tremendous prestige among them. That is necessary for anyone who commands, be he civilian or military.

It is remarkable that although he executed the Russian policy in the Kingdom of Poland and, sometimes, did so with a heavy hand, he was, nonetheless, respected by the Poles because he was firm, straightforward, and honorable. Poles would say: "We know that Gurko is an enemy of the Polish cause, but we respect him because he is a straightforward and honorable man whose word we can trust."

Gurko had one weakness—his wife, who exerted some influence on him.

Unlike him she often behaved improperly by being involved in shady deals.

They had three sons. The first is very intelligent, like his father, but takes after his mother with respect to probity.[2] When he was assistant minister, his career came to an end because of the nasty Lidval affair. Now he is being rehabilitated, to a degree, as is shown by the fact that he was appointed gentleman of the chamber a year ago by the Emperor.

The second son is a general who, by the way, is the author of the official history of the Russo–Japanese War. I have no personal knowledge of him, but I know of two black marks against him. First is the fact that a few months ago he married Countess Komarovskaia, a widow much older than he, a woman of questionable reputation. Second is the strange kind of courage he showed toward the third of the brothers.

This brother was a sailor who, as is well known, was afflicted with kleptomania and came to a terrible end. In Monte Carlo he sneaked into the hotel room of Alexander Aleksandrovich Polovtsov and stole a large sum of money from him, nearly strangling him in the process. He was caught and placed in a Parisian jail. His brother, the general, then visited him and persuaded him to take poison, from which he died.

Returning to Governor-General Gurko. He wanted his eldest son [Vladimir] to be appointed director of his chancellery. But the son even then had an unsavory reputation in financial matters: therefore the then minister of interior, Ivan Nikolaevich Durnovo, would not agree to the appointment. Governor-General Gurko then went to Petersburg, saw the young Emperor, and presented him with something of an ultimatum—in essence, either name my son director or I will leave my post. The Emperor chose the latter. Thus, this distinguished military and political figure left the scene. He settled down on his estate in the province of Tver and thereafter played no role in government.

The Emperor agreed to the departure of Gurko for two reasons. First, because Gurko put the matter in so harsh a manner. Second, it was in the nature of His Majesty to dislike persons who were firm in their opinions, their words, and their actions. The removal of Gurko was the first manifestation of this side of the character of His Majesty.

I do not justify Gurko. I believe that those who put things as harshly or firmly as Gurko did are somewhat to blame for what follows because they do not take into account the Emperor's nature and forget that, after all, they are dealing with His Majesty. I, too, have been guilty of the same offense. But there is some excuse for acting as Gurko did on the part of those who served Emperor Alexander III before serving Emperor Nicholas II. Emperor Alexander III never paid any attention to the use of harsh words in the expression of opinions; in fact, he greatly valued those who had strong opinions. In short, the character of Emperor Alexander III was completely different from that of Emperor

Nicholas II, and this each of his subjects, I among them, should keep in mind.

Count Shuvalov, whom I have mentioned earlier, was a member of Petersburg high society. His first wife was Princess Beloselskaia-Belozerskaia, who bore him several daughters and a son, Paul Pavlovich Shuvalov.* Following her death, he married Komarova, a very fine and beautiful woman, who is now mistress of the court to Grand Duchess Marie Pavlovna.

He had had no previous diplomatic experience before his appointment as ambassador to Berlin. He had been named to the post because he was a man of the world, very adroit, also very much the soldier, with a St. George around the neck, which he had won in the last Turkish war. He was a *persona gratissima* with Emperor William II, first of all because he was a very interesting and amusing man, secondly because he kept the embassy in brilliant order, and thirdly because he was a military man who liked everything military and got along well with the military circles in Berlin. But he had one weakness: he liked to drink heavily at festive military dinners, both with Russians and with Germans.

After many years as ambassador he began to weary of his post and sought a position of comparable importance in Russia. Thus, when General Gurko unexpectedly left his post, it was offered to Count Shuvalov, who gladly accepted it. He was not to distinguish himself as governor-general, in any way, good or bad. But he would be personally liked, particularly among the officers, with whom he enjoyed wining and dining.

Ministers of Ways and Communications

Four days after the appointment of Shuvalov came the dismissal of Krivoshein from the post of minister of ways and communications. I had been partially responsible for Krivoshein's appointment to succeed me as minister of ways and communications [in 1892]. Had I spoken very unfavorably of Krivoshein to Emperor Alexander III, he certainly would not have been appointed. But, as often happens, and I have experienced this many times in my career, those persons who obtained positions, quite often eminent ones, thanks to my schooling, my training, my support, then gradually sever their relations with me and, when the moment seems ripe, even become my enemies, seeking to demonstrate their independence of me by their nasty actions against me. There are, of course, exceptions, but Krivoshein was not one of them.[3]

When he became minister of ways and communications, he sought by every means to dissociate himself from me. But since he did not know railroading and was of no significance in government, he, or rather his ministry, came under the

---

*Paul Pavlovich Shuvalov was killed in 1904 by anarchists and revolutionaries while serving as prefect of Moscow. Even anarchists and revolutionaries recognized this as a senseless killing.

Before this he had been prefect of Odessa, an appointment that he owed in part to my recommendation. He earned an excellent reputation in that city.

influence of my ministry. In fact, he did not pay much attention to his work, leaving it, for the most part, to his subordinates, who knew the work of the ministry and knew railroading.

Krivoshein was marked by a weakness that I have noted in many of my fellow ministers, namely, that as soon as he became minister he began to live on a grand scale, e.g., spending government money on his official residence. Thus, although the residence of the minister of ways and communications was already palatial, he turned the quarters of the assistant minister into a household church, at government expense, of course.

His dismissal came as a result of using his position for personal profit. According to the then State Controller Filippov, and I have not verified it, Krivoshein sold railroad ties from his estates to the railroads at very high prices; also he arranged, through the Committee of Ministers, for the construction of a short railroad line that ran through all of his estates. It seems that the last is true. On the whole Krivoshein was a sharp dealer who was constantly engaged in such operations as selling and buying estates. He had no fortune to begin with, but was quite rich even before he became minister and continued his operations even while minister.

Filippov, who was probably not on good terms with Krivoshein, presented an obviously unfavorable report about Krivoshein's operations to the Emperor. I dare say that Filippov exaggerated the facts tenfold, but even the unvarnished facts would have shown Krivoshein to be a person unfit to be minister.

Thus, less than two months after ascending the throne, the Emperor had to come face to face with improper behavior by a minister. This, naturally, could not help but disturb the young and honorable Emperor, who had not yet had the occasion to witness and become accustomed to human corruption. Therefore, he dismissed Krivoshein. This action gave others of Krivoshein's type something to think about.

I had nothing to do with Krivoshein's dismissal and thus was taken by surprise when I read about it in *Pravitelstvennyi vestnik*. A few days later when I entered the Emperor's study, at Gatchina, to give my regular report, he asked me to listen to a decree naming Kazi as minister of ways and communications. This amazed me, for I knew that Kazi had never dealt with railroads.

It was clear to me that Kazi was being pushed forward for the post by that arch-intriguer Grand Duke Alexander Mikhailovich. The Grand Duke, one can say, had begun to dream of replacing Grand Duke Alexis Aleksandrovich as general-admiral as soon as Emperor Nicholas II had ascended the throne. Kazi, who shared the Grand Duke's view about the naval ministry (and being of Greek origin was no stranger to intrigue), was obviously to be used by Grand Duke Alexander Mikhailovich as part of his campaign against Grand Duke Alexis Aleksandrovich and the whole naval administration.

But, as is clear from what has been said earlier, the Emperor lacked the strength

218   VOLUME I ■ 1849-1903

of will to shake up the administration of the naval ministry if this entailed the sacrifice of Grand Duke Alexis Aleksandrovich. In this case the Emperor's weakness was to the good, for if the Emperor had replaced Grand Duke Alexis Aleksandrovich, who, whatever his faults, was a decent and honorable man, with Grand Duke Alexander Mikhailovich, who is neither, the naval ministry would have been turned into a hotbed of intrigue.

I told the Emperor that, as he knew, I held a high opinion of Kazi, was in sympathy with him, and was on the best of terms with him. Nonetheless, I believed it was out of the question to appoint him because he knew nothing of the work of the ministry and would be like Krivoshein, who, as my successor in the ministry, had quite disrupted its work. I told the Emperor that if Kazi were minister of ways and communications he would busy himself with matters that did not concern him, particularly naval ones. I said that if it were a question of giving Kazi a ministerial post, why not directly appoint him director of the Ministry of the Navy. In the naval ministry he would, at least, be dealing with matters he understood. So, I earnestly advised the Emperor not to make the appointment.

Although my opposition obviously did not please the Emperor, he nonetheless asked whom I would suggest. I proposed Anatolii Pavlovich Ivashchenkov, my assistant minister, and previously my assistant minister in the Ministry of Ways and Communications.[4] He said that he would think about it.[5] When I gave my next report His Majesty told me that after having thought the matter over he came to the conclusion that he should not be appointed. In the first place, if he were, everyone would say that as minister of ways and communications Ivashchenkov was simply acting under my influence. Moreover, Ivashchenkov did not please him.* Therefore, he said he was returning to the idea of giving the post to Kazi. After I had tried hard to change his mind, the Emperor asked whom I would suggest. It suddenly occurred to me that Prince Khilkov would do and I suggested him. When the Emperor said that he knew nothing about the man, I suggested that he ask his mother about him and added that if he would tell her that I was recommending Khilkov, she would "emphatically support me."†He said that he would ask her.

I then returned to the Ministry, about 12:30. By three that afternoon, Khilkov

*Ivashchenkov subsequently [1897] left me, to become assistant state controller, partly because he preferred the work of state control, with which he was familiar, and partly because he hoped to succeed Filippov as state controller, as he had every right to expect. But when Filippov died, he was succeeded by General Lobko, who had been one of the Emperor's instructors when he was still Heir; also Lobko was recommended by General Vannovskii, the war minister. As a result, Ivashchenkov became a member of the State Council, where he enjoyed universal respect because of his well-balanced character, his modesty, and his great knowledge of government finance and state control. He is no longer among the living.

†Empress Marie Fedorovna had first become acquainted with Khilkov during the war with Turkey, when he was in charge of a hospital train under her patronage. She liked him and permitted him to call on her after the war. And he continued to see her from time to time. She was favorably disposed toward him, and as much as she opposed the appointment of Ivashchenkov, so much was she in favor of the appointment of Khilkov. That explains why it was to take so little time between my suggesting him and the Emperor's offering him the post.

came to see me and told me that he had seen the Emperor, who, out of the blue, had offered him the position of minister of ways and communications. He said that he had told the Emperor that he was afraid to accept without knowing my attitude toward him, because I, as minister of finance, was able to exert considerable influence on the Ministry of Ways and Communications and also because I, having earlier been minister of ways and communications, had considerable authority in all matters relating to railroads. Khilkov told me that the Emperor had then said to him: "Oh, but Sergei Iulevich was the first to recommend you; see him and talk it over." That is why Khilkov came to see me.

Khilkov was very flustered because the offer had been so unexpected and he wanted to know if the Emperor really believed that he could be useful as minister. I reassured him on this score.

Needless to say, Khilkov took the post and served in it until October 17, 1905. When I became premier I asked him to give up his position, a matter about which I will speak later. Now I want to explain why I recommended him.

Khilkov was a remarkable man. He belonged to the highest aristocracy. His mother had been close to Empress Alexandra Fedorovna during the reign of Nicholas I. He had been an officer in the Semenovskii Guards. During the liberal period following emancipation he had chosen to distribute most of his land to his peasants and, being of a liberal frame of mind, had left for America, virtually penniless, to work on the railroads.

He began as a common laborer, then became a machinist's helper, then a machinist. When railroad construction began to accelerate in Russia he returned home, to work on the Russian railroads. He was chief of the locomotive depot of the Kursk–Kiev Railroad when I began to work for the Odessa Railroad. It was at that time that we became acquaintances and we maintained our acquaintance-ship. I tried to lure him to our railroad. At first he was willing, but then he changed his mind and went on to become the traffic chief on the Moscow–Riazan Railroad.*

When the war with Turkey broke out he went to Bulgaria, where he served on the military railroads and even, I believe, served for a time as head of the Bulgarian Ministry of Ways and Communications. Afterward, during the campaign in Central Asia against Khiva, he served under General Annenkov in constructing the railroad there. When I became minister of ways and communications, I persuaded him to accept a position as manager of the Orlovsko–Griazskaia line. When Krivoshein succeeded me, he appointed Khilkov senior inspector of the railroads, the position he was holding when I recommended his appointment as minister.

Khilkov was a fine man, extraordinarily well bred, with but one shortcoming— a weakness for the ladies, which cost him a few black marks on his record. He knew railroading exceptionally well, but as it turned out, he was not cut out for government service, proving to be more at home as a senior machinist than as a

*The chairman of the board was Derviz, whose widow (Mme. Dukmasova by her second marriage) was accused last year of having poisoned her husband.

minister. I didn't know this when I recommended him, although I had some premonition that this is the way it would turn out. However, at the time I felt that we were facing an emergency.

Minister of Foreign Affairs

Several months after the accession of Emperor Nicholas II, Giers, our foreign minister, died. Shishkin, the assistant minister, was temporarily put in charge of the ministry, but no one expected him to be appointed minister because, although he was a very fine and honorable man, he was quite unimpressive and more than a little dimwitted.[6]

It was not long after Giers's death when, to the astonishment of many, Prince Lobanov-Rostovskii, our ambassador to Vienna, was named acting minister of foreign affairs. This appointment showed how little the Emperor knew of the personnel at the upper levels of the civil service. Had he known what a poor opinion his father had had of the man, he would not have appointed him.* But he was not yet initiated in all of the matters he should have known about and, for the most part, did not know what his father had thought about many people or how he had felt on many issues. At that time, out of reverence for his father's memory, he tried to act in accordance with what he thought his father would have wanted. And his chief source in such matters was his mother.

Prince Lobanov-Rostovskii was a distinguished man, but it was unfortunate that he was appointed minister of foreign affairs, if only for the reason that he did not take a serious interest in his work.

Even as a youth I heard of his foibles. I recall one of my relatives relating how shocked he had been, while attending services at our embassy church in Constantinople, to see our ambassador, Lobanov-Rostovskii, enter the church in what appeared to be no more than a dressing gown. It was also said that in Constantinople he attracted attention by his links with women of dubious reputation.[7]

Also, I recall an incident going back to the 1870s, when Lobanov-Rostovskii was assistant minister of interior. I was visiting my Uncle Fadeev, who was then living at the Hôtel de France in Petersburg. With him were Count Vorontsov-Dashkov, Cherniaev, and Lobanov-Rostovskii's brother, who spent most of his time abroad.

When asked if he intended to remain for an extended period in Russia, the brother replied: "How can I remain in Russia when it has reached such a state that even my brother can become assistant minister of interior?"

After Prince Lobanov-Rostovskii became minister I had occasion to meet him

---

*Once, Emperor Alexander III wrote a scathing comment, in rather strong language, on a report by the prince, saying in effect that he was a frivolous man. When Price Lobanov-Rostovskii became minister, so Count Lambsdorff told me, the higher officials in the ministry were at a loss as to what to do with the report to prevent the prince from seeing it. Some favored destroying it; others favored hiding it in the archives; how they decided I do not know.

at close quarters. Later I will tell about many incidents that occurred in the course of our contacts, but here I will restrict myself to my evaluation of him.

Prince Lobanov-Rostovskii was very much a man of the world. I never had occasion to see him in the company of ladies, but I would guess that he had great success with them, for he was quite witty and elegant. Also, he was very well educated, had an excellent command of languages, could write very well, knew the minutiae of diplomatic life. He was interested in some serious matters, for example, genealogy, about which he wrote several books that earned him something of a reputation.

He had a brilliant, but not a serious, mind, and as long as he lived, his character remained the same, frivolous. Even though he was well along in years—past sixty—when he became minister, he showed no change. He was not accustomed to spending much time at his work and did not take a serious interest in it.

How did he come to be named minister of foreign affairs? He was recommended by Grand Duke Michael Nikolaevich, chairman of the State Council, who, as eldest of the tsarist clan, had some influence on the young Emperor during the first years of the reign. The Grand Duke, in turn, was influenced by A. A. Polovtsov, who had become quite friendly with Lobanov-Rostovskii during their trips abroad.

Prince Lobanov-Rostovskii and Polovtsov had much in common. They were educated men of the world. Both were interested in historical investigation and to a degree sought to gain reputations in the historical field. Both liked to live well and make the most out of life. Each cut quite a figure abroad, Polovtsov because of his wealth, Prince Lobanov-Rostovskii because of his position as ambassador of the Emperor of Russia.

The chief difference between the two was that Prince Lobanov-Rostovskii was more of a grandee than Polovtsov. When abroad, Polovtsov benefited from the friendship of a man who was a prince and an ambassador and Lobanov-Rostovskii benefited from the friendship of a man who was very, very rich.

So Polovtsov convinced Grand Duke Michael Nikolaevich that the man most suited to be minister of foreign affairs was Prince Lobanov-Rostovskii. On the record, Lobanov-Rostovskii was one of the most senior of our ambassadors and to all outward appearances was a brilliant man. The Grand Duke in turn recommended Lobanov-Rostovskii to the Emperor, who, not knowing what his father had thought of the prince, appointed him acting foreign minister. Lobanov-Rostovskii was deeply offended, as he told me when we met for the first time, at not being named minister at once, he an actual privy councillor and an ambassador of long standing. However, within a few weeks after his arrival in Petersburg, he was named minister, again the work of Polovtsov.

Prince Lobanov-Rostovskii obviously pleased the Emperor and the Empress. How could such a worldly, well-educated, witty, and elegant man have failed to please them?

Minister of Interior

In July 1895, just before I was to go abroad, I learned that Durnovo would be leaving the post as minister to replace Bunge, who had just died, as chairman of the Committee of Ministers.

As I have written earlier, Durnovo had begun to feel that his position was shaky toward the end of the reign of Emperor Alexander III because Empress Marie Fedorovna had thought he was perlustrating her mail.* After the death of her husband she continued to think so, and this apparently explains why Durnovo quickly lost favor with Emperor Nicholas II. Durnovo, as noted, had asked Emperor Alexander III to let him go and had suggested Plehve as his replacement, but it had been the late Emperor's wish that Sipiagin should ultimately replace Durnovo, and he had accordingly appointed him assistant minister of interior. But Sipiagin had left this position in April 1895 to succeed General Richter as director of the Chancellery of Petitions. (Richter had asked to be relieved because of ill health and had recommended Sipiagin, who considered his new appointment a step up, because it was equivalent in status to a ministerial appointment.) Sipiagin had been replaced as assistant minister by Ivan Loganovich Goremykin: this was not at Durnovo's recommendation. Durnovo had had other candidates in mind, among them Prince Cantacuzene-Count Speranskii.

Well, when Durnovo left his post the question arose of who would succeed him. At the end of my last report to Emperor Nicholas II before going abroad he asked me whom I would suggest as Durnovo's replacement.[8] I replied by asking the Emperor the names of those already recommended to him and the name of the man he had in mind for the post: I was prepared to give my opinion of those who had been suggested to him, but I preferred not to suggest anyone on my own lest I would have to assume responsibility for the person I suggested.

He replied that Plehve and Sipiagin had been recommended to him, but did not say who had recommended them. However, I could guess who. I was certain that Plehve's name had been put forward by Durnovo and Sipiagin's by either the Dowager Empress or Grand Duke Sergei Aleksandrovich. In addition, I surmised that the Emperor knew that his father had had Sipiagin in mind for the post.

I said that I knew both men well. Concerning Plehve I said that he was a jurist both by education and experience, that he was an able jurist, that he was very intelligent, hard-working, businesslike. But, I continued, if I were asked what his

---

*Durnovo told me he did not concern himself with perlustration. This was not true, nor was it true for later ministers of interior. I know for a fact that Stolypin, his denials to the contrary, spent much of his time reading other people's mail. And when I was premier, I was given many letters to read. I know how these letters affect one's nerves and arouse various emotions, which can be kept below the surface only when one is composed. For example, I would find myself reading a [perlustrated] letter written by some well-known person, belonging to the highest society, in which he wrote the most unbelievable things about me, unimaginable filth, and then, a few hours later, I would be receiving this same person, who would act in a friendly fashion, smile servilely, shake hands; naturally such incidents could not calm the nerves of a person who is called to be head of the government. I believe that many of Stolypin's stupid or ill-considered actions were done under the influence of reading other people's mail.

convictions were, it would be difficult for me to be definite, for he was a man without fixed political convictions.

As procurator of the Kharkov Superior Court he had had liberal ideas, and that is why Count Loris-Melikov had brought him in as director of the Department of Police. While he served under Loris-Melikov he had more or less sympathized with the count's constitutional ideas. Then, when Loris-Melikov was succeeded by Count Ignatev, Plehve had become Ignatev's righthand man and had adopted Ignatev's Slavophile views, which, as we know, were quite different from Loris-Melikov's Western constitutionalist views. Then, when Tolstoi, who stood for autocratic bureaucracy in the full sense of the word, succeeded Ignatev, Plehve had treated Tolstoi's opinions as Gospel and had implemented them. Then, when Durnovo, a man devoid of any fixed political principles, became minister of interior, Plehve adopted whatever position Durnovo was adhering to at a given moment. It was evident, I added, that Plehve would adopt any political principle that would advance his career.*

With respect to Sipiagin[10] I said that he had a sound mind, but was not well educated, not as experienced, not as intelligent as Plehve. Although he had graduated from a university faculty of jurisprudence, his knowledge of jurisprudence was weak, and, in general, he lacked breadth of knowledge. I said that he was well acquainted with provincial administration, having served as a marshal of the nobility, as vice-governor, and governor.

I noted that although Sipiagin was inferior to Plehve in some respects, he was a man of principle, of firm and sincere convictions. To be sure his convictions were those associated with the nobility, with the autocracy, with local administration of the patriarchal type, but he believed in them and did not change them. I said that he was a fine man, a solid and humane man who, in the true sense of the word, was a decent Russian nobleman.

Having given my views of the two, I parted with His Majesty and soon left for Vichy.

When I returned from Vichy, nearly two months later, Durnovo was already chairman of the Committee of Ministers, but he had not yet been replaced as minister of interior.

I found on my return that all the business of the Ministry of Finance which depended on agreement between my ministry and the Ministry of Interior had been held up because Goremykin, who was temporarily administering the ministry, naturally did not want to assume responsibility for deciding fairly important questions. Therefore, at my first report to the Emperor

*In the version of this conversation given in the handwritten memoirs (pp. 15 verso–16), Witte writes:

"I did not say to the Emperor that Plehve was a renegade who had changed his religion to further his career. I did not say that Plehve was by nature a lout (*kham*). I did not say that Plehve's support of the nobility's self-serving aspirations did not derive from tradition (his father was not a noble, had probably been an organist for some Polish landowner), but from the desire to use the noble clique at court to further his career. . . .[9]

"I was unwary enough to tell Durnovo of my conversation with the Emperor, and he, as I learned later, naturally passed on what he had heard to Plehve."

I called his attention to this state of affairs. He said to me:

> I waited for your return before deciding on a minister of interior. After I had talked to you, I consulted Constantine Petrovich Pobedonostsev and his opinion kept me from making a decision. When I told him the two candidates I had in mind, and asked for his opinion, he replied: "Plehve is a scoundrel, Sipiagin a fool."

The Emperor smiled when he told me this.

Then I asked whom Pobedonostsev had recommended. The Emperor replied that he had not recommended anyone in particular, but had mentioned my name. I said that I could guess what Pobedonostsev had said: he had probably said that I was the only person capable of reorganizing the Ministry of Interior, which was badly in need of reorganization, and that he had then paid me a lefthanded compliment, à la Sobakevich in *Dead Souls*, who had said that the procurator was the only decent man in town and that he was a swine.

The Emperor laughed loudly and said: "I told him that even if I should appoint you, it would not lighten my burden, for I would then have to find someone to replace you." He then added:

> Evidently Pobedonostsev believes that because Goremykin is temporarily administering the ministry he should become minister. He has no particular opinion about Goremykin, but feels that if the choice should be among Plehve, Sipiagin, and Goremykin, the choice should fall on Goremykin.

When asked what I thought of Goremykin as a potential minister of interior I told His Majesty that I hardly knew the man and could not say anything definite about him, but that on the whole he impressed me as being a decent man, an intelligent bureaucrat. I added that Pobedonostsev had probably supported Goremykin because they were both *pravovedy* [graduates of the Imperial School of Jurisprudence] and that it was well known that *pravovedy*, like lycéeists, and like Jews in their *kahals*, look after one another.

I then asked the Emperor if, having no one but the three in mind, he would appoint Goremykin. He said he would. With this, our conversation ended.

As I left the Emperor's waiting room, I encountered Taneev, the director of His Majesty's Personal Chancellery, who was scheduled to report after me. Later, when I met Taneev on the train back from Tsarskoe Selo to Petersburg, he told me how glad he was that I was back, because the Emperor had not made a decision about who was to be minister of interior while I was away, and no sooner had the Emperor seen me than he ordered Taneev to prepare a decree appointing Goremykin.

(It seems Plehve was not appointed in part because I had spoken out against his appointment. At any rate he believed that it was I who had prevented his appointment, and he was to bear a grudge against me for this reason.)

On my return to Petersburg I went directly to the Ministry of Interior to inform Goremykin of his new status. He was very delighted at the news.

Then, out of the blue, Goremykin told me how happy he was to stop being a *locum tenens*, caliph for an hour. One of his first acts as minister, he said, would be to end the annual 50,000-ruble secret grant that the minister, in his capacity as *ex officio* head of the gendarmerie, received for special police purposes. The practice of providing such a grant went back to the time when the Third Section was incorporated in the Ministry of Interior. He told me that his predecessors had taken to spending this money, for which they accounted only to the Emperor, for their personal needs. This was improper.

As it turned out, his good intention of ending the grant came to naught. Goremykin and his successors continued to receive the grant and to use it for their personal needs. All that has changed is that the grant was increased to 100,000 under Stolypin, as I learned from Kurlov, his closest aide in police affairs, and from Kokovtsev, the premier.

Goremykin was quite a liberal when he became minister of interior, but no sooner did he assume office than he began to cater to those higher up. And out of fear of compromising his position, he began to carry out a very reactionary policy.

Court Commandant

In March 1896, General Peter Pavlovich Hesse was named court commandant,* to succeed General Cherevin, who had died of pneumonia, a disease fatal to heavy drinkers. Cherevin had been in disfavor with the young Emperor and Empress for several reasons. In the first place Cherevin was a man with a large ego, and this inhibited the Emperor, who had, so to speak, grown up under his very eyes. Moreover, Cherevin used strong language and was rarely sober: none of this could please the young Empress, who was very demure, having been brought up in the Anglo-German tradition.

Consequently, Cherevin had been out of favor with the new Emperor from the beginning of the new reign. He had not been invited to dine with the Imperial couple, and when the Emperor had been in residence in Petersburg, Cherevin had to stay in private quarters rather than at the Winter Palace or the Anichkov Palace.

Hesse was a natural choice as Cherevin's successor. He had been close to Cherevin, having served under him. Moreover, the Emperor knew Hesse, who had instructed him in the manual of arms and, for a time, had been his superior in the Preobrazhenskii Guards.

*Cherevin had had the title of chief of court security, but Hesse was given a new title, that of court commandant: it was said in explanation that the Emperor no longer required a chief of security. How unjustified that explanation turned out to be! Just think about the present state of affairs, about the meaning of security as it was developed by Stolypin; just think of the Azefs, the Dubrovins, the Union of the Russian People, the Haymarket *lumpenproletariat*, the Bogrovs, the Kazantsevs, the assorted police agents.

General Hesse was not a bad sort. He was quite proper, but a very ordinary person, who could not be compared to Cherevin, who had an exceptionally sound mind and was very amusing. By the way, Hesse's career had been helped by the fact that he had married the daughter of General-Adjutant Kozlianinov, commander of the Kiev Military District during the reign of Emperor Alexander II. Kozlianinov was a man of some importance in the military world.

Although he was of Jewish origin, P. P. Hesse did not look Jewish. But his brother N. P. Hesse, who had served as governor of Kiev (the result of Kozlianinov's influence), was quite Jewish in appearance, which did not matter, since he, like his brother, was a quite decent person. Many think that if someone is of Jewish origin, he or she will display the shortcomings of that people, but that is not always the case, while some who are 100 percent Russian, like P. P. Hesse's wife, suffer from shortcomings that afflict many Jews. Thus, Madame Hesse, although quite decent, looked after herself very well, using her position at court for personal advancement, and had a finger in minor court matters.

XXIV

The Sino-Russian Treaty of 1896

Before turning to the coronation, on May 14, 1896, of Emperor Nicholas II and Empress Alexandra Fedorovna, I want to deal with a major political event that took place during the coronation, the rapprochement with China.

Russia and the Sino-Japanese War

The war that broke out between China and Japan toward the end of the reign of Emperor Alexander III was of concern to Russia. But at that time our Far Eastern forces, in Vladivostok, were few. After the war broke out, we sent these forces to Kirin in case the fighting spread north to an area in which we had interests. The Siberian Railroad had by this time reached almost to Trans-Baikalia and there was some question of whether the railroad should continue on our territory, in a long arc north of the Amur River, or go in another [more direct] route through Chinese territory, that is, Mongolia and northern Manchuria. But no decision had been made, and there was no expectation that China would give us permission to go through her territory.

Meanwhile the Sino-Japanese War ended in complete Japanese victory. The Japanese imposed the Treaty of Shimonoseki on the defeated, a treaty that, among other things, gave Japan the whole of the Liaotung Peninsula, and this was against Russian interests. Previously our Maritime Region had been separated from Japan by the sea. Now the Japanese were on the mainland, in a region in which we had very basic interests. Therefore, the question arose of how we should respond.

At this time [early 1895] Prince Lobanov-Rostovskii was already our foreign minister. As I have said, he was well educated and knew everything about the West but nothing about the East, in which he had never had any interest. He knew as much about Manchuria, Mukden, Kirin as a second-year *gimnaziia* student. As a matter of fact, there were very few in those days in the government or among educated people in general who had any knowledge of China, Korea, or Japan.

I was practically the only one who concerned himself with Far Eastern matters, because in carrying out Emperor Alexander III's legacy to me, of completing the Siberian Railroad linking Vladivostok and European Russia, I had come to know a great deal about the area.

Emperor Nicholas II wanted to expand Russian influence in the Far East, particularly because of his tour there, when he had been on his own for the first time, so to speak, but he had not yet developed any definite goals. Therefore, I had to think matters out thoroughly. How should we act about the Japanese acquisition of the Liaotung Peninsula? I arrived at the conclusion, to which I still adhere, that it was better for Russia to have a strong, but passive, China as her neighbor [than Japan]. This would ensure future peace and prosperity for the Russian Empire in the Far East. Therefore, it was evident that we could not permit Japan to acquire so important an area as the Liaotung Peninsula, which would give her a foothold near Peking itself and in a sense would bestow a position of dominance on her. Thus, it was my position that we must prevent implementation of the treaty.

The Emperor was kind enough to act on my recommendation by calling a conference to consider what our policy should be. It was held in the temporary quarters of Prince Lobanov-Rostovskii, under the chairmanship of Grand Duke Alexis Aleksandrovich, with me, General Vannovskii, General Obruchev, Admiral Chikhachev, and Prince Lobanov-Rostovskii as participants.[1]

At this conference I argued very emphatically that for a long time to come it was in Russia's interest to maintain the status quo in China, and this required that we use our power to support the principle of the integrity of the Chinese Empire. Vannovskii supported me. Obruchev was rather indifferent because he was more concerned over possible conflicts in the West. Admiral Chikhachev and Prince Lobanov-Rostovskii took no definite position. The chairman asked what steps we should take to implement my views.

I proposed that we present an ultimatum to Japan, giving her a choice between giving up the claim to the Liaotung Peninsula in return for a sizable indemnity that would compensate her, as victor, for her expenditures in the war, or being subject to military action on our part. Of course, this was not the time to decide what action to take, but it might extend as far as the bombardment of several Japanese ports. No conclusion was reached about my proposal: no one definitely opposed it, but few supported it. Prince Lobanov-Rostovskii said nothing.

The Grand Duke then informed the Emperor about the results of the conference. The Emperor in turn summoned another conference, over which he presided, to which only I, General Vannovskii, Prince Lobanov-Rostovskii, and Grand Duke Alexis Aleksandrovich were invited. Here I once more presented my views. The others either objected weakly or not at all. In the end the Emperor agreed to accept my proposal and charged Prince Lobanov-Rostovskii with carrying it out.

I must give Prince Lobanov-Rostovskii his due. He carried out his task skillfully. We immediately reached an agreement with Germany and France to support our demands. We then quickly presented our ultimatum, which Japan had no choice but to accept. We did not take a hand in determining the size of the indemnity or other questions, stipulating only that we would not permit impairment of the integrity of the Chinese Empire. Thus [the revision of] the Treaty of Shimonoseki was worked out.

The Russo-Chinese Bank

At the same time I entered into talks with China, proposing that we aid her in concluding a loan [with which to pay the indemnity]. Obviously, China didn't have the credit for obtaining a loan, without guarantees. In this case repayment would be guaranteed first from her customs receipts, then by her other resources, and if she still proved unable to repay, Russia would be the last resort as guarantor.

I then arranged for a group of Parisian banking firms—Banque de France et Pays Bas, Crédit Lyonnais, the Hottinguer banking house—to take part in the loan. Two of the individuals who took part in floating the loan, Noetzlin and Hottinguer, came to Petersburg in connection with this operation and asked that in return for their good offices to me in arranging the loan I help them in the expansion of French banking activities in China.

In response I established the Russo-Chinese Bank,[2] with our government as the major shareholder and the French playing a major role in the bank's operations. At first the Chinese took some part in the work of the bank, but their role in it subsequently declined. Following the unfortunate war with Japan and our loss of prestige in China, the bank went downhill: it was merged with the Northern Bank to form the Russo-Asiatic Bank.

After our show of support for China, Prince Ukhtomskii, then quite close to the Emperor, went to China, first of all to increase his knowledge of the country, secondly to become acquainted with the customs officials.

Li Hung-chang Comes to Russia

A sign of China's immense gratitude to our young Emperor for the assistance we had given her was her choice of so distinguished an official as Li Hung-chang to represent her at the coronation of our Emperor [which was to take place in May 1896, in Moscow].

As I have said, we were thinking at the time of the possibility of routing the Siberian Railroad through Mongolia and northern Manchuria, a step that would speed up construction.[3] When completed, this great Siberian line would provide a commercial link between the Far East, including Japan, and Europe. Our aim was to achieve this end by peaceful means for the mutual benefit of all parties concerned. I was enthused by this idea and succeeded in winning Prince Ukhtomskii over to it; also I had the opportunity of reporting on it to His Majesty.

By the way, it was at this time that Doctor Badmaev,* who had paid a visit to his Buriat homeland, was arguing for a route that would have taken the railroad through Kiakhta to Peking, his position being that the route to Vladivostok would way, first of all because I considered it imperative for us to be linked to Vladivostok and secondly because I believed, and for good reason, that a route to Peking would rouse all of Europe against us.

long footnote

It should be noted that both Emperor Alexander III and Emperor Nicholas II considered the Siberian Railroad as a purely economic undertaking, not as an instrument for annexing foreign territory. Consequently, they felt that the only military significance the railroad should have was as a means of defending Russia.

After Li Hung-chang had already left China (this was his first trip abroad) I learned that England, Germany, and Austria were attempting to induce him to stop off in their respective countries while he was en route to Russia. It was obvious to me that if he did stop off he would be the object of all sorts of intrigues on the part of these countries. It was obviously not in our interest for him to make any stops. So, I suggested that Prince Ukhtomskii, who was on good terms with him, meet him at the Suez Canal and escort him directly to Russia.

His Majesty agreed, but he wanted the prince to act very circumspectly. Prince Ukhtomskii and I then worked out the details very carefully. To avoid attracting attention to his actions, Prince Ukhtomskii took an indirect route, going first to Marseilles and then sailing from there to meet Li Hung-chang at the mouth of the Suez Canal, where the Chinese statesman (who had not accepted invitations to stop off in other countries) was transferred to a ship belonging to the Russian Steamship and Commercial Company that I had directed to be there. From there they sailed to Odessa. When Li Hung-chang debarked, he was met by a military honor guard.

It had been my idea that since Li Hung-chang would have his first contact with Russia in Odessa, he be met when he landed by a military honor guard, as

*I became acquainted with Badmaev through Ukhtomskii, whose favor he had gained while the prince had been on one of his visits to China. Prince Ukhtomskii had introduced Badmaev to Emperor Nicholas II while the latter was still Tsesarevich; during the first part of his reign the Emperor even received Badmaev and, in general, was favorably inclined toward him.

Badmaev is typically Asiatic. He has an excellent mind. As a medical man he is, to a large degree, a charlatan, although his treatment had been beneficial in several cases. He has used his profession to engage in shady undertakings for personal gain.

His medical work has given him an opportunity to meddle in politics. When Prince Ukhtomskii and I became aware that he was meddling in Far Eastern questions, we dissociated ourselves from him.

It has been many years since Ukhtomskii and I have permitted Badmaev to see us. I hear that Badmaev has somehow managed to creep into the favor of Kurlov, as well as the favor of Dediulin, the present palace commandant. Not long after, I heard that the Medical Council is considering the notion of establishing some sort of society for the application of Buriat medicine, with Dediulin, Kurlov, and Badmaev in charge. From this I conclude that Badmaev has again insinuated himself into the higher police circles.[4]

befitted a man of his rank. This would be his first view of our armed forces. In addition, knowing that there would be no time during the coronation festivities, in Moscow, I had proposed that he proceed first to Petersburg while there was still time. But there had been difficulties.

When, with the Emperor's permission, I wrote to the war minister about an honor guard, he replied that although he would carry out His Majesty's wishes, he wanted to know when I had become the one to report to the Emperor about matters which were in the jurisdiction of the Ministry of War. And Prince Lobanov-Rostovskii saw no point in having Li Hung-chang come to Petersburg: he preferred that our Chinese visitor remain in Odessa until it was time to go to Moscow for the coronation. I had to go to the Emperor to overcome the foreign minister's objections.

[On April 18, 1896] Li Hung-chang and his suite arrived in Petersburg, in a special train that I had provided. On instructions from the Emperor I was to negotiate with him for the right to carry the Siberian Railroad across northern Manchuria. Prince Lobanov-Rostovskii took no part in the negotiations at this time, when, as I have said, he was neither informed about nor interested in Far Eastern politics.

Negotiations

Soon after his arrival, Li Hung-chang paid an official call on me at the Ministry of Finance. Then I returned the call. This was followed by a number of meetings at which we discussed relations between our respective countries.

I had been told that in dealing with high Chinese officials it would be improper to hurry, that everything must be done very slowly and in accordance with Chinese ceremonial. So, when Li Hung-chang paid his first call, he was ushered into my reception room. I was in uniform. We greeted each other effusively, bowed low to each other. Then I took him into another reception room and ordered tea. I and he sat, but the members of his suite and my associates remained standing. Then I asked him if he wished to smoke. He thereupon began to make sounds like those of a stallion neighing. Immediately two Chinese came in from the other room, one carrying a hookah, the other tobacco. There followed the smoking ceremonial: with great reverence they lit the hookah, held the pipe to his mouth while he sat very still, making no motion except to inhale, have the pipe taken from his mouth, exhale, then permit the pipe to be put back into his mouth. He obviously was trying to make a strong impression on me with ceremonials of this kind, but I, naturally, reacted very coolly and gave the impression that I paid no attention to such things.

It goes without saying that we did not touch on business at all at this first meeting, but just chattered away. He asked about the health of our Emperor, then about the health of our Empress, then about the health of their children. I in turn inquired after the health of his Emperor and his closest relatives.

As Li Hung-chang came to know me better and to realize that such ceremonials made no particular impression on me, he began to be less formal and no longer performed such ceremonials. In fact later, in Moscow, we became closer and could unbend.

I have met many notable statesmen in my career and would rate Li Hung-chang high among them. In fact, he was a great statesman; to be sure, he was Chinese, without any kind of European education, but a man of sound Chinese education and what is more, a man with a remarkably sound mind and good common sense. For that reason he played a major role in the administration of China; in fact, he governed the country.

As we discussed Sino-Russian relations I stressed how we had helped China preserve her integrity, how committed we were to the principle of the integrity of the Chinese Empire. But, I went on to say, it would be difficult for us to assist China as long as we didn't have the railroads to transport our troops from European Russia or from Vladivostok. I pointed out that during the recent Sino-Japanese War the troops we sent from Vladivostok to Kirin did not arrive there until the war had ended, because of the lack of a railroad. For us to increase our troop strength in that region it would be necessary to have a railroad.

I argued that for us to support the integrity of China, there would have to be a railroad going by the shortest route to Vladivostok, that is, through northern Mongolia and Manchuria. I said, too, that such a railroad was necessary for economic reasons: it would benefit both the Chinese and Russian territories through which it passed. Moreover, I said, the Japanese would not be antipathetic to such a railroad because it would link Japan with Western Europe. As we know, Japan, for some time, had been assimilating European culture, at least its technological and other external aspects. Consequently, Japan might be expected to react favorably to such a railroad, and, as it turned out, I was right.

Li Hung-chang, of course, raised various objections, but I believed that he would agree to our proposal if our Emperor asked him to. Therefore, I suggested to the Emperor that he receive Li Hung-chang. This he did, but so circumspectly that the meeting went unnoticed and was not reported in our official organs. Not long after, at a reception at Tsarskoe Selo, as I reached the Emperor, his face lit up. He gave me his hand and said, almost in a whisper: "I saw Li Hung-chang and told him."

The Russo-Chinese Agreement

I subsequently saw Li Hung-chang and settled on the following basic points for an agreement between our countries.[5]

First, the Chinese Empire would permit construction of a railroad through its territory to connect Chita and Vladivostok, but it would have to be constructed and owned by a private [Russian] company. (Li Hung-chang would under no circumstances have agreed to permit the Russian government to construct or to own the railroad.) Like all [Russian] companies, it would be subject to the jurisdiction of our Ministry of Finance. Its employees would not be civil servants but would be in the same category as employees of privately owned railroad companies, in the same category as persons assigned to the company, such as engineers of ways and communication, who were under the jurisdiction of the Ministry of Ways and Communications and served with privately owned railroad companies in European Russia.

Second, we would be given the right of way necessary for the operation of the railroad. Within the area of the right of way, Russia, or more properly speaking, the Chinese Eastern Railroad, would exercise authority—have its own police, its own security guard for the railroad. (The actual route of the railroad would be determined after a survey had been completed, but it should be as close as possible to the direct line between Chita and Vladivostok.) China would not incur any risk in the construction and operation of the railroad.

Third, we, for our part, would assume the obligation of defending Chinese territory from any aggressive action on the part of Japan, i.e., we would enter into a defensive alliance against Japan.

It was soon time to go to Moscow. Li Hung-chang went there with his own suite and with the officials we had assigned to him.

When I informed the Emperor of the results of my talks with Li Hung-chang he authorized me to take up the matter with the foreign minister. When I saw Prince Lobanov-Rostovskii to tell him that I had been given such authorization, it was evident that he had already been so informed. I told him that all I had so far was an oral agreement and that it was not necessary to put it in writing. He asked me to tell him in detail what had been agreed. When I was through, he took up his pen and wrote. Here, I must give him his due. When I read what he had written, I was struck by the accuracy and orderliness of the statement; it was done in a superb fashion. After I had read it and had made no corrections, he expressed surprise that I had not. I told him that he expressed it all so superbly that it was as if he were the one who had conducted the negotiations and added that if it had been I who had done the writing, it would have taken me more time and I would not have done it as well as he had. He told me that he would present this draft to the Emperor on the following day and that, if it were approved, he would so inform me.

The next day I received the draft back from Prince Lobanov-Rostovskii. I saw, to my great surprise, that the article about a defensive alliance against Japan had been changed by the omission of any reference to Japan. In its revised form, the article stated that in the event of any attack on China, we were obliged to come to the defense of China and that in the event of an attack on the Maritime Region, China was obliged to come to our defense. The change frightened me, for there was a world of difference between a defensive alliance against Japan and a defensive alliance against all [third] powers. After all, China and England were neighbors, with a long history of misunderstandings and disputes (for example, concerning Tibet), which continue to this day; then China had disputes with our ally France, over Tonkin, in Indo-China. Moreover, there were other European countries with interests in China—colonies, concessions and the like. To undertake to defend China against any power that might attack her would be a commitment impossible to carry out. Moreover, if we made such a commitment and it became public knowledge, all the European powers would be roused against us.

Consequently I saw the Emperor and explained what had happened. He told me to go to Prince Lobanov-Rostovskii and persuade him to restore the original wording. I replied that I would prefer not to do so because the foreign minister, being old enough to be my father and, moreover, my senior in service, and not having taken part in the negotiations, might be deeply offended and might become hostile toward me. It was not that I feared his antipathy so much as I did not like the thought of his being made personally uncomfortable. It would be better, I suggested, if he would be kind enough to talk to the foreign minister. The Emperor agreed to do so.

Soon after these events it was time to go to Moscow. Li Hung-chang went before I did and I went before the Emperor did.

In Moscow much of my time was taken up with the coronation festivities, but I spent as much time as I could with Li Hung-chang, for I considered it of paramount importance to make certain of being able to use the route between Chita and Vladivostok, and I wished to establish firm relations with so great a colossus as China, Russia's neighbor.

After the Emperor had arrived in Moscow and had established himself, in accordance with custom, at the Neskuchnyi Palace, I immediately went to give him my [regular] report. As soon as I arrived he told me that he had spoken to Prince Lobanov-Rostovskii about restoring the original wording about our alliance with China and that he had agreed to do so. The Emperor told me this so positively that I was left in no doubt that the matter was settled, and when I saw the foreign minister subsequently neither of us brought up the matter.

Meanwhile I continued my talks with Li Hung-chang about the terms for building a railroad across Manchuria. What I wanted was an agreement whereby China granted a concession to the yet-to-be-established Chinese Eastern Railroad Company to build and operate the railroad, but the company could not be formed until the Chinese government had formally granted the concession. And the concession could not be drawn up quickly because some minor questions had arisen that had to be settled first. Since the Russo-Chinese Bank was already in existence and functioning, I felt that it would be best for our secret treaty of alliance with China to stipulate that the right to build the railroad would be granted to the Russo-Chinese Bank, the treaty to be supplemented by an agreement between China and the bank for the construction and operation of the railroad, and this agreement to be supplemented by an agreement between our government and the bank to make certain that the bank would transfer its rights to build and operate the railroads to the Chinese Eastern Railroad Company when it was established by our government.

The first step then was to conclude the secret treaty of alliance with China, which Li Hung-chang had been authorized by Peking to sign. A date was set for the Chinese and Russian officials to meet at the house which the foreign minister had rented for the duration of the coronation and there to go through all the formalities required by protocol in signing an agreement. On the appointed day [May 22] we met at the foreign minister's house. He had two copies of the treaty ready, which both parties had to sign, one copy for us, the other for the Chinese. When we sat down around the table for the ceremonies, he said that he presumed that it was probably not necessary for us to read the agreement since the text had already been read and since the copies had been carefully prepared, and checked by the secretaries; therefore, all that remained was to sign it. However, he added, perhaps Li Hung-chang's associates might wish to read the text of the agreement once more. So, one copy was handed over to Li Hung-chang's associates. I picked up the copy made for us, to make certain that the article concerning our alliance with China was in its original wording.

To my horror I found that it was not, that we were still obligated to defend China against attack by any power. I then went over to Prince Lobanov-Rostovskii and told him that the article had "not been changed in the way that the Emperor wanted." I thought the omission had been deliberate on the foreign minister's part, but suddenly, to my surprise, he struck himself on the forehead and said: "Oh, my God, I forgot to tell the secretaries to rewrite this article according to the first draft." He then showed great presence of mind.

He looked at his watch, which showed 12:15. Then he clapped his hands and when servants appeared, he ordered them to serve lunch. (Lunch was to have been served after the signing.) Then, turning to Li Hung-chang and the others, he suggested that since it was after noon, we should all eat lest the food be spoiled and leave the signing till later.

All of us, except two secretaries, went to lunch. While we were eating they recopied the treaty in the form in which I had given it to the foreign minister in Petersburg. By the time we were ready for signing, the old copies were gone and the new ones ready. Li Hung-chang signed for China; I and Prince Lobanov-Rostovskii signed for Russia. The treaty was subsequently ratified by our respective emperors and was to serve as the basis of all our relations with China and of our entire position in the Far East.

Had we been faithful to the terms of this important treaty, there is no doubt that we would have been spared the shameful war with Japan and our position in the Far East would now be a strong one. How we arrived at the position we are now in—either through bad faith or poor judgment—I will have occasion to explain later on.

Li Hung-chang remained in Moscow until the Emperor left the city, staying at the private quarters we had rented for him. I was to see him again in Moscow several times, either at his quarters or mine.

In my meetings with him I noticed that his bodyguards were not like our bodyguards, whose task it is to protect the person to whom they are assigned. In China, it appears, bodyguards not only protect the person but also look after his body. They are constantly beside the man whom they guard: in the morning they perform his toilet; during the day they massage him, with perfumed ointments; at night they undress him. And Li Hung-chang permitted many of these ministrations to be performed in my presence.

Once, while I was visiting Li Hung-chang, it was suddenly announced that the Emir of Bukhara had come to call. Li Hung-chang immediately dressed himself in full regalia, sat down pompously in an armchair. When the Emir and his suite entered, Li Hung-chang arose, walked a few steps toward him and greeted him. Since I knew both of them quite well, I did not leave. I saw that the Emir was quite taken aback by the airs that Li Hung-chang assumed and let him know that he was a sovereign and was calling out of respect for Li Hung-chang's master, the Emperor of China. During the conversation that followed, the Emir solicitously inquired after the health of the Emperor of China and the Emperor's mother, but at no point did he display any interest in Li Hung-chang himself, an omission that seems quite insulting to Chinese, with their sense of protocol.

For his part Li Hung-chang devoted the time to talking about religion. He explained that the Chinese follow religious principles established by Confucius and then wanted to know about the religion of the Emir and of his subjects. The Emir explained that he was a Moslem, a believer in the principles established by Mohammed, and proceeded to elucidate the essence of his religion.

When the time came for the Emir to leave, Li Hung-chang, either by his own initiative or because it was suggested to him, accompanied the Emir to his carriage, in a manner indicating that he was fully the Emir's equal. Just as the carriage started, Li Hung-chang shouted something. The carriage stopped and a Russian officer, who was accompanying the Emir as translator, asked what Li Hung-chang wanted. Li Hung-chang said to tell the Emir that the Mohammed, who had founded his religion, had been a convict in China, had then been expelled and gone on to Bukhara. The Emir was quite evidently taken aback by this sally, which clearly was in revenge for the latter's rudeness. Then, quite pleased with himself, Li Hung-chang returned to his reception room. Since it was rather late, I left.

If you look at the newspapers of the time, particularly at *Pravitelstvennyi vestnik*, you will find that although there were official announcements about every move of important personages at the coronation, there was little about the comings and goings of Li Hung-chang, including the fact that he had been received by our Emperor. And there was not one word in the newspapers about our secret, and most important, treaty with China.

The next step after the treaty was to negotiate a convention whereby China would grant the Russo-Chinese Bank a concession to construct the Chinese Eastern Railroad. (The convention was to be made public.) I could not participate in this round of negotiations because I was scheduled to go to Nizhnii Novgorod then to visit the provinces in the Volga region where the liquor monopoly was being introduced.

Acting under my instructions, Peter Mikhailovich Romanov (who died just a few months ago) negotiated the terms of the convention with Hsu Ching-cheng, the Chinese minister to Petersburg and Berlin, who spent part of the year in Petersburg, part in Berlin. Since he was then in Berlin, Romanov went there and successfully concluded negotiations. After the document was ratified, there were allegations in Europe that Li Hung-chang had taken a bribe for agreeing to the concession. This was not true.[6] While he was in Petersburg he neither mentioned taking a bribe nor did he take one.

The proposed Chinese Eastern Railroad would put into our hands an instrument of the highest political and commercial significance, one that we (I especially) insisted should under no circumstances be used as a tool for annexations. It was to serve as a means for bringing together the European and Oriental nations, both in a material and a moral sense, and was intended to serve as an instrument of moral influence to the degree that the new [to them] culture, the Christian one, would demonstrate that it was more powerful than the culture of the yellow nations, based on idolatry.[7]

Li Hung-chang, with whom I had become friendly, repeatedly advised me, for the sake of Russia, never to go south of the line followed by the railroad. If we did so, he said, it would gravely shock and antagonize the Chinese, who were entirely unacquainted with Europeans and, to a degree, looked on every white man as malevolent, and there would be surprisingly unfortunate consequences both for China and for Russia. For me this advice was redundant because I, as loyal executor of the ideas of Emperor Alexander III (whose son in a well-known manifesto called him "the Peacekeeper"), was and continue to be a sincere adherent to the idea of peace, and I believe that Christian teachings will grow and flourish only when mankind will carry out the highest precept of Christian teaching, that no human being has the right to kill another human being. I mention this advice, earnestly given, to indicate how exceptional a man Li Hung-chang was among Chinese statesmen.

At the time it seemed pointless to me to transmit Li Hung-chang's advice to our Emperor, for in those days he bore in himself the seeds of all that could be good in a man. And I was convinced that he regarded the treaty with China as having only peaceful goals. The treaty was secret not because it gave us the right to build a railroad but because it provided for a defensive alliance against a potential enemy and was designed to prevent the repetition of the defeat of China at the hands of Japan.

The Russo-Japanese Treaty of 1896

Also, during the coronation a treaty concerning Korea was signed with Japan. In this case the negotiations were carried out by Prince Lobanov-Rostovskii, while I took a secondary role in them.

Before the Sino-Japanese War, Korea had been an autonomous part of China, completely under her influence. As a result of the war Korea was declared independent. The Russo-Japanese Treaty, which I consider a favorable one for Russia, delimited the respective spheres of influence in the two countries.

Under the terms of the treaty we were permitted to have military instructors and several hundred soldiers in Korea and, in addition, were permitted to name a financial adviser to the Emperor of Korea, which was tantamount to naming the country's minister of finance. Thus, in military and fiscal matters, Russia, one could say, received the preponderant influence. Japan, for her part, received the right to establish industrial enterprises and engage in commerce in Korea. Some rights were mutual: we both enjoyed most favored nation treatment with respect to financial advantages *et sim*. I considered the treaty a favorable one for Russia, and it should be noted that the Japanese gladly agreed to it.

XXV

The Khodynka Tragedy

The Tragedy

I will not speak of the festivities that customarily take place on such a glorious occasion as a coronation, but I would like to say something about a very sad, very dispiriting event that was not planned for: Г am speaking of the events on Khodynka field on May 18.

Customarily, following the coronation there is a very large outdoor fête on Khodynka field, then just outside the Moscow city limits, for the common people, to whom various gifts, mainly edibles, are distributed during the morning in the name of the Emperor. Later that day there are various kinds of entertainment at which the Emperor is present. On this occasion the Emperor was scheduled to appear there at noon and, among other things, attend a concert at which a large orchestra, under the direction of the well-known conductor Safonov, was to perform a cantata composed for the occasion of the coronation.

I was on my way to Khodynka field when I learned that a tragedy had occurred there: that morning a fearful crush of people had left two thousand persons, most of them women or children, killed or maimed. Many anguishing questions came to mind. Were any of the maimed in condition to be taken to the hospital? Would the dead and maimed be removed from the field so they would not be seen by the remnants of the joyous crowd or by the Emperor and his foreign guests when they arrived? Then I wondered if the Emperor might not order the cancellation of the remaining events scheduled for that day and instead have solemn services for the dead at Khodynka field.

When I reached the site there was no evidence that a tragedy had occurred. All visible traces of the event had either been removed or cleaned up.[1] Nonetheless, as the guests arrived to take their place in the pavilion provided for them, it was evident that they were aware that a tragedy had taken place and that they were affected by it.

Among the guests that arrived was Li Hung-chang. When he saw me, he asked through his interpreter if it were true that a catastrophe had occurred, leaving two thousand dead or maimed. Since it was obvious that he knew the facts, I told him that he was correct. Then he asked if the Emperor had been informed of the facts. I said that I had no doubt that he had been informed immediately. At this he shook his head and said:

> Your officials lack experience. Now when I was governor-general of Pechili, we had a plague which killed tens of thousands, but I continued to write to the Emperor that all was well and when I was asked if we had any sick ones among us, I replied that the entire population was in the most normal of conditions.

Finishing this sentence, as if with a period, he asked me:

> Tell me, why should I pain the Emperor with news that people in my jurisdiction are dying? If I were an important personage serving your Emperor I would, of course, have kept all this from him. Why should I give pain to the poor man?[2]

Soon the Emperor and the Grand Dukes arrived. To my astonishment the festivities were not canceled and the program went on as scheduled; everything went on as if nothing untoward had happened. However, the Emperor's face showed grief; in fact he looked sick. It seems to me that if he had followed his own inclinations he would have canceled the remaining festivities and would instead have held services for the dead. But he had obviously received bad advice, and one didn't have to be very wise to deduce that this advice came from the governor-general of Moscow, Grand Duke Sergei Aleksandrovich,* his uncle and brother-in-law, who was then and would continue to be very close to the Emperor.

That evening the Emperor was scheduled to attend a ball given by the French ambassador, Count (later Marquis) Montebello. Thanks to his wife, the count was a very rich man; for this reason, as well as his personal qualities and even more so the qualities of his wife, he was very popular in high society. The ball was to be a very splendid one.

We wondered if the ball would be canceled. Then, when we learned that it would go on as scheduled, we wondered if the Emperor and Empress would attend.

*I had several occasions to meet the Grand Duke on business. Our views differed, for he was ultraconservative in his political views, and he was quite religious, but in a sanctimonious way. I should note that he was always surrounded by comparatively young men, who were excessively affectionate toward him. I do not mean that he had unnatural instincts, but there was evidently some psychological abnormality, which expressed itself in a marked liking for young men. Despite my disagreement with his political views, I do respect his memory for he remained true to these views, and, as a result, perished from a bomb thrown by a senseless anarchist who, so it is said, was induced to commit this act by Azef, the well-known police agent.

Perhaps I will have occasion to speak of certain circumstances, rather serious ones, on which I had occasion to meet him in connection with the decree of December 12, 1904.

At the appointed hour I arrived at the ball, together with Dmitrii Sergeevich Sipiagin and Grand Duke Sergei Aleksandrovich. As soon as we had met we naturally began to discuss the tragedy. The Grand Duke told us that many had advised the Emperor to ask the ambassador to cancel the ball, or, at the very least, not to attend, but the Emperor had categorically rejected such advice. His position had been that although what had happened was a tragedy, it must not be permitted to cast a shadow over the joyous occasion of the coronation. In this sense the Khodynka tragedy was to be ignored, and I could not help but think of the words I had heard that morning from the great Chinese statesman Li Hung-chang.

Soon the Emperor and Empress arrived. He danced the first contredanse with Countess Montebello, and the Empress danced with Count Montebello. It should be noted that the Emperor did not stay long at the ball.

He was obviously depressed, and if he had followed his own promptings, as he had on many other occasions, he would have acted differently with respect to the tragedy and all the festivities.

The Investigation

Although the tragedy was first treated as if it had not occurred, the question of how it could have happened and who was responsible could not be evaded. In the effort to fix responsibility, all sorts of intrigues and factional quarrels arose, principally between those who considered the Moscow police, and thus Grand Duke Sergei Aleksandrovich, their superior, to blame, and those who blamed the officials of the Ministry of the Imperial Court, who supervised the arrangements at the coronation, and thus indirectly Count Vorontsov-Dashkov, the minister of the court.

At this time the superintendent of police in Moscow was Colonel Vlasovskii, who earlier had served as head of the police in one of the Baltic cities, Riga, I believe. He had been recommended to the Grand Duke as an energetic official, capable of maintaining order in the city. One had to speak to Vlasovskii for but a few minutes to see that he was a lout, a Derzhimorda.[3] He was a sly, pushy man who could be ingratiating when necessary, which is why everybody at the court of the Grand Duke treated him like a lout who would carry out any wish they might express. Although Vlasovskii was able to maintain a semblance of order in Moscow, he promoted corruption among his men and spent all his free time wining and dining in restaurants.

Well, it was Vlasovskii who declared that the Moscow police had carried out its responsibilities in the area under its jurisdiction, which did not include Khodynka field, and that it was the Ministry of the Imperial Court that should bear responsibility for what had happened at Khodynka. On the other hand, those officials from the ministry who had supervised the arrangements at the field blamed the police, saying that the maintenance of order on the field was in the jurisdiction of the police.

Naturally, the Grand Duke came to the support of the police. Had he not been a grand duke, he would have been the first person to be called to account for the tragedy. And the second would have been Count Vorontsov-Dashkov.

As I have mentioned, Count Vorontsov-Dashkov had become minister under Emperor Alexander III and therefore enjoyed a special authority in the eyes of the young Emperor; also Count Vorontsov-Dashkov was in the good graces of the Dowager Empress. It goes without saying that he defended his subordinates and placed the blame on the Moscow police and the governor-general of Moscow.

Naturally, this dispute created quite a stir, with factions being formed among the highest officials, one favoring Count Vorontsov-Dashkov, who had the backing of the Dowager Empress, the other faction finding it advantageous to identify itself with Grand Duke Sergei Aleksandrovich. Some officials were neutral because they did not know which faction would have the greater influence on the Emperor.

When Nicholas Valerianovich Muravev, the minister of justice, was selected to investigate the Khodynka tragedy, it was seen as a plus for the Grand Duke, whose patronage Muravev enjoyed. The results of his investigation were printed in a small book, now secret, of which I have a copy in my archive. Muravev was quite objective in his description of the details of the tragedy, but he was far less objective, and was often evasive, in dealing with the question of responsibility.[4]

Soon, however, a new investigation was begun, this time under Count Pahlen, a very honorable man who had once served as minister of justice and had been the chief master of ceremonies at the coronation. In Moscow his selection was taken to mean that the Dowager Empress's influence was in the ascendant.

I have not read the report of Count Pahlen's investigation and I have no official knowledge of his conclusions, but he did tell me that the Moscow administration (meaning Grand Duke Sergei Aleksandrovich) in general and the Moscow police in particular were the guilty parties. Although he told me what the Emperor's reaction to his report was, I don't remember what it was.[5]

Count Pahlen's report did not endear him with the Grand Dukes. Nor did his remark, made shortly after the tragedy, that whenever a Grand Duke was given a responsible post there was sure to be trouble.

In the end only one person was punished for this tragedy, which killed or maimed two thousand Russians. That person was Colonel Vlasovskii, who was dismissed from the service.[6] In this way the entire affair was hushed up.

From this time on Count Pahlen was never to receive a substantial appointment. To be sure he was quite old and the Emperor continued to be kindly disposed toward him, but it appears that he was out of favor. As for N. V. Muravev, his career continued to flourish under the patronage of Grand Duke Sergei Aleksandrovich.

I left Moscow soon after the coronation for Nizhnni Novgorod, to open an exhibition which had been organized on my initiative. The Emperor was to go there some weeks later.

XXVI

May–October 1896

Liquor Monopoly, Nizhnii Novgorod Exhibition, the Gold Standard, the Bosphorus

Liquor Monopoly

On June 2, 1896, while I was in Nizhnii Novgorod, it was announced that the Department of Indirect Taxation of the Ministry of Finance was being transformed into the Chief Administration of Indirect Taxation and Government Liquor Sales, with Markov continuing as its head. As I noted earlier, he was an able man who had made his career in the excise service.

The change in name, and status, reflected the fact that ever since I had introduced the liquor monopoly on the initiative of Emperor Alexander III it had been the chief concern of the department. By this time the liquor monopoly was already in operation in several provinces; by the time I was to leave the Ministry of Finance, it was to be in operation in all but the most remote areas of the country.[1]

I was to encounter opposition when the time came to establish the liquor monopoly in the province and city of Petersburg, opposition from those whose interests were threatened—distillers and operators of establishments where liquor was sold. Some of these elements in the city were able to gain the ear of Grand Duke Vladimir Aleksandrovich, commander of the Petersburg Military District and the Emperor's uncle, a very fine man but with little knowledge of practical affairs. They warned him that there would be bloody riots in the city on the day [January 1, 1898] the liquor monopoly was introduced and that since he commanded the military there, this matter concerned him. He passed on this information to the Emperor, who asked me, just a few days before the date set, if the liquor monopoly should be introduced in the city. I had no difficulty in putting his mind

243

at rest, because in those days I still enjoyed the complete confidence of the young Emperor. As I expected, everything went quietly.

During my tenure as minister of finance, the chief aim of the liquor monopoly, in accordance with the intentions of Emperor Alexander III, was to curb alcoholism "insofar as possible." In my opinion general temperance can be achieved only among a prosperous, cultured, and educated people, but it was our task to do what we could to curb alcoholism by such means as were available to the government, and I so instructed Markov and the officials of the excise service.

When the war with Japan began, the then finance minister Vladimir Nikolaevich Kokovtsev began to use the liquor monopoly primarily as a means of increasing revenue, by raising liquor prices and increasing the number of liquor stores. And the work of excise officials was judged by increase in revenue rather than by decrease in alcoholism.

We all know that a steep increase in the price of liquor can bring down liquor consumption, although at the risk of encouraging illicit production. Kokovstev did not set the price high enough to discourage consumption but yet high enough to be ruinous for the poorer classes: the result was increased revenue from liquor sales and increased alcoholism.

Given the enormous cost of the war, no one can be blamed for seeking to increase revenue from liquor sales at such a time. Any minister would have done as Kokovtsev did. But, in my opinion, when the war ended and finances were restored to a good condition, it was the first obligation of the minister of finance to remember that the original purpose of the liquor monopoly was to curb alcoholism. But Kokovtsev did not remember and maintained liquor prices at their wartime level.

The Nizhnii Novgorod Exhibition

When I opened the Nizhnii Novgorod exhibition of commerce and industry on May 28, 1896, there was still some work to be done on it.[2] This was because Timiriazev, whom I had chosen to organize the exhibition because of his previous experience, was the kind of person who completes everything on paper, but is always late in getting things done. When I saw how things were going, I asked V. I. Kovalevskii, whom I have mentioned earlier, to lend a hand. Being an able and energetic man, he was able to have everything finished in a few days. Unfortunately, the exhibition was to be only moderately successful, perhaps because it came so soon after the coronation.

Soon after the opening of the exhibition, Li Hung-chang arrived as the guest of the Ministry of Finance and spent a few days there. He was amazed at everything, particularly the machinery and technology sections. From Nizhnii Novgorod he went on to visit several European countries. Their Majesties, accompanied by

Grand Duke Alexis Aleksandrovich, arrived in Nizhnii Novgorod on July 17. During his three-day stay, the Emperor visited the exhibition several times and looked attentively at everything, but it seemed to me that he and the Empress were a bit cold toward me. Being a seasoned bureaucrat I suspected that the coldness was the result of slanderous statements directed at me during the exhibition. I was not sure of the source, but I thought it might be Prince Lobanov-Rostovskii, because he was unhappy over my prominence in concluding the treaty with Li Hung-chang, yet it was difficult to believe because he was a decent man who was not involved in any kind of intrigue at court.

From Nizhnii Novgorod Their Majesties went to Peterhof, then, accompanied by Prince Lobanov-Rostovskii, to Vienna, to visit the aged Emperor Francis Joseph. After two days in Vienna they journeyed to Kiev. En route to Kiev the foreign minister died of a heart attack. The Emperor and Empress were deeply grieved by his death.

The foreign minister's death was to be of critical importance for Russia because, despite his shortcomings, he was too cultured and experienced a man to have permitted those developments in our foreign policy that produced the lamentable results we are now experiencing. His temporary replacement was Shishkin, about whom I have already spoken.

From Kiev, Their Majesties, now accompanied by Shishkin, went to Germany, to visit Emperor William. Then it was on to Copenhagen, to visit the Emperor's grandfather, King Christian. From Copenhagen they traveled to England, to spend some time with Queen Victoria, the young Empress's grandmother. Their next stop was in France, to visit President Félix Faure.

Their Majesties spent a week in Paris and its environs, a week that was called Russian Week, a period during which they were met with overwhelming enthusiasm. This was so for a number of reasons. First of all, they created a charming impression by their unspoiled youth, which was accentuated by the Emperor's great charm: he charmed by his kindly and attentive manner and by his exceptionally fine breeding.

In addition the visit produced an enthusiastic impression because it was the first visit by a Russian emperor since that of the great Emperor Alexander II [in 1867], who had been the target of a shot fired by the Pole Berezowski. What is more, by visiting France, the Emperor underlined his firm decision to follow in the footsteps of his father, the creator of the Franco-Russian agreement.

Also, the French tend to be fascinated by the magnificent. And they find a particular fascination in royalty, and here was the autocratic sovereign of a nation that encompassed one-fifth of the world's surface. Little wonder that the visit produced a kind of ecstasy.

From France the Imperial couple went to Darmstadt, the motherland of the Empress, to call on the Grand Duke of Darmstadt, her brother. By October 19, His Majesty was already in Tsarskoe Selo. Naturally, I returned to Petersburg earlier, at the beginning of September.

The Gold Standard

Even before the Emperor returned to Tsarskoe Selo I heard rumors from banking circles that while he was in Paris, Méline, the French premier, was intriguing against my determined efforts to establish the gold standard. Accordingly I wrote to the Emperor to find out if there were any truth to the rumors. He replied that what I had heard was no more than gossip.

However, when I saw him soon after his return, he handed me two documents, saying: "Here, I am giving you these statements concerning your proposal to establish the gold standard in Russia; I have not read them." These documents had been transmitted to the Emperor a few days earlier by the French ambassador, Count Montebello, who had been authorized by his government to do so.

When I had an opportunity to look over the documents I saw that in them Méline, supported by the well-known economist Theuriet, warned our Emperor that the gold standard would be harmful to Russia and urged that he adopt the silver standard instead, or, if that were not possible, that he accept a bimetallic standard, such as the one used in France.

I considered such an act by Premier Méline a highly improper act of interference in the internal affairs of Russia. I believe that one of his motives was to help France get rid of some of her large silver reserve, at a profit. He apparently wanted to see the price of silver rise and then foist off on Russia a large part of the French silver holdings, which would have brought his country a profit of several hundred million francs. I believe that Méline knew that the State Council was against me and therefore wanted to take advantage of its opposition by sending these documents to the Emperor in the hope of influencing his decision.

When the proposal to adopt the gold standard was placed before the various departments of the State Council, I encountered unexpected opposition, not in the form of nay-saying, but in the form of efforts to create obstacles that would slow things down. Most of the members of the council knew nothing about the question, but they were influenced by two of their number who opposed me and were known to be experts.

One was the eminently respectable Boris Pavlovich Mansurov, who raised objections chiefly because he did not believe that I could get the reform enacted and, also, because he was naturally a carping individual. The other was Vladimir Vladimirovich Verkhovskii, who had served as director of the Credit Chancellery under Bunge and was therefore listened to by his fellow members. His objections were motivated by pique over the fact that it was I and not he who had been chosen to be minister of finance. As a result of this opposition, the meetings of the departments of the State Council resulted in a set of questions to which I was expected to respond with detailed and factual explanations. I did not respond because I understood full well that I couldn't get the monetary reform through the State Council and therefore decided to bypass it, by going through the Finance Committee.[3]

Virtually all educated Russians opposed the reform. In the first place because of ignorance: even Russian economists and financial experts were, for the most part, uninformed about the theoretical aspects of the question. In the second place because of habit: ever since the Crimean campaign we Russians had lived with paper currency and had no understanding of the theory and practice of the metallic standard; all had become acclimated to paper money, just as one becomes accustomed to chronic sickness, however debilitating such a sickness may be. In the third place, because of mistaken self-interest among exporters, particularly landowners who believed that depreciated paper money provided them with favorable terms of trade. For example, exporters thought that the fact that the paper ruble was worth about two and a half francs, rather than four francs as it would have been if the paper ruble had been accepted at par, was to their advantage because they received more rubles for their exports than they would have had the paper ruble been exchanged at par. What these people did not see was that this advantage was offset by the fact that they had to pay more for most of the things they needed as a result.

So I had to go against the general current of opinion, which favored keeping things as they were. Of course, there were those who understood that a currency based on metal was preferable to one that was not, but they opposed me because they feared that with my well-known energy and determination, the reform would be carried out swiftly and decisively, and they preferred that it be done slowly and systematically. But I understood very well that if I did not act rapidly, the attempt at monetary reform would end in failure, for one reason or another. My experience in government had taught me that in Russia reforms had to be carried out in a hurry if they were to be carried out at all.

Among those who opposed me were some who, for one reason or another, sought to undermine my position. One such was my assistant minister Antonovich, about whom I have spoken earlier. When he had seen that public opinion was against me, he, who had written in favor of a stable metallic standard, now began to support those who favored the continuation of a monetary system based on paper money. So he had begun to intrigue against me, working with, among others, S. F. Sharapov, an able journalist, but a man of weak character.

As I have noted, I had become disappointed with Antonovich soon after he had become my assistant minister because in Petersburg it was soon evident that he was an ill-bred provincial who became a laughingstock among those with whom he had to deal. It was, however, his intriguing against me with respect to the gold standard that had finally forced me to part with him, in March 1896. (Naturally, he then became my enemy and began to attack me in memoranda directed to the Emperor, who ignored them.)

Antonovich's replacement was Vladimir Nikolaevich Kokovtsev, who had been serving as state secretary of the State Council's Department of State Economy. He was a meticulous and able state secretary, but he possessed some traits I did not like, among them the tendency to be a Zoilist. However, the members of the Department of State Economy, particularly Prince Imeretinskii, entreated me to appoint him. I agreed to his appointment because he was on good terms with the members of the department and could twist these old men around his little finger, men with whom he would have to deal as assistant minister. Also, he was well acquainted with government finance.

And then there were some—many of them competent and eminent financial experts—who opposed the gold standard because they favored the silver standard. Although silver had fallen in value by this time, there were many financial experts who believed, or tried to believe, that the fall in the price of silver was ephemeral, that the price would either be stabilized or would rise again. I, on the other hand, believed, correctly as it turned out, that silver would continue to fall in price and in time might cease to be a precious metal.

Fortunately, the Emperor, having complete confidence in me, was not swayed by adverse public opinion or adverse advice and supported me completely. Since, as I have said, I did not expect to get the monetary reform through the State Council, I decided to get it approved through the Finance Committee, which supported me, in part because appointments to it were largely determined by the minister of finance, in part because the members had some knowledge of financial questions. So, when I felt it time to bring the question of the gold standard to a conclusion, I asked the Emperor to assemble the committee, under his chairmanship, and invite, in addition to the committee members, Grand Duke Michael Nikolaevich, and such other members of the council as he considered it necessary to invite.

The Emperor agreed. On January 2, 1897, the enlarged Finance Committee met, with himself as chairman. And it was at this meeting that the decision was made to reform our monetary system, i.e., adopt the gold standard. The following day the decision was announced in a decree.

Under the monetary reform Russia was placed on the gold standard. The new gold ruble was given a value equivalent to that of two and two-thirds francs, not four, as would have been the case had we followed the urgings of the press and the State Council. Why? This was done to prevent disrupting the price structure. In this way the monetary reform was carried out without having any noticeable effect on the people. After the decree of January 3, everything remained as before: prices remained unchanged and the stability of things as they were on that date was assured for the future. And with this sound base any possible fluctuation in prices because of the instability of the currency was precluded. Had we set the ruble as being worth four francs, there would have been violent fluctuations and the reform would have been undermined, a reform to which I had devoted all my energy, and I have always been noted for my energy, particularly when I was young.

Some argued that a gold coin smaller than the ruble should have been introduced, it being asserted that in countries with smaller units, e.g., Germany with her mark and France with her franc, the cost of living was lower. The argument is unfounded with respect to wholesale and foreign trade: a smaller unit would not have made it possible to buy more cheaply. The argument does have merit with respect to daily life, particularly in the cities. A smaller unit might mean lower prices for individuals, would benefit certain classes, but I was concerned with the broad interests of the state.

Nonetheless, I had considered the creation of a smaller monetary unit, the rus: in fact, a few specimens of the rus were struck. But then I decided that in view of the many objections being raised against my monetary reform it would be wiser to give up the notion of introducing the rus and to devote myself to carrying out my reform as quickly as possible.

Had I replaced the ruble with the rus there would have been a sharp disruption of prices, which would have alarmed the peasantry and, so to speak, all other backward elements. As a result, there would have been thousands and thousands of complaints instead of the calm with which the reform was carried out. And had we adopted the rus amidst a storm of complaints and had the monetary reform failed, people would have singled out the decision to adopt the rus and would have said: ''See, he did this in the face of all sorts of warnings; consequently, the minds of all Russians are in a state of confusion.'' As it turned out, the introduction of the monetary reform went off without a ripple because of my decisive and energetic action.

The establishment of the gold standard was my greatest achievement as minister of finance. Thanks to the gold standard we firmly established Russia's credit and placed her on equal footing in financial relations with other great European powers. Thanks to this reform we were able to cope with the financial strains produced by our war with Japan, the disorders that followed the war, and our current perilous state. Had this reform not been carried out, we would have experienced a general financial and economic collapse at the very beginning of the war, and the economic achievements of the preceding decade would have gone up in smoke.

My predecessors, among them Bunge and Vyshnegradskii, had prepared our finances for this reform, but what they had done was comparatively insignificant. It was I who carried out this tremendous reform, which will be regarded by history as one of the bright spots in the reign of Emperor Nicholas II. I was able to bring it off despite broad opposition because I enjoyed the Emperor's confidence and support.

The Proposed Seizure
of the Upper Bosphorous

In October 1896, as we were moving toward the adoption of the gold standard, Alexander Ivanovich Nelidov, our ambassador to Constantinople, appeared in Petersburg, setting off a wave of rumors in the Ministry of Foreign Affairs and other government offices that some action against Turkey was imminent. Behind the speculation lay the fact that the Ottoman Empire was by then in an advanced state of decay that manifested itself in such acute symptoms as the recent massacres of Armenians in Constantinople and other parts of Asia Minor.

These rumors prompted me to send a memorandum to the Emperor on November 12, in which I presented my views about the state of the Ottoman Empire and urged that we refrain from any measures involving the use of force. His Majesty was kind enough to write on my memorandum that he would discuss the matter with me when I next reported to him, but when that time came he did not allude to my memorandum.

On November 21, I received a top secret note, written by Nelidov, in which, employing the obscure language typical of the seasoned diplomat, he spoke of the alarming condition of the Ottoman Empire, with particular reference to the sultan and to Constantinople and, in effect, proposed that we create incidents that would allow us to gain control of the upper Bosphorus. At the same time I received an invitation from Shishkin, the acting foreign minister, to take part in a conference, under the chairmanship of the Emperor, to be held two days later. He would be present, as would also Generals Vannovskii and Obruchev, Admiral Tyrtov, the recently appointed director of the Ministry of the Navy, and Nelidov.

At the conference Nelidov argued for the views expressed in his note. As I would have expected, Generals Vannovskii and Obruchev supported him. This was so because Vannovskii always tended to be guided by Obruchev and Obruchev had an *idée fixe* concerning the seizure of the Bosphorus and, if possible, Constantinople.* Shishkin contented himself with a few meaningless phrases. Admiral Tyrtov did not seem particularly taken by the Nelidov position, but, lacking the courage to voice a firm objection, he confined himself to pointing out, from the point of view of the navy, what conditions would be required for an attempted seizure of the upper Bosphorus to succeed.

It turned out that I was the only one at the conference who objected, and very strongly, sharply, and decisively, to the proposed venture. I pointed out that this undertaking would lead in the end to a European war that would undermine the

---

*Some years earlier Giers told me that the military gave him trouble by proposing schemes that could lead to war, but that, fortunately, Emperor Alexander III did not permit such schemes to be carried out. When I asked which of these schemes he considered to be most dangerous, he said that it was one put forward by Obruchev; to use soldiers, sent in by raft, to gain control of the Bosphorus. That scheme, he said, had gained support toward the end of Emperor Alexander III's reign: several general staff officers, led by Kuropatkin, then a colonel, carried out reconnaissance surveys to determine under what circumstances the Bosphorus could be taken. Giers said that documents concerning the Obruchev proposal were among the papers at the Ministry of Foreign Affairs.

excellent political and financial situation in which Emperor Alexander III had placed the Russian Empire.

His Majesty, chairman and absolute ruler of Russia, expressed no opinion during the conference, limiting himself to a few questions. But knowing my Sovereign I realized that in this case he was not in sympathy with my position. Then, at the end of the meeting, after many sharp exchanges between me on the one side and Nelidov, Vannovskii, and Obruchev, the Emperor stated that he shared the view of our ambassador to Constantinople.

In this fashion the question was in essence settled, and in effect it was decided to create those circumstances in Constantinople that would give us the opportunity and right to effect a landing on the Bosphorus and take its upper part; then we would enter into negotiations with the sultan and, if he sided with us, we would promise him our protection. In anticipation of action it was necessary to make immediate preparations for operations based in Odessa and Sebastopol. And, when Nelidov would consider that the proper moment for the landing had come, he was to send a dispatch to Tatishchev, our financial agent in London, empowering him to buy such and such a quantity of grain. Tatishchev would be under instructions immediately to transmit this dispatch to Pleske, the manager of the State Bank, who would then transmit it to the war and naval ministers.

Nelidov then left for Constantinople, aflame with the desire to carry out the idea to which he was dedicated—the taking of Constantinople or, at the very least, the Bosphorus. Events began to move so fast that I instructed Pleske to have an official on duty at all hours, so that if the dispatch arrived it would be sent on immediately and no time would be lost in dispatching troop ships from Odessa and Sebastopol.

Meanwhile, I received a draft copy of the minutes of the November 23rd conference from Shishkin in which, to my astonishment, it was stated that unanimity had prevailed there. I wrote him that I would not sign the minutes as they were under any circumstances, for steps had been proposed that would get Russia into great trouble. Therefore, I wished to have the consent of the Emperor either to have the minutes revised to show what my views were or to have a brief statement included to the effect that I did not share all the views expressed at the conference: I had no desire to assume responsibility before history for this adventure.

This placed Shishkin in a difficult position. Nonetheless, he wrote to the Emperor, who was gracious enough to permit the minutes to be changed to read: "It was the position of State Secretary[4] Witte that the taking of the upper Bosphorus at the present time and under present circumstances without the consent of the great powers was extremely risky and could have the gravest consequences."[5]

Since I feared that the proposed action would have the gravest consequences, I could not refrain from expressing my doubts and fears, in language that would not irritate the Emperor, to two persons close to him—Grand Duke Vladimir Aleksandrovich, his uncle, and Constantine Petrovich Pobedonostsev, his former tutor. Neither had any reaction to my doubts and fears when I expressed them.

But, when Pobedonostsev read the copy of the minutes, which I gave him, and acquainted himself with my position, he wrote me on November 28: "I hasten to return what you sent me and I thank you. *Iacta est alea* [The die is cast]. May God have mercy on us."

For some reason, either because of the influence of these two or because of that power which we call God, which rules the universe, the Emperor reversed himself. As soon as Nelidov had reached Constantinople, he received instructions forbidding him to carry out the undertaking that he had conceived.

Meantime I had to bear the Emperor's displeasure for some days after the conference of November 23. He showed it at a meeting of the Siberian Railroad Committee on November 27 or 28. After I had reviewed the draft of the concession for the construction of the Chinese Eastern Railroad, he uttered some kind words about the late Prince Lobanov-Rostovskii. I was deeply moved by these words, not only because they came from the Emperor but also out of my respect for the memory of Prince Lobanov-Rostovskii: when he was in office, Nelidov would not have dared present his proposal. But then the Emperor went on to bestow all the credit for the concession to Prince Lobanov-Rostovskii and to do so in a manner that made it evident to all those present, who knew through rumor that it was I who deserved all the credit, that he was displeased with me about something.

If the Emperor was, in fact, displeased with me, it was because of the sharpness of my actions and opinions, and on this score I admit my guilt with respect to him, but, unfortunately, I cannot change; so I always was, so I am now. Nonetheless, this did not affect the Emperor's attitude toward me in the realm of finance, for, as I have indicated earlier, a month and a half later he was to give me his complete support in carrying out the monetary reform; without his support it could not have been done.

XXVII

Some New Faces, Some New and Unfortunate Policies

1896–1898

The Caucasus

On December 6, 1896, not long after the events I have just described, General Sheremetev, governor of the Caucasus, was relieved of his post at his own request, because he was ill. His departure was to mark an important change, for the worse, for the Caucasus. As I have noted earlier, he was not an effective administrator, but he was kind and gracious and was considered a Caucasian by the inhabitants of the region, who liked him, something that could not be said of their attitude toward his successor, Prince Gregory Golitsyn, known in society as "Gri-Gri."[1]

Prince Golitsyn was a very decent, well-bred, honorable man, but like so many of our current ultranationalists, he tended to sail with the winds of so-called Russian nationalism.[2] What makes this strange is that his mother was Polish: under her tutelage he acquired some of the characteristics of the Poles—a well-known extravagance of behavior coupled with a gentle manner and an ability to act graciously. One could call him a "Russian Pole" or, better yet, "a true Russian of Polish blood." Although well educated, he was very limited, particularly for a government official.

I remember him from my boyhood, when he commanded a Georgian regiment stationed not far from Tiflis. He was a proper enough regimental commander, but he rubbed Caucasians the wrong way. They are straightforward people, who act as God prompts them, and they do not like wiles. He was too elegant and subtle to appeal to the outspoken Caucasians. Apparently it was to rid the Caucasus of him that his superiors transferred him to the command of the Finnish Regiment in Petersburg.

Thereafter he made his career under the patronage of Grand Duke Michael Nikolaevich, who, as I have said, had some influence with the Emperor. (Why the Grand Duke chose to help Prince Golitsyn I do not know.) Prince Golitsyn next received the post of ataman of the Orenburg Cossack region, subsequently was appointed to the Military Council and to the State Council. Next came his appointment, obviously with the help of the Grand Duke, to succeed Sheremetev.

Given his character, Prince Golitsyn would not have been well received in the Caucasus under any circumstances. But he ensured that he would be badly received by becoming the first chief of the Caucasus to follow the kind of ultranationalist policy so prevalent these days. He chose that policy because he divined that there was something in the air to indicate that the Emperor was being drawn to nationalistic ideas, but it should be said that the ideas that attracted the Emperor were those shared by all Russian people, not those of our self-styled "true" Russians, our contemporary so-called nationalists, whom Stolypin encouraged.[3]

Prince Golitsyn thought it would be to his political advantage to become the first chief of the Caucasus to act in the spirit of "true" Russian, rabble-rousing ultranationalism. Inevitably he drove the natives, who had hitherto been loyal to Russia, into opposition, goaded them into embracing those separatist ideas that gripped them during our so-called revolution.

If, in applying an ultranationalistic policy, he had shown any kind of ability, if he had shown himself capable of carrying out any administrative reform, then the antipathy aroused among the Caucasians by this policy would have been balanced by the goodwill produced by such reform, but there was no reform. Also, had he been firm, had he had prestige, particularly military prestige, had he shown that distinction of character displayed by General Gurko, also a Russifier, but one who gained the acceptance of the Poles, it would have been a different matter. But Prince Golitsyn had nothing on the credit side: he had no military talent; he did not have the reputation of being a valiant soldier (this is not to say that he was not brave); he had no administrative ability or experience. Finally, because of his mixed blood he lacked integrity of character. In short, all that he accomplished was to turn the whole of the Caucasus against him and indirectly against the Russian government. Finally [in 1904], after being wounded by a would-be assassin, he left the Caucasus disliked by all, even the Russians.

If I am "savage" in characterizing Prince Golitsyn it is because I am a Caucasian, hold the region dear, remember all its traditions, and therefore cannot be indifferent to that which Prince Golitsyn did to the Caucasus, just as all other Caucasians, whatever their nationality, be they native or Russian, cannot remain indifferent to what he did.

Kingdom of Poland

About the time that Prince Golitsyn was initiating what may be called a policy of gutter-nationalism in the Caucasus, a different kind of man, Prince Imeretinskii, was replacing Count Shuvalov (who had suffered a stroke) as governor-general of the Kingdom of Poland. Prince Imeretinskii was a fine and kindly man (a Caucasian by origin) who, after a solid military career, had been appointed to the State Council and had served in its Department of State Economy, where I had come to know him. I was very pleased over his appointment.

In my opinion he established very proper relations with the Poles under his jurisdiction. I believe that under his administration there was a good chance of establishing mutually acceptable relations between the Russians and those Poles who were well intentioned. And, it should be noted that he followed what was a civilized and conciliatory policy despite difficulties made for him in Petersburg.

He had one serious shortcoming—a passion for the opposite sex, which was partially responsible for his sudden death, in 1900. His death caused much weeping on the part of his lovely and adoring wife, Countess Mordvinova, and his numerous friends.

He was succeeded as governor-general by General-Adjutant Chertkov, who had not held an administrative office since leaving the post of governor-general of Kiev. Chertkov, who remained in office until his death, in 1905, neither strengthened nor weakened the policy of Russification in the Kingdom of Poland. On the whole, his wife, who retained her vivacity, was more popular than he.

Finland

Not long after Prince Imeretinskii became governor-general of the Kingdom of Poland, Count Heyden left the office of governor-general of Finland. Although Count Heyden had followed a policy dictated by Russian interests, he had done so with great tact and without violating the Finnish constitution or, at least, those parts of it which had been recognized by our emperors, beginning with Alexander the Blessed.[4]

He left office partly because of poor health, but chiefly because he was not in sympathy with the growing tendency, inspired largely by the Ministry of War, to Russify Finland. He felt that such an effort was not justified by the real state of affairs, nor was it in keeping with the dignity of the great Russian Empire.

Nowadays [1910] there are venal persons inside the government and out who, in attempting to justify Stolypin's attempts at Russifying Finland, seek to prove that past Emperors had acted unwisely in recognizing the Finnish constitution and, moreover, had been misled into doing so by some of their trusted advisers. But these people are trying to impute thoughts to the dead which cannot be proven.

In my view the most superficial study will show that a century ago Emperor Alexander I gave Finland a constitution, recognizing that Finland was a borderland of a special kind, because he recognized that he was both the Autocratic Emperor of Russia and Grand Duke of Finland, i.e., the constitutional monarch of that land, governing it in accordance with a constitution that he had granted. This constitution developed in the course of implementation by Emperor Alexander II. Every monarch since Emperor Alexander I has, on ascending the throne, addressed a special manifesto to the people of the grand duchy, recognizing the loyalty of its people to the throne and in effect undertaking to rule the grand duchy on the basis of principles followed in the past.

Emperor Alexander III once said in my presence: "The Finnish constitution is not to my liking; I will not permit its further extension, but that which has been given by my ancestors can't be taken away. I must rule Finland on the basis of what I affirmed on ascending the throne." He was a man of honor.

He often sailed to the Finnish skerries without any pomp, without any special security arrangements. He met the local inhabitants unpretentiously and liked many of their traits: their temperance, their stability, their loyalty, the quality of their simple way of life. For their part the Finns were aware that he did not like their constitution but that he would tolerate it, that, having given his word, he would not go back on it, that he was not the kind of man to engage in political sophistry, not the kind of man to say: "Even God himself would take back his word if he saw that it was necessary to do so in order to serve a higher good." Such words would have had no more effect on his direct nature than a rubber ball on a granite rock.

Within the limits of the Finnish constitution Emperor Alexander III sought to amalgamate the Finnish and Russian postal systems and to make Finnish criminal law, particularly with respect to state crimes, conform to Russian law. During his reign the question of incorporating the Finnish army into the Russian one was put. Also, the question was raised of how best to frame legislation on matters pertaining to Finland that at the same time impinged on the interests of the entire Russian Empire. On this matter commissions and conferences were created, which decided that it was necessary to move gradually in the direction of ending the complete separation of the Finnish and Russian legislative systems. But it does not follow that this Emperor would have approved the abrogation of the Finnish constitution, that he would have followed the path of political provocation toward Finland in order to justify the use of Russian power, be it physical or legislative, to end the Finnish constitution, that he would resort, as is the case nowadays, to political Jesuitry, to undermining the Finnish constitution while denying that such is the case.

N. Kh. Bunge, the chairman of the Committee of Ministers, served as chairman of the commissions which dealt with the question of linking Finland more closely with the empire. No question that he favored a strict and limited reading of the Finnish constitution. However, it suffices to read his memorandum on the condition of the Russian Empire, which he prepared for the Tsesarevich Nicholas Aleksandrovich, soon to be emperor, to understand that his Russifying tendencies in general and with respect to Finland differed sharply from the views of contemporary governmental Russifiers and those venal scribblers who work for them.[5] For my part I have always been of the opinion that Finland should be brought into closer union with Russia, but without violating the basic constitutional structure granted to Finland by Emperor Alexander I, the Blessed, and Emperor Alexander II, the Emancipator, a structure that Emperors Nicholas I and Alexander III maintained. I dare say that these four Emperors were as deserving of being called nationalists as are our latter-day nationalists.

Although Emperor Alexander III respected the Finnish constitution, he was vigilant in seeing to it that the Finns did not take steps that would adversely affect the interests of the empire. What follows will illustrate my point.

Almost a year or two before his death, the Finnish Sejm decided to build a railroad linking the Finnish and Swedish railroads at Tornea. General Dähn, the state secretary for Finnish affairs, himself a Finn, asked me what I thought of the proposal, because as minister of finance I was in charge of railroad policy. I replied that I saw no objection. A few days later he told me that the Emperor wanted to speak to me about this proposal at my next report to him. When that occasion came the Emperor told me that he was opposed to linking the railroads because "in the event of war this might prove disadvantageous to us." I told the Emperor that even without access to this line an enemy could reach the Finnish railroads across the narrow straits that divide Sweden from Finland. His Majesty replied that if we linked the two systems, an enemy would have a second route for an incursion from Sweden into Finland, and for that reason he would not affirm the decision of the Sejm. In the end I came around to his view.

When he ascended the throne, Emperor Nicholas II, in keeping with precedent, issued a manifesto confirming Finnish rights. At the time and for several years to come he was well disposed toward the Finns. Typical of his attitude is the manner in which he reacted to the proposal to link the Finnish and Swedish railroads, which was once more put forward in the first year of his reign.

General Dähn, knowing that I knew how Emperor Alexander III had viewed the proposal, asked me to inform the Emperor of his father's opinion. This I did. Nonetheless, the Emperor said that he favored the link because he considered the Finns to be among the most loyal of his subjects. Subsequently, the Emperor's attitude toward the Finns gradually became less sympathetic, partly because of the influence on him of some in high places, particularly people from among the military, partly, I must say, because the Finns themselves, as ever, did not behave with complete propriety. The Finns were loyal, but in keeping with their forthright character, they tended to act in an abrasive and tactless manner. Had they shown more restraint it is possible that the Emperor's attitude toward them might not have changed.

As I have said, when Emperor Nicholas II came to the throne, there were already those in high places, especially the Ministry of War, seeking to Russify Finland. As long as Count Heyden was governor-general, such pressures were held in check by this fine and honorable man, but once he was gone the situation was to change. First the Emperor offered the post of governor-general to General-

Adjutant Chertkov, who had been out of favor during the reign of Emperor Alexander III. But then the offer was rescinded after Chertkov had a frank talk with Plehve, in the course of which he said that while he would not tolerate license on the part of the Finns, neither would he violate the Finnish constitution. He declared that if he accepted the post he would support integration of Finland and the rest of the empire, but only on the basis of mutual agreement. As a result General Nicholas I. Bobrikov was appointed to succeed Count Heyden. (As I have noted earlier, General Chertkov was subsequently given the post of governor-general of the Kingdom of Poland.)

The appointment of General Bobrikov opened a new era in our policy toward Finland. In this connection I vividly recall a conversation I had with him during a state dinner for King Carol of Rumania, on July 1, 1898. I was sitting next to him. Having heard before dinner that he was to replace Heyden, I asked him if what I had heard were true. When he said that it was, I congratulated him.

He replied that there were no grounds for congratulations, because he expected his task to be as burdensome as the one Count Muravev had had as governor-general of Vilna. I replied that I couldn't understand the comparison: Muravev had been appointed during the Polish revolt, to suppress it, whereas he, Bobrikov, was going to an autonomous borderland, a thoroughly quiet, civilized region that did not display separatist or revolutionary inclinations. It seemed to me that his remark implied that while Count Muravev had been sent to put down a revolt, he was being sent to provoke one. Unfortunately, my interpretation was to be justified by subsequent events.

With the assumption of office by General Bobrikov, friction between Finland and Petersburg began to develop, because he undertook to violate the established order in Finland, an order, as I have said, based in part on the Finnish constitution, in part on traditions maintained by our Emperors for nearly a century. The appointment of General Kuropatkin as minister of war about this time was to make matters worse.[6]

General Kuropatkin does not have a creative mind, but he has a great capacity for work. On becoming minister he avidly examined various proposals which had earlier on been prepared in the ministry but which had been laid aside, for one reason or another. Among them he found proposals for integrating the Finnish and the Imperial armies. As early as the days of Emperor Alexander II, the war minister had put forth such a proposal, but the Emperor had not agreed to it. Kuropatkin's predecessor had raised the question of integration, but he had been frustrated because Emperor Alexander III, although favoring a closer tie than existed between the two armies, did not wish to violate the traditional principles according to which Finland had been administered. Also, it seems that the question of integration was not thought to be of pressing importance given the loyalty of the Finnish troops. General Kuropatkin seized on what he had found, but went much further in preparing a proposal for integration of the two armies. Emperor Nicholas II, who was at first much taken by his new war minister, proved amenable to what General Kuropatkin proposed.

In raising the question of integration anew, Kuropatkin was motivated in part by the desire to make a name for himself, in part by the fact that he had too much energy. He decided to urge the Emperor to take decisive action to achieve integration, which would require overcoming the objections raised by the Finnish Sejm when the idea of integration had been broached earlier. An obstacle to such efforts was General Dähn, who, as I have said, was a Finn, like preceding state secretaries for Finnish affairs. He would not have cooperated in such a venture. What was needed was a man in this post who was not a Finn and not a man of principle. Such a person was Plehve, who was appointed state secretary for Finnish affairs on August 17, 1899, following Dähn's departure from office.

First the proposal for integration had to be approved in Petersburg. Normally, it would have gone to the State Council, and if approved by it and the Emperor and then by the Finnish Sejm it would become law. Being an intelligent man, Plehve understood that the proposal might encounter opposition in the State Council. It had often been the case that when the State Council was expected to object to a proposal that proposal would be submitted to the Committee of Ministers or the Council of Ministers. But Plehve realized that in this case he might encounter difficulties in these bodies as well. Moreover, if he tried to move the proposal through either of these bodies, the hostile influence of the Dowager Empress or of countries such as Sweden or Denmark might come into play. And if this happened, the Emperor might have second thoughts about violating the Finnish constitution.

As a result, in this case the State Council, the Committee of Ministers, and the Council of Ministers did not participate. Instead, the Emperor, after consulting only a handful of people, Plehve among them, issued a manifesto declaring that he had the right to promulgate laws affecting Finland on matters that impinged on the interests of the entire empire.[7] The manifesto was accompanied by a decree that dealt with specifics.

According to the decree, matters affecting Finland but of concern to the empire as a whole should first be considered by the Finnish Sejm, then by the State Council, and, finally, by the Emperor, who would have the final word. As I recall, two (possibly four) members of the Finnish Senate could participate in the deliberations of the State Council in such cases. (There were about one hundred in the State Council at this time.) All this meant that Kuropatkin's proposed legislation could be enacted even over the objections of the Finnish Sejm, which had already opposed some of the general's proposals.

Obviously, the decree was not in accordance with the Finnish constitution, but it provided a way out for a ruler who was both Grand Duke of Finland and absolute ruler of the Russian Empire. In my view the decree was defective in not specifying which matters were of significance for the empire as a whole, but it was widely expected that another decree providing additional detail would soon follow.

I recall that a few days after the decree was issued, I met Boris Nikolaevich Chicherin, the noted professor of public law, at the home of Emmanuel Nikolaevich Naryshkin. Chicherin scolded me, saying the decree clearly violated the Finnish constitution and violated the obligations undertaken by successive Emperors. He criticized me and others around the Emperor for advising him poorly and thus leading him into actions that would have unfortunate consequences. I told him that I had not taken part in the discussions leading to the decree, but noted that I was in favor of it up to a point.

As would be expected, following the issuance of the decree, Kuropatkin submitted his proposal to the Sejm, where it met opposition. The views of the Sejm were then sent on to the State Council. In my capacity as minister of finance I was asked to submit my views concerning the Kuropatkin proposal for distribution in printed form to all members of the council.

Meanwhile, the proposal was considered by a conference, under the chairmanship of General-Adjutant Vannovskii, attended by me, Kuropatkin, Bobrikov, Plehve, Sipiagin (by then minister of interior), and several others. There I presented the following argument.

The Emperor, as unlimited ruler of the Russian Empire, has the obligation to enact laws on matters vital for all his subjects, even if these laws affect Finland. In my view the question at issue here was not a matter of law but of practicality. In my opinion what Kuropatkin had proposed was not of vital concern to the empire yet was certain to have unfortunate consequences in Finland. I argued that instead of the Kuropatkin proposal, which would, in effect, erase all differences between the Finnish and Imperial armies, a proposal be considered whereby the Finnish military system be modified to resemble ours, but that Finns serve in their own units, to be stationed in Finland in time of peace, but serve together with the Imperial army in time of war. I should add that what I suggested went further than the proposal concerning Finnish units made during the reign of Emperor Alexander II and rejected by him on the advice of the then governor-general of Finland and the then state secretary for Finnish affairs.

In stating my opinion at the conference I dealt harshly with the argument advanced by Kuropatkin in support of his proposal, namely, that he was carrying out the wishes of the late Emperor Alexander III. At the time the name of the late Emperor carried a great deal of authority, and a reference to his wishes would surely influence Emperor Nicholas II to be firm in support of Kuropatkin. Moreover, the claim that this is what the late Emperor had wished would mean that any odium produced among Finns by this proposal would be directed at the late Emperor, not his son. I pointed out that the reference to Emperor Alexander III's wishes was untrue and added that as long as the grand duchy had been united with the Russian Empire its army had always been loyal to Russia and to the Russian throne and had participated in virtually all the wars that Russia had fought during this period.

My views greatly troubled Kuropatkin, who complained to the Emperor. At the Emperor's request I softened my statement, without changing my principal arguments, and was then required to ask Plehve, the Imperial secretary, to destroy all the printed copies of my original statement and substitute my revised statement for it for distribution to the State Council. The destruction of the copies meant that news of anything embarrassing I said would not reach the West.

Then the Kuropatkin proposal, the views of the Sejm, and my revised statement were discussed by the State Council as a whole and by the departments concerned. As it turned out, the great majority in the council, among them Grand Dukes Alexis Aleksandrovich and Vladimir Aleksandrovich, supported my position. The minority included Bobrikov, Kuropatkin, Plehve, and Grand Duke Michael Nikolaevich (that this Grand Duke, who disliked Plehve but was often influenced by him, supported the minority suggested that the Emperor was wavering and that Plehve had gone running to the Grand Duke for his support). The majority and minority views were then presented to the Emperor, who invited Grand Duke Michael Nikolaevich, Bobrikov, Kuropatkin, Plehve, and Sipiagin to confer with him. Sipiagin said that all but he, who was still undecided, favored the minority view, which is what the Emperor had expected.

Sipiagin told me that he had expressed the fear that if the minority view were followed, there would be grave unrest in a borderland that had been quiet and loyal. When he had asked what harm would come if the Emperor approved the majority view, he was told that one could not be certain of the loyalty of the Finnish troops. In reply he had suggested that if the Emperor did not trust the Finnish army, the best course would be to ignore the majority and minority views and to disband the Finnish army and not conscript any Finns.

The Emperor thereupon made a complex decision: he affirmed the minority view, but did not implement it. At the same time [June 1901] he issued a decree disbanding the Finnish army except for a battalion of Finnish Guards, which was always stationed in Petersburg, and a regiment of Finnish dragoons that his father had established.

The decision to disband the Finnish army only heightened unrest in the grand duchy. And as unrest grew, Bobrikov and Plehve began to Russify the region in violation of its constitution, e.g., introducing the use of Russian, replacing members of the Finnish Senate with men who had nothing in common with Finland, and exiling those who, in one way or another, opposed such high-handed rule. And, to please the Emperor, Plehve began to employ police methods on a broad scale.

In conformity with the universal rule that every action produces a reaction and vice-versa, it follows that our policy would lead to some kind of reaction, and, as will be seen, it did, in the assassination of General Bobrikov.

I recall that during the discussions I have described, Plehve was cautious and reserved, but it was he who was working behind the scenes, directing events to lead to a preordained result.[8] As for Kuropatkin, he expressed disapproval of Bobrikov's actions on several occasions and argued that we were going too far in Finland. As for me, I took no further part in discussions of Finnish affairs because they did not concern the Ministry of Finance.

As it turned out, the decree issued in 1899, giving the Emperor authority to enact legislation concerning Finland that affected the empire as a whole, proved to be a dead letter. And what had been done with respect to the Finnish army was not in conformity with the Kuropatkin proposal or the wishes of the Sejm or in conformity with either the majority or minority views of the State Council. Why, then, was it necessary for the opinions of the highest legislative body in the empire to be heard?

Foreign Affairs

It was not until early in 1897 that the vacancy left by the death of Prince Lobanov-Rostovskii was filled, by the appointment of Count Michael Nikolaevich Muravev as foreign minister, an appointment that was to have the most unfortunate consequences for Russia.

He was named to the post because he had served as minister to Denmark, where like our other ministers to that country he had the opportunity of displaying his abilities as a courtier and thus impressing our Emperor, who, because of his familial ties with the royal house of Denmark, often visited that country.

Since the young Emperor did not know any other of our diplomats, it was quite natural that his choice should fall on Count Muravev. Moreover, Count Muravev knew the Dowager Empress, a frequent visitor to Denmark, quite well.

At the time I did not know him at all, so I asked Paul Andreevich Shuvalov, under whom Count Muravev had served as counsellor in Berlin, what he thought of him. Count Shuvalov was rather skeptical of Count Muravev's abilities and said: "All I can tell you about Count Muravev is that he is a playboy."

Like Prince Lobanov-Rostovskii, Count Muravev was a man of the world and was a bit frivolous, but there the similarity ended. Prince Lobanov-Rostovskii was a cultivated man, a witty and sophisticated man. Count Muravev was in many respects an ignorant man. True, he was amusing, but with a low kind of humor, and he was not witty. Moreover, he liked to wine and dine too well. For that reason he was very reluctant to work after dinner. In fact, he was lazy and devoted little time to his duties.[9]

In contrast, the man he wisely chose to be his assistant minister, Count Vladimir Nikolaevich Lambsdorff, was a tremendous worker.[10] Count Lambsdorff, who had spent his entire career in the Ministry of Foreign Affairs, worked night and day. He began his career under Prince Gorchakov; subsequently he was secretary to Giers and was close to him; later he rose to be counsellor of the ministry and was close to Prince Lobanov-Rostovskii. He was a walking archive of all the secret affairs of the ministry. Count Lambsdorff was a splendid person, kind hearted, very modest, a true friend. He was highly educated although he had not gone beyond the Corps des Pages.

He was a priceless treasure to Count Muravev, who knew little and understood little of world diplomacy and, as I have said, did not like to work, but preferred to spend his time amusing himself. For some reason Count Muravev pleased both the Emperor and the Empress. He boasted that he was often, in fact nearly always, invited to lunch with the Emperor after giving his reports and he would tell his colleagues, me among them, how he entertained the young Empress with his stories.[11]

Ministry of the Imperial Court

On May 6, 1897, Count Vorontsov-Dashkov was relieved of his post as minister of the Imperial court. This did not come as a surprise to those who understood the psychology of court life.

He had lost the favor of the Emperor in part because, like so many of the ministers who had served under Emperor Alexander III and had known Emperor Nicholas II from the cradle, he could not immediately accept the fact that this young man had become the unlimited monarch of the greatest empire in the world and did not always speak to the young Emperor with the necessary respect. And undoubtedly he used the tone of a teacher in speaking to his Sovereign, thus shocking him and the Empress.

But the most important reason for Count Vorontsov-Dashkov's loss of favor arose from the strained relations between him and Grand Duke Sergei Aleksandrovich, who exercised considerable influence over the Emperor. The bad blood between the two had developed as a result of the dispute between them over responsibility for the tragedy at Khodynka. Moreover, Count Vorontsov-Dashkov was rather independent in his relations with grand dukes, as he had been taught to be by Emperor Alexander III, and kept a sharp eye on the Grand Duke, who, for his part, was a proud man and did not take kindly toward such an attitude.

Count Vorontsov-Dashkov mistakenly thought that I had had a hand in his departure. Although I had always been on the best of terms with him, we had disagreed about the procedure for requesting appropriations for his ministry. At first he had been firmly opposed to my point of view.

That my differences with Count Vorontsov-Dashkov had nothing to do with his departure is shown by the following incident. Shortly after his appointment as Count Vorontsov-Dashkov's successor, Baron Freedericksz came to me with an Imperial order setting forth the manner in which money should be appropriated for his ministry. This order was based on Count Vorontsov-Dashkov's proposals, not mine.

In the memorandum accompanying the order it was stated that since the new arrangement had not gone through the State Council, it was necessary to insert it into the laws in such a way as to avoid attracting attention and thus avoid rumors and arguments. In this connection I recall that once when I told the Emperor that if appropriations for the Ministry of the Imperial Court were not to go through the State Council, in accordance with established procedures, they should be determined by agreement between the minister of finance and the minister of the Imperial court, he replied: "Do you think that I will waste any money?"

I replied humbly, but quite sincerely and correctly, that I was not concerned over the money spent by him and his family—for his scale of living was a modest one, more modest than that of his closest servitors and advisers, I among them—but that I was concerned over the money spent by the ministry on its various enterprises, money that it spent uneconomically, without proper auditing, and without regard to regulations.

Baron Freedericksz, the new minister, is a very honorable and fine man, a true knight, but that is all one can say of him.[12] Nonetheless, such qualities have always counted for a great deal, and they are especially important these days. But he obviously lacks the knowledge and ability to advise the Emperor in affairs of state or even in the affairs of his ministry; for that reason he is an ideal minister for this Emperor.

Ministry of Education

On December 29, 1897, the minister of education, Count Delianov, died. He was quite old, but hale and hearty. [As I have said], he was an Armenian, with a meek and ingratiating manner, and was a very adroit, but intelligent, decent, and honorable man.

The academic world, however, considered him a reactionary. During his tenure many professors were treated with such disfavor that they left their posts. Among them was Mechnikov. This scientist, with a European reputation, left Novorossiisk University to go to Paris, where he is still head of the Pasteur Institute. Among other professors who gave up their positions in anger I remember Chicherin, that well-known professor and public figure, whom I often met at the home of his sister, Alexandra Nikolaevna Naryshkina. He called Delianov a reactionary. Nonetheless, Count Delianov's administration seems heavenly when compared with that of his successors, who proved to be cynical men, indifferent to all laws and usage.

Count Delianov was succeeded by Bogolepov, about whose appointment I have spoken earlier.[13] Bogolepov was sincere and well intentioned, but he was to follow a reactionary policy, with unfortunate consequences.

Ministry of War

[In 1898] General-Adjutant Vannovskii asked to be relieved of his position as minister of war, ostensibly for reason of health, but in fact because he could not administer his ministry with the same authority he had had under Emperor Alexander III: as I have noted earlier, several grand dukes had begun to interfere in the operations of the ministry under the young Emperor Nicholas II, and General Vannovskii, being a strong, authoritative, and straightforward man, could not tolerate such interference. The result was constant friction.

The Emperor could not help but be pleased at the thought of parting with this minister, whom he had inherited from his father: Vannovskii had served as war minister during the entire reign of his father and therefore possessed such authority in the eyes of the young Emperor that the Emperor could not help but feel inhibited in the presence of this man, who often acted more like a teacher than a minister.

General Vannovskii told me that when the Emperor asked him to suggest a successor, he put forward three possible choices—Generals Obruchev, Lobko,* and Kuropatkin.[14] Each had both strong points and weak points. He told the Emperor that General Obruchev's weak point was that he had never held a military command and was more a military specialist and adviser than a commander. Concerning General Lobko, toward whom the Emperor was favorably inclined since the general had been one of his teachers, General Vannovskii pointed out that, like General Obruchev, General Lobko had never held a command. Concerning General Kuropatkin, he pointed out that here was a young man who had held many military commands, had spent almost his entire career with troops, and had a considerable reputation in the military world. However, in Vannovskii's opinion General Kuropatkin was not yet ready to be minister of war: he suggested that Obruchev be appointed minister for the time being and that Kuropatkin be appointed his chief of staff, with the expectation that he would replace Obruchev in a short time.

General Kuropatkin was then summoned to Petersburg, where he first saw General Vannovskii, then the Emperor, then General Obruchev. What the Emperor said to him I do not know, but I know that Obruchev expected to be named minister, with Kuropatkin as his chief of staff, and was amazed to learn when Kuropatkin called on him that the latter would be named acting minister. Kuropatkin then sought to persuade Obruchev to stay on as chief of staff, but Obruchev was hurt and soon left his post, to be appointed member of the State Council.

I could easily see how the Emperor came to appoint Kuropatkin, then a young general with a considerable reputation, a man who was very servile toward higher-ups. The public, too, was impressed by Kuropatkin. Had there been an election for the post, he would have won, but as it was to turn out, public confidence in him was misplaced, as was to be demonstrated in the war with Japan.

At first the new war minister was *persona gratissima* with the Emperor. He also found favor with the Empress. But he could not remain in good standing for very long, particularly in the eyes of the Empress, for although he moved in high society, he spoke and acted like a staff clerk, and this weighed against him with the young Empress.

The following episode illustrates the nature of the man. One evening, in the

---

*General Lobko was a very intelligent, sensible man, a man of character, although somewhat narrow. After state controller Filippov died, toward the end of November 1899, he was appointed in his place. Such knowledge as he had of state control came from his experience as director of the war ministry's chancellery and consequently of the ministry's budget.

summer of 1898, when I was living on Elagin Island, in a house belonging to the Ministry of the Imperial Court, and Kuropatkin was living nearby, also in a house belonging to that ministry, I called on him to discuss some business. He was scheduled to report to the Emperor the following day.

When I had finished my business and started to leave, he asked me to stay. When I expressed concern that I might disturb him in the preparation of his report, he replied:

> Not at all. I am adequately prepared. Right now I am reading Turgenev, because after my reports I always lunch with the Emperor and the Empress and I want gradually to acquaint Her Majesty with the various types of Russian women.

By the time the war with Japan broke out the Emperor had cooled toward Kuropatkin. He was to appoint him commander-in-chief of the army in Manchuria, not because he would be so inclined, but because of the demand by the public and the newspapers, particularly *Novoe vremia* and its staff member Menshikov.[15]

(Kuropatkin's appointment, like that of Count Michael Nikolaevich Muravev, would bring much harm to Russia.)

XXVIII

The Visiting Dignitaries, 1897

Emperor William II

During 1897 Emperor Nicholas received a number of visiting dignitaries, some of whom were returning visits he had made to them. The visit of Emperor Francis Joseph, in April, was not marked by any significant occurrences, nor was that of the King of Siam, in June. However, the visit of Emperor William II, in July, was marked by one event that was to have great significance for our future in the Far East.

Emperor William and Empress Augusta Victoria arrived in Peterhof on July 14 and remained until July 30. In accordance with custom, our Emperor gave a state dinner in honor of his guests soon after their arrival.

Just as I arrived in Peterhof for the dinner, a member of Emperor William's suite told me that Emperor William wanted to make my acquaintance and for me to go to his quarters before dinner. When I did, I found him not yet fully dressed. He told me that because I was a wise and eminent statesman he was bestowing the Order of the Black Eagle on me, an order, as he said, usually reserved for members of the Imperial family and for ministers of foreign affairs. Naturally, I was very flattered by this high honor and favor.

I had another opportunity to meet with Emperor William when I came to Petersburg for lunch at the German embassy. I was invited to attend by the ambassador, Prince Radolin, who told me that Emperor William wished to speak to me.

After lunch, Emperor William came into the reception room, where I, embassy officials, and Russian personnel, chosen to accompany the visiting Emperor during his stay, were standing. He was almost prancing as he entered the room; then, as he walked about he gesticulated in a manner not befitting an Emperor. I was astonished by his foppish manner: obviously he acted as he did because he felt himself to be in an intimate group.

He led me into the ambassador's study and when we were alone told me that he felt that the United States was growing at European expense and that Europe should employ protective tariffs to safeguard herself against American imports. I disagreed, saying that I did not believe that other European countries would agree to such a policy and that, moreover, if protective tariffs were to be imposed on American imports they should be imposed as well on the imports from all overseas countries, including those from England.

To this Emperor William replied that he did not consider England, with which he was trying to establish cordial relations, an overseas country. He added that England was not flooding Europe with her agricultural products, while America, in contrast, was lowering the prices of all her agricultural products destined for the European market.

I replied that it would be extraordinarily difficult for Russia to follow the policy he had in mind because she was on the best of terms with the United States and was not ready suddenly to alter relations with that country. I also pointed out that economic and political relations were inseparably linked, that good political relations could not exist without good economic relations and vice-versa.

I went on to say that to the rest of the world Europe seemed to be like a woman in her declining years, that if Europe continued on her present course, she would become totally enfeebled in a few centuries and lose her international primacy, while the overseas countries would become strong; in a few centuries the greatness of Europe would seem like a thing of the past, like the greatness of the Roman Empire, Greece, Carthage, and some of the states of Asia Minor. I added that the time might come when Europe would be treated with the respect shown to aging, well-bred beauties on their last legs.

The German Emperor was astonished by my prognosis and asked what should be done to prevent such a decline. I said:

> Imagine, Your Majesty, the European countries united in one entity, one that does not waste vast sums of money, resources, blood, and labor on rivalry among themselves, no longer compelled to maintain armies for wars among themselves, no longer forming an armed camp, as is the case now, with each fearing its neighbor. If that were done, Europe would be much richer, much stronger, more civilized, not going downhill under the weight of mutual hatred, rivalry, and war.
>
> The first step toward attaining this goal would be the formation of an alliance (*soiuz*) of Russia, Germany, and France. Once this were done, the other countries of the European continent would join the alliance. As a consequence Europe would be freed of the burdens created by existing rivalries: Europe would be mighty, would be able to maintain a dominant position for a long time. But, if the European countries continue on their present course, they will be risking great misfortune.[1]

His Majesty told me that he found my views interesting and original and then graciously took his leave.

This was in 1897. Almost fifteen years have passed since then. During that time Japan has become a mighty empire on God's globe, a new state has been established in Africa as a result of the Anglo-Boer war, and several South American countries have become markedly stronger. On the whole the overseas countries have gained in political, military, and economic power.

At my next report to our Emperor, he handed me a short note from Emperor William, in which he repeated what he had said to me about employing protective tariffs against the North American republic. I told the Emperor about my conversation on the subject with Emperor William. His Majesty told me that he agreed with me and asked me to prepare a note expressing our views. I did so, without signing the note, which Emperor Nicholas II later signed and sent on to the German Emperor.

After the departure of Emperor William, Grand Duke Alexis Aleksandrovich, in speaking of the visit, noted the German Emperor was rather idiosyncratic and told me in this connection about the following incident. After returning from a drive with the German Emperor, our Emperor told the Grand Duke about an unpleasant experience. In the course of the drive, Emperor William asked him if Russia had any need of the Chinese port of Kiaochow, for Germany would like to use it as a base for her ships, adding that he did not wish to act without the prior consent of the Russian Emperor. Emperor Nicholas II did not tell the Grand Duke whether or not he had given his consent, but had merely said that the request had put him in a difficult situation, for to refuse a request from a guest categorically would have been embarrassing.[2]

Our Emperor is very well bred. I can easily understand that it was not in his nature, particularly when he was younger, to reject the request of a guest categorically. As a result the German Emperor could assume, so to speak, that the Russian Emperor had given his blessing to the proposal.

The President of France

Twelve days after the departure of the German Emperor, the president of France, Félix Faure, accompanied by his minister of foreign affairs, Hanotaux, arrived to pay a return visit to our Emperor. During his visit there occurred a memorable event that highlighted the difference in character of Emperor Alexander III and Nicholas II.

Emperor Alexander III had come to an understanding with France and ended the traditional ties with Germany, breaking with tradition. And he had been faithful to this understanding, and although he was an absolute monarch he had even listened to the French republican hymn, when it was played in response to the Russian hymn, an act that the French had greeted with enthusiasm. But beyond an understanding he would not go.

But Emperor Nicholas II went further. In responding to Faure's toast, he declared the understanding to be an alliance and an alliance it has been ever since, with i's dotted and t's crossed. What significance this alliance will have history will reveal.

This result was achieved by the diplomatic efforts of Hanotaux, who did the thinking on such matters for President Faure.

Hanotaux, then a comparatively young man, is well known not only for his work as minister of foreign affairs but also as one of "The Immortals," a member of the Académie Française: he was elected to it for his outstanding scholarly and literary work, particularly his book on the Duc de Richelieu.

I spoke to Hanotaux several times while he was in Petersburg and subsequently met him when he was no longer minister of foreign affairs. There is no question that he was a gifted, educated, and intelligent person, but I did not find him a sympathetic individual. Thus, I recall his manner when he and Faure went to the Cathedral of SS. Peter and Paul to lay a wreath on the tomb of Emperor Alexander III. As he approached the tomb he saw that he was the only one present wearing an outer garment, in this case a cloak, and had enough sense to take it off, but instead of placing it on his arm, he unceremoniously handed it to a nearby Russian officer, who was quite taken aback, but who held the cloak until Hanotaux was ready to put it on. I was very annoyed by such tactless behavior on the part of this little Frenchman.

While in Petersburg Félix Faure visited the Government Printing Office, which is a superb institution, from a technological and artistic point of view. In my capacity as minister of finance I escorted him around the establishment, which he inspected attentively. We gave him several knick-knacks as mementos. While there we drank to his health and to the welfare of France, and he drank to the health of the Emperor and the welfare of the Russian Empire.

Although President Faure was a distinguished-looking man, getting on in years, he was not a man of distinction. I believe that earlier in life he had been a wholesale lumber merchant. His wife, who was of the same age as he, was an ordinary little bourgeois Frenchwoman, whose very unassuming manner on festive occasions must have shocked her husband.

I was to see him later, in Paris. In fact, on that occasion he was to give me a state dinner at Rambouillet, his official summer residence; afterward we sat on the balcony, listening to musical entertainment provided by local musical societies.

He was gracious, gallant, clever, but in the bourgeois sense of these words. He was quite haughty, making it obvious that in his heart he regretted that he was merely president and not king or emperor of France.

He had been handsome when young and had been something of a lady's man.

Even in his latter years he thought himself still handsome and continued to chase women. As a result he was to die, [in 1899], of a heart attack, under circumstances that were both tragic and scandalous, for a man of his years and position. He was with the very pretty widow of the well-known artist Steinheil (whom she had been accused of murdering a year or so earlier) when he died. She thereupon began to scream and when some people entered the room on hearing her screams, they found a scene difficult to describe: Faure, in a most improper state, lying there, grasping her luxuriant, beautiful hair and she on her knees before him.

I believe she was born in Bayonne, not far from Biarritz. Since I am often in Biarritz, I have heard a great deal about her. I believe that she is still alive and lives in England.

As soon as President Faure left Petersburg, the Emperor and Empress departed for Warsaw, stopping en route in Bialystok for the maneuvers, then in Belovezh. From Warsaw they went to Spala, where the Emperor hunted. Their next destination was Darmstadt, to visit the Empress's brother.

The Emperor's stay in the Kingdom of Poland raised hopes among the Poles that, although they could not expect the past to be buried, they might find life somewhat easier than in the preceding reign. This hope was inspired in part by the gracious and sympathetic manner in which the Emperor behaved toward the Poles he met, in part by the behavior of the governor-general, Prince Imeretin-skii, who followed, or rather began to follow, a policy of conciliation between Russians and Poles. Unfortunately, the hopes of the Poles were not to be realized.

The Emperor returned to Tsarskoe Selo around October 20.

Visit of the Abyssinian Delegation

On October 22 Emperor Nicholas II received a comic-opera delegation, consisting of N. S. Leontev[3] and the semiliterate Ato-Iosif. Leontev was one of a whole pleiade of Russian adventurers who have come into prominence in recent times, a pleiade that includes such men as Bezobrazov, Vonliarliarskii, Matiunin, and Captain Sanin. They differ among themselves with respect to education and social status, but their common link is their inclination to adventurism.

After serving in our army as an officer, Leontev engaged in small-time speculation, ending up in Abyssinia, where he managed to convince King Menelik that he had the backing of our government and our Emperor. At the same time he convinced highly placed Russians that he was practically the chief adviser and guiding spirit of King Menelik.

In fact, the king had no respect for him, hardly saw him, and tolerated him only because he thought that Leontev had the backing of our government. I know from several persons, among them Count Wielopolski of the Life Hussars, who were in a delegation we sent to Abyssinia, that Leontev played no significant role in that

country and was appointed governor-general of one of the most primitive provinces to keep him far away from the king and the capital.

Leontev, for his part, called himself a count and, when visiting other countries,
called himself Count Leontev of Abyssinia, while engaging in various shady
enterprises.

Abyssinia is half-pagan, but because her religion has traces of Orthodoxy, has
some connection with the Orthodox church, we are very anxious to take her under
our protection and at the proper moment to annex her. This desire is in keeping
with the tendency of some of our upper strata for conquering, or rather annexing,
areas that are in poor condition. For a thousand years, beginning in the time of
Rurik, we have been swallowing up non-Russian peoples. As a consequence the
Russian Empire is a conglomerate of nationalities. Despite this fact we now have a
semi-comic nationalist party in the State Duma which insists on Russia for the
Russians, i.e., for those whose surnames end in ''ov'' and who read *Russkoe
znamia* and *Golos Moskvy*.[4]

XXIX

Origins of the War
with Japan, 1897–1900

German Occupation of Kiaochow

In November 1897, during a meeting of the Plague Commission,[1] a dispatch was handed to our foreign minister, Count Muravev. Obviously affected by it, he handed it to me: it stated that German naval vessels had landed troops at Kiaochow Bay [in China] and that these troops had occupied the port of Tsingtao. I told Count Muravev that the Germans probably intended to stay only temporarily and that if they did not leave, we and other powers should compel them to depart. He did not reply, being evidently reluctant to say yea or nay. I was astonished at the German action, but, as I was to learn later, he was not. From subsequent German statements we learned that the action they had taken had been in reprisal for the murder of German missionaries some months earlier. It seemed odd to me at the time that the Germans should have reacted with as much force as they had.

Proposal to Occupy Port Arthur

Not long after the German action I received a memorandum from Count Muravev, in which he stated that the German occupation of Tsingtao provided us with a propitious opportunity to acquire a much-needed port for our navy in Chinese waters; he suggested that it be either Port Arthur or neighboring Talienwan. The memorandum was followed by an invitation to a conference under the chairmanship of the Emperor, to discuss the proposal suggested in the memorandum.

At the conference (also attended by General Vannovskii, Admiral Tyrtov, and, of course, Count Muravev), I argued strongly against the proposal, making the following points: If Germany planned to take the Kiaochow Territory and if such an action, in addition to being illegal, were against our interests, why not take steps against Germany? Why should we emulate Germany, by acting against our ally China?

If we took a port from China, I continued, we, who had helped her regain the Liaotung Peninsula (where Port Arthur and Talienwan are located) from Japan and had pledged ourselves to protect China against Japan, would be committing an act of treachery that would transform China into our enemy. Her enmity would be all the greater because if we took Port Arthur or Talienwan we would have to link either to the Chinese Eastern Railroad in order to ensure the security of the port, and such a link would arouse the Chinese against us because it would run through densely settled areas, including Mukden, the birthplace of the ruling dynasty. Moreover, I said, our taking a port would rouse England and Japan against us. In short, the gravest consequences would follow if we acted on Count Muravev's proposal.

Count Muravev did not share my fear that England and Japan would show hostility at our action. He was certain that neither would take countermeasures. He would, in fact, assume responsibility for arguing that we were not taking any risks.

Although he knew little of international diplomacy, General Vannovskii strongly supported Count Muravev, taking the position that if the foreign minister thought that the undertaking entailed no risk, he, as minister of war, would support the taking of either Port Arthur or Talienwan. Admiral Tyrtov did not deal with Count Muravev's proposal directly, but said that the navy preferred a Far Eastern port that would provide direct access to the Pacific, a port on the Korean coast.

Although I was the only one who objected strongly to the foreign minister's proposal, and although the Emperor clearly did not find my objections welcome, he accepted my position. Consequently, the minutes of the conference were to read that His Majesty would not agree to the proposal of the minister of foreign affairs.

It should be noted that although Count Muravev was a shallow man, he was not without ambition. He burned with eagerness to distinguish himself and was bitterly upset that Prince Lobanov-Rostovskii had been able to achieve as much as he did in the Far East and to do so without incurring the enmity of Japan.

A few days after the conference, while I was at Tsarskoe Selo giving my regular report to the Emperor, he said, obviously embarrassed: "Sergei Iulevich, I have decided to take Port Arthur and Talienwan because the minister of foreign affairs informed me that English ships were cruising near the two ports and planned to take them if we did not: I have already sent warships with a complement of troops there."

Of course, the information provided by Count Muravev was untrue, as I later learned from O'Connor, the English ambassador: while it was true that English ships were cruising near Port Arthur and Talienwan, this was in response to German actions, not for the purpose of occupying the ports.

I was greatly disturbed by what the Emperor had told me. When I encountered Grand Duke Alexander Mikhailovich as I left the Emperor's study, I said to him: "Remember this day, Your Highness: it is one that will be remembered for the terrible consequences it will have for Russia." I gathered from his response that he had known in advance of the decision to take Port Arthur.

When I returned to Petersburg I went directly to the German embassy, where I saw Mr. Tschirsky, the counsellor, who was in charge while Prince Radolin, the ambassador, was on leave. I told him that when Emperor William had been there he had told me that I could communicate with him on any matter through the embassy. Therefore, I asked him to send a telegram to his Emperor, informing him that I believed it in the best interests of both our countries for Germany to leave Kiaochow; I earnestly advised that Germany do whatever she felt necessary to do in reprisal for the killings—execute those they thought should be executed, exact reparations—but to leave once this were done, for to remain would lead to harmful consequences. Within a few days Tschirsky brought me the Emperor's reply, which read somewhat as follows: "Inform Witte that I see from his telegram that he is unaware of certain important and relevant facts in this matter; consequently I can't follow his advice." It was then that I recalled what Grand Duke Alexis Aleksandrovich had told me about Emperor William's conversation with our Emperor in Peterhof. Also, I recalled how quiet Count Muravev had been when he had received the news of the German landing. Obviously the Germans had acted as they had because we had carelessly given our consent to their action.

Although our Emperor had already made his decision, I felt it necessary, given the consequences that would come from taking Port Arthur, to attempt to reverse that decision. This led to several sharp exchanges between me and Count Muravev that resulted in his being on bad terms with me for the rest of his life. But once he and General Vannovskii had advised the Emperor—young and avid for glory and achievement—that it was in Russia's interest to take Port Arthur, it was not to be expected that my efforts to have reason prevail should succeed.

When Prince Radolin, with whom I was on friendly terms, returned from leave, he called on me to talk about what was taking place. When he asked what I thought about it all, I replied: "I regard it as childish behavior (I was referring to the actions of the German Emperor) that, unfortunately, will have evil consequences."

As it turned out, he deemed it necessary to report our conversation to Berlin. Exactly how he reported it I do not know,[2] but I know that our foreign ministry deciphered his telegram* and turned over a copy of it to Count Muravev, who then informed our Emperor.

---

*Our foreign ministry, like all such ministries, tries to decode telegrams sent by foreign ambassadors. At least in that time we were able to break nearly all codes, despite the fact that they were difficult and were often changed.

When I next saw the Emperor he was unusually cold toward me, and when the time came for me to leave, he stood up and said: "Sergei Iulevich, I advise you to be more careful in conversation with foreign ambassadors." I replied: "Your Majesty, I do not know what conversation you are referring to, but this I know, that I have never said anything to foreign ambassadors that could harm Your Majesty or my fatherland."

When our ships neared Port Arthur, Count Muravev instructed our minister in Peking to assure the Chinese government that our purpose was to defend China from the Germans and that as soon as the Germans left, so would we. At first the Chinese accepted our assurances, but when they learned from their minister in Berlin that we were acting in concert with Germany, they began to distrust us.

Kwantung

Meanwhile General-Adjutant Vannovskii was replaced as minister of war by Lieutenant General Kuropatkin. I hoped that the new war minister would support me in my efforts to reverse our decision concerning Port Arthur. This did not turn out to be the case.

About this time [February 1898], a conference, under the chairmanship of Grand Duke Alexis Aleksandrovich, was held to consider what demands to present to China. Kuropatkin not only favored our taking of Port Arthur and Talienwan but also argued for the acquisition of the Kwantung Territory, of which they were part, on the ground that without it we could not defend the two ports in the event of war; also he called for construction of a branch line to link Port Arthur and the Chinese Eastern Railroad.

The conference then decided that we demand that China lease us the Kwantung Territory for thirty-six years. (There was no reference to our paying rent.) China would be given time to agree; if she did not, we would order Admiral Dubasov, who was in command of our warships lying off Port Arthur, to land troops and occupy the Kwantung Territory.

At my next report to the Emperor, who by now had taken up residence in the Winter Palace, I asked to be relieved of my post in view of what he had said (about my being more careful in conversations with foreign ambassadors) and in view of my disagreement with what was taking place. He replied that this was out of the question: he said he had a high opinion of me as a person, had complete confidence in me as minister of finance. He said that I had no ground for complaining about my treatment as minister of finance (in this he was right): in short, he would not part with me and asked me to continue to serve him. As for the question of Port Arthur and Talienwan, he said, the matter was closed; whether or not there would be unfortunate consequences only time could tell. Meanwhile, he was asking me to help him implement his decision as expeditiously as possible.

When Pavlov, our *chargé d'affaires* in China, presented our demands, they were rejected by the Empress-Regent, who had been influenced to take this position by English and Japanese diplomats. In view of the fact that our Emperor was set on his course, it followed that if we could not get the lease by negotiation, as now seemed unlikely, we would have to use force. I therefore decided to take a hand in the negotiations.

I telegraphed Pokotilov, the agent of the Ministry of Finance in Peking, to see Li Hung-chang and another official, Chang Yin-huan, and to advise them, in my name, to exert their influence to have the lease granted. I promised a gift of 500,000 rubles to the former and one of 250,000 to the latter. This was the only time I resorted to bribery to influence a Chinese decision.[3] These two realized that the transfer of the Kwantung region was unavoidable since we had ships carrying troops in full battle readiness. Pokotilov telegraphed me that the two had been able, after much effort, to persuade the Empress-Regent to agree to the lease.

I then sent the Emperor a note to inform him of her agreement. Since he did not know what steps I had taken to bring this about, he wrote on the note: "I do not understand what all this is about." After I explained, something Pavlov had failed to do, the Emperor noted on Pokotilov's telegram: "I find it hard to believe that this is so." The agreement to lease the Kwantung Territory was signed on March 15, 1898, by Li Hung-chang and Chang Yin-huan for China and Pavlov for Russia.* Had China not yielded, Admiral Dubasov could easily have occupied the territory, for the Chinese had no troops there and the fortress at Port Arthur was a mere toy.

Thus was taken the fateful step, an act of unparalleled perfidy, that was to have the most unfortunate consequences.[4] Historians will undoubtedly explain the consequences of this step on the basis of the many documents which former government officials, I among them, have in their possession.

Without a doubt Emperor William provided the stimulus for our action by his seizure of Kiaochow. Although he may not have foreseen the consequences, there is no doubt that he and his diplomats sought by all possible means to involve us in Far Eastern affairs, to which we would divert all our strength, thus providing him with security on the Russo-German border. In this he succeeded completely. And during our terrible war with Japan he acted as if he were the defender of our western border, but at a price, a commercial treaty that favored Germany.

Repercussions

Our seizure of the Kwantung Territory led other powers with interests in the Far East, particularly England and Japan, to take similar action. England took Wei-

---

*After the seizure of the Kwantung Territory, Grand Duke Alexis Aleksandrovich raised the question with me of providing additional funds for ship construction, according to a program approved by the Emperor. I reacted favorably because it was evident to me that once we were in the new territory we would have to enlarge our Far Eastern fleet.

As a result the Emperor summoned me and the Grand Duke to join him in a small conference, at which it was decided to authorize an additional 90 million rubles for ship construction. The Emperor was quite pleased by this decision and became more favorably disposed toward me, as he demonstrated by issuing a very kindly decree in my name on February 28.

haiwei, and Japan began to press Count Muravev, who had assured the Emperor that all would go off smoothly. So he began quickly to make concessions to England and Japan.

When we declared that Port Arthur would be a naval port, closed to ships of other powers, the English protested sharply. Count Muravev then promised that we would construct a large commercial, free port, open to all ships, in Talienwan.* This promise reduced the disquiet produced by our actions, but it did not completely eliminate it. Japan, in particular, was not satisfied. So we began to retreat from Korea, where, under the terms of the 1896 agreement, we had acquired predominant influence.

Under the terms of the agreement I had sent K. A. Alekseev, who served under me in the Ministry of Finance, to act as financial adviser to the Emperor of Korea. Within a short time he had acquired such influence with the Emperor that he was minister of finance in all but name and in time would have gained complete control over Korea's economic and financial affairs. In addition we had military instructors and a small military detachment there.

Fearing a military conflict with Japan in Korea, Count Muravev gave in to her demands and removed Alekseev, our military instructors, and our military detachment. Then, on April 13, 1898, we signed an agreement with Japan recognizing her predominant influence in Korea. Had we faithfully adhered to the agreement, both in letter and in spirit, we certainly would have enjoyed peaceful relations with Japan for many years. But this was not to be, partly because we did not observe our commitments to Japan faithfully, partly because of the consequences of the Boxer Rebellion in China.

The Boxer Rebellion

The process of seizure of parts of China by European powers begun by Germany and accelerated by us, led, as I have mentioned, to the English seizure of Weihaiwei. Then France took areas in southern China. Even Italy presented demands to China.

These developments greatly aroused the national feeling of the Chinese. Thus, no sooner did Li Hung-chang sign the agreement of March 15, 1898, than his

---

*We wanted a Russian name for the port, which was to be constructed under my aegis. On the Emperor's instructions I asked Grand Duke Constantine Konstantinovich, the president of the Academy of Sciences[5]—a fine and honorable man, a grand duke in the true sense of the word—to canvass members of the academy for suggested names. This he did, sending a list of possible names: "Svetonikolaevsk," which incorporated the Emperor's name; "Port Slavsia," based on the word *slava* (glory); "Svetozar," based on the word *svet* (light); "Alekseevsk," in honor of Grand Duke Alexis Aleksandrovich.

When I submitted the list to the Emperor, he asked which I preferred. I said they were too pretentious for a place whose fate only God knew; it might be glory or sorrow. I thought a more modest name would be preferable. When he asked for a suggestion, I had a sudden inspiration and said "Dalnyi" (Distant), adding that our soldiers would probably pronounce Talienwan as if it were spelled Dalnyi, a fitting name, for it was far from Russia.

The Emperor was pleased. When I brought him the draft of a decree naming the port, with the name left blank, to be filled in when the name had been decided on, he wrote "Dalnyi" in the blank space.

prestige began to go down: he lost his status as the highest official in the land and was sent off to southern China to serve as governor-general. And later, during the so-called Boxer Rebellion, Chang Yin-huan, the other Chinese signatory of the agreement, was sent off to a prison in the depths of China, for some reason or other, and was either stabbed to death or strangled. And Hsu Ching-cheng, the minister to Berlin and Petersburg, a very fine and honorable Chinese, was to be publicly executed [by the Boxers] on his return to Peking.

The national feeling roused by the actions of the European powers, as I have indicated, resulted in the Boxer Rebellion, which began first in the south [in 1899] and then gradually spread north. Chiefly, it took the form of attacks on Europeans, destruction of their property, and threats to their lives. As the rebellion spread, the Chinese government felt impelled to take the side of the Boxers, if not openly at least covertly; in any event it had neither the desire nor the means to oppose the rebellion.

When the rebellion reached Peking, matters were made worse by the killing of the German minister. Finally, the European legations in the city came under siege. At that point the European powers and Japan agreed to act in concert to end the rebellion and punish the guilty.

When the rebellion broke out, Kuropatkin, who was then in the Don region, returned immediately to Petersburg, where he went directly from the station to the Ministry of Finance, to see me. His face was radiant. When I told him that the rebellion was the direct result of our taking the Kwantung Territory, he replied joyfully that he was very pleased with this result, for it gave us "grounds for taking Manchuria." When I asked if he proposed to make Manchuria a province of Russia, he said: "No, we will have to turn it into something like Bukhara."

Intervention in China

Once the European powers and Japan decided to act in concert, we, together with the English and Japanese, were the first to move. Our ships, under Admiral Alekseev, joined English and Japanese vessels at Chefoo. Then the English admiral Seymour led an expedition to prevent the legations in Peking from being overwhelmed by the Chinese, but his small force proved unequal to the task. So, it was decided to send a stronger detachment under German Field-Marshal Waldersee to relieve the legations, but before he could reach China, events were to take a new turn.

It was proposed that we send our own expedition to Peking even before he arrived. Kuropatkin insisted that we play the dominant role in punitive action against China. I was completely opposed. I tried first to persuade him to counsel the Emperor to leave the task of relieving Peking to those powers whose interests were directly affected by events in Peking. After this effort failed, I sought to convince the Emperor that since our only major interest in China was with respect to Manchuria, we should restrict ourselves to protecting our position in Manchuria and to do so without upsetting the Chinese. Despite my efforts and those of Count Lambsdorff (by now foreign minister), we sent an expeditionary force, under General Linevich, to Peking, as did the Japanese.

Thus we assumed a leading role in punitive action. Together with the Japanese we took Peking, from which the Emperor and the Dowager Empress had fled. Although we inflicted no bodily harm on the Chinese, our forces and those of other powers engaged in widespread looting of many buildings, including the Imperial Palace. I heard rumors that our ranking officers behaved no better than their colleagues in other armies; unfortunately, these rumors were unofficially confirmed by information supplied by Pokotilov, my ministry's agent in Peking. On my insistence and that of Count Lambsdorff we quickly came to our senses and withdrew our troops from the city.*

That would have marked the end of our intervention in the Boxer Rebellion if it had not spread to Manchuria. First there were a few isolated incidents in Manchuria—the seizure of some [Chinese Eastern] railroad employees and the burning of a few railroad buildings. Kuropatkin was ready and eager to send our troops into Manchuria in reply to such actions, but I was able to dissuade him. However, when the rebellion in Manchuria took on a general character, accompanied by terrible incidents and characterized by hostility against us for our earlier actions in China, I felt impelled to ask that we send in troops, from the Amur region. I believed that a small force would suffice to check all disorders.

Kuropatkin, on the other hand, in keeping with his frivolous and naive nature, insisted on sending large contingents, by land, from the Amur region, and by sea, from European Russia. Our first detachment, commanded by General Subbotich, to reach Manchuria quickly succeeded, despite its highhanded behavior, in quieting the local population. (For his efforts in Mukden, where there was a strong Boxer contingent, the general received a St. George, but if truth be told it was because he was on *tutoyer* terms with Kuropatkin.) As a result, when the seaborne troops arrived, at Port Arthur and Talienwan (Dalnyi), all was quiet and they were sent back immediately. However, the troops that had come by land stayed on and firmly occupied all of Manchuria.

Our occupation forces pursued a harsh policy toward the native population that was in sharp contrast to that pursued by the personnel, including the security guard, of the Chinese Eastern Railroad. In the brief time that they had been there, the railroad personnel had succeeded in establishing good

---

*General Linevich (who was to receive a St. George around the neck for leading the expedition) took ten chests of looted precious objects with him when he left Peking. Had I known what he was up to, I would have had the chests opened and would have made a big fuss over his action.

Among the things looted from the Imperial Palace were documents. One of these was the original of the treaty we concluded with Li Hung-chang in 1896, kept in a special chest in her bedroom by the Dowager Empress, because she attached great importance to the treaty. She had to leave it behind when she and her family hurriedly fled from the palace.

After this document was turned over to our legation in Peking, it was sent to Count Lambsdorff, who asked what I would suggest doing with it. I proposed that we return it. This would show that although we had violated the treaty we had not repudiated it and wished to continue our friendship with China. We did return it, but to no avail, for our continued maintenance of troops in Manchuria would make it impossible for China to trust us.

relations with the local population as a whole and with the local authorities. They believed that if we had refrained from taking the Kwantung Territory, if we had refrained from the expedition to Peking, the Chinese would have remained loyal to us. Kuropatkin, on the other hand, continued to believe that we should use the opportunity to take all of Manchuria, and the troops were behaving as if they were occupying an enemy country, a country that happened to be Asiatic. Thus, the ground was laid for inevitable catastrophe.

I and Count Lambsdorff attempted to convince the Emperor to remove our troops from Manchuria and to reestablish the friendly relations with China that had existed before our taking of the Kwantung Territory. We expressed the hope that sooner or later China would reconcile herself to our presence in the Kwantung Territory if only we refrained from highhanded measures, including the use of force.

As we expected, Kuropatkin took a different view, as did other higher officers, who were under his influence. Therefore it was in their interest that incidents continue to occur in Manchuria that would give us an excuse to retain troops there.

Consequently, there were constant disputes over Manchurian policy for the next eighteen months between two camps, one consisting of the Ministry of War and the ranking officers in Manchuria and the other consisting of the Ministry of Finance, the employees of the Chinese Eastern Railroad, and agents of the Ministry of Foreign Affairs. The Emperor took an ambivalent position with respect to these disputes; without categorically rejecting the positions that I and Count Lambsdorff advocated, he seemed to support the positions advocated by Kuropatkin. The explanation of this ambivalence was to be found not so much in our Manchurian policy as in changes in our Korean policy that were the result of a new influence, being exerted by a new and, so to speak, extra-governmental figure, Alexander Mikhailovich Bezobrazov, a retired captain of the Chevalier Garde, whose schemes helped lead us into war with Japan.

Bezobrazov and Korea

As I have noted, Bezobrazov belonged to that group of adventurers that came to the fore in those days, the only difference between him and the others being that he was an honorable man. Therefore it is natural to ask how such an honorable man could become involved in such schemes. The best answer probably came from his wife, a fine woman, who said when her husband began to become prominent and influential: "I can't understand how Sasha can have such a prominent role; don't they realize that he is half-mad?"

[Around 1898] he began to propagate the idea that we should not have given up our influence in Korea and should seek to regain it by covert means. What he proposed was that we obtain concessions from the Korean government to operate what appeared to be private undertakings (e.g., timber cutting) that in fact would be supported and directed by our government and, if necessary, buttressed by our military power.

Bezobrazov first presented this idea to Count Vorontsov-Dashkov, under whom he had served as a young officer.[6] Perhaps because he was at loose ends, having little to keep him occupied except for his membership in the State Council, Count Vorontsov-Dashkov was sympathetic to Bezobrazov's scheme. Bezobrazov then approached Grand Duke Alexander Mikhailovich, who also was sympathetic to the idea, because, to put it mildly, he had a weakness for all kinds of political adventures that could either help advance his career or satisfy his restless spirit. These two then took Bezobrazov to the Emperor, expressing their full support for his proposal to gain a dominant influence in Korea by spiderlike means.

The decision was made to implement Bezobrazov's idea. Once this was done, concessions were negotiated with Korea, and then expeditions, conducted in a childish manner, were sent to Korea to investigate commercial and, what was more significant, strategic possibilities there. As Bezobrazov's influence with the Emperor grew, he eased Count Vorontsov-Dashkov and the Grand Duke out of this undertaking.[7] They, for their part, left willingly after they had come to see that the undertaking might end in catastrophe. Thus Bezobrazov began, so to speak, to operate on his own responsibility. Of course, the Japanese soon realized what we were up to in Korea and began to use our continued presence in Manchuria as a means of exerting pressure against us.

Our Isolation

When we first sent our troops into Manchuria we stated unequivocally that we were there to support the Chinese government and that once the Boxer disorders were ended we would withdraw. However, we continued to stay in Manchuria after order had been restored and the Chinese government had been reinstalled in Peking, this despite repeated pleas from the Chinese that we leave. It is easy to see why China began to lose faith in us and then began to become friendly toward Japan, England, and America, which seemed to be protecting her interests by supporting her demand that we withdraw.

Also, Japan, after being pushed out of the Liaotung Peninsula by us, after seeing us establish ourself on part of the peninsula, the Kwantung Territory, and after seeing us violate our agreement to cede predominant influence in Korea to her, became hostile toward us, as did England and America, because of our actions in Manchuria. Thus a coalition of China, Japan, England, and America was formed against us as a result of the policies we had been following since our seizure of Port Arthur. All four stopped believing our promises; all vigorously demanded that we leave Manchuria.

Long-range Consequences

As I have said, the seizure of Port Arthur was a fateful step. It resulted in the elimination of our influence in Korea to placate Japan. It led to the destruction for all time of our traditional relations with China. It marked the beginning of the process of carving up China, by powers that used our seizure of Port Arthur and the rest of the Kwantung Territory as a pretext for their actions. This process of partition in turn led to the Boxer Rebellion, which in turn led to foreign intervention in China, all leading to the ultimate collapse of the Chinese Empire. The seizure of Port Arthur was the first step in a process that led us into war with Japan, a war that led in turn to revolutionary disorders in Russia, the consequences of which we are still experiencing.

And now there is a civil war being fought in China, which may lead to the replacement of the Imperial government by a republic. There is no question but that this civil war and the fall of the Imperial government will produce disruption in the Far East that will have consequences which we and Europe will feel for decades to come.

XXX

Foreign Affairs, 1898–1900

The Hague Peace Conference,
the Fashoda Incident,
a New Foreign Minister

The Hague Peace Conference

In the middle of 1898, Count Muravev, the minister of foreign affairs, with whom I had not been on good terms, came to ask my opinion about a matter that Kuropatkin had raised in a letter to him. It concerned the fact that Austria was strengthening her artillery at a time when we were reequipping our infantry at great expense and could not afford to spend enough to catch up with her artillery. Kuropatkin wanted to know if it were possible to persuade Austria to refrain from building up her artillery if we agreed to refrain as well or, failing that, could we persuade Austria to maintain the same pace in building up her artillery that we did.

I told Muravev that what General Kuropatkin proposed was not feasible: first of all, Austria would probably reject such a proposal and do so with delicate scorn; secondly, for us to make such a proposal would indicate to Europe that we were in financial straits. In short, it would be more harmful to make such a childish proposal than it would to increase our military expenditures. I added, in great detail and with considerable vigor, that I considered the armaments race harmful for the entire world, particularly Europe, because it was impoverishing the masses and providing a favorable soil for the spread of socialist ideas, which were beginning to gain support in Russia. For my part, said I, I would consider it the greatest blessing for the world if governments and people came to realize that they suffered as much from armed peace as they did from war and undertook to limit armaments.

Although my ideas were not novel, they evidently made a strong impression on Count Muravev, who, being a man with limited knowledge, found much of what I said new to him.[1] A few days later he sent me an invitation, sanctioned by the

Emperor, to attend a conference on an important matter. As it turned out, those who took part in it were Count Muravev, Count Lambsdorff, several other high officials from the Ministry of Foreign Affairs, Kuropatkin, and I.

Count Muravev told us that he had raised the question of disarmament, or, at the very least, of arms limitation, with the Emperor and had received a sympathetic response. Then he read us a note inviting the [European] powers to hold a peace conference. As expected, Kuropatkin, speaking for the Ministry of War, objected, while I, who favored the solution of international conflicts by peaceful means, gave my full support to the note. The note, which was issued on August 12, 1898, drew a favorable response, making possible the holding of a peace conference in the Hague in May 1899.

[When I had the opportunity] I congratulated the Emperor for assuming the initiative in such a great and beneficial undertaking, but added that one could not expect any practical consequences to result in the foreseeable future from the peace conference because it would take centuries to rid humanity of what might be called that universal depravity which had led it to resolve disputes through the spilling of blood. After all, it would be as difficult to do so as to persuade the human race to live up to the principles of the Son of God. We know that the truths and principles expressed by Christ and his apostles have been rejected out of hand by some and treated with complete indifference by many: it would take millennia for Christian principles to become ingrained in humanity. I added that His Majesty had, nonetheless, rendered a great service by raising the question of peace: he would be rendering an even greater service if the remainder of his reign could see practical results from his peace proposal.

I must say that it is a matter of deepest regret that thus far the idea of peaceful settlement of international disputes has not been honored in deed, not even by Russia, which later acted contrary to that idea and became embroiled in war with Japan.

The Fashoda Incident

The year 1898 was marked too by the Fashoda incident, which occurred when French travelers hoisted the French flag in the Fashoda region, to which England had laid claim. The resulting dispute between France and England became so intense that war seemed likely. At that point Delcassé, the French foreign minister, sent a note to Count Lambsdorff [then assistant foreign minister] to ask if we would support France in the event of an Anglo-French conflict.

When Count Lambsdorff asked me for my opinion, I said that we could not exert direct naval pressure on England because our fleet was too weak, nor could we exert direct military pressure because we had no common land frontier with England. I then went on to say that, of course, we could create a diversion in Central Asia by sending troops toward India, but, unfortunately, we could not send troops in time to be of any assistance because the railroad link between central Russia and Central Asia was not yet completed. Count Lambsdorff conveyed my opinion to the Emperor, who agreed with it. After France was informed that we could not offer any assistance, she felt compelled to come to terms with England by giving up the Fashoda region.

The Fashoda incident had an important consequence for us. Either in 1900 or 1901, Delcassé came to Petersburg to determine what we could do to aid France in the future if she clashed with England. He spoke to the Emperor, to our minister of foreign affairs, and, particularly, to me.[2] I said that all we could do would be to create a diversion in Central Asia, but to do that we would have to construct a direct link with the Trans-Caspian Railroad, preferably between Orenburg and Tashkent, adding that such a link was not high on our list of proposed railroad construction. Then Delcassé asked the Emperor to speed up construction of the link and the Emperor agreed. An agreement was then drawn up by which we committed ourselves to construct the link and France undertook not to hinder our floating a loan in that country in the near future. Both sides lived up to the agreement.

A New Foreign Minister

About ten in the evening of June 7, 1900, just about the time a courier arrived from my ministry with some papers, Count Muravev called on me. I was rather surprised because, for some time, we had been at loggerheads over our Far Eastern policy, so much so that we had not exchanged personal visits for some time.

I was staying then on Elagin Island. I invited him into my study, on the upper floor. He had just been at the home of Countess Kleinmichel and had obviously dined and wined well there; in fact he was a bit tipsy. He opened the conversation by saying that he had been wrong and I right about the wisdom of taking Port Arthur and Dalnyi, but what was done was done. He wanted to make peace with me and secure my cooperation in dealing with the Boxer Rebellion, particularly the grave disorders in Peking, where the European envoys were virtually under siege. I told him that what had happened was to have been expected, but that since we both served the same fatherland and the same Sovereign, it was obviously my duty to cooperate with him. He promised to give great weight to my advice, based as it was on experience.

When he arose to leave it was nearly eleven. He asked if Mathilda Ivanovna, my wife, were at home; I said that he could find her in the reception room, but excused myself from accompanying him because I had to look over and sign the papers that the courier had brought. I had a servant show him to the reception room and turned to the papers, which occupied me until nearly midnight. As I started to go downstairs I could hear my wife and Muravev laughing heartily. As I entered the reception room, Muravev was about to leave. He continued laughing and said that when he visited my wife he always enjoyed himself. With that he left. It was a hot night and I was very thirsty. When I reached for a large bottle of champagne, I found that Muravev had drunk it down to the last drop. I told my wife that Muravev was a fortunate man, to be able to drink as much as he had, without ill effects; had I drunk as much, I said, I would be dead by morning.

The next morning I arose early and as usual went riding, accompanied by a soldier from the border guard. When I returned, nearly two hours later, my manservant told me that Muravev had passed away. At first I did not quite take it in and asked what he was talking about. He said that Count Muravev had died that morning. I then got into a carriage and drove to his house, where I found him, lying dead, in his bed. I was told that when he had sat down for his coffee that morning he had collapsed and died, apparently from a stroke. Who would succeed him?

At the conclusion of my next report, the Emperor, his back turned to me, looking out of a window, asked whom I would recommend to replace Count Muravev. As usual, I asked whom he had in mind. He replied: "No one." I then said that my recommendation would depend on the kind of man he had in mind. If he wanted someone from outside the foreign ministry I would suggest one of the older, more experienced ministers: he might not know foreign affairs, but, in any event, he would be cautious and would not treat matters of extreme importance lightly, as Count Muravev and Prince Lobanov-Rostovskii, to a degree, had done. As for someone from the diplomatic corps, I said, I did not consider any of our ambassadors capable of dealing with the demands of the position. Accordingly, I suggested Count Lambsdorff, saying that although he had never served in an embassy, he had spent his entire career in the Ministry of Foreign Affairs, was its ambulatory archive, and, moreover, was a man of outstanding intellectual qualities. His Majesty was kind enough to act on my recommendation.[3]

Despite my high regard for Count Lambsdorff, I should state here that I find fault with him for having permitted Count Muravev to take Port Arthur and thus bring on a storm that led to the most terrible consequences in the Far East, the results of which are still being felt. I believe that he could have stopped Count Muravev, but had not done so because he had not wished to quarrel with his superior.

XXXI

A New Minister of Interior and Some Minor Developments, 1898–1900

Honors for Pobedonostsev and Miliutin

In August 1898 the Emperor and Empress went to Moscow for the unveiling of a monument to Emperor Alexander II. Although I was invited to attend, I chose instead to go with my wife to Karlsbad.

It was while in Moscow that the Emperor honored Constantine Petrovich Pobedonostsev and Count Dmitrii Miliutin for their services to Emperor Alexander II. [That Pobedonostsev should have been so honored seems odd] for he had done no more than serve briefly under Emperor Alexander II, as over-procurator of the Holy Synod, at the end of the reign, and even then his sentiments had been very much opposed to the spirit of the great reforms.[1] Pobedonostsev was awarded the order of St. Andrei.

Count Miliutin was awarded the rank of field marshal, on the recommendation of Kuropatkin. When the modest Count Miliutin had heard that this honor was being proposed, he had asked the Emperor to withhold it because the rank was traditionally reserved for generals who had won great victories and he was not such a general. Nonetheless, His Majesty was kind enough to bestow the rank on this fine old man, who is still among the living.[2] Because Count Miliutin was universally respected, there was no criticism of the Emperor's act.

The Northern Route to the Far East

On my initiative, construction was begun on the icebreaker *Ermak* toward the end of 1898. My immediate goal was to use the ship for keeping Petersburg and major Baltic ports open the year-round; my long-range goal was to use it to determine if it would be possible to sail the northern route to the Far East.

Construction was carried out under the auspices of the Ministry of Finance and under my direct orders. Admiral Makarov, a distinguished officer, provided close assistance during construction of the ship and its subsequent use. Mendeleev, the eminent chemist and the director of the Board of Weights and Measures of the ministry, assisted in the planning.

Mendeleev, a very able but quarrelsome man, had sharp differences with Admiral Makarov over which route to follow to the Far East: he favored a route that would cross the North Pole, while Makarov favored one that followed the Siberian coast, each arguing that his route was less hazardous than the one proposed by the other. After a very bitter argument, in my office, the two never met again.

Neither route was to be tried, partly because of the disagreement between the two, partly because Makarov soon left to take command of the port of Kronstadt. The *Ermak* did perform some service in clearing ice from Baltic ports, and Makarov once made a fairly long trip on it to the northern seas, once attempting to sail to Novaia Zemlia. He later sailed on another ship to the Far East, where he died heroically in the war with Japan.

My Tour of Smolensk and Mogilev Provinces

In the summer of 1899, while His Majesty was abroad, I visited Smolensk and Mogilev provinces, where the liquor monopoly had recently been introduced. This was in keeping with my custom of visiting those provinces where the monopoly had just been introduced: during such visits I impressed the fact on the local excise officials that the monopoly had been initiated not for the purpose of raising revenue but for the purpose of reducing alcoholism and that their performance would be judged by how well they achieved their purpose. I was accompanied on this trip by an inspector of the French financial administration, who had come to Russia with President Faure: the inspector, a fine man and a member of a very ancient and noble family, was related to Count Montebello, the French ambassador.[3]

In Smolensk, while visiting the residence of the local prelate, we came upon a reminder of the Napoleonic invasion. There, on the walls of a neglected room, we found barely legible inscriptions made by French soldiers who had been there in 1812. Some were quite moving, particularly one in which a soldier said that he was almost certain to die and expressed his admiration for his fiancée. Another sent his love to his aged mother. I advised the local authorities to see to it that these inscriptions were preserved.

At the end of the trip I asked my companion what he thought of the liquor monopoly. He wisely replied that from the point of view of public policy it was magnificent, and that it would be beneficial for France if she were ruled by a strong, unlimited monarch.

Emperor Alexander III was such a monarch. Had he not been strong I would never have been able to carry out the reform. Under parliamentary regimes, particularly republican ones, such a reform would be unthinkable because it hurts the interests of highly placed and well-to-do persons. And I have noted in my visits to France that persons involved in the sale and distribution of liquor play a leading role in electing members of the Chamber of Deputies.

A New Minister of Interior

After completing my tour in the two provinces, I went to the Crimea, where my wife and my young daughter Vera were waiting for me, for a brief rest. We stayed in a cottage at Nikitskii Sad that belonged to the Ministry of State Domains.

A few days after my arrival I met Nicholas Valerianovich Muravev, the minister of justice, who was staying some distance away in a cottage that belonged to Count Shuvalov. He said that he had been told by Grand Duke Sergei Aleksandrovich that Goremykin would soon be leaving the post of minister of interior because the Emperor considered him too liberal, too lacking in commitment to conservative ideas, particularly the idea of buttressing the nobility. Assuming that I knew what was up, he told me that the Grand Duke had recommended him for the post and said he would be obliged to me if I did not support the rival candidate, Sipiagin.[4] He said, too, that the dismissal of Goremykin would take place after the Emperor had returned from Darmstadt.

I said that this was the first I had heard of Goremykin's imminent departure from office and that, moreover, His Majesty was not likely to ask for my opinion concerning candidates for the post. I added that when Durnovo was being replaced the Emperor had asked for my opinion and I had supported Sipiagin over Plehve, but Sipiagin had not been appointed. Muravev evidently did not believe that I knew nothing about the matter and was convinced that I was working on Sipiagin's behalf.

For my part I found it hard to believe that Goremykin was being let go because he was not conservative enough, for, as I have noted, he gave up his liberal ideas very quickly after becoming minister of interior and became completely conservative. For example, he supported the institution of land captains. Also, he took a strongly conservative position with respect to student disorders at the University of St. Petersburg, when mounted police used excessive forces to disperse a group of students near the university and beat several of them.[5]

When a conference concerning the incident was held at Goremykin's quarters, he, as well as Bogolepov, the minister of education, fully approved what the police had done. In fact, Goremykin believed that the police should behave the same way in the future. I took an opposing view and asserted that the student disorders that resulted from the incident would end only after it had been determined who was at fault—the police or the students. I then prepared a memorandum, which is still in my archive, expressing this view. To everyone's amazement the Emperor in the end supported me and appointed General Vannovskii to carry out an investigation.

The Emperor chose General Vannovskii for those attributes to be found among the military—firmness, decisiveness, and severity. Consequently, my first reaction to the appointment was skeptical, but this honorable man proved very conscientious in carrying out his task. (Having served for a number of years as head of a cadet corps in Petersburg and thus having learned to deal with young people, he understood their psychology, something that many adults forget when they have to decide the fate of the young.) In his report he placed the major blame on the police. As a result several junior police officials were censured. In my opinion, it was Goremykin and the prefect of Petersburg who should have been censured.

After our return from the Crimea, Sipiagin, who had just come back from the country, stopped off to visit us. This was during the evening of October 19. Being on close terms with him, I asked if what Muravev had said was true. He replied that he knew nothing about the matter.

The following day Sipiagin's appointment as minister was announced. But, in the morning before I had read the news, Sipiagin stopped to apologize to me for having withheld the truth from me. He told me that the Emperor had summoned him in August, before leaving for Darmstadt, to tell him of what he intended to do, and bound Sipiagin not to tell anyone but his wife until the decree appeared announcing his appointment. That is why he had not told me the truth; Sipiagin had remained in the country so long to be sure he wouldn't let the cat out of the bag.

Muravev was very unhappy over Sipiagin's appointment, certain that but for me he would have become minister of interior. As I have noted earlier he was to be hostile toward me for many years to come. Thus, the appointment of Goremykin as minister of interior, in 1894, earned me an ill wisher in the person of Plehve, who felt I had blocked his appointment, and the departure of Goremykin, in 1899, earned me another ill wisher, Nicholas Valerianovich Muravev.

Goremykin and Rachkovskii

Before leaving the subject of Goremykin I want to say something about Rachkovskii, the head of our secret police in Paris, and his trip to England with Goremykin in the summer of 1899.[6]

Rachovskii had been named to his post by Emperor Alexander III. As our relations with France improved, so did his status, because the French, who had given Russian terrorists asylum, began to take a less kindly attitude toward them, thus helping Rachkovskii. Also, his position was strengthened by the fact that he was a remarkably intelligent man, in fact the most gifted and intelligent police official I have ever met, incomparably superior in ability, and character, to men such as Gerasimov and Komissarov, not to speak of scoundrels like Azef and

Garting. Rachkovskii's position in Paris was strengthened, too, by the insignificance of our ambassadors there, Mohrenheim and Urusov.

Consequently, Rachkovskii was able to exercise more influence on the course of our rapprochement with France than did our ambassadors: he exercised this influence with the help of our ministers of interior, our palace commandants, and our ambassadors. In what high regard he was held in France can be judged from the fact (which I learned from President Loubet) that when the president had to go to Lyons, where threats had been made against his life, he entrusted the arrangements for his security there to Rachkovskii because he had more confidence in him than he had in his own security force.

During the summer of 1899, while the Emperor was abroad, Goremykin went to England, accompanied by Rachkovskii, toward whom he was well disposed. Also traveling with Goremykin were the engineer Belinskii, whose father was a well-known psychiatrist (and later part-time literary figure, part-time police agent), and M. M. Liashchenko, who was to end up in an insane asylum; his father was a cavalry general.

Well, the members of Goremykin's party made agreements with various English industrial firms, among them an agreement to build a circular railroad on the docks near Petersburg. The "well-known" Tatishchev, our financial agent in Paris, reported to me (I filed the report in the archive of the Ministry of Finance) that there had been some improprieties in connection with these agreements and added that he could not believe that Goremykin was aware of them. But a reading of the report indicates that if Goremykin had not had a hand in these arrangements, he was certainly aware of them.

I say "well-known" about Tatishchev (he happens to have been a Catholic) because he was a brilliant diplomat in his earlier years. Although he was nominally the secretary of our embassy in Vienna, he, in fact, ran it. He opposed close relations with Germany and asserted, probably with cause, that he was forced out of his post, after we went to war with Turkey, because of Bismarck's influence. But there were undoubtedly other reasons as well for his fall: while in Vienna he lived with a prominent opera singer, whom he later married; also, he was accused of selling documents to foreigners, an accusation accepted as true by Emperor Alexander III and Empress Marie Fedorovna. After leaving his post in Vienna, he fought as a volunteer against Turkey and earned a St. George cross.

After I became minister of finance, knowing what an able and gifted man he was, I offered him the post of financial agent in London, a post he held until Plehve became minister of interior. Then he joined the Ministry of Interior.

Tatishchev is well known for his very important *History of the Reign of Alexander II* and for his articles in *Novoe vremia*.

As I have indicated, Goremykin was removed from his post following his return from England. He later told me that he had been informed in advance by the Emperor of what was in store. However, judging by the effects of the news on his wife, I can only conclude that the dismissal came as a complete surprise and that he professed otherwise *faire bonne mine à mauvais jeu.*

After Sipiagin became minister of interior it became apparent that Goremykin and his travel companions were intriguing against me, because on one occasion Sipiagin asked me if I knew Liashchenko. I said that I did and that I knew that he was the kind of gentleman one should avoid, a scoundrel who could repudiate what he had said and could swear that he hadn't done what he had done: later, when Liashchenko lost his mind, I had some inkling of the reasons for his behavior.

Also I told Sipiagin about Tatishchev's report, which he borrowed. When he asked if he could keep it for a few more weeks, I told him that I didn't need it and would not use it in any case. After Sipiagin's assassination, about which I will speak later, it occurred to me to get the report back. When I asked the officials of the Ministry of Interior in charge of sorting out papers if they had found the report, they said they had and not knowing how it had reached Sipiagin, they had turned it over to Zvolianskii, the director of the Department of Police and an intimate friend of Goremykin.* When I asked for the report, Zvolianskii pretended that it had been destroyed. Had I had this report at my disposal I would later have been able to stop all the intrigues that Goremykin would carry out against me in the conference for the study of the needs of agricultural industry.

My Trip to Paris

While the Emperor was abroad during the summer of 1900 I left for Paris, to attend the International Exhibition there, in my capacity as minister of finance.[7] En route I was informed that the Dowager Empress, Marie Fedorovna, who was visiting in Copenhagen, wanted me to stop off to see her. I took Grube, the ministry's agent in Persia, along with me because he was a Dane and knew the Empress and was on very good terms with Princess Marie of Denmark, who had helped considerably in the rapprochement of Russia and France during the reign of Emperor Alexander III.

I spent only a day and a half in Copenhagen because I was anxious to get to Paris. The Dowager Empress was interested in particulars about the Boxer Rebellion, about which I informed her and then assured her that if we would choose to

---

*The two were good friends, although they were both admirers of Mme. Petrova, wife of a former director of the Department of Police.

act wisely, we would experience nothing untoward as a result of the rebellion. Unfortunately, that was not to be the case.

While I was speaking with her, her sister Princess Alexandra, the future queen of England, entered the room. Then, after taking my leave from them, just as I was about to go out of the room, an adjutant of King Christian, the father of the Dowager Empress, told me that the king wished to see me.

I was taken to the king and presented to him. He was very kind to me and gave me his autographed picture, which still hangs in my study. As a rule he gave pictures of himself only to members of his family, but in my case he made an exception, he said, because this was the highest [mark of favor] he could bestow on me.

He then asked me if I had seen the Dowager Empress, his daughter. I told him that I had and briefly described our conversation. He then said that she had told him that I was giving instruction to her son Misha [Grand Duke Michael Aleksandrovich] and wanted to know what kind of a person Misha was. I informed him that it was the case that I had been given the high honor and pleasure of giving instruction to the Grand Duke and indeed knew him well, yet I found it difficult to describe his personality in a few words, because of the complexity of personality: I found it more useful to try to imagine how a given person would behave under various circumstances, that is, to write something like a story. The king, however, insisted that I try to do it in a few words, saying that he had known Misha only as a boy and had never "had a serious conversation with him." Then I took the liberty of saying that since the king knew Emperor Nicholas II and had known Emperor Alexander III, I could provide an approximate description of the Grand Duke's personality by saying that the Emperor Nicholas resembled his mother in nature and character, while the Grand Duke resembled his father. The king laughed heartily at this and we then parted. I was never to have the opportunity of seeing this worthy monarch again.

While in Copenhagen I and Grube called on Princess Marie, who was very interested in the formation of the Danish Asiatic Steamship Company and wanted my help in this matter.

When I arrived in Paris, I found that although the exhibition had opened a few months earlier, the Russian section and several others had not yet been made ready. Prince Tenishev, whom I had named our commissar at the exhibition, handled his task well because of his practical experience: he had built a fortune through his own labor, starting his career as a railroad technician at fifty rubles a month. His son is now a member of the State Council.

Naturally, I gave close attention to the exhibition. In addition I made the proper calls on important personages. President Loubet—a fine, even-tempered, modest old man, a contrast to his predecessor Faure—invited me to dinner at Rambouillet, his summer residence. I was accompanied there by our ambassador, Urusov, and found several ministers—Caillaux, Delcassé, and Dupuy, whose *Petit*

Journal had made him a fortune—among the guests. Premier Waldeck Rousseau was not there, because he was away at the time.

At dinner I sat to the left of the president and Caillaux to his right. The three of us argued calmly about money standards: Loubet was still in favor of bimetallism while I and Caillaux, the latter firing a few cautious shots at the president, favored monometallism. After dinner there were illuminations.

I saw Caillaux and Delcassé again on this trip. Delcassé, who was acquainted with my wife, took her and my daughter Vera on automobile drives to Versailles and other places near Paris.

XXXII

The Imperial Court

The Succession Question, Changing Mores

The Emperor's Illness and the Succession Question

From Paris I went on, by way of Petersburg, to the Crimea, where I stayed in a house belonging to the Ministry of Ways and Communications, on the road from Yalta to Livadia. [The Emperor was then in residence at Livadia] and also nearby were Count Lambsdorff, Kuropatkin, Sipiagin, Grand Duke Michael Nikolaevich, and, of course, Baron Freedericksz.[1]

On November 1 [1900], the Emperor became ill. As was customary with members of the Imperial family, he did not want medical attention. Moreover, his personal physician, the aged Hirsch, had forgotten whatever he had ever known, if, in fact, he had ever known anything. At my suggestion, Professor Popov, of the Military-Medical Academy, was sent for: his diagnosis—typhoid fever. On November 28, the Emperor began to recover.

During the course of the illness the question of who would succeed the Emperor if he died then arose. When the Emperor's brother and Heir, Grand Duke George Aleksandrovich had died the preceding year, the next one in line of succession, Grand Duke Michael Aleksandrovich, had been proclaimed Heir.[2] At the time I had felt such a proclamation improper since it was quite possible that the Emperor might still beget a son, who would then replace Grand Duke Michael Aleksandrovich as Heir. Well, one morning, at a time when the Emperor's condition gave cause for alarm, Sipiagin asked me by phone to come over to the Hotel Rossiia, where he was staying. There I found, in addition to Sipiagin, Count Lambsdorff, Baron Freedericksz, and Grand Duke Michael Nikolaevich. As soon as I arrived, a discussion began about how to proceed if a tragedy were to occur and the Emperor should die: what would be the procedure concerning the succession?

I was taken aback by such a question and pointed out that the law left no doubt about the succession: Grand Duke Michael Aleksandrovich would immediately succeed. My reply evoked the hint that the Empress was in an interesting condition (apparently Baron Freedericksz knew of it) and she might give birth to a boy: might it not be better if the succession would be postponed for a few months until she gave birth? I replied that the succession law did not take such a contingency into account. The law was clear: if the Emperor should die without having begotten a son, Grand Duke Michael Aleksandrovich must succeed. To act otherwise would be illegal and would lead to grave disorders. In any case, no one could predict that the Empress would bear a son. After checking the law, the others agreed with me.

Then the aged Grand Duke Michael Nikolaevich asked me what would happen if the Empress were to bear a son after Grand Duke Michael Aleksandrovich had ascended the throne. I replied that only Grand Duke Michael Aleksandrovich could answer the question definitely, but that I believed that he, being a very decent and honorable man, would give up the throne in favor of his nephew. After we had come to an agreement, we decided to inform the Empress privately about our meeting.

A few days after the meeting General Kuropatkin stopped off for lunch. (He was on his way back from giving a report to the Emperor, who, despite his illness, heard reports in special cases.) After lunch, when we were alone, he asked me about the meeting, saying that he had been invited, but had been unable to attend. I reviewed what we had said and remarked that it was unfortunate that he could not have been there. Striking a theatrical pose, he said: "I will not cause my Empress grief." Knowing him for a poseur, I did not attach any significance to this remark and asked why he assumed that he alone had the privilege of not "causing the Empress any grief."

Happily, the Emperor recovered and there was no further talk then of the succession question, but before leaving the Crimea I made it a point to advise Baron Freedericksz that it would be wise to issue new instructions, legally enacted, to avoid future ambiguities. A few years later, as I learned from Pobedonostsev and Nicholas Valerianovich Muravev, Their Majesties raised the question of whether or not their eldest daughter could succeed if they had no son; the two were instructed to look into the matter. Pobedonostsev was absolutely opposed to the notion of changing the succession, believing that the succession laws laid down by Emperor Paul had contributed to the stability of the throne. Nonetheless, Pobedonostsev and Muravev were instructed to prepare the draft of a decree providing for the succession of the eldest daughter, but the decree was not published and, in 1904, lost its validity with the fortunate birth of a son, Grand Duke

Alexis Nikolaevich, to Their Majesties. I know nothing more about the episode of the decree.

A legend was to arise that, at the meeting I have just described, I showed myself less than devoted to the Emperor. I heard about it not long ago, in Biarritz, from Alexandra Nikolaevna Naryshkina, whose only claim to fame is that she is the widow of Emmanuel Dmitrievich Naryshkin, the illegitimate son of Emperor Alexander I and the well-known Naryshkina, a Pole by origin. (See the memoirs dealing with this subject published a few years ago by Grand Duke Nicholas Mikhailovich.)

Well, during our conversation she asked if I knew why the Empress was unsympathetic, if not hostile, toward me. I said that I did not know how she felt about me, for I rarely saw her and had spoken with her on but a few occasions.

Naryshkina then said: "I know that her attitude arose from the fact that when the Emperor nearly died at Livadia, you insisted that Grand Duke Michael Aleksandrovich succeed to the throne."[3] I said that I had not insisted on anything and had merely explained the exact meaning of the existing laws and that the others present, including Grand Duke Michael Nikolaevich, son of Emperor Nicholas I, whom none could suspect of being less than totally devoted to the Sovereign, had agreed.

Grand Duke Michael Aleksandrovich

The unfounded and dishonorable legend about my motives in taking the position I did at the time the succession question was raised at Livadia may have arisen in part from the fact that I taught Grand Duke Michael Aleksandrovich and that he was well disposed toward me. Although I esteem the Grand Duke and hold him dear, my feelings toward him can in no way be compared to the feelings I have always entertained toward his brother and my Sovereign, Emperor Nicholas II.

I had the good fortune to instruct the Grand Duke in political economy and finance from 1900, beginning my work a few months before the Emperor's bout with typhoid fever, until 1902.[4] Because of my method and manner of teaching, and also for other reasons that I do not know, he was an eager student.

I often talked with him after my lectures or in the intervals between lectures. Sometimes we had lunch together. Sometimes we took automobile drives in the park. As a result I became well acquainted with him. I found that he was considerably less educated and intelligent than his brother, Emperor Nicholas II, but that his character, as I have indicated earlier, was more like that of his father than was the character of Emperor Nicholas II.

Changing Mores

As early as 1902 Grand Duke Andrei Vladimirovich began to stray a bit from the norms of propriety, norms that are of particular importance for such highly placed persons as grand dukes, whose behavior and activities are of interest to all of society, and particularly to that part of society devoted to gossip.[5] I had given instruction to the Grand Duke, at the request of his father, Grand Duke Vladimir Aleksandrovich, with whom I was on excellent terms. Knowing that Grand Duke Andrei Vladimirovich and Grand Duke Michael Aleksandrovich were on friendly terms, I once happened to tell the latter that Andrei Vladimirovich was beginning to act somewhat improperly and that I feared that such behavior would have unfortunate consequences. (My chief aim in saying this was to warn Grand Duke Michael Aleksandrovich against such passions.) He replied that he could not understand how a person could consciously act improperly; he certainly would not.

Grand Duke Michael Aleksandrovich is now thirty-three. There are rumors that he is entangled in some sort of romance.[6] I prefer not to believe them, but should they turn out to be true, I would say that the fault lies in his upbringing, which was very much like that given to young ladies, even when he was in his late twenties.

A few years ago he conceived a passion for a cousin, one of the daughters of Grand Duchess Marie Aleksandrovna and the Duke of Edinburgh, and wanted to marry her, but he was denied permission to do so because she was his cousin. Although I considered the denial justified, I regretted that he was not permitted to marry her.

Unfortunately, since then the rules governing grand-ducal marriages have been relaxed. Thus, Grand Duke Cyril Vladimirovich has been permitted to marry a cousin, sister of the princess whom Grand Duke Michael Aleksandrovich was forbidden to marry; not only is she his cousin, but she is also a divorcée and, what is more, the divorced wife of the brother of the Empress. Also, Grand Duke Nicholas Nikolaevich was permitted to marry Princess Anastasia Nikolaevna, the divorced wife of Prince George of Leuchtenberg.

[Then there is the case of] Grand Duke Paul Aleksandrovich, a nonentity, but not a bad sort. As we know, his first wife, the older daughter of the King of Greece, died at the summer home of Grand Duke Sergei Aleksandrovich. A few years later, defying the wishes of the Emperor, he married Olga Pistolkors, née Karnovicha, the former wife of one of Grand Duke Sergei Aleksandrovich's adjutants.

She is very beautiful, but she could not win a prize for proper behavior and morality. And she keeps him under her thumb. She was subsequently given the title of Countess Hohenfelsen, a Bavarian title. How this was arranged I do not know.

Because he married her in defiance of the Emperor's wishes, he was dismissed from the military and banished from Russia. Later, however, he was permitted to return and was restored to the rank of general-adjutant. Nonetheless, he chooses to reside mainly in Paris. This is so because the court will not receive his wife, and for good reason.[7] It should be noted, too, that his relations with his wife are such as to be unacceptable at court.

XXXIII

On the Road to War and Revolution, 1901–1903

Assassination of Bogolepov

On February 14, 1901, Karpovich, a former student at the University of Moscow, shot Bogolepov, our minister of education, in the neck. This anarchist attack was the prelude to all those events we experienced between 1901 and 1905 and are still experiencing, because of the Stolypin regime.

As soon as I learned that Bogolepov was wounded I went to his home, where I found his wife (née Princess Lieven), a fine woman, and Zverev, assistant minister of education, a shallow man, an extremely reactionary person of little learning or ability, but not a bad sort. I insisted that Bergmann, the famous surgeon, be summoned immediately from Berlin. This was done.

After Bergmann had come and had looked at Bogolepov he called on me, with a favorable prognosis. Unfortunately, he was not correct; a few days after his departure, on March 2, Bogolepov died.

Bogolepov was a decent and honorable man, but his views were very reactionary and, undoubtedly, contributed to unrest in the universities. But I should note that his policies were well intentioned, and legal, something that can't be said about the policies of the current minister of education, Casso.

Bogolepov was replaced by General Vannovskii, probably because he was known to be a man of extremely conservative views and because of his role in investigating student disorders.

"Occult" Forces at Court: Dr. Philippe of Lyons

In August 1901 the Emperor and Empress went abroad, to visit Denmark, Germany, and France. (While in France they did not visit Paris or Versailles because of the agitated state of mind among our revolutionaries who were living in Paris.)

Some of Her Majesty's ladies-in-waiting told me that while the Emperor and Empress were watching a cavalry exercise in France a man was seen in the square through which the cavalry was to ride. Some of those standing near the Empress expressed fear for the man's safety and called Her Majesty's attention to him and to what might happen to him. When the Empress recognized him—he was Philippe—she calmly remarked that he would come to no harm.

Philippe had been introduced to the Empress by Grand Duchess Militsa Niko-laevna, one of the daughters of Prince Nicholas of Montenegro and the wife of the sickly Grand Duke Peter Nikolaevich. Both the Grand Duchess and her sister Princess Anastasia Nikolaevna (then married to Prince George of Leuchtenberg, who lived with his mistress in Biarritz) are infected by that disease known by such names as spiritualism and occultism. Well, the Grand Duchess had become acquainted with Dr. Papius, one of the charlatans connected with spiritualism, who had then introduced her to another charlatan, Philippe.[1]

Philippe, whose education was slight, lived in the environs of Lyons. Although lacking any medical training (his son-in-law was a doctor), he began to practice medicine, employing wonder-working means. As often happens in such cases, he effected some successful cures and made some successful predictions. People who knew him said that on the whole he was a clever man with some sort of mystic power over people with weak or disturbed personalities.

Because he was denounced by some as a charlatan, he was prosecuted several times and forbidden to practice medicine. Nonetheless, Philippe attracted a small group of followers, primarily nationalists who were pro-Boulanger and anti-Dreyfus. One of his followers was Count V. V. Muravev-Amurskii (the younger brother of Nicholas V. Muravev, about whom I have spoken), our military attaché in Paris. This count, who was decidedly abnormal, was always trying to involve us in some scheme or other against the republic, which he hated. And because I was among those who prevented such adventures, arguing that we had no business interfering in French internal affairs, he was removed from his post; he hated me deeply even though he did not know me personally. He and other admirers of Philippe considered him a holy man, asserting that he had descended from heaven and would return there.

Philippe managed to get into the good graces of Grand Duke Nicholas Nikola-evich and Peter Nikolaevich and later of Their Majesties, through the efforts of Grand Duchess Militsa Nikolaevna and Princess Anastasia Nikolaevna. As a result, Philippe made several *secret* visits to Petersburg, staying chiefly at the summer homes of the grand dukes, where he met and had mystical seances with Their Majesties, the two grand dukes, and the two sisters. Apparently it was at the summer home of Grand Duke Peter Nikolaevich that the thought of canonizing Serafim of Sarov was born. (Serafim had been considered a holy man during his lifetime, but he had not been considered a saint, and it was not the practice to canonize a man unless the people believed him to be a saint.)

Constantine Petrovich Pobedonostsev told me about the circumstances behind the canonization. I well remember, it was in the summer of 1902, how he came to see me after having lunched at Peterhof with Their Majesties. He had been astonished to be invited to lunch since he had not been in their good graces for some years. He soon discovered the reason.

After lunch the Emperor asked Pobedonostsev to prepare a decree canonizing Serafim, the decree to be issued on the day of Serafim's anniversary, a few weeks hence. Pobedonostsev replied that it was the Holy Synod that proclaimed saints, and then only after a lengthy investigation of the candidate's life and the popular tradition surrounding him. The Empress reacted by saying that the Emperor could do anything. However, they finally accepted Pobedonostsev's judgment, but the Emperor directed that the canonization take place the following year, on the occasion of the consecration of the relics of Serafim.

Because Grand Duchess Militsa Nikolaevna was greatly impressed by Philippe, she sought to help him gain the right to practice medicine.[2] Once, while in Paris, she summoned Rachkovskii, the head of our secret police abroad, and asked him to arrange [for the French government] to give Philippe a medical diploma. Naturally, Rachkovskii told her how naive her request was and in so doing showed little respect for Philippe. His answer made her his dangerous enemy and would lead to the undermining of his position.

Kuropatkin, the minister of war, then came to Philippe's rescue. In disregard of legal procedure, he arranged for the man to receive the degree of doctor of medicine from the Petersburg Military-Medical Academy and the rank of actual state councillor. The holy Philippe then went to a military tailor and ordered the uniform of a military doctor. All this was done very quietly.

Shortly thereafter Hesse, the court commandant, acting with the permission of the Emperor, asked Rachkovskii to investigate Philippe. Rachkovskii's inquiries led him to conclude that Philippe was a charlatan. Rachkovskii carried the report to Petersburg, where he first saw Sipiagin, before reporting to Hesse. Sipiagin, having a better notion of the state of affairs than did Rachkovskii, advised him to burn the report, but his advice went unheeded. This is why Rachkovskii, who had long been in the bad graces of Plehve, was dismissed as soon as the latter became minister of interior and, what is more, dismissed under the remarkable condition that he would receive a pension only if he lived continuously in Brussels.

I saw Plehve soon after I had heard of Rachkovskii's dismissal. When he confirmed that what I had heard was true, I suggested that this was not a wise step for we would thereby be losing our whole network of information about what revolutionaries and anarchists were doing abroad. He did not react to this, saying only that the dismissal had been on orders from the Emperor.

To return to the Emperor's trip aboard, he came back to Russia in September. On October 27 it was my pleasure to inform him of the linking of the Chinese Eastern Railroad, which had been constructed under my direction, with both the lines running to Vladivostok in the east and trans-Baikalia in the west.

The Visit of Marquis Ito

Around October 15, [1901], the remarkable, perhaps even great, Japanese states-man Marquis Ito arrived in Petersburg to negotiate an agreement that, if com-pleted, would have prevented the unhappy war that was to come. What was offered, in diplomatic terms, was Japanese acceptance of our taking of the Kwan-tung region and our construction of a railroad linking Port Arthur and the Chinese Eastern Railroad in return for our recognition of the predominant influ-ence of Japan in Korea, the withdrawal, except for railroad guards, of our troops from Manchuria, and our maintenance of an open door policy in Manchuria.

Because the Japanese envoy to England was then negotiating with England for an agreement, Ito tried to speed up negotiations with us in order to avoid the conclusion of such an agreement or, at the very least, to modify its terms. He presented himself to the Emperor, saw Count Lambsdorff, and had several ex-tended talks with me because he knew that I fervently supported his efforts, foreseeing that if the agreement he sought were not concluded, there would be a catastrophe.

Unfortunately, he was received coldly. And we moved slowly. Count Lambs-dorff solicited opinions from the concerned ministers: navy, war, and finance. I was in favor of a speedy settlement, but the other ministers raised various objec-tions. In the end we countered his proposal with our own, which did not accept the basic wishes of Japan. We sent our draft proposal to Ito, who was by that time in Berlin: he did not respond to it, nor could he have, for seeing how his friendly proposals had been received in Petersburg, he no longer opposed having an agreement with England, by which she would pledge herself to support Japan in a quarrel with Russia, an agreement that would lead to a war that was disastrous for us. It was because of the influence of Bezobrazov and Co. that we presented such conditions to Marquis Ito that made an agreement with Japan unthinkable, even though we did not flatly say no to an agreement.[3]

The fact was that Bezobrazov and Co. had been gaining influence that permit-ted them to engage in adventurous schemes in Korea. As a result we were following two policies, one supported by me, Count Lambsdorff, and, in this case, Kuropatkin, and an opposing policy, the covert, unofficial policy of Bezobrazov, based on the belief that we must strengthen our position in Korea and establish, as Bezobrazov put it, a military buffer there, by covert means. They argued further that we must keep our troops in Manchuria to buttress our covert efforts in Korea; if we did not, our power in Korea would diminish and Japan would be left ensconced there. Although Kuropatkin disagreed with me and Count Lambsdorff about our policies in Manchuria, he supported us in arguing that we must accept the fact that we had ceded dominant influence in Korea to Japan, that to follow the Bezobrazov policy might lead to war with Japan.

In all fairness I must say that as long as the ministers agreed on the policy to be followed with respect to Korea, His Majesty, when all is said and done, was inclined to support the views of his ministers, despite the influence of Count Vorontsov-Dashkov, Grand Duke Alexander Mikhailovich, and Bezobrazov, although he was evidently sympathetic toward the views of the latter group.

It was to our advantage that Sipiagin supported me, Count Lambsdorff, and Kuropatkin. On several occasions, Sipiagin, who had access to all kinds of secret information, told me that he was concerned over the influence of Bezobrazov and Co., saying that they had "considerable influence in high places"; he was worried over "the consequences of the adventures on which they were embarked."

The Assassination of Sipiagin

On April 2, 1902, Sipiagin, that genuine nobleman, was assassinated. He was in the vestibule of the Marie Palace, which housed the Committee of Ministers, waiting for the committee meeting to begin. As he was waiting and other members were arriving, a man dressed in an officer's uniform, with the insignia of an adjutant, entered, carrying a parcel which he said was for Sipiagin. When the minister of interior asked from whom the parcel had come, the man said it was from Grand Duke Sergei Aleksandrovich and, as Sipiagin reached for it, shot him several times, with a Browning pistol. Sipiagin fell and was then taken to the nearby Maksimilianovskii Clinic, still conscious.

General Vannovskii was among those who rushed into the vestibule when the shots rang out. He said that this man was an officer. By the time I arrived on the scene, the man was in the next room, undressed. He was tall and blond. He admitted at once that he was not an officer, that he was an anarchist and ex-student and that his surname was Balmashev.

I was with Sipiagin to the last. As I have already had occasion to say, he was a fine and noble person.[4] I was deeply moved by his death.

He had known that he was in great danger. Just a few days before his death, I told him that I thought that he was pursuing excessively severe policies that, while serving no useful purpose, would alienate certain elements which, although not well intentioned toward the government, were at least moderate. He said that I was right, but that those at the top felt that he was not being severe enough.

Just a few weeks before he died, Sipiagin and I dined at the home of the notorious Prince Meshcherskii, to whom he was distantly related. There were just the three of us at dinner. Afterward Sipiagin talked about his situation, saying that he found his position so difficult that he had thought of asking the Emperor to let him go. When the question of a possible replacement arose, the name "Plehve" was uttered.

Sipiagin said that he had had an unfavorable opinion of Plehve even before becoming minister of interior, and that after becoming minister, his opinion had grown even more unfavorable because he had been able to become acquainted with Plehve's earlier activities [as director of the Department of Police] in the ministry. As a result he had become convinced that Plehve would pursue only personal aims if he became minister and that therefore his appointment would be a misfortune for Russia. Prince Meshcherskii agreed completely.

Nonetheless, immediately after Sipiagin's death, Prince Meshcherskii called on Plehve and then recommended him to the Emperor as the only man suitable to become minister of interior. Two days after Sipiagin's death, Plehve was appointed minister of interior.[5]

Plehve's appointment was to have a fateful effect on both domestic and foreign policy.[6]

He wanted to get rid of me and Count Lambsdorff. He undertook to achieve this end by supporting the views of Bezobrazov and Co., and since as minister of interior he had means, denied to other ministers, of influencing the Emperor, he would be able to tip the scales in favor of Bezobrazov. As a result, I was to lose all my influence, and my efforts—supported by Count Lambsdorff and to a degree by Kuropatkin—to prevent the deterioration of our relations with Japan were to fail.

The Ministry of Education

Shortly after the appointment of Plehve, General Vannovskii retired from the position of minister of education. It seems that Vannovskii—that ardent conservative, that quintessentially military man—could not get along with Plehve, because the new minister of interior presented demands that he considered unacceptable. Seeing that the Emperor was favorable to Plehve, he chose to retire.[7]

He was replaced by Sänger, a former professor at the University of Warsaw, a man of absolute probity, but not of this world. He was such an excellent classicist that he was able to translate Pushkin's *Eugene Onegin* into Latin, and very well at that. He administered the ministry in the spirit of order, but not of reaction: for that reason he was later to be replaced by General Glazov.

Kokovtsev, Plehve's Replacement

With Plehve's appointment as minister of interior the office of Imperial secretary became vacant. Vladimir Nikolaevich Kokovtsev, who had been one of my assistant ministers since 1896 and is now premier, asked me to help him win appointment to this post.

I knew that the chairman of the State Council, Grand Duke Michael Nikolaevich, was well disposed toward him and accordingly asked why he didn't turn to the Grand Duke for help. He said that he had and that the Grand Duke had agreed to recommend him but had also suggested that he ask me to put in a good word with the Emperor, because my recommendation might be more effective than his. (The Grand Duke had learned to fear Emperor Alexander III, and he feared Emperor Nicholas II; unfortunately, fear of the Emperor has disappeared among many Grand Dukes in recent years.) At my next report to the Emperor I found an opportunity to speak about Kokovtsev and was told that the Grand Duke had already spoken about him. On April 14, Kokovtsev was appointed Imperial secretary.[8] In my archive I have a letter from Kokovtsev in which he effusively thanked me for having had the opportunity to serve under me and for my help in assisting him to win appointment as Imperial secretary.

Visiting Dignitaries

On May 7, 1902, President Emile Loubet of France arrived in Petersburg to return the visit to France made by our Emperor the preceding year. I was among those presented to this very fine and sympathetic man at the Winter Palace. Since I had already had the honor of meeting him, he was very amiable toward me.

That same year Prince (now King) Ferdinand of Bulgaria came to Petersburg. I was then staying on Elagin Island, where he came to visit with me and we spent considerable time talking of this and that. I found him to be a very refined, intelligent, and cunning man into whose mouth one shouldn't place one's finger. But it should be noted that he employs his cunning for the sake of his people. In fact he has transformed Bulgaria from a small principality into a fairly important kingdom which will come to have some influence in international affairs.

He gave me an autographed picture of himself.

In June of the same year King Victor Emmanuel of Italy came to Petersburg to visit the Emperor. I had the opportunity of speaking with him at some length and found him to be a very refined and intelligent man, without that kind of cleverness that is unsuitable for the head of a great state. Also, I was impressed, in fact amazed, by his extreme leftism: although he makes no effort to hide his political opinion, he is respected and loved in his country. He told me that if he were an ordinary mortal and were a deputy to parliament, he would sit in the left side of the chamber.

While the king was still in Russia, Count Lambsdorff told me that the king was somewhat at a loss over what order to bestow on me, because the highest order of his country was reserved for members of ruling families and the next highest order might seem an insult to me. I laughed and told Count Lambsdorff to inform the king that I hoped he would not trouble himself over the matter, that I needed no order, but would be happy to receive an autographed picture of him. The next day I received a large, signed photograph of the king. Later, following his return to Rome, the king had a large oil painting of himself sent to me.

Imperial Travels

That same month, Emperor Nicholas II and Emperor William II met at Reval, where we were conducting naval maneuvers. In the course of the customary exchange of signals following the completion of the maneuvers, the German Emperor signaled: "The Emperor of the Atlantic Ocean salutes the Emperor of the Pacific Ocean."

I do not know how the Emperor—who was at a loss as to how to answer the signal—replied to it, but I know what it meant: "I seek a predominant position in the Atlantic and I advise you to seek a similar position in the Pacific; if you do, I will support you." As I have already noted, Emperor William lured us into Far Eastern adventures in the hopes of having a free hand in Europe; this signal was in keeping with the comedy he was playing.[9]

From this time on, particularly in 1903, our Emperor, in his dispatches to our viceroy in the Far East and in other documents, frequently expressed the wish that Russia acquire the dominant influence in the Far East. I do not know whether he did so under the influence of the German Emperor's signal or under another influence.

Emperor Nicholas II went from Reval to Peterhof, and from there to the maneuvers at Kursk,[10] where the opposing armies were respectively commanded by Grand Duke Sergei Aleksandrovich and General Kuropatkin. Although Kuropatkin had tremendous prestige at the time, the Grand Duke was declared the victor, as was only fitting in a contest between a grand duke and a minister.

From Kursk the Emperor returned to Peterhof, which he left on September 14 to take up residence in the Crimea.

Far Eastern Policies

[In August 1902 I went to the Far East, where I] visited Vladivostok, Port Arthur, and Dalnyi: I thoroughly acquainted myself with what was going on in that distant region and drew very sad conclusions from my observations. On my return [in October] I went directly to the Crimea, to convey my impressions to the Emperor. Because Bezobrazov, who had been out of favor, was now back in his good graces, His Majesty was not particularly interested in speaking with me about my impressions of the Far East. But he did ask that I send him my report on my trip. This I was to do after my return to Petersburg.

In my report I expressed myself forcefully about the abnormality of the situation in the Far East. I insisted that normality could return only if we withdrew our troops from Manchuria, thus permitting the area to return to a peaceful condition. Also, I spoke up once more about the need for an agreement with Japan, predicting that without it things would go very badly. Brief excerpts from the report were published in *Pravitelstvennyi vestnik* at the time, and a large part was published later, after the Treaty of Portsmouth. I will not deal in detail with the report, a copy of which is in my archive: one who reads it will recognize that if my views and suggestions had been paid attention to, we would have been spared the dreadful war with Japan and all its consequences.

As I have said, Bezobrazov had been out of favor. As I was to learn from General Hesse, the court commandant, more than a year before my trip to the Far East, His Majesty had been torn between following the direction represented by Bezobrazov, which would have meant getting rid of me, for he knew that I would not retreat from my views and would vigorously oppose those of Bezobrazov, or to follow the direction represented by me and get rid of Bezobrazov.

And although, as was evident, Bezobrazov was more to the Emperor's liking than I, His Majesty had decided to follow my policy, because Count Lambsdorff supported me. He had therefore decided to part with Bezobrazov, who had been obliged to return to Geneva, where his sick wife was living.

But while I was in the Far East, Grand Duke Alexander Mikhailovich had brought Bezobrazov back and had helped him to be restored in the Emperor's favor. Bezobrazov thus regained his power and, with the help of Plehve, introduced policies that would lead to catastrophe. I am telling all this in the most general and sketchy terms. Those who read these memoirs, when I am no longer among the living, will find in my archive the most circumstantial, factual, and fully prepared material on this subject.

It is often said that no matter what course we followed, Japan would have gone to war against us. Not so. Had we punctiliously lived up to our treaty with China, had we not engaged in that fantastic adventure in Korea, which can best be called "Bezobrazovshchina," after its author, had we accepted the sincere proposals made by Ito and the subsequent proposals made by Kurino, the Japanese ambassador, on the eve of the war, there would have been no war.

But it is argued that Japan was preparing for war and that therefore war was inevitable. Yet one can see from our relations with Germany that it is possible to prepare for war and yet not go to war. Ever since I entered railroad service our railroad and financial policies have been chiefly based on the expectation of war with Germany, just as German policy was based on the expectation of war with us. Even when we were on the brink of war with Japan, the thoughts of our military administration were centered on the possibility of war with Germany, so much so that we named Grand Duke Nicholas Nikolaevich to command our armies on the German front and General Kuropatkin to command our armies on the Austrian front in the event of war. But, the Lord be praised, we have thus far avoided war with Germany and Austria, and I am convinced that if we follow a wise, unprovocative, and honorable policy there will be no war for a long time to come.

Thus it follows that preparation for war does not make war inevitable. On the contrary, prudent preparation for war, accompanied by a wise policy, provides a guarantee that war will not break out except for the gravest of reasons.

Grand Duke Alexander Mikhailovich and the Merchant Marine

While I was at Yalta a disturbing event involving that arch intriguer Grand Duke Alexander Mikhailovich occurred. Following my report to the Emperor about my trip to the Far East, he raised the question of the construction and administration of our ports; he had information that these facilities, which were under the administration of the Ministry of Ways and Communications, were poorly managed and that there was a good deal of bribery going on. I said that major contractors involved with the ports made a great deal of money and that I thought there should be stricter controls in making contracts and stricter auditing, but I did not think that the ministry was guilty of impropriety in port construction. With that the conversation ended.

The following day, after lunch, the Emperor asked me what I thought of the idea of creating a new ministry with jurisdiction over commercial ports.[11] I replied that we already had a small section in the Department of Commerce and Industry in the Ministry of Finance that dealt with the merchant marine, and a Merchant Marine Council to deal with broad questions: I saw no point in transforming the small council into a ministry, but I could see merit in creating a Ministry of Commerce and Industry to which those divisions of the Ministry of Finance relating to commerce and industry could be transferred. In fact, I had made such a suggestion to the Emperor on an earlier occasion, but he had not been favorably disposed to the idea. After he had heard my opinion the Emperor left me.

That evening Count Musin-Pushkin, commander of the Odessa Military District, a fine old man and a close friend to my wife, came to see me. He had spent his whole life at court and knew its ins and outs. After asking and being told what the Emperor had spoken about with me, he said that it was odd that I hadn't noticed the Emperor's displeasure, as in fact, I had not.*

A few days later, while I was en route from Yalta to Petersburg, a courier from His Majesty handed me a packet containing a copy of a decree announcing the

---

*I should add, by way of background, that in 1898, recognizing the importance of the merchant marine, I had been instrumental in the creation of a merchant marine section in the Department of Commerce and Industry and in the formation of a Merchant Marine Council. In 1901 I was told that Grand Duke Alexander Mikhailovich would like to become chairman of the council. Not yet acquainted with his shortcomings, but knowing that he was a naval man, an intelligent person, and that he was the husband of the eldest daughter of Emperor Alexander III, to whose memory I was devoted, I told Emperor Nicholas II that I was agreeable to the Grand Duke's becoming chairman. This was done and the Grand Duke thus became my subordinate.

Soon he began to introduce innovations which many members of the council opposed. He managed to terrorize some of the opposition by virtue of his rank, but not all. Since it was my duty to approve or disapprove recommendations of the council, I often found myself agreeing with his critics. As a result, he often threatened to leave. Knowing that he would complain to the Emperor, I made it a point to inform the Emperor about our differences and about his talk of quitting his post, to which the Emperor had replied: "Well, let him."

formation of the Chief Administration of the Merchant Marine, with Grand Duke Alexander Mikhailovich as its chief. With this appointment he became a member of the Committee of Ministers. All this was the result of the Grand Duke's capacity for intrigue and the fact that he was the Emperor's brother-in-law.

Imperial Rescript

On January 1, 1903, the Emperor issued a rescript expressing his appreciation for my work in strengthening the government's financial position and also for my having given instruction to Grand Duke Michael Aleksandrovich.

Ministry of the Navy

On March 4, 1903, the director of the Ministry of the Navy, Admiral Tyrtov, a fine but undistinguished man, died. He was replaced by Admiral Avelan, who had until then been chief of naval staff. Like Admiral Tyrtov, Admiral Avelan is a limited man, but he is a very fine and honorable person. This is shown by the fact that after being removed from his office, following the disaster at Tsushima, he refused to accept an appointment to the State Council because he felt that the person in charge at the time of such a disaster should not play an active role thereafter, even though he was not responsible for what had happened. (He had opposed sending our fleet to the Pacific.) And to this day, even though he holds the rank of general-adjutant, he has refrained from taking any active role.

Admiral Rozhdestvenskii replaced Avelan as chief of naval staff when the latter became director of the Ministry of the Navy. Rozhdestvenskii was well known for his service on the *Vesta* in the war with Turkey. Also, he gained attention at the time of the naval maneuvers at Reval [in 1902]. During the maneuvers he was praised on all sides for the performance of our naval artillery, which he commanded.

I was to meet Admiral Rozhdestvenskii when I served as chairman of the Committee of Ministers. I was to find this man, who was to lead our fleet to disaster at Tsushima, a rather strange and limited man. For example, he strongly supported an odd proposal, one that had the backing of Grand Duke Alexander Mikhailovich, that no merchant ships be permitted to enter Kronstadt or Petersburg without being inspected. He argued energetically, and in dead earnest, that such inspection was necessary because Japanese vessels, disguised as merchant ships, might sneak mines into these ports. The proposal was not approved by the committee.

Death of Durnovo

On May 29, Ivan Nikolaevich Durnovo, chairman of the Committee of Ministers, died.[12]

Their Majesties' Journey to Sarov

In July Their Majesties went to Sarov,[13] for the consecration of the relics of Serafim of Sarov, for whom they had special reverence. During their visit there were several instances of miraculous cures, and the Empress herself bathed in a curative spring. It is also said that the Emperor and Empress believed that Saint Serafim would give them a son. Later, after they had a son, Grand Duke Alexis Nikolaevich, Their Majesties' faith in the saint became unshakable, and a large portrait of Saint Serafim was to be hung in the Emperor's study.

Among the many whose careers were to be advanced by their roles at Sarov were Plehve and Launitz. Both were to die at the hands of assassins. Although I oppose all assassinations, particularly anarchist ones, I must say in all candor that these two contributed to their own deaths by their lack of principle. Plehve was at least intelligent and well informed; Launitz was neither.

XXXIV

My Departure from the Office of Minister of Finance

The Ascendancy of Bezobrazov and Co.

Since the summer of 1902 the Emperor had been shifting to the side of Bezobrazov and Plehve, despite the opposing opinions of the ministers of finance and foreign affairs, the latter two being supported to some extent by the minister of war. I have told the whole story of the origins of the war with Japan elsewhere.[1] Therefore I am restricting myself in these memoirs to a sketchy account.

During this period, 1902–1903, when the influence of Bezobrazov and Co. grew,[2] there were several conferences dealing with our Far Eastern policy, at which I was an implacable critic, constantly expressing sharp and decisive objections to the course we were following, a course that I said would lead Russia and the Emperor to misfortune. His Majesty was kind enough to make an effort to change my mind or, at least, to persuade me not to object as emphatically and sharply as I did. (As I have noted, I am aware that I was too sharp with him and that loyal subjects should learn to control themselves in his presence.) But this kind of attention on the part of His Majesty could not alter my convictions, and I continued to express myself emphatically.

Also, I used the good offices of Prince Meshcherskii, who had some influence at that time, to persuade the Emperor that the course being urged by Bezobrazov and Co. was a dangerous one. Here one must give Prince Meshcherskii his due. He completely understood and supported my position and, at my suggestion, wrote in this vein to the Emperor.[3] In his reply, which expressed the great intimacy which then existed between the two, the Emperor rejected Prince Meshcherskii's warnings and said: "On May 6, they will see what my opinion on this matter is." Prince Meshcherskii had no idea of what was to happen on that date, and when he asked me if I knew, I replied that neither did I.

On May 6, [1903], Bezobrazov was given the title of state secretary of His Majesty and his associate General Vogak was appointed general à la suite of His Majesty. Both appointments were exceptional and significant. After receiving this appointment Bezobrazov began to play an increasingly important role and consequently brought his ailing wife from Geneva, to have her presented at court. [As I have noted earlier], his wife, a kind and educated woman, was quite taken aback and said: "It is difficult to understand how Sasha can play such an important role; don't people know that he is half-mad?"

Viceroyalty of the Far East

On July 30, [1903], ten days after the Emperor's return from Sarov, the news appeared of the creation of the Viceroyalty of the Far East.[4] The announcement was a surprise to all but Plehve. It was clear to me that the man appointed to be viceroy, Alekseev, who had been serving as chief of the Kwantung region, had decided to support Bezobrazov and Co., because he had seen that they were in the ascendancy, and had consequently been rewarded with the post of viceroy. To me the creation of the viceroyalty meant that the game in the Far East was lost and that war was inevitable.

Early in August Bezobrazov called on me in an effort—either on his own initiative or at the urging of someone higher up—to win me over to his side. I was surprised at the call because I had seen him no more than four times in the preceding period. He told me that on such and such a day, at such and such an hour, the Emperor would visit the Putilov plant (which was then under the supervision of the State Bank because it was insolvent) to inspect torpedo boats being constructed there. He suggested that I be there, to meet His Majesty.* I replied that I was obliged to meet His Majesty whenever it pleased him to have me do so, after informing me through official channels, but, I said that I would not go to the Putilov plant at his, Bezobrazov's, suggestion, or on my own initiative.

As it turned out, His Majesty did appear at the plant at the time that Bezobrazov had indicated. There he was received by a number of people, among them Pleske, manager of the State Bank, who was to succeed me as minister of finance.

The Emperor's Attitude toward Me

Principally because of my implacability concerning our Far Eastern policy, the Emperor had come to display an unfavorable attitude toward me. This is illuminated by an incident, involving Baron General Meyendorff, that occurred about this time.

---

*One of the directors of this plant, Albert, a man of Jewish origin, once came to see me to make fun of the extravagant conduct of Bezobrazov and Co., although he had been helped by the Bezobrazov faction and was subservient to it. When I asked how he happened to be one of them, he replied: "Fish swim where the water is deeper."

Baron Meyendorff—a very kind and decent man, but with very little up-stairs—was chief of the Imperial escort. His wife, née Princess Vasilchikova, on the other hand, was possessed of some sense, which she devoted to advancing their financial interests. Because neither had an independent income of any conse-quence, she was constantly on the lookout for opportunities to improve their finances. Well, a certain Zavoiko, in return for a favor* done for him by Baron Meyendorff, advised him that he could enrich himself by buying a certain estate, which could be had at a very low price.

The Nobles' Bank agreed to lend Baron Meyendorff all but 250,000 rubles of the sum required to buy the estate. Well, sometime in July he told me that he had an order from the Emperor for the State Bank to lend him that sum. I told him that only a state secretary or His Majesty or a general-adjutant could give me an [oral] Imperial order, and since he was neither and since, moreover, the matter was personal business, I could not act without a signed order from the Emperor. A few days later I received such an order and, although there was no provision in the charter of the State Bank for such a loan, it was granted immediately in view of the Emperor's request. I was to learn later that the incident was used by some to say to the Emperor and Empress that things had come to a fine pass when the minister of finance would not listen to the Emperor.

My Departure from the Post of Minister of Finance

During the evening of Thursday, August 14, I received a note from the Emperor asking me to bring Pleske with me when I came to give my regular report, the following day. The request surprised me. Did it mean that His Majesty wished to replace me with Pleske?

I was convinced that as matters stood, I could not continue as minister of finance, for to do so would mean that I would have to accept responsibility for all the consequences that would result from a war with Japan. To be sure, other ministers could use the justification that they were only carrying out the Emper-or's wishes, but public opinion would not accept such a justification from me, for Russia already knew my character, my decisiveness, my firmness too well to believe that if I stayed on it was only because I was bowing to the inevitable.

And if the Emperor chose to replace me, that was quite understandable, for if he retained a minister who was opposed to his Far Eastern policies, a minister with so important a role as mine was in our Far Eastern affairs, that minister would constantly serve as a hindrance in carrying out the new policy, and his continued presence would mean a conflict of policies. Nonetheless, it seemed to me that if His Majesty chose to part with me, he would do so in a conventional manner, by summoning only me and informing me of his decision. And if he were going to

*Because Zavoiko had been thwarted in his efforts to obtain large loans from either the Nobles' Bank or the Peasants' Bank, he prepared a memorandum, inspired by Plehve, which was transmitted to the Emperor by Baron Meyendorff. The memorandum resulted in the transfer of these two banks from the jurisdiction of the Ministry of Finance to that of the Ministry of Interior.

replace me, why choose Pleske, a man whom he had seen only once, at the Putilov plant, and whom he did not know at all?

Such were my thoughts when I read the Emperor's note.

I then asked Pleske to meet me the following day at my residence on Elagin Island. From there we sailed to Peterhof on the border patrol steamer that usually took me there. En route he asked me why he had been asked to go. I did not tell him what I thought, but said only that I presumed that the Emperor intended to appoint him to some new post. In Peterhof we went by carriage to the Emperor's residence. Pleske remained in the reception room when I went into the Emperor's study to give my report.

The Emperor received me kindly. As usual, my report lasted an hour. In the course of that hour I told him of my many ideas for the future and requested permission to use the time that he would be abroad to visit those provinces where the liquor monopoly was being introduced. He gave his assent, adding that it was good that I was giving so important a matter my personal attention.

As I arose to leave, he seemed somewhat disconcerted and asked if I had brought Pleske with me. I said that I had. Then he asked my opinion of Pleske. I replied that I thought highly of him, as in fact I did, for Pleske was a man of utmost rectitude, a close associate for many years, an outstanding man, with much experience and knowledge in several fields of financial administration.

The Emperor then said to me: "Sergei Iulevich, I am asking you to take the post of chairman of the Committee of Ministers and wish to appoint Pleske as minister of finance." This was unexpected, chiefly because of the manner in which it was done. Apparently noting an expression of astonishment on my face, he asked: "Are you dissatisfied with the appointment? Don't you know that the position of chairman of the Committee of Ministers is the highest in the Empire?"

I replied that if this appointment were not a sign of his disfavor I would naturally be very happy with it, but I ventured to suggest that I could be more useful in a post that offered more scope than this one did. I then took my leave of His Majesty, and, at his request, asked Pleske to go in to see him.[5]

Then I went from the Emperor's residence to that of the Dowager Empress, who had invited me to lunch with her. She was very kind and gracious to me, probably because she knew what was taking place. During my visit she did not talk politics except to remark that she feared that Plehve was leading her son into trouble, adding: "It was for good reason that my late husband didn't want to appoint Plehve to a responsible post."

She did not refer to the reason[6] for my dismissal—my opposition to the course we were following in the Far East—but she obviously understood, and that, I believe, is why she invited me and was so kind and gracious to me. Earlier on I had warned her, through Prince Shervashidze, her high master of the court and an old acquaintance of mine, that unless there were a sharp change in our policy, war with Japan was unavoidable, and had advised her to summon Count Lambsdorff.

This she did and was told, in a politic manner, that I was correct. I learned later that she had then spoken to her son, who assured her that he did not want war.

After I left her, I went to see Grand Duke Alexander Mikhailovich, at his invitation, at the so-called farm in Peterhof, where he was then staying.[7] His chief interest was in talking to me about Plehve's responsibility for labor troubles in Odessa. Also, he congratulated me on my new appointment, by which he was obviously pleased, because it meant, in effect, that I was being removed from an active role in government.

The Enigma of Count Lambsdorff

My transfer from the position of minister of finance to the eminent but meaningless post of chairman of the Committee of Ministers is, as I have said, largely explained by my rejection of a dangerous policy that was to lead to war with Japan. That being the case, I could not help but wonder why Count Lambsdorff had not been let go as well, for he had consistently taken the same position as I.

The answer is to be found in our differences in character and manner. I can illustrate my point by an imaginary tale about a man, well along in years, who wants to leave his wife and marry a young girl. His two children—a son and a daughter—are aghast. The son tells his father in a harsh manner that such an act would harm him as well as his family. The father, after repeatedly, but to no avail, telling his son to avoid this delicate subject, loses his temper and drives the son out of the house. The daughter uses different tactics. She says to her father: "Father dear, because I love you and fear that you will harm yourself, I beseech you not to do this." The father pats her cheek and says: "My darling, go for a walk: tonight I will take you to the theater." My manner was that of the son, Count Lambsdorff's that of the daughter.

Also, I could not help but wonder why Count Lambsdorff decided to remain in his post after my departure. Why did he not ask to be relieved of his post, as Prince Valerian Sergeevich Obolenskii and others strongly urged him to do? He told me frankly that he accepted the fact that our Sovereign was an autocrat and that it was his duty to carry out the Sovereign's decisions even if they were in contradiction to the advice that he had given him. I believe that there is some logic in such a position, for a person with an elastic ego.[8] Unfortunately, I do not have such an ego.

The Enigma of Pleske's Appointment

I do not know why the Emperor chose Pleske to succeed me, but I think that he did so on the recommendation of Bezobrazov and Co., who thought that Pleske would be suitable for their purposes, inasmuch as he did not appear to have a strong will and would, moreover, not feel secure in his new position for some time. However, he was to be a disappointment to these gentlemen, because he was a man of high principles and would not compromise with them.

XXXIV ■ MY DEPARTURE FROM OFFICE   317

Bezobrazov would have been better advised to have recommended Kokovtsev, a man who finds it easier to swim with the current than did Pleske, even though he has a firmer will than Pleske had. I was later informed that Kokovtsev was disappointed that he had not been chosen to succeed me. In fact, he was better qualified than Pleske in some phases of government finance and, what is more, was intelligent enough quickly to fill in gaps in his knowledge.

Appendix A

Some of My Achievements as Minister of Finance

Some General Comments

The wealth of a nation and, consequently, its power, depends on three factors: natural resources, capital (both material and intellectual), and labor.[1]

Russia is extraordinarily rich in natural resources, but those resources cannot be adequately exploited, because they are located in regions with a severe climate. Russia has little accumulated capital, in part because of the cost of frequent wars, in part for other reasons. Russia could be rich in intellectual and physical labor power because the healthy and God-fearing Russian is well-endowed by nature. All three—natural resources, capital, and labor—must work together to produce a nation's wealth.

It is possible to compensate for the lack of natural resources because improved communications makes shipping from one country to another feasible. Also, nowadays the capital of the whole world is, to a significant degree, internationalized, because of the availability of international credit. It follows that attention must be given to the formation and attraction of capital and even more to the effective use of labor.

Finance and Capital

The formation and attraction of capital requires the establishment of the nation's credit on a firm basis.

During my tenure as minister of finance, the financial position of the government improved markedly, permitting the accumulation of surpluses that enabled us to maintain free reserves of several hundred million rubles in the treasury. I was able to accomplish this with the Emperor's complete support and confidence.

I was under constant attack, particularly from the newspapers, for maintaining such large reserves. It was argued that such a practice was not to be found in countries with a strong financial position, such as France and England, and not even in Germany; it was said that it would be better to use these reserves for productive purposes.

But I believed that it was always useful, and sometimes imperative, for an empire with the peculiarities of Russia to maintain a large free reserve. First of all, Russia, unlike those three countries, has a large foreign debt, and that is one of the weakest features of Russian life. And in a country with such a debt it is important to be able to use the reserves in the event of a financial panic, to prevent a decline in the value of Russian bonds held abroad. Secondly, our agriculture is at a far lower technological level than the agriculture of those three countries. Because we are at such a level, we are more subject to crop failures: a few weeks of drought during a heat wave will destroy our crop, and it is important to have a reserve to deal with such a contingency.

An additional reason for my policy of maintaining large free reserves was to be able to meet the contingencies of war, this because in the latter years of my tenure I had reason to fear that, because of the interaction of two factors, we might be faced with a bloody drama someplace or other. One factor was the existence of a group, particularly among the military, notably represented by Alexis Nikola-evich Kuropatkin, which was influencing the Emperor to follow foreign policies that might lead to war. The second factor was the young Emperor, Nicholas II. He was not warlike, but he did not love peace or calm, and he was susceptible to the blandishments of some in his confidence who proposed foreign ventures that, so they assured him, did not involve the risk of war.

As it turned out, it was providential that I looked ahead. When I left the office of minister of finance, we had a reserve of 380 million rubles. This enabled us to weather the first months of war with Japan without having to borrow money and later, when we had to float a loan, we were able to do so under more favorable terms than would have been possible had our financial status been weaker.

Also, during my tenure as minister of finance, I was able to convert a large part of our debts, on which we were paying a high interest, to ones on which the interest was low. In addition, I was able to negotiate several direct loans for railroad construction and the building up of our gold holdings during the institution of the gold standard. In this work I had the complete support and confidence of Emperor Nicholas II.

Thanks to my efforts, which established foreign confidence in Russia's credit, our country received several (not less than three) billion rubles of foreign capital. There were then and still are many who criticize me for attempting to attract foreign capital. I have been and am still opposed to hindering the influx of foreign capital, if it will benefit Russia.

But there are some ultranationalists, self-styled "true Russians," largely from the nobility, usually nobles who have lost their fortunes and have gone into commerce or industry, who are not particularly in favor of the importation of foreign capital unless it is to their personal advantage, for example, by providing them a place on the board of directors of some company.

Of the thousands of examples I could cite of such nobles, I will cite only one here, that of Colonel Vonliarliarskii,[2] who like many ultranationalists, argued that our gold fields should be mined only by Russians, with the help of Russian capital. Well, at the wishes of the Emperor, he received a concession to operate gold fields on the Chukotskii Peninsula. Within a few months after receiving this concession, he sold it to foreigners and thus was able to pocket a substantial amount of unearned profit.

Another group opposed to foreign capital consists of Russian industrialists who do not want competition from foreigners.

There were many conferences at the Winter Palace under the chairmanship of Emperor Nicholas II on the subject of whether or not it was desirable to attract foreign capital, conferences at which I presented my views, arguing that foreign capital would help the fatherland and expressing the fear that if we placed obstacles in the way of foreign capital, obstacles not found in other civilized countries, we could frighten foreigners away from doing business with us. No one opposed me directly, because no substantial arguments could be presented in opposition; and whatever objections were raised, I demolished. Generally speaking, I have found that arguments advanced against foreign capital remind one of the atmosphere found in Ostrovskii's *The Bogeyman*.[3]

The Emperor, acting under influences that I cannot identify, did not seem sympathetic to my position, perhaps because he is not well acquainted with financial history or the field of finance and feared that the influx of foreign capital would mean foreign influence in Russia. Although the majority of the Finance Committee and the Committee of Ministers shared my views (men like I. N. Durnovo, Plehve, and General Lobko did not), they were afraid to speak up categorically on the subject because they sensed that foreign capital was not in special favor in higher circles. As a result of obstacles placed in the way of investment by foreigners, not as much foreign capital was invested in Russia during my tenure as finance minister as there might otherwise have been.

Railroads and Labor Productivity

As finance minister I gave considerable attention to raising the productivity of our labor force. Productivity was low for several reasons: the existence of barriers to the exercise of initiative on the part of the peasantry,[4] the bulk of our labor force; climatic conditions which leave millions of peasants with nothing to do for several months of the year; inadequate transportation.

As finance minister I was able to do something about transportation, by doubling our railroad network. Many said that I was going too fast, but now these objections are no longer heard, for everyone understands that the recently built railroads have been bringing us significant benefits. For that reason there has been energetic railroad construction in recent years.

Unfortunately, my work in extending the railroad system suffered from constant interference by military authorities, who generally were supported by His Majesty. Several railroads—among them the Trans-Caspian branch to Kushka and the Bologoe–Polotsk line—were built over my objection. Moreover, the routes of some new railroads were often changed for reasons that were unconvincing.

The military authorities supported me only when they thought that a railroad I proposed to build had strategic importance, but they disagreed among themselves: some would insist that it was imperative, for strategic reasons, that we build such and such a railroad immediately, while others argued that the proposed railroad would be harmful from a military point of view. Both General Kuropatkin, as minister of war, and General Obruchev, as chief of staff, created many difficulties for me and did much harm.

General Obruchev was an educated, gifted, and decent man, but strategic railroads were something of a mania with him. And it would happen that a railroad declared to be of strategic importance one year would be declared of no strategic importance two or three years later. And it should be remembered, as I have noted, that it was he who supported the construction of a worthless naval port at Libau. Obruchev, by the way, was constantly speaking of the need to give attention to the peasantry, but then contradicted himself by insisting on ever increasing military expenditures, some of which proved to be a waste of money.

After working with railroads for forty years, it is my conviction that all strategic considerations concerning the routing of railroads are chimerical, that the state will benefit far more if it is guided exclusively by economic considerations in such matters. How we have wasted money is shown by the fact that for thirty years we built railroads for use in a war in the West, but in the end we had to fight in the Far East.

Industry

During my tenure as finance minister, industry grew so rapidly that it could be said that a Russian national industrial system had been established. This was made possible by the system of protectionism and by attracting foreign capital.

I was criticized by some blockheads for building up industry too rapidly. Also, I was criticized for using "artificial means" in promoting industry. What does this stupid phrase mean? By what means other than artificial can industry develop? Everything that man does is, to a certain degree, artificial. Only barbarians manage to live without artificial means. Industry has always been developed by artificial means, and the artificial measures I employed were far weaker than those employed for the same ends by other states. This, of course, our salon ignoramuses do not know.

Our landed nobility attacked the protective tariff of 1890, but that tariff helped us build our industry, as did the influx of foreign capital. Unfortunately, in addition to the hindrances I encountered in attracting foreign capital, I encountered opposition in the Committee of Ministers—particularly from successive ministers of interior, notably Plehve—to my efforts to improve legislation regarding the establishment of corporations.

There is a common complaint that I was too liberal in handing out State Bank loans to industry. This is not so. In the first place, the total amount of money loaned came to no more than 50 or 60 million rubles. It is ridiculous to argue that such a sum of money could have provided the "artificial means" for giving birth to the industry of such a country as the Russian Empire. In the second place, a good part of these loans went to nobles turned industrialists, men who either belonged to the court camarilla or who had ties with that group.

Generally speaking, the importance of industry to Russia is not appreciated or understood. Only a few men, like Mendeleev—that great scientist and scholar and my devoted associate and friend—understood its importance and tried to enlighten the Russian public about it. I hope that his book on the subject will be of use to Russian society. Unfortunately, he was not appreciated while he was alive, for we Russians, more than other peoples, are inclined to wait with our appreciation until after a man is dead.

It should be noted that the growth of railroads and industry under my direction took some 4 to 5 million working adults (a total of 20-25 million persons, if one includes their families) off the land. This meant, in effect, an increase in the amount of available land of 54-67 million acres. Of course this meant only a slight increase in labor productivity. To raise productivity significantly we must see to it that the people, particularly the peasantry, have both the incentive and the opportunity to work more productively.

Labor Policy

The factory inspectorate was established when Bunge was minister of finance and had always been regarded with suspicion, because it allegedly favored the interests of the workers against the capitalists. This has never been true. The factory inspectorate supported the position of the workers only when they were treated unfairly. But, since many capitalists belong to noble families and have greater entrée to the higher spheres than do the workers, they have spread the legend that the factory inspectorate is concerned only with supporting liberal tendencies among the workers. In my efforts to protect this institution I had less than complete support from Emperor Nicholas II.[5]

Toward the end of the last century, as unrest began to grow among our workers, as socialist ideas, originating in the West, slowly gained support among them, a movement began among the liberal intelligentsia, as well as among workers, to introduce labor legislation similar to that found in the West, laws concerning insurance for workers, length of the workday, workers' associations, employer responsibility for workers' medical care, and workmen's compensation. These laws were enacted in many countries as a result of the growth of socialist influence among the workers. They were even enacted in Germany, when the unquestionably conservative Bismarck was in power.

However, in Russia efforts to enact such legislation met with strong opposition from reactionary circles. Thus, it was only with great difficulty that I was able to have a workmen's compensation bill approved by the State Council.[6] And the provisions of this law were much less liberal than those in comparable laws abroad.

Because we lagged in such matters, relations between workers and capitalists became embittered: a socialist, even revolutionary, view began to gain support among our workers, as I have noted.

Instead of using rational means, based on foreign experience, to direct the minds of Russian workers away from extremism, a different method was devised by Zubatov, head of the Moscow secret police, a man who had once been an anarchist-revolutionary. This was at a time when the governor-general of Moscow was Grand Duke Sergei Aleksandrovich and that city's police superintendent was Dmitrii Trepov.

Zubatov, with the support of these two, decided to deal with the labor question by forming workers' associations under the patronage and control of the secret police. In order to attract workers, these associations would give limited support to workers in their struggles against factory owners, the police assuming that they could control the workers. Such support would, of course, be at the expense of the owners.

From the police point of view this policy had some initial success. Thus, on holidays, workers took to the streets and greeted the Grand Duke and other officials with enthusiasm. As far as the police were concerned, the workers were behaving properly, but this was achieved by giving them unfair and illegal support at the expense of the factory owners.

Naturally, the factory inspectorate protested, and I supported its protests, but Grand Duke Sergei Aleksandrovich was then almighty. When Sipiagin was minister of interior he tried to persuade the Grand Duke not to continue with the Zubatov system, but both his predecessor, Goremykin, and his successor, Plehve, aware of the Grand Duke's powerful position, professed to find this system inspired and gave it their blessing.

When Plehve became minister, he transferred Zubatov to Petersburg, to serve as the head of the secret police there. When the Zubatov system, which came to be known as the Zubatovshchina, began to take root in Petersburg, my quarrels with the Ministry of Interior increased. Both I and the factory inspectorate predicted that the Zubatovshchina would produce dire results, but these efforts led nowhere, for the Emperor generally supported the Grand Duke and the Ministry of Interior or did not give me any support. Meanwhile Plehve and the Grand Duke introduced the Zubatov system in other localities.

In the end that system was to lead to the tragic events of January 9, 1905, about which I shall have occasion to speak later. In Moscow, where the Zubatovshchina originated, the workers were to break away from police leadership at the first opportunity and were to become a significant force in the events of 1905.[7]

My Role in the Expansion of
Commercial and Technical Education

As minister of finance I was able to expand commercial and technical education in our country. Much of this expansion was carried out by the educational section of the ministry's Department of Commerce and Industry, the work of which was broadened by my efforts. I placed Anopulo, the former director of the Tsesarevich Nicholas Trade School,* at the head of the section.[8] A statute on commercial education, for which I was able to gain the approval of the State Council, enabled me to encourage businessmen to establish commercial schools and to take part in their administration. As a result they willingly began to contribute to the establishment and support of such schools.

The promotion of commercial education led me to the idea of establishing polytechnic schools, for advanced commercial and technological education, these to be organized like universities rather than narrow specialized higher schools. What I envisioned were schools where there would be contact among students from various specializations, contact that would enable them to acquire a broader, more humanistic education than would be possible in a narrow higher school.

In 1899 I raised the question of establishing what was to become the St. Petersburg Polytechnic Institute. Then, with the aid of my colleagues, I prepared the charter of this institute. When it was submitted to the State Council I encountered some opposition, but thanks to my influence in the council and with the Emperor I was able to gain approval for the charter. The institute is now one of the major institutions of higher learning in the city. (I was also able to establish similar institutions in Warsaw and Kiev.)

I was very enthusiastic about the St. Petersburg Polytechnic Institute and was able to provide it with a magnificent building, thanks to the fact that as minister of

*That school is one of two maintained by the House of Charity and Trade Education for Poor Children in St. Petersburg, of which I became director when I assumed the office of minister of finance. I became acquainted with Anopulo through the Tsesarevich Nicholas Trade School.

finance it was easier for me than it was for other ministers to get the funds I needed. I was criticized for being liberal with money for something I thought of doing while stinting when others asked for money. I was also criticized for establishing such an institute at a time of widespread disorders in the universities: many said that I was providing an additional site for student disorders.

Because of such criticism I was very careful to see that the man appointed as director of the new institute should be someone who would not arouse any misgivings in the higher spheres. Such a man was Prince Gagarin, who was suggested to me by General Petrov (now a member of the State Council and honorary academician).

Prince Gagarin was considered to be one of our ablest artillery specialists. He was and continues to be interested in scholarly technological investigation. He is a man of the utmost probity. (Sipiagin, who had known Prince Gagarin from childhood, had no criticism of him except that he was a bit too good [*blazhennyi*].) Moreover, he had good ties at court: his mother had been held in high esteem in the days of Empress Marie Aleksandrovna, and one of his brothers-in-law, General à la Suite Nicholas Dmitrevich Obolenskii, was, and is, very close to the Dowager Empress. The Emperor gladly accepted my recommendation and appointed Prince Gagarin as director. He turned out to be an excellent choice: he enjoyed the respect not only of the professors—despite the fact that they were much older than he and possessed all kinds of academic qualifications—but also of the students. Nonetheless, he was to be dismissed as a revolutionary by Premier Stolypin [a matter I shall discuss later].[9]

Peasant Legislation

As minister of finance I succeeded in initiating the abolition of collective responsibility of peasants [for payments of taxes and redemption dues]. Collective responsibility had been established after emancipation partly for administrative reasons (it is easier to manage a herd than to manage individuals), partly for fiscal reasons. What collective responsibility meant was responsibility of the punctual for the unpunctual, of the energetic for the lazy, of the sober for the drunkards. It meant, in short, a grave injustice that demoralized the peasantry and destroyed any basic sense among them of law and civic responsibility.

Since the Ministry of Interior always defended collective responsibility as being in the interests of the Ministry of Finance, I informed the State Council that this was not the case. I proposed that collective responsibility be abolished and that, moreover, the task of collecting taxes from the peasantry be transferred from the hands of the police to those of tax inspectors from the Ministry of Finance. Naturally, I encountered strong opposition.

Goremykin, then minister of interior, could not object to my proposal on substantive grounds, so he urged that the task of collecting taxes from the peasantry be given to the land captains. This would have meant, in effect, that the police, employing arbitrary power, would continue the process of "squeezing out taxes."

The majority of the State Council supported me, although it made some changes in my proposal that would have weakened the legal basis of individual responsibility and the legal basis for the collection of taxes. Goremykin, however, held to his position and complained to the Emperor that I wanted to weaken the position of the land captains in the eyes of the peasants.

His Majesty accepted Goremykin's position. Then Prince Obolenskii, assistant minister of interior, came to see me to persuade me to retreat. I refused and wrote to the Emperor that if the proposal supported by the majority of the State Council were rejected, I would ask to be relieved of my post. Solskii, the chairman of the State Council's Department of State Economy—a fine man but a typical "conciliator"—then intervened in the affair. In the end, collective responsibility was abolished and the collection of taxes from the peasantry was transferred to tax inspectors, but in the process my original proposal was so modified as to retain the notion that the peasant was somehow different from other beings.

Also, I was responsible for the enactment, in 1894, of new passport regulations for the peasantry that would significantly increase its freedom of movement. The Ministry of Interior argued for retention of the old regulations on the ground that the passport tax was necessary for the Ministry of Finance. In proposing the new regulations I declared that the Ministry of Finance was ready to give up the tax. My proposal was adopted, but with some modifications insisted on by the Ministry of Interior: these were connected with the Jewish question (the Pale of Settlement) and the need for means of guaranteeing punctuality of tax collections from the peasantry.

Appendix B

My Work on the Peasant and Nobility Questions, 1893–1905

Origins of the Peasant Question

The difficulties faced by our peasantry derive for the most part from the manner in which they were emancipated by that great Emperor Alexander II and the manner in which the legislation applying to the peasantry subsequently evolved.

Emancipation of the serfs was a great historical act. And in freeing them, Emperor Alexander II did not violate civil [property] law. However, in forcing their former lords to allot them land after they had been emancipated, the Emperor acted against the principle of the inviolability of property, a principle embodied in civil law since the days of the Roman Empire.

One might applaud the allotment of land to the emancipated serfs, but one must recognize that the principle of private property was thus violated for the sake of political necessity. One must recognize that such an act set a dangerous precedent, a precedent for such demands as we hear today, when peasants say that if Emperor Alexander II could force landlords to part with their land, why can't our present government do the same? But it was not understood at the time that the principle of private property had been dealt a blow. Many still do not understand that a dangerous precedent had been set at the time of emancipation.

Even more important for an understanding of the origins of the peasant question is a knowledge of how the land taken from the landlords was allotted to the emancipated serfs. At the time there was debate over the question of whether this land should be allotted to peasants as individuals or to the peasants collectively through their village communes. The decision, in favor of the village commune, was made in haste, as a result of influence from two quarters. There was influence from administrators who favored the village commune because it is easier to deal with herds than it is to deal with individual members of a herd. Then there was the influence of Slavophiles, and other lovers of the past, who proclaimed the village commune to be uniquely Russian, of ancient origin; they said it was the backbone of Russian life and to infringe on the village commune was to infringe on the Russian soul.

Once this "lofty and patriotic" Slavophile view was accepted, whatever conclusions that were required could be drawn from it, for paper will endure anything. And if it is written on by a talented and experienced hand, it will be read zealously. One such supporter of the village commune and one of the "last of the Mohicans" of the group that helped prepare the emancipation legislation is the aged and honorable Semenov-Tian-Shanskii. During the winter of 1906–1907 I heard him admit, in the drawing room of A. N. Naryshkin, that, in the light of what had happened in the preceding two years, a great mistake had been made in preparing the emancipation legislation; he said that he and others had been too entranced by the idea of the village commune and had not given enough attention to the principles of private property.

Love of the old ways is laudable and understandable; it is an essential element in patriotism, but it is impossible to exist on such love alone. One must temper it with reason. Everyone knows that everything changes, that only that which is obsolete or dead does not change, and that if a living organism does not change, it soon begins to decay.

The institution of communal property is not peculiarly Russian: it is to be found everywhere at a primitive stage in the evolution of landholding. With the development of culture and political organization, it gives way to the institution of private property. But if this process is retarded, particularly by artificial means, as has been the case with us, then the people and the state decay.

In contemporary life everything is based on individualism, which has become particularly strong in the last two centuries and is responsible for both the great and the weak aspects of the contemporary world. Without respect for the individual, the "I," there would have been no Shakespeare, no Newton, no Pushkin, no Napoleon, no Alexander II, and so on. Nor would we have experienced the marvelous growth of technology, wealth, commerce, and so on and so forth.

The chief cause of the revolution we have experienced is the artificial retardation in our country of the development of the principle of individuality, of private property, of equal civil rights. But life must follow its own course, and as in the case of a badly constructed steam engine there must be an explosion unless the engine is rebuilt.

In the last fifty years, socialism, in its many shapes and forms, has gained support. And among the socialists there are some who see in the village commune the practical application of theoretical socialism. Such people amaze me. They do not understand that the village commune bears little resemblance to collective ownership as it is envisioned. They remind me of the horticulturalist who confuses a pear that comes from an uncultivated tree with one that comes from a well-cultivated modern orchard. If collective ownership of the land in the modern sense ever comes to Russia, it will come only after the village commune has been replaced by individual ownership and after the peasantry has gone through the crucible of individual ownership and has come to believe that "we," collective ownership, can better serve his welfare than the "I," individual ownership.

Although the principle of private property was dealt with unceremoniously at the time of emancipation, the emancipation legislation did provide the peasantry with some means of increasing their understanding of the inviolability of property and the meaning of civil rights. Unfortunately, the attempted assassination [in 1866] of the Tsar-Liberator strengthened the hands of those at court, and among the nobility generally, who were unsympathetic to his reforms. As a consequence the original intentions behind this legislation did not receive the necessary implementation and the peasants continued to be denied full equality of civil rights, for example, they continued to be subject to corporal punishment.

And then, after the damnable event of March 1 [the assassination of Alexander II], reaction gained the upper hand. As a result, the Ministry of Interior came to regard the village commune as sacred—for administrative-police reasons. In addition peasant participation in the zemstvos was reduced, and justices of the peace for the peasantry were replaced by land captains. Generally, the peasants, constituting the bulk of the population, were looked upon as children who needed to be looked after, but only with respect to their behavior, not their stomachs, children who unlike other children were expected to feed themselves. The land captains, who were supposed to be judges, administrators, guardians, acted in fact like pre-emancipation landlords, with this difference: the good landlords in pre-emancipation days were concerned with the welfare of their serfs, but the land captains are more interested in their own well-being.

To sum up, when I became minister of finance a large part of the land was still collectively held by village communes and was thus excluded from the possibility of being intensively cultivated. And the land belonging to individual [peasant] households was ill defined, because it had not been surveyed and laws defining property rights to such holdings were imprecise. Moreover, the peasant's economic situation was bad. His savings were negligible, for how could he have savings in a country that was almost always at war, for the Russian Empire has been, in essence, a military empire.

And, as we have seen, the peasantry was under a special civil and criminal jurisdiction, that of the land captain, a kind of serf owner. In the eyes of the law the peasant was a semi-person, no longer a serf belonging to a landlord, but, in effect, a serf of the peasant administration, subject to the guardianship of the land captain.

Because I was born in the Caucasus and my previous experience had been on the periphery of central Russia, I knew little of the heart of the country, particularly the Russian peasant, when I became minister of finance. And I still had something like the Slavophile enthusiasm for the village commune.

But once I was placed in charge of the finances of the Russian Empire, I would have had to be a fool not to understand that a machine cannot operate without fuel, which is provided by the economy, even though the economy was not in my jurisdiction. And since the peasantry constitutes the bulk of the population, it was necessary to know the peasant economy. In this I was helped by Bunge, the former minister of finance, who had been involved in the peasant reforms of the 1860s. It was he who directed my attention to the fact that the chief obstacle to the economic development of the peasantry was the medieval village commune.

Above all, it was the statistics, with which the Ministry of Finance is so well endowed, that opened my eyes. When I studied these statistics I fairly soon began to see that while more and more was being demanded from the peasant to fuel the state machine, his life was so organized as to make him unable to meet the demands put on him. I came to the conclusion that a state like the Russian one cannot be strong when its chief pillar—the peasantry—is weak. I saw where the trouble lay and what was necessary to cure it.

The peasantry is our main source of labor. [Our peasantry] labors the way it drinks. It does not drink much, but it gets drunk more often than do other people. It works little, but sometimes it is overworked. To make sure that the peasantry does not starve, that its labor becomes efficient, it must be given the opportunity to work, it must be freed from tutelage, it must achieve equality under the law, it must be assured that it can enjoy the fruits of its labor. But why should a man work hard and show initiative if he knows that his allotment from the village commune, which he has cultivated for some time, may be exchanged for other land? Why should he work hard when he knows that the fruits of his labor will be inherited on the basis of custom rather than on the basis of law? Why should he work hard when, because of collective responsibility, he may be responsible for the payment of taxes others have failed to pay? Why should he work hard when his existence is not under the protection of the general law but that of the land captain, when he cannot leave his home, often a miserable hovel, without a passport? In short, his life is somewhat like that of a domestic animal, with this difference, that the owner of a domestic animal is interested in its welfare, but at the present state in the development of the Russian state, there is such a surplus of peasants that no value is attached to them. This is the essence of the peasant question. The essence is not in the taxes the peasant has to bear; it is not in our protective tariff system. It is not in the lack of land. And the solution to the question is certainly not to be found in confiscation.

The peasantry falls back on [specious] arguments about how its problems should be dealt with, because the government has neglected to provide it with the means of becoming productive, of being able to enjoy the fruits of its labor, because the government has exercised a function no longer found in contemporary states, that of police guardianship over the peasantry. If the peasantry is starving, it feels that the obligation to feed it rests on its guardians. If it finds the burden of taxation too high, it says: if you do not permit us to enjoy the fruits of our labor then lower our taxes, for we have nothing to pay them with. The peasantry says to the government: if you regulate our land holdings by law in such a way that we can't farm our land efficiently, give us more land, in proportion to our numbers. If the peasantry is told that there is no land available, it points to the large holdings of the Imperial family, the state, and the landlords. If the peasantry is told that property rights are sacred, it replies that under Emperor Alexander II private property was taken when it was needed and then was given to it. Such is the reasoning of the peasantry, and it is the government which is responsible by its policies for such reasoning. Such are the policies which were to come to white heat in the revolution.

The Peasant Question in the
Last Years of Emperor Alexander III

During the last years of the reign of Emperor Alexander III, Durnovo, the minister of interior, raised the question of renewing the application of that article[1] of the redemption statute which permitted peasants to acquire individual title to their allotments, an article that had been virtually abrogated. The question was raised because by that time the redemption dues still owed had declined considerably, making it financially possible for many peasants to buy their allotments.

In raising this question it was impossible to avoid returning to the question of the desirability of the village commune. As I have noted, the Ministry of Interior, particularly under Dmitrii Tolstoi, preferred to deal with the peasantry as herds, rather than as individuals, and consequently was committed to the village commune for administrative-police reasons. It was the estimable Nicholas Khristianovich Bunge, chairman of the Committee of Ministers, who raised the question, which was then put before the State Council.

As minister of finance I was required to express my views before the State Council on the subject rather specifically. But, [as I have noted], I had not yet studied the peasant question thoroughly and had not yet come to a firm conclusion, except on one point, that if it were decided that individual peasant landholding was superior, one should not implement that view in haste but one should proceed systematically in conformity with definite rules. And since I had not yet come to a firm position I presented the arguments both for and against the village commune, without expressing a definite position of my own. I urged that the article in question should not be enforced until the complex peasant question had been thoroughly investigated. The State Council voted in favor of my view. Unfortunately, the primary responsibility for investigating the peasant question was placed in the hands of the minister of interior.

Earlier on the day of the State Council's vote I had been to Gatchina to report to the Emperor. On the return trip to Petersburg, the Tsesarevich Nicholas, who was on the train, invited me to his carriage. He had evidently not read the material concerning the matter and was not acquainted with it. I said that I favored temporarily suspending the application of the article, provided that it was understood that the peasant question would be studied in the near future, and that a decision would be made about the question, in all its complexity. It was evident to me, from this conversation and others, that the Tsesarevich, when he ascended the throne, was sympathetic to the needs of the peasantry and considered the peasant question to be one of primary importance.

For that reason I assumed when he became Emperor that a new period was opening, one that would see a return to the attitudes of the Great Emperor-Liberator Alexander II, a period that would be characterized by greater fairness toward and concern for the peasantry. And I, for my part, tried to impress on him the necessity for dealing quickly and seriously with the peasant question, for one did not have to be very clever or have the gift of prophecy to know that if the peasant question were neglected, if a satisfactory solution to that question were not found, the seeds of serious trouble for the future would be planted.

But evidently the forces that were unsympathetic to the spirit of Emperor Alexander II's reform inspired doubts in the young Emperor's mind about the wisdom of giving primary attention to the peasantry. It appears also that these doubts were intensified by addresses presented to him by representatives of the zemstvos and the nobility shortly after his accession, in which they expressed aspirations similar to those later embodied in the Manifesto of October 17.

I feel that the addresses were hardly tactful. I believe that the representatives of society should have acted more seriously than they did, at a time when the young Emperor had just come to the throne and was not yet able to reach mature judgments by himself. Their tactlessness was exploited by Durnovo, the minister of interior, probably aided by Pobedonostsev, to persuade the Emperor to include the phrase "vain, senseless dreams" in his reply to these addresses.[2] On the whole his reply was perfectly justified, but the phrase "vain, senseless dreams" might better have been left unsaid, because happily or unhappily for Russia these "vain dreams" stopped being dreams after October 17, 1905.

The Special Conference on the Needs of the Nobility

I was disappointed in my expectation that among the first things to be studied in the new reign would be the peasant question. Instead it was the needs of the landed nobility, as was shown by the formation of the Special Conference on the Needs of the Nobility, with Ivan Nikolaevich Durnovo as chairman and Alexander Semenovich Stishinskii as chief administrative assistant.[3] This was the same Stishinskii who had been associated with the introduction of various reactionary laws under Count Dmitrii Tolstoi, laws hostile to the spirit of Emperor Alexander II's reforms. And clearly the composition of the conference showed its only purpose was to improve the condition of private landowners, primarily those belonging to our debt-ridden and artificially supported landed nobility.

As minister of finance I was *ex officio* a member of the body. At its first meeting I said that the nobility and the peasantry were interdependent, that the well-being of one depended on the well-being of the other, and that therefore the conference should give primary attention to finding ways of improving the well-being of the peasantry. The chairman closed the meeting after my speech, saying that he would ask the Emperor for a directive on this question. At the next meeting he informed us that the Emperor had established the conference to seek means for improving the conditions of the nobility, that the peasant question was not the concern of this conference.

This was a death sentence for the conference. Although it continued its operations for many years, it accomplished virtually nothing in its efforts to restore a moribund organism to health by artificial means. True, a few crumbs were thrown to the impoverished nobility and other private landowners, but nothing of moment was accomplished, nor could it have been accomplished, because I repulsed all its efforts to line the pockets of the nobility at the expense of the treasury, that is to say, the people. This I did despite the fact that the majority opposed me. At every turn I so clearly revealed the ugly tendency of the nobility to reach into the coffers of the state that the members of the conference, despite their fury at me, still had enough feeling of shame to restrain themselves from purposefully trying to grab the people's monies.

Plehve, it goes without saying, was the soul of the conference because he believed that he could advance his career by catering to the nobility. Here he showed himself in all his glory, making speeches in which he ventured into the history of Russia, seeking to show that the empire owed its existence chiefly to the nobility. I was constantly arguing with him, without sparing his pride, so much so that on several occasions he turned to Durnovo for help.

The minutes of the conference are undoubtedly in some archive or other, probably in that of the State Council. Even though Mr. Stishinskii prepared the minutes in such a way as to misrepresent what was said, particularly Plehve's speeches, which were not fully recorded, these minutes have never been published, because they are so embarrassing that even such members of the Third Duma as Mr. Guchkov and Count Bobrinskii would blush for shame if they were published.

Speaking of our nobility, I feel impelled to say again that I am a hereditary noble and have among my ancestors many historically famous nobles of great lineage and that I am aware that some nobles are truly noble, men who are concerned for the entire people, particularly the weak. Such nobles were the ones who worked out the reforms of Emperor Alexander II, but, unfortunately, they are in the minority. Politically speaking, the majority of the nobles constitute a band of degenerates who are concerned solely with their own interests, their own appetites, and it is they who direct their efforts at extracting favors from the government at the expense of the people.

Conflicts with the Nobility

Naturally, the conference on the needs of the nobility sought first of all to gain new privileges for the Nobles' Bank and to limit the operations of the Peasants' Bank.

The Nobles' Bank had been established by Emperor Alexander III over Bunge's objections, its essential purpose being to provide government credit for the nobility. This was a minor evil that was compounded when, on various pretexts, the interest nobles had to pay the bank was reduced to less than what the government had to pay when it borrowed money. This was done over the objections of Bunge's successor, Vyshnegradskii.

Thereafter the history of the bank was one of an unbroken succession of petitions for favors to nobles and complaints that the administrators of the bank were hostile to the nobility. The first manager of the bank, Kartavtsev, one of Bunge's students, was dismissed, as I have noted earlier, because he was charged with being a "red."

The four men who successively served under me as managers of the bank— Count Arsenii Arkadeevich Golenishchev-Kutuzov (poet, ultrarightist); Prince Alexis Dmitrievich Obolenskii (later assistant minister of interior and then over-procurator of the Holy Synod, now member of the State Council); Prince Alexander Andreevich Lieven (a man of the highest moral caliber, very hard working, the owner of large estates); Count Vladimir Vladimirovich Musin-Pushkin (married to Countess Vorontsov-Dashkova)—were all to be accused of being "reds," of oppressing the nobility. The notorious Prince Meshcherskii was always seeking favors for one or another of his acquaintances or for one of his "spiritual sons" (as he called his favorites). In the event of a refusal, he would write slanderous denunciations in his newspaper.

Prince Meshcherskii, of course, demanded that the government take steps to improve the condition of the nobility, that is, benefit it at the expense of the rest of the population. Such a medieval policy could not be followed in our times because the people's consciousness has changed. Not to understand this is to prepare the way for revolution, which breaks out when rulers lose their prestige and power, as happened following the war with Japan.

The Peasants' Bank was established on Bunge's initiative, almost as compensation for the injustices of the creation of the Nobles' Bank.[4] It could lend money to peasants for purchase of land, but it could not buy land for later sale to the peasants. On my initiative Count Golenishchev-Kutuzov (who also served as manager of the Peasants' Bank) sought to revise the charter of the bank so that it could buy land for resale. He thought that the nobility would benefit, while I favored such a step because it would enhance peasant ownership.

To my astonishment, I encountered objections from several members of the State Council, objections that were inspired by Durnovo and Plehve. Also, the conference for the nobility especially objected to the proposed change, as did many others who sent statements to the Emperor declaring that it would weaken noble leadership. However, in those days I still had power and was able to have the State Council approve the revised charter, with some emendations.

By this time Plehve had become minister of interior and tried with all his might to end, or at least limit, sales of land by the Peasants' Bank, but I would not give in to him. It is worth noting that such sales, which met so much opposition then, have in recent times become the basis of the government's agrarian policy, but it may be too late, for now there are demands for compulsory sale and even outright confiscation.

Our revolution was caused by the fact that the rulers did not understand that our society and people (*obshchestvo i narod*) have changed and that if the government strives to prevent all change instead of controlling it, to keep it within bounds, there will be a revolutionary upheaval. In Russia such an upheaval is even more likely under such circumstances than it is elsewhere because 35 percent of its population is not Russian and everyone who knows history knows how difficult it is to knit together peoples of different origins into a whole, particularly in an age that has witnessed the growth of nationalism. Our rulers have still not learned the lesson.

Land Captains

At the beginning of Emperor Nicholas II's reign I tried to convince the then minister of interior, Durnovo, that land captains should be deprived of their judicial power. He replied that he would rather let his right arm wither than put his signature to any change in the statute concerning land captains.

His successor, Goremykin, was at first in favor of limiting the arbitrary power of land captains. Accordingly, I was hopeful when Goremykin invited me to a meeting at his residence to consider peasant affairs. I was joined at the meeting by several of my colleagues, among them that fine man Alexander Aleksandrovich Richter, who was well acquainted with peasant affairs and was considered something of a liberal by the standards of those days, but who would be found in the *right* wing of the Octobrists if he were alive. When he pointed out that it was necessary to change the statute on land captains, Goremykin cut him off rudely, declaring that as long as he was minister of interior he would not permit the institution of land captain to be touched. Following such a rejoinder to this fine, old man, I and my associates from the Ministry of Finance left the meeting.

The Peasant Question Yet Again

In 1898 the Committee of Ministers reviewed the State Controller's report for 1896. Next to the passage in the report in which it was noted that the peasantry's ability to pay its obligations was almost exhausted, the Emperor was good enough to note, "I, too, am concerned."

This provided me with an opportunity to suggest to the Committee of Ministers that we take up the peasant question, to complete the work that Emperor

Alexander II had left unfinished. I proposed the establishment of a special commission, with extraordinary authority, to deal with the peasant question, reminding my colleagues that this was the peasant question that had been dealt with in the 1860s. My proposal was discussed at the meetings of April 18 and May 5. After some argument, the Committee of Ministers proposed the formation of a special commission to review legislation concerning agricultural conditions; it would be chaired by a person appointed by the Emperor from among the highest officials and would present its conclusions directly to him. The Emperor neither approved nor disapproved the recommendation of the Committee of Ministers, but directed the chairman of the committee to ask him later, in the fall, for "further direction in this matter."

It was clear that the Emperor was being subjected to two opposing influences, one coming from me and the majority of the Committee of Ministers and the other coming from the chairman of the committee, Durnovo, whose views are represented nowadays by the conference of the "united nobility."[5] Such nobles have always looked on the peasant as being somewhere between a human being and an ox. This is the view held by the Polish gentry from time immemorial and helps explain the partitions of Poland.

Whether or not there would be a peasant commission depended on how the Emperor would look at the matter when he returned from the Crimea in the fall. While he was residing there I felt obligated to write him a letter [in which I pointed out the gravity of the peasant question and the need to appoint suitable people to participate in and to direct the work of the proposed commission].[6]

What kind of impression my letter made on the Emperor I do not know, since he never discussed it with me. But it was evident when he returned from the Crimea that he had not yet made up his mind, thus bringing delight to Durnovo and to men like Mr. Stishinskii and the ill-starred Plehve, who thought as he did.

As a result no action was taken to deal with the peasant question. After a while I tested the water several times at meetings of the State Council by raising the question of abolishing redemption dues, but when I did so, I noticed an evident antipathy for such a measure. It was argued that if such a large source of revenue were eliminated it would be necessary to impose new taxes, and it was feared that such taxes would have to be borne by the upper classes as well as the peasantry. One must remember that in those days in the State Council, just as today, there were members who beat their breasts when speaking about the "poor" peasantry, yet were in full accord with those who felt that the peasantry had been pampered and had gone out of control.

Special Conference on the Needs
of Rural Industry

It was only after that honorable man Dmitrii Sergeevich Sipiagin became minister of interior that I was again able to raise the question of establishing a peasant commission. It was he who spoke to the Emperor about it and persuaded him to establish the Special Conference on the Needs of Rural Industry. When the Emperor asked him to recommend a chairman for that body, Sipiagin said that I was the only suitable candidate.[7] Then His Majesty invited me to see him and informed me of his decision to establish the conference and to have it deal with the peasant question in the spirit of the principles laid down by Emperor Alexander II.

Although the appointment added to my work and worries and was of no personal benefit to me, I was glad to receive it because the peasant question has always been of great concern to me. And not for sentimental reasons, but rather because I believe that Russia's past as well as her future are bound up almost exclusively with the interests, the way of life, the culture of the peasantry. I have always regarded Russia as more democratic than all the states of Western Europe, but democratic in a special sense, democratic as a *muzhik* (peasant) state. And if I still believe that Russia has a great future, despite all the misfortunes we have experienced and may yet experience, it is precisely because I believe in the Russian peasantry, in its world significance.

The Special Conference on the Needs of Rural Industry was charged with investigating everything relating to the needs of rural industry, the chief need being, of course, to improve the life of the chief agricultural group, the peasantry. Among the members were I, the successive ministers of interior, and Kokovtsev (after he became minister of finance). Also it included Count Vorontsov-Dashkov, the present viceroy of the Caucasus; General-Adjutant Chikhachev, chairman of the State Council's Department of Industry; Gerhard, chairman of the body's Department of Civil and Spiritual Affairs; Prince Dolgorukii, high master of the court; Count Sheremetev, huntmaster of the court; State Secretary Kulomzin; and Semenov-Tian-Shanskii; although no one could question their conservatism, they were to support me throughout. There were other members, also conservative, who, as I shall indicate, were to oppose me, overtly or covertly.

The conference functioned more than three years, from January 1902 to March 1905. During the first year and a half of its life, district and provincial committees were organized to collect information concerning the needs of the rural economy. Although these committees were formed in such a way as to limit their freedom of judgment—the provincial ones being chaired by governors and the district ones by marshals of the nobility—for the first time in Russia there was the opportunity to express oneself freely.

I noticed that the Emperor and the Ministry of Interior thought that in organizing these committees I had unwittingly set a trap for myself because it was assumed that the committees would attack my fiscal and economic policies. To their astonishment it turned out that in general there was little complaint against my policies, although the court camarilla, which was demanding more and more favors [for the nobility], was working against me. Instead there was widespread complaint at domestic policy in general and at the lack of rights for the peasantry in particular.

During this initial period the conference itself dealt only with questions of secondary importance, rather than with the broader questions, particularly those concerning the needs of the peasantry, which were to be considered when the data from the provincial committees had been collected.

By the time we were ready to come to conclusions and to make decisions on substantive matters, Sipiagin, who had been in complete sympathy with our work, was dead and in his place was that careerist and police type Viacheslav Konstantinovich von Plehve,[8] who was not in sympathy. He had been unsympathetic toward the conference from the beginning. As soon as he became minister he took action against some leading figures in these committees who had expressed themselves frankly and sharply, and sometimes unfairly. Thus, Prince Peter Dmitrevich Dolgorukov, chairman of the district zemstvo board in Kursk province, was removed from his post. The fairly well-known statistician Shcherbin was exiled from Voronezh province, and less important personages were treated less ceremoniously. Also Plehve employed repressive measures against local committees that went beyond the limits set for their work and dealt with political questions.

In my archive is a letter from the well-known writer Count Leo Tolstoy defending a peasant member of a committee who had been banished for expressing his liberal opinions.[9] He accused me, not without some foundation, of being guilty of provocation.

When the information provided by the local committees had been collected, the conference settled down to the discussion of the chief needs of rural industry and particularly of the needs of the peasantry that arose from their unsettled state.

Naturally, in the course of such discussions there was criticism of certain legislation enacted during the reign of Emperor Alexander III that basically altered certain features of the reforms of Emperor Alexander II. Unlike the conference on the nobility, this conference, on the whole, recognized that the needs of the peasantry must be looked after, that both the sheep and the shepherds have needs, and that if the sheep are in good health the shepherds will benefit. There was, however, some opposition to recommendations for the repeal of certain laws, such as those establishing the institution of land captains, that had been enacted under Emperor Alexander III. And there was some opposition to some proposals to change Emperor Alexander II's peasant legislation.

Some of the opposition was, at least, expressed openly, in writing, by such men as Count Sheremetev (an honorable but abnormal man, a pillar of the court camarilla, later one of the covert chiefs of the Black Hundreds), Count Tolstoi (also of the same stripe), Count Shcherbatov (later one of the visible chiefs of the Black Hundreds), and Senator Khvostov.

But there were many others, some of whom professed to be in sympathy with the work of the conference, who covertly began to intrigue against it, insinuating that it was untrustworthy. Among them were that egregious careerist Krivoshein, Gurko (subsequently involved in the Lidval affair), and Stishinskii. They were led by Goremykin (who was ostensibly on our side) and supported by Plehve.

APPENDIX B ■ PEASANT AND NOBILITY QUESTIONS

One effort to undermine the conference was made by Plehve. He prepared plans for a conference, under the auspices of the Ministry of Interior, to consider the question of peasant administration. The possibility was created that the Emperor might order our conference not to consider the needs of the peasantry, and because I was convinced that his conference would accomplish nothing, our conference turned to general questions (rather than peasant needs) such as those concerning grain trade, railroad spur lines, and small-scale credit. After his death, our conference turned to the consideration of the peasant question. *

On the whole our conference favored individual ownership of land by the peasants. In this the Ministry of Interior and reactionary elements among the nobility detected signs of extreme, liberal, even revolutionary, tendencies. This was because the higher police authorities saw the village commune, that is, the herd organization of the peasantry, as the guarantee of order.

But we were not proposing that peasants be forced to leave the village commune. Rather we called for the right of free exit for those who wanted it. We favored measures that would gradually lead the peasant to regard individual ownership of land as significantly superior to the system of ownership represented by the village commune.

Also, the question of abolishing redemption dues was raised at our conference. Kokovtsev, by then minister of finance, was opposed, and the Emperor decided to postpone action on this issue until after the war.

Before private ownership of land could be properly established among the peasantry, it was first necessary to establish the peasants' civil rights, particularly those relating to property, on a firm basis. Because customary law prevailed to some degree among the peasantry, it would be necessary to codify customary law and to draw up a special civil code for the peasantry. Further, if individual peasant proprietorship were to be established in fact, as well as on paper, it would be necessary to provide the peasantry with courts that would guarantee complete enforcement of laws provided for them. This would mean the reintroduction, with some modification, of the system of justices of the peace that had existed before the establishment of the system of land captains.

Some members of the conference saw such proposals as an infringement, if not something worse, of some of the statutes enacted in the reign of Emperor Alexander III. Others, among them Goremykin, aided by Trepov, found in these proposals a useful tool for intrigue, a means of insinuating to those higher up that the conference favored measures that were virtually revolutionary.

Thus, the basis for closing the conference was laid, although its work was far from done, its final recommendations not yet drafted and edited for the Emper-

*Plehve's successor, Prince Sviatopolk-Mirskii (a decent man, but too weak to be minister of interior), was sympathetic to our conference, but the intrigue against it was well under way. Plehve's plans for a conference on peasant administration could not help but produce a rift among the members of our conference and could not help but encourage those intriguing from within against our conference. This intrigue was the work of an insignificant minority, but Prince Sviatopolk-Mirskii proved unable to stop it.

or's approval. Although I was an active chairman and reported on the work of the conference to the Emperor, I had no inkling that the end was near. As late as two days before the conference was ordered closed, the Emperor approved the minutes of the conference, which contained statements about its future work. Needless to say, he never said a word to me about being dissatisfied with the work of the conference, nor did he let me know in advance about the closing of the conference. Nor did he subsequently ever utter a single word to me about the conference. Such was his nature.

On March 30, 1905, as I was drinking my morning coffee, I was called to the telephone and found myself speaking to Ivan Pavlovich Shipov, the chief administrative assistant for the conference. He asked if I had read the Imperial decree. When I asked what decree he was talking about, he told me that it was the one closing the conference. There was a rebuke in his words at my not having been forewarned, but I did not respond to it because it would have been odd for me to admit that this was the first I had heard of the matter.

Although the conference was able to settle some minor questions concerning the needs of the rural economy, generally those dealing with the provincial way of life, it had not settled the major questions when it was closed.

The conference left behind a whole library of serious studies by distinguished members of the conference. It left behind a whole library of materials collected by the provincial committees, materials that were later put together in systematic form, providing a rich source for further investigation.

From the materials produced by the conference it is evident that in 1903–1904 thoughtful persons in the provinces were becoming convinced that it was necessary to carry out a number of reforms in consonance with the spirit of the times, in order to guard against the evils of revolution.

In fact, it was this aspect of the conference that was perceived as a threat to the foundations of the state and thus led to the closing of the conference. It is unfortunate that the conference was prematurely closed, for had it been permitted to complete its labors, it is possible that some of the excesses which took place in the last months of 1905 and early 1906 might have been avoided. During these excesses the government proposed to go even further than the conference had intended to recommend, but by that time it was too late. A hungry person may be placated if he is fed in time, but a single portion will not suffice to placate a person brutalized by hunger. He wants vengeance on those whom he considers, rightly or wrongly, to be his tormentors. Subsequent to the reign of Emperor Alexander II, the nobility exhausted the peasantry to such a degree that in the end the backward peasantry turned on the nobility without distinguishing between the innocent and the guilty. Thus was mankind created. Those who are absolute rulers "by the grace of God" must accept whatever responsibility they bear for such consequences.

Unfortunately, our Emperor says that he is answerable only to God when it comes to making decisions, but when it comes to answering to mortals, he responded that this one had deceived him, that one had undermined him, and so forth. If an unlimited monarch wishes to hold his servants responsible for their official actions, he should be bound by their counsel and opinions. Otherwise he should consider himself responsible for his actions and hold his servants responsible only for carrying out his orders exactly.

The Goremykin Commission

Just as the Conference on the Needs of Rural Industry was closing, another conference or, more properly speaking, commission, with Goremykin as chairman, was opened. It was to deal exclusively with the peasant question. But because the chief figures in the commission were such men as Krivoshein and Stishinskii—who favored the village commune and police administration—it was clear that if the commission made any changes in peasant life, these changes would not affect the interests of the nobility adversely.

But because Goremykin was the chairman, the commission, naturally, did not accomplish anything, for although an intelligent man and not a bad sort, he was extremely passive, if not lazy, possessed of the kind of equanimity that is characteristic of every inactive organism. Soon the so-called revolution came along and everybody forgot about the Goremykin commission. By that time I was premier and, at my suggestion, the commission was closed and immediately forgotten, for it left no traces.

Appendix C

Letter from Witte to Nicholas II Concerning the Proposed Conference on the Peasant Question

MOST GENTLE SIRE

Forgive me for presuming to disturb YOUR rest with this most humble letter. I do so because I consider it my duty as the devoted minister of YOUR IMPERIAL MAJESTY and as a son of my fatherland to write to you: for there may not be an opportune occasion to express myself orally.

YOUR MAJESTY was good enough to decide on the question concerning the appointment of a peasant conference to improve the welfare of the rural population. This took place without friction. It is the first step. Whether or not the effort succeeds will depend on the kind of persons selected to participate in the work.

But what is the nature of the problem with which they will have to deal? In my memorandum to the Committee of Ministers on this subject I could not deal with the problem in its entirety. The essential question we face is this: will Russia continue to grow stronger, as she has since the emancipation of the serfs, or will she retrogress?

The Crimean War opened the eyes of those capable of seeing: they recognized that Russia could not remain powerful under a regime based on slavery. YOUR great autocratic GRANDFATHER cut the Gordian knot: HE ransomed the spirit and body of HIS people from their owners. This unparalleled act created that colossus which is now in YOUR AUTOCRATIC hands. As a result of that act Russia was reorganized, and her strength, her mind, her understanding increased tenfold. And this was done despite the fact that certain factions, fascinated by liberalism in the years following emancipation, disturbed the AUTOCRATIC power and threatened to undermine the foundation of the Russian Empire—AUTOCRACY. The might of YOUR AUTOCRATIC FATHER put Russia back on the rails. Now we have to move forward. It is necessary to complete that which EMPEROR ALEXANDER II began but could not finish, but that can now be completed because EMPEROR ALEXANDER III guided Russia on a straight path by the exercise of AUTOCRATIC power.

It was not the emancipation of the serfs, which made Russia as great as it is, that led to the crisis of the 1880s. The crisis was the result of the corruption of minds by the printed word, by the disorganization of the schools, by liberal administrative bodies [the zemstvos], and, finally, by the undermining of the authority of YOUR ministers and officials, by the attacks, some intentional, others not, on the part of people some of whom are well meaning and others who are not. Who does not curse out the bureaucracy? These causes did not further the progress of peasant life: in fact, they hindered such progress.

EMPEROR ALEXANDER II redeemed the soul and body of the peasantry, but he did not turn them into free sons of the fatherland; he did not organize their lives on the basis of firm legality. And because EMPEROR ALEXANDER III was preoccupied with restoring our international status and with the strengthening of our armed forces, he did not have the opportunity of completing the work begun by HIS AUGUST FATHER. This task he bequeathed to YOUR IMPERIAL MAJESTY; it must be carried out and it will be. Otherwise the grandeur of Russia will not continue to grow as it has in the past. For this it is necessary to understand the indispensability of completing the great work, to have the firm determination to complete it, and faith in the power of God.

YOUR MAJESTY has 130 million subjects. Barely more than half of them can be said to live; the rest vegetate. Before the emancipation our budget was 350 million rubles; emancipation provided the opportunity of raising it to 1,400 million. But the weight of taxation is already being felt. Meanwhile France, with 38 million inhabitants, has a budget of 1,260 million rubles and Austria, with a population of 43 million, has a budget of 1,100 million. If our tax-paying capacity were equivalent to that of France, we would have a budget of 4,200 million rubles, or if it were equivalent to that of Austria we would have a budget of 3,300 million. Why do we lack tax-paying ability? It is because of the lamentable state of our peasantry.

It is natural for a human being to seek to improve his lot. This is what distinguishes the human from the animal, and it is this trait that makes for economic and political development, that makes for social order. But for man to make use of this impulse, suitable conditions must exist. They do not exist under slavery, which extinguishes this impulse in the slave because he realizes that it is impossible for him to improve his own lot and that of his close ones; as a result he becomes immobile. But liberty restores him to the condition of a human being. However, it is not enough to free men from being enslaved to owners; they must be freed from the slavery that arises when officials have arbitrary power over them. The peasant must be freed from such power; he must enjoy the protection of law and come to understand the nature of legality; he must be enlightened. As C. P. Pobedonostsev has expressed it, the peasant is now a "semi-person" and must be turned into a "person."

344   VOLUME I ■ 1849–1903

At present the peasant is the slave of arbitrary authority. His rights and obligations are not precisely defined by law. And his well-being is determined by the whim of many officials, some of them men of the most questionable character: he is subject to the whim of such local authorities as the land captain, the *ispravnik*, the *stanovoi pristav*, the *uriadnik*, the *feldsher*, the village elder, the *volost* clerk, the teacher, and, finally, to every "gentleman." He is virtually slave to his village commune meeting and to those who shout loudest at it. Not only is his well-being dependent on the whim of these people; even his body is dependent upon them, for his is subject to flogging. The question of whether or not peasants should be subject to such punishment is a moot one. I, for one, think that flogging as a normal practice insults the God in man. When EMPEROR ALEXANDER II abolished flogging in the army there were false prophets who were certain that the army would collapse as a result. Who would now dare say that the spirit and discipline of YOUR troops has declined as a result? If flogging is still necessary for the peasantry, it should be done according to law, not, as at present, at the discretion of *volost* courts, which consist of his ignorant fellow-peasants, sometimes led by the worst elements among them. It is odd that if a governor has a peasant flogged, he is brought to judgment before the Senate, but if a peasant is flogged as a result of the chicanery of a *volost* court, that is considered proper. Thus the peasant is a slave of his fellow villagers and of the rural administration.

Further, the land allotment that was given the peasantry [after emancipation] is not precisely defined by law. Under the village commune form of ownership the peasant does not even know which land is his. Also inheritance rights are determined by ill-defined custom, and today's peasants, the second post-emancipation generation, cultivate land without knowing precisely which land is theirs. Moreover, the law does not deal with the family rights of peasants.

EMPEROR ALEXANDER II granted Russia [reformed] civil and criminal courts. However one may criticize them, one cannot deny their greatness, that they provide subjects with protection of their rights and obligations under law. Unfortunately, this reform did not deal with the civil and criminal cases in which peasants are involved: such cases are decided by peasant courts and not according to the general laws of the country. The peasants are subject to special laws, to custom, and to put it plainly, to the exercise of arbitrary authority, to caprice.

The system of taxation for the peasantry is in poor condition. Often direct taxes are imposed arbitrarily on peasants as collective bodies, not, as should be, according to time-honored law, on individuals, based on individual norms. Sometimes governors and police may double taxes, sometimes they may exact nothing.

Collective responsibility [for the payment of taxes and redemption dues], which is linked to the village communal form of landownership, makes the peasant responsible for everyone, not just for himself; this sometimes leads to complete irresponsibility. The zemstvos have the power to set some of the taxes at their own discretion and thus may burden the peasant beyond his capacity; such rights are not given in ultraliberal countries. And as for the taxes imposed by the village communes, they have risen unbelievably in recent years and are arbitrarily imposed, without being subject to the control or supervision of higher authorities.

What of education? It is widely known that it is still in an embryonic stage, that our educational system lags not only behind the educational systems of Europe but also behind those of many Asiatic and trans-Atlantic countries. Of course, this is not an unmitigated evil, for there is education and education. What kind of education would the [common] people have received during the two decades following emancipation, a period of social turmoil? Nonetheless, one must push on with education and do so energetically. Just because a child falls and hurts itself does not mean that it should not be taught to walk. But it is necessary that education should be entirely in the hands of the government [and not the zemstvos].[1] Our people, with their Orthodox soul, are ignorant and backward. And a backward people cannot mature. And not to progress is now to retrogress, for other peoples are moving forward.

To sum up. The peasantry was freed from its master, but it is now in thrall to the exercise of arbitrary power, to illegality, to ignorance. Under such conditions the peasantry loses the motivation to improve its situation by legal means. The vital nerve of progress is paralyzed in it: the peasantry becomes disheartened, apathetic with all the vices that result from such a state. This sad condition cannot be ameliorated by isolated, although powerful, measures of a material nature. Above all what is needed is to raise the spirit of the peasantry, to transform peasants into YOUR genuinely free and loyal sons.

Under the present condition of the peasantry the state cannot move strongly ahead, will not be able in the future to enjoy that international importance for which it has been marked by the nature of things and perhaps even by fate. The sad state of the peasantry results in minor annoyances which, like warts, are endured. But suddenly there comes famine. A big fuss is made over it; huge sums of money are spent on the victims of famine; money is collected for the famine victims from those who some day may be or have been victims, and people fancy that something is being done. The famine-stricken of today are only being made more accustomed to being the famine victims of the future.

People speak of a land crisis. A strange crisis when the price of land is rising everywhere! Appetites are whetted. The question of which classes make the greatest contribution and of which classes are more loyal to the THRONE is raised. As if the AUTOCRATIC THRONE could base itself on anything but the entire Russian people; on this unshakable base it will rest forever. GOD preserve RUSSIA from a throne that is based on individual classes, not on the entire people.

The essence of the problem is not to be found in the land crisis or in the crisis of private landownership. It is to be found in the poor organization of peasant life, in peasant impoverishment. Where things are bad for the sheep, they are bad for the shepherds.

The destiny of Russia requires ever increasing expenditures. These are small considering the size of our population. That they seem excessive arises not from poverty but from disorganization. Demands for money are made on the minister of finance while he is at the same time attacked for attempting to increase revenue to satisfy pressing demands. Also the open and covert enemies of the AUTOCRACY find a fertile field for their activities in the disorganization of peasant life and ill-intentioned publishers of newspapers, magazines, and illegal leaflets take joy in and capitalize on that disorganization. In short, SIRE, it is my deepest conviction that the most pressing question facing Russia is that of the peasantry.

YOUR IMPERIAL MAJESTY, the Committee of Ministers had recommended the formation of a preparatory commission and a conference to put peasant affairs in order. The conference should consist of the highest officials and should be YOUR MAJESTY'S immediate instrument for dealing with the question. In my opinion, the conference should have a limited membership if it is to be effective.

The commission, under the chairmanship of a member of the conference, should do the preparatory work and prepare proposals. It should consist of high-ranking representatives of the governmental agencies concerned and of prominent local personages.

But every undertaking depends on personnel. It is essential that consideration of the peasant question be entrusted to *enlightened* persons who know and understand the era of the emancipation. Because the ministers of interior, justice, agriculture, finance, and, perhaps, education should *ex officio* be members of the conference, only a few others need to be added to their number. As I have earlier taken the liberty of indicating in an [oral] report to YOUR IMPERIAL MAJESTY, these additional members should be chosen from among the following enlightened, wise, and experienced men: Solskii, Pobedonostsev, Kakhanov, Frisch, Thörner, Derviz, Golubev, and Semenov. The chief burden will fall on that member of the conference who is chairman of the commission. In my opinion the man most suitable for such an appointment is Prince Obolenskii, the assistant minister of interior. He is young, a hard worker, intelligent. During more than ten years as marshal of the nobility he dealt with the peasantry. The chairman of the conference should be someone older. The man most suitable for this appointment is D. M. Solskii,[2] an outstanding man who is well balanced and temperate, a man who worked closely with EMPEROR ALEXANDER II, who has served as assistant chairman of the State Council.

Naturally, even if so important an undertaking is entrusted to enlightened men, it cannot succeed unless they are inspired by the firm wish of the FATHER of the Russian people to transform the peasant into a truly free person. This is a heavy burden to bear. It was borne fearlessly by YOUR MOST AUGUST GRANDFATHER, but it was not given to HIM to carry it to its final destination. YOUR MOST AUGUST FATHER having eliminated the obstacles to completing the work, it now falls on YOU, SIRE, to make the people entrusted to YOU by GOD happy and thus open new opportunities to enhance the greatness of YOUR EMPIRE.

I respectfully ask, SIRE, that you forgive me for expressing myself with the utmost frankness about that which troubles my soul. But if YOUR ministers are not impelled by their consciences to tell you what they think, who will speak to YOU of such matters?

YOUR IMPERIAL MAJESTY'S
most loyal subject,

Sergei Witte
Petersburg, October 1898

Appendix D

The Origins of the Russo-Japanese War

Excerpts

Some believe that credit for the first suggestion for a trans-Siberian railroad belongs to Court Muravev-Amurskii, who served as governor-general of eastern Siberia, but this is hardly the case. . . .[1]

. . . [A] radical turn in the conduct of our affairs in the Far East occurred. Without the knowledge and participation of the ministers of foreign affairs, finance, and war, who, at this time, shared the chief responsibility for the conduct of our affairs in the Far East, there appeared on July 30, 1903, an IMPERIAL decree establishing the position of viceroy of HIS IMPERIAL MAJESTY in the Far East, in whose hands would be concentrated supreme military-administrative authority over all the territory east of Lake Baikal and with the responsibility for conducting diplomatic relations with China, Japan, and Korea concerning matters relating to the territory under his jurisdiction. The decree was prepared by the minister of interior in conjunction with State Secretary Bezobrazov. Given these new circumstances, the views concerning the direction of our policy in the Far East expressed by the ministers of foreign affairs, finance, and war at a conference held on August 1 were to have a purely academic character, as soon would become evident.

In a personal letter, dated August 4, Count Lambsdorff informed S. Iu. Witte:

> Yesterday the Sovereign completely approved the conclusions reached at our conference and gave me permission to send the minutes, via the war minister, to him at Pskov [where major maneuvers were to take place]. In this connection HIS MAJESTY expressed himself in favor of removing our troops from the disputed territories to Kwantung. When I informed him that you and I are of the same opinion, the Sovereign said: ''I know that Kuropatkin is opposed to this step, but I

will arrange it for you: I will note on the margin of the minutes that, except for the railroad guards, the troops should be transferred to Kwantung.'' A laconic telegram, known in diplomatic jargon as ''télégramme de patience'' was sent to Alekseev. . . .

Despite the fact that Japanese actions were far from provocative, and despite the fact that their demands were considered essentially acceptable by the chief ministers in Petersburg, negotiations did not lead to a successful outcome. For no good reason these negotiations dragged on. Failing to receive any reply to their final proposals, the Japanese decided finally on a rupture (*razryv*), which took place on January 24, 1904.

The degree to which the SOVEREIGN EMPEROR did not expect this rupture can be seen from the fact that in September he left for Darmstadt and did not return to Petersburg until the late fall. When Emperor William warned HIM in Darmstadt that the Japanese were energetically preparing for war, HIS MAJESTY replied that there would be no war because he did not want to fight.

VOLUME II

1903–1906

I

On the Eve of War

The Committee of Ministers

As I have related earlier, my opposition to the dangerous policies we were following with respect to Japan led to my being shifted to the chairmanship of the Committee of Ministers, "the highest administrative post in the Empire," according to the Emperor, but, in fact, an utterly inconsequential position.

Although the committee was the highest administrative institution in the Empire, it was of little importance in coordinating the administration of the country. To it came all kinds of administrative rubbish—everything that was not clearly defined in law, as well as important bills that had encountered or might encounter opposition in the State Council, bills such as those providing temporary restrictions on Jews, Poles, Armenians, and foreigners.[1] Of the same ilk were measures providing all sorts of privileges and favors, not sanctioned by law, for persons in high places.

The committee consisted of ministers or their assistant ministers, representatives from the departments of the State Council, as well as others appointed by the Emperor. Usually only two or three individuals who enjoyed the complete favor of the Emperor played an active role in the committee, while the rest merely listened. During the course of my experience with the committee, those who played an active role were Count Dmitrii Tolstoi, an exceptional man, a powerful personality, politically on the far right; Ivan N. Durnovo,* a very limited individual, but

*I can't help recalling a conversation I had with him at the time of the accession of Nicholas II, when he predicted that "this one will be something of a copy of Paul Petrovich, but in modern form." I was to think of this conversation often.

Of course, Emperor Nicholas II is no Paul, but he has some of Paul's traits and some of Alexander I's (mysticism, slyness, and even craftiness), but without his education. Alexander I was one of the sly and worldly wise; Plehve, an intelligent secret police agent, not a bad jurist, an opportunist with a superficial education, an adroit bureaucratic careerist, but in no sense of the word a statesman; Pobedonostsev, a man of remarkable education and cultivation, completely honorable, possessed of a statesmanlike mentality, but a nihilist by nature, a negativist, hostile to creative thinking; General-Adjutant Vannovskii, not a bad sort, an upright man, with a soldier's character, poorly educated, but not without common sense; Abaza, a man of exceptionally good sense, a heavy gambler, bone lazy, who learned little after leaving the university, who, thanks to his good sense, his Petersburg bureaucratic tact, and social connections played a major role in the State Council and the Committee of Ministers. Sometimes the sensible opinions of the more intelligent members of the committee carried some weight, but only with reference to questions that had not been decided in advance, at least not in principle.

Like some of my predecessors, I tried to shift as much of the distasteful business that came to the committee to other bodies so as not to have a hand in it. I did this by handing over such business to the State Council and arguing either that such and such a matter was within its jurisdiction or that such and such a matter was the responsibility of the individual ministers.

As a rule the chairman of the Committee of Ministers did not report directly to the Emperor and since I was somewhat out of favor I was [virtually] never alone with him during my tenure as chairman of the committee.

Shortly after appointing me chairman of the committee, the Emperor and his family left Petersburg, going first to Libau, then to Belovezh, then to Darmstadt, where they remained from about September 10 to October 25, visiting with the Empress's brother. Soon after the Emperor's departure I, too, went abroad, stopping for a few days in Berlin, before going on to France, where I was to spend a month.

Intimations of War

I was firmly convinced that we were on the brink of war with Japan because of the policies followed by the Emperor. I was even more alarmed by the fact that while we were following a policy that would lead to war, we did not prepare for it, because we believed that no matter what we did, the Japanese would not go to war. In fact, our concern at this time was over who would command what army in the event of war with Germany and Austria-Hungary.*

---

best educated of Russians, while Nicholas II, by the standards of his time, has no more than the average education of a guards colonel from a good family.[2]

As minister of interior, Durnovo avidly engaged in perlustration of letters by or to members of the Imperial family and consequently had trouble with Empress Marie Fedorovna, who believed that he was reading her mail. I think that he learned something about Nicholas II from his perlustration.

*Grand Duke Nicholas Nikolaevich would command the army on the western front and General-Adjutant Kuropatkin would command the army on the Austro-Hungarian front. The Grand Duke and Kuropatkin, in his capacity as war minister, quarreled over preparations for a war in the west. For example, the Grand Duke favored construction of certain railroad branch lines. Kuropatkin would not support him. I heard Kuropatkin criticize the Grand Duke's proposals and, what is more, speak very critically of the Grand Duke's military qualifications. I agreed completely, being convinced that the Grand Duke, who is very certain of himself, is, to put it mildly, unbalanced.

When I arrived in Paris I was amazed that everyone believed that there would be no war with Japan. This was because Delcassé, the foreign minister, said so, claiming that he had reliable information on which to base himself. In fact he had no information from his diplomatic service in the Far East upon which to base his assertion; his so-called reliable information came from Urusov, our ambassador to Paris.[3]

When I saw how optimistic the mood was in Paris, I tried to avoid saying anything undiplomatic, and as soon as I could, I left for Vichy.

Occult Forces at Court

While I was in Paris I spoke to Baron Alphonse Rothschild, head of the House of Rothschild, a well-educated and knowledgeable old man, with whom I was on excellent terms. He knew much, had seen much, had read much. He had been friendly with Napoleon III and with most of the other leading personages of the Second Empire. In his heart he favored restoration of the Bonaparte dynasty, but he had made peace with the republic.

At this time he was the only outstanding Rothschild. His son Eduard is a very personable young man, but he has not shown the business acumen of his father. Many of the other Rothschilds are very decent people, all of them men of the world, but none of them is outstanding. Perhaps one of the younger members will one day rise to the stature of Baron Alphonse. Who knows?

At one of our meetings, the baron told me that the preceding night Delcassé had asserted that the rumors about a possible war between Russia and Japan were absurd, but I would not be drawn into speaking about the Far East.

Most of all, he spoke of the bizarre mysticism, an evil phenomenon in his opinion, that had crept into our court.[4] He pointed out that history teaches that when, usually through the agency of an influential charlatan, mysticism gains a hold at court, it portends major changes, particularly on the domestic scene. Later, he sent me a book in which this thesis is demonstrated on the basis of the historical record.

When I asked why he was raising this subject, he said that there was much talk in France about the influence of Doctor Philippe of Lyons on Their Majesties and other members of the Imperial family. He told me of some of the rumors he had heard, admitting that they were probably exaggerated, but adding that it was a fact that Their Majesties had been seeing and had come under the influence of this charlatan, whom they considered a holy man.

That such accounts were making the rounds in France was depressing. Of course I had already heard much about Philippe in Petersburg. I shall note here what I know to be true or believe to be true about the man.

Philippe was a man of slight education, from the environs of Lyons. Although without medical training (something his son-in-law had), he began to practice medicine, employing wonderworking means. As often happens in such cases, he made some accurate predictions. And he effected some successful cures, through his mystic power over weak or disturbed personalities. Denounced by some as a charlatan, he was prosecuted several times and forbidden to practice medicine.

Nonetheless, he attracted a small group of followers, primarily nationalists who were pro-Boulanger and anti-Dreyfus. One of his followers was Count V. V. Muravev-Amurskii, our military attaché in Paris. This count, who was decidedly abnormal, was always trying to involve us in some scheme or other against the French Republic, which he detested. Because I was among those who thwarted him, on the ground that we had no business interfering in French internal affairs, he was removed from his post. Although he did not know me personally, he hated me. Well, he and other admirers of Philippe considered the man holy and avowed that he had descended from heaven and would return there.

Philippe was introduced to one of our Montenegrin princesses, Grand Duchess Militsa Nikolaevna, by Dr. Papius, another charlatan-mystic. And it was through her and her sister, Princess Anastasia Nikolaevna, that Philippe came to the attention of Their Majesties. But first a word about these two Montenegrins. What harm they have brought Russia! To tell of all the harm for which they are responsible would fill a book. The Russian people will not remember them kindly.

They are the daughters of the notorious Prince Nicholas of Montenegro, so widely renowned for his cupidity and lack of scruples.[5] During the reign of Emperor Alexander III he placed these two as students in the Smolnyi Institute and thereafter paid little attention to them. Because the prince did what he could to earn the Emperor's good will, it was only natural that the Emperor should show some attention to these young ladies upon their graduation from the institute. And this was enough to encourage some of the young men of the Imperial family to seek their hands in marriage.

As we know, we had a whole flock of unmarried grand dukes and princes of the Imperial blood in those days. One of them, the weak-chested Grand Duke Peter Nikolaevich (brother of Grand Duke Nicholas Nikolaevich the younger), married Montenegrin No. 1, Militsa Nikolaevna, and Prince George Leuchtenberg (the third son of Grand Duchess Marie Nikolaevna) married Montenegrin No. 2, Anastasia Nikolaevna. This was his second marriage. Soon after the ceremony he returned to Biarritz, where he spent most of his time, to resume his liaison with the courtesan with whom he had been living. And so, thanks to Emperor Alexander, the two princesses married lesser members of the Imperial family. With this the Emperor felt he had done his duty toward the young ladies.

Their position at court improved with the ascension of Nicholas II to the throne and his marriage to Alix. Although the new Empress was warmly received at court, only the two Montenegrin princesses showed her the deference due an Empress. They were not only deferential but also boundlessly devoted.

Thus, when the Empress came down with a stomach disorder they were right on the scene. They took over the work of the chambermaids, carrying out the unpleasant duties associated with illness. In this way they gained the Empress's favor, but the Emperor paid little attention to them as long as he was under the influence of his mother, but as her influence waned, the Montenegrins' status with him grew.

Like their father, the Montenegrins were greedy and tried to get as much money as possible out of the Emperor. After all, the apple falls not far from the tree. It was because of this trait that I came into conflict with the sisters, first with Montenegrin No. 2, who came to see me and complained that she and her husband could not get along on their income. She had already asked the Empress to help get the Emperor's agreement to an annual grant of 150,000 rubles and wanted my assistance.[6] As far as I was concerned a grant was out of the question. Therefore it had to be taken care of by an order from the Emperor that the budget of the Ministry of the Imperial Court be raised by 150,000 rubles a year, which would permit the ministry to pay out the money.

[I had a similar problem with Montenegrin No. 1.] When her husband fell into financial straits (his business manager, Demmeni, had gambled with his money, but evidently without his knowledge, and lost) he asked for my help with the State Bank. Naturally, I refused because the State Bank's charter prohibited such action. The Grand Duke therefore turned to the Emperor, who helped him, from appanage funds, I believe. The Grand Duchess could not forgive me for my "insolence."

But one must give the Montenegrin princesses credit for being loyal to their father by supporting him in his efforts to wheedle money out of the Emperor. When I became minister of finance, Prince Nicholas was already receiving a subsidy, from secret funds, for his army. Because the appetite grows with the eating, he was constantly asking for and receiving increases in the subsidy, which he justified on the ground that when the inevitable war between Russia, on behalf of Slavdom, and Germany broke out, Montenegro, as Russia's only friend, would provide invaluable aid. Undoubtedly there was a particle of sincerity in his rhetoric about Slavs versus Germans (I have a letter from him in my archive that contains a very uncomplimentary remark about Emperor William), but his only loyalty was to his pocketbook.

Because I had reliable information that much of the money we gave him for military and educational purposes was used for the personal needs of the prince and his family, I tried to persuade the Emperor to end the subsidies. Although I failed, I was able to see to it that the prince received less than he asked for.

Usually a request for an increased subsidy was preceded by a supporting letter or visit from Anastasia Nikolaevna. My efforts to curb her father's appetite only increased her ill will toward me, and, needless to say, he was not kindly disposed toward me. Thus, he avoided meeting me while I was minister of finance.

Prince Nicholas was particularly annoyed with me over an indirect clash between us in connection with his sudden visit to Petersburg in 1901 or 1902. Shortly after he had returned to Montenegro, Montenegrin No. 2 called on me to let me know that the Emperor had agreed to her father's request for more money and that I would soon be receiving an order from the Emperor to provide the money. She assured me that this money would not come out of the pockets of the

Russians. When I asked for an explanation, she told me that an arrangement had been made to turn over to her father the annual installment (3,600,000 rubles) which Turkey paid us on her indemnity.[7] Her father had been certain that I would agree and so was she, but I told them that such an arrangement was impossible.

At my next report to the Emperor, he explained that when Prince Nicholas had asked for more money, he had replied that if the request were for money from the Emperor's personal funds it would have been granted, but that since what was asked for would be coming from the Russian people, he could not oblige even so devoted a friend as the ruler of Montenegro. At that, according to the Emperor, the prince had said that transferring Turkey's annual indemnity installment to Montenegro would be the solution.

I told His Majesty that the indemnity installment was listed among our revenues and that its disappearance from the list was sure to be noted. I went on to say that this money was as much Russian as any of our other revenues because Turkey was reimbursing us, and then only in part, for what we had spent during the war. If that money were transferred to Prince Nicholas, we would have to make up for it. Moreover, I added, the sum in question, wherever it might come from, was excessive.

The Emperor said his hands were tied, he had already agreed. He often disarmed me with such an argument, but not this time. I explained that since Prince Nicholas's explanation was misleading, whether intentionally or not, the understanding with him could be considered null and void. After convincing the Emperor, I took care of the matter with the help of our foreign minister. However, then the annual subsidy for Montenegro was increased by several hundred thousand rubles. After this episode Montenegrin No. 2 told me in a furious tone that she would not forget. I can imagine how she and her sister subsequently defamed me before the Empress.

Montenegrin No. 2 also interceded on behalf of another relative, Prince Peter Karageorgevich, the present ruler of Serbia. Shortly before he was due to arrive in Petersburg, she asked that I receive and help him. When he came to Petersburg he asked for an appointment and I gave it to him.

He was on time, but I had to keep him waiting for fifteen minutes. I found him to be an elderly, modest, unhappy-looking man. Truth to tell he was a nobody in those days. He had served in the French army in the 1870s and after returning to civilian life had remained in France because his family was barred from living in their native land.

What he wanted was a government loan, to be secured by an estate in Rumania that he owned. I could not agree to such a loan, even though this would displease the Montenegrin sisters, but I made arrangements for a loan from the Bessarabian Bank. Since that bank's charter did not permit it to make loans secured by land held abroad, I had to ask the Emperor's permission to make an exception. Obviously informed in advance by the sisters, he agreed. Prince Peter repaid the loan when he sold the estate.

It never occurred to me that this ordinary-looking man would soon be ruler of Serbia. It is said that Prince Peter knew in advance of the plot to oust and murder the ruling Obrenovich family so as to permit him to ascend the throne.* Be that as it may be, once on the throne Prince Peter adhered to his country's constitution. Perhaps this was a result of his long residence in France, where, living the life of an ordinary citizen, he became accustomed to constitutional government.

And now to return to Philippe. Montenegrin No. 1 was so impressed by him that she tried to help him gain the right to practice medicine. Once, while in Paris, she summoned Rachkovskii, the head of our secret police abroad, and asked him to arrange that the French government grant Philippe a medical degree. Naturally, Rachkovskii told her how naive her request was, in words that showed little respect for Philippe. He thus earned her enmity, which would help undermine his career.

General Kuropatkin came to the rescue. In disregard of legal procedure he arranged that Philippe be granted a medical degree from the Petersburg Military-Medical Academy and the rank of actual state councillor. The holy Philippe then bought himself the uniform of a military doctor. All this was done very quietly.[8]

It was not long after this that Hesse, the court commandant, acting with permission of the Emperor, asked Rachkovskii to investigate Philippe. In his report Rachkovskii branded Philippe a charlatan. When he arrived in Petersburg to deliver the report, he first spoke to Sipiagin about it. The minister of interior, having a good notion of which way the wind was blowing, suggested that Rachkovskii burn the report, but his advice went unheeded. That is why Rachkovskii, who had long been in the bad graces of Plehve, was dismissed as soon as the latter succeeded Sipiagin and, what is more, dismissed on the remarkable condition that only if he took up residence in Brussels would he receive a pension. When I learned from Plehve that the rumor of Rachkovskii's dismissal was true, I pointed out that with his departure we would be losing our intelligence network abroad that informed us about what the revolutionaries and anarchists were doing. He did not react to this, but he did say that Rachkovskii had been dismissed on orders from the Emperor.

The Montenegrin sisters helped Philippe get into the good graces of Grand Dukes Peter Nikolaevich and Nicholas Nikolaevich. The latter, who would later marry Montenegrin No. 2, was inclined toward mysticism [spiritualism?] and easily fell under the spell of Philippe. With such friends, Philippe was able to visit Petersburg secretly and conduct nocturnal seances with Their Majesties, the two Grand Dukes, and the two sisters. Under the influence of messages he received at these seances, Grand Duke Nicholas Nikolaevich ended his liaison, of many years standing, with Burenina, a break, it is said, that led to her madness.[9] Slowly Philippe gathered a small sect of believers who, when he died [in 1905],

*This is a good place to mention that when Prince Alexander Obrenovich contracted a mésalliance by marrying his mother's lady-in-waiting, Montenegrin princess No. 2 said that he would come to a bad end. When Prince Alexander and his wife sought to visit the Emperor, then in Yalta, the Montenegrin sisters connived to keep them from being received.

believed that he bodily ascended to heaven, his work on earth completed.

To what extent Philippe was able to influence our neurasthenic Empress can be seen from the following incident, which I know to be true. In 1901, in France, while our Emperor and Empress were watching a cavalry exercise, a civilian was seen to enter the square through which the cavalry was to charge. When some of those standing close to the Empress expressed fear for the man's safety, the Empress, on recognizing that this was Philippe, calmly remarked that he would come to no harm.

The Dowager Empress was quite disturbed about the seances conducted by Philippe. In replies to questions from their friends about Philippe, Prince George Leuchtenberg and Grand Duke Nicholas Nikolaevich categorically asserted that, whatever might be said about him, he was a holy man.

Apparently, it was at Grand Duke Nicholas Nikolaevich's summer home, near Peterhof,* that the idea of canonizing Serafim of Sarov was conceived. Unquestionably Serafim was a holy man, but although his holiness had been recognized in his lifetime, he had not been considered a saint, and it is not the practice to canonize a man unless the people of the time considered him a saint.

Constantine Petrovich Pobedonostsev told me about the events leading to Serafim's canonization. It was in the summer of 1902 that he came to see me after having lunched with Their Majesties at Peterhof. He had been astonished at having been invited to lunch, for he had not been in their good graces for some time. He soon discovered the reason for the invitation.

After lunch the Emperor asked him to prepare a decree canonizing Serafim, the decree to be issued on the day of the holy man's anniversary, a few weeks hence. Pobedonostsev replied that it was the Holy Synod that proclaimed saints, and then only after a lengthy investigation of the candidate's life and the popular traditions about him. The Empress responded that the Emperor could do anything, but in the end His Majesty agreed that canonization could not be done immediately, but directed that it be done the following year, on the occasion of the consecration of Serafim's relics.

In the summer of 1903 Their Majesties went to Sarov for the consecration of Serafim's relics. During the courses of these ceremonies there were several instances of miraculous cures. I was told that Their Majesties believed Saint Serafim would enable the Empress to have the son and heir they had so long sought after having four daughters. One night the Empress bathed in a curative spring there. And it happened that she bore a son the following year.[10] As a result their faith in Saint Serafim was reinforced. Indicative of this faith was a large portrait of the saint that hung in the Emperor's study and his reply to a later overprocurator of the Holy Synod, Prince A. D. Obolenskii. When the prince mentioned Saint Serafim in connection with a complaint about the interference of the Montenegrin princesses in synodal affairs, he said: "I have indisputable evidence

*It was here that Philippe met Father Ioann of Kronstadt, the well-known priest.

of the holiness and miraculous power of Saint Serafim; I am certain that no one can ever shake my faith in that power.''

Among those who advanced their careers as a result of their participation in the ceremonies at Sarov was "Cutlet Colonel" Prince Putiatin, assistant to the high marshal of the Imperial court, who did a painting of the consecration ceremonies. He earned the special favor of the Emperor and later became the secret messenger between the court and the Black Hundreds. I did not know him well, but I can affirm that he was always deferential to me.

Another whose career was advanced was Father Serafim, who had been an artillery officer before becoming a monk. Subsequently he was ordained a priest and advanced in the hierarchy, although he did not have a good reputation. [In 1907] Varnava, the estimable abbot of Poliostrovskii Monastery, told me that Father Serafim was being pushed to take the place of Antonii, metropolitan of Petersburg, and to make this possible the Black Hundreds newspapers were carrying on a campaign of defamation against Antonii. According to Varnava, there were those in the highest circles who believed that it was necessary for the tranquility of Russia that Serafim become metropolitan.[11]

That such things could be believed can be judged from the fact that even after Tsushima the cutlet colonel could express amazement that any *decent* person could believe that we would be crushed by the Japanese. Had not Father Serafim predicted that we would conclude a victorious peace in Tokyo?

Still another whose career was helped by the events at Sarov was Prince Shirinskii-Shikhmatov, procurator of the Moscow synodal office, who made the arrangements for the consecration of the relics. He was soon appointed a governor, of Tver, where he became known for requiring that priests inform him about the political views of their parishioners. When Prince Sviatopolk-Mirskii became minister of interior, he insisted that the governor be dismissed because of this practice. The Emperor reluctantly agreed, but received Shirinskii-Shikhmatov as soon as he came to Petersburg and quietly listened to his insinuations about the new minister of interior. Then, in violation of the rules, the Emperor appointed Shirinskii-Shikhmatov to the Senate. When I left the office of premier, the Emperor appointed Shirinskii-Shikhmatov (a man with all of Pobedonostsev's defects but none of his virtues) as over-procurator of the Holy Synod. When Stolypin became premier, the prince had to give up his post, but was immediately appointed to the State Council, where he became a leader of the Black Hundreds.

Others whose careers were advanced by their work at Sarov were Plehve and Launitz, but in the end both died at the hands of assassins. Although I condemn all assassinations, particularly anarchist ones, I must say in all candor that these two contributed to their own deaths by their lack of principle. At least Plehve was intelligent and well informed. Launitz was neither.[12]

A Visit from a Police Agent

While I was in Paris, I. F. Manuilov, who together with Rataev had assumed Rachkovskii's duties in Paris, came to see me. A clever fellow, of Jewish origin, he had been appointed to the secret police on the recommendation, or rather on the insistence, of Prince Meshcherskii, who regarded him as one of his "spiritual sons." (This was the term used by the prince for those young men who amused him.)[13]

Well, Manuilov was very apologetic and assured me that the police agents who followed me around were not acting on his orders or those of Rataev. They were, he said, Plehve's men and had been on my heels ever since I left Petersburg. Their task was to find out whom I was seeing and what I was doing while abroad. I had not noticed that I was being followed, but after I received indirect confirmation from the French government, on the following day, that this was so, I became more observant. I noted that I was kept under surveillance until I reached the Russian border on my way home. As soon as I could, I caused Plehve some embarrassment by thanking him for being so concerned about my safety.

Lopukhin and the Zubatovshchina

Another visitor I had while in Paris was A. A. Lopukhin, director of our Department of Police, who was abroad on official business. His purpose in calling on me was to find out if I had had anything to do with the recent dismissal of Zubatov. The background of this query is as follows.

After Plehve became minister of interior, I spoke to him at our first meeting about the danger of the Zubatov scheme of organizing labor associations under police direction.[14] He agreed that it was dangerous, as well as stupid, and said he would talk about it with Grand Duke Sergei Aleksandrovich [under whose aegis Zubatov had been operating].

Nonetheless, Zubatov's influence in the Department of Police became greater. He established new security sections,[15] which came under his jurisdiction, thus giving him control over the entire secret police operations of the department. In fact he rose in Plehve's favor, as can be seen from the following incident. When in the spring of 1903 I happened to ask Plehve what he planned to do that summer, he replied that he was thinking of spending some time in the country. I expressed surprise that he could take leave at a time when, so I heard, Lopukhin would be out of the country. Plehve declared that the entire police apparatus, i.e., the responsibility for the maintenance of tranquility, was, in fact, in the hands of Zubatov, in whom he had confidence.

A few weeks later Zubatov, who had hitherto avoided me because he knew of my opposition to his labor organizations, called on me.[16] Citing secret sources, he told me, at length, that Russia was in turmoil and that it was impossible to hold revolution back by the repressive methods that Plehve was following. Plehve, he said, was only driving the disease inward and this would lead to dire consequences, one of which would be the killing of Plehve, whose life he had already saved on several occasions.

I asked why he had not gone to Plehve with this warning. He had, he said, but had failed to sway Plehve from his dangerous course. I told Zubatov that although I felt obliged to report this conversation to Plehve, I would pretend that it had never occurred because I did not wish him any harm, but I did advise him to plead once more with the minister of interior to adopt a new course.

In telling Lopukhin about this conversation with Zubatov, I assured him, when asked, that I had told no one before about it. As far as I knew, I said, Zubatov had come a cropper because he was held responsible for the strikes in Odessa and other Black Sea ports early in July.

That arch intriguer Grand Duke Alexander Mikhailovich, in his capacity as head of the Chief Administration of the Merchant Marine, had learned from his subordinates that the trouble in Odessa had been organized by a Jewess (whose name I can't recall) and "Doctor of Philosophy" Shaevich,* who had organized workers' associations on the model of those created by Zubatov. The Grand Duke assumed that this had been done with the blessing or support of the Factory Inspectorate, which was under my jurisdiction, and expressed surprise that my people should be involved. I told him that the associations had been organized under the aegis of the Department of Police, without informing the inspectorate. I then gave him the reports I had received from my factory inspectors about the recent events in Odessa and about the Zubatov associations.

Later I informed the Emperor about the episode, reminding him of the danger represented by the "Zubatovshchina." He listened calmly but did not respond. But, as I was to learn, he told the Grand Duke that I must have been mistaken because both Grand Duke Sergei Aleksandrovich and Plehve had complete confidence in Zubatov.

At the time of my dismissal from the post of minister of finance, in August, I was told by Grand Duke Alexander Mikhailovich that the Emperor had recently said to him:

> You know, Witte was right: Zubatov had arranged the strike and had created those labor organizations, but Witte was wrong in thinking that Plehve knew all about it. Plehve has just recently uncovered everything and has recommended that Zubatov be dismissed.

Lopukhin told me that the associations had been authorized by Plehve.

It was on my return to Petersburg that I learned more about Zubatov's dismissal. After being coldly received by me, Zubatov had gone to Prince Meshcherskii and told him what he had told me. The prince, who was quite close to Plehve, then told the minister of what Zubatov had said to him. It was for this reason that

*To put a good face on things, Plehve had Shaevich, a police agent, and the Jewess arrested and exiled to the north, but once they arrived there they were freed and sent abroad at government expense. Naturally, they later returned to Russia.[17]

Plehve had recommended Zubatov's dismissal, using the trouble in Odessa as justification for his request.

Departure of Dragomirov

It was during the Emperor's stay abroad that Dragomirov was relieved of his posts of governor-general of Kiev and commander of the Kiev Military District.* Ill health played a part in his departure, but the chief reason he left was his sharp criticism of our foreign and domestic policies and of our war minister, Kuropatkin. He held Kuropatkin in low esteem and expressed his opinions of him in a witty but inelegant manner. On several occasions I heard him say of the policies in Finland and Manchuria favored by the war minister: "I am afraid that we are chasing several rabbits at the same time and will catch none." And so it turned out.

At this time Dragomirov was the only one left in the country with a distinguished record as combat general. He gained renown in the war with Turkey during the crossing of the Danube, when he received a leg wound that left him with a limp, of which he made something of a show. He loved to eat and drink, and there were always friends and associates who indulged him in this weakness. No question that he was witty, gifted, original, and well educated in the military arts, but he clung to the old tradition that military art consisted of courage and effective use of the bayonet, the old Suvorov teaching. Recent wars, particularly the one with Japan, have shown that technology, as well as courage, is necessary for victory.

General Kleigels, who had been serving as prefect of Petersburg, was named to replace Dragomirov. Everyone was amazed by this appointment, for although he had not been a bad prefect, at least no worse than those who had preceded him, General von Wahl, for example, and was undoubtedly better than those who succeeded him, that was no recommendation. He was a very limited man, poorly educated, with a greater knowledge of horses than of men. He was not a bad sort and could be quite amusing. Evidently he had been handsome when a young grenadier, and although he was by now well along in years, he still had the proud carriage of a grenadier conscious of his good looks. When he spoke, it was very deliberately, with a generous employment of lofty words, often of foreign origin. He was addicted to certain pompous phrases, which most Petersburgians associated with him. As governor-general of Kiev he was neither loved nor hated. [I shall have more to say about him when I deal with the events of October 1905.]

*When Dragomirov was given the command of the Kiev Military District, Count Alexis Pavlovich Ignatev, brother of our ambassador to Constantinople, was named governor-general of Kiev. Usually when the military and civilian commands are thus divided, there is conflict, with the victory going to the military. Such was the case in Kiev. Count Ignatev, an aggressive man who owed his career more to his ties than to his ability, had the backing of Goremykin, the minister of interior, but General Dragomirov had the backing of war minister Vannovskii, who was more powerful than Goremykin. As a result, Dragomirov later replaced Count Ignatev as governor-general.

Meanwhile in Darmstadt:
The Drift to War

It was while the Emperor was in Darmstadt that the statute establishing the Special Committee for the Far East was confirmed and Bezobrazov and Admiral Abaza were appointed members of that body. In fact, our entire Far Eastern policy was now in the hands of Bezobrazov, Abaza, and their satellites, men such as Vonliarliarskii and the director of the Putilov factory, Albert. Admiral Abaza, Bezobrazov's myrmidon and relative, a knave and a scoundrel, was appointed chief administrative assistant of the committee. It was men such as these who now prepared the policies that our viceroy for the Far East, Admiral Alekseev, a man with the mentality of a sly Armenian rug dealer, was to carry out, while Count Lambsdorff, our foreign minister, was ignored.*

Baron Freedericksz, who visited Paris while I was still there, told me a good deal of what was going in Darmstadt: the Emperor was in fine spirits, going for automobile rides, taking long walks. The baron was a bit unhappy that the Emperor was unable to wear certain German uniforms while he was there, because these uniforms called attention to his short stature. He wished the Emperor had the height that one expects in a sovereign.

When our talk turned to the Far East, the baron said that although Count Lambsdorff was in Darmstadt, His Majesty did not communicate through him with Admiral Alekseev, but through his Military Field Chancellery,[18] which was now very busy at enciphering and deciphering telegrams. When I remarked that such a state of affairs was dangerous, the baron told me that he had said so to both the Emperor and Count Lambsdorff and that the count had then spoken to the Emperor about this. As a result, the foreign minister was permitted to see some, but not all, of the telegrams that passed between His Majesty and that egregious careerist Admiral Alekseev.

On a later occasion I learned more about the count's conversation with the Emperor from the count himself. The Emperor told him that he had entrusted all matters concerning the Far East to Alekseev, who now bore responsibility for carrying out our policies in that part of the world. When he agreed to send the count copies of telegrams between himself and the viceroy, he asked him to draft a reply to Alekseev's latest telegram, urging that since Japan's insolence made further talk futile, we turn to force. Count Lambsdorff told me that he was able to prevent this resort to military action.

His Majesty told the foreign minister that he did not want war. What this meant was that he had accepted the view of Bezobrazov and his gang of adventurers, that we could achieve what we wanted in the Far East without the risk of war because the Japanese would not dare to fight, that the only way to deal with the likes of Japan or China was to be direct and unyielding, and that if we made any

---

*I do not wish to insult the Armenians by such a characterization: what I mean is that his was the mentality of a dishonorable, petty tradesman, not that of a statesmanlike diplomat. To think of Alekseev as being typical of Armenians is to defame them.

concessions it would be only because of the grace of the white Russian tsar.[19]

It was because His Majesty accepted the views of a Bezobrazov that we were pursuing a reckless policy in the Far East without being prepared to fight there.[20] But it should be noted that in his heart he thirsted for the glory that would come from a victorious war. I am convinced that had there been no war with Japan there would have been a war at the border of India [over Afghanistan] or, more likely, war with Turkey, over the Bosphorus, and such a war would, of course, have turned into a larger war.

The Emperor's conviction that the Japanese would not dare to attack us is even better illustrated by what I learned from Count Bülow, the German chancellor. It appears that the German foreign office had received foreboding news that Japan considered war inevitable and was preparing for it because Witte, the chief force for restraint, had been removed from office, and because the conduct of negotiations between Russia and Japan had been taken out of the hands of Count Lambsdorff.* On receiving this information, Emperor William wrote to our Emperor, then in Darmstadt, of what he had learned, declaring that he considered it his duty to inform him. His Majesty's reply was that there would be no war, because *he* did not want war.

Another warning about the imminence of war came from Baron Rosen, our minister to Tokyo, an honorable and sensible man, but with a Germanic cast of mind. He warned that Japan was becoming aroused and advised that we give up our schemes on the Yalu and come to an agreement with Japan concerning Korea. However, he believed, with Germanic tenacity, that Manchuria should be ours.

But Manchuria could not be ours. We should have been content with the Kwantung Peninsula that we had taken so perfidiously and with the Chinese Eastern Railroad. Not America, not England, not Japan, not any of their open or secret allies, not China would ever have agreed to let us have Manchuria. Therefore, to argue for gaining control over Manchuria by any means possible made war inevitable. Baron Rosen did not understand this and therefore was not the proper person to be dealing with Japan at such a critical time, particularly under the direction of a man like Admiral Alekseev.

An Aborted Trip to Italy

The Emperor had planned on visiting King Victor Emmanuel of Italy while abroad, the king being the only monarch [of a major European country] to whom he had not yet paid a visit. But he was advised by some around him that a call then

---

*When its political ventures fail, the court camarilla inevitably seeks a scapegoat upon whom to let loose a pack of half-mad dogs. After the absurd, senseless, and most unfortunate of wars, with Japan, it sought to make Count Lambsdorff, that fine man, its scapegoat, just as it was to make me the scapegoat after October 17 [1905].

This is typical of the Emperor, as it was not of his father, a simple man but a tsar, who gave Russia thirteen years of tranquility. Only a genuine tsar can bring happiness to his country. Craftiness, unspoken lies, the inability to say yes or no and to live up to what one has said, to be possessed of an optimism born of fear (i.e., optimism used to shore up one's nerve) are harmful traits in a ruler.

might be unwise because he might encounter hostile demonstrations in Italy, perhaps even be the target of a Russian anarchist assassination attempt. The advice was based on the fact that Italian left-wing parties (which were then, as now, of considerable influence) were very hostile because of our domestic policy, particularly as it was under Plehve. Most Italian newspapers protested against the proposed visit, referring to our ruler as a "despot." Some Roman newspapers predicted that the Emperor would be received with hostile demonstrations.

The king wrote to assure the Emperor that he assumed personal responsibility for his safety while in Italy and that the outcries against the proposed visit were of no importance. At worst, he wrote, there might be some demonstrations, but there was no possibility of danger. Nonetheless, Lopukhin was summoned to Darmstadt and instructed to go to Italy and see for himself what the facts were. He told me that after visiting Italy he informed the Emperor that the necessary steps to protect him would be taken, but that he could not guarantee that there would be no demonstrations. The upshot was that the Emperor decided to cancel the visit, thereby deeply insulting King Victor Emmanuel, who accused our ambassador to Rome, Nelidov, of duplicity, of telling him one thing and reporting another to Darmstadt. He demanded that Nelidov be withdrawn.

The Emperor then decided to give Nelidov an appointment to the State Council, which was tantamount to sending him into retirement, at which point Count Lambsdorff stepped into the breach by requesting that Urusov, our ambassador to Paris, trade places with Nelidov. The Emperor agreed. The count told me that although he did not have a high opinion of Nelidov, he would not permit a man with such a long tenure as ambassador to be sent into virtual retirement.

It was not until 1909 that the Emperor was able to visit King Victor Emmanuel.

The Emperor's Return to Russia

During his lengthy stay on German soil our Emperor showed no desire whatever to call on Emperor William, much to the German monarch's embarrassment. The explanation may lie in the fact that our Emperor resented William's stern and patronizing manner toward the Grand Duke of Darmstadt, the Empress's brother.

During a stop in Berlin on my way home, I was told of the German Emperor's embarrassment by Ernest Mendelssohn-Bartholdy, who was friendly with the chancellor and was held in such high esteem by Emperor William that the two sometimes dined alone. I suggested that he tell the chancellor that I suggested that Emperor William take the initiative. So, a meeting was arranged.

The two Emperors met, alone, for a few hours in Potsdam, and at William's suggestion they went for a ride in the park. The German Emperor later expressed astonishment that during their meeting Emperor Nicholas did not utter a single word about the Far East or about politics in general. Perhaps this was so because Emperor Nicholas felt that Emperor William had led him into a trap by getting his agreement on Kiaochow. Or perhaps it was because he thought that he would be giving misleading advice.

En route home Emperor Nicholas and his party spent several weeks at [his hunting lodge] in Skierniewice. In the party were the Grand Duke of Hesse and the latter's daughter, who died during the stay there, an event that could not fail to sadden our Emperor and Empress.

Meanwhile, Count Lambsdorff had returned to Petersburg, knowing that with Alekseev in charge of the negotiations with Japan there was no need for him to be at the Emperor's side. The count still hoped that war could be avoided. I had to tell him that such hopes were based on emotion rather on reason. Only a person who did not know the Emperor's character, or lack of character, and did not know what had been happening could believe that war was avoidable.

I suspected that the prime mover behind the scenes was Plehve. And it turned out, after his death, when his papers were examined, that all the documents concerning the Far East were in his office, either in the original or in copies. At the Emperor's orders all such papers were turned over to that scoundrel Abaza.

His Majesty returned to Tsarskoe Selo on November 21. At the end of December he took up residence at the Winter Palace, and in January the season of court balls began, as if everything were normal.

A Little Victorious War

Not long after my return to Russia, Kurino, the Japanese minister to Russia, came to see me. In July 1903, while I was still minister of finance, he had presented a proposal to me and Count Lambsdorff that would have made a peaceful settlement of our differences possible. I favored acceptance, but to no avail, because it was sent to Viceroy Alekseev and became the subject of endless and fruitless discussion.

This intelligent man told me how my country was dragging out negotiations while his was acting with dispatch. Japan would make a proposal, Lambsdorff would say that matters were in Alekseev's hands, while Alekseev and Rosen would say that their hands were tied because the Emperor was away. To Japan this sort of tactic meant that we wanted war, and he felt it a matter of honor to do what he could to prevent a conflict. Time was short, he argued. Japanese public opinion was becoming increasingly aroused and was therefore difficult to keep under control. After all, he declared, Japan was a sovereign state, and it was humiliating for her to have to negotiate with some sort of "viceroy of the Far East," as if the Far East belonged to Russia and Japan was but a protectorate. I said there was nothing I could do, being out of power.[21] When I suggested that he turn to Count Lambsdorff, he said that the count was no more than a messenger now.

[On January 19, 1904] at a court ball at the Winter Palace, Kurino picked up the subject of the imminence of war. He asked that I warn our foreign office that if we did not reply quickly to Japan's latest proposal war would break out within a few days, because Japan had lost patience. He was telling me this, he said, as a friend of Russia.

We did not reply in time. On January 26, Japanese warships attacked Port Arthur and sank several of our ships. We were at war. The following day a solemn service was held in the Winter Palace chapel, amidst a mood of depression. I was not far from His Majesty as he returned from the chapel to the family quarters. As he passed, General Bogdanovich shouted "hurrah," but few followed his example. Later that day, as I watched from my home, the Emperor and Empress drove by, in a carriage, to call on Princess Altenberg. As they passed my house, the Emperor looked up and evidently saw me: his expression and manner were those of one who had evidently triumphed. Obviously he did not see that what happened did not bode well for Russia.

During the next days the government arranged several popular demonstrations to show support for our cause, but they did not come off well. It was evident from the start that the majority of the people abhorred the war. For this reason alone, no good could have been expected from the conflict.

It was not long after the outbreak of war that Kuropatkin reproached Plehve for being the only minister who had wanted war and had allied himself with that band of political adventurers. In a tired voice, Plehve replied: "Alexis Nikolaevich, you do not know Russia's internal situation: we need a little, victorious war to stem the revolution."[22]

Such are the words that came from Plehve's "sharp" and "statesmanlike" mind! Such was the way this all-powerful minister looked at the situation! And it was thanks to him that His Majesty had allied himself with Bezobrazov and Co.

There was no question in the Emperor's mind that Japan would be soundly beaten, even if it might require some effort. As for the cost of the war, he saw no cause for alarm since Japan would have to indemnify Russia for her cost.

Thus a terrible period began, with the most unfortunate of wars leading to a revolution for which the police-*cum*-nobility regime, or rather police-*cum*-court camarilla regime, had paved the way. Then revolution would turn into anarchy. What does God have in store for us? There is still so much to endure. One's heart and soul are deeply burdened. How sad for Russia! How sad for the Emperor, that poor, unfortunate man, who has had to endure so much and has so much still to endure. He is a good man, and is by no means stupid, but he has no will. It is from his lack of will that his political sins, i.e., sins that he commits in his capacity as an autocratic and *unlimited* ruler, who feels that he is responsible only to God, derive.[23]

II

My Differences with Plehve

After my return to Petersburg [in the fall of 1903], I found myself at odds with Plehve on several occasions in the State Council.[1] This led him to think that I was trying to replace him.[2] I tried to persuade him that his fears were unjustified, that if I sometimes opposed him it was because we disagreed on most political questions. I told him that for someone in my position to seek the post of minister of interior would be stupid, and no one had yet accused me of being stupid. Also I tried, unsuccessfully, to convince him that the policy he was following would end badly for him and for the state.

It should be noted that the atmosphere of Petersburg is such that it attracts many who spend their time trying to undermine each other through defamation in order to gain some fleeting advantage. And many, including the Emperor, are easily taken in by such defamatory reports. As for Plehve, he had worked so long to become minister of interior that, having achieved his aim, he was ready to destroy anyone he suspected of trying to have him removed from his position. He held a grudge against me, in the mistaken belief that I had twice prevented him from becoming minister of interior.

As I told the Emperor in 1895, when Plehve was being considered for the post, I considered him a very able man, but with no fixed political convictions, a man who would adopt any political principle that would advance his career. What I did not tell the Emperor was that Plehve was a renegade who had changed his religion to further his career, that he was a low police type, that his support of the nobility's self-serving aspirations did not come from his status (his father was not a noble, had probably been an organist for some Polish landowner); it came from his desire to further his career by helping the court clique. A religious renegade and a non-Russian, he acted like most renegades and made himself out to be "true Russian and Orthodox,'' ready to impose all sorts of restrictions on those of His Majesty's subjects who were not Orthodox. I think that Plehve had greater faith in the devil than he did in God, but he feigned great piety: for example, when he became minister, he made a trip to worship at the Sergei-Trinity Monastery, near Moscow, to gain favor with the extremely pious governor-general of Moscow, Grand Duke Sergei Aleksandrovich. That is why Pobedonostsev, who acted out of conviction and not expedience, despised him.

As I have noted elsewhere, Plehve was passed over for the post again in 1899. For some reason he believed that on this occasion, as on the previous one, I had a hand in blocking him. He never forgot and he never forgave me for what he thought was my role in twice preventing him from attaining his goal of becoming minister of interior.

People and Nobility

It was my conviction that a Russian Sovereign should shape his policies for the benefit of the people, whereas Plehve thought it should be for the benefit of the nobility. During my tenure as minister of finance I was unable to do much for the economic well-being of the people because, despite verbal support for my efforts from the ruling circles, I encountered covert opposition, encouraged from behind the scenes by Plehve.

As I have noted elsewhere, my first conflict with Plehve over the need to help the people rather than the nobility alone took place at the Special Conference on the Needs of the Nobility. And a bitter conflict it was. When, after the closing of this conference, I tried once more to raise the needs of the peasantry with His Majesty, I was frustrated because of the influence of Plehve and the Minister of Interior Durnovo.

When I tried to help the peasantry by revising the charter of the Peasants' Bank, Plehve and Durnovo were behind the objections to revision that I encountered in the State Council. But in those days I still had influence, and, despite all objections, I was supported by His Majesty and the revised charter, with some changes, was adopted. As I have said, when Plehve became minister of interior he tried to undercut the bank, but I would not yield to him, making for new unpleasantness between the two of us.

And then when I served as chairman of the Special Conference on the Needs of Rural Industry, which I tried to direct toward helping the peasantry, that careerist strove both overtly and covertly to undermine the work of the conference.

I should note that Plehve was prominent among the successive ministers of interior who tried to impede my effort to eliminate barriers to the formation of corporations as a means of increasing the wealth of the Empire and thus of the people.

In addition to disagreeing with Plehve on the most basic of questions, whether to serve the needs of the people as a whole or the special interests of the nobility, I disagreed with him on other questions, notably the policies to be followed toward non-Russians in general and Finns, Jews, and Armenians in particular.[3]

The Finns

As I have stated earlier, Plehve, acting, as always, out of expedience, supported the efforts, which emanated chiefly from the War Ministry, to undermine the Finnish constitution. I, for my part, believed that certain aspects of Finnish administration should be assimilated into the general administration of the Empire, but it should be done without violating what was in effect the constitution of the grand duchy.

With Bobrikov as governor-general of Finland and Plehve as state secretary for Finnish affairs, the Emperor imposed the heavy-handed, centralized rule of Petersburg on the grand duchy and, in so doing, drove the hitherto loyal Finns into open resistance. Even so the Finns shunned the method of assassination, so favored by many of our revolutionaries of the extreme left and right. During this period there were only two assassinations in Finland, both the work of Finnish nationalists rather than of revolutionaries. One victim was a procurator, the other Bobrikov. It is regrettable that there were as many as two Finnish assassins, for assassination is an abhorrent crime—against religion, against mankind, against the state.

General Bobrikov was killed by the son of a former Finnish senator. The son then killed himself. From what I heard Bobrikov died honorably, as any official with self-respect should.

The Emperor's choice of a successor caught everyone by surprise. Acting on the advice of Plehve, he appointed Prince Ivan M. Obolenskii, who had distinguished himself as governor of Kharkov by his successful suppression of peasant riots, in the course of which he had personally supervised the flogging of rioters. For this an anarchist later tried to kill him, but failed, fortunately. That the prince had peasants flogged severely was taken as proof of his youth and decisiveness: "what a solid young man," "what a fine fellow," "who else but he should become governor-general of Finland."

What was particularly surprising was that Prince Obolenskii was immediately given the rank of general-adjutant, even though his only service had been in the navy, and then for only a short time. Nothing like this had taken place since the reign of Emperor Paul Petrovich.

The prince is a good man, and not at all stupid, but he is not a serious person and is a great chatterbox who confuses fact and fancy. He is called "Vania Khlestakov"[4] by his family.

After he received his appointment as governor-general, he came to see me for advice. I urged that he avoid Bobrikov's harsh policy of Russification and return to the earlier traditions, but at the same time continuing to bring under Russian administration matters that affect the entire Empire.

Naturally, Plehve counselled him to continue Bobrikov's policies.[5] This Prince

Obolenskii did, but since he is not a serious person, he did not act with the firmness of his predecessor. When revolution broke out in Russia, he shifted to a more moderate policy, but by then it was too late.

It goes without saying that if we had not had an emancipation movement,[6] if we had not suffered from the searing effect of that most shameful of wars, if we had not had a rebellion in the interior of Russia, then the borderlands would not have raised their heads, would not have begun to advance demands, some justifiable, some arrogant, and would not have begun to avenge themselves for policies directed against them—some of these policies constituting persecution, others perfectly justified—all, however, repugnant to the national feelings of the aroused non-Russians.

From the Russian point of view such feelings on the part of non-Russians are base and seditious, but they are human feelings. The error of our recent policies toward non-Russian subjects derives from our forgetting that since the days of Peter the Great we have been not "Russia" but "the Russian Empire." When thirty-five percent of our population is non-Russian and when the Russians themselves are divided into Great Russians, Little Russians, and White Russians, it is impossible to follow a policy that ignores the language, religion, et sim. of the non-Russian nationalities that have become part of the Russian Empire.

The aim of such an Empire cannot be to turn everyone into a "true Russian." Rather than attempt to reach such a goal, it would be better to part with our borderlands. But you see, neither this Tsar nor his predecessors would have accepted such a thought. And not satisfied with having Poles, Finns, Germans, Letts, Armenians, Georgians, Tatars, et al. as subjects, we have dreamed of annexing territories inhabited by Mongols, Chinese, and Koreans.[7]

That is what brought us into the war with Japan that has shaken the foundations of the Russian Empire. For the present we are still experiencing shocks. Given the current policy, given the Tsar's covert ideals, those of the half-mad party of "true Russian men," one does not have to be a prophet to see great tragedy ahead. God have mercy on us.

The Dowager Empress,
the Empress, and the Emperor

Before leaving the subject of Finland I must point out the role played by the Dowager Empress. Marie Fedorovna is not specially intelligent, but she is very honorable, has experienced much in life, and has therefore learned much. She is sincere and very affable. She is truly an Empress.

I heard her say that Kuropatkin is not a serious person and that it is his misfortune that he wanted a monument erected in his honor while he was still alive. As for Plehve, she could not endure the man. As soon as Kuropatkin began to badger the Finns, she tried to persuade the Emperor to hold him back. But, as I have said, it was to no avail. In addition, her father, the king of Denmark, wrote to the Emperor in the same vein. The Emperor responded by discontinuing the practice of stopping off to see the king when he went abroad.

The Dowager Empress had been losing her influence on the Emperor for some time, and as it waned, the antipathy between her and the Empress waxed. This led to the dissemination of false rumors (disseminated, I have reason to believe, by self-appointed lackeys of the young Empress) to the effect that the Dowager Empress was encouraging anarchists and revolutionaries to assassinate the Empress. And after the October Manifesto rumors were spread that she had opposed it and that she later tried to get her son to rescind it. I know for a fact that she favored a constitution.

It is not she but Empress Alexandra Fedorovna who conspires with the Union of True Russians, with such political scoundrels and pathological types as the Dubrovins and the Father Iliodors. It is not the Dowager Empress who provides them financial help and it is not the Dowager Empress who brought the Emperor to his present shameful position. The one who is most to blame is Empress Alexandra Fedorovna. Those courtiers who happen to be intelligent know this and speak of it privately, but before her they bow and scrape and act like lackeys.

Be it noted that the Dowager Empress is brave. Despite warnings not to, she travels freely in Petersburg and abroad, while Empress Alexandra Fedorovna and her crowned spouse immure themselves in fortresses—the palaces at Tsarskoe Selo and Peterhof. From their fortresses they send telegrams of condolence to the wives of men who have fallen at the hands of foul revolutionary assassins, praise the fallen for their courage, and declare "my life does not matter to me as long as Russia is happy." (Telegram to the State Council this year in connection with the uncovering of a plot against the Emperor and several bigwigs, a "plot" that turned out to be a provocation arranged by Azef, a police agent.)[8]

When a wife was sought for the present Emperor, while he was still Tsesarevich and Heir, Princess Alice of Darmstadt was brought to Petersburg to be looked over. She did not please. For the next two years no serious effort was made to find a bride for the Tsesarevich, and that was a grave political mistake.[9] Naturally, he found a mistress, the Polish ballerina Kshessinskaia.[10]

The Emperor did not know of the affair, but some of those around him nosed it out and began urging that the Tsesarevich be married off as soon as possible. When the Emperor became gravely ill, he decided that the Tsesarevich be married off quickly. So they thought once more of Princess Alice and sent the Tsesarevich to propose to her.

In speaking of Princess Alice, that strange person, I recall what Count Osten-Sacken, our ambassador to Berlin, told me when I saw him in 1904. He had known her as a young girl while he was *chargé d'affaires* at Darmstadt. Years later, when the Tsesarevich went to Darmstadt to propose, Osten-Sacken was sent there too, for the occasion, and used the opportunity to ask the marshal of the court of Hesse-Darmstadt how Princess Alice had turned out. After making sure that no one could overhear, the marshal said: "How lucky we are that you are taking her from us."

Of course the princess accepted the offer of marriage. How could she refuse it? Yet she expressed regret that she would have to change her religion. No one finds conversion easy, but it was especially difficult for a person with Princess Alice's narrow and obstinate character. Conversion is especially difficult for a person who is not motivated to do so out of conviction. And it was not out of conviction that she accepted Orthodoxy. She had no more comprehension of the sublimity of that faith than children have of the complexity of the motion of the heavenly spheres.

Having decided to change her faith, she had to convince herself that Orthodoxy was the only true religion in the world. Soon she was smitten by the beautifully and poetically elevated aspects of Orthodoxy, particularly as they are presented in the services she attends at court, but she still did not grasp the essence of the faith. How many do?

Given her dull, egotistical character and narrow world view, given the intoxicating effects of the luxury of the court, it is not odd that she should have completely succumbed to what I call Orthodox paganism, i.e., worship of the form without understanding of the spirit. She succumbed, too, to the conviction that the faith can be propagated by compulsion rather than by persuasion and the belief that, if you do not bow before me, you are my enemy, against whom I will use my autocratic power because what I wish represents the truth, and I have the right to act on the basis of what I know to be the truth. Given her psychology, given the fact that she is surrounded by lackeys and intriguers, it is easy to see why she should fall into such illusions.

It was this kind of soil that was favorable for the appearance of the kind of mysticism represented by Philippe, Father Serafim, and all sorts of soothsayers and hysterical women believed to have special powers. The worse things are, the greater the sorrow. The greater the sorrow, the more the soul must seek surcease in divination. And there will always be soothsayers—especially for tsars—who say: "Be patient, you will be victorious and all will be at your feet, all will recognize that only that which comes from you represents truth and salvation."

Alexandra Fedorovna is pretty. She is a good mother and undoubtedly loves her husband and seeks her happiness through him. She might have been a suitable wife for a German prince or for a tsar with a backbone, in which case she would have been the tsar's wife and nothing more. But sad to say, this Tsar has no will,[11] and Alexandra Fedorovna is the only person close to him who exercises a continuing influence on him. It is fatal for the Russian Empire that a person such as this should be adviser to its Autocratic Master, able to affect the fate of tens of millions of human beings.

I can illustrate the fact of her influence from my own experience. On several occasions while I was premier, the Emperor disregarded my advice. When I asked him on one such occasion who had advised him, he replied: "The person whom I trust without reservation." When I took the liberty of asking who that person might be, he told me it was his wife.[12]

No question that she, her poor husband, those of us who are obliged to be his loyal servants unto the grave, and, above all, Russia, would have been happier if she had married a German prince.

The Armenians

I disagreed with Plehve about our policy in the Caucasus, particularly with respect to its Armenian inhabitants, many of whom had come to ally themselves with the growing opposition to the government. In part Armenian attitudes were affected by the emancipation movement that was creating a mood of rebellion in the interior of the Empire, a movement that was being transmitted to the Caucasus by Russian newcomers to the region, also by long-term Russian residents of the area, and by Caucasian natives who had studied in the interior of Russia. An additional stimulus came from the thousands of Turkish Armenians, many of them seasoned revolutionaries, who had migrated to the Caucasus to escape Turkish persecution. It should be noted, too, that rebellion[13] in the Caucasus has a peculiar character, because the natives are in essence Asiatic, with their own psychology, their own conception of what civilization means, particularly with respect to the value of human life. To be sure, popular unrest was exacerbated by the growing venality and arbitrariness of our administration in the Caucasus, but until Prince Golitsyn was appointed its chief administrator, in 1897, the policies of his predecessors had made for peaceful relations between the government and the natives.

Had the man I had suggested for the post, Count Vorontsov-Dashkov, been appointed, we would have been spared the chaos that Prince Golitsyn created and the Caucasus would now be much calmer than it is. The prince [as I have said elsewhere] is a man of good character but a confused mind. He came to the region with a program of Russification, which he carried out in a vigorous but confused manner. He wished to Russify all the natives of the region, but he was especially hostile toward the Armenians, partly because they engaged in commerce of an exploitative kind, partly because they were being influenced by the revolutionary Turkish Armenians who had settled among them. But until Plehve became minister of interior he was frustrated in his efforts at Russification.

First, he proposed to confiscate the property of the Armenian churches, a proposal that could not help but antagonize the Armenians, for to them the church is a living thing, an essential feature of their lives, the center of their educational activities, the focus of their charitable efforts. To consider his proposal a conference was summoned, consisting of E. V. Frisch (chairman), Pobedonostsev, Foreign Minister Count M. N. Muravev, and Justice Minister N. V. Muravev, Minister of Interior Sipiagin, Prince Golitsyn, and I.

At our meetings I protested against this outrageous proposal, on both political and ethical grounds. I argued that such a step would be impolitic because it would rouse Armenians at home and abroad against us. I said it would be unethical because Armenians were not only Christians but also Christians linked to our Orthodox church. Pobedonostsev, who first favored the proposal, came over to my side after hearing my argument about the ethical implications. In the end only Prince Golitsyn supported the proposal. When the Emperor received the minutes of the conference, he approved neither the majority nor the minority opinion.

After Plehve was appointed minister of interior, Prince Golitsyn came to Petersburg to make another attempt to gain approval for his proposal. Plehve, sensing that the Emperor was sympathetic to the prince's views, immediately began to support him. This time the proposal was submitted to the Committee of Ministers.

In cases such as this, when the majority of the Committee of Ministers, or the State Council, is opposed to a proposal of relatively lesser importance and has reason to believe that the Emperor is in favor of it, the tactic used is not to express opposition but to seek ways of temporizing, or, as Pobedonostsev would put it, putting the matter "into the sand." Such was the case this time, at least in the sense that although the majority was opposed, I was the only one to speak at length in opposition, while Plehve strongly urged that we vote in favor. In the end he was joined in voting in favor by Prince Golitsyn and Education Minister Sänger (a decent but weak man who probably misunderstood the issue), while the majority, including Grand Duke Michael Nikolaevich, voted with me. Although the Grand Duke entreated him to confirm the majority view, the Emperor confirmed the minority view, and Prince Golitsyn was able to go ahead with his plans.[14]

As could have been expected, the Armenians reacted violently. And the struggle between them and the administration was heightened by conflict between them and native Moslems, the work, it was said, of the local administrators. Late in 1904, after an attempt on his life, Prince Golitsyn left the Caucasus never to return. It is remarkable that this essentially honorable and decent man could have roused everyone in the Caucasus, civilian and military, Russian and non-Russian, against him.

His successor, Count Vorontsov-Dashkov, returned to the policies of Prince Golitsyn's predecessors, but by that time it was too late and the Caucasus became one of the major centers of revolutionary upheaval.

The Jews

Also, I disagreed with Plehve on the Jewish question.

At the beginning of my tenure under Emperor Alexander III, he asked if it were true that I was sympathetic toward the Jews.

I said that it would be difficult for me to answer directly and asked if I might answer in the form of a rhetorical question. He agreed.

I asked if he could drop all the Jews of Russia into the Black Sea. If he could, the Jewish problem would be solved.[15] But since that was impossible the only choice as a means of solving the Jewish question was the gradual elimination of all discriminatory laws against the Jews. His Majesty did not reply, [and although he did not share my views on this subject] he remained favorably disposed toward me until the day he died, a sad day for Russia.[16]

I have consistently held to the view concerning the Jewish question that I expressed to Alexander III. As minister of finance I opposed all legislation that discriminated against the Jews, but it was not in my power to compel review of the discriminatory laws already in force. Many of these were extremely unjust and, what is more, were harmful to the Russians. And I have always approached the Jewish question from the point of view of the interests of the Russians and the Empire rather than from the point of view of the interests of the Jews.

Most of the discriminatory laws had been enacted by the Committee of Ministers and were presented as "temporary" laws, always accompanied by the pharisaical phrase "pending the review of all laws concerning the Jews." This phrase was intended to suggest that they would be reviewed with the aim of expanding, not restricting, Jewish rights, but the reverse happened.

The reason that such legislation usually went through the Committee of Ministers was that the ministers who proposed such laws knew that the majority of the State Council would either openly oppose the laws or else try to bury them "in the sand," and those ministers did not have the civic courage to face the State Council. Such laws, as I have suggested, had a much better chance of getting through the Committee of Ministers than through the State Council. And if there were danger of opposition even in the Committee of Ministers, one could get such legislation enacted by having the Emperor call a special conference to deal with it or have the Emperor approve a recommendation made by a minister. Thus, Grand Duke Sergei Aleksandrovich, while governor-general of Moscow, was able to secure the enactment of measures against the Jews of the city, by such means.[17]

If Alexander II's policy of gradually eliminating laws discriminating against Jews had been followed by his successors, Jews would not have become the evil factor they have been in our damnable revolution, and the Jewish question would be no more acute in Russia than in other countries with a sizable Jewish population. It will take decades, probably centuries, to consign the Jewish question to oblivion because the racial characteristics of the Jews can be modified only gradually.

Unfortunately, the policy toward the Jews changed after the death of Alexander II from one of gradual elimination of discriminatory legislation toward one of adding more legal restrictions. And because this great mass of laws is shot through with ambiguity, these laws have been interpreted in arbitrary and contradictory ways, thus providing abundant opportunity for bribing the officials who administer these laws. In fact, the greatest incidence of bribery in our administration is to be found in the enforcement of laws against Jews. In some localities bribery is no more than open and direct taxation. It goes without saying that the chief burden of anti-Jewish legislation falls on the poorest Jews, for the richer the Jew, the easier it is for him to buy his way out. Moreover, rich Jews can acquire some influence over local officialdom.

In the early 1880s, many senators opposed arbitrary interpretation of anti-Jewish legislation, but steps were taken against them by the Ministry of Interior, which spread slanderous insinuations that they were opposed to the government. As a result some of these senators were passed over for honors, some were transferred to other departments of the Senate, some were even deprived of their places in the Senate and replaced by servile appointees. Such tactics made the Senate tractable.

Anti-Jewish legislation, arbitrarily interpreted, reinforced by the [negative] influence of the Russian schools, helped drive the Jewish masses, particularly the youth, to become extreme revolutionaries. In the course of a generation many Jews were transformed from timorous creatures into bomb throwers, assassins, brigands—revolutionaries—willing to sacrifice their lives for their cause. To be sure, not all Jews became revolutionaries, but there can be no question that no other nationality has produced so high a percentage of revolutionaries as the Jews. A very high number of them joined the most extreme revolutionary parties, while nearly all of the Jewish *intelligenty*[18] with a higher education were to join the Party of People's Freedom (Kadets), which is, to a considerable degree, beholden to the Jews for its influence, for they have nourished it with their intellectual efforts and material support. These Jewish *intelligenty* looked to the emancipation movement for improvement in their lot and, when the Kadet party was formed, identified themselves with it because it promised them immediate freedom.

I have often warned Jewish leaders, both in Russia and abroad, that to follow the road of extremism would only make the lot of the Jews in Russia more difficult. I advised them that the route to amelioration of the Jewish condition in Russia was through the Tsar, whose good will they can earn by being models of loyalty, by asking not for every freedom they can think of, but only that they not be discriminated against. But in the heat of the emancipation movement and the revolutionary upheaval, Jewish *intelligenty* paid not the slightest attention to my advice: believing as they did in the Kadet leaders, they thought that equal rights could be achieved immediately.

Naturally, the behavior of the Jews in the last troubled years turned many non-Jews who had either been neutral or sympathetic toward the Jews into anti-Semites, and bitter ones at that. Never have Jews had as many enemies as they do now; never have the conditions for solving the Jewish question been as unfavorable as they are now, a situation that makes life hard for the Jews. I am convinced that until the Jewish question is dealt with humanely, sympathetically, and properly, Russia cannot return to a state of normalcy.

But I am afraid that if Jews received equal rights at one fell swoop, there would be new disorders and the atmosphere would become even more strained than it is. Such questions as those relating to the Jews, which impinge on traditional prejudices (which are based to some degree on the negative racial characteristics of the Jews), can only be solved gradually, because sudden, extreme solutions are upsetting. The state, after all, is a living organism and should not be subjected to radical surgery. It is better to move so as to produce a temporary equilibrium, even if it is arbitrary and unfair.

Count N. P. Ignatev, the minister of interior, who was the official author of the anti-Jewish law of 1882, did great harm to the state by his stupid policy toward the Jews. His successor, Count D. A. Tolstoi, although an ultra-conservative, was too intelligent to have been guilty of such stupidity. Although he was unable to correct Ignatev's mistakes, he followed a more sensible policy. His successor, I. N. Durnovo, resumed the stupid policy initiated by Ignatev, even though he was on the best of terms with several Jewish Croesuses and not out of venality, for he was an honorable man in money matters. It was simply that he was not very bright and was servile, so he followed the course that was pleasing to the court camarilla.

Plehve, who served under all three, was the soul and the author of all the anti-Jewish projects and administrative measures implemented under Count Ignatev and Durnovo. Yet, as I learned from many talks with Plehve, he had nothing against Jews and he was intelligent enough to understand that the official Jewish policy was incorrect, but he knew that this policy pleased Grand Duke Sergei Aleksandrovich and evidently His Majesty as well, and he tried to please.

Pogroms were one aspect of the Jewish question. Under Count Ignatev they were particularly violent. When Count Tolstoi took office, he put an immediate stop to them. After Plehve became minister of interior there was a new round of pogroms. I am not asserting that he was directly responsible for them, but I do believe that he tolerated them because they seemed to have an anti-revolutionary character.[19] The most barbarous and disgraceful of these pogroms was the one that took place in Kishinev.

General-Adjutant Count A. I. Musin-Pushkin, then commander of the Odessa Military District, who was sent to investigate the bloody events there, told me of the terrible things that were done there to defenseless Jews. The count, a soldier of the old school, claimed that the soldiers on duty could not act to stop the pogrom because they were under orders of the civilian authorities and these authorities would not issue any orders. He did not like Jews, but he was an honorable man and was consequently very disturbed by this terrible episode. Also, he felt that events such as these could result in the demoralization of the troops.

The policy that led to the pogrom was even more idiotic than it was terrible. The pogrom drove the Jews to despair, providing the final stimulus that pushed them to the side of the revolution. Also, it aroused public opinion throughout the civilized world against us, especially so in America. This marked the beginning of a turn to unfriendly relations between us.

Yet Plehve used the following language to Jewish secular and religious leaders: "Order your people to refrain from revolution and I will put an end to pogroms and begin to eliminate restrictions against Jews." Their response was: "It is not in our power to do so, for the majority—the youth—is crazed by hunger and we have no control over them, but we are certain that if you begin to ameliorate their conditions, they will quiet down.'' Shortly before his death, Plehve did ease some restrictions, for example, permitting Jews to reside in many villages from which they had been barred.

It is obvious that I disagreed with Plehve on many matters. As one would expect from him, he passed on the most slanderous accusations about me, even going so far as to say that I was virtually a revolutionary who conspired against the life of the Emperor, a life that every honorable Russian holds sacred. (That he did such things was learned after his death from the archive of the Department of Police.)[20] He knew I was opposed to his police-type policies, which were rapidly driving Russia to revolution. To retain his post he used whatever means he could to get rid of me. Perhaps that is why he took such a leading part in the schemes of Bezobrazov, expecting that I would give up the post of minister of finance rather than be party to such a ruinous adventure.

III

The First Months of War, January–July 1904

The High Command

When the war broke out, His Majesty appointed Admiral Alekseev, our viceroy in the Far East, to be commander-in-chief of our forces in the theater of war. The admiral was as qualified for his new post as I. He knew nothing about the army and little about the navy: he had achieved his rank by diplomatic acumen rather than by his ability as an officer.

His rise in the navy began as a result of the acumen he displayed when as young officer he accompanied Grand Duke Alexis Aleksandrovich on a round-the-world trip designed to bring the Grand Duke to his senses about Zhukovskaia.[1] It is related that on a stop in Marseilles the Grand Duke and some of his companions behaved in such a disorderly fashion at a house of joy that he was ordered to appear before the local authorities. Alekseev appeared in his place, claiming that it was he who had been at fault and that the Grand Duke had been mistakenly charged because of confusion between the names "Alexis" and "Alekseev"; the authorities accepted the explanation and let him go with a fine.

The Grand Duke was grateful and thereafter helped Alekseev rise in position. It was on his recommendation that Alekseev was appointed chief of the Kwantung region. That Alekseev could possibly rise to become viceroy and then also commander-in-chief of our forces there probably never occurred to him.

There were many unflattering stories about Admiral Alekseev's relations with his troops in Manchuria, to which I can add one. When I was in Port Arthur, in 1903, I was invited to attend a military review. Expecting that Alekseev would review the troops from horseback, I, in my capacity as [ex officio] chief of the

Border Guard, was there mounted and in uniform. To my surprise he was on foot, because, as I later learned, he was afraid of horses.

I was amazed too that General Stössel should have been appointed to command Port Arthur. What I learned about him in Port Arthur convinced me that he would make a bad situation worse. Several people told me that he reminded them of a stallion from poor stock.

Shortly before my arrival a fellow officer had tried to kill him. When Admiral Alekseev asked what I thought should be done with the offending officer, I said that whatever kind of person General Stössel might be, the officer who had tried to kill him should be tried and shot, for such an action could not be tolerated in a border region.

Public opinion, as expressed in the press, did not consider Alekseev equal to his task and unanimously called for Kuropatkin, the popular war minister, to be given command of the army in Manchuria. Although he had become hostile to Kuropatkin by this time, the Emperor bowed to public opinion and on February 8 gave the command of the army in Manchuria to the war minister, but retained Admiral Alekseev as commander-in-chief of the military and naval forces in the Far East.

At the beginning of his tenure as war minister, Kuropatkin won the hearts of the Emperor and Empress. He was, after all, the holder of the St. George, a man with a solid reputation for personal courage, an eloquent general staff officer. The "honeymoon" between Emperor and the war minister did not last, because Nicholas II has a feminine character. Someone once remarked that it was only by a whim of fate that he was born with the [physical] traits that distinguish male from female.

Initially, ministers (particularly those who owe their appointment to him and not his father), and others who report directly to him, enjoy considerable favor, favor that goes beyond the bounds of moderation. But fairly soon the Emperor becomes indifferent, and even antipathetic, toward such people and is sometimes even bitter that persons whom he had once favored should come to seem unworthy.

That is what happened to Kuropatkin, with the help of Bezobrazov and Co. When they appeared on the scene, he aligned himself with me and Count Lambsdorff, either because he feared that the kind of policy they supported would inevitably lead to war or because he was envious of the influence that these "fine fellows" gained. Then, when he saw that they were too strong for him, he tried to come to terms with them, but it was too late. They repaid him by seeing to it that when he was appointed to command the army in Manchuria he would lose his position as war minister.

At the time he was given the command, General Kuropatkin believed that he was only taking a leave of absence from his ministerial post, when in fact the

Emperor had decided that General Sakharov, whom he had chosen to replace Kuropatkin, would stay on in that post even after Kuropatkin's return. But the Emperor being the man he was would not be candid.[2] He asked General Kuropatkin to suggest some candidates to replace him. The general suggested a few men who might be suitable as temporary replacements. General Sakharov was not one of them. When the Emperor asked what he thought of Sakharov, Kuropatkin said he considered him quite unfit. Sakharov was immediately appointed after this conversation.

Before the appointment of Sakharov was announced, Kuropatkin, expecting to resume his duties as war minister when he returned, suggested a number of measures to be taken in view of the fact that the country was at war. When he talked to the Emperor about them following the announcement of his replacement, His Majesty said he would ask Sakharov to carry them out. Knowing that Kuropatkin kept a diary (the parts that he read to me showed he garbled accounts of conversations), he asked the general to let him see those parts of his diary that contained his suggestions so that he would have the information on which to base an order to Sakharov. That day Kuropatkin sent him two of the notebooks in which he kept his diary, the first listing suggestions, the second containing an account of the conversation about generals being mentioned as replacements for him, in which he recorded the following: "I do not recommend the appointment of Sakharov: he has never held a major field command, he is terribly lazy and is getting fat." The Emperor intended to send the first notebook to Sakharov for his guidance, but instead sent both.

That General Kuropatkin would serve under Admiral Alekseev meant in effect that there would be a dual command, a clear violation of the most basic principle of military science, an arrangement certain to produce chaos. The night before the general's departure for Manchuria, when he came to see me, the subject came up when he asked me, as a person he considered an expert on China and Japan, to advise him about the conduct of the war. I asked that he first give me his views.

He said that since we were not ready to engage in large-scale operations, he would retreat slowly toward Harbin, doing no more than slow the Japanese until our forces were at full strength. As for Port Arthur, by then under siege, it could hold out unaided for several months. Meanwhile a new army would be forming near Harbin. When our retreating troops joined it, he would take the offensive, destroy the Japanese forces, and conclude peace in Tokyo.*

I told him that the notion of concluding peace in Tokyo was nothing but a marvelous fantasy, because to do so we needed naval power and we didn't have it. However, I expressed approval of the rest since Japan was prepared for war and was close to the theater of war while we were not prepared for war and the bulk of our men and materiel was in Europe.

*How optimistic were our views then can be seen from the fact that the day war was declared, Kuropatkin told Vannovskii that we would require a ratio of two Russian soldiers for every three of the enemy in the theater of war, while Vannovskii argued that a ratio of one Russian to two Japanese would suffice! This from a war minister and a former war minister.

As he made ready to leave, Kuropatkin said: "Sergei Iulevich, as a person of great intellect, you can surely give me some farewell advice." I told him I could, but knew that he would not follow it. When he insisted on hearing it, I asked if he had complete confidence in the staff that would accompany him. After receiving reassurances that he had, I said:

> If I were you, as soon as I arrived in Mukden, I would send several of my officers to Admiral Alekseev's headquarters to arrest him and put him on the train on which I had arrived and have him sent back to Petersburg, under arrest. Given your prestige among the troops, I am sure that no one would protest. Also, I would send a telegram to the Emperor saying: "Your Majesty, in order to carry out the great task with which you have entrusted me, I have deemed it imperative to arrest the commander-in-chief and send him back to Petersburg, because otherwise victory would be impossible. Your Majesty, either have me shot for my insolent action or forgive me for the sake of the fatherland."

Kuropatkin burst out laughing and, as he left, said: "You are right."[3]

The next day General Kuropatkin left for Manchuria, with great pomp, as if he were certain of victory. It would have been more prudent if he had departed quietly and saved the pomp for a victorious return. Unfortunately, there was to be no victory to celebrate.

When he arrived in Manchuria, Kuropatkin wisely chose not to make Mukden his headquarters, but instead of locating them to the north of that city, he chose the south. And, instead of carrying out the plan he had described to me, he sent some forces to relieve Port Arthur, in deference to Admiral Alekseev's wishes. It was easy enough for the admiral, sitting in his luxurious office, to call for relieving the fortress by land, but where were the necessary forces? The fact is that Alekseev had no campaign plan. All he tried to do was anticipate the Emperor's wishes. And the Emperor, you see, still clung to the insane ideas of Bezobrazov and Co., that the Japanese were nothing but "baboons" who could easily be destroyed.

With good cause Kuropatkin considered Alekseev an utter nonentity, a land-lubber not a sailor, and, above all, a careerist. For his part, the admiral hated Kuropatkin and wished him nothing but misfortune. Both took their cases to Petersburg, each sending his own version of what had happened and of what should be done. But because Kuropatkin did not want a break with Alekseev, he compromised, while the latter took refuge behind orders from the Emperor, some of which he inspired.

Under these circumstances it was the capital that directed the fighting, a guarantee of failure, particularly when one has an Emperor who vacillates between calling for offensive and defensive action. After the war Kuropatkin showed me telegrams from Petersburg that proved that such vacillation was the real reason for the failure of the first part of the campaign. When he told me that he had been hampered by the interference of Petersburg in his conduct of operations and by being forced to accept unqualified generals, I told him that if he had made it clear immediately that he would not tolerate interference, as I had advised, and if he had failed, as one might expect with this Emperor, then he could have asked to be relieved of his command. By failing to act decisively, he had assumed responsibility for what followed.

I do not know the details of the first part of the campaign, so I cannot say with certainty that if there had been no division of command things would have taken a completely different turn, but I am certain that we would have been better off. The early setbacks in turn affected the second part of the campaign.

The Course of the War in 1904

The war, as I have said, began with the Japanese attack on Port Arthur. The chief events that followed during the remainder of the year were as follows.

On March 31, the battleship *Petropavlovsk* was sunk. With it went down part of the crew and the commander of our Far Eastern fleet, Admiral Makarov. The loss of this ship, on the heels of other naval losses, meant that our Far Eastern fleet was of no further use.

On land things went badly. On April 17–18 we lost the battle of Tiuerenchang (Chiu-lien-cheng). On April 28 the Japanese landed at Bidzivo (Pi-tzu-wo). This marked the beginning of the end for Port Arthur. A month later we lost more of our ships in a naval battle off Port Arthur. In August we suffered a major defeat at Liao-yang and began to retreat toward Mukden. In his order of the day Kuropatkin said we would not retreat another step. The year ended with the fall of Port Arthur.

Meanwhile the Emperor and Empress were seeing our troops off to the Far East, visiting cities throughout European Russia. In the course of these visits, they distributed icons, one of which pictured Serafim of Sarov. Given the fact that we were suffering defeats, General Dragomirov uttered a biting remark, which gained wide currency, that we were answering Japanese bullets with icons.

The Mood at Home

Against this background of defeat, the mood of opposition, which had already existed before the war, grew steadily. The masses, as well as the educated classes, were appalled by the lightmindedness with which we had entered the war and by the inadequacy of the military. The educated class was particularly rebellious and united almost as one under the slogan "It is impossible to live like this any longer; absolutism must be replaced by a government in which the educated and the masses have a voice." Even men like Prince Meshcherskii, publisher of *Grazhdanin*, and the prominent journalist Menshikov joined the cry. Both, staunch supporters of absolutism hitherto, told me with tears in their eyes that Russia would perish unless she were given a constitution.

Ominously, there was trouble in the army. Not only reservists, but regulars as well, who were en route to Manchuria would often refuse to obey orders, and their superiors would hide from them. Sometimes soldiers departing for the front ravaged railroad stations. One of the reasons for this lack of discipline was our lack of preparation for war. For days on end troops en route to Manchuria had to go without food or with inadequate food.

Meanwhile, workers were becoming more hostile toward their employers and the government. Some were now joining students in presenting demands to the government, all of this to the accompaniment of constant meetings at which revolutionary speeches were delivered. Revolutionary propaganda was being distributed in the army and in the countryside as well as in the cities. This revolutionary sentiment would continue to grow until October 17 [1905].

Plehve tried desperately to cope with the rapidly mounting revolutionary mood, but being no more than a dishonorable police type, despite his intelligence and cultivation, he could only conjure up measures in keeping with his police mentality, i.e., the use of fraud, e.g., the Zubatovshchina, or force. And to divert the minds of the masses he had raised the Jewish question in its most disgraceful form, a form that led to pogroms. Also, he used repressive tactics in dealing with disorders in the schools and with opposition among the educated classes.

It was obvious to me that the growing revolutionary mood would culminate in either a catastrophe or radical change, such as was to occur on October 17. Moreover, it was absolutely clear that, given the policies he followed, he was sure to be assassinated. Wherever he drove in his carriage he was guarded by police agents on bicycles, a form of protection so clumsy that his comings and going attracted widespread attention. And there were thousands of people who were ready to give up their lives for the privilege of killing a major official. A few months before his death I warned him that unless he changed his policies he would sooner or later be killed.[4]

The Russo-German Commercial Treaty of 1904

In the midst of the mounting turmoil I had to go to Germany to negotiate renewal of the commercial treaty I had negotiated with Germany in 1894.[5] I went at the request of His Majesty. Since my journey brought me indirectly in touch with Emperor William II, I want to digress to say a few words about his relations with our Emperor before returning to the negotiations.

When Nicholas II came to the throne, he did not take a kindly view of William II simply because that had been his father's view of this foppish and ostentatious man. This distaste was reinforced by our Emperor's resentment of the fact that the German Emperor was considered a more important personage than he, not only by foreigners but also by Russians. He was annoyed, too, that William II was a head taller than he. For that reason, postcards of the two clearly showing their difference in height were confiscated in Russia when they appeared, following the first meeting between the two.

Also contributing to our Emperor's unfriendly feeling toward William was the latter's manner toward Empress Alexandra Fedorovna and her brother, Ernest-Louis, Grand Duke of Hesse-Darmstadt. Emperor William sometimes treated our Empress as if she were still the little German Princess Alix he remembered from earlier years. As for the Grand Duke, William II tended to be quite unceremonious toward German princes and princesses, especially toward those he did not respect. Illustrative was an incident that occurred during maneuvers near Frankfurt, when William said to the Grand Duke: "I know how anxious you are to receive the Order of the Black Eagle, first class; if you can tell whether a hussar mounts his horse from the right or the left, I will confer it on you at once."

It was early in 1904 that Chancellor Bülow and the German ambassador to Petersburg complained to me that our Emperor had for some time ignored letters from their Emperor and had not acknowledged minor acts of kindness and marks of attention. Such behavior, they said, could not but affect relations between our two countries. Could I help? I suggested that it would help if their Emperor would be very attentive toward our Empress and her brother. The advice was heeded. William was especially kindly toward the Grand Duke during the latter's divorce from Grand Duchess Marie Aleksandrovna.[6]

As a result, our Empress's feeling toward William changed completely, and that change in turn influenced Emperor Nicholas II's attitude toward William, particularly after the latter came to realize that his didactic manner toward Nicholas was sure to produce resentment. Thereafter William affected the manner of a younger man toward an older one. (Emperor Nicholas II does not feel comfortable with men who are mentally or morally superior to him and feels at ease only with people he considers more poorly endowed than he, and that includes people who, knowing this weakness, act as if they were more poorly endowed.)

Thereafter correspondence between the two Emperors took on a friendlier tone and William began to exert a marked influence on our Emperor, directed toward undermining our relations with other powers, notably France. I learned about this from Count Lambsdorff, who sought to blunt William's influence. That was probably the reason William could not endure him. The count told me that if secret papers in his possession were ever published, they would create a sensation.*

*In his private archive, Count Lambsdorff had a large collection of piquant, highly secret unofficial and semi-official political papers, dating back to the early 1880s. When I asked him, shortly before his death, what he intended to do with these papers, he said that he wanted them handed over to his friend Prince Valerian Sergeevich Obolenskii after his death. The count, as we know, died recently, in San Remo, and was buried in Russia. Immediately after the funeral, His Majesty sent one of his generals-adjutant and an official from the foreign office to sort out Count Lambsdorff's papers, at which point Prince Obolenskii stepped in to indicate what Count Lambsdorff's wishes had been. He was permitted to assist in the sorting, but died a few days afterward. What will happen to these papers? One can expect that the more piquant ones will be destroyed, and with them will go many secrets.

To return to the negotiations. Profiting from my experience with the 1894 treaty, I began negotiations by letter many months before the expiration of the treaty. My position, approved of by the Emperor, was that the treaty should be renewed for another ten-year term with no change in its provisions. But Emperor William wanted the provisions to be based on the tariff recently passed by the Reichstag, which sharply raised duties, particularly on raw materials.

Although Germany had been informed that we would make no concessions, it was suddenly decided, apparently as a result of the intervention of the German Emperor, that the matter required the attention of a conference, of which I was to be chairman. The other members were Count Lambsdorff, Plehve, Kokovtsev (the recently appointed minister of finance), Grand Duke Alexander Mikhailovich (head of the Chief Administration of the Merchant Marine), and, if I remember correctly, General Sakharov and Admiral Avelan, director of the naval ministry. We gave particular attention to a statement from Emperor William addressed to our Emperor, that Germany badly needed to have the treaty based on the tariff. In that statement he attempted to coat the pill by assuring the Emperor that he need have no concern about his western frontiers for the duration of the war, one in which we were doing badly.

The Grand Duke insisted that we accept the German position, to prevent a strain in our relations. Plehve, sensing that the Grand Duke was speaking for the Emperor, argued that any losses suffered by our agriculture as a result of increased German duties could be made up by other means. Kokovtsev took a different tack: he argued that the reserve funds (which I had accumulated while minister of finance), now being used to finance the war, would soon be depleted. Therefore, he said, we should accept the German terms if we were assured access to the German money market when the time came to float a loan. Contradicting advice we were receiving from our ambassador to Berlin, Count Lambsdorff took the position that there was no compelling reason to give in to Germany. I said that to do so was against our economic interests, that if Germany insisted on raising duties levied against imports from Russia, we should retaliate, to maintain the existing balance of trade. But, I said, if we had to make concessions in order to float a loan or for political-strategic reasons, we should do so with a clear understanding of the economic costs.

The vote went in favor of concessions, provided we were assured of access to the German money market. Also, the conference recommended that the German guarantee of our western frontiers for the duration of the war and the question of German moral support be discussed further by the two monarchs, since such matters were in the realm of personal relations. The minutes of the conference (one copy of which is in my archive) were approved by the Emperor and given to me for my guidance in further negotiations.

As I have said, I had been negotiating by letter, but Chancellor Bülow, evidently at the request of Emperor William, decided on face-to-face negotiations because I was in charge for my country.[7] Because it was summer we decided to meet on the island of Nordeney. At the beginning of July, accompanied by Timiriazev, assistant minister of finance, I left for Germany. Among the chancellor's associates in the negotiations was Count Posadowsky, secretary of state for internal affairs, the only one of these associates who was notable for knowledge and industry. It was Posadowsky with whom I had most to do.

I spent two weeks at Nordeney, most of that time in the company of the chancellor, engaged during the day in official business and dining and chatting with him and his wife in the evening.

She was of Italian birth, had evidently once been very good-looking, was well educated and an accomplished musician. At this time she was reading a book about the Decembrists. She was fascinated by Count Leo Tolstoy and expected to find in me one of his devotees. But as much as I respected his talent as a writer, so much did I reject his political and religious teachings, which are nothing more than the product of a second childhood. He has not contributed a single new idea but has merely restated what the Gospels and the philosophers have already said, doing so in a talented and popular fashion. A great artist, a naive thinker, very much in love with himself.

When the chancellor and I were alone, we spoke mainly about the war. He told me that my dire predictions about the consequences of the taking of Kiaochow and Port Arthur were in a dossier which his Emperor had recently asked to see, to refresh his memory. He told me that my prediction had at first been treated skeptically, but that it had become evident that I had been right.[8]

Probably at Emperor William's behest, Bülow showed great interest in my views of the war. I said that I expected us to be defeated at sea, but that, even though I had no confidence in Kuropatkin, I expected that we would in the end prevail on land.

Bülow told me that William was doing all he could to be pleasant to my Emperor and that in recent times relations between the two monarchs had become very intimate because William had shown that he was a genuine friend to Russia.

Chancellor Bülow was obviously aware of the fact that I had argued forcefully for our position when negotiating the treaty of 1894 and seemed afraid that I might use sharp words this time, but I sensed that he was convinced that I would not break off negotiations this time, because he probably had had word from Petersburg that I was under instructions to conclude the treaty amicably. To be sure, we bargained a great deal, but our freedom of action was limited by the fact that we were at war and that consequently our western frontier was vulnerable.

As the talks neared the end, I said that I hoped we could count on the German money markets for floating loans once the terms of the treaty were settled. Bülow told me that he had no objections, but that his Emperor had recently said that he felt that only Germans should have access to the German money market and showed me several telegrams from Emperor William on the subject.

Once we had agreed on the terms, I suggested that we sign the treaty in Berlin and then departed. Bülow arrived there the next day. With the treaty on the table, ready for signature, I said I would not sign without official assurance that the

German money market would be open to us. At first he would not agree, but, seeing that I was determined, provided me with his Emperor's commitment within a short time, and I signed the treaty. (William was sailing in the waters off Norway at this time and Bülow was in daily telegraphic communication with him. On my arrival in Berlin and at the conclusion of the negotiations, I received kindly telegrams from Emperor William.)

My impression of Bülow was that he is not a bad sort, is not particularly industrious or clever, but is able to speak well. His chief trait as a diplomatist is his slyness, in the good sense of the word, if you will, and the chief use he makes of it is in dealing with his Emperor. Knowing his Sovereign's weaknesses, he makes good use of them, but in the process he often pockets not only his personal pride, but also the dignity befitting a first minister. Obviously he is no Bismarck, nor can he even be compared to the straightforward and honorable Caprivi. He can best be compared to Count M. N. Muravev, who died while serving as our foreign minister, but is a more intelligent and far better educated man. All in all, I consider Bülow to be a second-rate political figure.[9]

While I was still in Berlin I received a letter from Actual State Councillor Rutkovskii, the finance ministry's agent in London. Accompanying it was a report to our ambassador concerning a proposal for peace negotiations from Hayashi, the Japanese ambassador to England. This proposal, transmitted through a former German diplomat living in London, suggested that on my way back to Russia I meet with Hayashi to discuss possible terms of peace, while Port Arthur was still holding out, implying that if negotiations were conducted after the fall of Port Arthur, the Japanese terms would be harsher.

This was a most opportune time to end the awful war. I should note here that it was about this time that General Kondratenko, the hero of Port Arthur, had the courage to ask General Stössel to write frankly to the Emperor about the true state of affairs and to recommend that Russia should begin peace negotiations so as to avoid great misfortune.

Had I been authorized to negotiate at the time, we would have been forced to give up the Kwantung region, including Port Arthur, as we had to later, but we would have been able to retain the southern branch of the Chinese Eastern Railroad and all of Sakhalin Island. Most important of all, we would have been spared the shame of Liaoyang, Mukden, and Tsushima. But I received no authorization.

On July 6, as I was walking on Unter den Linden, past our embassy, I learned that Plehve had been assassinated by Sazonov on the preceding day.[10] Who would replace him?

IV

The "Political Spring" and Bloody Sunday

The Hayashi Proposal

After my return to Petersburg, Count Lambsdorff told me that His Majesty had been given the report on the Hayashi proposal but had not acted on it. When [on July 21] I reported to the Emperor, he thanked me, coldly, for negotiating renewal of the treaty with Germany, but he made no reference to the proposal because I was out of favor and he would not talk to me about affairs of state. I left immediately for my summer home, in Sochi, in the Caucasus.[1]

The New Minister of Interior

With Plehve dead, intrigue began about a successor. Some recommended Stürmer, director of the Department of General Affairs of the Ministry of Interior, and, in fact, he was presented to the Emperor. What they talked about I do not know. Others suggested General von Wahl, assistant minister of the interior.[2] In the end the Emperor settled on Prince P. D. Sviatopolk-Mirskii, largely because of the influence of Mme. E. G. Milashevich (Gendov), who had been married to Vladimir Alekseevich Sheremetev, commander of Emperor Alexander III's convoy. Because she had spent much time with our present Emperor while he was Heir, she had come to be on good terms with him and thus was able to exercise some influence on this occasion.[3]

Prince P. D. Sviatopolk-Mirskii was born in the Caucasus, where his father, a general, earned a reputation for courage. The prince is a rare soul—a man of the highest principles, an intelligent and cultivated general staff officer. His intentions are good, but he is physically frail, is not a firm administrator, and did not have adequate experience for the task he was given.

Early on he served as district marshal of the nobility in the province of Kharkov. He went on to become governor of Penza. In 1900, while Sipiagin was minister of interior, he was named assistant minister in charge of the Department of Police and the Corps of Gendarmes. This appointment did Sipiagin proud, because this post was rarely filled by someone who was above reproach.

When Sipiagin began to adopt measures that enflamed public opinion, Mirskii wanted to leave his post, but decided to stay on because he and the minister were close friends. Illustrative of the spirit of the time was the fact that a man so eminent as Prince L. D. Viazemskii—a very rich man, a former head of the appanages, a general who had been wounded in the war with Turkey—was exiled to his estate for protesting against police brutality in connection with the disorders at Kazan Square.[4] I told Sipiagin, in the presence of his wife, that such measures as exiling Prince Viazemskii would only alienate men of good will, without ending disorder. But he defended himself, adding: "If you only knew what the Emperor demands of me: he thinks I am too weak."

When Plehve succeeded Sipiagin, Mirskii, knowing what the new minister represented, told him straight out that he could not serve under him and wished to leave. Plehve tried to dissuade him, telling Mirskii candidly that his departure would produce an unfavorable impression, would be taken to mean that an honorable man such as Mirskii would not serve under him. Would he not stay on, for a brief period at least? Mirskii refused, but was persuaded to accept the post of governor-general of Vilna, the post he occupied at Plehve's death.

Obviously, his appointment to succeed Plehve was taken as a sign of change. Mirskii confirmed that impression on assuming office, when he asserted that the country should be governed on the basis of confidence in society (*obshchestvo*),[5] a view that he repeated to a deputation that called on him, and one which quickly became the slogan of the day. He expressed himself in the same vein, but with some embellishments, in an interview with a foreign correspondent. When I read about it, I thought to myself that it would do Mirskii no good. I was right, as I learned from letters sent to me while I was still in Sochi telling me that the Emperor was unhappy over the interview.

For some reason, Mirskii thought that I should have been the person to replace Plehve. At least that is what I gathered from the telegram he sent me at the time of his appointment, in which he justified his acceptance of the post. In my reply I expressed my deepest and most sincere approval of his appointment.

Unfortunately, he assumed office at a time when revolutionary ferment had reached the stage when, because of domestic developments and military setbacks, it was not longer possible for one in his position to effect change,[6] all the more so because the Emperor continued to listen to the advice of extreme reactionaries. It is evident that even if Mirskii had a firmer will and more experience than he had, he would not have been a suitable minister of interior for the circumstances under which he took office.

Since I was on friendly terms with him, I called on him when I returned to Petersburg, in October. When I asked him about the Emperor's attitude toward his policies, he told me that when he was offered the post, he tried to decline, on the grounds that he had a conception of the course to be followed with which His Majesty might not agree, adding that he did not feel qualified for the post and that, moreover, his health was not up to the demands of a position such as that of minister of interior. In explaining the course that he felt must be followed, he told His Majesty that in his view the long-simmering conflict between government and society had been brought to a head by the unfortunate war and that it had to be resolved. He felt reconciliation between the two could be achieved only by satisfying the considered and justifiable desires of society. Also, the legitimate desires of non-Russians should be satisfied.

Mirskii told me that His Majesty insisted that he take the position, assuring him that he shared his views of what had to be done and would see to it that he would encounter no difficulties in following the course he had set. Mirskii believed him. In addition the Emperor promised Mirskii several months of rest each year.

It was around the time of my conversation with Mirskii that the so-called congress of public men[7] was scheduled to meet. It was to consist of zemstvo members, members of municipal dumas, certain politicos (Miliukov, Hessen, Nabokov, et al.),[8] who were later to lead the so-called Kadets. Many of those who were to participate in the congress have since moved to the far right, but in those days all educated people, including the so-called *intelligenty*, with few exceptions, were at war with the bureaucracy and demanded radical change. When asked what they meant by bureaucracy, they privately said "the unlimited supreme power" [absolute monarchy], which they could not say in print because of censorship and repression.

Plehve had prohibited such meetings because it was known that they would call for a constitution, but such meetings were held secretly, in private dwellings, and what they decided later became public. Now the public men were asking Mirskii for permission to meet openly and he had agreed, provided that they accept certain conditions, among them that they meet in Petersburg.

I told Mirskii that by granting permission he was opening the door to unpleasant consequences because, in one way or another, the congress would demand a constitution and their demand would certainly be rejected. Rejection, I noted, would thwart the aim of reconciling government and society by creating even greater antagonism between the two. And so it was to happen.

When he asked me if I would support him in his efforts, I said that I would do what I could, but that given the Emperor's feelings toward me, what I thought was of no practical consequence. I assured him that if the Emperor were to summon a conference, I would express myself with complete candor because that is what I always did, with no concern about whether or not my views pleased the Emperor or the others at the meeting.

The Search for My Pamphlet
on Far Eastern Events

Not long after my return from Sochi, an official of the Ministry of Interior told me that the Department of Police was busily hunting for a pamphlet that I was supposed to have written about events leading to the war. Several days later, when I saw Mirskii, I asked just what this pamphlet was. He was taken aback by the question, saying that he had no idea.

The next day he came to see me and told me that, without his permission, General Hesse, the palace commandant, had given Lopukhin, the director of the Department of Police, an order from the Emperor directing him to find a pamphlet that I had written about our Far Eastern policy. He told me that the department had learned that such a pamphlet had been printed by the Ministry of Finance but could find no more than a few corrected pages from that publication. Mirskii showed me the pages, adding that he had expressed his displeasure to Lopukhin for acting without his knowledge.[9]

Realizing now what the object of the search had been, I burst out laughing. It was a pamphlet, of an academic character, written in official style, that had been prepared by the Chancellery of the Ministry of Finance while I was still minister, a pamphlet documenting our Far Eastern policy from 1900 to 1902. It was the practice of the ministry to prepare such documentation concerning important events and projects in which the ministry was involved. Under ordinary circumstances copies of it would be distributed.* But by the time the pamphlet was printed, it was clear to me that war was inevitable, and therefore, although it contained no secrets and was of an innocent character, I felt that if the facts became public knowledge, the people responsible for the madness leading to the war would be harmed. With this thought in mind I had all but a few copies, to be retained for my personal use, destroyed.

I went to a bookcase, took out a copy of the pamphlet, and handed it to Mirskii, asking that he give it to the Emperor the next time he saw him and to tell him that Lopukhin could call off his search. I asked, too, that he tell His Majesty that I regretted that he had not asked me directly for a copy.

When I next saw Mirskii I asked if he had done what I requested. He had. And what had the Emperor said? Nothing, except to ask if it were true that copies of the pamphlet had not been distributed. Mirskii said that the fact that the Department of Police, after much effort, had been unable to find it was the proof.

Events in the Far East

It was now October, and as I have noted earlier, the war was going badly for us. Admiral Alekseev and the court camarilla were trying to blame the war on me, and articles in this vein began to appear in the newspapers, notably *Moskovskie vedomosti*.

*The pamphlet appears as an appendix to my history of the origins of the Russo-Japanese war.

By this time the conflict between General Kuropatkin and Admiral Alekseev had reached such a point that the admiral had to be recalled, leaving the post of commander-in-chief to Kuropatkin. Whatever faith, a faith perhaps based on wishful thinking, that I might have had in Kuropatkin was gone, and I found myself thinking of A. A. Abaza's prophetic words about Kuropatkin, that he was a "clever general, a brave general, but with the soul of a staff clerk."[10] When General Kuropatkin retreated according to plan I was not upset, but I was disturbed when the plan called for advance and he retreated under pressure, and with heavy casualties.

Reluctantly I came to the conclusion that the war was lost. So I began to urge that we negotiate for peace, but with no success. The evidence that we had lost had to be much more convincing before those in high places were ready to begin to negotiate.

The Decree of December 12, 1904

As soon as he became minister, Mirskii began to exert a liberal influence on the Emperor, or, to be more precise, he began to try to get the Emperor to pursue a sensible course, for there was nothing about Mirskii's origins, his career, or his way of thinking that justified calling him a liberal. He was simply an intelligent, honorable, sensible, and loyal servant to the Emperor.

Late in November, as a first step in achieving the changes he had in mind, Mirskii appended to the report he gave to the Emperor the draft of a decree providing for various ameliorative measures, among them the addition of elected members to the State Council and the granting of complete freedom of religion to the Old Believers. The report and the draft were in fact the work of Kryzhanovskii, an official in the Ministry of Interior, who was acting under the influence of Prince A. D. Obolenskii.[11] (Obolenskii is an intelligent and well-intentioned Dobchinskii,[12] who sticks his nose into everything, expressing ideas that are not stupid but that, for the most part, are the expressions of a restless and basically neurasthenic soul.) No one spoke about the report at the time or knew anything about it then, but after Mirskii's departure Prince Obolenskii gave me a copy of it, which is now in my archive.[13]

To consider Prince Mirskii's recommendations, the Emperor called a conference to which he invited all the ministers, as well as Budberg (director of the Commission of Petitions), General-Adjutant Richter, Count Vorontsov-Dashkov, Count Solskii, E. V. Frisch, Baron Nolde (director of the Chancellery of the Committee of Ministers), and me. Prince Obolenskii told me that the Emperor had not wanted to invite me but was persuaded to change his mind by Mirskii.[14] At the time I received the invitation I did not know exactly what would be discussed at the conference.

In opening the deliberations His Majesty stated that, given the mounting revolutionary spirit, he had summoned us to consider whether to take steps to meet the wishes of that part of society that was moderate and well intentioned or to continue with the reactionary policies that had led to the deaths of Sipiagin and Plehve.[15] That he should even raise such a question showed how far he had moved in his political outlook.

In the past when I used the term "public opinion" in reports, he would ask in anger: "How does public opinion concern me?" Justifiably, he believed that what was called public opinion was really the opinion of the *intelligenty*. And what he thought of them was related to me by Mirskii, who as governor-general of Vilna had accompanied the Emperor through the provinces under his jurisdiction. At one stop, when someone uttered the word *intelligenty*, the Emperor said: "How I dislike that word" and added, undoubtedly in jest, that the Academy of Sciences should be directed to expunge the word from the language.

His Majesty was constantly being told that the common people, i.e, all of the non-intelligentsia, were for him. It is true that the people are always for a tsar who is on their side. But one cannot expect the people to be loyal to a tsar who rules through a "court-nobility camarilla" which considers itself the salt of the Russian earth, for which everything is done, and through which everything should be done.

The Emperor could have retained the loyalty of the people if, after the Treaty of Portsmouth, he had, on his own initiative, enacted a broad reform in the spirit of Alexander II for the benefit of the peasantry or had boldly taken a stand in favor of complete religious toleration, for example, had lifted all the limitations on the Old Believers and had removed the manifestly unjust restrictions on non-Russians. Had he done so, there would have been no need for the Manifesto of October 17,[16] for it is a general rule that if a government refuses to meet the demands of the people for economic and social reforms, the people will begin to demand changes in the political structure. And if a government does not meet such demands and at the same time engages in such madness as the war with Japan, revolution will break out.

Unfortunately, the Emperor, while failing to meet the demands of the people, would continue to believe that the people were behind him. In this he has been abetted by Empress Alexandra Fedorovna, who, since she directs him, is more responsible than anyone else for the fact that her husband's reign has been unfortunate for him and for Russia.* Illustrative of her conviction that the people were solidly behind her husband was her reply to Mirskii when he told her that all Russia was against the existing order. As he told me, she said in anger: "Yes, the intelligentsia is against the Tsar and his government, but the people as a whole support him and will continue to do so." To which Mirskii responded: "Yes, but the intelligentsia is a creative force, while the people are an elemental force: today

*May God grant that what is to come not be for the worse, especially for him. I, who know the Emperor since he was a youth, love him warmly and sincerely as a person. If I am angry at him, it is because I am disappointed in him, in the fact that he harms himself, his dynasty, his country, when he could have followed a different course.

the people could slaughter the intelligentsia in the name of the Tsar, but tomorrow they could destroy his palaces.''

To return now to the conference, which conducted its work without any prepared material before it.

I was the first to speak following the Emperor's introductory remarks. I said that it was impossible to continue with a reactionary policy, for to do so would lead to disaster. I was supported by Count Solskii, Frisch, Ermolov, Muravev, and Kokovtsev. Frisch and Muravev spoke of the need to restore legality [rule of law], which had been badly violated. Kokovtsev supported me in the sense of arguing that if we did not change our domestic policy foreign bankers would lose confidence in us and that might spell financial disaster, given the fact that we were doing badly in the war. Others spoke of the need to end the harsh restrictions on the Old Believers and, in general, of the need for complete religious toleration. Still others spoke of the need to broaden the powers and scope of the zemstvos and municipal dumas. Pobedonostsev was critical of those who urged reform, but he was equivocal, suggesting that it was best to do nothing. Baron Nolde said nothing because of his position. Prince Mirskii hardly spoke up, evidently because he had already presented his views to the Emperor.

Most of the discussion thereafter centered on Mirskii's proposal to add elected representatives to the State Council. The majority supported him, but Pobedonostsev opposed him, speaking intelligently as always, making some good, critical points, but vague in his conclusions. I did not speak to this subject until called upon by the Emperor. I stated that the existing political structure did not meet the needs of the state and, moreover, was in conflict with the views of all educated people and that therefore I supported the proposal. However, I went on to warn against accepting the view that the fundamental nature of the state would not be changed if the proposal became law. I was not implying, I said, that those who advanced such a view were disingenuous, but I was convinced that any properly organized system of participation in the legislative process by elected representatives must lead to what is usually called a constitution.

As usually happens at meetings working without prepared materials and presided over by the Emperor, no specific recommendations were made. However, at the conclusion of the session His Majesty expressed agreement with the opinions of the majority and empowered me, as chairman of the Committee of Ministers, and Baron Nolde to prepare a draft of a decree embodying what had been proposed at the session. Also, since such a decree would require changes in existing law, the Committee of Ministers was charged with recommending the changes that would be required. It was advised that it ask for instructions from the Emperor when necessary.

I and Baron Nolde then prepared a draft, which was submitted to the conference on the following day.[17] Pobedonostsev said neither yea nor nay. The others, except for Count Vorontsov-Dashkov and General-Adjutant Richter, supported it. These two objected to the wording of the point in the decree about elected representatives.[18] Because of the absence of unanimity, the Emperor called another session, which took place on either December 6 or 7. There the draft was edited and signed by all, as I recall, although it is possible that Pobedonostsev, who created difficulties, refused to sign.

Most of the participants were exhilarated by the thought that His Majesty was good enough to permit the adoption of a new direction for our great motherland. At the end of the conference, the aged Count Solskii, speaking for us all, in a heartfelt tone, thanked the Emperor on our behalf for taking the initiative that he had taken. He added that all Russia would share this feeling. The scene was so moving that several, notably Ermolov and Prince Khilkov, wept.

On the morning of December 11, I received a note from the Emperor asking me to see him that evening. That evening I took the train to Tsarskoe Selo and was received by His Majesty, as usual, in his study, where I found Grand Duke Sergei Aleksandrovich, the Emperor's brother-in-law, also present.[19] His Majesty asked me to sit down. After we were seated, he told me that he had changed the third point of the proposed decree concerning the participation of elected public men in the legislative process: they would be selected by the administration rather than be elected. What did I think?[20]

I replied that I approved of the decree in essence and felt that the time had come to implement it. But, since I was being asked for my advice, I had to state once more, in all conscience, that the admission of representatives, particularly elected ones, to legislative institutions was the first step toward representative, i.e., constitutional, government, for which all civilized countries were instinctively striving. Surely this first, modest step on the road toward constitutionalism would be followed by others. Therefore, I continued, my advice was to retain point three if His Majesty had come to the irrevocable conclusion that it was impossible to go against world history, but if he felt that the representative form of government was so intolerable that he could never resign himself to it, then, as an act of prudence, he should delete point three.*

After hearing me out, His Majesty looked at the Grand Duke, who was obviously pleased by my answer, and said: "I will never agree to the representative form of government because I consider it harmful to the people whom God has entrusted to me; consequently, I will follow your advice and eliminate this point." At that he rose and thanked me profusely. I took my leave and returned to Petersburg with the amended decree. I was never to see the Grand Duke again.

Since this decree (dated December 12, 1904) "Concerning Plans for the Improvement of the Social Order" can be found in *Sobranie uzakonenii* (Collection of Laws), I shall not give the text here.

On December 12, during a session of the Special Conference on the Needs of Rural Industry at which Prince Mirskii was present, I sent him a note telling him

---

*During the course of this conversation, the talk turned to *zemskie sobory*. I said that they belonged to the venerable past and could not be used in our times, given the present makeup of Russia, her relations with other countries, the level of her self-awareness (*samoznanie*) and education. I said that, on the whole, the ideas of the sixteenth and twentieth centuries were quite incompatible.[21]

that the decree, minus the point at issue, had been signed. This news obviously disturbed him. After the meeting I told him in detail what had happened.

As the year 1904 drew to a close, rebellion was on the minds of all levels of society. The mood became even more intense at the news of such shameful disasters as the surrender of Port Arthur. The focal point of rebellion, or, as it is now customary to call it, the revolutionary movement, was Moscow, whose governor-general was Grand Duke Sergei Aleksandrovich, who, as I have said earlier, was a good man at heart, but a very limited, stubborn, and reactionary man. To make matters worse, he was surrounded by equally limited individuals, notably General Trepov, the police superintendent, who followed in the tradition of an earlier police superintendent, Vlasovskii, of Khodynka "fame." All levels of society were deeply embittered by the Grand Duke's (or rather General Trepov's) policies, resulting in an untenable situation. Because the Grand Duke received no support at all from Mirskii, he gave up the post of governor-general on January 1, 1905, but retained command of the Moscow Military District.

Even without the provision for elected representatives, the decree of December 12 might have blunted the revolutionary mood if it had been implemented quickly, fully, and, most importantly, sincerely. Unfortunately, that was not to be the case, and, as will be seen, the decree not only failed to mollify society but in fact antagonized it, because society, for the most part, soon became aware that they [the powers that be] wanted to rescind what had been given.

The Blessing of the Waters Incident

On January 6, 1905, a near-catastrophe occurred. On that day the Emperor, accompanied by members of the clergy and his suite, were in a summer house outside the Winter Palace at the river's edge to watch the traditional blessing of the waters by the metropolitan. After this sacred rite was completed, cannon at the Fortress of SS. Peter and Paul, across the river, fired the traditional salute, but this time one of the cannon fired live ammunition, not the customary blank shot. Had the live ammunition hit the summer house, the results would have been tragic.

The resulting inquiry disclosed that use of live ammunition was the result of an oversight. With his customary indulgence toward the military caste, the Emperor treated those responsible mildly. Although he regarded it as an accident and did not attach any importance to it, many, at various levels of society, thought it was deliberate, intended either to alarm him or to kill him.

The Bloody Day of January 9

Three days later, on Sunday, January 9, there occurred the well-known march under the leadership of Father Gapon. The tragic events of that day were the consequences of that misguided effort known as the Zubatovshchina, to which I have referred earlier. After Zubatov was transferred to Petersburg, he helped establish a workers' association which came under the leadership of the priest Father Gapon, in whom Plehve, as well as the prefect of Petersburg, General Fullon, had complete confidence.

The general had been appointed to succeed Kleigels solely because of his friendship with General Hesse, with whose help he had at first enjoyed the Emperor's favor. The general is a well-bred, very decent, gentle man but he lacks the temperament and character to be in police work. He would have been more suitable as a director of a young ladies institute. It is small wonder that he should have complete faith in Gapon and his organization. That faith continued even after Plehve's death.

I had predicted that the time would come when the Zubatov organizations would throw off police direction and adopt some form of socialist struggle against the capitalists, i.e., they would resort to force and would become a danger to the social fabric. Unfortunately, I was correct.

As early as 1903, when the seditious and revolutionary mood was beginning to affect both high and low, it was natural that the Zubatov workers' associations, including the one led by Father Gapon, should have been caught up by this mood. Father Gapon could not have stood up against it even if he had wanted to, but there were few in those days who did not seem to have become infected by the madness sweeping Russia, with so many demanding the reconstruction of the Russian Empire on the basis of extreme democratic principles. If hitherto conservative journalists like Prince Meshcherskii and Menshikov could be espousing such ideas at this time, it is small wonder that Father Gapon could not, or would not, resist being affected by such ideas.

Under his leadership his workers' association, during the first week of January, prepared a petition that consisted in part of requests, in part of what might be called demands. Of course the demands were extremely one-sided and exaggerated and not without a certain revolutionary tinge, although they were couched in respectful language. A plan was prepared whereby thousands of workers, led by Father Gapon, would march to Palace Square on Sunday, January 9, bow to the Emperor, hand him their petition, and quietly disperse.

The Emperor could have chosen to be there and to accept the petition, but had he wished to do so and had I been asked for my advice, I would have advised him not to meet the marchers. I would have suggested that Mirskii or one of his generals-adjutant be there to accept the petition, tell the crowd that it would be studied and acted upon, one way or another, and, having said this, tell the crowd to disperse. Also, I would have advised that if the workers refused to leave, force be used to make them do so. However, the Emperor was to follow a different course.

For days General Fullon was completely in the dark about what was being planned. When he learned about it, he assured Mirskii that nothing serious would come of it. The minister was of course aware of how inadequate Fullon was, but because he himself was weak, he did nothing.

Father Gapon did make an effort to see the minister of justice, Muravev, and the minister of interior. I do not know whether he was received, but I do know that they were given copies of his petition. I, too, in my capacity as chairman of the Committee of Ministers, received a copy, which was sent to my home. I should note that since my departure from the office of minister of finance I had virtually no information about what the Zubatov organizations were doing, but my successors, Pleske and Kokovtsev, certainly had such information.

On January 8, I had some business with Muravev. As we parted, he remarked that we would be meeting again that evening.[22] When I asked where it was that we would be meeting, he said that it would be at Mirskii's place, to consider what to do about the proposed march. When I told him that I had not been invited, he said: "Of course you will be invited: I told Mirskii that it was important to invite you because you have a good knowledge of the labor question and have been in contact with workers all your life." But I received no invitation. I was told that Kokovtsev had asked Mirskii not to invite me because I would surely take the workers' side.

That evening at my house I received a delegation of men who had asked to see me, on what they said was a matter of greatest importance. I was not acquainted with any of them,[23] but I recognized Honorary Academician Arsenev and the writers Annenskii and Gorky from their pictures. They urged me to try to persuade the Emperor to appear before the workers and accept their petition. I told them in my position there was nothing I could do. They charged me with relying on a formalistic argument and left in an angry mood. As soon as they were gone, I phoned Mirskii about their visit.[24]

As I learned later, at the meeting at Mirskii's, in which a representative from the Ministry of War participated, it was decided to prevent the workers from reaching Palace Square by intercepting their columns at designated points, where they would be told to turn back and that if they would not obey they would be dispersed by force. Also, it was decided that the petition would not be accepted.

On the morning of January 9, just after I got up, I looked out of my window and saw a crowd of workers, *intelligenty*, women, and children marching along Kamenno-Ostrovskii Prospekt, carrying church banners, pictures, and flags. As soon as this crowd, or, rather, procession, passed by, I went to my balcony, from which I could see Troitskii Bridge, toward which they were marching. I got to the balcony just in time to hear shots, a few of which whizzed close by. One of these killed a porter at nearby Tsarskoe Selo Lycée. Then came a series of salvoes. Within ten minutes a large crowd came running back, some of them carrying dead and wounded, among them children. What happened at Troitskii Bridge and at other points was this: as planned, the columns of marchers were intercepted at designated points by military units and warned that if they did not turn back they would be shot. But the marchers would not believe that the military were in earnest and pushed on. They were, of course, fired on, and, as far as I can recollect, over two hundred were killed or wounded.[25] As for Gapon, he went into hiding, then fled the country. Thus the first blood, in great quantity, of the so-called Russian Revolution of 1905 was spilled.

This episode was most unpleasant and, in my opinion, badly handled. What made matters worse was that the accounts of what happened were exaggerated: all over Russia it was said that thousands had been killed, only because they wanted to present a petition, describing their difficult lives, to the Emperor. Naturally, the revolutionary leaders used the events of that day to further arouse the people. But even among reasonable people this episode created a most unpleasant impression.

This Gaponian catastrophe produced unrest not only in society, but also within the ranks of the government. Everyone began to criticize Mirskii, accusing him of weakness. Despite my respect and friendly feelings for him, I cannot deny that he behaved ineffectually in this case by placing his trust in General Fullon, a man even weaker than he.

Trepov, Mirskii, and Bulygin

The popular reaction to the Gaponian catastrophe spurred the powers-that-be to look for a strong man to restore order. That man was Trepov.

As I have noted, Grand Duke Sergei Aleksandrovich gave up his position as governor-general on January 1. It goes without saying that Trepov, who had been governor-general in all but name, could not stay on as police superintendent. He left very dramatically, declaring that he could not continue to serve under this minister of interior, whose views he did not share.

A former Horse Guards officer, General Trepov announced that he wished to go to Manchuria to take part in the fighting and would accept a command, which would have to be at the very least command of a brigade. But while waiting for an offer, he went to Petersburg to see if he could get a major appointment in the capital through his connections, of whom the chief was Baron Freedericksz, who had once commanded the Horse Guards.

The baron believed that the highest credential a man could have was to have served with the Horse Guards, particularly when he was in command. As a result, the highest positions in the Ministry of the Imperial Court were filled by former Horse Guards officers, men such as General à la Suite Mosolov, who happened to be Trepov's brother-in-law, and Prince V. N. Orlov.

Trepov let it be known through his connections that a man such as he—strong, decisive, dependable, and loyal—should not be overlooked in such troubled times, for he was especially well suited for the task of combatting disorder, sedition, and revolution. He would show them "where the crayfish winter." Baron Freedericksz was easily convinced that only a gallant alumnus of the Horse Guards such as Trepov could carry out the necessary task of reestablishing respect for order among the subjects of the Emperor.

A few days after the Gaponian catastrophe, the post of temporary governor-general of Petersburg was created and Trepov was named to it, on the recommendation and insistence of Baron Freedericksz and with the help of former regimental comrades. In addition, he was assigned quarters in the Winter Palace.

Why did the Emperor accept the baron's suggestions? In the first place, because with Mirskii's prestige battered, it was only natural for him to choose a man such as Trepov, whose views were opposed to those of Mirskii. For you see the Emperor continually swings from one position to another. His entire system of governing, if one can call it such, is to seesaw. A second reason for the Emperor's decision was that he was impressed by Trepov's manner and appearance, that of a gallant officer with piercing eyes and simple, straightforward, soldierly speech, the speech of a political ignoramus for whom everything is simple and clear. And simple and clear answers, rather than the woolly ideas of the intelligentsia, are what the Emperor prefers.

What sort of a man was Trepov? Prince Urusov would later call him "a sergeant major by training and a *pogromshchik* by conviction." But a human being cannot be disposed of in a phrase or even in several pages. There is no scoundrel who has never had a decent thought or who has never performed a decent deed. And there is no man so honorable or noble, except a saint, who has never had an ignoble thought, or who has never committed a vile act, given the right circumstances. Also, there is no fool who has never said anything wise and no wise man who has never said anything foolish.

To explain a man fully one must tell the story of his life, because every characterization of an individual is no more than a sketchy outline. A sketch may suffice for one who knows the person and can fill in the rest through his imagination and knowledge, but for one who does not know the person, a sketch leaves only a skimpy, and often distorted, impression.

It is fair to say that Trepov was "a sergeant major by training," and that was Russia's misfortune. A product of the Corps des Pages, he probably never read a serious book in its entirety. He received his real education in the barracks and officers' club of the Horse Guards, primarily the former, because being a serious soldier and an honorable officer he suffered no harm from the latter. His first contact with political life was when he became police superintendent in Moscow.

To Trepov, as to every ignoramus, everything seemed simple: if people riot, you beat them; if people are free thinkers, you take them in hand; if workers are attracted by the revolutionary movement, you divert them to your side by acting as a policeman-revolutionary. For the likes of Trepov there are no complex questions, for such questions are the inventions of *intelligenty*, "kikes," and Freemasons. All one has to do is to be guided by one's judgment and that led to . . . a cesspool.

"A *pogromshchik* by conviction"? Hardly. But he accepted the use of pogroms when he, "a sergeant major by training," saw them as necessary to defend the state as he, with his mind, understood its needs. But was he the only one to take such an attitude toward this bloody political game? Was Plehve opposed to teaching the "kikes" a lesson at Kishinev, Gomel, and elsewhere? And did not the

Counts Ignatev think likewise? And do not the Black Hundreds, the so-called Union of the Russian People, openly preach violence against "kikes," and does not the Emperor invite us to rally under the banner of this party of rabid fools?

Such then was Trepov.

Given the change in policy represented by the appointment of Trepov, Mirskii felt obliged to leave a week after the appointment.[26] When he presented himself to the Emperor to take his leave, he was kindly received, but he was not given the appointment to the State Council customarily given to departing ministers. However, he was given the impression that he would fill the post in the Caucasus that Prince Golitsyn had recently vacated, but that did not happen.

As soon as Prince Mirskii left office, he was subjected to abuse from the extreme right—that he was a Pole, a friend of the "kikes," a traitor whose policies had opened the door to revolution. In short he was showered with all the sewage from all the cesspools that represent the minds, hearts, and consciences of the self-styled "true Russian people," led by that petty swindler Dubrovin.

Mirskii left Petersburg, to spend the next eighteen months or so at his estate or abroad. On his return to Russia, in August 1906, he asked by virtue of his title of general-adjutant to be presented to the Emperor and Empress but was refused. He thereupon asked permission to leave the service. At that both Baron Freedericksz and Premier Stolypin intervened. Their Majesties received Mirskii and, as is usual in such cases, were very pleasant to him, as if nothing untoward had happened.

Since leaving office Mirskii has avoided politics and lived the usual life of a member of high society. But if he is asked for his opinion on a political question he answers candidly. For example, when I spoke to him once about the sad, if not terrible, state of affairs in our country, he said that the trouble came from the fact that we lived under a vacillating and untrustworthy ruler.

Because he enjoyed great favor at court, Trepov was able to decide who would be the next minister of interior. On his recommendation, Bulygin, who had been assistant to Grand Duke Sergei Aleksandrovich, received the appointment.

Bulygin is a very decent man, far from stupid, a man with a broad knowledge of statecraft, but a placid personality who dislikes unpleasant situations of any kind. Such a man suited Trepov, who took over control of the principal and controversial business of the ministry, relegating secondary and noncontroversial business to Bulygin.[27] Naturally, only someone with Bulygin's great store of apathy could endure such a situation and put a good face on it. Often, when he was asked about business of his ministry, he would calmly reply: "I don't know, they haven't spoken to me about it" or "I just read about it in the newspapers." Being an honorable man he did not approve of Trepov's erratic policies, but he did not quarrel with the man who was nominally his subordinate. As long as the Emperor was willing to keep him on, he was content to sit events out placidly, learning about what was going on from the newspapers, devoting his time to administrative details and, when the time came, to preparing a bill to establish a state duma.

It was Trepov who in fact controlled the Ministry of Interior. It could be said that Trepov became dictator, in fact, if not in name, because of his power over the Ministry of Interior and, even more so, because of the favor he enjoyed at court. He was in special favor with Grand Duchess Elizabeth Fedorovna, the Empress's sister. The Grand Duchess, a very worthy but exceedingly unhappy woman, looked kindly at Trepov because of his long service under her husband, Grand Duke Sergei Aleksandrovich. Her attitude disposed the Empress to be favorably disposed to Trepov. And the Empress's favorable feelings in turn reinforced those of the Emperor, who would for some time enjoy a honeymoon relationship with the quasi-dictator.

Trepov was also helped by his friends Baron Freedericksz, General Mosolov, and Prince Orlov. The baron, as we know, had too dim a mind to evaluate what Trepov was doing and therefore had to rely on Mosolov, a clever man who was able to convince him that what the quasi-dictator wanted was what was needed. And Prince Orlov, as unpaid chauffeur[28] to Their Majesties, was very close to the Empress; a nice man, but utterly incompetent, yet sometimes an intimate adviser or, if necessary, an informer. It was gentlemen such as Mosolov and Orlov who served as Trepov's messenger boys in communicating with the Emperor. It was not long before Trepov had the Emperor under his thumb, communicating with him almost daily on all sorts of matters, offering advice on both domestic and foreign affairs.

In his new role this sergeant major by training became a kind of political Hamlet because he found himself in very deep waters. His military background inclined him to think first of relying on military orders such as "Look lively" or "Don't spare the bullets." But as he faced the stormy waves of the raging Russian ocean, he soon perceived that such orders were not enough. And because he had no political acumen, education, or training, he moved from one extreme to another. For example, at meetings of the Committee of Ministers he would argue for harsh measures against both students and instructors, while at the same time arguing that all institutions of higher learning be shifted from governmental to private operation. Later he would be responsible for the ill-considered granting of autonomy to the universities. In short, he could move easily from right to left and back again on major political questions.

An example of Trepov's odd way of thinking was the manner in which he tried to undo the horrible impression produced on workers by the events of January 9. It was to have the Emperor receive a "margarine" [ersatz] deputation of workers.

It goes without saying that after what had happened on January 9, it was not altogether safe to permit workers freely to elect a delegation because the ones they chose might be extreme in both word and deed. So, after getting a list of reliable workers (who could, if need be, also serve as informers), he selected a dozen from that list and presented them to the Emperor as the voice of the workers of Petersburg. The delegation assured His Majesty of their deep loyalty, and he, in turn, read them a prepared speech, assuring them that he was aware of their needs and that he would do everything he could for them. They were then given lunch and returned to the city.

This effort to soften the impression created by January 9 was a complete failure. The mass of Petersburg workers disowned the delegation, some of whose members were beaten up. In contrast, a more nearly genuine delegation, sent by workers of the Government Printing Office to be received by the Emperor, was given a somewhat favorable treatment by moderate workers of that office.

Implementing the Decree of December 12, 1904

Several circumstances affected work of the Committee of Ministers in its implementation of the decree of December 12.

The first of these was the revivification of the Council of Ministers, a body which met, on the rare occasions that it did, under the chairmanship of the Emperor.[29] Well, in January 1905, the Emperor, for some reason or other, called a session of this body. At the end of the meeting he turned, almost offhandedly, to Count Solskii and said: "Count, I ask that hereafter you summon meetings of the council on all questions brought up by the Committee of Ministers and on such other matters as I shall indicate."

This order left everyone in a state of confusion because the council had never met except under the chairmanship of the Emperor. Also, it was not clear whether this meant that the Committee of Ministers was abolished, and if it was not abolished whether or not it should continue to deal with the decree of December 12.[30] Count Solskii later asked the Emperor for directives to enable him to carry out the order, but, I believe, he received none. [However, the count was later to hold meetings of the Council of Ministers, and the Committee of Ministers continued to function and to deal with the decree of December 12.][31]

What soon became apparent, though, is that the Emperor no longer attached any importance to the reforms he had just promised in the decree and that, moreover, he was under the influence of persons hostile to me, an influence that went back to the taking of Port Arthur. I was constantly being told that the Emperor did not like me, some even going so far as to say that he hated me because of the sharp manner in which I spoke to him, a manner that had been acceptable to his father. But aside from the anger that my manner might arouse, aside from the effect of the intrigues against me, there was an additional and more important explanation of the Emperor's hostile feelings toward me: that everything I had said would happen had come to pass, precisely because he had not listened to me.

Another relevant circumstance was the participation of Peter Nikolaevich Durnovo, assistant minister of interior, in our deliberations. I had already come to know him as a firm, intelligent man who had learned much in the course of his work with the judiciary. In the course of our work, he showed knowledge, acumen, and candor. I was favorably impressed, but the Emperor evidently thought of him as somewhat of a liberal, which explains his later reluctance to appoint Durnovo as minister of interior when I became premier.

Another circumstance that affected our work was the replacement at this time of Muravev by Manukhin as minister of justice. As I have related elsewhere, Muravev scented that things would get much worse and, like a rat deserting a sinking ship, was able to obtain an ambassadorship that would take him away from the scene of trouble. Although undoubtedly superior to a later minister of justice like Shcheglovitov, Muravev had not held the banner of judicial independence sufficiently high. His successor, Sergei Sergeevich Manukhin, is an excellent jurist, a man of highest probity, a very enlightened, intelligent, and moderate person. After I became premier, I was glad to retain him as minister of justice.

Finally, I wish to mention three men, subsequently leaders of the Kadet party, whose help I sought in our work. They were I. V. Hessen, V. D. Nabokov, and Professor L. I. Petrazhitskii. The first two were associated with the periodical *Pravo*, which impressed me with its serious articles. At the time it did not show revolutionary tendencies. I found Hessen, a former official in the Ministry of Justice and the chief figure in the periodical, to be an intelligent and knowledgeable person. He spoke to me about current unrest and especially about how Muravev had debased our judicial institutions, but I received no particular benefit from these conversations.* As for Nabokov, whose father had served as minister of justice under Emperor Alexander II, he told me frankly that he would not assist the present regime in any way. However, Professor Petrazhitskii, with whom I became acquainted about this time, was to be of some help. Subsequently, like the other two, he was to be caught up in the turbulent spirit of the times and would become a Kadet, but a more reasonable one than the other two, who, together with other Kadet leaders, were to declare war on me when I became premier.

In implementing the decree of December 12, the Committee of Ministers was instructed to strengthen legality, extend freedom of the press and religion, broaden the authority of local self-government, eliminate unnecessary disabilities of non-Russians, do away with exceptional laws. Also, the decree called for the satisfactory completion of the work of the special conference on rural industry.

The task of the Committee of Ministers was to establish the basic principles for carrying out the decree, but the amending of old legislation or the framing of new legislation was to be the work of special conferences, whose chairmen and regular voting members were to be appointed by the Emperor, though the chairmen could add members with a consultative vote. The chairmen of the special conferences would not report to the chairman of the Committee of Ministers but to the Emperor [or to Count Solskii].

On occasion the Committee of Ministers invited experts from outside the government when dealing with matters within their competence. One such was

*When he was later imprisoned, his wife told me that he could not survive incarceration. I was able to secure his release, for which he thanked me.

His Grace, Antonii, Metropolitan of Petersburg and Ladoga. Sometimes we invited members of the State Council who had special knowledge about a subject under consideration. Our decisions were published immediately, and our minutes were published later so that anyone interested in our work would be informed of what we were doing.

I worked hard to see to it that all the reforms promised in the decree of December 12 would be carried out as quickly and fully as possible. It was I who provided the initiative on every question. The committee's chancellery provided the necessary documentation. I, of course, hoped that speedy enactment of reforms would reduce discontent, but, as might be expected, I encountered obstacles from the beginning: First there was apathy in high places, then intrigue and hostility, particularly after the departure of Mirskii, finally, lack of faith on the part of the Emperor in the promised reforms.

Consequently, our accomplishments were to be limited to partial extension of religious toleration, and partial lifting of the ban on publication in the Little Russian [Ukrainian] language and on instruction in non-Russian languages in the western provinces and the Kingdom of Poland. All the other proposals for reform were put on the shelf, under the influence of succeeding events. However, some of the work that we did that had no immediate results was to prove useful to me later, when I became premier.

In accordance with its agenda, the Committee of Ministers began with the question of strengthening legality. The only opposition during these deliberations came from Pobedonostsev.

Our first task was to demarcate clearly the respective spheres of the legislative and administrative bodies. Basing themselves on what was said in the committee, several ministers took up the question in the State Council. The view expressed by the majority in that body concerning proper procedure in the issuance of laws was affirmed by the Emperor and published on May 23, 1905.

Also of concern to the committee was the buttressing of the independence of the Senate and the enactment of a statute on administrative justice, of the kind found in other countries with a system of administrative justice distinct from the judicial system. In view of the complexity of these subjects, the committee recommended the formation of a special conference to deal with them. On my recommendation, the Emperor appointed A. A. Saburov, a former minister of justice, as chairman and Golubev, Koni, Tagantsev, and other eminent members of the State Council as members. At the end of 1905 all the papers prepared by this conference were turned over to the Emperor and then to me, in my capacity as premier, but after my departure from office nothing further was to be done to carry out the work of the conference.

Next we turned to the question of freedom of the press. In our deliberations we had at our disposal materials from the committee's chancellery, as well as materials from the Academy of Sciences, whose president, Grand Duke Constantine

Konstantinovich (a well-known poet, well educated like his father, a fine man, far from stupid, but no eagle), took part in the discussion of this question at the academy. Pobedonostsev and Sabler, his assistant, took a skeptical view of what we were doing and soon stopped attending meetings.

The Emperor approved the committee's position that reasonable freedom of the press, within clearly defined and strict limits, did not constitute a danger to the state, but was in fact a necessary attribute of any modern civilized society and agreed to create a special conference to prepare a new press statute. At my suggestion, he appointed as chairman Dmitrii Fomich Kobeko, director of the Public Library, my former associate in the Ministry of Finance, and, more to the point, the author of *The History of Emperor Paul I*, a work of which His Majesty approved. I recommended men of diverse views as members, among them Arsenev, Count Golenishchev-Kutuzov, Koni, Prince Meshcherskii, and Pikhno. They were appointed, but soon they were joined, without my having been consulted, by Prince Golitsyn, who wrote under the pseudonym of Muravlin, and Iuzefovich,* both later prominent in the extreme right.

That these two became members was in and of itself of minor importance. But the fact that the Emperor selected them was a sign that he was wavering, as usual, that tales were being brought to him from dark corners that a step forward was being made, when he had already decided to make a step backward. It was evident that what was being said in the Committee of Ministers was being presented to him in a distorted form, a form that those who favored a constitution would call obscurantist.

Kobeko and his conference did manage to do its work and prepared the details of the draft of a new press statute, which did not go into force until after October 17, when I made use of it in preparing a temporary press statute.

The Committee of Ministers then examined that plague known as the Law on Exceptional Measures, which gave administrative officials unbridled power. Peter Nikolaevich Durnovo, basing himself on what he had learned as director of the Department of Police, dwelt on the evil that this law represented and concluded that the law had done Russia more harm than good.

After expressing its views about what should be done with the law, the committee recommended the formation of a special conference to deal with it. His

*Iuzefovich, a scoundrel with an unnatural passion for young boys, to whom I have referred earlier, served for a time as censor in Kiev, but had to give up his post because of his constant quarrels with the local editors, among them Pikhno. Finally, he was able to find a niche with his childhood friend General-Adjutant Hesse, who provided him with a stipend of 12,000 rubles a year from money allocated to the palace police. In return, Iuzefovich used his gifts as a writer to prepare memoranda for Hesse to submit to the Emperor.

After Hesse died [July 1905], his successor as palace commandant, Prince Engalychev, immediately got rid of Iuzefovich. Then, at the request of Rachkovskii, by now the power within the Department of Police, Trepov sent Iuzefovich on a police assignment to Paris. I warned Trepov that he was sure to create a scandal because of his unnatural passions, and so it happened, ending in his recall. Subsequently Iuzefovich became head of the Black Hundreds organization in Kiev and began to send dispatches to the Emperor in the name of his despicable party.[32]

Majesty agreed and, on his own initiative, selected Count Alexis Pavlovich Ignatev as its chairman. This was the same Ignatev whom General Dragomirov had succeeded in ousting from the governor-generalship of Kiev. The count was not stupid, but he was crafty rather than clever, the product of Petersburg high society and the military-bureaucratic environment.

The choice of Count Ignatev, upon whom selection of the members of the conference depended, clearly indicated what those who opposed our work wished to be done with respect to the Law on Exceptional Measures. This is shown by the fact that by the time I became premier the conference had done virtually nothing. After I left the post of premier, some of the materials it had collected were turned over to the Ministry of Interior, where they were filed away and forgotten.

In dealing with the sixth point[33] of the December 12 decree, the Committee of Ministers gave special attention to the question of religious toleration, with Metropolitan Antonii taking part in these deliberations. When Pobedonostsev noted that the metropolitan was expressing views that clashed with the concept of a church acting as policeman that he had cultivated during his tenure as over-procurator, he stopped attending meetings and sent Sabler, the assistant over-procurator, in his place. Although Sabler worked hard to impede Metropolitan Antonii, and although the metropolitan was quite moderate in the positions he took, Pobedonostsev continued to be very dissatisfied with the tone of our sessions.

The committee agreed unanimously on an interpretation of religious toleration that was in keeping with the spirit of the times as well as in keeping with the spirit of genuine Christianity. This would mean the end of governmental supervision of any faith but the Orthodox one and the elimination of police intervention in the operations of the church.

The question of toleration was particularly important in the case of the Old Believers, to whose difficult position the committee gave special attention. This group has always been quite conservative and very loyal to tsar and fatherland, a fact that Emperor Alexander III recognized and that made him well disposed toward them. That he failed to do anything for the Old Believers was because of the narrow views of his advisers, notably Pobedonostsev. How often I tried to change the over-procurator's attitude on this subject and failed! As for Emperor Nicholas II, although he was also on the side of the Old Believers and wanted to help them, he lacked the will to overcome the obstacles put in his way by C. P. Pobedonostsev, A. P. Ignatev, A. A. Shirinskii-Shikhmatov, *i tutti quanti*.

The members of the Committee of Ministers as well as others—notably Kulomzin, Saburov, and Tatishchev—agreed on the need to act decisively with respect to religious toleration. In this spirit, the committee drafted a decree, subsequently approved by the Emperor, establishing norms of toleration for those not belonging to the Holy Orthodox church.[34] This decree, issued on April 17, is in the same class as documents such as the Manifesto of October 17: it can be damned, but it cannot be annulled. It is engraved in the hearts and minds of the great majority of the inhabitants of the great country that is Russia.

Since the decree dealt only with principles, it was necessary to delineate the freedom that would be enjoyed by non-Orthodox Christians as well as by non-Christians and the relation of officialdom to them. Therefore, the committee recommended the formation of a special conference to deal with the subject. His Majesty agreed. And whom did he appoint as chairman? None other than Count Alexis Pavlovich Ignatev, who would thus be serving as chairman of two special conferences. His appointment made clear what could be expected from this body. Nothing. It lived up to expectations, accomplishing nothing in the time before I became premier or during my tenure as premier. Subsequently it was disbanded and some of its papers were turned over to the Ministry of Interior.

By freeing all faiths but the Orthodox one from governmental supervision, the decree of April 17 created an anomalous situation that many in the Orthodox church found painful. Metropolitan Antonii expressed this view when he asked of the committee why the Orthodox church alone was being denied freedom from state control. Such a question could not be received with anything but complete sympathy by the committee and could not fail to arouse the saddest of feelings, at least in my soul. We agreed that we should examine the relations between the Orthodox church and the state, with a view toward allowing the church adequate freedom of action and administration. In informing His Majesty about the work of the committee of the decree on toleration I could not refrain from informing him of Metropolitan Antonii's position and of our reaction to it. He gave his approval.

I then informed the committee that we were free to consider measures to change certain aspects of the relations between the Orthodox church and the state, noting that any recommendations we might make would have to be carried out at best with the participation of the Holy Synod or at worst exclusively by that body. To aid the committee in its deliberations on this subject I had one of my associates prepare a memorandum. I took a considerable and deeply felt part in this because of my strong lifelong ties with the church that were part of my family tradition.

After copies of the memorandum had been distributed to the committee members, it was attacked in writing by Pobedonostsev, then allegedly ill. I replied in kind.[35] At the same time, Metropolitan Antonii prepared a statement for the committee concerning the issue under discussion. He did so at my request and, I am told, with the help of faculty of the Theological Academy. After giving the committee members time to read all the materials, I set a date for a meeting. The night before we were to meet, I received a letter from Pobedonostsev informing me that consideration of the relations between the Orthodox church and the state was shifted, on orders from the Emperor, to the Holy Synod, which had jurisdiction over such questions. Obviously the order was the work of our opposition, led by Pobedonostsev.

Oddly enough, the Holy Synod, with Pobedonostsev absent, at this time went much further than the Committee of Ministers would have gone if given the opportunity. It took the bold step of calling for a church council to consider the state of the church and to reestablish the partriarchate.[36] This decision was taken with the support of Sabler, when it was his duty, as Pobedonostsev saw it, to have opposed it. Consequently, the assistant over-procurator had to leave his post. Metropolitan Antonii, also, fell into the bad graces of the over-procurator as a result of the Holy Synod's action. As for the Emperor, he neither approved nor rejected the call for a council, saying only that the question of whether or not to hold a council would be decided later. After I became premier, with Pobedonostsev out of office, preparations were made to call a council, but they came to nothing after I left office.

If one takes a long-range view of the future, then, in my opinion, the greatest danger facing Russia comes from the sad state of the Orthodox church and the decline in genuine religious spirit. If Slavophilism performed any real service for Russia, it was in its revelation of the deplorable condition of the church.

Our so-called revolution of 1905 demonstrated even more clearly that which had been evident before: that no state can exist without lofty spiritual ideals. The masses can embrace such ideals only if they are simple yet lofty and inspiring, that is, of divine origin. Without a truly living church to give it expression, religion becomes philosophy and is unable to influence life. Without religion the masses turn into beasts, worse than four-legged beasts because humans possess intelligence.

Our church has turned into a dead, bureaucratic institution, and its services are conducted to celebrate not God in heaven but the earthly gods. Orthodoxy has turned into a kind of paganism. Herein lies our greatest danger. We have gradually become less Christian than adherents of other Christian religions. The Japanese defeated us because they have incomparably greater faith in their god than we have in ours. This is as palpably true as is the statement ''Germany was victorious over France in 1870 because of her schools.''

When we turned to point four of the December 12 decree, which dealt with the need for government insurance for workers, Kokovtsev said that this was under consideration by the commission on labor questions, of which he was chairman. Consequently, the committee did not pursue the matter further, except to stress the need for broad insurance against illness and industrial accidents for the workers and to deal with several proposals that had come to us from the commission.

In dealing with point two of the decree, which called for broadening the authority of local self-government, we recommended the calling of a conference of representatives from the municipal dumas and the zemstvos. But this effort was blocked by the Ministry of Interior.

As I have noted earlier, we had some success in removing restrictions on the right to publish in the Little Russian language. Until then, even publications of the Gospels in that tongue had been forbidden. Grand Duke Constantine Konstantinovich, who favored permitting publication of the Gospels in Little Russian, at our invitation attended a meeting at which we considered the matter and helped us end the restriction.[37]

Also, as I have said, we were able to accomplish something with respect to instruction in non-Russian languages in the western provinces and the Kingdom of Poland. Some of our recommendations were put into effect with Imperial approval; others were turned over to the ministries concerned with such matters, and some of these were acted upon.

Once it became evident that the efforts of the Committee of Ministers to implement the December 12 decree were encountering increasing disfavor and obstruction, I felt it necessary to end our work in this matter.[38] We had been able to achieve only a few of the modest goals embodied in the decree.

Meanwhile seditious and revolutionary sentiment was growing stronger, stimulated by our disgraceful defeats in the Far East. The government's vacillation between reaction and quasi-liberalism only made matters worse. These quasi-liberal interludes, instead of calming the opposition, as was intended, had only the opposite effect.

The Labor Question

One of the consequences of January 9 was the decision to form a commission to consider such demands of the Petersburg workers as seemed reasonable, with Shidlovskii, a member of the State Council, as chairman. Toward the end of January, at the Emperor's request, addressed to me in my capacity of chairman of the Committee of Ministers, I informed Shidlovskii that the Emperor wished to see him. [Afterward] I suggested some people to Shidlovskii who could help him.

Shidlovskii is not a stupid man. He is a good, businesslike, and decent bureaucrat. But he is mediocre and, to boot, of a somewhat bilious disposition. This assignment was beyond his capacity, a fact that he himself recognized. I do not know who recommended him. Had he been better equipped for the task, he still would have had a double handicap, one of having to work with Kokovtsev, who was so jealous about his prerogatives, and two, having to work under Trepov, meaning that he had to bear responsibility for the governor-general's activities in this field. Moreover, it was impossible to deal with the labor question in Petersburg without considering the rest of the country.

As it turned out, the commission was stillborn because the workers by this time were up in arms, incapable of making calm and reasonable decisions and therefore would not elect representatives to the commission with the kind of mandate Shidlovskii wanted. Evidently he was frightened by the mood of the workers and with his characteristic prudence wanted to be rid of this assignment. The commission accomplished nothing and was disbanded on February 20.[39]

As a result, a new commission to investigate the labor question, the one under

Kokovtsev that I referred to, was formed.[40] It accomplished virtually nothing except for the proposals that were examined by the Committee of Ministers.

February 18—Manifesto, Rescript, Decree

On February 3, while the Committee of Ministers was still at work on implementing the December 12 decree, at a time of defeat abroad and disorder at home, the Emperor presided over a meeting of the Council of Ministers, at Tsarskoe Selo, to consider the question of giving elected representatives a voice in the making of laws. Bulygin, Ermolov, Manukhin, and Kokovtsev were in favor, Kokovtsev arguing that if this were not done it would be impossible to borrow money for the prosecution of the war. Bulygin said he was increasingly convinced that the internal situation required such a step. I said nothing and nothing definite was recommended by the participants, but the Emperor directed Bulygin to prepare a draft of a law providing for elected representatives. A second meeting was then scheduled [for February 18] to consider the draft.

[On the morning of February 18], as the train taking us to Tsarskoe Selo was beginning to move, one of the ministers asked if we had read the manifesto and the decree to the Senate that had been published earlier that day.[41] The only one of us who was not astonished by the news was Manukhin, to whom we turned for an explanation of how these documents had come to appear so unexpectedly.

He explained that the night before the manifesto and the decree had been sent to the Senate Printing Office for publication, but the office would not comply without his permission and got in touch with him. Under the impression that the documents could not be published until the necessary formalities had been attended to, he got in touch with Taneev, the director of His Majesty's Chancellery, who informed him that an Imperial order authorizing publication was on its way. Thereupon Manukhin permitted publication.

Who was the author of the manifesto? Not Trepov. Not any of us on the train. When we arrived at Tsarskoe Selo, we learned that the manifesto had been sent to Pobedonostsev (who was at home, allegedly ill) the day before for his opinion. It was his opinion, we were told, that the document was so well composed he would not change a single word in it.

Later we learned that the document had been given to the Emperor by the Empress, who had received it from "Cutlet Colonel" Prince Putiatin. I do not know who the author was, but it was evidently one of the pillars of the Black Hundreds.[42]

When we met, the Emperor acted as if there had been no manifesto. Evidently he was secretly gloating, for he liked to throw his advisers off balance with surprises.

Bulygin then took the floor to read his draft of a rescript providing for fairly broad participation of elected representatives in the legislative process, a proposal diametrically opposed to the spirit of the manifesto published a few hours earlier.

During the discussion that followed, more or less serious observations were made about the wording of the document. I did not utter a word. Then we adjourned for lunch: as was customary, the Emperor lunched with the Empress, the rest of us lunched separately.[43]

During lunch, when someone asked for my opinion about the draft, I replied that it seemed to me that the participants were permitting themselves to be carried away by arguments over a document sure to be a dead letter. As for the manifesto, everyone was so upset over the trick represented by the manifesto that we agreed to accept Bulygin's wording in the draft without arguing any further.

When we met after lunch, the Emperor was obviously surprised to find that none of us had any comments about the draft and proceeded to sign the rescript. Prince Khilkov was so moved that he cried. Count Solskii thanked the Emperor on our behalf.[44]

So, on the same day the Emperor issued a manifesto concerning disorder and signed a rescript to Bulygin providing for elected representatives. Such contradictory steps had been taken before and would be taken again, as, for example, the Imperial manifesto of June 3, 1907, which affirmed the Manifesto of October 17 and the Emperor's letter a few days later to that scoundrel Dubrovin, chairman of the Union of the Russian People, which, in essence, renounced the October 17 document.

It was obvious that when the affairs of state are thus managed there can be no tranquility, despite the desire of our country to be done with revolution.

They play with Russia as if it were a toy. They are not evil. They are merely childish. Take the war with Japan: they saw it as a war played as if with toys. Such is their state of mind, one of complete irresponsibility, with respect to both this world and the world to come.

As for the decree to the Senate concerning the right to petition, it was completely impractical, because if everyone could submit petitions to the Council of Ministers and every petition had to be looked at, it would require the transformation of that body into one equipped with a large staff and in continuous operation. The thought behind the decree was based on the age-old belief that if the people could communicate directly with the Emperor then all would be well. As it turned out there were so many petitions that the decree had to be rescinded within a few months.

I took little part in the drafting of the law implementing the rescript to Bulygin, i.e., the law establishing the Bulygin duma.[45] And I had little to say at the sessions of the Council of Ministers, presided over by Count Solskii, to consider the draft. As will be seen, I would be in America when the final deliberations on the law took place.

Unquestionably, the vacillations of our Emperor and the camarilla that surrounds him were linked to our misfortunes in the Far East.

V

**War and Peace,
February–September 1905**

The End of Hope

Between February 15 and 20, our army, led by General Kuropatkin, suffered a striking defeat near Mukden. (Meanwhile, on February 17, General Stössel, who had so shamefully surrendered Port Arthur, was the Emperor's luncheon guest, despite what had happened.) The battle was remarkable, both for the number of troops involved and for the severity of our defeat, the worst, as far as I can recall, in the history of our army. In an order of the day Kuropatkin had vowed not to retreat beyond Mukden under any circumstances, but retreat he did, in disorder.

Because the debacle at Mukden revealed General Kuropatkin's complete inadequacy as commander-in-chief, he was replaced by General Linevich, whose subordinate he became. The aged, poorly educated Linevich's only claim to fame was his role in pillaging Peking during the Boxer Rebellion. He had attained his position by courage on the field (but Kuropatkin was also brave) and adroitness in his dealings. Perhaps he had been a good regimental commander and, had he been appointed commander-in-chief at the beginning of the war, he might have given a better performance than Kuropatkin had, but by now it was too late.

The chief reason for our failures in Manchuria was our lack of preparation for a war which we had provoked. Matters were made worse, as I have explained, by the division of authority between Kuropatkin and Alekseev and between Kuropatkin and subordinates who had been appointed without his knowledge or consent. General Rödiger, later to be minister of war, openly said that we could not win the war because we lacked competent generals. Had Kuropatkin been able to act with a free hand, without interference from Petersburg, his operations might not have ended as disgracefully as they did.

Our defeats, especially that at Mukden, roused all levels of the Russian population, in varying ways to be sure, against a regime that had shown itself to be weak and incompetent. Our people were growing frenetic and, in the end, one can say that they lost their mind. The revolutionary mood at home, which became stronger with the news of each defeat, a mood that revealed itself in proclamations, meetings, and strikes, spread to our troops in Manchuria and at home.

Our prestige abroad fell, because, let us face the facts, the semi-Asiatic tsardom of Muscovy had not been transformed into the dominant European power by virtue of our bureaucratic church or our wealth or our well-being but by our bayonets. And it was to our might that foreign states bowed their heads. Now when they were hearing reports, somewhat exaggerated, of our defeats, they concluded that Russia was "a giant with feet of clay." Even our friends abroad were beginning to have second thoughts about us.

While it was possible to argue about why we had experienced defeats, no sensible person could argue after Mukden that there was any hope for victory in Manchuria, any hope that we could reach the point where we could dictate terms of peace, and we needed peace desperately.

My view that a land victory was no longer possible was supported by an article in *Russkoe slovo*, one of a series of sensible articles on the course of the war. In it the anonymous author (who, as I recall, turned out to be Mikhailovskii, a Moscow zemstvo statistician) clearly demonstrated that it was impossible to expect any victories from Linevich. I sent a copy of the article, with an accompanying letter of advice, to Count Heyden, the chief of the Emperor's field chancellery, suggesting that he direct His Majesty's attention to it. The count, informing me that he was writing with the Emperor's knowledge, sent a tart replay. I answered in kind, saying that having opposed the war, I had consistently believed that the sooner we would be rid of this political crime the better off we would be.[1] I also stated that there was no point in believing that Admiral Rozhdestvenskii and his fleet (then en route to Far Eastern waters) could possibly succeed. (Copies of both letters are in my archive.) I know that His Majesty read both my letters.

With his characteristic optimism the Emperor believed that the admiral could change the course of the war. Had not Father Serafim predicted that peace would be concluded in Tokyo? Only "kikes" and *intelligenty* thought otherwise. And some newspapers, progenitors of the current Black Hundreds press, were certain that as soon as the admiral appeared in Chinese waters, Japan would be seized by panic.

I was convinced that the plan to send our Baltic ships, under the command of Admiral Rozhdestvenskii, almost all the way around the world, would end in disaster. Even if they managed to escape destruction in European waters and managed to arrive at their destination, it would do no good and would provide additional evidence of our incapacity. I held this view because even before the war I knew that our navy was inadequate, and the war confirmed my belief. Also, I had information (now in my archive) from Admiral Dubasov that the Baltic ships were obsolete as well as defective. Further, I had a very unfavorable opinion of Rozhdestvenskii, based in part on what I had been told about his "exploits" during the war with Turkey[2] and in part on what I learned about his strange character when I dealt with him in the Committee of Ministers, where I learned that he believed the Japanese would send fighting ships disguised as merchantmen to Petersburg. It was this strange belief that led to the tragi-comic Dogger Bank incident.

My misgivings were reinforced by what I heard from Count Lambsdorff and Grand Duke Alexander Mikhailovich about the conference that considered the plan to send the admiral to the Far East. At this conference, presided over the Emperor, I was told, virtually all the participants, chiefly ranking naval officers, evidently doubted that the undertaking could succeed, and some were certain that it would not. Having participated in many such conferences, I could easily imagine that those who expressed any critical opinions did so very cautiously, knowing that if they were frank they would sooner or later lose favor with the Emperor and have to leave their posts, as witness my experience. This lack of courage to speak up was one factor in the Emperor's decision to send Rozhdestvenskii; another was his light-minded optimism.

I was told that when Rozhdestvenskii was asked for his opinion, he said that he considered the proposed undertaking a difficult one, but that if the Emperor ordered him to carry it out he would. Shortly before he was due to leave, the Emperor, as a sign of favor, presented him to the infant Heir Alexis Nikolaevich, from whose hands, it is said, he received a blessing in the form of an icon.*

While the Baltic squadron was en route to the Far East, it was proposed to reinforce it with our rather modest Black Sea Fleet. Grand Duke Alexander Mikhailovich and Count Heyden favored the idea strongly, and the Emperor was inclined toward it. When Count Lambsdorff asked for my opinion, I told him that such a venture would not help us in the Far East and would surely hurt us in Europe, for it would be an invitation to the English to send their warships into the Black Sea. More to the point, such a step would violate international agreements. The count was also opposed, very much so, but since he had to speak as foreign minister, he relied on arguments concerning international relations and did so diplomatically. In this case his arguments prevailed. (A copy of his memorandum dealing with this matter is in my archive.)

Another scheme connected with the Rozhdestvenskii expedition was the stupid and abortive effort to purchase the Argentine Fleet.[3] It was politically stupid because had it gone through, the pro-Japanese powers would have interpreted it as a violation of neutrality by Argentina and would have used this act as a pretext for sending some of their own warships to reinforce the Japanese fleet.

Even more stupid was the way in which this scheme was handled. The negotia-

---

*The Heir was born on July 30, 1904, and christened on August 11. His birth was an outstanding event in the history of the Russian Empire. I often ask myself Hamlet's question and wonder what the fate of this boy will be. I pray to God that through him Russia will find peace and the basis for a new life, a life filled with the greatness that the Russian people have earned by their spirit and strength. May God grant that this be so.

tions were carried out in great secrecy by such gentlemen as Admiral Abaza, who went abroad disguised and incognito, and Kotiu (Panama): in other words, it was a conspiracy that attracted dozens of shady characters. Of course it came to nothing, but millions of rubles were wasted or stolen in the course of negotiations. This was but one of many instances in which the Bezobrazov operations were linked with the embezzlement of public monies.

The details of Rozhdestvenskii's voyage to the Far East, which culminated in the disastrous battle of Tsushima during May 14–15, are well known. This was the climax of the unfortunate adventurism that had led us into war. After Tsushima everyone, even the Emperor, recognized that peace must be negotiated.

In response to his disaster, Grand Duke Alexis Aleksandrovich, general admiral of the navy, and Admiral Avelan, director of the Ministry of the Navy, asked to be relieved of their duties. This was to their credit, for they were in effect accepting responsibility for the low state of the navy. Admiral Birilev, who had been sent to Vladivostok to replace Admiral Makarov as commander of the Far Eastern squadron, was appointed minister of the navy.[4]

Another consequence of Tsushima was that the Special Committee for the Far East, which had never met, was dissolved. Admiral Alekseev was relieved of his post of viceroy without being given another assignment: in effect the disastrous adventure produced by Bezobrazov and Co. was being buried.

But Admiral Alekseev was awarded a consolation prize, the St. George, although he had never heard a shot fired in anger and had spent the war in his office in Mukden, more concerned about his creature comforts than about the condition of the army, and a good thing, too, because the army was better off without his attention to it. It was a good thing, too, that the St. George was hidden by his beard because this kept people from being upset at the notion he had been given a high honor denied to most of the generals who had distinguished themselves in this war.

The news of Tsushima fanned the seditious and revolutionary movement at home. Consequently, a few days after the news of the defeat had been received, General Trepov was given an additional post, that of assistant minister of interior, with special power over the police, making his extraordinary power even greater than it had been.

Preparations for Peace

Not long after Tsushima, the newspapers began to report rumors that President Roosevelt wanted to mediate peace talks between Russia and Japan.* I knew little of what was going on because Count Lambsdorff had been keeping me in the dark. But one day he happened to tell me that the Emperor had agreed to

---

*In my archive is a collection of documents showing how the idea of peace negotiations arose, what instructions the chief plenipotentiaries received, and why these led to a peaceful settlement. Consequently, I will not deal with these matters here, but restrict myself to more or less secondary events and incidents not touched upon by these documents.[5]

negotiations, the place still to be decided, Roosevelt favoring an American site, Count Lambsdorff a European one. I suggested that a site close to the theater of war would be preferable, but that if one had to choose between Europe and America, the latter would be better because it would be less subject to European intrigues.

The foreign minister told me that Muravev, our ambassador to Rome, had been summoned posthaste to Petersburg so that the Emperor could ask him to serve as our chief plenipotentiary in the peace negotiations. Muravev was the Emperor's third choice for the post.

Count Lambsdorff told me that he had recommended me for the post as being the one most qualified for it, but the Emperor had not reacted to the recommendation.* And I can understand why. After all, I was in disfavor, particularly so since everything I had predicted about the consequences of following the policies of Bezobrazov and Co. had come true, with a vengeance. Knowing the character of our gentle, delicate Emperor, I could understand that after everything that had happened, His Majesty would not find it very pleasant to bring me close to him once more by appointing me chief plenipotentiary.

The count told me that the Emperor had first offered the assignment to Nelidov, our ambassador to Paris, but that Nelidov, pleading advanced age and poor health, had declined. (Nelidov became ill because he was afraid of the responsibility.) Then the Emperor had offered the post to Izvolskii, our envoy to Denmark, but he, too, had declined, recommending me as the person most qualified for such a difficult task, insisting further that I was the right choice because of my prestige in the Far East as well as in Europe.[6] At that, according to the foreign minister, His Majesty decided on Muravev.[7]

Soon after his arrival in Petersburg, Muravev called on me at my summer residence, on Elagin Island, and spent the entire evening with me. He told me that he had accepted the Emperor's offer of the post of chief plenipotentiary and he had talked to those ministers who could help him prepare for his mission. He had come to see me because of my considerable knowledge of Far Eastern affairs. He said he had frankly told the Emperor that, given existing conditions, we must end the war. He went on to say to me that his would be a thankless task: if peace were concluded, he would be mercilessly attacked on the ground that if peace had not been concluded, we would have won the war, but if he failed to negotiate a peace settlement, he would be attacked for the consequences of failure to conclude peace. Nonetheless, he had decided to make a personal sacrifice by performing this service for his Emperor.

Muravev confided to me how glad he was to be away from Petersburg while all

---

*When the Emperor agreed to peace talks, the Japanese assumed that I would be the chief plenipotentiary for our side because it was I who had supported a policy of accommodation and I who was best acquainted with the situation in the Far East. Therefore, they chose Marquis Ito, their leading statesman, as their chief plenipotentiary. But when they heard that someone else had been chosen, they replaced Marquis Ito with Komura, their foreign minister. By the time I was chosen, Komura was already on his way to America. All that Marquis Ito could do then was send me a telegram expressing regret that he would not be the one negotiating with me.

the nonsense we were experiencing was going on. Living abroad, he told me—even in a country such as Italy, with its large number of socialists and anarchists—he had decided, after all that had happened, that Russia could save herself only through a constitution. In passing, he told me that he had asked for 100,000 rubles to cover the expenses that his mission would entail. When he asked whom I would recommend to accompany him, I suggested Pokotilov, our minister to China, and Shipov, the director of the Treasury, as men who had been associated with me in Far Eastern affairs. There was no indication that evening that he was ill. In fact, he said that he felt very well.

Several days later, on June 28, at the conclusion of a meeting of the Committee of Ministers, at the Marie Palace, Count Lambsdorff, who had been unable to attend, arrived, in uniform and sash, an obvious indication that he had just come from giving a report to the Emperor.[8] Because he wanted to talk to me, we went into my office, where he told me he had just come from the Emperor to sound me out about becoming chief plenipotientiary. He said that the Emperor had given him this task because he knew how close we were. He told me that the Emperor would not offer me the post unless he knew in advance that I would accept.

When I asked about Muravev, the count told me that the day before, Muravev had gone to the Emperor and, bursting into tears, had told him he was too ill to carry out the mission with which he had been entrusted. The Emperor told Count Lambsdorff that Muravev had in fact seemed ill.

Why had Muravev withdrawn? According to the foreign minister, Muravev had apparently realized that he knew nothing of the subjects he was to deal with and also, being an intelligent man, understood the danger to which he would be exposed if he carried out his mission. Moreover, Muravev had been quite put out when he had learned that, at Lambsdorff's suggestion, the Emperor had decided he would be given not 100,000 rubles but 15,000 to cover expenses. Count Lambsdorff had not been happy over Muravev's appointment because he felt that he was not sufficiently informed about what he would have to do.

I asked Lambsdorff if he couldn't go instead of Muravev or, if he could not, how about Prince Obolenskii, his assistant minister and closest friend. The answer was that he could not go and that he did not consider the prince suitable for the task.[9] Appealing to my sense of duty, he said that I could not refuse. I agreed that, given my position, I could not refuse, but would not accept unless the Emperor personally asked or ordered me to go. With that Count Lambsdorff left me.

On returning home I received a note asking me to present myself to the Emperor the next day. I did as I was asked and was offered the post. I told the Emperor that I was always willing to be of service. He thanked me and assured me that he sincerely wanted peace, but not at the cost of even a kopek in indemnity or the cession of even a square inch of our soil. He then suggested that I call on Grand Duke Nicholas Nikolaevich (the chairman of the Council of State Defense) to be briefed about our military position in the Far East.

On my return from Tsarkoe Selo, I called on Count Lambsdorff immediately and told him of the instructions I had received. He asked if I were willing to be accompanied by those already chosen to go with the chief plenipotentiary: Pokotilov, Shipov, Baron Rosen (our ambassador to Washington), to serve as second plenipotentiary, Professor Martens (a well-known specialist on international law), three men from the Ministry of Foreign Affairs—Korostovets, Nabokov (these two to act as secretaries), and Planson—and three selected by the Ministry of War and the high command of the army in Manchuria—General Ermolov, Colonel Samoilov, and naval Captain Rusin. I said that I did not wish to offend anyone and would therefore suggest no changes. Did I wish to be bound by the instructions that had been prepared for Muravev? I said that it was a matter of indifference to me, but we agreed that I would adhere to them only to the degree that seemed necessary.

As we parted, he told me that Kokovtsev was not very friendly toward me and asked how we got along. When I asked the reason for the question, he told me that on the preceding day, after he had spoken to me at the Marie Palace, Kokovtsev asked why he had come. He had assumed that the finance minister would be pleased at the news, but when he told him why he had come, Kokovtsev said: "Too bad: peace is assured because Sergei Iulevich will agree to all the conditions." This from Kokovtsev,[10] who, during my stay in America, sent me telegrams favoring a position that would lead to peace. Such behavior was typical of this man whose career I had done so much to advance.*

The following day I called on Grand Duke Nicholas Nikolaevich. He said he

---

*In speaking earlier of Kokovtsev's appointment as minister of finance, I forgot to mention some of the circumstances attending the event, which show how much he owed me.

After my successor, Pleske, became ill, Romanov was named as his temporary replacement. It soon became clear that Romanov would not remain long in this post, because Count Solskii was quite critical of him. (When the count spoke to me about Romanov he spoke favorably because he knew that I did not agree with his criticism.) It soon became obvious to me that the count's criticism was inspired by Kokovtsev, then serving as Imperial secretary, a post he had obtained with my help. Count Solskii was under the thumb of his wife and of Kokovtsev, who planted critical ideas about Romanov in her mind and thus in her husband's.

When Count Solskii, and possibly others, told the Emperor that although Romanov was a fine man he would not be a suitable minister, the search for someone to replace Pleske began. State Controller Lobko, another of Romanov's critics, recommended his assistant state controller, Filosofov, a young, very intelligent, and knowledgeable man. Lobko's recommendation carried weight with the Emperor because the general was known as a man of integrity and, moreover, had been one of the Emperor's teachers. Had Filosofov been appointed, it would have taken him many months to become acquainted with his work.

Kokovtsev, for whom it was natural to consider himself a candidate to fill any important vacancy and for whom intrigue was second nature, told me that it was all but settled that Filosofov would be the next minister of finance and that the Emperor had ordered Count Solskii to draft the necessary decree. Would I do him, Kokovtsev, a good turn by intervening? I said that once the Emperor had made up his mind and had ordered the necessary decree prepared, there was nothing I could do. Not so, said Kokovtsev. He suggested that I enlist the help of Prince Meshcherskii, who still had some influence with the Emperor, to write His Majesty a letter suggesting the appointment of Kokovtsev. Still on good terms with Meshcherskii, I told him that Kokovtsev would be a better choice than Filosofov and persuaded him to write a letter to that effect to the Emperor. This he did, in my presence. I learned later that, under the influence of this letter, the Emperor then ordered Count Solskii to prepare a decree appointing Kokovtsev.

Kokovtsev had intrigued to get me to help him become my assistant minister of finance, then Imperial secretary, and now minister of finance. It was because Count Lambsdorff was a decent man and knew of how I had helped Kokovtsev that he had found Kokovtsev's attitude toward me so strange.

would not offer any opinion on whether or not peace should be negotiated or under what conditions it should be made, except to say that under no circumstances should we cede a square inch of our soil. He said that all he would do would be to inform me of the conclusions about our military situation arrived at by the conference of the military over which he had presided.

In his usual precise way, and in considerable detail, he told me that the army could not endure another defeat of the magnitude of the ones at Liaoyang and Mukden. With General Linevich at the helm, we were not likely to suffer such defeats, and given favorable circumstances and time to reinforce our army in Manchuria, we would be able, within a year, to force the Japanese back to the Kwantung Peninsula and the Yalu River, but, lacking naval power, we could push them no further. Such an operation would probably entail the loss of up to 250,000 dead or wounded, and would probably cost a billion rubles. We could also expect that while we drove the Japanese back in Manchuria they would take Sakhalin Island and parts of our Maritime Region. Admiral Birilev, our new minister of the navy, added that Japan was now master of the Far Eastern waters.[11] He said that we should not accept humiliating conditions as the price of peace, but he saw no objection to our yielding some of the territory [in the Far East] that we had taken in more favorable times. The next day when, as I was taking leave of the Emperor, I started to tell him of what I had learned from the Grand Duke, he interrupted me to say that he had already been told.*

I had no information about General Linevich's thoughts about our military situation, but I did receive a brief letter (now in my archive) from Kuropatkin, written shortly before my appointment as chief plenipotentiary, in which he expressed confidence that we could be victorious, "providing no more mistakes are made." This is the same Kuropatkin who had long been predicting victory, who had assured us that Port Arthur would not surrender, that we would not retreat beyond Mukden. I am convinced that both Kuropatkin and Linevich knew that their only hope lay in peace and were praying that I would be able to conclude a peace. Then when the war was over, they would be free to lament that if peace had not been negotiated, they could have won the war.

Our financial situation was as desperate as our military one, in part because of Kokovtsev's mistakes. He is a hard worker, but he is hampered by a narrow, bureaucratic mind, by the lack of feel for government finances. When the war began, he did not hurry to borrow abroad, thinking that he could get better terms if he waited until we had demonstrated our military strength.[13] The minutes of the Finance Committee, of which I was a member, will show that I was alone, except

---

*The Grand Duke gave me the conclusions [of the conference] in writing. Also, after our talk I prepared a resumé of what had been said; it is now in my archive. In connection with my polemic later on with General Kuropatkin, I provided both the Ministry of Foreign Affairs and the War Ministry with evidence of what the Grand Duke had told me before my departure for America. Sazonov, the foreign minister, directed that my letter be filed with the relevant papers of the Grand Duke, and I know that Sukhomlinov, the war minister, informed the Emperor about my letter and that the Emperor confirmed that what I said was correct.[12]

for the weak support of Count Lambsdorff, in expressing pessimism about our military prospects. Because we waited too long for victories that did not come, our credit rating abroad fell. And we could not float loans at home.

Because of his inexperience and conceit, Kokovtsev was guilty of another major error, that of unjustifiable recourse to the printing press to finance the war. Nations with a sound gold or silver standard rely heavily on paper only in the case of major wars and then only when expenditures cannot be covered by borrowing and when there is a sudden and sharp economic crisis that requires the central bank to provide immediate help, the kind of crisis I experienced when premier.[14]

None of these conditions existed. Moreover, the State Bank did not grant credit to commercial undertakings during the war. Thus, neither the war nor the needs of commerce called for an increase in the obligations of the State Bank, yet Kokovtsev managed to double the amount of paper money in circulation, from 600 million to 1,200 million and, in addition, issued 150 million rubles' worth of treasury notes, which were the equivalent of paper money. When it later became possible to borrow money, he did not contract the money supply, thus threatening the gold standard.

After my return from America, I privately explained all this to Kokovtsev. Then we wrote memoranda to each other. The material concerning this exchange of views, which is in my archive, will be of interest to those interested in the theory and practice of finance.

En Route to America

On July 6, I left Petersburg with my wife, my infant grandson, Lev Kirilovich Naryshkin, and several servants. Some members of my suite were scheduled to meet me at Cherbourg, our port of departure. Others were to meet me in New York.

A few words now about the members of my suite. Professor Martens is a fine man, a very knowledgeable professor of international law with many years of service at Petersburg University, an honorary member of the faculties of many foreign universities. However, the reputation he enjoys abroad is inflated. He is a limited person, in a number of respects, to say the least, a man afflicted with a pathological vanity. Planson, a typically obsequious bureaucrat, had served under Viceroy Alekseev as servile executor of a policy that had led us into this war. Pokotilov, a very intelligent, gifted, and fine man, with a good knowledge of the Far East, had been opposed to the war from the beginning and was convinced that we must make peace to save us from new disasters. He arrived from China only after the negotiations had begun and took virtually no part in them, but as an unqualified supporter of peace he exercised a beneficial effect on Baron Rosen. I became well acquainted with the baron only after our arrival in America. He is a decent man, a gentleman to his fingertips, with the average intelligence of a logical Baltic German. He was quite out of touch with what was going on in Russia.[15] He vacillated on the question of peace until he learned what Colonel

Samoilov and Captain Rusin had to say. Or to put it another way, he supported peace when he saw what the terms would be. He took no part in the negotiations, but he gave me his complete support. Then there were our talented secretaries, Nabokov and Korostovets.[16] Shipov,[17] accompanied by two minor officials, represented the Ministry of Finance.

General Ermolov, our military attaché in London, with jurisdiction over all other military attachés, was the ranking officer among the military and naval personnel in my suite. A fine, intelligent man, although somewhat weak, he had little faith in the possibility of victory and believed that peace was desirable. He was anxious to be treated with great honor lest the dignity of our valiant but leaderless army be wounded while we were negotiating. Also, he was very concerned that the military high command be kept *au courant* with the course of negotiations.

I met Colonel Samoilov on the ship taking us to America. I found him to be a very intelligent, educated, and knowledgeable man. Although he came to us from General Linevich's headquarters, he brought neither instructions nor information from the general. The colonel told me categorically that because there wasn't the slightest hope of victory, peace must be concluded, even if it entailed a large indemnity.

Captain Rusin, who spoke for the naval ministry, joined us only when we were in Portsmouth. Like Colonel Samoilov, he was attached to the headquarters of General Linevich. He held the same views as the colonel, but expressed them more cautiously and with greater restraint.

When we arrived in Paris we turned our grandson over to his parents. At our arrival we were greeted by Nelidov, who seemed in perfect health, by the prefect of police, Lépine, and by a large crowd that included virtually all of the Russian colony in that city. I spent several days there so as to have time to talk to Premier Rouvier and President Loubet.

I told Rouvier that once peace was concluded we would require a loan. He told me that we could not count on the French money market until we made peace, as we had to. He added that according to his information we would have to pay an indemnity. He assured me that France would help us pay because it was in her interest to extricate Russia from this unfortunate war, for so long as Russia was embroiled in the Far East she could be of no help in the event of complications in Europe.

I replied that although I was unreservedly in favor of peace, I would not agree for us to pay as much as a sou because Russia had never paid and would never pay an indemnity. Rouvier pointed out that after the Franco-Prussian War, France had paid an indemnity without injury to her pride. My response was that if the Japanese army reached Moscow, we might reconsider.

The aged President Loubet, who made a special trip from his summer residence to see me, also urgently advised us to conclude peace, saying that he spoke as a sincere friend of Russia. He told me that French officers who had visited the theater of war reported that it was unlikely that we could improve our military position by continuing to fight. The longer we waited to make peace, he said, the harsher the terms we would have to accept. Also, he told me in confidence that he had reliable information that Japan was supporting disorder in Russia.[18]

To understand the mood of Premier Rouvier and President Loubet, one must consider the circumstances that had weakened the Franco-Russian alliance and had pushed France toward England.

For several years before our disgraceful war with Japan, Anglo-French relations had been very cool, largely because of the rivalry between the two countries in North Africa, which culminated in the Fashoda incident, in 1898, when the two countries came close to war and we could not help our ally. Relations remained cool until we became embroiled in war, one we could have avoided if France had behaved wisely.

Delcassé, the veteran foreign minister of France, with whom we dealt both before and after the Fashoda incident, is an intelligent and honorable man, but he is far from foresighted. He should have been aware that the insane policy of Alekseev and Bezobrazov must lead to war, yet, as I have noted, he was assuring everyone as late as the summer of 1903 that there would be no war. If he had been able to foresee the consequences of our adventurous Far Eastern policy he could have informed our government of what the consequences of war would be, that no matter how the war turned out, it would weaken Russia on her western borders during hostilities, giving Germany increased influence, if not power, in European affairs.

I am certain that an energetic word from France, our ally, would have led us to conduct negotiations quite differently, with more maturity and caution. Our shameful defeats in the war did not cause the makers of French foreign policy to abandon the alliance with us, but they sought new friendships. Rapprochement with Germany was out of the question because of the adverse effect that a Franco-German entente would have had on French and Russian public opinion. Therefore, France agreed to an *entente cordiale* with England [in April 1904.][19] This was done with the knowledge and consent of Russia. Even if Russia had had reason to object, she was not in a position to do so at a time when she could not have provided her ally with any help had the need arisen. Moreover, the terms of the *entente cordiale* had no direct bearing on Russian interests.

Meanwhile, Emperor William II gained from our involvement in a war that would weaken us for years and thus hurt his most hated rival, France. And he had been able to achieve this position by diplomatic efforts alone, because of his thorough understanding of our Emperor. Despite William's restless character, Germany might have felt comfortable at this point if not for the *entente cordiale*, which provided for division of influence in Morocco between France and England. Because Germany had some commercial interests in Morocco, the German foreign office responded by playing its own game. Emperor William, accompanied by a brilliant suite, visited that country, to show that he was on friendly terms with its sultan and that France and England could not ignore German interests there.

The presence of Emperor William in Morocco could not fail to impress its government and people and thereby reduce the influence of France. A series of diplomatic exchanges followed, with Germany presenting various demands to France, sharply worded demands because Germany knew that France could not count on Russian support. When Germany let it be secretly known that as long as Delcassé remained in office she would be obdurate in her demands, the French foreign minister lost his portfolio, which was assumed by Premier Rouvier, an able financial expert, an intelligent man, one of the pleiade of Gambetta's associates.

All this took place a few months before my arrival in Paris and helps explain the mood I encountered there, a mood of apprehension. Did Emperor William intend to take steps that would weaken France for a long time to come? Could France count on Russia? France was disappointed in Russia, which had followed policies leading to weakness and disgrace. She wanted to count on Russia as an ally, which meant that Russia should get out of the war and transfer her troops as well as her attention from Manchuria to the Vistula basin.

An example of French anxiety that I witnessed while in Paris was the furor produced by the news that Emperor Nicholas and Emperor William had met at Björkö, in the Finnish skerries. Despite the official announcement that this had been a purely personal meeting, devoid of political significance, as demonstrated by the fact that neither the German chancellor nor the Russian foreign minister had been present, French newspapers expressed alarm. And not without cause, for they had learned from experience that the German Emperor always mixed business and pleasure. They suspected that he would exploit our Emperor's pride and vanity to play such a trick on us that we would be scratching our head in puzzlement for years to come.

I had no advance knowledge from Count Lambsdorff because he had not known that the meeting was planned. Nor had the Emperor said anything to me about it when I last saw him, although he obviously knew what was afoot.[20] Although I put a good face on the news, assuring those who asked me that the meeting had no political significance, I did feel it necessary to send a telegram of inquiry to our foreign minister, who informed me that the meeting had been exactly what it purported to be, personal and of no political significance. When I showed the reply to Premier Rouvier, he was both thankful and reassured. He told me that President Loubet had also been alarmed by the news from Björkö and said that he would immediately inform him of my visit and of Count Lambsdorff's reply.

Throughout my stay in Paris I was under the protection of the secret police, who accompanied me on bicycles. It appeared that the French government feared that Russian anarchist-revolutionaries might try to kill me to prevent the conclusion of peace. In this connection let me note that while in Paris I received a letter from Burtsev, a major revolutionary figure, expressing the view that autocracy must be destroyed and that if its destruction could be avoided by the conclusion of peace, then peace should not be concluded. I sent this letter (now in my archive) to Count Lambsdorff, who showed it to the Emperor.

At this time, for whatever reason, the European powers held me in high esteem and unanimously agreed that if anyone could conclude peace it was Witte.

During my stay I was depressed, perhaps excessively so, by the public attitude toward me, the chief plenipotentiary of the Emperor and Autocrat of Russia. The tone was so markedly different from the one I encountered years earlier when, as minister of finance, I had visited Paris. This time, most Frenchmen seemed indifferent toward me, as if I represented *une quantité négligeable*. Only a few displayed sympathy, while a small minority actually expressed delight at our troubles. Typical of the public mood were the shouts of *"faites la paix"* hurled at me at the railroad station both when I arrived in Paris and when I departed. The left-wing newspapers referred to Russia and to our Emperor in a contemptuous and insulting manner, in sharp contrast to the cordial treatment I received from President Loubet, who spoke with sincere love and loyalty about my Sovereign.

It was galling to represent a great military power that had acted stupidly and been defeated badly. But it was the infantile regime under which we had been living for some years past, not Russia, not the Russian army, that had been beaten. This was the view I expressed in my letter to Count Heyden, about which I have already written. Of course, they hated me for uttering the kind of truth that the Tsar seldom heard and never grew accustomed to hearing.

It was precisely the conviction that it was the regime and not Russia that had been defeated that permitted me to hold my head high in Paris, despite the public attitude toward me. It was this conviction that gave me the strength to gain a moral victory in America. Perhaps it was because I took too much pride in my position as representative of Russia that I was so angered by the attitude I encountered in Paris. In Cherbourg, our port of departure, the attitude was even worse.

There my party (which included my wife, my daughter, my son-in-law, many members of my suite, as well as journalists who accompanied me from Paris to Cherbourg) was met with complete indifference. My mood was not improved when a storm kept our ship, *Kaiser Wilhelm der Grosse*, from leaving that night, as scheduled. As a consequence we had to spend the night at a hotel near the pier that was so crowded that we were barely able to get two very uncomfortable rooms.

My spirits rose the next morning when I was welcomed aboard with great pomp by the captain and his crew and when I heard the orchestra play "God Save the Tsar," our national anthem, and saw all the Russians aboard (Colonel Samoilov, Planson, Nabokov, Korostovets, and Martens among them), as well as many of the non-Russians join me as I bared my head. The demonstration of such an attitude toward Russia could not help but raise my spirits. My family, I should note, did not accompany me to America.

It is appropriate to say something at this place about the journalists (several of whom I already knew) who accompanied me on the ship. Two were Russian. The first, Brianchaninov, a young man, is the son of a former governor and the husband of Princess Gorchakova. He writes fairly well, is not without ability, sticks his nose into everything, is quite immature and frivolous, but may mature in time. He was convinced that Russia must have peace at any price. His chattering, insofar as the words of this young chatterbox could have any influence, did not help us in our negotiations. Nowadays he is a Kadet, is on the staff of its newspaper, *Rech*, and as the husband of a Gorchakov dreams of becoming chancellor of a Russian Empire governed by a ministry led by Miliukov and Hessen, those misguided bourgeois revolutionaries.[21] As for the other Russian, Boris Suvorin, there is nothing to say except that he is a nice young man.[22]

The English press was represented by Joseph Dillon, with whom I was acquainted,[23] and Mackenzie Wallace. Dillon is a very decent, trustworthy, and talented man, with a considerable reputation in England and America. He holds a doctorate from a Russian university, taught comparative philology at Kharkov University, speaks and writes Russian well, has an excellent knowledge of contemporary Russia, and has ties with all parties and all levels of society. Midway in our voyage he sent a report by wireless telegraph of an interview with me about the forthcoming negotiations. This report, which was published in all the European newspapers, was the first in the history of journalism to be sent in this fashion from mid-ocean.

Mackenzie Wallace was a different sort. Formerly director of the foreign department of *The Times*, he was with us to keep King Edward informed of the progress of the negotiations. Misinformed would be a better word because until the actual signing of the treaty Wallace insisted that the negotiations would fail. Perhaps he is an able journalist, but as far as Russia is concerned he has provided his countrymen with the most misleading reports. He speaks Russian well, but what he knows about Russia comes from the aristocracy, for whom he has a weakness. In Russia, he associates only with that class and accepts as bona fide everything he hears from it. He is not taken seriously in England.

In his book about the Russian peasantry, he gave high marks to our village commune.[24] As late as six months before our revolution, he issued a new edition of this book in which he asserted we could not possibly have a revolution because of the beneficent effect of the village commune.

I am told that when he was in Petersburg last winter, he spoke of me in an uncomplimentary fashion.[25] Undoubtedly this was a reflection of the circles in which he moves, as well as of the fact that while in America I did not treat him seriously. On one occasion I told him that his book about our peasantry shows how even intelligent persons can fall into error if their information comes secondhand.

Le Matin was represented by Hedeman, a gifted, quick-witted man, a true professional, who was sympathetic to Russia. In addition to reporting for his newspaper, he kept various officials of his country abreast of what was taking place.

The German press was not well represented, probably because Germany was not anxious for us to conclude peace. For example, a few months earlier Chancellor Bülow had sent me a message through the banker Mendelssohn that "if he were merely a friend of Russia (an allusion to France) he would advise the speedy conclusion of peace, but since he was more than a friend, he would advise against it."

There were other correspondents as well, whom I will not discuss. As things turned out, Dillon and Hedeman were in charge of all the reporting to the European press.

We had a fairly calm voyage and I hardly suffered from seasickness. Except for two meals, I dined privately with my suite and, on occasion, with a few correspondents. As I learned, many of the passengers were making the voyage solely out of interest in the sensational, hoping to be on the spot when I and Komura would have our political match.

Only two weeks had passed since my unexpected appointment as chief plenipotentiary. During that time there had been so much excitement that I had been unable to organize my thoughts and prepare for the dreadful diplomatic battle I would soon face. So I used my six days at sea to work out the following plan of action: (1) I would give the impression that we had agreed to negotiate not because His Majesty wanted peace, but because the rest of the world wanted the war to end; (2) I would act in a manner befitting the representative of the greatest of empires, an empire that had suffered no more than a minor unpleasantness; (3) in view of the power of the American press, I would be very pleasant and accessible to all its members; (4) I would behave in an unaffected and democratic manner so as to win over the American public, which is very democratic; (5) I would not display hostility toward Jews (not a difficult task given my views on the Jewish question) in recognition of their considerable influence in New York and in the American press. In furtherance of this plan I sought to make a favorable impression on my fellow passengers, an impression that was communicated to the press and then to the American public.

From New York to Portsmouth

As we approached New York, we were met by a virtual flotilla, filled with people who wanted to greet and see Russia's chief plenipotentiary.[26] Among these people were several American journalists, who came aboard. To them I expressed my joy at being in a country that had always been on the most friendly terms with Russia. From that moment on, until my departure from the country, I was under the eyes of newspapermen. In Portsmouth, possibly by design, I was given two small rooms, one with windows so placed that everything I did in that room could be seen. In short, all during my stay I felt as if I were always on stage, before a full house. Because I followed the plan I devised aboard ship, I helped win us a favorable peace, a fact recognized by educated people throughout the world. I will go further and say that until a few days before the signing of the peace treaty no one believed that we would win such favorable terms as we did.

From the day of my arrival in America the curious were constantly taking pictures of me with their Kodaks. Everywhere I went I was asked, particularly by women, to let them take my picture, to give them my autograph, or both. In addition, I received constant requests from all over the country for my autograph. I fulfilled all such requests in a friendly spirit. And when I traveled by train I made it a point at the end of a trip to seek out the engineer, thank him, and shake his hand. The first time I did this all the newspapers expressed approval and made much of this. This was so because Americans had come to expect ambassadors and other prominent personages from Europe to be standoffish, yet here was a man who, despite the fact that he was the chief plenipotentiary of the Emperor of Russia, the chairman of the Committee of Ministers, state secretary of His Majesty, behaved unaffectedly, being more accessible than the very democratic President Roosevelt, who makes good use of his democratic simplicity. In short, I acted an equal among equals. This meant that I had to bear the heavy burden of constantly playing a role, one that helped me gain public support.

As can be imagined, I gave special attention to the press, going out of my way to be accessible to newspapermen. Of course, I had to guard my tongue, measure every word, refrain from saying what should not be said, while emphasizing that which served my ends. By following this policy I was gradually able to win the press over to supporting me in the task set for me by my Sovereign. This change could be seen by following the American press from day to day. By the time I left New York almost the entire press was on my side.

Komura helped us unwittingly. Although he had been educated in America, he not only shunned the press but also made it difficult for the press to learn about the course of negotiations. I took advantage of his coolness toward the press by proposing that the press be thoroughly informed about negotiations, on the assumption that the Japanese would not agree. Even if they had I would not have been unhappy because the chief plenipotentiary of the Tsar of Russia was prepared to shout out to the whole world what he had to say. As I expected, the Japanese refused, so it was decided to issue a brief communiqué, edited by the secretaries and approved by the plenipotentiaries, after each session. The press soon learned that the brevity of the communiqués was entirely the responsibility of the Japanese and accordingly reacted unfavorably toward them.

As a result of my efforts to influence the powerful American press, public opinion gradually shifted away from Komura and his country toward me and my country.[27] The shift in public opinion is demonstrated by the telegram that Roosevelt sent to Japan toward the end of the negotiations, in which he stated that under no circumstances would Witte agree to such Japanese demands as the one calling for an indemnity and that if the negotiations should fail because of Japanese obduracy, the American public would be less sympathetic toward Japan than it had been. He showed me a copy of this telegram when I last saw him before leaving the country.

The president's sympathy was clearly for the Japanese. He showed this by supporting them from the very start of negotiations, as well as by the fact that he permitted his daughter to accompany Taft, the war minister, to Japan at this time. But being a clever man he knew the danger of going against the current, and as American public opinion began to incline toward us, he began to urge the Japanese to make concessions.

In keeping with my plan of action, I made it appear that we regarded what had happened in Manchuria as no more than a minor unpleasantness. I acted this way with the public and with President Roosevelt and the Japanese. This attitude once provoked Komura into exclaiming: "You talk as if you were the victor." My answer: "Here there are neither victors nor vanquished."

It was unbearably hot when we arrived in New York and the city was almost deserted. Baron Rosen and his staff took us directly to [the St. Regis], the best hotel in the city, located on the city's chief thoroughfare. From the balcony of the hotel hung the flag of the chief plenipotentiary and ambassador extraordinary of the Emperor and Autocrat of All the Russias.

I was shown to my suite, consisting of a bedroom, a room for my manservant, two studies, a large dining room, and a bathroom, for which I had to pay the fantastic sum of 380 rubles a day. Dinners, which cost from 30 to 50 rubles a person, were vile, but no more so than those generally served in America. I soon discovered that Americans will eat anything placed before them, even if it is not fresh, provided it has the proper sauce and appearance. I was to come to the conclusion that it is dangerous to eat the food ordinarily available in America.

Wherever we ventured in public from the time I came ashore, I was supposed to have a guard of secret policemen, first two, then four, provided by President Roosevelt. Unlike Russian and other secret policemen, who can usually be spotted by their umbrellas and bowler hats, these secret agents did not look the part: they looked like gentlemen—in appearance, manner, and speech. I did not like the idea of such protection, but Baron Rosen justified it by telling me that there were rumors that agents of a Japanese party opposed to peace might attempt to take my life. These rumors increased in intensity after peace was signed. Also, there were rumors that some of the many Russian Jews in New York might try to assassinate me. There were about half a million Jews in that city. Some of them had left Russia after such pogroms as the one that Plehve had arranged at Kishinev, and some (the majority) had left Russia because they could not earn a living there.

Although I had been warned not to visit the Jewish quarter, I did so the day after my arrival, accompanied by one of our embassy officials. Several of the Jews to whom I spoke, in Russian, recognized me, some reacting favorably, others with hostility. When I returned to the hotel I found that the secret agent who was to have accompanied me was rather alarmed, because he had been told that the local Jews were very hostile toward the Russian chief plenipotentiary.

Later that day I and Baron Rosen went to Oyster Bay, to be presented to President Roosevelt. His home and its furnishing were rather modest, the kind one associates with a bourgeois of moderate means. All his servants were negroes. He is widely regarded as a friend of the negroes and for that reason is held in respect and affection by them. He does believe in genuine equality and for that reason is attacked by some of his fellow Americans.

Before lunch I talked to the president about the forthcoming negotiations.* What I had to say did not please him at all. He said that my views indicated that agreement was out of the question. Not to offend him, since it was he who had initiated the negotiations, I suggested that the meetings could be ended with propriety by having the plenipotentiaries meet, state their positions, admit that they were irreconcilable, and then go home.

The meal that followed was more than modest. There was no tablecloth. The food was barely digestible, at least for a European. Except for Baron Rosen, who was provided with some sort of wine, the rest of us had to be content with ice water. Subsequent meals with the president were no better. As I have said, Americans are poorly fed, and the service at meals is very simple.

I was astonished to see that the president preceded his wife into the dining room, sat at the head of the table, was the first to be served and the first to get up from the table. This seemed out of keeping with European practice, particularly in a family setting. To be sure, the French president walks ahead of his wife on state occasions, but then his wife usually does not take part. For the rest, the wife of the French president is still *madame* and *monsieur le président* is still *monsieur*.

After lunch I talked with the president, but since his wife was present, our conversation was semi-official. We agreed that on the next day I and my suite would meet Komura (who arrived in New York the day after me) and his suite on the president's yacht, in Oyster Bay. Then I, Baron Rosen, and the rest of my suite would leave for Portsmouth, the site of the peace conference, on one warship and Komura and his suite would leave on another.

Of course, our first meeting with the Japanese would have to be difficult, for, despite the fact that I represented the most powerful nation on earth, I knew we had been defeated. I was anxious that the Japanese not be given precedence over us and told Baron Rosen that I would not take it lightly if at lunch on the yacht the president would first toast the Mikado and then our Emperor. I said this because I was afraid that the president, having little experience and being a typical American, would commit a blunder by paying little attention to formalities.

The following morning I left my hotel at the appointed hour for the dock from which we were to sail. There we found a large, friendly crowd waiting to see us. During the hour-long trip to Oyster Bay we received salutes from passing ships and from the factories on shore. When I asked what all this meant, I was told that

*I am not relating the details of this conversation, nor will I deal with the details of the negotiations that followed, because they can be found in the documents in my archive, which have been systematically organized.

these were expressions of friendship. When we docked at Oyster Bay, we again were met by a large, friendly crowd. We noted the Japanese were not greeted in this fashion when they arrived. We were then rowed to the president's yacht, where we and the Japanese were saluted as we went aboard.

Introductions were made aboard the yacht. I had met Komura when he was minister to Petersburg, and I already knew some members of his suite. Undoubtedly Komura has many outstanding qualities, but he is not particularly sympathetic in manner or appearance, far less so than other Japanese statesman, among them Ito, Yamagata, Kurino, and Motono, whom I have met. Lunch was served immediately. When the time came for a toast, the president offered one that did not give precedence to either of the monarchs.[28] This was so because Baron Rosen had alerted the assistant foreign minister [Pierce], a man with six years' service in the American embassy in Petersburg, who had been put in charge of supervising the details of the conference.

At the president's request, a group photograph was taken of me, Baron Rosen, the president, Komura, and Takahira, the second Japanese plenipotentiary. Copies of the photograph were given to each of us and to the American newspapers. Then, we set sail for Portsmouth on our respective warships.

Because I have no special love for sea voyages, and because I wanted to see Boston, I and one of the secretaries went ashore more or less secretly at Newport, planning to go on from there by train to Boston and then from there to Portsmouth. Of course, my arrival in Newport quickly became known.

I called on the port commandant, with whom I had tea and lunch.[29] Then I took a tour around the city. One part is rather small and not very affluent. The other part is the summering place of all the New York multimillionaires as well as of some of the rich from other parts of the country, and of European guests. This part is the site of very luxurious villas that are really palaces.

Although it was still early, many of the wealthy residents were out riding. I was astonished by their costumes. The men wore light-colored shirts, tucked in their trousers, a contrast to the Russian style. They wore light breeches, their legs shod in light boots and leather leggings. Despite the strong sun they rode bareheaded. The women too wore light and very short riding habits and rode bareheaded.

Two years later, while I was in Bad Homburg, the port commandant, who was there with his wife, asked to see me, to return my call. He told me that his government had first intended to hold the peace conference in Newport, which is more luxurious and has better recreational facilities than Portsmouth, but had decided against Newport to save the Japanese from embarrassment. He explained that although Americans favored the Japanese cause, they looked down on them because of their race, whereas they thought of us as equals since we were white and European. Newport society would have been friendly toward us and cold toward the Japanese because of two additional factors: the novelty of our presence and the great prestige I enjoyed among American financiers. And that would not have done.

From Newport I went by special train to Boston, where I was put up at [the

Hotel Touraine], the best in the city. The following morning I visited Harvard, which is considered the best university in the country.[30] There I was received by its president (Roosevelt told me that it was his great ambition to serve as president of the university after completing his term of office) and several professors, who invited me to lunch with them at the university club. After lunch I returned to Boston, went sightseeing, and returned to my hotel for dinner.

After dinner I drove to the railroad station, where a special train was waiting for me. The secret policemen, who followed me in another car, asked me to use a back entrance to the station and once in my carriage to remain there. Evidently my protectors feared an attack or a hostile demonstration by the large, evidently Jewish, crowd. As I approached, those close by took off their hats and so did I. When I drew close several addressed me in Russian. Some were recent immigrants, others had come here as boys, still others were the children of immigrants. When I asked how they were getting along, they said they enjoyed complete freedom and full equality, which enabled them to make a living with comparative ease. When I asked if this meant that they were content with their lot, they replied:

> No, not completely. Although we are American citizens, we can never forget Russia, where our ancestors are buried. We have no love for its regime, but we love the country. So, if you hear that we wish the Japanese success at the conference, do not believe it. We all wish you, as representative of the Russian people, success and we will pray for you.

After I had boarded the train and it had begun to move I heard a loud "hurrah" from the crowd. I was to find the same attitude among the Jews in Portsmouth.

Portsmouth

When I arrived in Portsmouth I found that both delegations would be housed in [the Hotel Wentworth], a huge, wooden resort hotel located outside Portsmouth. The city itself is small, comparatively old, by American standards, a rather modest place for year-round living, inhabited for the most part by members of the middle class. The conference itself was held in the Portsmouth Navy Yard, located in the adjacent state.

Because the news of the forthcoming conference had attracted many visitors, accommodations at the hotel, a place for people of modest means, were so scarce that the chief plenipotentiary of the Russian Emperor was given only two, rather small rooms for himself, and a third, equally small room for his two menservants.

Moreover, one of the rooms, the study, was virtually glassed in and, as I have said, I could not have privacy in it because everything I did there was visible from outside the hotel as well as from rooms, verandas, and balconies of the hotel. Because of my visibility, large crowds of the curious were constantly streaming by to see what the chief plenipotentiary of the Russian Emperor was doing, to observe my meetings with my associates and with the hordes of journalists who came to see me. It must have been a joyous occasion for the hotel owners.

As for the journalists, they were always talking to my secretaries, but that was not enough for them. All wanted to speak to me, and those who represented major newspapers wanted exclusive interviews.

At Portsmouth, both delegations were guests of the American government. Lunches were provided at the Navy Yard. At these meals I, Baron Rosen, Komura, Takahira, and two secretaries ate separately. The secretaries were there to act as translators in the event that Japanese rather than French was spoken.

The food served at lunch was plentiful and varied, but it consisted entirely of cold dishes, prepared in advance, and kept in refrigerators. As I have observed, it is dangerous to eat the food ordinarily available in America. But with cold dishes one faces an even greater danger than with hot ones. When I became ill after a few days at Portsmouth I stopped eating anything at lunch but bread and vegetables. Komura, however, ate everything, with a good appetite. More than once I asked him if he were not afraid to eat all that food. Obviously seeking to demonstrate that his people were courageous, he said that he feared nothing. By the time he returned to New York after the conference he had come down with a serious form of what some called intestinal flu and others called nervous shock.

The food at the hotel was almost as bad. During the first days I and my suite ate in the public dining room, at a separate table, but later, after this had proved unsatisfactory, we ate in a private room, not far from my quarters. And we were served specially prepared food, because of the danger represented by the food generally to be had in America.

In the course of our stay in Portsmouth I was struck by several other peculiarities of American life. Among them was the fact that most of the waiters and busboys in the local restaurants and hotels were students who did this work (work that paid well—the equivalent of two hundred rubles a month) to help them go to school. They did not feel demeaned by such labor and were not considered socially inferior for doing it. At work they wear the costume appropriate to their tasks and punctiliously serve and clear tables, but they do not perform the dirtiest work. After work they resume their usual costume, which is often embellished with college insignia. They pay court to young ladies and women staying at the hotels. When the time comes to return to work, they change back to their working clothes.

I was amazed at this aspect of American life because I could not conceive of any of our students, even hungry ones with no more than ten or twenty rubles a month, performing such tasks. They would feel demeaned to be waiters, dressed like lackeys, even in the best restaurants. The same can probably be said of other European students.

Also, I was amazed that young ladies of good family were not considered to be behaving improperly if they went walking after dark with them, if they spent hours with them unobserved, be it in the parks, in the woods, or in rowboats. No one considers such behavior improper; on the contrary, it is considered improper to say anything critical of such behavior. I was particularly struck by this attitude on the two occasions I and some of my suite had tea at the homes of two very respectable young ladies who lived with their mothers near the hotel. No one thought anything of the fact that young men visited with them until late in the evening, for such was the reputation of the young ladies that no evil could be thought of them.

When there was time I would be taken for an outing at the beach. The beach, the open sea, the high waves, reminded me of Biarritz across the Atlantic, but the waves here were more impressive.

While in Portsmouth I had an unexpected visit from Jeremiah Curtin, whom I had seen briefly in New York.[31] An American with an excellent command of Russian who had written much about my country, he was well known in American literary circles. He was on good terms with Pobedonostsev, was interested in the Orthodox church, and loved Russia. He tried very hard to win the American press over to my side.

I became acquainted with him in Tiflis, when I was a boy. He was friendly with my Uncle Fadeev and often visited our family. For a time he was secretary of the American legation in Petersburg. After he left the diplomatic service he continued to visit Petersburg, where I met him again. At the time of his visit to Portsmouth he seemed in good health, although he was quite old. I did not see him again and learned a few months later that he had died.

Among the delegations I received in Portsmouth was one of prominent American Jews—among them Schiff, one of the richest men in America, the banker Seligman, Dr. Straus, a diplomat—to speak to me about the difficult position of the Russian Jews, how pressing was the need to grant them equal rights. (I was to meet with this delegation again.)[32]

I responded in a friendly fashion, saying that, of course, Russian Jews were in a difficult position, but adding that some of the allegations about their status were exaggerated. Also, I told them that I was convinced that the sudden granting of equal rights to the Jews of Russia would do them more harm than good, which evoked a very sharp response from Schiff. His sharpness was offset by the more judicious reactions of the others, notably Dr. Straus, who impressed me very favorably. (Schiff and Straus were on good terms with President Roosevelt, who would later talk to me about the status of the Russian Jews.)

I kept Petersburg fully informed about my conversations with these representatives of American Jewry. All the official material on this subject will be found among the documents on the Portsmouth conference to which I have referred.

The Conference

Early on the morning following my arrival in Portsmouth, the warships provided for the two delegations arrived. I went incognito to the heavily guarded conference site and was taken by sloop to our ship, which was at our disposal for the remainder of our stay. When I, Baron Rosen, and the rest of my suite disembarked, we were greeted with full military honors. We then walked to the building in which the conference was to be held, followed by the Japanese delegation, which disembarked after us.

One wing of the building was for our delegation, the other for the Japanese. Between the two wings is a large hall, in which the negotiations took place. Nearby are rooms in which we had lunch and tea during breaks in the sessions and rooms for other purposes.

First, Portsmouth society and officialdom, which had been waiting for us in the conference building, were presented to us. Then we all went to lunch, after which we left for the City Hall in open carriages, the assistant minister of foreign affairs in the lead, followed by the Japanese and Russian delegations. The streets were crowded with people who were more friendly toward us than to the Japanese. As we drove along, I heard some shouts in Russian of "Good health to Your Excellency" from some soldiers of obvious Russian Jewish origin, who were part of the honor guard lining the route. At City Hall we were welcomed by the governor of the state and by the city officials. After the governor had delivered a speech and a group picture had been taken, we returned to our hotel, this time in automobiles, which were faster and more comfortable than the horse-drawn carriages. The actual negotiations began the following day.

It was an agonizing and depressing time. I felt myself under a heavy responsibility, understanding full well that if I did not return to Russia with an olive branch, fighting would be resumed. And I knew, from official sources, that if fighting were renewed, we could expect new disasters. All Russia would condemn me if I did not make peace, yet my Russian heart was heavy at the thought that we were negotiating as vanquished, not as victors.

Shortly after our arrival, we and the Japanese exchanged calling cards. Beyond that, with one exception, we had no social contacts with the Japanese during the course of the conference, although we stayed at the same hotel. The exception occurred toward the end of the conference, when, at my request, Takahira came to see me so that we could agree on the time of one of the last meetings.

The Japanese behaved stiffly but properly during the negotiations, but they often interrupted sessions to confer among themselves. Also, they made our work unnecessarily difficult by insisting that only the first and second plenipotentiaries and their respective secretaries be permitted to attend the sessions. I was opposed to the idea, but Komura, for some reason or other, was adamant on this point. It was I and Komura who did most of the talking. Professor Martens was very upset at being excluded. At only one session were all the members of the delegations permitted to be present.

I should note that those in the Japanese delegation who were excluded from the sessions stayed in nearby rooms during these sessions. One of them was an American [Henry W. Denison], a former lawyer living in Japan, with whom

Komura was constantly taking counsel. The American later entered the service of the Japanese Ministry of Foreign Affairs, in which he was to play an important, but not highly visible, role.

As the days went by, we managed to reach agreement on most issues, but when I would not agree to any further concessions, a dispute arose between Komura and his government over whether to agree to my position or to break off negotiations: one party in Tokyo, led by Ito, was insisting that my proposals be accepted, while another party, led by the military, was insisting that fighting be resumed unless we agreed to pay an indemnity.

This was the occasion on which President Roosevelt telegraphed the Mikado advising him to agree to my proposals. The president did so because he was fearful that American public opinion was moving toward Russia and would turn against him and the Japanese if negotiations were broken off. As I learned later from journalists who were in touch with Komura's suite, he then received a directive to give in, but since he opposed any concessions, he insisted that the directive come directly from the Mikado. It was this that caused the brief suspension of negotiations.[33]

The day before we were to resume negotiations was a very tense one for me. I did not know what reply Komura would receive, but I knew that peace was indispensable for us, that without it we would be threatened with new troubles, with the prospect of the fall of the dynasty, to which I was devoted with every fiber of my being. I was deeply distressed at the thought of having to conclude a peace so shocking to Russia's self-esteem. I don't want to share with anyone what I went through during those last days at Portsmouth. I was very ill, yet I had to play the part of one who had triumphed. Only a few of my close associates knew of my condition.

All Portsmouth knew that the tragic question of whether or not blood would continue to flow on the fields of Manchuria would soon be decided. When I went to bed that night I did not know what tomorrow would bring, what instructions the Japanese would receive. Roosevelt had been warning me that if I did not make additional and major concessions the Japanese would break off negotiations, and when that tactic failed to affect me, he tried to influence the Emperor to yield. As I said, I did not know at the time that he was warning the Japanese of the need to compromise.

When I went to bed that night my soul was torn. On the one hand reason and conscience told me that if peace were arrived at the following day, it would be cause for rejoicing. But then a voice inside me would whisper: "How much happier you would be if fate kept you from signing a peace treaty, for if you do sign, you will be blamed for everything, since no one, not even a Russian Tsar, particularly a Russian Tsar like Nicholas II, is willing to admit his sins toward God and fatherland." I spent a restless, nightmarish night, sobbing and praying.

When I went to the Navy Yard the next morning I did not know what to expect. During the night Komura had received instructions to agree to my conditions. I was overjoyed: we had peace. In the city, bells were rung and whistles blown to mark the joyous news. [During the next week three members of my suite worked with three members of Komura's suite to prepare the final text of the peace treaty.][34]

[On the afternoon of August 23/September 5, I, Baron Rosen, Komura, and Takahira signed the treaty of peace[35] in the room where we had held our sessions.] As planned, cannon were fired at the Navy Yard as we signed, and when the shots were heard in town, flags were raised everywhere. I had told the pastor of the church [Christ Church], which I attended while in Portsmouth, there being no Orthodox church there, that following the signing of peace I would go directly from the conference site to his church. Meanwhile Orthodox priests had arrived during the night from New York to be there for the conclusion of the tragedy we had endured. Under the influence of similar feelings, clergy of various other faiths began to arrive from nearby localities.

As soon as the treaty was signed, I and my associates left for the church. Along the way we were warmly greeted and congratulated by the waiting crowds. Everyone wanted to shake our hands, a customary sign of attention among Americans. The crowd was so thick that it was difficult to reach the church. And when Baron Rosen and I reached the church we found it so full that we had to stand behind the rail at the altar. And then we witnessed a wonderful scene: a procession to the altar led by an excellent choir of amateur singers, followed by Orthodox, Catholic, Protestant, and even Jewish clergymen. Then the Orthodox priest, followed by the pastor of the church, offered brief prayers of thanks for the conclusion of peace and the end to the spilling of innocent blood. During the service a senior bishop arrived from New York to take part in the service. He and the Russian priest gave brief sermons. Then the assembled clergy and the church choirs offered a hymn of thanksgiving.

It was evident during the course of the service that all felt a sense of Christ's great teaching: "Thou shalt not kill." This sense of Christian unity was confirmed in me as I watched the Americans thanking God with tears in their eyes for the granting of peace, thus answering my unspoken question: of what concern was the Portsmouth Peace to them? The answer of course was: we are all Christians. As I left the church, the choir sang "God Save the Tsar." It was with these sounds in my ears that I pushed my way through the crowd, waiting till the end of the hymn before getting into the waiting automobile.

As I left, various people, apparently following local custom, slipped gifts into my hands and pockets. Later, at the hotel, I found some precious stones among the gifts.

That I should have been able[36] to conclude a comparatively favorable peace treaty, given the defeats we had endured, was unexpected. Even the Emperor felt a moral obligation to recognize my achievement and would do me the extraordinary honor of bestowing a title on me. This despite the dislike he and the Empress felt for me and despite the most insidious intrigues of a pack of courtiers and higher officials who are as contemptible as they are unendowed. Why did I succeed?

First, because from the very moment I arrived in America I was able to rouse in the Americans the recognition that we Russians, who are related to them by blood, culture, and religion, had come to compete with members of a race that was alien to them in all the elements that shape the nature and spirit of a nation.

Also, the Americans saw in me a man who, despite his high position as representative of the Emperor and Autocrat of All the Russias, behaved as their equal, behaved as unpretentiously as did their public figures. And my associates strengthened this impression by following my example. And, as I have said, our cause was helped by my attitude toward the press. The Japanese, as I have noted, helped in their own way. As for the American Jews, they did not help me, but neither did they hinder me, for it was in their interest to support the kind of Russian statesman who, as they knew from my record, thought of them as human beings. Such statesmen are still rare in Russia.

Roosevelt wanted the conference to succeed for the sake of his self-esteem, for it was he, after all, who had inspired the conference. Moreover, its success would enhance his popularity. But if he desired peace, it was on terms favorable to the Japanese, in ignorance of the fact that strengthening Japan was not in America's interest. That the terms were not as favorable to the Japanese as he might have wished was the result of my intractability and the shift of American public opinion in my favor.

As I became acquainted with the president and other major figures in America, I was astonished at how little they knew of the international situation in general and of the European situation in particular. I was amazed at the very naive opinions they expressed, e.g., that since Turkey was a Moslem country it should disappear from the face of the earth or, at the very least, from Europe. When asked what should take the place of Turkey they expressed indifference. Another naive opinion I heard was that it was only natural and desirable that a separate and powerful Poland be reestablished.

France wanted peace out of self-interest as well as out of sympathy, at least on the part of her chief officials.

England too wanted peace, because her leaders, past masters in international politics, realized that Russia had been taught a lesson that would make her more tractable when the two countries next dealt with questions over which they were at odds. And although England wanted Japan to leave Portsmouth with favorable terms, she could not ignore the fact that a greatly strengthened Japan was not in her interest. It is relevant to note that the English and the Japanese were negotiating renewal of their treaty of alliance at this time and that the English made the wording of the final text dependent on what took place in Portsmouth. I called Count Lambsdorff's attention to what was going on, but we could not discover why the negotiations in London should be affected by the results of the negotiations in Portsmouth.

An additional force for peace was the money market, which had been disturbed by the war and wanted it to end.

Also, those of the Christian faith and their leaders favored the conclusion of peace, for whatever else the war might have been, it was a war between Christian and heathen. That the Japanese represented a special kind of heathen, with a firm belief in the afterlife and with a deep faith in a god, was something that was not understood then, nor is it understood now.

Finally, there was the influence of Emperor William, who had come to feel after Björkö that peace was in his interest. That he should think this way is understandable because he thought that he had succeeded at Björkö in getting Russia into more trouble than she would have been as a result of failure to conclude peace. Of course, he did not realize at the time that Björkö would come to nothing.

It should be noted here that Emperor William and President Roosevelt agreed on many things. When Roosevelt told me that the whole world wanted peace, I asked if that included the German Emperor. His reply was an unequivocal "yes." By this time they were maintaining close contact by correspondence.

They are both patriots. They are both young, original, *restless*, rash, yet able to keep their own counsel.[37] Each represents the spirit of his nation. This does not mean that the two countries will become close. A president is but caliph for a day, president one day, private citizen the next. And it should be remembered that it was not many years ago that William wanted to form a European alliance against America.

As for the Japanese, once they decided that we were gaining an advantage they came to the conclusion that they stood to gain more by concluding peace then, than by continuing the war.

As we learned after the signing of the peace treaty, when members of the two delegations began talking informally among themselves, Komura signed the treaty against his convictions and, moreover, knew that an unenviable fate awaited him in Japan.

And so it turned out. When the terms of peace were announced, rioting broke out in Tokyo, leading to the destruction of a monument to Ito. Troops were summoned, the city was placed under martial law, and there were many casualties. Komura received no honors on his return and was forced to leave government service. It was only later, when the mood became calmer, that he was named ambassador to England.

In contrast, I was enthusiastically received when I returned home and was made a count. Later, when I left the office of premier I was given some honors, but was soon in disfavor. Such are the tricks that fate plays with human beings.

Intrigue

Seeing that public opinion in America began to shift in favor of Russia from the first day of my arrival, Baron Rosen strongly urged that once the conference was over I should visit the chief cities of the country to strengthen our relations with the Americans. I pointed out the value of such a trip to Count Lambsdorff.

Petersburg was already aware of my favorable reception in America, and this led to the spread of hostile stories about me. It was whispered in the Emperor's ear that I, who was no more of a threat to Nicholas II than I was to Roosevelt, aimed at becoming president of a Russia turned republic. I can imagine his being told that I was attracting the masses and his replying: "Witte is a hypnotist; wherever he speaks he wins over his enemies." In short, they were insinuating that I must not be permitted to gain popularity.

It was such insinuations that seemed to lie behind Count Lambsdorff's reply that the Emperor agreed to my visiting the major American cities, but with conditions attached that made me realize at once that they were afraid of my making such a tour. I sensed this because I knew the atmosphere in which the Emperor lived. Another plenipotentiary might not have been shocked, as I was, by this reply, but I am not the kind of person who is accustomed to receiving such instructions. In my answer, one that perhaps was not delicately couched, I told the count that I did not care to make the trip.

Precisely the same thing happened to me before the war when I was in the Far East and the Mikado invited me to visit Japan. Izvolskii, who was then our minister to Tokyo, urged me to accept and I did. It was clear to me that Izvolskii so urged me because, knowing my role in our Far Eastern affairs, he thought that by visiting Japan I could apply a brake to the tendencies in Tokyo that were leading to war. But I received word from Petersburg that I was free to make the visit, but only in a private capacity. Yet there I was in the Far East on the Emperor's orders. Would my making the short voyage from Port Arthur to Tokyo make me a private person? Obviously they feared that I was trying to dampen the warlike fires burning in their hearts.

While I was in America they were also intriguing to turn Count Lambsdorff against me by insinuating that I was aiming to become chancellor and then get rid of him. This was evident from several of his personal dispatches to me, which I have in my archive, together with my replies. It was only our genuine friendship and his noble character that made these intrigues fail. Their contemptible authors believed that if I and Lambsdorff could be set at odds, the Emperor would lose confidence in what we were doing and I would fail. It was not for nothing that enemies said when I left for America: "We have tossed him into the fire."

Also, I surmised from Lambsdorff's telegrams and from a telegram from the Emperor that the intriguers (of whom Kokovtsev was a leading figure) were insinuating to the Emperor that I was trying to circumvent his rejection of an indemnity in order to feed my vanity by concluding peace. The fact of the matter is that my only deviation from the instructions I received at the beginning was the agreement to cede half of Sakhalin, and the honor for that deviation belongs to the Emperor himself. Had I been free to choose, I might not have agreed to the cession, but I believe that the Emperor acted correctly: without this concession there would have been little chance of concluding peace.

When the peace treaty was finally signed, it came as a surprise to everyone, even the Emperor. Evidently, when he received my telegram announcing the fact, he did not at first know how to react to it. It was only after he had received congratulations from all over the world, including an enthusiastic communication from Emperor William, that he sent me a telegram expressing thanks.[38]

As for General Linevich, our commander-in-chief in Manchuria, I received not a single word, directly or indirectly, from him during my service as chief plenipotentiary. When I began negotiations I refrained from suggesting an armistice to keep from tying his hands. Did he reciprocate by giving me any support for my task? Not in the least!

But after the war was over, after he had to be replaced because he had given in to the gang of revolutionaries who had come to demoralize his army, this sly old man insinuated on his return to Petersburg that if I had not concluded peace, he would have shown the Japanese what for. What was he doing on the battlefield while I was negotiating peace? Nothing! He let the Japanese take the southern part of Sakhalin without a struggle. And when our detachments encountered the Japanese between Harbin and Vladivostok they retreated after the first exchange of fire.

Recently, in Biarritz, where I am writing these lines, I had the opportunity of talking to General Palitsyn, chief of the General Staff. Asked if Linevich had asked the Emperor to conclude peace and why he had not gone into action during the peace negotiations, Palitsyn replied that, as far as he knew, Linevich had never communicated with His Majesty about peace negotiations, but he did know that the general had informed the Emperor he was preparing a plan to assume the offensive and was sending it for approval, only to be told that no approval was necessary, that he was authorized to proceed with the offensive. This reply drove Linevich into total inaction and into remaining quiet until he could return to Petersburg and whisper his insinuations about me. General Palitsyn added: "Now Linevich finds it convenient to say that if we had not concluded peace, he would have been victorious. That is to be expected from petty people. Kuropatkin goes even further to claim that everyone but he is responsible for our defeats."

New York and Washington

As soon as our work was concluded in Portsmouth, some of my associates left to visit Niagara Falls and other sights. As I have noted, I might have toured major cities around the country had I not sensed a hostile attitude in Petersburg toward such a journey, but I was able to spend some time in New York and Washington.[39]

Immediately after the conference I returned to New York, where I was put up once more at [the St. Regis Hotel]. This time my situation there was different. Once the peace treaty was signed, I was no longer chief plenipotentiary and ambassador extraordinary of His Majesty. Accordingly, I was given cheaper accommodations, on the seventeenth floor, at eighty-two rubles a night. The food was as vile as before.

Because the cost of living in America is extraordinarily high, my allotment for expenses—15,000 rubles, later supplemented by another 5,000—did not suffice, forcing me to spend tens of thousands of rubles of my own money. Illustrative of the high cost of living was the fact that the least one could tip the hotel elevator operator was a dollar, i.e., two rubles. Generally speaking, there is no such thing as small change at the large hotels.

While in New York I made an unscheduled appearance at the Stock Exchange, where trading was suspended in honor of my visit. The reception was friendly and attentive.

Then, at his invitation, I visited General Grant, son of the famous president and father of Princess Cantacuzene.[40] I was glad to accept the invitation because my wife and I were on excellent terms with the princess, who was married to an officer in the Chevalier Garde. When I visited with him on [Governor's Island], where as commander of the New York Military District [Department of the East] he has his residence and headquarters, I was received with military honors.

I spent one morning at Columbia University, which conferred an honorary degree of doctor of laws on me.[41]

I was well received at the university. As several professors showed me around the library, I asked to see the collection on economics. When I asked a professor of political economy if he dealt with the teachings of Henry George (quintessential agrarian socialism, according to which all land should be publicly owned, teachings that have attracted our gifted but naive Leo Tolstoy), he replied: "Of course, in the first place because Henry George is one of our most gifted writers and in the second place because I consider it useful to acquaint my students with his views so that they can see how fallacious they are." It would be useful for our homegrown economists, as well as for Tolstoy, to attend this professor's lectures.

I asked the professors who were showing me around if they thought that the kind of student disorders we had experienced in our universities could be experienced by their American counterparts. They told me they had never thought about such an eventuality because they had never had to deal with such problems. They were certain that if any students made the slightest attempt to concern themselves with anything but learning, they would immediately be thrown out of the school by their peers.

By this time classes had begun, so I was able to see the students. I was struck by the fact that in all American universities a great deal of attention is given to gymnastics and sports. At Columbia one large building is set aside for physical exercise.

By the way, Columbia is wealthier than Harvard.

[That evening] I and Baron Rosen dined with President Roosevelt and his family at Oyster Bay. Both before and after dinner I and the president talked at length.

Among the subjects we touched on was the American tariff discriminating against our sugar. It had been imposed while I was minister of finance, and I had protested, in vain, that such discrimination was a violation of the most favored nation policy. At my suggestion the Emperor had imposed discriminatory tariffs on several American products, much to the displeasure of America. Shortly before I left for America, we decided to rescind these tariffs and I was given permission by the Emperor to inform President Roosevelt of the fact.[42] I did not make use of this permission during the conference lest it be thought that I was currying favor with the Americans, but now I felt it appropriate to inform the president, who was very pleased at the news, which was published the following day and was well received.

In the course of our talk, particularly before dinner, President Roosevelt obviously tried to smooth over the differences between us that led to his dealing directly with Petersburg. He assured me that he had acted the same way toward the Japanese and showed me the copy of the telegram to which I earlier referred as proof.

Then we talked about various subjects in a most friendly manner. When I asked him for an autographed photograph he gladly complied.

In the course of the evening, the president asked me to transmit a letter to the Emperor, which opened with an acknowledgment of the thanks he had received for his efforts in negotiating peace. The letter went on to deal with the article in the Russo-American Commercial Treaty which stipulated that Americans could travel freely in Russia except under certain circumstances applicable to all Americans. The United States, the letter continued, had no objection to the barring of Americans who represented a danger to Russia, but it objected to the fact that Americans of the Jewish faith were singled out for exclusion and declared that the United States could never reconcile itself to the idea that the trustworthiness or decency of individuals depended on their religion. The letter concluded by urging that, as a means of improving the friendly feelings between Russia and America that my visit had produced, the Emperor stop interpreting the article of the treaty referred to in a manner prejudicial to Americans of the Jewish faith. On my return home I transmitted the letter to the Emperor, who turned it over to the Ministry of Interior for consideration.

[After returning from Oyster Bay, I went by train] to Washington, the official capital of America, arriving there early on a Sunday.

I saw the White House, the Senate, the House of Representatives, and several libraries, but my chief interest was in seeing the house in which the great George Washington, the creator of the present United States of America, lived and died. It is located outside of Washington, on the Potomac River. It is remarkable that every ship that passes this house salutes it and that everyone who walks or drives by it takes off his hat. Obviously, Americans pay homage to this place as if it were sacred.

Unfortunately, the George Washington home is usually closed on Sundays, as is nearly everything else in America. Since I could not stay on for another day, I asked the president if an exception could be made for me. He replied that unfortunately there was nothing he could do, because historical monuments of this kind were administered by an organization of wealthy ladies who maintain them at their own expense and who therefore do as they please. They would refuse him if he asked them to make an exception, but if I were to get in touch with the president of the organization, she would undoubtedly make an exception for me, because of my great popularity. I did as he suggested and she made an exception. I then sailed to [Mount Vernon] on a navy ship.

As we looked around the first president's home, I was struck by how small the rooms seem by present standards, yet in his day they were considered spacious. I was shown the room in which Lafayette, the French general who helped in the establishment of the United States of America, stayed. Also, I was shown the room in which Washington died.

In touring the estate I saw the graves of Washington and his wife. One area in the estate is set aside for trees planted by famous and not-so-famous visitors. I, too, planted such a tree. In what condition it is now, I do not know.

While in New York I had several meetings with J. P. Morgan, one of the richest men in America.[43] He is evidently the most influential Christian financier and industrialist in America, with Schiff ranking as the richest and most influential Jewish financier in the country. Consequently, there is some enmity between the two.

Morgan graciously invited me and my suite to sail up the Hudson with him on his yacht to visit the military academy that trains almost all the officers of the American army.

Although he owns a mansion in New York, he tries to spend as much time as possible at sea, believing, and not without reason, that life at sea is more healthful than life on land. We had lunch on the yacht on the way up and dinner on the yacht on our way back. These were the only two decent meals I had while in America.

On our arrival at the lavishly built academy, we were greeted with military honors. Then, after looking over the school, we went to a large parade ground, where we witnessed a magnificent parade of the entire cadet corps. I noted that the cadets, who wore resplendent uniforms, were much older than our cadets. During part of the parade they marched to the strains of "God Save the Tsar." As the sounds of this wonderful hymn resounded, I took off my hat, as did everyone else.

During our visit I noticed several officers from Komura's suite, whose presence there was probably coincidental. Seeing that they were put out because nobody paid the slightest attention to them, I invited them to join our group. This they did, gratefully.

Recalling Kokovtsev's urging that I try to arrange a loan, I used the occasion of being with Morgan on his yacht to ask if he would participate in floating a loan to help Russia pay for her wartime expenditures. He responded very favorably, and said that while he and his group were not in a position to arrange a loan in America, they were ready to participate in a loan floated in Europe. At the same time he urged me not to negotiate with the group of Jewish financiers led by Schiff. I complied. Later, when the opportunity arose to float a loan in Germany, Morgan went back on his word and would not participate, apparently under the influence of Emperor William. I will deal with this episode later on.

Speaking of Morgan, I am reminded of an interesting conversation I had with him about a disfiguring growth on his nose that looked like a red beet. When we were alone, off the yacht, I said to him: "Permit me to thank you and, by the way, to do you a favor. Professor Lassar, of Berlin, a good friend of mine, once treated me successfully for a skin disease. While at his clinic I saw many patients with disfigured noses whom he was able to help."

Morgan thanked me, then told me that he already knew this famous professor, but that, unfortunately, he could not have an operation on his nose. When I asked if it were fear of pain that would keep him from having an operation, he said that fear was not involved, nor was it lack of confidence in the professor. The reason, he told me, was that everyone knew of his disfigurement: "If I should appear in public with a normal nose, every street urchin that saw me, would stop, point at me, and burst out laughing." It seemed a strange reason, but he was obviously serious and apparently was sorry to have to forgo the operation.

During my last days in New York I saw its tallest skyscrapers and was taken by elevator to the top of a thirty-seven-story building. Atop the building, I noticed that it swayed slightly under the impact of a light wind. This is only natural, since the slightest movement at the base will result in perceptible swaying at the top.

While in New York, I was struck by the authority enjoyed by the secret police. Once, when we were driving on a street where traffic was so heavy at the intersection that we could not proceed, one of the police with me showed his badge to the traffic policeman on the spot. That policeman immediately stopped all other traffic to let us proceed. I was astonished, because in our monarchy the public would have been outraged by such an act on the part of the police and many, undoubtedly, would have refused to obey.

VI

Return to Russia
Paris, Berlin, Rominten

Paris

[I left New York on August 30 (our calendar) on the *Kaiser Wilhelm II*], a larger and somewhat faster ship than the *Kaiser Wilhelm der Grosse*. In addition to being luxuriously appointed and providing entertainment, it was equipped with a recently installed device at the bow to sound an alarm if the ship encountered an obstacle. Whether or not this device, which the captain demonstrated for my benefit, has been adopted by other ships I do not know.

When I boarded ship I was very ill. In fact, I had been in poor health even before leaving for America, but I had kept the fact to myself lest I be thought a malingerer like Nelidov and Muravev. Needless to say what I went through in America only made matters worse. The trouble centered in my lungs, and I kept myself going by adhering to a strict diet and receiving powerful cocaine massages, which completely upset my nerves. Even if I were well I would have wanted a rest, away from Petersburg, where I might find myself being "tossed into the fire" once more.

When we called at Southampton, I sought to ease my burdens by sending Planson on to Petersburg, to hand over to Count Lambsdorff all the documents concerning the conference, although they added nothing to the information I had already provided. In notifying the foreign minister that the documents were on the way, I requested that he ask the Emperor to grant permission for me to spend several weeks in Brussels, with my daughter, before returning to Petersburg. The reply, which was waiting for me when I reached Paris, was that he had not passed my request on because it was obvious that the Emperor wanted me to return to Petersburg.

When our ship docked in Cherbourg I deliberately waited there a few hours before going on to Paris, so as to arrive there very early in the morning when there would be few people, especially the curious public, about. Also I resolved not to talk to reporters and with one exception stuck to this resolve until October 17. The exception was Tardieu of *Le Temps*, to whom I granted an interview that I was to regret, at the strong urging of Nelidov.*

I arrived in Paris on September 6 (our calendar), as I recall, and was to spend several days there. My first call was, of course, on Premier Rouvier. After warmly congratulating me for concluding peace, he went on to complain about the difficulties he was experiencing with Germany over the Moroccan question. He told me that if he met their demands, his opponents in Parliament would bring his government down. It was not Prince Radolin, the German ambassador, who was making things difficult for him but Rosen and Kaufmann, who had been sent from Berlin to negotiate about Morocco. Rouvier felt that the differences over Morocco between his country and Germany were of less importance than the manner in which Germany was pushing its demands, a manner that was creating fear of war in his country.

In fact, I found some talk of the possibility of war in the French newspapers, and I learned that the government had already begun large and costly military preparations. Rouvier told me that it would be difficult for us to get a loan at a time when the press was talking of possible armed conflict with Germany. This was the sentiment of leading French bankers, who would tell me that although they were eager to float a loan, their hands were tied until "the Moroccan nightmare was over."

When he asked for my aid[2] in settling the dispute, I suggested that France leave the settlement of thorny questions to a conference of concerned powers. If France had to make concessions as a result of such a conference, he would face less opposition in Parliament than if he were to make concessions on Germany's insistence. He said that this was his view, too, but that the Germans would not agree to a conference. I urged him not to argue with the Germans about substantive questions for the time being and to concentrate instead on arranging a conference. He promised me that if the Moroccan question were settled he would fully support our efforts to float a loan, both as head of the government and as a financial expert.

I was so assured by Rouvier's promise that I went from the Quai d'Orsay to see Prince Radolin, with whom I had been on good terms when he had served in Petersburg, to see what I could do to patch things up between the two countries. After he had congratulated me about Portsmouth, I turned to business. I told him

*Because I was still in the dark about what had been agreed to at Björkö, I told Tardieu that in contrast to the French left-wing press, Emperor William had behaved properly toward Russia during the peace negotiations. At the same time I spoke kindly about both the government and people of France. Nonetheless my criticism of the French left-wing press provoked a very hostile reaction from it, this at a time when France was moving markedly toward the left. The hostile reaction was used against me by my enemies, among them Muravev, who was afraid that I would get the post he was seeking, the ambassadorship to Paris. It was alleged that I hate Frenchmen, and even now I hear echoes of this legend from decent, but credulous, Frenchmen.[1]

frankly that it was against Russia's interest to permit the dispute over Morocco to end in war, and that if it did, Russia was obliged to help France. He told me that the dispute had been made to appear more serious than it was by Rosen and Kaufmann, who were interfering with his efforts. In fact, he was considered a Francophile in Berlin. Couldn't I exert some influence over Chancellor Bülow, who had asked that I call on him on my way back to Petersburg? (Bülow was then in Baden, taking the cure, and I had informed him that it would be inconvenient for me to go to Baden, but that I could see him in Berlin, where I would be stopping off for a few hours.) When I saw Rouvier the following day, he repeated that the French mood was such that if he gave in to German demands his government would fall. I advised him to agree only to minor demands and leave the rest to the proposed conference.

Soon after my arrival in Paris I was informed by the English embassy that King Edward would be glad to receive me. I replied that I did not feel that I had the right to call on him before I had presented myself to my Emperor. Shortly thereafter, I received a visit from the secretary of our embassy in London, Poklewski-Koziell, a clever and hardworking man who was an intimate friend of the king. He assured me that he was calling on his own initiative, but with the knowledge of our ambassador, but it was obvious that he had come at the behest of the king.

Poklewski-Koziell told me that both the king and his people wanted me to visit their country. I told him that much as I wished to accept the invitation, I could not do so without permission from the Emperor. Had I asked for permission, I would have been refused, because the Emperor was still under the influence of Emperor William, as a result of Björkö. Even if King Edward had addressed himself directly to our Emperor he would have been refused, because Emperor Nicholas II still considered England our sworn enemy and more than once had said in my presence that there was no difference between "kikes" and Englishmen.

My visitor then came to the point of his visit, that the time had come for Russia and England to end their senseless quarrels over Persia, Afghanistan, and other matters. I told him that rapprochement had to be viewed in light of our major goal—several decades of peace. I favored good relations with England, but not at the expense of good relations with the continental powers. Moreover, to achieve our goal we must make an honest effort to establish good relations with Japan. Undoubtedly, the entente we subsequently established with England demonstrated the influence of King Edward on Poklewski-Koziell and the latter's influence on his friend Izvolskii, the foreign minister.

I received another invitation from a monarch, from Emperor William, to visit him. My reply to this one was the same I gave to the English, but shortly thereafter I received instructions from our Emperor to call on Emperor William, who was then at his hunting lodge in Rominten. I informed Rouvier and Radolin that I would be seeing Emperor William and promised I would try to persuade him to permit the more substantive questions concerning Morocco to be dealt with by a conference.

Aware that if I saw the German Emperor without having called on President Loubet there would be an unfavorable reaction in France, I told Rouvier that I would like to visit the president. I received an invitation immediately and that evening left for Montélimar, in the south of France, to call on Loubet at his nearby estate. I spent the next day with him and his family and then returned to Paris.

When I had a chance to be alone with Loubet, and I always enjoyed talking with this fine old man, he congratulated me once more on my achievement at Portsmouth. (He had sent me a congratulatory telegram, one of the multitude I had received, while I was still in America.) He spoke briefly about the Moroccan crisis and at length about my country's domestic situation, arguing that without a constitution and representative government Russia was in grave danger. Had he ever spoken about this subject with the Emperor? He had. And what was the response? The response, said Loubet, was: *"Do you really think so?"* Loubet told me that he replied: "Not only do I think so, I am convinced of it," and added that recent events had borne him out.

When I asked if he considered the growing, and militant, socialist movement in France a threat, he said with conviction: "It is nothing but hot air. As soon as the socialists come to power, they will gradually cease being socialists. The French are too level-headed and politically mature to permit socialist fantasies to be put into practice." When I tried to steer the conversation toward his government's anti-clerical policy (which had gone beyond the kind of reasonable limits which Gambetta, an extremist but a great man, had set), he obviously did not want to talk about it. When he told me that he had decided not to seek reelection, I thought to myself that he was concerned not about the remote possibility he might not be reelected but about the uncivilized anticlerical war which his government had been conducting under pressure from the Chamber of Deputies.

I was accompanied part of the way to Montélimar by Noetzlin, director of the Banque de Paris and Pays Bas. Speaking for a French syndicate that wanted to float a loan for us, he told me that it would be impossible to do so until the Stock Exchange calmed down. After my return from seeing President Loubet, Premier Rouvier once more assured me that his government was committed to help with a loan once the Moroccan question was settled.

Berlin

Because our embassy had informed me that there would be a large crowd waiting to see me at my hotel, the Bristol, when I arrived in Berlin, I chose to walk rather than ride from the railroad station so as not to be noticed. In this I was successful, but when it was learned that I was at the hotel a large crowd gathered outside demanding to see me. In response I appeared on my balcony, several times.

The next day I called on the minister of foreign affairs, Bülow not being in town.[3] Also I saw the French ambassador, whom I promised to inform about my conversations with Emperor William so that he could pass it on to Rouvier.

Rominten

That evening I left on the Berlin to Petersburg train. Close to the German side of the border I changed trains for one that would take me on the short trip south to Rominten. I was met at the Rominten station by Prince Philipp Eulenberg, an elderly man reputedly very close to the Emperor and one of the chief figures in the court camarilla. During the automobile ride to the lodge, the prince told me that his Emperor had a high opinion of me, was delighted at my success in America, and was anxiously waiting to see me. When we arrived, Emperor William and his rather small suite were waiting. He greeted me very kindly and then directed Count August Eulenberg, Prince Philipp's cousin and chief marshal of the Imperial court, to show me to my quarters.

The lodge is located on a small hill, in the middle of a forest where the Emperor hunts every day. The lodge consists of two wooden two-story buildings connected at the second story by a covered gallery. Surrounding the lodge are smaller buildings for the servants. Their Majesties occupy all of the larger of the two buildings and the second story of the other. Members of the suite and guests are lodged in the first story of the second building. The Emperor, his suite, and his guests wore hunting clothes. The rooms are rather small, but as is always the case with the Germans, everything was clean and in good order. Life at the lodge is very plain.

Shortly after I had settled down in my room, Prince Philipp Eulenberg came in and took up the conversation we had begun in the automobile. We talked about the international situation, including Russo-German relations. He told me that Emperor William still remembered the conversation he had with me in 1897 on his visit to Russia, in the course of which I had suggested that the major European powers drop their conflicts and unite in order to preserve Europe's preponderant position in the world.[4] I expressed regret that this conversation had not led to any practical results. The prince replied that my hopes might be realized somewhat sooner than I thought.

We then went to lunch. The Emperor presented me to the Empress, whom I had met when she and her husband had been in Russia eight years earlier. Then I greeted the princess, a rather plain but extremely pleasant girl whom her parents obviously adored. Next I was introduced to those of the suite I had not yet met— the former minister of the navy (Hollmann, if I remember correctly), a general, and two young aides-de-camp. All in all, a small, friendly group. The Empress, who sat on my right, did not talk politics. Among other things, she said that her husband, who at one time had disliked automobiles, was now very taken up with them and drove too fast for her peace of mind.

After lunch the Emperor spoke privately to me. After congratulating me on my success at Portsmouth, he returned to the conversation we had years earlier in Russia. I told him I was still firmly convinced that the idea I had put forward then was the correct one to follow. He said he agreed completely and was happy that I had remained committed to it. He allowed as how what had been agreed to at Björkö between him and my Emperor was a step in the right direction. He said he was informing me about the agreement with my Emperor's agreement, but he did not share the details of it with me, i.e., he did not give me the text to read, leaving that to my Emperor.[5] When he asked if I were pleased about Björkö, I replied, in all candor, that I was. Then after some small talk, he left to go hunting.

Soon Prince Eulenberg came to see me, on the pretext of wanting to know if I had everything I wanted, but in fact to tell me that because his Emperor had complete confidence in him I could communicate with his master through him concerning matters of great confidentiality. I could be certain, he said, that whatever I sent would be given immediately to Emperor William and he would then send the reply directly to me. He added that I could send letters meant for Emperor William to him through the German embassy in Petersburg if I had no other channel I considered reliable.

After the prince's departure I went for a walk, during the course of which I saw the princess at play. Shortly after returning to my room I looked out the window and saw the Emperor returning from the hunt. It was not long after his return that I was told he wanted to see me.

I told him that if Europe were to be united the first step would be rapprochement between Germany and France. First, it would be necessary to prepare French public opinion for such a shift, and this would not be easy, as I had noticed while I was in France. I ventured to say that neither we nor Germany was preparing the way for such rapprochement and that after Björkö nothing could be done toward that end. He remarked that although nothing had been done so far on behalf of rapprochement, Björkö would help get things going.

William then took another tack, going on to complain that the French government was continually behaving badly toward him and his country. He had, he said, attempted several times to improve relations with France, but without success. He was particularly incensed over the way in which Delcassé had negotiated the entente with England. Germany, he told me, had assumed that if her interests were affected by the agreement being negotiated, she would be consulted by France or, at the very least, be informed before the agreement was concluded. But even though the agreement affected German interests in Morocco, his government had been neither consulted nor informed.

I countered by saying that since then France had shown that she wanted to smooth things over. Granted that the Rouvier government was still in power, but Delcassé had been replaced by Rouvier, who was trying to settle the dispute over Morocco amicably. I then noted that His Majesty's ambassador to Paris, Prince Radolin, told me that Rouvier was making all the concessions he could and was behaving very correctly toward Germany. I also talked about the difficulties that Rouvier was encountering from Rosen and Kaufmann, suggesting that he, the

Emperor, was not being adequately informed about what the two were doing. It seemed to me, I said, that it was in Germany's interest to have a sensible government, like that of Rouvier, in office and that the two were endangering the government with their unreasonable demands. If the Rouvier government should give in to them it might have to give way to one averse to seeking friendly relations with Germany. Moreover, if Rouvier capitulated, other countries with interests in Morocco, e.g., America, could argue that France had acted improperly in coming to terms with Germany without consulting them.

I urged that the more serious questions impinging on interests of several powers be left to an international conference. After listening carefully, Emperor William said he was convinced and wrote a telegram to Bülow, which he showed me.

Turning to his complaints about the French ambassador in Berlin, I suggested that if he were unacceptable, he could be replaced by someone more likely to help improve Franco-German relations. To this suggestion, the German Emperor responded: "The present ambassador is a nonentity, but at least he is courteous and calm. His replacement might be worse."

To illustrate how improperly the French government behaved toward him, the Emperor told me that after he had been attentive to a very proper and excellent officer attached to the French embassy, he learned that Paris was planning to recall the man. At the first opportunity he asked the French ambassador if the rumor were true. Upon being told that it was, William expressed regret, to which the ambassador replied that his government had the right to place its officers wherever it chose. I had to acknowledge that the Emperor had the right to feel offended by this reply, but suggested that Paris was either not aware of the facts or was acting on inadequate information.

The Emperor then spoke sarcastically about our ambassador to London, Count Benckendorff. The count's importance in London, he said, derived solely from the fact that King Edward liked him because he was a good bridge partner. He was unhappy, too, over the fact that the count, because of his ardent Catholicism, was hostile to Germany.

He then shifted the conversation to the situation in Russia, saying that he had heard that things were very unsettled. I observed that our government had driven many of our classes into opposition both by an incorrect domestic policy and by a foreign policy that had provoked war with Japan. I said that our government had lost all authority with its people and could not avoid granting a constitution.

It was Emperor William's opinion that our Emperor should grant some of the reforms demanded by society at once, but that having done so, he should make no further concessions. He told me that he had suggested this to our Emperor. But he did not say a word about the war with Japan, obviously remembering my prediction about what would happen if Germany seized Kiaochow.

After I returned to my room, Count Eulenberg brought me a gold-framed portrait of the Emperor, personally inscribed with the following: "Portsmouth-Björkö-Rominten. Wilhelm Rex" and the chain of the Order of the Red Eagle.

"Portsmouth-Björkö-Rominten" summarized the policy that William had followed from the time that Emperor Nicholas had agreed to a negotiated peace until
that moment. Apparently, his conversation with me had convinced him that the
war with Japan had weakened Russia to the degree that he could regard his
eastern border as secure and that Portsmouth and Björkö strengthened him on his
western border at the least and at best made it possible that he could receive
Russian aid if need be. All this without spilling a drop of German blood or
spending a single German pfennig! But man proposes and God disposes.

Why had the Emperor bestowed an order on me that is reserved for members
of ruling families? Apparently he decided to grant me this extraordinary honor
because, after having made me a member of the Order of the Black Eagle, there
was nothing else he could do. This remarkable honor probably helped prompt
Emperor Nicholas to grant me a title in recognition of my accomplishment at
Portsmouth when I returned to Russia.

When I asked Count Eulenberg if I could thank his Emperor for the honor he
had bestowed on me, he said that the best time to do so would be before dinner.
Then he added that if I wanted to please His Majesty I should wear the chain at
dinner. I told him that this would be difficult because I had taken neither uniforms
nor decorations with me to America in the knowledge that neither would be
required there. And I had not expected to be presented to any monarch during
this trip. It was agreed that I would wear the chain with my dress coat and that he
would explain the matter to the Emperor.

After dinner all of us, except the princess and an aide-de-camp, went into an
adjoining room, where we sat around a table, drank coffee or beer, and were
free to smoke. Soon, apparently as was the custom, those present took turns telling funny stories and anecdotes, the Emperor laughing more heartily than the
others.

I was particularly struck by the Emperor's attitude toward Prince Eulenberg.
He sat on the arm of the prince's chair, his right hand on Eulenberg's shoulder,
almost as if he were putting his arm around him. The prince was the most relaxed
person there. Had a stranger been asked to point out who in that company was the
Emperor, he would have been amazed by the question, but, upon being assured
that one of those present was in fact the monarch, he would probably have pointed
to Prince Eulenberg. William's attitude toward the prince assured me that the
prince was in his complete confidence. Around ten o'clock the Emperor said good
night and we all left. My visit was to end the following day.

The next morning I was up early, went walking, and saw the princess at play.
To catch the fast train to Petersburg I would have to leave Rominten before one.
When I returned to my room, Count Eulenberg told me that the Emperor would
lunch earlier than usual in order to be able to join me. Shortly after eleven I was
called to lunch, at which the mood was a lively one.

All in all I was favorably impressed by the great simplicity with which the
Emperor and Empress lived at Rominten. Also I was struck by her kindly manner,
as well as by the fact that the Emperor is much more charming in private than he is

in public, where he is harsh and arrogant in the manner of a fine Berlin guards officer.

After lunch I took leave of the Empress, the princess, and the members of the suite. When I started to take leave also of the Emperor he astonished me by saying that he would ride with me to the station. During the ten-minute trip Prince Eulenberg sat in the front seat of the automobile and I sat in the back with the Emperor, who told me that I could have complete confidence in the prince, who had informed him of our conversation.

When we arrived at the station the Emperor insisted on waiting for the train. At the station a courier sent by our financial agent in Berlin was waiting for me. On a scrap of paper I wrote a short note to the French ambassador in Berlin asking him to inform Rouvier that I had spoken to Emperor William about the Moroccan question and had been assured by the Emperor that he did not intend to create any difficulties and that the question of holding a conference was settled. I told the courier to deliver the note as soon as possible.* When I said goodbye to the Emperor I thanked him once more for his kindness and hospitality. Of course, he had his reasons for being so kind.

When my train stopped on the Russian side of the border, at Verzhbolovo, I was greeted by all the officers of the local brigade of border guards, a body toward which I have had a special regard from the time I established it as a special corps.[7] I take great pleasure in the fact that this creation of mine was in top military form during the war with Japan and that it never wavered during our time of revolution and anarchy.

After lunching with the officers I boarded the train for the completion of its trip to Petersburg, where I arrived on September 15.

---

*Some time later, when I told a French statesman that I had succeeded in preventing conflict between France and Germany over Morocco, he expressed doubt. That prompted me to try to get hold of the note, for my archive. In this I failed, but I was able to get an official copy of the note sent by the French ambassador in Berlin to Rouvier, giving the substance of my note.[6]

VII

General Strike

My Welcome

My friends, who learned of the date of my return to Petersburg only the evening before my arrival, took care not to spread the news, particularly not to the press, because the city was already in a revolutionary fever and my arrival might spark demonstrations and counter-demonstrations. Nonetheless, a large crowd was waiting when I arrived at the station, so large that I had difficulty in reaching the waiting automobile. Someone in the crowd delivered a welcoming speech, praising me for my service to the fatherland in negotiating peace. I felt obliged to respond to this unexpected welcome with a few words of thanks.

Because it was still early in the morning, there were few people about as I drove home. Those who recognized me, strangers as well as acquaintances, took off their hats as I passed and made signs of thanks. Not a soul showed any hostility. Later, when I had an opportunity to speak to my acquaintances, they said, almost to a man, that having prevented "the spilling of more Russian blood in Manchuria," I must now prevent the spilling of Russian blood at home, where things were ready to boil over.

Later that day I called on Count Lambsdorff, to share with him my impressions of Portsmouth, particularly about the future of our relations with Japan. It had been my feeling that a treaty of peace with Japan should include a provision for a postwar alliance whereby each of us would undertake to defend the other if the interests of either, as defined in the treaty, were menaced. When I suggested this to Komura he was evasive, but implied that the treaty might include something less binding than an alliance. Accordingly, I sent a telegram from Portsmouth to Count Lambsdorff saying that it would be desirable to move in this direction in our talks and asking for instructions.

A few days later I received a reply that was both evasive and discouraging. Consequently I did not raise the question with Komura again, resulting in a treaty that did not guarantee that the peace would be more than an interlude between wars. Although I had received a discouraging reply from the foreign minister, I now repeated what I had said in my telegram about the need of establishing some kind of *entente cordiale* with Japan. As I learned from the count, the reason for his discouraging reply was that some of our generals and higher civilian officials were talking about a war of revenge, an idea that was being widely supported by widely read newspapers, notably *Novoe vremia*. This desire to settle scores, naturally, had some influence on the Emperor himself.

I felt that we should give signs to Japan that we considered her important and that we were willing to treat her as a great power. In that vein I suggested to Count Lambsdorff that we raise the rank of our envoy in Tokyo from that of minister to that of ambassador.

When the foreign minister told me that the Emperor was planning to appoint Bakhmetev as minister to Tokyo, I said that he knew nothing about the Far East and was, reputedly, a silly person to boot. When asked to suggest someone else, I recommended Pokotilov. The count felt that he would be quite suitable, but he knew that, for some reason, the Emperor was set on Bakhmetev. The foreign minister said he would defer raising the question of the need for a suitable person for the occasion when the proposal to raise the rank from minister to ambassador arose.[1]

We barely talked about my conversation with Emperor William at Rominten on this occasion.

I of course informed the Emperor of my return immediately on my arrival. The next day he invited me to see him aboard his yacht, *Shtandart*, anchored off Björkö. I was taken to the yacht aboard the *Strela*, arrived at my destination about noon, and was shown to the Emperor's cabin. He thanked me sincerely and warmly for my successful completion, both in *letter* and *spirit*, of the very difficult commission he had given me and told me that in recognition of my service to him and the fatherland he was bestowing the title of count on me. I must admit that I was very moved by this extraordinary honor and, accordingly, thanked him profusely and kissed his hand.[2]

He then turned to my stay in Rominten. He told me that Emperor William had written him enthusiastically about me and informing him how pleased I was by the idea of the Björkö agreement. I said that I favored an alliance of Russia, Germany, and France, to which His Majesty replied that he remembered my conversation with Emperor William about that subject.

I then asked the Emperor: "Your Majesty, do you still have any doubts about my loyalty to you and do you believe those who have tried to persuade you that I am a revolutionary?" His answer: "I trust you completely and have never believed those slanders." This implied that he was admitting that he had received slanderous statements about me, slanders coming chiefly from

Plehve. I shall never forget what the Emperor said on this occasion.

After leaving the Emperor I went to the lounge, where the Empress and the entire suite were already assembled for dinner. During the meal Admiral Birilev, a fine man, but a bit of a character, was very amusing. After dinner I spent some time with the admiral, Baron Freedericksz, and some members of the suite. Their attitude toward me was cordial, even respectful.

After spending the night aboard ship, I returned to Petersburg. On the vessel taking me back to the city was a young officer, a professor at the Naval Academy, who had also been presented to the Emperor. He told me that Tsushima had been inevitable because our warships were poorly constructed.

The news that I had been granted a title, and what it represented, aroused a range of reactions. The traditionally silent majority of society expressed approval in the belief that I had earned the honor. Many, some of them strangers, even asserted that the honor was redundant because everyone knew what I had done for the fatherland.

The left reacted unfavorably because it had wanted us to be forced to sign a peace that was as disgraceful as our defeat. Therefore its press minimized my contribution and gave President Roosevelt all the credit. For, after all, he was the president of a republic and the left wanted a republic. And what kind of a republic!

Needless to say, the rightist press, which had incited us to go to war in the first place, in the spirit of Plehve's "we need a little victorious war," was now saying that we could have won the war had I not concluded peace. And after revolution began to rear its head, this press began to scream that I was a traitor, that I had deceived the Emperor and had made peace against his wishes. *Novoe vremia*, in particular, harped on this theme because its publisher, the mercenary A. S. Suvorin, and M. O. Menshikov,[3] his talented but unbalanced associate, were now trying to prove that their earlier prediction that we could smash the Japanese was correct. Suvorin had the audacity to say in print that the Emperor had let it be know that he, the Emperor, had been the only one opposed to concluding peace. Obviously Suvorin would not have dared print such a story if he had not known that the court would react favorably to it.

Whether or not the Emperor uttered these words I do not know, but if he had, it would have been in character. Suvorin's "revelation" was, of course, picked up by the extreme rightist gutter press, which began to scream: "You see, we were right in calling 'Count Semi-Sakhalin'[4] a traitor." And the monk Iliodor, their prophet, immediately wrote a lead article demanding that I be publicly hanged. And it is this press that received subsidies, channeled through "Cutlet Colonel" Prince Putiatin, the confidant of the "hysterical" Empress Alexandra Fedorovna.[5] That she is "hysterical" can be seen from the following.

The Empress wanted a son, but God had given her four daughters. Then along came that charlatan Dr. Philippe, who convinced her she would bear a son.[6] So she decided she was in an "interesting condition." After several months she stopped wearing a corset. Everyone noticed that she was growing fatter and believed her to be pregnant. The Emperor was overjoyed. Finally, it was officially announced that she was expecting and that, consequently, she would no longer hold receptions.

When she was in what was presumed to be her ninth month, everyone in Petersburg expected to hear the cannon of the Fortress of SS. Peter and Paul signal that she had given birth and to learn from the number of shots whether it was a boy or a girl. By this time the Empress had taken to bed and Professor Ott, her personal obstetrician, and his assistants, had taken up residence at Peterhof, waiting for the event to come at any hour. But nothing happened. When she finally permitted him to examine her, he found that she was not pregnant. Then the appropriate announcement was made.

If a charlatan like Dr. Philippe can convince her that she is pregnant and if she remains convinced for nine months, she is capable of believing anything. And once she is convinced of something, she convinces her spineless but good husband. And this is the man who has unlimited power over mighty Russia, over the fate and welfare of 140 million subjects with God-given souls.

The news that I had been granted a title stirred the muck in the depths of the souls of the Russian ruling class. At court the cry that I had prevented Russia from winning the war was taken up by the military types at court—generals-adjutant, aides-de-camp, and ordinary colonels and generals, who had advanced in rank by looking after the court kitchens, automobiles, horses, dogs, and the like. This view was also convenient for all the generals who had gone to war for plunder and debauchery. It was particularly convenient for those chiefly responsible for our military disgrace—General Kuropatkin ("with the soul of a staff clerk") and that old fox General Linevich, who might have been an adequate sergeant major in a good regiment fighting guerrillas in the Caucasus.

But those who were most disturbed by my new title were to be found in the top ranks of the Petersburg bureaucracy, men like Kokovtsev, Budberg, and Taneev, who could not forgive me for receiving this honor and have therefore intrigued against me indefatigably ever since. Also, I heard that Muravev, our ambassador to Rome, fell into a black melancholy on hearing the news and never recovered from it. He, too, became my avowed enemy.

The Annulment of Björkö

After returning from seeing the Emperor I called on Count Lambsdorff once more. He was genuinely pleased at the honor I had received. He told me that the Emperor was very satisfied with my conduct of the peace negotiations, with me in general, and, in particular, with my visit to Emperor William, from whom he had heard that I agreed completely with what the two Emperors had decided at Björkö.

I said that I had agreed and was convinced that the correct policy for us to follow was to form an alliance among Russia, Germany, and France, to be joined later by other continental powers. The foreign minister demurred: he preferred that Russia stand alone, obligated to no one. I said he was right in principle, but the fact was that we were allied, to France. I argued that an alliance of the three powers would give our unhappy motherland a long period of freedom from the ravages of war, a long breathing time.

Had I read the text of the treaty signed at Björkö? I told him that neither of the Emperors had given me the opportunity to do so. Looking very upset, he told me that until very recently he, too, had been denied the opportunity, and saying "how charming," he showed me the text. In essence it obligated each power to go to the aid of the other if the other were attacked by a third European power. It stipulated that Russia would make every effort to have France join this alliance, but whether or not she succeeded, the treaty would be binding, but would not go into force until peace were signed between Russia and Japan. (From the German point of view, the longer the war the better.) The treaty was signed by the two Emperors and countersigned for Germany by a bigwig whose surname I could not make out[7] and for Russia by Admiral Birilev.*

In effect the treaty obligated us to go to the aid of Germany if she were at war with France, yet we were obligated to defend France against Germany. And from whom would Germany defend us? France, with whom we were allied? Italy? Austria? But these two were allied with Germany. The only possible case in which Germany would be obligated to defend us would be a war between us and England, but England could not attack us on land. And if Russia should find herself again at war with Japan, Germany would not be obliged to help us under the terms of this treaty.

When I was finished reading, I told the count that it imposed heavier obligations on us than it did on Germany, that, moreover, it was incompatible with our obligations to France and therefore was unacceptable. How, I asked, could he have been kept in ignorance of the text for so long? And was not our Emperor aware that we had a treaty with France?

Count Lambsdorff replied that the Emperor certainly knew of our alliance with France, but that it might have slipped his mind, or, if it had not, his mind might have been so befogged by William that he had not grasped the implications of what he was agreeing to. He assured me that when he had telegraphed me in Paris to say that the meeting at Björkö was of no political significance, he had done so in good faith.

I told him: "The treaty must be annulled, by whatever means necessary, even postponement of the ratification of the Treaty of Portsmouth. It is your duty." We then considered how best to persuade the Emperor to annul the treaty. One could use the argument that the treaty was not valid because it had not been countersigned by the minister of foreign affairs. Or, it could be pointed out that when the Emperor had signed the treaty, he did not have at hand the text of our treaty with

---

*When I saw the admiral, I asked if he knew what he had countersigned. The answer was "no"; the Emperor had asked him to sign it on trust and he had. He was aware that it was important since the Emperor told him he needed his signature because the Germans wanted a minister to countersign it for the Russian side.

France, which was completely incompatible with the Björkö treaty. Another line of argument would be to suggest that the treaty not go into force until France agreed to it. All this would require time. We agreed that the only acceptable point in the treaty was the one urging an alliance among Russia, Germany, and France, something to which we should bend every effort.

After our conversation I thought of how best to influence the Emperor to annul the treaty. It was unlikely that he would listen to me even if I had a chance to talk to him, and as chairman of the Committee of Ministers I had very few such opportunities. The chances were that even if I could see him and tried to talk about the treaty, he would tell me that it was none of my business. As for Count Lambsdorff, what kind of influence could a man who had been kept in the dark about the treaty exert?* Given these facts, it occurred to me to work through Grand Duke Nicholas Nikolaevich because he was in good favor with the Emperor, partly because of his personal qualities, chief of which is his personal loyalty to Emperor Nicholas Aleksandrovich, both as a monarch and as a person.

When I had the opportunity of speaking to the Grand Duke, he did not admit to knowledge of the terms of the treaty, but, from what I learned later on, I am certain that he knew. I say this because General Palitsyn, chief of the General Staff, had already been permitted by the Emperor to see the text, and since he owed his position to the Grand Duke, I am sure that he would have shown the text to the Grand Duke or, at least, have informed him of its terms. When I explained to His Highness why the treaty must not be allowed to go into force, he accepted the argument that the treaty would put the Emperor in a dishonorable position and he would not have agreed to it had he understood the implications. I said that it was necessary to annul the treaty before we ratified the Portsmouth pact. As for me, I could not raise the subject with the Emperor since it was not in my jurisdiction. Count Lambsdorff would do what he could. The Grand Duke promised to help.

A few days later I was summoned to Peterhof, where I, the Grand Duke, and Count Lambsdorff were received by the Emperor, who turned at once to the subject of the Björkö treaty. We explained to His Majesty why the treaty should be annulled and suggested that, if he wished, it could be replaced by another treaty compatible with our treaty with France. We said that it would obviously be difficult for him to disown what he had signed, yet it had to be done and suggested that he authorize Count Lambsdorff to take the necessary steps.

Toward the end of September I asked the foreign minister how he was faring and was told that we had sent a note, which had elicited a reply that, for the most part, was evasive, but firm in its conclusion that "what is signed, is signed." We responded with a strong note. After I became premier, I asked Count Lambsdorff,

---

*I think that even before he knew, he guessed at the truth because, as he often told me, William was always trying to get our Emperor into trouble, relying on the personal letters between the two, about which the count was kept in the dark. Only when something resulted from this correspondence could he take steps to undo the mischief, and, being a gentle soul, he did so very slowly and diplomatically. William knew what the count was up to and therefore hated him and tried to have him put out of office.

not as a friend but in my official capacity, how things stood with the treaty. His reply: "Rest assured. The treaty no longer exists."

After these events Emperor William's hostility toward Count Lambsdorff was even greater than ever, and, as for me, it was said that he was no longer enthusiastic about me, although I continued to believe in an alliance with both Germany and France, while maintaining good relations with England and other powers. Unfortunately, we have since moved to a triple entente with France and England.

University Autonomy

While I was away much had been happening that contributed to or was symptomatic of the growth of the revolutionary spirit. One such event was the granting of autonomy to the higher schools by a decree issued on August 27.

I first learned of the decree while still in Paris, at the home of Alexandra Nikolaevna Naryshkina, a widow whom I had come to know while her husband was still alive. One reason for my call was that she was related, distantly, to my son-in-law, Cyril Vasilevich Naryshkin. Known in society as "Auntie Sasha," she was known for her loose tongue and odd ways. Although capable of fine feelings and thoughts, she was more noted for her ability to be embarrassing.

Turning to me with a radiant face, she asked if I knew of the decree granting autonomy to the higher schools, an act that would permit restoration of calm in these schools. I was surprised by this news and could not share her expectation that the decree would restore calm in the higher schools, which had been "on strike" and closed for half a year. But, being out of touch with what had been going on back home, I did not express my reservations.

It was obvious to me that those involved in the preparation of such a decree, the likes of General Glazov, minister of education, and the quasi-dictator General Trepov, were acting not under the spur of enlightenment but under the spur of fear, and that once fear had passed, the decree would become a dead letter. Moreover, it was obvious to me that autonomy unaccompanied by revision of the charters of the higher schools would lead to all sorts of difficulties. In fact, prior to my departure for America, when the state of the higher schools had been discussed in the Committee of Ministers, I had insisted on the need to revise these charters in order to make it possible to calm the professors and the students.[8] During the discussion Trepov and Glazov reacted to what I said with that ignorance of university life common to most higher officials, who were either military types such as Trepov and Glazov, about whom the less said the better, or graduates of elite higher schools, such as the Tsarskoe Selo Lycée or the Imperial School of Jurisprudence, who, even if enlightened, had little knowledge of what a university represents.

As I learned on my return to Russia, the decree of August 27 was prepared at a conference that Trepov initiated and dominated. Among those who participated were General Glazov, Kokovtsev (Tsarskoe Selo Lycée) and Schwanebach (Imperial School of Jurisprudence). When I saw the text of the decree I realized how vague it was, how little it reflected what had happened since the issuance of the university charter of 1884.

As I soon learned, the effect of the decree was to open the higher schools to ceaseless revolutionary meetings, attended not only by students, but also by workers (some genuine, some bogus), teachers, officials, enlisted men and non-commissioned officers in uniform, *kursistki*,[9] and even ladies from high society, who went to see these astonishing goings-on, to find the kind of thrills there that one could get from champagne, bullfights, and risqué entertainment. At these meetings anarchists and socialists delivered subversive speeches attacking the Emperor and higher officialdom, while their hearers responded with shouts of "Down with autocracy." It is unthinkable that such speeches would be tolerated even in the kind of republic that would have [an anarchist like] Prince Kropotkin for a president. But Trepov and other higher officials, aside from stationing troops to prevent disorder spreading from these meetings to the streets, did nothing except tell the professors (now in charge of these institutions as a result of the decree) that such meetings were impermissible. The professors and the school administrators admitted that what was going on was disorderly, but they argued that if Russia had freedom of assembly, as enjoyed in all civilized countries, students would not have to share with outsiders the freedom of assembly that they alone enjoyed. In short, they said, if all Russians enjoyed freedom of assembly, they could prevent outsiders from entering university grounds. As for the students, they announced that they were ending their "strike," not to return to their studies but to use the privilege of "autonomy" for revolutionary purposes.

Thus, the decree of August 27 opened the first crack through which the developing revolution could break through to the open.

Freedom of Assembly

Apparently the government accepted the view that the only way to deal with these disgraceful meetings was to grant some form of freedom of assembly. I say this because, on my return to Petersburg, the chairman of a conference on this subject invited me to attend one of its sessions,[10] at which I learned that a law dealing with the right of assembly had been drafted, but there were still minor differences to be resolved. When I learned the details of the proposed law I said that it would do little to keep the public from attending meetings in the higher schools, because its version of freedom of assembly was in stark contrast to the freedom being enjoyed within the walls of the higher schools. I said also that it would have been better to have issued a law on the right of assembly before granting ill-defined autonomy to the universities.

A few days later legislation granting the right of assembly was issued as a decree rather than as a law, thus bypassing the State Council. The decree would turn out to be a dead letter, in no way limiting the stormy and uncivilized meetings being held in the higher schools as well as in the halls of such learned bodies as the Technical Society and the Free Economic Society. This situation would continue until most higher schools were closed because of the growing strike movement in October.

Representative Government

The major event that occurred in Russia while I was in America was the law of August 6, providing for the establishment of an elected State Duma with consultative powers, usually called the Bulygin Duma, because Bulygin had drafted the law, in accordance with the Imperial rescript to him of February 18. Once he had prepared the draft of the law, the aim of which was to permit popularly elected deputies to participate in the legislative process, he turned it over for editing to the so-called Solskii Conference, that is, the Council of Ministers meeting under the chairmanship of Count Solskii.

One of the major questions facing those who were working out the details of the proposed duma was which class to give preference to in representation in order to guarantee a conservative body. Hitherto the government had considered the nobility the pillar of conservatism. But now, in the months following January 9, even in the highest ranks of the nobility, the song of the intelligentsia was being echoed, namely, that the existing order must be ended because Russia had been led into a disgraceful war and into utter chaos thanks to an autocracy which had come to mean nothing more than an irresponsible administration directed by the bureaucracy.

To be sure, the song that the nobility, or, at least, its prominent representatives, was singing was different in some important respects from that sung by the majority of the intelligentsia, which wanted a bourgeois constitutional monarchy that denied representation to the masses for still being too backward. And some *intelligenty* even had no objections to a bourgeois republic.[11] The nobility, on the other hand, felt that power should pass from the monarch to them, the self-styled "salt of the earth."

The peasantry, however, had remained truly monarchist, true to its traditional belief that the people could not exist without a tsar, one, it went without saying, who spoke for the people. In contrast to the nobility and the intelligentsia, the peasantry did not dream of political change, but only of social and economic change—the transfer of most, if not all, of the land to them, who were no better than drones, exploited by those who owned the land, be they nobles, merchants, or *intelligenty*. The ordinary people, particularly the peasantry, could not believe that their Tsar was responsible for any of the evils, the war included, that had been visited on Russia, and instead placed the responsibility on his advisors, i.e., nobles of various categories. Therefore, the peasantry felt that it was far better to dream of social and economic changes than of political ones.

It was possible to hold to such a belief in the days of Emperor Alexander II and his great reforms, because he governed under the slogan that Russia exists for the benefit of the weak, not the strong. But that no longer held true. Experience here and abroad has shown that there can be no economic reform without political reform above. It is remarkable that the Russian masses should have continued to cling to a shortsighted belief when its fallacious nature had been recognized in all the civilized countries of Europe.

[Given the fact that much of the nobility was now in opposition to the government, given the fact that the peasantry still seemed firmly loyal to the Emperor], many at the top levels of government and at court had come to believe that the peasantry should be favored in awarding representation to the duma.

[As weeks and months following the rescript of February 18 dragged by without signs of progress in implementing it, many in society sought assurance from the Emperor that some kind of elected legislature would come to pass. Accordingly a congress of zemstvo and municipal duma leaders elected a deputation to ask the Emperor for such assurance.] The deputation, led by Prince S. N. Trubetskoi, was received by the Emperor on June 6. It told him unequivocally that Russia expected a change in the structure of government that would give the people and society a role in the making of laws. His Majesty responded kindly but equivocally.

Nearly two weeks later, on June 18, Count V. V. Gudovich, marshal of the nobility of Petersburg province, and Prince P. N. Trubetskoi (brother of S. N. Trubetskoi), marshal of the nobility of Moscow province, presented a letter to the Emperor, signed by twenty-six provincial marshals of the nobility, which expressed much the same view as the delegation led by Prince S. N. Trubetskoi, but in a more restrained tone. In effect, it stated that Russia could not continue to live any longer as it had been living.

The situation in June was such that the Emperor felt it imperative to take some drastic steps to stave off a complete breakdown that would threaten his dynasty.

During the meetings to implement the rescript of February 18, C. P. Pobedonostsev and State Controller N. L. Lobko, both pillars of conservatism, led in the effort to give the peasantry preponderant representation in the proposed State Duma on the ground that it was a reliable bulwark of the dynasty and the government. Other participants did not express disagreement with this position. I had reservations not only about this position but also about what was the accepted view of the kind of body the State Duma would be.

What was being proposed was a body modeled on Western European parliaments in all respects but the essential one, the power to enact laws. It would be a body that would permit those in power to say, in effect: We will always listen to what you have to say, but then we will do as we please. I was certain that such a monstrosity would either go out of existence in a few months or develop into a genuine parliament that could enact laws and limit the power of the monarch. I did not speak during the sessions under Count Solskii because I felt that it was best for one in my position not to air my views unless asked for them.[12] However, I did intend to speak up when the time came for a special conference under the chairmanship of the Emperor to complete preparation of the law establishing a State Duma. But, as it turned out, I was in America when the conference was held, at Peterhof.[13]

I learned something of what went on at the Peterhof conference from Kokovtsev, with whom I was in touch while in America, and from Shipov, who was receiving information from the Ministry of Finance, and from other reliable sources. I learned that Pobedonostsev and Lobko continued to argue for preferential treatment for the peasantry, that to implement this view Kokovtsev thought up a scheme to increase peasant representation by giving peasant electors at the provincial level two votes each, once when electing one of their own as deputy to the State Duma and again in voting with other electors to choose the other deputies from the province.[14]

As I learned, the dim-witted exponents of noble rights, among them Count Vladimir Alekseevich Bobrinskii, who had been invited to participate in the conference, took a different tack, arguing for preferential treatment for the nobility in the election process. This provided Grand Duke Vladimir Aleksandrovich with the opportunity of saying in strong, but justified, language that while the nobility shouted its devotion to the Autocratic Sovereign in words, it acted systematically to limit its powers.

It was a fact that, for nearly a century, following the Napoleonic wars, the nobility was the class that sought liberal change. Under the influence of France and her ideas, the nobility, being the most enlightened and naturally most humane of all the classes, sought equality of rights and the enactment of a constitution that would limit the powers of the emperor. This movement caused Alexander the Blessed much unease during the last years of his reign.

Then, following his death, came the bloody Decembrist revolt, which gravely affected the reign of Nicholas I. Who led the revolt? Nobles, and what nobles they were! Not the present variety, which overtly or covertly participates in the infamous Union of the Russian People. The Decembrist nobles are now honored, even by tsars, as exceptionally dedicated men.

When the long reign of Nicholas I ended in the Sebastopol debacle (the responsibility of his regime, not of our valiant army), the liberal regime of the Great Liberator Alexander II began. The zemstvos that he established provided the nobility with an instrument for pressing for a constitution. That was to be expected, as I have pointed out in a memorandum that is still quoted in the press,[15] since the zemstvo was an institution that could gradually lead to a constitutional form of government. This could have come about peacefully had the zemstvos and municipal dumas been given autonomy from the beginning and not later been hamstrung by the administration.

No question that over the years the nobility wanted to limit the powers of the

Emperor, to share power with him, for its own benefit. For was it not the nobility that predominated in the congresses of zemstvo and municipal duma leaders in 1904 and 1905 which demanded a constitution?

The bourgeoisie, which had begun to crystalize in the reign of Emperor Alexander II as a thoughtful and class-conscious stratum, joined in the movement for a constitution in the latter years of the century. And this gave the nobility reason to realize that it would have to divide the pie with the bourgeoisie. What the myopic leaders of both classes failed to foresee was the emergence of a class-conscious proletariat with appetites of its own. And when the culturally backward proletariat, aware that it had nothing to lose, burst upon the scene in October 1905 like an elemental force, it began to tear at the pie with unbridled animal appetite. At this point the nobility and the bourgeoisie became frightened and began to sing a different song.

The State Duma established by the law of August 6 was, as I have said, to have only consultative power in the making of laws. The franchise was open to men of all religions and nationalities. As planned, the system of elections to this body was designed to give peasants the preponderance of seats in it. It should also be noted that the electoral system was not subject to change by administrative action.

The new body would in effect be a lower house [with the State Council becoming the upper house].[16] It was naive, as I have suggested, to believe that such a body—parliamentary in form but with no power to enact laws—could accomplish anything or long endure. It would either turn into a genuine parliament or collapse amidst revolutionary chaos. To put it bluntly, a parliament with no more than consultative power is the invention of bureaucratic eunuchs.

The expectation that the law of August 6 would have a calming effect on the public was not realized. Instead, the announcement that there would be a consultative State Duma seemed to be an invitation to open wide the door to the bedroom of Madame Constitution, and the weeks that followed saw revolutionary eruption seeping out of the cracks. These cracks were now being forced wide open as a result of decades of dissatisfaction over our government's failure to satisfy the psychic and material needs of the people and as a result of that most shameful of wars we had just been through.

Toward a Cabinet?

Among the matters being dealt with by the Solskii Conference while I was in America was a proposal to turn the Council of Ministers into something like a cabinet, i.e., a unified body that would coordinate the work of the several ministries. Count Solskii preferred that the name "Council of Ministers" be retained because the name "cabinet" smacked of Western parliamentarianism.

I have reason to believe that behind the proposal to change the functions of the Council of Ministers was the fact that Count Solskii knew that a storm was brewing and did not want to find himself acting as chairman of the council when the storm broke. This was understandable and forgivable, for he had been quite ill for many years, in fact, was unable to walk. It is a wonder that he was able to bear all the responsibilities with which he was saddled: chairman of the State Council, chairman of the Finance Committee, *locum tenens* for the Emperor as chairman of the Council of Ministers, chairman of various conferences.

When I returned to Petersburg, consideration of the proposal was still in an early stage. Virtually all the members of the conference but Kokovtsev were in favor of a unified body, at least in principle. But because of his *amour propre* and his pettiness, he was opposed because he knew that he would not be chairman of the new Council of Ministers. The few who supported him did so, not because they opposed the idea of unification, but because they feared that the chairman would be regarded as the equivalent of a premier, and that would lower the significance of the Emperor in the eyes of the people. In the end, the majority prevailed, resulting in the decree of October 19. Like everything that came out of the Solskii Conference, the decree was vague, the result of the compromises the count liked to make to keep from troubling His Majesty with disputes.

As will be seen, I became chairman of the Council of Ministers, i.e., in effect premier, the day before the decree appeared. Because the old name of the body was retained, I was to find myself held responsible for what had been done by it before October 19, e.g., the law on the Bulygin Duma. To this day most people are unable to distinguish between the pre–October 19 Council of Ministers and the post–October 19 body.

Freedom of the Press?

On my return to Russia I was struck by how unbridled the press had become, given our very reactionary censorship laws. With each defeat in the Far East our press had become more daring, until by mid-October the liberal, and even the conservative, press had come to ignore the constraints of censorship. The Petersburg press, which, and even now but to a lesser degree, set the tone for the press of the entire country, organized a union to defy the censorship rule, and even the conservative press joined the union.[17]

By this time the entire press had, in a sense, become revolutionary, opposed to the regime that had brought Russia to the pass in which she found herself. Later, of course, the right-wing press, notably *Novoe vremia*, would rant against the government for not showing enough vigor in dealing with the "dissolute" left-wing press. In those days, when the press proclaimed that "it was seizing the right to freedom of the press," it appealed especially to that part of the public that belonged to affiliates of the Union of Unions,[18] offering full coverage of some unions like the Union of Professors, partial coverage of others, and very limited coverage of the rest.

All these unions, whatever their political coloration, agreed on the need to end the existing regime. And many of their leaders believed that the end justifies the means, including the printing of lies. But the left-wing press was to be outdone in the dissemination of lies, slander, and deceit by the right-wing press, e.g., *Novoe vremia* (Suvorin),[19] *Russkoe znamia* (Dubrovin), *Moskovskie vedomosti* (Gringmut),[20] *Veche*, and even *Kievlianin*, once it became frightened by the anarchy following the October strike.

Also, there was an underground press that was doing what it could to stir things up by printing and distributing millions of copies of revolutionary leaflets and pamphlets of every description. Some of the underground publication was the work of the secret police because Trepov still could not free himself of the Zubatov idea of "fighting fire with fire," i.e., of using revolutionary weapons and tactics in the struggle with the revolutionaries.

Confusion at the Top

The government, i.e., Trepov, reacted belatedly, when it did, to all this ferment. To be sure, not enough was known abut the goals of the Union of Unions and its affiliates. Thus, the naive and somewhat senile minister of ways and communications, Prince Khilkov, asserted (according to Trepov) that the railroad employees union, which was to lead the railroad strike in October, was only concerned with working conditions and was in no way hostile to the government.

In those days General Trepov was in a tizzy, alternating between left and right. He complained to me that the responsibilities laid on him were more than he could bear. I sensed that he wanted to escape from the incomprehensible chaos in which we found ourselves, partly because he was ill, partly because he sensed the storm that was coming. As for that wise and skeptical old man Pobedonostsev, he no longer sought to exert any influence, at least not openly. Other ministers, colorless bureaucrats like Bulygin, Kokovtsev, General Glazov, and General Rödiger did nothing. Schwanebach, although another colorless bureaucrat, offered a proposal, a harebrained one, for distributing land to soldiers returning from Manchuria as a way of insulating them from revolutionary influence. [I shall have more to say about this proposal later on.]

The Revolution Gathers Strength

[By late September] several parts of the. country were falling into the grip of revolution.

The Baltic provinces were especially hard hit. Mitau, and districts adjoining it to the south, were virtually under martial law, with troops from the Vilna Military District called in to deal with the trouble. General Freese, the commander of that district, was accused of being indecisive as well as of being too indulgent toward Jews and Poles and was quickly replaced and appointed to the State Council. The turmoil in the Baltic provinces was such that some Baltic nobles with influence at court—General-Adjutant Richter and Baron Budberg—called for the establishment of a temporary governor-generalship for those provinces.[21]

In the Caucasus, the well-intentioned efforts of the viceroy, Count Vorontsov-

Dashkov, to undo the harm caused by his predecessor, Prince Golitsyn, particularly with respect to the Armenian church, came too late. Entire districts and cities were by now in open rebellion. Although the count is a well-intentioned man, as I have oft noted, he is no eagle and, more important, does not choose his subordinates wisely. Accordingly, in his efforts at a good-will policy he shifted between very liberal and very reactionary policies, for example, first imposing martial law on a locality, then lifting it.

Another troubled area was the southwestern region—Kiev, Podolia, and Volhynia—whose unqualified governor-general, Kleigels, responded to unrest by sitting with his arms folded. In Moscow, where the Zubatovshchina had originated, there was a new and also unqualified governor-general, Peter Pavlovich Durnovo, who had recently been appointed to the post with the help of Count Solskii. Durnovo's predecessor, General Kozlov, a universally respected man, vacated his post because he could not get along with Trepov.

We were more fortunate in the Kingdom of Poland, where General Skalon, no eagle but a straightforward and honest man, had just been appointed governor-general. His predecessor, General Maksimovich, had received the governor-generalship as a reward for a favor done for Baron Freedericksz: the general, a close friend of the baron's and like him a former Horse Guardsman, had somehow been of service when the baron had contracted what some considered a *mésalliance*. The general had reacted to the state of near rebellion in the Kingdom of Poland by departing for a summer home near Warsaw and refusing to budge from there. But General Skalon, thanks to a strong military force and his own courage, was able to keep rebellion from breaking out into the open except in a few localities.

Siberia, too, was in a state of near rebellion. In part this was the result of the fact that from time immemorial restless and vicious persons had been sent there as exiles. Another factor was its proximity to the theater of war, which enabled the inhabitants to know more about the shameful war than did the inhabitants of European Russia. In addition, the troops in transit through Siberia contributed to its unsettled mood.

The governors-general of the region were of no help. One, Count Kutaisov, governor-general of Irkutsk, is not a stupid man, but he is a chatterbox and does not take his work seriously. Everyone has been amazed that such as he should have been appointed to such a post. It was said that he owed it to Empress Alexandra Fedorovna, who had become acquainted with him as a girl, while visiting Queen Victoria, when he was serving as our military attaché in London. General Sukhotin, the governor-general of Omsk, was strong, straightforward, and intelligent, but he was inclined to be hasty, particularly after he had eaten. He and Kutaisov had long been at odds, a condition that undermined authority.

Revolutionary ferment was especially marked in Odessa, where Jews were in the majority. Noting the general unrest and the fall in the government's prestige, they decided to use revolutionary means to get rid of the disabilities under which they had long suffered. Of course, only a minority of the Odessa Jews were revolutionaries, but most of them, having lost patience because of their unfair treatment, were sympathetic to the so-called liberation movement and looked with tolerance on revolutionary acts, even of the most extreme kind. Neidhardt, the city's prefect, made matters worse. He is not stupid, but he is very frivolous, superficial, ill informed, yet has a high opinion of himself. He was arrogant and coarse toward his subordinates and was thoroughly hated by most Odessans. After becoming premier I would have to remove him from his post.

The revolutionary threat was growing in other cities as well, particularly in Moscow. Particularly rebellious were the students, not only university students, but also the older students in the secondary schools. Those students now listened only to those who preached the most revolutionary ideas. Most of the professors were also opposed to the regime, as were the zemstvo and municipal duma leaders, who saw salvation only in a constitution. They and the professors were supported by both merchants and industrialists, some of whom (Morozov, Chet-verikov, and Tereshchenko's widow) gave money to the liberation movement, while some, e.g., Savva Morozov, even gave money to the revolutionaries. And the workers had fallen completely under the sway of revolutionary leaders and could be counted on where physical force was called for.

All the non-Russians (thirty-five percent of the population) raised their heads on realizing how weak the empire had become and decided the moment was at hand to achieve their goals: for some, e.g., the Poles, it was "autonomy," for others, e.g., the Jews, it was "equal rights." Mainly the non-Russians wanted the end of the restrictions to which they had long been subject, restrictions that in many cases were outrageous and un-Christian and in some cases merely stupid.

The peasants were violently condemning their oppressed condition in general and their lack of land in particular.

Civil servants, aware of how the patronage system in government had grown to gigantic proportions during the reign of Nicholas II, began to turn against the regime they were supposed to serve.

The soldiers were restless and susceptible to the revolutionary message for two reasons: first, because they were unjustly blamed for our disgraceful defeats; second, because, contrary to law, reservists were not being demobilized following the conclusion of peace. Reservists were being kept in the army in European Russia because troop strength was low there. Another reason for delay in demobi-lization was fear of the reservists among the troops returning from Manchuria because some of them had given some slight support to revolutionaries.

In short, I found a country in complete turmoil on my return from America, with revolution beginning to break out into the open, with a government unable to act, crumbling in some places, and losing authority. Sedition was growing not by the day, but by the hour. One can say without exaggeration that all Russia echoed to the *cri de coeur* that "It is impossible to live this way any longer." In short, the cry was for the end of the regime. To achieve this goal, thousands and thousands, from all classes, engaged in struggle, some with the pen, some with the sword. Of course, the majority was passive, but its sympathies were with the activists. Subsequently, the united front of hatred for the regime would be broken, but in September and October all seemed united.

This period is described in a manuscript prepared by a civil servant while I was premier. Entitled "On the Eve of October 17," it is now in my archive.[22]

In late September and early October what was to become a general strike began in the industrial areas of the country. When the Moscow railroads struck on October 8, Prince Khilkov went there, rode on a locomotive in an effort to win over the engineers, but they only smiled at his naiveté. On October 10, the Kharkov area railroad workers struck. On October 12 it was the turn of the Petersburg railroadmen. By October 17 virtually the entire railroad and telegraph systems were shut down. During the same period the factories in the major industrial areas were shut down by strikers. Chaos increased by the hour.

Since I was only a bystander at the time, my knowledge of what was going on outside of Petersburg came from the newspapers, but there were few of these because many newspapers had been closed down by strikes. But I did have first-hand knowledge of what was going on in Petersburg.[23] There the workshops and factories began to go out on strike on October 12. By October 15 normal activities in the city were virtually at an end: streetcars were immobile, the water supply was cut off, the telephone system was shut down, the only communication between the city and Peterhof, where the Emperor and his family were staying, was by government steamer. The idled workers spent their time either at meetings or marching in the streets, where they were joined by so-called hooligans. At first, the higher schools provided forums for revolutionary meetings. Then, when they were closed, students, like workers, spent their time at street meetings or in marching. And the press, as I have said, "seized the right to the freedom of the press" by ignoring censorship.

It was in this setting that a soviet of workers' deputies was formed in Petersburg. The idea of such a body had been broached early in October and soon spread among the workers. On October 13, the first meeting of the soviet was held in the Technological Institute. At that meeting an appeal calling on workers to join and setting forth extreme political demands was adopted. At the second session, on October 14, again at the Technological Institute, a Jewish lawyer named Nosar (under the name of Khrustalev he had taken a job at the Chesher factory to propagandize the workers) was elected chairman. Virtually all the workers in the city unconditionally accepted the decisions of the soviet. On October 15 another meeting was held at the Technological Institute, this time with professors and members of other professions taking a lively part. The next meeting was held at the Free Economic Society building because, in accordance with the recently enacted decree concerning the right of assembly, educational institutions were closed to outsiders.

Day by day the movement against the government became more widespread and brazen. The Union of Unions, and its constituent units, spoke solemnly of revolution. Under the influence of revolutionary propaganda there were disorders in some army units and demonstrations of soldiers on leave demanding to be demobilized. And the navy, particularly the Black Sea Fleet (in which the incredible mutiny of the *Potemkin* had occurred a few months earlier), was in a rebellious state.

What was so dangerous about all this was that everyone seemed to be on the side of change and the few who professed to be defenders of the government did not do so sincerely. Those who spoke in defense of the Emperor against charges that he was to blame for our troubles included many who are now to be found on the extreme right. Publicly they defended him, but privately, in keeping with their baseness, they were even sharper in their attacks on him than the revolutionaries. In recent times they have gone so far as to hatch the most stupid and contemptible plans for replacing the Emperor with someone like Grand Duke Dmitrii Pavlovich, with Grand Duchess Elizabeth Fedorovna serving as regent. And some of the Black Hundreds are so bold as to say privately that they would like to see that utter numbskull Prince Shcherbatov on the throne. All this, of course, belongs to the realm of the strange and mindless stories that came out of the revolution.

What was not sufficiently understood then and is not sufficiently understood now is that the power of the tsar, like that of any monarch, is, in a sense, an incomprehensible mystery, a secret expressed in the word "legitimacy." No one knows Nicholas II, with all his defects as ruler, better than I, yet I say, as God is my witness, that I pray to God that nothing happens to him. Loving Russia as I do, I beseech God every day to keep Emperor Nicholas Aleksandrovich well, for so long as Russia does not find a safe harbor in the world, so long as everything is unstable, it can maintain itself only because he is our legitimate Tsar, our Tsar by the grace of God. In this lies our strength and in this strength, pray God, Russia will soon find stability.

In the weeks before October 17 I was out of the swim. Aside from Trepov, with whom I spoke briefly, Count Lambsdorff, and Count Solskii, there was hardly anyone in the upper reaches of the government with whom I spoke about what was going on. But I did talk to several persons outside the government who were to play a significant role in later months.

One of these was General Kuzymin-Karavaev, a graduate of the Corps des Pages and the Military-Juridical Academy (where he was to serve as professor *ordinarius* for a time), an hereditary noble with some land, a publicist, a well-known zemstvo activist in the province of Tver.[24] Known in those days as a liberal, he had taken part in the zemstvo and municipal duma congresses, would later be elected to the First and Second State Dumas, but he would not join the Kadets, because of what he considered its extremism, and instead would join the small Democratic Reform party. This brief review of his career shows that he was no *sans-culotte*, nor a revolutionary, but simply an educated man in touch with the times. Moreover, he had never done anything in his life for which he could be reproached.

I saw him twice, on my initiative.[25] When I asked him for his frank opinion about the state of affairs, he said, ·in great detail, that the only way out was constitutionalism, although such a turn was so long overdue that it might be accompanied by excesses. I asked him to put his ideas in writing, and within two days I received a short memorandum summarizing what he had told me.

Another person with whom I spoke was a man to whom I have already referred, Menshikov, of *Novoe vremia*. I asked him, as I did the general, for a brief summary of his belief that a constitution was necessary. In response he provided me with a draft statement expressing views slightly to the left of the spirit of the October 17 Manifesto.

Unfortunately, I have been unable to find this document, which provided an example of how opinions were shaped by events.[26] Then he joined with the left, but this talented journalist would later become an ardent rightist, like so many others shifting from left to right. May God grant that the Russian wagon that was dragged close to the edge of a precipice by the left not now be pulled into the mire by the right and sink in it.

Another who sailed with the wind was that mendacious and meretricious Prince Meshcherskii, publisher of *Grazhdanin*, of whom I have spoken earlier. He, too, came to see me in those days before October 17. He was very depressed and said that he was "convinced" that there was no choice but to grant a constitution. Later, after the danger of revolution had passed, this man, who considers it his right to be subsidized by the government, would return to his old reactionary tune. They pay him well for this.

During this period I also had several visits from Peter Nikolaevich Durnovo, who had spoken in a somewhat liberal vein when we were working on the implementation of the December 12 decree. In his view, Trepov was the chief cause of the current breakdown, and if Trepov did not go we would experience the most frightful troubles. He, like so many others, was certain that there was no choice but to grant liberal reforms, which necessitated repeal of the exceptional laws. His opinion carried weight for he had served as director of the Department of Police. Later, like so many others, he would move to the right.

The only person from whom I heard rightist views in those days was A. P. Nikolskii, who had served under me while I was minister of finance. In his view all our trouble came from the press. Therefore, the only wise policy for dealing with the revolutionary movement was to show no mercy to the press. I was amazed that he, a longtime contributor to *Novoe vremia*, should take this view when that newspaper was taking an editorial opinion hostile to the government.

As the strike spread and authority crumbled, the revolution "seized" the rights that had for so long been sought. This had come to pass because the government had for so long ignored the needs of the people, and then, when unrest began to break out into the open, it had tried to bolster its power and prestige by means of "a little, victorious war" (Plehve's expression) that resulted only in disgraceful defeat, proving to the Russians that the regime under which they lived was inadequate and rotten. Then disorder broke out and even the more sensible elements lost their senses. In the glow of the revolutionary fire the question was "What is to be done?" The answer to that question was that great document, the October 17 Manifesto. How it came into being I will describe in the next part of my memoirs.

VIII

The October Manifesto

Call to Duty

It was evident by the first days of October that Russia required action and leadership, but it seemed to me that there was nothing I could do and that under the circumstances I should leave the country for a while.[1] I knew I could not rely on the weak and irresolute Emperor, who, despite his analytic mind, was incapable of grasping broad issues. In thinking of leaving the country I was not seeking, as Muravev had, a comfortable haven in time of storm, but seeking to avoid being exploited again, as I had been in my mission to Portsmouth. I did not want to be sent to put out a fire after those responsible for starting it saw that it was out of control and could find no volunteers to put it out.

It was in these days, with revolution in the ascendant, that a very depressed Count Solskii came to see me, insisting that I was Russia's only hope. In this he was seconded by his wife. When I told him that I had every intention of going abroad for a rest after my labors at Portsmouth, he began to cry and said: "Well, go and let us perish, for without you I can see no future for us."

On October 6, in response to the count's pleas, I asked the Emperor to receive me so that I could present my views on the situation in which we found ourselves. Two days later I received a reply informing me that he would receive me the following day, at 6 p.m.

At the appointed time I read to him from a hastily prepared memorandum that explained why the desirable course at this time was the adoption of constitutionalism but offering an alternative if this were unacceptable: the appointment of a reliable person with virtually dictatorial power to employ implacable force against disorder of whatever variety. In my opinion the first course was the better one, but I admitted that I might be mistaken and suggested that His Majesty might find it advisable to consult with other officials as well as with other members of his family. As usual, His Majesty seemed calm, but he did not express an opinion about what I had to say.

On my return from Peterhof, I and N. I. Vuich, who was serving as chief administrative assistant of the Committee of Ministers in the absence of Baron Nolde, reviewed the memorandum and made some corrections in it. We also amended it to say that adoption of the second course meant going against the current, meaning that for it to succeed it would have to be carried out by someone who was committed to it as well as firm of will.

At the Emperor's request, I returned to Peterhof the following day to meet with him about my suggestions. When I entered his study I expected to find several grand dukes with him but I found only the Emperor and the Empress.* That no grand dukes were present may have been partly the result of the Emperor's reluctance to take the initiative to invite them, partly the consequence of the Empress's alienation of all grand dukes but Nicholas Nikolaevich and Peter Nikolaevich, which meant that only these two were eager to come to the aid of the Emperor. As for these two, the first was at his estate, hunting, and the second was, I believe, in the Crimea. Baron Freedericksz later criticized Grand Duke Vladimir Aleksandrovich for not offering advice to the Emperor at such a difficult time. I suspect that if he had offered unsolicited advice, he would have been told to mind his own business, for, as a rule, His Majesty does not tolerate those whom he does not consider mental inferiors nor those whose opinions differ from those of the court camarilla, i.e., his household slaves.

During this meeting with the Emperor and Empress I explained the edited memorandum and presented my views in detail. As on other occasions when I was in her presence, the Empress sat stiff as a ramrod, her face lobster-red, and did not utter a single word. His Majesty did not react to what I said except to suggest that it might be desirable to issue an Imperial manifesto based on the memorandum.

On my return home I thought seriously about the proposed manifesto. It seemed to me such a document, emanating from the Emperor, would have a disquieting effect on both the educated and the masses. It was my conclusion that it would be best not to issue a manifesto but to carry out the proposed changes by legislative means, either through the State Council or the State Duma, which was to be elected in accordance with the law of August 6. Because I had been out of the swim for the last two years I used the time to get my bearings, waiting to hear again from Peterhof, but during the two days following the meeting I had no word from the Emperor.

On October 11 or 12 I was told that the Emperor was consulting with people who were not identified. I did not ask, nor was I interested in learning, who these people might be, but I suspected that they might be people like General-

---

*The Dowager Empress was in Denmark at this time. A few days later she sent Izvolskii, our minister to Copenhagen, to deliver a message to the Emperor saying she believed a constitution to be necessary. Because of the strikes, Izvolskii was unable to reach Petersburg until after October 17 had come and gone. Whether or not he delivered the message I do not know.[2]

Adjutant Chikhachev,[3] Count Pahlen, or Count A. P. Ignatev. I suggested that he might want to take counsel with Count Ignatev and the count might be suitable as a dictator, if the Emperor rejected the constitutional course.

Although I had advised the Emperor against a dictatorship, I privately wished, for selfish reasons, that he would ignore my advice, for, if he did, I would be spared the burden of becoming head of government in a time of crisis under an Emperor and court with whose charms I was already familiar. I knew that if I became head of government I could not count on decency or gratitude: if I were successful those who feared my success would destroy me, and if I failed they would be only too happy to turn the extremists loose on me.

I believe that the Emperor would have preferred a dictatorship, for, being a weak man, he believes above all in the use of force (employed by others, of course) to destroy his real or fancied enemies, and he considers those who oppose the unlimited, arbitrary, serf regime to be his personal enemies. When he later decided against a dictatorship it was probably because he was advised by the military (among them Grand Duke Nicholas Nikolaevich, who, it seems, had been summoned to Peterhof by the Emperor) that the troops could not be relied on for use in the restoration of calm.

From what I heard, my proposals were discussed with the Emperor on October 11 and 12. On October 13 I received a telegram from His Majesty directing that in the interim before the issuance of a decree changing the nature of the Council of Ministers I was to coordinate the work of those ministers responsible for reestablishing order and pointing out that it was not until order was restored that the still-to-be elected State Duma could engage in constructive work. In response to the telegram I saw the Emperor the following day to advise him that the coordination of the work of ministers holding varying views would not of itself be sufficient to stop disorder, that in my view a clear choice between constitutionalism and dictatorship had to be made.[4]

On this occasion I submitted a short report summarizing my October 9 memorandum. I pointed out that if my recommendations were adopted, the responsibility for carrying them out would fall on me as their author. It was my view that it would be most prudent to publish the short report but not an Imperial manifesto because a document of that kind, which could not go into detail about proposed changes, a document that would be read in all churches, would not be advisable.

By this time, as I have noted earlier, the strike movement was in full swing. Acting on His Majesty's instructions of October 13, I met with War Minister Rödiger, General Trepov (commander of the Petersburg garrison in addition to his other duties), Prince Khilkov, and others to consider means for returning the railroads to service, at least between Petersburg and nearby points. Generals Rödiger and Trepov claimed there were enough troops in Petersburg to put down an armed rising in the city or in the vicinity of nearby Imperial residences, but not enough even to restore railroad service between Petersburg and Peterhof. General Rödiger then offered the gloomy appraisal that the morale among the troops in

European Russia was poor, because many of their commissioned and noncommissioned officers had been sent to Manchuria and replaced by reserve officers. Another reason for demoralization, he said, was that troops had been used so frequently to carry out police functions.[5]

Preparation of the October Manifesto

Despite my advice against issuing a manifesto, I received an order during the evening of October 14, transmitted by telephone by Prince Orlov, to prepare a draft of a manifesto and to have it with me the following day for a conference presided over by the Emperor. He told me that the point of a manifesto was "so that everything would emanate personally from the Emperor and that the measures mentioned in the report move from the realm of Imperial promises to the realm of Imperial deeds."

What was behind Prince Orlov's words? From my subsequent conversations with him I realized that he had some part in the maneuvering that was going on, but I did not know what part, nor could I credit him with playing an important role because I knew him to be nothing more than an agreeable after-dinner companion, a frivolous, poorly educated man. As I learned much later from Prince N. D. Obolenskii, director of His Majesty's Office,[6] Prince Orlov had carefully written out his message to me.

What all this means is that those who had the ear of the Emperor were certain that I expected the monarchy to be replaced by a republic, of which I would be president. To circumvent me they planned to use my ideas and then dispense with me. To make certain that I would not realize what they considered to be my goal, they decided to limit my role to that specified in my instructions of October 13, to restore order. But they were taken aback when, on October 14, I told the Emperor that steps to restore order must be supplemented by confirmation of my proposed program of reforms. They feared that if only my report were published I would receive credit for the reforms recommended in it. Therefore, it was important in their eyes that an Imperial manifesto be issued, permitting the Emperor to receive the credit.[7]

All this may seem incredible, but, unfortunately, is true. That Prince Orlov and His Majesty's other highly placed lackeys (not genuine lackeys, of course, for the lackeys who minister to the Emperor's physical needs are honorable servants) should believe in such mad ideas and that the Emperor should be influenced, however slightly, by their insinuations graphically illustrates into what an abyss Russia had fallen in the eleven years since the death of Emperor Alexander III.

Prince Obolenskii told me later that when he realized that Prince Orlov was suffering from an almost mad dilemma about me—that if I became head of government I would try to overthrow the monarchy, but that if I did not the monarchy would fall—he decided that he had to protect the Emperor from such dangerous influences. Knowing that the Empress had her husband completely under her thumb, and being in her good graces, he decided to act through her.

Going to his knees, he implored her to dissuade the Emperor from naming me head of government. Why? Because the Emperor did not trust me and I was not the sort of man to serve as someone's tool. It was certain, the prince argued, that as soon as things calmed down, the Emperor would begin to take advice from others, something I would not tolerate. I would then become even more obstinate than usual and less able to compromise than I could where mutual confidence existed. It would all end, he said, with my leaving office after a short tenure, with the Emperor feeling vindictive and hateful toward me, with consequences that would harm him and the country. Her Majesty, he told me, listened in silence.

The consequence of this intervention was that Prince Obolenskii fell out of favor with the Emperor and the Empress. Illustrative of his fall from their grace is the following. In the past, when he was in their palace on business and it was early enough, he would be invited to lunch with them. Since then, if occasion required that he report to the Emperor, his appointment would be set for 2 p.m., to spare His Majesty the embarrassment of not inviting him to lunch. How petty is the Great, Most Blessed, Most Autocratic Emperor Nicholas II.*

Acting against my better judgment I agreed to draft a manifesto, but, feeling under the weather, I asked Prince A. D. Obolenskii,[8] who was visiting me, to prepare the draft which I would be taking with me the next morning to Peterhof. I also asked him and Vuich to accompany me.

On the ship taking us to Peterhof the following morning was Baron Freeder-icksz, who, together with Vuich and me, listened as Prince Obolenskii read what he had prepared. There was only enough time for me to suggest some changes by the time we were ready to dock. So, I asked him to revise the draft on the basis of what had been said while I and the baron talked to the Emperor. When we two arrived at the palace we found Grand Duke Nicholas Nikolaevich and General-Adjutant Richter there, also waiting to see the Emperor. At eleven o'clock His Majesty received the four of us. At his request I again read my report setting forth the choice of courses. As I read, the Grand Duke asked many questions, to which I replied in detail and adding my opinion that while a constitution would not guarantee immediate calm, given the bloody war we had been through and the disorders we were experiencing, it would restore calm more quickly than would a dictatorship.

When I was through, the Emperor asked if I had prepared a draft of the manifesto. I said it had been done but that I had become acquainted with it only aboard ship and that it was being revised. I repeated my view that it would be better to publish only the report I had just read. At one he adjourned the meeting, asking us to return at three and for me to bring the revised draft of the manifesto. When the meeting resumed there was further discussion of my report. Then I

*Illustrative of the panic in those days was a remark made to Vuich by Count Benckdendorff, chief marshal of the court and one of the Emperor's loyal servants. He said that he was sorry the Emperor had so many children because they would be a hindrance if the Emperor had to flee to a foreign haven.

read the proposed manifesto. No one expressed an opinion and we then adjourned.

"Byzantine" Methods

On our way back to Petersburg that day, someone said that Goremykin would be aboard the ship on its return voyage to Peterhof. It was then that I learned that His Majesty was holding two sets of meetings, one in which I participated, the other with Goremykin and Budberg.[9] This was typical of the Emperor's penchant for "Byzantine" methods, but, devoid of the talents of a Metternich or a Talleyrand, his use of such methods leads to bloody or shameful results.

Although the news made my blood boil, I derived some pleasure from it, because it provided me with a justification for declining the "honor" of becoming head of the government. Accordingly I telephoned Baron Freedericksz and Prince Engalychev, the palace commandant (I needed the latter's help because the baron did not hear well on the phone), to tell the baron of my feelings about the news that the Emperor was meeting with Goremykin and Budberg concerning changes in the draft of the manifesto. I told him once more that this was not the time for a manifesto, but that I had no objection to changes being made in my draft as long as it was understood that I would not be asked to be the head of the government. However, if, despite my wish to decline the "honor," I was forced to accept it, I wanted to see what kind of changes were being made. Baron Freedericksz assured me that the changes were only editorial in nature and hoped that, in the interest of speed, I would not insist on seeing them. I insisted, nonetheless, and was told that he would call on me that evening to show me the revisions.

It was not until midnight that he, accompanied by General Mosolov, arrived at my house. He admitted that he had erred in saying the changes were only editorial ones, that, in fact, substantive changes had been made. He then gave me two drafts of the manifesto, the one submitted by me and the other, meant to be a final draft, prepared by Goremykin and Budberg, and told me that the Emperor wanted me to look at both.

I asked if General Trepov, whom I had seen only once during these days, had been informed of all that was happening. After all, it was he who was responsible for the maintenance of order in the Empire; if he were not informed in advance of any major step, there might be unfortunate consequences. The baron said that he and General Mosolov had just come from seeing Trepov and that is why they were so late. Subsequently, the baron was to assert that he had told me that Trepov had made some comments about the wording of the manifesto. Neither I nor Princes A. D. and N. D. Obolenskii (who were visiting with my wife that evening) recall this, but it is possible that I did not pay attention to this remark, given my preoccupation with how to end this game of hide-and-seek. In any case, Trepov's political opinions were of no matter to me.

After I had looked over the two drafts, I told Baron Freedericksz I could not accept the one prepared by Goremykin and Budberg for two reasons: first, because their version had the Emperor bestowing rights immediately, whereas mine had His Majesty ordering the government to prepare the legislation specifying what these rights would be; second, because this draft did not include certain substantive measures included in my report. If their version of the manifesto were published simultaneously with my report, the differences between the two would at once raise doubts in the public mind about the Emperor's commitment to the principles enunciated in my report.

All this evidence of equivocation, of backstairs meetings, added to the fact that I had been ill for some time, upset me completely. I would have felt less distraught if things had been done honorably, in a manner befitting a tsar, so that I and Goremykin and that Baltic chancellery type Baron Budberg had been brought together openly to discuss the drafting of the manifesto. After all, despite our differences of opinion, we did share a sense of responsibility and would have been able to come to a reasonable agreement. However, courtiers like Prince Orlov and Prince Engalychev, who had also been advising the Emperor, were of a different stripe: they could not be taken seriously because the only useful advice they could offer the Emperor was on household affairs.

I then repeated what I had told the Emperor several times, that it was not necessary to publish a manifesto. When the baron told me that the Emperor had decided to publish a manifesto and that the decision was irrevocable, I asked him to inform His Majesty that, in that case, I could not agree to a manifesto that was not in accord with my program and that unless my program were affirmed I could not agree to become head of government. Further, I asked the baron to inform the Emperor that I sensed from what was happening that he had no confidence in me and that, consequently, it would be a great mistake to appoint me head of government. It would be better, I said, to appoint either of the two men, Goremykin and Budberg, with whom he had been consulting behind my back. I asked that he inform His Majesty that if my services in another capacity were needed I was ready, as I had already informed the Emperor, to serve even in a secondary position such as provincial governor.

When General Mosolov and Baron Freedericksz left, at 2 a.m., both the baron and I were in a rather agitated state. (The baron took both drafts of the manifesto with him and I was never to see them again.) When I was finally alone, I prayed to the Almighty that He deliver me from this morass of cowardice, blindness, treachery, and stupidity. I prayed that what I had said would result in my being left in peace.[10]

Decision

A few hours later I was summoned back to Peterhof. When I landed I asked Baron Freedericksz if he had informed the Emperor of what I had said. He had. I said: "Thank God. Will I now be left in peace?" He shocked me by telling me that the Emperor would sign my version of the manifesto and affirm my report. When I asked how this had come to pass, he replied:

This morning I reported our conversation in detail, but the Emperor said nothing, probably because he was waiting for Grand Duke Nicholas Nikolaevich.

As soon as I returned to my quarters, the Grand Duke came to see me. I told him about what had happened and said that this meant he must assume the post of dictator. On hearing this he took a revolver out of his pocket and told me he would beg the Emperor to sign your version of the manifesto and affirm your report. If the Emperor refused, he said, he would shoot himself. With this he left, but returned after a while with an order for the report and the manifesto to be copied for the Emperor's signature and then to take them to His Majesty, who would sign the manifesto and affirm the report in your presence.

Some time later General Mosolov told me how disappointed Baron Freedericksz (who was on *tutoyer* terms with Grand Duke Nicholas Nikolaevich) was in the Grand Duke. He told me that after the Grand Duke had left him, the baron had said to him:

I see now that there is no choice but to accept Count Witte's program. I had been acting on the assumption that in the end the Emperor would decide on a dictatorship and that he would, of course, give the post to the Grand Duke, who is utterly devoted to him and who, I thought, was the right man for the task. I see now that I was mistaken in the Grand Duke: he is a weak and unstable person. In fact, everyone has lost his head; everyone shies away from power. Therefore, whether we like it or not, we must yield to Count Witte.

General Mosolov said he did not know what Baron Freedericksz and the Grand Duke had said to each other. On another occasion the general told me that he had learned that the agitated Grand Duke had torn the manifesto out of the Emperor's hand and had insisted that he affirm my report.

On that historic day I did not understand why Grand Duke Nicholas Nikolaevich, unqualified believer in absolutism that he was, should have insisted that the Emperor agree to the dramatic change in the nature of our government that the manifesto represented. Obviously, it was not logic or reason that moved him, for he had long been under the influence of spiritualism and, moreover, was, so to speak, not quite right in the head. His version of absolutism, I should add, meant the kind of license that permits the Sovereign to say: "I have spoken, the matter is closed." It was no accident that the Grand Duke would later come close to the revolutionary right, which, like the revolutionary left, believes that the end justifies the means.

It was about a year later that the matter was explained to me by P. N. Durnovo, whose ties with the Department of Police gave him access to facts not available to others. He told me that Ushakov, the head of a small labor party, was the one responsible for convincing the Grand Duke to argue for the manifesto.[11]

My knowledge of Ushakov goes back to my days as minister of finance, when he was one of the prominent workers in the Government Printing Office. After my return from America he called on me to congratulate me for what I had done. Later, during my tenure as premier, he would see me about questions concerning wages of workers in the Government Printing Office. He was not one with the revolutionary labor leaders. His party was, in fact, considered quite conservative for the time and would not support the so-called workers' soviet led by Nosar, Trotsky, *et al.*

Well, after hearing about Ushakov's role, I sought him out and asked if what I had heard was true. It was. So, I asked him to give me a written statement about what had happened. The next day he brought it to me and it is now in my archive.[12]

In it he declared that in the days before October 17, when he and other workers were opposing the revolutionary labor movement, he was introduced to Grand Duke Nicholas Nikolaevich by a certain Naryshkin, whom he had met through the offices of Prince M. M. Andronikov, and he had been able to convince the Grand Duke that a constitution was the only way out of the current difficulties and that it was necessary to convince the Emperor of this.

To this day I do not understand Prince Andronikov. He is a contemptible person, quite unlike his father, Prince M. A. Andronikov, an honorable man, who served as adjutant to Grand Duke Michael Nikolaevich.

Prince M. M. Andronikov attended the Corps des Pages. He is not stupid, has a good knowledge of languages, but can hardly be considered an educated man. After leaving school he entered on his chosen career—swindler and police agent. He works hard at insinuating himself into the good graces of grand dukes, ministers, and other persons in high places, doing favors for them, offering them information they may find interesting, hoping that they will reciprocate with information he may find useful and by opening their doors to him. When I was minister of finance he managed to worm his way into my favor, but I never received him at my home. He is, shall we say, a troublemaker who is always up to petty tricks and obviously enjoys his work greatly. When people speak of this worthless being, they do so with a puzzled smile on their faces.[13] As for Naryshkin, he is not a genuine Naryshkin (my daughter is married to one), who have nothing in common with him. In essence he is a *"jeune premier"* who squandered his fortune, never turned a hand at anything useful, is part of Petersburg high society, is a sportsman, a hunter, is good company at hunts, and therefore was close to Grand Duke Nicholas Nikolaevich.

A few weeks ago, here in Vichy, where I am writing these lines, P. N. Durnovo told me that it appears that Prince A. D. Obolenskii was the one who arranged to have Naryshkin introduce Ushakov to the Grand Duke and, on this basis, claims credit for the appearance of the October 17 Manifesto. I doubt it and am inclined to believe it was Prince Andronikov who was the intermediary.

Of course, in writing about this period one should remember that ordinarily level-headed people behaved strangely then.

[To return to my account of the events of October 17.] Later in the afternoon, Grand Duke Nicholas Nikolaevich, Baron Freedericksz, and I were ushered into the Emperor's study, where we found him sitting at the table at which he works rather than at the table at which he sits when he listens to reports. After telling us that he had decided to sign the manifesto, he stood up, crossed himself, sat down once more, signed the manifesto, and affirmed my report.

We left the palace and the Grand Duke, Baron Freedericksz, I, Prince A. D. Obolenskii, and Vuich were soon aboard ship on the way back to Petersburg, where we arrived about dinnertime. Prince Obolenskii was overcome with joy. After all, he had been insisting that all would be lost if the manifesto were not issued immediately. (Yet, later, when things were calmer, he would say that the greatest sin of his life was to have argued for the manifesto.) The dimwitted baron was in excellent spirits, as was the Grand Duke, who said to me "This is the second time that the Imperial Family has been saved on an October 17."[14] I tell this to show the mood at the time, a mood I could not share because I knew there was rough sailing ahead, under an Emperor who would make a difficult situation even more difficult. I knew that in the end we would have to part.

During the days leading up to October 17, I told the Emperor that the movement toward freedom and self-rule was irresistible, that sooner or later the striving for reasonable freedom had to be satisfied. In Russia it was later rather than sooner, and that was the chief cause of the pathological phenomena we were experiencing. The war had accelerated this movement. Now, I said, there was no choice but to grant major reforms, sufficient, at least, to bring most of society back to the side of the government.

As I have said, I knew that, whatever course was chosen, we could not count on a speedy return to normalcy. Aware that His Majesty did not understand how complex was the situation we were facing, I tried during these days to show him what difficulties lay ahead. And, when I saw that, *faute de mieux*, he had decided to place the entire burden of power on me, I felt obliged to illustrate what lay ahead by an allegory. I said that it was as if we were about to cross a stormy sea and that no matter how good a ship we took and no matter how carefully we plotted the course, we would be taking risks. I went on to say:

> I am convinced that my ship and my course will involve the fewest risks and the course chosen is the one most suitable for the future of Russia. But I must warn you, Your Majesty, that if you sail on my ship and agree to my course, you will find that as soon as the ship leaves shore it will begin to roll and pitch. Machinery will break down. Part of a deck may break off. Passengers will be washed overboard. Then you will be told that all this could have been avoided if you had taken another ship. Such assertions can't be proved, and under the circumstances it is possible to believe anyone. You will begin to have doubts. There will be intrigues. Undoubtedly, things will end badly for me and, what is more important, for the voyage.

The Emperor would listen and assure me that he believed what I said, but I knew that one can't rely on his assurances, because he doesn't believe in himself. Unable to believe in himself and to follow his own judgment, he sails with the wind, usually an ill wind.

And, difficult though it was for me to tell him so, I had to remind the Emperor that he, too, was mortal. We are all in God's hands and if, God forbid, anything should happen to him, we would have a boy for an Emperor and the poorly prepared Grand Duke Michael Aleksandrovich for a regent.* We would then be experiencing the first regency since the days of Biron, at a time when the country might still be turbulent. Against such a contingency, I told the Emperor, it was necessary for the dynasty to reestablish a broad base of support by putting its house in order.

In short, I was trying to convince the Emperor that if he appointed me head of government he should do so on the basis of confidence in me and my program. But, despite his assurances, I did not believe that I could rely on him because I knew him too well. An additional reason for doubting his assurances was that I believed, as I have said, that he would have preferred to deal with the problem by force, but when he saw that those who also would have preferred force had lost their nerve, he decided to sign the manifesto out of fear that, if he did not, he would go under. Like most optimists, he recognizes danger only when it stares him in the face, but when danger seems to recede, he regains his confidence and returns to his convictions.

During that fateful day of October 17, everyone in Petersburg was waiting to see what was coming. It was known that talks were being conducted in Peterhof, with me, as well as with others. It was known that some kind of struggle was going on there. Would Count Witte, who stood for liberal reforms, or the reactionaries, who sought to preserve the old regime, emerge victorious? The revolutionaries hoped that the reactionaries would prevail, for if they did it would be easier for them to topple the dynasty. It would not have been difficult to bring the dynasty to an end because the Emperor aroused repulsion, hatred, indifferent pity, or contempt, and none of the grand dukes seemed to offer a better alternative either because they lacked prestige or because their reputations were tarnished. And if the revolutionaries had been able to apply more pressure, the government could not have stood up to them because, lacking sufficient money and reliable troops, it had lost its head.

Within hours of our return it was known in Petersburg as well as in the provinces that the manifesto had been signed. The dramatic news was unexpected. Everyone felt instinctively that a divide in the life of twentieth century Russia

---

*When I had the opportunity to talk to the Dowager Empress after her return from Denmark, I told her how difficult it was for me to do my work under an Emperor who did not trust me, to which she replied: "You are saying the Emperor has neither will nor character, but what if he should be replaced by Misha [Michael Aleksandrovich]. I know you like Misha very much, but the fact is he has an even weaker character."

had been crossed. Those who were enlightened, of good will, with faith in the honor of those in charge, understood that society had been granted everything it had sought, everything for which so many fine people, from the Decembrists on, had made sacrifices. Such people expected the dynasty to survive. But ill-willed and unstable persons who had lost their faith in those at the top were convinced that not only the regime but also the Sovereign, who had inflicted so much harm on Russia, would fall.

It is true that he had toppled Russia from her pedestal because his was not the character worthy of a tsar. Many believed that he had acted out of fear and would, as soon as he felt confident again, rescind what he had given with the explanation that he had been deceived. Or, perhaps, he would find in the great mountain of Russian laws a loophole through which to squirm. And, once he started wallowing in the swamp of lies and deceit, he would find hundreds, perhaps thousands, of eager helpers.

On the other side were most, if not all, non-Russians, who had endured so much during the last years of Emperor Alexander II and had endured even more during the reign of Emperor Alexander III, and still more under the mindless first eleven years of the reign of Emperor Nicholas II. They would, of course, be happy over Russia's misfortune. With that passion always found in times of turmoil, they were yearning for their own kind of emancipation from the "Russo-Mongol yoke."

[A major role in the long series of events leading to October 17 was played by the educated youth.] They, particularly the university students, are inclined to react with passion, are susceptible to all sorts of intellectual and spiritual sicknesses, and are capable of all kinds of excesses. This is explained in part by Russia's backwardness, in part by the principles followed by our administration, principles that are in contrast with the progressive ideas they were exposed to in school, particularly the higher schools, and in the writings of popular authors. Many of these writers were very popular among students not so much because of their talent as because of the ideas they espoused. It is enough to recall the so-called age of Pisarev (the 1860s and 1870s), when Pushkin was consigned to the dust heap while Nekrasov was put on a poetic pedestal, not so much for his poetry as for the political aspirations expressed in his verse.

Turbulence among the students became even more pronounced in the 1890s, during Goremykin's tenure as minister of interior, and still more in the years that followed. Our youth is a mirror that reflects, sometimes in distorted form because of their passionate nature, the spiritual state of society, i.e., thinking Russia. And to understand this state it is enough to study the life of the higher schools under Emperor Nicholas II, when conditions reached the stage of an abscess ready to burst at the slightest touch. What did the trick was not a touch but a blow, that childish war with Japan.

That war had such an effect that turbulence spread from the higher schools to male and even female secondary schools. The entire [educated] youth, as has been noted, played a major role in the disorders that preceded October 17. It was a period when the youth could be said to have been in a state of revolutionary bewilderment. Educated youth, like society, were divided in their reaction to the October 17 Manifesto. Some showed their bewildered state by reacting to the suggestion that the manifesto was nothing but a maneuver by singing "God Save the Tsar," while others chose to sing the "Marseillaise."

Note should be made, too, of the influence of socialist ideas, deriving from Karl Marx and Leo Tolstoy, on workers and peasants in the period leading up to October 17, as well as in the months that followed. Socialism, which rejects the principle of private property as found in Roman law, spread from the West to Russia, where it found a favorable soil in the last fifty years, partly because of the lack of respect shown by the powers-that-be for law in general and for property laws in particular, partly because of the cultural backwardness of the masses.

The influence of socialism has been reinforced by the simple belief in the right of "expropriation" and pillage. Thus, when revolutionaries promised the factories to the workers, the workers engaged in savage strikes. And when revolutionaries promised peasants the land of the landlords, the peasants naturally took to what some call the "Red Cockerel" and others call "illuminations" [torchings] (which Herzenstein, a Kadet deputy to the First State Duma, called for in a seditious speech largely plagiarized from one made during the French Revolution). Such promises and calls were to incite outbreaks after October 17.

IX

My First Ten Days as Premier

I am sure that the only man who can help you now and be useful is Witte, because he should be well disposed again *now*, and besides he certainly is a man of genius, *energetic* and clear-sighted.[1]

—Marie Fedorovna to Nicholas II

A New Chapter

The Emperor's approval of my program placed Russia irrevocably on the constitutional path, meaning that he now had to share power with the elected representatives of the people, this after several years of turmoil had shown how impossible it was to have an autocratic regime without an Autocrat, after Russia's prestige had fallen, after all the hostile passions that had been aroused at home. It was the fact that we were entering a new era that drove me to accept the post of premier[2] against my wishes. I was, of course, aware that I found myself in power because those who were really close to the heart of the Emperor had declined to accept the burden of office, either because they feared assassination or because they were completely demoralized by the rush of events. Goremykin had declined the honor, Count A. P. Ignatev was frightened, and General Trepov was bewildered. Now, as he had in sending me to Portsmouth, the Emperor was throwing me into the fire with a light heart, thinking to himself: "If he survives, we can get rid of him later, but if he perishes, so be it. He is an unpleasant person: he does not yield on anything; he understands everything better than I, and this I cannot endure."

For the next ten days or so I continued to reside at home and conduct my business from there. At my insistence, I received no police protection. The only outsiders on duty were a courier and an official from the Committee of Ministers.

The door of my house was always open and no special effort was made to check the many people who came to see me.*

About ten days after I became premier, the Department of Police suggested that I take up quarters in the Winter Palace, where the police could provide adequate protection for the many ministers and other high officials who came to see me. I did not like the prospect of leaving home, where I was comfortable, but I had no choice. Accordingly, I took up residence in the guest building of the palace, which the palace commandant had occupied. Believing that I would soon be returning home, dead or alive, I took nothing with me.

Near my new quarters rooms were provided for my office, my chancellery, and for cabinet meetings. The Committee of Ministers, of which I continued to serve as chairman, met, as before, at the Marie Palace.[4]

Because there was no separate chancellery for the cabinet, at first I had to rely on the staff of the Committee of Ministers to deal with the day-to-day details of cabinet operations. Although Baron Nolde, the committee's chief administrative assistant, was intelligent, hard-working, decent, he was a typical Petersburg bureaucrat, and I therefore arranged to have as little as possible to do with him, relying instead on Vuich. Vuich, an exceptionally honorable man, was more to my liking, and I worked closely with him, sometimes far into the night.

Oddly enough, his father-in-law was the late Viacheslav Konstantinovich Plehve. Out of loyalty to her husband, Vuich's wife found herself at odds with some members of her family, one of whom, N. V. Plehve, was close to the Black Hundreds.

Partial Return to Normalcy

I expected that the promises made in the October 17 Manifesto would satisfy the aspirations of reasonable people, making it possible for a new and better order to come about, but not without the stormy experiences about which I had warned the Emperor. The return to normalcy was to take longer than I had expected, but the effect of the manifesto was such as to permit the reestablishment of calm in a few days in some cities, in a few weeks in others.

In many cities there were large demonstrations to express joy over the manifesto. These in turn led to counter-demonstrations by gangs of so-called Black Hundreds. In some places the growth of the Black Hundreds was made possible by support that came at first from local authorities and later also from some in high places, among them Grand Duke Nicholas Nikolaevich.[5]

Because the manifesto did not satisfy the working masses, the Petersburg soviet called for continuation of the general strike, but in view of the subsidence of the

---

*Among them was a group of workers, come to complain of the unjust arrest of one of their comrades. When I told them to see Governor-General Trepov, they insisted that I give them a note urging Trepov to listen to their complaint and to help them if they seemed in the right. And both here and in my next residence I received Ushakov and his comrades, who spoke for the conservative minority of workers opposed to the soviet.[3]

strike in Moscow and elsewhere, it decreed on October 19 that the strike end on the 21st.

Petersburg was one of the cities in which calm returned quickly. In short order the city began to resume its accustomed character, with water supply, lighting, transportation, and all other municipal facilities returning to fairly regular operations despite efforts to the contrary by the soviet.

For a time there were street demonstrations, under various banners. I asked General Trepov not to interfere with them as long as they did not violate public order or incite revolution. (I considered funeral processions for victims of clashes between revolutionaries and Black Hundreds as deliberate attempts at disturbing public order.) Also I asked that troops be kept out of sight, in their barracks or in the courtyards of palaces or public institutions, and not be used except to preserve order. Trepov complied.

Throughout my tenure order was maintained in the city without recourse to special security measures, in contrast to what has happened since I left office. When demonstrators saw that the authorities paid no particular attention to them they began to quiet down. During the transition to accustomed life in Petersburg there was no looting, no use of arms against demonstrators, with one exception, at the Technological Institute [on October 18].

That day the director of the Technological Institute, with whom I was not acquainted, telephoned me for my help to avoid a bloody clash between a unit of the Semenovskii Guards and a large crowd that had gathered outside the building demanding that someone they claimed was hiding inside be turned over to them. The soldiers had been sent there to disperse the crowd, and he feared that they would use deadly force in carrying out their mission. When I told him that I could not interfere because I knew nothing of the matter, he put the officer of the day on the phone. The officer told me he had tried unsuccessfully to convince the crowd that the man they wanted was not there. He was afraid that the guards would not use good judgment in trying to break up the crowd and would inflict heavy casualties.

I agreed to call the commander of the military of the district, who was, I was told by the officer, General Min, commander of the Semenovskii Guards. I knew the general only by reputation, that of being an honorable soldier. When I called him to ask what was going on, he replied in an offended tone that under the law he was in charge. I informed him that I knew the law, too, and was not questioning his authority, but that I was speaking only on the basis of morality. I asked that he spill no blood if it were at all possible, adding: "Of course, I am not presuming to give you orders, but am simply making a request to you as a man to whom His Majesty has seen fit to show his confidence." That was the end of the conversation.

As I recall, the incident ended with only minor casualties, among them Professor Tarle, who received a light head wound.[6] I did not feel particularly sorry for him because during these troubled times instead of acting with the restraint befitting an eminent professor he was making things worse, as, for example, by the tendentious lectures on the French Revolution that he was delivering.

My Failure with the Press

Because I considered the press an important instrument for helping restore calm, one of my first acts was to invite representatives of the Petersburg press to see me. The most detailed account of this meeting, which took place in my home during the morning of October 18, appeared in *Birzhevye vedomosti*.[7] That is so because its publisher, Propper, was the spokesman for all but the extreme left at this meeting.

Propper is a Jew who came to Russia with little money and little knowledge of Russian and managed to work his way up in the press until he gained control of *Birzhevye vedomosti*. This is the man who hung around my anteroom, as he did around the anterooms of other influential persons, on the lookout for favors. This is the man who managed to get me to arrange for him to receive the title of commercial counselor.[8] It was Propper who, speaking in the insolent tone characteristic of educated Jews, particularly Russian ones, did most of the talking, making a number of declarations and presenting outrageous demands. (A spokesman for the extreme left, from *Bogatstvo* I believe, also took an extreme position, but, unlike Propper, he used a different tone and spoke out of conviction.) What was especially shocking was that the representatives of such right-wing newspapers as *Petersburgskie vedomosti* (Ukhtomskii), *Novoe vremia* (Suvorin), *Svet*, and *Grazhdanin* gave support to his insolence by their silence.[9]

When such an individual could be permitted to use such language, without being disavowed by the others present, it could be said that Russia, and especially the rotten city of Petersburg, had gone mad. The future historian of this amazing period should look at the account of this meeting, which undoubtedly can be found in the Public Library. Accounts such as these are not objective, but they illustrate the psychic condition of Russian society in those October days.

In essence what Mr. Propper said to me, in the presence of the press representatives, was: "We do not trust the government." To be sure, there are regimes, such as that led by Stolypin, whose hypocritical professions of liberalism do not merit trust, but it was not for the likes of a Propper to tell me after October 17 that he did not believe the professions of the government and to do so in that insolent tone used by certain Russian kikes.[10]

Among other things, Propper demanded that all troops be withdrawn from Petersburg and that its protection be turned over to a municipal militia. This was, of course, a revolutionary demand, which no person entrusted with power could accept: had I done so, the city would have been given over to murder and pillage. And this would have forced me to bring in troops, with a consequent heavy spilling of blood. For a socialist or anarchist sheet to make such a demand was to be expected, but I took it as a sign that the rest of the press had lost its senses when it acquiesced in such a demand. I should note here that it is to my credit that during my tenure as premier no one was executed and no more than a few dozen people were killed in Petersburg. In fact, fewer people were executed in all of Russia during those six months than are now executed in a few days by Stolypin's so-called constitutional regime.

Another demand presented by Propper was for the immediate removal of General Trepov. It goes without saying that one of my first goals was to get rid of that dictator, but to have done so immediately after receiving such a demand would have been taken as a sign of weakness. Therefore I had to hold on to Trepov for another week or so.

Still speaking in an insolent tone, Propper also demanded that universal amnesty be granted.

Then he demanded complete freedom of the press, to which I replied that until a new press law could be issued, the old law would be enforced, but, as I would require of the censors, in the spirit of press freedom as promised in the October 17 Manifesto.[11] The press must admit that never in the history of Russia has the press enjoyed as much freedom as it did during my days as premier, when not one retaliatory action was taken in response to attacks on me or my associates, no matter how coarse or dishonest these attacks might be. The only action taken against the press was against those newspapers that published the manifesto of the Petersburg soviet which sought to undermine the government's financial stability. This was something that no government, however liberal, could tolerate.[12]

Given the hostility of the press demonstrated at that meeting of October 18, given the incendiary tone of the press, I quickly realized that I could not count on the press to help me establish a new order in Russia. But the press counted on me, either to do its bidding or to help it financially, whether by direct subsidies or by paying it to print official announcements.

Except for newspapers of the extreme left, which alone spoke out of conviction, the Petersburg press was demoralized. The entire semi-Jewish press, typified by Propper, fancied that power was now in its hands and that, consequently, it could be as insolent as it wished.

As for the right-wing press, it was running with its tail between its legs, because it now realized that the principles of autocracy (as interpreted by a juvenile mind) which it had for so long celebrated had led the fatherland to its present disgraceful condition. For the time being the right-wing newspapers of the "how can I be of service"[13] type were following a leftist line, for two reasons. First, because, given the leftist mood of the reading public, it was profitable, and profit was the chief aim of most of the press. Second, as I later learned, because of fear of the printers, who had become unionized and seditious and would not permit the publication of an issue of the newspaper of which they disapproved. In truckling to their printers, the publishers were in effect encouraging revolutionary tendencies.

Later, when it became profitable and possible to do so, these "how can I be of service" newspapers shifted to a Black Hundreds line. A striking example of this is the well-edited and influential *Novoe vremia*, which, although devoted to profit, is a comparatively decent and, in some senses, patriotic newspaper. It is still one of the best of our newspapers.

Amnesty

[On October 21] there occurred one of those extraordinary events that separates one era from another, in this case the era of absolutism from the era of constitutionalism (or "the era of popular government," as Stolypin and his ministers like to say, lest that foreign word "constitution" offend the Emperor or provoke obscene abuse from Dr. Dubrovin's *Russkoe znamia*). That event was the issuance of an amnesty decree.[14]

Although there was no reference to amnesty in the October 17 Manifesto everyone expected it. Immediately on taking office, I asked the minister of justice, Manukhin, to study the question of an amnesty and to call a meeting to consider it. We met at Trepov's official residence (formerly that of the minister of interior) because it was conveniently located. I recall that among those present were Trepov, P. N. Durnovo, Shcheglovitov, Baron Uexküll, Kokovtsev, Schwanebach, Baron Freedericksz, Filosofov, and Lukianov.

The only opponent of an amnesty was Trepov, but, in the end, he came out for a sweeping amnesty, with no exclusions. Manukhin favored a broad amnesty, but one that excluded revolutionaries guilty of murder, and for these he proposed reduction of sentences. It should be noted that P. N. Durnovo sensibly favored such an amnesty and that Shcheglovitov, the rapporteur for the session, spewed forth the views of *Rech*, the Kadet organ. Manukhin's view prevailed, with my support. An amnesty decree was drafted, approved by the Emperor, and issued immediately. This was the first broad political amnesty in the history of Russia, marking a step in the transition from a police state to one based on law, a transition requiring the division of power between the Monarch and a reasonably genuine legislature.

I must admit that at the time I was apprehensive about the consequences of amnesty, but I accepted it as as an inescapable consequence of the manifesto. Looking back, I believe that we acted correctly.

Restoration of Finnish Autonomy

As I have related earlier, Finland, which had already been brought to the edge of revolt by our mistaken policies, was swept by the so-called revolution of 1905. Its governor-general, Prince I. M. Obolenskii, compromised in the face of revolt, but by then it was too late for him to regain his authority.

Very shortly after October 17, a delegation of Finnish political leaders, headed by L. Mechelin, called on me. They assured me that Finland was beginning to calm down, would forget the past and behave correctly if our government would return to its earlier policy, and would, in good faith, recognize the rights and privileges that Emperor Alexander I and Emperor Alexander II had granted to Finland.[15]

For my part, I informed the Emperor that it would be most dangerous to create another Poland on the outskirts of Petersburg, that we must return to the policies of his forebears with respect to Finland. I pointed out that as long as we had behaved correctly toward the Finns, so had the Finns, most correctly indeed. Moreover, I noted, Finland was the only borderland that owed us nothing, the only borderland for which we had not paid with the blood of our peasant soldiers. It was not for me to suggest what proper policy should be because Finland was not in my jurisdiction, but I did stress that we had to come to terms with the Finns. How this was to be done was for the next governor-general to decide, for Prince Obolenskii clearly could not remain in office.

[Shortly after the Mechelin visit] Linder, the state secretary for Finnish affairs, came to me with a draft of an Imperial manifesto, which in effect said that all that had been done under the Bobrikov regime was annulled and that the Finnish constitution would be liberalized, almost to the point of being ultrademocratic. What did I think of the document? When I told him that I could not give him an official opinion without consulting my cabinet, he asked for my personal opinion. Before saying what I thought, I asked who had proposed the document and was told that it was Governor-General Obolenskii. When I asked Linder if he agreed with him, he said that he did. To this I replied that if the two of them considered that a document of this sort must be issued, I would offer no personal objections, but I would say that I found certain expressions in it imprudent and that, moreover, I was distressed by sharp shifts in our policy toward Finland, from a constitutional regime to the Bobrikov regime and now from the Bobrikov regime to an ultrademocratic constitutional one. [On October 22, the manifesto was issued.]*

Forming a Cabinet, Initial Steps

The day after the October 17 Manifesto I returned to Peterhof to discuss ministerial changes. The Emperor agreed that Bulygin, Glazov, and Pobedonostsev would have to leave. He also agreed to my attempting to bring some public men into the cabinet if doing so would help calm society. Accordingly I immediately telegraphed two public men—Dmitrii N. Shipov, a well-known figure among zemstvo activists, and Prince Eugene N. Trubetskoi, a professor at the University of Kiev—to come to Petersburg. I will talk about my meetings with them and other public men subsequently.

Bulygin, that honorable and well-balanced man, had long wanted to leave, but

---

*In 1910, in connection with the discussion of the Finnish question in the State Duma and the State Council, some newspapers alleged that I was the one who initiated the manifesto and had written a memorandum in favor of it, which Linder then submitted to His Majesty. I did not initiate the manifesto and I do not remember writing a memorandum about it. At the time I was sending notes and memoranda to the Emperor every day, and it is possible that, at Linder's request, I put in writing my brief comments to him. When I say that I do not remember whether or not I wrote such a memorandum, people ask incredulously how could I not remember what I wrote to the Emperor. *If I did write a memorandum, it can probably be found in the Emperor's archive.*

the Emperor, naturally, had not agreed, undoubtedly because he valued the minister as a kind of buffer [for Trepov]. Now the Emperor was willing to part with him, but no decision was made at the time about a successor.

As for General Glazov, he had been appointed minister of education in 1904 only because of "autocratic" misunderstanding or understanding.* At the moment I did not have a successor in mind.

Pobedonostsev could not stay on because he represented that part of the past that was inconsistent with the new order that the times demanded. For him to have remained would have made my task impossible. I recommended Prince Alexis Dmitrevich Obolenskii as his successor, and the Emperor agreed.[16]

Because the Emperor parts easily with people who have served him, I took it upon myself to arrange that Pobedonostsev continue to receive the same salary he had been receiving and to continue to reside for the rest of his life, at government expense, in the official residence he had been occupying. Also, I asked Baron Freedericksz that this aged man be treated with as much consideration as possible, for example, by having His Majesty personally impart the news to Pobedonostsev that he was parting with him. Had I not intervened, the outgoing over-procurator would have learned of his fate from the newspapers.

Pobedonostsev was the last of the Mohicans of the old political persuasion which was defeated on October 17. But he was a great Mohican. He was distinguished from other officials not only by his considerable intelligence but by his indifference to storing up treasures on earth. He was the best educated and most cultivated Russian official I ever dealt with. I should add that, as I have noted elsewhere, he did not have a high opinion of Emperor Nicholas, perhaps because he had known him from the cradle on.

Bulygin, Glazov, and Pobedonostsev left office soon after October 17. P. N. Durnovo was to serve as acting minister of interior and S. M. Lukianov as acting minister of education. Bulygin and Pobedonostsev continued to serve in the State Council. General Glazov found a place as assistant to the commander of the Moscow Military District.

In addition to these three who had to leave there were two others of ministerial

*When Sänger was relieved of the post in January 1904 at his own request (because, as he told me, His Majesty did not fulfill a justified request), several candidates were proposed to replace him. Grand Duke Vladimir Aleksandrovich, president of the Academy of Arts, recommended the vice-president, Count Ivan Ivanovich Tolstoi, but the Emperor did not agree. I know that His Majesty offered the post to General Shilder, then director of the Cadet Corps in Pskov, but the general, an honorable man, would not accept because he considered himself quite unsuited for such a position.

As one would expect, Prince Meshcherskii had several people to recommend. One of these was Kristi, governor of Moscow, who was, in fact, offered the post, but who declined, not out of principle, but, I believe, out of fear. Another was Gerasimov, director of the Nobles' Institute in Moscow. Prince Meshcherskii suggested Gerasimov because he had the approval of Prince Peter N. Trubetskoi, marshal of the Moscow nobility, and, more to the point, of Count Sheremetev, a pillar of mindless Russian conservatism. Also, Gerasimov was well thought of by Grand Duke Sergei Aleksandrovich. In short, his credentials showed him to be considered reliable by the right. In the end, General Glazov, head of the General Staff Academy, was given the appointment.

rank with whom I felt it necessary to part. The first was that archintriguer Grand Duke Alexander Mikhailovich, who could not be permitted to serve in the cabinet of a government based on popular representation. Fortunately, the Grand Duke chose to give up his post,[17] leaving Rukhlov, his assistant, in charge. Rukhlov knew, of course, that he could not remain long in my cabinet, because I would not tolerate a man there who would serve as the Grand Duke's spy.

With the Grand Duke leaving it was possible to consider what to do with that concoction of his, the Chief Administration of Merchant Marine and Ports, of which he had been head. As I have noted earlier, it had been created out of units from the Ministry of Finance and the Ministry of Ways and Communications. I could return them to the ministries from which they had been taken or combine them with the Department of Commerce and Industry of the Ministry of Finance to form a new body, the Ministry of Commerce and Industry, an idea I had proposed to the Emperor a few years earlier.

I decided on a new ministry and the Emperor agreed, but I could not act until I had first informed Kokovtsev, who, like so many Petersburg bureaucrats, has an overblown estimation of his own worth. For that reason the decision to act was held up for a few days.

The second person with whom I felt it necessary to part was Prince Khilkov, minister of ways and communications, whom I had known for several decades. It was I who recommended him for the post, in 1894, but I later became convinced that I had made a mistake, that although an excellent railroad man, he was not suited for the responsibility of being a minister. We parted amicably and remained on good terms.

I suggested to the Emperor that Nemeshaev, chief of the Southwestern Railroad, replace Prince Khilkov. Although I was not personally acquainted with him, I heard from officials on the railroad who had also served under me that he was a very able railroad engineer and an experienced railroad administrator. When I managed the Southwestern Railroad I built up its reputation and Nemeshaev maintained it. I thought the Emperor would accept my recommendation because after traveling on the railroad he had spoken well of Nemeshaev. I was right. His Majesty quickly agreed to make the appointment. Nemeshaev proved himself by soon being able to deal effectively with the strikes and disorders on the railroads and to get the trains moving again.[18]

As for the other incumbents who would be in my cabinet, I had no objections to their staying on.[19] I considered the minister of war, General Rödiger, a hardworking and knowledgeable man and still do. I thought of Admiral Birilev, the minister of the navy, as unobjectionable, not a stupid man, but one more given to chattering than to working. I considered Baron Freedericksz dimwitted, but very honorable. As for Count Lambsdorff, he was an excellent foreign minister and there could be no thought of replacing him. I thought highly of the incumbent minister of justice, Manukhin—an excellent jurist, an honorable man—and was strongly in favor of his staying on. I did not think highly of Kokovtsev, the minister of finance, or of Schwanebach, the head of the Chief Administration of Land Organization and Agriculture,* but I was prepared to endure them as long as they refrained from intrigue and behaved themselves.

My Efforts To Recruit Public Men

It seemed to me very pressing to find a new minister of education because all the schools under the jurisdiction of the Ministry of Education were either on strike or given over to politics rather than education. A good choice for such a time seemed Professor Tagantsev of Petersburg University:[21] he had a reputation as an authority on law, was a member of the Senate, was a man of liberal but well-balanced ideas who enjoyed considerable popularity in the university community.

With the Emperor's permission I offered him the post, suggesting at the same time that Posnikov, dean of the economics division of the Petersburg Polytechnic Institute, might do as his assistant minister. Saying that he was under great nervous strain (Who was not under great nervous strain in those days?) he asked for a day in which to consider my offer. Meanwhile I told Posnikov that I intended to offer him the post of assistant minister and suggested that he meet with Tagantsev.

When both men came to see me, the following day, Tagantsev, obviously under great strain, said he did not feel strong enough to accept the responsibility. I tried to persuade him to change his mind, but, after a few minutes, he put his hand to his head, cried out: "I can't, I can't," ran into the next room, grabbed his coat and hat, and ran out so rapidly that I was unable to catch up with him. Posnikov then told me that he had made an effort to persuade Tagantsev to accept, but obviously had failed. Clearly, in those days, fear of assassination made people reluctant to become ministers.

At this point I decided that, before settling other questions relating to the cabinet, I would talk to public men whom I had in mind for ministerial posts: Dmitrii N. Shipov—state controller; Prince Eugene N. Trubetskoi—minister of

---

*In the spring of 1905 the Ministry of Agriculture was transformed into the Chief Administration of Land Organization and Agriculture as a means of getting rid of its minister, Ermolov, whereupon Schwanebach, who had been serving as assistant minister, was named head of this body.

I first became acquainted with Schwanebach while director of the Department of Railroad Affairs of the Ministry of Finance. Although a cultivated, well-bred man, with a good knowledge of many languages, he was a frivolous, superficial person, unsuited for any serious work, and was consequently held in low esteem in the Ministry of Finance, where he held a position. Vyshnegradskii, the then minister, would not give him any responsibilities, nor would I when I became minister, but to keep from humiliating him I appointed him to the ministerial council. When the Emperor suggested that he be appointed to the Finance Committee, I objected on the ground that he was incapable of dealing with serious financial questions and the Emperor abandoned the idea.

Schwanebach was, however, able to rise in the bureaucratic hierarchy because of influence. At one time he served Grand Duchess Catherine Mikhailovna as major domo-*cum*-secretary and managed to use this post to ingratiate himself with the Montenegrin princesses, with whose influence he succeeded in advancing himself. It was with their help that he had become assistant minister under Ermolov.

It is one of the shameful facts of our bureaucratic life that when people like Schwanebach succeed in becoming assistant ministers, they try with all their might to trip up their superiors and replace them. That is what he did to Ermolov, working with Goremykin against the man under whom he was serving.[20]

education; Alexander I. Guchkov—minister of commerce and industry; Prince Sergei D. Urusov—minister of interior; Michael A. Stakhovich—an assistant ministerial post.[22]

I was barely acquainted with Shipov, but I knew that he was well known among zemstvo activists and had a remarkably honorable record in public life. I might disagree with some of his views, but I admired him.

I was not acquainted with Prince Trubetskoi. Less well known than his brother Sergei Nikolaevich, he, nonetheless, had an excellent reputation in the academic world. My first conversation with him convinced me, unfortunately, that from the top of his head to the tip of his toes he was a naive professorial type who knew only theory.

Guchkov was another with whom I had had no personal acquaintance, but I knew that he belonged to a prominent Muscovite merchant family, had attended university, was a gallant man, that he was well thought of by the so-called congress of zemstvo and municipal duma leaders. Later I was to learn that this was the Guchkov whom I had dismissed from the Border Guard while I was minister of finance and that the episode had evidently left him with a sour feeling toward me.

I had never heard of Prince Urusov (whose brother-in-law Lopukhin had recently left the post of director of the Department of Police) until Prince A. D. Obolenskii vigorously recommended him for the post of minister of interior. When I inquired about his career, I learned that he had served in the Ministry of Interior, had held the posts of governor of Bessarabia and then of Tver, that his record was flawless, unless one considers it a flaw that he could not accommodate himself to Plehve's unconscionable police methods. But his lack of experience in police work—particularly Russian police work, tainted as it was by the use of such *agents provocateurs* as Azef and Harting[23] in the Plehve and Trepov periods—made me doubt that he could fill so responsible a post as minister of interior. In expressing my doubts to Prince Obolenskii, I asked him not to inform Prince Urusov that I was thinking of making him an offer of the position. Prince Obolenskii agreed, but tried to convince me that Prince Urusov, being a shrewd man, was quite capable of mastering the police operations of what was virtually a police state.

When I met Prince Urusov I was favorably impressed by him, but I was confirmed in my premonition that he would not do as a minister of interior because it was quickly evident that his was not a commanding personality. Later meetings with him convinced me that he was a decent, fairly intelligent man, but one easily roused to enthusiasm, in this case for the cause of "liberty." But at least it was based on conviction, whereas the enthusiasm for "liberty" of men like Guchkov, as it turned out, meant the kind of liberty that was in the interests of their class.

I was well acquainted with Stakhovich[24]—a well-educated, warm-hearted, gifted, honorable man, but like Prince Urusov given to enthusiasm and, what is more, a frivolous man who enjoys life in the Russian manner. Like other public men, he had participated in the zemstvo and municipal duma congress. He had let me know that because he expected to be a candidate for a seat in the State Duma he could not accept a ministerial portfolio, but he agreed to talk with me.

There are many accounts in circulation of what was said at my meetings with the public men, none of them correct. Only the participants can record exactly what was said on these occasions and why we disagreed. Undoubtedly, some of the participants will someday publish their accounts of these meetings, but since I am older than they, I probably shall not live long enough to read them.

At my request, Prince Obolenskii invited the public men to meet with me as soon as possible.[25] Some were able to come quickly, but others were delayed, either by the railroad strike or by distance, as was the case with Prince Urusov, who was then in Yalta. With Prince Obolenskii present, I met with these men several times over the course of two or three days. As will be seen, we agreed on virtually everything but the choice of minister of interior.

Mainly we discussed suffrage. The public men wanted the coming State Duma to be elected by direct and universal suffrage. I pointed out that the second article of the October Manifesto tied my hands by its stipulation that the question of universal suffrage should be left to the State Duma while promising broadening of the franchise in the interim to the degree consistent with holding elections as scheduled. The implication of the article was that, except on the question of limited extension of the franchise, I was bound by the electoral law of August 6 [which provided for limited and indirect suffrage]. Also, I was bound by the circular issued on September 22 by Bulygin, with the Emperor's approval, setting the deadline of October 15 for completion of lists of eligible voters and the middle of January for convening of the State Duma. (That the State Duma did not open till April was the consequence of broadening the franchise.) The circular, I should add, also required that the officials supervising the elections in no way interfere in those elections.

I told the public men that the cabinet had not yet completed consideration of broadening the franchise* and that if they entered the cabinet they would have a voice in arriving at a decision. There was no disagreement thereafter on the question of the suffrage.

Moreover, the public men raised no questions about those already in the cabinet or about to enter it and declared that they could work with them.†

---

*Shortly after October 17 I discussed extension of the franchise with my cabinet. Prince Obolenskii favored making as many eligible to vote as possible, whereas Schwanebach wanted to exclude workers and members of the professions. My remarks about the latter's arguments made it clear to him that he could not remain in my cabinet.

†By this time it was clear that the extreme left would not accept a bourgeois constitution, much less the October Manifesto, and that its views were so seditious that we could expect extremist actions from it. But even more disturbing was the fact that the Constitutional-Democratic (Kadet) party (which also called itself the Party of People's Liberty to gain popularity), a party that included the most cultivated and educated men in Russia, had not yet decided to cut its ties with the extreme left, which preached the use of force, of bombs and Brownings.

I raised this question with I. V. Hessen, by this time a leading figure among the Kadets, when he came to see me shortly after October 17. When he asked what my attitude toward his party would be, I

Where we differed, as I have said, was over the question of who would be the next minister of interior. By this time, even after a brief acquaintance, I was certain that Prince Urusov did not have the experience necessary for a post that required a knowledge of police operations, particularly at this time, when demoralization was widespread among the police. Even Prince Obolenskii began to have some doubts about his suitability. This impelled me to tell the public men that I was coming around to the view that Peter Nikolaevich Durnovo, then assistant minister of interior, was the man for the job. It seemed to me that he combined the experience necessary for the post with sympathy for the program on which we were embarking. He was not a paragon, but his pluses were greater than his minuses.

He had a great deal of valuable experience behind him. After serving in the navy, he entered the judicial service during the period of court reforms, reaching the position of assistant procurator of the Kiev Court of Appeals. Count Pahlen, who served as minister of justice in those days, spoke highly to me of Durnovo's ability and energy. Durnovo went on to succeed Plehve as director of the Department of Police. From what I heard from those who had the misfortune, whether merited or not, to come to the attention of this body, he was comparatively humane.

After a number of years in this position he was forced to leave because of a scandal. Then, as later, he had a weakness for the ladies, but, be it noted in his favor, his attachments were fairly enduring ones. According to what I heard, his trouble began when he became enamored of a lady of rather easygoing ways, for whose upkeep he paid. When he learned that she was also giving her affections to the Spanish ambassador, he had his agents rifle the envoy's desk, where they found letters from the lady in question, with which Durnovo then confronted her.

An angry Spanish ambassador informed the then Emperor, Alexander III, of the entry into his embassy. The Emperor, not one to countenance impropriety, used an expression in his comments about the case that resulted in Durnovo's immediate removal from his powerful post, one, I should add, that placed at his disposal a good deal of money for which he did not have to account. Durnovo would probably have been forced out of government service altogether if the then minister of interior, Ivan Nikolaevich Durnovo (no relation), had not persuaded the Emperor to appoint him to the Senate.

---

told him that I was sympathetic with many of its views and was therefore prepared to support it, but only on one ironclad condition, that it stop being the tail to the revolutionary kite and openly come out against the extreme left. He replied that for the Kadets to do so would be the equivalent of the government's renunciation of the use of force. After this exchange of views our paths diverged and there would be no more serious discussions between the Kadets and me while I was premier.

I believed that our task was the honorable implementation of all that was promised in the October 17 Manifesto. I was aware that every radical change in the life of the state produces a reaction and that, consequently, one must proceed with discretion. The Kadets, however, believed in immediate and radical transformation that would give Russia a monarch with as little power as, say, the French president, and that would give Russia a cabinet responsible to the State Duma, which would, of course, be dominated by them. Therefore, as a matter of principle, they were opposed to any cabinet responsible to the Emperor.[26]

Durnovo served many years in that body, where he commanded attention and respect. Unlike most of his colleagues he expressed liberal, but reasonable, views. Consistent with these views, he regularly defended the rights of Jews against an administration that was casuistically attempting to narrow their already limited rights.

It was during Sipiagin's tenure as minister of interior that I first became acquainted with Durnovo. At the minister's request I received him. He wanted a grant of 60,000 rubles to save him from the sad fate that would befall him if he could not cover his stock market losses. I told him that I could not ask His Majesty for such a grant. What if the request came from Sipiagin? Again my answer was "no"; I told him that although I was on good terms with the minister of interior, I would still refuse, and that even if he were able to put the request directly to the Emperor, I would advise His Majesty to refuse. Fortunately for Durnovo, Sipiagin was able to dip into the funds of the Department of Police for the money requested.

The day after Durnovo's call on me, Sipiagin asked what I thought of him. My only basis for comment, I said, was his work in the Senate, which caused me to think of him as sensible and intelligent. What would I think of Durnovo as one of his assistant ministers? My opinion was that he needed an intelligent, hardworking, and experienced assistant minister and that Durnovo was well acquainted with the ministry. I advised him, however, not to entrust Durnovo with any duties related to the police or any other duties not subject to scrutiny, in short, not to entrust him with any work that was not done in broad daylight. Sipiagin said he understood.

So, Durnovo was appointed assistant minister, with jurisdiction over the Chief Administration of Postal and Telegraphic Services. It was about this time that Prince Sviatopolk-Mirskii was appointed as an assistant minister. Prince A. D. Obolenskii (Sipiagin was on *tutoyer* terms with him and thought well of him, except in one respect: the prince was too anxious to advance his career to be trustworthy) was already an assistant minister.

Durnovo carried out his new duties ably and behaved very correctly toward Sipiagin and his successors, whether he liked them or not. When Sipiagin fell ill, he would not join Prince Obolenskii and the others who were intriguing against the minister. And although he hated Plehve (and was hated in return), he behaved with propriety toward his superior. Although sharply critical of Trepov, as I have noted, he behaved correctly toward him, too. In the days following the departure of Bulygin, Durnovo continued to tell me, as he had on the eve of October 17, that Trepov must go and indirectly put himself forward as candidate for the post of minister of interior.

To repeat, I believed that Peter Nikolaevich Durnovo had the necessary experience and the proper attitude toward the work of implementing the October 17 Manifesto to be minister.

When I informed the public men that I was coming around to the view that

Durnovo should be the next minister of interior, most objected, but only one, Shipov, I believe, suggested an alternative—Stolypin. Some reacted favorably to the suggestion of Stolypin, others did not, saying that it was difficult to know what he stood for. I said that all I knew of him was that he was reputed to be an able governor.

Several of the public men then urged me to accept the portfolio of minister of interior. I declined, citing, first of all, the sixteen- to eighteen-hour day that I was already working. I went on to say that even if the circumstances were such that I had to accept such an additional burden, I would insist that police operations be assigned to a body other than the Ministry of Interior. As I have noted, the minister of interior in our police empire is also a minister of police, and I knew nothing about police operations except that there was something unclean about them. But, if a separate ministry of police or something like the old Third Section[27] were to be established, it would produce a most unfortunate impression on society, which would take such a step to mean that the government did not intend to abide by its promise of civil rights. I concluded my argument by saying that, given the times we were experiencing, a man with Durnovo's credentials seemed satisfactory to me and that, in any case, I preferred him to others associated with the Ministry of Interior, men like Rachkovskii, Zvolianskii, Lopukhin, Stürmer, and Garin.

Prince Obolenskii took my side and, surprisingly, so did Prince Urusov, who said that in order to demonstrate that he had nothing against my nominee and because personal feelings should not stand in the way at such times of doing what had to be done, he was willing to serve as assistant minister under Durnovo. At this we adjourned to permit the public men to decide whether or not they would serve with Durnovo.[28]

While waiting for their reply, I told Durnovo that the only issue on which I and the public men disagreed was over my proposal that he be the next minister of interior. This upset him. Did it mean that if he were not appointed minister he would be relieved of his duties as acting minister? And what was it that the public men objected to? I said I didn't know, but that I suspected that it had something to do with his relations with the ladies, a matter that had attracted some attention. He admitted that he had erred.

By this time I had made up my mind that I would insist on Durnovo no matter what the response of the public men because I felt that the next minister must already be familiar with the duties he would assume and yet not be a puppet in the hands of General Trepov, who was by now more influential than ever. Early on I had sensed that the general wanted to direct the Ministry of Interior, or rather its police operations, from behind the scenes and for that reason wanted a minister who was ignorant of the inner operations of the police or one who would do as he was bid. This suspicion had been strengthened when I had mentioned to him that I was thinking of either Prince Urusov or Durnovo as candidates. He had reacted with hostility toward the former and quite unkindly toward the latter, suggesting I take the portfolio myself, to which I had demurred. The Emperor's reactions to the two was another factor in my decision. When, before my meeting with the public men, I mentioned Prince Urusov as a possible candidate, the Emperor was noncommittal but when I mentioned Durnovo, he was hostile to the idea, but suggested no other candidate. The antipathy of both General Trepov and the Emperor toward Durnovo convinced me that he would not be a puppet.

When the public men returned, a few hours (or it may have been a day) after adjournment, Shipov, Guchkov, and Prince Trubetskoi told me they could not serve with Durnovo, but Prince Urusov said he was willing to serve under him.[29] I said once more that I could not accept the portfolio and that I could not think of anyone but Durnovo as being suitable for such times. I must say in all candor that it seemed to me that the real reason for the refusal of the public men to join the cabinet was fear, fear of the violence being experienced at the time by the proper-tied classes.

We parted on outwardly friendly terms. In parting, I asked that they submit their proposals for extending the franchise, subject to the limitations I had mentioned. The public men said they would find it more convenient to do this work in Moscow. I asked them to move quickly because elections could not be scheduled until the electoral law of August 6 was revised.

Completion of My Cabinet

The action of the public men left me with the task of selecting men to fill the posts of minister of interior, minister of education, minister of commerce and industry, and state controller.

When I asked the Emperor to appoint Durnovo as minister of interior and member of the State Council, he agreed to the latter, but would only agree to making him acting minister, in effect saying to him: "If you please me, I will forget about your past, including your liberal record in the Senate, but if you do not please me, you will not be in office long." And to please the Emperor it was necessary to please Trepov.

Durnovo quickly realized that the Emperor had appointed me unwillingly and would gladly get rid of me as soon as he could do without me. Consequently, he decided it was better to be *persona gratissima* with the Emperor than with Count Witte because life is short and the tenure of a minister even shorter. So he set out to please. He got along with the Emperor, with Grand Duke Nicholas Nikola-evich, with Dubrovin, and even with Trepov, whose zigzags he followed with equanimity.

Among other things, Durnovo dealt with the Emperor behind my back,* not

---

*How the Emperor dealt with ministers behind my back is illustrated by the following:

About the middle of December, while I was waiting to see the Emperor, Trepov told me that it would be desirable for the State Bank to grant a loan to Skalon (an officer in the Life Hussars and the son-in-law of N. A. Khomiakov). I replied that although such loans had been made, as exceptions, on Imperial orders, it would be against the spirit of October 17 to do so now, even if we were not in financial straits. Even if a loan were justifiable, I doubted that Skalon was a good risk. I did not know because he wanted to trip me up and replace me (he knew that there was not the slightest chance of his becoming premier), but because he wanted to please the Emperor, who has been called a *charmeur* for good reason.

Durnovo never spoke to me about conversations with or his reports to the Emperor, but knowing His Majesty very well, I can imagine what kinds of conversations took place.

> Durnovo: Your Majesty, so and so should be appointed to such and such a position because he would show the liberals what for.
>
> Emperor: That would be an excellent appointment. Why don't you propose it?
>
> Durnovo: I don't know how Count Witte would react. He calls such people Black Hundreds types.
>
> Emperor: That is none of Count Witte's business. His task is to preside over the cabinet and nothing more.

Or a conversation might go as follows:

> Durnovo: Your Majesty, we decided at a cabinet meeting that Count Podgorichani would have to leave the Corps of Gendarmes because he organized a pogrom against Jews in Gomel.
>
> Emperor: I haven't seen the minutes yet. Did you, in your capacity as minister of interior and chief of the corps, agree to such a step?
>
> Durnovo: Yes, Your Majesty, I can't oppose Count Witte in such matters.
>
> Emperor: Why not? It is none of Count Witte's business. In general, each minister should act on his own and come to me for directives.

By acting as he did, Durnovo survived his probationary period and was rewarded, first, by being made minister, with the civil service rank of actual privy councillor, without my having been consulted, and by having his daughter honored with the title of lady-in-waiting.

---

him, but on the basis of my experience and on the face of things I would predict that if a loan were granted, Skalon would either default or ask for an extension of the loan.

Some time later, the minister of finance, I. P. Shipov, told me that knowing my state of health he did not want to upset me, but felt he had to tell me that the Emperor had ordered him to have the State Bank lend Skalon 2 million rubles but not to tell me.

I promised to keep what he had told me a secret, but I wanted to know how he had responded to the order. Shipov told me that when he returned to his office, he wrote to the Emperor saying he would carry out the order, but felt it his duty to point out that the charter of the State Bank did not sanction such loans and, moreover, that no security had been offered for repayment. How had the Emperor responded? By telling him to carry out the order. Shipov was to pay for his temerity at a later date.

Durnovo is not a model husband, but he adores his daughter, who isn't rich, isn't pretty, is not of high social status. For many years he had been trying to secure the title of lady-in-waiting for her, but the Dowager Empress, remembering what her husband thought of him, had put her foot down against such an appointment. Undaunted, Durnovo had sought the help of Sipiagin and others, but with no success until now. That he finally succeeded obviously meant that he had served the Emperor well enough to get His Majesty to change the mind of so upright a person as the Dowager Empress. (I understand that the assent of both the reigning Empress and the Dowager Empress is required for appointment as lady-in-waiting.)

Have I changed my mind about Durnovo? I still think of him as an intelligent, experienced, energetic, and hardworking man, but my opinion of his character, not very high to begin with, fell as a result of my association with him. He would have been the kind of minister I needed if the Emperor, from the start, had made it clear to him that as long as I chose to keep him in my cabinet it was I who answered for him and that he was to do nothing of consequence without my knowledge and consent. All in all, I consider my part in having him appointed as one of my major mistakes, a mistake that made my difficult position even more difficult.

To fill the position of minister of education I now looked for a man whose record would disturb neither society nor the court, a man who was competent, had a university education, some knowledge of the educational system, and the courage to accept the responsibility. The acting minister, Lukianov, was not such a man. In fact, he was not qualified even to be assistant minister in such troubled times. Well-educated, gifted, not stupid, he should have stuck to his calling, medicine, in which he was very competent. I even consulted him when my wife was very ill. But instead of continuing to make his career in the field he knew best, he chose to advance himself in the bureaucracy. He had managed to advance to the rank of assistant minister because of the fact that for many years he had been a welcome guest in the salon of Countess Marie Aleksandrovna Solskaia, where he recited verse of his own composition.

To my mind the man who had the qualifications then needed was Count Ivan Ivanovich Tolstoi, the vice-president of the Academy of Arts, who, as I have mentioned, had been recommended in 1904 for the post of minister by that fine man Grand Duke Vladimir Aleksandrovich. As the man who administered the academy at a time when heads of other higher schools had lost their nerve and had become putty in the hands of distraught youth, the count had been able to maintain his authority, refuse to be terrorized, and yet retain the respect of his students. His standing at court, where he had friends, and in high society was good. I did not think that the Emperor would object to him. Despite Count Tolstoi's standing in court, he was his own man, and that was to the good.

When I offered him the post, he said that he did not feel qualified for it and suggested that I seek another candidate. But when I told him that other suitable candidates shied away from accepting such a post in times like these and that I was under pressure to fill the many vacancies in the cabinet, he agreed, stating that he considered it his duty to accept what amounted to a front-line assignment and to help carry out the principles of the October 17 Manifesto. As I expected, His Majesty agreed to the appointment, immediately.

Since the new minister would not keep Lukianov, with his thwarted ambition to be minister, he asked me to suggest a replacement for the assistant minister. I recommended Gerasimov, to whom I have also referred earlier, for two reasons, first because of his long experience in the Ministry of Education, second, because he stood well with those pillars of the right who might consider Count Tolstoi as too liberal. After meeting Gerasimov, Count Tolstoi said he was favorably impressed by him and added, knowingly, that the Emperor approved wholeheartedly of Gerasimov.

Both men turned out well. The new minister showed balance and solidity, did nothing of which I disapproved. The new assistant minister proved to be an intelligent and well-informed man. Yet both were later to be charged with being too far to the left and would lose their positions as a result!

I regretted that D. N. Shipov would not join my cabinet because I needed a man such as he, who had the absolute confidence of society, to help adapt an office created during the period of absolutism to the needs of a constitutional era.

Following Shipov's decline I offered the state controllership to D. A. Filosofov, the acting state controller. He was highly respected in the bureaucratic world but as yet little known to society. He accepted on condition that before the State Duma convened the office be reshaped to conform to the principles of the new times, something that has yet to be done. During my tenure Filosofov behaved irreproachably, always adhering to a moderate liberal position.

To be head of the newly established Ministry of Commerce and Industry I selected Vasilii Ivanovich Timiriazev, who had been with the Ministry of Finance for many years and had been assistant minister of finance in charge of the Department of Commerce and Industry since I had chosen him for that post while minister of finance.

My acquaintance with him went back to the days when I was director of the Department of Railroad Affairs in the ministry and he was vice-director of the Department of Commerce and Industry. During our common service on the commission that prepared the first protective tariff I learned a good deal about him, that he was not stupid, knew the details of his work, could write in a good chancery style, had a broad knowledge of foreign languages, but was a man from whom one could not expect initiative or originality.

Shortly after I became minister of finance and the post of director of the Department of Commerce and Industry became vacant I chose not to promote Timiriazev because I wanted to strengthen our commerce and industry and he lacked the talent and energy for what I had in mind. Since it would have been uncomfortable for Timiriazev to stay on under the new man, V. I. Kovalevskii, he was sent to Berlin as financial agent for the ministry. When Kovalevskii had to give up his position I had no qualms about appointing Timiriazev as his replacement, first, because I felt that I knew the business of the ministry very well and, second, because I was appointing the very knowledgeable M. M. Fedorov as his assistant.

It was Fedorov who, just before the announcement was made that Timiriazev would be the minister of commerce and industry, warned me that the man was guilty of political improprieties. To my regret, I paid no attention.

I did not expect Timiriazev to show great ability or initiative, but I did expect him to behave with propriety. This did not turn out to be the case during his service in my cabinet. That he expressed ultraleftist opinions at cabinet meetings did not disturb me. But I was upset when I learned, too late, he had daily contact with reporters from left-wing newspapers and spoke to them as if he were an ultraliberal giving them confidential information he had picked up at cabinet meetings. When such information appeared in the press, I did not know the source and admonished my colleagues not to divulge what was said or decided at our meetings. Timiriazev would listen to such admonitions as if they did not concern him.

The reason for his ultraliberalism, I discovered, was that he had spent so much time abroad that he had forgotten what the real Russia was like and believed that we would soon become a democratic republic. Being a servile man, he was trying to ingratiate himself with those he thought would soon be in power. (While I was minister of finance he was servile toward me.) But when it turned out that the monarchy was far from dead, he changed his tune, with nothing to show for his erstwhile liberalism, but more of this later, except to say that he would leave my cabinet under very unpleasant circumstances.

In addition to having to fill the vacancies left by the refusal of the public men to enter my cabinet, I found myself with two other vacancies, caused by the unexpected departure of Schwanebach and Kokovtsev.[30]

When Schwanebach chose to leave I decided on Nicholas Nikolaevich Kutler as the next head of the Chief Administration of Land Organization and Agriculture. He was one of the ablest of the men with whom I had worked in the Ministry of Finance, and I knew him to be an honorable man. Had Stakhovich chosen to join me, I would have proposed him as Schwanebach's successor.

There was some unpleasantness about Kokovtsev's departure. It was during the meeting to discuss amnesty that I learned of the finance minister's desire to leave office from Baron Uexküll, when he asked if I knew that the minister had submitted a request to the Emperor asking to be relieved of his duties. I said I had not, had no idea why he should have done so, and, in any event, had no thought of parting with him, although I would have no difficulty in replacing him. I told the baron that all that I had done was to tell Count Solskii I was planning to remove from the finance minister's jurisdiction those parts of his ministry dealing with commerce and industry.

The following day Kokovtsev asked me to write a note to the Emperor asking him to ignore his request. I said it would be awkward for me to do anything at this point and reproached him for not informing me in advance of what he had in mind. He told me he had submitted his request because Count Solskii told him I wanted him to leave. After I succeeded in convincing him that I had said nothing of the kind to the count, Kokovtsev expressed regret over his action and began to cry, saying: "What shall I do? When you are out of the swim, you read and write, but such things do not interest me; I shall die of boredom."

But it was too late. On my recommendation the Emperor appointed my old colleague Ivan Pavlovich Shipov as minister of finance. Shipov is an intelligent man and, aside from being a bit disingenuous, is a worthy man.

Shortly after Kokovtsev's departure from office I learned that Count Solskii intended to ask the Emperor to appoint Kokovtsev as chairman of the Department of State Economy of the State Council. By that time I had seen Kokovtsev's request to be relieved of his post as minister of finance, and because I found certain insinuations in it about October 17, I saw to it that he did not receive the appointment as chairman.[31]

All in all, the process of replacing the men who left my cabinet took ten days. At the end of that period, my cabinet stood as follows: Baron Freedericksz—Imperial court; Count Lambsdorff—foreign affairs; General Rödiger—war; Admiral Birilev—navy; Manukhin—justice; Prince Obolenskii—Holy Synod; Count Tolstoi—education;[32] Shipov—finance; Timiriazev—commerce and industry; Nemeshaev—ways and communications; Kutler—land organization and agriculture; Filosofov—state control.

X

Impediments to My Work

General Trepov and
Grand Duke Nicholas Nikolaevich

[In the last days of October, just as I was completing the formation of my cabinet, the Emperor made two appointments that were to hamper me seriously. The first was that of General Trepov as palace commandant and the second was that of Grand Duke Nicholas Nikolaevich as commander of the Petersburg Military District.]

A New Palace Commandant

Within a few days after I became premier, General Trepov—governor-general, assistant minister of interior, commander of the Petersburg garrison: in short, dictator—told me, first by phone and then in writing, that he wished to leave his posts. That was what I wanted, but because, as I have said, I did not wish to appear to be yielding to the demand of the Petersburg press for his removal, I did not give him a definite answer.

It was about October 27[1] that he officially informed me that he wished to be relieved of his posts. I told him, over the telephone, that I would not stop him. Inasmuch as I was scheduled to report to the Emperor the following day, I planned to tell him of Trepov's request when I saw him.

The following morning, when I arrived at the dock to take the boat to Peterhof, I was surprised to find Trepov there also. When I asked if he would be returning with me later that day, he replied that he would be staying on at Peterhof, as palace commandant. (In fact, he did not even return to Petersburg for his things, but had them sent to him at his new residence.) I was somewhat taken aback by the news, first, because I had not been given advance notice of the change and, second, because his departure from the capital might be interpreted as flight.

During my report to the Emperor, I mentioned that I had intended to inform him of Trepov's request, but, in view of what I had just learned, that was no longer necessary. I remarked that I was pleased that Trepov's only duty would now be that of protecting His Majesty, a duty for which his police experience fitted him.* I added that I was pleased, too, that Trepov would be sharing the burden of protecting His Majesty with me and my cabinet. The Emperor did not respond, but changed the subject. The next day the appointment of Trepov was officially announced, much to the surprise of his closest associates.

It was not long before Garin, the director of the Department of Police, gave up his post and joined Trepov. The Emperor informed Manukhin, the minister of justice, that he was appointing Garin to the Senate. When the minister objected that others with a better claim to such an appointment had been passed over, the Emperor said that he had already given his promise and the appointment was made.[2] Garin's unofficial function was to serve as aide and chief secretary to Trepov, who, in addition to being responsible for the protection of the Emperor, began to serve as his advisor.

Once Trepov and Garin were ensconced at Peterhof, I noted that the Emperor's comments on documents returned to me were being written in a long-winded chancery style, e.g., "This opinion does not agree with the cassational decisions of the Senate of such and such a date concerning such and such case, which explained the true sense of article such and such, volume so and so, part so and so." The handwriting was the Emperor's but the words and style were not his. Never in his life had he read anything on Russian law, and he never really understood how the Senate operated. In his eyes the Senate is a body of more or less experienced men—appointed by him, not for their qualifications, but for their many years of service or because he feels sorry for them or because they have influential supporters—whose chief task is to decide issues for the benefit of the state and especially for the benefit of the Emperor and his family on the basis of equity. And he considers the minister of justice as a kind of inspector for legal matters whom he can ignore when the law has to be bent, in which case he turns to the director of his Commission on Petitions or the head of a section of his chancery. Knowing the Emperor's ignorance of legal niceties I was puzzled by the new style until I learned that virtually all reports from ministers and the like, except those dealing with foreign affairs or defense, went to General Trepov, who, with the aid of Senator Garin, drafted the Emperor's comments and notations.†

It was quickly evident that, far from having lost power by giving up all his

---

*Under Emperor Alexander III, when things were called by their proper names, the post was called "His Majesty's chief of security." All that has changed is the extent of undercover operations carried out by palace commandants, which has increased, and the quality of those responsible for the Emperor's safety, which has declined.

†After Goremykin became premier, a friend of mine, who is in favor at court, asked Baron Freedericksz for his impression of the new cabinet. The reply: "I respect and admire Count Witte, but I must say that under Goremykin, cabinet meetings are calmer and greater attention and respect are shown for the Emperor's notations. Just yesterday, his notations, which included references to various articles of the law, were read at a cabinet meeting, after which Goremykin, with tears in his eyes, told me how dazzled he was by His Majesty's memory and knowledge."

That prompted me to ask if Senator Garin were still working with General Trepov.

previous posts for the comparatively lowly one of palace commandant, he had become even more powerful, answerable to no one, an Asiatic eunuch in a European court.[3] His power was enhanced chiefly because this decisive and imposing man was now in a position to exercise great influence on the weak-willed Emperor, whom he was seeing every day. Also, the fact that he was responsible for protection of the Emperor gave him power. Then, too, he controlled expenditures for which he did not have to account. Note, moreover, that he was privy to all the counsel that reached the Emperor. And it should be remembered that all confidential material intended for the Emperor went through his hands, a fact of particular importance given the Emperor's passion for secret documents and meetings.

It was Trepov who now decided what was worthy of the Emperor's attention and what was not. After all, didn't His Majesty have more than enough to read? And if one of the documents that passed through Trepov's hands provided material for getting rid of an undesirable minister, it could be touched up in a beautiful and humble style to make the point very evident.

In addition, Trepov was now able to influence the Emperor's political views. Wavering as he did between ultraconservative and ultraliberal sentiments, Trepov was especially susceptible to the arguments of powerful and propertied persons who, now that the threat to the throne had lessened thanks to the October 17 Manifesto, had, in accordance with the inexorable laws of history, shifted from liberalism to reaction. He was especially open to influence from careerists who, seeing how the political winds were blowing, tried to influence the Emperor through him. And there was that clique of foreign correspondents who thought it their duty to exercise a similar influence. All this helps explain how, in the dim recesses of his soul, the Emperor came to regret that he had signed the manifesto and now sought to abrogate it, if not openly then indirectly, by hook or by crook.[4] [I will deal later with how Trepov, responding to pressure from such people, helped push two of my cabinet out of office.]

Trepov and the Police

Trepov could be said to have been born and raised in a police environment, ending his career as chief of what could be called His Majesty's police headquarters. And in his new capacity he retained his links with the police, as shown by the Captain Komissarov case.

The captain was chief of a special section of the Department of Police engaged in the printing of inflammatory literature, largely of an anti-Semitic character, that had been organized under the aegis of Rachkovskii[5] while Trepov was assistant minister of interior. When Durnovo became minister of interior he stripped Rachkovskii of his major responsibilities and assigned duties to him that would keep him out of Petersburg. But, as Durnovo told me, Rachkovskii neglected his new responsibilities and, instead, spent most of his time with Trepov, providing the new palace commandant with a link to the police. This was so because, although Rachkovskii was in disfavor with Durnovo, he retained many ties, among them the tie with Captain Komissarov, about whose activities I was informed by Lopukhin.[6]

Lopukhin was a man with a grievance. After Trepov became assistant minister of interior, Lopukhin was removed from his position as director of the Department of Police and named governor of Estland. During the turbulent October days, so it was charged, Lopukhin virtually abdicated his authority in the face of revolutionary outbursts. The charge was filed with Grand Duke Nicholas Nikolaevich by a divisional general stationed in Revel, the capital of Estland. The Grand Duke immediately informed the Emperor of the charge, and the Emperor, in turn, demanded that Durnovo immediately remove Lopukhin. Had the minister of interior been made of stronger stuff he would have supported the governor. As he told me, Durnovo did suggest an investigation before any action should be taken, but the Emperor would not agree. So Lopukhin was removed and assigned to a minor post in the ministry.

After Lopukhin's removal, which took place without my participation, I learned that it was the divisional general who had acted in a cowardly fashion and so informed the Grand Duke. He said that he knew the general very well and therefore believed that what I had heard could not be true. Nonetheless, he dispatched a general (Bezobrazov, former commander of the Chevalier Garde, I believe) to investigate. What he found agreed, on the whole, with what I had been told. As a result the divisional general was deprived of his command.

It was in January or February 1906 that Lopukhin came to see me with information about Captain Komissarov and his special section, about which I had not been aware at all before this. He told me that inflammatory leaflets were being distributed in large quantities in various places, most recently in Kursk, Vilna, and Moscow. Since I considered Lopukhin untrustworthy, particularly so in this instance, given his enmity for Trepov and Rachkovskii, I asked for proof.

He returned a few days later with copies of leaflets that had already been distributed or were about to be and warned me that if I did not surprise the captain at his work the whole operation would be concealed from me. Ignoring his advice, I sent an official from my chancellery the next day in my carriage with orders to bring Captain Komissarov to me from wherever he might be and whether or not he was in uniform. About a half an hour after the official left, the captain, dressed as a laborer, was brought to my office. I asked him to take a seat, inquired about his work, told him that I considered it interesting and important. When he realized that I knew what he had been doing, he obviously lost his head and spoke freely about his work. He told me that he was using printing presses taken from revolutionaries and that these presses had been placed in the basement of the Department of Police. He claimed that the number of leaflets distributed was not as great as alleged.

When I asked who had organized the operation and who was in charge, he claimed that he had acted on his own, without the knowledge of his superiors, because he believed that what he did had to be done. (His story was plausible because E. I. Vuich [brother of N. I. Vuich, who worked with me] was new to his work.) I then said sternly to Captain Komissarov:

> What you have been doing is utterly reprehensible. Promise me that you will immediately destroy your stock of leaflets, throw the presses into the Fontanka Canal, and never engage in such work again. If by tomorrow I find that you haven't destroyed the leaflets and gotten rid of the presses, I will turn you over to the law.

He gave me his word that he would do as I said.

After talking to Durnovo the following day about the Komissarov operation, I was convinced that he had known nothing about it and that he was opposed to such activities. Obviously puzzled by what I had told him, he quickly ordered an investigation. The report, of which I have a copy in my archive, agrees with what I learned but tends to minimize the importance of this case, which was subsequently discussed in the State Duma, by Prince Urusov, and in the press.[7] As far as I can tell, both the press and the prince exaggerated the facts. In any case, it was improper for Prince Urusov (Lopukhin's brother-in-law) and Lopukhin, who obtained their information through their positions, to make it public.

At my first opportunity I informed the Emperor of the Komissarov case, asking that the captain not be disciplined. His Majesty, obviously already informed, said he had no intention of doing so, in view of the captain's service with the intelligence in the war with Japan.

Another instance of the role played by the Department of Police in instigating pogroms is provided by what happened in Gomel, where a cruel attack on Jews took place in December. The investigation, conducted by the Ministry of Interior, at my request, revealed that the police, acting under the direction of Count Podgorichani, the local gendarme chief, had organized the pogrom. I asked Durnovo to inform the cabinet of what the investigation had uncovered. The cabinet was shocked. When the Emperor read the minutes of this cabinet meeting, minutes that understated the facts, he wrote this comment: "How does this concern me? Responsibility for the disposition of the case of Count Podgorichani rests with the minister of interior."[8] A few months later I learned that the count had been appointed chief of police in some Black Sea city.

Trepov and I

Those who knew how Trepov's influence on the Emperor made it impossible for me to function as head of the government later suggested that I should have tried to weaken his influence by seeing the Emperor every day, given the fact that he is easily influenced by those who are constantly with him, which explains the influence of the Empress. To have followed this naive advice would have meant my taking up residence first in Peterhof, then in Tsarskoe Selo, to be near the Emperor and devoting all my time to gaining influence over him. Had I tried to see the Emperor every day, it would have been under circumstances dictated by Trepov, who could be with him several times a day. Had I followed such advice I would have neglected my work, yet I would have failed in my effort, and, most important, I would have demeaned myself.

As things turned out, Trepov had more influence over the Emperor than I did and was virtually the head of the government for which I bore responsibility. During my six months as premier I had to do battle with him over every question about which we disagreed. This was the chief reason for my not being able to do what I considered necessary and leaving the post of premier a few days before the opening of the First State Duma. I will refer to this abnormal state of affairs as I go along.

Grand Duke Nicholas Nikolaevich

Like Trepov, Grand Duke Nicholas Nikolaevich exercised considerable, and harmful, influence over the Emperor.[9] This influence, as will be seen, enabled the Grand Duke to amass considerable power over military and, to some extent, naval affairs, to the detriment of the state. I, too, was affected by the Grand Duke's power.

As I have said earlier, the Grand Duke's influence was linked to that abnormal interest in mysticism from which he had long suffered and with which the Emperor had been infected by the Empress.

One cannot call the Grand Duke mad. Neither can one call him normal. Like others with Oldenburg blood in their veins, he inherited some of the abnormal characteristics of Emperor Paul.[10] Typical of his mentality is a remark he made to me while I was chairman of the Committee of Ministers. The matter concerned allegations that malicious stories about my wife were being bandied about at his brother's home. Now, I pay no attention to gossip, however loathsome, about me, but I could not permit her name to be sullied. I took advantage of my acquaintance with him (I became acquainted with him in Kiev in the 1880s, and while I was minister of finance he would either leave his card at my home on holidays or send it to me) to call on him and tell him of what I had heard. He assured me that he had heard no such talk at his brother's home, but that if he ever did, he would speak up.

Then we spoke of the Emperor. Rather abruptly he asked if I considered the Emperor human or divine. I replied: ''He is my Sovereign and I shall be his devoted servant as long as I live, but although he is the Autocratic Sovereign, whether given us by God or by nature, he is, nonetheless, a human being, with all the attributes of other human beings.'' The Grand Duke responded that the

Emperor was neither human nor divine, "but something in between." With this we parted.

The Grand Duke is an honorable man, utterly devoted to the Emperor. His intentions are good, but he has done Russia much harm and will probably do so again. However, he is capable of doing good for Russia, as he did in helping me annul the treaty concluded at Björkö. He has *some* military abilities and, as I have mentioned earlier, has the distinction of being the only Grand Duke to have attended the General Staff Academy, but how seriously he took his studies there I do not know.[11] All in all, he is a man of limited ability.

His ambition was to exercise influence in military affairs and he was able to do so because of his close ties to the Emperor. Even while Kuropatkin was war minister, the Grand Duke, who was allied to a degree with him, improved his position, for example, by being designated to command the German front in the event of war.

Then, when General Sakharov—a decent and intelligent man, but not a strong one—replaced Kuropatkin, the Grand Duke began to gain even more ground, as a result of two important changes which had the support of the Grand Duke. The first was the creation of the Council of State Defense, a kind of Areopagus, to deal with matters of national defense, subordinate only to the Emperor, with the Grand Duke serving as its chairman. The Grand Duke was thus placed in a position superior to those of the war and navy ministers, a position that he was to exploit.

The second change was the division of the military establishment into two parts: one administrative, under the war minister, and the other concerned with military operations, under the chief of the General Staff, who would answer to the Emperor, not the war minister.

When this change was proposed, General Sakharov, who showed me a copy of the proposal, opposed it. I told him that I, too, thought it unwise, because what was proposed was a truncated version of the German system, under which the division between the administrative part and military operations started at the bottom, making the division at the top logical and workable, while what was proposed followed the German model only at the top, while continuing to adhere to the traditional French model lower down. Such a system, in my opinion, was sure to fail. The result would, in effect, be dual power—the War Ministry and the General Staff.[12]

General Sakharov was not strong enough to oppose the Grand Duke, who won the day. The General Staff was removed from the jurisdiction of the Ministry of War, and General Palitsyn, who was beholden to the Grand Duke, was named as its chief. As for General Sakharov, he was replaced by General Rödiger, whom the Grand Duke mistakenly considered more likely to be docile.[13]

General Palitsyn is a decent sort of person, far from stupid, with a detailed knowledge of military administration, but he is not a man of stature in the military world. The appointment of such as he to a position corresponding to that of Field

Marshal von Moltke in Germany could not be taken as a wise response to our problems.

In fact, the changes I have mentioned only exacerbated the demoralization brought on by our disgraceful war with Japan. They would be proven worthless and in the end would be undone.

The Grand Duke's power in the military was further enhanced when, shortly after I became premier, he succeeded Grand Duke Vladimir Aleksandrovich as commander of the Imperial Guard and the Petersburg Military District. It was as commander of the Petersburg Military District that he was to create difficulties for me.

Grand Duke Nicholas Nikolaevich used his position in the military not only to influence military and naval affairs but also to find high positions for those close to him as well as for those close to the lady he held dear, Mrs. Burenina, those who had been close to his father and to the one his father had held dear, the dancer Chislova, and those close to Princess Anastasia Nikolaevna, his sister-in-law.[14] In bestowing such favors he was displaying a weakness common to all grand dukes.

During the first weeks after October 17, the Grand Duke behaved in a fairly normal fashion, but as it became evident to him that calm would not return immediately, his composure and his judgment began to decline, leading him to become friendly with the Union of the Russian People, that gang of paid thugs that was just gaining strength with the support of Prince Orlov, Count Shereme-tev, and, possibly, P. N. Durnovo. (I include Durnovo because, following my departure from office, he said in response to my characterization of Dubrovin as a good-for-nothing that the man was "a most fine and honorable man.") From what I soon learned, General Rauch, the Grand Duke's chief of staff and his most trusted general, was seeing Dubrovin in a building not far from the English Club and belonging to it.[15] The Grand Duke himself visited the club and probably met Dubrovin, even while I was premier. And then, after I left office, the Grand Duke did little to hide his ties with Dubrovin and the Union of the Russian People. At one point the Petersburg branch of that organization even thought of electing the Grand Duke as its honorary chairman, but decided that that might be too risky. But because he could count on the support of the Grand Duke and Durnovo, Dubrovin held a meeting of his thugs in a riding hall at which he delivered an inflammatory speech which moved his audience to shout as it left the hall, "Down with the rotten constitution, death to Count Witte." But they did not dare stage a march.

Also illustrative of how the Grand Duke's judgment was adversely affected in those days was the decision to reduce the term of compulsory military service, which was made on the recommendation of the Council of State Defense, without my participation or that of the cabinet. At a time of stability, such a step might have made sense, provided that the reduction in service was accompanied by compensatory measures such as providing our peasant and worker soldiers with adequate training in modern military techniques. But it was fear, the need to placate the lower ranks, not the good of the army, that motivated the reduction in service. It was as if we were saying to the Russian people: "We admit our responsibility for the disgraceful war and for the slaughter of so many Russian soldiers, and we are therefore going to make things easier for you in the future, and, in return, we ask that you forget what happened and observe discipline." Yes, what happened in those post-October days showed me that stupidity, more than any other human trait, is nourished by cowardice.

And now another example of how the Grand Duke's judgment was warped by the events of those days. Shortly after he was given command of the Petersburg Military District, I turned to him in my belief that "God helps those who help themselves," meaning, in this case, that one must prepare for any eventuality. Accordingly, I asked the Grand Duke that, to be prepared for the possibility that it might be necessary to place the capital and its environs under martial law and to provide military protection for the Emperor and his family, plans be made so that every unit under his command know exactly where to go and what to do in order to restore calm quickly. He listened carefully. A few days later, General Rauch informed me that everything necessary had been done. I asked him to thank the Grand Duke and to assure him that I was certain that the need for martial law would not arise but had wanted to be prepared for trouble, however remote the possibility of it. That was not the end of the story.

A few weeks later, General Hasenkampff, who had just been appointed assistant to the Grand Duke, called on me, on behalf of his superior, to ask that, should an emergency arise, I should declare a state of "extraordinary protection" rather than a state of "martial law." When I asked why, he told me that if it became necessary to impose death sentences the man responsible for imposing death sentences in the first instance would be the minister of interior, but that the man responsible in the second instance would be the Grand Duke. And the man who imposed the death sentences would become the target of assassins. I told him to tell the Grand Duke that as long as I was premier such emergency measures would not be required in Petersburg and its environs.

I shall speak subsequently of the difficulties I had with Grand Duke Nicholas Nikolaevich in my efforts to put down the Moscow uprising.

XI

The Restoration of Order

Everyone said that Witte was so clever, but in the end the Cossacks once more had to save the state.[1]

—Empress Alexandra

The Problems

As I warned the Emperor when he was considering whether or not to sign the manifesto, we could expect some stormy weather before reaching a safe harbor, and for some two months after October 17 the sailing was very rough indeed. As I have observed, the strike that had paralyzed the country was soon over, but seditious and revolutionary ferment continued. In Petersburg, despite the quick return of comparative calm, the soviet continued to command the support of the workers. In Moscow, where the troops were unreliable, there was trouble. The Caucasus was still aflame. Much the same can be said of Finland, the Kingdom of Poland, and many parts of the Baltic provinces. Disorder was prevalent in the southwestern provinces (Kiev, Volhynia, and Podolia). Unrest among the peasantry was on the rise. In Siberia the region served by the railroad was out of hand, and the bulk of our million-man force that had been sent to Manchuria was still east of Lake Baikal.

Throughout my tenure as premier there were outbreaks in the army, but these were little more than minor symptoms of a fairly sound organism fighting off a mild infection. Mutinies and riots were comparatively few. In Voronezh a mutinous disciplinary battalion had to be taken in hand by reliable troops. In Kiev a company of the Fifth Pontoon Battalion took to the streets in a demonstration. In Petersburg there was unrest in the Military Electro-Technical School and among

522

the sailors in the naval barracks on Morskaia, near the Horse Guards barracks. In this case Grand Duke Nicholas Nikolaevich acted energetically, taking a personal part in the operations, when his troops surrounded the naval barracks at night, herded the mutinous sailors on barges, and shipped them off to Kronstadt.

The fact is that there was more trouble in the navy than in the army because the navy was badly administered and, more to the point, its lower ranks were filled with men who were better educated than their counterparts in the army and hence more easily influenced by revolutionary ideas, which these men, in turn, disseminated among civilians. Kronstadt, which was administered by the Ministry of the Navy, was the scene of revolutionary disorders that began on October 26 and continued for three days. Also, there were mutinies in the Black Sea fleet and at its base, in Sebastopol.

Several of the mutineers, among them Lieutenant Schmidt, were sentenced to death. Schmidt's lawyer, Pergament (subsequently elected to the State Duma from Odessa), assured me that his client was insane and should be put into an asylum. Because the lieutenant was tried by a naval court I could not intervene, but I did inform the Emperor of what Pergament had told me. His Majesty's response was that if Schmidt were insane, the court would have said so.[2]

The task of restoring order was made difficult, as I have indicated before, by the fact that the viceroy of the Caucasus and many of the governors-general, governors, and prefects were not equal to the tasks they faced. The task was made even more difficult by the lack of police and troops.

The police were too few in number, were demoralized, lacked arms. For example, in Moscow, even at the height of the troubles there, there were not enough revolvers to go around, so that police going off duty had to turn their revolvers over to those reporting to duty. During my tenure, the urban and rural (particularly the rural) police were strengthened.[3]

More important was the lack of troops for use in troubled parts of European Russia. One reason for the shortage was the policy, going back to the days when Count Miliutin was war minister, of concentrating our troops near the German, Austro-Hungarian, and Turkish frontiers, leaving few troops in the interior. This is as it should be, if one believes that the army exists for use against a foreign enemy, not our people, but now we were paying a price for that policy.

The only military districts up to strength were those of the Caucasus, the Kingdom of Poland, and Petersburg, the first two because of their proximity to frontiers, the last because of Grand Duke Nicholas Nikolaevich's determination to hold on to as many troops as he could in order to protect the Imperial residences in the environs of Petersburg. And the commanders in the Caucasus and the Kingdom of Poland were very reluctant to give up troops because of dangerous unrest in their areas.

One reason, I was told, for the below-strength state of our troops in European Russia lay with General Kuropatkin. Both as war minister and as commander-in-chief in Manchuria he assumed that we would need no more than 400,000 men in

Manchuria, but as it turned out we required a million men, resulting in a heavy drain on our numbers in European Russia. Kuropatkin was like an unskilled fire chief trying to put out a fire with a small stream of water, a fire that I had to put out in the end.

Even our Ministry of War did not know how few troops we had in European Russia and often did not have precise information about their location. When we would inform General Rödiger that so-called battalions sent to deal with peasant riots turned out to have fewer than fifty men, he would reply that many units were under strength because the new levy of recruits had not arrived (railroad strikes delayed the autumn call-up of conscripts by as much as two months). It was as if the depleted units in European Russia had suffered heavy casualties without having been in action. To make matters worse, stores of medical supplies and uniforms were depleted.

Although we lacked sufficient manpower to cope with violence, I favored demobilization of reservists because they were especially susceptible to revolutionary influence. There were some who felt that demobilization should be delayed in view of the uncertain situation we faced, but I, who had to deal with disorder, won that day. Grand Duke Nicholas Nikolaevich, I am glad to say, did not create any difficulties in this case.

Thus, with insufficient manpower, I had to cope as best as I could with the disorder I encountered in my first months in office.

The Kingdom of Poland

For several years the Kingdom of Poland had been the scene of considerable disorder,[4] which became more widespread and intense during the war with Japan, as the government lost both moral prestige and power. These disorders had a social character, peasant against landowner, worker against factory owner. Labor unrest was particularly intense as a result of industrial growth in recent years.

The disorders also had a political character, which accounted for much of the widespread unrest, because of the so-called Polish question, which to this day is a burning issue among the supporters of the so-called Slavonic cause. In part because of Polish historical tradition, in part because of the actions of the heavy-handed Russian bureaucracy, Poles of all classes (Russian nationalism, in contrast, has a class character, because of economic self-interest) united around one goal, "emancipation" from Russian influence, although they were divided about the kind of "emancipation."

Some dreamed of a return to the old Kingdom of Poland, linked to Russia only by a common sovereign.[5] But the great majority asked for no more than administrative autonomy for the Kingdom of Poland, while some, mainly of the upper class, asked for no more than that they be treated as equals, not as "negroes," by the Russians and be relieved of arbitrary administration at the hands of bureaucratic sons of priests, of the Pobedonostsev stripe.[6] Because they were fighting for "emancipation," the Poles were sympathetic to the Russian emancipation movement, which in a display of bad sense tended to forget its own national heritage, to forget Russia's glorious heritage in its ardor for denigrating the arbitrary Russian bureaucracy and the cretinous court camarilla.

As I have said earlier, I found the Kingdom of Poland in a state of near rebellion when I became premier. The circumstances were such that I felt it imperative to take decisive steps. Therefore, I asked the governor-general, General Skalon—a loyal servant of the Emperor and a man of good breeding, strong character, and sound principles—if he did not agree that the region should be placed under martial law. Evidently he had already thought about it, but those in positions of authority had not wanted to take the initiative. So, [on October 29] without Tsarskoe Selo being involved in the preliminaries, the Kingdom of Poland was placed under martial law.

To my surprise this step aroused more disapproval from the Russian left than from most Poles. For example, it provided Russian anarchists and socialists with a pretext for calling a new general strike, one that had little success. Another example was the condemnation of martial law by a congress of zemstvo and municipal duma leaders.

I was particularly disturbed by the appearance at the congress of Polish spokesmen, among them the well-known lawyer Dmowski, Wrublewski, and Count Tyszkiewicz, who on his return to Warsaw disseminated such extremist propaganda that General Skalon exiled him to the northern provinces. (Later, at my suggestion, the count was expelled from the country.) At this congress the self-appointed representatives of Poland were supported by most of the delegates (but not Guchkov) in their criticism of Russian policies and their demand for autonomy for the Kingdom of Poland.

On their way back home, these Polish spokesmen called on me in an effort to convince me to end martial law.[7] Count Tyszkiewicz uttered only generalities, which did no more than confirm what I already knew from conservative and reasonable Polish aristocrats (e.g., Count Czapski), namely, that all Poles wanted emancipation from the Russian yoke (or rather from the yoke of a certain kind of Russian administration) and that all Poles, ranging from conservative magnates to anarchists, were united in this desire.

In contrast to the count, Dmowski spoke in a serious and thoughtful vein. He admitted that separation of the Kingdom of Poland from Russia was an unattainable dream and recognized that the Russian government had to take strong measures to deal with violence in the kingdom, but went on to say, roughly as follows:

> But to whom are we indebted for all this violence? To Russian ways and culture, from which all Poles seek to dissociate as much as possible. The infection from which we suffer came from you Russians.
>
> After the Kishinev pogrom, organized by Plehve, and other pogroms that took place with the consent of government organs, large numbers of Jewish artisans and factory workers came to the Kingdom of Poland, where the policy

toward Jews is more humane than among you. By bringing with them militant anarchism, the use of bombs and Brownings, they changed the nature of our labor problem, which had been developing along Western lines. Your Russian Jews turned our Jews into savages, just as wild animals affect domesticated animals. But how could Russian Jews keep from being savages when Russians would not consider them as truly human?

Also, your teachers, your professors, your educational methods have infected our children with the political and socialist venom of Russian nihilistic propaganda. Under our traditions children were taught to respect their families, their elders, their religion, their culture, their national past. Our students studied and learned and were imbued with the feelings and traditions of a strong nation. Then you began to Russify our schools. You sent us seminarists to serve as teachers, teachers who bowed to Mammon rather than to God. You corrupted our students, turned them toward nihilism and democratism. You systematically drove what you call the Polish spirit from their hearts and replaced it with Russian religious, governmental, and political nihilism.

He concluded by saying that if we *sincerely* acted on the principles proclaimed in the October 17 Manifesto, Polish society was ready to enter on the path of reconciliation with us. But first martial law had to be lifted.

When I communicated with General Skalon about ending martial law, he informed me politely that as long as he was governor-general it would not happen. A few days later I had the opportunity of talking to Iachkevskii, director of his chancellery, whom I had known for a long time. A moderately liberal young man who knew the Kingdom of Poland well and was no enemy of the Poles, he surprised me by opposing my idea of ending martial law. He informed me that most Poles did not sympathize with the revolutionaries, that those with property had not felt safe before the imposition of martial law and would privately be unhappy if it were lifted. This argument persuaded me to accept the governor-general's position.[8]

End of the Petersburg Soviet

Although Petersburg quieted down after October 17, the Petersburg soviet remained alive and continued to be a thorn. Superficially, it seemed a major force because the working masses, including the printers, blindly followed its direction. That the printers did so was of particular importance because the decision of the soviet determined whether or not the printers would permit newspapers to appear on time, if at all. Yet, I attached little importance to the soviet, because its influence was limited to Petersburg and I knew that I could deal with it when it became necessary to do so. For the time being I tolerated it despite the problems it created.

Thus, on October 27, the workers of Petersburg began to impose the eight-hour day. Shortly thereafter, the soviet, which felt that it was losing its influence, decided to strengthen its hand by calling a general strike, to begin on November 1, in protest against both the imposition of martial law in the Kingdom of Poland and the steps taken to end the disorders in Kronstadt.

On October 31, when I learned of the strike call, I sent a message to the workers, through the factory administrators, warning them against paying heed to those who were leading them to ruin. In my message I used the phrase "comradely advice." *Novoe vremia* and several other newspapers scoffed at my use of the word "comradely," one not in common use among high officials, but labor leaders were extremely upset by it because they realized what effect it had on their followers.

By this time the workers of Petersburg were no longer listening to their leaders, and few heeded the strike call. Consequently, the Petersburg soviet terminated the strike as of November 5. By and large the strike movement in Petersburg and elsewhere ended by November 7.[9] It was on November 7 that the Emperor wrote me: "I am happy that the senseless railroad strike is over; that is a great moral victory for the government."* For my part I believed that the strikes and disorders we experienced had their origin in the times when Trepov, Bulygin, Kokovtsev, *i tutti quanti* were in power and that the end of the movement was the effect of October 17.

When factory owners in Petersburg saw that the government was regaining its strength and moral authority, they went over to the offensive. They warned workers they would not be paid for time lost by strikes, that part of their wages would be withheld if they chose to work no more than eight hours a day, and they were as good as their word. The workers then began to realize that they had been misled and that it was they, not their leaders, who had to bear the cost of following bad counsel. On November 13, the Petersburg soviet considered calling yet another strike, but decided against it. Also, it felt obliged to order the "temporary" suspension of the eight-hour day.

I had long thought of having Nosar, the head of the Petersburg Soviet,† arrested but had held my hand on the wise advice of Litvinov-Falinskii, of the Ministry of Commerce and Industry, who suggested that we could avoid a bloody conflict with the workers if we waited until the soviet had lost its authority over them. By late November the time was ripe. On November 26 Nosar was arrested. Direction of the soviet was then placed in the hands of a three-man presidium, which had to meet secretly. The soviet considered calling a strike to protest the arrest, but the idea met with little support from the workers.

*A strike by telegraph workers, which broke out unexpectedly [in mid-November], was a great inconvenience for governmental operations. It is remarkable that Durnovo, who had once directed the postal and telegraph system, did not anticipate the strike.

†*Novoe vremia*, that "how can I be of service" newspaper, originated the stupid saying that at this time there were two governments, one directed by Count Witte, the other by Nosar, and that it was hard to predict who would arrest whom. Oddly enough, it was a rumor that Nosar, at the head of a detachment of workers, was coming to arrest me, that led the police to summon a detachment of Preobrazhenskii Guards to protect me in my quarters at the Winter Palace. Naturally, I asked to be relieved of this guard.

After my departure from office, some newspapers spread the story that Nosar and deputies from

I was ready to have the remainder of the soviet members taken into custody following Nosar's arrest, but Durnovo preferred to wait until the soviet met, to be able to take all its members at one swoop. The soviet delayed meeting out of fear, but when it finally convened, on December 3, at the quarters of the Free Economic Society, Durnovo had all 190 of its members arrested, without incident, *without the shedding of a single drop of blood.*[11]

With this the story of the soviet of workers' deputies came to an end, a story that had been blown up by the press out of fear of the printers. Of course there were some journalists who supported "the workers' revolution" out of principle, not fear, but these were penniless men, most of them given to fantasizing, a type produced in great supply by the revolution.

The Baltic Provinces

The Baltic provinces experienced greater disorder than most other parts of Russia both before and after October 17. As with other phenomena, this one had more than one cause.

The first was the harsh, almost medieval manner in which the German landed nobility treated the Lettish peasantry, which constitutes the lower class. The second was our government's policy of Russifying the Letts, thereby undermining the authority of the German nobility, which had instilled a sense of order and discipline in their peasants. The Russian schools that we introduced undermined the hold of the German culture, whatever its shortcomings, that the educated Baltic Germans had created, on the Lettish lower class, without substituting a solid Russian culture in its place. Instead our Russian schools infused the Lettish peasantry with many of the liberal ideas current in Russia. Under the influence of these imported ideas, the Lettish peasantry, which tends to be direct and forceful, engaged in violent and widespread agrarian disorder, including burning landlords and homes.

The disorders led me to suggest the creation of a temporary governor-generalship for these provinces, with General Sollogub—a hardworking man, one of the most intelligent, best-educated, and upright men to come from our General Staff, as governor-general. The appointment was delayed because of the initial opposition of Grand Duke Nicholas Nikolaevich. General Sollogub did not disappoint me. Unlike so many other high officials of that period, he did not lose his nerve,

<hr/>

the soviet had been to see me. Some even asserted that I was a puppet of the soviet. And some scoundrels from the Union of the Russian People spread rumors that I had criminal ties with the soviet and with revolutionary workers. All lies! I have never seen Nosar nor had any ties with him or with revolutionary or anarchist workers. Had any workers from the soviet tried to see me, I would have referred them to the prefect.[10]

Such defamatory statements were widely diffused. For example, Stolypin's daughter, who was married to Lieutenant Bok, our naval attaché in Berlin, claimed that the Ministry of Interior had compromising documents about my alleged relations with the soviet and with Nosar. She probably heard this from her mother or from her mother's brothers, the Neidhardts. What a fine lot!

acted decisively and firmly, without succumbing to an urge toward senseless brutality against peasant rioters, as so many others did.

In the Baltic provinces, more so than elsewhere, there were not enough troops to deal with unrest. Early on, as I have mentioned, units from the Vilna Military District were brought in. Then, without my knowledge, General Alexander A. Orlov, commander of the Uhlan Guards Regiment, was sent with an expeditionary force to deal with the disorders along the route to Riga.

But additional troops were needed to deal with the trouble in and around Revel. When, at General Sollogub's request, I asked the war minister and Grand Duke Nicholas Nikolaevich for men, they said they could not help. When I mentioned the problem to Admiral Birilev, the navy minister, he suggested that the sailors who had been sent under arrest from Petersburg to Kronstadt be formed into a battalion and sent to Revel. Might they not join the revolutionaries? He assured me that such a unit would be commanded by reliable officers and that its men would "prove to be the most loyal defenders of order." At my request he informed the Emperor of the suggestion. His Majesty approved, and the battalion was formed and sent off.

Shortly after the battalion went into action, General Sollogub telegraphed me that one of its officers, Captain-Lieutenant Richter (son of the honorable General-Adjutant Otto Borisovich Richter), was ordering the execution, without trial, of persons who had peacefully surrendered, and asked that I see to it that the officer act in accordance with the law. I passed the telegram on to the Emperor, who returned it with the notation that Richter was doing a fine job.[12] Nevertheless, I asked Admiral Birilev to reprimand Richter, and he did, but it is possible that Richter received a different kind of reprimand from Tsarskoe Selo.*

General Orlov also behaved savagely in carrying out his assignment. General Sollogub told me later that it had taken a great effort to get Orlov to behave reasonably and also to keep him from entering Riga, because, had Orlov gone into that city, he would have put some of it to the torch and, what is more, would have harmed many innocent people. Sollogub's removal from office shortly after my departure was probably in retaliation for his efforts to hold General Orlov in check.

I should say a few words here about General Orlov and the Empress. He was the widower of a wealthy woman, was a jaunty, gallant line officer with a passion for strong drink. An outstanding officer, he had risen to become commander of the Uhlan Guards, of which Empress Alexandra was colonel-in-chief. As a result, he became involved in spiritualistic activities.

Also, the Empress decided to marry him off to Anna Taneeva, one of her

---

*After I left office, the Emperor asked that I return all memoranda and telegrams on which he had made notations. I regret that I returned most of them, for they reveal the soul, mind, and heart of this truly unfortunate Emperor, with his weak mental and moral nature, the result of corruption by his training, his experience, and particularly the abnormality of his spouse.

ladies-in-waiting, a typical, stupid Petersburg lady, who also happened to be ugly and shapeless, like a blob of dough, a young woman who happened to be in love with the Empress, at whom she would gaze with ardent, honeymoon eyes and sigh. General Orlov managed to avoid this "blessing," and, as a result, so I am told, the Empress cooled off toward him. However, the Empress relented about the time she managed to marry Anna Taneeva off to Lieutenant Vyrubov. With this, secret ties among the Empress, Anna Vyrubova, and General Orlov were resumed.

Admiral Birilev, who attended the wedding of Anna Taneeva to the lieutenant, told me some of the piquant details of the event. At the festive ceremony, at Tsarskoe Selo, the Empress wept freely, like a merchant's wife marrying off a daughter. Some of those present thought it would have been better if she had waited to shed her tears privately. Anna kissed the hand of the Emperor as well as that of the Empress. After the wedding, the couple returned on the Imperial train to Petersburg.

The admiral concluded his account by saying: "The devil knows what kind of filth was going on." When I asked what he thought was going on, he asked if I were being discreet or naive.[13] As I see it, as far as the Empress is concerned, we are dealing with nothing other than psychological illness. She is a decent person who loves her family, but that is of no account weighed against what she has done.

Within a year Anna Vyrubova and her husband were divorced. Why is a matter of dispute, but the fact is that they were divorced and that he is on sea duty all the time, while Anna is now closer to the Empress than anyone else and has certain ties with her. Not only the courtiers, but also their wives and daughters, try to get into her good graces. Also, she helps some officials gain access to the Emperor.[14]

The mysterious ties among the Empress, Anna Vyrubova, and General Orlov continued until his death, a year ago. Shortly before going abroad this summer, the Empress and Anna, so I was told by eyewitnesses, went to the general's grave, left flowers, and wept.

Peasant Disorders

Late October saw the growth of peasant unrest and violence in the central and eastern provinces. In view of the absence of troops in those areas, the idea, not a bad one, was put forth of sending three of His Majesty's generals-adjutant, with small detachments, to the most troubled regions, in the expectation that their mere presence would serve to calm the peasantry and reassure the local authorities. If the need arose, they were empowered to use extraordinary measures to establish order.[15] The three selected were: the former war minister, General-Adjutant Sakharov, General-Adjutant Strukov, and General-Adjutant Admiral Dubasov, who commanded our Pacific squadron at the time of the seizure of Port Arthur, in 1898.

General-Adjutant Sakharov was dispatched to Saratov, whose governor, Peter Arkadevich Stolypin, had proved unable to cope with the violence in his province. Poor Sakharov—an honorable and decent man, incapable of any brutality—was assassinated in the governor's office by anarchists. They spared Stolypin because he was considered a liberal, or, if not a liberal, then a governor who was not brutal. It would be interesting to know how anarchists would now behave toward Stolypin, who had thousands of persons, many of them quite innocent, shot or hanged, if he were not protected by an army of police and detectives.[16]

General-Adjutant Strukov was sent to Tambov and Voronezh, where he proved nothing about his abilities. No doubt that he acts according to regulations and is a good cavalry man, but on this mission he drank excessively, even in the company of telegraph operators. When we learned about this, the minister of interior felt obliged to inform Baron Freedericksz orally about the general's drinking.

General-Adjutant Dubasov was sent to Chernigov and Kursk, where he did very well in dealing with the extremely intense peasant outbreaks. With only a handful of troops he appeared everywhere, brought the riotous peasants to their senses, and achieved almost total pacification without earning reproach from any direction.

Obviously, the peasant outbreaks impressed him deeply because, when he returned to Petersburg for a few days during this period, he urged vigorously that I see to it that a law giving peasants title to the land they had seized be enacted before the State Duma convened. When I objected, he replied that such an act would therefore be in the interests of the landlords. This was an extreme and inappropriate suggestion, but Dubasov, unlike others in the propertied classes, was speaking out of prudence, not fear. What he said was typical of the mood then prevalent in conservative circles.

By the time he was finishing his mission in Chernigov and Kursk serious trouble was brewing in Moscow.

The Moscow Uprising

Of all the mutinies that occurred during my tenure, that of the Moscow Grenadiers [in early December] had the most serious consequences—a major uprising that would have to be suppressed by extreme measures.[17]

I was very concerned about Moscow because it was the source of the opposition which led to the excesses of 1905. This was the result of the misguided policy of Grand Duke Sergei Aleksandrovich during his tenure as governor-general. As a consequence of that policy virtually all of Moscow was in a state of overt or covert opposition on the eve of 1905 and during 1905.

A substantial part of the Muscovite nobility was identified with opposition to the government, among them Princes Peter and Paul Dolgorukov, Princes E. N., P. N., and S. N. Trubetskoi, Prince Golitsyn, D. N. Shipov, and F. A. Golovin.

Many of the local nobility, among them Shipov and Golovin, were prominent in the zemstvo movement.

It was Moscow that set the tone and provided the leadership for the zemstvo movement throughout the country. It was Moscow that served as the site of the so-called congresses of zemstvo and municipal duma leaders. Associated with these congresses were many who were to be closely identified with the Kadet party (e.g., Miliukov, Nabokov, Herzenstein, and A. A. Stakhovich) and the Octobrist party (e.g., Guchkov and M. A. Stakhovich). The congresses were, in effect, the general staff of the Russian opposition, which gave rise to the so-called revolution of 1905.[18]

Prominent in the opposition were also leading Muscovite merchants and industrialists, some moderate in temper, others less so. And then there was Morozov, who funneled several million rubles to the revolutionaries with the help of Gorky's mistress, an actress, whom he admired.

I recall how Morozov, early in 1905, called on me to tell me how imperative it was to do away with the Autocracy, to replace it with a parliamentary system based on universal, equal, secret, and direct suffrage, how impossible it was to let things go on as they were, etc., etc. When he finally calmed down, I put my arm around Morozov, whom I had long known, and said to him:

> Let me give you some friendly advice. Stick to your own business, do not become involved in the ongoing political drama, do not become involved in the revolution. And pass my advice on to your colleagues, particularly Krestovnikov. (He was then either chairman of the Stock Exchange Committee or a candidate for the post.)

My advice obviously took him aback. Clearly embarrassed, he thanked me and left. That was the last I saw of him. He got into trouble with the police, who, to avoid a scandal, suggested that he go abroad. He left the country and became completely involved with the revolutionary network abroad. In the end he took his own life.

Toward the end of 1905, while we were preparing a new electoral law, at a time when the government was in financial crisis, Krestovnikov came to see me. Speaking for his fellow merchants and industrialists in Moscow, he complained that the State Bank was charging excessively high interest rates. Without going into detail about our difficult financial position, I told him that it was impossible to lower interest rates at this time. He put his hand to his head, cried out that the State Duma must be convened as soon as possible, and then, in a very agitated state, he left my office.

This episode illustrates how poorly the spokesmen of educated public opinion understood our situation. All moderate elements, as well as that barometer of public opinion *Novoe vremia*, demanded immediate elections on the assumption that the State Duma would act in their behalf. In Krestovnikov's case, the expectation was that the new body would help capitalists such as he. But when these elections produced a radical State Duma, the moderate elements began to sing a different tune.

Because Moscow was the source of tendencies making for revolution, it was natural that I should pay attention to what was going on there in the troubled period after October 17.

At that time, as I have noted, the governor-general there was General-Adjutant P. P. (known to his friends as Pepe) Durnovo (no relation to the minister of interior). A very wealthy man, with excellent social connections, he sought high office not for the sake of money or social prestige but for the sake of a career. In the days of Loris-Melikov he served as governor of Kharkov. Early in the reign of Emperor Alexander III he held the post of director of the Appanages Department of the Ministry of the Imperial Court, but, not being in the good graces of the Emperor, he soon left government service and did not return to it until the next reign, when he was appointed to the State Council with the help of Count Solskii, or rather Countess Solskaia. Then, in the summer of 1905, he managed to have himself appointed governor-general of Moscow.

General-Adjutant Durnovo was not a stupid man, but he preferred chattering and arguing to serious work. What I knew about him indicated that neither he nor the prefect, General Medem (a typical gendarme general, distinguished only by the fact that his wife was the object of the unnatural love of Princess Kochubei, née Princess Beloselskaia-Belozerskaia, wife of the director of the Appanages Department), was equal to the tasks they had to deal with in this seething city.

An instance of the governor-general's inadequacy was his loss of nerve after October 17. I was told that when a crowd, carrying a red flag, appeared before his official residence, he stepped out on his balcony, in uniform, took his cap off as if in deference to the red flag, and made an inappropriate speech.[19] As soon as I learned of this incident, I informed the Emperor about it.

Although Moscow was in turmoil, I had no information from official sources about what was going on there. Because I had little contact with the Department of Police I received no information from that quarter, nor, for that matter, from the minister of interior. He complained that the secret police were pretty well demoralized. What that meant I did not know, but I was convinced that he did not know what was afoot in Moscow, or elsewhere for that matter. But even without information from official sources I was able to get some help from the press. And by chance I was able to learn what was being planned by anarchists and socialists for the city.

I acquired this information from a woman I had met in the late 1870s, while I was working with the Baranov Commission in Petersburg. During this period I would sometimes visit Zolotnitskii, director of the commission's chancellery, a former officer who had been forced to leave the army because of a scandal over his action in stealing the wife of a fellow officer. At this time he was living with this sweet, young lady, whom he passed off as his wife. She had a pretty but cross-eyed sister, who would be the source of my information.

Well, some time after I had moved to Kiev, to be director of the Southwestern Railroad, the sister came to me for help. She had fled Petersburg to escape from Zolotnitskii's efforts to seduce her. She had no resources. Would I help her earn her daily bread? I found her a position in one of the railroad offices. I met her a few times thereafter in Kiev, but did not see her or think about her once I left Kiev.

About fifteen years passed before I saw her again. It was a few weeks after I had become premier that a lady was shown into my office whom I recognized as the one I had helped in Kiev. She had aged, but, then, so had I. She said she had come to repay my kindness to her.

First, she told me of what had happened to her since I had seen her last. She married a rich landowner and bore him a son. Her husband turned out to be an improvident man who left her so little when he died that she had to leave the estate on which they lived. She then went with her son to Moscow, where she married an older man, named Chirikov. Although her chief motive in marrying him was to find someone to support her, their marriage had turned out well.

Mrs. Chirikova then came to the point. She was very grateful to me because without my help she would have had to take to the streets to earn a living. Now, she was in a position to help me with vital information she had learned from a friend, a wealthy widow she had known some time. The widow had fallen in love with a young lawyer, a member of the landed nobility, who was in the thick of the revolutionary movement. The widow was so smitten that she gave him all she had for his cause. He, in turn, took her into his confidence about what he was doing.

What Mrs. Chirikova had learned was that the anarchist party to which the young man belonged was planning an armed uprising in Moscow. The party planned to strike as quickly as possible because it knew that the police had no information about what it was doing, that the civilian and military authorities were frightened and demoralized, and that both the police and the military were below strength.

She was telling me all this not only out of gratitude but also out of conviction, because she was out of sympathy with the anarchists. Moreover, she wanted to save her friend and her friend's lover from the ruin that would befall them if the uprising took place. The only way they could be helped would be if they were forced to flee the city. She then promised to keep me informed of what she learned when she returned to Moscow.[20]

Thanks to her I knew more about what was going on in Moscow than did the minister of interior or the Moscow secret police. Because I was convinced that there would be an uprising in Moscow unless steps were taken to prevent it, I urged the Emperor to replace the governor-general with an energetic and decisive man. Also I wrote to His Majesty asking if one could depend on the military command in Moscow. He assured me that we could rely completely on the commander of the Moscow Military District, General Malakhov.

When I next saw the Emperor, he asked whom I would suggest as a replace-

ment for Governor-General Durnovo. I recommended General-Adjutant Dubasov. What did I think of Bulygin as a replacement? I said he was a fine man who
would be suitable for the post because he knew Moscow well and was well known
there. He had, of course, served in Moscow under Grand Duke Sergei Aleksandrovich, but he was not a decisive man, as I have indicated.

While waiting for the Emperor to take some action, I received such alarming
information from Mrs. Chirikova that I asked the minister of interior to order the
arrest of her friend's lover. A few days later I learned from her that when the police
searched the young man's quarters they found nothing incriminating because he
had received advance warning from someone in authority.

It was about this time that I learned that a peasant congress would soon be held
in Moscow.[21] The day before the congress was to open, I telegraphed the governor-general to keep an eye on the meetings, because, as was evident from newspaper reports, the congress would be attended by men who wanted to exploit it for
revolutionary purposes as well as by those who were sincerely interested in the
welfare of the peasantry. I received no reply.

As I learned from the newspapers, the speeches given at the congress were of a
purely revolutionary character, and once the revolutionary slogans uttered there
had been sufficiently publicized, the session was ended on the initiative of the
organizers. It was only after the congress closed that I received a telegram
from the governor-general informing me that the congress was over. Such behavior showed how fear of bombs and bullets produced passivity in those
days.

Time was running short. On November 9, after a cabinet meeting at Tsarskoe
Selo, presided over by the Emperor, I stopped him as he was leaving to tell him
how urgent it was that he replace Governor-General Durnovo. He was obviously
not happy at being held up, but he responded in a kind voice to tell me that
Bulygin had declined the post on the ground that he was unsuitable for the task in
Moscow. Then he asked me once more to suggest a replacement for P. P. Durnovo. Once more I proposed Admiral Dubasov and asked permission to summon
him from Kursk, where he was at the time, and offer him the governor-generalship. Permission granted, I telegraphed immediately to Dubasov to return to
Petersburg and present himself to the Emperor. Within a few days he was back in
the capital.[22]

When he came to see me I noted that his attitude toward the minister of interior
was, if not distrustful, then, at least, unsympathetic, or, to use a stronger word,
contemptuous. As for the minister's attitude toward Dubasov's appointment, it
seemed to be one of indifference. Also, I guessed that the Emperor's hesitation
about giving Dubasov the post was explained by Trepov's opposition.

I urged the new governor-general to leave immediately for Moscow. Soon after
he arrived there he called to ask for my help in getting troops from Petersburg to
bring the military in Moscow up to strength. He assured me that he had complete
confidence in the troops there and in their commanders, but much later, when we

could speak face to face, he said that actually he had had no confidence in the Moscow military, but felt that if he said so at the time he would be compromising the military command in Moscow. It was not long after the telephone call that the uprising began.[23]

After receiving the call from Dubasov, I telephoned the war minister, who informed me that a regiment from Poland was on its way to Moscow and would be there in three days. But the regiment, as it turned out, was delayed when revolutionaries derailed several of the cars on the train. While the regiment was still en route, Dubasov called to say his situation was critical, he had only enough troops to guard the railroad stations, leaving the rest of the city virtually unprotected. If he did not receive reinforcements, the city would fall to the revolutionaries. He had, he said, asked Tsarskoe Selo for more men but had received no reply. I telephoned General Trepov immediately, asking him to inform the Emperor of the emergency, adding that if Moscow fell there would be terrible consequences for His Majesty's government.

It was toward evening that Trepov telephoned in the name of the Emperor to ask me to persuade Grand Duke Nicholas Nikolaevich to release some of his troops for use in Moscow. Later that evening I was at the Grand Duke's residence explaining why troops had to be sent immediately to Moscow. He agreed that the troops in Moscow were too few and too demoralized to be counted on, but argued that the regiment from Poland would be there soon if it was not there already. As for releasing any of his men, he said that he could not spare a single soldier, adding, and these are virtually his words:

> Our immediate task is to protect Petersburg and the environs in which the Emperor and his family reside. We have barely enough troops for this task. If we released even a small detachment and, God forbid, there were an uprising in Petersburg and its environs, we would be shorthanded. As for Moscow, let it fall. Once Moscow was indeed the heart and mind of Russia, but now it is the center from which all antimonarchist and revolutionary ideas spread. No harm would come to Russia if it were destroyed.

I tried to convince him that Moscow must be saved and assured him that rumors about the danger of an uprising in Petersburg only served to prove that the eyes grow larger with fear. At midnight, while we were still talking, an adjutant brought in a note for the Grand Duke that had just been delivered by courier. He read the note, then told me that it was the Emperor's wish that he send troops to Moscow. I asked that this be done as soon as possible.

I then telephoned Dubasov to give him the news and express the hope that he would put down the uprising as energetically as possible. In passing, I asked why it was so difficult to reach him at his residence. He explained that General Malakhov (an elderly and honorable man) was not well enough to come to his residence for meetings, forcing him to go often to Malakhov's residence. With this telephone call my role in the pacification of Moscow came to an end.

XI ■ RESTORATION OF ORDER   537

General Min and most of the regiment he commanded, the Semenovskii Guards, plus a cavalry squadron and some light artillery, to protect the two trains carrying the force, were sent to Moscow. General Min carried out the pacification without a plan. Even after the uprising was crushed, some of his men continued to use force and, in so doing, committed many acts of brutality.

The general was quickly publicly condemned for the atrocities committed by his men, and less than a year later revolutionaries struck back by assassinating him. I feel that the general and his men should not have been blamed for their actions, considering their situation. Here they were, thrust suddenly into a strange, dangerous place, without proper leadership. If anyone is at fault, it is those who did not act in time to deal with the problem, who lost their nerve, who permitted their troops to become demoralized.[24] Later, when it became safe to do so, many were critical of the government for having been irresolute in these times, forgetting that they themselves were behaving then like a flock of frightened crows, fearful for their pocketbooks and privileges. In those days such people not only held their tongues, but also winked at what the revolutionaries were doing, in order to protect their hides.

No question but that Admiral Dubasov was the only one who did not lose his head. He saved the day by his courageous and honorable behavior. It should be noted that the minister of interior, P. N. Durnovo, played little part in the pacification, chiefly because it was not he who had recommended Dubasov. That did not prevent him, years later, from remaining modestly silent when his followers gave him the credit for suppressing the uprising.

Once the fighting was over and General Min and his men were back in Petersburg, the governor-general recommended to the Emperor that, as a gesture to show that the emergency was over, those civilians who were to be tried for their role in the uprising be placed before regular courts, not courts-martial.[25] When asked for his opinion by the Emperor, the minister of interior favored the use of courts-martial, but I supported Dubasov. And as long as the two of us remained in office, the regular courts were used in such cases.

General-Adjutant Dubasov's recommendation in this case, as in others, apparently did not sit well with the Emperor. This apparently explains why an Imperial rescript expressing gratitude to Dubasov for his work in Moscow that I and the minister of interior drafted at the Emperor's request was never issued. The failure to do so was of a piece with the coldness that the Emperor showed Dubasov after his recommendation of moderation.

It was the Emperor's coldness, I believe, that led Dubasov not long after I left office to ask to be relieved of his post. The official explanation for his departure was that his health was poor—he had suffered a concussion from a bomb that had exploded in his carriage—but had he been treated kindly he probably would have chosen to stay. Evidently, no such effort was made. To forgive, you must realize, is regarded as a sign of weakness, unless the culprits are right-wing thugs who murdered "kikes" or liberals. This way of thinking was further illustrated by something that occurred a year after Dubasov left his post.

As he was strolling in the Tauride Garden in Petersburg, a young man fired at him, but, fortunately, missed. The youth, who was immediately caught, stated that he, and other anarchists, had been selected to repay Dubasov for what he had done in Moscow.

As soon as I heard the news of the attempted assassination I rushed to see Dubasov. He seemed calm, except about the probable fate of the would-be assassin, who, most likely, would be tried by a court-martial and executed. He said: "I cannot be calm because I can still see his childish, frightened eyes; it would be a sin to execute such an irresponsible youth." He told me that he had written to the Emperor asking him to show mercy by having the young man tried in a regular court.

The following day, when I saw Dubasov, he read the Emperor's handwritten, well-organized reply to me. After congratulating General-Adjutant Dubasov for escaping harm and delivering himself of a few kindly phrases, the Emperor dealt with Dubasov's request. The law is the law, he wrote, and no one, not even the Emperor, should interfere with the course of justice.

I don't know whether to characterize this reply as childish or Jesuitical. The Emperor was ignoring the fact that the law to which he was referring had been enacted by him as a part of the military code of law after the State Duma had revoked a similar law. And it should be remembered that at this time the Emperor was granting pardons to assassins belonging to the extreme right, at a time when the police made little effort to apprehend such assassins or to turn such men over to the courts. Wasn't the Emperor aware of all this?

Before turning to another subject, I will finish the story of the rich widow and her revolutionary lover. I learned later from Mrs. Chirikova that the two managed to escape from Moscow and take refuge nearby with a landowner whom the young man knew. When police arrived to arrest him, the young man, having been alerted, was able to escape and go abroad, where he was later joined by his lady.

The Caucasus

As I have noted earlier, Count Vorontsov-Dashkov was appointed viceroy of the Caucasus early in 1905, succeeding the unfortunate Prince Golitsyn. Also noted was the fact that, despite the count's efforts at conciliation, the Caucasus was out of control.[26]

Count Vorontsov-Dashkov is one of the very finest men in the upper circles, but he was not a strong enough administrator for the challenges of the so-called revolution of 1905. The question of appointing a more energetic man was raised, but nothing was done in view of his importance at court. As I have indicated before, his strengths outweigh his weaknesses. He is a Russian *boiar*, in the true sense of the word. And, as I have said before, he should be given credit for returning to the sound policies of earlier viceroys such as Prince Bariatinskii and Grand Duke Michael Nikolaevich.

Finland

As I have already said, it was clear when I took office that Prince I. M. Obolenskii could not continue as governor-general of Finland. When I was asked by the Emperor, or perhaps it was on his behalf by Grand Duke Nicholas Nikolaevich, to recommend a successor, I said that he should be a man of moderate views, one accustomed to respecting the law, one who did not trim his sails to advance himself. Such a man, I said, was N. N. Gerhard, a member of the State Council.

My only contacts with Gerhard had been of an official nature—in the State Council and in the Conference on the Needs of Agricultural Industry, of which he had been a member. The views he expressed in these bodies were those of a conservative who respects the law. More important in motivating my recommendation was what he had accomplished in the Kingdom of Poland when introducing the reformed Russian court system there. In carrying out his mission, he earned the respect of both Russians and Poles. The latter, as a matter of principle, were hostile to the new courts, but once the new courts had begun to function, the Poles had to admit that they were incomparably better than the old ones. For these reasons I suggested Gerhard, but I did not care particularly who replaced Prince Obolenskii as long as he was competent.

Some time passed before the Emperor, having made inquiries about Gerhard, wrote me on November 6 saying that he had decided to appoint Gerhard, asking me that I have Gerhard see him the following day. Gerhard was taken aback when I told him that the Emperor intended to name him governor-general of Finland and wanted to see him. After seeing the Emperor, Gerhard told me that he expressed great reluctance to accept the post, but that His Majesty had asked him to take two days to decide one way or the other. In those days many who once would have mortgaged their souls to become a governor-general now trembled at the thought. Gerhard was not such a man: I think he was motivated by modesty rather than fear. In any case, he accepted. General Böckmann, who would later succeed him, was appointed to command the troops stationed in Finland.

Because the governor-general of Finland was not subordinate to the premier and because the Emperor, who liked to bypass the premier, would have looked with disfavor at me, to put it mildly, if I had made any claim to influence over Finnish affairs, I had few dealings with Gerhard. I saw him on a few occasions in connection with the need to find places for several of the late Governor-General Bobrikov's associates, because he would not have them in Finland as a result of their identification with Bobrikov's policies. Also, I saw him in connection with the drafting of the article on Finland in the Fundamental Laws.[27]

Governor-General Gerhard lived up to my expectations. An intelligent, patriotic man, with good political sense, he followed a wise policy of respecting the historical rights of Finland while strongly supporting the interests and the prerogatives of the Emperor in the grand duchy. By following such a policy he earned the admiration of the Finns. Unfortunately, he was to be ousted by Stolypin, but that is another story.

The Return of Our Troops from Manchuria

One of the major tasks I had to accomplish as premier was to assure the early return of the nearly one million men we had sent to Manchuria. Under any circumstances their speedy return and the speedy demobilization of the reservists among them would have been an urgent task. But in the weeks following October 17 the task became even more urgent, both because we needed more troops to cope with disorder and because the longer the delay the more demoralized these troops would become.

Following the ratification of the peace treaty with Japan, which came after October 17, all the men in Manchuria were in a frenzy to return home. According to my information the scenes along the Chinese Eastern Railroad were like those at railroad stations at home, at the end of weekends, when people who had been in the country were fighting for places on trains taking them home. But as a result of the railroad strike that began early in October, movement on the Trans-Siberian Railroad virtually came to a halt as self-constituted organizations [soviets] and gangs took over. If they wished, trains moved; if they did not, nothing moved. The revolutionaries deliberately prolonged the strikes along the Trans-Siberian Railroad because they soon realized that the field army[28] would remain in a revolutionary frame of mind only as long as it was kept away from home.

Well before October our men in Manchuria knew there was unrest at home, something that could only lower their morale, which was further depressed by their eagerness to return home. And what they heard was a wild exaggeration of the facts, because the railroad, telegraph, and postal strikes meant delays of weeks before reliable news could reach them. For example, Prince Vasilchikov, head of the Red Cross with our field army, later told the Emperor, who told me, that on the basis of what he had heard in Manchuria he fully expected that on his return to Petersburg he would find that the Imperial family had fled the country and that I and my colleagues were hanging from gallows on Mars Field. It was not until he reached Cheliabinsk, he said, that he was able to get reliable news.

What was then taking place in the field army has been concealed to this day, to protect the reputation of the military. To do so represents a misguided form of patriotism. The Russian army has a glorious tradition, and to maintain that tradition by preventing a repetition of what took place in our war with Japan we must face the truth that after October 17 our field army was in a revolutionary mood. I doubt that anyone in the military could accurately describe the mood even if he wished to. However, although a civilian and an outsider, I knew the facts from the vantage point of my high office.

There was trouble from top to bottom in the field army. One would have thought that iron discipline would prevail in an army located in a foreign land, but discipline was in fact worse in Manchuria than it was in European Russia. As for General Linevich, the commander-in-chief, he had turned into a sort of kindly uncle in the eyes of his men. Many of his commanding officers were apathetic or frightened or both and gave in to the lower ranks just as many of their counterparts did back home. I should say once more that the lower ranks were in a revolutionary mood, especially those stranded along the Trans-Siberian Railroad by the strike.

There were bureaucrats in Petersburg who feared the return of the field army. One such was Schwanebach, then still the head of the Chief Administration of Land Organization and Agriculture. At a meeting of the Committee of Ministers, shortly before October 17, when we were already beginning to receive alarming reports about the low morale in the field army, Schwanebach, possibly at the suggestion of the Emperor, proposed that soldiers who did not wish to return to European Russia be given government-owned land in Siberia, on favorable terms. As one would have expected, the committee rejected this "original" proposal in language so sharp as to explain possibly why Schwanebach soon asked to be relieved of his post.

I, for one, felt, correctly as it turned out, that once the troops were back they would help establish order, because they would want to see Russia so strong and powerful that if the need arose their country could regain its prestige on the field of battle. But as long as the field army remained east of Lake Baikal it would grow more restive. Of course, the source of its infection was European Russia, but, as I informed the Emperor, it was probable that as calm was returning in European Russia the infection would spread from the East to the West, from a demoralized field army.

Time was precious, but weeks passed with little prospect of getting our troops back soon because of the troubles along the Trans-Siberian Railroad I have mentioned. To add to the trouble, the telegraph strike in November made it difficult to learn the facts about the chaos in the field army. Moreover, the fact that our men had not yet returned hurt us both at home and abroad. When I spoke of the need for speed to Grand Duke Nicholas Nikolaevich, General Rödiger, and General Palitsyn, they put all the blame on General Linevich,* who, they said, should be replaced.

Something had to be done, so I decided to take the initiative.[29] Early in December I wrote to the Emperor about how dangerous it was to leave the field army east of Lake Baikal and how dangerously short of troops we were at home. I suggested that he appoint two reliable and decisive generals, provide each one with a detachment of reliable men, dispatch one from Harbin westward bound

---

*Just as was the case when I was at Portsmouth, so it was after I became premier, that I never heard from him, with one exception. The exception came shortly after October 17, when he sent me a telegram that went roughly as follows: "Fourteen (I remember the number well) anarchist-revolutionaries have come to the field army to incite rebellion." I sent the telegram to His Majesty, who returned it with the notation: "I hope that they will be hanged." I informed the war minister about the telegram and the Emperor's notation. I do not have this document because, unfortunately, it was among the papers I returned to the Emperor after I left office.

and the other eastward bound from European Russia, with instructions to reestablish order and regular train movement by *whatever means necessary*. I suggested
General Kuropatkin as commander for the expedition originating in Harbin,
hoping thereby to give him a chance to demonstrate his efficiency.

The Emperor responded immediately by sending General Palitsyn to talk to
me about what needed to be done. The general told me that His Majesty would
not agree to Kuropatkin because he had no confidence in him. General Palitsyn
then proposed that General Rennenkampf command the westward expedition
and General Meller-Zakomelskii command the eastward one. I was not acquainted with the two, but I had heard that they were decisive men. General Palitsyn
and I then discussed and agreed on details.

Before his departure, General Meller-Zakomelskii came to ask for my instructions. I repeated what I had written the Emperor, that the mission must be carried
out by *whatever means necessary*. The same instructions were sent to General Rennenkampf, but to reach him by telegraph it was necessary to send the message
from Petersburg to London, from London to Peking, from Peking to Harbin,
because the overland connections had been cut off by strikes.

The two detachments started off early in January and met in Chita several
weeks later. To restore order they had to make many arrests and order the
execution of several dozen persons. General Meller-Zakomelskii had several telegraph operators flogged for disobedience.*

One incident in particular that suggests the spirit of the times occurred when
several revolutionary leaders were sentenced to death following the arrival of
General Rennenkampf in Chita. The day the sentence was imposed my wife
received a telegram from Russian émigrés in Brussels threatening that if the
sentences were carried out my daughter Vera (whose husband served in our
legation in Brussels) and her son would be killed. When my wife, in tears, showed
me the message, I told her that if no threats had been made I might have
interceded, but that I could not do so in face of a threat. The sentences were
carried out, but the threats were not. It is evident from the incident that the
revolutionaries in Chita had close ties with their comrades abroad.

With the meeting of the two generals in Chita, orderly train movement was
soon reestablished, and our troops began to return home.

About the time that the two generals left on their missions, it was decided to
replace General Linevich. I was astonished when Grand Duke Nicholas Nikolaevich told me he had recommended General-Adjutant Baron Meyendorff as a
replacement because, although a fine man, the baron was even less qualified for
the post than Linevich. At my suggestion the post was given instead to General
Grodekov, a member of the State Council. He performed ably, restoring discipline

*Evidently the floggings were regarded with approval in higher circles because later, when a brutal
man was wanted as temporary governor-general of the Baltic provinces, he was chosen.

He is, it turned out, a rather sinister man. Had he not been a general, he would have made a good
jailer, particularly in those jails where corporal punishment is administered. He would also have made
a good police official, in the sense of being able to maintain the appearance of law and order.

in the field army and completing the return of our men. He went on from that task to become governor-general of Turkestan (succeeding Subbotin), but he did not get along with Grand Duke Nicholas Nikolaevich and resumed his seat in the State Council. When he met me there and asked if I felt satisfied at having recommended him, I said "absolutely."

The prospect that our troops would be returning soon at a rapid pace from the East, the fact that by mid-December normal traffic had been restored on the railroads in European Russia, and the fact that we would be profiting from a new levy of conscripts meant that we could look forward to bringing up our forces to full strength. And that would make it easier to cope with disorder, providing our troops were properly distributed. We had learned that whenever troops appeared in villages where there was trouble, order was quickly established, but that in regions where no troops were available, disorder was endemic. The problem then was to arrange for proper distribution of our troops.

Accordingly I brought up the matter with the Emperor, and, on December 24, he agreed to a special conference, over which I would preside, and to which Grand Duke Nicholas Nikolaevich, War Minister Rödiger, General Polivanov, General Palitsyn, and Interior Minister Durnovo were invited.

At the meeting that followed we worked out a plan for distribution of troops as well as the procedures to be followed by them in dealing with local uprisings.[30] The basic principle to be followed, a principle to which I adhered after October 17, was that force be met with force, with no regard for niceties, but that once order was restored there would have to be a return to normal procedures. Not so under Stolypin, with his wholesale executions. I have a premonition that those responsible, particularly the chief one, for such egregious brutality, will answer for their actions with blood. I hope that my premonition will not be realized.[31]

Afterthoughts

After order was restored there were many who said of my policy in dealing with disorder that I had lost my nerve, that I did not shoot or hang enough people, and that, moreover, I prevented others from taking life when they should have been permitted to. The conclusion: that because I was too queasy I shouldn't have accepted the responsibility of office. No one has yet told me whom I should have hanged or shot.

In this vein, an old acquaintance, Mechnikov, the director of the Pasteur Institute, counseled after the fact that I should have abandoned Petersburg, Moscow, and several provinces to the revolutionaries for a few months, then, like Thiers, in dealing with the Paris Commune, should have used mass force to retake them and, having retaken them, should have shot a few thousand people. Some delighted Russians listened with open mouths to such counsel.

I consider it dimwitted, the product of ignorance. Thiers did not create the Paris Commune, and when he acted against it, it was with a mandate from a national assembly elected by all of France on the basis of universal suffrage. Moreover, it was not he who demanded repressive action, but the national assembly, which he tried to restrain.

If we had had a national assembly elected by universal suffrage after October 17, it would have demanded that I stop the shooting, not intensify it. It would have demanded the end of the Romanov dynasty or, at the very least, the abdication of Emperor Nicholas II. It would have demanded that those responsible for dragging us into that shameful war with Japan be handed over to the highest tribunal. This would have led to a civil war and would undoubtedly have resulted in the secession of several of our borderlands and the seizure of some of our provinces by foreign armies while our troops were still stranded east of Lake Baikal.

After 1905 there were no major strikes, because the workers learned from their experience with revolutionary strikes to be skeptical of men like Nosar, under whose leadership they suffered greatly. The industrialists also learned something from the revolutionary strikes and, as a result, improved the conditions of their workers, to a degree. And the government also learned something. This year [1912], a workers' insurance law was enacted, despite covert opposition from industrialists, a law which had been proposed while I was minister of finance.

The gendarmerie and the secret police, however, seemed to have learned nothing. Recently, a certain gendarme officer named Treshchenkov was responsible for the shooting of more than two hundred workers in the Lena minefields, where workers had been attempting for years to improve their wretched conditions.[32]

It appears that the entire local administration was directly or indirectly in the pay of the wealthy mine owners and catered to their rapacious appetites. Makarov, the minister of interior, offered a far-fetched and misleading explanation of the incident in a speech which he closed by justifying the mass killing with these words: "Thus it has always been and thus it will always be." One does not have to be a prophet to say that what has been will continue to be. After all, October 17 marked the beginning of the end of the kind of administration under which such slaughter was possible. Of course, no government can tolerate uprisings. Force must be met by force. But in this, the twentieth century, no government can long endure that tolerates officials who blink at unconscionable policies that provoke workers into actions that end with the slaughter of these workers. Such a government must surely perish.

XII

Cabinet Changes

Trepov, Pressure from the Right, and Manukhin

Following the completion of my cabinet at the end of October I had to part with three of the members of my cabinet—Manukhin, Kutler, and Timiriazev. The first two had to leave because of pressure from the right, exerted through General Trepov. The third had to leave because of a scandal resulting from the reappearance of Father Gapon. First, S. S. Manukhin, the minister of justice.

Manukhin is a man of high principles, an excellent jurist, an expert on the judiciary, who gave a good account of himself as minister of justice. However, he had a slight bent toward doctrinaire Slavophilism and also was perhaps inclined to see things from the point of view of what ought to be, rather than from the point of what had to be. This was not a plus in those disorderly, revolutionary days.

Because he saw things through rose-colored glasses, he was often at odds with P. N. Durnovo, the minister of interior. But the chief of his ill-wishers was General Trepov, who while governor-general of Petersburg had been rebuffed when he had asked Manukhin to take certain illegal actions. Another reason for Trepov's animosity was Manukhin's objection, mentioned earlier, to Garin's appointment as senator. Soon after his appointment as palace commandant, Trepov began to complain that we could not cope with the revolution because the Ministry of Justice, under Manukhin, was not acting with sufficient vigor. Manukhin, in turn, said that the chief source of trouble was Trepov, whose baneful influence over the Emperor was increasing.

But, in all fairness to His Majesty, I must say that as long as Trepov was the only powerful enemy of Manukhin, the minister was safe. But when Manukhin incurred the displeasure of other influential personages, chief among them some Baltic barons, his position became tenuous. These personages, many of them very honorable officials, were frightened by the revolution and deeply disturbed by the way in which it affected their pocketbooks. It did not seem to them that the Ministry of Justice was protecting their interests. They were upset because officials of the ministry were either biased toward the left, whether out of conviction or fear of retribution from the revolutionaries, or, if not biased, were following the letter of the law with Olympian calm at a time when vigorous action was required to maintain order and protect life and property.

The Baltic barons were especially frightened because, as I have noted, the revolution was so intense in their region. There the local population had stopped obeying the law and the officials. The lower classes robbed and murdered landlords. Also they established revolutionary substitutes for established local administrative entities.

Illustrative of the temper of the times was what happened to the aged Count Pahlen, who, when minister of justice, himself had helped carry out the legal and judicial reforms upon which our system of justice was based. Well, it was about the end of October that I was told that this fine, well-balanced man wished to see me. I, of course, received him immediately. He told me that he had received a telegram from the manager of his estate that spokesmen for revolutionary Lettish gangs demanded money, claiming that they were acting on the authority of the government. Should he yield to their demands? I asked him if the governor-general (who had very broad power in the area because it was under martial law)[1] had been informed of the demand. On being told that he had, I said that it was for him to decide whether or not to pay. Visibly shaken by my answer, the old man left.

On November 7, I received a note from the Emperor that on November 9, at 11 a.m., he would preside over a cabinet meeting that would open "with *a personal report by the minister of justice.*" His Majesty also said in the note: "I consider this innovation necessary and useful for all the ministers." (This "innovation" was still-born, at least during my tenure.)

At the meeting, held at Tsarskoe Selo, I was surprised to see that, in addition to the cabinet, there were three others—Count Pahlen, E. V. Frisch (vice-chairman of the State Council), and someone whose name I don't recall.

The Emperor opened the meeting by stating that because the Ministry of Justice had come under criticism, he had thought it advisable to hear what its chief had to say. In a dignified manner, Manukhin defended the officials of his ministry, arguing that they were adhering to the principles upon which the courts had been established, that proceedings be open to the public, that the judiciary be independent, that it was better to have some who were guilty go free than to punish a single innocent person. Granted that a few officials had acted improperly, but they were being dealt with, in accordance with the law.

When his turn to speak came, Durnovo attacked the Ministry of Justice for alleged weakness in dealing with disorder. Also, he asserted that something like a strike was going on in its offices. When I spoke, I admitted that the minister of interior was, unfortunately, correct, up to a point, but that he was talking about exceptional cases and that to generalize on the basis of exceptions was to do a disservice to one of the most enlightened agencies of the Empire.

A few days later Manukhin told me that at the first opportunity he would ask His Majesty to let him go, because it was obvious that his views did not please the Emperor and equally obvious that he would not change them. Not many days passed before he told me that the Emperor had agreed to let him go and for him to inform me of the fact.

At my next report to the Emperor I urged that he follow the custom of appointing ministers to the State Council with respect to Manukhin. He agreed, but not with pleasure. When I asked whom he had in mind as a replacement, he told me it was S. A. Lopukhin (procurator of the Kiev Court of Appeals, one of A. A. Lopukhin's relatives).[2] The candidate was also related to Prince Obolenskii, the over-procurator of the Holy Synod, leading me to conclude that the prince, who has a weakness for finding posts for his relatives, was behind this. After telling the Emperor that I did not know S. A. Lopukhin, I asked for and received permission to make inquiries about him.

On my return to my residence I found Samofalov, professor of criminal law at the University of Kiev, waiting to see me. A rather conservative person, and himself a former official with the Ministry of Justice, he complained that many of the officials of the ministry were not acting with the firmness required by the times.

When I asked if he knew S. A. Lopukhin, Samofalov told me that he was an honorable, well-liked, and well-respected gentleman. What kind of minister would he make? Samofalov, who regarded Manukhin as too liberal for the times, said that Lopukhin would be another Manukhin, but without his authority, broad judicial knowledge, and capacity for hard work. This led to our looking through the register of members of the Senate for men with Russian surnames, unassailable reputations as conservatives, and sound experience in the judiciary. Three such were found: Akimov, Ivanov, and Shcherbachev.

The following day I told the Emperor that I had reservations about Lopukhin. When he asked for my recommendations, I gave him the three names, explaining how I had selected them. Did I know them? I replied that I knew only Akimov (Durnovo's brother-in-law) from my days as manager of the Southwestern Railroad, when he was assistant procurator of the Kiev Court of Appeals. The Emperor said he did not know Akimov, to which I took the liberty of replying that he didn't know Lopukhin either. He was not pleased with the conversation and ended it by telling me to have Akimov see him, without letting on that he was being considered for the post.

When I returned to my residence I telephoned Akimov, asking that he come to see me. It was not long before he arrived. This was our first meeting in twenty years. He told me that he intended to retire, but that there was some dispute over the size of his pension. When I told him that the Emperor wanted to see him, he asked if I knew the reason for the summons.

Later that day, the Emperor sent me a note that he had seen Akimov, was very pleased with him, and would I draft a decree naming him minister. When I told Durnovo that his brother-in-law would be the next minister of justice he did not seem overjoyed, perhaps because he feared competition in the area of extreme conservatism. (As Durnovo's position became more entrenched, as he drew closer to Trepov, and as he became more certain of the Tsar's favor, he became increasingly unsympathetic to the principles of the October 17 Manifesto.)

I must say Akimov behaved splendidly as minister. Although he expressed conservative opinions, he did so with more restraint and with more respect for the law than did Durnovo. I cannot think of one instance in which Akimov went beyond the limits logically set by the October 17 Manifesto, which he interpreted from a conservative point of view, but without straining its meaning. It was such good behavior, if I may put it that way, that led me, when the time came for me to leave my post, to say to the Emperor that if he wanted a conservative premier, Akimov would be a good choice. And he did offer the post to Akimov, who declined. The Emperor soon appointed him chairman of the State Council. I will deal subsequently with how he abused the chairmanship to serve the Emperor and demean the State Council.

An inkling of what kind of person Akimov could be should have come to me when, on becoming minister, he decided that Shcheglovitov should be his assistant minister. I was amazed at the choice because here was a conservative insisting on the appointment of a man who expressed such hackneyed and ultraleftist views that I had asked Manukhin not to bring him to cabinet meetings. Yet, when I asked Akimov if he knew Shcheglovitov, he said that he knew him very well.

At the time I did not realize what an insincere man Shcheglovitov was, how little he believed in his professions. This became evident after he succeeded Akimov as minister of justice, and it was only then that I understood why Akimov chose him as assistant minister.

Trepov, Pressure from the Right, and Kutler

Typical of the way in which Trepov, like a favorite Asiatic eunuch, won the upper hand is the story of how Kutler, the honorable, intelligent, and hardworking head of the Chief Administration of Land Organization and Agriculture, was driven out of office. The issue over which he was forced to leave was whether or not to take land from the landowners for the benefit of the peasantry.

It should be realized that the most important aspect of the Russian revolution of 1905 was not labor unrest but the peasant demand for land, which is beginning to be realized.* In the first weeks after October 17, as unrest and violence grew in the countryside, as peasants, who had never clearly understood the meaning of

---

*The latest developments in the history of the peasant question were accurately described in *Vestnik Evropy*, early in 1909.[3]

private property, stopped paying heed to those in authority, many noble landowners lost their heads and out of fear began to talk of letting peasants have some of
their land so that they might save the rest. It goes without saying the General
Trepov shared their fears.

For example, on one occasion when I was in the Emperor's reception room,
waiting to give my report, Trepov was there, too. As we talked about the wave of
peasant uprisings, he said that the only way to restore quiet in the countryside was
to give some of the nobles' lands to the peasants. I replied that it would be unwise
to take such an action before the State Duma convened. He assured me that all
noble landowners favored such a step and that he would be ready to give up half
his land if he could keep the rest.

When I gave my report to the Emperor, he did not raise the question of
expropriation directly, but did so indirectly by handing over to me a memorandum and some proposals, which, he said, came from Professor Migulin. He asked
that I discuss the material with the cabinet. After I left His Majesty, Trepov told
me that what was proposed in the memorandum—expropriation of land, by
Imperial decree, for the benefit of the peasantry—needed to be carried out as
quickly as possible to prevent peasants from taking matters into their own hands. I
now understood who it was that had given the material to the Emperor. (A copy of
the memorandum and a letter to me from Professor Migulin are in my archive.)[4]

Who is this Professor Migulin? The most important fact about him is that he is
the son-in-law of M. M. Alekseenko, former professor of business law at Kharkov
University and at this time superintendent of the Kharkov School District. Alekseenko is an intelligent and cultivated man who has not strayed beyond the
bounds of propriety, yet because of his unwillingness to live on his salary alone, he
is better known as a shrewd, small-town operator than as a scholar. Migulin, a
lawyer and an able and clever publicist, profited doubly from marrying [Alekseen-
ko's] daughter, first because she was a rich prize and second by assuming, as if by
right of inheritance, the chair that his father-in-law had held.

Migulin had written many books, which are nothing more than clever, shallow
pamphlets, the obvious product of his effort to advance himself in those troubled
times. Although he is not taken seriously by those with even a modest knowledge
of his field, he has a name as one of the younger men in his academic field and has
some prestige in petit-bourgeois circles and among people like his father-in-law,
shrewd small-town operators. It is easy to see how he came to the attention of
General Trepov.

When the cabinet considered the Migulin proposal, all, including Kutler,
opposed taking immediate action on it because we thought that a proposal as
important as this required careful consideration and, in any case, should not be
decided without the participation of the State Duma and the State Council.
However, we felt that some steps should be taken immediately to ease the peasants' burdens by abolishing the redemption dues they had been paying for so

many years and by having the Peasants' Bank make more land available for purchase by peasants. In addition, we proposed formation of a commission, with Kutler as chairman, to consider other measures to help the peasantry, these to be submitted to the State Duma when it convened. The Emperor agreed. He issued decrees abolishing redemption dues and broadening the operations of the Peasants' Bank. And a commission, under Kutler, was created.

By January, as quiet began to return to the countryside, noble landowners began to recover from their fears and to have second thoughts about the wisdom of expropriation, even with compensation. In the end they denounced the whole idea as criminal and began to brand those who supported such "heresies" as revolutionaries.[5]

But while their mood was shifting away from expropriation, Kutler's was moving in favor of it. I recall that after a cabinet meeting he told me that the more he thought about it, the more convinced he was that the only way to provide the peasants with more land was through some form of expropriation, with compensation for the owners. What was my opinion, he asked? I told him that only very exceptional circumstances would warrant such a step.

A few days later I found on my desk a packet of copies of the Kutler commission's statement of major principles to be followed in preliminary consideration of peasant landholding. Because His Majesty had called for speed in dealing with the peasant question, I ordered distribution of the copies without first reading the statement. Copies went to members of the cabinet as well as to three others who had dealt with the peasant question—Semenov-Tian-Shanskii, that estimable survivor of the group that prepared the legislation emancipating the serfs, and Kutler's predecessors, Ermolov and Schwanebach. I kept one copy.

Late that evening, as I was clearing my desk, I picked it up and read it.[6] I was taken aback by the strong recommendation of expropriation in it. Such a proposal was, to say the least, inopportune after the cabinet had rejected a similar, although somewhat more radical proposal from Migulin, and in view of the noticeable shift to the right in higher circles, particularly among the nobility. Consequently, I told the official on duty to halt distribution of the copies. When he told me that they had already been sent out, I ordered their recall and asked that Kutler see me the following morning.

The next day I told Kutler that I would not submit the statement to the cabinet even if I thought it would be well received because I did not consider it adequately prepared. I asked if he had taken steps to assure that the statement would not fall into the wrong hands, because it could provide ammunition to hostile parties.[7]

He replied that he had not taken such steps because it had not occurred to him to do so. He did not insist that his commission's statement be accepted, but did ask for a private meeting of the cabinet so that he could be guided by its views in going on with his work.

When the meeting he asked for was held, all opposed expropriation, largely in the name of the "sanctity" of private property. I could not help pointing out that

XII ■ CABINET CHANGES 551

although I, too, believed in the sanctity of private property, I remembered that its sanctity had been breached when the serfs were emancipated, thus creating a precedent to which the common people could look back.[8] Also, I said that in addition to violating the principle of private property, expropriation would also further weaken Russia's already battered finances and economy. I went on to say that I would support expropriation only if Kutler could demonstrate that it would not weaken Russia. He answered that he couldn't give such an assurance, but, nonetheless, remained convinced that expropriation was the only measure that could effectively calm the peasantry. I should note that although he said he was convinced of this, he did not present his view with great conviction.

In the end the Kutler commission was asked to revise its proposal, with the help of additional members—V. I. Gurko, from the Ministry of Interior, and A. P. Nikolskii, an old acquaintance of mine, from the Ministry of Finance. Both were influential men, known to be strongly opposed to expropriation. Kutler did not object to what the cabinet called for. In fact, he seemed pleased, and he thanked me for being given the opportunity to discuss the matter with his colleagues. It is of some interest that the following day I received a memorandum (undoubtedly now in my archive) from Semenov-Tian-Shanksii expressing support of the Kutler commission proposal.

A few days later I received a note from the Emperor asking to see the proposal. I did as requested, including with a copy of the proposal my summary of what the cabinet thought of it and what it had recommended.

It was not long thereafter, during the course of my report, that the Emperor told me that everyone was against Kutler and that he wished to replace him. I asked that, if Kutler had to go, he be appointed to the State Council. His Majesty did not object, but no sooner had I returned to Petersburg than a note, in his own hand, was delivered to me, informing me that he had found it inappropriate to make such an appointment. A few days later, when in the course of my report the question of Kutler's departure was once more raised, I urged that he should at least be appointed to the Senate. His Majesty agreed, but no sooner had I returned to Petersburg than I received a note informing me that after thinking about it, he had decided that such an appointment was inappropriate. The imperious explanation he gave for his decision, prompted me, on February 6, to write the following letter, of which I have a copy:

> Your Majesty has informed me that you consider both the retention of Kutler in his present post and his appointment to the Senate undesirable. To refuse him such an appointment means departing from the custom of giving appointments to the State Council or the Senate to departing ministers. Your Majesty stated that we should profit from the experience of Western governments in such matters. I believe that it would be useful to borrow much from such governments in appointing and dismissing ministers, as well as in other areas of governmental service, but we must not forget that their practices are based on

law or constitutional principles. Here the state is governed by an Autocratic Monarch and our practices have therefore been different. But whatever system is followed, it must be based on equity.

In recommending that Kutler be appointed to the Senate I have not gone beyond what is equitable and possible. After all, before assuming the office he now holds at your wish, he had successfully served as assistant minister of interior and assistant minister of finance. And it is customary to appoint [departing] assistant ministers to the State Council, as was the case not long ago with Rukhlov, who did not have a long record of service. Neither did Garin, who had not served long as director of the Department of Police when he left office, at the same time that Trepov did. Yet Garin was appointed to the Senate.

Does Your Majesty wish that I ask Kutler to request permission to leave the service or would you prefer another method?

The Emperor replied that he did not consider it desirable for Kutler to stay, and would I recommend several candidates for his post. Thereupon I advised Kutler that, in view of the misunderstandings produced by the proposal for expropriation, he request permission to leave his post. He did so immediately, convinced, so I gathered, that I had not defended him adequately and that it was I who was responsible for his leaving. (This is the way persons in my position earn hostility and sometimes enmity.) I believe that he subsequently came to see that I had defended him, but that my defense had been to no avail.

At a subsequent occasion, while reporting to the Emperor, I asked that Kutler be given a pension. He kindly agreed to one of 7,000 rubles a year. He went on to say that he would like Krivoshein, who had been serving under Kutler, to replace him.

I was acquainted with Krivoshein, whom I had first met in the 1880s. At the time he was serving as lawyer to the Donets Railroad, a post he had received through his close ties with Moscow merchants that had resulted from his marriage into the Morozov family. He is far from stupid and works hard. All that I knew to his discredit was that he was a rather shrewd careerist.* That he was proposed alerted me to what was afoot, and I objected strongly to his appointment.

When the Emperor asked if I objected to Krivoshein because he was a conservative, I replied:

You do not know Krivoshein, Your Majesty, and want to appoint him on the recommendations of persons who do not have responsibility. I cannot have persons in the cabinet over which I preside who seek to advance themselves by improper means. I am prepared to see Kutler replaced by a man of very

*Incidentally, Krivoshein was the indirect source of some of the things I learned about Trepov. After October 17, Privy Councillor Shapirov, our family doctor, sometimes spoke to me about Trepov. When I asked for the source of his information, he told me that it was Krivoshein, who had it from one of Trepov's brothers.

conservative views, providing that he hold them on the basis of conviction, not expediency.

When asked for my recommendation, I suggested Fedor Samarin, a notable public man. I said that I knew him only by his reputation as an extremely honorable man whom I respected even while realizing that we would undoubtedly disagree about many things. The Emperor agreed that Samarin would be suitable, but wanted Krivoshein to serve as acting head. Sensing that this made me apprehensive, he told me not to worry, that Krivoshein would serve only until a permanent appointment were made.

At my invitation Samarin came to Petersburg to see me. When I offered him the post he declined, explaining at great length, and very candidly, why he could not accept. In the first place, because he was a Slavophile, he considered the October 17 Manifesto a disaster for Russia because it spelled constitution. In the second place, his health was not good enough nor his experience and knowledge sufficient for him to accept so important and responsible a position. After failing to change his mind, I asked that he explain his decision in writing, first to confirm what I would report to the Emperor, who might doubt my account, and second so that he could be assured that I was reporting him accurately. I should note that Samarin was to continue to be true to his principles and to act honorably.

Following Samarin's declination, I suggested Ermolov, the former minister of agriculture, but the Emperor would not agree. I then suggested Prince Kochubei, chief of the Appanages Department, a man with large landholdings, a conservative, but a decent man. I believe that he was offered the post, but refused. In any case, he was not given the appointment. Next I suggested Prince Urusov, assistant minister of interior, who was well acquainted with the life of the noble landowners, but the Emperor demurred. At that point I asked for time to discuss the matter with my colleagues and for me to think some more about possible candidates.

As the days and weeks went by the air grew thick with intrigue. General Trepov and others like him, who, as I said, had favored expropriation out of fear, were now trying to compensate for their cowardice by going after Kutler as a way of showing what "true Russian men" they were. I was informed by friends and sympathizers that the general was transmitting denunciations of me and others to the Emperor and that, as things grew calmer and fear receded, such documents carried increasing weight at court.

Nemeshaev, the minister of ways and communications, who had recently been inspecting the railroads, informed me of one such document he had encountered during his journey. It was a petition being circulated for signature among landowners calling for my removal and denouncing Kutler, Shipov, the minister of finance (a man very much to the right but definitely not one of the Black Hundreds), and Putilov (his assistant minister) as holding revolutionary beliefs. By this time my relations with His Majesty had become extremely strained and I was continuing in my post only out of loyalty to the monarchical principle, as will become evident if I manage to finish these memoirs. The nature of these relations is illustrated by a letter, of which I have a copy, that I wrote to the Emperor on February 2:[9]

> I am enclosing a copy of a petition which is being circulated among landowners for their signature. It was printed in Kiev, but the initiative for it obviously came from Petersburg. I first learned about its content a few weeks ago and again, just now, from K. S. Nemeshaev. Of course I could find out who inspired and wrote it, but I consider such an effort a waste of time, for, like all who are active in public life, I know that the initiative for this undertaking comes from what we in the State Council call "the Black Hundreds of the State Council." Whether or not the inspiration came from Count A. P. Ignatev or Stishinskii or Goremykin or Stürmer or Admiral Abaza or from some other member of the group is of no consequence. By the way, I doubt that this illustrious group wishes to attain power, because they don't care to gamble with their lives. They prefer instead to act furtively, by spreading all sorts of lies in the drawing rooms of Petersburg, with the help of certain members of the press, e.g., V. A. Gringmut, B. V. Nikolskii (docent), and S. F. Sharapov.

The lengthy petition which I enclosed, opens as follows:

> Despite the generous bestowal of rights on the people under your scepter, revolutionary unrest and governmental paralysis continue gradually to grow worse. All Russia looks with hope at the energetic and wise measures being employed by the minister of interior and the minister of justice, aided by the loyal army, to establish law and order.

Concerning agrarian proposals the petition says:

> Both landowners and peasants are disturbed by the rumor that has been reported in the newspapers about a legislative proposal drafted by Actual Privy Councillor Kutler, one of Count Witte's closest associates, that provides for the expropriation of privately owned land above a set maximum, for the *benefit of the peasantry*.

There was no such legislative proposal, and the authors of the document knew this very well. The petition then went on to say:

> Because it is hard for people to believe that those who have received the reins of power from Your Majesty lack knowledge and practical experience, it is no wonder that there are some in society who are convinced that what appear to be utopian legislative proposals emanating from Count Witte's office are secretly designed to spread revolution, which failed in the cities and among workers, to the villages and the countryside.

The petition concludes by saying:

> We consider it our sacred duty as loyal subjects to inform Your Majesty that
> the present government, as personified by Count Witte, does not have the
> country's confidence and that *all Russia* expects from Your Majesty the replace-
> ment of the all-powerful Count Witte with a person of more solid political
> principles, a person more experienced in the selection of reliable and experi-
> enced associates who have earned popular confidence.

From this example of the intrigue directed against me and from the way in
which I reacted to it, it is evident that I was in an untenable position. That I was
permitted to continue in office for another two months is explained by the fact that
I was still needed, to conclude a huge and indispensable foreign loan and to ensure
the swift return of our troops from east of Lake Baikal. After I had completed these
two tasks and had arranged for the convocation of the State Duma, it was possible,
as they say, for any fool to deal with the Russian revolution of 1905.[10]

The intrigue of which I was the object also helps explain the manner in which I
reacted to the Emperor's note of February 10, informing me that he was appointing Krivoshein to replace Kutler and Rukhlov to replace Timiriazev.[11] I was so
upset that I decided to ask permission to leave government service, but out of
consideration for my colleagues, I talked to them before doing anything. After
listening to their arguments, I agreed to send the following report, which they
helped edit, to the Emperor:

> The criticism, accusations, and animosity which are now being directed at
> the government, are, in fact, directed primarily against me, as is to be expected,
> given the law that established the cabinet. Yet, although I am the premier, I do
> not know about some important measures, particularly those taken by local
> authorities, until I see the newspapers. All this places me in a most difficult
> position. Yet, despite fatigue and poor health, I continue to endure the difficul-
> ties out of a sense of loyalty to Your Imperial Majesty and out of love for the
> motherland.
>
> But now I am to be deprived of the opportunity of coordinating the activities
> of the ministries when I shall soon have to answer to the State Duma and the
> reorganized State Council. It will be difficult for me to justify actions for which I
> do not bear responsibility, the adoption of measures that I cannot execute, and
> proposals with which I am not in accord.
>
> As circumstances grow more difficult, it is impossible for a cabinet to do its
> work if it is not of one mind, or, at the very least, if it is not animated by a sense
> of solidarity. I do not have the basic feeling for Krivoshein and Rukhlov that
> would enable me to work with them.
>
> I have twice had the honor of reporting to Your Imperial Majesty about
> Krivoshein, and each time you have been kind enough to inform me that he
> would serve as acting head for no more than a few days. After receiving

your note today about your intention of appointing Krivoshein and Rukhlov, I felt it incumbent upon me to learn what my colleagues feel about these two men.

At a private meeting today with the ministers (General Rödiger, Admiral Birilev, Durnovo, Count Lambsdorff, I. I. Tolstoi, Filosofov, Prince Obolenskii, and Akimov), it was unanimously agreed that Krivoshein and Rukhlov would not meet the requirements of the posts for which they are being proposed and that their appointment would make the work of the cabinet more difficult. For that reason they authorized me to bring the above to the attention of Your Imperial Majesty and ask that the cabinet be permitted to carry out the difficult task confronting it before the convening of the State Duma without obstruction.

This report was sent on February 12. I received a reply the same day, asking whom I would propose, aside from those he had already "rejected." Because I had heard a few days earlier from Dr. Shapirov that Krivoshein was very anxious for the appointment, I was convinced by the Emperor's reply that as long as I continued suggesting candidates unacceptable to Krivoshein, Trepov would criticize them and they would be rejected, permitting Krivoshein to continue in office. Consequently, I suggested A. P. Nikolskii to replace Kutler.

The son of a deacon, with some of the characteristics of the priestly caste, Nikolskii has a good head and writes well. He graduated from Petersburg University, but is poorly educated by European standards: he knows nothing of foreign countries and if he knows any language besides Russian, he knows it poorly. I first became acquainted with him while I was working with the Baranov Commission in Petersburg and he was a junior reporter with *Novoe vremia*. I took him under my wing and gave him a few assignments. After I left for Kiev I lost touch with him for a time. When I returned to Petersburg as director of the Department of Railroads, I found a post for him in the department as official on special assignment. After I became minister of finance I had him appointed head of the savings banks, a position he was still holding in February 1906.

While working for the Ministry of Finance he continued writing for *Novoe vremia*, doing most of its articles on financial matters, although he is not much of a financial expert. For the most part, though, he wrote fairly interesting articles about the peasant question, concerning which he has a good practical and theoretical knowledge. He favored individual peasant ownership and therefore opposed the village commune. I should add that he helped me while I was chairman of the Conference on the Needs of Rural Industry. Since early 1904 he strongly supported the conservative position that had been characteristic of *Novoe vremia*. As I have noted, he was the only person from whom I heard rightist views on the eve of October 17.

No objections were raised against him, probably explained in part by the fact that he was on good terms with Krivoshein. His Majesty therefore agreed to appoint him, but only as acting head.

The Return of Gapon and
the Departure of Timiriazev

I can now turn to why I had to replace Timiriazev as minister of commerce and industry.[12]

Not long after I became premier, Prince Meshcherskii, with whom I was still on reasonably friendly terms, urged me to find a place for I. F. Manuilov[13] in my newly formed chancellery. My only contact with the man had been when he had come to see me in Paris in 1903, as I have mentioned. At the time I did not know Manuilov's reputation, and in a moment of weakness I told Prince Meshcherskii that I had no objection to having his candidate assigned to the chancellery, but remaining technically on the rolls of the Department of Police, providing that the minister of interior agreed. I asked Vuich, director of my chancellery, to take the matter up with the minister. Durnovo agreed, so Manuilov came to work, under the supervision of Vuich, who soon informed me that the newcomer had a bad reputation.

A few days after he had started work in the chancellery, Manuilov asked, on behalf of Prince Meshcherskii, that I receive Gapon. He declared that Gapon was repentant for his role in the events leading to January 9, and now that the majority of workers were under the influence of anarchist-revolutionaries and now that a constitution had been granted, he would like to help the government bring the workers back to their senses.

I was surprised to hear that Gapon was in Petersburg. Manuilov told me that in fact Gapon had been here since August. I had never met Gapon and had never had any connections with him. Nor did I want to have any connections with him. I told Manuilov that if Gapon did not leave Petersburg within twenty-four hours he would be arrested and tried for his role in the events that led to January 9. That evening, when I asked Durnovo if he knew Gapon was in the city, he expressed surprise and asked if I knew where he was staying. I did not.[14]

The next day Manuilov told me that Gapon wished to leave the country, but had no money. I gave Manuilov 500 rubles to be used to take Gapon to Verzhbolovo [a border station] and see that he actually left the country. Two days later Manuilov reported to me that he had carried out his mission and that Gapon had promised never to return to Russia. Perhaps things would have turned out better if I had had Gapon arrested and tried, but at the time it seemed best to let him go, given the fact that he still had considerable popularity among workers and that workers were still turbulent and also given the fact that it was so soon after the October 17 and the declaration of amnesty.[15]

Later Prince Meshcherskii tried to convince me to permit Gapon to return to Petersburg and for me to receive him. He assured me that Gapon had completely broken with the anarchists and the revolutionaries as a result of what he had learned about them while abroad, that given the fact that Gapon still had some influence among workers, he could be useful in the struggle with the anarchists and revolutionaries. I told the prince I did not trust Gapon, wanted nothing to do with him, and asked him to leave me alone.

It was around November 10 that Vuich told me that two journalists named Matiushenskii and Pilskii wanted to see me. In those days I would not receive people I did not know and so I asked who they were. Vuich told me that they worked for *Novosti*, a liberal but moderate newspaper and that the Department of Police did not consider them dangerous. Their aim, he told me, was to wean workers away from the anarchist unions.

When I received Matiushenskii a few days later, he told me he had a plan to remove workers from anarchist influence by reopening the workingmen's libraries and reading rooms that had been closed following the events of January 9. I said I had no objection, but knew nothing about the matter, and suggested that he take it up with Timiriazev, the minister of commerce and industry. He then asked that I arrange for a pardon for Gapon. I categorically refused.

At Matiushenskii's request I wrote a note asking the minister to receive him. Because he did not appear trustworthy, I decided not to let him get his hands on anything in writing and therefore asked Manuilov, who happened to be present in the chancellery, to accompany Matiushenskii to Timiriazev's office and deliver the note.

Around November 20 Timiriazev told me that he approved of Matiushenskii's proposal, but that it would take money to carry it out. I said that I had no objection to the proposal, but suggested that he also consult the minister of interior about it. As for money, he should ask the Emperor for it, from the special contingency fund. I suggested that he not ask for much, no more than 6,000 rubles, as I recall.

I heard no more about all this until about the end of January or early February, when I read in the newspapers that Timiriazev had given Matiushenskii 30,000 rubles, of which the journalist had stolen and hidden all but 7,000. Naturally, I wrote to the minister asking for an explanation. He replied that he had asked for and been given 30,000 rubles, which he turned over to Matiushenskii, and went on to say that some politically moderate workers had learned that most of the money had been stolen, and had located its hiding place, with the help of the gendarmerie. What he failed to tell me then, or later, was that he had been seeing Gapon, as I learned, after his departure from office, from the judicial report of the investigation of the case.*

My correspondence with Timiriazev about the case and Manuilov's explanation, which are in my archive,[16] shows that the minister was not telling me the truth. His behavior in the case—his secret contacts with Gapon, the fact that he gave money to Matiushenskii without my knowledge or that of his other colleagues, his failure to tell me the truth—was the immediate cause of his dismissal.

*In March, after Timiriazev's dismissal, Durnovo told me that Gapon had been living secretly in Finland, also that he had offered to betray the fighting organization of the central revolutionary committee for 100,000 rubles. When I asked what he was going to do about the offer, he said he had nothing to do with Gapon and that the matter was in the hands of Rachkovskii, who offered him 25,000 rubles. I said I did not trust Gapon and that the amount of money was irrelevant. Subsequently I learned of the death of Gapon.

But the indirect cause was his indiscreet relationship with left-wing journalists, about which I have already written.

By the way, he was not particularly sorry to leave a government that did not share his expectation that before long Russia would virtually become a democratic republic. And, as will be seen later, when he left he was able to find a comfortable berth for himself.[17]

When it became evident that a replacement would have to be found for Timiriazev, I thought of Academician Ianzhul, professor of business law at Moscow University and former chief inspector of factories in that city. But before suggesting his name to the Emperor, I sounded him out. Obviously the fear of bombs and Brownings still had a chilling effect, because he declined to be a candidate.

As I have related earlier, when it became clear that we would have to find a new minister, the Emperor wrote that he wished to appoint Rukhlov and I objected. What were my objections to Rukhlov, a man, whom, it will be recalled, I would not tolerate in my cabinet from the day one?

Rukhlov is an intelligent and sensible bureaucrat, but not a very cultivated man, in the European sense of the word. More to the point, he belongs to the "how can I be of service" school and tends to sail with the prevailing political wind. In 1902, when there was an opening as assistant minister of finance, he sought, through Count Solskii's help, to get the post, but I would not agree. Later, however, when another assistant ministerial post became vacant in the ministry, I made the gesture of offering Rukhlov the post, to please Count Solskii, but to my delight was refused.

Rukhlov then went on to succeed Admiral Abaza as chief administrative assistant in Grand Duke Alexander Mikhailovich's ill-famed Chief Administration of Merchant Marine and Ports. Here, too, he had Count Solskii's assistance. This agency, which did not smell of roses, was the right place for Rukhlov. As an accommodating man, he acceded to the slightest wish of his grand ducal chief, and as a good bureaucrat he provided the veneer of propriety and seriousness to an agency that was neither proper nor serious.

As I have noted, neither I nor my colleagues wanted him in the cabinet. I did not want him in my cabinet because of his character defects, but also, and more compellingly, because I knew that he was one of Grand Duke Michael Aleksandrovich's tools and that, by bringing him in, I would take the risk of having to face even more intrigue than I already was. The Emperor knew Rukhlov only through the latter's ties with the Grand Duke.

With Rukhlov rejected and Ianzhul refusing to be a candidate, I turned to Fedorov. He is a very decent, unaffected, rather cultivated (but not in the European sense) man. He is a liberal, but moderate, and therefore did not agree with Kutler's agrarian proposal. His experience was considerable. He had served as editor of the Ministry of Finance's *Vestnik finansov, torgovli, i promyshlennosti*, as head of the commerce and industry section of the Ministry of Finance, and then as assistant minister under Timiriazev. It was he, it will be recalled, who had warned me about Timiriazev's lack of principles. The Emperor agreed to appoint him, but only as acting minister. As I have stated, Fedorov is a man of principle, and therefore, when I left office, he declined the offer of the rank of full minister, because he did not share the views of my successor, Goremykin.

XIII

The Loan That Saved Russia's Financial Strength

I have already spoken of our desperate need for a huge loan and of my efforts both before the peace negotiations and immediately after to arrange for such a loan, of the fact that our chief hope for a market in which to float such a loan was France, and of the promise of the French government that it would aid us in our effort after its differences with Germany over Morocco were amicably settled.[1] I have also related how at Rominten I persuaded Emperor William to agree to an international conference to deal with the question. Time was of the essence, but we had no choice but to wait for the successful conclusion of the conference, which did not begin until January 1906, in Algeciras.

I was convinced that for Russia to survive the revolutionary crisis and for the Romanov dynasty to remain in power it was necessary quickly to bring back the troops that had been in Manchuria and to borrow enough money to tide us over several years. I felt that once we had the money in hand, once the troops were back, and once we had in good conscience carried out the promises made in the October 17 Manifesto and in my report to the Emperor published on that day, we could return to the state of normalcy that our 150 million people required.

Moreover, the loan had to be arranged and most of the troops brought back before the opening of the State Duma if the government of Emperor Nicholas II were to avoid difficulties with the new body, which was likely to be vengeful and unreasonable. If we did not conclude the loan in time and had to permit the State Duma to deal with the loan, there would be delays, which would result in our having to accept more onerous conditions from the bankers with whom we were dealing. Without the loan, the government might lose the freedom of action that it must have under any circumstances, especially circumstances such as the ones we were experiencing.

As I have indicated earlier, Noetzlin, director of the Banque de Paris et Pays Bas, led the syndicate that planned to float a loan for us as soon as the French government gave the signal to do so. Some called his syndicate "the Christian syndicate," because no Jewish banking houses had participated in it since the Kishinev pogrom.[2]

The title "Jewish syndicate" was given to the Jewish banking houses in France that had been led by Baron Alphonse de Rothschild until his death, which occurred shortly before my return from America. It was because of his death that I had not called on the Rothschilds while I was in Paris in September. Because with the death of Baron Alphonse de Rothschild leadership passed to the head of the English branch, Lord Nathan Rothschild, I now had to turn to London to see if I could get support from the House of Rothschild. Although I was aware that the chances of getting such support were slim until the situation of the Jews in Russia improved, I commissioned A. G. Rafalovich,[3] our financial agent in Paris, to go to London to sound out the English Rothschilds. Their response, as he informed me, was that they admired me and would gladly support my efforts if Russia would improve its treatment of the Jews. Since I considered it improper for us to make concessions for financial reasons, it meant that we could not count on help from the Rothschilds.

Our efforts to borrow money abroad were hindered, too, by the left, which wanted to weaken the government. That the socialists and anarchists would engage in such efforts was to have been expected, but I had hoped that the Kadets would have seen the wisdom of cooperating with the government; however, my efforts to persuade their leaders to do so had failed, as I have noted, and they chose instead to continue to serve as the tail to the revolutionary kite. It goes without saying that the left understood that in order to weaken the Imperial government, of which I was head, it was necessary to deny it the troops and the money it needed.

The revolutionaries did their part by working among the troops, while Messieurs les Kadets tried to impede my efforts to arrange a loan by trying to persuade the French government not to permit the floating of a loan until the State Duma could decide whether or not to authorize the government to borrow. Without such authorization, they argued, a loan would not be considered an obligation of our government.

Among those who carried out this mission were Prince P. D. Dolgorukov, basically a decent man but not very gifted politically, and V. A. Maklakov, also a decent person, and a gifted and intelligent man.[4] I am certain that they came to regret this action, which can hardly be called patriotic. In their defense it can be said that they, like so many educated Russians of the time, were acting like men who had become drunk from the effects of the shameful war and from biting the apple of political freedom (October 17), of which so many had dreamed since the days of the Decembrists. Theirs was a temporary lapse from ingrained decency, but there were so many other men who were also bawling about freedom in those days who were not decent, as they showed later, when they sold their principles for money, honors, and comfortable positions.

The efforts of the Kadets to undermine my efforts to negotiate a loan were abetted, willy-nilly, by our press, which painted so gloomy a picture of our situation that the foreign public had reason to wonder how stable our government was. In acting as it did, the press reflected the confusion that had seized the minds of educated Russians. The press also hurt our efforts by publishing the Petersburg Soviet's revolutionary "financial manifesto," about which I have spoken earlier. As I have written earlier, some journalists were sincere in the opinions they expressed at the time, but others, like A. S. Suvorin, of *Novoe vremia*, were not.

The alarm about our stability that our press created was to the taste of that large part of the foreign public that took pleasure in our difficulties. This was shown in a report that Rafalovich sent from Paris at the end of December informing me that the hostile attitude of much of the foreign business and financial press provided a clue to the difficulties we were encountering in negotiating a loan. He reported that while such financial experts as Paul Leroy-Beaulieu and Kergell, editor of *Revue économique*, were trying to "reassure the public" about us, there were many publications, notably the London *Economist*, which were doing the opposite. That publication predicted that we would leave the gold standard and, in general, wrote about our financial position with the pleasure that some have on viewing the corpse of an enemy. Rafalovich concluded that these were "the war cries of the enemies of Russian credit."

While we were waiting for the time when the loan could be concluded, our finances were deteriorating. Consequently, early in November, I decided that the Finance Committee[5] be kept abreast of the state of our finances. With my consent, the committee authorized two of its members, Kokovtsev and Schwanebach, and I. P. Shipov, the minister of finance, to report on gold prices and on the operations of the State Bank. This they did, but, as was to be expected, they were unable to suggest any measure to improve our financial position.

Although our financial situation was critical, I knew we had no choice in our efforts to get a loan but to wait until the Moroccan question was settled, but I could not reveal what I knew. But because several members of the Finance Committee believed that it was possible to borrow money at this time and because I knew that Kokovtsev wanted to go abroad to make an attempt, I suggested that he make the journey, and I provided him with the necessary authorization.

He arrived in Paris around December 20 and was told by Premier Rouvier, as I expected, that the loan would have to wait until the satisfactory conclusion of the conference at Algeciras. Also, after receiving permission to do so, granted on my recommendation, he called on President Loubet.[6] All that he was able to accomplish in Paris was, again with my authorization, to obtain 100 million rubles as an advance from the bankers with whom I was negotiating.

Unfortunately, some short-term obligations held by Germans were about to come due, and the advance would be of no help if we had to meet these obligations as scheduled. Therefore I asked Kokovtsev to stop off in Berlin to see if he could get the date extended for a few months. He had no difficulty in doing so because the German government had not yet decided whether to help or hinder me in my activities in the field of foreign affairs.[7] In my favor was the fact that I was continuing to work for a Franco-Russian-German alliance. (That it was not to be realized would be because of lack of wisdom on our side and Emperor William's, who would be more to blame than we.) On the debit side was my part in the annulment of the Treaty of Björkö. The German Emperor was so angry with me over this that he would have withdrawn his agreement to an international conference concerning Morocco, but by now it was too late and the game was about to begin at Algeciras.

It is not necessary to repeat why it was in our interest that the conference complete its work as soon as possible. Also, I had a personal stake in reestablishing financial stability. It would have been deeply distressing to me, who had established the gold standard and thus provided Russia with a sound monetary system, who had put our finances on a solid footing, if we had had to abandon the gold standard as a result of not receiving a loan.[8] It need hardly be said that it was not I but those who had dragged us into the senseless war and Kokovtsev, for his lack of foresight during the war, who were responsible for the sad state of our finances.

Germany's interest, on the contrary, was to delay a settlement, for two reasons. First, German diplomacy operated on the beloved principle that the more you bargain, the more you obtain. Second, Germany wanted to place the Tsar's government in as difficult a position as possible in order to make it more tractable.

The French aim, quite understandably, was to win such terms at Algeciras as would permit her to retain paramount influence in Morocco. France counted on English support and even more so on ours, both because we were an ally and because of our urgent need of money.

Once the conference opened, in January, I recognized that it was desirable to go beyond the general terms of a loan on which I and Noetzlin had agreed on in September, when I was in Paris, and to deal with specifics. Unfortunately, I could not go to Paris, nor could I send anyone in my place: I. P. Shipov lacked the necessary experience, and Kokovtsev, who had the experience, had not been successful in his efforts in December.[9] It followed then that Noetzlin had to come to Petersburg, to talk to me.

But if it were known that he was in Russia, the negotiations at Algeciras would be impeded. Also, such news would lead to speculative trading in Russian bonds, which had already fallen by twenty percent since my departure from the office of minister of finance. So I asked Noetzlin to come incognito and arranged for him to stay secretly at Grand Duke Vladimir Aleksandrovich's guest house in Tsarskoe Selo. This was done with the gracious agreement of the Grand Duke and the knowledge of the Emperor, who was kept informed of all that was going on.

Noetzlin arrived on February 2 and remained for five days. I saw him several times and with I. P. Shipov's assistance worked out the details of the loan. The first question was when the loan would be concluded. Noetzlin wanted to wait until the State Duma convened. I would not agree, pointing out that if we waited, precious time would be lost, because that body, with no experience to rely on, would be certain to move slowly. Also, it would be sure to exploit the occasion to raise irrelevant political questions that would only serve to confuse foreign public opinion. We agreed that as soon as it was evident that the conference at Algeciras was drawing to a successful close we would conclude the loan.

Another major question was the size of the loan. I wanted it to be large enough to repay the advance that Kokovtsev had arranged and our short-term German loans and yet leave us enough to be free from the necessity of having to borrow for a long time. I insisted on a sum of 2,750 million francs. Also, there was the matter of interest. Noetzlin insisted on six and a quarter percent; I would agree to no more than six percent.

Further, we decided that the loan could not be converted for at least ten years, that it would be floated by a syndicate of French, Dutch, English, German, American, Russian, and, possibly, Austrian banks and banking houses. The money raised would remain with the participants at one and a quarter percent interest until it was transferred to our government, to be done in installments within a year. Also, the syndicate would agree to assume half the loan. These matters out of the way, we dealt with minor details.

Toward the end of his stay, Noetzlin asked if I did not think he should see Kokovtsev, as a matter of courtesy. I had no objections. I informed Kokovtsev of Noetzlin's presence and a meeting was arranged.

After he returned to France, Noetzlin worked out the broad terms of the loan with other members of the syndicate. Once that was done, we kept in touch until the loan was concluded, I giving him instructions on all questions and he speaking for his syndicate.

Unfortunately, things did not go as rapidly as I hoped because of delays at Algeciras caused by German intransigence, which was so excessive that even her allies, Austria and Italy, supported France on some questions. In my report of February 10 to the Emperor I felt obliged to say that Germany, far from trying to improve relations with us and France, as it professed to be doing, was, in fact, using the conference for devious purposes. I said:

> No doubt the present situation provides Germany with a rare opportunity to exert pressure on France, in the knowledge that under present circumstances if war broke out France could not count on substantial aid from Russia or England. The temptation is there, but even if it does not come to war, Germany may find it tempting to act in such a way as to prevent Russia from getting the loan she needs to recover from the war and to demonstrate to France that it is in her interest to seek rapprochement with Germany rather than to rely on Russia, her ally.

Unwillingly, the suspicion arises that Germany is playing a clever game by using the Moroccan question, which does not affect her vital interests, for political machinations. In any event, we must remember that Germany is kindly and obliging only in words.

A few days before this, at my insistence, Count Lambsdorff, our foreign minister, had sent a letter to Count Osten-Sacken, our ambassador to Berlin, stating that France had made all the concessions she could and that it was now up to Emperor William to demonstrate the love of peace about which he and his chancellor had so often spoken. Count Lambsdorff also pointed out that it was difficult to believe that Germany was seeking to provoke the breakup of the conference by creating unnecessary difficulties, because such an event would not only hurt efforts to bring Germany, France, and Russia together but would "sow alarm among the European powers, alarm that would be no less harmful in its effects than war itself." Such an event, he added, would hinder Russia's efforts to borrow money, and without money she would not be able "to root out the revolutionary movement, which had already spread to neighboring monarchies and had forced them to recognize the need for common action to deal with the danger created by international anarchist organizations." The telegram concluded with the following:

> Despite the widespread belief that Jewish agitation is hindering the conclusion of a loan to Russia, there is indisputable evidence that the only bar to concluding the loan is the uncertainty over the outcome of the Algeciras conference; it is this uncertainty that is restraining French bankers.
> If Emperor William or the Chancellor should happen to touch on the Moroccan question in talking to you, you may speak with the utmost candor about the position taken in this telegram.

The allegation about "Jewish agitation" was raised because I had learned from the Emperor that Emperor William had informed him that the real obstacle to a loan was the refusal of Jewish money kings to take part in the operation. To scotch this allegation I asked Rafalovich to get Premier Rouvier's opinion. He reported that Premier Rouvier said the Germans were mistaken and concluded that Berlin had the power to decide whether or not we would get the loan. I showed the report to the Emperor.

Count Osten-Sacken, in his reply, of February 9, to this telegram, reported that Germany was trying still another tack. He said that Chancellor Bülow was now arguing that the chief obstacle to a loan was the fact of the revolutionary movement in Russia and once more urged us to use our influence to make France more tractable. Count Lambsdorff answered Count Osten-Sacken immediately, emphasizing the need to make it clear that France had shown her readiness to make concessions and that if the conference failed, the blame would be attributed exclusively to "Germany's aggressive designs."

Despite our efforts, Germany continued to be difficult. So, with the Emperor's consent, I sent a letter by special courier to Prince Eulenberg (who, it will be recalled, had assured me that I could communicate confidentially with his Emperor through him) for delivery to Emperor William. In this letter (a copy of which is in my archive, but is not at hand) I asked that he inform Emperor William that I earnestly requested that he use his good offices to bring the conference to a conclusion, to emphasize to him that while the Moroccan question was of substantial importance to France, it was but of minor significance to Germany, that by using his good offices he would promote the drawing together of Germany, France, and Russia and would help Russia meet her financial needs. The reply came swiftly: Emperor William had been informed of what I had written, but continued to feel that he could not yield on certain issues without harm to German prestige, this followed by the by now customary advice that we prevail on France to be more tractable.

Naturally I was disturbed by this response, and when Schön, the German ambassador to Russia, came to see me about some business I let him know how I felt, informing him in no uncertain terms how amazed I was at Germany's failure to give France credit for her conciliatory efforts. Schön replied that Germany had acted properly and that if the conference failed it would be France's fault. On February 20 he sent a telegram to Prince Bülow about this conversation. The following day he received a reply which ended with the following: "Instead of speaking of Russian interests being endangered, Count Witte would be better advised to persuade the French government to desist from her intrigues." Neither Schön nor Bülow knew that I was informed of what was in this exchange.[10]

Illustrative of the intrigue in which Germany engaged at this time and of the way in which such intrigue inflamed passions was the following. Some German newspapers reported that Cassini, our plenipotentiary at the Algeciras conference, had received instructions to support the German position concerning Casablanca.[11] This nettled the French, causing Nelidov, our somewhat frivolous ambassador to Paris, to inform Tardieu of Le Temps that the report was incorrect. Tardieu then prepared a story giving a garbled version of what allegedly had been the instructions. When this was published, several German newspapers engaged in polemics with Le Temps over which version was correct. All this required the foreign offices of Russia, Germany, and France to offer diplomatic explanations of the "facts." All this fuss could not help but produce bewilderment among the French and the Germans and make the work at Algeciras more difficult.

On February 23, while all the furor was going on, the Rouvier government fell, over domestic issues. A new government was formed with Sarrien as premier, Poincaré, whom I did not know personally, as minister of finance, and Bourgeois as minister of foreign affairs. I immediately instructed Noetzlin and Rafalovich to call on the new finance minister and inform him of where we stood with respect to the loan.

About a week later Rafalovich called on M. Henry, director of the Commercial and Consular Section of the Ministry of Foreign Affairs, and very close to Bourgeois, and then on Poincaré, to whom he pointed out the nature and details of the agreement between Rouvier and me. Rouvier, too, had briefed the new government, which was favorably inclined to our efforts. This was especially true of Poincaré, but he felt that he needed time to become acquainted with the details. In any event we would have to wait until the end of the conference, which had been dragging on and on because of German obstructionist tactics.

But there is an end to everything. With all the moot questions considered, with increasing evidence of her isolation at Algeciras, Germany had to accept the fact that the conference must come to a close. As early as March 16, Count Lambsdorff wrote me: "We know from a completely secret source (a communication from the chancellor to Schön) that Bülow considers the conference at Algeciras to be reaching a satisfactory conclusion and seeks only to convince Germany that she has achieved everything that could be desired."

In the meantime Noetzlin was getting ready for the conclusion of the loan. On March 12 he wrote about proposals for additional terms and suggested that when the conference ended we send our representatives to Paris to work with the syndicate in editing and concluding the loan contract. He had also made many suggestions about dealing with the French press during this period, and I had turned these over to Rafalovich.[12]

In the letter of March 12, as in others, Noetzlin informed me that Poincaré wanted to know if our government had the right to conclude the loan without the participation of the State Duma. I informed him that when the time came to sign the contract, I would present proof of our right to do so without the State Duma. I then asked Professor Martens, who, as I noted earlier, had a considerable reputation abroad as an expert in international law, to prepare the requisite justification.[13]

As the end of the conference drew near, I suggested to the Emperor that we appoint a plenipotentiary to meet with the representatives of the syndicate: he would settle some minor details that had not been dealt with and sign the contract. It would be more convenient for the representatives of the syndicate, I said, to do the final work in Paris, rather than come to Petersburg, because they would be coming from various countries. When asked whom I would suggest as plenipotentiary, I nominated Timashev, the manager of the State Bank, explaining that I. P. Shipov could not go because of his obligations here and that Timashev would be suitable because I had already negotiated the basic terms and all that remained to be settled was trifling. His Majesty said that, if I had no objections, I should send Kokovtsev, to keep from hurting his feelings. I replied that it didn't matter to me who was sent, because the negotiations were virtually completed. (Since Kokovtsev's return from Paris, in December, I had not discussed the loan with him, nor had he had any role in the negotiations.)

Toward the end of March Noetzlin went to London to talk to Fischel (of the Mendelssohn house), representing Berlin banking interests; Revelstoke, speaking for London banking interests; and J. P. Morgan. In his telegram of March 22, Noetzlin informed me that Fischel expected to receive definite permission on the following day from the German government to participate in the loan, but that Morgan seemed less inclined to participate than he had been. The next day he let me know that the German government had just told Fischel that German firms would not be permitted to participate. So, having failed to drive us off the gold standard by its delaying tactics at Algeciras, the German government now resorted to this treacherous step.

In my reply to Noetzlin, sent on March 23, I wrote:

> I had already alerted you to German intentions. Germany was waiting for an excuse to create difficulties. Not finding one, she created one by deciding to float a loan for which there was no urgent need. Basically, this is in reprisal for Algeciras and for our drawing closer to England. This act should lead other countries to increase their share in the loan rather than the contrary. Moreover, this action should lead to speeding things up rather than causing delay.

At the same time I sent the following telegram to Rafalovich about what had occurred:

> In reprisal for Algeciras and out of fear that the loan will strengthen our links with France and provide the basis for the start of rapprochement between us and England, the German government at the last moment refused permission to its bankers to participate in the international syndicate. In order to provide a plausible excuse for such a hostile act, the German government unexpectedly floated a loan. Yet two weeks earlier when Mendelssohn had been in Petersburg, armed with instructions from his government, there was no hint of abstention. * (He had come to discuss several matters concerning the loans.) The German government decided to take this step on the spur of the moment in order to create trouble for us and in effect to say to us: "You have supported France throughout, now you must see that you acted unwisely." In suitable language, inform the French newspapers of this machination.

Following Germany's lead, Morgan went back on his word and refused to participate in the syndicate. He acted as he did because Emperor William was well disposed toward him and, despite his American democratic feelings, Morgan set much store on receiving the attention of so exalted a monarch. But neither his treachery nor that of Germany succeeded.

As Noetzlin informed me, the German and American actions had no effect on the English in their commitment to participate. On the whole, Algeciras, where Russia and England had firmly supported France, was the first expression of the thawing of Anglo-Russian hostility.

*Despite the action of his government, I was confident that Mendelssohn would participate in the loan because his banking house, the most important one in Germany, had for nearly a hundred years supported Russian financial interests, and the head of its house and I were on very friendly terms.

Nor was Austria, Germany's ally, dissuaded from permitting its bankers to participate in the syndicate. That the other ally, Italy, did not take part was explained by the fact that, having recently adopted the gold standard, she was not in a strong financial position. (On a visit to Russia a few years earlier King Victor Emmanuel gave me the first gold coin to be struck at the Italian mint, saying that it was a gift to the man who had established the gold standard in the great Russian Empire.)

Looking back it is evident that, for the most part, German policy at Algeciras misfired, as I have indicated. Yet I cannot believe that the cause was lack of foresight. Certainly there was foresight at Rominten when Emperor William showed me such extraordinary personal kindness and expressed such sympathy for my dream of a Russo-Franco-German alliance. These were efforts to charm me in the knowledge that whether or not the notorious Treaty of Björkö was implemented depended on me. And although Emperor William was disappointed by the annulment of that treaty following my return to Petersburg, he was not ready to write me off completely, as was shown on the occasion of New Year's Day 1906, when he sent me a greeting card depicting his meeting with Emperor Nicholas at Björkö, with an inscription in his own hand. His intention was to indicate that the ideas expressed at Björkö and Rominten needed to be realized, but in a different form. I, of course, have continued to favor the idea of a Russo-Franco-German alliance, and had I remained in power I would have sought to bring it about. The German foreign office, too, thought I might still change my mind about Björkö, but it had thoughts of revenge for what had been done, thoughts that were intensified as it saw how we were supporting the French at Algeciras. It was the thought of revenge that led the German foreign office to try to take advantage of our difficult financial position to force us off the gold standard and thereby weaken France, the ancient enemy.

It is very probable that as Emperor William began to guess that my position was not secure, he no longer felt bound by the promise he had made at Rominten that when I needed help I should let him know, through Prince Eulenberg. Thus, when I asked for his help in bringing the Algeciras conference to a satisfactory end, he refused. And then he treacherously refused to let German bankers participate in the syndicate, thinking that his action would leave me in a completely untenable position, but he did not succeed.

And now to deal with the last step. On March 20, at my request, Kokovtsev came to see me. I explained where we stood and provided him with detailed instructions. About a week later I sent him off to Paris, accompanied by A. I. Vyshnegradskii (son of my predecessor as minister of finance), who had worked with me when I was minister of finance, in the credit chancellery. I could rest easily, in the knowledge that there would be no slip-ups because Vyshnegradskii knew all the ins and outs of credit operations.

On April 3 Kokovtsev signed the loan contract.[14] On his return he turned it over to me. I passed it on to our minister of finance, who, in accordance with established procedures, submitted it to the Finance Committee, which examined the contract and approved it. Then Shipov presented it to the Emperor for his approval.

Vyshnegradskii brought back with him a letter of congratulations from Ernest Mendelssohn-Bartholdy, head of the Mendelssohn banking house. In this letter, dated April 5/18, he not only congratulated me warmly for having secured the loan, but also expressed regret that after all his efforts on behalf of the loan he had not been permitted to take part in the syndicate. He assured me that he was trying by acts as well as words to ensure success, by secretly investing in the loan in Paris, London, Amsterdam, and Petersburg, a fact that he was revealing to me in the utmost confidence. It was thus obvious from the actions of Germany's foremost banker that his government had failed in its efforts to sabotage the loan.

In a letter dated April 17/30, Noetzlin also affirmed our success:

> Yesterday the last step was taken. The international loan is an accomplished fact. Today this great financial victory constitutes the major news. Russian credit is on the way to becoming more firmly entrenched.
>
> Thanks to Your Excellency I have had the honor of participating in this undertaking from the very beginning. I deeply appreciate the confidence you have shown me throughout. When, at Tsarskoe Selo, you gave up the plans you had already made, you finally demonstrated your approval, which sustained and encouraged me during the critical moments we experienced during the negotiations.

This was the largest foreign loan ever floated. To be sure, Thiers floated a larger loan after the Franco-Prussian War, but it was primarily subscribed to at home, not abroad, as ours was. Our loan was of extraordinary financial and political importance. Thanks to it Russia was able to maintain the gold standard, which I established. Thanks to the maintenance of the gold standard, our fundamental financial structure, for which I was chiefly responsible, and which Kokovtsev later maintained with admirable fortitude, enabled Russia to recuperate from the ravages of war and revolution, providing the government with a monetary reserve that enabled it to cope with the problems it had to face in succeeding years. The financial strength made possible by the loan and the return of our troops from the East permitted the restoration of order and the government's recovery of self-confidence.

The Emperor fully understood the importance of the loan. He knew what ills would have followed had the loan not been concluded. As always in connection with financial matters, he showed me complete confidence and did not interfere with my work, contenting himself with the role of a spectator, but a deeply concerned one, watching a chess game. He expressed his appreciation in a handwritten letter, dated April 15, in which he wrote: ''The successful conclusion of the loan represents the finest page [in the record] of your activities. It represents a great moral success for the government as well as a guarantee of Russia's peaceful development in the years to come.''

Unfortunately, he did not show me the same kind of confidence in other matters. When I began to find my position as head of the government undermined, during February and March, and suggested that it might be better if I made way for someone who was more in his confidence than I, the Emperor told me straight out that until the loan was completed I would not be permitted to leave. That was because he fully understood that only I had sufficient experience and a high enough prestige in foreign financial circles to complete the loan. And it would be shortly after the completion of the loan, with our troops returning from beyond Lake Baikal, with the promises made in the October 17 Manifesto largely carried out, with the preparations for the convening of the State Duma completed, that I would ask to be relieved of my burdensome post.

In concluding my account of the loan, I should note that, on his return, Kokovtsev, after congratulating me and being thanked for carrying out his task exactly, asked that he be given 80,000 rubles as a gratuity, to come from the money raised by the loan. This request, coming as it did at a time of great financial difficulty, left me virtually speechless. All I could say was that he should talk to the minister of finance, this because I knew that the two were on good terms. I quickly told Shipov that Kokovtsev apparently was not aware that the practice of giving gratuities to ministers of finance and their associates on the completions of loans had been abolished by Emperor Alexander III. I advised Shipov, who was very shocked when I told him of the request, that he explain to Kokovtsev how things stood and to suggest that he never raise the question again. When this request was rebuffed, Kokovtsev turned to Count Solskii, with whom he had great influence, to arrange that he be given an honor in recognition of his work. When the count spoke to me about this request I raised no objections. Kokovtsev was then awarded the Order of Saint Alexander Nevskii.

When Kokovtsev returned to the office of minister of finance following my departure from office, he told the State Duma how difficult it had been for him to make the final arrangements for the loan. That most ''honorable'' man assumed that neither the deputies to the State Duma nor other Russians knew the facts and could be persuaded that he, Vladimir Nikolaevich, was Russia's savior. There you have Kokovtsev!

Because of his remarks I went to the trouble of collecting all the relevant documents in my archive and placing them in one packet. It was these documents that I have used in preparing this account of how the loan was made.[15]

XIV

Fulfilling the Promise of the October 17 Manifesto

The Electoral Law

One of the major tasks of my government was to carry out the promise of the October 17 Manifesto to extend the right to vote in the election of deputies to the State Duma as far as possible, "leaving the further development of the principle of universal suffrage to the new legislative order."[1] This meant preparing a revised version of the Bulygin electoral law of August 6, 1905, that extended the suffrage to various groups not enfranchised by the Bulygin law. In carrying out the task, I had to deal with two proposals.

The first came from D. N. Shipov, Guchkov, and Prince Trubetskoi, the three public men from Moscow who had refused to enter my cabinet, but who had agreed to submit a proposal for extending the franchise within the limits that I had indicated to them, i.e., that suffrage could not be universal nor the elections direct. As will be recalled, they had said that they could best accomplish this task in Moscow, and I had asked them to complete their work as soon as possible because until the electoral law was revised, elections could not be scheduled. As it turned out, their participation caused delay in holding the elections. In carrying out their task they were assisted by other public men.

When their proposal finally arrived it was clear that they were approximating the Kadet ideal of universal, direct, equal, and secret suffrage, known as the four-tail system. It was probably called "four-tail" because, if realized, it would have represented something like flogging the rich and the powerful with a four-tailed knout.

The second proposal was the work of Kryzhanovskii, of the Ministry of Interior, who had prepared the electoral law of August 6. Acting under my direction and instructions, he revised the law only to the extent of widening the suffrage by giving the vote to workers, renters, and members of the so-called free professions.[2]

Both proposals were then examined at a special session of the Committee of Ministers,[3] to which two members of the State Council, A. A. Saburov and Tagantsev, and six public men—Shipov, Guchkov, Stakhovich, Muromtsev, Kuzmin-Karavaev, and Count V. A. Bobrinskii—were invited. Of the six public men the first five had helped draft the first proposal and were invited for that reason. I invited Count Bobrinskii because he had expressed rather conservative views to me about what kind of electoral law we should have.[*]

The count and most of the government officials at the meeting favored the Kryzhanovskii proposal, with minor reservations. A few officials supported the proposal of the public men. Filosofov, a convinced liberal, gave his support on the basis of principle, Prince Obolenskii on the basis of expedience. There may have been as many as two other officials who supported the first proposal.[4] As expected, the men who drafted the first proposal argued in its favor, none more vigorously than Muromtsev, who was to serve as chairman of the First State Duma. This was my first glimpse of this fine old man.

The two proposals were then considered at a special conference, presided over by the Emperor, that was held at Tsarskoe Selo in December. The conference was attended by members of the cabinet, officials who had attended the meeting of the Committee of Ministers but who were not members of the cabinet, and several grand dukes (Michael Aleksandrovich among them), who were there at the Emperor's invitation. Also present, at my suggestion, were D. N. Shipov, Guchkov, Baron Korff, and Count Bobrinskii. I advised the Emperor that Shipov and Guchkov would support the first proposal and that Baron Korff and Count Bobrinskii would oppose it, the former because he was known as a moderate among zemstvo leaders and because he was acquainted with the Empress (and consequently with the Emperor) through his philanthropic work and the latter on the basis of the opinions he had expressed to me.

After the Emperor opened the conference, I offered some brief explanations, trying to be as objective as possible. Then the Emperor gave the floor to the public men. To my astonishment and the Emperor's, both Baron Korff and Count Bobrinskii supported the first proposal. I was not astonished that D. N. Shipov and Guchkov supported that proposal, as they had before. After they had spoken, the Emperor closed the morning's meeting and excused the four public men from further attendance.[5]

I was perplexed by Count Bobrinskii's change of position. When I asked him for an explanation, after the meeting, he replied: "Your Excellency, after the meeting of the Committee of Ministers I spent some time in the country, talking to

---

[*]I had served under his father in the Ministry of Ways and Communications but I knew little of him other than that he had been in the Hussar Guards and had at one time, in the 1890s, been considered such a "red" that when the Emperor was at Yalta he would not receive him because of his leftist reputation. Like many wealthy landowners, the count moved to the right later as a result of the fears induced by the unrest of 1903–1905.

the people there, and came to the conclusion that no proposal except an extremely democratic one would satisfy Russia and therefore decided to support the proposal of the public men.''

In the discussions that took place when the meetings were resumed, the majority favored the Kryzhanovskii revision of the electoral law, but the session ended without a decision by the Emperor. I could see that he was wavering. The next day, when because of some sort of holiday I had the opportunity of speaking to the Empress, I told her what we were doing and suggested that the Emperor would be making a mistake if he agreed to the first proposal. This was the only occasion on which I ever attempted to persuade the Empress to use her influence in connection with a matter of state.

During the remaining sessions of the conference, several spoke in support of the first proposal, but most, as before, favored the government's proposal. Among the latter were Tagantsev and Saburov, who were considered, for good reason, to be thoughtful liberals. As for me, when I had the opportunity to speak I pointed out the arguments for and against both proposals, but favored the second, i.e., my own. As a result, the Emperor assented to the one which I favored.[6]

The revised electoral law was criticized by the press for not providing for universal suffrage and consequently for not meeting the expectations of either the educated or the masses. And yet there were some liberals who recognized that we had acted wisely. Take Count Heyden, with whom I had become acquainted when he served as head of the chancellery of the Imperial Commission of Petitions. Count Heyden, whom I had thought of as an honorable but dried-up bureaucrat, had surprised me by suddenly becoming one of the leading figures during 1904–1905 among those striving for a constitution. Yet liberal though he had become, he recognized earlier than most liberals the meaning of the phrase ''the people are raising their heads'' and shifted to the right, but in doing so he continued to act calmly and decently, as he was to demonstrate as a deputy to the First State Duma. In speaking to me of the revised electoral law against which so many liberals ranted, he said that he approved of it because ''if the project of the 'public men' had been enacted, it would have produced the kind of Duma that would have had to be dissolved immediately.''

Many liberals took longer than he to realize what he saw immediately, that the law was as democratic as was then possible. They came to learn this after the elections, which although based on a law they considered too restrictive, permitted the election of a State Duma that ''opposed the powers-that-be.''

Why was a State Duma elected that ''opposed the powers-that-be''? It was because the revised electoral law had to retain those features of the law of August 6 that gave a preponderance of representation to the peasantry, on the mistaken assumption, accepted by such archconservatives as Pobedonostsev and General Lobko, that this was the only class on whose loyalty the state could rely. The assumption was mistaken, as I have said, because it left out of account the fact that the peasants are loyal to their Tsar when they believe that he is acting justly, as they did of Emperor Alexander II. They believed that justice required the completion of the division of the land begun by "the Great Emperor Emancipator." But when peasants, elected in great number to the First State Duma, saw that what the Autocrat Alexander II considered just was not considered just by the Autocrat Nicholas II, when they heard my successor, Goremykin, declare to the State Duma that private property was inviolable and that consequently there would be no distribution of land, the peasant deputies gave their support not to the government of the Tsar but to those who said: "The first order of business will be for us to give you land, as an adjunct to freedom," i.e., they gave their support to the Kadets (Miliukov and Hessen) and to the Trudoviki.[7]

I was criticized from above for not trying to influence the outcome of the elections, but to have done so would have meant acting against the spirit of the new order and contrary to the clear instructions of the Emperor in the circular that appeared not long after the appearance of the electoral law of August 6, 1905. In that circular, Bulygin, still minister of interior, instructed all provincial authorities that it was the Emperor's wish that local authorities make free elections possible by not attempting to influence their outcome.

It seemed obvious to me that this circular remained in force after October and therefore my government did not try to influence the elections, acting only to see that election rules were observed. The minister of interior, P. N. Durnovo, showed no inclination toward interference. Had he done so, I would have stopped him. Clearly, the Emperor, in accordance with the Bulygin circular, did not indicate to Durnovo that interference was desirable. It is true, however, that Durnovo, and temporary governors-general acting under his direction, were responsible for many illegal and arbitrary actions, about most of which I was informed only after the fact.[8] The public, antagonized by such acts, was more inclined to vote for leftist candidates than it would have been under better circumstances, tending to vote for candidates whose slogans were: "Down with bureaucracy," "Down with its arbitrary actions," "Down with the death penalty," "Down with administrative sentences of exile and imprisonment," "Subordinate the Imperial power to that of the legislature."

Unfortunately, His Majesty refused to recognize that it was such actions on the part of his officials that helped produce a leftist State Duma. It was in that spirit that he wrote to me after the elections, on April 15: "It seems to me that the extremism of the Duma is the consequence of the total restraint shown by all officials during the election campaign, something not found in other countries, rather than of reactions to repressive actions on the part of the government."

In other words, the Bulygin circular had been issued merely for the sake of appearance. In deeds the government was supposed to act *sub rosa* to influence the elections. In other words, the law is one thing, its execution another. "Who knows what the law means?" That was the slogan introduced by Stolypin and is still in vogue, although it is now expressed with less insolence than it had been by Stolypin, and it will continue to be in vogue until something drastic happens.

Legislative Power

In conformity with the promise made in the October 17 Manifesto, it was necessary to revise the statute of August 6, 1905, in order to transform the State Duma provided for in that act from a consultative into a lawmaking body. Likewise, it was necessary to revise the older legislation concerning the State Council to give it power to participate with the State Duma in the making of laws and to change the composition of the State Council.[9]

Recently [1912] I read in a Russian publication that the State Council should either have been castrated or done away with. This view is not justified in the light of the documents of October 17, nor was any question raised in the process of changing the State Council about its right to share in the making of the laws. All that can be said was that it was assumed that there would be a division of responsibility between the two houses, the State Duma being responsible for the drafting of legislation and the State Council for examining the basic features of the bills submitted to it by the State Duma. It was not envisaged that both houses would be performing identical tasks, concerning themselves with the details of bills. This is explained partly by the fact that the State Duma lacked experience in the editing of bills and partly by the fact that the right wing of the State Council, being opposed in principle to the [very existence] of the other body, tended to say "black" if the State Duma said "white."

To deal with the State Council a commission was created by Imperial order, with Count Solskii as chairman, working with the ministers, the chairmen of the departments of the State Council, and some other members of the State Council. Count Solskii was given the appointment because he was chairman of the State Council and because the cabinet had too many other tasks. However, mine was the dominant voice in the deliberations of the commission both because of my position as premier and because of my influence over the count.

In connection with our discussion of the roles of the State Council and the State Duma in the drafting of legislation, A. A. Polovtsov suggested that because neither would be capable of editing bills, the task be entrusted to a commission representing both bodies. I thought that it was a good suggestion and that, if followed, it would help eliminate many disagreements between the State Duma and the State Council. Unfortunately, this proposal was not acted upon because we were pressed for time.

Among the questions dealt with was the term that deputies to the State Duma should serve. I supported the view that the term be fairly long, to permit the development of tradition in that body as well as to avoid the problem of having to deal with newcomers. A five-year term was decided on.

Also, I proposed that the term of elected members of the State Council be nine years, with the provision that of the first contingent to be elected, one third be replaced, by lot, at the end of three years, and another third replaced, also by lot, at the end of six years. However, the term for members elected by the zemstvos was set at three years, at the suggestion of Prince A. D. Obolenskii. He argued that because the zemstvo statute then in force was unpopular, the public would not look kindly at deputies elected for nine-year terms while that statute was in force; better to elect deputies from the zemstvos for a shorter term, during which the zemstvo statute could be revised to permit the return to the original conception of the zemstvos. Once this was done, he argued, deputies from the zemstvos should be elected for nine-year terms. But six years have gone by and there has been no word of changing the statute.

Another problem we dealt with in our deliberations about the State Council and the State Duma was the power to issue emergency legislation when the legislative bodies were not in session. In his manifesto of February 20, 1906, issued in conjunction with the new laws concerning the two bodies, the Emperor said the following about emergency legislation:

> If *extraordinary* circumstances require consideration of legislation, the cabinet will submit it to Us directly. Such legislation may not, however, make changes in the fundamental laws, nor in the statutes dealing with the State Council and the State Duma, nor with elections of members of these bodies. Such legislation will cease to have force if the minister or head of the chief administration concerned does not submit it to the State Duma within two months after it resumes work, or if the State Duma or the State Council rejects it.

This statement became part of the Fundamental Laws, about which I shall soon speak, as Article 87. This article was intended to be employed only in emergencies, but, unfortunately, Stolypin was to exploit this article as a means of circumventing the State Duma on questions of substance not of an emergency character.

The Power of the Purse

Regulations concerning the adoption of the annual governmental budget were issued at about the same time that the revised statutes concerning the State Duma and the State Council were published. This legislation was prepared by the commission under the chairmanship of Count Solskii, but its major features were suggested by me.[10] They are the following.

First, the budget was to be published on the first day of the year. To meet this deadline, the proposed budget was to be submitted to the State Duma the preceding October, which, in turn, was to send it to the State Council by December 1. Second, if the budget could not be published on schedule because of the absence of the Emperor or for unforeseen circumstances, the government could operate on the basis of temporary appropriations within the limits of the proposed budget. I assumed, of course, that any delay in the adoption of a budget would be exceptional and short. Third, legislative approval would not be required for expenditures from the 10 million-ruble contingency fund, but the minister of finance would continue the practice of providing the State

Council with monthly reports about expenditures from the fund.

When the draft of these regulations was brought to me by a state secretary from the State Council and I had read it, I told him that since what appeared there expressed the views I had expressed, I agreed with them, but I found the wording confusing in places. He replied: "I can't pass on what you said to Count Solskii because he would feel deeply insulted if I told him that you had said that the editing, which he had approved, was not satisfactory, but he would not feel insulted if I told him that you thought he had done something unwise." The editing was corrected somewhat in a few places, but what was published was essentially what had been presented to me.

I must note with regret that to this date [1912], none of the basic features of the budget regulations has been adhered to.

Revision of the Fundamental Laws

One of the most important pieces of legislation with which my cabinet dealt was the revised code of Fundamental Laws.[11] This code has provided significant protection to the changes in the political structure resulting from the October 17 Manifesto, this despite the distortion created by Stolypin's extralegal actions of June 3, 1907.[12]

The idea of revising the code was anticipated either at the end of 1904 or the beginning of 1905, when zemstvo leaders, participants in the well-known conference of zemstvo and municipal leaders, prepared a draft of a new, basic state law for the Russian Empire. The draft, deeply democratic in spirit, called for the four-tailed vote and the transformation of the Emperor into little more than a figurehead, such as the president of the French Republic.

In fact, revision of the Fundamental Laws was necessitated by the changes in the structure of the state resulting from October 17, e.g., the new State Duma, the new State Council, the new budget rules, but during the first months of my tenure the question of revision did not enter my head, nor was it raised by my colleagues in the cabinet. The idea came instead from another quarter.

Early in 1906 Count Solskii advised me unofficially that His Majesty had authorized Baron Uexküll, the Imperial secretary, and Kharitonov, the assistant Imperial secretary, to prepare a draft of a revised code of Fundamental Laws. Once the draft was completed, it would be reviewed by an unofficial commission of which the count would be chairman. He was anxious that I serve on that commission.

Although I was on excellent terms with the count, I declined the invitation in no uncertain terms. When he tried to change my mind, I told him that I had decided not to participate in such bodies because I had learned from sad experience that I was the one held responsible for any shortcomings of laws I had helped frame. Now, given my position as premier, my mere presence in such a body would place a heavy burden of responsibility on me toward my contemporaries as well as to future generations for what the commission did. I said also that in any case the revision of the Fundamental Laws should have been the task of the cabinet, whose members, including me, would be the first to be held responsible for the new laws. My reply obviously displeased him.

I learned later what lay behind the devious tactic of entrusting the task to men like Baron Uexküll (a well-meaning liberal, a cultivated and honorable man, with considerable bureaucratic experience, but a bit malicious and devoid of broad ideas), Kharitonov (an intelligent, cultivated man, an able official, but inclined to sail with the wind), and Count Solskii (a product of the Tsarskoe Selo Lycée, a well-meaning liberal, like so many others of its alumni, and a talented hierarch of Petersburg's aristocratic bureaucracy) and in so doing bypassing me and my cabinet. As I learned, the initiative for revision of the Fundamental Laws came from General Trepov, the quasi-dictator, who wanted the task done without my participation or that of my cabinet, or, to put it more accurately, with me in the role of *"tête de turc,"* i.e., the one who would bear responsibility.[13] In general the whole episode is typical of the disturbed psychological condition in which not only Russian society, with a few notable exceptions, found itself in those days, but also its representatives.

At the end of February Count Solskii, acting on orders from the Emperor, sent me a draft of the revised Fundamental Laws, which Baron Uexküll and Kharitonov had prepared and he had edited, for consideration by the cabinet. Because I had declined to play the role of *"tête de turc"* by refusing to serve on Count Solskii's commission, the draft, which the Emperor obviously had not read, was not accompanied by any instructions from him.

Had the draft, which bore the stamp of Count Solskii's well-intentioned liberalism, been accepted without change, the government would have been castrated, a prey to the blows that would have been delivered by the many unbalanced deputies elected to the first two State Dumas. The power of the Emperor would have been even less than that of the president of the French Republic. And who would have been held accountable for such toothless laws that could only encourage new sedition? None other than Witte!

There were other shortcomings in the draft as well, about which I wrote to His Majesty as follows:[14]

> In my opinion, the draft contains some articles which, if enacted, would be dangerous. In addition the draft fails to deal with the crucial distinction between laws and decrees issued in the execution of the laws. As matters now stand, a literal reading of the statute which established the State Council leads one to conclude that virtually all decrees are treated as laws and have to pass through the State Council. Such an arrangement may have been to the advantage of the Monarch while the State Council was only a consultative body, but it would create very serious difficulties under the new order. Although I have spoken many times about this matter at sessions dealing with the new statutes concern-

ing the State Council and the State Duma, the draft given me by Count Solskii contains nothing on this subject.[15]

Also I have some doubts about the provisions for a regency. C. P. Pobedonostsev and N. V. Muravev have informed me that at one time Your Majesty considered revising the law concerning a regency.[16]

In the course of several meetings the cabinet hastily reviewed this most important document.[17] The basic question, as I saw it, was whether or not the new political structure that had been proclaimed on October 17 would be able to survive. To ensure survival it was essential that the revised Fundamental Laws be published before the State Duma convened, for if they were not, that body would transform itself into a constituent assembly and this would lead to the use of armed force to stop such an effort. The use of force would spell the end of the new political structure. That would be no tragedy if we had a Peter the Great at hand, but that was most unlikely. For that reason I urged publication before the opening of the State Duma. The only cabinet member who disagreed was Prince Obolenskii, who by now was at his wit's end, wavering between extreme liberalism and extreme conservatism. But I had come to ignore him, as did other members of the cabinet, some of whom addressed him sarcastically, others of whom spoke to him patronizingly as if to a *bon enfant*. Although my colleagues could not see as far ahead as I (and I did not share all my forebodings with them), all, expect Prince Obolenskii, could see the danger of permitting the State Duma to become a constituent assembly.

When we discussed those articles in the draft that limited the Emperor's powers with respect to the armed forces and foreign affairs, I was astounded that the ministers most concerned—General Rödiger, Admiral Birilev, and Count Lambsdorff—said that they had no objections, in principle, to the articles as they stood. I did not share their view and argued that the conduct of foreign affairs and the command of the armed forces should be in the exclusive jurisdiction of the Emperor, with the only power in these fields for the legislative bodies to exercise being that over the budget.[18] My arguments led the three ministers to change their minds and to argue successfully at a subsequent special conference for my position.

I believe now , as I believed then, that given the circumstances in which the country found itself, circumstances that have not changed, the State Duma should not interfere in such matters because to do so would diminish Russia's world influence. Of course, reference will be made to the great mistakes committed under the present Emperor, and I pray God that they will not be repeated. To err is human, but in saying this one should remember to look at the map to see how Russia grew between the days of Ivan the Terrible and Nicholas II, and that hardly any other country in the world has expanded as much.

In the course of the cabinet discussions of the draft, I turned to the question I had raised with His Majesty—the need to distinguish clearly between laws and decrees. To preclude ambiguity over the distinction, we decided to specify areas with respect to which the Emperor had the exclusive power to issue decrees: these included the establishment of governmental agencies, the maintenance of law and order, and the promotion of the common welfare.

In this connection the cabinet considered it desirable that the Fundamental Laws also affirm the Emperor's exclusive powers in other respects: to coin money, to place localities under martial law or other forms of exceptional status, to grant pardons and reduce sentences, to limit the right of residence and the right to purchase property in areas of military significance, to exercise jurisdiction over property belonging to the Imperial family, to decide on the structure of the Imperial court, to decide whether or not proceedings should be instituted against members of the privileged classes for the purpose of stripping them of their status or against higher officials, and to exercise authority over government employees, notably the authority to dismiss any of them, including members of the judiciary. I should note that a minority of the cabinet favored retention of the principle of irremovability as embodied in the statutes issued by Alexander II, but the majority, I among them, voted for removability of members of the judiciary.[19]

Also, taking advantage of the fact that only the Emperor had the power to initiate changes in the Fundamental Laws, the cabinet proposed inclusion in these laws of the budget rules recently approved by the Emperor. In the same vein, to preclude obstructive action by the legislative bodies with respect to the armed forces, a vital matter, the cabinet proposed that these laws stipulate that if by May 1 the legislative bodies had not yet approved the number of recruits to be called up that year, the government would have the right to use the figure of the preceding year. And, while proposing that the legislative bodies have some authority over ministers, the cabinet called for inclusion in the Fundamental Laws of a provision that the cabinet was answerable only to the courts for dereliction of duty, and it was responsible only to the Emperor [in the sense of holding office solely at his pleasure]. The cabinet also called for reaffirmation in the Fundamental Laws of the principle of freedom of conscience, as stated in the decree of April 17, 1905.

These, in sum, were the major changes in the draft submitted by Count Solskii that the cabinet proposed.

I should note here that no sooner had I received the draft of the Fundamental Laws from Count Solskii than Mechelin, vice-chairman of the Finnish Senate, came to see me. Mechelin, who, as I have noted, had called on me just after October 17, seemed an intelligent and educated man and an ardent Finn. That he was an ardent Finn was not a fault, but it was a fact that a Russian official had to take into account.

He told me that the reason for his visit was his alarm over a report, supposedly from reliable sources, that the revised Fundamental Laws would abolish the Finnish constitution. He warned me that if the Finns heard rumors about such a change we would see a return to the kind of unrest in Finland that had broken out during "the Bobrikov nightmare."

That such an unfounded report could be spread was typical of the times. Fearing that its dissemination might arouse not only the Finns but also other inhabitants of the Empire, I told Mechelin that what he had heard was untrue. I read the draft article concerning Finland to him in return for his word (which he kept) that, for the time being, he would not reveal what I had read to him and that on his return to Finland he would try to prevent the spread of misinformation by troublemakers.

The article in question read: "The Grand Duchy of Finland, being a possession of and inseparable from the Russian Empire, is administered in its internal affairs according to special laws." Mechelin was obviously relieved by the wording and asked that I dictate the text to him. After I had done so, he said that the language was not precise enough, asked for permission to submit a substitute. On receiving it I sent it (it is in the cabinet archive now), together with the original article, to Governor-General Gerhard, and invited him, Frisch (vice-chairman of the State Council), and Professor Tagantsev to attend a cabinet meeting at which the article would be discussed. (I invited the last two because for more than a decade they had served on every commission that dealt with linking Finland and the rest of the Empire more closely. Both, but Tagantsev more than Frisch, had supported the elimination of many constitutional rights that the Finns had enjoyed.)

At this meeting, Mechelin's substitute wording was unanimously rejected, but the original wording of the draft article was changed to read: "The Grand Duchy of Finland, being an inseparable part of the Russian Empire, is governed in its internal affairs by special institutions, on the basis of special legislation." This version met with Gerhard's complete approval.[20]

Just before Easter, on March 20, I sent the cabinet's revision of Count Solskii's draft of the Fundamental Laws to the Emperor. He then called a special conference, over which he would preside, to deal with the revised draft, to meet after the holidays.[21] Invited to participate were the members of the cabinet, several members of the State Council (among them Count Pahlen, Goremykin, and Count Ignatev), also Grand Dukes Vladimir Aleksandrovich, Nicholas Nikolaevich, and Michael Aleksandrovich. (The last was accompanied at the conference by General Pototskii, who served him as part-tutor, part-advisor.)

Among the revealing discussions that took place in the conference was one that dealt with the article concerning the number of recruits to be called up each year. Grand Duke Nicholas Nikolaevich saw no reason why the legislative bodies should have any voice in this respect, that it should be decided by the Emperor alone. Grand Duke Vladimir Aleksandrovich objected, arguing that this was an issue affecting the entire population and should therefore be within the purview of the legislative bodies, which, after all, had been given the authority to pass laws and that meant that they should not be bypassed when it came to decrees that had the character of laws: if we had no faith in the State Duma being elected we should not permit it to convene, but if we had faith in it, we could not deny it the right to participate in deciding as important a matter as the number of recruits. He concluded by declaring: "For my part, I believe in Russia, in the Russian people. I believe that the Duma will be patriotic because it will consist of Russians, and consequently I do not look at the future with apprehension." The Emperor was convinced by this argument and rejected Grand Duke Nicholas Nikolaevich's proposal.

Another revealing discussion dealt with the question of irremovability of judges. The minister of justice, Akimov, argued for removability, as did I. It was my view that the principle of irremovability in the statute concerning the courts issued by Alexander II was meant as a limitation on the power of the minister of justice, and other higher officials, and not on the power of the unlimited Monarch.[22] I believed that now, because the Monarch no longer had unlimited power, it was necessary to make explicit what had been implicit, that only the Emperor had the power to remove judges, for cause. Such a provision in the Fundamental Laws, it seemed to me, would assure the independence and impartiality of the judiciary.

Count Pahlen spoke vehemently for irremovability, obviously forgetting that while minister of justice he had circumvented the rule by making provisional appointments of judicial investigators, permitting him to remove them easily. Goremykin, who next took the floor, supported Count Pahlen. In the end, the Emperor agreed with the minority, which favored irremovability, but the practice nowadays, under Minister of Justice Shcheglovitov, flouts that principle.

Still another revealing, and important, discussion dealt with the article concerning inviolability of private property. Here Goremykin and I disagreed strongly, not over the article, but about what should be done if the State Duma chose to consider confiscation of land for the benefit of the peasantry. He took the position that the State Duma should be prohibited from even discussing such a matter and that, if it ignored the prohibition, it should be immediately dissolved. This view, presented rather forcefully, obviously pleased many of those present, including the Emperor, it seems.

I, too, believed in the inviolability of property rights, but argued that the State Duma had the right to consider a proposal that infringed on those rights, providing it observed proper procedures. Even if it passed an unacceptable bill, the State Council could dispose of it. With this the exchange of views between Goremykin and me ended. As it was to turn out, this disagreement would be one of the causes for my leaving office, providing Goremykin, aided by General Trepov, the opportunity of succeeding me.

The Emperor brought the conference to an end by accepting the draft of the Fundamental Laws as revised by the cabinet, except for minor, chiefly editorial, changes decided on at the conference. He then signed the draft. I then fully expected to see the document published before the opening of the State Duma, which was set for April 27.

But, as the date approached it was not published. On April 22, as I shall relate, the Emperor, at my request, relieved me of the premiership. I then returned to my home, on Kamenno-Ostrovskii Prospekt, and it was from there that I telephoned General Trepov when I became alarmed over the nonpublication of the laws. I said to him:

> Everyone knows that I am no longer premier and therefore do not bear responsibility for what is to come. Nonetheless I feel obliged to ask that you go immediately to the Emperor and tell him that I, as a loyal subject, humbly advise him to publish the Fundamental Laws at once, because the State Duma will open in a few days; if the laws are not published by then and the Duma begins to function without limits set by these laws, many unfortunate consequences will follow.

He soon called back to tell me that he had given the message, verbatim, to the Emperor. On April 24 the laws were published, identical in text with the draft the Emperor had signed, except for a few changes that I will discuss very shortly.[23]

Why the delay? It was obvious to me that General Trepov, who could shift from left to right and back again within the space of twenty-four hours, was behind it.[24] It was not until 1907, however, that I learned the facts, from Vladimir Ivanovich Kovalevskii, who had served under me as assistant minister of finance. At first I did not want to believe him, but he then convinced me with documentary proof, which is now in my archive.

It appears that immediately after the cabinet had sent its revision of the draft of the Fundamental Laws to the Emperor, General Trepov asked V. I. Kovalevskii to study the document. V. I. Kovalevskii then asked M. M. Kovalevskii (a cultivated, liberal scholar, now a member of the State Council) and three Kadets— Muromtsev, Miliukov, and Hessen—to join him in the task. The result of their efforts was a memorandum, which V. I. Kovalevskii submitted on April 18, to General Trepov who obviously then showed it to His Majesty.

The memorandum opened with these words: "The draft of the Fundamental Laws presented by the cabinet creates the most painful impression. Under the guise of preserving Imperial prerogatives, it seems to assure that the ministers are responsible to no one and have the power to act as they please." What followed was in the same vein, followed by the recommendation that: "To avoid a complete redoing of the draft, it should be retained except for some more or less substantive changes and a few alterations in wording." The "more or less substantive changes" would have reduced the power of the Emperor to that of a French president and would have made the cabinet responsible to the State Duma. Moreover, the memorandum dealt in a frivolous and liberal manner with many questions of fundamental historical importance.[25]

It is clear that the memorandum so disquieted the Emperor that he held off publishing the Fundamental Laws until he was informed by General Trepov of what I had said on the telephone. Even so, several changes were made in the document, as a result of General Trepov's influence and to placate the backstairs advisors.

One of the major changes was the limitation of the right of the Emperor to issue decrees on his own authority, resulting in the burdening of the legislative bodies with so-called legislative vermicelli. Another major change was the requirement that decrees be countersigned by the premier or the minister in whose province the decree fell. These changes meant that the ministers were responsible to the legislative bodies as well as to the Emperor, in short, a kind of parliamentarianism. Also, the force of the article on toleration was substantially diminished, probably under the influence of the church prelates, acting through the Empress.

The facts I have related demonstrate how, under the influence of fear, people vacillated in those days, going from one extreme to another. They also illustrate the behind-the-scenes intrigues that went on at the time. Had I not insisted on the publication of the Fundamental Laws before the opening of the State Duma, we would have witnessed the use of force to dissolve that body and the end of the era opened by October 17.

How do I feel about the Fundamental Laws, as published on April 27, 1906? Of course, they would have been better had there been enough time for more thorough work on them. In essence they constitute a constitution, a constitution that is conservative—without parliamentarianism, one that preserves many of the prerogatives of the Emperor. This document makes it possible to hope that a return to the old regime is no longer possible and that the new regime, established by the October 17 Manifesto, will endure.

Is the passing of the old regime a good thing? I think so, because the conditions necessary for an absolutist government to function no longer exist. All will be well if the Fundamental Laws are observed.

But if the arbitrary use of Article 87 continues, if Russia continues to be administered under the exceptional laws, if what was granted in the decree of December 12, 1904, including toleration, is rescinded, if, despite the so-called constitution, we continue to have a police regime, the likes of which was not experienced even in the days of Plehve, it is naturally pointless to enact laws of any kind.

I should add that some of the Fundamental Laws have been either ignored or completely misinterpreted. In order to keep the State Duma and all of Russian society from learning these facts, the minutes of the meetings at which they were discussed under the chairmanship of Count Solskii or the Emperor have been kept secret.

Had I foreseen what would occur, I would have retained copies of these minutes, but I did not foresee. In fact, I did not know that the minutes were being kept secret until recently, when I wanted to look them up because of an incorrect interpretation of the laws made at the State Council. When I was permitted to look in the State Council Archive for the minutes I was told they were not there. I learned a bit later from Kryzhanovskii, the Imperial secretary, that only three copies of the minutes existed and that they were being kept secret, because if they were published, the Fundamental Laws and the laws concerning the State Duma and the State Council would be interpreted in a manner quite different from that of the hypocritical Stolypin.[26]

The Death Penalty

Among the other important legal matters I dealt with was the death penalty, a subject that aroused strong feelings and concerning which there are sound arguments on both sides. When I assumed office the law permitted [civilian] criminals to be tried by courts-martial, which had the power to impose capital punishment.[27] In areas with governors-general, the governor-general had the power to turn such criminals over to courts-martial; elsewhere, this could be done only with the consent of the ministers of justice and interior. Until 1904 this law was rarely employed, but as the revolutionary threat grew greater, its use grew rapidly. And as the number of such cases increased, the tendency to apply the law in an arbitrary and uneven fashion grew, particularly after the establishment of temporary governor-generalships in troubled areas and after Durnovo, the minister of interior, began catering to the growing reactionary sentiment.

To assure that the death penalty would be imposed in an evenhanded manner, I proposed enactment of a temporary law making it mandatory that [civilians] charged with politically motivated physical attacks on government officials or with the preparation or use of bombs be tried by courts-martial. The death sentence for those found guilty would be mandatory except when special, mitigating circumstances called for reduction of the sentence to hard labor. The sentences would not require administrative approval, i.e., approval by governors-general or the minister of interior. Because it was mandatory that such cases be turned over to courts-martial and because the sentences did not have to be reviewed, the courts could act independently and evenhandedly. Had the law been enacted, the number of cases turned over to courts-martial would have been reduced.

When I submitted this bill to the cabinet, Prince Obolenskii and Timiriazev opposed it, obviously to demonstrate liberalism in a liberal-revolutionary period. However, the cabinet voted in favor of it, but to spare the Emperor from having his name associated with such a painful subject in this troubled time, it proposed that the bill be presented first to the State Council.

The majority of that body voted in favor of my bill. Among those who opposed it was Professor Tagantsev, who objected to the death penalty on principle. Other opponents argued that, given the fact of October 17, it was better to have the old law live out its days than to replace it with another that still called for the death penalty.

His Majesty did not discuss the majority and minority views of the State Council concerning this bill with me, but apparently acting under the influence of Prince Obolenskii and Metropolitan Antonii he chose to approve the view of the minority, thus letting the old law stand. I regretted that in so doing the Emperor permitted the continuation of the unfair and arbitrary use of the death penalty, but I could at least interpret his action as a sign that in his heart he opposed the death penalty.

Unfortunately, worse was to come. After I left office, Durnovo's successor as minister of interior, Stolypin, persuaded the Emperor to agree to the use of Article 87 for the enactment of a law instituting field courts-martial, which resulted in even more arbitrary, extensive, and barbarous use of the death penalty.[28] (By the way, General Pavlov, the chief military procurator, had presented a proposal for field courts-martial to my cabinet, but we had found it unacceptable and had unanimously rejected it.)[29]

Civil Rights

In the October 17 Manifesto, the Emperor pledged that he would grant civic freedom—inviolability of person, freedom of conscience, speech, assembly, and association—to his people. Where such freedom exists, it is guaranteed by laws and an independent judiciary against arbitrary action on the part of officialdom. Under Emperor Alexander II one can say that there were some laws, appropriate to the stage of development of the nation, that protected the civil rights of the people. But under the influence of the events of March 1, Emperor Alexander III weakened these laws through temporary legislation enacted by the Committee of Ministers.[30]

One such temporary law was the one dealing with exceptional measures, the essence of which was to permit a locality to be placed more or less outside the law, subject to the arbitrary power of a civilian or military administrator. This law, enacted for a three-year period, continued to be renewed for successive three-year periods. After I became premier it was again renewed, as before, by the Committee of Ministers,[31] in the expectation that by the end of that period there would be no necessity to extend the law. Unfortunately, Stolypin was in power when that time arrived, and, with Imperial approval, relying on Article 87, he renewed the law for another three years, and when those three years were over, the law was once more renewed. What is worse, Stolypin interpreted the law far more broadly than had his predecessors, with the result that the guarantee of personal inviolability and other civil rights was honored in the breach.[32] And now I shall deal with what was done during my tenure to establish civic freedom.

During the course of the unpleasant meeting with the press immediately after October 17, to which I have referred earlier, I was asked by some of the more responsible journalists to explain the meaning of the phrase "freedom of speech" in the October 17 Manifesto. I said that it referred primarily to freedom of the press. I am still of the same opinion. Freedom of the press, like other phenomena, has both good and bad sides, but the good outweighs the bad. A free press, even when it exceeds its rights, is essential to prevent abuse of power by the administration, to guarantee that it acts within the law.

As I have noted earlier, a commission under the chairmanship of Kobeko had been at work for some time, in accordance with the decree of December 12, 1904, in preparing new press laws, but it had not yet completed its task when I took office. Accordingly, as a temporary measure, the Chief Administration for Press Affairs, acting on my instructions, issued regulations on October 19 easing limitations on the press: all previous instructions to the censorship authorities that were not based on existing press laws were rescinded, and these authorities were instructed to act in the spirit of the October 17 Manifesto by using restraint and by refraining from any action *not based on law*.

Unable to draft new press laws quickly, Kobeko provided help in the form of temporary press regulations, which were considered by the cabinet, then the State Council, and finally enacted by Imperial decree on November 24, 1905.* The decree reaffirmed the commitment to freedom of speech and stated, among other things, that, pending the enactment of a new press law by the legislative bodies, violations of the press laws would be dealt with by the courts and not by administrative authorities.

Unfortunately, many of the recently established newspapers refused to obey some of the new regulations. As a result, a new decree was issued [on March 18] amending the decree of November 24, but without changing its substance.[33] Then on April 26, the day before the opening of the State Duma, regulations dealing with nonperiodical publications, regulations prepared by my cabinet and reviewed by the State Council, were promulgated.

Although six years have passed since my departure from office, the temporary press regulations prepared under me have not been replaced by a permanent legislation. To be sure, Stolypin considered the temporary press regulations to be too liberal, but he did not seek to replace them with permanent ones, instead relying on other means to deal with the press. This I learned in 1907 from Kokovtsev. I was informed that when Kokovtsev, then minister of finance, and Kaufmann, then minister of education, suggested preparing a new press law for consideration by the legislative bodies, Stolypin and other ministers objected and undertook instead to deal with the press by relying on the law on exceptional measures. Although some ministers protested against such highhanded action, Stolypin followed his own counsel. Accordingly, when something in a newspaper displeased a minister or other higher official, the prefect or governor in the area involved would receive a phone call directing that the offending newspaper be fined. Then, if it appeared the fine were not enough, the prefect or governor would be directed to jail the editor of the newspaper for a few months, by administrative action. Even when editors were taken to court, in accordance with the temporary press regulations, these regulations were interpreted to suit the

---

*Poor Kobeko! After fifty years of service to the fatherland, he fell into Imperial disfavor because of his work on the press laws and was excluded from the list of active members of the State Council. A courtier, whose name I do not remember, told me that the Emperor in speaking of Kobeko said: "I will never forget the manner in which he handled the matter of the press law."

wishes of the administration, this as a result of the influence of the minister of justice, Shcheglovitov.

Thus, the solemn promise of freedom of the press remains unfulfilled. And the press interprets "freedom of the press" to suit its interests. The right-wing newspapers cry about the irresponsibility of other newspapers and of the need to curb them, but the moment action is taken against them, usually for stepping on the toes of highly placed persons, they scream about "unheard of" restriction on the press. The moderate press, particularly of the "how can I be of service" kind, shifts in all directions: sometimes it argues that some newspapers owned by competitors (particularly if they are Jews) should be bridled, but if their own rights are infringed they immediately call for enactment of a permanent press law. As for the left-wing press, it considers any limitation, even if it be in accordance with law, as a political crime, an infringement on its right to present the news as it sees fit, a right it uses to imperil the Russian Empire.

Because the temporary regulations concerning the right of assembly issued a few days before October 17 were not enough to fulfill the promise made in the October 17 Manifesto of freedom of assembly and association (including the right to form trade unions), my cabinet drafted temporary legislation, which resulted in two Imperial decrees issued on March 4, 1906. The first dealt with the right of association, the other with the right of assembly, and both were to remain in force until the legislative bodies could prepare permanent legislation.

These decrees were received in the same spirit as were the press regulations: most of society and most newspapers did not deem these decrees sufficiently liberal and hoped that the State Duma and the State Council would do better. Well, in the years that followed the State Duma produced neither a law concerning the right of assembly nor one concerning the right of association. And Stolypin, particularly after the *coup d'état* of June 3, 1907, paid even less heed to the decrees of March 4, 1906, than he did to the temporary press regulations, acting on the expressed view that the law means what the administration wants it to mean.

With respect to the promise of freedom of conscience, the decree of April 17, 1905, remained in effect.[34]

Thus, under my leadership the most essential promises made in the October 17 Manifesto were fully carried out. The promise of inviolability of person was assured because the law on exceptional measures could not be applied without consent of the State Duma and the State Council. Temporary legislation providing for freedom of the press, freedom to form associations, including unions, and freedom of assembly was enacted. As for freedom of conscience, the principle of toleration had, as I have indicated, already been established by the decree of April

17, 1905. Also, the legislative bodies were provided with adequate checks on the work of the administration.[35]

I have already indicated that what was accomplished during my tenure in establishing civic freedom has been undermined since I left office. In fact, because of administrative abuses, there is less freedom now than before October 17. Why?

First of all, because all the revolutionary and virtually all the liberal parties have acted shortsightedly and irresponsibly, literally throwing off all restraints and unrealistically rejecting the October 17 Manifesto as inadequate and then rejecting all that was done to carry it out. Second, their senseless attack on the existing structure of our great nation and Empire produced, as similar attacks in other countries have done, a counterrevolutionary attack, a reaction supported by those in high places unhappy over the new order created by October 17. Third was the contribution of the Stolypin regime, which professed to believe in the October 17 Manifesto, but which in fact did whatever suited its interests.

How will it all end? I am convinced that in time Russia will become a truly constitutional state, like other civilized states. The October 17 Manifesto marked an irreversible change. Once its call was heard in Russia, neither military force nor administrative machinations could restore the old order. What is not certain is whether more blood will have to be shed before Russia becomes a truly constitutional state. As a true monarchist, as a loyal servant of the Romanov dynasty, as one who has served Emperor Nicholas II loyally, is deeply devoted to him, I pray God, for his sake, that this be accomplished peacefully.

The Peasant Question

I cannot deal with all the other legislation enacted during my tenure as premier, but I do wish to say something about my efforts to establish the basis for the complete reorganization of peasant life. As will be recalled, much of the groundwork had already been laid by the Special Conference on the Needs of Rural Industry, of which I was chairman, for the gradual transition to individual peasant landownership and the establishment of full legal equality between the peasantry and the rest of the population. Unfortunately, as I have noted, this conference was closed, in March 1905, as a result of the intrigues of Goremykin and Trepov, before it could complete its work. Also, I have already noted Professor Migulin's proposal for confiscation of privately owned land for the benefit of the peasantry and the fate of that proposal. Although I had little time given to me, I, working with my cabinet, was able to provide some aid to the peasantry.

Although we were in the midst of serious financial difficulties, about which I have spoken, and we could therefore ill afford to reduce revenues, I felt it was necessary to end the payment of redemption dues by the peasants for the land allotted to them by Emperor Alexander II. The cabinet prepared recommendations that resulted in the Imperial manifesto and decree of November 3, 1905, which terminated the payment of such dues and enabled the Peasants' Bank to make it easier for peasants to purchase privately owned land.[36]

Subsequently the Chief Administration for Land Organizations and Agriculture and local authorities were provided the means for studying the condition of the peasantry and finding means to help it. All these efforts created a solid foundation for easing the condition of the peasantry and for reorganizing its way of life, but because my government felt that fundamental changes should be left to the State Duma and the State Council, it considered its task to be that of providing these bodies with the material necessary for them to conduct their deliberations.

Accordingly, the cabinet worked out a carefully detailed program for the reorganization of peasant life, based largely on the work of the Special Conference on the Needs of Rural Industry. This program was phrased in the form of questions and was to be transmitted to the State Duma as soon as it opened. It was based on the principles I have already mentioned: the gradual and voluntary transition from communal to individual ownership among the peasantry and the establishment of legal equality between the peasantry and the rest of the population. These materials provided the basis for the agrarian program carried out by the Stolypin government, which, unfortunately, perverted the program by making the transition neither gradual nor voluntary.

The Jewish Question

Very soon after I became premier I agreed to receive a Jewish delegation led by Baron Ginzburg (a fine man and a very rich one). Among those who accompanied him, as I recall, were Vinaver (a lawyer and a leading Kadet), Sliozberg (also a lawyer), Kulisher (also a lawyer, whom I knew from my Kievan days, when he took a prominent part in *Zaria*, a very liberal newspaper for its day), Varshavskii (a fairly rich man whose father was a member of the notorious firm of Gorvits, Kogan, and Varshavskii).[37] Their object: that I plead with the Emperor to grant Jews full legal rights.[38]

I told them that they must be aware, as everyone was, that I was no Judeophobe. I said that I believed that in the long run the Jewish problem in Russia would have to be solved as it had been in all other civilized countries, by granting Jews legal equality with the rest of the population. For the short run, however, I believed that the transition to legal equality must be gradual, because if it were abrupt we would see genuine, not government-inspired, pogroms in some rural areas.

I said, moreover, that before I could argue for equal rights for Jews, they would have to show by their behavior that they deserved them. To do so they would have to state publicly to the Emperor that they asked him for no more than to be treated like other subjects, and then they would have to support their words by deeds, i.e., by giving up their prominent role in the opposition movement. (That Jews played such a prominent role in it is explained, and possibly justified, in large part, by their lack of rights, as well as by the pogroms carried out against them by the rabble, pogroms that were not only tolerated by the government but in fact organized by it, but it is true, nonetheless, that Jews played a prominent role in the unrest and revolutionary turmoil of recent years.)

Referring to this role, I said: "That is not your business. Leave it to those who are Russian by blood as well as by law. It is not your business to teach others. Your business is to worry about yourselves, for you can see how much you and your children have suffered from your behavior."

Baron Ginzburg, Sliozberg, and Kulisher agreed with me. The rest, particularly Vinaver, did not. Vinaver declared that the time had come for Russia to achieve civic freedom and full rights for all and that Jews should support with all their might those Russians struggling against the government to achieve these goals. With this the meeting came to an end.

Later, in the summer of 1907, I had occasion to repeat my advice to a group of Jewish leaders in Frankfurt-am-Main, which included Ashkenazi (a citizen of Frankfurt, a fine, rich man, of Russian origin, whom I had long known), the chief spokesman for German Jewry, and the well-known Dr. Nathan, who had come there from Berlin. Dr. Nathan reacted to my words as Vinaver had. However, when I was subsequently in Paris and repeated my advice to Baron Eduard Rothschild and several other French Jews, they agreed with me, but said they were unable to influence Russian Jewry.

Jews can decide whether I or their tactless (a mild word in this case) advisors were right. Nowadays [1912], the Jewish question in Russia is as acute as it ever was. In fact, Jews are now subject to fiercer persecution than ever before. I don't think that the persecutors themselves know where they are going, nor what they hope to accomplish.

One may dislike Jews. One may consider them an accursed people, but one must recognize that they are human and that Russian Jews are subjects of the Emperor. There is only one way to deal with them, and that is by gradually assimilating them, as has been done in all other civilized countries, e.g., Germany, France, England, Italy, and America.

Some Afterthoughts

I have been dealing at some length with events over which I had some control while I was premier. I will now return briefly to events and forces over which I had no control.[39]

As I have noted, when I assumed the reins of government the country was virtually in a state of madness. The most evident sign of the breakdown of public and governmental life was the universal dissatisfaction with the status quo that united all classes of the population.

They all wanted changes in the political structure, but their aspirations differed according to class and status. The nobility had no objection to limiting the powers of the Emperor, if this were for its own benefit, by the creation of an aristocratic, constitutional monarchy. The merchants and industrialists dreamed of a bourgeois, constitutional monarchy, under the hegemony of capital, of the Russian

Rothschilds. The intelligentsia, i.e., the members of the various professions, dreamed of a democratic, constitutional monarchy that would ultimately be transformed into something like the French bourgeois republic. The workers thought of filling their bellies and were therefore easily attracted by socialist ideas. And then there was the peasantry, the bulk of the Russian people, which wanted more land and sought liberation from the arbitrary power exercised over them by bureaucrat and landed noble: they dreamed of a Tsar acting on behalf of the people in the manner of an Alexander II, who emancipated the serfs and violated the sanctity of private property in giving them land. The peasantry was inclined to fuse the ideal of a constitutional monarchy with the socialist principles of the Trudoviki, who believe that the land belongs to those who till it.

In any case, everyone wanted change. Everyone attacked the power of the Autocracy and its tool, the bureaucracy. Then came October 17, which split society into parties that fought among themselves, some of them seeking support from the autocratic regime and the bureaucracy against their opponents, a situation that still exists.

Even more disturbing to the government were the anarchistic attacks on officials, particularly the police, and the disorders in the armed forces, among peasants and workers, in all schools, and even in some secondary schools, all accompanied by attacks on person and property.*

Although there were few anarchistic attacks on higher officials during my tenure, in contrast to the experience under Stolypin, there was a continuing hunt after me, and even more so against Durnovo, the minister of interior. He defied danger and visited a female acquaintance every day, much to the dismay of his small guard. As for me, I was constantly receiving warnings from the Department of Police, first of all that I not leave my guarded quarters at the Winter Palace and, secondly, that if I had to venture out I was to avoid certain places. But I paid no attention, not because I had no fear of death but because I felt that my position required me to be visible and appear unafraid. I left my residence every day on

---

*During my tenure virtually all higher schools remained closed. Most professors had turned liberal and many no longer showed good sense, but I was certain that given the respect that Count I. I. Tolstoi, the minister of education, enjoyed, quiet would soon return to the academic world. As it turned out, the October 17 Manifesto helped calm the professors down, making it possible for the higher schools to reopen in the fall of 1906, but by that time there was a new minister of education, Kaufmann.

Officialdom had been so engrossed with the disorders in the higher schools before October 17 that it ignored what was happening in the secondary schools. When I became premier it was evident that the spirit of disorder had also enveloped the secondary schools, and Count Tolstoi took measures to correct matters. He introduced the so-called parents' committee into these schools, giving them the right to check on the behavior of the students and the general order of these institutions. These committees proved useful by helping the schools go on about their business, but the current minister of education, the reckless Casso, is trying to eliminate them, evidently in the belief that they are liberal in spirit.

Among other things, Count Tolstoi submitted a proposal to the cabinet for ending the quotas for entrance of Jews into educational institutions. He argued, and I agreed, that the most natural way of solving the Jewish question is to bring Jews into the national educational system. After lengthy consideration, the cabinet voted for the proposal, but the Emperor withheld approval, informing us that he would provide us appropriate instructions at a later date [but never did].

foot. And on the occasions I rode in my automobile I could easily be spotted because of the noise made by the vehicle. God made me so that while I feared danger when it was remote, I was without fear when danger was at hand.

By the way, a good friend of mine, the late Prince Melikov, who had served as marshal of the nobility in Tiflis, told me after I left office that, had I stayed on, a member of one of the extreme revolutionary-anarchist groups in the State Duma would have tried to kill me. He told me that he had learned from two members of the group that lots had been drawn for the task, but that the task had been joyously abandoned when I left office; they would have been sorry to see me killed because I was a native of the Caucasus and, like my relatives, enjoyed respect and affection among its natives.

In short, I inherited a nightmare from my predecessors. As I have noted, the October 17 Manifesto brought some calm to the country. Under my administration order was slowly restored by late December, by which time the troops were being brought back from beyond Lake Baikal and the loan that would save the country was being negotiated and the legislation necessary for the fulfillment of the promises made in the manifesto was being enacted.

Unfortunately, in carrying out my difficult task I had to contend with the shortcomings of the Emperor—his weak character, his unfortunate marriage to a woman who not only failed to compensate for his shortcomings but in fact enhanced them, whose abnormality was reflected in the abnormality of his actions. It was his errors that had led to the necessity for issuing the October 17 Manifesto.

As I have shown, he never would have agreed to it had he not seen that he had no choice, as I showed him. Then, under the influence of highly placed persons in Russia and of world opinion, he forced me to assume the reins of government.

However, it should be said that no matter how unappetizing the manifesto was to the Emperor, no matter how malign the influence of the clique that surrounded him at court and of those nobles who had existed for so long at the expense of the people, he would have carried out the promises made on October 17 if the educated classes had shown the good sense of immediately parting company with the revolutionaries. But, as I have shown, they did not rise to the occasion, something that requires considerable political experience.

Had they been sensible, the educated classes would have realized that unless the political system is altered step by step, chaos will result. Instead, they used the occasion of the manifesto to present extreme demands while the left-wing revolutionaries engaged in violence. Such actions led to the creation of right-wing revolutionary parties, which soon found support at court, and ultimately from the Emperor himself, support that remained covert as long as I was in power, but not thereafter.

Another fact to be kept in mind is that as the Emperor saw the country becoming calmer his fear of a revolutionary overthrow began to diminish and he began to ignore my advice and act behind my back on his own, notably in dealing with members of my cabinet. His view was that the role of premier was limited to coordinating rather than directing the ministers, who remained responsible to him. As early as January 31 he made this view explicit in a comment on one of my reports. This meant that the premier could be ignored or circumvented when it seemed desirable and that the Emperor felt free to deal directly with individual ministers without informing the premier of what he was telling them. The minister who especially lent himself to such circumvention was Durnovo. As will be recalled, the Emperor had objected to the appointment of Durnovo because he had considered him too liberal, but when he came to realize that the minister was ready to advance his career by trying to trip me up and by dissociating himself from me while drawing closer to General Trepov, he began to pay less attention to what I had to say.

XV

The End of My Tenure

Although the Emperor and many others increasingly circumvented me because I was insufficiently docile, they were afraid to see me go until the loan necessary to save the government from bankruptcy was completed and the troops were back from beyond Lake Baikal. Although I felt it my duty to stay on as premier at least until these two goals were reached, there were many occasions when I felt that I could not stay under the anomalous conditions in which I found myself, nothing more than quasi-premier. Because General Trepov and Grand Duke Nicholas Nikolaevich were the men whom the Emperor most trusted, I took occasion to tell them of my feelings. I told the Grand Duke that although I was prepared to take responsibility for what I did, I was not prepared to take responsibility for what others did and wished that the Emperor would relieve me of my duties. He said nothing. Several days after I had spoken to General Trepov in a similar vein, the general told me that the Emperor categorically refused to let me go. And when I spoke directly to the Emperor about my wish he either changed the subject or told me that there were still two major tasks for me to complete, the conclusion of the loan and the return of the troops.

Subsequently, when I had decided that I could no longer endure the abnormal position in which I had been put, I decided to send a formal, written request to the Emperor asking to be let go.[1]

Before taking this step I informed several colleagues, among them Admiral Birilev, the minister of the navy, of my intention. The following day he tried to change my mind. As he argued it became evident, as he admitted, that he was acting at the behest of the Empress, whose favor he enjoyed. He insisted that as long as the Emperor had not told me that he had lost confidence in me it was my duty to stay on. He told me that when he had accepted his appointment, he did so on one condition, which the Emperor accepted, that if the

Emperor ever lost confidence in him, he would tell the admiral so frankly.
In reply I said:

> My relations with the Emperor are now completely abnormal because I will
> not agree to be a puppet, with the strings nominally in his hands, but actually in
> the hands of another. As soon as I was able to arrange the loan and the troops
> began to return from Trans-Baikalia, as soon as they felt they could get along
> without me, relations began to become even more abnormal. You say that I
> should stay on, if not for the sake of the Tsar, then at least for the sake of the
> fatherland. If I stayed on I would in effect serve as a puppet to General Trepov,
> Grand Duke Nicholas Nikolaevich, and a host of Black Hundreds figures who
> are now making their appearance on stage, and then I would be of no use to Tsar
> or fatherland. And even if I stayed on under such conditions, the Emperor
> would get rid of me the first time I showed opposition, an act from which he now
> refrains for fear of a repetition of the events that led to October 17.[2]

The admiral argued that I had the duty to remain at my post as long as the
Emperor did not tell me he had lost confidence in me, but a contrary view was to
be presented to me after I had left office by several people, that it was my duty to
leave office the moment the Emperor disagreed with me on a major issue. They
were wrong, for to have done so would have meant inflicting severe, possibly
irreparable, damage on Russia. Also, I would have imposed a very heavy burden
on the Emperor, who, whatever his shortcomings, is my Sovereign. As I have said
earlier, if he were to fall, the monarchy would be shaken to its foundations. And I
was born and raised a monarchist and hope to die one. Moreover, as I have said, I
am bound by close ties to the dynasty: I was one of Emperor Alexander III's most
cherished ministers, have known Emperor Nicholas II since he was a young man,
have served him for many years. I have a duty to him.

Although I expected to leave office before the opening of the State Duma, I felt
obliged to have ready for its consideration all the legislative proposals necessary
for fulfilling the promises made in the October 17 Manifesto and for repairing the
damages wrought by war and sedition. Consequently, I devoted many sessions of
the cabinet to this matter.

The most important of these meetings took place on March 5, when I once
more raised the question of preparing the necessary legislative proposals. I said
that it was imperative that the State Duma's activities should from the start be
directed toward *definite and broad, but realistic and relevant questions so as to make certain
that its work would be productive. The most pressing and important of these questions*, I told
the cabinet, was the reorganization of the peasant way of life, and therefore we
had to move as rapidly as we could in preparing the material we would present to
the State Duma. Also, I told my colleagues, it was imperative for the government
to appear before that body with a *well-organized* program.

By the middle of April, this program was ready, including the thoroughly prepared proposal for the reorganization of peasant life about which I have already spoken. Because each deputy had to be provided with a copy of each proposal, a joke went around that my government had prepared a whole trainload of proposals for the State Duma.

At this point I felt ready to make a formal request to be relieved of my burdensome position. On April 14 I sent His Majesty the following letter:

Your Imperial Majesty:

At the time I concluded the loan I had the honor of most humbly requesting Your Imperial Majesty to release me from my duties as premier before the opening of the State Duma in order to help matters. Your Imperial Majesty listened most kindly to what I had to say then. Now I am taking the liberty of most humbly enumerating the reasons behind my request:

(1) I am worn out from the badgering from all sides that I have experienced and have become so nervous that I cannot maintain the equilibrium required of a premier, particularly under new circumstances.

(2) With all due respect to the firmness and energy shown by the minister of interior, I am convinced, as Your Imperial Majesty is aware, that the course of actions he and several local officials have followed is improper, particularly the actions of the last two months, following the suppression of large-scale revolutionary activity. In my opinion, such actions have antagonized most of the population, many of whom then voted for extremist candidates as a means of registering protest.

(3) It would be difficult for me to appear side by side with the minister of interior before the Duma. If I did, I would have to remain silent while he was being interpellated about actions of the government which were taken either without my knowledge or without my consent, for I have no executive power. Also, it might be embarrassing for him to offer explanations of his actions with which I did not agree.

(4) There is no agreement in the cabinet or in influential circles about major political questions such as those concerning the peasantry, the Jews, and religious toleration,[3] and I do not agree with the views of the extreme conservatives which have *recently* become part of the political credo of the minister of interior.

(5) At the recent conference concerning the Fundamental Laws, State Councillor Count Pahlen and State Councillor Goremykin (chairman of the peasant conference, who is considered by some an expert on the peasant question) spoke not only about the nature of the peasant question but about how the government should deal with it.* It is a fact that the peasant question will be the chief one facing the Duma. Therefore, if their views are correct, they should have the opportunity of implementing them.†

*Goremykin said that if the Duma raised the question of confiscation, it should be immediately dissolved.

†It might appear that I inspired the appointment of Goremykin to succeed me.

(6) During my tenure I have been attacked by all those in Russian society who can scream and write, as well as by the extreme elements that have access to Your Imperial Majesty. The revolutionaries curse me because I have strongly and conscientiously favored the use of the most decisive measures that were taken during the period of active revolution. And liberals attack me because, in keeping with my sense of duty and my conscience, I have defended, and will continue to defend, as long as I live, the prerogatives of the Emperor. As for conservatives, they attack me because they have mistakenly blamed me for all the changes in our political system that have taken place since the appointment of Prince Sviatopolk-Mirskii as minister of interior.* It is evident that as long as I remain in office, I shall be violently attacked from all sides. What has made the conduct of government especially difficult for me is the lack of confidence in me of extremely conservative nobles and high officials who naturally have had and will continue to have access to the Tsar and consequently will continue to be able to inspire doubts about the actions, and even the intentions, of those who displease them.

(7) When the Duma opens, the government should either come to terms with it or else follow a very firm and decisive policy toward it, being ready to use the most extreme measures. If the first course is chosen, it will be easier to carry out if those ministers who have become objects of attack and the premier, who has become a source of bitterness for this or that influential group during this time of stress, should be replaced. If the second course is followed, the principal persons in carrying it out will be the ministers of interior, justice, and war, in which case I would be in the way, for no matter what I did, the extreme conservatives would criticize me bitterly.

There are other cogent reasons I could present to support my request to be released from my post before the opening of the Duma, but it seems to me that the ones I have presented should suffice to persuade Your Imperial Majesty to accede to my request. I would have submitted it earlier, as soon as I became aware that my position as premier was shaky, but I did not believe that I had the right to do so as long as Russia's financial position was as perilous as it was. I considered it my duty to save Russia from financial ruin or, what was even worse, from circumstances that would have permitted the Duma to exploit the needs of the government to force concessions that would be in the interests of the party making the demands but not in the interests of the state, which are identical with those of Your Imperial Majesty.

All the revolutionary and antigovernmental parties have good reason to attack me, because I had the chief, if not exclusive, role in concluding the loan. Now that the loan, granted under favorable terms, is a fact, and now that the country has reached a fair degree of calm and Your Imperial Majesty can turn His Imperial attention to domestic affairs, free of the need to find the means of meeting the costs of the recently concluded war, I believe that I have the moral

*I approved of his appointment, but had no part in it because I was then in disfavor.

right to renew my request to Your Imperial Majesty. Therefore, I take the liberty of placing at the feet of Your Imperial Majesty my most humble request that you show me the kindness of acceding to my request.

On the evening of April 14, with my request already on the way, I held a meeting of the cabinet at which I read the text of my letter. P. N. Durnovo listened quietly. It was obvious that all were disturbed by my request to leave office because it brought their futures into question. Several wanted to follow my example, but I dissuaded them in the belief that by joining me they would be creating a precedent for a parliamentary form of government. Count I. I. Tolstoi approved of my decision, saying he knew what kind of intrigue against me was going on at court and, that no matter what, once the Emperor could do without me, he would get rid of me because of my intractability.

Two days later, in the evening, I received the following hand-written letter from the Emperor:

Count Sergei Iulevich:
Yesterday morning I received your letter asking to be released from your duties. I accede to your request.[4]

The successful conclusion of the loan constitutes the finest page in your list of accomplishments. It is a great moral victory for the government and constitutes a guarantee of a calm future and the peaceful development of Russia. It is evident that the prestige of our fatherland is high in Europe.[*]

How things will go after the opening of the Duma only God knows. But I do not take as dim a view of the future as you do.[†]

It seems to me that we have an extremist Duma not because of the reaction to repressive measures on the part of the government, but because of the breadth of the electoral law of December 11, the inertness of the conservative majority, and the total failure of all authorities to try to influence the elections, something that does not happen in other countries.

Sergei Iulevich, I thank you sincerely for your devotion to me and for the great zeal you have shown during the very difficult six months of your tenure. I hope that you will rest and regain your health.

Gratefully,
Nicholas

The following day I saw the Emperor, who asked me whom I would suggest as my replacement.[5] I replied that this would depend on which course he intended to follow. If His Majesty were thinking of following a liberal policy, in the spirit of the October 17 Manifesto, I would suggest Filosofov—young, intelligent, and ener-

---

[*]Apparently the Emperor thought that our prestige in Asia was particularly high after the recent, disgraceful war with Japan. Several courtiers told me that the Russians had smashed the Japanese.
[†]Subsequent events justified me.

getic. But if His Majesty proposed to follow the line recently propagated by the extreme right, I would advise him to appoint Akimov, the minister of justice. As I learned later he did, in fact, offer the post to Akimov, who declined to accept it. Meanwhile, Goremykin, aided by Trepov, was scheming behind the scenes.

On April 22, the following Imperial rescript was published:

> Count Sergei Iulevich:
>
> The weakening of your health brought on by the extraordinary tasks you have carried out have impelled you to ask to be released from the post of premier.
>
> When I summoned you to this major position, I was certain that your abilities and your governmental experience would facilitate the preparation of the new electoral bodies created for the purpose of implementing the rights I granted to the people. Thanks to your determined and enlightened efforts, these institutions have been established and are ready to begin work despite the obstacles created by the seditious groups in the struggle with which you have demonstrated your characteristic energy and decisiveness. At the same time, thanks to your experience in financial matters, you have helped assure the government's financial stability through the conclusion of a loan for Russia.
>
> In granting your most humble request, I feel obliged to express my sincere recognition of the many services you have rendered the fatherland, in recognition of which I appoint you knight of the Order of Saint Alexander Nevskii [these words in his own hand] with diamonds. I remain inalterably well disposed toward you [also in his own hand] and sincerely grateful.
>
> Nicholas

The following day, in uniform, I paid an official call on the Emperor, to thank him for granting my request. Since the Empress was with him I had the opportunity of paying my respects to her as well. Both behaved kindly toward me. (Her Majesty, of course, had never been favorably disposed toward me, and I am told that when she heard that I was leaving, she uttered a sound of relief.)

In the course of our conversation,* the Emperor asked me to accept the first ambassadorial post that would become vacant. I asked if he were thinking about Tokyo,[6] a post so distant that I could not have accepted it because of my poor health. He said that he had in mind a European appointment and added: "Please remind me as soon as an ambassadorial post becomes vacant so that I can appoint you immediately." I replied that I was ready to carry our His Majesty's orders and would be happy to spend a few years away from Russia.

He then asked if I would mind serving under a foreign minister much younger than I. I found the question puzzling. I said that although I outranked Count

---

*During this conversation he asked that I return the letters and notes he had written me while I was premier. I complied but regret that I did because these documents reveal so much about the Emperor's mental processes and because they help explain my actions, which became the subject of later criticism, stemming, for the most part, from court circles.

Lambsdorff, he was my senior in length of service and that, in any case, we were such good friends that the difference of rank was inconsequential. The Emperor then said that Count Lambsdorff would be replaced by Izvolskii, to which I replied that I knew that ambassadors were subordinate to the Emperor and not to the minister of foreign affairs. The Emperor said: "Exactly." (A year later I informed the Emperor of a vacant ambassadorial post, but received no reply.)

The Emperor went on to tell me that he had decided to appoint one of my enemies as my successor, but that I was not to think that he was appointing the man because he was my enemy. I asked which of my enemies the person might be—Schwanebach, Prince Shirinskii-Shikhmatov, Goremykin?[7] The answer was "Goremykin." (I believe that the choice was inspired by Trepov, and I already knew that the choice had been made.) He told me, by the way, that he had thought of offering the post to Muravev, our ambassador to Rome, but had decided against it because of the man's poor personal reputation.

On April 27 I attended the ceremonies marking the opening of the sessions of the First State Duma and the reorganized State Council. These ceremonies took place at the Winter Palace, where the members of the two bodies, as well as higher officials and members of high society, assembled.

The Emperor, accompanied by the chief officials of the court and his suite, entered the hall in solemn procession. It was an historic occasion, the first and only meeting of the Emperor with the representatives of the people. His Majesty then took his place. Looking quite pale and solemn, but calm, he welcomed the members of the two bodies in a short, thoughtful speech, which was based on a draft given to Trepov on April 25 by V. I. Kovalevskii, who had prepared it with the help, among others, of some of the pillars of the Kadet party.[8] I will not give the text of the speech here, but one sentence remains in my memory: "My deepest desire is to see my people happy and my son heir to a strong, well-organized state. May this wish be fulfilled." It is very unfortunate that several of His Majesty's instructions were not carried out faithfully. I believe that a painting was made of this occasion.

During the next weeks I attended sessions of the reorganized State Council, then left for Brussels to visit my daughter. My second period of being out of favor had begun.

Appendix

Origin of the October Manifesto
The Witte, Vuich, and Obolenskii Memoranda

During my tenure as premier I did not consider it proper to relate how the October Manifesto came into being.[1] But I changed my mind after I left office and began to hear rumors that the notion was being spread at court that I had forced the Emperor to issue the manifesto. These rumors are of a piece with what appears daily in such Black Hundreds' organs as *Russkoe znamia* and *Moskovskie vedomosti*, accusing me of being a traitor, a Mason, of being in the pay of the Jews and the like.* It is well known that such papers receive support from some members of the court, with the backing of Empress Alexandra Fedorovna. This means that such newspapers are subsidized by the government, with money that comes chiefly from the lower classes.

Then I heard that the Empress herself took the liberty of saying that I had forced the manifesto on her husband. Although he does not take such liberties, he appears to lend support to such allegations by his attitude toward me, which intimates that I had somehow acted improperly toward him, and by his silence when members of his suite chatter about such things. A clue to his thoughts is supplied by the incautious phrases uttered by the Empress. I use the word "incautious" because I do not consider it proper to use a more accurate word. Those who try to protect the Emperor by suggesting that this unlimited monarch signed so important a document under duress or that he began a most shameful and terrible war because he was misinformed by people who told him that we would "destroy the baboons" do not understand that in trying to protect the monarch by such means they are dealing a dangerous blow to his power.

*In spreading these rumors the court camarilla was also trying to incite the hooligans of the Union of the Russian People against me. In this they twice succeeded, but God spared me as He had on similar occasions when I was in dreadful danger.

604

Even though they have titles, such persons are both stupid and contemptible.

It was this atmosphere of foul rumors that finally forced me to prepare a memorandum setting forth my account of the origins of the October Manifesto. I prepared it on the basis of a brief accoùnt that Vuich, who was *au courant* with the events, prepared. I first asked Vuich to read the memorandum. He found no errors. I next sent it to General Rödiger, the minister of war, who replied by letter (now in my archive) suggesting only one editorial correction, which I accepted.

Then, on January 30, 1907, I mailed the memorandum to Baron Freedericksz, who was also acquainted with the events described, asking him to point out any inaccuracies he might find. Also, I told him that I did not feel it right to disturb the Emperor by submitting it to him. I asked the baron "to be *sure* to return the memorandum to me with any observations you might make."

A few days later I saw General Mosolov, director of the Chancellery of the Court, who told me that my memorandum had been found to be accurate and that a reply was being drafted. A few days later he told me that he had submitted the draft of the reply to Baron Freedericksz, together with a suggestion that he show the memorandum to His Majesty. Prince N. D. Obolenskii told me that the memorandum was given to the Emperor, who kept it for two weeks, then returned it to Baron Freedericksz, saying that it was accurate.

Because I did not hear anything from the baron, I asked him on March 25 when I might expect a reply. He told me that he had found the memorandum to be accurate except on one point: as he recalled it, when he saw me during the evening of October 16, he told me that Trepov had suggested certain changes in the manifesto. I did not recall this, nor did Prince Obolenskii, who was there. Nonetheless, the baron would not give me a written reply because, as I learned subsequently from Prince N. D. Obolenskii, who had it from the baron, the Emperor had told the baron: "The memorandum prepared by Count Witte is correct, but do not tell him so in writing." What do you think of words such as these, coming from the lips of the Emperor and Autocrat? Can you believe that this is the son of Alexander III, that most noble and upright of monarchs? Herewith is the text of my memorandum.

Memorandum Concerning the Manifesto of October 17, 1905

In view of the severe disorder that broke out in late September and early October of 1905 throughout Russia, but particularly in Petersburg and several other major cities, Count Witte, chairman of the Committee of Ministers, inquired on October 6 if His Majesty would be kind enough to listen to his explanation of the current extremely grave situation. He did this at the insistent request of Count Solskii, chairman of the State Council. On October 8, His Majesty wrote that he would receive Count Witte on the following day, October 9, at 6 p.m., to hear his views concerning the current events.

On October 9, the chairman of the Committee of Ministers had the pleasure of appearing before His Majesty to present a hastily prepared memorandum outlining his view of the current situation. In his opinion His Majesty had two choices: either to follow the course proposed in the memorandum (and presented orally as well) or to appoint a responsible person (a dictator) with complete authority to use unrelenting force to suppress disorder in all its forms. For such a purpose it would be necessary to select a decisive military man. The first course seemed more appropriate, but it might very well be that such an opinion was in error. Therefore, it would be desirable to discuss this matter at a conference with other officials and with those members of the Imperial family who might be concerned. His Majesty listened kindly to Count Witte but did not express his opinion.

On his return from Peterhof, Count Witte and N. I. Vuich, the acting chief administrative assistant to the chairman of the Committee of Ministers, reviewed the hastily prepared memorandum, made some corrections in it, and added to it that there was another course of action. That was to go against the current, but to do so required decisive and systematic action. Count Witte doubted that such a course would succeed. In any event, whatever course was chosen, it should be implemented by a person who believed in it.

On the following day, October 10, at 1 p.m., Count Witte had the pleasure of presenting to the Emperor, in the presence of the Empress, the revised memorandum, explaining it in detail and speaking once more about the second possible course. Their Majesties did not express their opinion about the document, but His Majesty suggested *that it might be best to publish a manifesto based on it.*

During the following two days Count Witte received no news of any kind from Peterhof. It was about this time, at a meeting under Solskii, at which, among other things, there was discussion of the very dangerous situation produced by current unrest that was approaching rebellion, that General-Adjutant Chikhachev and Count Pahlen insisted that the first priority was to put down all disorder by force of arms. Count Witte did not fail to report this opinion in writing to His Majesty, recommending that he hear the views of these high officials. General-Adjutant Chikhachev later asked Count Witte if it had been at his suggestion that the Emperor had been kind enough to summon him. Count Witte replied that he did not know, but said that he had considered it his duty to inform the Emperor of the views of certain high officials about how to deal with the existing situation and to suggest that it would be very useful if His Majesty would hear them out.

Count Witte was informed that on October 11 and 12 his program had been discussed. On October 13, Count Witte received the following telegram from His Majesty:

> Even before I confirm the law concerning a cabinet, I am instructing you to coordinate the activities of the ministers to whom I entrust the task of reestablishing order everywhere. It is only when the work of government is on a calm course that constructive work in concert with the still to be freely elected representatives of my people can go ahead.

As a consequence of this telegram Count Witte went to Peterhof on October 14 and informed the Emperor that coordination of the work of ministers holding varying views would not of itself be sufficient to stop the disorders, that, in his opinion, circumstances demanded decisive measures of one kind or another. In this connection, in view of His Majesty's suggestion on October 10 that it would be useful to express the principles outlined in the memorandum in the form of a manifesto, Count Witte presented to His Majesty a short report summarizing the memorandum. At the beginning of the report it was stated that it had been prepared on the instructions of His Majesty and that it was subject to Imperial confirmation. With respect to the proposed manifesto, Count Witte stated that because it was the kind of document that would be read in all churches it should not be burdened with great detail. On the other hand, an imperially approved report would signify the Emperor's acceptance of the program contained in it, with responsibility falling on Count Witte and not the Emperor. It would be more prudent, therefore, to issue the report rather than a manifesto.

Meanwhile the strike of factory workers in Petersburg and in many cities, as well as the strike of most railroad employees and employees of other establishments, was already in full swing. Many commercial establishments in Petersburg were without lights; streetcars were not running, nor were the railroads. Telegraph service had stopped. On the basis of the instructions he had received from the Emperor, Count Witte felt obliged to hold a meeting with several other ministers—among them General Rödiger, minister of war; General Trepov, assistant minister of interior, governor-general of Petersburg, and commander of the Petersburg garrison; and Prince Khilkov, minister of ways and communications—to consider how best to reestablish railroad communications, at least with nearby cities. Generals Rödiger and Trepov said that, while there were enough troops to put down an armed rising should it break out in Petersburg or in the nearby Imperial residences, there were not enough to reopen railroad traffic even between Petersburg and Peterhof. General Rödiger stated further that the reservists in European Russia, who comprised a large part of the troops there because so many of the regulars had been sent to the front, were restless at not being demobilized now that peace had been concluded. Also contributing to low morale among the troops in European Russia was the fact that they had been used so frequently for police duty.

During the evening of October 14, Prince Orlov telephoned Count Witte to attend a conference at Peterhof the following day, at 11 a.m., under the chairmanship of His Majesty, and to have with him the draft of a manifesto "so that everything will come personally from the Sovereign and so that we can move to translate the measures noted in the report from promises to facts emanating from the Sovereign." Feeling a bit under the weather, Count Witte asked Prince A. D. Obolenskii, who was visiting him, to prepare the requested draft.

When he sailed for Peterhof the following morning, Count Witte, at his request, was accompanied by Prince A. D. Obolenskii and Vuich. Also aboard the ship was Baron Freedericksz. Prince Obolenskii read the draft to the others.

Count Witte made some suggestions for changes. By this time the ship was approaching Peterhof, so he asked Prince Obolenskii to revise his draft on the basis of what had been said, while he and Baron Freedericksz were with the Emperor. When the two arrived to see the Emperor, they found Grand Duke Nicholas Nikolaevich and General-Adjutant Richter already there. At eleven the Emperor received the four of them and asked Count Witte to read the report he had submitted earlier on. After doing so, Count Witte said that it was his deepest conviction that under existing circumstances there were only two courses of action, either a dictatorship or a constitution, the latter being the course that His Majesty had already embarked upon in the manifesto of August 6 and in the laws which accompanied it. The course favored in Count Witte's report would lead to legislation broadening the law of August and would result in a constitutional regime.

With the Emperor's permission Grand Duke Nicholas Nikolaevich asked Count Witte many questions during the reading of the report. Count Witte answered these in detail, adding that he did not believe that it would be easy to restore calm quickly given the cruel war they had been through and the profound unrest they were experiencing, but he believed that the course he favored would produce the desired results more quickly than the other one.

When Count Witte was finished, His Majesty was kind enough to ask Count Witte if he had prepared the manifesto. Count Witte said that a first draft was ready and that he had read it en route to Peterhof and that it was being revised, but that he was still of the opinion that it would be advisable for the Emperor to limit himself to confirming the report just read. At 1 p.m. His Majesty kindly permitted the group to leave and asked that it return at three and that Count Witte have the draft of the manifesto with him.

When the meeting was resumed, opinions were offered about Count Witte's report. Then he read the draft of the manifesto. No one expressed an opinion. Then the Emperor was good enough to adjourn the meeting.

During the evening of October 16, Count Witte was informed that Baron Freedericksz would be calling on him to discuss the manifesto. Not long after midnight the baron, accompanied by General Mosolov, arrived and proceeded to inform Count Witte that the Emperor had consulted various people and that Goremykin and Budberg had prepared two drafts of a manifesto, with which His Majesty wanted him to become acquainted. Count Witte asked immediately if General Trepov had been informed of all that had occurred: after all, the general was responsible for the maintenance of public order throughout the Empire, and any measure taken without his prior knowledge might have unfortunate consequences. Baron Freedericksz replied that he had just come from seeing General Trepov and that was why he was so late. He then gave Count Witte the two drafts to read.*

Count Witte declared he could not accept the draft to which his attention was directed as being the more suitable for two reasons. First, this draft would have the

---

*Baron Freedericksz took the drafts with him, and I was never to see them again.[2]

Emperor grant all the civil and political rights as of the day of publication of the manifesto, whereas in his draft the Sovereign only ordered the government to proceed to implement the Emperor's irrevocable commitment to grant these rights. Second, because in this draft certain substantive measures enunciated in the draft of Count Witte's report were omitted: to publish a manifesto based on this draft together with the report would immediately raise doubts about the strength and soundness of the very principles stated in the report.

For these reasons he asked Baron Freedericksz to inform His Majesty that in his opinion, as he had already had the honor of stating more than once, it would be prudent for His Majesty to do no more than confirm Count Witte's report. To this Baron Freedericksz replied that the matter had already been decided, to publish both the manifesto and the report. On hearing this, Count Witte asked that since it appeared that His Majesty appeared to have some reservations about his, Count Witte's, views, it would be preferable for him to appoint a premier with a more suitable program, assuming that the course of appointing a dictator had been definitely put aside. Perhaps one of the coauthors of the draft in question might be the suitable person. In any event Count Witte asked that the Emperor be informed that he was ready to serve his Sovereign in any capacity, even a secondary one, such as governor of a province.

[By now it was in the early hours of October 17.] A few hours after Baron Freedericksz and General Mosolov had left, Count Witte was summoned to Peterhof. On arriving there he was taken to see Baron Freedericksz, who informed him that it had been decided to accept his draft of a manifesto and his report and that Grand Duke Nicholas Nikolaevich had categorically supported this decision on the ground that there were not enough troops to permit the establishment of a military dictatorship. At 6 p.m., Count Witte and Baron Freedericksz, who had with him the manifesto which had been copied in the chancellery, went to the palace. Grand Duke Nicholas Nikolaevich was already there. In their presence His Majesty was good enough to sign the manifesto and confirm Count Witte's report. Later that day both documents were published, with General Trepov's knowledge.

After having shown the preceding memorandum to Baron Freedericksz, I asked Count Pahlen, who had served as minister of justice under Emperor Alexander II, to read it. He then asked permission to show it to General-Adjutant Richter, who returned it to me several days later with a noncommittal note. When I met the general the following day in the State Council, I asked if he had found any inaccuracy in the document. He replied that he had found it completely accurate. Then I asked Grand Duke Vladimir Aleksandrovich to read it. He returned it within a few days. I learned of his reaction through a letter (now in my archive) from Count I. I. Tolstoi, who is close to the Grand Duke:

> The day after receiving your memorandum the Grand Duke happened to meet Freedericksz and Mosolov while dining at his club. Because you men-

tioned the two in your memorandum, he asked them what they knew about it. Mosolov replied that the memorandum had been submitted to the Emperor for [written] confirmation, but that he would permit Freedericksz to do no more than confirm it orally in general.

Before preparing my memorandum I had received two sets of recollections concerning the events leading to the October 17 Manifesto from men worthy of complete confidence. The first is N. I. Vuich, about whom I have already spoken. The second is Prince N. D. Obolenskii, who was Emperor Alexander III's favorite aide-de-camp, who accompanied the present Emperor when he was Heir on his Far Eastern trip, who is, in all but title, assistant minister of the court and was very close to the Emperor. Also he was close to Empress Alexandra Fedorovna because when she first came to Petersburg he was the only man at the court who showed her any attention. We are close acquaintances. Because he knows everything that goes on in court, including everything that goes on around the Emperor, his brief recollections, which follow those of Vuich, are of value.

N. I. Vuich's Memorandum
(Recollections)

Because Baron Nolde, chief administrative assistant of the Committee of Ministers, left for the Caucasus on September 21, his duties were temporarily assumed by N. I. Vuich, his assistant. It therefore fell to Vuich to inform Count Witte, the chairman of the Committee of Ministers, about the business before that body. The count was extremely preoccupied during those days and several times during our conversations discussed how difficult a situation we were in. He said there were only two courses of action possible, either to declare martial law or to grant a genuine constitution. In this connection he said that uncoordinated actions would not lead to satisfactory results and that repressive actions against the press would be useless because the underground press would immediately grow stronger.

On October 6, Count Witte was asked speedily to prepare a report [for the Emperor] that would suggest that prior to review of the proposal for reorganizing the Committee of Ministers,[3] which was being considered by Count Solskii's conference, its chairman should be given provisional authority to coordinate the activities of the ministers. S. Iu. [Witte] spent the following day at work on this. During the evening he gave Vuich a memorandum[4] which he had prepared on the subject and asked that it be copied. The following morning the copy was given to S. Iu. In the conversation that followed Vuich remarked on the speed with which events were leading to the idea of establishing a constitution. S. Iu. said, with some feeling, that recent times had witnessed Mukden and Tsushima; that because the agricultural conference [the Special Conference on the Needs of Rural Industry] had been closed, the liberal elements who had some ties with it were now looking for a different course of action; that he had come to the conclusion that the means offered them were absolutely inevitable. The chairman asked for a brief report [for the Emperor] based on the memorandum that could be published if the need arose.

On October 9 the chairman made some changes* in the introductory part of the report to indicate that it had been prepared at the direction of His Majesty. Also, the concluding part was revised to read that there was another course of action, to go against the current and that to do so it would be necessary to act decisively and systematically. S. Iu. doubted that such a course could succeed, but acknowledged that he could be mistaken. In any case, whatever course of action was adopted, the person entrusted with its execution should believe in it. On October 10 he saw the Emperor and probably presented the memorandum to His Majesty.

The brief report [for the Emperor] was once more recast and during the evening of October 13 was given a final reading by S. Iu. He said that he would be going to see the Emperor the next day and invited Vuich to accompany him. October 14 was rather unpleasant, marked by snow mixed with rain, and the journey to Peterhof was a bit rocky. Aboard ship the report was read once more. S. Iu. said he would not accept the office of premier if this report were not confirmed.

En route we talked of what a shameful situation we were in, when loyal subjects virtually had to swim to reach their Emperor. When we landed, S. Iu. went directly to the palace, where he remained until one o'clock. During lunch he said that he could have insisted on immediate confirmation of the report, but that he did not wish to force agreement and therefore had been asked to return to the palace for a second audience with the Emperor, from which he came back at five. We returned to St. Petersburg in darkness. S. Iu. said that a decision would be made the following day.

The following day, S. Iu. and Vuich left at 9 a.m. Also aboard were Baron Freedericksz and Prince Alexis D. Obolenskii. It turned out that the prince had with him the draft of a manifesto, about which nothing had been heard from S. Iu. before. After the draft, with its eloquent preamble, was read, S. Iu. said that the draft was not specific enough.

The first point of the body of the draft dealt with freedom of speech, assembly, *et sim.* and stated that the government was to prepare legislation dealing with these freedoms for submission at a time to be specified. Then came the point about broadening the suffrage. This was followed by discussion of the point dealing with the workers, which was immediately deleted in view of the comments by S. Iu.

While we were trying to smooth out the language in the first points, it was suggested that they could be linked to the decree of December 12, 1904, by describing them as a continuation of that decree, but by this time we were ready to debark. So it was decided that for the time being only a rough outline of the substance of the points in the manifesto would be put down, with three points being selected, two of them points proposed by Prince A. D. and a third, concerning the powers of the State Duma. All of this was put down, in brief form, in

*It was recopied the same day and two copies were given to S. Iu.

writing. S. Iu. said that brevity was in order at this point because he would be explaining it all in his report to the Emperor. No particular objections were raised by those present to what was proposed.

Then it was decided that while S. Iu. was at the palace, Vuich and Prince A. D. would try to prepare a final draft of the manifesto. In the course of this preparation virtually all of Prince A. D.'s draft was set aside, and the chief emphasis was placed upon the suggestions that had been made aboard ship.

S. Iu. returned from seeing the Emperor at one, by which time the revised draft was ready. He said that a final decision had not yet been reached and that it might be necessary to wait another day or two. Prince A. D. said anxiously the delay was undesirable, a view with which the others present agreed.

Then the revised draft was read. The first point, stating that the Sovereign had decided to grant freedom of speech *et sim.* and that the government's first task was to implement them was clear and did not elicit any comments. But there was considerable discussion of the two succeeding points. Although Prince Obolenskii argued that changes in the revised draft would lead to unnecessary delay, discussion continued. One question at issue was whether extension of the franchise should be limited to the workers or extended to include other elements of the population that had not been given the vote [under provisions of the law of August 6].

There was also discussion about the statement that elections to the State Duma could be held as already scheduled. S. Iu. agreed with Prince A. D. that changing the legislation concerning the franchise might make it necessary to postpone elections. In the end, however, it was agreed that the statement about holding elections as scheduled should be retained, because delay might not be desirable. Some discussion followed about the part of the manifesto dealing with the legislative powers of the State Duma. It was suggested that it was too specific, but it was recognized that this precision was in keeping with the sense of the report to the Emperor.

At three S. Iu. left to go to the palace and returned after five. He said that Grand Duke Nicholas Nikolaevich, Baron Freedericksz, and General Richter had taken part in the conference with the Emperor. He reported that the Grand Duke had at first called for strong measures but had come to agree with the ideas of S. Iu., as had General Richter. He recounted that the Emperor said: "If I agree, I will let you know tomorrow."

The next day passed without S. Iu. receiving any word from Peterhof. At 10 p.m. he crossed himself and said that there was obviously no point in waiting for the document and that he considered himself freed from further obligation in that matter because he had learned that Goremykin and Budberg had been summoned to see the Emperor at six and that it was for that reason that he had received no final answer that day.

There was no further news until the morning of October 17, when it was learned that during the preceding night there had been talks to the effect that S. Iu.'s report not be published at all and that the manifesto had been revised to state that the Sovereign was immediately granting reforms, omitting any reference to the need for preparing legislation to implement the reforms. S. Iu. said he could not agreed with such wording.

That afternoon he sailed for Peterhof, where he went directly to see His Majesty and returned from him with a signed manifesto and confirmation of his report. On the return journey he declared that if it were possible to hold out until the convening of the State Duma all would be saved, but that if it turned out that it was impossible to hold elections he could guarantee nothing.

On October 20, at the direction of S. Iu., an official announcement was published in *Pravitelstvennyi vestnik* to the effect that implementation of the reforms listed in the October 17 Manifesto would require legislative definition as well as several administrative decisions and that until all this was accomplished all existing laws would remain in effect.

Nicholas Vuich
December 31, 1906

The Memorandum (Recollections) of Prince N. D. Obolenskii

October 1905 will appear in future annals of Russia as a decisive month, during which the first real recognition occurred of the unavoidability (at the time not completely recognized in the higher circles) of taking the last step on the road of reform and renewal begun in the reign of Emperor Alexander II.

During that momentous month all of Russian society was deeply saddened. That was so because of the unsuccessfully conducted war that fully revealed the unpleasant truth of the inadequacy of the governmental machinery. The dissatisfaction, tinged with the deepest shame, that arose among the members of society then spread to all other classes, each explaining our domestic and foreign failures differently.

Thus was created a seedbed for those individuals of various political hues whose point of view was internationalist [rather than nationalist], who sought, by whatever means possible, to undermine an unpopular government. This complex evolution of society's thoughts, having many causes and taking many forms, expressed itself in the form of strikes, rebellion, looting, and assassinations before the very eyes of a Russian society that was becoming increasingly hostile to the government.

Admission of the futility of this sadly led, cruel, and unsuccessful war with Japan was somewhat tempered by the victory won at the peace table in Portsmouth, where somehow or other, with minor concessions, the fruitless bloodshed was ended, bloodshed that might have cost us Vladivostok, Kamchatka, and the islands off Siberia, which had completely fallen into Japanese hands. Under the influence of this act of belated wisdom on the part of the government, the mood of society softened somewhat, and the name of the individual who had won peace for the fatherland naturally came to mind as the man equipped to undertake the task of bringing enduring domestic tranquility to the country, that of State Secretary Count Witte, chairman of the Committee of Ministers.

Physically exhausted by the pressures he had experienced, Count Witte returned to Russia, where, in resuming his duties, he found a country in chaos, torn by discord, conditions that cried for solid answers and firm leadership. In the course of meetings of the Committee of Ministers and of sessions of various conferences under Count Solskii, it became abundantly clear that it was necessary to infuse the government with a fresh spirit and to proceed to a thorough overhaul of the governmental machinery.

On October 6, S. Iu. Witte wrote to the Emperor requesting permission to deliver a report in which he would express some of his observations about the existing disorder—the many gatherings of public men, the political demonstrations and strikes, which were assuming a character of open hostility to the government. By this time the railroads were on strike and Peterhof was accessible only by ship.

On October 8 Count Witte received the Emperor's reply, stating he had already thought of summoning him for an exchange of opinions concerning the current disorder and asking Count Witte to be in Peterhof the following day at 6 p.m. With the help of Actual State Councillor Vuich, Count Witte prepared a program of reforms that had already been proposed, together with an explanation of those pressing questions with which the future Council of Ministers should concern itself. It appeared that, on the basis of such a program, Count Witte, if appointed chairman of the Council of Ministers, could expect to satisfy and calm part of Russian society.

On October 9 Count Witte sailed to Peterhof and at 6 p.m. was received by His Majesty. Count Witte explained to the Emperor that there were only two courses that could be followed in dealing with the extremely difficult situation in which the government found itself: (1) to confer unlimited dictatorial power on a trusted person, who could then decisively strike at the root of antigovernmental manifestations, however high the cost in blood; (2) to yield to public opinion and instruct the future cabinet to proceed on the path of constitutionalism, meaning that His Majesty would decide in advance to grant a constitution and to affirm the program worked out by Count Witte. Count Witte stated that he did not consider himself prepared to carry out the first course. He went on to say that he felt morally obliged to point out to His Majesty the gravity of a decision to accept limitations on his power as well as to point out that it was out of the question to return to the situation that had existed.

In view of all this, Count Witte suggested that before coming to a final decision the Emperor should consider the matter at a special conference, inviting to it those who took a different view, of the kind expressed in recent meetings and conferences. It would be understood that if the Emperor in due course agreed to the proposed program, Count Witte would not be limited in his choice of associates, that he would be free to offer portfolios to public men. Further, Witte, pointing out the gravity of a decision that at one stroke of the pen would change the entire structure of government, the gravity of a decision voluntarily to have his power limited, suggested that the Emperor invite the Empress and the grand dukes to such a conference.

Count Witte was invited to return to Peterhof on the following day, October 10. This he did and, in the presence of Her Majesty, repeated all he had said the preceding day and set forth his program.

October 11 and 12 came and went, during which time Count Witte's program was carefully considered by persons close to the Emperor, persons who reported directly to him. As a result of these deliberations, a dispatch was sent to Count Witte on October 13 that read roughly as follows: "I am appointing you chairman of the Council of Ministers for the purpose of coordinating the work of all the ministers." But there was no word about Count Witte's program.

Quite properly Count Witte concluded that the program he had presented had not been approved. On October 14 he went to Peterhof and informed His Majesty that he could not in good conscience carry out the Imperial order to become premier unless his program was approved. He repeated his recommendation that the program be considered at a conference by persons whom the Sovereign would be good enough to invite and stated that the situation was growing worse by the day, making it imperative to come to a decision about which course to follow. After this the Emperor instructed Prince Orlov (Count Heyden being on leave) to invite certain persons to discuss Witte's program. Also, it was decided before the meeting took place that a manifesto was to be drafted that would make it evident that everything expressed in Count Witte's program came personally from the Sovereign.

Grand Duke Nicholas Nikolaevich, General-Adjutant Baron Freedericksz, General-Adjutant Richter, Count Witte, State Secretary Goremykin, and Baron Budberg were invited to the conference. Then Count Orlov was informed by a servant that it was His Majesty's wish that Goremykin and Budberg travel on a separate ship, not attend the conference, and await further instructions at the palace. The conference was to begin at 11 a.m., October 15.

Count Witte was asked to bring with him a draft of a manifesto that would move reforms from the realm of promises to the realm of concrete action by the Sovereign. Count Witte had from the first intended to revise the introduction to his program to make it clear that the program had been prepared on the orders and under the personal direction of His Majesty. Count Witte considered it difficult and possibly premature to express the program in the form of a manifesto. Since Prince A. D. Obolenskii happened to be visiting him, Count Witte asked him to prepare the draft of a manifesto and to accompany him and Actual State Councillor Vuich to Peterhof the following day, October 15.

The conference at Peterhof opened at 11 a.m., on October 15, the Emperor presiding. Declaring that he was not well acquainted with the subject matter and wanted matters that were unclear to him explained, Grand Duke Nicholas Nikolaevich asked and was given permission to put some questions to Count Witte. In the course of the conference Witte described the general situation in the country, emphasizing that even moderate elements in Russian society were hostile to the government and concluding that at that time there were only two choices, dictatorship or a constitution. Count Witte also discussed specific points in his program, among them the granting of legislative power to the State Duma and the granting of freedom of speech, assembly, and conscience and affirming inviolability of person. Grand Duke Nicholas Nikolaevich interrupted Count Witte several times to ask for clarification of specific details that were being explained. At one the conference was adjourned until 2:30 p.m. The Emperor stated that when the session was resumed a draft of the proposed manifesto would be presented, this despite Count Witte's objections to a manifesto, which had been repeated on this occasion.

The conference resumed at 3 p.m. Count Witte was somewhat late because he had been busy revising the draft of the manifesto. After the manifesto was presented, no objections were raised, but Count Witte asked the Emperor not to sign the document without a full understanding of its extraordinary historical importance and of the fact that even after such a document was signed there would be no immediate return to calm. His Majesty adjourned the conference, placed the draft of the manifesto on his desk, thanked Count Witte, saying that he would pray to God, would give the manifesto some more thought, and would let him know his decision.

After Count Witte's departure, the Emperor asked General-Adjutant Freedericksz to summon State Secretary Goremykin and Baron Budberg and ask them to review the manifesto. They went to work immediately and concluded that the document was not acceptable. State Secretary Goremykin disagreed in principle with the idea of a manifesto. Baron Budberg, on the other hand, criticized the wording of the draft and felt that it had been poorly edited. Goremykin agreed to help edit the draft.

While these two were at work, Count Witte happened to learn what was afoot. Because he did not wish to be bound by revisions made without his participation, he telephoned Baron Freedericksz and Court Commandant Prince Engalychev, asking them to inform His Majesty that either he be informed about the changes made in the manifesto or that the authors of the changes be given the responsibility of power. He was informed that the changes in the manifesto were minor, editorial ones. Nonetheless, Count Witte insisted that before the manifesto was signed he should have the opportunity to read it.

On Sunday, October 16, rumors spread throughout Petersburg that Count Witte's proposal for governmental reorganization had not been approved and that another proposal, by State Secretary Goremykin, had been approved and adopted. The effect of such rumors was depressing.

Around midnight that day, after calling by telephone, General-Adjutant Baron Freedericksz and Major General A. A. Mosolov, his chief of chancellery, called on Count Witte. Baron Freedericksz apologized for informing Count Witte that the changes in the manifesto had been merely editorial in nature. In fact, he said, there had been substantive changes, but he asked Count Witte to accept the manifesto in its changed form because the changes represented even greater concessions than the ones made in Count Witte's draft.

After having read the new [Budberg-Goremykin] draft, Count Witte noted that it presented the promised reforms as already granted, whereas in his draft His

Majesty was represented as stating that it was his irrevocable will that the reforms listed be implemented, also that in the new draft there was no reference to the exercise of legislative initiative on the part of the State Duma.[5]

Count Witte once more asked Baron Freedericksz to implore the Emperor not to issue any manifesto but content himself with publishing the program that he had prepared, then revised, and to indicate that the program was based on the initiative, direction, and will of His Majesty. Baron Freedericksz explained that the decision to proclaim reforms by a manifesto was final.

Count Witte replied that he clearly realized that, despite all the attention shown him by the Emperor, the fact was that the Emperor did not have complete confidence in him, making it difficult for him to coordinate the work of the ministers and that under such circumstances it would be more advisable for the Emperor to select one of the authors of the new draft as premier. He suggested too that the Emperor be advised that he was ready to accept a position of secondary importance if that would serve the common good.

Count Witte had good reason for saying what he did. There were persons close to the Emperor who did not believe in the sincerity of Count Witte, being convinced that he wished to see Russia become a republic, with himself as its president.[6] Such persons suggested that Emperor William II showed Count Witte extraordinary kindness recently because he saw in him the future president of republican Russia.

At 9 a.m. on October 17 Baron Freedericksz reported to the Emperor about what had been happening. As a result, Grand Duke Nicholas Nikolaevich and Count Witte were summoned to Peterhof. The Grand Duke, who was the first to arrive, had come to the conclusion that the explanations earlier given by Count Witte were sound and that, given the insufficiency of troops, it was impossible to establish a military dictatorship. Prior to the arrival (at 4:30 p.m.) of Count Witte, the Grand Duke and Baron Freedericksz were received by the Sovereign, who decided that he would affirm the program prepared by Count Witte and sign the manifesto prepared by him. Therefore the Chancellery of the Ministry of the Imperial Court, which had been temporarily transferred to Peterhof, was instructed to transcribe the manifesto. That task was completed by 6 p.m.

Some time after his arrival in Peterhof, Count Witte went to Alexandria, where, in his presence, the Emperor signed the manifesto and affirmed Count Witte's program. Thus, not without some conflict, doubt, and questions, the Sovereign was good enough to return Russia to the path of reform, from which she had strayed because of various foreign and domestic circumstances, and to complete the great undertaking begun by his Most August Grandfather.

On the return trip to Petersburg, Grand Duke Nicholas Nikolaevich, who seemed happy and pleased, said to Count Witte: "Today, October 17, is the seventeenth anniversary of the day when the dynasty was saved at Borki. It seems to me that today the dynasty has been saved from no less a danger as a result of the historical action that has just taken place."

August–September 1906

VOLUME III

PART I

My Life ▪ *1906–1911*

PART II

My Times ▪ *1906–1912*

I

Exile?

A Visit with Prince Napoleon

In May 1906, following my departure from office, my wife and I[1] went to Brussels to visit with my daughter and her family (her husband was with our legation there). During the ten days we spent in the city I had the opportunity of talking with Prince Napoleon, the Imperialist[2] pretender to the French throne. I met him at a dinner at the home of Lambert, the leading banker in Belgium. The prince then invited my wife and me to lunch with him at his home.*

At his home I was astounded to note that he was treated there as if he were on the throne of France. All who addressed him called him "Your Majesty," and although the meal was a rather simple one, the etiquette appropriate for dining with an emperor was observed. Moreover, as I learned, he maintained a small court, in which elderly supporters took turns serving as his high marshal, and officers of the French army, both active and retired, took turns as his adjutant.

After lunch the prince invited me to his study. When we were alone he told me that like so many others in Europe, he knew a great deal about me and my career. Having said this, he told me that he wanted my counsel. The matter was this.

The situation in France was so bad that many feared that Clemenceau, an extremist with socialist leanings, would come to power. Given the growing strength of extreme socialists, his advisers suggested that he return to France and proclaim himself ruler. What did I think?

I replied that since he had shown confidence in me, I must be frank: What he

---

*The prince later married the daughter of King Leopold. The king, who spent much of his time in France, amusing himself, had at first objected to such a marriage lest it hurt his relations with the French, but then relented.

had been advised to do had not the slightest chance of success. Why? Because once socialists in France gained power they would have to realize that it was impractical for them to base their policies on their theories. It was for this reason that France, although a republic, was more conservative in her economic and social policies than monarchies like England and Germany.[3] It was certain therefore that a Clemenceau government would not turn out as feared and would in fact prove bourgeois in orientation. My answer pleased the prince, who shook my hand and told me that in his heart he held the same view.

Events proved me right. The government of Clemenceau was succeeded by the extreme socialist government of Briand, which, once in power, functioned within the confines of sound governmental principle. To this day [1912] France does not have such things as an income tax, which has been adopted in England, Germany, and other European states.

Family Problems

While we were still in Brussels, word came that my son-in-law's father, Vasilii Lvovich Naryshkin, had died in Aix-les-Bains. I, my daughter, and my son-in-law left immediately for Aix-les-Bains, while my wife and my grandson went on to Paris. My daughter and her husband then left for Petersburg, accompanying the body of Vasilii Lvovich, who was to be buried in one of the cemeteries of the Alexander Nevskii Monastery. I went on to Paris and with my wife and grandson went from there to Vichy.

A Visit from Mechnikov

While in Vichy, I received a telegram from Mechnikov, the renowned director of the Pasteur Institute, asking if I would see him. I agreed. My acquaintance with him went back to my days at the university, where he had just begun to teach zoology. At that time he was too far to the left for my tastes, but although we were not close, I had come to know him fairly well.

His reason for seeing me, it turned out, was to ask for advice. He wanted to know if I would advise him to accept the offer of a chair at Oxford, at a salary of 3,000 pounds, plus free quarters, heat, and light, i.e., compensation equivalent to about 30,000 rubles. I asked what his salary was at the institute: it was 3,000 francs a year, with no perquisites. I told him that obviously he should accept the chair at Oxford, but what he said next indicated that the choice was not as simple as it appeared.

His salary at the institute was inadequate, but the 8,000 rubles a year that came in from his wife's property in Russia made it possible for them to live on an adequate scale in Paris, and he preferred to remain in his present position because it gave him a worldwide reputation. If he could be certain that his wife's property would not be confiscated he would reject the offer from Oxford. Should he take all the talk about land expropriation at home seriously?

I told him that widespread expropriation was unlikely, but that even if it should come to pass, owners of confiscated land would be compensated. Therefore he could rest assured of continuing to receive the supplementary income on which he relied. He accepted my word, and as it turned out, he had no cause to regret having done so. As a result of this meeting our relations became friendlier.[4]

Police Protection

From Vichy my wife, I, and our grandson returned to Aix-les-Bains to meet our daughter and her husband, now back from Petersburg. After taking the cure there, we separated. Our daughter, her husband, and our grandson went on to Brussels. My wife and I set out to follow the Rhine to Cologne and then go on to Brussels, but at Mainz my wife fell ill, so we went to Frankfurt for medical attention. The doctor there decided that I too required an operation, so we took up residence in nearby Bad Homburg, where we remained for about a month.

At Bad Homburg I visited Prince Melikov, an old friend of mine from the Caucasus, who was taking the cure at the neighboring spa of Soden for an illness from which he was to die a few years later. It was on my way back from seeing the prince that I was surprised to note that I was being followed by men whom I could not identify. Then when I took my seat on the train (Kovalenskii, a former director of the Department of Police, who was to commit suicide a few years later, sat next to me), I found two strangers in the compartment who virtually surrounded us. This I found quite perplexing.

After returning to Bad Homburg, I became aware that I was being followed by German police agents. When I asked our local consul for an explanation, he told me that the local chief of police had received orders from Berlin, with no reason given, that I be provided with police protection.

It was in Paris, after a stopover in Brussels, that I learned the reason for the orders. On the first day of our stay in Paris, at the Bristol Hotel, several acquaintances warned me to exercise caution because an attempt on my life might be made. Then, when Rachkovskii, the former head of our secret police in Paris, came to see me, I told him about my experience in Germany and about the warnings I had received. How seriously should I take these warnings? He promised to get the facts from Rataev, who, as I have mentioned elsewhere, had replaced him.

The next day Rachkovskii returned to show me some documents that explained what had happened. It seems that a revolutionary Jewish student, whom I had actually encountered while in Soden, wanted to assassinate me and that the German police had found out about it by accident. The story was as follows.

The student, a consumptive, who was staying in Soden, had written to Gotz, the head of his party [Socialist Revolutionary], declaring that he had only a few months to live and was prepared to assassinate me if the party deemed such an act desirable: he had learned that I sometimes visited Soden, and, when I did, he could kill me. The student had then sent the letter on to a party leader, a Jewish doctor named Rabinovich or Gurovich, who was with a hospital in Paris, for forwarding to Gotz. The party leaders in Paris could not decide whether or not to give the student permission and so sent the letter on to Gotz, who was in Berlin for a major operation, but the letter was withheld from Gotz because he was about to undergo surgery, from which, as it turned out, he did not recover. After Gotz's death, the letter was turned over to the Berlin police, who knew who he was. Upon reading it they ordered the Frankfurt police to protect me and, knowing that I would be visiting Paris, also informed Rataev of the facts. According to Rachkovskii, Rataev then took steps to assure that no harm would come to me.

Suggestion or Order?

While I was still in Aix-les-Bains I received a letter, dated July 17, forwarded to me by our Paris embassy, from Baron Freedericksz, the minister of the court.[5] In it he informed me that in the course of a conversation with the Emperor, His Majesty had "expressed the opinion" that, "given the present political situation" (a situation, I should note, that had become very grim thanks to the policies of Goremykin and Trepov), my "return to Russia at the present time would be most undesirable." He closed by saying, "I feel obliged to inform you of His Majesty's opinion so that you might take account of it in planning the rest of your trip."[6]

This was, in effect, an Imperial order not to return. It upset and offended me deeply, particularly in view of my conversations with His Majesty at the time of my departure from office. I reacted by sending an immediate request that I be permitted to leave government service.[7] But when the news came a few days later that the State Duma had been dissolved, I sent a telegram to the director of the Post Office requesting that the letter be returned to me. Thus, the letter did not reach its destination.

Subsequently, around August 20, while I was still in Bad Homburg, after the atmosphere in Russia had cleared and Stolypin had succeeded Goremykin as premier, I wrote to Baron Freedericksz as follows:

> The day following receipt of your letter of July 17, with its kindly advice "not to return to the motherland at the present time," I wrote you a letter asking permission to leave the service. But, recognizing the bloody consequences that would follow the dissolution of the Duma, I did not consider it patriotic to raise personal questions at such a time and had the letter held up in Petersburg. Now, a month later, I consider it possible once more to speak up concerning this episode.
>
> When I asked to be relieved of my post as premier, . . . His Imperial Majesty was good enough to agree graciously and to inform the country of my services in an extremely kindly rescript and by bestowing an honor on me. Then a cabinet was formed of persons who, given their record, could not meet with anything but disdainful hatred on the part of the Duma and most of society. This cabinet has been described as solid as a rock.* At least it had the characteristics of a rock, silence in the face of blows, inability to answer ideas with ideas.

Finally, the revolutionary Duma was dissolved prematurely, in response to its decision to turn to the country concerning the agrarian question, a question made all the more acute by the impolitic attitude, to put it mildly, toward this question on the part of the cabinet. . . . As you will recall, at the last session to deal with the Fundamental Laws, I had the honor to inform His Imperial Majesty about my view of Goremykin's position that if the Duma chose to discuss confiscation of land it should be dissolved, my view being that in this matter the attitude of the government should be temporizing and conciliatory, not provocative, as proved to be the case. It is most unfortunate that the government gave the peasantry good reason to believe that, if not hostile toward the peasantry, it was, at the very least, not on its side. . . .

After taking the unfortunate step of dissolving the State Duma, Goremykin and several parts of the ministerial rock vanished into thin air. One who remained was Stolypin, who, as far as I know,[8] is an honorable and decisive man, who rode into power on the basis of the October 17 Manifesto and my most humble report approved by the Emperor, which accompanied it, and also a whole set of laws issued during my tenure. For the present the horse prances and the government has enough funds thanks to that largest of loans which I succeeded in arranging before my departure. May God grant Stolypin complete success, but this horse will not stay on its feet for long without the necessary care.

As for me, no sooner had I left the post of premier than the official attitude toward me changed radically. . . . Thus, the purportedly privately owned newspaper *Rossiia*, which everyone knows is an official newspaper, began to make insinuations of every kind against me, not without the blessings of several ministers. And some members of the cabinet, too cowardly to let their names be used, anonymously ("a member of the cabinet states") † inform foreign correspondents of their political "credos," never missing an opportunity to shoot arrows at me, which, to my good fortune, are tipped with childish spit rather than with the poison of pure reason. The honorable Stolypin and General Trepov have felt it proper to inform foreign correspondents that my actions had been in error. And foreign correspondents reprint this, knowing the weakness of their readers for the piquant and the comic. Recently Premier Stolypin's drunkard brother, the journalist, who is on good terms with the premier, has referred favorably to my talents (just think, what an honor), saying that he has it on good authority that I helped spread the legend about Trepov's influence.‡ This is even more serious.§ May such stories be on the conscience of their author and on those who inspired this drunken newspaperman.

*His Majesty permitted himself to use this expression when I went to say farewell, following my departure from office.

†Schwaneback, whom I forced out of my cabinet and who was appointed to Goremykin's cabinet.

‡This alleged "legend" was generally known to be true even before October 17 and is now accepted as *established fact*. In what way is Trepov worse than the French doctor Philippe, the "holy man" Rasputin, and the rest?

§Because this was done to turn the emperor against me, because these observations were sent on to him by Stolypin.

Just today there appeared in almost all newspapers a telegram to Emperor William from so-called "true Russian" (popularly known as Black Hundreds) parties, who, at least in my time, were in the good graces of some of the government, in which all the ills of Russia are ascribed to me and which virtually labels me as one of the Jewish hierarchs. Moreover, I am informed that members of the Imperial family close to the Emperor permit themselves to accuse me of being responsible for all that is now occurring in our fatherland.* You, as an honorable witness of the events of October 17, know of my role in the preparation of the manifesto, and later, as a colleague in my cabinet, know to what degree this is true.

Moreover, I have been informed that entire dissertations are being prepared, not without help from government officials, which try to show that I am responsible for the rebellion [smuta] and for the unfortunate war which was its main cause. Yet I must remain silent in the face of all this because of my official position.

All that I have said explains why I feel impelled to return to my original wish, induced by your letter "advising" me not to return to the fatherland at "the present time," despite the fact that at "the present time" Russian revolutionaries and bomb throwers have returned, to find havens, be they legal or illegal.†

You know me well enough to be certain that it would go against my conscience to do anything for personal reasons that would be unpleasant as well as uncomfortable for the Emperor. But, if my complete withdrawal from government service would be in accordance with his wishes and views, my feeling of self-esteem would not let me waver for even a moment, and I would immediately ask to be released from all government service.

Then, because I do not have the financial resources on which to live and because I do not wish to deprive my family of all the comforts to which they were accustomed while I was in office, I would be able to earn the necessary income from private employment and indirectly be of service to society.

Perhaps it is not inappropriate at this point to affirm that no change in my position could ever shake my feelings of complete loyalty to my Sovereign and those principles which I acquired with my mother's milk, principles that His Imperial Majesty, as Russian Monarch, personifies. I hope that your chivalrous spirit will spur you to reply to my letter most quickly.

After some three weeks had passed without a reply, I wrote the baron once more, this time from Frankfurt, reminding him of my letter and asking that he immediately present my request to the Emperor. I then went to Brussels, where the following letter, dated September 10, was delivered to me:

*After my departure, Empress Alexandra Fedorovna told those close to her that I was responsible for all the unrest. If this is what the emperor was told, it is not surprising that grand dukes like Nicholas Nikolaevich, Nicholas Mikhailovich, and Alexander Mikhailovich have begun to spread such stories far and wide.

†Obviously the baron's letter was written on orders of the Emperor, and that is why I called it an Imperial order.

I informed the Emperor of the contents of your letter as soon as I received it, but I did not discuss it fully with him at the time but waited for a more favorable opportunity to do so. This occurred during our voyage to the skerries.

I can assure you that the Emperor's suggestion that you should not return to Russia was solely a reflection of the situation as it then existed, when he felt that your return at that time might be undesirable because of the danger that persons of ill-will might use your presence as an opportunity for making the work of the cabinet, which was already difficult, even more difficult. But not for a moment was this an expression of personal animosity. His Majesty looks favorably [?][9] at your wish to return to Russia to attend to your personal affairs [?] and believes that *at present* your return would not create any serious [?] political difficulties. He has authorized me to inform you that he sees no obstacles to your return. I am particularly pleased to inform you that when you return you will be well received by the Emperor and that he is unequivocally in favor of your remaining in government service.

The baron also asked if he should show my letter to the Emperor and suggested that my reply should be "no."

Whether this letter was written before the receipt of my second one I do not know for certain, but I do know that Kokovtsev spread the word that as soon as European banking circles heard that I was thinking of leaving government service, I would be inundated with offers of well-paying positions. I know too that he passed on this word to Stolypin. Also I know that before deciding on a favorable reply, the Emperor consulted with Stolypin and other members of the government.

In reply to the baron's query I sent him a telegram that it would be better not to show the Emperor my second letter. Given the circumstances and the person, I suspect that he did show the letter to the Emperor.[10] (The correspondence I received is in my archives.)

Not long afterward, while I was in Paris, after leaving Brussels, the baron was there, providing us an opportunity to talk. (Our families have long been on friendly terms.) It was obvious that he did not wish to discuss our exchange of letters, but he did say that if he were in my place he would try to live abroad as much as possible. To this I replied that even if I didn't prefer to live in Russia, I did not have the means to live abroad in the style I enjoyed at home.

Warning Ignored

It was while I was in Paris that I received a telegram, written in French, from the notorious and contemptible Prince Michael Mikhailovich Andronikov, about whom I have spoken earlier. It read: "Having learned that you plan to return soon, I beseech you, out of genuine concern for you, to prolong your stay abroad. The danger to you here is greater than you think. Return if you wish to die. This is my last word." (After I returned to Petersburg, I asked him what had occasioned the warning. He replied that he had learned from Dubrovin, the head of the Union of the Russian People, and from Launitz, the prefect of Petersburg, that there was a plot to kill me on my return and that he had documentary proof of it. When I asked to see that proof, he promised to show it to me, but has not done so to this day [1912], claiming that he has it somewhere under lock and key.)[11]

My feelings on reading the telegram were very unpleasant. It was evident that because the Emperor's effort to induce me to remain abroad had failed, an attempt was now being made to frighten me into remaining abroad. My resolve to return was all the more fortified by this warning, and return I did, with my wife, in October.[12]

After returning I used my first meeting with Stolypin to speak once more about my leaving government service. I did so because I felt that since the state no longer felt any need to avail itself of my energy, my experience, and my knowledge and because, as a result of my having given up private employment at the request of Emperor Alexander III, I had not been able to accumulate an estate, making me and my family almost solely dependent on what I received from the government, I had the right to devote my declining years to the benefit of my family. And this I could easily have done given the huge number of offers I received to accept private employment at salaries running into the hundreds of thousands of rubles a year.

Stolypin did not react then, but at our second meeting he told me (probably after having spoken to His Majesty) that, of course, I was free to do as I pleased, but my leaving government service, particularly at a time like this, would be the equivalent of an anarchist bomb. I replied that if His Majesty's government believed that my departure would have an untoward effect, I would, of course, withdraw my request.[13] Since that day I have not raised the question again despite all that had been done to me.

Soon after this meeting I was received by the Emperor, as usual, in his study. And, as usual, he was very kind. Not a word was said during the twenty-minute audience about the suggestion that I not return to Russia. The only subject we touched on were the plans for a monument to Emperor Alexander III.[14] I was told that after this meeting, he said to some intimates: "Witte is a clever man after all: he did not say a word about what has taken place."

Since then I had no occasion to speak to the Emperor until my audience with him this year [1912]. During the interval I was sometimes in the same room with him, at official receptions and dinners, but he did not speak to me about anything. As for Stolypin, we exchanged formal visits for about two years, but then the visits tapered off and finally came to an end, because I had occasion to say things at the State Council that the government found disagreeable.

As a result of my decision to remain in Russia I was to be hunted as if I were a wild animal.

II

Attempts on My Life

The First Attempt

As I have said, I was to be hunted as if I were a wild beast, hunted by thugs at the behest of the extreme right, which was led by scoundrels like Dr. Dubrovin and Purishkevich, men with ties to the police, many high officials, and even the Imperial court. My first brush with death was to come on January 29, 1907, but before I deal with it, a few background details.

When I returned from abroad in October 1906, several Okhrana (secret police) agents were assigned to my house, taking turns at sitting in my vestibule.[1] They were a sign that Stolypin and the secret police, who were under his direction, were interested in me. Presumably their assignment was to protect me, but I did not want the presence of Okhrana agents to be noted by the many visitors to my house, so I had them sit in a small room instead of the vestibule.

And there were signs of attempts either to kill me or to frighten me with threats. Shortly after my return I began to receive threatening letters—some marked with crosses, some with skeletons—warning me that such and such a party had decided to take my life, but I chose to ignore the letters and destroyed them.

Came the night of January 29. My wife had gone to the theater, but I had remained home, to wait for my doctor, who came twice a week to swab my throat. (I had been having trouble with my throat for many years.) While I was waiting, it was now nine o'clock, Gurev, a former associate in the Ministry of Finance, who had been helping me prepare a work dealing with the Far East, came to see me.[2]

He had come to look at some relevant documents from my archive, which I did not want taken out of my home.

Before I go on with my story, let me tell about an incident that took place in connection with Gurev's visits to my home. Several months after the night of January 29, Baron Freedericksz came to see me. It seems that His Majesty had heard that I was preparing to publish a critical book dealing with our finances and with the work of V. N. Kokovtsev, the then minister of finance. Would I please decide not to publish the book? I answered that His Majesty had been misinformed, that no such book was in progress.

Uncertain that the baron would relay my answer exactly, I wrote a letter to the Emperor repeating what I had told the baron and adding that I had been working with Gurev on a different kind of subject and that if the work resulting from it were ever published, it would be after my death. I added that I would be obliged if in the future His Majesty would attempt to verify reports about me by inquiring directly of me. What I was hinting at was that if he acted as I suggested, he would not believe the many slanderous stories about me that he then accepted and still accepts as fact.

How did this unfounded story arise? I think that it came from Kokovtsev, who on learning that Gurev had been to see me must have inferred that we were planning to write something about the current administration of finances. Kokovtsev may have been concerned because when he because minister of finance, following my departure from office, Gurev had published an article referring to the new minister, expressing the opinion that things had reached a point where persons ill-prepared for the task could become ministers of finance and saying that he was reminded of cooks who advertised themselves as chefs. Another person might have ignored such an article, but Kokovtsev is a bit touchy and therefore could not forgive Gurev.

I return now to the events of January 29. About ten, with Gurev still looking over the documents, my doctor arrived and I asked Gurev if he would mind finishing his task another day. He asked if he could remain and continue his work in another room while the doctor was with me. I agreed and asked my manservant to show him to an unoccupied room on the top floor that my daughter had used before her marriage. The room was rarely heated. This time it was cold, so my manservant instructed the furnaceman to light up the stove in the room. Meanwhile Gurev went to work making excerpts from the documents.

While the doctor was looking at my throat my manservant, quite alarmed, asked that I go upstairs with him on an urgent matter. I asked the doctor to complete his work another time and went upstairs. I was taken to the stove, in which the fire had not been started. Inside the stove was a rectangular package with a long piece of twine attached. When I asked what this meant, the furnaceman told me that when he had opened the stove he had found some twine and had pulled on it. After pulling on it, he had found this package at its end. The discovery had been the occasion for alarm. There was little soot on either the package or the twine.

Gurev suggested taking the package out of the house and then opening it. I demurred because having been warned of an attempt on my life I suspected that the package might contain an explosive device. Therefore I told Gurev and the servants not to dare touch it and then telephoned the Petersburg Okhrana, which was then under the command of Colonel Gerasimov.

Before long the first of many Okhrana officers arrived. This was Captain Komissarov, head of the most secret of the sections of the Petersburg Okhrana. Then came Colonel Gerasimov, followed by an examining magistrate. Then came Trusewicz, the director of the Department of Police, who was succeeded by a swarm of other police and judicial personnel.

Captain Komissarov took the package to the garden and opened it, revealing an explosive device that was meant to be detonated by a vial of sulfuric acid, which was supposed to be broken by the action of an alarm clock set for nine o'clock. It was now eleven. It was about this time that my wife returned from the theater, to be shocked by the sight of all these officials in our home.

After the inspection of the device, the taking of statements began—from me, my manservant, the furnaceman. (Gurev was gone by this time.) When Colonel Gerasimov asked if I suspected anyone I naively replied that I suspected no one, that I had no personal enemies and that my political enemies at this moment were not on the left but on the extreme right and I could not imagine such people trying to assassinate me or of doing it in such a way that my wife and my manservant might be killed as well.

In the course of their questioning, our groundskeeper told the police that he had been asked earlier on by a man in a fur coat, his face partly concealed by a turned-up collar, on which side of the house my bedroom and that of my wife were located. When told that he didn't know, the stranger suggested that if we ordinarily slept on the lefthand side of the house we should shift to the right.

I suspect that this gentleman was a member of the gang that had placed the device. What I do not understand is why he suggested that we move to the righthand side of the house when the device had been placed on the left. I thought at the time that the groundskeeper's recollection of the exchange was confused. I learned the facts later on.

Although their search and inquiry seemed thorough, the fact is that it occurred to none of the officials present to check our roof for footprints leading to the chimney serving the stove in which the device was found, but it did occur to Nicholas Karasev, who had come to see me that night. A very bright fellow who had served me as courier both when I was minister of finance and when I was premier, he checked the roof, which was covered with snow, and found footprints from this chimney that indicated that someone had come from the neighboring house, which belonged to Lidval. Karasev then suggested that we inspect all the other chimneys, but it was too late at night to do so. He did inform the examining magistrate of what he had found on the roof, but no effort was to be made to corroborate this until the following day. The Okhrana men did not seem interested.

It was under such circumstances that my wife and I finally went to bed. Sleep was certain to be difficult, but fortunately, because my wife is a strong and decisive woman, there was no need for me to calm her. On the contrary, it was I who needed calming.

The next day, following Karasev's suggestion, we decided to have all our chimneys inspected. We were afraid that if we used our chimney sweeps and they found such devices it might be suggested that they had planted them there. So my wife asked General Speranskii, commandant of the Winter Palace, to send us chimney sweeps from the palace. He complied and they found another package in the chimney next to the one down which the first package had been lowered. This package was in the chimney of our dining room.

We immediately informed the Okhrana of the discovery. Once more it was Captain Komissarov who opened the package, to find an explosive device identical with the first one. I was beginning to think that those who had come the night before to investigate had little concern for my safety or for the safety of others in my home but had other aims in mind, as I was to discover.

Meanwhile, the investigation continued. Experts at the artillery laboratory to whom the devices were turned over reported that they were well made. Had either or both gone off, the adjacent walls would have collapsed and nearby rooms would have been damaged. The experts reported that either the alarm clocks or heat could have set off an explosion. That no explosion occurred was explained by the fact that the devices were packed too tightly to permit the hammers on the clocks to go their full course and because there was not enough heat to detonate the explosives. Those responsible for placing the devices in our home erred in assuming that our bedrooms were on the lefthand side of the house. Had the first device gone off we would not have been harmed, but our maid who occupies one of the rooms on the left side would have been. Had the second device gone off while we were in the dining room we would, of course, have felt the force of the explosion.

Of course the attempted assassination was reported the following day in the newspapers. Many of our friends and acquaintances came to see us to express concern and relief. Among these was Baron Freedericksz, who came as a close acquaintance, not in his official capacity. As for His Majesty and his family, no gesture of any kind was made as a result of the news.

I should note that on the day following the discovery of the first device I received an anonymous letter, directing me to send 5,000 rubles in an envelope to a designated room at the People's Palace.[3] I put the letter back into its envelope and sent it to the director of the Department of Police but never received a reply from him.

A few days later there came a second anonymous letter warning me that my failure to reply to the first letter would result in another attempt on my life. [If I wished to live] I was to have someone take my reply and turn it over to someone who would be standing on one of the streets adjacent to Nevskii Prospekt. I turned this letter over to an Okhrana agent who was stationed in my house, told him what was going on, and asked that he catch the criminal who wrote the letter. I never saw the agent again because the agents at my house were frequently replaced by others. The criminal was not caught. The letter was not returned to me.

The Investigation

Investigation of the attempt on my life was to continue for some time both by Okhrana agents and by an examining magistrate from the Ministry of Justice. It soon became evident that they rejected the notion that the devices had been lowered down our chimneys, deciding to believe that they had been put there from inside the house, this because the packages and the twine attached to them were free of soot. But the answer to this hypothesis was a simple one: there was no soot because the stoves in question were rarely used and the chimneys, even the ones not in use, were cleaned by the sweeps every time they came, but the examining magistrate paid no attention to this explanation. Obviously the idea was to find that the attempt had been staged.

Early on when the examining magistrate first questioned me he had asked if I suspected anyone, my manservant perhaps? I replied that I could vouch for him and all the other servants. When I then turned to Colonel Gerasimov and asked who he thought was the culprit, he replied that it could be someone from the right. But the line of inquiry was to be directed to finding that the attempt had been staged.

I was not kept informed of the results of the investigation as it progressed, but I did hear from some of the judicial authorities about the line that the investigation was following. Also, I learned from reliable (I wish they hadn't been) sources that during the first days of the investigation the Emperor toyed with the idea I had planted the devices in order to draw attention to myself and thus increase my popularity and that, when he was told that such an idea was inconceivable, he said that perhaps some of my well-wishers had placed the devices there at my suggestion. As will be seen, the Emperor would later take a somewhat different view, his views obviously depending on what he learned from Stolypin and from the minister of justice, that egregious good-for-nothing Shcheglovitov.

That it was Shcheglovitov who was chiefly responsible for the notion that I had staged the attempt on my life I learned from several members of the State Council, notably from Stakhovich, a good friend of mine. Stakhovich, also a good friend of the minister's, told me that once during a recess at the State Council several members had expressed concern to the minister about the attempt on my life: smiling, he had responded by saying that it might turn out to be the case that the attempt had been made by persons living in my house and with my knowledge. What is one to think of a man who could say such a thing?

A few months after the attempt on my life I happened to meet Shcheglovitov at the State Council and asked if the investigation had resulted in the apprehension of the criminals. He told me "not yet" and went on to say that he had spoken that day to the Emperor about the case. When I asked how the case had come up in their conversation, he told me that he had informed His Majesty about the findings of the artillery laboratory. The experts there became interested in the kind of dynamite used in the devices. It was a kind they had never seen before, and they discovered that it had been manufactured in Vienna. With permission of the Ministry of Justice the experts had then exploded the dynamite at an artillery range, discovering that the force of it was such that had it exploded in my house it would have destroyed the house and damaged several of the neighboring houses as well, including Lidval's.

How had the Emperor reacted to this information, I asked. Shcheglovitov replied that the Emperor had then taken a plan of my house out of a drawer and said, "Well, the explosive devices weren't placed there for fun." From this I concluded that His Majesty no longer believed that I, or someone from my house, had staged the attempt and that he would no longer permit anyone to express such a thought. That he could have for a moment entertained such a thought is very painful. It is difficult to believe that His Majesty, knowing how much I had sacrificed for him and his father, could know so little about me as ever to permit such a thought to be expressed in his presence without ordering the person who uttered it to shut up and never say anything so foul again.

Now I would like to turn to how I learned the identity of the man who had told my groundskeeper to advise me that my wife and I should move to different sleeping quarters. The story is this.

The man was V. N. Kazarinov, by that time perhaps vice-chairman of the Union of the Archangel Michael, another of those Black Hundreds groups, or possibly still linked with the Union of the Russian People. Well, a general of the Border Guard, whose sister-in-law was married to Kazarinov and with whom he was staying at the time, happened to discover that this man was preparing two explosive devices, and when he asked what was the purpose of them, he was told that they were to be used to blow up Count Witte and his house. Well, because the general was one of my many well-wishers among the officers of the Border Guard, of which I had once been the *ex officio* chief, he told Kazarinov that if not for the fact that they were related he would immediately inform the police, but, in any event, he could no longer stay with him and immediately left the house and would not visit it thereafter.

A few days before the fateful day of January 29 Kazarinov took up residence in a house opposite mine that had some cheap furnished rooms above a tavern. His intention was to see the explosion that was set for the night of January 29. Not long before that date his child came down with diphtheria and came close to dying. As a result Kazarinov had some kind of religious experience that left him conscience-stricken about what he was trying to do to me. But being unable to prevent the explosion, he tried to prevent our deaths by giving the advice he did to our groundskeeper.

I learned all this from an acquaintance who had been told the story, under a pledge that he not repeat what he heard, by the son of the general. The son was a student at the Polytechnic Institute, which I had helped establish, many of the students of which, both past and present, are among my admirers. I cannot name my acquaintance because he was under a pledge of secrecy. Also, I could not inform the investigators about this because this episode, about the advice to the groundskeeper, was not under investigation and [besides] because I did not wish to compromise either the student or his father, the general, for by doing so I would create discord in the Kazarinov family, and, in any event, it was widely known that Kazarinov was capable of anything.

All this reminds me that I soon came to realize during this whole affair that the Okhrana agents ostensibly detailed to protect me were really there to keep an eye on me and, if possible, put me in a compromising position. Not only were such agents stationed in my house but several had quarters in a neighboring building to keep my house under surveillance, in the hope of noting something improper that could be used to put me in a compromising position, but I have no fear of such efforts. Early on I asked that the Okhrana agents be removed from my house. However, for some time I was aware that I was under surveillance by other Okhrana agents. It is only in recent months that I am no longer aware of being watched by such men, but I cannot be sure that my doorman does not report the comings and goings at my house to the Okhrana.

This reminds me of an experience about which Count Miliutin, the former war minister, told me. When the time came for him to leave office he wanted to take his courier, who had served him for many years, with him to the Crimea where he planned to live. When the courier refused, he was upset, but then someone close to the Department of Police said to him: "Why be upset? You should know that he can't go with you because while he was serving you he was also serving the secret police, who paid him a higher wage than he received as courier and he doesn't want to lose the money." Just think, here was a man who was close to Emperor Alexander II yet had been kept under surveillance, probably at the behest of Count Peter Shuvalov, the head of the Gendarmerie. Count Miliutin told me this story in sorrow, but I wouldn't care if my doorman turned out to be an Okhrana agent because in him I have a good servant to whom I pay low wages.

A Second Effort To Kill Me

Four months after the first attempt on my life there was to be another plot to kill me. Because of information received by Akimov, chairman of the State Council, that a terroristic act might take place, the May 26 session of that body was canceled and the next session set for May 30.[4] On the eve of the thirtieth, Ivan Pavlovich Shipov, with whom I had long been associated, called on me to warn me not to attend the next session because if I did, while I was en route to the State Council, an attempt would be made on my life. He had this information from

Lopukhin, a neighbor of his although not a close acquaintance.* I told Shipov that I appreciated his concern, but wished that he hadn't warned me. Without the warning I might not have chosen to attend the May 30 session, but having been warned I had to attend lest I be suspected of cowardice, because if Lopukhin knew what was afoot, many of his party comrades in the State Duma would know as well. If it were known that he passed the word on to Shipov, my failure to attend the session would be widely noted and ascribed to fear.

So I decided to attend, but at my wife's insistence I changed my routine. Instead of leaving my house after lunch, I left earlier and had lunch at the home of Bykhovets, her brother-in-law, and went from his house to the State Council in his carriage, not in my automobile. Nothing happened on the way there, nor did anything untoward occur during the session of the State Council. Now I had to face the trip home. When I left the State Council building I couldn't find the Bykhovets carriage because I couldn't remember what the coachman looked like, didn't know his name, and probably he did not know me by sight. So I started for home on foot, hoping to find a decent-looking cab on the way. It was not until I had gone past the Hœtel de l'Europe, on Nevskii Prospekt, that I found such a cab, took it, and arrived home safely. I concluded, prematurely it turned out, that the warning had been a false alarm.

The next day the newspapers reported that on May 29, an as yet unidentified person had been killed while preparing a bomb, at a place outside Petersburg, Porokhovoe, in the woods of a correctional colony, near the Irinovskii Railroad. The newspapers also reported that rumor had it that he had been preparing a bomb intended for a member of the State Council. Thus, I could assume that nothing had happened to me on May 30 because the chief participant in the preparation had been killed.

The Investigation

The investigation of this case and of the previous case concerning the events of January 29 took three years. There were in fact three investigations, conducted independently of one another, with frequent changes in the personnel carrying them out. The first concerned the facts surrounding the event at Porokhovoe, the second dealt with the first attempt on my life, and the third concerned links between Moscow and the event at Porokhovoe. During these years I received such documents from the authorities as I was entitled to receive under the law, i.e., depositions of those questioned and of the investigators. From these documents and from what I heard I soon concluded that it was intended that the investigations lead nowhere.

*As I have mentioned earlier Lopukhin had once been director of the Department of Police and upon leaving government service had gone over completely to the Kadet Party, on whose behalf he gave special attention to what the secret police were up to, because it was known the police were unscrupulous about dealing with people it considered enemies or who were hated by persons in high positions. That the warning came from Lopukhin meant, of course, that the attempt on my life would not be coming from the left.

Consequently I turned for help and information to Kamyshanskii, the procurator of the Petersburg Court of Appeals, whose appointment to that post had been made possible by me while I was premier, something for which he was grateful. He belonged to the right politically but he was meticulous in carrying out the law. When I told him in what a scandalous way the investigations were being conducted, he told me that the investigators' hands were tied because if they were given a free hand action would have to be taken against such "pillars of society as Dr. Dubrovin, who have emerged as saviors of Russia, and this we cannot do." When I asked why, he told me that if they arrested Dr. Dubrovin, it would probably mean that the trail would take them to people in high places, and this the officials of the Ministry of Justice did not dare do without assurance from the minister of justice that they would suffer no harm if they went where the evidence took them, but "since we have received no such indication, and will not, it follows that we must snarl the investigation in order to cover up the truth."

Kamyshanskii's words prompted me to call on Shcheglovitov. Without bringing the procurator's name into the conversation, I told the minister that the investigations were being conducted in a scandalous fashion, that they were designed to hide the truth, not to uncover it. He then made some excuses and said he would ask for the files. He also asked Kamyshanskii for a memorandum about the entire case. This the procurator did, sending me a copy of it: in the memorandum he indicated where the guilty parties were to be found and what means should be used to find them. Nonetheless, the minister refrained from taking the necessary steps. This provoked me into calling on him again and warning him: "You should know that you are pushing me to a point where I will create a scandal, a very unpleasant scandal for you and the government." This was my last meeting with Shcheglovitov. After this I had no further personal relations with him.

Despite the government's efforts to conceal the truth, a great deal about the efforts to kill me came to light, from various sources, during the three years of the investigation. A major source consisted of articles by Fedorov, about whom I shall have more to say, that appeared in the newspaper *Le Matin*. I collected a large file of official documents dealing with the case. The file is in my archive. Copies of it have been deposited in several places, for assurance that the facts can be known. The documents I have establish the following facts beyond question.

A central figure in the efforts to kill me was Kazantsev, a retired guardsman, who worked with the Okhrana in gathering intelligence and in assassinating persons whom the secret police considered leftist and, generally, dangerous to the reactionary cause. He was one of those persons whom Stolypin called "ideological volunteers."

Illustrative of Kazantsev's work was his participation in the assassination of the State Duma deputy Herzenstein in July 1906. This act was carried out by agents of the Okhrana and of the Union of the Russian People, which was so closely linked to the Okhrana that it was difficult to mark the boundary between the two bodies.

After this killing the thought of assassinating me occurred to Dr. Dubrovin, the head of the Union of the Russian People. He then discussed the idea with his chief associates and, probably, with Launitz, the prefect of Petersburg. It is obvious that it was from them that the notorious Prince Andronikov, who had wormed his way into their confidence, learned of what was in store for me if I returned to Russia and then sent me the warning telegram to which I have referred. Dr. Dubrovin not only wanted to have me killed but also to gain possession of or destroy the documents I had in my house, telling his associates that he had an order (something I do not believe) from the Emperor to destroy the documents. (This comes from the evidence which Prussakov, Dr. Dubrovin's ex-secretary, gave an examining magistrate after breaking with Dubrovin.)

To cover the trail that might lead to them if the operation against me were organized in Petersburg, Dr. Dubrovin and his associates decided to entrust the preparations to their Moscow associates. It appears that Kazantsev was ordered to Moscow for that purpose, where he worked under the direction of Count Bux-hoevden, whose title was "official on special assignment" in the office of the governor-general of Moscow. It was from the former governor-general Dubasov that I heard that the count was a man of limited intelligence and was married to a rich woman. From what I learned, the count did not concern himself with his official duties but had other interests, including a foundry near Moscow, where projectiles, among other things, were produced. He worked with the Okhrana and the Union of the Russian People.

Kazantsev first recruited Fedorov—a convinced revolutionary, an anarchist although a worker, intellectually semi-cretinous—to take part in his work. He convinced Fedorov that he would be helping the revolutionary cause. He did the same with another worker, Stepanov, also an extreme leftist.

These three then repaired to Petersburg, where they rented furnished rooms near Nevskii Prospekt. Then Kazantsev got in touch with Dr. Dubrovin and with the Union of the Archangel Michael. It is likely that it was Kazarinov who supplied Kazantsev with the explosive devices to be used in my house. On January 29 they [Kazantsev, Fedorov, Stepanov] climbed to the roof of the neighboring house, belonging to Lidval, then crossed over to the roof of the wing of my house where the kitchens and servants' quarters are located, and from there to the roof of the main wing of my house and there lowered the explosive devices down the chimneys. The following day, when it was learned that the explosive devices had not gone off, Fedorov was sent to drop heavy weights down the chimneys to set off the devices, but when he arrived he was informed by Kazarinov that the devices had been removed.

Frustrated, the three returned to Moscow, at which time it was suggested to Fedorov and Stepanov that the directive to kill me came from the head of the revolutionary-anarchist [Socialist Revolutionary] party on the ground that I was an extreme reactionary who had suppressed the revolution. Kazantsev also told the two that Iollos, a Kadet [Constitutional Democratic] Party leader and deputy to the State Duma, should be assassinated because he had stolen large sums of money intended for the revolutionary cause. In March, Fedorov, acting under the direction of Kazantsev, assassinated Iollos. With this accomplished, they returned to the task of removing me from the living. This time they were going to throw a bomb at me. Then, having prepared several bombs, they returned to Petersburg. All this planning, I should repeat, was being done under the direction of Count Buxhoevden.

By the time the three had returned to Petersburg, the Second State Duma had opened. Stepanov told several of the left-wing deputies of how Iollos had been killed and of what was being planned, still believing that he was acting for the revolutionary cause. He and Fedorov were soon told the truth, that they had been acting as puppets for the Black Hundreds. Angered by this revelation, Fedorov decided to kill Kazantsev.

As was revealed, Kazantsev's plan was to have a bomb thrown at me on May 30, while I was en route to the State Council. On May 29, at Porokhovoe, as Kazantsev was making a bomb ready for use the next day, Fedorov came up to him from behind, plunged a dagger into his neck, and killed him. Thus, for a second time, the good Lord came to my rescue.

Obviously, the Petersburg Okhrana was well informed about Kazantsev, after all he was its agent, yet when his body was found the police pretended to be unable to identify him, in order to give Fedorov and Stepanov time to go into hiding. Had they been arrested, all would have been revealed. Stepanov went into hiding in this country and is still here, I believe, but the police, under Stolypin, pretended that they could not find him. As for Fedorov, he fled to Finland and from there to Paris, where, as I have said, he gave his story to the press.

As a result of my continued insistence with the Ministry of Justice, Aleksandrov, the examining magistrate in the Kazantsev case, asked the French to extradite Fedorov, but they refused. Later, when I had the opportunity, in Paris, to ask the French government why, I was told that under international law political criminals, such as Fedorov, could not be extradited, but that, truth to tell, they would have returned him to us in view of the fact that he was truly no more than an ordinary murderer and in view of the respect they had for me, but they had not done so because our government had let the French know orally that it would be obliged if he were not extradited.

I was certain that Kazantsev was an Okhrana agent and equally certain that the government would deny it, so I tried to lay my hands on evidence to prove my point. Thinking that the note demanding 5,000 rubles of me, which I so unwisely turned over to the director of the Department of Police, might shed some light, I asked Aleksandrov to intercede, but after many requests to the department for the note, he was fobbed off with various excuses. Then I took a hand in the matter and wrote to the director of the department. After a long delay, he replied that he had handed over the note to the Okhrana, which could not locate it.

Evidently Aleksandrov's conscience was troubled because he had to conduct the investigation in a manner designed to bring it to naught. That is probably why, the last time he saw me, he helped me with evidence. On that occasion he showed me a photocopy of a note and asked if this was the document in question. I said that it was and asked how he had come upon it. The following are his exact words:

> I have another case, not a political one, that required my seeing the handwriting of an agent of the detective division of the Petersburg Prefecture. When I made my request to the head of the division, he said: "We have samples of the handwriting of the agents of the Okhrana and the detective division because under Launitz the two were fused: if you wish you may look at the files."
>
> After finding a sample of the handwriting of the agent with whom I was concerned, it occurred to me to check if there were a sample of Kazantsev's handwriting. I looked under the letter "K," Kazantsev. I then had a photo made of what I found, showed it to the man in charge and asked whose handwriting it was. He replied: "it is that of the well-known Okhrana agent Kazantsev, who was killed by Fedorov near Porokhovoe."

Aleksandrov then agreed to my taking the photocopy for a few hours. I had it photographed and thus obtained fairly decisive proof that Kazantsev was an Okhrana agent.[5]

What I have related thus far proves that the attempts on my life were the work of agents of the extreme right and the government. Yet, after three years of work, the examining magistrate concluded that since Kazantsev was dead and the other culprits who had tried to take my life could not be apprehended, the case was closed.

But the case was not closed as far as I was concerned. In a letter [to Premier Stolypin] dated May 3, 1910, I explained what had happened, by reviewing the scandalous behavior of both judicial and police officials in the investigation of the case and in conclusion expressing the hope he would take steps to end the terrorist and anticonstitutional activities of secret organizations, which received money from secret funds of the government and in which government officials participated. I pointed out that if I were a private citizen, I could appeal to public opinion, but since that was not the case, I had no choice but to make my appeal to the government.[6]

The text of the letter was prepared for me by Reinbot, a well-known lawyer, but its thought and, in some places, its expressions, are mine. Before sending it off, I showed it, together with documentary material I had collected, to such jurists as Koni, Tagantsev, Manukhin, and Count Pahlen, all of them members of the State Council.[7] All agreed that from the standpoint of the law, the letter was proper, but did say that it did contain some strong language, which was my personal business.

Shortly after receiving this letter, Stolypin met me in the State Council and said: "I received your letter and it disturbs me very much." I said: "I advise you, Peter Arkadevich, not to reply to the letter in any way because I have documents that confirm everything in it and because before sending the letter I showed it to several top-notch jurists, among them so competent an official as Count Pahlen." To this he replied: "It is possible that Count Pahlen has taken leave of his senses." (This remark provided some insight into the moral level of the premier.) And then, in an exasperated tone, he said: "I must conclude from your letter that either you consider me an idiot or that you believe that I had a hand in the attempt on your life. Which is the correct answer?" My answer was: "Spare me from replying to so delicate a question."[8] I never spoke to him again after this exchange.

In December of the same year, after I had returned from abroad, I received a very insolent reply from the premier to my letter of May 3. In it he cavalierly denied the truth of some of my statements and also made some nasty insinuations. I did not let this pass and replied in a harshly worded but quite justified letter, ending it by urging that since there was obviously a difference of opinion about the manner in which the investigation had been conducted between me on the one hand and the premier and the minister of justice on the other, that the matter be turned over for review by several members of the State Council who were qualified by training and experience to decide who was right: I, who believed they were concealing the truth, or they, who denied it. I included the names of several members of the State Council who were qualified to conduct such a review, the results of which would be given to His Majesty. The men I suggested came from the left as well as the right, in the conviction that as members of the State Council they would not permit their political views or their attitudes toward me to keep them from reaching the inescapable conclusion that I had.

This correspondence was discussed in the cabinet. Some time after receiving my second letter, Stolypin sent me a brief note saying that His Majesty had been kind enough to take an interest in the matter and that after reviewing what he had received from the cabinet, he had written that he saw no impropriety in this case on the part of his officials and that the correspondence should therefore be closed. It goes without saying that His Majesty had neither the knowledge of judicial matters nor the time to go thoroughly into this case and that he wrote what he did at the request of Stolypin. All this shows how poorly Stolypin looked after the interests of the Emperor and in what a remarkable position, to say the least, he placed him.[9]

Copies of my letters to Stolypin and his replies are in my archive.[10] Now that he is dead, there is no reason to keep them secret and I may have them published in my lifetime.[11] Then society will see to what a disgraceful level the judiciary and the administration had fallen during Stolypin's tenure. It was only under his administration that such cases could occur. It was only during his tenure that people of standing as well as defenseless people of the lower classes were killed when it was thought their removal served the government's purposes.

It was just recently that I received additional confirmation of what I have said. It was at a reception for the recently arrived ambassador from Austria-Hungary that an elderly man asked if I would see him. I said that I would, with pleasure, and set an hour for the following day.

When he saw me, he told that his name was Psheradskii, that he was a privy councillor, a member of the council of the Ministry of Interior, to which he had been appointed by Stolypin, to whom he had been close. He told me the following story, often stopping to cry as he told it.

The events occurred after the Emperor refused to accept Stolypin's request to leave office after the controversy concerning the proposal to the western provinces. It was said that the chief reason he had refused was because he valued the premier for his accomplishment in ending revolutionary activity, including revolutionary terrorism, and believed that with Stolypin in office such terrorism would not reappear. Therefore it was in Stolypin's interest to make it appear that there were no new revolutionary terrorist acts.

Well, not long after the Emperor's refusal, what was evidently the work of revolutionary-anarchists, the killing of a procurator while he was traveling on a train, was treated by the investigators as an ordinary murder, done by a robber, but when someone who admitted having carried out the killing on behalf of a revolutionary committee was jailed, in Sebastopol, the authorities were embarrassed. So, it was arranged that he be permitted to escape, and no sooner had he succeeded then the guards shot him, thus erasing the evidence that the killing of the procurator had been politically motivated.

Psheradskii went on to tell me about another incident that affected him personally. In 1905, Kurosh, a naval officer stationed off Helsingfors, had fired at revolutionaries in the city who had raised the red flag. The revolutionaries swore they would kill him in retaliation and so informed him, but for some reason did not carry out the threat at that time. Some years later, when relations between the Russian government and Finland had again become strained, the revolutionaries decided to take their revenge on him by killing his seventeen-year-old son, a student in Petersburg. They reasoned that by so doing they would make the father suffer for the rest of his life.

The deed was carried out while Psheradskii and his wife, whose sister was married to Kurosh, were staying at the naval officer's villa near Riga. Kurosh himself was at sea at the time. Young Kurosh, however, was there. When he went to close a window facing the garden, someone appeared there, fired several shots, killing him on the spot. Ironically, given what later happened, the Emperor sent the elder Kurosh a telegram of condolence about the killing of his son.

Aleksandrov (the same Aleksandrov whom I have mentioned earlier) conducted the investigation. It was quickly apparent that the investigation was being conducted to prove that young Kurosh had killed himself. Psheradskii, himself a jurist, noted, among other scandalous things, that material aimed at proving a suicide was substituted for several pages of testimony taken by the examining magistrate.

This fine old man said plaintively that what he had seen happen before his very eyes was being turned into a suicide. When I asked him why this was being done, he replied that it was Stolypin who had ordered that politically motivated killings be treated as ordinary murders. Why, I asked, hadn't he gone with the facts to the minister of the navy or the minister of justice? He had gone to the former, who had reacted in indignation, but he had chosen not to call on that good-for-nothing Shcheglovitov because that man was nothing but Stolypin's lackey, who had turned the Russian system of justice into a police agency serving the premier.

III

Personalia, 1907–1911

1907–1908

Following the end of the session of the State Council, not long after the events of May 30, 1907, I went abroad with my wife.[1] I do not have to describe our state of mind.

We went first to Frankfurt, where I was to have a minor throat operation, taking up residence at nearby Bad Homburg, where the air was better.[2] My daughter and her family, who were to spend the summer with us, came to be with us at the spa. After a short stay there, I and my son-in-law went to Cauteret by automobile, while my wife, daughter, and our grandson traveled there by train. From Cauteret we went on to Biarritz, I and my son-in-law by automobile, the others by train, to spend some time at our villa.[3] After several weeks, my son-in-law left to return to his post in Brussels, taking his wife and their son with them.

My wife and I remained in Biarritz for a while longer, then made our way to Paris, where we stayed at the St. James and Albany Hotel. Then I decided to go on to Brussels, while my wife was to remain in Paris for another ten days, to look after her wardrobe.

While we were still in Bad Homburg we had all noticed that she was quite nervous and did not look at all well. I ascribed her condition to the terrible strain under which we had been the preceding months, and, possibly, to the return of a stomach ailment which she had contracted while we resided on Elagin Island.

After I had left Paris, she had what appeared to be an epileptic seizure and lost consciousness. Her maid immediately called Mechnikov, who looked after her better than a nurse would have, and spent much time with her, acting like a true friend. I did not learn of the episode until she arrived in Brussels. I was shocked by how her appearance had changed in the ten days since I had last seen her, but I was reassured by a letter from Mechnikov about her condition.

After our return to Petersburg [in November], my wife had another seizure, which led me to turn to Bekhterev and his assistant, Karpinskii. A consultation was arranged—with Bekhterev, Karpinskii, Professor Veliaminov (a close acquaintance), our family physician Shapirov, and Dr. Vestfalich, a well-known specialist on internal [gastro-intestinal] ailments.[4] Bekhterev was certain that she was suffering from epilepsy. Karpinskii agreed, but with reservations, as did Dr. Shapirov. Veliaminov thought that her seizure may have been brought on by diseased tonsils. In the end they prescribed bromides and other medications for nervousness and insomnia. Nonetheless, she continued to have seizures during the winter, but there might have been more of them if not for the medications, which she was given in increasing doses.

I was, naturally, anxious, even desperate, about my wife's condition. It was in this state of mind that I wrote to Mechnikov, whose reply provided me with some reassurance. He said that although he did not know what my wife's ailment was, he was certain that it was not epilepsy, certain too that the ailment would eventually be diagnosed correctly and that she would improve.

My anxiety was thereby relieved somewhat, but was far from dispelled because my wife's nervousness increased. Already under strain from the assassination attempts of the preceding year, her nerves were further frayed during the winter of 1907–1908, as a result of the campaign of slander directed not only against me but also against her. There were foul attacks made against her on the floor of the State Duma by such scoundrels and good-for-nothings as Purishkevich. Of course she could not be kept ignorant of these attacks. And as she grew more nervous, I began to fear that I was doomed to outlive her.

It was in this condition that we went abroad in the summer of 1908. With our grandson we went first to Vichy and then to Ouchy, near Lausanne, on Lake Geneva, for her to be treated by Dr. Combe, a well-known and fashionable doctor, who had an office in Lausanne, where he practiced his real specialty, pediatrics. In Ouchy he treated stomach disorders, and at the time we thought my wife's illness might be gastro-intestinal in origin.

Dr. Combe had a large financial interest in the Beau Rivage Hotel in Ouchy, and that is where his patients stayed. In my opinion, he is a second-rate doctor, but the hotel was comfortable and had a good dining room, which probably provided more help to the patients who ate there than did his treatment.

While we were in Ouchy, Kokher, the famous surgeon, was also there, for a vacation. My wife and I knew him from Petersburg, where he had come to perform an operation. While in Petersburg he had participated in a consultation about my wife's illness.

Well, when he visited with us in Ouchy, I talked about my wife's illness. He asked if her gastric juices had been analyzed. We told him that this had not been done because no one had been able to insert a tube to get a sample of the juices. Dr. Kokher then advised us that if we would spend a few days at his clinic in Berne, he would be able to analyze her gastric juices and make a diagnosis.

My wife asked if in addition he could remove a rather large growth on her forehead, above her right eye that had been increasing in size. Another doctor had previously dismissed the growth as of no relevance to my wife's state of health. Dr. Kokher was of the same opinion, suggesting that the growth was of no more than cosmetic significance, but if she wished, he could easily remove it. She did wish it. Dr. Kokher agreed, but said we would have to wait a bit before he could see her at the clinic so he could finish his vacation.

During our wait, I decided to go to Rome to attend memorial services, on the anniversary of the death of Emperor Alexander III, October 20. There I had occasion to talk with our ambassador to Italy, Muravev, who was to die under scandalous circumstances a while later.[5]

Not long after we arrived at Dr. Kokher's clinic, he decided, after consultation with Sali, a well-known professor of medicine in Berne, that since there was probably nothing seriously wrong with my wife's stomach and since she was rather weak, he would not try to get a sample of her gastric juices. But he did remove the growth and did it so skillfully that no trace of the surgery remained. Immediately after the operation my wife's quasi-epileptic symptoms disappeared and never returned, even after she stopped taking bromides. It is evident that those symptoms had been produced by pressure of the growth on the nerves above the eye. Mechnikov was thus vindicated: she did not have epilepsy and the cause of her troubles was uncovered.

It was now November. From Berne we went directly to Petersburg, where my wife returned very swiftly to complete health and, glory be to God, has remained in that state to this day.

1909

Early in the summer of 1909, we made our yearly trip abroad, first to Vichy, then to Biarritz, where we spent several months in Biarritz with my grandson, my daughter, and her husband. At the end of November we returned to Petersburg.

1910

[Witte deals with his stay abroad in 1910 in another context.][6]

1911

In May I [and my wife] went abroad and did not return until December.

For medical reasons we had to spend some time in Frankfurt. The preceding summer I had been compelled to take to bed because of a very painful inflammation of the middle ear. Well, in Frankfurt I was told by several professors of medicine, men in whom I had complete confidence, that if I did not wish to have more trouble with my ear, I should be operated on, the sooner the better because if I waited too long I might not have the strength to undergo [surgery]. I decided not to wait and I was operated on for an hour and a half, under chloroform. A month later I had another operation, this one a minor one, that has left me with no sensation in parts of my face.

In August we visited with our daughter in Biarritz.[7]

IV

Formation of the Goremykin Government

Out with the Old

As I noted earlier, several of my colleagues in the cabinet wanted to join me when I told them I was asking to be relieved of my post as premier, but I dissuaded them lest their departure serve as a precedent for establishing a parliamentary system. Consequently, I assumed that most of them would be asked to stay, but to my amazement only three did, Baron Freedericksz, the minister of the court, Admiral Birilev, the minister of the navy, and General Rödiger, the minister of war. The last two would leave sometime later because of differences with Grand Duke Nicholas Nikolaevich. Only one other cabinet member, Fedorov, was asked to stay. Goremykin, the new premier, was anxious to keep him and offered to have his status changed from that of acting minister of commerce to that of minister, but Fedorov, a very fine man who did not share Goremykin's views, chose to leave government service.

Count Lambsdorff, the foreign minister, wanted very much to remain, but after hearing that I intended to submit my request to be allowed to go, he asked me if he shouldn't follow my example. I advised him not to for the reason given above, as well as because I was aware of how anxious he was to stay on. Prince V. S. Obolenskii, his bosom friend, strongly urged him to do as I did, but Count Lambsdorff did not submit a request until a few days later. This occurred because of my conversation with the Emperor on April 22, when I learned that Izvolskii would be the new foreign minister. As soon as I returned to Petersburg from Tsarskoe Selo I called on the count to inform him of what was in store and advised him to submit his request to be relieved of his duties immediately so that it would appear that his departure had been at his request. This he did, and, as he later told me, he was then graciously received by His Majesty, who shed some tears over parting with him. Following the announcement of the count's departure, Baron Freedericksz cynically told me that Count Lambsdorff had been let go ''as a sop to public opinion for the Japanese war and as a means of getting rid of the last traces of that catastrophe.''[1]

What most surprised me was the replacement of Durnovo as minister of interior. I had felt certain that he would be kept because he had been at odds with me and had been following the wishes of General Trepov. In fact, the Emperor told him that he wished him to continue in office after my departure. He was, of course, overjoyed, as was his wife, who called on my wife with the good news, informing her that she was on her way to look at the summer residence of the minister of interior, on Aptekarskii Island, because they would be moving into it in a few days.

However, two days later there appeared a decree announcing Durnovo's departure from office.[2] But he was given a grant of 200,000 rubles, this on top of the many honors and favors he had already received—state secretary of His Majesty, actual privy councillor, appointment as lady-in-waiting for his daughter—in return for services rendered the Emperor at my expense. And now a consolation prize of 200,000 rubles! Obviously another reward for his treachery toward me. Obviously, fate does not always punish traitors.

Another person who would have stayed on in office, given a choice, was Prince A. D. Obolenskii, the over-procurator of the Holy Synod. Toward the end of my tenure, when he realized that my departure was imminent, he said bluntly that the over-procurator's position should not be tied to the fate of the cabinet and, in fact, asked that the law be changed to separate the Holy Synod from the cabinet, but wanted to continue to attend its meetings as usual. Naturally, I did not show any sympathy for such an idea. I should say that he was not a bad over-procurator. To be sure he was torn between seeking his own advantage and adhering to the principles of gentry liberalism with which he had been inculcated in his younger days, but had he stayed on he would not have permitted what we now have, the infection of the Orthodox church by the unholy spirit of the Black Hundreds.

When it became evident that most of my cabinet colleagues would be leaving office, I wrote the Emperor asking him to provide them with suitable appointments, e.g., to the State Council or to the Senate.[3] This was the custom when a minister left office. And the Emperor adhered to this custom, with those who were not already state councillors or senators, except in the case of Count I. I. Tolstoi, the outgoing minister of education, who has received no honor or appointment to this day [February 1912], apparently because he was under attack by the Black Hundreds, the servile newspapers, and right-wing state councillors, as being, if not a revolutionary, then at least a ''kike-loving'' Kadet.

In with the New

Goremykin replaced the outgoing men with the following.

Kokovtsev was to be his new minister of finance. Undoubtedly, he was one of the most suitable candidates available, meaning that the appointment was a very appropriate one. Before accepting the post, he had shown me the courtesy of asking if I advised him to do so, but, subsequently, in a true Kokovtsev fashion, he expressed his gratitude by implying to the State Duma that it was he, not I, who had arranged the loan that saved Russia.

The appointment of Schwanebach as state controller was a different matter. He was as qualified to be a state controller as he was to be a metropolitan. His sole qualification was that he was in the good graces of the Montenegrin princesses.

Stishinskii, who replaced Nikolskii as head of the Chief Administration of Land Organization and Agriculture, is an untrustworthy man, and a reactionary to boot. He has the ability to serve as an official, but he has all the traits of a renegade. I have no doubt that he was born a Pole or is of Polish origin.

Why Kaufmann was given the portfolio of minister of education is difficult to determine. His only experience with educational institutions was as assistant chief of the Institutions of Empress Marie.[4] In this capacity he dealt largely with girls' institutes, the pupils of which have little in common with genuine students. Moreover, because he studied at the Tsarskoe Selo Lycée he had no understanding of university life, and he was, in addition, far removed from the worlds of science and scholarship. Yet it must be granted that he is not stupid and that he is a very decent man, which was to lead later to his falling out with Stolypin and his removal.

General Schaufuss, a railroad man whom I knew from my Odessa days, was chosen to be minister of ways and communications. He was [he died in 1911] a very fine man with a good knowledge of railroading, but he lacked initiative and had no bent for governmental work. I believe that the reason for his choice was that he had once been head of the Nikolaevskii Railroad and had then become acquainted with Goremykin, who has an estate in Novgorod province and often traveled on that line.

The man chosen to replace Prince Obolenskii as over-procurator of the Holy Synod was Prince Shirinskii-Shikhmatov, whom even Pobedonostsev had considered a reactionary! As I related earlier he had served under Pobedonostsev as assistant over-procurator and had had to leave office when I became premier.

Count Lambsdorff, as noted earlier, was replaced as foreign minister by Izvolskii, who was appointed for the same reason that Count Lambsdorff's predecessor, Count Muravev, had been appointed—that he had served as minister to Denmark, the Dowager Empress's birthplace.

Stolypin was the new minister of interior. I was aware that he had little book learning and no governmental experience.[5] Therefore I did not expect him to be an outstanding minister, but on the basis of what acquaintances and friends said about him, I thought him a decent person and was not upset by his appointment. I will deal later with my bitter disappointment in him.

The worst appointment of all was that of Shcheglovitov, as minister of justice. In fact it was the worst appointment made in all the years since my leaving office because he undermined the judicial system that Emperor Alexander II established, so much so that is it difficult to determine nowadays where the courts end and the Azefs begin. I am certain that he will be remembered unkindly in the judiciary for decades to come.[6]

In Preparation for the New Era

In the days between my departure from the office of premier and the opening of the First State Duma, the decrees concerning the reorganization of the State Council and the enactment of the Fundamental Laws, which provided the basis for reform of our political structure, were published.

Also, during this interval a decree was issued abolishing the Committee of Ministers. With the establishment of the cabinet, the Committee of Ministers had become redundant and it was soon suggested that it be abolished. I, however, opposed such a step, believing that the Committee of Ministers should be retained until the reorganization of the government had been completed. It seemed to me that until that time came there would be matters with which the Committee, a body neither exclusively administrative nor legislative, a body which included not only ministers but also representatives from the departments of the State Council and other persons appointed by His Majesty, would be better equipped to deal. The abolition of the Committee of Ministers might have done no harm had the cabinet not begun to consider, without proper checks, legislative matters that previously had gone through the Committee of Ministers.

V

The First State Duma

I will deal only briefly with the First State Duma and the reasons for its failure and dissolution.

A major reason for its failure was the electoral law which resulted in a State Duma opposed to the government. Although I was responsible for the drafting of the law, I was not, as I have stated before,[1] responsible for the basic and erroneous assumption upon which the law was based, that the peasantry was a pillar of conservatism and hence should be favored in the electoral process.

As it turned out, the peasant deputies elected to the State Duma favored confiscation of privately owned land[2] and its distribution to the peasantry, to some degree what Emperor Alexander II had done when he liberated the serfs. In this desire the peasant deputies had the support of the large number of liberal and radical middle-class and working-class deputies.

Of course, confiscation would mean a violation of the basic principle of private property and could not have been countenanced by the government, but there was no danger of the proposal becoming law, for even if the State Duma had passed a bill calling for confiscation, the conservative State Council (with half its members appointed by the Emperor) would have rejected it, and even if that unthinkable event should have occurred, the Emperor could have refused to sign the bill. Had the State Duma been permitted to debate such a bill, its members would have come to recognize the complexities and difficulties of enacting a law calling for confiscation, a law far easier to frame than it would be to put into effect. Such debates might have had a sobering effect and might have prevented the peasant deputies from becoming allied to the liberal and radical urban deputies and the State Duma might have become a sensible, even conservative, body.

But Goremykin had long been determined that if a confiscation bill were taken up in the State Duma, then that body should be dissolved. This determination had unfortunate consequences. It strengthened the leftist tendencies in the State Duma, creating a strain between it and the government, a strain that could only be aggravated by the presence in the cabinet of men known throughout Russia as reactionaries and adherents of a police regime. As a consequence one could expect no constructive work from the State Duma, this at a time when most Russians seemed to have taken leave of their senses. At the same time the mere rumor that the State Duma would consider a confiscation bill provoked a rightward trend among noble and other private landowners, a trend reflected in the rightward-shifting composition of the zemstvos.

The State Duma opened on April 27. As early as June the government decided to dissolve it, but held off for fear that such a step might provoke a revival of the kind of unrest experienced in the preceding October. Thus, Stolypin asked local officials, among them General Rheinbott, the prefect of Moscow (Stolypin was particularly concerned about Moscow), if the State Duma could be dissolved without creating widespread disturbances. This was a time, it would be noted, of many terrorist acts.

Another illustration of how the government at this time had lost its head was General Trepov's abortive negotiations with Miliukov to form a Kadet cabinet that would replace that of Goremykin. Stolypin dissuaded the Emperor from carrying out Trepov's idea, either because he feared the direction a Kadet cabinet might take or because he was afraid that he would not be invited to join it.

Stolypin, as noted, was afraid that dissolution of the State Duma would have revolutionary repercussions and hence opposed such a step. When it was finally taken, it was on the insistence of Goremykin, who told the Emperor that it would be impossible to get anything constructive out of the State Duma and that if it continued to sit it would serve only to fan revolutionary sentiment. His Majesty agreed and on July 7 signed the decree that dissolved the First State Duma.

On returning to Petersburg from Peterhof, Goremykin sent the decree to the Senate for publication, then went to bed, leaving orders that he not be disturbed. While he slept an order arrived for him not to have the decree published, but he was not awakened. After the decree was published on the following morning, malicious gossips let it be known that the State Duma had been dissolved because of the premier's well-known desire not to be disturbed.[3]

In advance of the dissolution of the State Duma, Petersburg and Kiev were placed under martial law, but the publication of the decree of dissolution did not provoke the dreaded disorders. A large number of opposition deputies, chiefly Kadets, did try to arouse the country against the closing of the State Duma. Fearing that they would not be able to meet in safety elsewhere, they journeyed to Vyborg, in Finland. Even there they were soon warned by the governor that if they did not disperse, he would take action against them. But they met long enough to issue the famous Vyborg Manifesto calling on the peasantry to react against the high-handed dissolution of the State Duma by refusing to pay taxes and dues to the government as well as by other means. Of course, such a call was totally unpatriotic and revolutionary.

Several of the signatories, among them Professor Petrazhitskii and the engineer Mikhailov, were wholly out of sympathy with the manifesto, but signed it rather than be thought cowardly by their comrades. Some would-be signatories could not sign because they did not know when the meeting was to be held. They were in luck because, as will be seen, the signatories were later punished.

A New Government

Goremykin did not expect that the dissolution of the State Duma would mark the end of his tenure, but it did. Not without foundation he ascribed his fall to the intrigues of Stolypin, who wanted to succeed him, and Trepov.

It was Trepov, we should remember, who had recommended Goremykin, that tin-type bureaucrat, distinguishable from other bureaucrats only by his mutton-chop whiskers, for the post of premier. General Trepov had expected Goremykin to follow his instructions and the premier had done so, but only to the degree that his desire for quiet and rest permitted him to do so. Being a *m'en fichiste*,[4] he rarely appeared at State Duma sessions and then only to read prepared statements of a kind that could only irritate that body.

This dissatisfied General Trepov, who advised the premier to attend State Duma sessions more often and generally to keep a close eye on the Duma's activities and by reacting vigorously to what it did, when vigor was called for. So, as I learned from Goremykin toward the end of the First State Duma, Trepov prepared something in the nature of written instructions to guide the premier in his behavior toward the Duma, instructions on which the Emperor would note his concurrence. All this quickly chilled relations between the premier and the general. Sometime later, when I had the opportunity, I asked Goremykin why he had to leave office. He replied that he could not function with Trepov in the wings and that the final straw was having to accept instructions from the general. These provoked Goremykin into complaining to the Emperor that to follow the instructions would do no good, that what was necessary was to dissolve the State Duma. The Emperor accepted the premier's advice, then soon turned around and accepted Trepov's advice to dismiss Goremykin. In relating this story, Goremykin said: "Of course, you are acquainted with the character of our unfortunate Emperor." I nodded. When I asked what he thought of his successor, he said: "A typical, adaptable provincial noble, who was fortunate that Trepov soon died, because he could not have gotten along with him."

It appears that Trepov advised the Emperor that the government would get along better with the next State Duma if Goremykin, Stishinskii, and Prince Shirinskii-Shikhmatov were replaced by men of a more liberal stamp. Accordingly, Stolypin replaced Goremykin, while retaining his portfolio of minister of interior; Prince Vasilchikov replaced Stishinskii; and P. P. Izvolskii replaced Prince Shirinskii-Shikhmatov.

Stolypin seemed quite the liberal at the time of his appointment as premier.[5] In speaking to the State Duma he advocated complete religious toleration, the removal of legislation that discriminated against the peasantry, the extension of education, amelioration of the status of non-Russians, and the like. Trepov expected with the aid of liberals such as Stolypin to throw dust in the eyes of the Russian electors and to ensure the election of a State Duma that was more conservative than its predecessor.

There had been some thought of appointing Krivoshein as successor to Stishinskii, but given the possibility of widespread unrest following the closing of the First State Duma and given the desire to placate the peasantry, they fixed on Prince Vasilchikov, a decent man, a thorough gentlemen, and reputedly a liberal.*

Indicative of Prince Vasilchikov's reputation as a liberal is the fact that Prince Sviatopolk-Mirskii had considered having him as one of his assistant ministers, but the Emperor had rejected the idea because Prince Vasilchikov had presented as requirement for his acceptance of the post the government's commitment to a number of political changes, including respect for the Finnish constitution, something that did not sit well with the Emperor. I had occasion to talk with Prince Vasilchikov during this time and discovered that he considered my views too conservative for his taste. But after joining the Stolypin government he moved to the right: not long ago he was elected chairman of the Nationalist Club of Petersburg, a group with a marked point of view, particularly with respect to non-Russians. Typical of the change in him is the fact that not too long ago he voted for the complete abolition of constitutional guarantees for Finland.

It is possible that Prince Vasilchikov was not conscious of how much he has shifted, for it seems to me that he does not have firm convictions and that, like many officials and public men in recent times, he followed Stolypin's example of changing convictions to suit the times. The exceptions can be counted on one's fingers.

According to my information, Stolypin suggested Prince A. D. Obolenskii, a close relative and, as I have noted, something of a liberal, as over-procurator of the Holy Synod, but the Emperor would not agree. Then, at a cabinet meeting, when Stolypin said that he had no one but Prince Obolenskii to suggest, the foreign minister, A. P. Izvolskii, put forward his brother, P. P. Izvolskii, then assistant minister of education, and so the appointment was made. No question that P. P. Izvolskii is a very decent sort, with many fine qualities, but not those required for such a high position, nor did he have the requisite experience.

---

*Krivoshein then tried, but failed, to get another ministerial portfolio, but he later managed to become assistant minister of finance.[6]

VI

The Opening of the Stolypin Era

The New Premier

When I heard about Stolypin's appointment, while I was abroad, I was pleased by the news because, according to those acquainted with him, he held liberal opinions and was a man of strong character and an iron will, but not possessed of great ability. Had he had the mind, the education, and the experience to match his strong character he might have turned out to be a statesman, and whatever mistakes he might have made would have been forgiven him and he would still have held on to the reputation of a statesman.[1]

But he lacked the mind, the education, and the experience to match his audacity and courage, and that condemned him to be at best no more than a bayonet Junker.[2] But at least he would have gone to his death with a reputation for integrity had he remained a bachelor.

Unfortunately for him, and for Russia, he married. Those who dealt with him said the only person toward whom he did not show his strong will was his wife, who could do anything she pleased with him. As a result her numerous family (she was born a Neidhardt) acquired considerable influence in Russia. Also, according to those who knew him, Stolypin's acquiescence to his wife's desires gradually corrupted him, so much so that by the end of life he had lost interest in his work and even in the maintenance of his reputation, being concerned only with using his position for amassing honors and material advantage, in ways that would have been unthinkable under his predecessors.[3]

Another negative influence on Stolypin's career, an influence almost as unfortunate as that of his wife, was the attempt on his life on August 12, when a bomb was thrown into the reception room of his summer residence, on Aptekarskii

Island, killing several persons and wounding his poor son and daughter. (I was in Paris when I heard the news. I was so upset by the news that I sent him a telegram of sympathy, to which he sent a kindly reply.)

The attempt on his life helped erode that liberalism which had provided him a path to the premiership. First his liberalism waned, then it disappeared. During the last two or so years of his tenure he not only instituted a reign of terror but also undermined the rule of law. Never before in the history of the autocracy was there such a disregard for law as in the last years of the Stolypin era, when he became more and more an obscurantist, more and more a police type, who employed the most brutal and treacherous methods both toward persons he considered dangerous to the state as well as toward persons whom, for whatever reason, he considered ill disposed toward him. From several sources I heard that when later in his tenure he expressed views clearly in contradiction to those he had expressed earlier in his career, he would respond: ''Yes, but that was before the bomb on Aptekarskii Island; now I am a different person.''

Stolypin was a brave man, almost irrationally so, but, in contrast to the slim (by my choice) measures taken to protect me while I was premier, millions were to be spent to protect him. His residences became fortresses, and he was surrounded by almost an army of guards, disguised as coachmen, lackeys, employees of the State Council and the State Duma. These senseless expenditures did not save him; in the end he was to fall before an assassin's bullet.

In the short run the attempt on Stolypin's life helped him. It helped him at court, where he was already admired for his audacity and courage. Now he was in addition an object of kindly sympathy from the court, naturally, since the attempt on his life could not fail to arouse sympathy for him.

He was aided at court too by what was his good fortune, the death of Trepov, from a heart attack, about the time he became premier. No doubt had Trepov lived, he would have undermined Stolypin, as he had me and Goremykin.[4]

Stolypin's Misuse of Article 87

In the interval between the First and Second State Dumas, Stolypin set a precedent for later abuse of Article 87 of the Fundamental Laws by using the article to carry out both quasi-liberal and repressive measures. And he did so without a twinge of conscience. As I have stated earlier, this article, of which I was the author, was intended to be used exclusively for questions of extraordinary importance when the legislative bodies were not in session. It was not intended to be employed in dealing with substantive questions that did not require immediate action, questions like that of the organization of peasant life.

As will be seen, Stolypin proposed to deal with the question of the organization of peasant life before the opening of the Second State Duma, employing Article 87 to do so. In so acting, he tied the hands of the next State Duma, for a law of this kind, dealing with a question of the gravest importance, already in force for several months, becomes virtually impossible to rescind without causing chaos. What he was to do in this case, as well as in other cases where he invoked Article 87, was to preclude the careful consideration of such legislation by the legislative bodies.

The Velvet Glove

One of the quasi-liberal measures that Stolypin had enacted by the use of Article 87 permitted Old Believers and sectarians to leave the Orthodox church and form their own congregations, with rights and obligations specified by law.[5]

Several of his seemingly liberal measures enacted under Article 87 were aimed at placating the peasantry, but they were ill conceived, harming some peasants and doing little good for the rest. Thus, a considerable portion of appanage lands and state domains were turned over to the Peasants' Bank for sale to the peasantry.[6] Also, some of the unpopulated land in the Altai Region belonging to the Emperor was made available for peasant settlement. The amount of land made available for peasant use was too little to bring any substantial benefit to the peasantry, but the loss of appanage lands reduced the income of the Imperial Family, and the loss of state domains meant a reduction in the state's reserve of useful land, a reserve required by Russia's size and her rapidly growing population. All in all these measures were not sensible from an economic point of view.

Among other quasi-liberal measures for the benefit of the peasantry were decrees lowering the rate of interest that peasants paid on loans from the Peasants' Bank and liberalizing the conditions under which that bank could grant loans where appanage lands were offered as security.

As indicated, the replacement of Stishinskii by the reputedly liberal Prince Vasilchikov was intended to please the peasantry.

During this period Stolypin's major effort for dealing with the agrarian problem, using Article 87, was designed for the benefit of the large landowners, not the peasants. When he took office he undertook to carry out the childish idea of protecting the large landowners from the peasant movement to confiscate their land by turning part of the peasantry into private landowners, so that instead of tens of thousands, there would be hundreds of thousands, perhaps a million, private landowners. This large-scale conversion of part of the peasantry into private landowners, he reasoned, would give the new landowners a stake in defending the interest of noble and bourgeois landowners as well as their own against the peasant masses.

This simple, childish idea, having taken root in a police mentality, bore fruit in the law of November 9, 1906, which later, much later, was approved by the State Council and the State Duma and is supposed to provide the basis for shaping the future structure of the peasant economy. The basic goal of the law, that all land be held individually, was borrowed from the work done by the Special Conference on the Needs of Rural Industry, of which I was chairman.[7] Our intention was that the shift from communal to private, individual ownership be gradual and voluntary but the Stolypin law distorted our intention by calling for the use of compulsion. Moreover, the Stolypin law failed to provide for necessary changes in the law codes defining peasant property rights.

In the final analysis, the Stolypin law means that the village commune is to be broken up by compulsory methods to create a sufficiently large number of so-called individual peasant proprietors to enable the private landowners to protect themselves. Stolypin cynically expressed what was on his mind when he later told the State Duma that this law is not for the benefit of the weak, i.e., the ordinary peasant, but for the benefit of the strong.[8]

Of course, it is possible that with the passage of time this law will be revised to provide satisfactory conditions for the peasantry. But I believe that before this occurs, we will see much disorder and the shedding of innocent blood as a consequence of the short-sighted police mentality behind this law. I hope that I am mistaken.*

The Iron Fist

At the same time that he was taking quasi-liberal steps, Stolypin employed repressive measures to stifle disorder, for example, by increasing the penalty for disseminating antigovernmental propaganda among the troops and by instituting field courts-martial.

The idea of establishing field courts-martial, i.e., extraordinary military courts, presided over by officers of the line rather than by military judges, with the power to try civilians and sentence them to death, was put before the cabinet by General Pavlov, the military procurator, while I was premier, but my cabinet would not agree to an institution that was so egregiously brutal, an institution that no country with the slightest claim to respect for legality would countenance. Even Goremykin, during his brief tenure, did not establish field courts-martial, but Stolypin did.

The regulation establishing these odious courts was enacted under Article 87. When it was later submitted to the State Duma for approval it was voted down. Stolypin then circumvented the Fundamental Laws by having the regulations included in the code of military laws, which is not subject to review by the legislative bodies. The regulation establishing field courts-martial is still in force, permitting *murder by the administrative powers* to continue.

As very competent jurists informed me, Stolypin used exceptionally repressive

---

*It is remarkable that one of those who defended the law in the State Council was Mr. Stishinskii, the very Mr. Stishinskii who ardently defended the village commune in the days of Count Dmitrii Tolstoi and enforced measures contrary to the spirit of the law he now defends. He acted as he did to show how loyal he was to Stolypin, or rather how much of a lackey he was.

Also, I am grieved that the implementation of the Stolypin Law was entrusted to Krivoshein [who succeeded Prince Vasilchikov in 1908]. This is the same Krivoshein who was out of sympathy with the ideas expressed at the Special Conference on the Needs of Rural Industry and had a hand in having the conference terminated to make way for Goremykin's special conference, which favored the rural commune.

and extra-legal methods in dealing with the signers of the Vyborg Manifesto.*
That document, as I have said, was clearly seditious, and its signers should have
been tried, but in accordance with the law. But Stolypin directed matters through
his compliant minister of justice, Shcheglovitov, so that the signers should receive
the kind of jail sentences that would deprive them of the right to be elected to the
State Duma. Moreover, he also had those that had not come to trial by the time of
the elections prevented from being candidates. All this was unfortunate, not only
from the point of view of legality, but also from the point of view of political life:
most of those thus deprived of the right to be elected to the State Duma were
Kadets. Whether or not one agrees with their program, one must recognize that
the Kadet Party includes some of the most cultivated members of our intelligentsia, men who enjoy great prestige. As a consequence some of the most prominent
Kadets lost the opportunity of representing their party in the Second State Duma.

A Glimpse at Stolypin's Character

Stolypin's behavior in the Gurko-Lidval affair, which provided sensational material for the public in November 1906, gives us an insight in his character. The facts
of the affair are as follows.[10]

A bad harvest that year compelled the government to purchase grain. Gurko,
an assistant minister of interior, gave the purchase contract to a certain Lidval, a
foreigner, in violation of various laws and regulations, and apparently did so for
mercenary motives. When Lidval proved unable to carry out his contract, a
public uproar broke out. With elections to the Second State Duma imminent, the
government was unable to hush up this affair, which after all affected the stomachs
of the peasantry. Gurko tried to explain matters away to the press, but it became
necessary to conduct a senatorial investigation, a task entrusted to V. N. Varvarin. He found that the affair was of such gravity that Gurko should be tried by
the Senate.

A trial was held despite all efforts to prevent it, and Gurko was sentenced to
leave government service. I was told that the sentence would have been more
severe had his name not been Gurko.[11]

Earlier, during my premiership, when Gurko was appointed assistant minister,
I was aware that although he is an able, intelligent, well-rounded man, he is not a
man of principle. I did not oppose the appointment because I believe it should be

*After Stolypin became premier, several noble assemblies [reflecting their shift to the right] either
boycotted or expelled those of their members who had signed the Vyborg Manifesto as well as leading
liberals who had not been signatories. The Kostroma noble assembly defied this trend by accepting
several of those expelled in its ranks. This in turn drew a protest on December 20, 1906, from the
Council of the United Nobility, a body that is still [1912] functioning.

This council, like other noble organizations, has not served Russia, because it is devoted to highly
reactionary aims, largely those that serve their class. These organizations hold to the old view that the
peasantry should be treated as a class apart. That many leading nobles should still cling to such a
medieval view is remarkable.

It should be noted, however, that in recent times some of the noble organizations have become
more sensible.[9]

the prerogative of a minister to select those working closely with him and I knew that Durnovo was as well aware of Gurko's defects and virtues as I.

Stolypin showed his true colors in the Gurko-Lidval affair by shifting all responsibility for it to Gurko and dissociating himself from Gurko, despite the fact that he had some share of responsibility for what happened. It is certain the Gurko kept Stolypin informed about the negotiations with Lidval and that if there had been anything questionable about the contract he should have been aware of the fact, but it was characteristic of Stolypin to be unaware of the smell of scandal even in matters in which he is involved. Whether or not the premier approved of what Gurko was doing because he trusted his assistant minister or because the assistant minister was doing what he was told to do was Stolypin's business, but he should have known what was going on and, in any case, bore a share of responsibility. But as I have noted, Stolypin immediately washed his hands of his subordinate, as if the matter did not concern him at all.[12]

There is a sequel to this story which I wish to relate here.

Senator Varvarin was very anxious to be appointed to the State Council, but as Shcheglovitov told me the Emperor was furious with Varvarin for permitting the Gurko case to go to trial and would not agree to such an appointment. Shcheglovitov, who felt that Varvarin had acted properly, said, somewhat naively to me: "I am looking for a case for Varvarin to prosecute that will rehabilitate him."

The opportunity came later, when Lopukhin, the former director of the Department of Police, was tried for revealing to the revolutionaries that Azef, who was one of their leaders, was also a police agent. The law was not clear about such offenses. In my opinion, as well as that of competent jurists, Lopukhin should have been sentenced to a few months of imprisonment at most, but Varvarin, to whom the case was entrusted, in an effort to distinguish himself, was able to have the defendant sentenced to a long term at hard labor, a sentence later commuted to exile in Siberia. It is not because I approve of Lopukhin that I say this, but what is right is right. Incidentally, I recently learned from a member of the council of the Ministry of Interior, a person who had been close to Stolypin, that after the sentence had been pronounced the premier gave Varvarin 5,000 rubles from the Ministry of the Interior's secret funds.

Assassinations and
Assassination Attempts

As I have said earlier, during my tenure as premier, there were hardly any assassinations, but under Goremykin and Stolypin they became almost daily occurrences. Most of the killings of officials were done on orders of the revolutionary-anarchist [Socialist Revolutionary] party, who, it appears, had drawn up a list of reactionaries in high places whom they considered most harmful. Although I oppose all such killings, believing that they do more harm than good to the state, I must say that when a party decides that only by killing such persons is it possible to obtain a government based on human principles, then it is quite natural that it should act on its convictions. Of course, such killings are reprehensible and cannot be justified on the basis of morals or practicality.

In June Count Alexis Pavlovich Ignatev, a member of the State Council about whom I have spoken earlier, was killed by an anarchist-revolutionary while on his way to Tver for a zemstvo meeting. As I have written earlier, he was not a bad person, but was very much of a high society careerist. Because of his reactionary views, he subverted much of the work undertaken to carry out the decree of December 12, 1904: thanks to him we do not have legislation normalizing the use of the law on exceptional measures; thanks to him we do not have adequate legislation concerning religious freedom.

I was very upset by the news of his death and sent a telegram of condolence to his widow, whom I had met at the home of my friend Sipiagin, but I received no reply. When the count's body was brought to Petersburg for burial, his widow, having heard that I might be attending the services, was upset by the idea, and I received a note from Mme. Dubasova (Sipiagin's sister) advising me that my presence at the services might have an untoward effect on Countess Ignateva.

The killing of her husband naturally had a very unsettling effect on the countess, an unstable person of limited intelligence. Thereafter she busied herself with church politics, her salon providing a haven for many connected with the decay that has been evident in the higher levels of the Orthodox church, with the rise of such people as Illiodor, Hermogen, and Rasputin.

Then came the attempt on Stolypin's life, in August. The following day, General Min, commander of the Semenovskii Guards, was assassinated in revenge for his role in suppressing the Moscow rising in December 1905. He deserves credit for his work in suppressing the rising, but the unfortunate excesses that followed cannot be condoned.

On December 22, Launitz, the prefect of Petersburg, was assassinated while attending the ceremony marking the opening of a new branch, for skin diseases, of the Institute of Experimental Medicine. He was among the many eminent persons invited to attend. I, too, had been invited but was not there, in keeping with my practice, following my departure from office, of not accepting such invitations. It was after the religious services that Launitz was shot and killed by a revolutionary anarchist. The assassin was, in turn, killed on the spot, by a member of either the military or the police.

Because the assassin could not be identified, the strange step was taken of displaying his severed head that had been placed in a jar of alcohol. Whether or not this resulted in his identification I don't know, but I am certain that he was a member of the revolutionary-anarchist party and acted on its orders.

I was not one of Launitz's admirers. Although I had misgivings about him, I did not protest against his appointment as prefect while I was premier. He was given the post on Durnovo's recommendation and at His Majesty's wish. I did not intervene because I felt that the prefect of Petersburg was directly subordinate to the minister of interior.

Unfortunately, my misgivings proved to be justified. Once in office, Launitz associated himself with the Union of the Russian People and served as its protector. In return, that organization began to do him favors as it gained strength. Such reactionary actions on his part had to lead to a bad end.[13]

Five days after Launitz's death, General V. P. Pavlov, the chief military procurator, was assassinated. He was, as I have noted, the man who had proposed establishment of field courts-martial while I was premier. By the time of his death he had earned a reputation for being very unfair and merciless in cases involving civilians and, as a consequence, had received many threats to his life. Because of these threats he had stopped taking walks in public, and when he felt the need for fresh air, he would walk in the garden of his residence. It was on such an occasion that an unknown assailant entered the garden, killed him, and fled.

I have dealt earlier with the attempt on Dubasov's life in reprisal for his role in putting down the Moscow rising. An equally unsuccessful attempt was later made on Hörschelmann, his successor as governor-general of Moscow. I did not know the man, but I heard that he was a gallant soldier, without any political sense. He was the son of a Jewish renegade and like so many others in this category he became a "kike-eater" and spiritual ally of the Union of the Russian People.

As is already evident, assassinations were not the monopoly of the left, which shared this field with the extremists of the right, i.e., the Union of the Russian People. In this connection I have already spoken of the killing of Herzenstein and Iollos and the attempts on my life.

I should note that as early as the time of the First State Duma, Stolypin, in his capacity of minister of interior, was protecting the Union of the Russian People. This body of thugs and hooligans began to grow strong because the government supported it with subsidies as well as the use of police force. As will be seen, it was only after the election of the Third State Duma, which provided Stolypin with a compliant legislative body, that he no longer felt the need of the support of the Union of the Russian People.

Stolypin and the Borderlands

Shortly after becoming premier Stolypin began taking steps that were not completely consistent with the Finnish constitution. Because the Finnish Sejm was not indifferent to such actions, it was closed on September 5, 1906. Subsequently there were more attacks on the Finnish constitution as Stolypin gave in to pressure from Russian nationalists.[14]

Little more than a month after the closing of the Finnish Sejm came a change in the administration of the Baltic provinces, with the replacement of General Sollogub by General Meller-Zakomelskii as governor-general. It will be recalled that on my initiative General Sollogub had been named to the post. A decent well-balanced man, he had fulfilled all my expectations. When Stolypin asked him to take measures toward the inhabitants of the Baltic provinces that were not in keeping with his convictions, friction arose that ended with his removal.*

His successor is a rather sinister, strong-willed man. As I have recounted earlier, I chose him, on General Palitsyn's recommendation, to direct the punitive expedition on the Trans-Siberian Railroad, and he carried out his task rather well.

It would be correct to say that if General Meller-Zakomelskii had not been a general, he would have made a good prison warden, particularly in prisons where corporal punishment is permitted. He would also have made a good police official, in the sense of being able to maintain the appearance of law and order.

He was chosen by Stolypin because the Baltic nobility was afraid of a new outburst of unrest. Although General Sollogub had dealt effectively with unrest in my tenure, the local nobility did not trust him to use whatever means necessary if the need arose. What they wanted was someone who could be a holy terror, who would not worry about legal niceties. Stolypin believed that the new governor-general filled the bill, that he would use whatever means necessary to put an end to the hydra of unrest.

Himself a native of the area, the general could be counted on to use arms and corporal punishment wherever it was necessary to deal with unrest. He suited the Baltic nobility, but it turned against him after it became evident that a man such as he was not needed and after it was learned that he had been guilty of irregularities, many of them of a pecuniary nature. Collectively, the local nobility did not have the influence to have him removed, but several of their number had access to the court and for that reason could help determine what Petersburg did in their region. In the end General Meller-Zakomelskii had to leave office.

Two years ago I met him and his young daughter in Vichy. She looked jaded, more like a young woman of easy manners than a young lady. I was told she was capable of keeping a beast like her daddy in hand.

A year ago I saw him again in Biarritz, where he gambled heavily. Accompanying him was a young lady whom he introduced as his daughter, but she bore no resemblance to the real daughter I had seen the year before. His heavy gambling and his living with a spurious daughter shocked the Russians, for, after all, he was a member of the State Council, to which he had been appointed on leaving the

---

*I consider General Sollogub to be pre-eminent among our generals in the knowledge of military science. At present he is a member of the board of directors of the Chinese Eastern Railroad, on which he had served as representative of the War Ministry during my tenure as minister of finance.

post of governor-general. I was told that he left Biarritz after heavy losses at gambling, but that he did pay his debts.

After his return to Russia he engaged in some shady dealing that landed him in trouble, as I learned from Akimov, the chairman of the State Council. It seems that he did something that verged on forgery in selling an entailed estate of his in the Kingdom of Poland, after receiving permission from the Emperor to do so. What he did was arrange matters so that he could sell the estate for a larger sum than he had said it would bring, this to reduce the tax he would have to pay. When this was uncovered he was ordered not to touch the money he had received, but he still managed to pocket some of the money.

How it all ended I don't know, but I do know that the general did not appear in the State Council again and that his name did not appear on the list of active members of the body when it appeared on January 1 of this year [1912].

VII

The Second State Duma

The Short-Lived Second State Duma

The Second State Duma, which opened on February 20, 1907, was elected in accordance with the same electoral law by which the First State Duma had been elected and like the first had a majority of deputies opposed to the government, but by this time political passions had cooled somewhat and revolutionary ferment was dying down. Also many of the opposition figures who had been so prominent in the First State Duma were absent from the second because of the manner in which Stolypin had dealt with the signers of the Vyborg Manifesto.

I could not understand why the government, after its experience of the elections to the First State Duma, had troubled to hold elections again under the same electoral law that had produced such disappointing results in the preceding election. It was obvious that the Second State Duma would have to be as hostile to the government as the first, that those elected under the electoral law of December 1905 would not be servile to the government, would not wait politely in the anterooms of the premier and other ministers who served a government that clearly did not intend to rule in accordance with the wishes of the people, but would instead serve the egotistic, and unrealistic, interests of a small group close to the throne.

That was what I thought. But Stolypin was unable to come to terms with reality. He chose to believe that this Duma would come to accept his program, with its fantasies and experiments that reflect not the wishes of the Russian people but those of the higher-ups he was trying to please. He was, of course, mistaken.

As a means of diverting the Second State Duma's attention from controversial subjects, the first task assigned to it was to review the budget for 1907, a budget that was already in effect for the following reasons.

According to the law governing the state budget, for which I was largely responsible, the budget for the next fiscal year, to begin on the same day as the calendar year, should be submitted to the State Duma early enough so that this body could review it and send it on to the State Council by December 1. The State Council would then act on it in time for the budget to go into effect on January 1. The budget law was based on the assumption that the State Duma would be in session by early autumn, but that was not the case in 1906, following the dissolution of the First State Duma. There was no provision in the budget law for such a situation. So the government took the extralegal and extraordinary step of declaring on January 1, 1907, that the draft budget it had prepared would be in effect until June, by which time it was expected the State Duma and the State Council would have approved it.[1]

It became quickly evident, even to Stolypin, that this Duma would not cooperate with him, and he found himself in a dilemma about what to do about the various laws he had enacted in the preceding months under Article 87. According to that law, as I have said, a law issued under Article 87 would lapse if it were not approved by the State Duma [and State Council] within sixty days after the opening of the legislative session. Seeing the mood of this State Duma, Stolypin chose not to present most of the controversial legislations issued under Article 87, but decided to keep them in force by one subterfuge or another. He did, however, send one law—which dealt with "Responsibility for Fomenting Criminal Acts Through Speech or the Press"—to the State Duma, which promptly rejected it.

As relations between the government and the Second State Duma became more strained, it became evident that something had to be done. So, Stolypin began to prepare to have this Duma dissolved on the basis of some convenient pretext and then have a new State Duma chosen on the basis of a revised electoral law that would assure the government a cooperative State Duma. To change the electoral law without the consent of the legislative bodies was, of course, in violation of the Fundamental Laws and would amount to a *coup d'état*, but Stolypin, whose position at court was now solid, was prepared to do so.

During the tense period preceding the dissolution of the Second State Duma, I twice saw Baron Freedericksz, the minister of the court. On the first occasion, which concerned a personal matter, he told me that a new electoral law was being considered. I suggested that when the cabinet dealt with this matter it consult with officials acquainted with the history of the law.

On the second occasion Baron Freedericksz came to see me, whether on his own initiative or at the suggestion of someone else I don't know. He wanted my advice on what should be done at this time. I replied that without knowing all the circumstances I could not be of help. He evidently took this to mean that I refused to be helpful. It had become fashionable after October 17, 1905, to say that I knew how to save Russia, but that I did not wish to do so.

The baron responded by saying that, surely, I knew what should be done and asked me to give my view. At that I became angry and replied that to do so would be pointless because what I would suggest could not be realized. When he insisted that I speak up, that perhaps what I would advise could be done, I pointed to the portrait of Emperor Alexander III, hanging in my study where this conversation took place, and said, "Bring him back to life." Baron Freedericksz was taken aback by this, and on this note we parted.[2]

A new electoral law intended to assure a subservient State Duma was prepared by the "famous" Kryzhanovskii, one of Stolypin's assistant ministers of interior and the man who did the thinking for Stolypin. I was told that the cabinet met only once to consider the new law and that Akimov, Bulygin, and Goremykin were invited to this session because of their experience in the framing of the old law. I was told that some of the invited disagreed with cabinet members concerning the law. In any case the law was prepared hastily, so hastily, and this I know for a fact, that parts of it were altered while type was being set.[3]

Following the dissolution of the Second State Duma, in the presence of P. N. Durnovo, I asked Kryzhanovskii, who had prepared the new electoral law, why it gave some elements of the population disproportionately higher representation. Somewhat naively he replied that it had been done to assure the election of desirable deputies.

I do not believe that the revised electoral law will long endure. Either it will be replaced by a more reasonable law, based on principle, or the State Duma will go out of existence. For what is the purpose of such a body? It is to express the wishes and will of the people, or at least of the majority of those who care and think. If it does not do so, it is redundant and the work of legislating could in that case better be left to the State Council, which, although it does not speak for the people, has among its members a large number with sufficient experience and knowledge to frame legislation. The State Council, as is the nature of upper legislative chambers, is less subject to fears and fancies than a popularly elected lower chamber: that, after all, is why upper chambers were established. Therefore, to have a lower chamber which does not represent the people yet is more poorly equipped to legislate is to no purpose. In such a case the upper chamber will pay no attention to the lower one. And that is precisely what happened under the revised electoral law. Whereas the State Council feared the First State Duma, it neither fears nor heeds the present State Duma. And because the two bodies now go in separate directions, the government pays little attention to the legislative bodies and governs as it pleases, paying no heed to the Fundamental Laws or to the spirit of the October Manifesto.

In hastily preparing the new electoral law, Stolypin and his government decided to give the appearance of preserving the gains resulting from the October Manifesto, but in fact subverted the spirit of that manifesto. But first it was necessary, as I have said, to find seemingly plausible justification for dissolving the State Duma.

That justification was made on June 2 with the official announcement that on May 5, in the course of the search of the home of a deputy to the State Duma, documents revealing a conspiracy on the part of the fifty-five Social Democratic members to overthrow the government were found.[4] The following day, June 3, after the announcement had created the desired impression, an Imperial manifesto and a decree appeared announcing the dissolution of the Second State Duma and setting the date for the election of a new State Duma. On the same day the revised electoral law was published.

Not long ago, at a closed session of the State Duma, it was revealed that the alleged conspiracy was largely a figment of the imagination of the Ministry of Interior. I believe that some of the Social Democratic deputies to the Second State Duma did have some thoughts about an uprising and that Stolypin blew up what he learned to create the allegation of a conspiracy that threatened the security of the state, this so that public opinion would be induced to swallow what was in essence a *coup d'état*.[5] It was a coup because it violated the Fundamental Laws, which I helped frame.

The coup meant that thereafter the State Duma would not be the voice of the people but the voice of the subservient parts of the upper strata—the nobility, the bureaucracy, the merchants, and the industrialists. It meant that the State Duma would express only the wishes of the rich and the powerful, and then only to the extent that those on high did not object.

Changes in the State Council

While the Second State Duma was living out its short life, a noteworthy change, for the worse, took place when, following the death of Frisch, Akimov was appointed to replace him as chairman of the State Council. Frisch was not a distinguished official, but he was a decent and honorable man and an excellent jurist. The appointment of Akimov came as a surprise. True enough, he was considered an honorable man, but he was a person of limited capacity and lacking in the broad governmental experience required in a chairman. He had served with me as minister of justice, following the departure of Manukhin. And I had suggested him to the Emperor as my successor if what His Majesty wanted was a conservative. At the time of his appointment as chairman there were dozens of others with a better claim to the position than he. I thought he was the Emperor's choice, selected because he was a reactionary, a man with a police fist, a man who would do what the Emperor told him to do. I learned later that I had been mistaken, that he was not the Emperor's choice, but Stolypin's.

It appears that Stolypin wanted the next chairman to be a person who would accept his direction. While there were many in the State Council better qualified to be chairman, there were few among these who would be subservient. Goremykin conceivably could have been such a candidate had he not been so much better informed, so far more experienced in government than Stolypin that he could not have accepted intellectual and moral subordination to the new premier. In the end Stolypin decided to recommend Akimov, after having been assured, so it is said, that he could count on Akimov's help, i.e., subservience. As it turned out Akimov took his direction from Tsarskoe Selo, from the Emperor, and a disappointed Stolypin would tell intimates that Akimov had taken him in and that if he had known what kind of a man Akimov was he would not have recommended him.

Once installed as chairman, Akimov used his power to see to it that bills favored by the Emperor received a majority and that those to which the Emperor was opposed were rejected. In so doing he often acted in a high-handed and unworthy manner. At meetings of the State Council he sometimes abuses his powers as chairman, cutting off speakers who displease him with no justification or for inadequate reasons, while permitting those following a line that pleases him to talk at great length or to use unparliamentary language.

Most of all he uses his powers to influence the voting of those members of the State Council who are appointed by the Emperor. Sometimes he will let them know what the Emperor's wish is or intimate that His Majesty will be displeased if they do not vote "correctly." And so as to make appointed members accept such direction he interpreted, or rather misinterpreted, the legislation concerning appointed members to frighten them into submission. According to the law, members of the State Council are designated either as "active" members (with the right to participate in the work of the State Council) or as "inactive" members at the time of their appointment. And the status of "active" member may not be changed to that of "inactive" thereafter. Akimov, however, used the legal require-ment that each year a list of members, both "active" appointed and elected members, be published. The list of "active" appointed members is brought up to date by omitting from it the names of those who have died, who have asked to be transferred to an "inactive" status, or, simply, those who have offended the powers that be by the speeches they have made or the manner in which they voted.

Consequently, an appointed member of the State Council may unexpectedly find his name missing from the next yearly list. Those so excluded, even men whose loyalty, conservatism, and propriety are beyond question, are often ex-cluded in a tactless and offensive manner. These are men such as Butkovskii, Kobeko, Steven, and General Kosich, men with long records of valuable service to the state. Such exclusions mean that every "active" appointed member of the State Council lives under a sword of Damocles, in the knowledge that he may be excluded if his behavior meets with disapproval. Naturally, this threat has the most demoralizing influence on such persons, most of them aged officials, with no source of income other than their salaries as state councillors.

Akimov knows not only how appointed members vote and what they say at general sessions of the State Council but also—through informants (some state councillors and some officials in his chancellery)—which caucuses appointed members attend and what they say there.

All in all, the Emperor has reason to be satisfied with Akimov, but the State Council is being debased. And I am certain that on many important matters the vote would have been different from what it was had unworthy means not been used to influence the results.[6]

Two False Alarms

As I have written earlier, when the Polytechnic Institute was established, on my initiative, I made certain that this director would be not only a man qualified for the position, but also one whose social status and political background were such that no objection could be raised to him by the Emperor.[7] That man, Prince Gagarin, lived up to my expectations by being an excellent director who enjoyed the respect not only of the professors but also of the students. Nonetheless, Stolypin found it expedient to consider Prince Gagarin a revolutionary.

On February 18, 1907, the authorities searched the dormitory at the institute and claimed to have found a bomb. As a result, the dormitory was closed shortly thereafter and has remained closed since then. Proceedings were then instituted against the administration. As I learned, the bomb was placed in the dormitory by the police so that they would have a pretext for closing the dormitory and putting the administration on trial.

Without such a pretext it would not have been possible to charge so socially prominent a man as Prince Gagarin with being a revolutionary, because no one would have taken it seriously. In the end he was subjected to an artfully arranged trial before the Senate, resulting in his dismissal. The sentence in no way diminished the respect in which he was held by acquaintances and society.

After the trial I saw his wife—a very fine woman and a close relative of Stolypin, who had known him since childhood. After she told me the whole story, explaining that the charges had been fabricated, I asked if she and her family had not spoken about the case to Stolypin. She replied that she had no desire to speak to such a person and added: ''Who would have thought that Petia [Peter] would turn out to be such a scoundrel.'' Naturally, the Gagarin family severed all relations with Stolypin after his display of such police-type brilliance.

On May 7, 1907, the State Duma and the State Council were informed of the detention of members of an alleged criminal organization charged with conspiring to take the lives of the Emperor, Grand Duke Nicholas Nikolaevich, and Stolypin. In August the case was heard in the Petersburg Military District Court. Because the trial took place behind closed doors, it was difficult to learn the facts.

The left-wing press claimed that the charge was false. I was assured that if the charge was not completely false, it had little or no substance and had been made to influence society in favor of the government.

I do not necessarily accept the view that the charge was wholly, or in large part, fabricated, but given the activities of such *provocateurs* as Azef and the activities of the secret police and of Stolypin himself, I am not prepared to put my hand in the fire to demonstrate my confidence in the truth of the government's charge.[8]

I was particularly struck by the fact that Stolypin's name was associated in this instance with the names of the Emperor and Grand Duke Nicholas Nikolaevich.

Two Deaths

On March 10, 1907, Constantine Petrovich Pobedonostsev died. He was the last of the Mohicans, the last of the group defeated on October 17, 1905. But, as I have already asserted, a great Mohican, far more intelligent than other officials, distinguished for his learning, for his lack of interest in storing up treasures on earth, unlike many officials, especially those of the Stolypin period. I felt morally obliged to attend the services for him as well as his funeral. His death keenly reminded me of the past, particularly of the glorious years in which Emperor Alexander III reigned.

On September 28, 1907, the well-known journalist Gringmut died. He was a renegade Jew whose ancestors had emigrated to Russia. He looked Jewish but was blond.

He was a typical renegade. It is a fact that a nationality or a religion has no greater enemies than those who have left their fold. There is no greater Judeophobe than a Jew who has adopted Orthodoxy, no greater enemy of the Poles than a Pole who has adopted Orthodoxy, particularly a Pole who entered the Russian secret police.

Early in his career Gringmut taught Latin at the Katkov Lycée, later became inspector and virtual director of the institution. Also, he was associated with *Moskovskie vedomosti*, the newspaper which belonged to the University of Moscow and had been leased to Katkov.

While I was minister of finance, Gringmut would make it a point to call on me when he visited Petersburg, and that was often. I found him intelligent, fairly well educated, a man of well-composed manner. During the turmoil that began in 1904, he did not know with which side to associate himself and for a time forsook politics completely.

After I became premier, the Ministry of Interior decided to entrust the editorship of *Moskovskie vedomosti* to him. I was rather dubious about the wisdom of this decision. He soon chose to associate himself with the right and declared himself head of the Moscow branch of the Union of the Russian People.[9] To make sure of acceptance by the right he had to prove himself an enemy of the Jews, and he did, for that was the way to win credentials as a true conservative. But it should be noted that a few years earlier he had not considered it beneath him to be very friendly with Rothstein, director of the International Bank, and to accept favors from him.

Even though he knew of my feelings about his appointment as editor, he at first came to me to ask for directives. But relations soon changed. After he identified himself with the Union of the Russian People and began to attack the October

Manifesto and all that followed from it, I demanded that Durnovo, the minister of interior, take energetic steps against Gringmut's newspaper, i.e., that he take the same steps against the revolutionaries of the right, at whose head stood Gringmut, as he had against the revolutionaries of the left. Gringmut could not forget what I had done and after I left office attacked me vigorously.

Stolypin and the Secret Police

As I have related elsewhere,[10] when it was suggested after I became premier that I accept the portfolio of minister of interior in addition to that of premier, I refused, saying that I might agree if the secret police were removed from the jurisdiction of the Ministry of Interior because I knew nothing about the secret police and had no time to learn; and, since it would have been impolitic to make the separation, I could not accept the post of minister of interior. Stolypin, although he had neither the knowledge nor the experience, acted with his usual courage and, without batting an eyelid, accepted the post of minister of interior and quickly began to concern himself with the operations of the secret police. To make matters worse, he took on as his assistant for the administration of the police the procurator of the Saratov Court of Appeals, with whom he had become acquainted while governor of Saratov.[11] This man knew as little of police work as did Stolypin.

The fact that police administration fell into the hands of completely inexperienced people enabled the likes of Azef and Landezen[12] to become so powerful and prominent that, for example, Landezen accompanied the Dowager Empress on one trip she made abroad and, so I am told, was invited to lunch at the Imperial table on train trips. These men were double agents, occupying influential positions in both the revolutionary-anarchist party and the secret police. On one occasion when I pointed out that those two and others had gained exceptional power in the secret police under Stolypin, I was reminded that they had been with the secret police while I was premier and Durnovo minister of interior. To this I replied, true enough, but there was a difference between their status under Durnovo and under Stolypin. In homes lacking in modern plumbing there are servants whose duty it is to clean necessary places [privies] and one cannot do without them, but one doesn't invite them to dinner. Under Stolypin they were given more elevated duties and treated as equals. This was, as I have suggested, because secret police work for Stolypin was *terra incognita* and this at a very difficult time. Given such a state of affairs it was not at all surprising that many officials were assassinated in Stolypin's time by revolutionary anarchists and, as I have already suggested, it was difficult to distinguish between genuine assassinations and acts of provocation.

One such assassination was that of Maksimovskii, chief of the prison administration, in October 1907. The choice of Kurlov to succeed him set into operation a chain of events that further weakened the secret police.

I believe that Kurlov was a graduate of the Nikolaevskii Cavalry School. He received a commission, then attended and completed the Military-Juridical Academy and subsequently, as I recall, served in the Border Guard. He then left the military, entered the service of the Ministry of Justice, and somehow managed to go on to become governor of the province of Minsk, a position he occupied when I became premier. I soon heard charges that when there was trouble in Minsk he behaved like a coward, hiding in his residence; I also heard that he ignored laws which he found inconvenient. My unfavorable impression of him was reinforced by accounts along these lines I heard from a very decent Polish noble from Minsk, the father of a Preobrazhenskii Guards officer who had been sent to protect me soon after I became premier.[13]

Because of the charges made against him, Kurlov had to leave office during my tenure. It was not on my initiative that he left, but I was pleased to see him go. I learned later that the charge of cowardice was unfounded.[14] Kurlov is not without ability, but he is not a man of principle.

As soon as I left office Kurlov was appointed governor of the province of Kiev, probably just because he had been dismissed during my tenure. His stay in Kiev was brief and unmarked by any accomplishment. Then when Maksimovskii was killed, Shcheglovitov, the minister of justice, chose Kurlov to replace Maksimovskii. I was not surprised because, as they say, birds of a feather flock together, although Shcheglovitov is even more of a liability to sound government than Kurlov.

As it turned out, Kurlov was in the good graces of the Union of the Russian People, which was then far more influential in governmental affairs than it is today [1912]. It was the Union of the Russian People that campaigned for Kurlov's appointment and after they had succeeded began to urge that he replace Makarov as assistant minister of interior and director of the Department of Police.[15] When the party falsely calling itself the Party of October 17, which supported Stolypin, heard rumors of what was afoot, it objected to such an appointment, and Stolypin assured the party leaders that he would never agree to the appointment of Kurlov because he thought poorly of him. Of course, this did not prevent Kurlov from being appointed because Kurlov had support from higher up and Stolypin wanted most of all to retain his position and with it all the advantages that came with it. He might pretend to be taking a firm stand, but it was only pretence. Like Marshal MacMahon he might say "*j'y suis et j'y reste*," but then he might add "*et je m'en fiche.*"[16]

First it was necessary to shift Makarov, who it should be noted had some knowledge of the Department of Police and, although not particularly able or distinguished, is a decent, firm, and well-balanced man. To do this Baron Uexküll was relieved of his position as Imperial secretary and given an appointment as member of the State Council and Makarov appointed in his stead. I know that when His Majesty informed Makarov of his new position, which, he said, was a step up, Makarov said he was grateful but that he preferred to remain where he was. However, since His Majesty made it evident during the course of the conversation that he wanted Makarov to vacate his post immediately, Makarov raised no further objections.

It was in this wise that Kurlov became assistant minister of interior and head of the Department of Police, about whose work he knew nothing. Being in favor at court he was given a court title, gentleman squire (*shtalmeister*), and was soon appointed commander of the Corps of Gendarmes and promoted to the rank of general.

His position as director of the Department of Police gave him free access to the large sums provided for the maintenance of the secret police under the rubric "for expenditures known to His Imperial Majesty." In Stolypin, who spent government money for his own needs and for such things 'on which his predecessors would never have spent government money, he had a model, which he followed by squandering secret funds for many purposes, among them his own needs and desires. He had long been married to a rich woman, a fine person from the merchant class considerably older than he. Shortly after attaining his new office he was attracted to the youthful wife of his adjutant and he acted with dispatch. Using his power and the favor of His Majesty he had no difficulty in arranging a divorce from his wife, whose fortune he had already spent, and a divorce for the adjutant's wife, whom he married as soon as he could. Members of the Imperial family have no use for the rules and customs of marriage, so God forgave Kurlov for following their example.

In his ignorance Kurlov completed the job of demoralizing the secret police. The climax was to come with the assassination of Stolypin on September 1, 1911, in Kiev.

VIII

Stolypin in the Ascendant, 1907–1910

The Third State Duma

By employing the electoral law of June 3, 1907, and by the liberal use of government funds, Stolypin was able to make certain that the elections to the Third State Duma produced a docile group of deputies,* consisting largely of members of the falsely named Party of October 17, the party that Stolypin now favored. Now that he could rely on the Octobrists to provide him with a majority in the State Duma, he could dispense with the services of the Union of the Russian People, which had received financial and other support from his government. (A. A. Stolypin, his brother, would use a quotation from Schiller in writing in *Novoe vremia* to indicate the change: "Depart, Moor, you have done your work.")[1] Because he could now count on good relations with the State Duma, Stolypin felt free to give a reception for about 200 of the deputies shortly after the opening of the State Duma.

The man on whom Stolypin now relied in the State Duma was Alexander I. Guchkov, the leader of the so-called Party of October 17 (the Octobrists), who was elected chairman of that body. Under the old electoral law Guchkov had failed to be elected to either the First or Second State Duma. And he might not have been

*Many conservatives and reactionaries who could not have been elected under the old electoral law managed to gain seats in the new Duma. One of these was Count A. A. Bobrinskii, under whose father I had served when I was a young man. I know little of Count A. A. Bobrinskii except that he served in the Life Hussars, then left the army. Before the troubles that began in 1904 he was considered such a "red" that when the Emperor was in Yalta in the 1890s he would not receive the count. But once the troubles began, in 1904, troubles that threatened the pocketbooks of the rich, especially of the large landowners such as Bobrinskii, this honorable count began to panic. He was elected to the Third State Duma as an Octobrist, but then joined the Nationalists and began to make reactionary speeches à la Purishkevich. It is said, and with good reason, he was rewarded for his excellent behavior [in the State Duma] with a huge loan from the State Bank, a loan without which he would have been ruined.

elected to the Third State Duma if Stolypin had not arranged, through bribery, to have him elected, a fact that I learned from General Rheinbott, the Moscow prefect. Once elected, Guchkov served Stolypin well and as a result was able to become a major shareholder in *Novoe vremia*.[2]

Guchkov, it will be recalled, was one of the public men I had tried to recruit for my cabinet after my appointment as premier. In those days he was all in favor of "liberty," but then when he felt his class interests threatened by the masses he came to interpret "liberty" to suit his own interests. Thus, by the time he was elected, he had moved sufficiently far to the right to be able to serve Stolypin.

As was to be expected, the Third State Duma, for several years at least, did Stolypin's bidding. And for that reason the promise of the October Manifesto has not been realized, because the Third State Duma was in fact not elected, but rather selected by Stolypin.

Even after the election of so docile a body as the Third State Duma, Stolypin continued to use Article 87 of the Fundamental Laws in an irresponsible and improper manner to bring about changes that had been waiting for decades to be effected. This was to be the case with the introduction of zemstvos in the western provinces.[3] And the accommodating and largely lackeyish State Duma has borne this.

This body has made no effort to exercise one of the chief powers a legislature has, the power of the purse. Stolypin did not follow the budget rules that I had prepared. Because he did not convene the State Duma early enough for a proper review of the budget for the coming year, and by not insisting on rigid adherence to the timetable for budget considerations, he was able to operate for many months of the year without a legally approved budget. Moreover, the State Controller's office has been dilatory in submitting its accounting to the State Duma and chary in its explanations of the figures it submitted. And often it omitted figures when such omissions served the government's purpose. In dealing with the State Controller's accounting, the Third State Duma proved itself indifferent, partly from lack of experience, partly from servility, being guided perhaps by the proverb "What has fallen from the wagon is lost." This year [1912] the State Duma finally prepared a bill to change the budget rules, which have never been enforced, but it did not pass because of differences with the State Council.

The Third State Duma has proved itself delinquent, too, in dealing with the 10 million-ruble contingency fund. According to the budget rules, the use of contingency funds was not subject to review if the limit set for the fund was not exceeded, but it was assumed that an existing law requiring the minister of finance to submit monthly reports to the State Council about such expenditures would remain in force. However, such reports have not been made on the grounds that the law referred to applied to the pre-1906 State Council and not to the reorganized one. The Third State Duma has silently agreed to what is at best a very lame explanation.

In dealing with the question of my efforts to carry out the promise of the

October Manifesto with respect to civil rights, I noted that I had to agree to the renewal of the temporary law on exceptional measures while I was premier. This was done because of the unrest we were experiencing, but we assumed that by the time three years were up the country would have returned to a peaceful state and the law would not be renewed. But at the end of the three-year period Stolypin presented a bill for a new law on exceptional measures to the Third State Duma. Because it did not have time to review the law, he invoked Article 87 to renew the old temporary law. He did this with Imperial approval, and the State Duma chose not to regard his act as illegal. And he chose to interpret that law more loosely than had any of his predecessors.

Matters have reached such a state that the authorities can, without a how-do-you-do, enter your home, accompanied by a phalanx of gendarmes, turn your house inside out, rummage through all your papers, seize whatever they find interesting, then perhaps arrest you and ship you off to exile in Siberia. This is what happened only recently to Rumanov of *Russkoe slovo*, a man who gets along well with the new premier, Kokovtsev. After ten days he was released from political prison (Kresty). Then the minister of interior apologizes to this stunned and humiliated man for the mistake committed by the Department of Police!!

In speaking of Stolypin's relations with the Third State Duma, I should note that in most parliaments, ministers who cannot answer a direct question without lying usually resort to circumlocution. But Stolypin in such a situation had no hesitation about lying to the State Duma, or the State Council for that matter. A case in point is his response to an inquiry about the newspaper *Rossiia*. The story is as follows:

When I became premier, the entire press, as I have noted, opposed the government, distorted the facts, reported events tendentiously, and sometimes even fabricated stories. We needed to be able to explain matters correctly to the public, but the government newspaper, *Pravitelstvennyi vestnik*, was not designed to carry out such a task. When Tatishchev, a writer, among other things, with whom I had long been acquainted,[4] suggested that the government establish a newspaper that could appeal to the public, I acted by establishing *Russkoe gosudarstvo*, which was to be published by *Pravitelstvennyi vestnik* but was better written and more like a daily newspaper than the latter. My first choice for editor of the new publication was Tatishchev, but his death intervened. I appointed N. A. Gurev as acting editor, but His Majesty, acting on the basis of an unfavorable report by General Trepov about Gurev, would not agree to have him named editor but did agree to permit him to act as editor as long as someone else, someone from *Pravitelstvennyi vestnik*, would be listed on the masthead as editor.

Russkoe gosudarstvo performed its task ably, but when Stolypin became premier, he ended its publication on the ground that it did not adequately influence public opinion. To carry on its work the government took over an existing but faltering newspaper, *Rossiia*, and subsidized it. S. N. Syromiatnikov was appointed its editor, but the chief figures in publishing it were Gurev and I. Ia. Gurliand, a renegade Jew, the son of an Odessa rabbi, who had been converted to Orthodoxy and had advanced himself through the favor of the police.

Ostensibly *Rossiia* continued to be a privately owned newspaper. Stolypin maintained this fiction the better to influence public opinion, but everyone knew that it was financed by money from secret government funds and from *Pravitelstvennyi vestnik*, which enjoyed large revenues from printing official notices. When the State Duma raised questions about the cost of operating the newspaper and the sources of its funds, Stolypin brazenly had Kryzhanovskii, one of the assistant ministers of interior, blandly inform the legislature that *Rossiia* was a private publication. Since then, *Rossiia*, which has no influence on public opinion, has been sarcastically referred to as "*Rossiia*, a private publication."

Civil Rights Under Stolypin

Even before June 3, 1907, but much more so after the election of the Third State Duma, Stolypin was able to make a mockery of the civil rights I tried to establish while premier.

With respect to inviolability of person, one of the worst infringements of this right was the practice of perlustration. It had been going on long before October 17, but not on the scale of the Stolypin era.

When I became premier, an official, whose name, I believe, was Timofeev, asked, on behalf of Durnovo, the minister of interior, if I had any instructions about being given perlustrated letters. I gave no instructions, nor did I discuss the matter with Durnovo, but every day I received a packet of such letters from the minister, who, naturally, had selected what he wanted me to read. I used to skim through them, but not once did I see a letter which provided anything useful to the government or the police.

But there was many a letter in which I was attacked. The author of one such letter was Count S. D. Sheremetev, a man who had served as adjutant to Emperor Alexander III, who now holds the court title of senior master of the hunt, and who has a seat in the State Council, where he has nothing to say. Everyone knows that he is not completely normal, but he is generally believed to have a noble character.

My wife and I had become friendly with him through the Sipiagins, to whom he was related. While I was minister of finance he, it goes without saying, turned to me for favors. My relations with him had their ups and downs. After my return from Portsmouth he seemed very friendly and expressed his respect and admiration for me in effusive letters to my wife. Although he was very upset by the October 17 Manifesto—in his home he turned the picture of the Emperor to the wall when he learned of the manifesto—he continued to be friendly toward me, at least on the surface, and continued to keep up his ties with the Imperial court. After reading a letter from him in which he referred to me in unflattering terms, I found it unpleasant to shake hands with him and I tried to avoid him thereafter.

Clearly the perlustrated correspondence serves no useful purpose and, in fact, does harm, because it permits the administration to learn purely personal matters, which is none of its business, knowledge that often has unfortunate consequence. I know that if Stolypin had not been attracted to the reading of such letters by the narrowness of his character he would have gotten along better with many people and might not have made so many personal enemies. Yet, although perlustration was carried out energetically under him, one of his spokesmen called the belief that perlustration was being carried out a fairy tale when a question was raised in the State Duma in connection with the appropriations for the postal and telegraph services.

And perlustration has continued under Kokovtsev, the present premier, who told me, when I brought up the subject, that he receives a packet of perlustrated letters every day, that in one of them Krivoshein, head of the Chief Administration of Land Organization and Agriculture, was quoted as having said unkindly things about the premier. To embarrass the man, Kokovtsev telephoned him and advised him, in a friendly fashion, to be more careful in the future. Krivoshein said he had been misunderstood by the author of the perlustrated letter. In telling me all this, Kokovtsev, smilingly said: "Of course, Krivoshein is contrite."

As I have already related, it was not possible to prepare the permanent press regulations necessary to carry out the promise of freedom of the press made in the October 17 Manifesto.[5] It was expected that the temporary press regulations prepared under my direction would sooner or later be replaced by permanent legislation. When Kokovtsev and Kaufmann presented a draft of a permanent press law, Stolypin, supported by the majority of the cabinet, rejected it. And instead of working for a permanent press law with which he could be comfortable, he chose to permit the temporary press regulations to remain on the books, while honoring them in the breach by the use of the law on exceptional measures, which permitted him and his government to use high-handed methods toward the press. To be sure, Stolypin did not dare be too harsh toward the press before the *coup d'état* of June 3, 1907, but thereafter he acted freely, in the knowledge that there would be no objection from a compliant State Duma.

As will be recalled, during my tenure temporary regulations concerning freedom of assembly and freedom of association were issued. These were received in the same fashion as the temporary press regulations, i.e., most of society and most newspapers of the time considered these regulations too restrictive and placed their hopes of achieving full freedom of the press, assembly, and association on the State Duma and the State Council. Well, their hopes were not realized. And since the *coup d'état* of June 3, 1907, the government has dealt even more cavalierly with the alleged freedom of association (including the right to form unions) and with freedom of assembly than with the promised freedom of the press. Stolypin cynically stated that what the law says and what the administration chooses to do are two different things. And in this he was supported by the Third State Duma, particularly Guchkov's so-called Party of October 17, so much that it will require major surgery to cleanse the blood vessels of Russian public life.

The Orthodox Church

It will be recalled that while I served as premier, preparations were being made to call a council (*sobor*) of the Orthodox church to consider its condition and to move toward the reestablishment of the patriarchate.[6] These preparations had not been completed at the time I left office. Later, on September 14, 1907, with Imperial approval, rules were issued for the convening of a council and the setting of its agenda. Reference was made to the imminence of it, but to this date [1912] there has been no council and, as far as one can judge, there is no intention of calling one. The fact is that the publication of the rules was simply one of the many ruses used during the Stolypin regime to distract public attention.

Meanwhile, with each passing year the higher church administration has become demoralized and has lost authority and influence in the eyes of its Orthodox sons. In part the trouble has come from the fact that after Pobedonostsev a series of dillentantes served as over-procurators. I have already mentioned Prince Obolenskii, Prince Shirinskii-Shikhmatov, and P. P. Izvolskii. Lukianov, who succeeded Izvolskii in February 1909, was, as I have noted earlier, an able medical man but nothing else.* Adding to the weakening of the Orthodox church was the fact that many of the higher and lower clergy began to dabble in politics, by working with the Union of the Russian People and consequently engaging in actions unworthy of men who claim to look after the souls of Orthodox Christians.

What we see as a result of the decay of the church are people like Rasputin, the monk Iliodor, Archbishop Hermogen, and hysterical types like Mitka, whose prominence shows to what depths the higher administration of the Orthodox church has sunk.[7] What is happening in the higher circles of the church cannot help but weaken the influence of the church, which, as we know, played such an important role in the shaping of Russia. It still plays a major role in our life, and what is happening to it cannot help but arouse fears for the future of Russia.

I think that the recent replacement of Lukianov by Sabler may improve matters. I may have had a hand in Sabler's appointment. About two months before he was named over-procurator I spoke at length about him to a very fine prelate who does not engage in political intrigues, a man far removed from the likes of Father Ioann of Kronstadt,† Hermogen, Iliodor, and Rasputin. I suggested that, given the current state of affairs, it would be better if Sabler were named over-procurator. I learned later that this fine prelate presented this view at Tsarskoe Selo as his own.

*He was appointed on the recommendation of the minister of education as a "firm" man. It was the fashion then, as it still is, to appoint so-called firm men.

†I became acquainted with the late Father Ioann early in my tenure as minister of finance. I was inclined to respect him because Emperor Alexander III thought highly of him, and when the Emperor died, Father Ioann was summoned to Livadia. Like all Russians I knew that he exercised considerable influence on the common people by his preaching and his commanding appearance. Early in my tenure as minister I saw him at his request: he visited me and conducted services in my official

I believe Sabler's appointment to be a proper one because unlike some of his predecessors he has enough experience, having served long in the Holy Synod and having been assistant over-procurator under Pobedonostsev, to be well acquainted with the organizational details of the religious institutions. What are his principles? I think that like his colleagues he generally sails with the wind.[8]

Stolypin and the Jewish Question

When Stolypin took office he, as I had, proposed eliminating some anti-Jewish restrictions and proceeding gradually to remove all restrictions. After reading the cabinet minutes proposing such a policy (I have a copy of the minutes in my archive), the Emperor withheld his approval.[9] When Stolypin realized that his prospects would be enhanced if he bore down on Jews and other non-Russian subjects, he began to follow a neonationalist course, which included the imposition of new restrictions on the Jews. The first substantive action in his war on Jews was a set of regulations concerning Jewish quotas in the schools issued in September 1907 by Imperial action, without approval by the legislative bodies, although these regulations were legislative in character. Other restrictions were to follow.

As I have said before, one does not have to like Jews to argue for their admission to civic equality. The attack on Jews launched by Stolypin was politically unwise and morally unjustifiable.

Stolypin and Finland

I have already written about how Gerhard was appointed governor-general of Finland following October 17, 1905, on my recommendation. Under his wise administration, the grand duchy began to calm down, and if he had been permitted to remain in office, Finland would have become completely calm. But he soon came under attack from the press of the extreme right, particularly by *Novoe vremia*, for allegedly being too indulgent toward the Finns, so much so, they claimed, that the grand duchy was virtually separated from the Russian Empire.

Such accusations were slanderous. True, the manifesto of October 22, 1905,

residence. He made a strong impression on my wife but not on me. He did not seem well educated.

In the course of the unrest of 1905, Father Ioann apparently lost his sense of balance and instead of remaining politically neutral, as befits a priest, he fell under the influence of Dr. Dubrovin and the Union of the Russian People. As a result he began to engage in many activities that, in my opinion, are unworthy of any intelligent human being, let alone a man who claims to look after the souls of Orthodox Christians.

All of this derives from the fact that, although not a bad person, he was a man of limited intelligence whose judgment became clouded by the fact that he had access to higher circles, including the Imperial family. As I have observed, such access tends to corrupt persons lacking in firm principles.

There were many who considered him a holy man, as was shown by the pomp of his funeral and the fact that a cathedral was erected where he was buried, acts that had more to do with politics than with the spirit of Orthodoxy.

Was he a holy man? To say so is to utter blasphemy. He was an ordinary priest, had not taken monastic vows, had not given up family life or anything else that monks renounce. However, on balance I must admit that he did more good than harm in his life, particularly to the common people, and that he stood out among other priests, but that is not enough to make him a holy man.

granted too much autonomy to Finland, but that was not Gerhard's fault. An intelligent man, more patriotic and with more political sense than his critics, he followed a wise policy of respecting the historical rights of Finland, while strongly supporting the interests of the Empire and the prerogatives in the grand duchy of the Grand Duke of Finland and the Emperor of All the Russias. By following such a policy he earned the admiration of the Finns. I believe that if he had been given enough time he could have established a proper relationship between the grand duchy and the rest of the Empire, but this was not to be. Stolypin, it seems, decided to undermine his position and in November 1907, against the governor-general's wishes, arranged for the appointment of General Seyn as Gerhard's assistant. General Seyn, it should be noted, had worked closely with Bobrikov, who had so much to do with provoking the Finns to revolution, and it was Gerhard who had insisted that Seyn and other associates of Bobrikov had to go. General Seyn was not very able, but was quite high-handed. Stolypin decided that Seyn, who would do whatever he was told, would be a desirable replacement for Gerhard.[10]

When I saw Gerhard after his removal from office [in 1908], I asked what the Emperor's attitude toward him had been while he was in office. He replied that he had made it clear to the Emperor what he intended to do at the beginning of his tenure and the Emperor had approved. During the course of it he had enjoyed the good will and support of the Emperor. Therefore, he said, he did not think that his departure from office had anything to do with the Emperor, that his fall had come about from disagreements with the clique of former associates of Bobrikov and Plehve with whom Stolypin had surrounded himself.

When I observed that Stolypin could not have acted as he had without the Emperor's approval, Gerhard asked: "Do you really know His Majesty?"

The talk then shifted to Stolypin. At the time I still believed that Stolypin was a man of principle, that if he behaved oddly it was from lack of experience. When I said: "Stolypin has his limitations, but he is an honorable and gallant man," Gerhard replied: "Believe me, Stolypin is not as limited as you think and, what is more, is far from being as honorable as you describe him. I say this on the basis of my relations with him while I was governor-general, and I have the evidence to prove it." I know that Gerhard was not given to loose words, but for a time I chose to believe that in Stolypin's case he was mistaken. Unfortunately, I subsequently had many occasions on which to note to myself that Gerhard had been right.

General Böckmann, who had served under Gerhard as chief of the military, became the new governor-general [with General Seyn staying as assistant]. Following his appointment he called on me, in full uniform. I was surprised at this courtesy, for such courtesies had become rare following my departure from office and the Emperor's evident contemptuous disfavor toward me.

This was my first sight of the general, who impressed me as a straightforward, honorable man. When I asked what he thought of Gerhard, he said that he had gotten along very well with him and that he respected him. When I asked what kind of policy he intended to follow, he said: "That which is indicated by my Grand Duke." At first I thought he was speaking of the Emperor, the Grand Duke of Finland, as was to be expected from a military man, but it soon became evident he was referring to Grand Duke Nicholas Nikolaevich, commander of the Petersburg Military District.

After General Böckmann had suffered the same fate as Gerhard [and had been replaced by General Seyn], he called on me again, this time on the occasion of his appointment as an inactive member of the State Council. When I asked why he had had to leave his office, he replied that although, unlike Gerhard, he believed that the Emperor had the right to change the laws governing Finland, he could not as an honorable soldier interpret and execute the laws of Petersburg to suit the convenience of Petersburg. Not long after this encounter, the State Duma and the State Council, acting at the government's behest, passed a law which made it legal to ignore the Finnish Sejm in cases concerning Finland if those cases could be taken to have significance for the entire Empire. When I heard this law defended in a Jesuitical manner to make it appear that it was in accord with the Finnish constitution, when it clearly was not, I thought to myself: "Apparently a soldier's honor is a special kind of honor."[11]

Tolmachev, the Scourge of Odessa

On October 2, 1907, a misfortune befell my very own Odessa,[12] with the appointment of General I. N. Tolmachev as its prefect. Before I tell of the harm he wrought, I should tell how he came to be selected for the position.

When I became premier the prefect of this city was D. B. Neidhardt, who owed his position to the fact that while he commanded the Preobrazhenskii Guards the present Emperor had served under him as battalion commander. Because of complaints that Neidhardt had provoked much of the violence and unrest that was gripping Odessa, a senatorial investigation under Kuzminskii was conducted,[13] resulting in a report so unfavorable that I had to replace him, thus making an enemy of him and, what is more important, of his sister, the wife of Stolypin. Because of Neidhardt's ties to the Emperor, he was appointed to the Senate.

Because of the continuing unrest in Odessa it seemed to me that the next prefect should be a military man like General Grigorev, whom I knew from my days with the Odessa Railroad. He had been serving for some time on the staff of the commander of the Odessa Military District and had earned a good reputation for himself. He was, moreover, associated with Odessa, owned a home there, was married to the daughter of a wealthy Odessa merchant. When I asked General Kaulbars, commander of the Odessa Military District and temporary governor-general of Odessa, if he would approve of the appointment of his subordinate as prefect, he agreed, saying that his would be an excellent appointment.

General Grigorev was given the post and lived up to my expectations, making an excellent record for himself. But after Stolypin became premier, the prefect became the object of constant sniping from Petersburg directed by Neidhardt, who felt greatly aggrieved because he had had to leave Odessa. In the end General Grigorev found the constant friction with Petersburg too much and retired.

His successor, General Novitskii, former chief of the gendarme administration in Kiev, was able, quite energetic, on the whole a decent man, although not without his faults. He was getting on in years and suffered from heart trouble. The position of prefect of Odessa then was no sinecure anymore than it is today, when unrest, in a covert form, is strong as a result of the Stolypin regime. Well, under the stress of his work General Novitskii suffered a heart attack and had to leave after only a few months in his post.

Thereupon General Tolmachev, a man who deserves to be remembered, unkindly, appeared on the face of God's earth. He had been serving in the army in the Caucasus and had left, if not at the request of Count Vorontsov-Dashkov, the viceroy, then to his delight for, as he told me, he considered Tolmachev an impossible individual. It appears that Tolmachev went from the Caucasus to Petersburg, where, it is said, he ingratiated himself with that rogue and good-for-nothing Dr. Dubrovin, the chairman of the Union of the Russian People, then enjoying great influence in higher places. I have been told that it was Dr. Dubrovin who recommended Tolmachev for the position of prefect of Odessa.

When he first took up his new position, he seemed full of good will toward all, but soon he showed himself in all his unmitigated nastiness. He not only paid no attention to the law but also openly flaunted his contempt for it. He vigorously persecuted the Jewish inhabitants and, because they constitute a large part of the population, began to consider all inhabitants as "kikes" and treated them accordingly. He interfered in all aspects of the city's life, whether they were his business or not. For example, he forbade the hospitals to use any anesthetic but chloroform. He told the university and other schools what to do and gradually by defamation and denunciation drove decent and independent people out and replaced them with his protégés, for the most unqualified or conscienceless men. He did much the same with the municipal administration. And that was not all: he made a spectacle of himself by appearing in public with prostitutes. In short, Tolmachev administered Odessa in a manner which even today's Asiatic despots could not manage to do.

It goes without saying that he was embraced by the local Black Hundreds and their head, Count Konovnitsyn.* Gradually the dark Black Hundreds atmosphere fell over the city and normal, honorable life became impossible. These Black Hundreds types, like their colleagues elsewhere, lost all sense of honor and

---

*Count Konovnitsyn is a former naval officer. I met him in Kiev while I was manager of the Southwestern Railroad. There he met Professor Mering's daughter. (Sonia, my first wife's daughter, married the professor's son.) After he had run through her money, he divorced her and married their governess. Through good connections he became a land captain (zemskii nachalnik) but was forced out of that position because he embezzled public money. Again his connections enabled him to find a position, this time with the Russian Steamship and Commercial Company, in Odessa, for which I had once worked. When the revolution came to Odessa, he became head of the local branch of the Union of the Russian People and found himself in the company of people as contemptible as he.

gradually became thoroughly depraved, like prostitutes. Naturally they soon fell out among themselves, quarreling like hyenas over carrion.

Tolmachev had so much power that he fell out with General Kaulbars, who himself was identified with the Black Hundreds. The conflict between them grew out of trouble between the prefect's police and the general's troops. It began with a bloody episode. An army officer while walking in Odessa noticed that a policeman was abusing a young lady and came to her defense, virtually knocking the policeman down. A second policeman then intervened and killed the officer. At the subsequent inquiry this policeman justified his action on the ground that the prefect had decreed that if a policeman's orders were not obeyed he had the right to shoot, particularly if the person physically resisted the officer.

This incident made the military in Odessa very restive and made for extremely strained relations between Kaulbars and Tolmachev. I was in Odessa in 1908 when General-Adjutant Panteleev arrived to investigate the troubles between the civilian and military authorities in the city and see if he could smooth relations between them. When General Panteleev returned from Odessa, he reported his findings to His Majesty, with the recommendation that martial law, then in effect in Odessa, be lifted, and that the city be placed under "reinforced protection" or "extraordinary protection" in consonance with the law on exceptional measures. Stolypin, who at this time still held a high opinion of Tolmachev, approved of the recommendation, but was reluctant to give his personal support to it in view of the high esteem in which the Odessa prefect was held by the Emperor. When he learned of Stolypin's reluctance, the Emperor expressed surprise, saying that whatever the status of Odessa, Tolmachev was the kind of prefect who would do what was necessary to be done, without being hampered by existing laws.*

The upshot of the conflict was such that General Kaulbars was removed from his command. I must confess that when I heard the news I said that it served him right.

While temporary governor-general he had permitted the sentence of death that had been imposed by a court-martial to be carried out against two young Jews, one nineteen, the other seventeen. Their elderly mother then went to my sister, who lives in Odessa, and, crying constantly, told her that the two had not even been on the scene of the incident for which they had been shot. My sister could not believe the story of this old Jewess and went to Kaulbars to ask if it were true. It was, he said, but not to worry, he had found the real culprits and had them shot. When my sister asked how he could have such an "attitude toward human life" he replied that it was all my fault. "Why?" she asked. He answered:

*The states of martial law, "reinforced protection," and "extraordinary protection" give governors and prefects and governors-general a broad range of arbitrary power, but this was not enough for Stolypin. He thought up a fourth category for areas for which one could not justify any of the preceding statuses. Under this status the prefect, governor, or governor-general would be given the right to issue binding rules on his own authority when it was necessary to restore calm to an area. Such a status would be worse than the other three because it would not set legal limits on the official's authority. Such an idea went with Stolypin's behavior, to appear to be acting in a liberal manner when doing the opposite.

Because while he was premier, I proposed to him that court-martials [for civilians] be abolished and that the right to impose death sentences on such people be given to governors-general. Had he agreed, it would have been I who would have heard the case of these two innocent Jews and they could not have been executed. But as it was, they were sentenced by a court-martial and I had to confirm its sentence.

Tolmachev also fell out with Count Konovnitsyn and again was the victor. The count was forced to leave Odessa, conferring a blessing on the city by his departure. But he was able to help bring down Tolmachev in the end, with the indirect assistance of Stolypin.

At first, as I have said, Stolypin held Tolmachev in high regard, but gradually became less approving as Tolmachev, his head turned by his successes and the praise he received from Petersburg, became increasingly conceited and began to ignore the premier. It goes without saying that Stolypin could not endure to be treated in this fashion and tried to edge Tolmachev out, but he could not do so on his own, for the prefect after several years in office had powerful support at court.

The erosion of that support came about through the intervention of Flag Captain Nilov,[14] to whom, one might say, Odessa owes a debt of gratitude. Count Konovnitsyn and Nilov had served together in the navy many years earlier, had become good friends, and shared several interests, among them the worship of Bacchus. This explained why Nilov was able to arrange for Count Konovnitsyn to be invited to lunch with His Majesty in Yalta. This occurred about two years after Tolmachev had become prefect, at a time when the first battle between Konovnitsyn and the prefect had taken place. The report that the count had lunched with His Majesty, which appeared in the newspapers, astonished those who knew him because ordinary, decent mortals would not shake hands with such a creature, much less sit at the same table with him. Everyone assumed that the Emperor did not know what sort of a person his guest was and probably still does not know. This minor fact is one of a multitude that shows what kind of times we experienced under the dictatorship of Stolypin. I mention it not to put blame on the Emperor, but to show how he could be deceived and put in a false position.

In any event, the fact that Count Konovnitsyn could be invited to lunch with the Emperor helped turn opinion in the higher circles against Tolmachev. In the end, shortly after Stolypin's death, Tolmachev lost his place and is now [1912] in retirement, on a pension. As expected, once he was out of office, we learned more about his misdeeds. In addition to having been involved in financial improprieties, it came to be known that he had arranged for the killing of many persons whom he suspected of trying to kill him: he would have such persons arrested, then arrange to have them transferred from one place of detention to another, permitted to "escape" during the transfer, and once they were in flight, having them shot.

Naturally, everyone in Odessa was greatly relieved to be freed of this man and thanked God for their deliverance from him.

I cannot leave the subject of Tolmachev and Odessa without telling about an episode that affected me. Because I had played a substantial role in Odessa, Dvorianskaia, the street on which I had lived while a student at the university, one of the streets on which the institution is located, was renamed after me. This had happened many years earlier. Well, Tolmachev, who pretended to be friendly to me when I was in Odessa, was in fact quite hostile to me: on one occasion when it was proposed that Grand Duke Alexander Mikhailovich be named honorary chairman of an exhibition to be held in the city, he wrote to Stolypin, who then informed the Emperor that it would be inappropriate for the Grand Duke to accept because several undesirable individuals, among them, Witte, "a well-known Kadet," were honorary members of the exhibition's committee. In 1908, in keeping with his attitude toward me, he directed the city's Municipal Duma to change the name of Witte Street. Because permission from the Ministry of Interior is required for the renaming of streets and because such permission is almost never given when the street in question is named after a living person, the members of the Municipal Duma, Tolmachev's henchmen, passed an ordinance changing the name to Emperor Peter I Street. Such a change, they reasoned, would have to come to the attention of the Emperor. This would ensure approval and, once approval was granted, the fact that the street was named after Emperor Peter I would guarantee that it would not be renamed Witte Street. After all that is what the people of Odessa were used to calling it, and who knows, the time might come when a less reactionary Municipal Duma might want to restore the old name.

Before going abroad that year, I informed Stolypin about the ordinance and was assured that he had not heard of it, doubted that it could be passed, and that, if by any chance it had passed, it would not be implemented because he would not permit it. Knowing that he was influenced by Gerbel and Kryzhanovskii, his associates, I spoke to them and was told that such an ordinance would not be affirmed by the Ministry of Interior. In any event, when I visited Odessa on my return to Russia I found that the street name had not been changed. But that is not the end of the story.

Early in 1910 Prince A. D. Obolenskii informed me that a few months earlier the Emperor had given his approval of the ordinance. I then asked Stolypin if in presenting the legislation to the Emperor he had told him that the action proposed was unprecedented and impermissible. He assured me that the name of the street would not be changed, but, as I learned later, he had not advised the Emperor to reject the ordinance.

Emperor Alexander III acted in quite a different manner when confronted with an analogous case. When Grand Duke Sergei Aleksandrovich replaced Prince Dolgorukov as governor-general of Moscow, the local Municipal Duma passed an ordinance changing the name of the street running by the governor-general's residence from Dolgorukov Street to Grand Duke Sergei Aleksandrovich Street, this to curry favor with the Grand Duke. Even though Emperor Alexander III took a dim view of the outgoing governor-general because of the latter's sympathetic attitude toward Jews, he wrote "how contemptible" on the legislation when it was submitted to him. This was in keeping with his noble and straightforward manner.

Rheinbott and Stolypin

The case of General Rheinbott, who was relieved of his post of prefect of Moscow in December 1907, provides another illustration of Stolypin's character. An energetic and intelligent man, Rheinbott had performed well in his post. To be sure, like most prefects and governors he could be high-handed, but he had enough sense not to go too far and acted with greater moderation than most in comparable positions. On balance, his positive attributes outweighed his negative ones.

He fell into trouble because he earned the favor of the Emperor, who appointed him to his suite and even gave him permission to call on him without asking prior assent. Consequently, General Rheinbott began to visit Petersburg frequently and to call on the Emperor. On such occasions he probably told His Majesty things about the premier which Stolypin learned only later. Such a situation could not fail to irk the premier, who began to see a potential rival in the prefect, and with good cause, because Rheinbott was an intelligent, well-educated, and decisive man. So, Stolypin instigated a senatorial investigation of this man's conduct in office.

The investigation was entrusted to the "well-known" Senator Garin, about whose connection with General Trepov I have spoken earlier. Garin, a man servile to those in high places, conducted a biased investigation, in the course of which negative findings were grossly exaggerated. Of course, there is no smoke without fire. The prefect was guilty of some improprieties, but far fewer than those committed by Stolypin and those who served him. As a result of the investigation, General Rheinbott was forced to retire and was dropped from the Emperor's suite. Subsequently, General Rheinbott was tried by a criminal court for alleged improprieties in office. (In the course of the trial, Rheinbott told how Stolypin had used money to assure victory of Octobrist candidates to the Third State Duma. He also told me some of the details.) The court, as was common in the era of Stolypin and Shcheglovitov, was far from independent and imposed a severe sentence on the former prefect, but at the same time recommended that the sentence be reduced. Although the Emperor had taken the findings of the senatorial investigation more seriously than the facts warranted because Garin had worked so closely with Trepov, he acted mercifully when the recommendation came before him by giving Rheinbott a pardon.

I am certain that most of those acquainted with the case were pleased by this act of mercy on the Emperor's part. After all, under Stolypin's influence he had pardoned members of the Union of the Russian People who had either incited or committed murder.

Cabinet Changes: State Controller

As he consolidated his power in the years following the *coup d'état* of June 3, 1907, he, Stolypin, was able to have a number of his ministers replaced, usually by men further to the right than their predecessors or, at least, by men who were more docile. The first to go was Schwanebach, the state controller, who left office a few weeks after the dissolution of the Second State Duma. He was let go partly because he could not get along with the premier, partly because he went beyond the bounds of reactionary policies considered reasonable at the time (bounds beyond which Stolypin was himself to go thereafter), and finally, because he meddled in foreign affairs, in a way that ran counter to the policy that our foreign minister, Izvolskii, was following.[15]

He was replaced by P. A. Kharitonov, then serving as assistant Imperial secretary, an intelligent, able man, an excellent jurist with great experience, but like others tempered by experience in the Petersburg chancelleries, particularly the chancellery of the State Council, his motto was, "How can I be of service?" He had no trouble in being for a constitution, then against a constitution, for Finland and now against Finland. Because he took part in the drafting of the Fundamental Laws he knew what they were intended to mean, yet serving under Stolypin he was capable of taking the floor to interpret these laws to mean the opposite.

Moreover, although he has a good mind and knows a great deal, he is pretty much the narrow bureaucrat. I recall that during the drafting of the Fundamental Laws, when I would ask why he had phrased a certain article in a given way, he would not deal with the substantive question but explained that this article came from the Japanese constitution, that one from the Swedish constitution, and a third one from the Italian constitution. That was typical of him.

Cabinet Changes: Ministry of Education

At the beginning of 1908, P. M. Kaufmann was replaced as minister of education by A. N. Schwarz. The explanation is somewhat convoluted.

Kaufmann, as I have said before, lacked the background to be minister of education and as a result permitted his assistant minister, Gerasimov, to guide him. As may be recalled, I had chosen Gerasimov to be assistant minister of education when I became premier for two reasons: first, because he had the necessary experience, second, because he had the kind of solid conservative credentials and support that could help balance the liberalism of that excellent man Count Ivan Ivanovich Tolstoi, whom I had chosen to be minister. Gerasimov, an intelligent and able man, had acquitted himself well, shown himself to be also a convinced, reasonable conservative. But with the change in the temper of the times, he was considered to be too far to the left! And since it was generally, and justifiably, believed that he was the one in charge at the ministry, pressure grew for his dismissal.

Stolypin thereupon put it to Kaufmann that he could remain in office if he would agree to having Gerasimov go, but the minister turned out to have too much character to agree to such an arrangement, so they both went. Stolypin sweetened the pill for Kaufmann by arranging to have him appointed to the first rank at court. Gerasimov received no such favor.*

The new minister, Schwarz, held on to office for more than two years, but in the end he had to leave his post because, as it turned out, he was insufficiently infected with the ideas of the Union of the Russian People and therefore could not agree with Stolypin. With all his affectation of liberalism, Stolypin required from Schwarz such measures and such indifference to the law to which the minister of education could not agree. As a result, he had to leave his post.

When the name of the next minister of education, L. A. Casso, was announced, everyone was astonished because he was virtually unknown. It turned out that he was of Greco-Moldavian origin, a product of French and German secondary and higher schools, and was somehow distantly related to Renan. Who had recommended his appointment? After a few weeks it was learned Stolypin's aunt, who lived in Moscow, knew the man and that it was through her that the premier had become acquainted with Casso. What form her recommendation took was, of course, a secret, but one can guess that knowing nothing about Casso's professional qualifications, she convinced her nephew that Casso was a gentle person, an excellent neighbor, a man who as minister of education would be bothered by nothing, least of all the laws of Russia.[16] Such a recommendation could not fail to be attractive to Stolypin or fail to sway him to recommend this man to be placed in charge of the Russian educational system. It is said that the Emperor had never heard of this man, but apparently when he came to know him was pleased with him and soon raised him from acting minister to minister.

At the time of Casso's appointment I was in Biarritz and Kokovtsev was in Paris. In a letter I asked him, among other things, what was going on, particularly with the strange appointments being made. He replied that he knew nothing about the appointment of Casso and was somewhat puzzled by it, but added later in the letter, which I have in my possession, that we were witnessing the flowering of unlimited autocracy, but a reverse kind of autocracy, signifying that the premier, not the Emperor, was the autocrat.

---

*Gerasimov, who had enjoyed the support of the late Grand Duke Sergei Aleksandrovich, had talked to His Majesty many times. Therefore, when he was let go he asked for and was given an audience with the Emperor, who received him kindly and told him that he had been dismissed at the request of the premier. In the course of the audience, His Majesty had something to say about me, which I learned from one of my friends, M. A. Stakhovich, who learned about this from Gerasimov. Gerasimov told the Emperor that he had not had a chance really to get to know me but that he did have the opportunity of becoming acquainted with Stolypin, trusted and admired him, and so was astonished that Stolypin would act kindly toward him, yet arrange for his dismissal. According to Stakhovich's report, the Emperor replied: "Well, I know Count Witte well and therefore do not trust him."

I would like to believe that these words were not spoken because so much importance is attached to each word he utters that it is not fitting to give such language currency.

Cabinet Changes:
Ministry of Ways and Communications

In 1909 Schaufuss, minister of ways and communications, was replaced by Rukhlov, the man I would not accept as minister of commerce and industry when His Majesty tried to impose him on me. Schaufuss left partly because he could not get along with Stolypin, partly because of poor health.

The decline in health was brought on by General Wendrich, with whom I had had difficulties when I was minister of ways and communications.[17] After I had been able to shunt him out of authority, he went abroad, spending the next decade or so writing about German railroads, and did not return until Stolypin came to power, this at a time when Schaufuss was unable to cope with the seditious spirit among railroad men. It was at this point that Grand Duke Nicholas Nikolaevich recommended that Wendrich be brought in to help the minister: after all, the Grand Duke argued, Wendrich had effectively dealt with railroad problems under Emperor Alexander III. Accordingly Wendrich was asked to help.

For an entire year, in keeping with his character, General Wendrich made a nuisance of himself by proposing grandiose schemes, the most grandiose of which was the establishment of a railroad corps, patterned after the Corps of Gendarmes, that would consist of men drawn from the armed forces. Apparently Wendrich submitted this scheme to the Emperor without Stolypin's knowledge. According to the general, the Emperor approved and indicated that Wendrich would be the chief of the new railroad corps.

Although the alleged appointment was not announced, Wendrich told everyone about it, thereby arousing opposition from everybody, particularly from the Ministry of Ways and Communications, where it was felt that the establishment of the proposed corps, with a chief reporting to the Emperor, would disturb the organization of railroad operations. The upshot was that Wendrich was eased out of the ministry and given an appointment to the Senate.

All this furor seriously undermined Schaufuss's health, and he had to give up his post. There were those who thought that General Wendrich would succeed him, but this was not to be because of the opposition of Stolypin and virtually the entire ministry. As I have said, the Emperor appointed Rukhlov as the new minister of ways and communications.

Rukhlov is of peasant stock, which is to his credit. He is intelligent, has some experience and considerable knowledge, but he was not acquainted with railroading. He is not without character, but he tends to sail with the wind and, as I have noted, was at one time one of Grand Duke Alexander Mikhailovich's creatures.

Cabinet Changes:
The Ministry of Commerce and Industry

Following the death of Filosofov, the minister of commerce and industry, at the end of 1907, Ivan Pavlovich Shipov,[18] with whom I had long been associated, was asked to replace Filosofov. At the same time he was offered the post of ambassador to Japan, because the incumbent, Bakhmetev, did not seem suitable, at least from the point of view of foreign minister Izvolskii. Shipov had some knowledge of the Far East: he had been with me at Portsmouth during the negotiation of peace with Japan and had recently visited China and Japan, at Kokovtsev's request, to become better acquainted with the situation and particularly to become acquainted with matters affecting the Russo-Chinese Bank.

When he asked me which of the offers to accept, I urged him to take the post in Tokyo. I advised against accepting the ministerial portfolio for two reasons: first, he did not have the background to be minister of commerce and industry; and second, because it seemed to me that a decent and independent person could not serve under the regime as it had come to be, particularly under Stolypin. In favor of accepting the ambassadorship, I said, was the fact that it would give him a degree of independence and he would not be affected by politics at home. Without telling me his reasons, he ignored my counsel and accepted the ministerial portfolio. I learned later that he did not want to leave the country because he was in love with a nice young lady on the staff at the Smolnyi Institute. I felt that he had made the wrong decision and would not be in his new office very long. I was right. A year after his appointment, Shipov was replaced by Timiriazev, an old colleague of mine.

While he was serving as minister of commerce and industry, Shipov did not call on me, like my other former associates who felt it wiser when in office to avoid me because of my differences with Stolypin. Once out of office he came to see me, and when I asked why he had to leave it he told me that he found much about the Stolypin regime to be unpalatable. For one thing he said, he found Stolypin petty and vain. The first time he called on the premier, he was shown a carefully organized collection of congratulatory telegrams which Stolypin had received on coming into office. I, on the other hand, said Shipov, had simply torn up the thousands of such telegrams that I had received, first on becoming minister of finance and then on becoming premier.

Surely, I said, he had more weighty reasons for asking to be relieved of his position. He replied that the immediate reason for his request was that he was being asked to distribute government-owned oil-bearing lands to persons to whom these lands had been promised by His Majesty, and he could not in good conscience carry out such a request. Then, he said: "Let us see how Timiriazev gets out of this situation." I replied: "I know Timiriazev. He will get out of it simply by distributing the lands to those designated as recipients and, in addition, will suggest to the Emperor other recipients who might be useful to him." And that is exactly what happened.

I have related earlier the disgraceful conduct of Timiriazev that had compelled me to have him replaced as minister of commerce and industry while I was premier.[19] On leaving office he found a position with the Russian Bank for

Foreign Trade as well as additional posts and was elected, under the liberal banner, to the State Council, representing commerce and industry. During the period of the First and Second State Dumas he continued to play the liberal, but by the time of the election of the Third State Duma he realized that espousal of liberal ideas was not to his advantage. It was evident to him his liberal attitudes might cost him his seat in the State Council because the time for the drawing of lots for the end of the terms of one-third of the elected members was drawing near and he was afraid that if, by mischance, his name should be drawn, he would not be reelected by those speaking for commerce and industry.[20] Therefore he began to try to strengthen his position by earning the favor of Stolypin, by acting as his spokesman and staunch supporter in the State Council.[21]

Stolypin was well pleased by such accommodating behavior, and when Shipov left the post of minister of commerce and industry, he offered it to Timiriazev, who accepted it. As he feared, he was chosen by lot to leave the State Council, but then used his new position to good effect and was elected to a new term.

During his short tenure as minister he sought and obtained all sorts of honors and honorary official positions for persons on whom he had been dependent while with the Russian Bank for Foreign Trade and other companies. Before long he regretted leaving private employment, because as minister he could not receive compensation (at least not in monetary form) from all the enterprises with which he had been associated. Therefore once reelected to the State Council and once having obtained honors for the persons on whom he had been dependent while privately employed, he began to seek a pretext for leaving his post.[22]

As they say, good fortune can come in the form of misfortune. In this case it was the death of his wife, which provided him with the excuse that grief prevented him from carrying on his work. He prepared a petition asking to be permitted to leave his post, to be transmitted by Stolypin to the Emperor, who was then in Yalta. At the same time he asked the premier to intercede for him to get him an appointment to a court title of the first rank (*chin*). After all, Kaufmann had received such a title on leaving office. Moreover, Timiriazev argued, he needed the title for the sake of his orphaned daughter, who would not be able to find a suitable husband if he did not. If he received the title, she would be able to attract a suitor from the Imperial court.

It was at this time that the State Duma was reviewing the estimates of the Department of Mines, in connection with the proposed budget for 1910. The review provided the occasion for raising questions about illegal distribution of government oil fields, in which Timiriazev had participated.

It was this speech which helped Stolypin in his plea that the Emperor grant Timiriazev's request for a title. He pointed out that the bereaved Timiriazev had capped his loyal service to the crown with his speech, that he had been well liked at court. How could he be denied this title? The Emperor acceded and signed an order which named Timiriazev high master of the court (*ober-hofmeister*).

This was not enough for Timiriazev. Although he knew that by law he could not keep the title and engage in private employment, that is precisely what he sought to do. As soon as his appointment as high master of the court was made official, he bought the appropriate uniform for his new rank and left for Yalta, to present his case. His plan was to influence Baron Freedericksz, the minister of the court, either to support him in his efforts or, at least, not to oppose him. As part of his strategy he worked on General Mosolov, director of the baron's chancellery, to serve as his ally. In his effort to influence the baron, he pleaded that Stolypin had not informed him in advance that he was acting on his behalf to gain the title, that had he known he would have told the premier that he was not worthy of such an honor and that in any case he had to seek private employment to support himself and his orphaned daughter. He asked for and was given an audience with the Emperor.

Meanwhile Kokovtsev, who was in Yalta, intervened in his usual envious and spiteful manner. He informed Baron Freedericksz of Timiriazev's wily strategy, that the man was not telling the truth when he said that he had not known that Stolypin would plead on his behalf for a court title. When Timiriazev was received by the Emperor he was told that he would have to give up his court title if he accepted private employment. A few weeks later a decree was issued releasing him from his position of high master of the court but at the same time promoting him to the [civil service] rank of actual privy councillor.

Thus, Timiriazev did not come out of all this empty-handed. He was still an elected member of the State Council, now had the rank of actual privy councillor (retired), and was able to earn a good living in various banking and other commercial operations.

Death of Leo Tolstoy

The death of our great writer Count Leo Tolstoy at the end of 1910 was a major event which aroused various kinds of reactions and attracted widespread notice.

His Majesty noted on the report of his death that he was a great artist but that God would be his judge. For my part I believe that Russians, both the educated and uneducated, consider him a great man and will continue to do so. He was indeed a great artist but he was also great because of his moral influence not only on Russians but on all Europeans.

As I have noted elsewhere, I considered many of his political views naive, but that cannot be said of his moral views. His moral influence derived from the fact that he could rise above egotistical concerns. In the final analysis, his greatest service derived from the fact that he genuinely believed in God and was able to use his great talent to instill this belief in the hearts of thousands and thousands and thus fight against atheism and Russian nihilism, which had been a major influence on the minds of the Russian youth of the 1870s.

The death of Count Tolstoy put the government in a difficult position. It did not know which leg to dance on. It was impossible to ignore such a major event. It was impossible to attack him. It was undesirable to permit large-scale demonstrations of sorrow. The government dealt with the problem by feigning sorrow while at the same time taking covert steps to restrict public expressions of sorrow as much as possible.

It is remarkable that not one Russian writer, or for that matter foreign writer, has had such universal influence as Tolstoy. That fact alone demonstrates what kind of talent he possessed.

IX

Foreign Affairs, 1907–1911

Rapprochement with Japan

On July 17, 1907, Izvolskii, our foreign minister, signed a convention with Japan delimiting our respective spheres of influence in the Far East. This was his first step toward rapprochement with Japan, and it was in the spirit of what I had tried to do at Portsmouth.

I attempted to have included in the treaty we were to sign at Portsmouth a provision for a postwar alliance between the two countries, whereby one would defend the other if the interests of either, as defined in the treaty, were menaced, this to assure that the treaty would mean more than an interlude between wars. When I discussed my idea with Komura, the chief Japanese plenipotentiary, he was evasive, but implied that the treaty might include something less binding than an alliance. So I sent a telegram to Count Lambsdorff, our foreign minister, asking for instructions. Because his reply was both evasive and discouraging, I did not raise the matter with Komura again.

I learned the explanation for our foreign minister's reply when I returned to Russia: that some generals and higher officials had begun to think of a revenge and that this idea was being supported by *Novoe vremia* and other widely read newspapers. Naturally, the Emperor himself was influenced by expressions of such a sentiment. That Grand Duke Nicholas Nikolaevich, chairman of the Council of State Defense, was among those supporting the idea meant that this absurd notion would be blown up and taken seriously. It should be noted that most of those calling for revenge for our disgraceful defeat had in some way profited financially from the war, chiefly through speculation, but had not shed their blood in the war or had relatives who had shed blood.

The Council of State Defense proceeded to consider various measures to enable us to get back at Japan. Of course, Premier Stolypin gave his support, and he, together with several military men, proposed that we construct a railroad line north of the Amur, which, they argued, would be safe from seizure by foreigners, i.e., the Japanese.[1] When the proposal for this expensive line was submitted to the Third State Duma it was defended with the proposition that war with Japan was inevitable and would probably come as early as 1911, a prediction that demonstrates how reason had been eroded by the idea of revenge. The proposal for construction of this line was approved by the State Duma and sent on to the State Council.

Once it came before this body, I had the opportunity to express my vigorous opposition.[2] I advanced several arguments. First, that in the event of war, the proposed line could be taken just as easily as could the Chinese Eastern Railroad. Second, such a line would encourage immigration of Chinese, Koreans, and other foreigners into the Amur basin when it was to our advantage to leave the region sparsely settled and half savage.[3] Third, and most importantly, the money that the line would cost, paid for by the poor Russian people, could be put to better use in strengthening our defenses east of Lake Baikal, including the defenses of the Chinese Eastern Railroad. Recent events have proved me right.

One must give Izvolskii credit for being perhaps the only one in the government to understand that our defeat in the Far East and the resulting weakening of our influence in Europe required us to assure our security in the Far East by coming to terms with the Japanese, thus permitting us to concentrate our attention on regaining that authority in Europe which Emperor Alexander III, of sacred memory, had established. That was the reason Izvolskii had concluded the convention which obligated us and Japan to observe the status quo except in permitting Japan to annex Korea.[4]

At Portsmouth, it should be recalled, we had merely recognized Japan's preponderant influence in Korea. If I had been given permission at Portsmouth to negotiate a treaty of friendship and alliance with Japan and if we had then agreed to Japanese possession of Korea (an idea which did not even enter my mind then, an idea that would have been branded as treacherous if it had), then we would not have had to cede the southern half of Sakhalin and we would have been able to retain part of the southern Manchurian railroad, perhaps as far south as Mukden.

Yes, Izvolskii did well by giving Russia the opportunity to be free of concern about our position in the Far East and to concentrate on European affairs, thus preventing us from sinking to the status of a second-rate power, with an influence comparable to, let us say, that of Spain.

To be sure we are at present playing second fiddle to Japan in the Far East, but we have peace of mind there. However, if we once more act in an adventurist spirit in that part of the world, then whatever we gain in territory will be more than matched by Japanese gains. It is in our interest to try to maintain the status quo and refrain from any risky ventures. Unfortunately, I have received information in recent months that we are becoming involved in adventurist actions in Mongolia, that the detachment of Mongolia from China, exploiting the disorder in China, is taking place under our covert influence and, if you will, our provocation.[5]

Rapprochement with England

The Anglo-Russian Convention signed on August 18, 1907, marked a sharp turn from our policy of rapprochement, or rather flirtation, with Germany to one of rapprochement, or rather flirtation, with England. Since such ladies as Germany and England are inclined to be jealous, and since they are as clever as we, we put ourselves into an ambiguous position from which we try to escape by assuring each in turn that we love only her and are only flirting with the other. We have already paid for this ambiguity, and we may have to pay again in the future.

Taken by itself the rapprochement with England has no special significance, but taken in context it is important because both we and England are allies of France. Therefore, the conclusion of a convention that deals with some important differences between us and England signified if not the formation of a triple alliance then at least something which the diplomatic world justly calls an *entente cordiale de trois puissances* directed against the Triple Alliance of Germany, Austria, and Italy.[6] Moreover, as I shall show, the convention gave England more than it did us.

As I have related elsewhere,[7] the idea of such a convention was first broached to me by Poklewski-Koziell, of our London embassy, while I was returning from America. In reply I had said that, even if I had the power to see that such a convention were concluded, I would not do so because if we did, a jealous Germany would be able to cajole us into signing a comparable agreement with her and I did not believe that Russia should become entangled in commitments to various powers. Russia, I said, needed a free hand to regain her proper status as a great power. So, as long as I was premier, England did not raise the question of a convention again, but once I left office Poklewski-Koziell, acting as go-between for England and Izvolskii, was able to negotiate the convention.*

As I have said, this convention gave England more than it did us. This was especially true with respect to Persia. From time immemorial we had exercised the dominant influence in northern Persia, the most densely populated and most productive part of the country, and the shahs of that country had been completely subordinate to us. Given the blood we had shed to annex the southern part of the Caucasus, it seemed to me to be inevitable that the neighboring region, northern Persia, should either be annexed by us or turned into a protectorate. Consequently, I felt and still feel that our hands should not be tied in Persia, that instead events should be permitted to take their own course.

*Poklewski-Koziell was close to Izvolskii, first because he had served under him and second because, according to unkind rumor, Izvolskii was always short of money and Poklewski-Koziell, a rich man, could be of help.

Our policy toward Persia should be one of benevolent protection, with the aim of incorporating the northern provinces of Persia, just as we incorporated the provinces of the southern Caucasus. But this requires that the inhabitants of the Caucasus, who shed so much blood on our behalf, be treated as sons of the Russian Empire, and not as aliens, as that so-and-so Stolypin tried to do.

The convention hurt our interests in northern Persia by stipulating that, although England recognized our predominant economic influence in the north, both powers would share political influence over the whole country, meaning sharing influence in northern Persia, where the capital, Teheran, is located.* It could be argued that one could live with the convention, but such an agreement for division and sharing of influence rested on the mistaken assumption that no other major powers had aspirations in Persia, on the assumption that we could divide influence without the consent of other interested major powers.

Germany, for one, is such a power. She had had economic aspirations in Persia for some time. Thus, as early as 1904, when I was in Germany to renew our commercial treaty, Chancellor Bülow complained that we were preventing the free entry of German goods into Persia, primarily by prohibiting transit through Batum, by our economic presence in Persia, particularly the northern part: we had built streets in Teheran and Tabriz, had opened many consulates, and had gained virtual control over Persian customs receipts by having them serve as guarantee of repayment of what we had arranged. We should have foreseen that Germany would not accept the division of economic influence between us and England. It did not. Once the convention was concluded, she began to seek free entry into Persia for her goods. In the end, in 1910, during the meeting of the Russian and German Emperors at Potsdam, an agreement concerning Persia was reached which provided that we place no obstacle in the way of entry of German goods into northern Persia and that we make no difficulties for German financial and commercial activity in that region. Also, it was agreed to link the railroads in northern Persia with the proposed Berlin to Baghdad railroad.

What do we have left in Persia? We cannot annex northern Persia because that would be in contravention of our convention with England. We have lost our economic advantages in northern Persia by allowing Germany to compete on an equal footing with us. In short, the convention has meant that we have no future in Persia, that we experience nothing but trouble, without any compensating gain, in exercising political and economic influence there.[8] Russia can play no more than a police role in Persia until that country has an administration capable of restoring order.

The provisions in the convention respecting Afghanistan also represent a minus for us. It is in our interest that Afghanistan serve as a buffer between Russia and England. Beyond that we have no interest in that country. True, the convention stipulates that Afghanistan remain a buffer, but gives England certain

*We renounced the right to exercise influence in southern Persian ports, a provision to which no objection can be made.

advantages by obligating us not to send diplomatic agents, even temporary ones, to Afghanistan, and to deal with that country only through England. This leaves Afghanistan as a buffer, but one under total English influence, a fact of dangerous significance to us.

The provision in the convention concerning Tibet, which obligates both parties not to send troops or diplomatic missions into that country, seems redundant, because there would be no sense in our seeking influence in Tibet.

To repeat, we lost more than we gained by signing the convention.

The Bosnian Crisis

In July 1908, the Young Turk revolt began, culminating in the replacement of Abdul Hamid II by his brother Mohammed V, who proved to be no more than a pawn in the hands of the military, the men behind the revolt. It seems to me that the constitution that was enacted and is still in force has no solid foundation and Turkey has lost more than it has gained from the Young Turk revolt. Bompard, the current French ambassador to Constantinople, with whom I have spoken about these events at length, does not agree with me, and he is not the only one. On the other hand, he is not positive that the present Turkish regime will endure. [One of the consequences of the revolt was the Bosnian crisis, which resulted from an agreement reached between Izvolskii and Baron Aerenthal, the foreign minister of Austria-Hungary.][9]

In September 1908 Izvolskii, who was fond of going abroad, visited with Baron Aerenthal at Buchlau, the estate of Berchtold, the Austro-Hungarian ambassador to Petersburg. Aerenthal alleges that there he told Izvolskii of his country's intention to annex Bosnia and Herzegovina, to which the Russian foreign minister replied that he had no objection, provided that the Straits be opened to Russian warships. Aerenthal claimed that he had made no commitment to Izvolskii about the Straits. Izvolskii's version was that he had offered objections to Austro-Hungarian annexation and that Aerenthal had looked favorably at opening the Straits to Russian warships.

Aerenthal, who had been shown the cards in our hand by our own Schwanebach and some of Schwanebach's colleagues, was well informed about our weaknesses, and accordingly he could risk annexation. To make his task easier he agreed to have Prince Ferdinand of Bulgaria declare his country independent of Turkey and assume the title of tsar. Prince Ferdinand proceeded to do so in late September, thus becoming the second tsar on the face of the earth. Immediately thereafter Austria-Hungary announced its annexation of Bosnia-Herzegovina.

The immediate consequence was severe diplomatic strain, of which V. N.

Kokovtsev took advantage for his own purpose.[10] Greatly overstating the gravity of the situation, he persuaded the State Duma, which had not yet reviewed the budget, to agree to his floating a loan of 450 million rubles. In arguing for the loan before the Finance Committee, of which I was and am a member, he painted a grim picture, arguing that we needed the money because we might soon be at war. Although it was evident that the proposed terms for the loan were unfavorable, the committee declared that it could not judge how serious the threat of war was, but was willing to agree to the loan. Before we considered the loan proposal I told Davydov, director of the Credit Chancellery, that because the terms for the proposed loan were unfavorable we should wait until we could bargain for better terms, to which he replied that Kokovtsev had virtually committed us to the loan when he had been to Paris in the autumn and that it was now too late to back down. He admitted that the terms were unfavorable.

Thus the loan was floated. Whether or not Kokovtsev really believed in the imminence of war I do not know. I did not, being convinced that Russia would do what she could to avoid war. I was right. Russia swallowed the pill of the annexation and of Prince Ferdinand's declaration of himself as tsar. As a result our prestige in Europe suffered greatly, and in the end Izvolskii would have to leave office because of the irresponsible manner in which he had acted.

After the shameful episode was over, Izvolskii told me that he had asked the Emperor to relieve him of his post because his position had become untenable. Izvolskii said that the Emperor had agreed and told him that he would be going to Madrid as our ambassador. When I asked who would replace him, he said that several candidates, all unsuitable, had been mentioned. One of these was Prince Engalychev, who had served as military attaché in Berlin: if he is known for anything in higher court circles, it is for his highly developed capacity for intrigue, a trait he has probably inherited from his mother, the sister of Alexis Pavlovich and Nicholas Pavlovich Ignatev.

I expressed amazement that there were no suitable candidates, to which he replied: "What can one do when there are none." I mentioned several possible candidates, among them Hartwig, the present minister to Serbia. He responded that under no circumstances would the Emperor appoint a man with a non-Russian surname as minister of foreign affairs.

Then I told Izvolskii that he had erred in not choosing as associates men capable of succeeding to high posts, something I had done as minister of finance. He replied that he did not see anyone in the diplomatic corps who could be appointed assistant minister, as a way of preparing that person to become minister. I suggested one such person, Sazonov, our diplomatic agent to the Vatican, with whom I had become acquainted when visiting Rome recently. To be sure, I said, Sazonov lacked broad experience, but if he were appointed assistant minister he could get the training necessary for him to become minister. Izvolskii was very cold to the suggestion, arguing that Sazonov's diplomatic experience was limited to minor posts in our London embassy and to service with the Vatican and that he did not have a broad enough knowledge or understanding of foreign affairs, particularly those relating to Eastern and Central Europe.

Nonetheless, he decided somewhat later to have Sazonov appointed assistant minister, as a way of winning favor with Premier Stolypin, Sazonov's brother-in-law.[11] To make this appointment, a vacancy had to be created. This was done by relieving Zinovev, our ambassador to Constantinople, and replacing him with Charykov, assistant minister of foreign affairs.

At first the replacement of Zinovev by Charykov seemed puzzling, for Zinovev was very competent and prominent, while Charykov was known even to those who barely knew him as second-rate, a mediocrity—not a bad sort, but very limited, a man taken up by numismatic and other scholarly pursuits which helped calm his nerves, but without that brilliance of mind and other gifts required of an active diplomat.* The excuse given at the time of Zinovev's departure—that he was very old—turned out to be very thin, for even now [1912] Zinovev, who is a fellow member of the State Council, appears to be hale and hearty. The real explanation soon became apparent, to create a vacancy for Sazonov.

Sazonov received the appointment. A few months later, the decision to replace Izvolskii with Sazonov was made. At the time the Emperor was staying in Friedberg, while Izvolskii was nearby in Frankfurt. By this time Izvolskii wanted to be named ambassador to London. Accordingly Count Benckendorff, our ambassador to London, was sent for and urged to accept the ambassadorship at Paris, but he would not agree, so Izvolskii was given the latter post and Sazonov was named acting foreign minister.

In my opinion Sazonov is a decent sort of person, but rather inexperienced, of modest abilities, and not in the best of health.[12]

Russo-American Tensions

In November 1907 Taft, then the war minister and now [1912] the president of the North American republic, visited Petersburg. As I have noted earlier he was away from America when I was there. I recall Roosevelt speaking highly of him. It was Roosevelt who enabled Taft to succeed him, expecting loyalty in return, but as usually happens the two fell out and are now [February 1912] vying for the Republican presidential nomination. There is no question in my mind that Roosevelt is more gifted than Taft.[13] As is well known, Roosevelt had a military command in the Spanish-American War, but neither of the two is a military man.

It is said that when Taft was here and was presented to His Majesty he brought up the question of our interpretation of the article in the Russo-American Commercial Treaty of 1832 concerning the right of subjects of each country to travel in

---

*In today's [28 February 1912] newspaper I read that Charykov has been appointed to the Senate, which means that he is leaving the post of ambassador under a cloud, for departing ambassadors are usually appointed to the State Council, not the Senate.

the other country. At issue was our practice of creating difficulties for American subjects of the Jewish faith wishing to visit Russia, a practice America refused to countenance. I do not know if Taft in fact spoke to His Majesty about this matter, but I do know the following.

As I have stated earlier, before I left for home, Roosevelt gave me a letter to transmit to His Majesty asking that the dispute be settled so as not to disturb the good relations between America and Russia that had been created during my visit. I transmitted the letter to His Majesty, who probably sent it on to the minister of interior, who probably informed His Majesty that the question was already under consideration and therefore it was not necessary to take any further steps in response to the letter.[14]

The matter was this. Even so conservative a man as minister of interior Bulygin recognized the need to eliminate obstacles against foreign Jews visiting Russia. A commission under Peter Nikolaevich Durnovo, needless to say also a conservative, prepared a report that recommended that in the preparation of a new passport law all restrictions on the entry of foreign Jews be eliminated because they served no useful purpose but only served as an irritant in our foreign relations. This report was submitted to the State Council on the eve of my departure for America. When the law establishing the State Duma was enacted [in August 1905], many of the reports which had been submitted to the State Council were returned to the ministries from which they had come so that they could be resubmitted to the State Duma. Thus the report of the Durnovo Commission was returned to the Ministry of Interior. During my tenure as premier, with unrest at its height, there could be no thought of dealing with the issue, all the more so given the fact that the State Duma had not yet been convened. After Stolypin became premier he did not submit the report, and it remained buried in the Ministry of Interior.

Thus many years passed without any reply to Roosevelt's letter. I do not know whether any reminders came [from America], but the fact is that the Russian government did nothing to placate the American government and continued to restrict the entry of foreign Jews—among them Oscar Straus, who served as American ambassador to Turkey—and showed no intention of changing its ways. The consequence was the American denunciation of the commercial treaty of 1832.[15]

Our nationalists reacted with bitter recrimination, but I feel differently. If our government had taken the matter seriously and responded positively to the Roosevelt letter, without compromising Russian interests, we would have been spared this unpleasantness.

Appendix:
Schwanebach, Aerenthal, and I

When he could, Schwanebach tried to counter Izvolskii's policy of friendship with France and England by trying to strengthen relations with Germany and

Austria-Hungary. By blood and inclination he was completely German. It is noteworthy that he was staying in a German city when he died, a city close to the place where Emperor William was staying, the man to whom he had sought to gain access.

Schwanebach had absolutely no qualifications for meddling in foreign affairs, but meddle he did. It was his friendship with Baron Aerenthal that contributed in a significant way to Austria's actions in the Bosnian crisis. That friendship was formed while Aerenthal served as ambassador.

The baron was married to an aristocratic Austrian lady who was no longer young, but who still retained traces of her youthful beauty. Because she was of higher social status than he, as well as because he was of Jewish origin, she had several times rejected his proposals of marriage but when he was named ambassador she, the years slipping by, accepted.

While I was chairman of the Committee of Ministers and especially after I became premier, the baron attempted to establish social ties between our two families. But our relations remained purely formal and our meetings few, in the first place because I was very busy and in the second place because Austro-Russian relations were not of major importance at the time. Then Aerenthal became friendly with Schwanebach.

It was during the summer of 1906 that the friendship between the two was cemented. The two lunched regularly. By this time Schwanebach was state controller, in a position to know much of what was going on in the government. And so, by being close to Schwanebach, Aerenthal was to become well acquainted with the true state of affairs in Russia. Even now [1912] the Austrian foreign minister has sources which keep him well informed about us.

After my departure from office, while Aerenthal was still ambassador and later, while foreign minister, he sought to please our government by systematically disseminating the most reactionary views concerning Russia, namely, that the Russian people were still too primitive for representative government to be successful in their country and could be governed only by an absolute monarch, then going on to say that I had committed a grave error by insisting on a constitution. Such talk was pleasing to the ears of the gentlemen who served as our ministers and to the higher circles at court. As a result he became *persona gratissima* and was thereby able to learn about the state of our country. What he thought he learned was that our government was trying by all means, fair or foul, to take back what had been given by the October 17 Manifesto, that because of the disgraceful war we had fought and the rebellion that had followed it Russia would be a negligible quantity in foreign affairs for a long time to come. It followed that the great powers would not have to take Russia into account when carrying out their schemes.

When Aerenthal was preparing to leave to assume his new post, that of foreign minister, he was given the text of a kind of memorandum, prepared by Schwanebach, that was directed against me, with the request that it be presented to Emperor William. The Goremykin government, which gave the memorandum to Aerenthal, was tacitly asking him to do it as a favor in return for the cordial treatment he had received.[16]

You see, I was a thorn in the flesh of the Goremykin and Stolypin governments and am a thorn in the flesh of the present government. Those in power have lived in fear that I might return to office. Because they are the kind who hang on to power, they find it difficult to believe that there are those who do not treasure power. Moreover, they were afraid that if I should return to office I would pay them back for all the rotten things they did in my absence or, that if I did not seek to pay them back, I would be unable to conceal the crimes they had committed. Aware of the great respect in which I continued to be held abroad and of the great interest in me that Emperor William continued to have, these gentlemen thought of denigrating me in the eyes of the German Emperor.

That was the ugly mission that Baron Aerenthal accepted. After being installed as foreign minister in Vienna he went to Berlin to present himself to Emperor William and used the occasion to turn over the memorandum to him. About a year later it was published in the French periodical *La Revue*, whose editor is a certain Finot.

Essentially the memorandum repeated the views that Aerenthal had so energetically propagated while ambassador, that the granting of a constitution had been a mistake. Of course, such a view could not be presented in such naked form, and therefore it was put this way: the constitution was a great blessing but the manner and means by which it was granted were unfortunate, and for this I was responsible because I am like Herostratus of ancient times, who put an entire city to flame for the sake of his glory; that I gave a constitution and started a conflagration in all of Russia for the sake of my own glory.[17]

Later, while in Paris, I asked Finot how he had obtained this memorandum. He told me that it had been given him by Schelking, with the request that it be published. Schelking is an able man who was dismissed from our diplomatic service for some reason or other. Then, to make a living he had turned to journalism, first in Paris, then in Petersburg. His sister, a great beauty, was married to Sementovskii-Kurilo, an official in our foreign office. Schelking is well acquainted with Goremykin, or, to put it more correctly, he performs all kinds of services for Goremykin.

I have reason to believe that this memorandum made no impression on Emperor William other than to reinforce in him the impression that Emperor Nicholas would rather that he paid no attention to me. He already had this impression as a result of hints from highly placed sources and from a document, signed by Iuzefovich, that he had received from the Kievan branch of the Union of the Russian People.[18] Because of this impression he has not received me since then, but I know that when he refers to me he calls me the wisest man in Russia. For my part I have made no efforts to see him.

Finally, I should repeat that Baron Aerenthal acted as he had in the Bosnian crisis, as if Russia did not exist, because he had been able to see all our cards, which had been shown to him in Petersburg by Schwanebach and some of his colleagues.

X

Court Calendar, 1907–1911

1907

In July the Emperor sailed to Swinemünde to meet the German Emperor.[1] I am told that His Majesty was advised by Emperor William not to permit the October 17 Manifesto to keep him from acting decisively against all liberal and, especially, revolutionary manifestations.[2]

On August 19, the Emperor attended the consecration of the Church of the Resurrection, which had been erected on the spot where the Great Tsar Liberator Alexander II was assassinated on March 1 [1881].

Later that month, while the Emperor was aboard his yacht *Shtandart*, en route to the Finnish skerries, the ship struck an underwater rock. The first thought was that the accident was the result of some terrorist plot, but it was soon decided that it was the consequence of lack of experience of our sailors, particularly Admiral Nilov, Flag Captain of His Majesty.[3]

This Nilov is a handsome fellow, a heavy drinker, always under the influence of Bacchus, is very loyal to the Emperor, who likes him. As a youth he was very well liked by the "famous" Prince Meshcherskii. The prince still has a variety of pictures of Nilov as a very handsome young midshipman on his table. Nilov is married to Princess Kochubei, a former lady-in-waiting to Grand Duchess Marie Pavlovna.

Thanks to Nilov, Meshcherskii, who had been ignored by the Emperor since the war with Japan, managed to worm his way once more into His Majesty's good graces, is able to see him, give him advice on many subjects, and write to him. I don't think that Prince Meshcherskii has much influence on the Emperor, but what he writes in his newspaper, *Grazhdanin*, is pleasing to His Majesty.

As in the past, Prince Meshcherskii's chief aim in his relations with the throne and with others who have power is to get subsidies for his newspaper, subsidies which he uses for his own needs and those of his young men. Also, he continues to use his influence to enable his favorite young men, chief among them Burdukov, to enrich themselves at the expense of the government.[4]

1908

With the return of the appearance of domestic calm to our country (in reality the spirit of rebellion had been driven underground), it was once more possible for the Emperor to receive members of foreign ruling houses and other foreign dignitaries.

Late in March Prince Nicholas of Montenegro arrived in Petersburg, apparently to ask for a large sum of money, as usual. On April 13, the heir to the throne of Rumania arrived here. At the same time Gustav Adolph, the new king of Sweden, came to Tsarskoe Selo.

Among the festivities arranged for King Gustav Adolph was a state dinner, to which I was invited because of my seniority in government service. I had the pleasure of sitting at the head table with the Emperor, the Empress, other members of the Imperial family, the king of Sweden, the Rumanian heir, and the highest officials of our government.

As was customary, a *cercle* was organized after dinner in the neighboring hall, in the course of which the Emperor invited various people to be presented to the king. Although I had attracted the attention of the king's suite, all of whom wanted to meet me, quite understandably so, given Portsmouth and October 17, I was not among those invited to be presented. This was done in such a form that it could not fail to attract the attention of those present.

On May 27, Their Majesties met with the king and queen of England at Reval. This was the first visit of an English monarch. It seemed to be a natural consequence of the Anglo-Russian convention of the preceding year, a sign of Anglo-Russian rapprochement. In that sense the meeting had historical significance.

On October 1, Grand Duke Alexis Aleksandrovich died in Paris. He was a good-looking, nice person who never did anyone any harm. He was very gracious to all, a quality that the well-born, and especially grand dukes, should have. His appearance befitted his status. But in essence, particularly in political matters, he was very, very weak.[5]

In any event, his death grieved not only his friends but all who had been close to him. In his relations with me and, especially, my wife, he was extremely attentive and kind, even after I had left the post of premier, when it became fashionable to attack me from all sides.

1909: The Alexander III Monument,
the Anniversary of Poltava

In 1909, after many frustrating years of preparation, the equestrian statute of Emperor Alexander III was unveiled. At this point I would like to tell the history of the construction of this monument.

Immediately after the death of the Emperor it occurred to me that a monument in his honor should be constructed and the sooner the better, for delays can sometimes be very long indeed. I need only say that to this day there is no monument to Emperor Alexander II in Petersburg. In the case of Emperor Alexander III it was especially necessary to act quickly given the spell of extreme liberalism in the country, which would make for hostility to the idea of a monument to so absolute a ruler. And future generations would probably be even less inclined to support the idea of a monument to him. It stood to reason that once his contemporaries were gone, no one would even think of such a project. So I assumed the initiative and talked to the new Emperor, who responded very favorably because of the respect and love he had for his father.

At my suggestion a competition was held in which sculptors anonymously submitted designs, which were exhibited at the Winter Palace and inspected by the Emperor, his mother, and other members of his family. A group of specialists selected the winner, Prince Paul P. Trubetskoi, the illegitimate son of an Italian mother and an impoverished member of the Trubetskoi family, who was living in Italy.

The winning sculptor was an instructor in a Moscow art school at this time. Although he bore a Russian surname he was in essence Italian, born in Italy, raised there by his mother, and did not come to Russia until he was twenty-four. He had come to live in Moscow because one of the Trubetskois there, Prince Peter Nikolaevich Trubetskoi (who died recently at the hands of his nephew Kristi under tragic circumstances), was related to him and took him under his wing. After talking to Paul P. Trubetskoi I saw that he had little breeding or education, but he had great talent and was already well known in Italy and France.

He was presented to the Emperor and his mother and impressed them favorably. That he had been received by them was enough to enable him to get anything he needed. It was natural that they should feel kindly toward him because they still felt the death of Emperor Alexander III keenly.

An artistic commission was formed to supervise the work. It consisted of Prince B. B. Golitsyn, then in charge of the Government Printing Office, which has an excellent art section, Count Ivan Ivanovich Tolstoi, the vice-president of the Academy of Arts and later my minister of education, and A. N. Benois, the well-known artist. But the ultimate responsibility for supervision was mine, and I felt so committed to it that after I left the post of minister of finance I asked Emperor Nicholas to permit me to carry on with this obligation although I asked to be relieved of my *ex officio* obligations, such as my chairmanship of a home for poor children.

A large studio on Nevskii Prospekt was provided for the sculptor and he went to work. He quickly showed himself to be quarrelsome and undisciplined. He would not accept decisions by the commission, circumvented Prince Golitsyn's instructions and mine, wasted money on fantastic schemes, and was constantly redoing his work. I did not attempt to express any artistic judgment, lacking the competence to do so, but Benois and Tolstoi were qualified. However, Trubetskoi would not recognize their authority.

He did, however, listen to the Emperor and the Dowager Empress, who, with me present, sometimes inspected the work. Both approved of what they saw, and the Dowager Empress made some suggestions for change, to which Trubetskoi acquiesced. When the model was completed the Emperor and his mother gave their approval. Grand Duke Vladimir Aleksandrovich, the president of the Academy of Arts, felt differently at first when he saw what Trubetskoi was doing, declaring that it was a caricature of his brother. Although he never became completely satisfied, he gradually became reconciled to what was being done.

As for me I saw my role as peacemaker between Trubetskoi and the commission. I felt that I should support him. After all, he had a considerable reputation abroad, particularly in Paris. I succeeded in keeping relations between him and the commission in hand, an effort that often led me to see how the work was going. Every time I looked at the likeness I could not help thinking what a remarkable man Emperor Alexander III had been.

About a year before the casting of the statue was begun I decided to view the model on the spot where it would be, in Znamenskaia Square, opposite the Nikolaevskii station. A temporary enclosure was erected, and one night the model was placed on a temporary, wooden pedestal. One morning, at four, just as the sun was rising and there were no passersby, the enclosure was removed to permit us to form an impression of how the statue would look in its permanent site. I was upset by what I saw, feeling that the Emperor appeared deformed. I felt so strongly that I told Grand Duke Vladimir Aleksandrovich that I would never agree to acceptance of such a representation. Trubetskoi himself admitted that there were serious shortcomings to the model when he saw it on location. He thanked me for making it possible to see what was wrong and made some changes, resulting in the Grand Duke's declaring that although the altered model was not without defects it did justice to his brother.

By the time I left the post of minister of finance, Prince Trubetskoi was ready to begin casting the statue. He insisted on bringing in assistants from Italy, and this was agreed to after Prince Golitsyn had gone to Italy to make certain they were qualified. It goes without saying that there were many quarrels during the course of the casting. Then followed a quarrel about the pedestal. The sculptor objected to the proposal that it be a block of stone, arguing that the proper stone was not available. His idea, a rectangular pedestal that looked something like a tomb, was approved by the Emperor.

Thereafter, my responsibility was limited to the supervising of the financing of the work. My successor as minister of finance raised questions about the cost, and he was right. A million rules or so had already been spent, and it was understandable that authorization of additional money to satisfy Trubetskoi's fantasies would be resisted. After leaving the post of premier, it seemed to me that since my only responsibility in this matter was supervision of the finances, Kokovtsev, the new minister of finance, might assume that responsibility. Accordingly, on my return to Russia in the fall of 1906 I said as much to His Majesty when he received me. He replied that he would think about it. A few days later I received a letter from Kokovtsev informing me that His Majesty wanted me to retain the responsibility. Nonetheless, I had no further opportunity to report to the Emperor about the work in progress because both the sculptor and Prince Golitsyn were able to bypass me by gaining direct access to the Emperor or by going through various ministers.

Not long before the unveiling of the monument, Prince Golitsyn gave me a list to submit to the Emperor of those who should receive remuneration for their work and the sums they should receive, the sum for him being exceptionally large. I told him I couldn't do so because I hadn't given any financial, or other, reports to the Emperor since the fall of 1906. He replied that it would be awkward for him to submit the list because he and the other members of the commission were on that list. I then offered to deal with the matter through Baron Freedericksz, the minister of the court, and I did. A few days later the baron told me that the Emperor had agreed to payment of the sums requested and then wanted to know how it was that I was still involved when I had disassociated myself from the operation in 1906. I then showed him the letter I had received from Kokovtsev and also explained why I had not been able to report to His Majesty since then. On a later occasion he informed me that he had passed on to the Emperor what I had said and had been told that the facts were as I had related them.

When the time (May 23) came for the unveiling of the monument I was of two minds about attending the ceremony. On the one hand, I would have preferred not to be there because of the Emperor's attitude toward me since 1906 in connection with the monument. On the other hand, if I did not make an appearance it would be said that I was disassociating myself from the monument because of all the difficulties encountered along the way. So I decided to attend and stood at the head of the commission that had supervised the work. The sculptor himself was not there because he had not been informed in time of the date.

The ceremony was a festive one. The Emperor commanded the troops which marched by the monument. In the course of the ceremony he addressed a few words of appreciation to me, words that I did not feel were heartfelt. I believe that he uttered these words because the Dowager Empress, who was present, insisted that he do so and also because, if he had failed to do so, the huge crowds that were there would have drawn a conclusion he did not want to have drawn.

At last the burden of this responsibility was off my shoulders, but I still had to live with the fact that there was so much criticism from society concerning the monument and the work on it, criticism on aesthetic grounds, on personal grounds because of my connection with it, and on political grounds that here a monument was being erected so quickly for the reactionary Emperor Alexander III where there was still no monument in Petersburg to Emperor Alexander II.[6]

Fortunately, with the passage of a little time people made their peace with it and some began to find artistic merit in it. Repin, the famous painter, even called it an outstanding artistic achievement.

As for the sculptor, Prince Paul P. Trubetskoi, he now lives in Paris, where he has a studio. He is an ardent vegetarian. He denies that art can be taught, arguing that art instruction only destroys inborn talent. He is given to absurd theories and fantasies, is a bit sly, and loves to squander money. But there is no question that his considerable reputation as an artist is deserved.

On May 30 the Emperor and his family sailed for the Finnish skerries, where they met Emperor William. From there they went to visit the king of Sweden and returned to Peterhof on June 22.

They soon departed for Poltava, to celebrate the two hundredth anniversary of the famous battle that occurred there.[7] It was an expensive trip. It was said that Kurlov, the one most responsible for protecting the Emperor and whose standing with His Majesty was still growing, received 250,000 rubles for security arrangements, money for which he did not have to account.

In connection with the celebration, the Emperor conferred several honors, among them the rank of general-adjutant on Prince Kochubei, the present chief of appanages, and a descendant of the famous Kochubei. The Stolypin family had hoped for an honor for one of its own and had started rumors that there would be an honor for the Neidhardt in the military. This rumor caused smiles because it was not clear which Neidhardt was being referred to: the Neidhardts after all had come from Finland and probably were of Jewish origin with no military men among their forebears.[8]

His Majesty returned to Peterhof on June 29. On July 2 King Frederick of Denmark, brother of our Dowager Empress, and his wife arrived in Peterhof. Again there was a state dinner, to which I had the good fortune of being invited. Again, as in the case of the dinner for the king of Sweden, I sat at the head table, not far from the Emperor and the guests of honor.

During the course of the dinner the king frequently looked at me and spoke about me to the Dowager Empress. After dinner there was the usual *cercle*, but because I had received an undeserved slight on an earlier occasion such as this and did not want a repetition, I chose not to go to the room where the *cercle* was being held. I was later told that several highly placed persons were astonished that I had not done so and that King Frederick had wanted to have me presented to him.

On July 11 His Majesty sailed on his yacht for Cherbourg to meet the president of the French republic. He then went on to England to visit with King Edward VII. On the way back to Russia he stopped off at Rendsburg to see the German Emperor. He returned to Peterhof on July 28.

Less than a month later the Emperor left for the Crimea. From there he left for a much delayed visit to King Victor Emmanuel of Italy at Raccognigi, the king's summer residence. Because of security considerations, the visit was arranged with little publicity or fanfare.[9] Neither in his journey to Raccognigi nor on his return trip to the Crimea did he pass through Austria-Hungary, by way of protesting the annexation of Bosnia-Herzegovina.

On October 16 the Emperor reached the Crimea. Two months later he returned to Tsarskoe Selo, for the funeral of Grand Duke Michael Nikolaevich.

1910: Persons and Politics

The arrival of a French parliamentary delegation in Petersburg in February aroused mixed emotions. Society was jubilant but our higher officials, including the State Council, did not know what foot to stand on. On the one hand, the delegation represented an allied government; on the other hand, they represented the French parliament. The result—a reception by officialdom that was no more than civil.

Also in February Tsar Ferdinand and Tsaritsa Eleanor of Bulgaria came to visit the Emperor. I was not invited to the state dinner in their honor, probably because some in high places had considered my behavior at the dinner for King Frederick inappropriate. But I did attend a ball in their honor at the home of Countess Shuvalova, née Bariatinskaia. I kept my distance from the Bulgarian Tsar, but as soon as he saw me he approached and said: "Everything that you foretold came about just as you said." What he meant by this I don't know, but I remember having two long talks with him some years earlier, one at my official summer residence on Elagin Island, when he called on me, and the other at the residence of the Bulgarian minister, to which I had been invited for an intimate dinner in his honor.[10]

I have never been to Bulgaria and do not have a close knowledge of what goes on there, but as I have said before, he is a clever and intelligent man who through his ability has transformed Bulgaria from a small principality into a fairly important kingdom. It seems to me that although he strives to preserve good relations with us he is much closer to Austria than to us.

On March 9 King Peter of Serbia, whom I had met while he was still in obscurity, came to Tsarskoe Selo on March 9. I did not see him during this visit because I was not invited to the state dinner which the Emperor gave for him.

The death of King Edward VII of England on April 23 was an event of international importance. He was, beyond question, an outstanding ruler, partly because of his innate ability, partly because he had learned life and had learned to know all sorts of people before ascending the throne, at an advanced age.[11]

Thanks to him England established what was virtually an alliance with France and thanks to him the Triple Entente was formed. He was a formidable rival to Emperor William, and although he could not do with the German Emperor what he wanted, he was able to block him on the world diplomatic scene. No question but that his death was a great political stroke of luck for William.

Some months later an English envoy extraordinary came to inform our Emperor of the accession of King George V to the throne. The two monarchs are cousins and bear an extraordinary likeness to each other, but it seems to me that Emperor Nicholas II is handsomer and, as far as is known, abler than the king.

On June 2 Their Majesties sailed for the Finnish skerries and went on from there to Riga for the unveiling of a monument to Emperor Peter I, as part of the bicentennial celebration of the annexation of the Baltic provinces.

In anticipation of this event, Stolypin and his entourage had started a rumor that he would be made a count at the festivities. This was simply a maneuver to turn a hope into a reality, but it was off the mark.

From Riga Their Majesties sailed for the Finnish skerries, then returned to Peterhof, to prepare for their voyage to Friedberg, to stay at the castle of the Empress's brother, the Grand Duke of Hesse-Darmstadt. One purpose of the trip was to permit the Empress to take the waters at nearby Bad Nauheim, this for a heart ailment, of psychosomatic origin, from which she had suffered for many years.

My wife and I had been staying in Frankfurt, an hour's journey from Bad Nauheim, since July, well before Their Majesties were to arrive in Friedberg. Even if it had not been announced that they were coming, it would have been guessed from various preliminary signs. First was the influx of highly placed Russians who had suddenly discovered the need to take the waters at Bad Nauheim or Bad Homburg, which were fairly close. These were the types who lick the boots of those above them. Then there appeared in Frankfurt and Bad Nauheim hundreds of Russians who were unmistakably agents of the Russian secret police.[12] Some of them noted me with astonishment and practically wanted to say hello to me. Also there was an influx of German policemen sent from Berlin. We left Frankfurt for Vichy before the arrival of Their Majesties at Friedberg, partly to avoid meeting members of the Emperor's suite.

Not long before the arrival of Their Majesties a political incident occurred. This concerned the inclusion in an exhibition at Frankfurt of a fairly able painting by a Polish artist depicting the pogrom against Jews in Kiev following October 17, 1905, a painting in which the Emperor was clearly evident. The painting dealt with real events, but with some exaggeration. It must be admitted that it was provocative.

The Frankfurt police tried, unsuccessfully, to convince the organizer of the exhibition to close it. Then the municipal authorities took a decisive hand in the incident. They argued that whatever one thought of the government of Russia and of its ruler, simple courtesy required a polite attitude toward him and that, moreover, it was not in the city's interests to forget that the visit of the

Russian Emperor to Friedberg meant a good deal of money for nearby cities.

The stay at Friedberg did not bring the Empress the wished-for medical results. That was because, as I was told by some in Frankfurt in a position to know, her treatment did not follow wholly rational lines. This seemed to be the result of poor choice of doctors. The best medical men in Frankfurt were of Jewish origin, and the Empress's brother recommended one of them, but given the atmosphere of kike-eating (*zhidoedstvo*) in which we find ourselves, it was naturally found inappropriate to be treated by a doctor who, however well known, was a Jew. The consequence—the Empress was treated by a local gentile doctor and Dr. Botkin, her personal physician, neither of them men of any standing. Moreover, Dr. Botkin did not have any experience with the Nauheim waters. By the way, the Empress did not go to Bad Nauheim to bathe there in the mineral springs; instead, mineral water was brought from there to Friedberg for her use.

While Their Majesties were still at Friedberg several diplomatic matters were being dealt with. One, as I have noted earlier, was the replacement of Izvolskii by Sazonov, who was made acting minister of foreign affairs. Second was the protocol of a meeting with Emperor William. Our emperor and his suite wanted a meeting near Bad Nauheim. The German Emperor felt, and not without reason, that since our Emperor was on German soil he should call on Emperor William at the latter's residence in Potsdam. Our Emperor agreed.

As will be recalled, it was at Potsdam that Emperor Nicholas II agreed to German wishes regarding northern Persia and to the linking of the proposed Berlin-to-Baghdad railroad with northern Persia. If there were any other agreements concluded at Potsdam I am not aware of them. I think there were none. All in all, the talks there between the two Emperors and between Sazonov and the German foreign minister and chancellor were friendly ones. To keep the diplomatic consequences of the meeting at Potsdam secret it was decided that there would be no speeches of any kind at the state dinner held in honor of our Emperor. Had there been any speeches it would have been necessary to say something that concealed the truth, that this had been no more than a family meeting between the two monarchs. No one would have believed this. After the completion of this visit, Sazonov was promoted from acting minister to minister, evidently a sign that Emperor William was pleased with him. To what extent Sazonov will justify the hopes and confidence of Emperor William remains to be seen.

All in all the visit to Potsdam marked a shift of the pointer on our compass from England toward Germany. At present [February 1912] the pointer has moved back toward England, as was demonstrated a few weeks ago by the enthusiastic welcome given visiting English dignitaries by both society and government, as if the English had been our friends from time immemorial. Forgotten was the fact that during the last century the English were hostile to us everywhere and did us a great deal of harm.

I think that the German Emperor will pay us back for this shift. He has not yet done so because he faces a recently elected Reichstag which is quite leftist and therefore out of sympathy with his views and with the traditions of his government.

From Potsdam Emperor Nicholas II returned to Darmstadt, where he was visited by Emperor William. This meeting was of a purely family nature. On November 3 Their Majesties returned to Tsarskoe Selo.

At the end of December the Emir of Bukhara, whom I had met some twenty years earlier, died. His successor had served in the Russian army for a time and had also studied in this country.

1911

February 15 marked the fiftieth anniversary of the emancipation of the serfs. The government would have preferred to make nothing of this event, but fearing that opposition groups would use this occasion, the government decided to control what was done by taking matters into its own hands. So the government did whatever it considered had to be done to mark the event.

On March 2, the two hundredth anniversary of the Senate was celebrated. His Majesty was good enough to take note of the excellent behavior of the Senate in recent years (excellent in the sense of paying more attention to the wishes of those in high places than to the law) by attending the official celebration in the Senate itself and then giving the senators a state dinner at the Winter Palace.

It is remarkable that the venerable Count Pahlen, who had served as minister of justice under Emperor Alexander, was a high chamberlain at court, was a member of the State Council, and still continued to receive visits from the Dowager Empress, was not invited to these festivities. True, he was not a senator, but that was an oversight, particularly when one recalls that Shcheglovitov, the present minister of justice, had been appointed to the Senate and that many others with less claim to the honor that Count Pahlen had been appointed to that body.

Early in May Crown Prince Frederick of Germany and his wife came to Tsarskoe Selo. They were followed by the new Emir of Bukhara, who, in turn, was followed by Prince Chakrabon of Siam.

I had met the prince in Petersburg on an earlier occasion and had become personally acquainted with him. So I was puzzled when he ignored my presence at a reception in his honor, at the residence of the German ambassador, that I attended. Whether this was accidental or deliberate I do not know.

On June 23 Grand Duchess Alexandra Iosifovna, the widow of Grand Duke Constantine Nikolaevich, died at an advanced age.

On July 2 Their Majesties sailed for the Finnish skerries, returning on the twenty-seventh, when the Emperor reviewed the so-called boy soldiers (*poteshnye*).

Boy soldiers are much in fashion because it is believed that boys who play at being soldiers will develop a patriotic spirit. How seriously all this is taken is shown by the fact that the review was quite elaborate and that the Emperor himself reviewed these boys on parade. But this whole business of boy soldiers is comical (*poteshnyi*), at least as far as adults are concerned.[13]

On August 19 King Peter of Serbia and his son arrived in Petersburg. On August 27 His Majesty left for Kiev for the unveiling of a monument to Emperor Alexander II. As will be seen, it was during this visit that Stolypin was to be assassinated.

XI

Politics and the Armed Forces, 1907–1911

Ministry of the Navy

As I have recounted, Admiral Birilev, the minister of the navy, was one of the few cabinet members who remained in office after my departure. Also, as will be recalled, he had tried to persuade me to stay on, saying that one should stay on as long as the Emperor did not say directly that he had lost confidence in that person. Before a year had passed following my departure his turn would come.[1]

Admiral Birilev is an honorable, knowledgeable naval man. He is not stupid, has a sharp tongue, a sharp pen, and can be amusing. For the most part the Emperor likes amusing people. The admiral amused both the Emperor and the Empress and enjoyed their favor.

After my return to Russia in the fall of 1906 we continued to see each other. On one occasion I asked if he still believed that I had acted improperly in leaving my post because of the behind-the-scenes influence of Trepov, Grand Duke Nicholas Nikolaevich, and the rest. He replied emphatically, ''As long as the Emperor has not told you that he has no confidence in you, you should believe him, and continue to carry out your policies.'' (I should note that he was quite critical of the Grand Duke, who as chairman of the Council of State Defense had some influence on the operations of the Ministry of the Navy, and referred to him as an obstinate fool.)

On January 10, 1907, I heard a rumor that the admiral was going to be replaced by Admiral Dikov and quickly called on him to ask if the rumor were true. He said it was not as far as he knew. Then he told me the following.

On the preceding day he had received a draft of a proposal to remove the navy from the direction of the Ministry of the Navy, which would henceforth have responsibility solely for administrative matters. The navy would henceforth be directly subordinate to the Emperor, who would have under him a chief of the naval general staff and a naval chancellery. Moreover, the commanders of the three fleets—Far Eastern, Baltic, and Black Sea—would each report to the Emperor, i.e., to the head of the Emperor's Military Chancellery, General à la Suite: Count Heyden, a decent man but not exactly a ball of fire. The result would be that instead of one head of the navy there would be five men of roughly equal authority—the minister, the chief of the naval general staff, and the three fleet commanders, all subordinate to the Emperor.

Admiral Birilev said that the proposal was absurd and expressed surprise that this was the first he had heard of such an idea, which was to be discussed the following day at Tsarskoe Selo, at a conference to which he had been invited. (As I learned later the proposal had been prepared by Count Heyden, who had served in the navy.) I saw the admiral the following day after his return from Tsarskoe Selo, and he told me what had happened.

He told me that when he arrived at the station to take the train to Tsarskoe Selo he was surprised to find that he would be accompanied to the conference by the notorious Admiral Alekseev, Admiral Dikov, Admiral Dubasov, and, as I recall, some others whose names escape me.

At Tsarskoe Selo they were taken to the Emperor's reception room, where a large table had been brought in for the meeting. The Emperor then entered the room. Count Heyden opened the proceedings by reading the text of a statute based on the draft that Birilev had received and the text of a decree concerning the statute, both to be published at once. The count then added that what was proposed was similar to the division of functions between the war ministry and the general staff in Germany.

His Majesty then said he had worked hard on this proposal and was completely committed to it.[2] Nonetheless, he wanted to hear the reactions of those present.

Birilev spoke critically of the proposal, saying that the Emperor could not coordinate so many disparate parts as the proposal would have him do. His Majesty replied that Emperor William had been able to do so, to which Birilev replied that it seemed to be the case that the existence of a parliamentary regime in Germany relieved its ruler of many responsibilities that the Emperor of Russia still had to fulfill and that, moreover, Emperor William had had the opportunity while young to acquire a sound knowledge of naval science, as attested by a plan for a battleship which the German Emperor had drawn up, a plan which Birilev had in his possession. (The Emperor tolerated such language but would not forgive it, whereas his father would not tolerate such language, but if it had been uttered would forgive it.)

Admiral Dubasov, as usual direct and precise, said that having been a naval attaché in Berlin, he knew that the proposed reorganization had nothing in common with the kind of naval organization found in Germany. Only Count Heyden supported the proposal. The others, among them Alekseev the courtier, who was acting in character, were evasive.

The result of the meeting was that the Emperor did not sign the statute and the decree as he had intended. He thanked those present for attending, saying that he would think things over and make up his mind. Then in his customary well-bred, kindly manner he took leave of each one separately.

As the Emperor was saying goodbye to Birilev, the admiral asked permission to speak privately to him. The Emperor clearly was not pleased by the request, but acceded to it. When they were alone, Birilev said: "Your Majesty, when you made me minister of the navy, I set only one condition: that when I lost your confidence you would let me know. Therefore, I cannot stay on as minister of the navy."

The Emperor declared that he had not lost confidence in him. Birilev replied that when a proposal such as the one they had been discussing could be prepared without his knowledge and shown to him only when it was ready for publication, he knew that His Majesty had lost confidence and therefore wished to be relieved of his post, and the Emperor agreed.

As I learned from Admiral Dubasov, the Emperor quickly summoned him and offered him the post vacated by Birilev. He declined, citing poor health among other reasons. But, as the admiral told me, the real reason for his refusal was because he considered it impossible to put the naval ministry in order, because of the poor state of the ministry resulting from our defeats in the war with Japan, the lack of confidence in the ministry of the State Duma and the State Council, and the malign influence exerted by Grand Duke Nicholas Nikolaevich.

Admiral Dubasov may be no eagle and is slow in mastering ideas and information, but he is a strong and decisive character, as he showed in Moscow. Once he has assimilated what is before him, he deals with whatever the problem is and he does what has to be done. He is a decent and independent man. No wonder that he believed he could not get along with the Grand Duke, of whom it would be said, if he were not of such exalted status, that he is hare-brained.

On hearing Dubasov's refusal, the Emperor said that in that case he wanted to offer the post to Admiral Alekseev. Dubasov told me that he could not keep from expressing dismay at the idea, saying that after what Admiral Alekseev had done in the Far East his appointment as minister would be considered a slap in the face of society. To this the Emperor replied that many of the accusations directed against Alekseev were made in ignorance of the kind of instructions Alekseev had received from him, the Emperor. Admiral Dubasov replied that even if one ignored Alekseev's record in the Far East, one could not conceivably think of him as the man to revitalize the navy.

In the end the Emperor settled on the aged Admiral Dikov, a very decent man, with a spotless reputation, the holder of the St. George. The Emperor chose Dikov not for his abilities but for lack of a suitable and willing candidate. Given Dikov's age, it was not expected that he would remain long in office. At the same time the Emperor appointed Admiral Boström as assistant minister of the navy. He had served as naval attaché in England during the construction there of our warships. He was said to have some ability. I heard him speak in the State Council on several occasions: what he said was to the point but was delivered in an ill-bred tone. Subsequently, after he had left the post and had been appointed commander of the Black Sea Fleet, he was removed from his command because he was responsible for one of his ships going aground and, I believe, going under.

In letting Admiral Birilev go, the Emperor ignored precedent by not conferring the rank of general-adjutant on him, as had been the case with preceding naval ministers who left office. Of course, the Emperor has the right to ignore precedent, but he should not have done so and was acting like Emperor Paul, who conferred the rank of general-adjutant on his barber.

As for the proposal to reorganize the navy, that was tabled. And the man who prepared it, Count Heyden, lost his position and was virtually cut off from access to the court not because of having prepared the proposal but because of his indiscretion in forming an attachment with a lady-in-waiting, whom he married after divorcing his wife. As I have said, he is a decent but limited man: his missteps in his official capacity and in his private life were the result of not recognizing them for what they were.

Two years after his appointment, in January 1909, Admiral Dikov was replaced as minister of the navy by rear admiral of His Majesty's suite Voevodskii.

Their Majesties had become acquainted with Voevodskii during a voyage to the Finnish skerries and had been pleased by him. He looks more like a guards officer than a sailor. His manners are excellent and he is very proper. All very good, but not enough to make for a good minister of the navy. It was evident to all who met him, even if only for a half an hour's conversation, that he was not to be taken seriously. He just was not the man to deal with a navy that was in shambles.

Admiral Voevodskii remained in office for two years. Then he was relieved of his post and given an appointment to the State Council.

His successor, Admiral Grigorovich, who had been assistant minister, enjoys great favor with the Emperor. To what degree he justifies such favor remains to be seen. It is said that the new minister is a sensible person who knows his business. One needs but a few words with Admiral Grigorovich to recognize that he is a more serious person than his predecessor. But it is said that he takes risks, that he makes promises and proposes projects that will never be carried out, that there is more graft in the ministry than ever before. But all this, so far, is talk.

The State Duma and the Armed Forces

As will be recalled, when the Fundamental Laws were being prepared, I insisted that with respect to the armed forces the legislature be given jurisdiction only over the appropriations, but that all other matters relating to the armed forces be reserved to the Emperor, the Supreme Commander.[3] I did so not because I doubted that the deputies elected to the State Duma would be lacking in patriotism, but because, given the fact that the State Duma would be something new under the Russian sun, I doubted that the deputies would have the political maturity and exercise the necessary discretion to deal wisely with such matters as the administration and operation of the armed forces.

With the *coup d'état* of June 3, 1907, and the election of the Third State Duma, dominated by the Octobrist Party, came a perversion of the October Manifesto and the Fundamental Laws. Russia would no longer continue on the path marked out by the October Manifesto. Legislative power would in fact be transferred to a largely servile clique, the self-styled Party of October 17, which in return for ignoring Stolypin's white terror, his abuse of power, and his disregard of civil rights would be permitted to concern itself with military and naval matters beyond its proper jurisdiction. It was as if Stolypin had reached an agreement with Guchkov, saying: "You Duma leaders can play at soldiers and I will not bother you, particularly since I know nothing about such matters, providing you, in turn, will not interfere with me in my bloody game of executing people, with no regard for the most elementary principles of justice, using the field courts-martial as my instrument."

The role of the Party of October 17 would be to divert attention from the way the October Manifesto was being subverted by pretending to restore national pride, which had been so severely wounded by the disgraceful war with Japan. In this spirit the Octobrists could deliver speeches in the State Duma concerning the defense of the realm and could, with some justice, criticize the role of the grand dukes in the armed forces.** Such speeches were unprecedented in Russian life and were well received in society, where it was said: "Although the Party of October 17 has done nothing so far in the State Duma, we still place our hopes in its leaders: see what bold and decisive speeches the leaders of the party make with respect to military and naval affairs, what a bold fellow Guchkov is, how adroitly Zvengintsev takes care of the naval minister, with what authority and knowledge Savich speaks."

But those who knew something about these men and the subjects under discussion expected nothing from their chattering. What kind of experts are they? What were the sources upon which they relied in speaking with a ridiculous air of authority? These men have no competence in military or naval matters, yet when the Third State Duma, shortly after its opening, created the Committee of State Defense, the three were elected to that committee and Guchkov was chosen chairman. Members of the opposition were excluded from this body out of fear that the so-called left wing might jeopardize defense, when the record shows that, except for the extreme left, all men are true sons of the fatherland. The Octobrist leaders did not consider that the time might come when the opposition might

*Although it is true that some fine and enlightened grand dukes have been of service in both civilian and military matters, everyone knows that grand dukes have occupied high military and naval positions for which they are not qualified and that such men have done more harm than good, if they did anything at all. This has been particularly true in the reign of Emperor Nicholas II.

again be in the majority, as it had been in the First and Second Duma, and might exclude the right wing from the committee and then perhaps endanger the fatherland.

What did people like Guchkov know about military and naval affairs?

Guchkov, the chief orator in the Third State Duma, has only peripheral knowledge of the military and this the result of love of thrills. A fairly well-educated man, he, like others of the Moscow merchant class, is a thrill-seeker. There was, for example, Khludov, who hunted tigers in Central Asia, where he served under Cherniaev, and then brought back several live tigers which slept with him, until one night he had to shoot a tiger that attacked him.

As I recall, Guchkov first saw service as a volunteer[4] in the military with the Trans-Caspian Railroad. Since this was peacetime, the only living things he fired at were tigers. It was there that he became acquainted with Colonel Gerngross, who went on to become, on my selection, the commander on the security guard of the Chinese Eastern Railroad, then under construction. Because of his love of adventure Guchkov went to Manchuria to serve under Colonel Gerngross as a captain in the guard.

At that time, with construction of the railroad in its early stages, there was tension between engineers and others engaged in construction and officers of the security guard, resulting in a number of duels. When I learned of these, I ordered Iugovich, the chief engineer, and Colonel Gerngross to inform their subordinates that duels between their subordinates on Chinese soil would not be tolerated, because of the unfavorable impression of us that they made on the Chinese, that if they must duel, they should settle their scores on Russian soil and accept the [legal] consequences of dueling there.

Not long after I issued this order, I received a telegram saying that Guchkov (this was the first time I had heard of him) had, in an argument over quarters, challenged an engineer, but that the latter, in accordance with my orders, had not accepted the challenge, whereupon Guchkov saw fit to slap him. I reacted to this information by ordering Gerngross to dismiss Guchkov from the service, but my telegram criss-crossed a telegram saying that Guchkov had already asked to be released from the service and his request had been granted. Subsequently, he fought on the Boer side in the Anglo-Boer War. During the war with Japan he was in the theater of operations as representative of the Red Cross and behaved gallantly.

This is the sum total of Guchkov's military education and experience, yet he deludes himself into believing that he is an expert on military matters. If he has any serious interests, it is with commerce, as befits a member of the merchant class.

It is said that he wanted to play a major role in the State Duma in everything that concerns the armed forces because he believed that the War and Navy ministries had shown themselves completely inadequate in the war with Japan. Therefore, it is said, he considered it his duty to act as the savior of our army and thus of the realm.* As for Zvengintsev, he had served briefly in the navy and briefly in the Chevalier Garde. The offspring of an estimable noble family, he was Guchkov's superior both by education and upbringing. These are his credentials. While I was minister of finance I knew his father, a fine man, then the governor of Voronezh. I first heard of the son during the Bezobrazov period, when a commission was organized ostensibly to go to Korea for economic investigation, but with the covert purpose of extending our power there. Because of its nature it had to recruit outsiders. One of these was the son.

Savich knew even less of military matters than Guchkov or Zvengintsev. His specialty was natural science, anatomy, I believe. When I asked how he came to be one of the State Duma experts on military and naval affairs, I was told that he was an avid reader of military pamphlets.

Guchkov was the only one who had ever heard gunfire, but he was ignorant of the subject on which he professed to be an expert, as were the other members of the committee, thus producing a comic spectacle. Nonetheless, because this committee together with the Budget Committee reviewed all military and naval appropriations, it became necessary for the War and Navy ministries to stay on the good side of Guchkov and the State Defense Committee.

It took just one instance to reveal what kind of danger the State Defense Committee represented. This occurred in March 1909, when a bill concerning personnel of the Naval General Staff, which had been approved by the State Duma, was sent on to the State Council. The bill itself was of secondary importance, but the question it raised—that of the prerogatives of the Emperor in his role as Supreme Commander—was of extraordinary importance.[6] As I have said, the Fundamental Laws are clear on this point, that the Emperor has exclusive authority over everything affecting the armed forces except appropriations, which he shares with the two legislative chambers. But this bill violated the clear meaning of the Fundamental Laws because it dealt not only with the appropriation for the Naval General Staff, but also with its organization, table of organization, and the rank and salary for each position on it. Had the bill become law it would have set a precedent whereby not only the appropriations for but the organization of the armed forces would have come under the purview of the two chambers and the Supreme Commander would have become but the executor of their will.

When the bill reached the State Council and was considered in the Finance Committee, before going to a general session, several committee members asked

---

*It is worth noting that when he returned from a visit to Turkey, following the Young Turk Revolution of 1908, he spoke with great admiration of the Turkish constitution and compared the Young Turks with the Octobrists. I think that such a comparison is not flattering to the Young Turks.

Also the comparison between the two is not quite apt for another reason: in essence the Young Turks betrayed their ruler, Sultan Abdul Hamid. As far as I know Guchkov does not have treasonable thoughts, but last summer [1911] while I was in France a Russian told me that Guchkov had said to him that the revolution of 1905 did not succeed because the army had remained loyal to the Emperor and that if there were another revolution the army would have to be won over to the side of the revolution. According to my informant Guchkov then went on to say that it was for this reason he was concentrating exclusively on military questions, against the time when it might be necessary to win over the army. I report this without vouching for the reliability of the information.[5]

me for my opinion concerning the moot question of whether or not the bill violated the Fundamental Laws, doing so in view of the fact that I had played a major role in preparing these laws. In presenting my view, I pointed out that in countries with parliamentary systems, the legislative bodies, like ours, were limited to dealing only with the appropriations for the armed forces. And I pointed out, too, that the Japanese constitution gave the Mikado even greater authority over the armed forces than did our Fundamental Laws.

V. A. Maklakov (Kadet, member of the State Duma) and M. M. Kovalevskii (in the extreme left of the State Council) both told me that my interpretation of the Fundamental Laws was correct. When P. M. Romanov, my former assistant minister, at this time chairman of the Finance Committee, came to see me about this matter, I told him where I stood and that I felt obliged to explain my position at the State Council session.

When I asked him where Stolypin stood with respect to the bill, he told me that because there were differences about it in his committee, he had gone to ask the premier for his opinion. He said that Stolypin told him he was aware of the arguments pro and con but had not yet made up his mind. To this I replied that the Octobrists would not have acted as they had in the State Duma if they had not sensed that Stolypin supported them. Then I went to Akimov, the Chairman of the State Council, to find out what he knew of Stolypin's position. He told me that he had been to see the premier, who told him that he had not made up his mind about the merits of the arguments, but, nonetheless, urged that the State Council pass the bill as it had come from the State Duma.[7]

When the bill was considered on the floor of the State Council, two sessions were required. The minister of the navy delivered a speech, prepared, as I later learned, in the cabinet's chancellery; speaking for the government, he urged passage. At the first session I explained in detail the intent of the relevant article in the Fundamental Laws, making it clear that the State Duma leaders were either playing games or engaging in a diversionary tactic. In so doing I unmasked Stolypin, demonstrating that he was willing to limit the supreme power of the Emperor if it were necessary for his ties with the State Duma majority. At the second session, following much debate, Kokovtsev (acting for Stolypin, who was ill) spoke in his stead, urging passage.

Before my speech at the first session it had been expected that the bill would pass by a large majority, but as a result of my arguments, as well as of others who opposed the measure, it passed by only a slim majority and even then only because the ministers, *ex officio* members of the State Council, voted for it.[8]

I assumed that the Emperor would then sign the bill into law for surely his government would not have argued for its passage if he had not approved of it in advance. (This view was later reinforced when I learned that the Emperor had read the speech that the minister of the navy was to give and that as a result of his reaction to it some changes had been made in the draft.) Also, those newspapers which were subsidized in part or whole by the government indicated that they expected the bill to pass easily when they said that Stolypin felt that my speech had played into the government's hands because the Emperor would surely take a position contrary to mine and would therefore sign the bill. (Stolypin was confident of such an outcome because of his insinuations against me, which he undoubtedly made in the course of reporting on police matters.) However, because my speech created such a strong impression and so clearly elucidated the issue, the Emperor refused to sign the bill. I am certain that it was no pleasure for him to be agreeing with me.

As soon as he learned of the Emperor's refusal, Stolypin asked to be relieved of his post, the only course for him: this was a defeat for him, his first, with respect to both the Emperor and the public. But his request was only a maneuver to get the Emperor to say some kind words to him and ask that he withdraw his request.

Stolypin tried to win public support for his retention by having the newspapers he controlled create the fear that if he left he would be succeeded by someone far to his right, perhaps P. N. Durnovo, the leader of the right wing in the State Council. In light of his attempts to represent himself as a defender of the October Manifesto, the opposition, including the more or less liberal wing of the press, was frightened into believing that his departure would be a loss. But by this time I had come to see through him. Therefore when liberals, for whom I had not lost respect, came to see me out of anxiety about what might happen, I explained the facts. I told them what the debate over the bill signified with respect to the Fundamental Laws, also that the debates revealed the tacit agreement between Stolypin and the Octobrist leaders, whereby they could play soldier and he made free use of the gallows. Moreover, I told them, Stolypin was bluffing. In the end he would not only swallow the Emperor's refusal to sign the bill, but would also go on to gain support from the extreme right as a means of guaranteeing his position. In short, this meant, I said, that what we would witness was the unmasking of Stolypin and the self-styled Party of October 17, thus revealing that both represented an unpleasant type of Russian constitutional opportunist that had sprung up after October 17. This type, I said, did not have the experience or knowledge possessed by bureaucrats, had the convictions neither of genuine liberals and extreme leftists, who are willing to suffer for their convictions, nor of those members of the right who genuinely hold to their beliefs, however primitive they might be, and are not afraid to speak out for what they believe.

As I predicted, the Emperor had only to say a few kind words to Stolypin and the premier immediately withdrew his request to be relieved. To make sure that the kind of incident represented by that of the Naval General Staff bill did not occur again, the Emperor, on April 27, ordered his premier to prepare rules governing legislative consideration of naval and military matters, about which of these should be considered by the legislature and which not. On the insistence of the war minister, the new rules actually gave the Emperor broader powers with respect to matters affecting the armed forces than had been intended in the Fundamental Laws. Thus, Stolypin found himself having to move from a position in which he was undermining the Imperial prerogative in violation of the Fundamental Laws to one in which he was broadening that prerogative beyond what the law had intended.

These new rules were then published in the *Collection of Regulations* and would find their way later into the new edition of the *Collections of Laws*, without having been approved by the legislative bodies. This was in violation of the constitution.[9] When questioned about his action, Stolypin said that the new rules did not change existing law, this in contradiction to the position he had taken with respect to the Naval General Staff bill.

The party upon which he had relied, the so-called Party of October 17, would not accept his explanation. Thereafter he could no longer maintain the pretense of being a liberal, a defender of the constitution, and pursuing the path of personal advantage he began to follow a course that such predecessors of his as Count Dmitrii Tolstoi, I. N. Durnovo, and Plehve would have been too ashamed to take. Although such men had turned to extreme conservatism and were often not squeamish about the means they used, they did not pose as politically chaste Benjamins.

The State Duma, the Military, and Grand Duke Nicholas Nikolaevich

As will be recalled,[10] Grand Duke Nicholas Nikolaevich, that somewhat unbalanced man, had gained a dominant influence in the military in early 1905, as a result of the favor his sister-in-law Grand Duchess Militsa Nikolaevna and her sister, Princess Anastasia Nikolaevna (his wife-to-be), enjoyed with the Empress.[11] He was able to bring about the creation of the Council of State Defense, with himself as chairman. He was able to bring about the removal of the office of chief of the General Staff from the authority of the war minister and to install General Palitsyn, his tool, as chief of the General Staff, and was able to replace War Minister General Sakharov, who opposed his plans, with General Rödiger, whom he mistakenly expected to be amenable to his direction. As noted, the Grand Duke's position was further strengthened when he was appointed commander of the Petersburg Military District in October 1905.

Two factors were to contribute to the undoing of much of the Grand Duke's work and the departure of General Rödiger. The first was the establishment of the State Duma, which was certain to challenge the lack of accountability of the Grand Duke's Council of State Defense and of the Ministry of War to the State Duma and was likely to raise questions about the independence of the chief of the General Staff from the war minister. The second was the gradual loss of influence that Grand Duke Nicholas Nikolaevich had with the Emperor and Empress. This decline began after Princess Anastasia Nikolaevna divorced her husband, Prince George Leuchtenberg, and married the Grand Duke [in 1907], after which the Empress's passion for her died down and was transferred to Mme. Vyrubova.[12] But this loss of influence was not immediate.

It was not long after the opening of the Third State Duma that Guchkov and

Savich delivered speeches sharply critical of the Council of State Defense and the General Staff on the ground that they were not accountable [to the legislative bodies]. As a result, efforts were made to subordinate the chief of the General Staff to the war minister. Palitsyn balked at this and was relieved of his post in 1908 and appointed to the State Council. To sweeten the pill he was sent to represent Russia at the accession of the infant emperor in China. He was replaced by General Sukhomlinov, the chief of the Kiev Military District and the governor-general of Kiev.

When Palitsyn was relieved I predicted that Grand Duke Nicholas Nikola-evich would blame General Rödiger, the war minister, for this defeat, and would pay him off at the first convenient moment. That moment arose early in 1909.[13]

In the course of the State Duma's review of the military budget, Guchkov declared the commanders of the military districts were not equal to their tasks. General Rödiger admitted that this was true of some of the commanders, but added that the government was aware of this and that in his good time His Majesty would take steps necessary to correct the situation. The war minister was criticized for daring to say what he did, was called before the Emperor, who was quite severe with him and who told him that it would be difficult under such circumstances to retain him as war minister. For that reason Rödiger left his post and was replaced by Sukhomlinov.

Rödiger, as I have said, is an intelligent, sensible, and energetic general, a man of strong character, but more of a desk than a field general. He is still [1912] robust and still has a great capacity for work.

I know comparatively little about his successor. While I was premier, I found General Sukhomlinov to be dealing with his duties as governor-general of Kiev in a calm and balanced way. He seems like an able man, but a superficial and frivolous person. He likes the ladies. He was divorced from his first two wives. His present wife is ill, perhaps fatally ill. I do not think that Sukhomlinov is capable of bringing our army up to the status required by a power such as Russia.

Sukhomlinov, like many a new minister, was apparently able to acquire consid-erable influence over the Emperor, probably because in the early stage he and the Emperor enjoyed a "honeymoon" period, such being the Emperor's nature, and partly because he likes to joke and is found amusing. Sukhomlinov set about truly subordinating the General Staff to the War Ministry and undermining Grand Duke Nicholas Nikolaevich's influence on military affairs. In the course of the year following Sukhomlinov's appointment as war minister, the Grand Duke lost all his influence with the Emperor. One sign of the war minister's victory was the abolition of the Grand Duke's Council of State Defense in August 1909. It seems, however, that in recent times [1912] the Grand Duke has begun to regain his influence.[14]

Although Guchkov and his men had some hand in bringing about the subordi-nation of the chief of the General Staff to the war minister, I have no doubt that this absurd division of power would still be in effect if Grand Duke Nicholas

Nikolaevich had not fallen from grace. Such a division is not absurd in Germany, where it is organic, goes from top to bottom, with the combatant parts of the military separated from the administrative components at all levels. In contrast, the system established under the Grand Duke's influence was a hybrid, combining parts of the French system of military organization upon which our army had been based from the 1860s to 1905 with parts of the German system. Neither system is perfect, but at least they have an internal consistency. But what we had from 1905 to 1909 was something like one trunk with two heads, the war minister and the chief of the General Staff. Naturally, nothing could come from such an experiment.[15]

XII

The End of the Stolypin Era

The Western Provinces Crisis

[The first serious blow, as I have shown, to Stolypin's position resulted from the conflict over the Naval General Staff bill. The second, and final, blow came from the turmoil arising from the issue of how the southwestern and northwestern provinces should be represented.[1] The turmoil began when] in May 1909, my old acquaintance Pikhno,[2] about whom I have spoken earlier, was able to collect enough signatures to permit him to introduce a bill in the State Council to change the system of electing members to that body from these western provinces. The background of Pikhno's effort is as follows.

According to the electoral law, provincial zemstvos are each permitted to elect some members of the State Council. In provinces with no zemstvos, as was the case with the southwestern and northwestern ones, a temporary law gave the right to elect to landowners of the respective provinces. Since most landowners in these provinces are Poles, it follows that almost all the deputies they chose were Poles (an exception was Count Bobrinskii, elected from the province of Kiev).

It should be noted that the Polish landowners in these provinces tend to remain on their estates and look after them because it is difficult for them to enter government service. The few landowners who are Russian in this area have, for the most part, bought their estates for speculative purposes, do not live on them, and are in government service. Consequently, the Polish landowners exercise considerable influence in their localities.

Pikhno's bill called for a permanent law to replace the temporary one, a law that would guarantee that most landowners from the region elected to the State Council would be Russians. I opposed the bill, as did many other members of the State Council.

In the course of our debates over the Pikhno bill, Stolypin appeared and tried to prevent passage of the bill. Speaking in a rather restrained manner, he expressed agreement with the intent of the bill, to reduce the number of Poles elected from the area and to increase the number of Russians, but, he assured us, the Pikhno bill was unnecessary because he was planning to introduce a bill to establish zemstvos in the provinces in question. As a result, the Pikhno bill was defeated, but I am certain that it would not have passed even if Stolypin had not intervened.

While the Ministry of Interior was preparing the bill about which Stolypin had spoken, it came under pressure from Nationalists[3] and Black Hundreds members in the affected areas, whose constituency was small but whose influence was considerable, to frame a bill that would give Russian landowners a preponderance of power in the local affairs of the regions. After considerable hemming and hawing, Stolypin yielded to these influences because he realized that they were regarded sympathetically in higher circles.

Therefore the bill sent to the State Council by the government virtually excluded not only Polish landowners but also peasants—the great majority of them Russian and Orthodox—from representation in the proposed zemstvos.[4] This was in keeping with the principle earlier proclaimed by the premier that the state exists for the benefit of the strong (i.e., the noble landowners) and not for the weak (i.e., the peasantry). A law giving the peasantry just representation in the zemstvos would have meant zemstvos with a great majority of peasant deputies and a sprinkling of Polish landowners.

Various groups in the State Council voiced vigorous opposition to the bill. The extreme right felt that zemstvos should not be established in the region because of its strategic importance and because of the ethnic heterogeneity of its population. Moderate nobles opposed the bill because of its divisive character, which would pit Russian nobles against Polish nobles, when in fact the two groups shared common interests.

In the course of the heated debate, I said many things to Stolypin that he found most unpleasant. As a result the bill was defeated, in March 1911, despite the fact that Stolypin and his ministers took part in the vote. He was shocked by this defeat and believed, justifiably, that I was the one most responsible for his setback. I was effective because of what I said and proved, not because I spoke for any faction in the State Council. I have never belonged to any faction and have always spoken only for myself.[5]

Stolypin was put out not only by what I said during the debate on the floor of the State Council but also by what I said and proved at the preceding committee hearings on the bill. At these I proved that the figures presented by the Ministry of Interior in support of its arguments were false. At first Gerbel, speaking for the ministry, vigorously disputed what I had to say, but subsequently admitted by his silence that what I had asserted was true.

Gerbel's performance only added to Stolypin's anger against me. From that time I haunted his thoughts. Thereafter, when anyone spoke to him of his enemies, he said that the only enemy to whom he paid attention was me, Count Witte, whom he feared.

When I heard this I asked friends of mine to inform the premier that I was not his enemy but simply a person who was able to distinguish between his high-blown, quasi-liberal speeches and his actions as premier and minister of interior, actions characterized by a degree of indifference to the law and by such a lack of conscience that not even a Viacheslav Konstantinovich Plehve had attained, a phenomenon explained by the fact that earlier reactionary ministers were intelligent men, something that could not be said of him.

The Threat of Resignation

Stolypin reacted to his defeat in the State Council by immediately submitting a petition to the Emperor to be permitted to leave unless His Imperial Majesty gave him his support, backed him up. The Emperor listened coolly, showed no interest in the conditions set by Stolypin for staying on, and told him he would think his request over.

Those who knew of Stolypin's petition assumed that it would be accepted. It would have been if not for the unfortunate intervention of Grand Dukes Alexander Mikhailovich and Nicholas Mikhailovich, both well known as intriguers. They worked on Stolypin to withdraw his request and tried to frighten those close to the court that if Stolypin left chaos would follow. It was doubly unfortunate that that most worthy woman the Dowager Empress supported the two Grand Dukes. It is said that she was able to influence the outcome because the Emperor visited her at the Anichkov Palace at a crucial time in the consideration of Stolypin's request. And it should be recalled that because he was the Emperor's brother-in-law Grand Duke Alexander Mikhailovich had some influence with him.[6]

Sensing this support, Stolypin dug in his heels and demanded the following of the Emperor if he were to stay on. First, that the State Duma and the State Council be prorogued for a few days, during which period the rejected bill would be enacted by power of Article 87 of the Fundamental Laws. (This condition was conscienceless because it violated the constitution. Moreover, it placed His Majesty in a most unpleasant situation with respect to the legislative bodies and his loyal ultra-rightist subjects.) Second, that Durnovo and Trepov—extreme rightist members of the State Council who, in the premier's opinion, had intrigued against the bill—take leave for the remainder of the year.

Stolypin wanted to have Durnovo and Trepov removed from active membership in the State Council, but loosely as the law was interpreted an active member could not lose his status during the year following his inclusion in the list of such members. By forcing them to go on leave he could ensure that they would not attend sessions of the State Council for the rest of the year, and he clearly intended that they be excluded from the list of active members for the coming year.

Obviously forcing the two to take leave was not only inconsistent with the

Fundamental Laws but also an insult to the two men. Of course, I do not agree with their ultra-rightist views, but I believe that they had acted within their rights as members of the State Council.

The suspense over whether or not the Emperor would agree to Stolypin's conditions continued for about a week, during which time the two Grand Dukes and other members of society carried on a desperate propaganda campaign to convince people that it was only thanks to Stolypin that revolutionary-anarchist activity, i.e., assassinations, had stopped and that if he were let go the assassinations would resume. Naturally, such a prospect could not fail to influence the higher circles. The Emperor gave in.

I have it on good authority that the Emperor could not forgive Stolypin for demeaning him by putting him in a position where he felt forced to keep the premier on and accept his conditions[7] and that he said to Stolypin: "I have another appointment in mind for you." According to my source, Stolypin was taken aback by this statement. What appointment the Emperor had in mind I do not know: some say an ambassadorship, others the viceroyalty of the Caucasus. But the fact remains that the Emperor yielded.

The State Duma and the State Council were prorogued for three days, during which interval the disputed bill was enacted by virtue of Article 87. Durnovo and Trepov were invited to apply for leave. Stolypin and his Myrmidons had triumphed, but anyone capable of looking ahead could realize that his triumph was but the prelude to his political downfall.

Everyone, especially the members of the legislative bodies, was indignant at Stolypin's actions. He tried to mollify the State Council by speaking in a deferential tone to it while making unflattering remarks about the State Duma, and in the State Duma he repeated this performance but said unflattering things about the State Council. Neither chamber was taken in. The State Council held his actions to have been irregular. The State Duma, showing greater independence than it had previously, held his actions to have been both irregular and illegal.

Guchkov, head of the so-called Party of October 17, and hitherto Stolypin's tool, criticized the premier's action, resigned his chairmanship of the State Duma,* and wisely left Petersburg, for a trip to the Far East, until the storm blew over. If Stolypin fell he would not be involved, but if the premier rode out the storm, he, Guchkov, would not have compromised himself in Stolypin's eyes and, by his complacence, could enjoy the premier's support and good will.

Durnovo took leave from the State Council without demur. Trepov, however, showed more spirit. Being in the good graces of the Emperor, he had been given the privilege of asking for audiences with the Emperor and used such audiences to share his impressions of what was going on with His Majesty. He availed himself of this privilege at this time.[8] Goncharov, also a member of the State Council, a

---

*Rodzianko, his successor as chairman, is not stupid, is, in fact, quite sensible, but he is more distinguished for the quality of his voice than of his mind.

very honorable man, who had preceded Durnovo as leader of the right-wing group in the Council, was so upset that he asked to be relieved of membership in the State Council.

At the time there were rumors that I, like Durnovo and Trepov, would be ordered to ask for leave, and one newspaper called me to ask if there was any foundation to the rumors: nothing happened to justify the reports.

Because Grand Dukes Alexander Mikhailovich and Nicholas Mikhailovich were so instrumental in having Stolypin kept, it was said after Stolypin's assassination, and for good reason, that they rather than Bogrov, the one who pulled the trigger, were the ones who killed the premier. If they had not intervened in something that was not their business, Stolypin would have been permitted to leave office. And had he done so, he would almost certainly still be alive, happy, and at peace with himself, respected as the kind of statesman who when his honor was at stake would have chosen to leave his position rather than compromise it. Something of the role of these Grand Dukes in the episode can be seen from the following.

Not long after the events I have described Grand Duke Nicholas Mikhailovich was a guest at a soirée given by Prince Platon Obolenskii. My wife was there, but I was not. Stakhovich—a member of the State Council and one of my close friends—was among those present. Naturally, there was much talk about recent events. The Grand Duke, who spoke strongly in support of Stolypin, told Stakhovich that if he had been in Stolypin's place he would not have contented himself with asking that Durnovo and Trepov be ordered to take leave; he would have asked that the State Council be dissolved.

Some time after this soirée Stakhovich, who was on good terms with Guchkov, talked with him about all that had taken place. In the course of the conversation Guchkov told Stakhovich that Stolypin had told him that he had asked that Durnovo and Trepov be excluded from the list of active members of the State Council to be published on January 1, but that the Emperor had not agreed. Stolypin also told Guchkov that if he, however, asked that I be excluded, the Emperor would have agreed, but that he had not been asked in view of my reputation abroad and the consequent stir that my exclusion would have created.

The Death of Stolypin

Knowing that I knew about Stolypin's record, I was certain that anyone who had done what he had done and who still clung tenaciously to his post would perish at his post. I was so certain of what was to come that when the well-known English journalist Dillon[9] visited me in Biarritz and asked for my opinion about the current state of affairs, I told him that I was certain that there would soon be a catastrophe that would result in changes.

I was certain Stolypin had aroused millions of people against him by his cruel and deceitful actions. Among them were millions of non-Russian subjects. He had lost the respect of all who had any spark of decency in them. He had even roused his former allies, the Black Hundreds, against him by his cynical dissociation from them once he no longer found any use for them. Never had a government official made as many enemies for himself as he had.

As I have said earlier, the Emperor left for Kiev on August 27, 1911, to attend the unveiling of a monument to Emperor Alexander II. In his entourage was Stolypin. The premier tried to use the occasion to his advantage. Before the unveiling ceremonies and the accompanying festivities, stories appeared in the newspapers hinting that Stolypin would be given the title of count while in Kiev. Also, the recently established zemstvos were to thank His Majesty for the boon conferred on them, with the implication of thanks to Stolypin, even though he had made a mockery of the constitution in arranging for this "boon."

Such things were in keeping with Stolypin's love of theatrical gestures and resounding phrases. He was to die under theatrical circumstances, on September 1, in the Kiev Opera House, during the intermission in a festive spectacle at which he, the Emperor and his daughters, as well as many bigwigs were present. Bogrov (whom newspapers refer to nowadays as a revolutionary-anarchist) shot Stolypin with a Browning pistol, in the presence of the Emperor.

On learning that her husband was wounded, Mrs. Stolypin hurried to Kiev, where, as Kokovtsev told me, she put on a theatrical scene. As the Emperor entered the room where her husband lay dying, she walked stiffly, like a soldier, up to him and said: "Your Majesty, the Susanins have not yet disappeared from Russia,"[10] and returned to her place. Stolypin died a few days later.

I am quite certain that had the Emperor's life been at risk, Stolypin would have acted like Susanin, ready to lay down his life for that of his Sovereign. But so would hundreds of thousands of the Emperor's other loyal subjects, seeing in him not Nicholas Aleksandrovich, an individual, but the embodiment of the spirit of Russian tsardom, under the inspiration of which Great Russia had been created.

As I have said, Stolypin was a man of courage, a strong character, and had been an honorable man until he was corrupted by power. But he did not die like a Susanin, for his Tsar, but died like hundreds of officials who had used the power bestowed on them for their own gain rather than for the benefit of the state and the people. In the case of Stolypin it should be added, as I have said, that he used his position not so much for himself as for his numerous relatives, many of them not of the first quality. Stolypin's widow, I was told, also behaved tactlessly during the funeral services.

Under the influence of the furor raised by Nationalists and other followers of

Stolypin, the newspapers were filled with articles declaring that Stolypin's departure was a great tragedy.* Then there followed a campaign to raise money for monuments to honor Stolypin. Naturally, this artificially created mood could not endure. Before six months had passed the attitude toward the late premier had changed completely, and Russia could judge the man for what he was.

Stolypin had the courage and temperament to do some good for the country, but the good he did was minuscule compared to the bad he wrought. He completed the debauching of the administration. He debased the State Duma, reducing it to no more than an administrative agency. He corrupted the press. He debauched many strata of society. And by having as his minister of justice so unprincipled and hypocritical a man as Shcheglovitov, he completely destroyed the independence of the judiciary. I am certain that when the country is once more ruled according to legal norms, when Russians no longer have to live in fear, that what I have said will be thoroughly proven.

It came as no surprise that Stolypin's supporters blamed Kurlov, the director of the Department of Police and commander of the Corps of Gendarmes, for the late premier's death; they charged the secret police, under Kurlov, with having committed unforgivable blunders.[12] Be that as it may, those who make such charges forget that Stolypin was the minister of interior, to whom the secret police was subordinate, and that he was therefore responsible for its actions.

I agree that our police, particularly the secret police, had become completely disorganized and demoralized under Stolypin, but who was responsible for this condition? Stolypin. As I said, he had no preparation for the position of minister of interior, but unlike me, when I was premier, he accepted the responsibility. This means that if the police bore sole responsibility for allowing the assassination, it was Stolypin who was responsible for his own death by assuming a responsibility which he did not understand, one which he administered with

---

*About the time of Stolypin's death, Guchkov, one of his satellites, returned from the Far East. Although he had dissociated himself from Stolypin's policies before his departure, he now found it expedient to pay tribute to the late premier, in order to help his party in the coming State Duma elections. At an assembly of party supporters he delivered a speech extolling Stolypin. In doing so he made some offensive and untruthful remarks about me.

The speech was reported by *Novoe vremia* on September 15. Because there were several inaccuracies in the report, a brief notice appeared in the paper the following day that Guchkov wished it to be known that the report was not wholly accurate. But the publication of the report had served the purpose for which it had been intended, and the subsequent statement amounted to no more than a clever ruse.

Therefore I replied to Guchkov's speech in a letter to *Novoe vremia* on September 25. My letter provoked a reply from Guchkov, which was published two days later. I then sent a reply, which *Novoe vremia* promised to print on the day [after its receipt]. However, my letter did not appear in the next day's edition. Instead my secretary was asked to remove some passages from it, but acting on instructions which I sent him from Biarritz where I was staying, would not agree. However, my letter was subsequently published simultaneously in several other newspapers, among them *Rech* and *Russkoe slovo*.[11]

the kind of audacity possessed by men not conscious of danger and by grown men whom God begrudges the wisdom to comprehend what it is they are doing.

It goes without saying that Stolypin's slaying was abhorrent. But, although one can't approve it, one can understand why it happened. No assassination can be justified on moral grounds. But it should be remembered that many such killings are carried out by persons who have power. Among the thousands executed during Stolypin's tenure, there were dozens, possibly hundreds, who were guilty of nothing, yet they were killed by Stolypin's government. The great Napoleon said: "A statesman's heart should be in his head." Stolypin never had a heart, either in his chest or in his head.[13]

A New Premier, Kokovtsev

During the last days of Stolypin's life, as he lay wounded, Kokovtsev acted in his place as premier, and Kryzhanovskii, assistant minister of interior, acted as minister of interior. Meanwhile the Emperor had gone to Chernigov to worship at a shrine there. By the time he returned, Stolypin was dead. On the following day, after appointing Kokovtsev premier, he left for the Crimea, where he would remain for several months. What took place during these days may be judged from the following.

About the end of July 1911, while Stolypin was still alive and well, a letter was delivered to me, not through ordinary channels, in Biarritz, from a certain George Petrovich Sazonov in which he asked for my assistance to get financial help for a newspaper, but his chief aim in writing was to ask if I would accept the post of premier. He said that the Emperor had decided to replace Stolypin, no later than the end of the festivities in Kiev, and that the Emperor had decided to appoint Khvostov, the Nizhegorodskii governor, to assume Stolypin's portfolio of minister of interior. After praising Khvostov and his family, Sazonov went on to say he and Rasputin had been to Nizhnii Novogorod to discuss the matter with the governor. They felt, he said, that Khvostov would make an excellent minister of interior but that he was too young also to serve as premier. If I accepted the post of premier I would provide the new government with the necessary authority. I had no idea whether Sazonov was serious.[14]

I first became acquainted with Sazonov while I was traveling with Vyshnegradskii in Central Asia.[15] At the time he spoke like a leftist yet tried to curry favor with Vyshnegradskii and me, as well as with Grand Duke Nicholas Konstantinovich, who was living there, in disfavor with the court.

Sazonov is somewhat abnormal, as well as being dishonest. I have tried to keep my distance from him.

He is a writer and a journalist, the author of several books, in some of which he fervently supported the village commune. With the help of M. O. Albert of the

Nevskii Shipbuilding Yard, he was able to get funds from several Muscovite industrialists to establish *Rossiia*, a leftist newspaper, which attracted several well-known contributors, among them Doroshevich and Amfitreatov. It was the latter's feuilleton "*Semeistvo obmanovykh,*"[16] that resulted in the newspaper's closing and Amfitreatov's flight to foreign soil, where he still lives and writes for several Russian newspapers. As for Sazonov, he was exiled to Pskov, but soon was able to return home and for a while he was close to Plehve.

In the period from 1903 to 1905, Sazonov participated in several leftist newspapers, but after October 17 found it to his advantage to become close to the Union of the Russian People and its leaders. It is said that while he was young he was friendly with Zheliabov, who took part in the assassination of Emperor Alexander II.[17]

Toward the end of 1906 he asked me to intercede with Metropolitan Antonii to get help in overcoming obstacles to his marrying the lady of his choice. This I did. It was at this time that he told me how he had once doubted my loyalty to the Emperor and had been among those who wanted to kill me, but that he had since become convinced of my loyalty.

By associating himself with the Union of the Russian People he was able to advance himself, but did not accumulate any money. So, to make more money, he established ties with Migulin and Alekseenko, about whom I have written elsewhere. And as the fortunes of the Union of the Russian People declined he sought to improve his position by associating himself with several religious figures, among them Archbishop Hermogen, the monk Iliodor, and Rasputin, particularly Rasputin.

He became so friendly with Rasputin that he was Sazonov's house guest when he stayed in Petersburg. And high society ladies would come there to see this so-called holy man. Gradually Sazonov came to act toward Rasputin like the curator of a museum with an outlandish creature on exhibit.

Sazonov made much of his connections with these religious types, particularly Rasputin, who had a great deal of influence. All this enabled him to publish a weekly called the *Ekonomist*, a strikingly mediocre publication, in which Migulin and Alekseenko participated. At first it attacked Kokovtsev. Being sensitive to such attacks the minister of finance bought the publishers of the weekly off both by direct subsidies and by indirect ones, in the form of using the publication for official announcements. These subsidies enabled the feeble publication to survive. In return it shifted from criticizing the minister of finance to praising him for "financial acumen."

But these subsidies were not enough to buy the influence of Sazonov and, consequently, of Rasputin. So Sazonov and Migulin presented a proposal to the Ministry of Finance for something to be called the Grain Bank, the business of which would be to remove rotten grain that had piled up on the railroads after the harvest. Of course, the ministry would not have given anyone else a charter for such a bank, but it did so in the case of these two. But their scheme died because the bankers and speculators to whom they turned said that they would be pleased to invest in a regular bank but not one of this kind, which could not possibly survive. The ministry then obliged by changing the charter to make it for one called the English Bank. They turned around and sold the charter for, I believe, 250,000 rubles. Perhaps they shared some of it with Alekseenko.

Sazonov decided to use part of the money to create a newspaper that would support Kokovtsev, but needing more financing, he turned to the Ministry of Finance for a grant of some kind. The director of the ministry's Credit Chancellery summoned the directors of the English Bank and told them that the ministry was very anxious to help Sazonov establish his newspaper. They agreed to underwrite it and, in addition, provided a sum of 100,000 rubles.

Thus, Sazonov established his newspaper, *Golos zemli*. He was able to do so because Kokovtsev wanted his support rather than opposition, and Sazonov made it appear that through Rasputin he had considerable influence at Tsarskoe Selo. The newspaper follows a progressive line. It has many contributors, of the type of Professor Khodskii, who feel at home in it, men who are baked from the same moral dough as Sazonov, i.e., when all is said and done, men who will use the printed word to deceive.

Difficult as it may be to believe, it is, nonetheless, a fact that someone like Sazonov can exercise great influence, through the instrumentality of Rasputin, and that Rasputin should have had considerable influence at Tsarskoe Selo. (Whether or not Rasputin still has influence I do not know.)[18]

This then is the Sazonov who wrote to ask if I were willing to become premier.

As I have said, I had no idea whether Sazonov was serious or not. In my reply, sent through the same channels he had used in writing to me, I said that his letter left me in a quandary: Were the ones who made such a proposal mad, or did it seem that I was such a madman that they could make such a proposal to me?

Before leaving this subject I should note among the many rascals who served as governors under Stolypin, Khvostov took the prize for rascality, being a man for whom law does not exist. I happen to know that he sent a memorandum to the Emperor, via Sazonov and Rasputin, asserting that Stolypin had not succeeded in extinguishing revolution, but had only driven it underground, that revolution would flare up again unless decisive steps were taken. One of the steps he proposed was to destroy all those suspected of being revolutionaries.

Now, to return to the appointment of Kokovtsev, which took place on September 9, the day of the Emperor's departure for the Crimea. What I have to relate I learned from Kokovtsev himself.[19]

The ministers and the local officials were at the railroad station, waiting to see Their Majesties off. The Emperor had not, as far as they knew, made a final decision about Stolypin's successor. Suddenly a courier arrived, walked toward the ministers, and seemed to hesitate in front of Shcheglovitov, but did not stop and went up to Kokovtsev to inform him that His Majesty wished to see him at the palace. Kokovtsev was then rushed there by automobile.

When he arrived at the palace, the Emperor and Empress were ready to leave for the station. The Emperor led Kokovtsev into the study and told him that after thinking matters over he had decided to appoint him as premier and Khvostov as minister of interior.

Kokovtsev told me that he pleaded with the Emperor not to appoint Khvostov, saying: "Your Majesty, you are standing at the edge of a precipice. The appointment of Khvostov would signify that you had decided to jump off the precipice." The Emperor, seeing that the Empress was already wearing her hat and was waiting for him, said: "In that case I ask you to take the post of premier and as for the post of minister of interior, I will think about it." At this Kokovtsev suggested Makarov.

No question that the new premier made the suggestion because Makarov belongs to the extreme right, and, although a person with limitations, was evidently a sincere man, with no stain on his record. But Makarov was not of the stuff required in a minister of interior at the time, chiefly because he was not and never could be a commanding personality.

Kokovtsev supplemented his oral recommendation of Makarov with a written one. When the Emperor arrived in Yalta, he appointed Makarov. Kryzhanovskii was offended by the choice and refused to stay on as assistant minister. He is morally inferior to Makarov, but stands head and shoulders above him in knowledge, ability, and intelligence. A clever man, Kryzhanovskii had done the thinking for Stolypin. He inspired the late premier to do things that he himself would not have done had he been minister. It was he who inspired the course of action that Stolypin followed after the State Council rejected the bill to establish zemstvos in the western provinces. Since he had been assistant minister throughout Stolypin's tenure as minister of interior, he knew all the secrets of this corrupt police period. Therefore, he had to be given a satisfactory appointment: he replaced Makarov as Imperial secretary.

I was told that during the five days that Stolypin lay wounded, Shcheglovitov, Krivoshein, and Kokovtsev all intrigued for the post of premier. If anything, Kokovtsev is more adept at intrigue than even the other two, but he is a more serious worker than they.

The Investigation of Stolypin's Death

Following the appointment of Makarov, it was announced, on September 17, that Senator Trusewicz, who had been head of the secret police until Kurlov had come along, would conduct an investigation into the death of Stolypin.

As I have related, I became acquainted with Trusewicz the day the explosive device was found in my house and had quickly realized that he was untrustworthy, that he was a typical police detective provocateur.

Kurlov was forced into retirement and replaced as head of the police of the Russian Empire by Zologarev, procurator of the Novocherkassk Court of Appeals.

A New Broom?

When the State Duma opened its sessions [in the fall of 1911], there was great curiosity in society about what direction the new premier would follow because it was known that he had not agreed with Stolypin, especially in recent years. Among other things he had not agreed with him concerning the policy followed toward Finland, the introduction of zemstvos in the western provinces, and the policy of pseudo-nationalism. It was generally expected that Kokovtsev would not be as zealous as Stolypin had been in urging the passage of some bills that the government had sent on to the State Duma, that he might even recall them.

But knowing Kokovtsev as I did, I knew that he did not give his support or offer opposition on the basis of conviction but on the basis of convenience, of what was to his advantage. Once he had achieved his goal, of replacing Stolypin—under circumstances that he could not have foreseen—he would pursue the policies favored by those above for the same reason that Stolypin had done, to keep his position. But there is a difference between the two: In pursuing a nationalist policy on orders from above, Stolypin became caught up in it emotionally and carried this policy out with ardor. Kokovtsev, on the other hand, did not become emotionally involved because he has better judgment, is more intelligent and knowledgeable than Stolypin. He has tried to soften the nationalist policy but not enough to be suspected of liberalism by those above and thereby forfeit the smallest fraction of Imperial good will.

Therefore, when the new session of the State Duma turned to the bill on Finland that Stolypin had introduced earlier on, Kokovtsev, who, when a mere minister of finance, had opposed it, now sang a different tune. Speaking at length (he loves to speak, at length, and can speak well and is therefore called "the gramophone" by Moscow merchants), he said in effect that policies are determined from above, not by the ministers, and that while as minister of finance he could disagree with the premier, once he became premier he had to follow the same policies as his predecessor and was amazed that he should be expected to follow a different course.

Thus I have reached 1912 in my stenographic memoirs. For the time being I am discontinuing this work. . . .[20]

March 2, 1912

VOLUMES I-III

Editor's Notes

Sources

Bibliography

Indexes

Editor's Notes

Introduction

1. *The Secret Letters of the Tsar* (New York, 1938), p. 221.

2. One copy is in the Bakhmeteff Archive, Columbia University; another in the Soviet archives. The opening and the conclusion of the work are excerpted here in Appendix D. *See below* pp. 348–49.

3. Witte faltered somewhat in his resolve that these works not be published during his lifetime by permitting B. B. Glinskii to publish his work on the origins of the Russo-Japanese War, in bowdlerized form, in *Istoricheskii vestnik* in 1914, but without any attribution. After Witte's death Glinskii published this material in book form, citing Witte as the source of the material but not as the author. Glinskii, a friend of Witte's, failed in his efforts to persuade him to permit publication of parts of the memoirs during his lifetime. B. B. Glinskii, "Graf Sergei Iulevich Vitte," *Istoricheskii vestnik* 140 (1915): 233.

4. "Two Russian Statesmen," *Quarterly Review* 236 (1921): 408. On the title page of his *Leaves from Life* (London, 1923), Dillon describes himself as Witte's "private adviser" from 1903 to 1914. This well-known journalist was close to Witte, knew a great deal about Witte's work on the memoirs, and, in fact, was able to use material from them in his *Eclipse of Russia* (New York, 1918).

5. I. V. Hessen writes that when Countess Witte retrieved the texts of the memoirs, she told him she was going to New York to remind Jacob Schiff of a million-dollar offer he had once made for publishing rights. He goes on to say that with the fall of the old regime the memoirs could no longer fetch such a sum, but that Schiff helped her sell the publishing rights. *Gody izgnaniia* (Paris, 1979), pp. 18–19. The papers of Jacob Schiff in the American Jewish Archive do not corroborate this account. Fanny Zelcher (American Jewish Archive), Cincinnati, letter, December 1, 1977, to the editor. In any case, this is what Hessen recalls.

6. Pyke Johnson, Jr. (Doubleday), New York, letter, September 22, 1976, to the editor; Avrahm Yarmolinsky, New York, letter, September 24, 1966, to the editor.

7. *Publishers Weekly*, March 19, 1921, p. 894. Doubleday, Page and Co. sold the French rights to Plon-Nourrit, the Spanish rights to Editorial Saturnino Calleja, and the German and Russian rights to Ullstein. Evidently they were supplied with Yarmolinsky's translation and were to use it for their translations.

8. The Slovo files were not preserved. Abram Kagan (International Universities Press), New York, letter, November 14, 1979, to the editor. The Ullstein files do not have the information required for explaining the decision not to use the Yarmolinsky text. Gabriele Rosche (Verlag Ullstein), Berlin, letter, December 8, 1977, to the editor. A clue may be found in Otto Hoetzsch's introduction to the German translation of the memoirs.

Hoetzsch, who was selected by Ullstein to supervise the translation and who worked closely with Hessen, writes critically of the Yarmolinsky translation, saying that it was difficult to determine what in it belonged to Witte and what to Yarmolinsky. Witte, *Errinerungen* (Berlin, 1923), p. 7.

9. Hessen is usually treated as if he were the editor of this redaction and that is because his is the only name identified with it, as author of the introduction. A very busy man, engaged in several types of publishing, he probably did not have much time for the minutiae of editing. In his recollections he states that the text used for this edition was prepared by a stepson, a "young historian," whom he does not name. *Gody izgnaniia*, p. 19. Apparently the stepson he refers to was named Semen. I. V. Hessen, *V borbe za zhizn* (New York, 1974), pp. 4–5.

10. There are several bits of evidence that the third volume was an afterthought, chief among them the fact that logically it should have appeared first, not last.

11. Countess Witte was evidently unhappy over the Yarmolinsky redaction. According to I. V. Hessen, Countess Witte found his redaction acceptable, but was very angry over his introduction to the memoirs, in which he raises questions about Witte's character. *Gody izgnaniia*, pp. 19–20. One gets the impression that Countess Witte's venture into the world of publishing left her with a sour feeling, which may be why she placed her late husband's papers under lock and key after her dealings with Hessen.

Countess Witte's Foreword

1. While it is true that Witte was quite limited in what he could publish under his own name, it is not true that he stood above the battle. A man of fierce passions, he was assiduous in having his views presented in print, sometimes under his own name, sometimes under the name of "a hired pen" to whom he supplied the necessary documentation. *See* B. V. Ananich and R. Sh. Ganelin, "Opyt kritiki memuarov S. Iu. Vitte," in *Voprosy istoriografii i istochnikovedeniia istorii SSSR: Sbornik statei* (Moscow: 1963), pp. 298–374. *See also* A. A. Spasskii-Odynets, "Vospominaniia," Bakhmeteff Archive of Russian and East European History and Culture, Columbia University, pp. 27–28. A list of books inspired by Witte will be found in the Bibliography.

2. Countess Witte is obviously referring to the table of contents of Witte's dictated memoirs. One copy of that document is in the Columbia Archive. Another is in the Soviet archives and was published in S. Iu. Witte, *Vospominaniia* (Moscow, 1960), I, 464–510. In his memoirs Witte is constantly referring to documents in the archive that he maintained in his home in St. Petersburg. In addition, he kept various documents—some originals, some duplicates—in various places abroad, obviously for safekeeping. As Countess Witte indicates, his precaution was justified.

It is probably the case that most, if not all, of the documents that Witte kept abroad are in the Bakhmeteff Archive. As for the documents he kept in his home in St. Petersburg, it seems that all of these that were not destroyed are in the Soviet archives. M. A. Tkachenko, "Fond S. Iu. Vitte v TsGIA i zadacha kritiki vospominanii S. Iu. Vitte," in *Nekotorye voprosy istoriografii i istochnikovedeniia SSSR: Sbornik statei* (Moscow, 1977), pp. 186–97; B. M. Vitenberg, "K istorii lichnogo arkhiva S. Iu. Vitte," *Vspomogatelnye istoricheskie distsipliny* 17 (1986): 248–60.

Editor's Notes to Volume I

Chapter I

1. Witte was born on June 17, 1849. If he began dictating his memoirs at the end of 1910, as there is good reason to believe, he was not yet sixty-two and presumably meant by "I am sixty-two" that he was in his sixty-second year.

2. Witte was not born into the hereditary nobility but was admitted to it in 1855, when his father acquired the status of hereditary noble. Theodore von Laue, *Sergei Witte and the Industrialization of Russia* (New York, 1969), p. 39, n. 9.

3. The Witte family may have been of Dutch origin, but Witte's immediate forebears were part of the Baltic German community, a fact that apparently did not suit him, for he had a marked bias against Baltic and other Germans and did not want to be identified with them.

4. P. Nikolaev, a friend of Rostislav Fadeev, describes Julius Witte "as one of the best educated men in Tiflis." "Vospominaniia o kniaze A. I. Bariatinskom," *Istoricheskii vestnik* 22 (1885): 623. E. Seraphim writes that he was unable to find Julius Witte listed among the students at the University of Dorpat. "Zar Nikolaus II und Graf Witte," *Historische Zeitschrift* 161 (1940): 279. (Student directories have been known to be in error.)

5. Viceroyalty (*namestnichesto*)—the territory administered by a viceroy (*namestnik*), an official with broad civilian and military authority. Until 1883 the Caucasus was administered by a viceroy. There were no viceroys between 1883 and 1905, a period in which civilian and military authority were separated; in 1905 the two were once more united and a viceroy appointed.

6. Andrei M. Fadeev speaks of Alexander as the second son. If he is correct, the first son must have died in infancy. *Vospominaniia* (Odessa, 1897), pt. 1, 200. Because he wrote largely from memory, Witte is often fuzzy on details. Had he consulted the above work, as well as others available to him, he could have provided more precise details about himself, his background, and his career.

7. The Order of St. George, to which Witte frequently refers, was established in 1769 for officers who had shown singular courage in combat or who had otherwise distinguished themselves.

8. Witte's description of Madame Blavatsky's wanderings between 1848 and 1858 disagrees markedly with her own, often self-contradictory, accounts of her life during that period. Because his version is unflattering, to say the least, it is an important source for writers hostile to her. *See*, for example, C. E. Bechofer-Roberts, *The Mysterious Madame* (New York, 1931). As Witte indicates, his mother shared Helen Blavatsky's belief in spiritualism. After she was widowed, Witte's mother firmly believed that her late husband's spirit was in the house. Jeremiah Curtin, *Memoirs of Jeremiah Curtin* (Madison,

Wisc., 1940), p. 250. Among the many who defended Helen Blavatsky's credibility was her sister, Vera Zhelikhovskaia, who wrote in her defense in *Rebus*, in the 1880s. Witte gives no indication of being acquainted with this work or other contemporary literature defending or attacking Helen Blavatsky.

Chapter II

1. As one would expect from an account written from memory and colored by sentiment, Witte's account of his uncle's life is in error on some details. *See* "Rostislav Fadeev," *Russkii biograficheskii slovar* (St. Petersburg, 1901), 21, 6–10.

2. Witte later refers several times to the alleged paternity of Grand Duchess Olga Fedorovna as a way of attacking her son Grand Duke Alexander Mikhailovich, whom he disliked intensely.

3. *See* Alfred J. Rieber, ed., *The Politics of Autocracy* (Paris, 1966), pp. 101–53, for the correspondence between Alexander II and Bariatinskii for the period 1857–1864.

4. Alexander II was apparently not as annoyed by the marriage as Witte suggests. *See* ibid., p. 151.

5. In presenting the conflict between Bariatinskii and Miliutin, Witte does not give enough attention to the larger questions in dispute. *See* P. A. Zaionchkovskii, *Voennye reformy* (Moscow, 1952).

6. Strictly speaking, *Svet* was not a continuation of *Russkii mir*, except in spirit. Incidentally, *Svet* was one of the few Russian newspapers that Nicholas II found endurable.

Chapter III

1. Membership in the Order of St. George was divided into four classes. Members of the second and third classes wore the order's badge around their necks.

2. *See below*, I, ch. XXVII.

3. Baron Nikolai may have been opposed to the new university rules, but he left office before their promulgation, not after, as Witte states.

Chapter IV

1. *Diadka*: diminutive for uncle. Often used, as in this case to refer to a retired soldier or sailor hired to serve as a low-grade tutor for young boys of upper-class families.

2. Parts of pages 104 and 106 of this excerpt from the dictated memoirs (pp. 102–54) are missing (cut out by Countess Witte?). It is likely that the excised parts deal with Witte's "loss of innocence."

3. Maurice Bompard, who as ambassador to Russia had come to know Witte, writes of his claim to excellence in French: "If his French was rough (*rugueux*), it was at least perfectly intelligible." "Les Mémoires du Comte Witte," *La Revue de Paris* 28 (1921): 21. Witte placed a high value on the knowledge of French. Of those who did not have it, he would say "They are not well educated in the Western sense of the word."

4. In 1837 the Lycée Richelieu began offering instruction at the university level. That part of the *lycée* which had been providing secondary instruction was thereafter called the Richelieu *Gimnaziia*.

5. Witte fails to mention that Andrei Zheliabov, one of those who plotted to assassinate Alexander II, was a fellow student. An anonymous fellow student states that Witte led a

circle to which Zheliabov belonged. *Odesskie novosti*, no. 9635, cited in Glinskii "Graf Sergei Iulevich Vitte," *Istoricheskii vestnik* 140 (1915): 235. Even if the assertion were not true, it is difficult to believe that Witte had not met him, given the fact that there were only 250 or so students at the university in those days. When he does mention Zheliabov later (dictated memoirs, p. 2420; *see below*, p. 739) he gives no indication of ever having known him. Was Witte feigning ignorance, or had he unconsciously erased any memory of the man who had aided in the assassination of Alexander II, an act that Witte calls one of the most tragic and dastardly in the history of Russia?

6. The Odessa English Club was a modest version of the English Club in St. Petersburg, whose members belonged to the Russian aristocracy. The designation "English" was used because English clubs provided the model for Russian clubs.

7. After Witte obtained high office, he helped many Odessans find fairly important government positions. Among those he helped were members of the Rafalovich family, with which he was fairly closely connected.

8. Father Petrov, who was unfrocked for his leftist political activities, was elected to the State Duma under the Kadet banner.

Chapter V

1. According to the anonymous fellow student cited earlier, Witte changed his mind about an academic career because his first scholarly effort did not come off. Glinskii, "Graf Sergei Iulevich Vitte," *Istoricheskii vestnik* 140 (1915): 235.

2. Why was he living in a hotel, rather than at home with his mother? Perhaps because living at a hotel enabled him to enjoy the freedom of bachelor life, a life that involved association with actresses, presumably of dubious reputation.

3. He is obviously referring to the pogrom of March 1871. Here, as elsewhere in the memoirs, Witte asserts that officials in those days acted properly in their dealings with Jews, in contrast to latter-day officials. In so doing he is too charitable. Thus, Count Kotzebue did not act immediately, as Witte says, but waited four days before taking steps to halt the pogrom. S. Dubnow, *History of the Jews in Russia and Poland* (Philadelphia, 1918), II, 191–93. It is noteworthy that Witte first used the word *razgrom* to describe the attack, then changed it to *pogrom*. The difference in denotation is slight, but the difference in connotation is considerable, because "pogrom" has come to be associated almost exclusively with attacks on Jews.

4. Witte's official biography disagrees on some details with the account he presents in his memoirs of the early stages of his career. According to that biography, he entered the service of the Odessa Railroad on May 1, 1870, then, on July 1, 1871, received a concurrent appointment to the chancellery of the governor-general of New Russia and Bessarabia and held that appointment until March 1, 1874. (The governor-generalship of New Russia and Bessarabia was abolished in 1874.) Then, on June 7, 1874, he was attached to the Department of General Affairs of the Ministry of Ways and Communications with the rank (*chin*) of titular councillor. This biography goes on to note that he left government service on April 1, 1877, "to devote himself exclusively to railroading." Russia, Ministerstvo Finansov, *Ministerstvo Finansov 1802–1902* (St. Petersburg, 1902), pt. 2, 323–24. (Witte writes later that his departure from the ministry was occasioned by his "insolence." His position with the ministry, like his position with the governor-general, gave him civil service status but did not impose any duties on him.)

5. Witte's account of the manner in which the Odessa Railroad was built is somewhat

fuzzy. For a short, clear account, *see* A. M. Soloveva, *Zheleznodorozhnyi transport Rossii vo vtoroi polovine XIX v.* (Moscow, 1975), pp. 90–92.

6. In January 1871, Prince A. I. Bariatinskii wrote to Chikhachev asking him to help Witte's career if he seemed worthy of confidence. Witte, *Vospominaniia*, I, 518, n. 19.

7. Witte was to change his views about Serbs and other Balkan Slavs. After the outbreak of World War I, he told Maurice Paléologue that the Balkan peoples were not Slavs, but rather "Turks christened by the wrong name," and added that the Serbs needed to be taught a lesson. *An Ambassador's Memoirs*, (New York, 1924), I, 122–23. Unfortunately, Witte does not tell us how he came to abandon many of the ultranationalist, almost Pan-Slav, views he held in those days.

8. Here, as elsewhere, Witte, like many of his contemporaries, uses the term "anarchist" very loosely, making no distinction between anarchists and socialists.

9. Mother Superior Mitrofania was charged with and found guilty of forgery and theft.

10. A prereform court was one that had not yet been reorganized in conformity with the judicial reform of 1864.

11. *See* International Railway Congress, Brussels, 1885, *Congrès des chemins de fer. Bruxelles: 8–15 août 1885. Compte rendu général*, 2 vols. (Brussels, 1886).

12. Elsewhere, Witte says that this hospital train was built at the expense of Derviz, chairman of the board of the Moscow–Riazan Railroad, and was taken under the Dowager Empress's patronage.

Chapter VI

1. Much of pp. 219–22 of the dictated memoirs, dealing with Witte's first marriage, was cut out (by Countess Witte?), but not destroyed; the cut-out material was tucked away elsewhere in the memoirs.

2. Elsewhere Witte says that the order came within a few hours.

3. Witte gives a very sketchy and unbalanced summary of the work of the Baranov Commission, the finds of which were recorded in a six-volume work. For a short summary, *see* Soloveva, *Zheleznodorozhnyi transport Rossii vo vtoroi polovine XIX v.*, pp. 153–57.

4. For more on the charter, *see* chapter IX.

5. The Radstockites were followers of the teachings of Lord Radstock, "a Victorian revivalist of the Plymouth Brethren variety." Serge Bolshakoff, *Russian Noncomformists* (Philadelphia, 1950), p. 116.

6. In suggesting that the old boy network of graduates of such elite institutions resembled the Jewish *kahal* (Jewish communal associations abolished in 1844), Witte was expressing a widespread, but unfounded, belief that the *kahal* had continued to exist in secret as a Jewish mutual aid network.

7. General-adjutant was the highest rank in the Emperor's suite. After 1881 only full generals could be named to that rank. As Witte implies, the title of general-adjutant was a prestigious one. Lesser ranks in the imperial suite were general à la suite, admiral à la suite, and aide-de-camp (*fligel-adjutant*).

In 1890, Alexander III said that he had cut his suite from 500 to 250 and that he intended to keep cutting it, designating those who remained as "trash." A. A. Polovtsov, *Dnevnik gosudarstvennogo sekretaria A. A. Polovtsova* (Moscow, 1966), II, 303.

Chapter VII
\

1. Witte errs. Vyshnegradskii was appointed acting minister of finance subsequent to Witte's appointment as manager of the railroad, not before. *Ministerstvo Finansov, 1802–1902*, pt. 2, 324, 652.

2. Peter Bark was to serve as minister of finance from 1914 to 1917. After the revolution, he emigrated to England, where he continued his banking activities and was knighted for his services.

3. That a man's surname ends in "skii" is not proof of Polish origin, but it raises the possibility.

4. Demchinskii can be classified as one of Witte's "hired pens," a term used for many men, holding official position, whose major function was to do Witte's writing. Some of the writing was for official purposes, some for nongovernmental publication. He relied on "hired pens" partly because he did not have the time to do much writing, partly because, as he acknowledged, he did not write well or easily.

5. Here, as elsewhere, Witte cannot refrain from unfavorably comparing the political atmosphere at the time of writing with that of the period he is writing about.

Chapter VIII

1. Witte's account of the Holy Brotherhood, slight though it is, is the major primary source for the history of this body, because he is the only participant to have left an account. A slightly different version of what he had to say on the subject will be found in Countess Marie Kleinmichel's *Bilder aus einer versunkten Welt* (Berlin, 1922), pp. 99–107. This version, based on what Witte told her in Biarritz in 1911 (not long after he had dictated this account), is in conflict on some minor points with what he dictated.

Witte's version of his role in inspiring the Holy Brotherhood has been questioned, but two careful scholars, B. V. Ananich and Sh. Ganelin, argue for the reliability of what he tells. *See* their article, "R. A. Fadeev, S. Iu. Vitte, i ideologicheskie iskaniia 'okhranitelei' v 1881–1882 gg.," in *Issledovaniia po sotsialno-politicheskoi istorii Rossii: Sbornik statei Pamiati Borisa Aleksandrovicha Romanova*. Trudy Leningradskogo otdeleniia Instituta Istorii, no. 12 (Moscow, 1971), p. 299.

2. A copy of the letter from Fadeev is in the Soviet archives and is reprinted in Witte, *Vospominaniia*, I, 521–22. This letter provides some confirmation of the reliability of Witte's account.

In his handwritten memoirs (p. 53 verso), Witte writes:

> At the beginning of his reign Emperor Alexander III assented to the formation of the Holy Brotherhood. It was something like the Union of the Russian People, but as soon as it began to take incorrect measures, ones that would be considered childishly innocent compared to those cooked up nowadays by the Union of the Russian People, . . . he immediately and completely shut the brotherhood down, despite the fact that many highly placed persons close to him were members. . . .

3. Gartman (Hartmann) was not in France at the time, having recently been expelled from the country. Witte's error may be the result of a slip in memory or an error in identification on the part of those from whom he received orders.

4. A. Cherikower argues, as others have, that the Holy Brotherhood probably inspired the anti-Jewish pogrom of 1881, but admits that he cannot prove this to be the case. "Naie

materialn begn di pogromen in Rusland in onhoib die 80er yohrn,'' *YIWO Historishe Shriftn* 2 (1937): 444–45.

5. Even after he ended his association with the organization Witte continued, under the influence of General Fadeev, to carry out activities in the spirit of the goals of the organization, that is, of shoring up the monarchy. *See* Ananich and Ganelin, "R. A. Fadeev, S. Iu. Vitte." *See also*, by the same authors, "S. Iu. Vitte, M. P. Dragomanov i 'Volnoe Slovo,'" in *Issledovaniia po otechestvennomu istochnikovedeniiu: Sbornik statei posviashchennykh 75-letiiu professora S. N. Valka*, pp. 163–78, Trudy Leningradskogo otdeleniia Instituta Istorii, no. 7 (Moscow, 1964).

Chapter IX

1. Chertkov was accused of employing improper measures in his campaign to stamp out revolutionary activities in the period immediately preceding Witte's arrival in Kiev.

2. Witte mistakenly had Drenteln preceding Chertkov as governor-general. I have reversed the order.

3. Witte is obviously referring to the pogroms that followed the assassination of Alexander II. According to General V. D. Novitskii, chief of the gendarmerie for the province of Kiev at the time, Drenteln bears some responsibility for provoking the pogrom and, moreover, was loath to stop it. *Iz vospominanii zhandarma* (Moscow, 1929), pp. 179–87.

4. Through the offices of Hesse, Iuzefovich was able to send memoranda, on educational matters, to Nicholas II, who regarded Iuzefovich as a "trustworthy" and "loyal" subject. Alexis N. Kuropatkin, "Dnevnik," *Krasnyi arkhiv* 2 (1922): 59. After Witte became premier, he was openly attacked by Iuzefovich. This may account for Witte's frequent references to the man's "abnormal passions."

5. Apparently a pun. In Russian, *takt* means both tact and time.

6. Many shared Witte's view that the Russian Oldenburgs had a hereditary psychological taint. *See* A. A. Mosolov, *At the Court of the Last Tsar* (London, 1935), p. 99.

7. The grand duke suffered from a violent temper that bordered on the irrational. Empress Marie Fedorovna, not one of his admirers, is quoted as saying of him: "Il est malade d'une maladie incurable. . . . Il est bête." Bogdanovich, *Tri poslednikh samoderzhtsa* (Moscow, 1924), p. 454.

8. A. A. Polovtsov speaks of the prince as "a good, but somewhat mad (*shalyi*), man." *Dnevnik*, II, 211.

9. Witte was fairly close to I. S. Aksakov and contributed to his publication *Rus*.

10. This is the Vasilii V. Shulgin who, together with Guchkov, traveled to Pskov in 1917 to ask Nicholas II to abdicate.

11. Bunge was already assistant minister of finance when Witte spoke to Loris-Melikov about him.

12. Witte is apparently referring to the student disturbances of 1884, concerning which he wrote an article in *Rus* that was sharply critical of the administration, thereby earning the hostility of much of the faculty. Glinskii, "Graf Sergei Iulevich Vitte," *Istoricheskii vestnik* 140 (1915): 245–56.

Novitskii provides an eyewitness account of the incident between Trepov and Subbotin. *Iz vospominanii zhandarma*, pp. 156–59.

It is interesting, but not surprising, that Witte makes no reference to Ukrainophile sentiment among Kievan students at that time. He, like most Russians, seemed oblivious to the growth of Ukrainian nationalism.

13. Here the Russian term *kontrakty* (contracts) refers to the *kontraktovaia iarmarka* (contract fair) held in February, where contracts for leases, land sales, sales of grain and such were drawn up.

14. Although Witte has some harsh things to say about those members of the Imperial family with whom he was at odds, he shows greater restraint in relating defamatory information about other members of the family than he does with ordinary mortals. Surely he was aware of the rumor that Polovtsov's wife was the illegitimate daughter of Grand Duke Michael Pavlovich, yet he neglects the opportunity to mention it.

15. Polovtsov's feelings about Witte are indicated in the following diary entry: "19 Feb. 1892. On the occasion of his appointment as minister of ways and communications, Witte called on me, in uniform. I explained to him that one appears in uniform only when calling on a superior and that I am not his superior. He appears to be very intelligent and reserved. He will perform well in his office, but he does not inspire any confidence with respect to honor and conscience." *Dnevnik*, II, 424.

16. Concerning Gorchakov's fortune, Polovtsov writes: "I know of no other Russian official who accumulated so great a fortune without in any way being accused of corruption." Ibid., I, 87.

17. Pliushkin: a character in Gogol's *Dead Souls*.

Chapter X

1. Witte tells the same incident with a slightly different emphasis in his handwritten memoirs (p. 48). There he makes the point that William acted as he did because he believed an emperor to be a superhuman being to whom obsequious behavior is due.

2. Many saw the hand of providence in the fact that Alexander III did not die at Borki and believed that had he died that day, October 17, 1888, the dynasty might have been in mortal danger.

3. Witte forgets that he first met Koni in the course of his work with the Baranov commission, a fact that he himself noted earlier. Koni, it should be noted, contradicts Witte concerning some of the details of the Borki wreck. *See* his "Sergei Iulevich Vitte," in *Sobranie sochinenii* (Moscow, 1968), V, 239-40, 243-46.

4. In stating that Alexander III supported the carriage roof on his back, Witte is repeating a widely circulated story that some have questioned. His reference to the emperor's "tremendous strength" contradicts his description elsewhere of the emperor as a large but flabby man. Witte probably contributed to the exaggerated notion of the emperor's strength, which grew in the telling until he was described as "Herculean" in Grand Duke Alexander Mikhailovich's *Once a Grand Duke* (New York, 1932), p. 168. (The grand duke almost certainly had the help of a ghostwriter, who probably was responsible for the liberties taken with the truth in the book.)

Chapter XI

1. Koni ("Witte," pp. 243-46) contradicts Witte. He writes that during the course of the investigation of the Borki wreck, Witte had a private talk with him in which he said that there was a prospect of his receiving a high position, providing he did not earn the ill will of Vyshnegradskii or Poset. Witte, we are told, felt his "entire future" would be hurt if he told the truth, for the truth would earn him the enmity of Poset. Koni writes that he advised

Witte to tell the truth no matter what, but that Witte tried to avoid damaging Poset in his findings. Since neither Witte's version nor Koni's version can be corroborated by other sources, it is difficult to tell where the truth lies. But it can be said that Witte, like most humans, understates the degree to which he was guided by ambition. Also, Koni seems rather fair-minded.

2. In the original Russian, *v otstavke*, commonly translated as "in retirement," but that is not what the phrase means in this context.

3. In 1722, Peter the Great established the Table of Ranks, with fourteen classes of ranks, for civilian officials, military and naval officers, and officials of the Imperial court. The Table of Ranks remained in use, with some modifications, until 1917. Normally an official remained in a rank for several years before being promoted to the next higher rank. Witte's promotion to the fourth class, comparable to promotion from major to major general, was indeed exceptional.

4. Witte's first wife, as far as we know, bore him no children.

5. On occasions such as presentation to the Emperor, a civil servant appeared in the appropriate uniform, wearing the insignia of the orders to which he belonged. Had he been a full-time civil servant for several years, he would probably have had the Order of St. Stanislas by this time. Ultimately Witte was to be admitted to the Orders of St. Vladimir, St. Stanislas, St. Anne, and St. Alexander Nevskii, as well as to many foreign orders.

6. Kovalevskii was a prisoner at the Fortress of SS. Peter and Paul from 1875 to 1877 for his connection with Nechaev.

7. This was among the first institutions for higher education of women in Russia.

8. Savva Mamontov, the well-known entrepreneur and Maecenas, was charged in 1889 with illegal conduct in the operation of several enterprises he controlled. *See also below*, I, ch. XVII, n. 10.

A. A. Lopukhin, who participated in the prosecution of Mamontov, has some uncomplimentary things to say about Witte's conduct in the Mamontov affair. *Otryvki iz vospominanii* (Moscow, 1923), pp. 60–65. These comments are part of his critique of Witte's memoirs, in which he, Lopukhin, does not figure well.

9. Witte does not refrain completely from mentioning names. He deals later on with the "wheeling and dealing" of Princess Iurevskaia, the morganatic wife of Alexander II, and Prince Alexander Dolgorukii, a high court official.

Chapter XII

1. The State Council (*Gosudarstvennyi Sovet*) was charged with examining and voting on the budget and on all legislative proposals. Although the emperor generally approved the majority view, he was not obliged to, and on many occasions he approved the minority view. By law the emperor presided over the body. In practice the task was performed by the chairman, whom he appointed. During Witte's tenure as minister of ways and communications and minister of finance, Grand Duke Michael Nikolaevich was the chairman. He left much of the responsibility for managing the operations of the council to the imperial secretary, the chief of the council's chancellery. When Witte first became a minister the council had three departments—state economy, legislative affairs, and civil and ecclesiastical affairs—which carried out the preliminary work of examining the budget and legislative proposals. (A fourth, with jurisdiction over science, industry, and commerce, was created in 1899.) Most of Witte's dealings were with the Department of State Economy.

2. The title *upravliaiushchii delami* is usually translated as *business manager*. However,

here, and elsewhere where it seems appropriate, the title is translated as *chief administrative assistant.*

3. The general-admiral was nominally in "supreme control" of the Ministry of the Navy, but the chief administrative responsibility in the ministry was in fact exercised by its *upravliaiushchii.*

4. Elsewhere the title of *upravliaiushchii* of a ministry is translated as *acting minister,* which accurately reflects the status of the person holding the title. Such a translation would be misleading in the case of the *upravliaiushchii* of the Ministry of the Navy, for during this period the nominal head of the ministry, as noted, was the general-admiral and hence there was no minister or acting minister of the navy. Under these circumstances it seems best to translate *upravliaiushchii* as *director.*

5. *Chief of staff* in this context is the translation of *nachalnik glavnogo shtaba,* sometimes translated *chief of the general staff,* which is misleading because the General Staff at this time was a subordinate part of the *Glavnyi Shtab.* A literal translation of *nachalnik glavnogo shtaba* is *chief of the main staff,* but it is a cumbersome one.

6. *See above,* I, ch. IV, n. 7.

7. The grand duke was arrested in 1874 for stealing jewels from his mother to give to Fanny Lear, a dancer. Had a panel of doctors not found him to be of unsound mind, the emperor would have had the unpleasant duty of permitting him to be tried. The grand duke's behavior while in exile was abnormal at times, to say the least. *See* Dmitrii Miliutin, *Dnevnik* (Moscow, 1947), I, 152–53.

8. Witte does not say, but it appears that Rafalovich credited Abaza's account with what he would have gained had Rafalovich carried out his orders.

9. Because Witte's account of this episode is very digressive, it is given here rather than in the body of the memoirs:

> About the time of the Abaza scandal, Durante, a Simferopol landowner, asked me to have the State Bank grant George Rafalovich, his son-in-law, a loan of either 300,000 or 400,000 rubles. Durante's estate would serve as security. I told him that this was not my business, but that of the State Bank. In the end the loan was granted, and, subsequently, the State Bank had to sell the estate.
>
> Durante then claimed, falsely, that the estate had been illegally sold at my behest, either for my benefit or that of the Rafalovich family. Later on, financially ruined, he tried to blackmail the Rafaloviches. Because this was a family case it was submitted to an arbitration tribunal, which found against Durante, but recommended that he be provided with a means of earning a living. The Rafaloviches then offered him a position in the Bessarabian Bank. But before accepting the position, Durante made certain demands on Rafalovich and threatened to shoot him.
>
> Also, Durante decided to submit a claim to the Emperor, alleging that his estate had been illegally sold. By this time (it was soon after our so-called revolution) he was a member of the Odessa branch of the Union of the Russian People (whose chairman, Count Konovitsyn, was as big a scoundrel as he) and promised to turn half of what he would recover to the branch. Although most of the members of the Union of the Russian People are men *sans foi, ni loi,* the Emperor chose to believe the charge and to have it investigated. He turned the claim over to Kokovtsev, who declared it to be an invention. (While the matter was being investigated, Durante was writing the most scandalous articles about me in *Russkoe znamia.*) The Emperor then asked Akimov, chairman of the State Council, to look into the case. He, too, concluded that the allegations were untrue, but suggested that the case be referred back to Kokovtsev, because he feared the power of the Union of the Russian People. Acting timorously, Kokovtsev suggested that the claim be referred to the Council of Ministers. Although the members of the council are no friends of mine, they too decided that Durante had no case.
>
> Thus, Durante's efforts came to naught. He has threatened to shoot me on sight, but we have never met. Had I met him I would have protected myself with the revolver I usually carry nowadays when I go walking.

An example of the attacks made on Witte in connection with the Durante affair is a pamphlet published in 1908, in Odessa, entitled *Byvshii ministr finansov Sergei Iulevich Vitte, kak glavnyi vinovnik . . . v dele ogrableniia krymskago pomeshchika K. A. Durante. . . .* (Odessa, 1908). Based on articles that had appeared in ultrarightist newspapers, it accused Witte of working with the enemies of Christendom, consistently referring to the Rafalovich in question as a "kike."

10. Witte was obviously repeating hearsay, most of it untrue. Rhodes was not a Jew. The princess did not live with him (a man whose lack of interest in the opposite sex was considerable), but she certainly did set her cap for him. It is true that she went to jail because of forgery. Brian Roberts, *Cecil Rhodes and the Princess* (London, 1969).

Chapter XIII

1. Witte devotes an inordinate amount of space to Wendrich, as he does to many others with whom he had difficulties. I have omitted some trivial material, although what remains is far from important. Witte, it should be noted, was not alone in considering Wendrich stupid, in some ways, and a sower of confusion. *See* Polovtsov, *Dnevnik*, II, 421.

2. In fact, Witte was appointed acting minister (*upravliaiushchii*). It was common for Emperors, particularly Alexander III, to first appoint a man as acting minister and then, after several months, to give him the title of minister.

3. Witte's statement leaves the mistaken impression that Nicholas had not yet been introduced to official duties. But it is correct to say that he was still a callow youth, who seemed younger than his years, probably because of his mother's influence on his development.

4. For more on the work of the committee, *see below*, I, ch. XIX.

5. Esper E. Ukhtomskii's book was translated into English as *Travels in the East of Nicholas II when Cesarewitch, 1890–1891*, 2 vols. (Westminister, 1896–1900.) Ukhtomskii was to serve as chairman of the board of the Russo-Chinese Bank and to work closely with Witte on Chinese affairs.

6. Witte elsewhere makes the point that it would have been fortunate if Nicholas II had come to know the real world in his formative years.

7. Ilia F. Tsion (Cyon) was a physiologist of some note when he involuntarily left academic life, in 1875, to become a publicist. Probably the most widely known of his works on Witte is *M. Witte et les finances russes*, 4th ed. (Paris, 1985), which appeared in many editions. There is evidence that, acting on Witte's behest, Rachkovskii, chief of the Russian secret police abroad, had some documents stolen from Tsion's home. "Karera P. I. Rachkovskago," *Byloe* 2 (1918): 80.

What lay behind the theft? George F. Kennan writes: "In 1896 his [Tsion's] villa . . . was raided, apparently by agents of the Russian secret police, and many of his papers stolen. From this point on, he appears to have ceased his attacks on Witte, at least the direct ones, a circumstance that has led to the occasional suggestion that prior to the disappearance of the papers he had held Witte under some form of blackmail." *The Decline of Bismarck's European Order* (Princeton, N.J., 1979), pp. 340–41.

8. Madame Juliette Adam (mistakenly spelled Aden in the dictated memoirs), publisher of *La Nouvelle Revue*. Princess Catherine Radziwill was among its contributors.

Chapter XIV

1. General Otto Borisovich Richter (1830–1908) enjoyed the confidence of both Alexander III and Nicholas II. He belonged to the category of those to whom heads of state turn for counsel not because of their knowledge or experience, but because they are trustworthy and close. He was to be one of the three to whom Nicholas II would turn when deciding whether or not to issue the October Manifesto.

2. It was widely believed that Witte paid Lisanevich to agree to the divorce. Stanislav M. Propper, publisher of *Birzhevye vedomosti*, and on good terms with Witte at the time of the divorce, offers the following circumstantial account: Lisanevich asked not only to be paid for his consent but also to be assured of a government position paying no less than 3,000 rubles; the cost of the divorce proceedings and the payment to the husband came to 30,000 rubles, a sum that Witte did not have; a certain Gravenhof, a "fixer," and a good friend of Mme. Lisanevich, was able to get the money from Fränkel, director of the Russian Bank for Foreign Trade, who apparently believed in casting his bread upon the waters. *Was nicht in die Zeitung kam* (Frankfurt am Main, 1929), pp. 165–68.

There were similarities in Witte's two marriages: both wives were pretty; both were divorcées; in both cases the husband was paid for assenting to a divorce; neither wife bore him a child. One dissimilarity: the first marriage was not a happy one, the second was, strikingly so.

3. Witte does not say so, but he seems to have hoped that he would not have to choose between marriage and position.

4. Both the bride and groom have a *shafer*. For want of a better term, *shafer* is here translated as "best man."

5. On the subject of the wild gossip surrounding Witte and his second wife, *see* Princess Julia Cantacuzene, *My Life Here and There* (New York, 1921), pp. 266–70.

6. Witte's account of his second marriage ends with page 564 of the dictated memoirs. There is no page 565, suggesting that this page was cut out.

Chapter XV

1. Iosif I. Kolyshko was one of Witte's many "hired pens." He prepared official documents for him and also, using one pseudonym or another, wrote newspaper articles defending Witte's views. After reading what appeared about him in Witte's memoirs, he published a pamphlet entitled *Lozh Vitte* [Witte's Lie] (Berlin, n.d.). The pamphlet, written in the form of a letter addressed to Witte in hell, is so wild in tone as not to be credible.

2. Khlestakov: the main character in Gogol's *Inspector General*.

3. Why Alexander III endured Meshcherskii as a person and why he subsidized *Grazhdanin* are related, but not identical, questions, although Witte treats them as if they were. There are some hypotheses that seem more credible than the one offered by Witte.

One, offered by A. A. Polovtsov, who cites Count N. P. Ignatev, Alexander III's minister of interior, is that although the emperor considered Meshcherskii a scoundrel, he felt that he owed him a debt for having thrown him down some stairs in a moment of outrage. He was angry because love letters he had once written to Meshcherskii's sister were stolen by the prince and shown to Empress Marie Fedorovna. *Dnevnik*, II, 197–98.

Polovtsov also offers a credible explanation of why the emperor subsidized *Grazhdanin*, namely, that he wanted the support of so conservative a newspaper as this one. He writes that the emperor justified providing a subsidy by citing Bismarck's practice of doing the same thing for newspapers he favored. Ibid., p. 140.

It was said that *Grazhdanin* was the only newspaper Alexander III read.

4. The scandal to which Witte refers became public knowledge in 1887 and nearly ended Meshcherskii's career.

5. Texts of letters from Alexander and Nicholas to Meshcherskii will be found in V. S. Frank's "Iz neizdannoi perepiski Imp. Aleksandra III i Nikolaia II s Kn. V. P. Meshcherskim," *Sovremennye zapiski* 70 (1940): 165–88 and I. Vinogradoff's "Some Russian Imperial Letters to Prince V. P. Meshchersky," *Oxford Slavonic Papers* 10 (1962): 105–58.

6. E. M. Feoktistov, a censor who had some unpleasant dealings with Meshcherskii, wrote about the prince and Alexander III in a similar vein. *Vospominaniia* (Leningrad, 1929), p. 247.

Chapter XVI

1. The word *khokhlatskii* is derived from *khokhol*, the epithet for Little Russian (i.e., Ukrainian).

2. *See above*, I, ch. XII, n. 5.

3. Why does Witte devote what seems a disproportionate amount of space to N. V. Muravev? Apparently because he was greatly nettled by the fact that Muravev was the Emperor's first choice to be chief plenipotentiary at the Portsmouth Peace Conference. Also, they seem not to have gotten along.

4. *See below*, p. 290.

5. Witte was not alone in believing that Giers had Jewish blood in him, but he was mistaken. Giers was, in fact, of Swedish origin on his father's side and largely of German origin on his mother's. Like Witte, he sought to minimize the German strain in his ancestry. Nicholas K. Giers, *The Education of a Russian Statesman* (Berkeley, Calif., 1962), p. 5.

6. Although he was sharply critical of Pobedonostsev's views, Witte obviously respected the man. Also, he behaved very kindly to Pobedonostsev and his family. *See* Robert F. Byrnes, *Pobedonostsev* (Bloomington, Ind., 1968), p. 367.

7. Witte's handwritten memoirs (p. 1 verso) include some criticism of Pobedonostsev not found in the typewritten memoirs. He says that Pobedonostsev was "inclined toward police measures because any other kind of measures would require change, and although he accepted the idea of change in his mind, his feeling of negativism and criticism made him fear change. Therefore he greatly strengthened the police regime in the Orthodox Church."

Witte adds another charge: "Thanks to him the embryonic constitution, put together at the initiative of Count Loris-Melikov . . . was aborted. This was Pobedonostsev's greatest sin; if not for him the history of Russia would have taken a different turn, and we probably would not have been experiencing dastardly and senseless revolution and anarchy."

8. *See above*, I, ch. XII, n. 4.

9. *Armiashka*: an ethnic epithet applied to Armenians.

10. A. S. Taneev had some reputation as a musician. Also, he had some claim to fame as the father of Anna Vyrubova, friend to both Rasputin and Empress Alexandra.

11. The Ministry of State Domains became the Ministry of Agriculture and State Domains in 1894.

12. *Bozhia korovka*: ladybird, ladybug, meaning a timid, mousy person; *navozyni zhuk*: dung beetle, i.e., a person predestined to work in dung.

13. Witte is apparently speaking of the circumstances leading to the issuance of the decree of May 6, 1884, which transformed the Committee on Imperial Honors into the Committee on the Service of Civilian Officials and on Honors. *See* P. A. Zaionchkovskii, *Pravitelstvennyi apparat samoderzhavnoi Rossii v XIX v.* (Moscow, 1978), pp. 60–65.

14. She was given the title following her marriage.

Chapter XVII

1. No doubt Witte was concerned about Vyshnegradskii's health, but he was also concerned about stepping into his shoes. Soon after he was appointed director of the Department of Railroad Affairs, we find him making derogatory remarks about his superior at the home of a well-known gossip. Bogdanovich, *Tri poslednikh samderzhtsa*, p. 102. That Witte did not feel kindly about Vyshnegradskii is quite evident from the memoirs. That Vyshnegradskii did not feel kindly toward Witte when he left office is suggested by his delay in vacating his official residence.

2. Witte is suggesting that Vyshnegradskii wished to give up the burden of office but not its powers and saw in Thörner a man who would do his bidding. Like Witte, Vyshnegradskii did not think highly of Thörner's mind. Polovtsov reports that when Vyshnegradskii was preparing to go to the Crimea in the spring of 1892, he designated Thörner to act in his place while he was gone, but took the precaution of locking up "the most important papers" and ordering Kobeko, director of the chancellery, "to see that no important papers be given Thörner by the departments." *Dnevnik*, II, 442.

3. Although Witte says later (p. 216) that he helped Krivoshein become minister, it is evident here that he would have preferred someone else, a man beholden to him, as minister of ways and communications.

4. The number of assistant ministers was raised to two shortly after Witte's appointment.

5. Elsewhere (dictated memoirs, p. 1126) Witte writes that Thörner suggested Ermolov as his replacement.

6. *See above*, I, ch. XVI, n. 1.

7. Although Witte, like other tsarist ministers, had little direct power over the selection of his associates, his assumption of office was quickly followed by a number of personnel changes that enabled him to begin building a cadre of subordinates whom he trusted and thought well of and to be rid of some with whom he was not happy. Thörner accommodated him by leaving. And as vacancies occurred or new positions were created, Witte was able to use his influence to surround himself with his men, men such as Romanov, Ivashchenkov, and Kovalevskii. Also, in the next years he was able to influence the operations of several other ministries through officials in those ministries who would be guided by him.

8. In his memoirs Witte mistakenly has Kobeko occupying the position of director of the Department of Direct Taxation when he became minister. Not so. Kobeko was director of the chancellery, and it seems likely that Witte helped kick him upstairs to make way for Romanov. Witte is guilty of a number of errors of detail regarding personnel changes during his first months as minister of finance. Perhaps they are the result of faulty memory.

9. *See below*, pp. 189–90.

10. Thus Witte is mistaken about the date of Maksimov's appointment. He was appointed director on September 26, 1892, several weeks after Witte took office, although it is possible that the appointment had been decided on while Vyshnegradskii was still

minister. *Ministerstvo Finansov, 1802-1902*, pt. 2, 685. There were rumors that N. V. Muravev, the minister of justice, having heard that Maksimov had been bribed by Mamontov, brought the case against the latter as an indirect way of discrediting Witte. V. T. Bill, *The Forgotten Class* (Westport, Conn., 1976), p. 132.

Chapter XVIII

1. Count Sergei G. Stroganov, a staunch conservative who opposed emancipation of the serfs and argued strongly against the so-called Loris-Melikov constitution, supervised the education of the sons of Alexander II, among them the future Alexander III.

2. V. M. Vonliarliarskii writes that he had it on good authority, which he did not cite, that the Tsesarevich was so outraged at his father's marriage to Princess Dolgorukaia that he wished to forsake Russia, but was persuaded to effect a reconciliation with his father. *Moi Vospominaniia* (Berlin, 1939), p. 102.

3. Unfortunately, Witte gives only a lick and a promise to the shift toward government ownership of the railroads. As minister of finance he had to negotiate the purchase of many major lines, including the Southwestern Railroad, still under the control of his old employer, Bloch.

4. The legislation concerning the imperial family was issued by Emperor Paul in 1797 and remained in effect, with some modification, until 1917. Under these laws the emperor had broad powers over the imperial family, which by the late 1880s had come to number some sixty grand dukes, grand duchesses, princes, and princesses of the imperial blood.

5. The Russian Leuchtenbergs were the issue of the marriage of Grand Duchess Marie Nikolaevna and Duke Maximilian of Leuchtenberg, the grandson of Empress Josephine Beauharnais. The couple made their home in Russia. The duke was made a member of the imperial family.

6. Alexander III was indulgent about the *amours* of Grand Duke Alexis Aleksandrovich, but then the grand duke was a bachelor; that apparently made a difference. What he thought about the premarital affair between his son Nicholas and the ballerina Kshessinskaia is a matter of dispute.

7. There was a sixth, Grand Duke Alexander Aleksandrovich, who was born in 1869 and died in 1870.

Chapter XIX

1. Apparently referring to the same incident, George F. Kennan writes that after refusing to permit Hoskier to join the consortium, Rothschild conceded a "personal share" to Vyshnegradskii that he could sell to Hoskier. *The Decline of Bismarck's European Order*, pp. 379-80.

2. The Corps of the Border Guard was established by the decree of October 15, 1893.

3. Witte is referring to his *Natsionalnaia ekonomiia i Fridrikh List*, in which he wrote favorably about List's ideas on promoting economic growth.

4. By the time of Alexander III's death, preparations had been made to institute the liquor monopoly in Orenburg, Perm, Ufa, and Samara provinces: the experience gained in those provinces would be used to guide the work of instituting the monopoly in other parts of the country. *See Ministerstvo Finansov, 1802-1902*, pt. 2, 192-203.

5. Additional details concerning the preparatory steps taken for the introduction of the gold standard will be found in ibid., pp. 99-120.

6. He wrote a description of the trip to Murmansk under the title *Po studenomu moriu* (St. Petersburg, 1895).

7. Elsewhere Witte writes that Kazi recommended Ekaterinskaia harbor and helped him write his report. Witte was to attach a great deal of importance to the report, in which he wrote that in the event of war with Germany, Libau would be useless as a base, but that Murmansk would prove useful in such a war, particularly with the support of the British fleet. When World War I broke out, his effort to have the report published was frustrated by the military censors. It was, however, read at a meeting of an historical society and was published a decade later by the head of the society. "Libava ili Murman?" *Proshloe i nastoia-shchee*, no. 1 (1924): 25–39.

Chapter XX

1. The Ministry of the Imperial Court had jurisdiction over the maintenance and security of members of the imperial family, the operation of the imperial court, and the many enterprises and institutions under imperial administration, including the appanages—the lands of the imperial family. *See* Mosolov, *At the Court of the Last Tsar*. *See also* the annual volumes of *Pridvornyi kalendar* and the sections on the imperial family in the annual volumes of *Almanach de Goth*.

2. Alexander III had the reputation of occasionally tippling, sometimes on the sly, with Cherevin. Count A. A. Ignatev refers to Cherevin as the emperor's "*sobutylnik*" (boon companion). *Piatdesiat let v stroiu* (Moscow, 1950), I, 90. *See also Golos minuvshago*, nos. 5–6, 1917, pp. 99–100.

3. Someone (Countess Witte?) apparently did not wish the material about Prince Dolgorukii and his sister to be published: not only were pages 979–84 of the dictated memoirs cut out (but tucked away elsewhere), but some of what appeared on these pages and on page 978 was inked out. Ellipsis points indicate inked out material that could not be deciphered.

4. It is noteworthy that neither here nor elsewhere is Witte critical of Russian policy in Persia, a policy that was carried out with the help of the Ministry of Finance.

5. Grand Duchess Catherine Mikhailovna, daughter of Grand Duke Michael Pavlovich, married George, Duke of Mecklenburg-Strelitz, in 1850. They made their home in Russia, and their male descendants, like those of the Russian Oldenburgs and Leuchtenbergs, made their careers in the Russian military and civil service.

6. *See below*, pp. 710–13.

Chapter XXI

1. Obviously a jibe at Nicholas II, who initiated the First Hague Peace Conference. *See below*, pp. 284–85. In the handwritten memoirs (pp. 255–58), Witte lets himself go in contrasting the views regarding war and peace of father and son:

> I had the greatest honor that a Russian could enjoy, of knowing and being one of the closest associates of the Peacemaker (*Mirotvorets*). This appellation was bestowed . . . in a manifesto issued immediately after his death and was written in the chancellery of Count Vorontsov-Dashkov, then the minister of the Imperial court. This appellation, which I consider entirely appropriate, was not entirely to the liking of his son.
>
> A few months after the death of Emperor Alexander III, when I had the occasion of giving Emperor Nicholas II a document in which the late Emperor was referred to as the Peacemaker, to sign, His Majesty asked if the appellation could not be crossed out, saying: "This appella-

tion does not quite suit the figure of my father; it creates an impression not commensurate with his strength, an impression that he feared war. When Vorontsov brought me the manifesto to sign, I was in such a state that I did not pay attention to this appellation, which is not fully suitable.''

In fact Emperor Alexander III reigned peacefully and significantly raised the prestige of the Empire not because he was a peacemaker, but because he was honorable and firm as a rock. . . .

Emperor Alexander III had seen war, as a commander of a detachment in the war with Turkey. He told me on one occasion: "One who has experienced war and seen its horrors cannot love war." For that reason his reign was peaceful, but not because he was weak. His character, his tsarlike honor, and his decisiveness raised Russia's international prestige higher than it had ever been. He would have been shocked to the core if he had been able to see how this prestige has fallen since his death.

Emperor Nicholas II is a different kind of military man. He has had no experience of war. His experience was as a commander of a battalion of the Preobrazhenskii Guards before he ascended the throne and that is all. His father was a proud Tsar and an equable and unaffected nobleman. Nicholas II is not a proud Tsar, but a very proud and affected guards colonel. . . .

In several other places in these memoirs, as will be seen, Witte, in one form or another, makes the point that Nicholas II professed not to seek war but did want the glory that comes with annexing foreign soil.

2. This is the first, but by no means the last, reference to Dmitrii F. Trepov, who was to rank high on Witte's list of enemies.

3. In his handwritten memoirs (p. 2 verso), Witte gives a somewhat different version of this conversation:

Ivan Nikolaevich asked if I knew the new Emperor well. I replied that I had rarely discussed affairs of state with him, that he was quite inexperienced, but not stupid, and that he had always impressed me as a fine and thoroughly well-bred young man. In fact, I had rarely met such a well-bred person as Nicholas II, and I still consider him remarkably well bred, but I think that his breeding has masked his shortcomings.

I. N. Durnovo reacted by saying, "You are mistaken, Sergei Iulevich. Mark what I say: this one will be something of a copy of [Emperor] Paul Petrovich, but in modern form."

I was to think of this conversation often. Of course, Emperor Nicholas is no Paul Petrovich, but he has some of Paul's traits and some of Alexander I's (mysticism, slyness, even craftiness), but without his education. Alexander I was one of the best educated of Russians, while Nicholas II, compared with his contemporaries, has no more than the average education of a guards colonel from a good family.

Chapter XXII

1. General de Boisdeffre, chief of the French General Staff, had been to Russia earlier in the year to review the terms of the Franco-Russian military convention of 1892. One of his tasks on this visit was to determine how committed the new emperor was to the alliance between the two countries. He was able to report that the alliance was "guaranteed for the duration of the reign." Boisdeffre to the Ministry of Foreign Affairs, November 17 and 22, 1894 (NS). France, Ministère des Affaires Étrangères, Archive, *Correspondence politique*, vol. 303.

2. In his handwritten memoirs (pp. 58–59), Witte has a somewhat franker version of the events leading to the decision in favor of Libau and its aftermath. What follows is an abridgment:

Grand Duke Alexander Mikhailovich, a navy man, had dreams of supplanting Grand Duke

Alexis Aleksandrovich as general-admiral. When Nicholas II ascended the throne, Grand Duke Alexander Mikhailovich believed that he would have the support of his brother-in-law and, with the help of Kazi, who had old scores to settle with Chikhachev, began a campaign against the general-admiral and Chikhachev. The general-admiral won the first skirmish, over Libau.

Knowing that the Emperor was displeased with Grand Duke Alexis Aleksandrovich, Grand Duke Alexander Mikhailovich began to exploit this displeasure by trying to have the general-admiral unseated. He did this by submitting memoranda, prepared by Kazi, for improving and reorganizing the naval ministry; these memoranda, it should be said, had some merit to them. When the Emperor turned one of these memoranda over to Grand Duke Alexis Aleksandrovich for study, the general-admiral demanded the dismissal of Grand Duke Alexander Mikhailovich from the navy.

With this the struggle became more intense. No question that Grand Duke Alexander Mikhailovich would have won if the Emperor had dared go against his mother [who favored the general-admiral]. So, the general-admiral won this skirmish as well, and Grand Duke Alexander Mikhailovich was forced to seek realization of his ambitions in other fields.

The Emperor could not vent his displeasure on the general-admiral, but he could do so, and did, by dismissing Chikhachev. However, Chikhachev's successor, Admiral Tyrtov, was the choice of the general-admiral, who thus remained in control of the ministry.

3. Stolypin died in September 1911.

4. A minor illustration. Once, looking out of the window of the Anichkov Palace, Alexander III saw one of the Grand Dukes riding by in a public conveyance, smoking a cigar, and promptly put him under arrest, presumably for conduct unbecoming an officer. Gabriel Romanov, *V mramornom dvortse* (New York, 1955), p. 129. Such a reaction on the part of Nicholas II would have been inconceivable.

5. In a franker statement in his handwritten memoirs (p. 352), Witte had the following to say about Nicholas II:

> From what has been said earlier it is as clear as the sky above that when Nicholas ascended the throne he was a kind man, who was far from stupid but lacked depth and who was weak-willed. When all is said and done, he is a good person, but he inherited all the qualities of his mother and some of the qualities of his ancestors (Paul) and hardly any of his father: he was not endowed with the qualities necessary for an emperor, particularly the absolute ruler of an empire such as Russia. The basic traits of Nicholas are kindliness (when he wishes to be) (Alexander I), slyness, and complete lack of character and will.
>
> . . . Things might have turned out differently if he had made a good marriage, i.e., if he had married an intelligent and normal woman, whose good qualities might have compensated for his shortcomings. . . .

Chapter XXIII

1. Witte opposed discrimination against Poles and other minorities, but he was clearly in favor of the harsh policy of Russification followed in what he calls the Kingdom of Poland since the suppression of the revolt of 1863. (The term "Kingdom of Poland" had no legal meaning after the revolt, but Witte, like many others, continued to use the term.) E. M. Feoktistov, a close friend of Governor-General Gurko, denies that Gurko asked to leave his post for the reasons cited by Witte, but he does agree with Witte in saying that the Emperor decided not to appoint Gurko's son, Vladimir, as director of his chancellery. *Vospominaniia* (Leningrad, 1929), pp. 402–03.

2. Much of what Witte had to say about Gurko and his family did not appear in the Slovo edition of the memoirs, but some of the derogatory material about Vladimir I. Gurko did appear. Vladimir I. Gurko wrote a lengthy critique of the published memoirs, entitled "Chto est i chego net v 'Vospominaniakh' grafa Sergeia Iulevicha Vitte," which appeared in

Russkaia starina, no. 2 (1922): 59-153. (The appearance of Witte's memoirs in the Slovo edition caused a sensation and elicited very quick responses from Gurko and other critics.) *See also* what Gurko had to say about the memoirs in his *Features and Figures of the Past* (Stanford University [Calif.], 1939), pp. 52-68.

3. *See above*, p. 163, where Witte, in a footnote, says that he did not oppose Krivoshein's appointment: not much of a cause for "gratitude."

4. For more on Ivashchenkov, *see above*, p. 120.

5. Nicholas II's refusal to appoint Ivashchenkov underlines the fact that, like his father, he guarded his power and sought to prevent ministers from building empires. Witte's later removal from the post of minister of finance was in part the result of the fact that Witte had become too powerful for the taste of the Emperor, who, although not a strong personality, did not like to be dominated by others and who protected his prerogatives very tenaciously.

6. Nicholas P. Shishkin was also to act as *locum tenens* when Lobanov-Rostovskii died, but on neither occasion was he seriously considered for the post of minister.

7. À propos of the fact that Lobanov-Rostovskii preferred that ambassadors be wealthy men, of eminent families, married to brilliant women, Count Vladimir N. Lambsdorff wrote in 1895 that the prince was "the son of a marketwoman (*torgovka*) and had not a farthing to his name when he started and has had romances all his life with women of questionable character to console himself for his unmarried state." "Dnevnik," *Krasnyi arkhiv* 46 (1931): 34.

8. Witte wrote three detailed accounts (handwritten memoirs, pp. 15-16; dictated memoirs, pp. 859-69, 1107-23) of the circumstances surrounding the appointment of Goremykin. The three are in substantial agreement among themselves, and what appears here is a conflation of the versions in the dictated memoirs.

9. Alexis A. Lopukhin, who served as director of the Department of Police, says that Plehve did not change his religion and that Plehve's father had not been an organist for a Polish noble, but had served as a school inspector in Kaluga province. *Otryvki iz vospominanii*, p. 11. *See also* Judge, *Plehve* (Syracuse, N.Y., 1983), p. 12. (Witte, it should be noted, hated Plehve more than he did any other man with whom he served and was ready to believe what he considered the worst about him. He considered converts to Russian Orthodoxy as "renegades" if he disliked them, assuming that they had acted not out of conviction but in order to further their careers.)

10. As Witte notes, he disagreed with Sipiagin on some major political questions, but the two were friendly enough for Witte to write frankly to him. In a letter written in 1900, Witte disagrees with Sipiagin's view that the emperor should not be bound by the laws and rules he had issued, saying that while an autocrat has the right to make the laws, he is bound by them if the state is to function properly. He goes on to say that Sipiagin's view is like that of the Catholics, who believe that to criticize the Pope is to criticize God. The Russians, says Witte, are of the Orthodox faith, not the Catholic faith, and do not accept the dogma of papal infallibility. "Pisma S. Iu. Vitte k D. S. Sipiaginu, 1900-1901 gg.," *Krasnyi arkhiv* 18 (1926): 31-32.

Chapter XXIV

1. Here Witte begins to deal with the origins of the Russo-Japanese War. What he has to say is long and, deservedly, served as a major primary source on the subject. He assumes that the reader has access to his "Vozniknovenie russko-iaponskoi voiny" and, as he puts

it, concerns himself in the memoirs with no more than the "external" (*vneshnie*) aspects of the subject, which means, in practice, providing less detail and being more personal.

2. The Russo-Chinese Bank was established in 1895, largely at the initiative of Witte. It was intended to serve as a means of lending money to China to pay her indemnity to Japan, in part to promote Russian economic influence in China. French banks were to provide five-eighths of the capital, Russian banks the rest, but five of the eight members of the board of directors were to be Russians, in whose selection the minister of finance played a dominant role. As noted earlier, the chairman of the board was Prince Esper E. Ukhtomskii.

3. Witte does not give enough credit to others for developing the idea of running the railroad across northern Manchuria. In this case, as in others dealing with the origins of the Russo-Japanese War, it is useful to supplement Witte's account with those found in Boris A. Romanov, *Russia in Manchuria (1892-1906)* (Ann Arbor, Mich., 1952), and Andrew Malozemoff, *Russian Far Eastern Policy, 1881-1904* (Berkeley, Calif., 1954.)

4. Zhamsaran (Peter Alekseevich) Badmaev is one of those "mysterious" figures, like Rasputin, who gained some prominence in the last decades of the Russian monarchy. He was a Russified Buriat Mongol who went to St. Petersburg, where he was converted to the Russian Orthodox faith, with Alexander III serving as his godfather. He was interested in Tibetan medicine and was credited with knowing "ancient healing secrets." It was his interest in Far Eastern policy that brought him into contact with Witte, who provided Badmaev with more initial support than he suggests in the memoirs. *See* V. P. Semennikov, ed., *Za kulisami tsarizma: arkhiv tibetskogo vracha Badmaeva* (Leningrad, 1925), pp. 75-83.

5. Texts of the treaty of alliance and of the railroad agreement will be found in *Sbornik dogovorov s drugimi gosudarstvami, 1856-1917* (Moscow, 1952), pp. 292-94, 297-302.

6. It is true that no money passed hands at the time, and it may be the case that Li Hung-chang did not ask for money, but he was promised a substantial sum for using his good offices. *See* B. A. Romanov, "Likhungchangskii fond," *Borba klassov* 1-2 (1924): 77-126; *see also* Romanov, *Russia in Manchuria*, pp. 84-85.

7. The Russo-Chinese Bank established the Chinese Eastern Railroad Co., whose charter was approved by Nicholas II in 1896. Although the chairman of the board was Chinese, appointed by his government, the headquarters of the company were in St. Petersburg, and its capital was guaranteed by the Russian government. In fact, the company was operated by the Russian government, i.e., Witte and his subordinates. Through the company Witte was able to establish his own quasi-diplomatic network in Peking and Manchuria and to become the dominant figure in his country's Far Eastern policy, at least until 1900. In fact, it may be said that from 1896 until his removal from the post of minister of finance, Witte was *the* major figure in the government, in part because of his role in Far Eastern affairs, in part because of the bold fiscal and economic policies for which he was responsible.

Chapter XXV

1. Alexis Lopukhin, who took part in the investigation of the Khodynka tragedy, disputes Witte's assertion that all traces of the victims had been removed by the time he arrived at the scene; according to Lopukhin the removal of bodies continued until 4 p.m. Also, Lopukhin disputes some of Witte's assertions about efforts to shift responsibility. *Otryvki iz vospominanii*, pp. 20-42.

2. In telling about this conversation with Li Hung-chang in his handwritten memoirs

(p. 17), Witte wrote, "After this observation, I thought, after all, we are ahead of China."

3. Derzhimorda: a nasty, brutish policeman in Gogol's *Inspector General*.

4. Excerpts from the Muravev report, which is in the Soviet archives, are reprinted in Witte, *Vospominaniia*, II, 585–86, n. 11. Other official material about the event will be found in "Dokumenty o khodynskoi katastrofe 1896 g.," *Krasnyi arkhiv* 76 (1936): 31–48, and *Otchet osoboi komissii, obrazovannoi dlia vyiasneniia lichnosti pogibshikh na Khodynskom pole* (Moscow, 1896).

5. Witte forgot what he had written four years earlier, in his handwritten memoirs (p. 17). There, in writing about Khodynka, he said that the Emperor commented favorably on the report, but that a few days later, after the arrival of Grand Duke Sergei Aleksandrovich, the Emperor completely changed his position.

6. Vlasovskii was given an annual pension of 3,000 rubles; survivors of breadwinners killed at Khodynka received annual pensions ranging from 24 to 60 rubles.

Chapter XXVI

1. For Witte's work on the liquor monopoly under Alexander III, *see above*, pp. 187–89. The liquor monopoly was introduced gradually, beginning in 1895. By 1901, it was in operation in all of European Russia, except the northern Caucasus. In 1902 the extension of the liquor monopoly to Siberia and Central Asia began, so that by the time he left office, Witte could feel that the task was virtually completed. To gain support for his efforts he sought to meet Leo Tolstoy, who was well known for his denunciations of the evils of alcohol. The writer saw no reason to meet Witte or to help him promote government-sponsored temperance societies. The struggle against drunkenness, said Tolstoy, required not the promotion of temperance, but the prohibition of the sale of alcohol. Tolstoy to Kuzminskii, November 13–15, 1896, in *Polnoe sobranie sochinenii* (Moscow, 1954), XIX, 205–06.

2. The exhibition was an important opportunity for Witte to demonstrate what the Russian economy had achieved under his leadership.

3. The Finance Committee was an important interagency committee that dealt with such subjects as foreign and domestic loans.

4. Witte was appointed "state secretary of his imperial majesty" on May 14, 1896, the day of the coronation. The position, awarded as a mark of favor, carried no specific duties with it, but a state secretary of his imperial majesty might be asked to carry out delicate missions for the emperor.

5. The text of the conclusions of the meeting of November 23, 1896, and of Witte's letter of November 24 to Shishkin will be found in "Proekt zakhvata Bosfora v 1896 g.," *Krasnyi arkhiv* 47–48 (1931): 64–68. Witte ignores the important role played by the French in preventing the seizure.

Chapter XXVII

1. Witte writes in his handwritten memoirs (pp. 42 verso–43) that he recommended Vorontsov-Dashkov to be Sheremetev's successor and that had his advice been followed much of the unrest in the Caucasus could have been avoided.

2. Witte ignores here the Russifying policies of Golitsyn's predecessor, Sheremetev, policies which, to be sure, were not as provocative as those of Golitsyn.

3. In this material, taken from the dictated memoirs, Witte seems to be walking on

eggshells in an effort to avoid identifying Nicholas II with the ultranationalists. But in his handwritten memoirs (p. 41 verso) he is less restrained, saying: "The ministers before Plehve kept Golitsyn in check to a degree, but when Plehve took office and sensed that the Sovereign supported Prince Golitsyn, he immediately began to support him."

4. This section on Finland is a conflation of material from the dictated and the handwritten memoirs, chiefly from the latter, in which Witte takes off the gloves in dealing with Nicholas II. Also, it should be noted that Witte was writing at a time when Stolypin, with the backing of Nicholas II, was seeking to restrict Finnish autonomy, which had been restored in October 1905, a fact that could only add to Witte's bitterness. It should be noted that by "Finn" Witte means a resident of Finland, not necessarily an ethnic Finn. Generally speaking, most of the Finns who served in the Russian government belonged to the Swedish-speaking upper class of the grand duchy.

5. In the memorandum Bunge declared that it was good that the status of Finland had not been tampered with, thus preventing Finland from becoming "another Poland, a country which is inimical to us and which we may hold onto only by relying on our army." "The Years 1881–1894 in Russia," *Transactions of the American Philosophical Society* 81, pt. 6 (1981): 41. *See also below*, vol. II, chapter IX, n. 15.

6. Kuropatkin, whatever his defects, was not quite as limited as Witte states. *See* Z. A. Zaionchkovskii, *Samoderzhavie i russkaia armiia na rubezhe XIX–XX stoletii* (Moscow, 1973), pp. 67–77.

7. The manifesto was issued in February 1899, several months before Plehve became state secretary for Finnish affairs. But even before he assumed the post he was already exerting influence on decisions concerning Finland.

The manifesto and decree meant, in effect, that the emperor had the authority to impose legislation on Finland against the wishes of the Finnish legislature on matters of concern to the empire as a whole. As Witte indicates, these actions aroused virtually unanimous opposition from the residents of the grand duchy.

8. As will be seen subsequently, both in the text and in the notes, Witte's hatred of Plehve made it impossible for him to be fair to Plehve. No question but that much of what took place in Finland in the years from 1898 to 1904 bore Plehve's stamp, but in all fairness to the man it should be recorded that he did try to deal with what he considered the moderate elements in the grand duchy and that he was aware of the extremely high costs of trying to Russify Finland.

9. Witte's low opinion of Count Muravev was widely shared by people who dealt with him. He was widely regarded as being both sycophantic and untruthful.

10. It is interesting that Witte makes no references to Lambsdorff's reputed homosexuality. His reticence seems motivated by friendship rather than by good taste. One such reference is in A. A. Polovtsov, "Dnevnik," *Krasnyi arkhiv* 3 (1923): 137.

11. Ministers were very rarely invited to lunch with the Emperor after giving their report, but lunched, as Witte notes elsewhere, at the so-called court marshal's table.

12. Alexander III is said to have agreed to Freedericksz's appointment as assistant to Vorontsov-Dashkov only if his duties were restricted to the care of the imperial stables and it was understood that there could be no thought of his ever becoming minister of the imperial court. Grand Duke Nicholas Mikhailovich, "Zapisi N. M. Romanova," *Krasnyi arkhiv* 49 (1931): 105.

13. *See above*, p. 36.

14. Witte's views at this point may have been affected by the public controversy he had with Kuropatkin not long before he wrote these lines concerning the latter's responsibility

for the war with Japan. *See* Ananich and Ganelin, "Opyt kritiki memuarov S. Iu. Vitte," pp. 323–24.

15. M. O. Menshikov wrote for *Novoe vremia*, where he was sharply critical of Witte. Nonetheless, Iuzefovich, an even harsher critic, charged, without offering proof, that at times Menshikov served as Witte's tool. *G[ospodin] Menshikov o gr. S. Iu. Vitte* (n.p., n.d.).

Chapter XXVIII

1. Witte and his family were in Biarritz when World War I broke out. Recalling what he had said to the Kaiser in 1897, he summoned his nine-year-old grandson, Lev Naryshkin, to his side and read him the passages in his memoirs describing the conversation, saying that if his idea had been implemented, war would have been avoided. What the boy thought of all this is not recorded. Vera Naryshikine-Witte, "Souvenirs sur le Comte Witte," *Revue politique et littéraire* 63 (October 1925): 157–59.

2. Apparently, Witte was not fully informed. Nicholas II did not consent to the German occupation of Kiaochow at the time, nor did he waive Russian interest in it, but he did give William II reason to believe that Russia would not object to German men-of-war calling at Kiaochow Bay. Germany would later use this as an opening for getting Russian consent to Germany's leasing of Kiaochow, but that is a different story. *See* Romanov, *Russia in Manchuria*, p. 132. Dillon's *The Eclipse of Russia*, pp. 245–52, provides an account of the Kiaochow episode that is almost identical in detail, but not in phrasing, with that provided by Witte. Dillon says that Witte dictated the account to him so that he, Witte, would be vindicated by history, "should that prove necessary."

3. There was more to Leontev's work in Abyssinia than Witte indicates. For example, he took part in a geographical expedition to that country in 1894–1895. M. V. Rait, "Russkie ekspeditsii v Efiopii v seredine XIX–nachale XX vv. i ikh etnograficheskie materialy," *Trudy Instituta etnografii*, n.s. 34 (Moscow, 1956), pp. 239–41.

4. Ultra-rightist newspapers.

Chapter XXIX

1. *See above*, p. 81.

2. Radolin wrote to von Bülow, secretary of state for foreign affairs, on November 14/26 concerning his conversation with Witte. (This means that the conversation occurred before the November 14th conference.) According to Radolin, Witte said that if Germany took Kiaochow, it would set off a chain of events that might end in a war between Russia and Japan and suggested that if Germany felt compelled to take a port, she should take one south of Shanghai, an act that would provoke neither Russia nor Japan to seek "compensations." Von Bülow then instructed Radolin to explain that Germany's action in Kaiochow was not against Russia's interests. On November 19/December 1, Radolin replied that he had succeeded in convincing Witte and that the finance minister had then suggested that Germany act in a manner calculated to spare Chinese feelings. *Die Grosse Politik der Europäischen Kabinette, 1871–1914* (Berlin, 1924), XIV, pt. 1, 104–05n.

3. The correspondence concerning the bribes will be found in *Krasnyi arkhiv* 2 (1922): 287–93.

4. Witte was sensitive to suggestions that it was he who had persuaded the emperor to take Port Arthur and was thus responsible, in part, for the Boxer Rebellion. In a letter to Sipiagin he remarked with pain that this allegation had reached the ears of Dowager

Empress Marie Fedorovna. *Krasnyi arkhiv* 18 (1926): 35. Also, there were those who argued that by having urged the construction of the Chinese Eastern Railroad, he bore responsibility for the subsequent taking of Port Arthur. He answered this charge by saying that if he had taken some guests to the Aquarium (a *café-chantant*), he would not have been responsible if they had become drunk, gone on to a brothel, and there created a disturbance. "Dnevnik Kuropatkina," *Krasnyi arkhiv* 2 (1922): 91.

    5. Witte was elected an honorary member of the Academy of Sciences in 1893.

    6. According to V. M. Vonliarliarskii, Bezobrazov had been Vorontsov-Dashkov's righthand man in the Holy Brotherhood of 1881. *Moi vospominaniia*, p. 106. Elsewhere, in another context (handwritten memoirs, p. 235), Witte has the following to say:

> The progenitors (*praroditeli*) of that Far Eastern adventure which led to the war with Japan and to general catastrophe were that very honorable Count Vorontsov-Dashkov, who naturally did not understand how it would end, and Grand Duke Alexander Mikhailovich, who is afflicted with an itch for adventure. (Nowadays [1910], he is interested in aviation, but, naturally, he himself will never fly.) The business began with the sending of a commission to the Far East which while pretending to study the Korean economy would focus on military-geographic aspects of that country. The commission would receive concessions from the Korean Emperor and lay the basis for gaining control of the country. It goes without saying that this commission went without some ministers (I, among them) being informed, despite the lack of sympathy for the venture on the part of the war and navy ministers, while the minister of foreign affairs and the minister of the court closed their eyes to what was going on.
>
> Baron Freedericksz, the minister of the court, told me that Bezobrazov, who at the start was Grand Duke Alexander Mikhailovich's righthand man, brought him an Imperial order directing that he be given 200,000 rubles from Imperial (*kabinetskii*) funds to finance the commission's trip. Baron Freedericksz did as he was told, but he wanted to have nothing to do with Bezobrazov and asked the Emperor to spare him from having anything further to do with such gentlemen. Consequently, no serious or sensible person in government service would serve on the commission and it became necessary to recruit outsiders, e.g., former guards officers.

    7. This statement appears to be misleading, for the two men were to help Bezobrazov subsequently. *See below*, p. 308.

Chapter XXX

    1. To round out Witte's account, *see* "K istorii pervoi Gaagskoi Konferentsii 1899 g.," *Krasnyi arkhiv* 50–51 (1932): 64–96.

    2. Witte is apparently referring to Delcassé's visit to St. Petersburg in 1901. Delcassé to Montebello, June 21, 1901, *Documents diplomatiques françaises*, 2nd series, (Paris, 1930), I, 338–39.

    3. Unlike Count Muravev, Count Lambsdorff was well thought of by the St. Petersburg diplomatic corps. In his handwritten memoirs (pp. 9 verso–10) Witte has the following to say about Lambsdorff:

> Since the public may some day read these lines, I feel a moral obligation to say a few words about Count Lambsdorff. He was a thoroughly decent, honorable man. Learned, an indefatigible worker, he spent forty years in the ministry and as the righthand man of a series of ministers of foreign affairs, he knew his trade inside and out. He was no eagle, but he was an efficient man. He enjoyed the respect of all diplomats because when he spoke, he told the truth. He was a refined aristocrat, but he did not like and, in fact, could not endure society. He could not speak easily before large groups, but he could express himself fully and knowledgeably face to face and with small groups. . . .

Witte then goes over ground covered elsewhere about the count's attitude and behavior with respect to the events leading to war. With respect to the count's avoidance of society, one Russian said to Maurice Bompard that Count Lambsdorff was like God: "all know he exists, but no one has ever seen him." *Mon ambassade en Russie, 1902–1908*, p. 2.

Chapter XXXI

1. Although Pobedonostsev had little to do with the reforms of Alexander II, he was sympathetic to them at first and only later came to the view that they had gone too far.
2. Miliutin died a few days after this was written.
3. Interestingly enough, the Montebello fortune came from champagne.
4. Witte has two accounts of Muravev's desire to become minister of interior, the first on pp. 850–54 and the second on pp. 1521–23 of the dictated memoirs. They disagree on only one point: in the earlier account Muravev asks Witte to support his candidacy, while in the later one he asks that he not oppose it. In his account of Goremykin's departure, Witte makes no mention of his memorandum of 1899 to the Emperor, while Goremykin was still minister, in which he attacked the minister of interior's proposal to introduce zemstvos into the western provinces. Somehow the opposition obtained a copy of this memorandum and published it, in 1901, under the title *Samoderzhavie i zemstvo*. The document is of interest both because it is an indirect attack on Goremykin, probably intended to undermine his position, and as a statement of Witte's views on zemstvos: although he did not call for abolition of the zemstvos, he did point out the contradiction between the principle of absolutism and the principle of representative government, as represented by the zemstvos. Also, it should be noted that with Sipiagin, a close friend of the Wittes, in the position of minister of interior, Witte's position became even stronger than it had been.
5. On February 8, 1898, the anniversary of the founding of St. Petersburg University, rowdy students at that institution clashed with the police. Witte in a memorandum (signed also by N. A. Protesov-Bakhmetev, N. V. Muravev, and M. I. Khilkov) characterized the incident as having no political significance. Tkachenko, "Fond S. Iu. Vitte v TsGIA i zadacha kritiki vospominanii S. Iu. Vitte," p. 193. However, police and university officials chose to take a more serious view. To prevent a recurrence of rowdyism at the succeeding anniversary, they employed heavy-handed preventive measures that led to a strike at the university. (Witte was one of the honored guests at the 1899 celebration.) *See* P. S. Vannovskii, *Doklad Vannovskago po povodu studencheskikh bezporiadkov 1899 g.* (St. Petersburg, 1900).
6. It is reported that Rachkovskii, after being involved with revolutionaries as a young man, had been arrested, been persuaded to act as a police agent among revolutionaries, then had worked with the Holy Brotherhood before being placed in charge of the Russian secret police in Paris. "Karera P. O. Rachkovskago," *Byloe* 2 (1918): 79–80.
7. Witte fails to note that his assistant minister V. I. Kovalevskii had an important role in Russia's participation in the exposition. It was he who was in charge of the publication of *Rossiia v kontse XIX veka* (St. Petersburg, 1900), a very useful handbook on Russia, issued on the occasion of the exposition.

Chapter XXXII

1. On occasion when the emperor was in residence in Livadia, his ministers would travel there to report to him.
2. Grand Duke George Aleksandrovich, Heir and Tsesarevich, died early in July 1899. Under ordinary circumstances, the next in line of succession, Grand Duke Michael Alek-

sandrovich, would have been proclaimed heir and tsesarevich as a matter of course, but this time there were complications because of the insistence of the Dowager Empress that Michael be given the title of heir but not that of tsesarevich. *See* letter from Pobedonostsev, whose task it was to prepare the manifesto, to Grand Duke Sergei Aleksandrovich, July 14, 1899, in *Pisma Pobedonostseva k Aleksandru III* (Moscow, 1926), pp. 356–58.

3. In the handwritten memoirs (p. 260), where Witte goes over the same episode, he has this to say:

> I then understood that the legend had inadvertently been started by Baron Freedericksz, a fine but hardly a brilliant man, who probably did not guard his tongue in speaking to the Empress about the meeting. It seems that the legend that I dislike Emperor Nicholas II was thus born. At times when I was not needed the legend was inflated. It could be taken seriously only by persons such as the Emperor and the Empress: they are fine people but one has a sickly will and the other an abnormal psyche. This fact explains my relations with His Majesty and with governmental activity.

4. It was the practice for young male members of the imperial family to receive private instruction from generals, ministers, and professors. Why someone like Witte, with no academic training in economics, should have been considered a more suitable instructor in the subject than a professor is a matter, but not a serious one, for speculation. An abstract of Witte's lectures to the grand duke (*Konspekt lektsii o narodnom i gosudarstvennom khoziaistve*) was published; it went through several editions in the original Russian and was also translated into German.

5. Witte may be hinting at a kind of *ménage à trois*, comprising Grand Duke Andrei Vladimirovich, Mathilda Kshessinskaia (one-time mistress of Nicholas II), and Grand Duke Sergei Mikhailovich.

6. The grand duke had formed an attachment for a woman who was both a commoner and divorcée. Despite Nicholas II's refusal to grant permission for the grand duke to marry her, he did so, in 1912, an act that infuriated the emperor. The grand duke was not restored to grace until after the outbreak of World War I.

7. Grand Duke Paul Aleksandrovich was also restored to grace after the outbreak of the war.

Chapter XXXIII

1. This account of Philippe comes from the dictated memoirs. A more candid account, from the handwritten memoirs, appears below in II, ch. I.

2. The emperor first asked Bogolepov, his minister of education, to grant Philippe an honorary medical degree. After Bogolepov stated that existing restrictions prohibited civilian but not military authorities from granting such a degree, the emperor turned to his war minister. The degree was granted by the Military-Medical Academy and privately bestowed on Philippe by the emperor. Zaionchkovskii, *Samoderzhavie i russkaia armiia na rubezhe XIX–XX stoletii*, pp. 45–46, n. 65. *See also* Bompard, *Mon ambassade en Russie (1903–1908)*, pp. 26–28. Philippe visited Russia on several occasions. His last visit was in 1903. He left under a cloud, possibly because his prediction that the empress would bear a son proved false. Nonetheless, we find Nicholas II writing in his diary on July 20, 1905 about "the sad news of the death of M-r. Philippe!!" *Dnevnik* (Berlin, 1923), p. 212.

3. Sir Charles Hardinge, the British ambassador to Russia, says of the failure of the Ito mission: "This was, I believe, the most crucial moment in the national history of Russia." *Old Diplomacy* (London, 1947), pp. 77–78.

4. In his handwritten memoirs (pp. 32–33) Witte writes:

In remembering Sipiagin, I will note the following incident, which will help illuminate the character of the Emperor.

When Sipiagin died, the first to go into his office was his assistant minister P. N. Durnovo, but he did not touch any of his papers. Then the Emperor had his court commandant, General-Adjutant Hesse, and Durnovo sort out Sipiagin's papers. Run-of-the mill ministerial papers were handed to the offices to which they pertained; official papers of a personal nature were handed over to Hesse, and purely private papers were handed over to Sipiagin's wife.

Alexandra Pavlovna Sipiagina knew that her husband kept a diary and that one part of it pertained to the period when he was director of the Chancellery for Petitions and the second to the period when he was minister. When she asked Durnovo where her husband's diary was, she was told that Hesse had taken it. A few days later she went to thank the Emperor and the Empress for their solicitude toward her. In the course of the conversation the Emperor told her that he had the diary and asked if he could keep it for a time, because he was interested in reading it. She, of course, agreed.

A few months passed without Sipiagina receiving the diary. She then turned to her nephew Count [D. S.] Sheremetev, an aide-de-camp and childhood friend of the Emperor, requesting that he ask one of the officers of the day to remind the Sovereign about her husband's diary. Some time later, at the end of a call on the Empress, the Empress asked her to wait because the Emperor wished to see her. A few minutes later he appeared, handed her a parcel, saying he was returning her late husband's memoirs with thanks, adding that he had found them very interesting.

When she returned home A. P. Sipiagina was astonished to find that only the first part of the diary was in the parcel. So she asked Count S. D. Sheremetev, her brother-in-law [father of Count D. S. Sheremetev], to get an explanation. He went to Hesse, who rather rudely asked why they were making such a fuss over the diary. Count Sheremetev thereupon broke off the conversation.

Some days later, in Moscow, where the Emperor had gone to spend the first few days of Easter, Count Sheremetev found himself seated next to Hesse at a dinner given by the Emperor, but would not speak to Hesse. The court commandant, however, spoke to him, saying that he had told the Emperor everything that had happened to Sipiagin's diary.

After returning to Petersburg, the Emperor summoned Count [S. D.] Sheremetev, and said that he knew he was concerned about the diary. He told Count Sheremetev that one part of the diary had disappeared. The count replied that Durnovo had assured him that he had turned over both parts to Hesse: he believed Durnovo and that, moreover, Hesse had not denied receiving both parts. Then the Emperor suggested that Hesse might have destroyed the second part because he had found something derogatory about himself there and did not want the Emperor to read it.

Count Sheremetev told me that he knew for a fact that it was the Emperor who had destroyed the second part.

I did not read the diary. Sipiagina told me that her husband wrote frankly in it. Sipiagin was a very decent and honorable man and an ultraconservative. During the last six months of his tenure as minister he told me with deep sorrow that one could not rely on the Emperor, that he was treacherous (*kovaren*) and untruthful. He had said the same to his wife.

My information about the incident with the diary comes from Sipiagina and Count [S. D.] Sheremetev.

5. A. A. Polovtsov wrote in his diary on April 15, 1902, that, according to Durnovo, the Emperor offered the position of minister of interior to Plehve within an hour of Sipiagin's death. "Dnevnik," 3 (1923): 138.

6. Witte's differences with Plehve over domestic policies are dealt with below in II, ch. 2.

7. In the handwritten memoirs (p. 218) Witte writes: "Difficult though it is to believe, it is a fact that the Emperor parted with Vannovskii because of his liberalism."

8. There is only a hint here of the intense dislike Witte developed for his former assistant minister. Kokovtsev in turn came to abhor Witte, to whom he referred as "ce batard d'un waguemestre allemand et d'une princesse circassienne." Bernhard von

Bülow, *Memoirs* (Boston, 1932), III, 148. It is a pity that Kokovtsev did not deal in his memoirs with the period when he served under Witte.

9. Illustrative is Emperor William's telegram of December 19, 1897 (NS), in which he wrote: "Please accept my congratulations at the arrival of your squadron at Port Arthur. Russia and Germany at the entrance of the Yellow Sea may be taken as represented by St. George and St. Michael shielding the Holy Cross in the Far East and guarding the Gates to the Continent of Asia. May you be able fully to realize the plans you often unrolled to me; my sympathy and help shall not fail in case of need." *Die Grosse Politik der Europäischen Kabinette 1871–1914*, XIV, pt. 1, 129–30. (The telegram was written in English.) Less than six years later, about the middle of 1903, William II allegedly advised the Japanese to attack Russia and promised "to observe benevolent neutrality" toward Japan if she went to war. Reportedly, the English advised the Japanese that no one could count on William, that he was only trying to muddy the waters. Cambon to Delcassé, January 12, 1905 (NS). France, Ministère des Affaires Étrangères, Archive. *Russie, politique Étrangère, dossier général*, II.

10. Witte does not mention here that it was at Kursk that the Emperor, reacting to recent peasant riots in the area, lectured a group of peasant elders on their responsibility for seeing to it that the peasants for whom they spoke behaved properly and respected private property. He does refer to the suppression of the peasant disturbances elsewhere. *See below*, p. 372.

11. Vonliarliarskii writes that the idea of establishing a separate ministry of the merchant marine was connected with plans for the East Asiatic Industrial Company, one of the enterprises with which Bezobrazov was associated. He adds that Grand Duke Alexis Alexandrovich had a hand in quashing the idea of a separate ministry. *Vospominaniia*, pp. 133–36.

12. Durnovo's death provided Nicholas II with a dead-end position into which to shunt Witte nearly three months later.

13. *See* Savelev, "Nikolai II v sarovskoi pustyni," *Golos minuvshego* 5 (1917): 211–20.

Chapter XXXIV

1. A reference to his unpublished "Vozniknovenie russko-iaponskoi voiny."

2. When Witte speaks of "Bezobrazov and Co.," he has in mind, in addition to Bezobrazov, the following: V. M. Vonliarliarskii, N. G. Matiutin, Admiral A. M. Abaza, and General K. I. Vogak. All were closely associated with Bezobrazov in his Far Eastern ventures; several had access to the emperor.

3. Earlier, Witte has a somewhat different version of this episode. *See above*, p. 140.

4. Of this event Witte writes in "Vozniknovenie russko-iaponskoi voiny," p. 835: "Without the participation of the ministers of foreign affairs, finance, and war, to whom the leading role in the formulation of our Far Eastern policy belonged, and without their being informed, there appeared on July 30, 1903, an Imperial decree establishing the position of viceroy of His Imperial Majesty in the Far East. . . . The decree was prepared by the minister of interior in agreement with State Secretary Bezobrazov."

5. In his handwritten memoirs, p. 11 verso, Witte writes that reportedly the Emperor said "uf" (what a relief) after the matter of Witte's departure from the post of minister of finance had been decided.

Pleske's account, as related by V. N. Kokovtsev, differs from Witte's on some details. *Iz moego proshlago*, I, 8–13. S. M. Propper writes that Witte saw him shortly after being told of his change in status. He reports that Witte, livid with anger, raised his right hand and said: "I swear by those I hold dearest in the world, my wife and my daughter, that I will never forget what he has done to me." *Was nicht in die Zeitung kam*, p. 28. Prince Bernhard von Bülow relates that when Witte saw him in July 1904, he told von Bülow that he showed his anger when the emperor informed him of his new post and that later that day he received a packet containing 400,000 rubles from the emperor, a "consolation prize." *Memoirs*, II, 50.

6. Why did Nicholas II consign Witte to what was a dead-end position? The question has aroused much speculation, has brought forth much evidence, but has not been fully answered. A look at what some who were fairly close to the centers of power said should be useful. General Kuropatkin, in his diary entry for August 19, 1903, explained Witte's fall as being caused by three mines exploding simultaneously under him: the first set by Grand Duke Alexander Mikhailovich, who persuaded the emperor that Witte had amassed too much power and was threatening the prerogatives of the throne; the second set by Bezobrazov, who argued that Witte was undermining Russia's efforts in the Far East; the third set by Plehve (possibly aided by Pobedonostsev and N. V. Muravev, the minister of justice), who sought to convince the emperor that Witte was a "red," that he gave comfort to opposition elements among the Armenians, Finns, Jews, and students. "Dnevnik A. N. Kuropatkina," *Krasnyi arkhiv* 2 (1922): 60.

A. A. Lopukhin, director of the Department of Police under Plehve, claims that the fall of Witte and the fall of Zubatov were connected, both resulting from their efforts, supported by Prince Meshcherskii, to get rid of Plehve, by doing unto Plehve what Plehve had been doing unto Witte. According to Lopukhin, Zubatov hatched a plan whereby he would pretend that in the course of reading opened mail he had come across a letter from one loyal subject to another alleging that Plehve was deceiving the Emperor, and this letter would be given Nicholas by Meshcherskii. Somehow Plehve discovered what was going on. On a Thursday, says Lopukhin, Plehve informed the Emperor what was afoot. The following day Witte was told his fate, and not long afterward Zubatov was let go. Lopukhin claims to have had all this information from Plehve. *Otryvki iz vospominanii*, pp. 73–75. In another context Lopukhin writes that Plehve showed letters from right-wing critics of Witte, linking him with Jewish-Masonic organizations, to the emperor. Ibid., pp. 12–14. *See also below*, II, ch. I, n. 15.

I. V. Gurko, who worked under Plehve, specializing in peasant problems, has a less lurid answer, that Witte's fall came as a result of some of the conflicts that arose from the work of the Special Conference on the Needs of Rural Industry. According to him, Nicholas II decided in the spring of 1903 to remove Witte and told Plehve that it was during a *Te Deum* service that he felt that God was urging him to act. *Features and Figures of the Past*, p. 225. Witte, in his memoirs, places the principal blame for his downfall on Bezobrazov and Plehve.

What we lack is the testimony of the key figure, Nicholas II. We have no documents in which he expresses himself on the subject or documents from those close to him telling us what he said to them. Even if we had such documents there would be room for dispute because people are not always clear about their motives and sometimes rationalize or simply lie. One more piece of evidence should be noted. In March 1903 Witte told General Kuropatkin that the Emperor had been cold toward him ever since the episode concerning the German seizure of Kiaochow, which Witte describes earlier in his memoirs. "Dnevnik A. N. Kuropatkina," *Krasnyi arkhiv* 2 (1922): 38. It may well be that it was then that the Emperor began to distrust Witte.

In any case there is no final answer as to why Nicholas II acted as he did toward Witte in August 1903. But it is reasonable to believe that the emperor believed he had reason to distrust Witte, that he had long chafed at Witte's overbearing behavior, his overwhelming personality, that he had come to see in Witte a threat to his prerogatives, that after listening to the insinuations of many who sought Witte's downfall, he finally steeled himself to do something he found exceedingly difficult, to tell Witte face to face that he was shifting him "to the highest post in the empire," a statement both knew to be nonsense. How difficult it had been for Nicholas can be seen from a statement he made to Kuropatkin shortly after dealing with Witte, that if a horse had had to experience as much mental strain as he had, the horse would have bolted. Ibid., pp. 58–59.

A final word. Witte's loss of office was unlike the experience of other ministers under Nicholas II. Others lost office but retained some measure of good will on the part of the Emperor. One has only to look at the careers of Count Vorontsov-Dashkov, I. L. Goremykin, I. N. Durnovo, and P. N. Durnovo. Toward no former minister did the emperor display as much distrust and hostility as he did toward Witte. If he did not suspect Witte of being a Mason in August 1903, it is certainly the case that he did so by the latter part of 1904. We are speaking here not simply about an allegation that Witte was a Mason, which if true would have meant automatic excommunication from the Orthodox church. We are speaking of the allegation that Witte was connected with Jewish-Masonic organizations, which meant in the eyes of those who made such an accusation that Witte was a partner in a revolutionary conspiracy directed against Russia. Even to suspect that this was true, as Nicholas II did, meant that he saw in Witte a man who might be a traitor. Such a thought, based on fantasy, could not help but poison his attitude toward Witte thereafter.

7. Elsewhere (handwritten memoirs, p. 12 verso), Witte writes, ". . . a day after I was dismissed I went to see Grand Duke Alexander Mikhailovich, who had sent me a telegram congratulating me on my appointment to the 'prestigious' post of chairman of the Committee of Ministers."

8. In his handwritten memoirs, page 10 verso, Witte writes:

> Count Lambsdorff did not have the courage to leave on his own accord, and there were no grounds for dismissing him, because although he expressed his views, he did not fight for them. The Sovereign knew that he would not go beyond expressing his views in the most diplomatic form and did not pay any attention to him. It was even suggested to the Emperor that Count Lambsdorff was simply repeating what I said and would change his views as soon as I was gone. This did not happen, but he limited himself to gentle, and sometimes contradictory, notes addressed to His Majesty.

Appendix A

1. Witte does not do justice here or elsewhere to his work as minister of finance. For an able account of his work, *see* von Laue, *Sergei Witte and the Industrialization of Russia*. *See also* Jürgen Nötzold, *Wirtschaftpolitische Alternativen der Entwicklung in der Ära Witte und Stolypin* (Berlin, 1966).

2. This is the Vonliarliarskii of "Bezobrazov and Co." He calls Witte "Russia's evil genius." *Vospominaniia*, p. 120.

3. Interestingly enough, *Zhupel* (Bogeyman) was the name of a satirical magazine that printed caricatures of Witte. Witte had these and other caricatures of himself collected and pasted up. Tkachenko, "Fond S. Iu. Vitte v TsGIA," p. 194.

In 1898 the emperor was receiving advice from some close to him about the need to limit the influx of foreign capital. At Witte's request a special conference on the subject was held by the emperor on March 17, 1899.

4. Concerning Witte's work on the peasant question, *see below*, Appendix B.

5. Witte may have in mind the emperor's implicit support of the critics of the factory inspectorate. For example, an investigation of the strikes of 1896 was critical of the factory inspectorate and led to an investigation that resulted in the recommendation that the inspectorate be transferred to the jurisdiction of the Ministry of Interior. This step was not taken, but that ministry's authority with respect to labor troubles was increased, with the emperor's approval. Subsequently, the question of how best to deal with labor unrest produced conflict between the Ministry of Finance and the Ministry of Interior.

A lengthy exposition of Witte's views on the history of government labor policy will be found in A. Morskoi, *Zubatovshchina* (Moscow, 1913). ("Morskoi" was the pseudonym of V. I. von Stein, who had worked for a time in the Ministry of Finance and then had become associated with *Istoricheskii vestnik*, whose editor had close ties with Witte.) Von Stein, as "a hired pen," wrote several books at Witte's request. Ananich and Ganelin, "Opyt kritiki memuarov," p. 326. *See also* "Iz istorii borby samoderzhaviia s rabochim dvizheniem," *Krasnyi arkhiv* 68 (1935): 154–57.

6. *See above*, pp. 150–51.

7. Elsewhere (handwritten memoirs, pp. 11 verso–12) Witte puts his thoughts about the Zubatovshchina in slightly different words:

> The rationale of the Zubatovshchina was a naive one, to fight fire with fire. "The way to weaken the hold of the revolutionaries on the workers is to do as the revolutionaries do, by organizing labor organizations, but under the aegis of the police, that will agitate on behalf of the workers and against capitalism. Of what concern are capitalism and industry to us? What we require is tranquility, i.e., the maintenance of a police-state regime that gives the appearance of tranquility." Obviously, the Zubatovs, the Trepovs, and the like could not understand the meaning of anarchistic socialism and thought they could use its means to achieve diametrically different ends.
>
> Grand Duke Sergei Aleksandrovich and Trepov were under Zubatov's thumb. Zubatov's schemes created a big sensation in Moscow. The factory inspectorate fought against the Zubatov organizations, and I supported the inspectorate, but did not accomplish anything of moment, because the Grand Duke did all he could to prevent any interference and Goremykin, then minister of interior, an inconsequential bureaucrat, did all he could to play up to the Grand Duke. When Sipiagin succeeded Goremykin, he reported unfavorably about the Zubatovshchina to the Emperor, but he could not fight what the Grand Duke was doing in Moscow.
>
> After Plehve became minister of interior, I took the occasion of my first meeting with him to point out the danger posed by the Zubatovshchina. He agreed that it was a harmful and stupid experiment and said that he would see the Grand Duke, hoping that would be sufficient. However, it was not long before Zubatov became the chief figure in the Department of Police.

8. Witte is apparently referring to Ivan Alekseevich Anopov, who was appointed head of the educational section in the ministry in 1900. "Anopov" is probably a Russified version of "Anopulo."

9. Elsewhere (handwritten memoirs, pp. 20 verso–21), Witte has the following to say about A. S. Posnikov, who would later become director of the institute:

> I recall that in the 1870s, after I had graduated from Novorossiisk University, I felt the need to become better acquainted with economics and finance. Having difficulty in getting a clear conception of the difference between "value" and "price," I turned to Posnikov, a professor at the university, a gifted man, the author of a well-known work on the village commune, who is to this day [1907] an ardent supporter of the commune. When I asked him to explain the difference between "value" and "price" to me, he replied: "Why should you waste time on such trifles? The entire theory of supply and demand, setting the value of goods and services, is a human invention. It was created by people who find it useful for the exploitation of labor. Only one thing can define price—labor—and prices will become fair only when they fairly represent the labor expended."

A few years later Posnikov had to leave the university. He then became a district marshal of the nobility. When I established the Petersburg Polytechnical Institute, I appointed him professor of political economy and later dean of the economics section. Recently he was appointed director of the institute.

While minister of finance I attended an examination of his students. He was a rigorous examiner. Also, he was a talented professor who taught his subject as far as I could tell by the historical method, thus avoiding theory, probably to avoid slipping into socialism, for he is somewhat tainted by the socialist point of view. In any case he is a worthy man.

Appendix B

1. Witte is referring to Article 165.

2. Nicholas II, in an address to representatives of the assemblies of the nobility, the municipal councils, and the zemstvos on January 17, 1895, declared his intention to adhere firmly to the principle of autocracy (absolutism) and used the phrase "vain and senseless dreams" to characterize the hopes that had been expressed for the extension of representative government. The phrase was to be thrown back at him for years to come.

3. The conference opened in 1897 and closed in 1901. At a session of the conference on November 29, 1897, Witte gave a major speech that tells much about his thinking and about why the landed nobility considered him an enemy. In that speech he dwelt on the inevitable growth of capitalism in Russia and predicted that within fifty years Russia would reach the stage at which Western Europe was then, one in which wealth and power would be in the hands of industrialists and bankers, and went on to say that for the landed nobility salvation lay not in shoring up their existing position but in shifting into industry and banking. It was not the kind of speech his listeners wanted to hear. Iu. B. Solovev, *Samoderzhavie i dvorianstvo v kontse XIX veka* (Leningrad, 1973), pp. 291–93. *See also* G. M. Hamburg, *Politics of the Russian Nobility, 1881–1905* (New Brunswick, N.J., 1984).

4. The Peasants' Bank was established three years earlier (in 1882) than the Nobles' Bank. Either Witte's memory slipped or he had something in mind that he did not make evident.

5. "United nobility," a reference to the Council of the United Nobility, established in May 1906, a body that was ultraconservative and very hostile toward Witte.

6. The text of the letter will be found in Appendix C, below.

7. It will be recalled that Witte and Sipiagin were on friendly terms.

8. The only instance in the memoirs that I have found in which Witte uses "von" in referring to Plehve. The "von" is correct, but it was hardly ever used in the case of Plehve except in official documents and in the publications of the left, which apparently believed that a "von" in a hated official's surname had a good ring to it.

9. Tolstoy to Witte, October 27, 1902, in Tolstoy, *Polnoe sobranie sochinenii*, LXXIII, 314.

Appendix C

1. Cf. what Witte says about zemstvo schools on p. 192.

2. Had Nicholas agreed to the formation of a conference on the peasant question and had he appointed Obolenskii and Solskii to the positions for which Witte recommended them, the conference would then have been directed by two men close to and under the influence of Witte.

Appendix D

1. As noted earlier, Witte assumed that the readers of his memoirs would have at hand a published copy of his "Vozniknovenie russko-iaponskoi voiny" (The Origins of the Russo-Japanese War), which would flesh out the exposition of the origins of the war contained in his memoirs. The reader who commands Russian does have at hand something like that work in the form of *Prolog russko-iaponskoi voiny* (Prologue to the Russo-Japanese War), edited by B. B. Glinskii, which is about two-thirds the length of "Vozniknovenie . . . ," from which it is taken. The reader who does not command Russian is out of luck.

To give readers a sense of what "Vozniknovenie . . ." is like, Appendix D provides a translation of excerpts from the work. The first paragraph is the opening and what follows is from the end of the work.

Editor's Notes to Volume II

Chapter I

1. This "temporary" legislation, most of it in force since the early 1880s, was a means of vitiating many of the reforms of Alexander II.

2. As noted earlier, Witte is "franker" in the handwritten memoirs than in the dictated memoirs, particularly with reference to Nicholas and Alexandra and, in some cases, other members of the imperial family. That greater "frankness" will be noted early on in volume II, when he deals with the "occult" forces at the imperial court. Also to be noted is the fact that in this volume, particularly in the case of his tenure as premier, Witte is dealing with events that bring back the most painful memories, and he is not reticent about expressing the pain he endured.

3. Elsewhere (handwritten memoirs p. 278 verso) Witte writes that if Delcassé had known the facts and had then warned Russia about the possible consequences of her Far Eastern policy, Russia might have acted with greater restraint.

4. This material concerning "occult forces" comes from the handwritten memoirs. Witte deals with the same subject in his dictated memoirs (*see below*, pp. 300–02). The chief differences between the two is that here he says frankly what he thinks of the "Montenegrin princesses."

5. *See above*, pp. 202–03.

6. Although Prince George Leuchtenberg and Princess Anastasia Nikolaevna lived apart most of the time, their marriage was not childless. Concerning the subject of how the "Montenegrin princesses" were able to get money from the Ministry of the Court, Witte has the following aside on pp. 8b–8b verso of the handwritten memoirs:

> When the Emperor Nicholas II came to the throne, the law specified that the budget of the Ministry of the Court be reviewed at a general meeting of the State Council. In practice, however, the budget was agreed to by the ministers of finance and the court, then simply approved by the State Council.
>
> Shortly after Baron Freedericksz became minister of the court, the procedure was changed by Imperial order. Thereafter the minister prepared the budget, subject to Imperial approval, then informed the minister of finance of the total amount, which was to be included in the budget without consideration by the State Council.
>
> To prevent the spread of rumors, this order, which changed the law, was not published at the time, but was quietly incorporated in the next edition of the law code. There had been no such orders since the days of Emperor Paul, and even he would not have undertaken to introduce a falsification in the new edition of the laws. Obviously such an act was committed on the initiative of the minister, not that of the Emperor, but that it was done at all just a few years before the revolution is remarkable.

7. Elsewhere (the dictated memoirs pp. 1691–93) Witte has the explanation coming from Nicholas II.

8. The Emperor first asked the minister of education to grant Philippe an honorary degree. After the minister replied that this could be done only by military authority, the matter was turned over to the war minister, who arranged for the granting of an honorary medical degree by the Military-Medical Academy. P. A. Zaionchkovskii, *Samoderzhavie i russkaia armiia na rubezhe XIX–XX stoletii* (Moscow, 1973), pp. 45–46 n. 65.

9. Grand Duke Nicholas Nikolaevich's affair with S. I. Burenina was of long standing. At one point he sought, in vain, for permission to marry her morganatically. He remained a bachelor until 1907, when he married Princess Anastasia Nikolaevna, following her divorce from Prince George Leuchtenberg. She believed that the Grand Duke was destined for high achievements and that it was fate that arranged for her marriage to the Grand Duke. A. A. Polovtsov, *Dnevnik* (Moscow, 1966), II, 68–72; Schoen to von Bülow, February 11, 1907 (NS). Germany, Auswärtiges Amt, Russland, no. 82, no. 1, vols. 54–55.

10. In his treatment of patients, Philippe used allopathy, spiritualism, prayer, and the laying on of hands, depending on his diagnosis. He achieved a reputation as a healer by selecting suggestible subjects. L. Maniguet, *Contributions à l'étude de l'influence des empiriques sur les malades . . . Philippe* (Lons-le Saunier, 1920), pp. 46–50. Apparently the chief reason for Philippe's access to the Empress was his claim to be able to influence the sex of the fetus, and as we know, the Empress desperately wanted a son. Reputedly she had sought help from others, in vain, to ensure that she would bear a son. It appears that Philippe fell out of favor after the failure of Alexandra to have a son and returned to France in 1903. He was not, however, in complete disgrace because in his diary, on July 20, 1905, Nicholas II wrote of receiving "the sad news of the death of Mr. Philippe." *Dnevnik* (Berlin, 1923), p. 212.

11. Witte was on friendly terms with Antonii, who, as metropolitan of St. Petersburg, was the ranking member of the Russian Orthodox hierarchy.

12. Apparently the Emperor was very pleased with the huge, enthusiastic crowds gathered for the ceremony and therefore felt kindly toward von der Launitz, the local governor, and Plehve for their role on this occasion. A. A. Savelev, "Nikolai II v sarovskoi pustyni," *Golos minuvshego* 5 (1917): 211–20.

13. For more on Prince Meshcherskii, to whom Witte devotes a great deal of attention, *see above*, pp. 134–42.

14. See *above*, pp. 323–24.

15. Zubatov was chief of the Moscow Security Section (*okhrannoe otdelenie*) from 1888 to 1902, then became chief of the Special Section (*osobyi otdel*) of the Department of Police, which was superordinate to the security sections. J. Schneiderman, *Sergei Zubatov and Revolutionary Marxism* (Ithaca, N.Y., 1976), p. 173.

16. A. A. Lopukhin asserts that Witte had met Zubatov even earlier, at the home of Prince Meshcherskii. The prince, according to Lopukhin, had become critical of Plehve and was working with Zubatov to have the minister of interior removed. He claims further that both he and Plehve knew what was going on. *Otryvki iz vospominanii* (Moscow, 1923), pp. 69–71. Lopukhin writes that when he saw Witte in Paris, the latter said in an ambiguous manner that the life of every Russian, including the Emperor, was in the hands of the director of the Department of Police, who could, if he chose, permit a terrorist group to assassinate the sovereign. If this were to happen, said Witte, Grand Duke Michael Aleksandrovich, whose favor he enjoyed, would become the ruler, and it might be that Lopukhin would enjoy his favor, too. Lopukhin writes that these ambiguous remarks only aroused his "disgust." Lopukhin, *Otryvki iz vospominanii*, p. 73. Witte may well have said something of the kind, but without knowing the full context and knowing Lopukhin's

hostility toward Witte, it is difficult to know how seriously to take the story. Even if the idea had occurred to Witte, it seems doubtful that he would express it seriously to a man who could pass on what he had heard to Plehve, who would surely inform the emperor.

17. Witte was apparently relying on hearsay. In fact, Shaevich was exiled to Siberia and released a year later. Schneiderman, *Sergei Zubatov*, p. 337 n. 13.

18. The Military Field Chancellery served the emperor, in his role of supreme commander, as his secretariat. It had been allowed to lapse, but was brought back to life at the beginning of the war with Japan. E. Amburger, *Geschichte der Behördenorganisation Russlands von Peter dem Grossen bis 1917* (Leiden, 1966), pp. 300–01.

19. In this context "white tsar" seems to have a racial connotation, i.e., that the Emperor saw himself as fighting for the white race.

20. Shortly after the beginning of the war, Grand Duke Alexis Aleksandrovich, the head of the navy, said that the war with Japan was a racial one and that it had been inevitable. A. N. Kuropatkin, "Dnevnik," *Krasnyi arkhiv* 5 (1924): 85.

21. Kuropatkin notes that Witte twice told him in January 1904 that he was very concerned about the country's finances and hoped to be summoned back to be minister of finance, while retaining the chairmanship of the Committee of Ministers. Ibid., p. 100, 105. It should be noted that Pleske, the incumbent minister, was terminally ill at this time.

22. This is the most quoted of all passages from Witte's memoirs. It came from page 14 of the handwritten memoirs. A slightly different wording will be found on pages 1753–54 of the dictated memoirs. I could not find this remark in the published portions of Kuropatkin's diary for the period in question, late 1903 to early 1904. I found one entry, for December 11, 1903, that may be of help. In it Kuropatkin wrote that he showed Plehve a dispatch indicating that war might be close and told him that war would not relieve the trouble at home and might, in fact, add to it. He noted that in reply Plehve said that Russia had come victoriously out of all "difficulties." Ibid., p. 93. It might be that in reporting Plehve's reply Kuropatkin might have put it in the words that Witte reports. There are some entries in the diary that indicate that Plehve thought war might help, but there are others in which Plehve is reported as being unhappy over the influence of Bezobrazov, as not wanting war, but being confident that if it came, it would be won without ill effect at home. Ibid., 83–93.

23. In his dictated memoirs, p. 1765, Witte writes:

> On July 30, 1904, there occurred an outstanding event in the history of the Russian Empire, the birth of the Heir Alexis Nikolaevich. He was christened on August 11. I often put Hamlet's question to myself. What fate awaits this boy? I pray to God that through him Russia will find peace and the basis for a new life, enjoying the greatness that is commensurate with the spirit and strength of the great Russian people. May God grant that this be so.

Chapter II

1. Witte's lengthy disquisition on his differences with Plehve is closely linked to Witte's thesis that the minister, having no principles, chose to serve as an instrument of policies that led to war and revolution. Witte's hostility toward Plehve is so great that although what he says about him is largely true, it is by no means all of the truth.

2. Whether or not the facts warranted it, Plehve believed that Witte wanted his post. E. H. Judge, *Plehve* (Syracuse, N.Y., 1983), pp. 147–48.

3. They also disagreed about policy toward the students, Witte taking a kindlier attitude than Plehve toward unruly students.

4. Khlestakov: an addle-brained character in Gogol's *Inspector General*.

5. Although it is true that Plehve supported Bobrikov, he was more willing than the latter to seek out Finns with whom some agreement was possible. Judge, *Plehve*, pp. 112–14.

6. Witte is referring to the liberal movement that began in 1901 with the aim of rallying broad support to compel the emperor to grant civil and political rights. Its leaders were far more aggressive than earlier liberals and far more willing to join hands with revolutionaries in the struggle against the regime.

7. Possibly a reference to what A. N. Kuropatkin spoke of as the emperor's "grandiose dreams of taking Manchuria, Korea, Tibet, Persia, and the Straits." "Dnevnik," *Krasnyi arkhiv* 2 (1922): 31.

8. This was written in 1907, two years before it became public knowledge that Azef, the head of the Socialist Revolutionary terrorist organization, was a police agent. Witte, it seems, learned about Azef while he was premier.

9. The key word is "serious." Others were considered, but whether or not they were considered seriously is questionable. In any case, Nicholas's heart was set on Princess Alice.

10. In her memoirs, Mathilda Kshessinskaia writes that her parting from Nicholas was on an amicable note. *Dancing in Petersburg* (London, 1960), pp. 50–52. However, a credible contemporary report has it that she made the parting difficult. "Dnevnik A. A. Polovtsova," *Krasnyi arkhiv* 67 (1934): 176.

11. It is true that Nicholas did not have a commanding personality, that he sometimes seemed irresolute, but he knew his own mind and could be quite stubborn in holding to a position.

12. The evidence indicates that Alexandra did not give her husband political advice until 1905. How much he listened to her is another question. S. Harcave, *Years of the Golden Cockerel* (New York, 1968), pp. 343–430 *passim*.

13. Witte, like other officials, preferred to use the word *smuta*, which is translated here as "rebellion," rather than the word *revoliutsiia* in referring to the unrest of 1904–1905. The reason for this choice seems to have been that the former had more of a pejorative sense than the latter.

14. A decree confiscating the wealth of the Armenian Orthodox church in Russia was issued on June 12, 1903.

15. It is reported that the first time he saw a Jewish cemetery, Alexander III said: "If they were all lying there, how quiet Russia would be." V. I. Mamontov, *Na gosudarevoi sluzhbe* (Tallin, 1926), pp. 210–11.

16. Witte was in the habit of telling anecdotes like this one to all manner of people, e.g., the journalist H. Bernstein (*Celebrities of Our Times* [Freeport, N.Y., 1968], p. 23); P. G. Kurlov, the police official (*Das Ende des russischen Kaisertums* [Berlin, 1920], p. 95); T. Herzl, the Zionist leader (*The Complete Diaries of Theodore Herzl* [New York, 1960], IV 1531). In Bernstein's account Alexander III refers to Jews as "*zhidy*" (kikes) and says to Witte at the end: "Perhaps you are right." Witte consistently took the position that Jews in Russia must eventually receive civic equality. Apparently because he took this position and because he was friendly with a number of Jewish bankers he had the unjustified reputation, especially among those on the political right, of being a Judeophile. He did not have quite the same reputation among Jews. After talking to Witte in 1903, Herzl wrote: "He has been in the government for thirteen or fourteen years, this friend of the Jews. Why hasn't he done a thing for the Jews?" Herzl, *Diaries*, p. 1533.

17. Witte, who so often accused others of sailing with the wind, occasionally did so

himself. On one occasion he offered help to the anti-Semitic Grand Duke Sergei Aleksandrovich against Jewish merchants in Moscow. L. M. Aizenberg, "Velikii Kniaz Sergei Aleksandrovich, Vitte i Evrei-Moskovskie Kuptsy," *Evreiskaia starina* 13 (1930), 80–99. Perhaps Witte made the offer to gain favor with the grand duke, who was close to the emperor.

18. *Intelligent* (pl. *intelligenty*): Russian for a member of the intelligentsia.

19. This was written in 1907, and Witte was being fairer to Plehve than he was in 1912, in his dictated memoirs (p. 1757), when he asserted that Plehve "organized" pogroms, including the one in Kishinev.

20. In the dictated memoirs (pp. 1763–64) he gives a more sensational account of what was found in the papers of Plehve:

> In the portfolio that Plehve had with him at the time of his assassination, P. N. Durnovo, his assistant minister, found a letter purporting to have come from a secret police agent, a Jewess (from Kissingen, in Germany, I believe), in which she alleged that I apparently had taken an active role in a revolutionary plot to assassinate His Majesty. I learned later that she had been told what to write. This was the product of a plan by which Plehve would receive letters from his agents, in which they would report that I was involved in revolutionary plots, some of them directed against the Emperor. Then, with an innocent face, he would show these to the Emperor, saying that although he felt the allegations to be lies, he considered it his duty to inform His Majesty of the existence of such reports. Obviously, his aim was to turn His Majesty against me.

Witte was apparently basing himself on widespread hearsay, which Lopukhin, who had firsthand knowledge, claims was untrue. What is true, he writes, is that after Plehve's death, among the papers in the late minister's office, were copies of letters from right-wing critics of Witte linking him with "*zhido-masonskie*" (kikish-Masonic) organizations, letters which Plehve had shown to the emperor. Lopukhin, *Otryvki iz vospominanii*, pp. 12–14. It may be that Nicholas's belief that Witte was a Mason came from these letters and may explain some of the mistrust he felt for his former minister of finance. There will be more on the emperor's mistaken belief subsequently. But it should be noted here that the legend of a Jewish-Masonic conspiracy, one in which Witte allegedly played a major role, was to become part of the stock in trade of the extreme right. That legend comes from the same tradition that produced the forged document known as the *The Protocols of Zion*, which was first published under another title in St. Petersburg in 1903. M. Vishniak, "Antisemitism in Tsarist Russia," in *Essays on Antisemitism*, ed. K. S. Pinson (New York, 1942), p. 102 n. 26.

Chapter III

1. Alexandra V. Zhukovskaia, daughter of the famous poet. A. Tarsaidze writes that the grand duke was sent on this trip to prevent his marrying her but that while en route he managed to see her and beget a son, who received the surname of Belevskii and the title of count. *Czars and Presidents* (New York, 1958), pp. 273, 281. *See also* Polovtsov, *Dnevnik*, II, 351.

2. Kuropatkin wrote in his diary that Nicholas gave him the choice of retaining the title of minister of war while serving in Manchuria and that he chose not to retain it, to make things easier for Alekseev and the emperor. "Dnevnik," *Krasnyi arkhiv* 2 (1922): 111.

3. This is from the handwritten memoirs. In the dictated memoirs (pp. 1749–50) Witte tells the same story with a slightly different ending, with Kuropatkin saying: "Sergei Iulevich, you are always joking" and Witte replying: "I am not joking: I am certain that

there will be division of power as soon as you arrive and that will guarantee military failure." Kuropatkin's version of the conversation has no reference to arresting Alekseev, but has Witte counseling him to silence the admiral if he tried to interfere in operations. "Dnevnik," *Krasnyi arkhiv* 5 (1924): 88.

4. Did Witte at this point have an alternative program that he would have implemented had he been given the authority? The evidence is slight, but what there is suggests that Witte still believed that the only government suited to Russia was absolutism, but an absolutism based on the monarch's adherence to the law, a capacity and willingness to know what his subjects think, and the wisdom to rely on competent and honest ministers. Nicholas II obviously did not fit Witte's bill of particulars.

5. *See above*, pp. 182–86.

6. The divorce took place in 1901, before Witte gave this advice.

7. Von Bülow writes that he used the good offices of the banker Mendelssohn-Bartholdy, in whom Witte had confidence, to find out whether Witte would be willing to negotiate directly with him. *Memoirs*, (Boston: 1932), II, 47.

8. *See above*, pp. 267–79.

9. What did von Bülow think of Witte? Writing after the appearance of Witte's memoirs, which he presumably read, he stated:

> Though Witte may not have been born to be a constitutional Chancellor, he at least saw in time that autocracy was no longer possible in Russia, above all with a feeble Tsar like Nicholas II. His manners were very bad indeed. He was always inclined to brutality, often rustic, but never really malicious. His love for his Matilde had something really simple and touching in it.

Ibid., III, 146.

10. Von Bülow again. He writes that while riding in the Tiergarten in Berlin he passed Witte who called out to him: "Good news: Plehve has just been murdered." Ibid., II, 54. An almost savage note is found in a letter from Witte to Kuropatkin, by now in Manchuria: "What happened to Mr. von Plehve was what had to happen, and it is remarkable that no tears have been shed over this crime." *Krasnyi arkhiv* 19 (1926), 71. Aerenthal, the Austro-Hungarian ambassador to St. Petersburg, reported that his talks with high Russian officials left him with the impression that they felt no shock over the killing of Plehve and like Witte felt that it was something that had had to happen. Aerenthal to Goluchowski, July 24/August 6, 1904, in "The Coming Storm" ed. by A. Ascher, *Survey* (October 1964): 154–66.

Chapter IV

1. Sochi: a resort town on the Black Sea with a subtropical climate.

2. V. I. Gurko claims that Witte, remote from the scene of action though he was, intrigued to have P. N. Durnovo chosen to succeed Plehve. *Features and Figures of the Past* (Stanford, Calif., 1939), p. 293. He was in a position to know because he was close to Durnovo, but one would like to know more before accepting what he says as fact. Unfortunately, I have found no corroboration.

3. Marie Fedorovna, the dowager empress, had a hand in persuading her son to appoint the prince. "Dnevnik Kn. Ekateriny Alekseevny Sviatopolk-Mirskoi za 1904–1905 gg.," *Istoricheskie zapiski* 77 (1965): 240. (Hereafter referred to as Sv.-Mirskaia, *Dnevnik*.)

4. A reference to the demonstration by workers and students at Kazan Square on March 4, 1901, held to protest the sending of some students into the army because of their role in disturbances. The demonstrators were dealt with in a brutal fashion.

5. A reference to the complaint that Plehve, even more so than his predecessors, dealt summarily with "public men" (*obshchestvennye deiateli*), i.e., elected leaders of zemstvos and municipal dumas, who claimed to speak for "society" (*obshchestvo*). Witte follows contemporary usage in employing the word "society" to mean the educated class, which had increasingly become alienated from the regime and was seeking, at the very least, some form of representative government and basic civil rights. Prince Sviatopolk-Mirskii mistakenly believed that if society could be satisfied the country would quiet down.

6. Witte thought kindly of the prince but did not believe that his efforts would succeed. There were those who thought that Witte was only professing to be on the prince's side and that in fact he wanted to trip him up, but no proof is offered. Be that as it may be, the prince later came to think of Witte as an ill-wisher.

7. A reference to what is usually called the first congress of zemstvo and municipal leaders, held in St. Petersburg early in November, which adopted a more liberal program than the minister of interior had expected.

8. In the original Russian, *politikany*, a pejorative term. Given the fact that Witte respected these men, it is not clear why he used the term.

9. The document referred to is apparently a kind of "white paper," using documentary material, that gave Witte's version of the recent course of events in the Far East, a document intended for very limited circulation. B. V. Ananich and R. Sh. Ganelin, "Opyt kritiki memuarov S. Iu. Vitte," *Voprosy istoriografii i istochnikovedeniia istorii SSSR: Sbornik statei* (Moscow, 1963), p. 309. Lopukhin claims that the search took place shortly before the prince's appointment and further that he was not reprimanded. More important is his statement that Admiral Abaza had called on him, at the behest of the emperor, to locate the document referred to, in which allegedly the emperor had been criticized, and to compare statements in it with those that had just appeared in an article entitled "The Tsar," published in the *Quarterly Review*. Lopukhin, *Otryvki iz vospominanii*, pp. 66–67. The article, which appeared in the July 1904 issue of the magazine, caused quite a stir, so much so that the German Foreign Office ordered thirty copies of it. Metternich to von Bülow, August 5, 1904 (NS), Germany, Auswärtiges Amt, Russland, no. 1, vols. 51–52.

"The Tsar" was published as an anonymous article allegedly by "a Russian official of high rank." In the name of defending a strong monarchy, the author sharply attacked the person and policies of Nicholas II, in language that could only deeply offend the emperor, who obviously suspected the anonymous official was Witte. In fact the author was Joseph Dillon (*Eclipse of Russia* [New York, 1918], p. 115). Dillon, who had only recently begun a close association with Witte, does not say whether or not Witte had any hand in preparing the article or even had any knowledge of its authorship. That Dillon was the author was not discovered. What is important here is that the emperor's suspicions of Witte in these two cases, coupled with the belief that the man was a Mason, added to earlier distrust of and annoyance with the former minister of finance made it most unlikely that he would ever rely on Witte again. Yet there was the impression that Witte was waiting to be summoned to assume an important role once more, an impression that he fostered and that was widely accepted because he was clearly the ablest man in the government.

10. *See above*, p. 107.

11. Lopukhin denies that Obolenskii had any hand in the preparation of the report, which, he asserts, was a collective work. Lopukhin, *Otryvki iz vospominanii*, p. 44. True, it was a collective work, but Kryzhanovskii, who did most of the work, believes that it was at Obolenskii's behest that he was chosen for the assignment. S. E. Kryzhanovskii, *Vospominaniia* (Berlin, n.d.), p. 16.

786   EDITOR'S NOTES ▪ VOLUME II

A word about Obolenskii is in order here. Although Witte did not think highly of the prince, and he was not alone in this, he had been associated with him for some time and would continue to be so for some time to come. At this time the prince was sympathetic to the liberal elements in society and seems to have provided Witte with information about the state of mind of society and may well have had a hand in the development of Witte's views about what needed to be done to placate society.

12. Dobchinskii: a character in Gogol's *Inspector General*.

13. Lopukhin, who took part in the preparation of the report, claims that Sviatopolk-Mirskii kept Witte *au courant*. Lopukhin, *Otryvki iz vospominanii*, p. 46.

14. When the prince called the attention of Nicholas II to the fact that Witte's name was not on the list of those invited to attend, the emperor replied: "He is a Free Mason and [besides] will say nothing definite." D. Shipov, *Vospominaniia i dumy o perezhitom* (Moscow, 1918), p. 287.

15. Witte's account of the events leading to the decree of December 12, 1904, is fuzzy in some places, inaccurate in others, perhaps the result of faulty memory, perhaps because he would just as soon not remember what he did or did not do.

16. It would have been useful if Witte had speculated about the influences that led the emperor to make such concessions.

17. Because of the absence of minutes of the conference, it is necessary to rely on accounts by participants or those to whom they spoke to supplement what Witte had to say. Chief among these are the diary of Princess Sviatopolk-Mirskaia and the memoirs of D. Shipov, who spoke to Prince Sviatopolk-Mirskii in 1906 about these days and, with his permission, made notes about the conversation. These two accounts are in close agreement, but occasionally differ on detail. V. N. Kokovtsev, a participant, is of no help. He contents himself with saying he "did not know a thing about the preparation of the decree of December 12, 1904." *Iz moego proshlago* (Paris, 1933), I, 49. The published diary of Nicholas II is useful here only on the matter of chronology.

Witte is wrong on his dates. The emperor writes in his diary of the first meeting being held on December 2, the next on the morning of the 8th and the third and last on the afternoon of the 8th. *Dnevnik*, pp. 184–86. It is probably the case that the session Witte has as occurring on the day following the first session took place on the morning of the 8th. Then there is the question of who opposed representative institutions. According to Princess Sviatopolk-Mirskaia, both Witte and Kokovtsev argued that autocracy and representative government were incompatible. Sv.-Mirskaia, *Dnevnik*, p. 260.

In this connection it should be noted that as early as November 16, Prince Sviatopolk-Mirskii was telling his wife that Witte was unconsciously playing a double game, urging him to stick to his guns about the admission of elected representatives to the legislative process and then saying that he would oppose such a reform if he could not be certain that the next ruler would be a wise person. She also quotes her husband as saying that one had to be cautious with Witte because he would not keep confidences. Ibid., p. 255. The last may be a reference to Witte's garrulity.

18. According to the princess, on the last day of the conference both Witte and Kokovtsev argued for appointment, rather than election, of "experienced public men" to the State Council. She writes that her husband felt that Witte had shifted his position from opposing the addition of public men to the State Council to adding some, by appointment, in an effort to gain power. Many believed that Witte was scheming to replace the minister of interior. If he were, seeing to it that the prince's proposal for the addition of elected members to the State Council failed would have have helped him by thus assuring the

prince's resignation. The allegation is plausible, yet it may be that Witte was simply expressing his inner conflict, to which he was to refer later, his heart telling him that absolutism "was the only form of government suitable to Russia," as he put it to the British ambassador (Hardinge to Marquess of Lansdowne, January 4, 1905 [NS], United Kingdom, Public Record Office, Foreign Office, 65/1698), and his mind telling him that sooner or later Russia would have some form of representative government, whether it was suitable or not. Witte, who was free in hurling the epithet "intriguer" at others, was himself an intriguer of no small caliber and certainly impressed people as being one. Yet the record shows that he was a man of strong convictions, that he stood up for what he believed at considerable cost to his career. In this case it may indeed be that what we are witnessing is ambivalence, not calculation. Chances are that Witte would rather have returned to the post of minister of finance than become minister of interior.

19. On December 11 Witte informed Prince Sviatopolk-Mirskii that he was being summoned to Tsarskoe Selo, and on the following day he visited the prince and his wife to relate what had happened there. The princess's account agrees with Witte's but includes some details not in the account: Witte told them the grand duke had wanted to know of what use the whole business [point three] was and that Witte had replied that it was of no use except, so Prince Sviatopolk-Mirskii believed, to calm society. *Dnevnik*, pp. 264–65.

20. In his dictated memoirs (p. 1783), Witte makes no mention of the emperor's having said that he had changed the wording, but quotes him as follows: "I approve of this decree except for one point about which I have doubts." This was point number three.

21. *Zemskie sobory* (assemblies of the land): advisory councils established in the sixteenth century to which tsars invited representatives of various classes. They met at irregular intervals at the pleasure of the tsars until the seventeenth century, when the practice of summoning these bodies was ended. Moderate liberals who were under Slavophile influence favored revival of the institution as a way of giving Russia a representative institution that was authentically Russian. Witte himself had some Slavophile leanings, but he obviously did not favor the revival of the *zemskii sobor* as an institution. But he did share, as will be seen, some Slavophile views: that the ruler should be a benevolent sovereign who listened to his people and that the Russian Orthodox church should be freed of its bondage to the state. Lopukhin relates that early in January 1905 Witte told him that he favored summoning a *zemskii sobor* to advise the Emperor about continuing the war and that Witte hoped to be asked to preside over such a body if it were summoned. Lopukhin, *Otryvki iz vospominanii*, pp. 56–57. If Lopukhin is reporting accurately, his account would suggest that Witte saw such an assembly as an *ad hoc* body rather than as the beginning of a permanent institution.

22. Elsewhere, in the dictated memoirs (p. 1797), he speaks of Muravev phoning him to ask if he would be at the meeting.

23. A slip of memory. Witte was acquainted with one of the group—Hessen.

24. Prince Sviatopolk-Mirskii was probably meeting with his colleagues at this time to discuss the procedures to be followed the next day.

25. The official figure was 96 killed and 333 wounded, of whom 34 later died. These figures do not include the dead and wounded removed from the scene by friends and relatives. S. Harcave, *First Blood* (New York, 1964), p. 193.

26. Actually, the prince had spoken as early as November 22 about being released and had even suggested Witte as his replacement. To this the emperor replied that he couldn't use a man like Witte, in whom he had no confidence and whom he suspected of being a Mason. Then, on December 13, when the prince insisted on being released, the emperor

asked him to stay on a month longer because he had no replacement in mind. Sv.-Mirskaia, *Dnevnik*, pp. 258–59, 265.

27. Witte is anticipating. Trepov may have acquired influence in the Ministry of Interior, but he was not appointed assistant minister until May.

28. For several months Prince Orlov would take the emperor and empress for drives in his automobile. The emperor enjoyed the experience so much that he then acquired several automobiles of his own. A. A. Mosolov, *At the Court of the Last Tsar* (London, 1935), pp. 250–51.

29. Witte neglects to mention that on January 17 he was appointed chairman of a conference to consider means of coordinating the activities of the government. On February 9 he submitted a proposal in this connection to merge the Committee of Ministers and the Council of Ministers under the name of the latter. Nothing came of it. *Krizis samoderzhaviia v Rossii, 1895–1917* (Leningrad, 1984), pp. 179–80, N. G. Koroleva, *Pervaia rossiiskaia revoliutsiia i tsarizm* (Moscow, 1982), pp. 29–32.

30. Being asked to implement the decree was something of a triumph for Witte. The British ambassador wrote home: "The success which he [Witte] has achieved in once more imposing his services on the Emperor, to whom, it is known, that he is personally distasteful, is an interesting example of his energy and ability, but it is not probable that his services will be long retained when order and calm have once more been restored." Hardinge to Marquess of Lansdowne, January 4, 1905 (NS), United Kingdom, Public Record Office, Foreign Office: 65/1698.

31. Russia, Komitet Ministrov, *Zhurnaly Komiteta ministrov po ispolnenii ukaza 12 dekabria 1904 g.* (St. Petersburg, 1908).

32. Iuzefovich was considered "a good patriot" by the emperor. *See above*, p. 75.

33. This point called for a review of laws concerning Old Believers and members of various sects considered heterodox or unorthodox. It also called for freeing "religious life from all limitations not prescribed by law." Harcave, *First Blood*, p. 284. Old Believers, also known as Schismatics (*Raskolniki*), were members of a group which did not accept changes in the ritual enacted by the Russian Orthodox church in the late seventeenth century. Numbering as many as 15 million, they in practice constituted a separate church, but the law considered them members of the established faith and hence in violation of the law which prohibited departure from that faith.

34. The decree gave Old Believers the legal status previously denied them. Also, it eased or removed restrictions on many religious groups outside the established church.

35. It is fair to say that the question of church reform stirred Witte more deeply than any of the other questions considered in connection with the decree of December 12, 1904, to the degree that he was willing to engage in a very bitter dispute that aroused considerable attention abroad as well as in Russia. Pobedonostev's reaction to the proposal for church reform was very bitter indeed. In his comments to the Emperor he stated that the speeches on the subject in the Committee of Ministers, with the exception of those of General Lobko, were "senseless." "Iz pisem K. P. Pobedonostseva k Nikolaiu II (1898–1905)," *Religii mira: Istoriia i sovremennost. Ezhegodnik, 1983* (Moscow, 1983), p. 189.

36. Until 1721 the Russian Orthodox church was technically a self-governing body, directed by a patriarch elected by the upper hierarchy. From time to time patriarchs held councils to consider major questions before the church. The last such council was held in 1682, and the last patriarch died in 1700. After delaying the election of a new patriarch for twenty-one years, Peter the Great abolished the office and entrusted the governance of the church to the Holy Synod, a body of prelates supervised by an over-procurator, a layman

appointed by and answerable to the emperor. The power of the over-procurator and the lay officials subordinate to him reached such a point under Pobedonostsev that the church could properly speaking be called an arm of the state.

37. At issue was whether Little Russian (Ukrainian) was a distinct language or merely a dialect and whether Ukrainians constituted a distinct nationality or merely a subgroup, and an inferior one at that, of the Russian nationality. The specific question was that of the right to publish works in Little Russian. In 1863 the Academy of Sciences approved the distribution of a Ukrainian translation of the Gospels, but the Polish revolt of that year, in which Poles found some support among Ukrainians, resulted in publication being held up, for four decades, as it turned out. In 1904, permission to publish the translation of the Gospels was once more requested. Prince Sviatopolk-Mirskii and the Academy of Sciences were in favor, but the Holy Synod, which had the power in this case to prohibit publication, was opposed. Witte took a hand in the matter and somehow was able to circumvent the Holy Synod. M. H. Voskobiynyk, "The Nationalities Question in Russia, 1905-1907" (Ph.D. diss., University of Pennsylvania, 1972), pp. 396, 397 n.

38. The termination of the work of the Committee of Ministers on the December 12 decree came at about the same time as the closing of the Special Conference on the Needs of Rural Industry, of which Witte had been chairman, i.e., the end of March. Some two weeks later the conference was brought to an end, leaving Witte with little to do but busy himself with the trivial work of the Committee of Ministers.

39. Witte does not mention that on January 14 he and Kokovtsev were received by the emperor to discuss the labor question. Five days later, the day on which the emperor received a workers' delegation, Witte, this time accompanied by Gerbel, was received once more by the emperor. Nicholas II, *Dnevnik*, p. 125.

40. A slip of memory. The Kokovtsev commission was already in existence when the Shidlovskii commission was formed.

41. The tone of the manifesto, which took to task those who were taking part in disorders, was clearly not in the same vein as the decree and the rescript, which promised reform. The manifesto was an expression of Nicholas II's anguish over the assassination, two weeks earlier, of Grand Duke Sergei Aleksandrovich. In his dictated memoirs, p. 1841, Witte takes note of the assassination, stating, "It was carried out on orders of the central revolutionary-anarchist committee and with the active participation of Azef, an agent of the secret police. . . . As is now evident, it was Azef, while serving as an agent of the secret police in the days of Plehve, who organized the assassination of Plehve."

42. This was written in 1907. Some five years later, in his dictated memoirs (p. 1845), Witte said: "As was evident from the editing, the style, as well as the thought, and, as was later confirmed, it [the manifesto] was prepared by C. P. Pobedonostsev, whose reactionary ideas were at variance with the spirit of the decree of December 12 and with all the measures taken to carry out the decree." If Gurko (*Features and Figures of the Past*, pp. 369-70) is correct, then Witte's earlier judgment is correct. Gurko writes that Iuzefovich, and others, working from an "outline prepared by the Tsar himself," prepared the text of the manifesto and that Pobedonostsev approved it.

43. According to the emperor's published diary, the group met before and after lunch on February 3, then before lunch on February 11, and then again on February 18, with no break for lunch indicated. *Dnevnik*, pp. 197, 199. Witte is the chief primary source we have for these meetings, making it almost impossible to check what he had to say. However, against his assertion that he said nothing (which could mean "practically nothing"), we have what appears to be a hearsay statement. In his diary entry for February 11, 1905,

Count A. A. Bobrinskii wrote that at a meeting (probably a reference to the meeting of February 9), General Lobko, Witte, and Grand Duke Vladimir Aleksandrovich spoke against the idea of an elected, representative body. "Dnevnik A. A. Bobrinskogo," *Krasnyi arkhiv* 26 (1928): 131.

44. This was written in 1907. In his dictated memoirs (pp. 1846–47), Witte presents a slightly different account of the meetings of the discussions:

> Even before the meeting many participants wanted to know what to make of it all. In reply to our questions His Majesty assured us that he continued to adhere to the views that had guided him in issuing the decree of December 12 and that he saw no conflict between the manifesto concerning dissent and disorder and the decree to the Senate concerning the right to petition on the one hand and the decree of December 12 on the other. But the fact was that the manifesto and the December 12 decree were clearly in conflict.
>
> At the meeting all the ministers expressed the view that sedition had reached such a point that it was necessary to take steps to restore tranquility in Russia and that the only possible step toward that end was the establishment of a representative body, even if it had no more than consultative authority. The Emperor readily agreed to a rescript to Bulygin in this sense.

45. It was common to refer to the proposed body as the Bulygin duma.

Chapter V

1. On May 7 (NS), Witte told Cecil Spring-Rice, secretary in the British embassy in St. Petersburg, that Russia had no hope of winning the war and that it was in the interest of all other European powers, Germany excepted, to have the war over with. Spring-Rice to Marquess of Lansdowne, May 7, 1905 (NS), United Kingdom, Public Record Office, Foreign Office, 65/1700.

2. *See above*, p. 310.

3. The ships belonged to Chile, not Argentina. Abaza's disguise did not work. A Parisian newspaper printed two photographs of him, one in uniform and bearded, the other of him in mufti and clean-shaven, and gave the address of the hotel at which he was staying. Kokovtsev, *Iz moego proshlago*, I, 66–68.

4. No successor to the grand duke was appointed, making it possible to reestablish the office of minister of the navy, to which Admiral Birilev was appointed. Amburger, *Geschichte der Behördensorganisation Russlands*, p. 353.

5. A packet of documents about the negotiations is in the Bakhmeteff Archive.

6. Izvolskii writes that the emperor thought of him only after Nelidov and Muravev had refused, but that Lambsdorff preferred Witte for the post. *The Memoirs of Alexander Izvolsky* (London, 1920), pp. 22–23.

7. With good reason Witte considered Muravev one of his enemies.

8. Civilian ministers wore their dress uniforms when reporting to the emperor. One of the most familiar pictures of Witte shows him in uniform.

9. In the dictated memoirs (pp. 1878–79) Witte has it that Lambsdorff did think of suggesting Obolenskii, but that the prince had begged off.

10. Shortly after being appointed chief plenipotentiary, Witte said to Kokovtsev: "When a sewer has to be cleaned, they send Witte, but as soon as work of a cleaner and easier kind appears, plenty of candidates will always be available." *Iz moego proshlago*, I, 73.

11. Witte does not say so, but he implies that Admiral Birilev was present at his conversation with the grand duke.

12. Witte is referring to a polemic with Kuropatkin that took place several years after the war, in the course of which he published a number of responses to General Kuropat-

kin's contention that given the resources and the time he could have defeated the Japanese on land. Ananich and Ganelin, "Opyt kritiki memuarov S. Iu. Vitte," pp. 323–24.

13. Kokovtsev, of course, does not agree. Kokovtsev, *Iz moego proshlago*, I, 59–62. For more on Witte's assessment of Russia's finances at the beginning of the war, *see below*, pp. 318–19.

14. Elsewhere Witte criticizes Kokovtsev for increasing liquor prices to get more revenues. As should be evident by now, Witte loses no opportunity to kick Kokovtsev in the pants. How much of this animus is based on considered judgment, how much on personal dislike, is not clear. Kokovtsev claims that he and Witte were on fairly good terms until the latter's return from America, when Witte turned against him. Why? Kokovtsev offers a number of suggestions, none of them flattering to Witte. *Iz moego proshlago*, I, 73–83 *passim*.

15. Rosen had a higher opinion of Witte than Witte had of him. He writes that Witte was "the greatest man Russia had produced in a century." *Forty Years of Diplomacy* (New York, 1922), I, p. 62.

16. At Witte's request, Korostovets kept a diary, which was published after the revolution of 1917 under the title "Mirnye peregovory v Portsmute v 1905 godu," in *Byloe* 1 (1918): 177–220; 2 (1918): 11–46; 3 (1918): 55–85; 12 (1918): 154–82. Other editions were subsequently published.

17. For Witte's assessment of Shipov, *see above*, pp. 166–67.

18. Evidently a reference to Japanese subsidies given to some opposition groups.

19. Russia's preoccupation with the Far East contributed to French rapprochement with England, but it was not the only factor.

20. Not so. On July 6, the day Witte left St. Petersburg, Nicholas received a message from William proposing that they meet. Nicholas suggested that they meet at Björkö. *Dnevnik*, p. 208.

21. A reference to Prince A. M. Gorchakov, the last person to hold the post of chancellor. If S. M. Propper is to be believed, Witte's head was so turned when he received the title of count on his return to Russia that he talked of some day becoming chancellor. *Was nicht in die Zeitung Kam* (Frankfurt am Main, 1929), p. 265.

22. Son of A. S. Suvorin, publisher of the influential *Novoe vremia*, with whom Witte was on fairly close terms and about whom he has much to say.

23. Not long before their departure, Dillon had gone to London at Witte's request to get Count Hayashi's help in having Marquis Ito replace Komura and in having Ito receive authority to negotiate something like an alliance as well as to negotiate the terms of peace. Dillon had failed on both counts and had so reported to Witte. *Eclipse of Russia*, pp. 301–02.

24. Apparently a reference to D. M. Wallace's *Russia*, which was first published in 1877 and has come to be regarded by some as a classic.

25. In May 1896, following an interview with Witte, Wallace described him as "having something of the overgrown boy about him. His features are rough hewn with an expression of determination and energy. In voice and manner he is rough and unsympathetic, and he has none of the *bonhomie* and suavity which are so common in Russia." Wallace Papers, Box 3, Cambridge University.

26. Since Witte chose not to deal with diplomatic details, the subsequent notes will deal primarily with what he has to say, rather than with what he could have chosen to say.

27. Korostovets writes that Witte quickly became familiar with details about which he had known little, that he was very effective in influencing American public opinion, and that, all in all, he did an excellent job. "Mirnye peregovory . . ." *Byloe* 1 (29) (1918): 179–80. Rosen provides an interesting sidelight. After the conference had been in progress for

some time, an American reporter told him that his colleagues had shifted from being 90 percent pro-Japanese to being 90 percent pro-Russian. When asked if the shift had anything to do with the discovery that the Russians were white, the reporter replied: "Well, that's about the long and short of it." *Forty Years of Diplomacy*, I, 169. A different view is provided by an American scholar who concluded from a study of the American press that, while Witte himself was favorably regarded, there was no marked shift in public opinion from a pro-Japanese attitude. He attributes the impression that there had been a shift largely to what is now called hype on the part of Dillon and Korostovets. "American Public Opinion and the Portsmouth Peace Conference," *American Historical Review* 53 (1948): 439–64.

Another sidelight is provided by the French *chargé d'affaires*, who wrote to Rouvier on August 8, 1905 (NS): "In a country where physical development is universally admired, the height and the broad shoulders of Witte have won him not only the sympathies of the crowd but also, it appears, the sympathy of the president, who is said to have said after their first meeting at Oyster Bay: 'He is a splendid fellow.'" France, Ministère des Affaires Étrangères, *Documents diplomatiques français*, series 2, (Paris, 1937) VII, 384.

28. The relevant words of the toast: "I drink to the welfare and prosperity of the sovereigns and peoples of the two great nations whose representatives have met one another on this ship." Rosen, *Forty Years of Diplomacy*, I, 265.

29. Apparently Witte found the voyage to America less pleasant than he indicates and decided to go by land to Portsmouth, thus causing a slight diplomatic flurry. The American government decided not to announce the change of plans and arranged for him to disembark quietly at Newport, where he would entrain for the rest of the trip. Once in Portsmouth he engaged in the face-saving expedient of boarding the *Mayflower* when it reached Portsmouth and then landing with his colleagues. Korostovets, "Mirnye peregovory . . ." *Byloe* 1 (29) (1918): 210; *The New York Times*, August 7, 1905, pp. 1–2.

30. In his text he sometimes refers to the institution as Boston University, an error that would not be forgiven in Cambridge.

31. Omitted from Curtin's published memoirs was a section from his manuscript (pp. 696–712) that according to the editors dealt with his conversations with Witte at Portsmouth, but that was not considered by his widow to be an "organic part of the Memoirs."

Jeremiah Curtin, *Memoirs* (Madison, Wisc., 1940). On examination this section turns out to be a review of Russo-Chinese and Russo-Japanese relations that may have been intended for publication as an article. Possibly it was based on notes taken by Curtin concerning what Witte told him. The manuscript is in the archives of the State Historical Society of Wisconsin.

32. Also in the delegation were Adolph Lewisohn, the philanthropist, and Adolph Kraus, president of B'nai Brith. Baron Rosen was present at the meeting. Straus, who was doing double duty at Portsmouth by acting as unofficial observer for President Roosevelt, states that the group was there at Witte's invitation. Oscar S. Straus, *Under Four Administrations* (Boston, 1922), pp. 189–90. This meeting was followed by another one in New York on August 30/September 12. *The New York Times*, September 13, 1905, p. 3.

33. Agreement had been reached on all issues except Sakhalin and indemnity. The Japanese insisted on receiving the southern half of the island and the payment by Russia of a large indemnity. On instructions from the emperor, Witte agreed to the former but not to the latter. At that point negotiations were suspended until August 16/29, to permit Baron Komura to receive instructions from Tokyo. On August 15/28, Count Lambsdorff telegraphed instructions from the emperor that when talks were resumed the following day

Witte was to break off negotiations rather than wait for Japan's "gracious concessions." The following morning Witte telegraphed Lambsdorff that it would be an error to end negotiations. That same morning Komura received instructions to agree to Witte's conditions.

R. A. Esthus asserts that Witte violated the emperor's orders "to end the parley tomorrow in any event." "Nicholas II and the Russo-Japanese War," *The Russian Review* 40 (1981): 410.

34. Both in his handwritten memoirs, pp. 99 verso–100, and in his dictated memoirs, pp. 1925–26, Witte writes as if Komura's agreement and the signing of the treaty occurred on the same day, and that is the way the story appears in both the Yarmolinsky and Hessen recensions. The facts are otherwise. Komura gave his agreement on August 16/29. Shortly thereafter a bulletin was posted at the Hotel Wentworth about this fact, resulting in a warm response from the crowd gathered to hear the latest news. In the late afternoon bells were rung and whistles blown on orders of the mayor. Meanwhile, at 3 p.m., the conference was reconvened, at which time it was decided to adjourn until a treaty was ready for signature. On August 23/September 5, 1905, the treaty was signed, and then the festive events that Witte described took place. I have corrected Witte's account by the insertion of bracketed material. Korostovets, "Mirnye peregovory . . ." *Byloe* 2 (30) (1918): 74–76; *The New York Times*, August 30, 1905, p. 1. What explains Witte's telescoping of events that occurred a week apart? Perhaps it was because he had virtually nothing to do during the period, when the work of drafting the treaty for his side fell to his associates. Perhaps, too, memory played him a trick by letting him remember a sequence of events that was more dramatic than what really happened.

35. The chief terms of the treaty were Russian recognition of Japan's paramount interest in Korea; simultaneous evacuation of Manchuria by the Russians and the Japanese, except for the leased Kwantung territory, which would be transferred to Japan; cession of the southern branch of the Chinese Eastern Railroad to Japan; cession to Japan of the southern half of Sakhalin Island; the granting of fishing rights to Japan along the Russian shores of the Sea of Japan, Okhotsk, and the Behring Strait. *Sbornik dogovorov Rossii s drugimi gosudarstvami, 1856–1917* (Moscow, 1953), pp. 337–44.

36. Witte is hardly the man to give Nicholas II credit where credit is due. By all accounts the emperor showed more firmness and played a greater role in influencing the negotiations than one would guess from reading Witte. Nor does he give sufficient credit to Baron Rosen, who, although he played a secondary role, was of considerable help.

37. Roosevelt took a less kindly view of Witte. One example is what he wrote to Cecil Spring-Rice: "Witte impressed me much while he was here, but by no means altogether pleasantly. . . he also impressed me as being more concerned with his own welfare than for the welfare of his nation, and as being utterly cynical, untruthful, and unscrupulous." *The Letters and Friendships of Sir Cecil Spring-Rice* (Boston, 1929), II, 8–9. What basis he had for this characterization is not evident, but we do know that Witte's manner aroused deep hostility in some people. In any case, Roosevelt's unfavorable opinion did not remain a secret, but Witte continued to profess a favorable view of the American president.

38. Witte may be unfair here. Consider what the emperor wrote in his diary on August 18, a day after receiving word from Witte that agreement had been reached: "Only today had the thought begun to sink in that peace will be concluded and that peace is truly a good thing, because that is the way it must be. I received several congratulatory telegrams." *Dnevnik*, pp. 214–15. This entry can be construed several ways, one way being that although he found the thought of making a peace on such terms abhorrent,

he accepted the fact that he had no choice.

39. Witte was booked to leave the country on August 30/September 12, giving him six free days. Interestingly enough the ship he was to sail on was *Kaiser Wilhelm II.*

40. This was on August 26/September 8. One of the guests at the luncheon was J. P. Morgan. Witte made part of the trip from his hotel to Governor's Island by subway. *The New York Times*, September 9, 1905, p. 2. Princess Julia Cantacuzene discusses her friendship with the Wittes in her *My Life Here and There* (New York, 1921), pp. 266–70.

41. En route to Columbia, his car was stopped in Central Park for speeding. The mounted policeman who stopped him permitted him to go on when the detectives in the car behind displayed their badges. *The New York Times*, September 10, 1905, p. 2. Witte forgets to note that Komura also received an honorary degree from Columbia University at this time. Columbia University, *Alumni Register, 1754–1931* (New York, 1932), p. 1184.

42. A dispatch from St. Petersburg carried in *The New York Times* on July 31, 1905, stated that negotiations for the end of Russian retaliatory tariffs were in progress and that it had been hoped that an announcement about this would be made during the course of the negotiations but that the announcement was being delayed, mainly, it was believed, to show Witte, "whose star is in the ascendant in Russia today," the courtesy of letting him give his approval.

43. In addition to having Witte as his guest aboard his yacht, J. P. Morgan also sent his private train to Portsmouth to take Witte back to New York. *The New York Times*, September 3, 1905, p. 1. Although Witte did not deal with Morgan before going to Portsmouth, he did talk with Perkins, who, as the French *chargé d'affaires* put it, "is considered to be Pierpont Morgan's righthand man." Desportes de la Fosse to Rouvier, August 8, 1905 (NS), *Documents diplomatiques françaises*, series 2, VII, 384. Witte arrived in New York from Portsmouth late in the afternoon of August 24/September 6. On August 26/September 8, he attended the luncheon on Governor's Island at which Morgan was also a guest. The following day he had what he called his "first business talk" with the financier. On August 29/September 11, the trip to West Point took place. "Portsmut," *Krasnyi arkhiv* 6 (1924): 46–47; *The New York Times*, September 12, 1905, p. 2.

Chapter VI

1. Following the publication of the interview, Count Benckendorff, the Russian ambassador to London, told the French *chargé* there that Witte talked too much to reporters. Geoffray to Rouvier, September 22, 1905, *Documents diplomatiques françaises*, series 2, VII, 562–63. Not only did Witte talk too much to reporters, but also he sometimes talked indiscreetly, a trait that could not help but offend Nicholas II.

2. Witte overestimates his role in influencing the outcome of the Moroccan crisis, as even Dillon admits. "Two Russian Statesmen," *Quarterly Review* 236 (1921): 404–05.

3. Witte's memory is at fault here. On the day in question, September 12/25, he spoke to von Bülow for two hours. In reporting the conversation, the chancellor said that Witte was in a very "anti-English mood" and told him that he had been able to prevent the floating of an Anglo-French loan to Russia in the belief that such a loan was not in the interests of France or Germany. Von Bülow to Emperor William II, September 25, 1905 (NS), *Die grosse Politik* (Berlin, 1927), XIX, pt. 2, 505–07. *See also* Bihourd to Rouvier, September 25, 1905 (NS), *Documents diplomatiques françaises*, series 2, VIII, 572. *See also* Kokovtsev, *Iz moego proshlago*, I, 86.

4. *See above*, p. 264.

5. The German emperor in a telegram from Rominten sent on September 25 (NS) told von Bülow that Nicholas II had given him permission to inform Witte about the treaty that had been signed at Björkö. *Die grosse Politik*, XIX, pt. 2, p. 505. If Witte is being candid in asserting that William II gave him only the sketchiest account of the treaty, the question arises: Why the reticence? According to Dillon, Witte's explanation was that the German emperor feared that if Witte learned all the facts then and there he "would flare up," become very difficult, and perhaps try to have the treaty annulled, whereas if Witte learned the terms of the treaty from his own sovereign or from Lambsdorff, "he would resign himself" given the fact that he had already agreed to the "principle" upon which the treaty was based. *Eclipse of Russia*, p. 397. In his telegram of September 27 (NS) to von Bülow describing his conversation with Witte, William implies that he informed Witte rather thoroughly about the contents of the treaty and that Witte was quite enthusiastic about it and suggested steps for making it work, notably by winning France over to it. The editors of *Die grosse Politik* insist that if Witte did not see the text of the treaty he certainly was thoroughly informed about its contents by William II. *Die grosse Politik*, XIX, pt. 2, pp. 508–11, 510–11 n. On this matter of what Witte knew and when he knew it, *see* chapter 7, n. 7.

6. M. Bompard, in writing about Witte's effort to lay hands on the document, in 1907, points out that Witte could not be disabused of the mistaken notion that he was responsible for the calling of the Algeciras conference. "Les Mémoires du Comte Witte," *La Revue de Paris* 28 (1921): 28–29. *See also* Bihourd to Rouvier, September 28, 1905 (NS), *Documents diplomatiques français*, series 2, VII, 585.

7. Witte deals with the establishment of the corps on p. 180.

Chapter VII

1. G. P. Bakhmetev was, nonetheless, appointed. He succeeded Baron Rosen as ambassador to the United States in 1911, to be succeeded in turn by B. A. Bakhmeteff, after whom the archive that now houses the Witte papers was named.

2. According to the emperor's diary (*Dnevnik*, p. 218), Witte arrived later, in time for dinner. In a letter to his mother, Nicholas II wrote: "At Biorkoe, Witte came to see us—he was very charming and interesting. After a long talk I told him of his new honor—I am creating him a count. He went quite stiff with emotion and then three times tried to kiss my hand." *The Letters of Tsar Nicholas and Empress Marie* (London, 1937), p. 179.

The title of count was often bestowed on ministers after long, usually twenty-five years', distinguished service and on generals who had won a major victory. In this case the rationale for the honor was neither lengthy service nor victory on the field of battle but what was perceived a victory in the field of diplomacy. What thoughts went on in the emperor's mind when he decided to bestow this honor, what counsel, if any, led him to this act we do not know. Nor do we know if he was telling the truth when he said he trusted Witte "completely," but we do know that he was not telling the truth when he said that he had never believed allegations about Witte's loyalty. But then it is not the business of heads of state to be completely candid. In any event, it is the case that for a time the emperor felt kindly toward Witte and Witte felt kindly toward his sovereign, but this *lune de miel*, as Witte liked to call periods of good will between Nicholas II and his ministers, was not to last long.

3. We will hear much more about Suvorin, who has, justifiably, been called Russia's first press lord. Witte had cultivated him, as he had other publishers. This publisher's good will was especially important for Witte because Suvorin's newspaper, *Novoe vremia*, tradi-

tionally ultramonarchist and jingoistic in tone, was one of the few St. Petersburg newspapers that Nicholas II approved of and read. Witte's pique at Suvorin probably arises from that the fact that *Novoe vremia* was critical of Witte's work as premier, a fact that is quite evident from the memoirs. Nonetheless, Witte did not cut his ties with Suvorin, as is evident from the publisher's published diary.

4. Generals who received a title in recognition of a victory were permitted to add the place where the victory occurred to their surnames, e.g., Count General Paskevich-Erivanskii. Those who referred to Witte as Count Witte Semi-Sakhalinskii were, of course, being very sarcastic, indicating that he was being "honored" for giving away half of Sakhalin.

5. This charge was widely believed, even in high society. General Mosolov, director of the chancellery of the Ministry of the Court, says that his investigation of such allegations proved them without substance, but he does acknowledge that the Black Hundreds had influence at court and that they had access to the emperor. Mosolov, *At the Court of the Last Tsar*, pp. 144–45, 167.

6. The false pregnancy to which Witte is referring took place before Philippe was on the scene. Harcave, *Years of the Golden Cockerel*, p. 322.

7. The "bigwig" was Heinrich von Tschirsky und Bögendorff. The treaty was signed on July 11/24, 1905. *Sbornik dogovorov Rossii s drugimi gosudarstvami, 1856–1917*, p. 336.

We are now faced with the question of when Witte and Lambsdorff learned the exact details of the treaty. The editors of *Die grosse Politik*, who are a bit partisan, argue, as we have seen, that, at the least, Witte had been exactly informed by Emperor William. They also argue, citing one of Lambsdorff's associates, Savinskii, that the foreign minister was shown the text of the treaty nearly a month before Witte's return, i.e., earlier than Witte would have us believe. The source is A. A. Savinskii, "Guillaume II et la Russie," *Revue des deux mondes* 12 (1922): 796. Savinskii does not provide conclusive evidence: he does not explain his sources; he was writing many years after and, moreover, was writing in a rather dramatic manner that invites a bit of skepticism. In support of Witte's account is Nicholas II's letter to William II of September 24/October 4, in which the emperor raised serious questions about the treaty, suggesting "that the coming into force of the Bjorkoe treaty ought to be put off until we know how France will look upon it." *Die grosse Politik*, XIX, pt. 2, 512–13. The timing of the letter and its content do not prove that Witte and Lambsdorff did not know the text of the treaty much earlier than Witte indicates, but they are consistent with what Witte writes. *See below*, n. 25, about Witte's abortive effort to be named ambassador to France.

8. A reference to the statute of 1884 which stripped universities of what little autonomy they had enjoyed and denied to their students the right to form any kind of association, even music clubs.

9. Students at what were called Women's Higher Courses, the equivalent of universities (from which women were barred).

10. A reference to the commission under Count Solskii that was to implement the law establishing the State Duma. One of the questions it dealt with was whether or not to permit meetings during the course of the coming electoral campaign. As a result of its work a decree was issued on October 12 permitting such gatherings under strictly defined circumstances. N. S. Tagantsev, *Perezhitoe* (Petrograd, 1918), p. 49.

11. "Intelligentsia" is variously defined. Usually it is taken to mean that part of the educated class that was at odds with the government and organized religion.

12. The assertion that he did not speak up at these meetings should be construed as meaning that he did not take a prominent part in the proceedings. But he did speak.

Although skeptical about representative government for Russia, particularly in the form proposed, he had something to say about the features of the proposed body and the process to be used in electing deputies to it. He opposed the proposal to deny the franchise to Jews. He argued against property requirements that would deny the franchise to workers. He called for broad representation for the peasantry, not because he considered it a pillar of conservatism, but because he considered it desirable that its voice be heard. *Krizis samoderzhaviia v Rossii, 1895–1917*, p. 199; Kryzhanovskii, *Vospominaniia*, p. 40. None of these positions is discreditable, but Witte ignores what he said apparently because he is trying to defend himself. His position here and elsewhere is that the mistaken belief in the peasantry as a pillar of conservatism resulted in giving the opposition a majority in the first and second State Dumas and that the responsibility for the electoral law that made this possible is not his but that of people like General Lobko and Pobedonostsev.

13. This special conference met at Peterhof from July 19 to July 26 under the chairmanship of the emperor to put the final touches on the law establishing a State Duma.

14. Although Kokovtsev took a lively role in the Peterhof deliberations, he barely touches on them in his memoirs.

15. A reference to his *Zemstvo i samoderzhavie.*

16. The law provided for an elective body, to be called the State Duma as noted, with the right to offer opinions on legislative proposals but not the right to pass legislation. Except in large parts of the Kingdom of Poland, the Caucasus, Siberia, and Central Asia, males over the age of twenty-five who met certain property qualifications were given the right to vote, indirectly, for deputies to the Duma. Jews were not denied the franchise. Workers were, for the most part, denied the franchise because of the property qualifications. Almost all peasants could vote and, because of the way in which the cumbersome electoral system was devised, were assured of broad representation in the State Duma. Properly speaking, one should refer to two laws, the first establishing the State Duma, the other establishing the manner in which it was to be elected, both issued on August 6, 1905. It was to fall to Witte to revise both in accordance with the promises made in the October Manifesto. *Gosudarstvennaia duma v Rossii: v dokumentakh i materialakh* (Moscow, 1957), pp. 30–54. For most of the opposition this State Duma was nothing but a sham and they undertook to boycott the elections to it, but moderate liberals were willing to participate in elections and to sit in the State Duma if elected, in the belief that half a loaf was better than none.

17. An apparent reference to the Union for the Defense of the Freedom of the Press, formed by publishers in the capital, which decided on October 16 to ignore the press laws by publishing news of the ongoing strike. C. A. Ruud, "The Printing Press as an Agent of Political Change in Early Twentieth-Century Russia," *The Russian Review* 40 (1981): 386–87.

18. "Union" (*soiuz*) is an association or federation. The Union of Unions was established in May 1905 as a federation of fourteen unions, representing trade unions, peasants, Jews, feminists, and various professions. It was led by liberals and was committed to rallying the opposition in a struggle to end absolutism and to the election of a constituent assembly to establish a democratic government. The assembly was to be elected on the basis of "four-tail (universal, equal, direct, and secret) suffrage." The Kadet party, about which Witte has much to say, grew out of the Union of Unions.

19. *See below*, pp. 495–97.

20. Gringmut was a leading figure in the Russian Monarchist Union, an extreme rightist group formed in April 1905. *Moskovskie vedomosti* was another of the small number of

newspapers that Nicholas II approved of and read. Of interest in this connection is the March 2, 1905, entry in the diary of L. Tikhomirov, one of Gringmut's associates. In noting what Gringmut had to say after a trip to St. Petersburg, Tikhomirov reports that "at the Imperial court there were those who believe that Witte pretends to be for autocracy but is in fact scheming to help create the kind of conditions that would permit him to appear as a savior and then proceed to establish a republic with himself as president, and that, of course, he is speaking for the Jews." He adds that those who are truly for the autocracy speak of stopping Witte but do nothing. "25 let nazad: Iz dnevnikov L. Tikhomirova," *Krasnyi arkhiv* 38 (1930): 67. Witte, as readers will note, was aware of such talk.

21. In areas of serious unrest, it was the practice to establish temporary governor-generalships that united civilian and military authority under one person, invariably a military man. This was the case in St. Petersburg under Trepov and in other areas during this period.

22. This might be called another of the many "white papers" that Witte commissioned during the course of his career to provide documentary support for his view of events with which he was involved.

23. It is evident that in writing this section Witte had detailed information at hand when describing events in St. Petersburg but did not have such information about other areas.

24. Witte appears to have been cautiously getting a sense of what "society" was thinking through people like Prince A. D. Obolenskii.

25. This is an appropriate place at which to consider whether or not Witte was anxious to assume the reins of government. It should be recalled that work had been proceeding for some time before Witte's return from America on the transformation of the Council of Ministers into something like a cabinet with a chairman occupying a position resembling that of a premier or prime minister. Even before Witte's return there was talk that the emperor would offer the chairmanship to him. Thus, on September 9/22 we find Bompard, the French ambassador, writing to Rouvier that the emperor "has decided to receive him [Witte] in a most gracious fashion," that he would bestow an honor on Witte, and adds: "Madame Witte to whom the doors of the court have been closed until now, will be presented to the Empress. It is expected that the chairmanship of the Council of Ministers will be offered to M. Witte." He went on to say that it was probable that Witte would accept the offer and that, if he did, there was sure to be trouble between him and the emperor. France, Archives de Ministère des Affaires Étrangères, Russie, Politique Intérieure, II.

We have little evidence of what Witte was thinking about in the period between his return and the outbreak of the crisis in early October, but we have some. One such piece of evidence comes from S. M. Propper, the publisher, who had been fairly close to Witte. He writes that very soon after Witte received the title of count, the two had a long talk, in the course of which Witte spoke in very warm terms of the emperor, indicated that he expected to be named chairman of the Council of Ministers, and asserted that he would be remembered by posterity not only for the gold standard, the Trans-Siberian Railroad, and the Treaty of Portsmouth but also "as the creator of the Russian State Duma." *Was nicht in die Zeitung kam*, p. 262. Propper may be exaggerating, but there is no reason to believe that he is making it up. Witte was an ambitious man, and the chairmanship of the Council of Ministers would provide him with an opportunity to employ his talent and energy and, as Cecil Spring-Rice, the English diplomat, wrote: "He is foolish to take the job; but he fears if he doesn't, the chance may not recur." Spring-Rice to Theodore Roosevelt, October 10,

1905 (NS), *The Letters and Friendships of Sir Cecil Spring-Rice*, I, 499.

An additional piece of evidence that Witte knew very early on that something was in store for him comes from the French *chargé d'affaires* in St. Petersburg, who in a dispatch to Rouvier dated October 21 (October 8 OS), wrote that when Witte at his audience with the emperor on his return from America asked for permission to go abroad for three months for a rest, he was told: "No, remain among us, I will have need of you." France, Archives de Ministère des Affaires Étrangères, Russie, Politique Intérieure, II. Unfortunately, Boutiron does not give his source, probably someone at court or in the Russian Foreign Office. But Witte's wife would have preferred that her husband find a haven as ambassador to France. In an undated letter, probably written shortly after their return to Russia, she asked their friend Ernest von Mendelssohn-Bartholdy to persuade his emperor to suggest to Nicholas II that Witte would be a good choice to replace the incumbent in Paris, with whom he was dissatisfied. She said that "within a few weeks all sorts of positions would be offered" to her husband and that, given the state of her husband's health and given the existing situation in Russia, it would be better for him to be out of the country. Von Bülow, *Memoirs*, II, 192–93.

Whether or not it was Witte's preference to go to Paris it is clear that he made an effort to do so. In a letter to Prince Eulenberg dated October 8 (probably new style), Witte pointed out that in order to implement the Treaty of Björkö it would be necessary to bring France into the projected alliance and to achieve that would require the right sort of ambassador in Paris. Evidently von Bülow was shown this letter with its not so subtle hint that Witte would be of help if he were in Paris. We find him writing on October 18 (NS) to Prince Eulenberg, urging him to keep up his ties with Witte but to keep them secret and "to spin the thread out skillfully and carefully because it is of the greatest importance that it not be broken." In his reply to Witte, which carried the date October 1905, but no day (but was clearly written before Witte became premier), the prince informed Witte that he had shown his letter to William II and expressed regret that given the internal situation in Russia it was not possible for Witte to be sent to Paris, concluding by saying: "But I am unable to refrain from thinking that Count Witte as the ambassador on the banks of the Seine would be exactly 'the right man in the right place.'" *Die grosse Politik*, XIX, pt. 2, 519–21.

A final note. Speaking of Countess Witte's letter, von Bülow wrote: "This faithful wife was quite justified in thinking that it would have been better for Sergei Yulevitch to be Russian Ambassador in Paris than to waste his strength on Russian domestic policy; but, as things were at the time, we were unable to satisfy her wish." *Memoirs*, II, 193. It is obvious that Witte was not of one mind about what he wanted for himself and his wife at this point. Pulling him in one direction was a combination of ambition and a sense of duty, and pulling him in another direction was a sense of prudence, the feeling that he and his wife would be better off in Paris than in St. Petersburg.

26. In a letter from Menshikov to Witte, dated October 7, 1905, it is stated that the two happened to meet on October 2, at which time Witte asked Menshikov to send him a draft on what he thought should be in a constitution. "K istorii sozdaniia manifesta 17 oktiabria," *Sovetskie arkhivy* 5 (1985): 60.

Chapter VIII

1. On September 28, A. A. Polovtsov noted in his diary that in the course of a discussion of the peasant question at the Solskii commission Witte said that current labor and student unrest was "negligible in comparison with the coming peasant Pugachev-

shchina.'' On October 1 he noted that Witte was very upset about current conditions, being of the opinion that the only way to cope with those conditions was by the appointment of a dictator, but he did not know of anyone suitable for such a responsibility. ''Dnevnik,'' *Krasnyi arkhiv* 4 (1923): 70–71.

2. Probably a reference to the letter of October 16, in which she said: ''I am sure that the only man who can help you now and be useful is Witte, because he should be well disposed again *now* and besides he certainly is a man of genius, *energetic* and clear-sighted.'' *The Letters of Tsar Nicholas and Empress Marie*, p. 184. The letter was delivered to the emperor on October 20. Nicholas II, *Dnevnik*, p. 222.

3. This is the Chikhachev who gave Witte his first position (*see above*, p. 42). Admiral Chikhachev, a member of the emperor's suite with the rank of general-adjutant, was well connected at court.

4. In his memorandum about the events leading to the manifesto (ms. pp. 129a and 129a verso), he offers a slightly different account:

> It was about this time, at a meeting chaired by Count Solskii, as we were discussing the current state of unrest, that General-Adjutant Chikhachev and Count Pahlen said firmly that the first priority was to put down all disorder. I reported their views to the Emperor, suggesting that he might want to listen to high officials who held such views. When General-Adjutant Chikhachev later asked if it had been at my suggestion that the Emperor had summoned him, I said I did not know, but I had suggested that he hear out high officials who held views such as his.

The emperor saw Chikhachev during the morning of October 13. *Dnevnik*, p. 221. A. A. Polovtsov apparently saw Chikhachev later that day. In his entry for October 13 he noted that the admiral told him that nothing much had happened during his talk with the emperor, except that the sovereign said he was almost ready to grant a constitution. ''Dnevnik,'' *Krasnyi arkhiv* 4 (1923): 76.

5. For more on the state of the army, *see below*, pp. 522–25.

6. Prince N. D. Obolenskii, the brother of Prince A. D. Obolenskii, was one of the few at court who was not hostile toward Witte and was apparently the source of much of the information about the court that Witte cites.

7. Although one might be tempted to discount what Witte says about the mood at court, the facts bear him out. The mood was one of panic. The attitude toward Witte was ambivalent, a combination of wild suspicion (of which more later) of him and the reluctant conviction that only he could take charge at this time.

8. Prince A. D. Obolenskii could justifiably be called Witte's righthand man during this period. It is a pity that he tells us so little about his ties with him and why he relied so much on a man about whom he had very mixed feelings. It is a pity, too, that we don't have the prince's version of his ties with Witte at this time.

9. The emperor met with Goremykin and Budberg during the evening of October 15. The next day he met again with these two and Freedericksz, to edit the manifesto. *Dnevnik*, pp. 221–22.

10. According to Mosolov, Witte was also shown a draft combining features from the Witte and Goremykin drafts, a draft prepared at the direction of Baron Freedericksz. Mosolov to Witte, December 23, 1905, *Krasnyi arkhiv* 11–12 (1925): 91.

11. Ushakov was the kind of worker considered reliable by the government and something else by radical workers. In 1904, with Witte's help, he had established the St. Petersburg Society of Mutual Help for Factory Workers, an organization analogous to that formed by Gapon, but far less popular. In the fall of 1905 he took part in the formation of the Independent Social Workers Party, which favored cooperation rather than conflict

between workers and employers. Schneiderman, *Sergei Zubatov,* pp. 181, 355–56; *Ocherki istorii Leningrada* (Moscow, 1960), III, 614 n. 10.

12. In asking Ushakov to prepare the statement, Witte obviously wanted to arm himself with evidence against allegations that he staged the meeting between Ushakov and the grand duke and that during the October general strike he had acted in concert with Ushakov and Nosar, the head of the St. Petersburg Soviet. The statement is in the Bakhmeteff Archive. Soviet scholars, working from a copy in their archives, published the text in *Krasnyi arkhiv* 4 (1923): 411–17.

13. Elsewhere, Witte says of the prince (dictated memoirs, pp. 2024–27.):

> He now lives at the Bellevue Hotel, across from the Hôtel de France, on Morskaia. His acquaintances are a varied lot. At present he is on very friendly terms with the war minister and frequently visits him and his wife. He is received by Markov, the minister of interior, and his wife. Kokovtsev permits the prince to call on him, but says of him: "He is a very bad lot."
> Andronikov has rarely come to see me since I left office. When he does, he is in dress uniform, behaves very respectfully, and sometimes provides me with interesting news. Evidently, he has managed to get into the confidence of Baron Freedericksz, for, not long ago, he gave me several interesting, intelligently written memoranda, which, he says, were transmitted to His Majesty by the baron. The memoranda were written by the late Sharapov, a man of considerable talent, but few principles.
> Recently, he let me read an interesting memorandum, written by the notorious Bezobrazov, concerning the causes of the war with Japan. He told me that there was a supplementary volume of documents that had been reproduced in twenty typewritten copies, one of which he had taken from the interior minister's desk. He offered to show me his copy and I expressed interest, but he never showed it to me. When I sent him a note reminding him of his offer, I received no reply.

Witte had a great interest, to say the least, in what Bezobrazov had to say about the origins of the war with Japan. While premier he stopped the publication of a brief work by Bezobrazov on this subject, a work of which he had a typewritten copy in his archive. Ananich and Ganelin, "Opyt kritiki memuarov S. Iu. Vitte," p. 318. A shortened version of the work was published many years later: "Les premières causes de l'effrondement de la Russie," *Le Correspondent* (May 1923): 557–615.

14. Alexander III and his family narrowly escaped death in a train wreck on October 17, 1887.

General Rödiger writes that he heard two versions of what happened on October 17, 1905, the first from Baron Freedericksz, on October 18, and the second from General F. F. Palitsyn, on October 19. The first agrees with the Witte version. According to the second, which General Palitsyn heard from Grand Duke Nicholas Nikolaevich, the decision to accept the manifesto had been made before the arrival of the grand duke. "Iz zapisok A. F. Redigera," *Krasnyi arkhiv* 45 (1931): 89.

An interesting sidelight about the events of October 17 comes from Grand Duke Andrei Vladimirovich, who wrote in his diary on March 9, 1917, that two days earlier Prince Vladimir N. Orlov told him the following: The prince knew that if Trepov advised the emperor to sign the manifesto, he would do so. Having served with Trepov in the same regiment, he knew that Trepov lacked "civic courage" and would advise the emperor to sign. Nonetheless he wrote Trepov, asking him to advise Nicholas against signing and warning him that their friendship would come to an end if he advised the emperor to sign. The prince went on to say that after the emperor had signed the manifesto, he summoned him to his study. The prince found his sovereign in tears, saying that in signing he had lost all. No, said the prince, it was necessary "to rally all right-minded people and all would be saved." The prince wrote to P. I. Rachkovskii (head of the political police), and that was how the Union of the Russian People came into being. "Iz dnevnika A. V. Romanova za 1916–1917 gg." *Krasnyi arkhiv* 26 (1928): 196–200. The prince's account, told nearly twelve years after the event, may contain some embroidering of the facts, but there is no reason to doubt that he found the emperor in tears or that he wrote to Rachkovskii. However, his explanation of the origins of the Union of the Russian People is too pat, although Rachkovskii, who had a hand in many behind-the-scenes operations, may have played some role in the establishment of the organization.

Chapter IX

1. *The Letters of Tsar Nicholas and Empress Marie*, p. 184.

2. Properly speaking, Witte's new title was chairman of the Council of Ministers, but I am adhering to the usage of Witte and others in calling him premier and the body over which he presided the cabinet. His position was analogous to that of premier or prime minister in other countries. Technically he was the head of government and the emperor the head of state, but in practice, as is evident from the memoirs, his authority was narrower than that of the typical premier.

3. *See above*, pp. 486–87 and II, ch. 8, n. 11.

4. Witte held his first cabinet meeting at General Trepov's quarters on October 18; he met with the cabinet at the Marie Palace on the 19th and 20th and thereafter at his quarters in the Winter Palace. A. F. Rödiger, "Iz zapisok A. F. Redigera," p. 90. Throughout his career, Witte worked at a frenetic pace, but especially so during his first weeks as premier, when he was like the proverbial one-armed paperhanger with the hives, dealing with the most critical of problems, meeting delegations of all varieties, reporting to the emperor, framing major legislation, forming a cabinet, trying to restore order, dealing with unforeseen problems.

5. The pejorative term "Black Hundreds" is applied collectively to ultrarightist organizations formed, for the most part in 1905, in reaction to the liberal and revolutionary movement. The largest, and most notorious, of these was the Union of the Russian People, led by Dr. Dubrovin, to whom Witte refers in season and out as a scoundrel. For Dubrovin's views on Witte, *see below*, II, ch. X, n. 15. These organizations considered the October Manifesto a betrayal of the "true Russian" spirit, which, in their view, meant autocracy, Russian nationality, and Russian Orthodoxy. In their eyes, the enemies of Russia and the ones responsible for revolution and the October Manifesto were "kikes, Poles, Russian fools and traitors, and assorted atheists and corrupters." Iliodor, *Pravda o Soiuze Russkago Naroda, Soiuze Russkikh Liudei i dr. monarkhicheskikh partiiakh* (Odessa, 1907), p. 1.

The term "Black Hundreds" was sometimes used in a more restrictive sense, for what might be called the fighting auxiliaries of the organizations referred to. These groups, which Witte refers to as "gangs of thugs," were often responsible for attacks on those they considered enemies of "the true Russians," notably Jews and students.

6. Not so. According to an official report, five were killed and twelve wounded. Akademiia Nauk SSSR, Institut Istorii, *Revoliutsiia 1905–1907 v Rossii: Dokumenty i materialy; Vserossiiskaia politicheskaia stachka v Oktiabre 1905 g.*, part I (Moscow, 1955), pp. 375, 381–82. Because Witte does not recall that there were any deaths, he does not recall that the left planned a major public funeral procession for the victims, to be held on October 24, but was forbidden to do so by Trepov, still the governor-general. This led to a visit to Witte by Hessen and other Kadet leaders to get him to intervene. He told them that he had tried,

unsuccessfully, to get Trepov to remove troops from the streets on October 24, and that if, despite this fact, they insisted on holding the procession, any blood that would be shed would be on their hands. The procession was not held. I. V. Hessen (Gessen), *V dvukh vekakh* (Berlin, 1937), pp. 208-10.

Also, Witte, or someone close to him, let the opposition press know of his conversation with Min, urging him not to shed "Russian blood." The officer corps took all this unkindly, accusing Witte of encouraging hostility toward the military. Trepov wrote to Witte deploring the attitude of the press. Apparently it was this letter that led to an official statement released by the premier's office defending the conduct of the military and insisting that untoward incidents were the exception, the product of extraordinary circumstances. "Iz bumag D. F. Trepova," *Krasnyi arkhiv* 11-12 (1925): 462-66. The facts that Witte does not recall do not show him in a heroic light, yet neither do they show him in a discreditable light. He was having a difficult time of it, trying to convince "society" of his good will yet having to get along with Trepov. Whether or not his lapse of memory was deliberate is moot. The period he is describing was chaotic, and it is possible that he forgot something he would rather not remember.

7. Propper relates that, at a meeting of newspaper editors the night before the session with Witte, all but one agreed that the premier was not to be trusted and commissioned Propper to speak in their names. He adds that after they had met with Witte, the premier asked Propper to remain behind and when they were alone asked for his cooperation by giving editorial support for his policies and calling on him more often than he had. Propper told him that he could not promise him his support and that to avoid compromising either of them he would not call on Witte as long as he remained in office. Apparently Propper and the others did not believe that Witte's record warranted faith that his deeds would match his words. *Was nicht in die Zeitung kam*, pp. 273-78.

8. An honorary title bestowed on persons in commerce and industry, placing the holder in the eighth rank of the civil service. L. E. Shepelev, *Otmenennye istoriei* (Leningrad, 1977), p. 54.

9. These were among the few newspapers that Nicholas II could stomach. It was in these newspapers that Witte attempted to place articles favorable to his policies. According to one of Witte's assistants, Suvorin of *Novoe vremia* would not publish articles supplied by Witte without identifying the source, but the publisher of *Svet* set no conditions. It is quite obvious that Witte was very concerned about the press, kept a close watch on what was being said about him, and, as can be seen, tried to influence the press. A. A. Spasskii-Odynets, "Vospominaniia," Bakhmeteff Archive, pp. 27-28, 48.

10. Witte deplored the use of the word *zhid* (kike), but in this case he let his anger at Propper get the best of him. In the Hessen redaction the epithet is enclosed by quotation marks, but these marks are not in the manuscript.

11. Hessen related that on October 18 he called on Witte at the premier's request and that, in the course of their talk, he told Witte it would be wise immediately to proclaim freedom of the press. The premier replied that he had been informed that it would take some time to prepare the necessary legislation, to which Hessen replied that it would take only five minutes to end preliminary censorship. *V dvukh vekakh*, pp. 206-07. Was it coincidence that the next day censors received instructions to use their powers with restraint?

12. *See below*, II, ch. XI n. 11.

13. This phrase, implying venality, was given currency by Saltykov-Shchedrin, who used it with respect to *Novoe vremia*. N. S. Ashutkin, *Krylatye slova* (Moscow, 1966), p. 719.

14. The decree on amnesty provided for the freeing of many political prisoners who had not committed acts of violence and reductions in sentence for those who had.

15. The text of Witte's report to the emperor about this conversation can be found in *Byloe* (February 1918): 108–09. Witte's reference to "another Poland" may have come from a memorandum prepared by N. Kh. Bunge for the Tsesarevich Nicholas Aleksandrovich, later emperor, in which he declared that it was good that the status of Finland had not been tampered with, thus preventing Finland from becoming "another Poland, a country which is inimical to us and which we may hold onto only by relying on our army." "The Years 1881–1894 in Russia," *Transactions of the American Philosophical Society* 71, pt. 6 (1981): 42. A copy of the Bunge memorandum is among the Witte papers at the Bakhmeteff Archive.

16. Prince Obolenskii was not particularly qualified for this office, but he was sympathetic, as was Witte, to the idea of church reform, and he was, at this time, very close to Witte.

17. Grand Duke Alexander Mikhailovich relates that he was away from the capital, and when he learned of the October Manifesto, which he refers to as a "cowardly compromise," he telegraphed his resignation to the emperor. *Once a Grand Duke* (New York, 1932), p. 225.

18. Apparently Witte was also motivated by the fact that Nemeshaev was popular among railroadmen. H. Reichman, "Tsarist Labor Policy and the Railroads, 1885–1914," *The Russian Review* 42 (1963): 64.

19. The incumbent state controller, General Lobko, was on leave at this time and died in November. Apparently Witte was acting on the assumption that the post would soon be vacant.

20. Schwanebach had long been critical of Witte's policies and considered the latter's appointment as premier a terrible mistake. After leaving office he was among Witte's most bitter enemies. *See below*, pp. 705–07.

21. N. S. Tagantsev, writing before the appearance of Witte's version of the circumstances, states that it was he who suggested Posnikov and goes on to say that he and Posnikov felt there was some question about where Witte was heading. Both felt they lacked the required experience. Tagantsev admits that he was concerned for his safety if he took the position. *Perezhitoe*, pp. 99–106.

22. The negotiations, it should be noted, lasted October 19–26.

23. In 1909 these two were exposed as being in the pay of the police.

24. V. I. Gurko asserts that it was through Stakhovich and Prince A. D. Obolenskii that Witte had earlier on become "acquainted with the work of zemstvo organizations." *Features and Figures of the Past*, pp. 207–08.

25. Because he was writing from memory in this case, he telescoped events. He and Obolenskii met with Shipov and Trubetskoi on October 19, at which time arrangements were made to invite other public men. Shipov, *Vospominaniia i dumy o perezhitom*, pp. 334–35.

26. I. I. Petrunkevich, the venerable liberal leader, relates that Witte tried, unsuccessfully, to get his help in persuading Guchkov to accept a ministerial post. "Iz zapisok obshchestvennago deiatelia," *Arkhiv russkoi revoliutsii* 21 (1934): 432. Witte and Guchkov subsequently engaged in sharp dispute over the events of these days. Witte reached out not only to moderate liberals in trying to form a cabinet but also to members of the recently formed Kadet party, even though it had denounced the October Manifesto as not going far enough. Around the end of October he sought, without success, to get the support of Paul Miliukov, the leader of the party. P. N. Miliukov, *Vospominaniia* (New York, 1955), I, 432.

27. Nicholas I created a Third Section in his Chancellery to act as "his eyes and ears," to learn what was going on in his country, particularly with respect to dissent and corruption. The body through which this information was to be obtained was the Corps of Gendarmes. In practice the Third Section and the Corps gave their chief attention to searching out dissent. In 1880 the Third Section was abolished and its duties assumed by the Department of Police of the Ministry of Interior, to which the Corps of Gendarmes was made subordinate.

28. D. Shipov gives a somewhat different version. According to him Witte said that only two men—Durnovo and Trepov—were qualified for the post. Under pressure from the public men, Witte proposed that Urusov become minister and Durnovo assistant minister. This proposal was accepted, and they adjourned until Prince Urusov could return to St. Petersburg. When they assembled on October 26, Witte shocked them by proposing that Durnovo become minister and Urusov assistant minister. Shipov states that the public men felt that they had been deceived and immediately stated, without asking for time to consider this, that they would not serve with Durnovo. *Vospominaniia i dumy o perezhitom*, pp. 343–47.

29. It is generally felt that Witte was not candid about his reasons for insisting on Durnovo, leading to much inconclusive speculation. One speculative explanation, furnished by V. I. Gurko, who was close to Durnovo but not to Witte, deserves some consideration. He writes that because the October Manifesto did not have as great a calming effect as Witte expected, the premier felt that he needed a man who knew police work and wanted Durnovo to serve as assistant minister, but, says Gurko, Durnovo insisted that he could not do the work required of him unless he were minister, at which point Witte decided that it was better to lose the support of the public men than the services of Durnovo because he was of the opinion that liberal support at that time was not enough to enable him to restore order. "Chto est i chego net v 'Vospominaniiakh' S. Iu. Vitte," *Russkaia starina* 2 (1922): 121–23.

30. Witte is clearly putting a gloss over the departure of Kokovtsev and Schwanebach. It is evident that he wanted them to go and that he made them so uncomfortable that they chose to go. Kokovtsev tells us that he and Witte were on fairly friendly terms before Witte went to Portsmouth but that on his return to Russia Witte turned against him and tried to make his life as difficult as possible. *Iz moego proshlago*, I, 81–99.

31. Witte wrote to the emperor that neither he nor his colleagues would continue to serve if Kokovtsev were appointed. This amounted to an ultimatum that led Nicholas II to write in the margin of the statement: "I shall never forget this insolence." "Graf S. Iu. Vitte i Nikolai II v oktiabre 1905 g.," *Byloe* 4 (1925): 107.

32. I. V. Hessen, the editor-in-chief of *Pravo*, a liberal weekly, writes that Witte asked him to help persuade Trubetskoi to accept the portfolio and that Trubetskoi took counsel with Miliukov and the editorial board of *Pravo*, as a result of which he decided to decline. *V dvukh vekakh*, pp. 207–08.

Chapter X

1. According to the diary of Nicholas II, it was on October 27 that Trepov was named palace commandant and that Grand Duke Nicholas Nikolaevich succeeded Grand Duke Vladimir Aleksandrovich as commander of the St. Petersburg Military District. *Dnevnik*, p. 223. Trepov was not replaced as temporary governor-general. Thereafter the principal responsibility for maintaining order in the capital fell on the prefect of the city and the commander of the St. Petersburg Military District.

2. At the time of his appointment to the senate, Garin was forty-four, comparatively young for such an appointment.

3. Trepov ranks very high on Witte's list of enemies and accordingly does not receive evenhanded treatment. But there can be no question that Trepov, who was completely devoted to his sovereign, enjoyed his confidence, as Witte did not, had his ear, and could influence him. The emperor wrote to his mother that Trepov was "absolutely indispensable" to him and that he "is acting in a kind of secretarial capacity. He is experienced and clever and cautious in his advice. I give him Witte's bulky memoranda to read, then he reports on them quickly and concisely. This is of course a secret to everybody but ourselves." *The Letters of Tsar Nicholas and Empress Marie*, p. 212.

4. This is not quite fair to Nicholas. Certainly he was unhappy about signing the October Manifesto, but he did stand by his commitment, as he understood it.

5. On Witte's connections with Rachkovskii *see above* I, ch. XIII, n. 7.

6. Supplementing Witte's account, Lopukhin writes that he saw Witte on January 22, 1906, at the premier's request. Witte was in the midst of negotiating a loan (*see below*, II, ch. XIII) and wanted some advice on how to get foreign Jewish bankers to participate in floating the loan, advice that Lopukhin was qualified to give because of knowledge of Jewish matters acquired while with the Department of Police. Would lifting of Jewish disabilities be enough to win these bankers over? Would such an act make a strong impression on Russian Jews? Which Jewish organizations might be of aid in persuading Jews not to engage in revolutionary activities? Lopukhin writes that he was shocked by Witte's apparent belief in some kind of international Jewish network that could influence Jewish behavior everywhere and told him that such organizations existed only in "anti-Semitic legend" and advised him that the best way to win Jewish support in Russia was by fulfilling the promise of the October Manifesto and granting Jews equality with other subjects. It was then that Lopukhin told Witte that the government was hardly in a position to talk about doing anything for Jews when pogroms were in the making and then went on to tell him about Captain Komissarov. *Otryvki iz vospominanii*, pp. 76–88.

7. A reference to a speech delivered by Prince Urusov in June 1906 concerning the Bialystok pogrom. Russia, Gosudarstvennaia Duma, *Stenograficheskie otchety* (St. Petersburg, 1906–07), II, 1129–32.

8. The text of the minutes and Nicholas's comment will be found in *Revoliutsiia 1905 goda i samoderzhavie*, ed. V. Semennikov (Moscow, 1928), p. 58.

9. Witte's picture of the grand duke as one of his heavier crosses seems excessive in the light of the evidence he presents here. However, if one also takes into account what he says of the grand duke elsewhere, one can understand why he took a dim view of the man.

10. *See above*, p. 79.

11. In the absence of any objective assessment of the grand duke's performance as a military figure, it is appropriate to note what A. A. Polivanov thought. This noted general wrote that the grand duke was abler than most other generals, that he did some good during these years and might have done more if he had a more stable personality and had not been averse to keeping up with military literature, a task he left to General F. F. Palitsyn. *Iz dnevnikov i vospominanii* (Moscow, 1924), pp. 120–23.

12. Witte had a longstanding interest in the question of which organizational model to follow, the French or the Prussian.

13. Concerning Rödiger's fall *see below*, pp. 728–29.

14. Concerning Mrs. Burenina *see above*, II, ch. 1, n. 9.

15. General Rauch's diary corroborates what Witte asserts and adds to it. In his entry

for December 16, 1905, the general writes that Dr. Dubrovin and Bulatsel called on him to arrange for a meeting with the grand duke so that they could warn him about the danger that Russia was in as long as Witte, acting "under the influence of the kikes," was in charge. They claimed that Witte was a member of a Jewish Masonic lodge. General Rauch told them that as a military man the grand duke could not engage in politics. However, the grand duke did agree to see them in General Rauch's quarters. In this entry General Rauch said that he believed what they said about Witte. "Dnevnik G. O. Raukha," *Krasnyi arkhiv* 6(19) (1926): 88–90. As a result of the meeting of the leaders of the Union of the Russian People with the grand duke, it was arranged that they meet publicly with the emperor, a meeting to which Witte refers with bitterness, as well he might. Did the grand duke believe the vicious nonsense that came from the Union of the Russian People? We don't know, but it is likely that he did, given the fact that he arranged for the meeting with Nicholas II. Did the emperor believe the allegations? We have no direct evidence, but the indirect evidence indicates that, at the very least, he thought it might be true. If Nicholas II even suspected it to be true, then we are faced with one of the more bizarre episodes in history, a ruler suspecting his chief minister of being a traitor yet retaining him, at least until this minister could perform certain essential tasks.

A minor point. In his handwritten memoirs (p. 188 verso), Witte wrote that General Rauch was staying at the English Club, yet the Hessen redaction has the general staying at the Yacht Club.

A final note. At this time there were many rumors, some based on fact, of plots to kill Witte. Whatever the grand duke may have thought about Witte by this time, December 1905, and thereafter, he opposed any attempt on the premier's life. When he saw the leaders of the Union of the Russian People, he apparently warned them not to have anything to do with any counterrevolutionary plots and apparently referred to a plot, about which there had been rumors, to seize Witte and some revolutionary leaders and kill them. "Dnevnik G. O. Raukha," pp. 88–90. General Rödiger wrote that toward the beginning of 1906 the grand duke told him that he was keeping General Parensov under surveillance because that general was plotting to replace Nicholas II with Grand Duke Michael Aleksandrovich and to arrest Witte. General Rödiger considered the allegation nonsensical. "Iz zapisok A. F. Redigera," *Krasnyi arkhiv*, 60 (1933): 100.

Chapter XI

1. The source of the epigraph is Hintze to William II, January 28, 1909 (NS), Germany, Auswärtiges Amt, Archiv, Russland, 82, no. 1, Geheim, vol. 6–7.

2. The text of Witte's note to the emperor, dated February 21, 1906, can be found in *Revoliutsiia 1905 i samoderzhavie*, p. 58.

3. As will be seen, the rural police often proved inadequate for dealing with agrarian disorders.

4. This seems to contradict what Witte said elsewhere about Skalon's ability to maintain order.

5. The name "Kingdom of Poland" was an anachronism at the time, given the fact that the kingdom lost its name in 1888 when it was renamed the Vistula Provinces, sometimes referred to as the Governor-Generalship of Warsaw, consisting of ten provinces administered by a governor-general who was also commander of the Warsaw Military District, which was coterminous with the Vistula Provinces. Nonetheless, the name "Kingdom of Poland" continued to be used, as in this case.

6. A reference to the fact that the Russian Orthodox church was an active participant in the effort to Russify the Poles and that many sons of priests who entered government service adhered to their fathers' views. Pobedonostsev was the son of a man who had studied for the priesthood but had not taken the vows and the grandson of a priest. Like many others he considered Polish nationalism and the Roman Catholic church in Poland as two sides of the same coin and agreed that as part of the effort to erase Polish national consciousness it was necessary to limit the influence of the Roman Catholic church.

7. Dmowski's recollection of the exchange differs somewhat from Witte's, but on the whole the two are fairly close. A. F. Fountain, *Roman Dmowski* (Boulder, Colo., 1980), p. 153.

8. Texts of the telegrams from Skalon to Witte will be found in *Tsarizm v borbe s revoliutsiei 1905–1907 gg.* (Moscow, 1936), pp. 150–51.

9. This might be amended by saying that the revolutionaries tried unsuccessfully to direct widespread political strikes that would finish off the work of the October general strike, i.e., bringing down the monarchy.

10. Witte was extremely touchy about any allegation that he was in league with the soviet and consequently tends to be too categorical in denying that he had any dealings, however aboveboard, with the soviet. He even assured A. S. Suvorin that there was a time when he didn't know the address of the soviet. *Das Geheimtagebuch* (Berlin, 1925), p. 251. Allegations that Witte had ties with Nosar continued for many years, leading to the publication in 1911 of a book by one of his "hired pens," A. Morskoi. It was entitled *Iskhod rossiiskoi revoliutsii 1905 i pravitelstvo Nosaria*. The work, as one would expect, gives Witte's view of the events.

11. In this account, Witte obviously forgot what he had written elsewhere about the "Financial Manifesto" issued by the St. Petersburg Soviet on December 2, an act which precipitated the arrest of the members of the soviet. What he said, in another context, in writing about his meeting with the press on October 18, was the following (ms. pp. 152–53).

> The only action taken against newspapers during my tenure was in response to the Petersburg soviet's manifesto calling on everyone to withdraw their deposits from the savings banks, to refuse to make payments to the government in gold, and wherever possible to undermine confidence in the government's ability to meet its financial obligations.
>
> No government, however liberal, could fail to act against such a subversive effort, one based on dishonest allegations, one that attempted to exploit the ignorance of the masses and the widespread intellectual and psychological confusion of the times. Accordingly, when I learned of the manifesto I called a meeting of the cabinet, at which it was decided to act firmly against any newspaper that published the document.
>
> Since I had known Alexis Sergeevich Suvorin for a long time and knew that his *Novoe vremia* sometimes acted thoughtlessly, I sought to keep him out of trouble by warning him in advance. When I phoned him to ask if he intended to publish the manifesto, he said he didn't know. I suggested that he find out and warned him that no good would come to his newspaper if it printed the manifesto. The next day *Novoe vremia* appeared without the manifesto. I learned later that it had already been set up in type when Suvorin, more fearful of me than of his printers, decided against publication. Those newspapers that did publish it were punished.
>
> The manifesto did some damage. Within a short time 150 million rubles were withdrawn from savings banks. These withdrawals, added to what had been spent on the war, placed our finances in a very difficult, almost disastrous position. I will deal later with how I was able to save us from bankruptcy.

12. The word that the emperor used was *molodets*, which can be translated as "fine fellow" or "good chap."

13. This seems to be a very cautious allusion to the rumor that Orlov and not Nicholas II was the father of Grand Duke Alexis Nikolaevich. A. A. Ignatev, who knew Orlov well, refers to the rumor in his *Piatdesiat let v stroiu* (Moscow, 1950), I, 176.

14. When Witte was writing this, in the summer of 1909, Anna Vyrubova was quite involved with Rasputin. Apparently the gossip about this had not yet reached Witte. *See* A. Spiridovich, *Les Dernières Années de la cour de Tzarskoïë Sélo* (Paris, 1928), I, 289–99.

15. Generals-adjutant, there were nearly sixty of them at this time, were usually full generals or admirals and formed the upper echelon of the imperial suite. The title was honorific, but bearers of the title were sometimes given special assignments, such as these, by the emperor.

16. This was written about three months before Stolypin was assassinated.

17. The reference here is to the mutiny of the second Grenadier Rostovskii Regiment.

18. Here, as elsewhere, Witte, like so many contemporaries, tends to overestimate the role of "society" in the events of 1905 and to underestimate the importance of the radicalized workers and the revolutionary parties.

19. He is probably referring to the incident following October 17, when a large crowd appeared at Durnovo's residence to demand that he free political prisoners.

20. Just what Mrs. Chirikova was referring to is not clear. Perhaps she was referring to plans among Socialist Revolutionaries to organize an uprising.

21. A reference to the Second Congress of the Peasants' Union held in Moscow, November 6–10.

22. Things did not happen as rapidly as Witte recalls. Dubasov was not appointed until November 24. He arrived in Moscow on December 4. L. Engelstein, *Moscow 1905* (Stanford, Calif., 1982), p. 70n.

23. In his report of December 15 to the emperor, Witte noted that the cabinet was of the opinion that the authorities should act "decisively and mercilessly" with those who oppose them with arms. *Revoliutsiia 1905–1907 gg. v Rossii: Dokumenty i materialy: Vysshii podem revoliutsii 1905–1907 gg: Vooruzhennye vostanniia noiabr-dekabr 1905 goda* (Moscow, 1955–1963), pt. 1, 156–57.

24. The savage manner in which General Min dealt with the uprising was widely condemned. Spasskii-Odynets, who was from Moscow, and seems to be reporting on the basis of good authority, writes that Grand Duchess Elizabeth Fedorovna broke into tears as she told the emperor and empress about what had happened in Moscow. Also he writes that Grand Duke Nicholas Nikolaevich was very disturbed by what he heard about General Min and proposed that he be either cashiered or given a minor command in the hinterland. He goes on to say that General Min then went to the emperor and showed him an order from Dubasov not to take prisoners and was told that he had acted properly in obeying orders. And that, says Spasskii-Odynets, is why Nicholas would not agree to a rescript thanking Dubasov. *Vospominaniia*, pp. 18–19.

Witte was not directly responsible for the bloody policy followed in suppressing the uprising, but he certainly encouraged it. For example, Witte, who felt that Dubasov was not acting decisively, called on the minister of interior on December 17 to complain. Durnovo then got Dubasov on the phone and told him to act mercilessly. Later that evening Durnovo received a telegram in which Dubasov reported that he had used artillery fire on one rebel stronghold and that in the course of the firing many women and children were killed. G. M. Vetlugin, "S. Iu. Vitte i dekabrskoe vosstanie v Moskve," *Byloe* 6(34) (1925): 225–26. In his account Witte tried to minimize Admiral Dubasov's responsibility for the brutality employed in suppressing the uprising and assigned whatever blame there was to General Min. He dealt with General Min not only in his account of the uprising but also in three other places in his memoirs:

> In putting down the uprising in Moscow, General Min may have acted with severity, but when there is open war, with barricades, then the military's first obligation is to act like military. A commander cannot require Bismarckian diplomatic abilities from his men. (Handwritten memoirs, p. 164 verso.)
>
> I approved of General Min's actions in Moscow. Force should be met with force, with no sentimentality, no quarter given. But as soon as the revolutionary activity or outbreak is put down, the spilling of the blood of innocent people is cruel and brutish. Unfortunately, General Min continued to permit aimless and heartless brutality after the rising was put down. (Handwritten memoirs, p. 276.)
>
> Unfortunately, after the rising had been put down, General Min permitted unjustifiable excesses. (Dictated memoirs, p. 2043.)

Witte was obviously very disturbed by the widespread disorder in December and reacted in an uncharacteristically fierce fashion, a reflection of the tense situation and, probably, of his psychological state. Writing to his mother in January 1906, Nicholas II said: "As for Witte, since the happenings in Moscow he has radically changed his views; now he wants to hang and shoot everybody." *The Letters of Tsar Nicholas and Empress Marie*, pp. 211-12.

25. The texts of some of the relevant correspondence will be found in *Revoliutsiia 1905 g. i samoderzhavie*, pp. 41-43.

26. Given the gravity of the situation in the Caucasus, particularly in December, when Tiflis was isolated by railroading strikes, the brevity of Witte's comments about Vorontsov-Dashkov is striking. This may be because Witte exercised no authority over the viceroy. From what Witte writes, it may be guessed that he recommended that Vorontsov-Dashkov be replaced by a younger and more vigorous man and was rebuffed.

27. *See below*, p. 582.

28. That part of the army detailed for use in the theater of operations was known as the field army.

29. Undoubtedly, Witte deserves most of the credit for suggesting these expeditions, but the credit is not his alone. For example, Nicholas II wrote to his mother that Grand Duke Nicholas Nikolaevich had suggested sending these two men to command the expeditions. *The Letters of Tsar Nicholas and Empress Marie*, p. 211. Meller-Zakomelskii gained favorable attention in high places for his work in suppressing the naval mutiny in Sebastopol. General Rödiger, the war minister at the time, asserts that Meller-Zakomelskii misrepresented what he had done in Sebastopol, that the man was a "thorough scoundrel" who had gained command of the expedition through influence in high places. "Iz zapisok A. F. Redigera," pp. 103-04.

30. In this period, late December, Witte was very concerned about having sufficient troops in places where trouble was likely to break out. In one report to the emperor he complained that neither he nor the minister of interior was being adequately informed by the minister of war about the movement of troops, their locations, their strength. He suggested, possibly with some malice, that thought be given to replacing him with a military man. *Revoliutsiia 1905 g. i samoderzhavie*, pp. 30-32.

31. This is not the only mention of such a premonition. Witte's words were prophetic.

32. This massacre helped speed up the growth in labor unrest that had begun to manifest itself in 1910.

Chapter XII

1. General Sollogub had not yet been appointed governor-general. Witte may be referring to General Böckmann, Sollogub's predecessor.

2. It is odd that Witte makes no comment about the fact that he had not been first consulted about this recommendation.

3. Apparently a reference to "Iz noveishei istorii krestianskago voprosa," *Vestnik Evropy* 44 (1909): no. 4, 631–37, no. 5, 99–115.

4. The documents referred to are among the Witte papers in the Bakhmeteff Archive. What Migulin proposed was the sale of some privately owned land and large tracts of state and crown lands to peasants, who would be enabled to buy through loans, primarily from the Peasants' Bank. Owners of land designated for sale would be compelled to sell at prices fixed by the government. Much of the privately owned land that he was talking about was land for which peasants were paying rent to nobles.

5. This was part of a general shift to the right among the landed nobility.

6. The text of the proposal and other relevant documents will be found in *Agrarnyi vopros v sovete ministrov (1906 g.)* (Moscow, 1924). Kokovtsev speaks of a conversation in which Kutler told him that Witte had suggested the proposal to him and then, when opposition to it arose, made him the scapegoat. *Iz moego proshlago*, I, 130.

7. Typical of the widespread hostility toward the Kutler proposal was the reaction of General Rauch, who noted in his diary entry for January 3, 1906, the need to enlist Grand Duke Nicholas Nikolaevich in the effort to have the proposal killed. Not long after talking to the grand duke he received a note saying that he, the grand duke, had spoken to the emperor and as a result could tell him that "nothing of the kind would take place" and went on to say, "Thank God, with God's help Russia and the Tsar will be saved." "Dnevnik G. O. Raukha," pp. 96–97.

8. *See above*, p. 327.

9. The text used for this translation comes from *Revoliutsiia 1905 g. i samoderzhavie*, p. 57. It is taken from the original received by Nicholas II, which differs slightly from the text that appears in Witte's memoirs. On Witte's letter is a notation from Nicholas, obviously meant for Trepov: "The count is angry," a fact that apparently caused the emperor no grief, another indication, if indication is needed, that Witte's outbursts, while of some cathartic value to him, were self-defeating.

10. In another context Witte writes:

> When I saw in which direction the camarilla was leading the Emperor, a direction I knew he approved of, I asked in February that His Majesty let me depart. Moreover, I was then in fact ill. But the Emperor, acting through Trepov, directly and indirectly asked me not to leave, in any event not before the conclusion of the loan and the convocation of the State Duma. (Handwritten memoirs, p. 249 verso.)

11. *See above*, p. 477.

12. Witte's diatribe against Timiriazev seems motivated by a desire to show that his hands are clean, but in presenting his case he doesn't tell all of the truth. *See* n. 15. It should also be noted that the two argued about their differences in public, through interviews given to journalists.

13. Manuilov, a bit of an adventurer, was, like Prince Andronnikov, later to be connected with Rasputin. For an earlier reference to Manuilov, *see* p. 16.

14. This account of the efforts to have Witte receive Gapon is from the handwritten

memoirs, pp. 223-24, and was written in 1909. Early in 1911, he dealt with the same episode in his dictated memoirs, pp. 673-75, in the following manner.

> Once Manuilov came to me and, speaking for Prince Meshcherskii, earnestly entreated me to receive the priest Gapon. I was astonished to learn that he was in Russia and within a few days sent him packing out of the country. But, before Gapon had left, Prince Meshcherskii tried to persuade me to receive Gapon, who, he stated, was repentant and would be of service to the government in the field of investigation.
>
> I replied that I had never seen Gapon in my life, did not want to see him, and would not receive him. I said that Gapon, by deceiving Sviatopolk-Mirskii and Plehve, was responsible for the events leading to January 9, as a result of which several hundred people were killed. I would not, I said, speak to this scoundrel.
>
> I was recently told by persons in a position to know that *Russkoe slovo* had bought the rights to Gapon's memoirs and would publish them this summer. They tell me that the memoirs contain an entry stating that Gapon was lying when he told Manuilov and Meshcherskii that he wanted to offer his help to the government, that, in fact, he wanted to see me because it had been decided that I was to be killed and that he was to do the shooting.

15. In suggesting that he wanted to have nothing to do with Gapon, Witte is not telling all. The fact is that he supported Gapon's efforts to revive the assembly of St. Petersburg Factory Workers as a way of winning workers away from the revolutionaries. That he did so was not necessarily a cause for shame, but because the whole affair with Gapon ended so shamefully he apparently tried to hide any connection, however innocent and well intentioned, with the Gapon undertaking. "K istorii 'Sobranie Russkikh Fabrichno-Zavodskikh Rabochikh g. S. Petersburg,'" *Krasnaia letopis* 1 (1922): 302; N. Petrov, "Gapon i Graf Vitte," *Byloe* 1(29) (1925): 15-27; W. Sablinsky, *The Road to Bloody Sunday* (Princeton, N.J., 1976), pp. 305-15.

Of passing interest is the fact that it was an N. A. Demchinskii who sought permission to reopen branches of the Gapon organization. He appears to be the N. A. Demchinskii who worked under Witte when the latter was minister of way and communications. Also of passing interest is the fact that Witte does not mention that Joseph Dillon told him of Gapon's presence in St. Petersburg. *The Eclipse of Russia*, pp. 164-65.

16. A folder on the Matiushenskii case is among the Witte papers in the Bakhmeteff Archive.

17. Kokovtsev, who likes to get his own back at Witte's expense, writes that in the fall of 1911 Witte quietly agreed to serve as adviser to the Russian Bank for Foreign Trade but then quietly changed his mind because he could not get a waiver of the rule that he could not remain in the State Council if he accepted the post. *Iz moego proshlago*, II, 94-96.

Chapter XIII

1. In the summer of 1911, while in Biarritz, Witte began writing about the background events relevant to the negotiation of the loan, intending to deal with the loan itself when he returned to St. Petersburg. He did not do so, as he notes, because of his fear that what he wrote might be taken by the police. As a result he waited until the summer of 1912, when he was at Bad Salzschlirf, to complete his account of the loan. Because much of what he included in writing about the background was repetitious, it is omitted here.

The chapter title is taken from the title of a pamphlet he published in 1913.

2. Although Witte managed to negotiate the loan without help from Jewish bankers, he would have preferred to have their help, and as indicated in an earlier note, he talked to Lopukhin about what he could do to get their support. But because he did not do what Lopukhin suggested, secure legal equality for the Jews of Russia, he closed the door to support from Jewish bankers.

3. As noted earlier, Witte was close to the Rafalovich family and had helped some of its members find positions with the Ministry of Finance.

4. Dolgorukii and Maklakov were acting without authorization from the Kadet party. O. Crisp, "The Russian Liberals and the 1906 Anglo-French Loan to Russia," *The Slavonic and East European Review* 39 (1961): 497.

5. This committee dealt with foreign loans.

6. Kokovtsev, as one might expect, tells a different story. He writes that Witte implored him to undertake this mission and in the course of doing so apologized for having been so hostile. He writes, too, that Witte told him he felt so desperate that he sometimes thought of suicide. *Iz moego proshlago*, I, 116–17.

7. Witte is being somewhat cryptic here. Elsewhere he makes clear that although William II was angry with him, the emperor still tried to be on good terms with him as part of his effort to wean Russia away from France.

8. In December, Russia's ability to maintain the gold standard was greatly weakened, so much so that there was some thought of temporarily abandoning that standard. "Finansovoe polozhenie tsarskogo samoderzhaviia v period Russko-Iaponskoi voiny i pervoi russkoi revoliutsii," *Istoricheskii arkhiv* 2 (1955): 127–32.

9. Witte is being a bit petty here, to make sure that Kokovtsev doesn't receive any credit.

10. Elsewhere Witte notes that the Russian Foreign Office was able to decipher telegrams to and from foreign embassies in St. Petersburg.

11. One can well imagine what effect such a report would have had on the French government, given the fact that it had been shown the instructions that Cassini had received. For the text of the draft of these instructions, *see Krasnyi arkhiv* 41–42 (1930): 2.

12. A reference to the use of bribery to gain the cooperation of French journalists.

13. Poincaré informed the French ambassador to Russia that he considered the argument a weak one. R. Girault, *Emprunts russes et investissements français en Russie, 1887–1914* (Paris, 1973), p. 442n.

14. The loan was to be repaid over a period of fifty years, and Russia was prohibited from floating another loan on the French money market within a period of two years. Ibid., 444 n. 69, 445.

15. Witte was to change his mind about not having the documents published, apparently because of his desire to weaken Kokovtsev's position by showing that the credit for the loan was his alone. In 1913 he published a forty-four–page pamphlet entitled *Spravka o tom, kak byl zakliuchen vneshnii zaem 1906 goda, spasshii finansovoe polozhenie Rossii* in forty copies labeled "confidential." At the end of 1913, Witte sent copies of the pamphlet, together with New Year's greetings, to Kokovtsev, Nicholas II, and others in high places. Ananich and Ganelin, "Opyt kritiki memuarov," p. 360.

Chapter XIV

1. When Witte set down the material on which this chapter is based, Stolypin was already dead, but he was very much on Witte's mind. As a result Witte digressed much too often to deal with the dead premier's alleged misdeeds. Much of the extraneous material has been removed in the process of editing.

2. How much importance Witte attached to broadening the suffrage in conformity with the promise made in the October Manifesto is shown by the fact that within hours after returning from Peterhof on October 17 he summoned Kryzhanovskii and asked that he

submit a draft of a proposal for broadening the suffrage the following day. Kryzhanovskii writes that it was who suggested that speed could best be achieved by starting with the Bulygin electoral law, which he had helped draft. *Vospominaniia*, pp. 53–55. Kryzhanovskii's statement does not necessarily contradict Witte's argument, and excuse, that he had no choice but to work with the Bulygin electoral law. The October Manifesto called for going ahead with the "scheduled elections," meaning that there would be little time to draft a completely new electoral law.

3. A reference to the sessions of the cabinet held on November 19–20. One can speak of three proposals on the table because there were two versions of the government proposal. Kryzhanovskii, *Vospominaniia*, pp. 61–64; H. D. Mehlinger and J. M. Thompson, *Count Witte and the Tsarist Government in the 1905 Revolution* (Bloomington, Ind., 1972), pp. 117–18.

4. As the record shows, Witte was more ambivalent about what kind of suffrage should be granted than he admits here, where he is defending the law that was enacted, the law with which he was identified in the popular mind. *See below*, n. 6.

5. The conference opened on December 5, then met again two days later, and closed on December 9. The holiday that Witte refers to was the name day of Nicholas II. The participants in the conference were invited to attend the services held on that day and to lunch. Tagantsev, *Perezhitoe*, pp. 93–94.

6. Witte's account of the proceedings is a bit fuzzy, partly, one can assume, because of faulty memory, partly because he is defensive. The minutes of the meetings show that he was more concerned with the short-range consequences of the electoral law than with its long-range consequences, concerned with the psychological effect of a broadened franchise. As he put it, there was a revolution in progress, and while it was easy to regain control of the cities, it was not at all certain that force alone would suffice in the countryside; it was necessary that the electoral law be the kind that would convince the people, particularly the peasantry, that its voice would be heard, yet not the kind of law that would permit the State Duma to turn into a constituent assembly. In this respect he argued that a revamped State Council could provide the necessary buffer between the emperor and the popularly elected body.

In discussing the merits of the government proposals and the Shipov proposal he showed ambivalence. Thus, he argued that the Shipov proposal would be more popular with the people than the other proposals, but it would be more dangerous for the state; reason told him that it was the one with the most merit, and if he had to choose he would cross himself and vote for the Shipov proposal. "Tsarskoselskie soveshchaniia," *Byloe* 3(25) (1917): 245–58 *passim*. Properly speaking, what issued from the special conference of December 5–9 was not a new electoral law but a decree, issued on December 11, that, while not enunciating the principle of universal male suffrage, made virtually all males over the age of twenty-five eligible to vote by adding new categories of those with the franchise. The decree modified the electoral law of August 6, 1905, but it did not rescind its provisions for indirect and weighted voting. The decree, which became popularly known as the Witte electoral law, was sharply criticized by the opposition, which, as we know, wanted universal, direct, and equal suffrage and the secret ballot.

It should be added that the position Witte took at this point was consistent with his position during the discussions preceding the enactment of the Bulygin law, that the masses should be made to feel that they would be heard, perhaps listened to, but that they should not exercise sovereign power.

7. *Trudoviki*: the name usually given to the *Trudovaia gruppa* (Labor Group), a group of deputies in the State Duma somewhat to the left of the Kadets and to the right of the

socialists. Led by members of the intelligentsia, it attracted the more radical peasant deputies and was primarily interested in having landlord-held land distributed among the peasantry. In his handwritten memoirs (p. 116 verso), Witte contemptuously refers to F. Aladyn, the leading figure in the Labor Group, as having been "a Russian commercial agent" at a London hotel.

8. Here Witte is once more defensive, blaming Durnovo. True, there was interference, but whether or not it produced the effect Witte ascribes to it is questionable. T. Emmons, *The Formation of Political Parties and the First National Elections in Russia* (Cambridge, 1983), pp. 181–93.

9. At the end of October, Nicholas II appointed Count Solskii as chairman of a commission to transform the State Council into a legislative body, in effect the upper chamber of the legislature. Witte argues that there had never been any question in the minds of the government that the State Council would be partners with the State Duma in the making of the laws. However, in the public mind the impression was formed that the October Manifesto meant that the laws would be made by a unicameral legislature, the State Duma. The Solskii Commission was also charged with rewriting the law of August 6, 1905, establishing a consultative State Duma, in conformity with the promise of the manifesto. The commission began its deliberations in November and concluded them in January 1906. Its recommendations were then considered at a special conference, presided over by Nicholas II, that met at the Great Palace of Tsarskoe Selo on February 14 and 16, 1906. To what Witte says about the conference the following should be added.

As on other occasions during 1905, Witte argued for protecting the powers of the monarch while giving the masses, particularly the peasantry, assurance that their voices would be heard by the monarch. Thus, at this conference he argued that since the State Council would be an "aristocratic" body, with no peasants in its ranks, the peasantry would consider the State Duma as their avenue to the emperor. Therefore, he proposed that if the State Council rejected a bill passed by the State Duma, the emperor could still consider such a bill if he felt there were reason to do so. His suggestion was not accepted by the emperor. "Tsarskoselskie soveshchaniia," *Byloe* 5/6(27/28) (1917): 305–06.

It should be noted that, although Witte refers to the October Manifesto as a constitution in his memoirs, he explicitly denied this to be the case at the conference, asserting that the emperor had granted the October Manifesto of his own volition. Ibid., p. 307. The emperor did not like the word "constitution," and Witte and his successors were not only careful not to use it, but also to contend that Russia did not have a constitution.

There was little for the conference to do with the recommendations of the Solskii Commission with respect to the State Duma other than to change the relevant articles in the law of August 6 to transform the State Duma into a legislative body.

10. These regulations were signed by the emperor on March 8, 1906.

11. In this section, even more so than in earlier ones in this chapter, Witte, in "trying to set the record straight," ignores much of the record and in so doing omits much that redounds to his credit. As is evident from the text, Witte concentrates on showing that Trepov was working against him and in trying to show that if not for his, Witte's, efforts the emperor would have been stripped of much of his powers.

12. Until April 1906, the fundamental laws consisted of those laws grouped together at the beginning of the Complete Code of Laws that dealt with the powers of the "unlimited, autocratic" emperor, those governing succession to the throne, and those dealing with the imperial family. The revised fundamental laws were to take into account the changes in the power of the emperor and the structure of the government resulting from the October

Manifesto. Most scholars consider the revised fundamental laws to be constitutional in nature, but, as noted, this was not the view of the emperor.

13. Witte is not being very explicit here. What he implies is that what people like Trepov and Solskii wanted was a liberal constitution that would permit the upper nobility to realize its ancient dream of sharing power with the emperor.

14. This is not the full text of the report. What Witte omits here is his recommendation that the revised fundamental laws be issued as soon as possible, certainly before the elections to the State Duma and the State Council. "Iz arkhiva S. Iu. Vitte," *Krasnyi arkhiv* 4/5(11/12) (1925): 115–16.

15. Witte also made this point at the special conference of February 1906.

16. *See above*, pp. 296–98.

17. On February 20, 1906, after receiving the draft of the revised fundamental laws from Count Solskii, Witte asked Baron Nolde to look at several conservative constitutions to see which of their features could be adapted for use in Russia. Because Russia had not made a distinction between decrees and laws, he was particularly interested in how these constitutions dealt with the distinction between the two. The Solskii draft was then revised to incorporate features of the Japanese and Prussian constitutions. Tagantsev, *Perezhitoe*, pp. 157–58, 157–58n.

18. Witte was to demonstrate his position on such matters during the third State Duma. *See below*, pp. 726–27.

19. *See below*, p. 584, n. 22 for Witte's interpretation of "independence of the judiciary."

20. Tagantsev argues that Mechelin was "anti-Russian" and for that reason wanted the revised fundamental laws to make it appear that Finland had voluntarily joined the Russian Empire and had not been annexed by it. Mechelin wanted the article in question to read that the Grand Duchy of Finland was "indissolubly united with the Russian Empire." The key word here was "united," to which Tagantsev objected. *Perezhitoe*, p. 170, n. 1.

21. This special conference, which was held at the Great Palace of Tsarskoe Selo on April 7, 9, 11, and 12, considered three drafts of the revised fundamental laws, the first being the one prepared by the cabinet, the second the one that had been submitted to it and which had been revised, and a third by Professor Otto Eichelmann, professor of public law at the University of Kiev. The last received short shrift. In the heated discussion of whether or not to retain the word "unlimited" in the article defining the power of the emperor, Witte argued that all emperors beginning with Alexander I had had to rule within the limits of the law and hence did not have unlimited power. At one point, however, he argued that there might be occasions when the sovereign might have to ignore the law because "it is necessary to reckon with the needs of the state, which are beyond logic." (Apparently what he feared was a State Duma that would be difficult to control.) "Tsarsko-selskie soveshchaniia," *Byloe* 4(26) (1917); 194, 205–06.

22. The weight of opinion is not with Witte. It is that Article 243 of the Statutes of Judicial Institutions promulgated by Alexander II made judges irremovable by anyone, except for cause. S. Kucherov, *Courts, Lawyers and Trials Under the Last Three Tsars* (New York, 1953), pp. 93–94.

23. The available evidence is insufficient for evaluating Witte's claim that his telephone call to Trepov was decisive in the emperor's decision to publish the revised fundamental laws before the opening of the State Duma. M. Szeftel, *The Russian Constitution of April 23, 1906* (Brussels, 1976), pp. 77–78.

24. Indirect evidence supports Witte's contention about Trepov's role. It appears that Trepov wanted Goremykin to serve as a *locum tenens*, while he, Trepov, would try to achieve what Witte had failed to do: form a cabinet that was liberal in composition, one that would be able to work with a State Duma.

25. In his introduction to the Slovo edition of Witte's memoirs, I. V. Hessen wrote that neither he nor any of the others mentioned took part in the discussion of the revised fundamental laws to which Witte refers. He asserts that a few days before publication of these laws, *Rech*, the newspaper he edited, was able to obtain a copy of the laws, which it then criticized sharply, criticisms that let to some changes in the laws. He argues that Witte must have remembered events incorrectly, basing what he said on his recollection of a "liberal manifesto" that he, Hessen, and Miliukov had prepared around 1902 at the request of V. I. Kovalevskii, a copy of which had been given to Witte at a subsequent date. But Hessen does not attempt to explain the provenance of the document Witte cites, which clearly refers to the revised fundamental laws. Witte, *Vospominaniia* (Berlin, 1922), I, 11-12. Hessen's statement does not close the case. Among Witte's papers were the document from V. I. Kovalevskii, dated April 18, 1906, to which Witte refers, also a copy of a memorandum from Kovalevskii to the emperor, dated April 7, 1905, detailing the critical situation in which the country found itself, the memorandum being accompanied by the draft of a "liberal manifesto" that the emperor might issue. "Iz arkhiva S. Iu. Vitte," *Krasnyi arkhiv* 4-5(11-12) (1925): 108-20.

Was Hessen mistaken in placing the "liberal manifesto" around 1902, or were there two proposed manifestos? More important is whether or not the kind of meeting referred to in the Kovalevskii document cited ever took place. Hessen says it did not. Miliukov in his memoirs says neither yea nor nay. M. M. Kovalevskii writes in his memoirs that V. I. Kovalevskii, who, as he notes, seemed to have had the confidence of General Trepov, asked him to look over a draft of the revised fundamental laws and to comment on them and so he did, alone. "Moia zhizn," *Istoriia SSSR* 4 (1969): 69. Where does all this leave us? In a state of confusion. All that can be said with reasonable certainty is that Witte was writing on the basis of information received from V. I. Kovalevskii, who, acting on behalf of Trepov, asked at least one of the persons cited to comment on the revised fundamental laws.

26. As is evident from the preceding notes, the minutes of the conference were eventually published, after the fall of the tsarist regime.

27. It should be emphasized that the question of whether or not to retain the death penalty was a highly charged one and that the opposition made the abolition of the death penalty one of its major demands.

28. *See below*, p. 659.

29. The text of Witte's report to the emperor about the meeting of the cabinet at which it was decided to recommend against the establishment of field courts-martial will be found in *Revoliutsiia 1905-1907 gg. v Rossii: Dokumenty i materialy. Vysshii podem revoliutsii 1905-1907 gg.*, pt. I, 156-57.

30. Witte is referring to the so-called temporary legislation issued following the assassination of Alexander II, legislation that, in effect, became permanent as a result of being renewed.

31. The Committee of Ministers was abolished shortly after Witte left office.

32. It should be recalled that the decree of December 12, 1904, called for examination of the law on exceptional measures.

33. As K. N. Mironenko points out, the press regulations of March 18 and April 26 still permitted the authorities considerable latitude in curbing the press. "Manifest 17

oktiabria 1905 g.,'' *Uchennye zapiski* 225, Leningradskii universitet, Seriia iuridicheskikh nauk, no. 10 (1958), 168.

34. As Witte pointed out earlier, a special conference under A. P. Ignatev had been established to deal with some of the questions that had not been settled by the decree of April 17, 1905, but it accomplished nothing. During Witte's tenure, Prince A. D. Obolenskii took an active part in the preparatory work involved in calling a church council to examine the state of the Russian Orthodox church and possibly call for the reestablishment of the patriarchate, but little had been accomplished by the time he and Witte left office. J. W. Cunningham, *A Vanquished Hope: The Movement for Church Renewal in Russia, 1905–1906* (Crestwood, N.Y., 1981), pp. 205–65.

35. He is referring to the power to interpellate ministers and similar powers given to the State Duma and the State Council which made it possible for the two chambers to make life difficult for the ministers.

36. The manifesto pledged improvement in peasant life, this in response to peasant unrest. The decree cut redemption dues for 1906 in half and freed peasants from the obligation to pay redemption dues after the end of 1906.

37. *See above*, p. 157.

38. At its second convention, in late November 1905, the Union for the Attainment of Equal Rights for Jews (in which Vinaver was the leading figure) voted against sending still another delegation to Witte and vowed to continue the struggle for equal rights by working together with the ''general movement for liberty,'' clearly ignoring Witte's advice. S. M. Dubnow, *History of the Jews in Russia and Poland* (Philadelphia, 1920), III, 131–32. *See also Voskhod*, December 1, 1905, cols. 21–30, and December 16, 1905, cols. 20–28.

39. This section is based on the handwritten memoirs, pp. 343–53. Some details are omitted because in these pages Witte repeated much of what he had said elsewhere. As is obvious, the theme of what he says is that he was constrained by events over which he had no control.

Chapter XV

1. One should add that the excellent showing in the elections to the State Duma made by the opposition hurt Witte badly in the eyes of Nicholas II, who had already lost confidence in his premier. Also, it should be noted that General Trepov and Grand Duke Nicholas Nikolaevich were hard at work to persuade the emperor to get rid of Witte. Koroleva, *Pervaia rossiiskaia revoliutsiia i tsarizm*, p. 106.

2. This is from the handwritten memoirs, pp. 230 and 354 verso. In the dictated memoirs, pp. 2084–85, in dealing with this conversation, Witte writes: ''I told him that I was ready to stay on if the conditions I considered indispensable for me to be able to appear before the State Duma were met and added that even if they were met and I stayed on the time would come when I would have to leave my post, but then it would not be at my initiative.''

3. Witte does not specify what these disagreements were, but it is evident from what he says elsewhere and from other sources that he had differences with those to the left of him, e.g., Prince Obolenskii, and those to the right, particularly Durnovo, who, toward the end, failed to attend cabinet meetings for a long time. In referring to ''influential circles,'' he meant what he and others called the court camarilla and the growing conservative wing of the landed nobility. From the evidence it is clear that he was not imagining things.

4. In his diary entry for April 15, Nicholas II wrote: ''Was very busy, accepted Witte's request.'' *Dnevnik*, p. 238.

5. This is from the handwritten memoirs p. 358 and was written between late August and early October 1912. A few months earlier, in February, he had dictated a slightly different account (typescript, p. 1978): "I asked him to tell me which of my enemies. He told me he had selected Goremykin. I replied: 'What kind of enemy is he? If the others are of the same caliber, they represent no danger.' He smiled at this." One version may represent what Witte recalls having said, the other what he wishes he had said.

6. Witte's chronology does not agree with the emperor's. From the account in his handwritten memoirs, as translated here, it appears that he saw Nicholas II on April 17 and April 23. The emperor's diary mentions accepting Witte's request to leave on April 15, but does not say that he received him on that day. In the entry for April 20, Nicholas says that he saw Witte that day. *Dnevnik*, pp. 238–39. To add to the confusion, Witte asserted in his dictated memoirs (p. 1977) that "when I submitted my request to leave and saw the Emperor, he asked whom I would recommend as my replacement." This seems to say that he submitted his request in person, and that might have been on April 15. Which dates are right is of no great moment, but the discrepancies have to be noted.

7. N. G. Koroleva writes, without giving a source, that Nicholas II preferred not to appoint Witte to the State Council but did so only at the urging of Count D. M. Solskii. *Pervaia russkaia revoliutsiia i tsarizm*, p. 106n.

8. To say that the speech delivered by Nicholas II was based on the Kovalevskii draft is stretching a point, as a comparison between the speech and the draft will show. The text of the draft can be found in "Iz arkhiva A. Iu. Vitte," *Krasnyi arkhiv* 4–5(11–12): 143–45.

Appendix

1. As should be quite evident by now, Witte was in the habit of collecting documentary material to support his version of events. The three documents translated here were typed and placed between pages 129 and 130 of the handwritten memoirs and numbered 129a, and 129b *et seq.*

2. In addition to the two drafts of a manifesto to which Witte refers there was a third, prepared separately by Baron Budberg during the night of October 14–15. In this one the State Duma would have been bicameral, with a lower house elected by universal suffrage and an upper house chosen in the manner adopted for the State Council after its reform. He also spoke of the ministers being chosen by the emperor, on recommendation of the chairman of the Council of Ministers, which would be responsible to the State Duma. Whether by this he meant "ministerial responsibility" in the Western sense is not clear. "Neizvestnyi proekt manifesta 17 Oktiabria 1905 goda," *Sovetskie arkhivy* 2 (1979): 63–65. In preparing this stillborn version of a manifesto, Baron Budberg said that it was needed to save Russia from revolution. Whether or not he thought at the time that Witte was a traitor and was thereby trying to circumvent him, it is a fact that soon after October 17 he was of that opinion and worked with a group of guards officers who were of the same mind and who were trying to collect evidence against Witte. Iu. B. Solovev, *Samoderzhavie i dvorianstvo v 1902–1907 gg.* (Leningrad, 1981), pp. 88–89.

A final note. Witte heard of the existence of a third draft and in December 1905 asked General Mosolov to see it. He was told there was no such draft.

3. At this time the Solskii conference was considering a proposal to reorganize the Council of Ministers into something like a cabinet, a corporate body with an appointed chairman at its head. The fate of the Committee of Ministers was also under discussion. It was expected that, if the Council of Ministers were reorganized as proposed, Witte would be its chairman.

4. In preparing the memorandum Witte obviously took it upon himself to deal with the state of Russia at the time and what needed to be done. The document runs to about 4,000 words. The report, based on the memorandum, which Nicholas II affirmed on October 17 is about 1,100 words long. The text of the memorandum can be found in "Manifest 17 oktiabria," *Krasnyi arkhiv* 11–12 (1925): 51–61. A translation of the report will be found in S. Harcave, *First Blood*, 289–92.

5. The reference to legislative initiative is puzzling because the final version of the manifesto does not mention it.

6. Witte himself makes reference to such allegations. At least as early as March 1905 there were those at court who were saying that Witte, working hand in hand with Jewry, wanted to act as if he were trying to save the monarchy but was in fact scheming to overthrow it and establish a republic with himself as president. L. Tikhomirov, "25 let nazad: Iz dnevnikov L. Tikhomirova," *Krasnyi arkhiv* 38 (1930): 67.

Editor's Notes to Volume III

Chapter I

1. Witte had the unfortunate habit of using the first-person singular when he should have used the first-person plural, as in describing his trips abroad with his wife. I have corrected him. A word about his grandson, Lev Kirillovich Naryshkin, to whom he dedicated his dictated memoirs. He was born in February 1905 and from all accounts was the subject of grandfather Witte's doting affection. Among the papers of Nicholas II was a letter from Witte, intended to be delivered after his death, requesting that the emperor permit Lev Kirillovich Naryshkin to inherit his grandfather's title and to be known as Lev Kirillovich Naryshkin Count Witte. Nicholas II obviously ignored the request. *Monarkhiia pered krusheniem, 1914–1917* (Moscow, 1927), pp. 100–01.

2. Imperialists: monarchists who favored the restoration of the empire, under Bonaparte rule. Prince Napoleon, it should be noted, was related to the Russian Leuchtenbergs. His brother served as an officer in the Russian army.

3. Witte is repeating what President Loubet told him a year earlier.

4. This, apparently, was the occasion when Mechnikov gave the advice, to which Witte refers earlier, about how Witte should have dealt with the revolutionaries.

5. Witte deals with this episode in his handwritten memoirs, pp. 359–61, and in his dictated memoirs, pp. 2020–24. What appears here is a conflation of the two.

6. I have abridged some of the exchange between Freedericksz and Witte because of its wordiness.

7. Witte was a member of the State Council and the Finance Committee. Also he retained the civil service rank of actual privy councillor and the title of state secretary of his majesty. Apparently his chief source of income was his stipend as member of the State Council.

8. Witte later changed his view of Stolypin, with a vengeance.

9. The bracketed question marks are Witte's.

10. The second letter is a good illustration of the intemperate, often coarse language Witte used when angered, language that served chiefly to irritate the recipient. There are insignificant differences between what Witte says in his handwritten memoirs, p. 361, and in his dictated memoirs, p. 2023, about the sequence of events. Copies of these letters are in the Columbia Archive.

11. Witte deals with this episode in his handwritten memoirs, pp. 358 verso–361 verso, and in his dictated memoirs, pp. 2021–28. What appears here is a conflation of the two.

12. The emperor's feelings about Witte's return are expressed in a letter to his mother:

To my great regret Count Witte has returned from abroad. It would have been more sensible of him and convenient for me if he had stayed away. As soon as he was back a peculiar atmosphere full of all sorts of rumors and gossip and insinuations began to form around him. Some of the wretched papers are already beginning to say he is coming back into power, and that only he can save the country. Evidently the Jewish clique is starting to sow sedition again, trying to undo all the good which my own and Stolypin's efforts for peace have been able to achieve. *As long as I live*, I will never trust that man again with the smallest thing. I had quite enough of last year's experiment. It is still like a nightmare to me.

Thank God I have not seen him yet.

The Letters of Tsar Nicholas and Empress Marie (London, 1937), p. 221.

What lay behind the assertion of utter mistrust and the reference to a Jewish clique? As we know, Nicholas had earlier on come to dislike and mistrust Witte but apparently had put these feelings aside when he appointed Witte to the post of premier. Then, within weeks after October 17, as he began to be disappointed with the results of the October Manifesto and with Witte's performance, he evidently came to accept, wholly or with some reservations, the accusations against Witte that so many around him fervently believed in, namely, that Witte was a power-hungry man who wanted to turn Russia into a republic, with himself as president, that he was a member of a Jewish Masonic lodge and part of a Jewish-Masonic conspiracy to subvert Russia, and that he was working hand in glove with people like Nosar, the head of the St. Petersburg Soviet. *See* Iu. B. Solovev, *Samoderzhavie i dvorianstvo v 1902–1907 gg.* (Leningrad, 1981), pp. 188–89.

It is apparent, too, that Premier Stolypin also believed that Witte was a subversive character, as Witte notes.

Nicholas was as good as his word. Aside from permitting Witte to complete the work of arranging for a monument to Alexander III, he never again entrusted Witte with any responsibility, however minor, thus depriving himself of the use of the talents of the ablest man to have served under him.

On the other hand, protocol was preserved in the treatment of Witte, a count, a member of the State Council, actual privy councilor and state secretary of his majesty. And when Witte died the official government newspaper carried a proper obituary, referring to Witte as "a remarkable Russian statesman" and listing all his positions, honors, and titles. *Pravitelstvennyi vestnik*, March 3, 1915. As we know, the news of Witte's death gave Nicholas II a sense of peace. All very bizarre.

13. What were Witte's aspirations when he returned? He could easily have found well-paid employment outside the government, but he preferred to remain in government service. He valued his seat in the State Council, where he spoke up on matters that lay within his competence. He took his work on the Finance Committee seriously. And he kept hoping that the emperor would give him an appointment as ambassador, as promised, preferably to a country such as France.

From time to time rumors would fly that Witte was about to be called back to power. And there were repeated insinuations that Witte was trying to "rehabilitate himself," i.e., trying to become *persona grata* at court. None of this was true. If anything, Witte chose to act as a gadfly to the powers that be. Perhaps in his heart of hearts he hoped that the emperor might find himself in a position where he had to offer Witte the premiership. Who knows? But we do know that he had a clear picture of how Nicholas and Alexandra felt about him, and the best he could hope for was something that would make use of his experience and keep him busy. An ambassadorship was his first choice, but he would have been pleased with a temporary assignment, like negotiating the renewal of the trade treaty with Germany in 1914. B. B. Glinskii, "Graf Sergei Iulevich Vitte," *Istoricheskii vestnik* 142 (1915): 907.

An interesting note. In 1913 the journalist Josef Melnik wrote to Witte about rumors that he might become premier. Witte replied that in the first place such an appointment would not be consonant with his "personal affairs" and that, in the second place, the country was not yet in such straits as to have to call on him. "Witte," *Century Magazine* 68 (1915): 690.

14. *See below*, pp. 710–13.

Chapter II

1. Okhrana: short for *okhrannoe otdelenie* (security section of the political police).

2. Probably a reference to the book on the origins of the Russo-Japanese War that Witte was working on with the help of former associates of the Ministry of Finance, among them Gurev. Joseph Dillon writes that he was present when the explosive device was found. His account differs in minor detail from Witte's. *The Eclipse of Russia* (New York, 1918), pp. 187–95.

3. There were several such institutions, which provided inexpensive entertainment of various kinds to the lower classes. The most prominent of these was the People's Palace of Emperor Nicholas II, and this is probably the one to which Witte was referring.

4. Dillon writes that he was about to have lunch with Witte on May 26 when the former premier received the telephone call advising him that the session had been canceled. *The Eclipse of Russia*, p. 190.

5. A folder containing information on the Kazantsev case is among the Witte papers in the Bakhmeteff Archive.

6. In his letter of May 3, 1910, reviewing the investigations into the attempts on his life, Witte remarked that if he were a private citizen he could appeal to public opinion, but since that was not the case, he had no choice but to appeal to the government to stop helping organizations that engaged in terrorist acts. *Soiuz russkogo naroda*, by A. Chernovskii (Moscow, 1924), p. 130.

7. A. F. Koni, after reading Witte's account of this episode, agrees for the most part with it. "Sergei Iulevich Vitte," *Sobranie sochinenii* (Moscow, 1968), V, 275–76.

8. Witte obviously believed that Stolypin had advance knowledge of the plan to kill him, but no evidence has been produced to support this belief. What can be said is that Stolypin bore some responsibility for what the Union of the Russian People did by subsidizing it and by not moving energetically to punish those who committed crimes in its name. As for the emperor, he showed no hostility toward the Union of the Russian People but was very upset with the Finnish police for permitting Russian revolutionaries to move freely within their jurisdiction. A. A. Gerasimov, *Der Kampf gegen die erste russische Revolution* (Frauenfeld, 1934), p. 146.

9. This account comes from the dictated memoirs typescript in which, as noted earlier, Witte is guarded in speaking of Nicholas II. In the manuscript, pp. 362 verso–363, where he also deals briefly with the attempts on his life, he speaks more openly:

> The killings of Herzenstein, Iollos, and others, as well as the attempts on my life, were the work of the Union of the Russian People, with the participation and permission of police agents and of the government generally. Of course, the Emperor did not take part in these bloody affairs, but if he was not pleased by them then they were, at least, a matter of indifference and curiosity to him. Those who carried out these acts knew that, at the very least, he would be indifferent toward them and that the authorities would do all in their power to conceal everything. Who is in charge? *(Kto takaia eta vlast?)*.

10. Writing about this correspondence in the manuscript, p. 362 verso, Witte said:

"This correspondence gives me the moral right to call Stolypin a great, big political scoundrel *(prokhodimets)*." Then he crossed the word *prokhodimets* out and put some ellipsis points in. Whether he did so because the word was too strong or because he thought ellipsis points would be more striking is not clear. That he considered Stolypin a scoundrel is more than obvious.

11. After the publication in February 1914 of an article on the attempts on Witte's life by A. M. Kliachko (L. Lvov), who used official documents, Witte permitted the author to copy his correspondence with Stolypin on condition that he withhold publication until after the count's death. Kliachko kept his word. "Perepiska Grafa S. Iu. Vitte i P. A. Stolypina," *Russkaia mysl* 36 (1915): 134–52.

Chapter III

1. As will be evident, Witte has little to say about his personal life from 1907 on. A pity.

2. As indicated elsewhere, it was in Frankfurt that Witte began to write his memoirs. It was also while there that he spoke to a Jewish deputation, to which he refers earlier, and it was in Paris that he spoke to another Jewish deputation, also noted earlier.

3. From this time on, Biarritz served as his summer residence. His routine was to leave St. Petersburg with his wife after the end of the sessions of the State Council and not to return until the State Council met again, in the late fall. He and his wife might spend part of the time at such spas as Vichy, Bad Homburg, and Bad Salzschlirf, but for the most part they stayed at their place in Biarritz with their daughter and her family.

4. This was a stellar group. Vladimir M. Bekhterev was a noted neurologist and psychiatrist. The Veliaminov referred to was probably N. A. Veliaminov, a well-known surgeon and a professor at the Military-Medical Academy. Their performance was less than stellar, reflecting the state of the art of medicine at the time.

5. While in Rome, Witte had an audience with the pope. *Times* (London), November 2, 1908, p. 13. Elsewhere Witte tells of his meeting in Rome with Muravev, the Russian ambassador.

6. *See below*, pp. 715–16.

7. Of interest is what Witte wrote to Herman Bernstein on July 20/August 2, 1911: "I am writing my memoirs, but I am writing very lazily. . . . Under no circumstances can they be published before my death. But if we meet next year in St. Petersburg I can let you have some very important documents." H. Bernstein, *The Celebrities of Our Time* (Freeport, N.Y., 1968), p. 33.

Bernstein, a correspondent for *The New York Times*, corresponded with Witte in Russian. The originals of the letters to him were, at last report, in the archive of the Yiddish Scientific Institute in New York.

Because Witte stopped dictating his memoirs in March 1912, the preceding item is the last one under personalia. He and his wife continued to go abroad in the late spring and to follow their customary routine while away from Russia. They were in Bad Salzschlirf at the time that the assassination of Archduke Franz Ferdinand roused the fear that war was near. Placing little faith in newspaper reports that war was imminent, Witte got in touch with a family friend in the Russian diplomatic service to find out what was going on. The reply prompted Witte quickly to make arrangements to return to Russia. Nicholas de Basily, *Memoirs* (Stanford, Calif., 1973), p. 101n.

By the end of August Witte was back in Russia, having taken a circuitous route, by way of Italy to Odessa, presumably to avoid having to travel through the territory of the Central Powers. Six months later he was dead. A. E. Kaufman, "Cherty iz zhizni S. Iu. Vitte," *Istoricheskii vestnik* 140 (1915): 229–30.

Chapter IV

1. Witte deals with Count Lambsdorff's departure in several places—ms. pp. 10, 55, 238–39 verso, and in the dictated typescript, pp. 1984, 1993–1904, and 2001. This account is a conflation of the various items.

2. Why was Durnovo let go? I. V. Gurko, who was close to Durnovo, suggests that Trepov thought that the State Duma would be pleased by the removal of a "reactionary" minister. The explanation is plausible, given the fact that Trepov was seeking an accommodation with those who led the State Duma. *Features and Figures of the Past* (Stanford, Calif., 1939), p. 457.

3. Witte does not mention that there was some question of whether or not he would be appointed to the State Council.

4. The Institutions of Empress Marie were a group of educational and charitable institutions, chiefly for girls, first placed under the jurisdiction and supervision of Empress Marie Fedorovna, the wife of Paul I, and then under succeeding empresses.

5. Stolypin was a university graduate and had had considerable government experience, but he did not have the kind of experience normally expected of a man chosen to be minister of interior.

6. Several members of the cabinet—Goremykin, Schwanebach, Prince Shirinskii-Shikhmatov, and Stishinskii—were enemies of Witte. Stolypin would soon become one. Kokovtsev, although superficially on fairly good terms with Witte, could hardly be considered his friend.

Chapter V

1. *See above*, pp. 575–76.

2. "Privately owned" land, it will be recalled, meant land owned by individuals as distinct from land held by village communes. Although some peasants owned land as individuals, it was not their land but land belonging to the landed nobility that was the primary object of peasants clamoring for more land.

3. I. V. Gurko claims to have had it on good authority that Goremykin's action was not the result of sloth but of the premier's determination to make sure that the emperor would not be able to countermand the decree. *Features and Figures of the Past*, p. 486.

4. Could be translated as "a man who doesn't give a damn."

5. As will be seen, Witte considers Stolypin's appointment to have marked the beginning of a new chapter in Russian history, one of retreat from the principles of the October Manifesto.

6. I. V. Gurko relates that later on, although hostile to Krivoshein, Witte sought his help in being appointed head of a commission to suggest plans for reorganizing the railroad system, a task for which Witte was certainly qualified. He goes on to say that Stolypin told Krivoshein he should be tried for treason for making such a suggestion. The remark may have been made in a jesting tone, but the thought it reflected was serious, that Witte was not a loyal subject of the emperor. *Features and Figures of the Past*, p. 458.

Chapter VI

1. This is an appropriate place to note the fact that Stolypin ranks at the top, alongside such men as Plehve, of those Witte most hated. As Witte notes, he was at first mildly pleased at the news of Stolypin's appointment as premier, but soon turned completely against him for several reasons, it seems: (1) he suspected Stolypin of being behind the

attempts on his life; (2) he came to believe that Stolypin was a scoundrel, willing to subvert the October Manifesto out of self-interest; (3) he knew that as long as Stolypin was in power he was a political pariah; (4) he felt that it was he, and not Stolypin, who should be guiding the affairs of Russia.

It is obvious that Witte could not write with any detachment about the man. Moreover, he had little inside knowledge of what went on in the Stolypin government. One of his few inside sources was Kokovtsev. It appears that Kokovtsev doled out some information to Witte as a sign that they were on friendly terms, but was both parsimonious and cautious about what information he passed along to him. Witte, of course, still had friends and acquaintances in high places and learned something from them about what was going on, but what he heard about Stolypin was not always reliable.

Consequently, Witte's memoirs are not a good source of information concerning the Stolypin regime except in instances where he himself was an eyewitness or had reliable sources. This is not to say that what Witte has to say about Stolypin is devoid of interest. For example, his evaluation of Stolypin's character, the influence of Mrs. Stolypin, and the changes in the premier's personality deserve serious attention.

2. Meaning, a courageous soldier but a poor commander.

3. On the subject of the discretionary funds of the minister of interior, *see above*, p. 225.

4. In another place and context (handwritten memoirs, pp. 76–76 verso) Witte writes:

> When Stolypin became premier he saw that he could not govern with Trepov around. Fortunately for him, Trepov's *"lune de miel"* was beginning to fade. Then before Goremykin's fall Trepov made a false move, not unlike the Zubatovshchina, of trying to woo the Kadets. With this thought in mind he was unwary enough to imply to a foreign correspondent that he was in fact the power behind the throne.
>
> Trepov's idea of bringing the Kadets into the government might have met with success if the Kadets had behaved sensibly. But they had acted so stupidly that it was easy for Stolypin to scuttle the plan and settle Trepov's fate.
>
> The Emperor decided to part with Trepov and, as usual in such cases, tried to do so deviously, like a spider spinning a web for a fly, in this case Trepov. Fortunately for the Emperor, Trepov's death saved him the trouble of administering the final blow.
>
> Of course, as I have said, Trepov was a political nincompoop, but he acted in good faith and out of loyalty to Nicholas II, the Emperor, and Nicholas Aleksandrovich, the man. Surely someone from Trepov's family will leave an exact account of the tragic situation in which this honorable man, so devoted to Nicholas Aleksandrovich, lived out his last weeks. I have learned only a few details of this story, from a reliable source.

5. A reference to the decree of October 17, 1906, which went beyond the decree of April 17, 1905 in recognizing the rights of Old Believers and Sectarians. *See* II, p. 97.

6. A reference to decrees issued in August and September 1906 making some appanage and state lands, as well as some land belonging to the emperor, available for sale to peasants through the Peasants' Bank. Appanage lands (*udely*) were lands which provided income for the upkeep of members of the imperial family.

7. *See above*, I, Appendix B.

8. A reference to Stolypin's oft-cited speech to the State Duma on December 5, 1908, in which, in explanation of the rationale of his major agrarian project, the shift from peasant communal ownership of land to individual proprietorship, he said that the government was wagering "not on the paupers and the drunkards but on the sturdy and the strong" as a means of shoring up the foundation of the monarchy. Russia, Gosudarstvennaia Duma, 3-i Sozyv, 2-ia Sessiia, *Stenograficheskie otchety* (St. Petersburg, 1908), col. 2282.

Witte obviously had no objection to the gradual shift to individual peasant proprietorship, but as he indicates, he objected to the means used by Stolypin effecting the change, and when he says "simple" and "childish" he is referring to the means.

9. The Russian population was organized on the basis of estates—nobility, merchants, artisans, peasants, *et sim.*—each theoretically with its own corporate structure. The landed nobility was organized on the basis of district and provincial assemblies of the nobility. Except in a few provinces, the noble assemblies had been quite conservative, but toward the end of 1904 and during 1905, at least until October 17, they had moved to the left. The rightward move to which Witte refers was largely a response to peasant unrest. That move was further demonstrated by the formation in May 1906 of the organization to which Witte refers, the Council of the United Nobility, which, for the most part, followed a conservative line.

10. As one would expect, Gurko sees the case in a different light. Moreover, he is less censorious than Witte in dealing with Stolypin's role in the affair. *Features and Figures of the Past*, pp. 506–09.

11. His father, General I. V. Gurko, won great distinction in the Russo-Turkish War of 1877–78.

12. This is a bit of "the pot calling the kettle black." Just think of how Witte dealt with his associates when they became involved in scandals.

13. Among other things, von der Launitz sent large numbers of copies of such publications of the Union of the Russian People as *All the Blame Is on Count Witte* and *Concerning the Jews* to be placed in the prison libraries of St. Petersburg. The director of prisons, to his credit, refused to comply. M. Agursky, "Caught in a Cross Fire," *Orientalia Christiana Periodica* 50 (1984): 177.

14. As Witte indicates in various places, Stolypin followed a retrograde policy with respect to the borderlands, particularly in the case of Finland, largely as a result of pressure from the nationalist side.

Chapter VII

1. The debates on the budget provided the opposition with a splendid opportunity to attack the government. Ironically, one of the sharpest attacks came from one of Witte's former colleagues, N. N. Kutler, by now a Kadet, who used his inside knowledge to make some telling points. Russia, Gosudarstvennaia Duma, 2-oi Sozyv, *Stenograficheskie otchety* (St. Petersburg, 1907), I, cols. 809–32. The electoral law of June 3, 1907, which favored the well-to-do over the less fortunate and the Russians over the non-Russians, was obviously a retreat from the ideal of one man, one vote. But it was successful in its aim of making certain of a cooperative State Duma. Even Kryzhanovskii concedes that the government violated the fundamental laws in enacting the new electoral law, but he argues that the alternative would have been to accept anarchy. *Vospominaniia* (Berlin, n.d.), pp. 114–15.

2. This is based on the dictated memoirs pp. 2182–86, dictated in February 1912. In his handwritten memoirs, p. 319, written in the summer of 1912 at Bad Salzschlirf, Witte gives a different version of this conversation:

> Prior to June 3 [1907], Baron Freedericksz came to see me to ask for my opinion. Whether he came on his own initiative or at the suggestion of higher-ups I do not know. I told him that there were two choices. The first was to observe the electoral law of December 1905 and wait patiently for the election of a reasonable State Duma. Such an eventuality was quite possible if one observed the spirit and the letter of the electoral law and kept on dissolving uncooperative State Dumas, as Japan had done following the introduction of its constitution. The second course was to revise the electoral law, on the basis of experience with the old law. If one decided on the second course, a temporary law should be issued empowering representatives of munici-

pal dumas and zemstvos to prepare a new electoral law, which would be submitted to the State Council. If such a step required a long time the representatives could fulfill the functions of the State Duma on a temporary basis. What I suggested would, of course, have to be refined. [Neither course was followed] and at the closing of the Second State Duma a new electoral law, prepared by the government was issued.

3. A. S. Suvorin wrote in his diary that when Witte saw him two days after the enactment of the law, he said that he had offered Stolypin advice about how to prepare a new electoral law (roughly the same advice that Witte says he gave Baron Freedericksz) before June 3 and that the premier had made some changes in the draft of the law that was issued on June 3. *Das Geheimtagebuch* (Berlin, 1925), pp. 244–45.

4. Witte's is a very shorthand and consequently simplified account of what is a very convoluted story involving the secret police and an informer, but the essential point is correct, that the government was looking for an excuse to dissolve the State Duma. A. Levin, *The Second Duma* (Hamden, Conn., 1966), pp. 307–49.

5. "*Coup d'état* of June 3, 1907," was a term favored by the left, presumably for its nice pejorative ring. It is noteworthy that in the section of the memoirs written during the summer of 1907, Witte, who was still not entirely hostile to Stolypin, does not use the term but does so later on after his feelings toward the premier became hateful, after he had come to feel that Stolypin had some share of responsibility for the attacks on his life.

What Suvorin notes about his talk with Witte on June 5, 1907, supports this view. He does not record that Witte blamed Stolypin for what happened on June 3, but quotes him as attributing the responsibility to Nicholas II, remarking according to Suvorin: "The Tsar is full of self-confidence. During the war with Japan he believed after each setback that we would win the next time and that all would be well. So it is now. He dissolved the Duma because he believes in God's blessing and the end of the revolution." *Das Geheimtagebuch*, p. 244.

6. This section is a conflation of the handwritten memoirs, pp. 242–243 verso, and the dictated memoirs, pp. 2172–74. Witte attended the sessions of the State Council faithfully and spoke frequently on issues that concerned him. Koni, who served in that body, writes favorably of his performance, but notes that when he began to speak many on the right would demonstratively leave the chamber. "Sergei Iulevich Vitte," pp. 258–75.

7. *See above*, pp. 324–25.

8. General A. I. Spiridovich, who was in charge of the security forces protecting the emperor, gives a very detailed account of the plot, which was directed by the Socialist Revolutionaries. According to him Azef had no connection with the affair. *Les Dernières Années de la cour de Tzarskoïë Sélo* I, 148–75.

9. Just as he tends to refer to those of the extreme left as "anarchist revolutionaries," regardless of their respective parties, so he tends to write as if all of the extreme right belonged to the Union of the Russian People. Although Gringmut was close to the URP, his affiliation was with the Russian Monarchist Union, in which he was a leading figure. It must have irked, but not surprised, Witte that services for Gringmut were attended by such dignitaries as Grand Duchess Elizabeth Fedorovna, the emperor's sister-in-law, and that the emperor referred to the late journalist as an "honest and manly fighter for the dignity and power of Russia." A. Levin, "The Reactionary Tradition in the Election Campaign to the Third Duma," Oklahoma State University Publications, no. 59 (1962): 9.

10. *See above*, p. 506.

11. May be a reference to A. A. Makarov, assistant minister of interior from 1906 to 1909.

12. Landezen: A. M. Garting-Landezen, who, together with Azef, was exposed in 1909 as having been a double agent. Witte, *Vospominaniia*, (Moscow, 1960), III, 665.

13. *See above* p. 493.

14. In his memoirs, which appeared before Witte's did, Kurlov tells a somewhat different story. He writes that when he was called back to St. Petersburg he was told by General Trepov that it was Witte who had demanded his dismissal and then goes on to say that upon further investigation Witte decided that the charges were unfounded. *Das Ende des russisschen Kaisertums* (Berlin, 1920), pp. 86, 94–95.

15. Actually M. I. Trusewicz was director of the Department of Police at the time and was succeeded in 1909 by N. P. Zuev. Makarov was assistant minister of interior with supervision of the police as his responsibility. Kurlov succeeded Makarov in that position and at the same time assumed the post of chief of the Corps of Gendarmes. E. Amburger, *Geschichte der Behördenorganisation Russlands von Peter dem Grossen bis 1917* (Leiden, 1966), p. 142.

16. Could be taken to mean: "I say that I draw the line here, but I really don't give a damn." The reference here is to MacMahon's reply to Gambetta in 1876, when the latter demanded that his authority be recognized. Witte, *Vospominaniia*, III, 647 n. 90.

Chapter VIII

1. The facts about Stolypin's relationship to the Union of the Russian People are more complex than Witte indicates. Even after the opening of the Third State Duma, Stolypin continued to make use of the extreme right, but the URP, with its high-handed and abusive leader, Dr. Dubrovin, had become a bit of an embarrassment and roused many enemies among the extreme right. By 1907 Stolypin was shifting his support to others, among them V. M. Purishkevich, who was to leave the URP to found the Union of the Archangel Michael. Even before the results of the election campaign for the Third State Duma were in, the URP was criticizing Stolypin for lack of support. A. Levin, *The Reactionary Tradition in the Election Campaign to the Third Duma*, Oklahoma State Publication, Social Science Series, no. 8 (Stillwater, 1963), p. 27; Agursky, "Caught in a Cross Fire," pp. 185–87.

And now a word about the quotation. Witte loved to quote from Dante, Schiller, and Shakespeare in both his speeches and writings. The quotation is from Schiller's *Die Verschworung der Fiesco in Genua*, Act III, Scene IV. "Der Mohr hat seine Arbeit getan, der Mohr Kann gehen."

2. It should be evident that Witte is almost as intemperate about Guchkov as he is about Stolypin.

3. *See below*, pp. 731–33.

4. *See above*, pp. 292–93.

5. *See above*, pp. 589.

6. In March 1906, while Witte was still premier, a commission began to make preparations for the convocation of a council and completed its work by the end of the year, expecting that the emperor would soon summon a council, but it was not until after the monarchy had been overthrown that the council met. Why the delay? Partly it was the reluctance of Nicholas II, who apparently was troubled by the thought of an independent church, partly the work of conservatives and the extreme right in the church and outside who feared "liberal" influences in the church. Partly it was the result of the opposition of Stolypin, who, like the emperor, was reluctant to see the church become independent. Another factor, an ironic one, was that many on the right feared that if the patriarchate were restored, the man chosen to fill the post would be Metropolitan Antonii, who was

considered a liberal and a friend of Witte. James W. Cunningham, *A Vanquished Hope* (Crestwood, N.Y., 1981), pp. 208–321 *passim.*

7. Witte is dealing with two phenomena, the alliance of some of the lower clergy and the hierarchy with the extreme right and the influence on the church of laymen like Rasputin. Witte has something to say about the influence of Rasputin, but surprisingly little given what was known and gossiped about at the time.

8. While Witte claims some "credit" for the appointment of Sabler, he does not mention the widespread rumors that Rasputin had more than a little influence in the appointment of Sabler and over the man's operations. Why the reticence, if it was reticence? Possibly it was because Witte was dealing with this subject in his dictated memoirs, which, he feared, might somehow be seized by the police. And it should be recalled he was careful not to speak his mind about Nicholas and Alexandra in the dictated memoirs. In this case a reference to Rasputin's alleged influence on Sabler impinged on the subject of Empress Alexandra's attempts to influence the church and to favor those in it who looked kindly on Rasputin.

9. In December 1906, when the cabinet recommended lifting many, but not all, restrictions on Jews, the emperor would not comply, saying that "an inner voice" told him that what they asked was wrong. V. N. Kokovtsev, *Iz moego proshlago* (Paris, 1933), I, 238. From whom did Witte get a copy of the relevant minutes? Kokovtsev?

10. This is a conflation of the handwritten memoirs, pp. 268–69, and the dictated memoirs, pp. 2237–38.

11. Witte is referring here to legislative efforts made in 1910 to curtail Finnish autonomy.

12. Odessa was close to Witte's heart, and he managed to visit the city about once a year, to visit with relatives, friends, and acquaintances. Odessa had produced many celebrities, but none like Witte, who as one admirer put it, had a dazzling rise to eminence, the kind that one might expect in America but not Russia. He did much for the city and was deeply mourned by that city when he died. Kaufman, "Cherty iz zhizni grafa S. Iu. Vitte," pp. 220–31; Glinskii, "Graf Sergei Iulevich Vitte," (1915): 243–45.

13. Kuzminskii reported that in the course of the pogrom against Jews that began in Odessa on October 19, the police actually helped the rioters in some instances and that the prefect was, at the very least, negligent, in carrying out his duty to stop the violence. H. D. Mehlinger and J. M. Thompson, *Count Witte and the Tsarist Government in the 1905 Revolution* (Bloomington, Ind., 1972), pp. 61–62.

14. For more on Nilov, *see below*, pp. 708–09.

15. *See below*, pp. 705–07.

16. Probably because he is concentrating on the shortcomings of Stolypin, Witte fails to mention Casso's repressive educational policies, with which he must have disagreed. It should be noted that one reason Casso was appointed was probably the fact that he had the kind of resolute attitude toward radical students and professors that was admired at court.

17. Witte had a good deal to say earlier on about Wendrich. *See above*, pp. 118–19.

18. Witte had mixed feelings about Shipov. *See above*, pp. 166–67.

19. Witte does go and on about Timiriazev, probably for reasons explained earlier. *See above*, pp. 557–60.

20. To ensure continuity among the elected members of the State Council, it was stipulated that one-third of the group elected in 1906 serve three years, one-third six years, the rest the full term of nine years. This meant that from 1909 on, all newly elected members would be able to serve full terms.

21. This is from the dictated memoirs pp. 2317–18. In the handwritten memoirs pp. 226 verso–227, Witte adds that Timiriazev was also currying favor with Kokovtsev, the minister of finance:

> Because Timiriazev had been elected a member of the board of a bank he had to earn the good will of the minister of finance in order to receive favors in return. This soon led to differences between Timiriazev and other deputies from commerce and industry in the State Council. This was because when the positions of the Ministry of Finance and those of big industry and commerce were at odds in the State Council, Timiriazev supported the former. Consequently they stopped electing him to committees. Some of the influential deputies for commerce and industry told me that they sought by one means or another to remove Timiriazev as deputy from commerce and industry. The time was approaching to replace two deputies from commerce and industry, and Timiriazev was afraid he would be one of the two. Consequently he hit on the tactic of acting as the unequivocal supporter of Stolypin on all occasions.

The two versions are somewhat contradictory, but agree on the main point—he decided to earn Stolypin's good will.

22. Timiriazev served from January to November 1909. He was succeeded by Sergei I. Timashev.

Chapter IX

1. The original plan for the Trans-Siberian called for it to be built completely on Russian soil. After the Chinese agreed to the Chinese Eastern Railroad going across Manchuria, the original plan for a section north of the Amur River, from Sretensk to Khabarovsk, was abandoned. Then, in 1908, construction on this section began and was completed in 1916. J. N. Westwood, *A History of Russian Railways* (London, 1964), pp. 110–15.

2. Witte also fought against building the Amur section in the Finance Committee, where he had some support, but not enough to constitute a majority. Those who argued for construction expected war with Japan, but the Japanese did not feel threatened by the line. Kokovtsev, *Iz moego proshlago*, I, 320–25.

3. Witte's prediction about immigration patterns was correct: there was no great urge among Russians to settle in the area, but there was immigration into this area from China.

4. The July 1907 convention did not provide for Russian agreement to Japanese annexation of Korea. That came later. Although Witte notes Izvolskii's motive in negotiating the July 1907 convention with Japan, he fails to make a connection between this agreement and the one negotiated with Great Britain in the same year. That connection was put vividly at a meeting concerning Afghan affairs in August 1907, when Izvolskii declared that Russia needed peace from Kamchatka to Gibraltar for a decade because events were moving rapidly in Europe and Russia must be ready to exert her influence there unless she were to become "a half-forgotten Asiatic power." For that reason, he argued, the convention with Japan made no sense without a concurrent agreement between Russia and Great Britain. A. A. Polivanov, *Iz dnevnikov i vospominanii* (Moscow, 1924), p. 32.

5. This material was dictated in February 1912. The "disorder" to which he refers was the revolution of 1911, which prompted the great powers to take advantage of Chinese weakness. In this instance Russia's energy was directed toward encouraging a movement for autonomy in Outer Mongolia, which was already within the sphere of Russian influence.

6. Witte continued to believe that the interests of Russia would be best served by a Franco-Russo-German alliance and consequently was distressed, as is evident, by the

conclusion of the agreement with Great Britain. He later told a reporter that if he had been ambassador to France in 1907, an alliance among France, Russia, and Germany would have been arranged. Melnik, "Witte," p. 688; V. Naryshkin-Witte, *Souvenirs d'une fillette russe* (Paris, 1925), pp. 229–36.

7. *See above*, p. 452.

8. Witte was dictating this material in February 1912, at a time of great turmoil in Persia, when Russian influence there was being challenged from several sides.

9. At the time Witte made no secret of his fear that Russia might be drawn into war over the Bosnian crisis. There was even a wild, and unfounded, rumor that when the emperor was thinking of ordering mobilization Witte was able to change his mind. A. Markow, *Rasputin und die um ihn* (Konigsberg, 1928), p. 98.

10. Witte is apparently referring to the loan concluded in January 1909, which included terms unfavorable to Russia. In negotiating the loan, the Russians spoke of using the money for naval construction and for the construction of strategic railroads. R. Girault, *Emprunts russes et investissements français en Russie, 1887–1914* (Paris, 1973), pp. 487–91.

11. Sazonov heatedly denies that Stolypin was influenced by family ties, but Kokovtsov suggests that Witte was correct. S. Sazonov, *Fateful Years, 1906–1916* (London, 1928), p. 21; Kokovtsev, *Iz moego proshlago*, I, 334.

12. This was dictated in February 1912, when, amid growing tensions, there were persistent rumors that Witte would be recalled to power. Thus, on October 14, 1912, *The Times* (London) reported a rumor that Sazonov and Witte had been summoned to Spala, where the emperor was in residence. Three days later it reported that the rumor had been true only with respect to Sazonov.

13. During the summer of 1911 a story appeared in the press that Witte had published a pamphlet attacking Roosevelt. In a letter to Herman Bernstein, then a correspondent for *The New York Times*, a letter printed in the newspaper, Witte declared that he admired Roosevelt greatly, that it was probably someone in the pay of Stolypin who had inspired the story. What had probably been referred to in the allegation, wrote Witte, was a pamphlet about Roosevelt written by Morskoi, a pamphlet about which he had learned only after its publication. *The New York Times*, August 18, 1911, p. 6. The letter was later included by Bernstein in his *Celebrities of Our Time*, pp. 33–34.

The pamphlet in question was *Razocharovaniia v chestnom maklerstve* (Disappointments in Honest Brokerage). The author, Morskoi, was well-known as being a spokesman for Witte. Witte's statement that he knew about the pamphlet only after its publication was probably at best only a half-truth.

14. *See above*, p. 447, where Witte states definitely that the letter was turned over to the minister.

15. Elsewhere Witte writes: "On June 2 [1911], a naval squadron from the North American United States called at Kronstadt, but was coolly received."

In December 1911 the United States informed Russia that the commercial treaty of 1832 would be terminated as of January 1, 1913. U.S. Department of State, *Papers Relating to the Foreign Relations of the U.S. 1911* (Washington, 1918), pp. 695–99.

16. Solid support for Witte's account is provided by Hans Heilbronner in his "An Anti-Witte Conspiracy, 1905–1906: The Schwanebach Memorandum," *Jahrbücher für Geschichte Osteuropas* 14 (1966): 347–61.

17. As every schoolboy and schoolgirl should know, Herostratus set fire to a temple, not a city.

18. This is apparently the document to which Witte referred in dealing with the circumstances of Kutler's dismissal. *See above*, p.550.

Chapter X

1. Much, if not most, of the material concerning the emperor's comings and goings adds little to our knowledge. That Witte writes about them indicates the extent to which the imperial court remained at the center of his interest.

The material used for this chapter comes from the dictated memoirs, in which, as has already been indicated, Witte is very careful in his use of gossip about the emperor and empress.

2. The meeting at Swinemünde took place in late July 1907. This one, like so many other meetings of Nicholas II with other monarchs, had a diplomatic as well as a social character. That Witte has little to say about what went on at these meetings suggests that he had few sources in the foreign office during these years. Among the topics discussed at Swinemünde were the Treaty of Björkö, Baltic problems, and German interests in Persia. M. Taube, *La politique russe d'avant-guerre* (Paris, 1928), pp. 123–46.

3. Flag captain: naval adjutant to the emperor, member of his suite. It was he who relayed the emperor's orders to the ship's captain and thus bore some responsibility for what happened.

4. Here, as elsewhere, Witte uses the opportunity to get his own back at Prince Meshcherskii.

5. For some detail on the grand duke's role as head of the navy, *see above*, p. 153.

6. The statue was to figure in the events of 1917, partly because of its location, partly because of its symbolic significance.

7. The emperor's visit to Poltava reflected the mood at court that the country was returning to normal. The emperor had not been to the interior of the country since 1904. Now it was felt safe for him to travel in the interior, and he and his entourage took such occasions to emphasize the monarchical tradition.

8. During the ceremonies at Poltava, honors were bestowed on the regiments that had fought there in 1709 and on descendants of officers who had participated in the battle.

9. It will be recalled that a visit scheduled for 1905 had been canceled because it had been feared that the safety of the emperor could not be guaranteed in Rome (*see above*, pp. 366–67). Even at this time, October 1909, it was considered prudent for the two to meet at the king's summer residence, in Raccognigi, which could be reached by sea. As it turned out, Nicholas II's plan to sail on his yacht from Yalta to Raccognigi had to be canceled because of Empress Alexandra's illness, but he did go to Raccognigi. There, among other subjects, there were discussions of Russo-Italian opposition to Austro-Hungarian expansion in the Balkans and Russia's perennial desire to have the Straits opened to Russian warships. Taube, *La Politique russe*, pp. 244–45; Spiridovich, *Les Dernières Années*, I, 387–91.

10. For Witte's views on Ferdinand, *see above*, p. 306.

11. For more of Witte's estimate of Edward VII as well as for his comparison of Edward and Nicholas, *see above*, p. 207.

12. Spiridovich, who was responsible for such operations, says that Witte was "hallucinating" in speaking of "hundreds" of Russian police agents in Nauheim when, in fact, there were no more than thirty-five. (Thirty-five agents scurrying around can seem like hundreds.) *Les Dernières Années de la cour de Tzarskoïë Sélo*, II, 34.

13. Boy soldiers (*poteshnye*): a quasi-military organization for boys sponsored by the

Ministries of Education and War for promoting patriotism. *Ocherki istorii Leningrada* (Moscow-Leningrad, 1956), III, 559. The word *poteshnyi* means both boy and comical. Witte's play on words does not survive translation.

Chapter XI

1. This account is a conflation of the handwritten memoirs, pp. 230–31, and the dictated memoirs, pp. 2086–96. The sharpest remarks come from the handwritten memoirs.

It should be noted that Count A. F. Heyden was a naval officer, that by the time referred to he had been replaced as head of the emperor's Military Field Chancellery and had been named head of the emperor's Naval Field Chancellery. Amburger, p. 301.

2. In the ms., p. 230 verso, Witte has the Emperor making these remarks before the reading by Count Heyden.

3. This account is a conflation of the handwritten memoirs, pp. 232 verso–238 verso, and the dictated memoirs, pp. 2338–44, 2351.

4. *Volnoopredeliaiushchii*: the term was applied to those who, with at least a secondary education, chose to meet their military obligations by volunteering for a six-month term of service.

5. Spiridovich says that Witte was too kind to Guchkov and goes on to say: "It was well known at Tsarskoe Selo that Guchkov was an adventurous revolutionary, that he claimed a competence in military affairs he did not possess and that he had a subversive effect on the army." *Les Dernières Années de la cour de Tzarskoïé Sélo*, II, 65. Witte's implication and Spiridovich's assertion that Guchkov was disloyal does not seem justified. Guchkov apparently did not feel that the army was in good hands, and his critical remarks appealed to some younger officers.

6. Concerning Witte's efforts to protect the emperor's prerogatives as supreme commander, *see above*, p. 581.

7. Not surprisingly, Witte's account of his role in the debate over the Naval General Staff bill inflates his role. Cf. G. A. Hosking, *The Russian Constitutional Experiment* (Cambridge, 1973), pp. 74–105.

8. In the course of his speech on the bill on March 18, 1909, Witte managed to get in a dig at the army, which, he suggested, should change its name from the Russian Imperial Army to the Army of Happenstance and Dilettantism. Russia, Gosudarstvennyi Sovet, Sessiia 4, *Stenograficheskie otchety, 1908–1909* (St. Petersburg, 1907–1912), III, col. 1364.

9. As noted earlier, the word "constitution" was officially eschewed, even by Witte, but he clearly believed that the revised Fundamental Laws, issued in April 1906, represented a constitution.

10. *See above*, p. 356.

11. This account is a conflation of the handwritten memoirs, pp. 232–32 verso, and the dictated memoirs, pp. 2289–90, 2336–68.

12. The grand duke gave up the chairmanship of the State Defense Council in August 1908, a year before the abolition of the body. It has been suggested that his departure had something to do with a speech that Guchkov had delivered in the State Duma decrying the role of the grand dukes in the armed forces and with a growing coolness between the grand duke and the emperor. Pourtales to von Bülow, August 1/14 1908, Germany, Auswärtiges Amt, Archiv, Russland, 82, No. 1, Geheim, vol. 57–58.

13. Witte does not explain what the grand duke's role in this was, assuming that it was self-evident he had a hand in the removal of General Rödiger.

14. Witte was right. The grand duke was regaining his influence and was subsequently given command of the army at the outbreak of war. Also, his evaluation of General Sukhomlinov was to prove fairly sound.

15. As indicated before, Witte's interest in the debate about the relative merits of the French and Prussian models of military organization was of long standing.

Chapter XII

1. In the background of all this was the power of the nationalist bloc in the State Duma, which sought to eliminate or, at least, restrict Finnish autonomy and to reduce Polish political influence in the western provinces (Kiev, Podolia, Volynia, Minsk, Vitebsk, Mogilev, Vilna, Grodno, and Kovno). What these provinces had in common was that until the Polish revolt of 1863 the landowning class had been Polish and, to a large extent, still was. Because the Polish landowners had supported the revolt, these provinces had been denied the right to have zemstvos. In 1899 Goremykin, then minister of interior, had attempted to introduce zemstvos in the western provinces but had been frustrated, in part by Witte's efforts. In 1903–1904 the first six of these provinces had been granted nonelective zemstvos that were referred to as "margarine" zemstvos. A. Ia Avrekh, "Vospros o zapadnom zemstve i bankrotstvo Stolypina," *Istoricheskie zapiski* 70 (1961): 65.

2. *See above*, pp. 82–84.

3. Nationalists: a bloc of about ninety deputies of the extreme right in the third and fourth State Dumas. They were chauvinistic Russians who expressed antipathy for Jews, Poles, Finns, and other minorities and who considered the October Manifesto to have been a grave error. For the most part they were landed nobles from the provinces of Kiev, Volynia, Minsk, and Bessarabia who probably would not have been elected if not for the electoral law of June 3, 1907. H. Jablonowski, "Die russischen Rechtsparteien 1905–1917," *Russland-Studien* (Stuttgart, 1957), pp. 42–55. As one would expect, the nationalists did not think much of Witte, and he did not think much of them. Referring to the nationalists, he said that he considered himself a nationalist but not one of their stripe; he thought of himself as an Aksovian (i.e. Slavophile) nationalist. Glinskii, "Graf Sergei Iulevich Vitte," *Istoricheskii vestnik* (November 1915), p. 895.

4. In referring to the peasants involved as Russian and Orthodox, Witte was following contemporary usage. Nowadays we would refer to the peasants in Kiev, Podolia, and Volynia as Ukrainians and those in Minsk, Vitebsk, and Mogilev as Belorussians. Moreover, the peasants in these provinces were, in large part, only nominally Orthodox but were, in fact, Uniates, i.e., members of the Uniate or Byzantine rite of the Roman Catholic church. As for the peasants of Vilna, Grodno, and Kovno provinces, they were Lithuanian and Catholic. Many of the legislative proposals dealt only with the first six of the western provinces, which may explain why Witte spoke of Russian and Orthodox peasants.

5. In a speech on January 28, 1911, concerning the zemstvo question, Witte remarked that the landed nobles in the western provinces had an exaggerated notion of peasant backwardness and suggested that many peasants knew more about their business than did many of the large landowners, especially those whom he referred to as "Russian landowning touring performers." Russia, Gosudavstvennyi Sovet, *Stenograficheskie otchety 1910–1911*, Sessiia VI, col. 816. Witte recognized that he didn't have many supporters in the State Council and at one point said he was not so "naive" as to believe that he would win many over. Ibid., col. 1308.

6. Grand Duke Alexander Mikhailovich does not deal specifically with this episode in his memoirs, but he does say: "Stolypin was a builder, a genius, a man who had choked

anarchy. . . . On one occasion I felt duty bound to have a serious talk with Nicky and warn him not to trust the enemies of Stolypin.'' *Once a Grand Duke* (New York, 1932), p. 239.

7. It should be recalled that when Witte had put Nicholas II in a similar position, the emperor had noted that he would "never forget this insolence." *See above*, II, ch. IX, n. 31.

8. Rather than ask for leave, Trepov asked to be released from government service. He was. Kokovtsov, *Iz moego proshlago*, I, 461.

9. Here, as elsewhere, Witte chooses to speak of Dillon as just another journalist, not as the close associate he was.

10. Ivan Susanin died a heroic death in 1613 in the struggle to rid Russia of Polish interventionists. His efforts helped make it possible for the Romanov dynasty to take power. The account of Spiridovich, who was an eyewitness, agrees for the most part with that of Witte. *Les Dernières Années de la cour de Tzarskoïë Sélo*, II, 124.

11. Clippings from *Novoe vremia* and *Rech* dealing with the Guchkov-Witte exchange were pasted on the pages following the end of the dictated memoirs and were reproduced in the Slovo redaction and in subsequent editions based on that redaction. What was at issue was how Guchkov recalled Witte's efforts to form a cabinet in October 1905.

12. Witte does not deal with the arguments concerning the assassination of Stolypin, particularly with the question of whether or not a person or persons in the secret police deliberately made it possible for Stolypin to be killed. The literature on the subject is voluminous, but the final verdict is not yet in and may never be, as if often the case in the assassination of prominent persons. On the whole what is known points to gross negligence on the part of those whose duty it was to protect him.

13. Note that Witte feels about the death of Stolypin pretty much as he does about that of Plehve, that he had no one to blame but himself.

14. I. V. Hessen writes that three months before his death, Witte assured him that he had seen Rasputin only once, in the company of Sazonov. He writes that he had documentary evidence that Witte had called on Rasputin more often than he admitted and suggests that Witte sought to regain power with the assistance of that man. He does not offer proof of what was in Witte's mind. *V dvukh vekakh* (Berlin, 1937), p. 320. We know that Witte was not candid about matters that might appear to be shady. That he called on Rasputin more than once is probable, that he sought his help is another matter.

15. *See above*, p. 108–11.

16. *Semeistvo Obmanovykh*: can be translated as "family of deceivers," the literal meaning, but was apparently meant to suggest *semeistvo Romanovykh*, meaning "the Romanov family, the family of deceivers."

17. Witte writes as if he had never been acquainted with Zheliabov, but it is almost certain that they had been acquainted as university students. *See above*, I, ch. IV, n. 5.

18. The time is February 1912. It is evident here as elsewhere that by this time Witte had very few sources of information at court.

19. Witte's account is consistent with that of Kokovtsev. *Cf.* Kokovtsev, *Iz moego proshlago*, I, 489–90.

20. As noted earlier, Witte did not take up this work again.

Sources

Texts Used in the Translation

Countess Witte's foreword is translated from Sergei Iu. Witte, *Vospominaniia: Tsarstvovanie Nikolaia II* (Berlin, 1922), I, xxxiii–xxxv.

The excerpt from I. V. Hessen's introduction is translated from the same volume, pp. xxii–xxvi. It presents a liberal's view of Witte's place in history and the value of his memoirs.

The excerpts from A. L. Sidorov's introduction are translated from Sergei Iu. Witte, *Vospominaniia* (Moscow, 1960), I, iii–viii and lxvii–lxviii. Sidorov presents the then current Soviet Marxist view of Witte's place in history and the value of his memoirs.

Volume I

Chapter I is translated from the dictated memoirs, pp. 1–30, 69.

Chapter II is translated from the dictated memoirs, pp. 31–62, 65.

Chapter III is translated from the dictated memoirs, pp. 63–101.

Chapter IV is translated from the dictated memoirs, pp. 102–54. Parts of pages 104 and 106 are missing. See chapter IV, n. 2.

Chapter V is translated from the dictated memoirs, pp. 155–212, 296–99, 390–94.

Chapter VI is translated from the dictated memoirs, pp. 212–45, 682–94.

Chapter VII is translated from the dictated memoirs, pp. 245, 275–95.

Chapter VIII is translated from the dictated memoirs, pp. 245–59. Part of p. 254 was inked out.

Chapter IX is translated from the dictated memoirs, pp. 124–26, 266–74, 295, 299–351, 740–44, 1334–46, 1597–98.

Chapter X is translated from the dictated memoirs, pp. 351–83, and the handwritten memoirs, p. 48 verso.

Chapter XI is translated from the dictated memoirs, pp. 259–60, 383–89, 413–37.

Chapter XII is translated from the dictated memoirs, pp. 439–504, 566–79, 987, and from the handwritten memoirs, p. 1 verso.

Chapter XIII is translated from the dictated memoirs, pp. 514–58, 580–88, 695–709, 942–50, 1083.

Chapter XIV is translated from the dictated memoirs, pp. 259–66, 559–64, 727. The account of the second marriage ends with page 564. There is no page 565, suggesting that this page was cut out.

Chapter XV is translated from the dictated memoirs, pp. 635–77, 727.

Chapter XVI is translated from the dictated memoirs, pp. 589–635, 854–59, 1093, 1107–08.

Chapter XVII is translated from the dictated memoirs, pp. 145–46, 339–42, 710–29, 738–39, 744–45, 765–68, 817–34, 1125, 1503–05.

Chapter XVIII is translated from the dictated memoirs, pp. 363–66, 769–816.

Chapter XIX is translated from the dictated memoirs, pp. 730–39, 756–64, 888–963, 968–74, 1032–34, 1079, and the handwritten memoirs, pp. 49–50.

Chapter XX is translated from the dictated memoirs, pp. 569–78, 976–1023, 1106–07, 1381–82

Chapter XXI is translated from the dictated memoirs, pp. 1004–20, 1022–26. These pages were dictated on May 18, 1911, after which Witte and his wife went abroad for several months.

Chapter XXII is translated from the dictated memoirs, pp. 1021–51, 1059–60. Witte began dictating these pages on December 12, 1911, following his return from a stay abroad, where he had undergone two serious operations.

Chapter XXIII is translated from the dictated memoirs, pp. 859–69, 1060–1124.

Chapter XXIV is translated from the dictated memoirs, pp. 1143–97.

Chapter XXV is translated from the dictated memoirs, pp. 390–92, 1197–1214.

Chapter XXVI is translated from the dictated memoirs, pp. 1221–73.

Chapter XXVII is translated from the dictated memoirs, pp. 72–73, 1273–1300, 1499–1500, 1514–15, 1551–57, and the handwritten memoirs, pp. 34 verso–37, 254–55.

Chapter XXVIII is translated from the dictated memoirs, pp. 1304–30.

Chapter XXIX is translated from the dictated memoirs, pp. 1326–27, 1346–80, 1394–1423.

Chapter XXX is translated from the dictated memoirs, pp. 1491–97, 1507–11, 1558–63.

Chapter XXXI is translated from the dictated memoirs, pp. 850–54, 1500–07, 1516–41, 1564–70.

Chapter XXXII is translated from the dictated memoirs, pp. 393–94, 1570–85.

Chapter XXXIII is translated from the dictated memoirs, pp. 1412–23, 1589–93, 1598–1639, and the handwritten memoirs, pp. 3–8.

Chapter XXXIV is translated from the dictated memoirs, pp. 1327, 160–66, and the handwritten memoirs, p. 13.

Appendix A is translated from the handwritten memoirs, pp. 23–26, and the dictated memoirs, pp. 1502–07, 1543–30, 1666–82.

Appendix B is translated from the dictated memoirs, pp. 1424–78, 1488–89 and the handwritten memoirs, pp. 18–32.

Appendix C is translated from the dictated memoirs, pp. 1446–57.

Appendix D is translated in excerpt from the opening and the conclusion of "Vozniknovenie russko-iaponskoi voiny."

Volume II

Volume II, which spans the period from August 1903, when Witte was appointed chairman of the Committee of Ministers, to April 1906, when he left the office of premier, is based primarily on his handwritten memoirs, which deal almost exclusively with this period, and pages 1715–1975 of his dictated memoirs, pages that cover the period from August 1903 to September 1905. (The dictated memoirs, by Witte's choice, do not deal with the period from September 1905 to April 1906.) In places the material in these pages of the dictated memoirs repeats what is said in the handwritten memoirs; in places it supplements; in places it contradicts, usually on minor detail.

Chapter 1 is translated from the handwritten memoirs, pp. 1–14 verso, and the dictated memoirs, pp. 1331–34, 1656–59, 1715–55, 1887–90.

Chapter II is translated from the handwritten memoirs, pp. 14–48 and 265–66, and the dictated memoirs, pp. 1753–58 .

Chapter III is translated from the handwritten memoirs, pp. 35, 54 verso–64, 291 verso, and the dictated memoirs, pp. 1741–60, 1763, 1772.

Chapter IV is translated from the handwritten memoirs, pp. 64 verso–81, and the dictated memoirs, pp. 1557–58, 1765–1849.

Chapter V is translated from the handwritten memoirs, pp. 83–102 verso, and the dictated memoirs, pp. 1634–35, 1850–1970.

Chapter VI is translated from the handwritten memoirs, pp. 103–09.

Chapter VII is translated from the handwritten memoirs, pp. 81-verso–83, 110–25 verso, 343–51, and the dictated memoirs, pp. 1953, 1966–67, 1871–73, 2053–57.

Chapter VIII is translated from the handwritten memoirs, pp. 126–144 verso, and a memorandum (see Appendix) by Witte dealing with the subject.

Chapter IX. Although Witte tried to write a coherent account of his first actions as premier, he frequently digressed, at length. Consequently, it was necessary to use materials from several places in his memoirs for Chapter IX: the handwritten memoirs, pp. 145–161 verso, 165, 207–08, 294 verso–295, and the dictated memoirs, pp. 1856–59.

Chapter X is translated from the handwritten memoirs, pp. 167 verso–175, 187 verso–189, 228–29, and the dictated memoirs, pp. 1859–63.

Chapter XI is a conflation of material from the dictated memoirs, pp. 405–12, and the handwritten memoirs, pp. 189 verso–199 verso, 250 verso, 266 verso–277 verso, and 343–350 verso.

Chapter XII is translated from the handwritten memoirs, pp. 175–85 verso, 222–26, 239 verso–250.

Chaper XIII is translated from the handwritten memoirs, pp. 277–311 verso.

Chapter XIV is translated from the handwritten memoirs, pp. 311 verso–52.

Chapter XV is translated from the handwritten memoirs, pp. 352–63.

Appendix. The three documents in the Appendix were translated from a typescript placed between pages 129 and 130 of the handwritten memoirs and numbered 129a, 129b *et seq.*

Volume III

Chapter I is translated from the handwritten memoirs, p. 358 verso, and the dictated memoirs, pp. 2008–28, 2097–2101.

Chapter II is translated from the handwritten memoirs, pp. 362–63, and the dictated memoirs, pp. 2105–64.

Chapter III is translated from the dictated memoirs, pp. 1696–1714, 2262–67, 2298–2302, 2403–05.

Chapter IV is translated from the dictated memoirs, pp. 1984–2008.

Chapter V is translated from the handwritten memoirs, p. 358 verso, and the dictated memoirs, pp. 1999–2000, 2029–47 *passim.*

Chapter VI is translated from the dictated memoirs, pp. 2048–85 *passim,* 2165–66.

Chapter VII is translated from the handwritten memoirs, pp. 242–43 verso, and the dictated memoirs, pp. 2167–91 *passim,* 2204–05.

Chapter VIII is translated from the handwritten memoirs, pp. 268–69, and the dictated memoirs, pp. 2218–2373 *passim.*

Chapter IX is translated from the dictated memoirs, pp. 2191–2201, 2206–17, 2238–44, 2289–94, 2306–15, 2345–51.

Chapter X is translated from the dictated memoirs, pp. 2201–2376 *passim.*

Chapter XI is translated from the handwritten memoirs, pp. 230–38 verso, and the dictated memoirs, pp. 2084–2104, 2335–45, 2284–90, 2302, 2355–56.

Chapter XII is translated from the dictated memoirs, pp. 2378–2438 *passim.*

Bibliography

The Witte Memoirs: Publishing History

The Yarmolinsky text, based on the translation by Avrahm Yarmolinsky

"Count Witte's Memoirs." *World's Work*, 16 (1920–21): 39–63, 132–52, 299–308, 370–79, 484–96, 587–93. Excerpts from the Yarmolinsky translation, published in advance of publication in book form.

"Memoirs." *Daily Telegraph* (London) November 15, 1920–January 21, 1921. Excerpts from the Yarmolinsky translation, published in advance of publication in book form.

The Memoirs of Count Witte. Trans. A. Yarmolinsky. New York and London, 1921. Reprinted 1967.

Mémoires du Comte Witte. Trans. F. Rousseau. Paris, 1921.

Memorias. Trans. M. Domenge. 2 vols. Madrid, 1921.

Paměti hraběte Sergěje Witte. Trans. T. Pistorius. Prague, 1922. Translation of excerpts from Yarmolinsky text.

The Hessen text, based on the Russian text published by the Slovo Publishing House, the head of which was I. V. Hessen (Gessen)

"Memuary S. Iu. Vitte" (Memoirs of S. Iu. Witte). *Rul* (Berlin) 1920–23. Excerpts from the memoirs. The first excerpts may have been based on the Yarmolinsky text, the rest, I assume, on the Hessen text. I. V. Hessen was one of the publishers of *Rul*.

Vospominaniia: Tsarstvovanie Nikolaia II (Memoirs: The Reign of Nicholas II). 2 vols. Berlin: Knigoizdatelstvo Slovo, 1921–22. Reprinted 1968.

Vospominaniia: Detstvo, tsarstvovaniia Aleksandra II i Aleksandra III (1849–1894) (Memoirs:

Childhood, the Reigns of Alexander II and Alexander III). Berlin: Knigoizdatelstvo
Slovo, 1923. Reprinted 1968.

Erinnerungen. Trans. H. von Hörner. Berlin, 1923. An abridged translation of the first two
volumes of the Hessen text.

Vospominaniia: Tsarstvovanie Nikolaia II. 2 vols. Moscow-Petrograd, 1923. The Hessen text,
edited to conform to Soviet orthography and capitalization.

Vospominaniia: Detstvo, tsarstvovaniia Aleksandra II i Aleksandra III (1849-1894). Leningrad,
1924. The Hessen text, edited to conform to Soviet orthography and capitalization.

Nichiro sensō to Roshia Kakumei (The Russo-Japanese War and the Russian Revolution). 3
vols. Tokyo, 1930.

Background for Chamberlain: A Turn-of-the-Century Plan for Peace. Trans. T. C. Wilson. Philadelphia, 1938. Translation of brief part of the memoirs. As far as can be told the only
English translation hitherto from the Russian.

Vospominaniia. 3 vols. Moscow, 1960. Text uses that of the Soviet 1923-24 edition, with
Vospominaniia: Detstvo . . . appearing as volume one of this edition and *Vospominaniia:
Tsarstvovanie Nikolaia II* as volumes two and three. Extensive annotation and excellent
index prepared by leading Soviet scholars. A printing of 75,000 sets.

Egy Kegyveszteit visszaemlékezései. (The Memoirs of One Who Has Fallen from Grace). Trans.
Vas Zoltan. Budapest, 1964. I have not seen this translation, but assume from place and
date of publication that this 750-page work is an abridged translation of the Soviet 1960
edition.

Nichiro sensō to Roshia Kakumei. Trans. Hirokichi Otake. 3 vols. Tokyo, 1972. Probably a
reprint of the 1930 edition, which I have not seen.

Commentaries Concerning the Memoirs

Ananich, B. V. "O rukopisiakh i tekste memuarov S. Iu. Vitte" (Concerning the Manuscripts and Text of the Memoirs of S. Iu. Witte). In *Vspomogatelnye istoricheskie distsipliny,*
vol. 12, pp. 188-204. Leningrad, 1981. Comments by one of the leading experts on
Witte following a visit to the Columbia Archive.

Ananich, B. V., and Ganelin, R. Sh. "Opyt kritiki memuarov S. Iu. Vitte (v sviazi s ego
publitsisticheskoi deiatelnostiu v 1907-1915 gg.)" (An Attempt at a Critique of the
Memoirs of S. Iu. Witte in Connection with his Publicistic Work from 1907 to 1915). In
Voprosy istoriografii i istochnikovedeniia istorii SSSR: Sbornik statei, pp. 298-374. Moscow,
1963.

Asheshov, N. "Nikolai II i ego sanovniki v vospominaniiakh grafa S. Iu. Vitte"
(Nicholas and his High Officials in the Memoirs of Count S. Iu. Witte). *Byloe* 18 (1922):
164-210.

Bompard, M. "Les Mémoires du Comte Witte." *La Revue de Paris* 28 (1921): 19-33.

Dehquist, J. "Graf Witte's Memoiren." *Preussische Jahrbücher* 191 (1923): 129-46.

Dillon, J. "Two Russian Statesmen." *The Quarterly Review* 236 (1921): 407-17.

Gurko, V.I. "Chto est i chego net v 'Vospominaniiakh' S. Iu. Vitte" (What is Included in
and What is Excluded from Iu. Witte's Memoirs). *Russkaia starina* 2 (1922): 59-153.

Harcave, S. "The Hessen Redaction of the Witte Memoirs." *Jahrbücher für Geschichte
Osteuropas* 36 (1988): 268-76.

Lopukhin, A. A. *Otryvki iz vospominanii (po povodu "Vospominanii" Gr. S. Iu Vitte)* (Frag-
ments from My Memoirs in Connection with the Memoirs of Count S. Iu. Witte).
Moscow, 1923.

Pokrovskii, M. N. "O memuarakh Vitte" (Concerning Witte's Memoirs). *Pechat i revo-liutsiia,* (January–March 1922): 54–58, (September 1922): 11–21.

Romanov, B. A. "Likhungchangskii fond." *Borba klassov,* 1–2 (1924): 77–126. Commentary on what Witte wrote about his dealings with Li Hung-chang.

Sidorov, A. L. "K voprosu o kharaktere teksta i istochnikov 'Vospominanii' S. Iu. Vitte" (Concerning the Character of the Text and the Sources of Witte's Memoirs). In his *Istoricheskie predposylki Velikoi oktiabrskoi sotsialisticheskoi revoliutsii,* pp. 187–216. Moscow, 1970.

Tarle, E. V. *Graf S. Iu. Vitte.* Leningrad, 1927.

Tkachenko, M. A. "Fond S. Iu. Vitte v TSGIA i zadacha kritiki vospominanii S. Iu. Vitte" (The Witte Papers in the Central State Historical Archive and the Task of Criticizing Witte's Memoirs). In *Nekotorye voprosy istoriografii i istochnikovedeniia SSSR: Sbornik statei,* pp. 186–97. Moscow, 1977.

Vasilevskii, I. *Graf Vitte i ego memuary* (Count Witte and His Memoirs). Berlin, 1922.

Vodovozov, V. V. *Graf S. Iu. Vitte i Imperator Nikolai II* (Count S. Iu. Witte and Emperor Nicholas II). Petrograd, 1922. Largely a commentary on the Yarmolinsky and Hessen texts and on the memoirs themselves.

Witte's Other Publications

Witte was no writer, as well he knew, but he did seek to express his views in print. One admirer claims that if Witte had not chosen another career he would have made a name for himself as a publicist. However that may be, he began to publish, under the pseudonym *Zelenoi Popugai* (The Green Parrot), in an Odessan periodical during the 1870s. In the 1880s, as he notes, he published a newspaper of his own, *Kievskoe delo.* During that decade he contributed to Aksakov's publication *Rus* and published two short works, noted below. After he entered government service in 1889, he was very limited in what he could publish. The list that follows includes only books and pamphlets.

Konspekt lektsii o narodnom i gosduarstvennom khoziaistve (Synopsis of Lectures on Economics and Government Finance). 2nd ed. St. Petersburg, 1912. Based on lectures he read to Grand Duke Michael Aleksandrovich.

"Libava ili Murman?" (Libau or Murmansk), *Proshloe i nastoiashchee,* 1 (1924): 25–39.

Natsionalnaia Ekonomiia i Fridrikh List (The National Economy and Friedrich List). Kiev, 1889. A second edition appeared in 1912 under the slightly altered title of *Po povodu natsionalizma: Natsionalnaia ekonomiia i Fridrikh List* (Concerning Nationalism . . .).

Printsipy zheleznodorozhnykh tarifov po perevozke gruzov (The Principles of Railroad Freight Rate Determination). Kiev, 1883.

Prolog russko-iaponskoi voiny (Prologue to the Russo-Japanese War). Ed. B. B. Glinskii. Petrograd, 1916.

Samoderzhavie i zemstvo (Autocracy and the Zemstvo). Stuttgart, 1901. This confidential document, written for official use, was "leaked" to the opposition, which published it abroad. In it Witte argued that zemstvos, being based on the principle of representation, were not compatible with autocracy. Some say that A. N. Gurev, who often helped Witte, should receive credit for the writing: others assign the credit to a professor at the Demidov Juridical Lycée, identified by the initial "M." There were several unauthorized editions of this work, culminating in an edition in 1914 authorized by Witte entitled *Po povodu neprelozhnosti zakonov gosudarstvennoi zhizni* (Concerning the Immutability of the Principles of Governmental Existence).

Spravka o tom, kak byl zakliuchen vneshnii zaem 1906 goda, spasshii finansovoe polozhenie Rossii (How the Foreign Loan of 1906, Which Saved Russia's Financial Position, Was Concluded). St. Petersburg, 1913.

Vynuzhdennye raziasneniia Grafa Vitte po povodu otcheta Gen.-Adiut. Kuropatkina o voine s Iaponiei (Unavoidable Comments by Count Witte Concerning General-Adjutant Kuropatkin's Account of the War with Japan). A rebuttal of some of the general's assertions about the war, first published in 1909 for limited distribution and then in another edition in 1911 for general distribution.

Zapiska po krestianskomu delu (Memorandum Concerning the Peasant Problem). St. Petersburg, 1904. An official document presenting Witte's conclusions as chairman of the Special Conference on the Needs of Rural Industry.

Witte's Published Letters, Reports, *et sim.*

"Borba S. Iu. Vitte s agrarnoi revoliutsiei" (The Struggle of S. Iu. Witte against Agrarian Revolution). *Krasnyi arkhiv* 31 (1928): 81–102.

"Dokladnaia zapiska Vitte Nikolaiu II" (Report of Witte to Nicholas II). *Istorik-Marksist* 2–3 (1935): 130–39.

"Doklady S. Iu. Vitte Nikolaiu II" (Reports of S. Iu. Witte to Nicholas II). *Krasnyi arkhiv* 11–12 (1925): 144–58.

"Graf S. Iu. Vitte i Leo Mekhelin" (Count S. Iu. Witte and Leo Mechelin). *Byloe* 2(30) (1918): 108–09.

"Graf S. Iu. Vitte i Nikolai II v oktiabre" (Count S. Iu. Witte and Nicholas II in October). *Byloe* 4(32) (1925): 107.

"Graf Vitte v borbe s revoliutsiei" (Count Witte at War with the Revolution). *Byloe* 3(31) (1918): 3–10.

"Iz arkhiva S. Iu. Vitte" (From S. Iu. Witte's Archive). *Krasnyi arkhiv* 11–12 (1925): 107–43.

"K istorii manifesta 17 oktiabria" (Concerning the History of the October 17 Manifesto). *Krasnyi arkhiv* 4 (1923): 411–17.

"K istorii 'Sobranie russkikh fabrichno-zavodskikh rabochikh g. S. Peterburga" (Concerning the History of the Assembly of St. Petersburg Factory Workers). *Krasnaia letopis* 1 (1922): 288–329. Includes correspondence between Witte and Plehve.

"K istorii sozdaniia manifesta 17 oktiabria" (Concerning the Genesis of the October 17 Manifesto). *Sovetskie arkhivy* 5 (1985): 62–63.

Korostovets, I. Ia. "Mirnye pergovory v Portsmute v 1905 godu" (Peace Negotiations at Portsmouth in 1905). *Byloe* 1(29): 177–220; 2(30) 110–46; 3(31) 58–85; 12(40) 154–82, 1918. A diary kept at Witte's request.

"Manifest 17 oktiabria," (The October 17 Manifesto). *Krasnyi arkhiv* 11–12 (1925) 39–106.

"Ob osnovakh ekonomicheskoi politike tsarskogo pravitelstva v kontse XIX-nachale XX v." (The Principles of the Tsarist Government's Economic Policy at the End of the 19th and the Beginning of the 20th Centuries). *Materialy po istorii SSSR* 6 (Moscow, 1959), 157–222. Contains statements by Witte concerning policy with respect to foreign capital.

"Perepiska Grafa S. Iu. Vitte i P. A. Stolypina," (The Correspondence of Count S. Iu. Witte and P. A. Stolypin). *Russkaia mysl* 36 (1915): 134–52.

"Perepiska o podkupke kitaiskikh sanovnikov Li-khun-chzhana i Chzhan-in-khuana"

(Correspondence Concerning the Bribing of the High Chinese Officials Li Hung-chang and Chang In-huan). *Krasnyi arkhiv* 2 (1922): 287–93.

"Perepiska S. Iu. Vitte i A. M. Kuropatkina v 1904–1905 gg." (The Correspondence of S. Iu. Witte and A. M. Kuropatkin, 1904–1905). *Krasnyi arkhiv* 19 (1926): 64–82.

"Perepiska Vitte i Pobedonostseva, 1895–1905 gg." (The Correspondence of Witte and Pobedonostsev, 1895–1905). *Krasnyi arkhiv* 30 (1928): 89–116.

"Pisma S. Iu. Vitte k D. S. Sipiaginu, 1900–1901 gg." (S. Iu. Witte's letters to D. S. Sipiagin, 1900–1901). *Krasnyi arkhiv* 6 (1924): 3–47; 7 (1924): 3–31.

Politicheskaia bezprintsipnost S. Iu. Vitte: Tainye tsirkuliary i doklady (S. Iu. Witte's Lack of Political Principles: Secret Circulars and Reports). Berlin, 1903.

"Popytki S. Iu. Vitte otkryt amerikanskii denezhnyi rynok dlia russkikh zaimov" (S. Iu. Witte's Efforts to Open the American Money Market to Russian Loans). *Istoricheskii arkhiv* 1 (1959): 123–40; 2 (1959): 115–35.

"Portsmut" (Portsmouth). *Krasnyi arkhiv* 6 (1924): 3–47; 7 (1924): 3–31.

Russia, Komitet Ministrov. *Zhurnaly komiteta ministrov po ispolneniu ukaza 12 dekabria 1904 g.* (Minutes of the Committee of Ministers in Connection with the Implementation of the Decree of December 12, 1904). St. Petersburg, 1908.

"S. Iu. Vitte, frantsuzskaia pechat i russkie zaimy" (S. Iu. Witte, the French Press, and Russian Loans). *Krasnyi arkhiv* 10 (1925): 36–40.

"Trebovaniia dvorianstva i ekonomicheskaia politika pravitelstva" (Demands of the Nobility and the Economic Policy of the Government). *Istoricheskii arkhiv* 4 (1954): 122–55. Witte's reply to statement presented in 1896 by marshals of the nobility concerning the needs of the nobility in the area of agriculture.

Works Inspired by Witte

Countess Witte notwithstanding, her husband did not "stand above the battle," particularly after 1906, when he found himself engaged in arguments concerning various aspects of the war and the revolution. Because of his position, and for other reasons as well, he often used the services of others, to whom he supplied the documentation, to present his side of the story. Following is a list of books inspired by Witte.

Demchinskii, B. *Rossiia v Manchzhurii* (Russia in Manchuria). St. Petersburg, 1908. Largely a defense of the policies with respect to Manchuria favored by Witte. The author is apparently the Demchinskii who served under Witte in earlier days.

Morskoi, A. (pseud. Vladimir I. von Stein). *Iskhod revoliutsii 1905 i pravitelstvo Nosaria* (The Denouement of the Russian Revolution of 1905 and the Government of Nosar). Moscow, 1911.

————. *Razocharovaniia v chestnom maklerstve: Ruzvelt i Portsmutskie soveshchaniia* (Disappointments in Honest Brokerage: Roosevelt and the Portsmouth Conference). Moscow, 1911.

————. *Voennaia moshch Rossii* (The Military Power of Russia). Petrograd, 1915. Presents more of Witte's criticism of General Kuropatkin.

————. *Zubatovshchina* (The Zubatov System). Moscow, 1913. A critique of the Zubatov system and a defense of Witte's views concerning labor while minister of finance. Has as an appendix the text of a memorandum to General D. F. Trepov from A. Tikhomirov concerning trade unionism which may have been included as representing Witte's views.

Articles and Books Concerning Witte

Aizenberg, L. M. "Velikii Kniaz Sergei Aleksandrovich, Vitte i evrei-moskovskie kup-tsy" (Grand Duke Sergei Aleksandrovich, Witte and Jewish Muscovite Merchants). *Evreiskaia starina* 13 (1930): 80–99.

Ananich, B. V., and Ganelin, R. Sh. "I. A. Vyshnegradskii i S. Iu. Vitte, korrespon-denty Moskovskikh vedomostei" (I. A. Vyshnegradskii and S. Iu. Witte, Correspon-dents for *Moskovskie edomosti*). In *Problemy obshchestvennoi mysli i ekonomicheskaia politika Rossii XIX–XX vv.*, pp. 12–34. Leningrad, 1972.

————. "R. A. Fadeev, S. Iu. Vitte, i ideologicheskie iskaniia 'okhranitelei' v 1881–1882 gg." (R. A. Fadeev, S. Iu. Witte and the Ideological Quests of the "Guardians" in 1881–1882). In *Issledovaniia po sotsialno-politicheskoi istorii Rossii: Sbornik statei pamiati Borisa Aleksandrovicha Romanova*, pp. 299–326. Trudy Leningradskogo otdeleniia Insti-tuta Istorii, no. 12. Leningrad, 1971.

————. "S. Iu. Vitte, M. P. Dragomanov i '*Volnoe slovo*'" (S. Iu. Witte, M. P. Dra-gomanov and Volnoe slovo). In *Issledovaniia po otechestvennomu istochnikovedeniiu: Sbornik statei posviashchennykh 75-letiiu professora S. N. Valka*, pp. 163–78. Trudy Leningrad-skogo otdeleniia Instituta Istorii, no. 7. Moscow-Leningrad, 1964.

Anspach, A. *La Russie économique et l'oeuvre de M. de Witte*. Paris, 1904.

Baian (pseud. I. I. Kolyshko). *Lozh Vitte* (Witte's Lie). Berlin, n.d. A defamatory work, obviously written after the appearance of Witte's memoirs, in which Kolyshko figures poorly.

Bernstein, H. "Sergei Witte." In his *Celebrities of Our Time: Interviews*. Freeport, N.Y., 1968.

Byvshii ministr finansov Sergei Iulevich Vitte, kak glavnyi vinovnik narushenii vysochaishego poveleniia ot 4-go Marta 1891 g. i ego sovmestnoe uchastie . . . v dele ogrableniia krymskago pomeshchiia K. A. Durante. . . . (Former Finance Minister Sergei Iulevich Witte, as Chief Culprit in the Violation of the Imperial Order of March 4, 1891, and His Participation . . . in the Theft of the Estate of K. A. Durante. . . .) Odessa, 1908.

Dillon, E. J. *The Eclipse of Russia*. New York, 1918.

Enden, M. N. "The Roots of Witte's Thoughts." *Russian Review* 29 (1970): 6–24.

Fadeev, A. M. *Vospominaniia* (Memoirs). Odessa, 1897.

Ganelin, R. Sh. "S. Iu. Vitte i peregovory o torgovom dogovore so Shvetsii i Norvegiei v 1895–1906 gg." (S. Iu. Witte and Negotiations Concerning a Commercial Treaty with Sweden and Norway 1895–1906). In *Istoricheskie sviazi Skandinavii i Rossii*, pp. 144–63. Leningrad, 1970.

Glinskii, B. B. "Graf Sergei Iulevich Vitte" (Count Sergei Iulevich Witte). *Istoricheskii vestnik* 140 (1915): 232–79, 573–89; 141 (1915): 520–55, 893–906; 142 (1915): 592–609, 893–907.

Golub, S. "Rabochie i ministry" (Workers and Ministers). *Sovremennik* 10 (1911): 387–92.

Grimm, C. *Graf Witte und die deutsche Politik*. Freiburg, 1930.

Gurko, V. I. *Features and Figures of the Past*. Stanford, Calif., 1939.

Heilbronner, J. "An Anti-Witte Diplomatic Conspiracy, 1905–1906: The Schwanebach Memorandum," *Jahrbücher für Geschichte Osteuropas* 14 (1966): 347–61.

Iuzefovich, B. *G. Menshikov o gr. S. Iu. Vitte* (G. Menshikov Concerning Count S. Iu. Witte). N.p., n.d. Example of the far-right defamatory pamphlets directed against Witte. This one alleges that Menshikov, the conservative journalist, was, in fact, one of Witte's tools.

Izvolskii, A. P. "Le Comte Witte." *La Revue de Paris* 19 (1922): 703–22.

Kaufman, A. E. "Cherty iz zhizni S. Iu. Vitte" (Some Aspects of the Life of S. Iu. Witte). *Istoricheskii vestnik* 140 (1915): 220–31.

Kitanina, T. M. "Programma ekonomicheskogo osvoeniia severa i tarifnaia politika S. Iu. Vitte" (The program of the economic opening-up of the north and S. Iu. Witte's tariff policy). *Trudy* (Institut istorii, Leningradskoe otdelenie) 13 (1972): 191–210.

Klein, A. *Der Einfluss des Grafen Witte auf die deutsch-russischen Beziehungen.* Bethel/Bielefeld, 1932.

Koni, A. F. "Sergei Iulevich Vitte." In his *Sobranie sochinenii* 5 (Moscow, 1968): 238–77.

Korostowetz, W. von, *Graf Witte.* Berlin, 1929.

Kutler, N., and Slonimskii, L. "Vitte," *Novyi Entsiklopedicheskii Slovar* 9, 827–50.

Laue, T. Von "Count Witte and the Russian Revolution of 1905." *American Slavic and East European Review* (February 1958): 25–46.

——————. "A Secret Memorandum of Sergei Witte on the Industrialization of Russia." *Journal of Modern History* 26 (1954): 60–74.

——————. *Sergei Witte and the Industrialization of Russia.* New York, 1969.

Lutokhin, D. A. *Graf S. Iu. Vitte kak ministr finansov* (Count S. Iu. Witte as Minister of Finance). Petrograd, 1915.

Lvov, E. *Po studenomu moriu* (Over the frozen sea). St. Petersburg, 1895. A description of Witte's trip to Murmansk.

Lvov, L. "Sem let nazad" (Seven years ago). *Russkaia mysl* 35 (1914): 48–84. Concerning the attempts on Witte's life in 1907.

Mehlinger, H. D., and Thompson, J. M. *Count Witte and the Tsarist Government in the 1905 Revolution.* Bloomington, Ind., 1972.

Melnik, J. "Witte." *Century Magazine* 68 (1915): 684–90.

Miliukov, P. N. "Vitte," *Entsiklopedicheskii slovar,* 7th ed. 10, 343–72.

Mironenko, K. N. "Manifest 17 oktiabria 1905 g." (The Manifesto of October 17, 1905). *Uchenye zapiski Leningradskogo universiteta* 255 (1958). Seriia iuridicheskoi nauki, no. 10. Voprosy gosudarstva i prava, pp. 158–79.

Naryshkin-Witte, V. *Souvenirs d'une fillette russe.* Paris, 1925. Recollections of Witte's adopted daughter. Includes material that had appeared in French and in Russian.

Nötzold, J. *Wirtschaftspolitische Alternativen der Entwicklung in der Ära Witte und Stolypin.* Berlin, 1966.

Petrov, N. "Gapon i graf Vitte" (Gapon and Count Witte). *Byloe* 1(29) (1925): 15–27.

Plavnik, L. B. "Vitte i revoliutsiia" (Witte and the Revolution). In *Muzei revoliutsii Soiuza SSR. Pervyi sbornik statei,* pp. 150–84. Moscow, 1947.

Romanov, B. A. "Vitte kak diplomat" (Witte As a Diplomat). *Vestnik Leningradskogo universiteta* 4–5 (1946): 151–72.

——————. "Vitte nakanune russko-iaponskoi voiny" (Witte on the Eve of the Russo-Japanese War). *Rossiia i zapad* 1 (1923): 140–67.

Rusov, A. A. "S. Iu. Vitte i ukrainskoe slovo" (Witte and the Ukrainian Language). *Utro zhizni* 3–4 (1915): 95–97.

Savitsky, N. "Serge Witte." *Le Monde Slave* 3 (1932): 161–91, 321–48.

Seraphim, E. "Zar Nikolaus II und Graf Witte." *Historische Zeitschrift* 161 (1940): 277–308.

Struve, P. "Graf S. Iu. Vitte" (Count S. Iu. Witte). *Russkaia mysl* 36 (1915): 129–52.

Szeftel, M. "Nicholas II's Constitutional Decisions of Oct. 17–19, 1905 and Sergius Witte's Role." In *Album J. Balon,* pp. 461–93. Namur, 1968.

————. "The Parliamentary Reforms of the Witte Administration." *Parliaments, Estates and Representation* 1 (1981): 71–94.

————. *The Russian Constitution of April 23, 1906*. Brussels, 1976.

Tompkins, S. R. "Witte as Minister of France." *Slavonic and East European Review* 11 (1933): 590–606.

Tsion (Cyon), I. F. *M. Witte et les finances russes*. 4th ed. Paris, 1895. The best known of the many published attacks by Tsion on Witte's work as finance minister.

Turnbull, D. "The Defeat of Popular Representation, December 1904: Prince Mirskii Witte, and the Imperial Family," *Slavic Review* 48 (1989), 54–70.

Vetlugin, G. "S. Iu. Vitte i dekabrskoe vosstanie v Moskve" (S. Iu. Witte and the December Rising in Moscow). *Byloe* 6(34) (1925): 225–26.

Vitenberg, B. M. "K istorii lichnogo arkhiva S. Iu. Vitte" (Concerning the History of Witte's Personal Archive). In *Vspomogatelnye istoricheskie ditsipliny* 17 (1986): 248–60.

Other Sources

Agrarnyi vopros v Sovete ministrov (1906 g.) (The Agrarian Question in the Council of Ministers, 1906). Moscow, 1924.

Agursky, M. "Caught in a Cross Fire: The Russian Church Between Holy Synod and Radical Right, 1905–1908." *Orientalia Christiana Periodica* 50 (1984): 163–96.

Akademiia Nauk SSSR. Institut Istorii. *Revoliutsiia 1905–1907 gg. Dokumenty i materialy*. 15 vols. Moscow, 1955–1963.

Alexander Mikhailovich, Grand Duke, *Once a Grand Duke*. New York, 1932.

Andreie Vladimirovich, Grand Duke. "Iz dnevnika A. V. Romanova za 1916–1971 gg." (The diary of A. V. Romanov for 1916–1917). *Krasnyi arkhiv* 26 (1928): 185–210.

Ascher, A., ed. "The Coming Storm." *Survey* (October 1964): 148–64.

Avrekh, A. Ia. "Vopros o zapadnom zemstve i bankrotstvo Stolypina" (The Western Zemstvos Question and the Bankruptcy of Stolypin). *Istoricheskie zapiski* 70 (1961): 61–112.

Basily, Nicholas de. *Memoirs*. Stanford, Calif., 1973.

Bechofer-Roberts, C. E. *The Mysterious Madame: Helena Petrovna Blavatsky*. New York, 1931.

Bezobrazov, A. M. "Les premières causes de l'effrondrement de la Russie: Le Conflit russo-japonais." *Le Correspondent* 291 (1923): 577–615.

Bill, V. T. *The Forgotten Class*. Westport, Conn., 1976.

Bogdanovich, A. V. *Tri poslednikh samoderzhtsa: Dnevnik A. V. Bogdanovich* (The Three Last Autocrats: Diary of A. V. Bogdanovich). Moscow, 1924.

Bompard, Maurice. *Mon Ambassade en Russie, 1903–1908*. Paris, 1937.

Bülow, Prince Bernard von. *Memoirs*. 3 vols. Boston, 1931–1932.

Byrnes, Robert F. *Pobedonostsev*. Bloomington, Ind., 1968.

Cantacuzene, Princess Julia. *My Life Here and There*. New York, 1921.

Chernovskii, A., ed. *Soiuz russkogo naroda* (The Union of the Russian People). Moscow, 1924.

Crisp, Olga. "The Russian Liberals and the 1906 Anglo-French Loan to Russia." *The Slavonic and East European Review* 39 (1961): 497–511.

Cunningham, James W. *A Vanquished Hope: The Movement for Church Renewal in Russia, 1905–1906*. Crestwood, N.Y., 1981.

Curtin, Jeremiah. *Memoirs of Jeremiah Curtin*. Madison, Wisc., 1940.

Dillon, Emile J. *The Eclipse of Russia*. New York, 1918.

Drezen, A., ed. *Tsarizm v borbe s revoliutsiei 1905–1906 gg.: Sbornik dokumentov* (Tsarism's Struggle against Revolution, 1905–1907: A Collection of Documents). Moscow, 1936.

Elkin, B. "Attempts To Revive Freemasonry in Russia." *The Slavonic and East European Review* 44 (1966): 454–72.

Emmons, Terence. *The Formation of Political Parties and the First National Elections in Russia.* Cambridge, Mass., 1983.

Engelstein, L. *Moscow 1905.* Stanford, Calif., 1982.

Esthus, R. A. "Nicholas II and the Russo-Japanese War." *The Russian Review* 40 (1981): 396–411.

"Finansovoe polozhenie tsarskogo samoderzhaviia v period russko-iaponskoi voiny i pervoi russkoi revoliutsii" (The Financial Situation of the Tsarist Autocracy during the Russo-Japanese War and the First Russian Revolution). *Istoricheskii arkhiv* 2 (1955): 121–49.

Fountain, A. M. *Roman Dmowski.* Boulder, Colo., 1980.

France. Archives de Ministère des Affaires Étrangères. Russie, Politique Interieure, II, III.

France. Ministère des Affaires Étrangères. *Documents diplomatiques français, 1871–1914.* 41 vols. Paris, 1929–59. 2nd ser., I, VII, VIII.

Gerasimov, A. A. *Der Kampf gegen die erste russische Revolution.* Frauenfeld, 1934. A translation from the Russian. Contains material not included in the 1985 Paris edition.

——————. *Na lezvii s terroristani* (The Struggle against the Terrorists). Paris, 1985.

Germany. Auswärtiges Amt. Archiv, Russland, 82, no. 1, Geheim, V-VIII.

Germany. Auswärtiges Amt. *Die grosse Politik der europäschen Kabinette, 1871–1914*, 40 vols. Berlin, 1922–26. XIV, pt. 1, XIX, pt. 2.

Girault, Ren', *Emprunts Russes et investissements français, en Russie, 1887–1914.* Paris, 1973.

Gosudarstvennaia duma v Rossii: V dokumentakh i materialakh. Moscow, 1957.

Harcave, S. *First Blood: The Russian Revolution of 1905.* New York, 1964.

——————. *Years of the Golden Cockerel: The Last Romanov Tsars, 1814–1917.* New York, 1968.

Herzl, Theodor. *The Complete Diaries of Theodor Herzl.* Vol. 4. New York, 1960.

Hessen (Gessen), I. V. *Gody izgnaniia* (Years of Exile). Paris, 1979.

——————. *V dvukh vekakh: Zhiznennyi otchet* (In Two Centuries: Autobiography). Berlin, 1937.

Hosking, G. A. *The Russian Constitutional Experiment: Government and Duma, 1907–1914.* Cambridge, 1973.

Ignatev, A. A. *Piatdesiat let v stroiu* (Fifty Years in Service). 2 vols. Moscow, 1950.

Ignatev, A. B. *S. Iu. Vitte—diplomat.* Moscow, 1989.

Iliodor (Trufanov, S. M.). *Pravda o Soiuze Russkago Naroda, Soiuz Russkikh Liudei i dr. monarkhicheskikh partiiakh* (The truth about the Union of the Russian People, the Union of Russian Men, and other Monarchist Parties). Odessa, 1907.

International Railway Congress, Brussels, 1885. *Congrès des chemins de fer. Bruxelles: 8–15 Août 1885. Compte rendu général.* 2 vols. Brussels, 1886.

"Iz bumag D. F. Trepova." (From D. F. Trepov's Papers). *Krasnyi arkhiv* 11–12 (1925): 448–66.

Izvolsky, A. *The Memoirs of Alexander Izvolsky.* London, 1920.

Jablonowski, H. "Die russischen Rechtsparteien 1905–1917." In *Russland-Studien: Gedenkschrift für Otto Hoetzsch*, pp. 42–55. Stuttgart, 1957.

Judge, E. H. *Plehve: Repression and Reform in Imperial Russia, 1902–1904.* Syracuse, N.Y., 1983.

Kleinmichel, M. *Bilder aus einer versunkten Welt*. Berlin, 1922.

Kliachko, L. M. *Povesti proshlogo* (Tales of the Past). Leningrad, 1929.

Kokovtsev, V. N. *Iz moego proshlago* (Out of My Past). 2 vols. Paris, 1933.

————. *Out of My Past*. Stanford, Calif., 1939. An abridged version of the above.

Koroleva, N. G. *Pervaia rossiiskaia revoliutsiia i tsarizm: sovet ministrov Rossii v 1905–1907 gg*. (The First Russian Revolution and Tsarism: The Russian Council of Ministers 1905–1907). Moscow, 1982.

Kovalevskii, M. M. "Moia zhizn" (My Life). *Istoriia SSSR*, (July–August 1969): 59–79.

Krizis samoderzhaviia v Rossii, 1895–1917 (The Crisis of Autocracy in Russia, 1895–1917). Leningrad, 1984.

Kryzhanovskii, S. E. *Vospominaniia* (Memoirs). Berlin, n.d.

Kurlov (Komarov-Kurlov), P. G. *Das Ende des russischen Kaisertums*. Berlin, 1920.

Kuropatkin, A. N. "Dnevnik A. N. Kuropatkina" (Diary of A. N. Kuropatkin), *Krasnyi arkhiv* 2 (1922): 5–112; 5 (1924): 82–101.

The Letters of Tsar Nicholas and Empress Marie. Ed. E. J. Bing. London, 1937.

Levin, A. *The Reactionary Tradition in the Election Campaign to the Third Duma*. Oklahoma State University Publication, Arts and Sciences Studies: Social Science Series, no. 8. Stillwater, Okla., 1963.

————. *The Second Duma*. 2nd ed. Hamden, Conn., 1966.

Long, J. W. "Organized Protest Against the 1906 Russian Loan." *Cahiers du monde russe et sovietique* 13 (1972): 24–39.

Louis, G. *Les Carnets de George Louis*. 2 vols. Paris, 1926.

Mamontov, V. I. *Na gosudarevoi sluzhbe: Vospominaniia* (Recollections of My Imperial Service). Tallin, 1926.

Markov, A. *Rasputin und die um ihn*. Königsberg, 1928.

Miliukov, P. N. *Vospominaniia* (Memoirs). 2 vols. New York, 1955.

Mosolov, A. A. *At the Court of the Last Tsar*. London, 1935.

Naryshkin-Witte, V. *À Petrograd pendant la Révolution*. Paris, 1925.

"Neizvestnyi proekt manifesta 17 oktiabria 1905 goda" (An Unknown Draft of the Manifesto of October 17, 1905). *Sovetskie arkhivy* 2 (1979): 63–65.

Nicholas II. *Dnevnik imperatora Nikolaia II* (The Diary of Nicholas II). Berlin, 1923.

Nikolaev, P. "Vospominaniia o kniaze A. I. Bariatinskom" (Recollections Concerning Prince A. I. Bariantinskii). *Istoricheskii vestnik* 22 (1885): 618–44.

Novitskii, V. D. *Iz vospominanii zhandarma* (From the Memoirs of a Gendarme). Moscow, 1929.

Paléologue, M. *An Ambassador's Memoirs*. 3 vols. New York, 1924–25.

Petrunkevich, I. I. "Iz zapisok obschchestvennago deiatelia" (From the Notebooks of a Public Man). *Arkhiv russkoi revoliutsii* 21 (1934): 5–467.

Pobedonostsev, K. P. "Iz pisem K. P. Pobedonostseva k Nikolaiu II (1898–1905)" (From the Letters of K. P. Pobedonostsev to Nicholas II). *Religii mira: Istoriia i sovremennost. Ezhegodnik, 1983*, pp. 163–93. Moscow, 1983.

————. *Pisma Pobedonostseva k Aleksandru III* (Letters of Pobedonostsev to Alexander III). 2 vols. Moscow, 1925–26.

Polivanov, A. A. *Iz dnevnikov i vospominanii* (From My Diaries and Memoirs). Moscow, 1924.

Polovtsev, A. A. "Dnevnik A. A. Polovtseva" (Diary of A. A. Polovtsev). *Krasnyi arkhiv* 3 (1923): 75–172; 4 (1923): 63–128; 33 (1929): 170–203; 46 (1931): 110–32; 67 (1934): 163–86.

—————. *Dnevnik gosudarstvennogo sekretaria A. A. Polovtsova (Polovtseva)* (Diary of Imperial Secretary A. A. Polovtsov [Polovtsev]). 2 vols. Moscow, 1966.

Propper, S. M. *Was nicht in die Zeitung kam.* Frankfurt am Main, 1929.

Rogger, H. "Russian Ministers and the Jewish Question, 1881-1917." *California Slavic Studies* 8 (1975): 15-76.

Rosen, R. R. *Forty Years of Diplomacy.* 2 vols. New York, 1922.

Russia. Gosudarstvennaia duma. *Stenograficheskie otchety Sozyv 1-2.* (Stenographic Reports, Session 1-2). 2 vols. St. Petersburg, 1907.

Russia, Gosudarstvennyi Sovet. *Stenograficheskie otchety, Sozyv 3* (Stenographic Reports, Session 3). 18 vols. St. Petersburg, 1907-1912.

Russia. Ministerstvo Finansov. *Ministerstvo finansov, 1802-1902* (The Ministry of Finance, 1802-1902). 2 parts. St. Petersburg, 1902..

Russia. *Polnoe sobranie zakonov rossiiskoi imperii* (Complete Collection of the Laws of the Russian Empire). 3rd comp. 1881-1913, 50 vols. St. Petersburg, 1885-1916.

Ruud, C. A. "The Printing Press as an Agent of Political Change in Early Twentieth-Century Russia." *The Russian Review* 40 (1981): 378-95.

Sablinsky, W. *The Road to Bloody Sunday: Father Gapon and the St. Petersburg Massacre of 1905.* Princeton, N.J., 1976.

Savelev, A. A. "Nikolai II v sarovskoi pustyni" (Nicholas II at the Sarov Monastery). *Golos minuvshego* 5 (1917): 211-20.

Savinsky, A. "Guillaume II et la Russie; ses Dépèches à Nicholas II (1903-1905)." *Revue des deux mondes* 12 (1922): 765-802.

Sazonov, S. *Fateful Years, 1909-1916.* London, 1928.

Sbornik dogovorov Rossii s drugimi gosudarstvami, 1865-1917 (Collection of Treaties between Russia and Other States 1865-1917). Moscow, 1957.

Schneiderman, J. *Sergei Zubatov and Revolutionary Marxism.* Ithaca, N.Y., 1976.

Semennikov, V. P., ed. *Monarkhiia pered krusheniem, 1914-1917; bumagi Nikolaia II i drugie dokumenty* (The Monarchy before Its Fall, 1914-1917; Papers of Nicholas II and Other Documents). Moscow, 1927.

—————. *Revoliutsiia 1905 goda i samoderzhavie* (The Revolution of 1905 and the Autocracy). Moscow, 1928.

—————. *Za kulisami tsarizma: Arkhiv tibetskogo vracha Badmaeva* (Behind the Scenes of Tsarism: The Archive of the Tibetan Doctor Badmaev). Leningrad, 1925.

Shepelev, L. E. *Otmennye istoriei: Chiny, zvaniia i tituly v rossiiskoi imperii* (Canceled by History: Ranks, Designations, and Titles of the Russian Empire). Leningrad, 1977.

—————. *Tsarizm i burzhuaziia vo vtoroi polovine XIX veka: problemy torgovo-promyshlennoi politiki* (Tsarism and the Bourgeoisie in the Second Half of the Nineteenth Century: Problems of Commercial and Industrial Policy). Leningrad, 1981.

Shipov, D. *Vospominaniia i dumy o perezhitom* (Recollections and Thoughts about the Past). Moscow, 1918.

Solovev, Iu. B. *Samoderzhavie i dvorianstvo v kontse XIX veka* (Autocracy and the Nobility at the End of the Nineteenth Century). Leningrad, 1973.

—————. *Samoderzhavie i dvorianstvo v 1902-1907 gg.* (Autocracy and the Nobility in 1902-1907). Leningrad, 1981.

Soloveva, A. M. *Zheleznodorozhnyi transport Rossii vo vtoroi polovine XIX v.* (Railroad Transportation in Russia in the Second Half of the Nineteenth Century). Moscow, 1975.

Spasskii-Odynets, A. A. "Vospominaniia" (Memoirs), Unpublished work. Bakhmeteff Archive of Russian and East European History, Columbia University.

852 BIBLIOGRAPHY

Spiridovich, A. I. *Les dernières années de la cour de Tzarskoïe Sélo*. 2 vols. Paris, 1928–1929.

Spring-Rice, C. *The Letters and Friendships of Sir Cecil Spring-Rice*. 2 vols. Boston, 1929.

Startsev, V. I. *Russkaia burzhuaziia i samoderzhavie v 1905–1917 gg: Borba vokrug "otvetstvennogo ministerstva" i "pravitelstva doveriia"* (The Russian Bourgeoisie and Autocracy 1905 to 1917: The Struggle over "Responsible Ministry" and "A Government of Confidence"). Leningrad, 1977.

Straus, O. S. *Under Four Administrations*. Boston, 1922.

Suvorin, A. S. *Dnevnik A. S. Suvorina* (The Diary of A. S. Suvorin). Moscow, 1923.

——————. *Das Geheim-Tagebuch*. Berlin, 1925. Translation of the above.

Sviatopolk-Mirskaia, E. A. "Dnevnik na 1904–1905 gg." (Diary for 1904–1905). *Istoricheskie zapiski* 77 (1965): 240–93.

Tagantsev, N. S. *Perezhitoe: Uchrezhdenie Gosudarstvennoi dumy v 1905–1906 gg.* (Experiences: The Establishment of the State Duma in 1905–1906). Petrograd, 1918.

Thorson, W. B. "American Public Opinion and the Portsmouth Peace Conference." *American Historical Review* 53 (1948): 439–64.

Tikhomirov, L. "25 let nazad: Iz dnevnikov L. Tikhomirova" (Twenty-five Years Ago: From the Diaries of L. Tikhomirov). *Krasnyi arkhiv* 38 (1930): 20–69; 39 (1930): 47–75.

Tolstaia, L. Il., "Vospominaniia I. I. Tolstogo kak istoricheskii istochnik" (The Memoirs of I. I. Tolstoi As an Historical Source), *Vspomogatelnye istoricheskie distsipliny* 19 (1987): 201–16.

"Tsarskoselskie soveshchaniia" (Conferences at Tsarskoe Selo). *Byloe* 3(25) (1917): 217–65; 4(26) (1927): 183–245; 5/6(27/28) (1917): 289–318.

United Kingdom. Public Record Office. Foreign Office, 65/1700 (1905).

Vishniak, M. "Antisemitism in Tsarist Russia." In *Essays on Antisemitism*, pp. 79–110. Ed. K. S. Pinson. New York, 1942.

Vonliarliarskii, V. M. *Moi vospominaniia* (My Memoirs). Berlin, 1939.

Wehrlich, R. *Russian Orders, Decorations and Medals*. Washington, D.C., 1968.

Westwood, J. N. *A History of Russian Railways*. London, 1964.

White, J. A. *The Diplomacy of the Russo-Japanese War*. Princeton, N.J., 1964.

Williams, R. C. *Culture in Exile: Russian Emigres in Germany, 1881–1941*. Ithaca, N.Y., 1972.

Witte Papers. Bakhmeteff Archive. Columbia University.

Witte, S. *My Love Affair*. Burlington, Vt., 1903. A novel, probably a translation of her "Pervyi opyt" (First Experience), which appeared in *Nabliud* in 1886. Of interest only because the author was Witte's sister.

Zaionchkovskii, P. A. *Samoderzhavie i russkaia armiia na rubezhe XIX-XX stoletii* (Autocracy and the Russian Army at the Turn of the Twentieth Century). Moscow, 1973.

Zhelikhovskaia, V. P. "Pravda o E. P. Blavatskoi" (The Truth about E. P. Blavatskaia). *Rebus* 2 (1883): 357–59, 366–68, 389–91, 397–400, 418–19, 428–30, 438–40; 3 (1884): 155, 263, 273, 465. The author was given as I. Ia. by the journal but obviously was V. P. Zhelikhovskaia, Witte's cousin. *See* A. P. Sinnett, ed., *Incidents in the Life of Madame Blavatsky*. London, 1886.

Name Index

Subject Index

Absolutism, 497, 510, 586, 705, 770n. 4,
784n. III 4, 787n. 18, 797n. 18
Abyssinia. *See* Ethiopia
Academic freedom, 144
Administrative justice, 409
Afghanistan, 366, 452, 701, 831n. 4
Africa, 269
Agriculture, 319, 335, 446, 554, 559, 592,
625, 658. *See also* Industry; Land;
Land captains; Ministry: of Agriculture; Peasantry; Redemption dues
Chinese method of, 66, 67
Special Conference on the Needs of
Rural Industry, 84, 336–41, 371,
399, 408, 591, 592, 610, 658,
659n, 774n. 6, 789n. 38
Americans
characterization of, 434, 437–38, 442,
791n. 27
racism of, 434, 435, 442, 792n. 27
Amnesty decree, 497, 804n. 14
Anarchists (anarchy), 47, 68, 171,
216n, 240n, 300, 302, 304, 311,
323, 359, 361, 367, 372, 374, 422,
428, 458, 466, 472, 525, 526, 531,
533, 534, 538, 541n, 557, 558,
562, 566, 594, 595, 638, 642, 662,
673, 750n. V 8, 758n. 7, 776n. 7,
828n. 9. *See also* Revolution; Socialist Revolutionary party; Terrorism
Anglo-Boer War, 269, 724

Anglo-Russian Convention of 1907, 699–
701, 709
Appanage, 213, 213n, 357, 658, 761n.
XX 1, 826n. 6
Appropriations, military and naval, 725–
26, 732
special commission to review, 106
Armed forces. *See also* Military; Navy;
Soldiers
control over, 722–28
organizational problems, 17–19, 519,
722–30
unrest in, 474, 522–23, 594
Armenians, 22–23, 76n, 153, 264, 353,
365, 376, 758n. 9, 774n. 6
church, 473
massacre of, 250
Asiatic Bank, 64
Assembly, freedom of, 466–67, 475, 590,
611, 616, 680
Assembly of St. Petersburg Factory Workers, 401–3, 812n. 15
Association, freedom of, 590, 680, 796n. 8
Austria-Hungary, 343, 354, 570, 699,
701–2, 833n. 9
relations with, 15, 18, 245, 308, 705,
714
Autocracy, 342, 345, 346, 429, 466–67, 492,
496, 532, 552, 594, 691, 777n. B 2, 784n.
9, 786n. 17, 798n. 20, 802n. 5
limitations of, 580, 581, 585–86, 722–
27, 775n. 6

Union
  of the Archangel Michael, 634, 638,
    829n. 1
  for the Defense of the Freedom of the
    Press, 797n. 17
  of Professors, 471
  Russian Monarchist, 797n. 20, 828n. 9
  of the Russian People, 34, 84, 115,
    225n, 405, 416, 469, 520, 528n,
    604n, 628, 634, 637, 638, 663,
    672, 674, 676, 681, 682n, 685,
    685n, 689, 691, 707, 739, 751n.
    VIII 2, 755n. 9, 801–2n. 14,
    802n. 5, 807n. 15, 823nn. 8, 9,
    827n. 13, 828n. 9, 829n. 1
  of Unions, 471, 472, 475, 797n. 18
Unions
  of railroad employees, 472
  right to form, 680
  trade. *See* Trade Unions
United Nobility, 336
United States, 268, 282, 366, 380, 447,
  569, 703–5, 794n. 42, 832n. 15
University, 38. *See also* Students
  autonomy of, 406, 465–66
  regulations, 25, 748n. III 3
  statutes, 144, 174, 796n. 8
  unrest in, 86–87, 144, 154, 466

Veche, 472
Vestnik Evropy, 548n
Vestnik finansov, torgovli i promyshlennosti, 559
Village commune. *See* Land
Volunteer Fleet, 123
Vyborg Manifesto, 653–54, 660, 666

War
  of revenge, 460, 697–98
  views on, 173

Western provinces
  introduction of zemstvos in, 82, 212,
    642, 677, 732, 736, 742, 770n. 4,
    835nn. 1, 5
  representation of, 731–33, 835n. 1
Workers, 150–151, 322–23, 387, 402,
  404, 466, 470, 474, 475, 491,
  493n, 503n, 522, 527–28n, 544,
  558, 594, 638, 776n. 7, 784n. IV 4,
  797nn. 12, 16, 799n. 1, 800n. 11,
  809n. 18. *See also* Labor; Soviets;
  Zubatovshchina
  workers' associations, 323, 401–2,
    776n. 7, 800n. 11
  workmen's compensation bill, 323
World War I, 750n. V 7, 761n. 7, 768n.
  XXVIII 1, 771nn. 6, 7

Xenia Institute, 204

Young Turks, 701, 725n

Zaria, 74, 592
Zemskii sobor, 399n, 787n. 21
Zemstvos, 144, 145, 329, 332, 343, 344,
  345, 394, 398, 413, 468–70, 474,
  498, 502, 525, 577, 579, 653, 731–
  32, 770n. 4, 777n. B 2, 785n. 5,
  828n. 2. *See also* Municipal dumas;
  Self-government; Western provinces
  statute of 1890, 174, 578
  Zemstvo movement, 394, 470, 532,
    785n. 7, 804n. 24. *See also* Liberals
Zhupel, 775n. 3
Zoilism, 248
Zubatovshchina, 324, 362–64, 387, 401,
  473, 776n. 7, 826n. 4. *See also* Labor;
  Soviets; Workers
Zukunft, 101

About the Translator and Editor

Sidney Harcave is professor emeritus of history at the State University of New York at Binghamton. His many books issued in numerous editions include *Russia: A History, First Blood: The Russian Revolution of 1905,* and *Years of the Golden Cockerel: The Last Romanov Tsars, 1914–1917.*